2016

Education for people and planet:

CREATING SUSTAINABLE FUTURES FOR ALL

UNESCO
Publishing

United Nations
Educational, Scientific and
Cultural Organization

This Report is an independent publication commissioned by UNESCO on behalf of the international community. It is the product of a collaborative effort involving members of the Report team and many other people, agencies, institutions and governments.

The designations employed and the presentation of the material in this publication do not imply the expression of any opinion whatsoever on the part of UNESCO concerning the legal status of any country, territory, city or area, or of its authorities, or concerning the delimitation of its frontiers or boundaries.

The *Global Education Monitoring Report* team is responsible for the choice and the presentation of the facts contained in this book and for the opinions expressed therein, which are not necessarily those of UNESCO and do not commit the Organization. Overall responsibility for the views and opinions expressed in the Report is taken by its Director.

© UNESCO, 2016
Second edition
Published in 2016 by the United Nations
Educational, Scientific and Cultural
Organization
7, Place de Fontenoy, 75352 Paris 07 SP, France

Graphic design by FHI 360
Layout by FHI 360

Cover and back cover photos: Fadil Aziz/
Alcibbum Photography

*The cover photos are of school children from the
Palau Papan Island in the archipelago of Togean
in Sulawesi, Indonesia. The children, from the
Bajo tribe, live in stilt houses and cross a bridge
spanning 1.8 kilometres to the neighbouring island
of Melange to go to school every day.*

Typeset by UNESCO
ISBN: 978-92-3-100167-3

Foreword

In May 2015, the World Education Forum in Incheon (Republic of Korea), brought together 1,600 participants from 160 countries with a single goal in mind: how to ensure inclusive and equitable quality education and lifelong learning for all by 2030?

The Incheon Declaration for Education 2030 has been instrumental to shape the Sustainable Development Goal on Education to "Ensure inclusive and equitable quality education and promote lifelong learning opportunities for all". It entrusts UNESCO with the leadership, coordination and monitoring of the Education 2030 agenda. It also calls upon the *Global Education Monitoring* (GEM) *Report* to provide independent monitoring and reporting of the Sustainable Development Goal on education (SDG 4), and on education in the other SDGs, for the next fifteen years.

The ultimate goal of this agenda is to leave no one behind. This calls for robust data and sound monitoring. The 2016 edition of the GEM Report provides valuable insight for governments and policy makers to monitor and accelerate progress towards SDG 4, building on the indicators and targets we have, with equity and inclusion as measures of overall success.

This Report makes three messages starkly clear.

Firstly, the urgent need for new approaches. On current trends only 70% of children in low income countries will complete primary school in 2030, a goal that should have been achieved in 2015. We need the political will, the policies, the innovation and the resources to buck this trend.

Secondly, if we are serious about SDG4, we must act with a sense of heightened urgency, and with long-term commitment. Failure to do so will not only adversely affect education but will hamper progress towards each and every development goal: poverty reduction, hunger eradication, improved health, gender equality and women's empowerment, sustainable production and consumption, resilient cities, and more equal and inclusive societies.

Lastly, we must fundamentally change the way we think about education and its role in human well-being and global development. Now, more than ever, education has a responsibility to foster the right type of skills, attitudes and behavior that will lead to sustainable and inclusive growth.

The 2030 Agenda for Sustainable Development calls on us to develop holistic and integrated responses to the many social, economic and environmental challenges we face. This means reaching out beyond traditional boundaries and creating effective, cross-sectoral partnerships.

A sustainable future for all is about human dignity, social inclusion and environmental protection. It is a future where economic growth does not exacerbate inequalities but builds prosperity for all; where urban areas and labour markets are designed to empower everyone and economic activities, communal and corporate, are green-oriented. Sustainable development is a belief that human development cannot happen without a healthy planet. Embarking upon the new SDG agenda requires all of us to reflect upon the ultimate purpose of learning throughout life. Because, if done right, education has the power like none else to nurture empowered, reflective, engaged and skilled citizens who can chart the way towards a safer, greener and fairer planet for all. This new report provides relevant evidence to enrich these discussions and craft the policies needed to make it a reality for all.

Irina Bokova
Director-General of UNESCO

Foreword

The 2016 *Global Education Monitoring Report* (GEM Report) is both masterful and disquieting. This is a big report: comprehensive, in-depth and perspicacious. It is also an unnerving report. It establishes that education is at the heart of sustainable development and the Sustainable Development Goals (SDGs), yet it also makes clear just how far away we are from achieving the SDGs. This report should set off alarm bells around the world and lead to a historic scale-up of actions to achieve SDG 4.

The GEM Report provides an authoritative account of how education is the most vital input for every dimension of sustainable development. Better education leads to greater prosperity, improved agriculture, better health outcomes, less violence, more gender equality, higher social capital and an improved natural environment. Education is key to helping people around the world understand why sustainable development is such a vital concept for our common future. Education gives us the key tools – economic, social, technological, even ethical – to take on the SDGs and to achieve them. These facts are spelled out in exquisite and unusual detail throughout the report. There is a wealth of information to be mined in the tables, graphs and texts.

Yet the report also emphasizes the remarkable gaps between where the world stands today on education and where it has promised to arrive as of 2030. The gaps in educational attainment between rich and poor, within and between countries, are simply appalling. In many poor countries, poor children face nearly insurmountable obstacles under current conditions. They lack books at home; have no opportunity for pre-primary school; and enter facilities without electricity, water, hygiene, qualified teachers, textbooks and the other appurtenances of a basic education, much less a quality education. The implications are staggering. While SDG 4 calls for universal completion of upper secondary education by 2030, the current completion rate in low-income countries is a meagre 14% (Table 10.3).

The GEM Report undertakes an important exercise to determine how many countries will reach the 2030 target on the current trajectory, or even on a path that matches the fastest improving country in the region. The answer is sobering: We need unprecedented progress, starting almost immediately, in order to have a shot at success with SDG 4.

Cynics might say, 'We told you, SDG 4 is simply unachievable', and suggest that we accept that 'reality'. Yet as the report hammers home in countless ways, such complacency is reckless and immoral. If we leave the current young generation without adequate schooling, we doom them and the world to future poverty, environmental ills, and even social violence and instability for decades to come. There can be no excuse for complacency. The message of this report is that we need to get our act together to accelerate educational attainment in an unprecedented manner.

One of the keys for acceleration is financing. Here again, the report makes for sobering reading. Development aid for education today is lower than it was in 2009 (Figure 20.7). This is staggeringly short-sighted of the rich countries. Do these donor countries really believe that they are 'saving money' by underinvesting in aid for education in the world's low-income countries? After reading this report, the leaders and citizens in the high income world will be deeply aware that investing in education is fundamental for global well-being, and that the current level of aid, at around US$5 billion per year for primary education – just US$5 per person per year in the rich countries! – is a tragically small investment for the world's future sustainable development and peace.

The 2016 GEM Report provides a plethora of insights, recommendations and standards for moving forward. It offers invaluable suggestions on how to monitor and measure progress on SDG 4. It demonstrates by example the feasibility of far more refined measures of education inputs, quality and achievement than the often crude measures of enrolment and completion that we rely on today. Using big data, better survey tools, facility monitoring and information technology, we can get far more nuanced measures of the education process and outcomes at all levels.

Fifteen years ago the world finally recognized the enormity of the AIDS epidemic and other health emergencies and took concrete steps to scale up public health interventions in the context of the Millennium Development Goals. Thus were born major initiatives such as the Global Fund to Fight AIDS, Tuberculosis and Malaria, the Global Alliance for Vaccines and Immunisation (now Gavi, the Vaccine Alliance) and many other examples. These efforts led to a dramatic upturn in public health interventions and funding. While it did not achieve all that was possible (mainly because the 2008 financial crisis ended the upswing in public health funding) it did lead to many breakthroughs whose effects continue to be felt today.

The 2016 GEM Report should be read as a similar call to action for education as the core of the SDGs. My own view, often repeated in the past couple of years, is the urgency of a Global Fund for Education that builds on the positive lessons of the Global Fund for AIDS, Tuberculosis and Malaria. The financing constraint lies at the very heart of the education challenge, as this report makes vividly clear through every bit of cross-national and household-based data.

This compelling document calls on us to respond to the opportunity, urgency and declared global goal embodied in SDG 4: universal education of good quality for all and opportunities for learning throughout life. I urge people everywhere to study this report carefully and take its essential messages to heart. Most importantly, let us act on them at every level, from the local community to the global community.

Jeffrey D. Sachs
Special Adviser to the UN Secretary-General on the
Sustainable Development Goals

Acknowledgements

This report would not have been possible without the valuable contributions of numerous people and institutions. The *Global Education Monitoring Report* (GEM Report) team would like to acknowledge their support and thank them for their time and effort.

Invaluable input has been provided by the GEM Report Advisory Board. We specifically wish to acknowledge the current Chairperson, Professor Jeffrey Sachs, and the Vice-Chair, Baela Raza Jamil. Special thanks also go to our engaged and committed funders without whose financial support the GEM Report would not be possible.

We would like to acknowledge the role of UNESCO, its leadership both at headquarters and in the field, as well as the UNESCO Institutes. We are very grateful to many individuals, divisions and units at UNESCO, notably in the Education Sector and the Bureau for the Management of Support Services, for facilitating our daily work activities. As always, the UNESCO Institute for Statistics has played a key role and we would like to thank its director, Silvia Montoya, and her dedicated staff, including among others Albert Motivans, Patrick Montjouridès, Elise Legault, Simon Ip Cho, Alison Kennedy and Pascale Ratovondrahona, Vong Shian and Peter Wallet. Additional thanks to many colleagues at UNESCO's Institute for Lifelong Learning, International Bureau of Education, International Institute for Education Planning and the UNESCO Bangkok Office.

An enthusiastic thank you to Radhika Iyengar, our special advisor, who worked with the team as the report began to take shape. She helped conceptualize key Report themes, emphasized engagement with other sector experts, and later provided extensive input and review of chapter drafts.

Several external experts, including Martha Ferede, François Leclercq, Edouard Morena, Fatou Niang, Ashley Stepanek Lockhart, Rosie Peppin Vaughan, Arjen Wals and Samuel Wearne also helped us during the development and drafting phases of this GEM Report and we would like to thank them for their critical contributions.

The GEM Report team would also like to thank the researchers who produced background papers and prepared key inputs informing the GEM Report's analyses: Bassel Akar, Sandy Balfour, Carol Benson, Patricia Bromley, Natalie Browes, Kenn Chua, James Cornwell, Luc Gacougnolle, Bryony Hoskins, Jeremy Jimenez, Julie Lerch, Marlaine Lockheed, Giorgia Magni, Yulia Makarova, Ismailou Maman Keita, Diego Martino, Dominic Orr, Amlata Persaud, Abbie Raikes, the late Anthony Read, Nicolas Read, Filiberto Viteri and Lisa Zaval.

We are also grateful to several institutions and their research staff: the Australian Council of Educational Research (John Ainley, Wolfram Schulz, Julian Fraillon), the Centre for Environment Education India Incorporated (Kartikeya Sarabhai, Rixa Schwarz), the Centre for Environment Education Australia Incorporated (Dr. Prithi Nambiar), Technopolis (Carlos Hinojosa, Annemieke Pickles), the Wittgenstein Centre for Demography and Global Human Capital (Bilal Barakat, Stephanie Bengtsson), Development Finance International (Jo Walker), the International Council of Adult Education (Katarina Popović), University of Haifa (Iddo Gal), Research Triangle Institute International (Amber Gove) and the Institute of International Education (Rajika Bhandari).

Two groups of students from the the MPA programme, London School of Economics also prepared papers for the Report as part of their Capstone project, and are to be thanked as well. The following individuals also provided valuable inputs: Mo Adefeso-Olateju, Ericka Albaugh, Nadir Altinok, Ian Attfield, Laura-Ashley Boden, Manuel Cardoso, Daniel Capistrano de Oliveira, Claudia Cappa, Eric Charbonnier, Christie Chatterley, James Ciera, David Coleman, Arlette Delhaxhe, Marta Encinas-Martin, Jarret Guajardo, Sonia Guerriero, Hiro Hattori, Fabrice Hénard, Ram Hari Lamichhane, Mitch Loeb, Esperanza Magpantay, Daniel Mont, Karen Moore, Sarah Pouezevara, Filipa Schmitz Guinote, Mantas Sekmokas, Tom Slaymaker, Paulo Speller, Andrzej Suchodolski, Susan Teltscher, Jair Torres, Lina Uribe Correa, Quentin Wodon and Gonzalo Zapata.

A group of independent experts also reviewed GEM Report chapters and provided valuable feedback. For their input we thank Farzana Afridi, Monisha Bajaj, Erica Chenoweth, Jessica Fanzo, Lloyd Gruber, Morgan Bazilian, Diego Martino, Aromar Revi, Guido Schmidt-Traub and Patience Stephens.

Special thanks go to Karen Fortuin, Keith Lewin, Mutizwa Mukute and Steve Packer who reviewed drafts of the full report and provided useful and insightful comments.

The report was edited by Andy Quan, who helped ensure a distinctive voice from the many perspectives and ideas advanced in this ambitious report. Our thanks also go to Andrew Johnston for writing the summary. Thanks also to Abracadabra for creating the new *Global Education Monitoring Report* logo and to FHI 360 for the design of the new templates.

We also wish to acknowledge those who worked tirelessly to support the production of the Report, including Rebecca Brite, Erin Crum, Shannon Dyson, FHI 360, Kristen Garcia, Phoenix Design Aid A/S, Melanie Tingstrom and Jan Worrall.

Many colleagues within and outside UNESCO were involved in the translation, design and production of the 2016 GEM Report and we would like to extend to them our deep appreciation for their support.

Several people provided support to the GEM Report's communication and outreach work, including Beard & Braid Ltd and Blossom snc. Finally, we would like to thank the interns and junior consultants who have supported the GEM Report team in various areas of its work: Farah Altaher, Fatine Guedira, Mobarak Hossain, Lidia Lozano, Kathleen Ludgate, Manbo Ouyang, Robin Sainsot, Laura Stipanovic, Ellen Stay and Kai Zhou.

The *Global Education Monitoring Report* team

Director: Aaron Benavot

Manos Antoninis, Madeleine Barry, Nicole Bella, Nihan Köseleci Blanchy, Marcos Delprato,
Glen Hertelendy, Catherine Jere, Priyadarshani Joshi, Katarzyna Kubacka, Leïla Loupis,
Kassiani Lythrangomitis, Alasdair McWilliam, Anissa Mechtar, Branwen Millar, Claudine Mukizwa,
Yuki Murakami, Taya Louise Owens, Judith Randrianatoavina, Kate Redman, Maria Rojnov,
Anna Ewa Ruszkiewicz, Will Smith, Emily Subden, Rosa Vidarte and Asma Zubairi.

The *Global Education Monitoring Report* (or GEM Report) is an independent annual publication. The GEM Report is funded by a group of governments, multilateral agencies and private foundations and facilitated and supported by UNESCO.

For more information, please contact:
Global Education Monitoring Report team
c/o UNESCO, 7, place de Fontenoy
75352 Paris 07 SP,
France
Email: gemreport@unesco.org
Tel.: +33 1 45 68 07 41
www.unesco.org/gemreport

New *Global Education Monitoring Report* series

2016	Education for people and planet: Creating sustainable futures for all

EFA *Global Monitoring Report* series

2015	Education for All 2000–2015: Achievements and challenges
2013/4	Teaching and learning: Achieving quality for all
2012	Youth and skills: Putting education to work
2011	The hidden crisis: Armed conflict and education
2010	Reaching the marginalized
2009	Overcoming inequality: Why governance matters
2008	Education for All by 2015: Will we make it?
2007	Strong foundations: Early childhood care and education
2006	Literacy for life
2005	Education for All: The quality imperative
2003/4	Gender and Education for All: The leap to equality
2002	Education for All: Is the world on track?

Any errors or omissions found subsequent to printing will be corrected in the online version at www.unesco.org/gemreport.

Contents

The references for the 2016 Global Education Monitoring Report can be downloaded at the following link: https://en.unesco.org/gem-report/sites/gem-report/files/2016ReportReferences.pdf

List of figures, tables, and text boxes

FIGURES

TABLES

TEXT BOXES

HIGHLIGHTS

Education for people and planet: key facts and figures

PLANET

Education is the most effective tool for reducing fertility rates: For example, one extra year of education in Madagascar increased spaces between births by 0.5 years.

Environmental education can increase green knowledge: 73% of 78 countries' curricula mention 'sustainable development', 55% mention 'ecology' and 47% 'environmental education'.

Sustainability practices continue outside of school: A 2008 survey reported that over 40% of global executives thought it important for their companies to align sustainability with their business.

Education is crucial for disaster preparedness: If education progress is stalled, it could lead to a 20% increase in disaster-related fatalities per decade.

Education systems should not encourage unsustainable lifestyles and can learn much from indigenous communities: They should respect local cultures and plural knowledge systems, and provide instruction in local languages.

PROSPERITY

Education can help increase agricultural productivity: Farm output needs to rise by at least 70% by 2050. Field schools and extension education help farmers increase productivity by 12% and net revenue by 19%.

Education can provide skills for green innovation: But sub-Saharan Africa's share of global expenditure on public agricultural research declined from 10% in 1960 to 6% in 2009.

Education reduces working poverty: It affects almost 90% of workers in low income countries. Increasing tertiary education in 10 recent EU member states would reduce numbers at risk of poverty by 3.7 million.

Tertiary education is required to sustain and expand high-skills occupations: In 2015, two-thirds of workers were employed in medium skills occupations.

Education needs to keep up with labour market needs: By 2020 the world could have 40 million too few workers with tertiary education, relative to demand.

PEOPLE

Millions, particularly the marginalized, lack access to basic services: In 2012, in low income countries, only 28% had access to sanitation facilities and 25% to electricity; 67% made it to the last grade of primary education.

Gender equality is a long way off: Only 19% of heads of state or government are women. Women in many countries do at least twice as much unpaid work as men.

Education improves health and reduces fertility rates: Educating mothers increased reliance on exclusive breastfeeding by 90% for the first six months. Four years more in school in Nigeria reduced fertility rates by one birth per young girl.

Health and nutrition improve education: Female literacy rates were 5% higher for those with better access to water in India. In Kenya, girls who received deworming treatment were 25% more likely to pass the primary school exam.

PLACE

Urbanization puts strain on education systems: In China in 2004, one-fifth of the 120 million internal migrants had less than a primary education. Of the more than 25 million refugees in 2015, 60% live in urban areas and half are under age 18. In Turkey, only 30% of refugees in urban areas were in formal education.

Education helps reduce inequality in cities by giving people vital skills for work: Street vendors make up one-third of urban employment in India and one-sixth in South Africa.

Education reduces crime in cities: In the United States, if 5% more men graduated from high school it would add US$20 billion to the economy via reduced crime and higher earnings.

Education improves cities' prosperity and makes them green: Some 18,000 firms created by Stanford University alumni are based in California, in urban areas. In countries with cycling cities, such as Denmark, Germany and the Netherlands, children receive safe-cycling training in school from an early age.

PEACE

Education can encourage constructive political participation: In 106 countries, people with higher levels of education were more likely to engage in non-violent protests. In 102 countries, adults with a tertiary education were 60% more likely to request information from the government than those with a primary education or less.

Education needs to be better recognized in peace agreements: It was mentioned in only two-thirds of such agreements between 1989 and 2005..

Only the right type of education works: In Rwanda, curricular content exacerbated Hutu-Tutsi divisions.

Conflict is destroying education: Of those out of school, 35% of children of primary school age, 25% of adolescents of lower secondary age and 18% of youth of upper secondary age live in conflict-affected areas.

Education helps people get access to justice systems: In 2011, in the former Yugoslav Republic of Macedonia, 32% of those with primary education understood the judicial system, compared with 77% with higher education.

PARTNERSHIPS

Aid is not being targeted to those most in need: Education aid received by 170 countries since 2003 has been associated less with need, and more with trade interests.

Poor quality education can decrease tax compliance: Low literacy was associated with reduced tax revenue in 123 countries between 1996 and 2010.

PROJECTIONS

On current trends, universal primary completion will be achieved in 2042, universal lower secondary completion in 2059 and universal upper secondary completion in 2084.

Rich countries are not on course either: Even at the fastest rate of progress ever seen in the region, 1 in 10 countries in Europe and Northern America would still not achieve universal upper secondary completion by 2030.

Universalizing upper secondary completion for women in sub-Saharan Africa by 2030 would result in 300,000 to 350,000 fewer child deaths per year in 2050.

In low income countries, universalizing upper secondary completion by 2030 would increase per capita income by 75% by 2050 and bring poverty elimination forward by 10 years.

Universal upper secondary completion by 2030 would prevent up to 50,000 disaster-related deaths per decade by 2040-2050.

Monitoring SDG 4

TARGET 4.1: Primary and secondary education

- In 2014, 263 million children, adolescents and youth were out of school.

- In 2008–2014, 84% of youth completed upper secondary school in high income, 43% in upper middle income, 38% in lower middle income and 14% in low income countries.

- Across the 15 countries in the TERCE study in Latin America, 60% of grade 3 students were at level 2 and above in reading.

TARGET 4.2: Early childhood

- Pre-primary education is free and compulsory for at least one year in only 38 countries.

- Children from the richest households are almost six times more likely to attend an early childhood education programme than those from the poorest.

TARGET 4.3: Technical, vocational, tertiary and adult education

- About 11% of secondary education students were enrolled in formal TVET in 2014.

- Across 76 countries, 20% of the richest 25- to 29-year-olds had completed at least four years of tertiary education, compared with less than 1% of the poorest.

- In European Union countries, 37% of adults participated in non-formal education in 2011.

TARGET 4.4: Skills for work

- In the European Union, in 2014, 65% of adults could send an email with an attachment and 44% could use basic arithmetic formulas in spreadsheets.

- According to one definition, one-third of adults are financially literate.

TARGET 4.5: Equity

- In low income countries, for every 100 of the richest youth who complete upper secondary education, only 7 do so among the poorest youth.

- In 2014, 63% of countries achieved gender parity in primary, 46% in lower secondary and 23% in upper secondary education.

- Across 30 education systems in Europe, 3.7% of pupils had a special educational need in 2010.

- Around 40% of people are not taught in a language they speak or fully understand.

- 50% of primary school-age and 75% of secondary school-age refugees are out of school.

TARGET 4.6: Literacy and numeracy

- In 2004–2011, only 6% of adults in 29 poorer countries had ever participated in a literacy programme.

- In 2005–2014, 758 million adults, 114 million of whom are aged 15 to 24, cannot read or write a simple sentence; nearly two thirds are women.

TARGET 4.7: Sustainable development and global citizenship

- Three-quarters of countries emphasized sustainable development issues in their curricula between 2005 and 2015; 15% included key terms related to gender equality.

- Close to 50% of secondary school textbooks mentioned human rights over 2000–2013.

TARGET 4.A: Education facilities and learning environments

- Three in ten primary schools lacked an adequate water supply in 2013.

- Schools were used for military purposes in 26 countries between 2005 and 2015.

TARGET 4.B: Scholarships

- An estimated 25,000 scholarships were offered in 2015 by government programmes to students from developing countries.

TARGET 4.C: Teachers

- In 2014, 82% of teachers had the minimum qualifications required to teach in pre-primary education, 93% in primary education and 91% in secondary education.

- In sub-Saharan Africa, less than three-quarters of pre-primary and half of upper secondary school teachers are trained.

FINANCE:

- In at least 35 countries, governments spent less than 4% of GDP and less than 15% of their total expenditure on education.

- Aid needs to increase at least sixfold to fill the US$39 billion annual education finance gap, but in 2014, levels were 8% lower than at their peak in 2010.

A young boy takes part in a reforestation project in Cape Town, South Africa, where children learn to reconnect with nature.

CREDIT: Sydelle Willow Smith/GEM Report

Sustainable development: a strategy for people, planet and prosperity

INTRODUCTION HIGHLIGHTS

Transforming our world: the 2030 Agenda for Sustainable Development

At the 70th Session of the United Nations General Assembly in September 2015, member states adopted a new global development agenda, Transforming our world: the 2030 Agenda for Sustainable Development.

The new Agenda unites global development and environmental goals in one framework.

There is no single definition of sustainable development: Most challenge the status quo, believing that human development means nothing without a healthy planet.

The Global Education Monitoring Report

The Incheon Declaration affirmed the mandate of the GEM Report as the mechanism for monitoring and reporting on the fourth global goal on education as well as on education targets in the other Sustainable Development Goals (SDGs).

The 2016 GEM Report is the first of a new 15-year series. It shows that education will not deliver its full potential to catapult the world forward unless participation rates dramatically improve, learning becomes a lifelong pursuit and education systems fully embrace sustainable development.

The thematic part of the GEM Report discusses the complex links between SDG 4 on education and the other 16 SDGs. It presents compelling arguments as to the types of education and learning that are vital for achieving other SDGs.

Monitoring SDG 4

The success of the SDG framework will rely on national policies, plans and programmes. However, the agenda's goals and targets will be monitored and reviewed using global indicators with a framework coordinated by the Inter-agency and Expert Group on SDG Indicators and agreed by the UN Statistical Commission.

To support country implementation of SDG 4 and its targets, the international education community adopted the Education 2030 Framework for Action in Paris in November 2015.

An important focus of SDG 4 is 'lifelong learning opportunities for all', which is a process that begins at birth and carries through all stages of life.

The SDGs, targets and means of implementation are universal, indivisible and interlinked

There is strong evidence of the importance of good quality and equitable education and learning in supporting social change, as well as the role of education as a cross-cutting means of advancing the 2030 Agenda.

The planet Earth is in a dire state. Natural resources have been overexploited. A significant loss of biodiversity is occurring while a massive rise of carbon levels is leading to climate change and associated extreme weather. Toxic substances are increasingly found in air, water, soil, and flora and fauna. The planet faces desertification, drought and land degradation. Human living conditions have not fared much better. Even though the number of people living in extreme poverty has declined by over 1 billion (United Nations, 2015a), disparities between rich and poor continue to rise. Oxfam recently reported that the world's richest 62 people possess as much wealth as the poorest 3.6 billion (Hardoon et al., 2016). Too many people are trapped in poverty, and lack clean air and drinking water as well as adequate food and nutrition. Many families are forcibly displaced or on the run due to protracted conflict. Wide disparities persist in access to education of good quality. It is out of these concerns that the concept of sustainable development was born.

WHAT IS SUSTAINABLE DEVELOPMENT?

Sustainable development is an organizing principle for global development that supports the well-being of both people and the planet. Since its emergence, the concept and term have expanded to bridge gaps among environmental, economic and social concerns, attempting to integrate environmental protection and

> 66
>
> Sustainable development is an organizing principle for global development that supports the well-being of both people and the planet
>
> 99

ecological integrity, economic viability, and social and human development. Intergenerational equity, balancing the needs of present and future generations, is also a key component.

Sustainable development was advanced in the 1960s and 1970s as a concept linking observed interactions between humans and the environment, as documented in literature such as *Silent Spring* (Carson, 1962), *The Population Bomb* (Ehrlich, 1968) and *The Limits to Growth* (Meadows et al., 1972). In 1972, the United Nations (UN) Conference on the Human Environment in Stockholm marked the beginning of a global conversation on sustainable governance, although the term was still in the making. Experts convened a global symposium in Mexico two years later and signed the 1974 Cocoyoc Declaration, which advocated harmonizing environment and development strategies through 'eco-development' (UNEP and UNCTAD, 1974).

The first use of the term 'sustainable development' in a major public document was the 1980 World Conservation Strategy, which confirmed that conservation of living resources was essential to sustainable development (IUCN et al., 1980). At the 1986 Conference on Conservation and Development in Ottawa, sustainable development was defined as: (a) integration of conservation and development, (b) satisfaction of basic human needs, (c) achievement of equity and social justice, (d) provision of social self-determination and cultural diversity, and (e) maintenance of ecological integrity (Lele, 1991).

The most common notion of sustainable development was popularized in the 1987 Brundtland Report, *Our Common Future*, which raised questions about the consequences of traditional economic growth in terms of environmental degradation and poverty (United Nations, 1987). The Brundtland Report referred to 'development which meets the needs of the present without compromising the ability of future generations to meet their own needs' and listed critical objectives for sustainable development: changing the quality of economic growth; meeting essential needs for jobs, food, energy, water and sanitation; ensuring a sustainable population level; conserving and enhancing natural resources; reorienting technology and managing risk; linking environmental and economic concerns in decision-making; and reorienting international economic relations to make development more participatory (Lele, 1991).

Global understanding of sustainable development has since evolved into a framework developed over decades by an international community of member state governments, UN agencies, multilateral and bilateral development partners, civil society organizations, researchers and scientists. It resulted in the 2030 Agenda for Sustainable Development, a value-based framework for action that reflects core beliefs and principles (Sachs, 2015).

Several key terms and values are essential to understanding the post-2015 agenda:

- **People, Planet and Prosperity:** The '3Ps' are interdependent and mutually reinforcing pillars that represent the social, environmental and economic aspects of progress for all life forms on Earth.

- **Good governance:** This dimension supports the 3Ps through responsible leadership and active engagement in both the public and private sectors. Good governance ensures peaceful societies and upholds human rights for the good of the planet.

- **Links and connections:** Sustainable development works as an organizing principle because it recognizes that complex natural and social systems are linked and interconnected. Changes that occur in one system may affect others in ways that result in something more than the sum of the parts.

- **Intergenerational equity and justice:** Fairness is critical to a world fit for future generations, where children can grow up to be healthy, well nourished, resilient, well educated, culturally sensitive and protected from violence and neglect, and with access to safe, unpolluted ecosystems. Equity and justice are also required for diverse groups in the current generation.

THERE IS NO SINGLE DEFINITION OF SUSTAINABLE DEVELOPMENT

The different perspectives of sustainable development include viewing it as a model to improve current systems (endorsed by those focusing on viable economic growth), a call for major reforms (supported by those who advocate for a green economy and technological innovation) and an imperative for a larger transformation in power structures and embedded values of society (supported by transition movements).

Some ecologists, such as deep ecologists, believe present-day human development focuses too much on people and ignores the plant, animal and spiritual parts of this world (Leonard and Barry, 2009). They believe humans must learn to be less self-interested and place the needs of other species alongside their own. Transformation advocates say societies should go back to ways of living that are locally sustainable – consuming and wasting less, limiting needs to locally available resources, treating nature with respect, and abandoning polluting technology that has become an integral part of modern society. Culture advocates believe sustainable living can happen only if communities truly embrace it as part of daily culture (Hawkes, 2001) so that it affects decisions about what to eat, how to commute to work and how to spend leisure time.

The South American *buen vivir* movement rejects development as materialistic and selfish, implying that living sustainably means finding alternatives to development (Gudynas, 2011). The *buen vivir* belief system comes directly from traditional values of indigenous people, and posits that collective needs are more important than those of the individual. In Ecuador, this concept is called *sumak kawsay*, the Quechua term for fullness of life in a community. It involves learning to live within boundaries, finding ways to reduce use or to do more with less, and exploring non-material values. Ecuador and the Plurinational State of Bolivia have incorporated *buen vivir* into their constitutions.

> 66
> Most definitions of sustainable development challenge the status quo, believing human development lacks meaning without a healthy planet
> 99

Most definitions of sustainable development challenge the status quo, believing human development lacks meaning without a healthy planet. This view requires people, communities and nations to reconsider basic values of daily living and change the way they think. Understanding one's own values, the values of one's community and society, and those of others around the world is a central part of educating for a sustainable future. This means education systems need to continuously evolve and change in order to identify what practices work best within a given context and how they need to change over time. Indeed, for many of its advocates in education, sustainable development is best understood as a journey, rather than a destination.

THE 2030 AGENDA UNITES DEVELOPMENT AND ENVIRONMENTAL SUSTAINABILITY

The 2030 Agenda for Sustainable Development unites global development and environmental goals in one framework. It is the result of decades of collective progress and failure and the articulation of future challenges. Since the Brundtland Report, three international meetings have played an instrumental role along the path to the 2030 Agenda: the Rio (1992), Johannesburg (2002) and Rio+20 (2012) Earth summits.

The 1992 UN Conference on Environment and Development, also known as the Earth Summit, established Agenda 21, an action plan intended for governments and other major groups. Participants at the conference in Rio de Janeiro hoped the plan's implementation would result in the widespread changes needed to integrate environmental sustainability and development. Agenda 21 included a special chapter (Chapter 36) on the need for education, public awareness-raising and training to reorient society towards sustainable development.

The 2002 World Summit on Sustainable Development (WSSD) in Johannesburg pledged to strengthen the mutually reinforcing pillars of sustainable development at the local, national, regional and global levels with the goal to 'banish underdevelopment forever' (United Nations, 2002). The WSSD agenda included fighting severe threats to sustainable development, including chronic hunger, malnutrition, terrorism, corruption, xenophobia and endemic, communicable and chronic diseases. Special emphasis was also placed on women's empowerment, emancipation and gender equality.

The 2012 UN Conference on Sustainable Development in Rio de Janeiro, commonly referred to as Rio +20, again evoked the three pillars – the social, environmental and economic dimensions of sustainability – as guides

for international development (United Nations, 2013). Importantly, Rio +20 acknowledged a lack of progress in achieving sustainable development, especially in integrating the three pillars. Therefore, Rio +20 emphasized the role of good governance and integrated planning in achieving sustainable development.

Despite these global meetings, over the past two decades the Earth's biosphere has continued to deteriorate, poverty has remained widespread and social inequality has increased. These harmful trends accelerated despite efforts to meet the Millennium Development Goals (MDGs), the 2000–2015 global development and anti-poverty agenda. After Rio +20, an inclusive intergovernmental process began to formulate the Sustainable Development Goals (SDGs) to succeed the MDGs, which were approaching their target date and had been subject to criticism (**Box 0.1**).

BOX 0.1

The Millennium Development Goals failed to ensure environmental sustainability

The eight MDGs – to eradicate extreme poverty and hunger; achieve universal primary education; promote gender equality; reduce child mortality; improve maternal health; combat HIV/AIDS, malaria and other diseases; ensure environmental sustainability; and develop global partnerships – saved millions of lives and helped improve quality of life for billions. But the final MDG review acknowledged uneven achievements and shortfalls in many areas.

Three critical factors hampered success. First, public agencies and private-sector firms were not held accountable for the environmental damage that economic growth causes. Rather, the damage was justified as the price of economic development, and the cost of damage was absorbed by society, not by polluters. Second, the cost to future generations of environmental damage during development was not evaluated, as it was commonly believed that countries could grow now and clean up later. Finally, the MDGs focused on developing nations, assigning rich countries the role of financial donors. By artificially separating rich and poor countries, the MDGs failed to recognize how all societies are interconnected, both reliant on and affected by changes to socio-economic and natural systems on Earth.

However, the experience of the MDGs taught global policy-makers to better recognize the differences between countries at the start of processes, and the need for context-specific goals, priority-setting and policy coherence between the global, regional, national and subnational levels.

Sources: United Nations (2012, 2015a); Zusman et al. (2015).

THE SDGS WERE CREATED THROUGH INCLUSIVE DECISION-MAKING

At the 70th Session of the UN General Assembly in September 2015, member states adopted a new global development agenda, *Transforming Our World: The 2030 Agenda for Sustainable Development*. At its heart are 17 SDGs, including SDG 4 on education. The SDGs establish development priorities to 2030 and succeed the MDGs and the goals of Education for All (EFA) – the global movement to ensure quality basic education for all children, youth and adults – both of which expired in 2015.

BOX 0.2

The Sustainable Development Goals

Goal 1: End poverty in all its forms everywhere

Goal 2: End hunger, achieve food security and improved nutrition and promote sustainable agriculture

Goal 3: Ensure healthy lives and promote well-being for all at all ages

Goal 4: Ensure inclusive and equitable quality education and promote lifelong learning opportunities for all

Goal 5: Achieve gender equality and empower all women and girls

Goal 6: Ensure availability and sustainable management of water and sanitation for all

Goal 7: Ensure access to affordable, reliable, sustainable and modern energy for all

Goal 8: Promote sustained, inclusive and sustainable economic growth, full and productive employment and decent work for all

Goal 9: Build resilient infrastructure, promote inclusive and sustainable industrialization and foster innovation

Goal 10: Reduce inequality within and among countries

Goal 11: Make cities and human settlements inclusive, safe, resilient and sustainable

Goal 12: Ensure sustainable consumption and production patterns

Goal 13: Take urgent action to combat climate change and its impacts

Goal 14: Conserve and sustainably use the oceans, seas and marine resources for sustainable development

Goal 15: Protect, restore and promote sustainable use of terrestrial ecosystems, sustainably manage forests, combat desertification, and halt and reverse land degradation and halt biodiversity loss

Goal 16: Promote peaceful and inclusive societies for sustainable development, provide access to justice for all and build effective, accountable and inclusive institutions at all levels

Goal 17: Strengthen the means of implementation and revitalize the Global Partnership for Sustainable Development

---

How did this come about? Almost immediately after Rio+20, various stakeholders began to plan a new agenda for sustainable development. With a mandate from the 2010 UN General Assembly, the UN Secretary-General led the Post-2015 Development Agenda process, which over three years, involved two main streams to develop specific goals in a transparent, participatory way – one more consultative, involving many stakeholders, and the other a more official intergovernmental process.

Among the other many initiatives and contributions that led to the final adopted Agenda 2030, the Sustainable Development Solutions Network played an important role. The UN launched it in 2012 to mobilize knowledge and help design and implement the post-2015 agenda, building on lessons learned from the MDGs and Earth summits. A 2012 report concluded that the MDG framework should be retained, but reorganized to guide international and national policy-making holistically along four key dimensions: (a) inclusive social development, (b) inclusive economic development, (c) environmental sustainability, and (d) peace and security (United Nations, 2012).

During the first half of 2013, the UN conducted a series of 'global conversations' that engaged almost 2 million people in 88 countries. They included 11 thematic consultations including one on education, activities at the national level and door-to-door surveys. The UN also launched the MY World survey, asking people which of 16 development goals mattered to them the most. Between July and December 2014, more than 7 million people responded online, by ballot or through SMS, of which over 5 million votes were collected offline via paper ballots and almost 500,000 through mobile phones (United Nations, 2014). MY World voters overwhelmingly chose 'a good education' and 'better healthcare' as top priorities. People chose education as the number one priority regardless of their gender, age, wealth or education level.

A concurrent process, involving discussions of the Open Working Group (OWG), was mandated in the outcome document of the Rio+20 conference in June 2012, which affirmed the role and authority of the UN General Assembly to lead the SDG process. In January 2013, member states established the intergovernmental OWG, with 70 member states sharing its 30 seats, to propose SDGs. Recommendations on the vision and shape of the SDG agenda were included in the report of the High-Level Panel of Eminent Persons on the Post-2015 Development Agenda, released in mid-2013. After 13 sessions, the OWG produced a document in July 2014 that put forward 17 goals with 169 targets (**Box 0.2**).

The two processes merged with the publication of the Secretary-General's synthesis report in December 2014, which led to a new intergovernmental process towards the adoption of the SDGs. Seven more rounds of negotiations during the first half of 2015 helped refine and finalize the formulation of the goals and targets.

The SDGs were designed using principles of good governance: accountability, transparency, and open participation in decision-making (Sachs, 2015). Overall, the success of the SDG framework will rely on national policies, plans and programmes. However, the agenda's goals and targets will be monitored and reviewed using global indicators with a framework coordinated by the Inter-agency and Expert Group on SDG Indicators and agreed by the UN Statistical Commission.

The UN Conference on Trade and Development estimates implementation in developing countries will cost US$2.5 trillion per year in public and private money over the next 15 years (UNCTAD, 2014), amounting to roughly 4% of world GDP. The UN Environment Programme recently reported that the cost of adapting to climate change in developing countries could rise to between $280 billion and $500 billion per year by 2050 (UNEP, 2016). But failure to make substantial progress towards the SDGs would be much more costly.

EDUCATION WITHIN SUSTAINABLE DEVELOPMENT

The 2030 Agenda unites global development goals in one framework. SDG 4 succeeds the MDG and EFA priorities for education. At the World Education Forum in Incheon, Republic of Korea, in May 2015, representatives of the global education community signed the Incheon Declaration, embracing the proposed SDG 4 as the single universal education goal, which commits countries to '[e]nsure inclusive and equitable quality education and promote lifelong learning opportunities for all' (**Box 0.3**). SDG 4 and its targets advance a model where learning, in all its shapes and forms, has the power to influence people's choices to create more just, inclusive and sustainable societies. To advance progress towards SDG4 and its targets, the global education community adopted the Education 2030 Framework for Action in Paris in November 2015 (UNESCO, 2015a).

Education within the sustainable development agenda is founded on principles drawn from a rich history of international instruments and agreements

---

BOX 0.3

SDG 4: the education goal and targets

Goal 4: Ensure inclusive and equitable quality education and promote lifelong learning opportunities for all

- **Target 4.1:** By 2030, ensure that all girls and boys complete free, equitable and quality primary and secondary education leading to relevant and effective learning outcomes

- **Target 4.2:** By 2030, ensure that all girls and boys have access to quality early childhood development, care and pre-primary education so that they are ready for primary education

- **Target 4.3:** By 2030, ensure equal access for all women and men to affordable and quality technical, vocational and tertiary education, including university

- **Target 4.4:** By 2030, substantially increase the number of youth and adults who have relevant skills, including technical and vocational skills, for employment, decent jobs and entrepreneurship

- **Target 4.5:** By 2030, eliminate gender disparities in education and ensure equal access to all levels of education and vocational training for the vulnerable, including persons with disabilities, indigenous peoples and children in vulnerable situations

- **Target 4.6:** By 2030, ensure that all youth and a substantial proportion of adults, both men and women, achieve literacy and numeracy

- **Target 4.7:** By 2030, ensure that all learners acquire the knowledge and skills needed to promote sustainable development, including, among others, through education for sustainable development and sustainable lifestyles, human rights, gender equality, promotion of a culture of peace and non-violence, global citizenship and appreciation of cultural diversity and of culture's contribution to sustainable development

- **Target 4.a:** Build and upgrade education facilities that are child, disability and gender sensitive and provide safe, non-violent, inclusive and effective learning environments for all

- **Target 4.b:** By 2020, substantially expand globally the number of scholarships available to developing countries, in particular least developed countries, small island developing States and African countries, for enrolment in higher education, including vocational training and information and communications technology, technical, engineering and scientific programmes, in developed countries and other developing countries

- **Target 4.c:** By 2030, substantially increase the supply of qualified teachers, including through international cooperation for teacher training in developing countries, especially least developed countries and small island developing States

(**Box 0.4**). These principles state that education is both a fundamental human right and an enabling right, i.e. it enables other human rights; that it is a public good and a shared societal endeavour, which implies an inclusive process of public policy formulation and implementation; and that gender equality is inextricably linked to the right to education for all (UNESCO, 2015a). These principles are inspired by a humanistic vision of education and development based on human rights and dignity, justice and shared responsibility.

BOX 0.4

Historical international agreements that affirm the right to education

- Article 26 of the Universal Declaration of Human Rights (1948)
- Convention relating to the Status of Refugees (1951)
- International Covenant on Economic, Social and Cultural Rights (1960)
- Convention against Discrimination in Education (1960)
- Convention on the Elimination of All Forms of Discrimination against Women (1979)
- Convention on the Rights of the Child (1989)
- UN Convention on the Rights of Persons with Disabilities (2006)
- UN General Assembly Resolution on the Right to Education in Emergency Situations (2010)

Source: UNESCO (2015a).

WHAT IS LIFELONG LEARNING?

One focus of SDG 4 is 'lifelong learning opportunities for all'. Lifelong learning comprises all learning activities undertaken throughout life with the aim of improving knowledge, skills and competencies, within personal, civic, social and employment-related perspectives (UIL, 2015). Lifelong learning has often been more narrowly associated with adult education, especially training to help adults compensate for poor quality schooling (UNESCO, 2000).

The post-2015 development agenda conceives of lifelong learning as a process, one that begins at birth and carries through all stages of life (**Figure 0.1**). This approach to education incorporates multiple and flexible learning pathways, entry and re-entry points at all ages, and strengthened links between formal and

FIGURE 0.1:
Lifelong learning opportunities for all

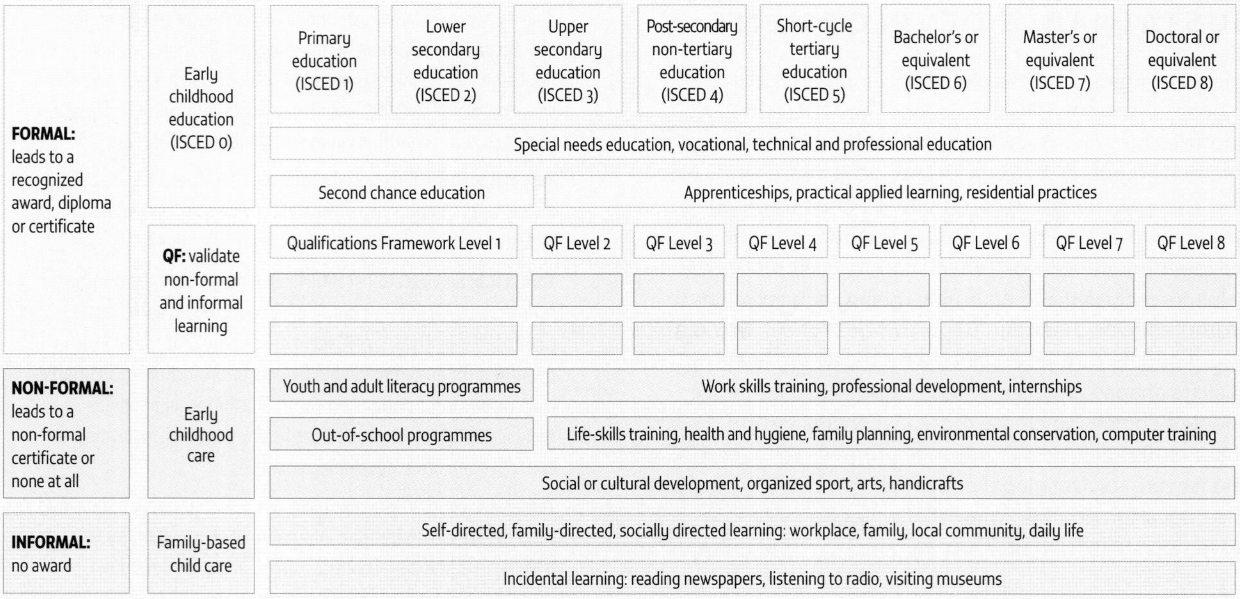

Source: GEM Report team.

> **Lifelong learning is a process, one that begins at birth and carries through all stages of life**

non-formal structures, including formal accreditation of the knowledge, skills and competencies acquired through non-formal and informal education.

Formal education occurs in institutions designed to provide full-time education for students in a system organized as a continuous educational pathway, from pre-primary and primary education to secondary and higher education. International education policy has historically focused on efforts to ensure the provision of universal primary education and reduce the numbers of out-of-school children. Non-formal education and training occur in planned learning settings but outside the formal system. Non-formal learning activities are often job-related but also provide training in life skills and other types of self-development. Both formal and non-formal education take place through organized programmes offered at schools, centres, associations or workplaces. Informal education takes place outside organized programmes and encompasses everyday activities such as reading a newspaper or visiting a museum. This kind of learning also includes intergenerational knowledge and skills passed through families and community members (UNESCO and UIS 2012).

SDG 4 is specific about the kind of education needed: inclusive, equitable and of good quality. The lesson that has emerged over the past 15 years is that progress in education cannot rest solely on increasing enrolment. About 38% of children old enough to have finished primary school have not learned the most basic skills they need to succeed in life (UNESCO, 2014a). Education of good quality cultivates the flexible skills and competencies that prepare learners for diverse challenges. The focus on quality ensures that foundation skills – literacy and numeracy – foster additional higher order thinking, creativity, problem solving, and social and emotional skills.

Local context and diversity shape both challenges and solutions. Rather than pushing individuals into a one-size-fits-all programme, a lifelong learning approach incorporates diversity into an inclusive, equitable system. Education for sustainability reaches out to serve marginalized communities by using all types of education, matching learning to context.

While it is a great global accomplishment that 91% of children are enrolled in school, reaching the last 9% requires different strategies. The children most likely to be out of school are those from the poorest households, ethnic and linguistic minorities, working children, those in nomadic or sparsely populated areas, orphans and children affected by HIV and AIDS, slum dwellers, children with disabilities, children displaced by conflict and those living in complex emergencies (UNESCO, 2015b). These groups have particular needs and require unique and flexible solutions.

Successful programmes for the marginalized are based on locally relevant solutions that foster social inclusion. For example, nomadic and pastoralist groups face challenges getting the basic education they deserve because their mobile lifestyles conflict with typical schooling formats. In addition, changes in weather, storms, droughts and conflicts decrease nomadic children's chances of staying in school. Governments and civil society have been challenged to understand first who these missing learners are and then what is exceptional about their nomadic livelihoods. Since 2000, nomad-specific education plans have emerged in Ethiopia, Nigeria, Sudan and the United Republic of Tanzania (UNESCO, 2015b). These programmes not only help targeted communities but also provide innovative examples for mainstream schools.

Lifelong learning is more than a longitudinal description of an education system that runs from cradle to retirement and beyond; it is an organizing principle, intended to improve people's quality of life.

EDUCATION IS INTERLINKED WITH OTHER SDGS

The SDGs, targets and means of implementation are thought of as universal, indivisible and interlinked. Each of the 17 goals has a set of targets. In each set, at least one target involves learning, training, educating or at the very least raising awareness of core sustainable development issues. Education has long been recognized as a critical factor in addressing environmental and sustainability issues and ensuring human well-being (**Table 0.1**).

The 2013/14 *EFA Global Monitoring Report* (GMR) analysed interdependencies and connections between education and other development goals. There is strong evidence of the importance of education and learning in supporting social change, as well as the role of education as a cross-cutting means of advancing the 2030 Agenda. Increased

TABLE 0.1:
How education is typically linked with other Sustainable Development Goals

Goal 1	Education is critical to lifting people out of poverty.	Goal 10	Where equally accessible, education makes a proven difference to social and economic inequality.
Goal 2	Education plays a key role in helping people move towards more sustainable farming methods, and in understanding nutrition.	Goal 11	Education can give people the skills to participate in shaping and maintaining more sustainable cities, and to achieve resilience in disaster situations.
Goal 3	Education can make a critical difference to a range of health issues, including early mortality, reproductive health, spread of disease, healthy lifestyles and well-being.	Goal 12	Education can make a critical difference to production patterns (e.g. with regard to the circular economy) and to consumer understanding of more sustainably produced goods and prevention of waste.
Goal 5	Education for women and girls is particularly important to achieve basic literacy, improve participative skills and abilities, and improve life chances.	Goal 13	Education is key to mass understanding of the impact of climate change and to adaptation and mitigation, particularly at the local level.
Goal 6	Education and training increase skills and the capacity to use natural resources more sustainably and can promote hygiene.	Goal 14	Education is important in developing awareness of the marine environment and building proactive consensus regarding wise and sustainable use.
Goal 7	Educational programmes, particularly non-formal and informal, can promote better energy conservation and uptake of renewable energy sources.	Goal 15	Education and training increase skills and capacity to underpin sustainable livelihoods and to conserve natural resources and biodiversity, particularly in threatened environments.
Goal 8	There is a direct link among such areas as economic vitality, entrepreneurship, job market skills and levels of education.	Goal 16	Social learning is vital to facilitate and ensure participative, inclusive and just societies, as well as social coherence.
Goal 9	Education is necessary to develop the skills required to build more resilient infrastructure and more sustainable industrialization.	Goal 17	Lifelong learning builds capacity to understand and promote sustainable development policies and practices.

Source: ICSU and ISSC (2015).

> Increased educational attainment helps transform lives by reducing poverty, improving health outcomes, advancing technology and increasing social cohesion

educational attainment helps transform lives by reducing poverty, improving health outcomes, advancing technology and increasing social cohesion (UNESCO, 2013, 2014b). It can also enable individuals to better cope with, and reduce their vulnerability to, the dangers associated with climate change.

Education is associated with increased environmental awareness, concern and, in some contexts, action. Across the 57 countries participating in the 2006 Programme for International Student Assessment (PISA) of the Organisation for Economic Co-operation and Development (OECD), students who scored higher in environmental science reported higher awareness of complex environmental issues. The more years of schooling, the more a person's concern for environmental protection increases, according to results from the World Values Surveys. Educated citizens with greater environmental awareness and concern are more likely to get involved in political action to protect the environment. Education also gives citizens skills needed to adapt to the adverse effects of climate change. Farmers in low income countries are especially vulnerable to climate change. A survey in Burkina Faso, Cameroon, Egypt, Ethiopia, Ghana, Kenya, Niger, Senegal, South Africa and Zambia showed that farmers with more education were more likely to build resilience through adaptation.

The links go both ways. Children living in poverty are more likely to have less education and less access to basic services. Access to clean water and improved sanitation is especially important for girls' education. It influences their education decisions and generates health gains, time savings and privacy. Sustainable consumption and production patterns, such as improvements to the physical environment, green government regulations and changes in consumer demand for greener products and services, increase interest in education for sustainable development. Tackling climate change is essential for overall progress on the SDGs, including SDG 4. SDG 13 aims to promote urgent action to combat climate change and its impact; sustainable development cannot be achieved without this.

The reciprocal ties between education and many SDGs have not been the focus of sustained research. A review of 40 flagship evidence-based UN reports found relatively weak coverage of links between education and SDGs 12 to 15, which address sustainable consumption and production, climate change, oceans and marine resources, and terrestrial ecosystems (Vladimirova and Le Blanc, 2015). Similarly, the evidence base on constraints and challenges to synergies between SDGs tends to be limited or non-existent. This clear gap in knowledge must be addressed: not only the nexus of links between development sectors, but also any unintended adverse effects between them, should be better understood.

WHAT KIND OF EDUCATION IS NECESSARY?

It is taken for granted that education of good quality can help develop citizens who are capable and mindful, which in turn improves their livelihoods and those of others around them. But the Incheon Declaration makes clear that certain knowledge and skills promote sustainable development more than others. Not all education brings the same benefits to everyone. Time, place, situation and context matter (Harber, 2014).

> **Not all education brings the same benefits to everyone. Time, place, situation and context matter**

Some scholars suggest that education systems that focus on preparing young people for a lifetime of work and consumption to serve mainly economic ends have adverse effects (Nussbaum, 2010; Orr, 1994). They argue that without critical reflection on the strengths, weaknesses and ultimate purpose of learning, education systems risk becoming an extension of an unsustainable globalizing economy. This concern is powerfully expressed by John Evans, General Secretary of the Trade Union Advisory Committee to the OECD (2015): 'There are no jobs on a dead planet.'

Education and lifelong learning can support the SDGs with at least two approaches. The first tends to focus on literacy acquisition and retention or on specific knowledge to generate behavioural change, showing that education can facilitate changes in values, world views and behaviour at the level of the individual, the community and society as a whole. This works particularly well when agreement exists on common values and the best and most desirable behaviours, e.g. the idea that reducing food waste and energy consumption is important for sustainability and that people can reduce food waste and conserve energy at home.

The second approach focuses on the development of agency, competencies and participation, showing that education can facilitate reflective or critical learning, knowledge and skills acquisition, and greater agency to address complex sustainability issues, e.g. how to create a sustainable school or a carbon-neutral city. This is particularly important where uncertainty exists over what needs to be done or when context-specific solutions need to be identified through collaborative and iterative processes. Both education approaches are complementary for engendering critical learning and sustainability outcomes (**Table 0.2**).

The transformation needed for a cleaner, greener planet requires integrative, innovative and creative thinking, cultivated jointly by schools, governments, civil society organizations and companies. This collaboration calls for education that goes beyond the transfer of knowledge and desirable behaviours by focusing on multiple perspectives – economic, ecological, environmental and sociocultural – and by developing empowered, critical, mindful and competent citizens. Such education can contribute to the realization of new forms of citizenship, entrepreneurship and governance that centre on the current and future well-being of people and the planet.

TABLE 0.2:
Learning outcomes in education for sustainability

Dimension of sustainability education	Associated learning outcomes
Learning to know Dynamics and content of sustainability	Sustainability literacy Systems thinking An integral view Understanding of planetary boundaries
Learning to critique Critical dimension of sustainability	Questioning of hegemony and routines Analysis of normativity Disruptiveness, transgression
Learning to bring about change Change and innovation dimension of sustainability	Leadership and entrepreneurship Unlocking of creativity, use of diversity Appreciation of complexity Adaptation, resilience Empowerment and collective change
Learning to be, learning to care Existential and normative dimension of sustainability	Connection with people, places and other species Passion, values and meaning-making Moral positioning, consideration of ethics, boundaries and limits

Source: Wals and Lenglet (2016).

> "
> The Incheon Declaration affirmed the mandate of the
> GEM Report as the mechanism for monitoring and reporting
> on SDG 4 and on education in the other SDGs
> "

READER'S GUIDE TO THE REPORT

In the Incheon Declaration, the international education community affirmed the mandate of the *Global Education Monitoring Report* (GEM Report) as an independent, authoritative report, hosted and published by UNESCO, to serve as 'the mechanism for monitoring and reporting on ... SDG 4 and on education in the other SDGs, within the mechanism to be established to monitor and review the implementation of the proposed SDGs' (UNESCO, 2015b). Relying on 14 years of monitoring experience as the GMR, the renamed GEM Report will continue to provide reliable, rigorous analysis of global progress on the education agenda through systematic and evidence-based reporting.

The 2016 GEM Report, the first of a new 15 year series, shows that education will not deliver its full potential to catapult the world forward unless rates of improvement dramatically shift, and education systems consider sustainable development in the way services are delivered.

Commissioned research for this report shows that, for 90% of industrialized countries, and for every single country in Southern Asia and sub-Saharan Africa, even expanding their education systems at the fastest rates ever observed in the regions would be too slow to meet the first target in the global goal on education, SDG 4.

Yet it also shows how crucial it is for education systems to expand at the rate reflected in the ambition of the 2030 Agenda. If the world were somehow to achieve universal upper secondary completion by 2030, income per capita would likely increase by 75% until 2050, and bring achievement of the goal of poverty elimination forward 10 years. Similarly, under-5 mortality rates in sub-Saharan Africa would drop by 13 deaths for every 1000 live births by 2050, and there would be globally up to 50,000 fewer disaster-related deaths per year.

In the thematic part of this report (Chapters 1-8), compelling arguments are given for the types of education that are vital for achieving the goals of poverty reduction, hunger eradication, improved health, gender equality and empowerment, sustainable agriculture, resilient cities, and more equal, inclusive and just societies. They highlight the evidence, practices and policies that demonstrate how education – broadly defined to include formal, non-formal and informal learning – can serve as a catalyst for the overall sustainable development agenda. At the same time, they recognize how other development challenges and success affect education systems and outcomes.

The many challenges concerning how to assess progress towards SDG 4 are tackled in the monitoring part (Chapters 9–23), including concrete recommendations for policy change in coming years. The report seeks to contribute to discussions of how best to respond to the proposed global education monitoring framework in a way that supports countries and their international partners.

This GEM Report is timed to contribute to the initial building blocks of the sustainable development agenda. Its findings show that equitable, good quality education and lifelong learning are vital to securing sustainable futures for all. How and what people learn not only influences their knowledge, skills, attitudes and world views, but also their respect for each other, along with investment and research choices that affect coming generations. The way education evolves over the next 15 years will have a tremendous impact on whether the world can achieve the ambitious vision of the international community of nations. It is necessary to think critically about education systems so they do not encourage unsustainable lifestyles but rather build resilient communities and enable individuals to become agents of change, working cooperatively to address the great challenges of this era. Humans must imagine, think and act differently in order to mitigate climate change and achieve sustainable development – and education is vital to that.

> " To achieve the SDGs, it is necessary to break down silos and build cross-sector collaboration that contributes to a shared vision "

Since 2000, experience has shown that only through a combined effort can humanity tackle the challenges facing it and the planet. To achieve the SDGs, it is necessary to break down silos and build cross-sector collaboration that contributes to a shared vision. Leaders in every area – from health, education and justice to environment, gender and urban development – must work together to create equitable policies and seek out synergies in order to ensure a decent and dignified life for all.

THEMATIC PART

The thematic part of the GEM Report discusses reciprocal ties between SDG 4 on education and the other 16 SDGs. It reviews education-oriented evidence, practices and policies that demonstrate education's role in achieving the overall 2030 Agenda for Sustainable Development. At the same time, it recognizes that changing realities in other development sectors affect education systems and outcomes.

The thematic part is made up of eight chapters. Six investigate the fundamental pillars and essential concepts of sustainable development – Planet, Prosperity, People, Peace, Place and Partnerships. The final thematic chapter, Projections, discusses how expected increases in educational attainment by 2030 will affect key development targets by 2050.

Planet focuses on the roles education can play in transforming society to move towards environmental sustainability. It discusses evidence on how education can develop the knowledge, skills and solutions to help increase concern for the environment, build awareness of climate change and other climate risks, and change individual behaviour to become more environment-friendly. It also acknowledges the importance of transforming education systems so that education helps foster sustainable lifestyles and rebalances the focus on individual economic and material gains. It addresses the need to encourage diverse perspectives so as to

achieve environmental sustainability – for instance, by learning from the knowledge and lifestyles of indigenous communities – and the need to educate and engage the private sector to achieve sustained transformation.

Prosperity explores the roles of education in fostering environmentally sustainable and economically inclusive development. It provides evidence on links between education and skills acquisition on the one hand, and long-term economic growth on the other. At the same time it discusses the importance of transforming economic processes to make them more environmentally sustainable through green industry and sustainable agricultural practices. The chapter examines the role of education in poverty and inequality reduction, making the case for closer integration of education, economic and employment policies to promote inclusion of all people in the economy.

People discusses inclusive social development as an aspiration to ensure that all women and men, girls and boys lead healthy, dignified and empowered lives. At a minimum, this implies that all people need access to essential basic services such as education, health, water, sanitation and energy. The chapter also focuses on the transformative social development needed to change social structures, institutions and relationships. It highlights the scale of the challenges in providing essential basic services to all, achieving gender equality and including diverse marginalized populations. It provides evidence on how education is important for female empowerment for positive outcomes in health, nutrition, sanitation and energy, and between generations. It also discusses how education as an institutional sector can improve the way other sectors function, such as through health-related interventions in schools. The education system is pivotal to inclusive social development, since education can equip people with knowledge, skills and values that can help improve social outcomes and change social norms. At the same time, ensuring inclusive social development requires recognizing the limits of education's role, understanding how other institutions and sectors affect education, and making sure there is integrated action between them.

Peace demonstrates the role of education in fostering peaceful, just and inclusive societies. It argues that stable peace is more likely in societies with democratic and representative institutions and a well-functioning justice system. Education has a key role in contributing to the participation and inclusion vital to ensure social cohesion and to prevent and mitigate societal tensions.

The chapter documents the links between education and politics, showing that education offers possibilities for participation, inclusion, advocacy and democracy. It also examines the multifaceted relationship between education and conflict and violence: if education is lacking, unequal or biased, it can contribute to conflict, but effective education can reduce or eliminate conflict. The chapter also shows how education can play a transformative role in peace-building and the alarming consequences of its neglect. In addition, it examines education and violence not related to conflict and wars, and provides evidence of how education initiatives, in particular driven by civil society organizations, can help marginalized populations gain access to justice.

Place highlights cities in discussing spatial dimensions of development, since urbanization is a defining population trend. It argues that cities are engines of knowledge-based innovation and growth. Conversely, education influences cities and is key to taking advantage of their physical and social capital. The chapter provides evidence that education can have positive effects, such as reducing crime, and be used in good urban planning, for example to encourage sustainable transport. At the same time, cities can be characterized by massive inequality, including in education, which can foster disillusionment, discontent and sometimes violence. Education needs to be viewed as a critical element of urban governance and planning arrangements to ensure that the opportunities of urbanization outweigh the challenges and result in more inclusive, environmentally sustainable and prosperous cities.

Partnerships describes how effective implementation of the SDGs requires integrated plans and actions. All government levels, sectors and types of national and international actors need to work together; they also require adequate financing and other enabling conditions (human capacity, effective institutions and political will) to meet the needs of the new agenda. These issues are addressed from the perspective of an education sector that must fulfil a much broader agenda – lifelong learning for all – and simultaneously work towards integration with other development agendas, given its instrumental role in other aspects of development. The chapter discusses the availability of domestic and external resources for education; concepts, evidence and implementation of integrated planning; and partnership arrangements.

Projections presents model-based scenarios for education attainment and describes education's role in attaining development targets. It projects likely scenarios for the increase in educational attainment between 2015 and 2030. Given that quantitative analysis usually views education as having longer-term intergenerational effects, it then projects how educational attainment by 2030 will affect key measurable development targets – infant and child mortality, adult life expectancy, economic growth, poverty rates and disaster-related deaths – by 2050.

MONITORING PART

The monitoring part of the 2016 GEM Report presents the wide-ranging challenges and debates involving monitoring for the Education 2030 agenda and how countries and the international community can move forward. It is organized into 15 chapters, including the introduction and conclusion.

The first 10 (Chapters 10–19) look separately at each of the 7 education targets and 3 means of implementation. They identify the concepts that are explicitly or implicitly embedded in the target formulation. Each chapter discusses how the concepts are articulated within the proposed global and thematic indicators. They focus primarily on the extent to which the methodology of the indicators is established, and on identifying tools currently available to collect relevant data. To the extent that methodology is established and information available for a sufficient number of countries, indicative baseline information is presented. Approaches for monitoring areas not yet covered by the proposed indicators are also discussed.

The monitoring part of the GEM Report tries not to be prescriptive but rather to make a timely contribution to the debate on what should be monitored and how. The state of global education monitoring is in flux. Many initiatives are under way to respond to the challenges of the proposed indicator frameworks. Given the time lag for information becoming available, it is still too early to provide baseline data for 2015 – or indeed definitive data for the end of the EFA period.

Chapters 20 to 22 address cross-cutting issues. Chapter 20 discusses education finance, for which there is no dedicated SDG target, though the Education 2030 Framework for Action gives a clear set of recommendations. Using a framework provided by national education accounts, the chapter discusses prospects for better data on public spending, aid and household expenditure. Chapter 21 reflects on the fact that some proposed indicators are about neither inputs nor outcomes but instead relate to growing interest in the role of education systems. It provides an overview of available mechanisms and the scope for better coordination, especially at the regional level. The short Chapter 22 looks at all targets under other SDG goals, as well as the corresponding global indicators, to identify those where education is mentioned directly or indirectly.

This comprehensive overview of the global education monitoring challenges offers insights, brings together disparate pieces of information and identifies stakeholders whose work needs recognition and coordination. Given that implementing such an agenda may be daunting and confusing, especially for countries, the GEM Report's monitoring part is meant to support countries and partners as they discuss and determine the best steps forward in achieving SDG 4. Chapter 23 draws attention to common themes and missing pieces in this discussion – and identifies building blocks and potential synergies for a more effective and efficient global education monitoring agenda over the next 15 years at the national, regional and international levels.

OVERALL CONCLUSION

To conclude, Chapter 24 reflects on the 2030 Agenda for Sustainable Development as a whole and the critical importance of follow-up and review processes. The 2030 Agenda sets out an ambitious collective vision for people and planet that requires political will, resources and collaboration. Thematic reports, such as the GEM Report, serve as a bridge between global dialogue and national initiatives, contributing not only to one sector but to broader efforts to identify effective policies that reduce poverty, improve health and create more inclusive, just and sustainable communities.

Here students in Indonesia learn about the animals and plants near the beach. The activity is designed to encourage the students to be more environment friendly.

CREDIT: Nur'aini Yuwanita Wakan/UNESCO

Planet: environmental sustainability

We are determined to protect the planet from degradation, including through sustainable consumption and production, sustainably managing its natural resources and taking urgent action on climate change, so that it can support the needs of the present and future generations.

– The 2030 Agenda for Sustainable Development

KEY MESSAGES

Living sustainably requires a huge shift in mindset.
Education has to be part of that change.

1   **Education can help people understand and respond to environmental issues.**
   a. It helps develop the right knowledge, skills and technical solutions that can change environmental behaviour.
   b. Education is clearly shown to be the best tool for climate change awareness.
   c. Education is the most effective means of curtailing population growth.
   d. Education improves disaster preparedness and reduces vulnerability to climate-related disasters.
   e. Green schools, well-designed curricula and hands-on learning outside of school can strengthen people's connection with nature.

2   **Outside of school, we must learn through communities and throughout our lives.**
   a. Learning among communities encourages people to reflect on their values, and participate more actively in shifts towards sustainable living.
   b. Traditional – and specifically indigenous – knowledge, passed down through the generations, is a major resource for adapting to climate change.
   c. Providing instruction in local languages in school helps knowledge be shared among generations and communities outside school.

3   **Education systems must be careful not to encourage unsustainable lifestyles.**
   a. Learning for economic growth alone will not bring sustainable solutions.
   b. Education systems and curricula must reflect the critical basis of indigenous communities' knowledge, which rests on deep intercultural respect, along with openness to plurality of knowledge systems and cultures.

4   **Schools need to take a holistic approach to tackling environmental challenges.**
   a. Both teachers and students need to learn about climate change and its underlying causes.
   b. Pedagogy needs to encourage collaboration and participation.
   c. Schools need to engage with their surrounding communities.
   d. Green operations and facilities need to be built.

5   **The private sector must encourage lifelong learning to fight climate change.**
   a. Efforts could include workplace learning, joining in multistakeholder partnerships to develop environmental solutions, reducing companies' ecological footprint, and funding greener schools.

A conclusive body of evidence built since the 1972 UN Conference on the Human Environment shows that the actions and habits of a single species, *Homo sapiens*, are leading to the planet's unprecedented dysfunction. An increasing part of the world's population lives beyond the ecological limits set by earth's finite natural resources and support systems.

Since human behaviour is clearly the problem, people are responsible for solutions to these planetary challenges. The 2030 Agenda for Sustainable Development emphasizes environmental sustainability issues, the need to transform consumption and production to restore balance to life on land and in water, and the need for urgent action on climate change. Furthermore, environmental sustainability is clearly intertwined with social and economic sustainability, as the challenges surrounding equitable and sustainable use of natural resources affect people's ability to lead peaceful, stable, prosperous and healthy lives.

The relationship between human development and environmental impact is not straightforward. On the one hand, people living in wealthy countries with higher levels of education are more likely to lead lifestyles that leave a harmful footprint on global ecosystems – from increased food waste to higher levels of carbon dioxide from car and airplane use. On the other hand, increases in environmental education and ecological literacy help people change their personal attitudes and behaviour in everyday ways such as recycling, reducing litter and conserving energy, as well as on issues including water sanitation and public health. This means some, if not most, kinds of education are effective tools in the fight towards environmental and planetary health.

This chapter outlines pressing environmental challenges and the kinds of policies proposed to move towards environmental sustainability. It explores various ways of understanding responsibility for the human behaviour that has contributed to the looming crisis, then turns to ways in which education and learning can contribute to solutions. Finally, it explores how integrated approaches to lifelong learning can help address climate change.

GLOBAL ENVIRONMENTAL CHALLENGES ARE PRESSING

Many climate scientists believe Earth has entered a new geological era, the Anthropocene, where human activities are undermining the planet's capacity to regulate itself. Until the Industrial Revolution in the late 1700s, global environmental changes were not strongly linked to human actions. They were essentially the product of slow-occurring natural causes, such as variations in the sun's energy or volcanic eruptions. But since the start of modern manufacturing, while humans have benefited from increased trade, economic growth and longer, healthier lives, the natural world has suffered environmental deterioration (UNEP, 2012).

The scale and pace of biodiversity loss, land degradation, stratospheric ozone depletion and climate change are attributable to human activities. Humans are responsible for the massive release of carbon dioxide and other heat-trapping gases into the atmosphere. Human behaviour has caused irreversible damage to some plant and animal species. The variety of vertebrates (mammals, birds, reptiles, amphibians and fish) has declined by 52% since 1970 (McLellan et al., 2014). The largest extinction is happening among freshwater species, mostly due to habitat loss and extensive hunting and fishing.

Experts developed the concept of planetary boundaries as a useful way to describe and measure the environmental limits within which humanity and other living organisms on the planet can safely operate (Rockström et al., 2009). Nine planetary boundaries are monitored via indicators for climate change, biodiversity loss, nitrogen and phosphorus pollution, stratospheric ozone depletion, ocean acidification, global freshwater consumption, change in agricultural land use, air pollution and chemical pollution. Six of the indicators have increased significantly since the pre-industrial era; five have remained at or entered high risk zones (**Figure 1.1**). Since all planetary boundaries are closely linked, these trends indicate a threat to the earth's land, water and atmosphere (Steffen et al., 2015).

HUMAN BEHAVIOUR HAS LED TO ENVIRONMENTAL CRISES

While the general consensus is that humans are responsible for global environmental crises, views differ as to the human-related factors most responsible. Experts have identified interrelated ways in which people are pushing planetary boundaries, each associated with a distinct set of policy options and solutions. This section reviews three of the most common explanations: overpopulation, modern lifestyles and individual behaviour.

The demographic problem

This idea proposes that there are simply too many people on the planet. More people use more natural resources, pushing planetary boundaries into risk zones. The global population tripled between 1950 and 2015 (United Nations, 2015), mainly due to improvement in public health, and is expected to grow by another billion to 8.5 billion in 2030. The population is not

> " The global population tripled between 1950 and 2015 "

FIGURE 1.1:
Global environmental health faces critical thresholds on several fronts
Nine planetary systems, pre-industrial and current levels

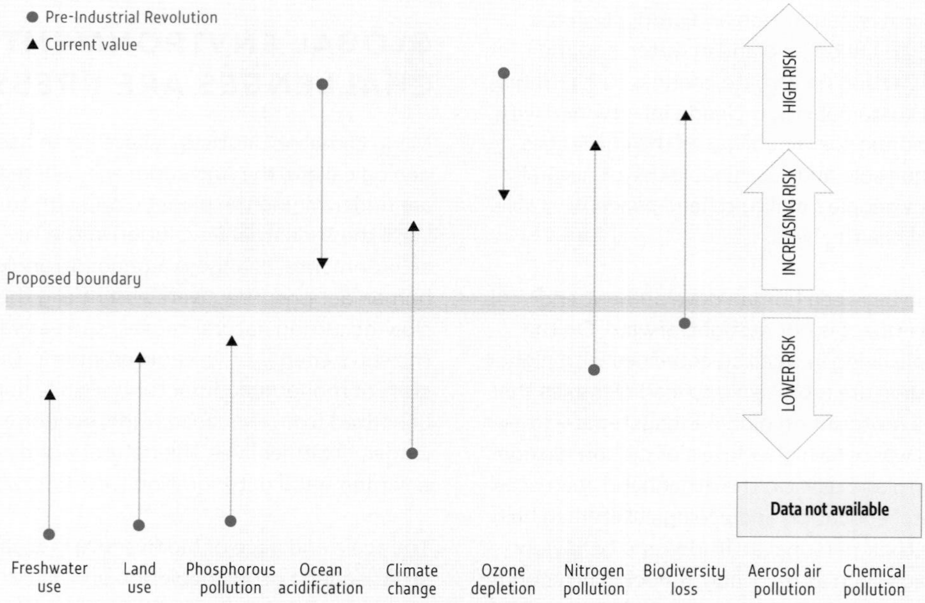

- ● Pre-Industrial Revolution
- ▲ Current value

HIGH RISK
INCREASING RISK
LOWER RISK

Proposed boundary

Data not available

Freshwater use | Land use | Phosphorous pollution | Ocean acidification | Climate change | Ozone depletion | Nitrogen pollution | Biodiversity loss | Aerosol air pollution | Chemical pollution

Note: One of the nine planetary systems, pollution, has two metrics, one for phosphorous pollution and the other for nitrogen pollution. This results in a total of 10 system metrics shown in Figure 1.1.
Source: GEM Report team analysis (2016) of data from Steffen et al. (2011).

TABLE 1.1:
Population growth is slowing but will remain a challenge in lower income countries
Total population and percentage change, 2000 to 2030 (projected)

	Total population (millions)			Change 2000–2015	Change 2015–2030
	2000	**2015**	**2030**	**%**	**%**
World	6 127	7 349	8 501	20	16
Low income	426	639	924	50	45
Lower middle income	2 305	2 916	3 532	27	21
Upper middle income	2 113	2 390	2 567	13	7
High income	1 254	1 373	1 447	10	5
Eastern and South-eastern Asia	2 001	2 222	2 352	11	6
China	1 270	1 376	1 416	8	3
Indonesia	212	258	295	22	15
Southern Asia	1 452	1 823	2 147	26	18
India	1 053	1 311	1 528	24	17
Pakistan	138	189	245	37	30
Bangladesh	131	161	186	23	16
Europe and Northern America	1 041	1 097	1 131	5	3
United States	283	322	356	14	11
Russian Federation	146	143	139	-2	-3
Sub-Saharan Africa	641	961	1 306	50	36
Nigeria	123	182	263	48	44
Latin America and the Caribbean	522	629	716	21	14
Brazil	176	208	229	18	10
Mexico	103	127	148	24	17
Northern Africa and Western Asia	340	463	584	36	26
Caucasus and Central Asia	71	84	96	18	15
Pacific	30	38	46	27	21

Notes: Data for 2030 are projections based on a median prediction interval. Regions and countries are listed by descending order of population in 2015. The countries listed are the ten with the largest populations in 2015.
Source: United Nations (2015).

evenly distributed: Nearly three-fourths of the increase will take place in low and lower middle income countries, especially in sub-Saharan Africa and Southern Asia (**Table 1.1**).

Not only are there more people, but they are also on the move. Two kinds of migration put pressure on the relationship between population and resources: internal migration from rural to urban areas and international migration from poor to wealthy nations. By 2050, two out of three people on the planet will live in urban areas; a large portion of future urbanization will be caused by rural–urban migration (Buhaug and Urdal, 2013). It will take place mostly in countries and regions where urbanization may cause serious environmental problems in cities including water scarcity and contamination, land shortage, polluted air and insufficient sanitation.

Meanwhile, high income countries received an average of 4.1 million net migrants annually from poorer countries between 2000 and 2015 (United Nations, 2015), a trend expected to continue. People living in urban areas and wealthier countries consume more resources per

person (UNEP, 2012), so these trends will put more stress on environmental systems.

The modern lifestyles problem

This approach focuses on the fact that people in urban areas and wealthier countries choose lifestyles entailing less environment-friendly consumption patterns. Resource consumption can be measured through the ecological footprint indicator, a calculation of a country's use of land and water resources compared to the stock of those resources (Ewing et al., 2010).

In 2012, most high income countries had an unsustainable ecological footprint, except those with very low population density . Most middle income countries of Eastern and South-eastern Asia, Northern Africa and Western Asia, and Southern Asia also had a deficit, particularly China. In sub-Saharan Africa, countries with large populations or middle income levels had a deficit. The only region where most countries lived within their environmental means was Latin America, owing to its lower population density and large biocapacity. With some exceptions, available natural resources per capita declined rapidly over 2000–2015, so that even countries with natural reserves in 2012 are expected to start running a deficit during 2015–2030 (Ewing et al., 2010; Global Footprint Network, 2016).

There is a clear relationship between modern lifestyles and resource consumption. Countries that perform better on the Human Development Index, measured in terms of education, living standards and health, are much likelier to have a much larger ecological footprint (**Figure 1.2a**).

The countries with the largest ecological footprints are mostly in Europe and Northern America. Countries that have experienced rapid increases in education, health and living standards, including the Republic of Korea and Singapore, have seen their ecological footprint nearly double as domestic consumption has expanded. In contrast, countries with low levels of human development, mostly in sub-Saharan Africa, have smaller ecological footprints. For instance, the ecological

footprints of Eritrea and Timor-Leste are less than 5% the size of the largest footprints.

Countries struggle to find balance between human development and sustainable practices. Some, including Cuba, Georgia, the Republic of Moldova and Sri Lanka, have begun to find it, managing to keep production and consumption within sustainable bounds (**Figure 1.2b**). Their citizens have relatively good health prospects, with life expectancy between 68 and 79 years. People go to school for 10 to 12 years, well above the global average of 8 years. Yet, their per capita income is less than the global average, from US$5,200 a year in the Republic of Moldova to US$9,780 in Sri Lanka (UNDP, 2015b).

It should be noted that the condition of a country's local environment is not taken into account in comparisons of human development and ecological footprints. Resources are not distributed evenly among countries or even among regions within countries. As a result, it may be

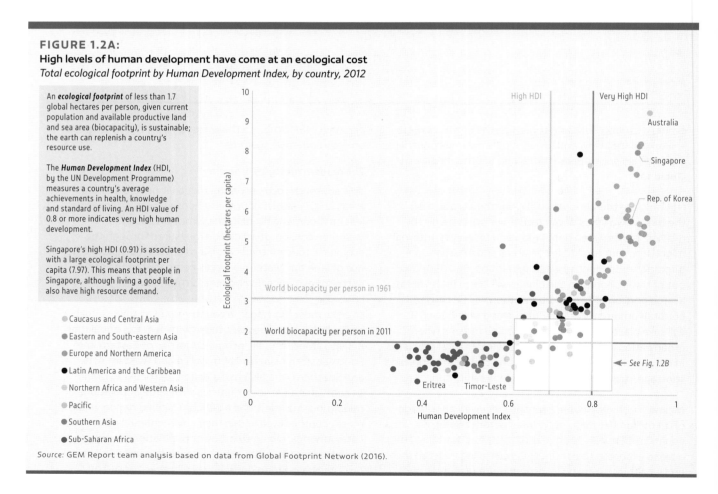

FIGURE 1.2A:

High levels of human development have come at an ecological cost

Total ecological footprint by Human Development Index, by country, 2012

An *ecological footprint* of less than 1.7 global hectares per person, given current population and available productive land and sea area (biocapacity), is sustainable; the earth can replenish a country's resource use.

The *Human Development Index* (HDI, by the UN Development Programme) measures a country's average achievements in health, knowledge and standard of living. An HDI value of 0.8 or more indicates very high human development.

Singapore's high HDI (0.91) is associated with a large ecological footprint per capita (7.97). This means that people in Singapore, although living a good life, also have high resource demand.

- Caucasus and Central Asia
- Eastern and South-eastern Asia
- Europe and Northern America
- Latin America and the Caribbean
- Northern Africa and Western Asia
- Pacific
- Southern Asia
- Sub-Saharan Africa

Source: GEM Report team analysis based on data from Global Footprint Network (2016).

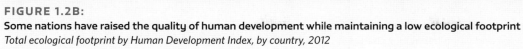

FIGURE 1.2B:

Some nations have raised the quality of human development while maintaining a low ecological footprint

Total ecological footprint by Human Development Index, by country, 2012

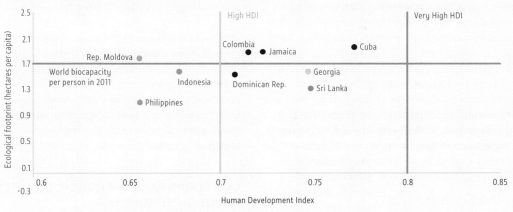

Source: GEM Report team analysis based on data from Global Footprint Network (2016).

easier for some countries, such as Colombia and Finland, to stay within the limits of their available resources than for others, such as Mongolia and Sudan.

The individual behaviour problem

A third explanation focuses on individuals as both the source of environmental problems and their solution. Yet, there is a mismatch between the scale of environmental problems, usually measured globally, and the scale of solutions, generally discussed at the individual or community level. While the impact of human behaviour on the environment can be seen on a large scale, it is necessary to analyse the individual level to see how this impact can be reversed through changes in personal behaviour. More careful analysis at the individual level can help identify factors that encourage or discourage particular types of behaviour.

Proponents of this approach believe large-scale change happens by targeting and influencing individual behaviour – getting individuals to buy fuel-efficient cars, insulate their homes and the like (Swim et al., 2011). Often, individual actions are interdependent. Adopting one type of environment-friendly behaviour can prompt adoption of others or deter negative behaviour, though it can also increase environmentally harmful behaviour (e.g. switching to hybrid cars may encourage people to drive more, offsetting emission reductions). Individual actions can also reflect social norms and cultural values. For example, in a European programme to increase the

use of carpool lanes, those who chose not to carpool often said they valued flexibility over reduced costs or emissions per person (van Vugt et al., 1996).

Because individual actions are interdependent and because they reflect social context, it is important to not only encourage behaviour change, but also provide people with the full set of knowledge, skills and attitudes they need to make comprehensive changes.

DIFFERENT PROBLEMS IMPLY DIFFERENT POLICY SOLUTIONS

The fact that experts emphasize different problems and come from varying perspectives affects their views on the solutions needed to resolve environmental crises.

Some believe technological innovations, such as renewable energy sources, sustainable infrastructure and cleaner production practices, are the answer. Others believe that since Western development trajectories have often caused environmental degradation, lower income countries need to find ways to avoid such paths while still improving quality of life. Those who believe population growth is the major driver of environmental challenges focus on ways to reduce fertility in poor countries, especially in sub-Saharan Africa.

There has also been a strong focus on making the problem an individual one, arguing that societies' success in responding to environmental challenges is based on how individuals act, separately and collectively. Proponents of this view believe that when individuals gain more knowledge and when behaviour change is in their self-interest, they start using their power as consumers and voters to support behaviour compatible with sustainable outcomes (Tietenberg and Lewis, 2012).

While differing perspectives on the problems lead to a range of proposed solutions, meeting the Sustainable Development Goals (SDGs) requires recognizing the need for cooperation and solidarity, despite contextual and ideological differences. All people in low and high income countries have to contribute in their own ways to ensure environmental sustainability for all. Changing the population pressure faced by the world requires significant emphasis on improving life chances and reducing inequality between and within countries. Changing how economies function, whether through technological innovation or using local solutions, requires commitment at the national level, with global and local actors also doing their share. The most important task is to recognize that revolutionary changes in lifestyle, not just incremental adjustments, are required (Senge et al., 2008).

> Meeting the SDGs means that all people in low and high income countries have to contribute in their own ways to ensure environmental sustainability for all

TO MEET THESE CHALLENGES, LEARNING IS ESSENTIAL

Education has a key role to play in addressing environmental challenges, whether their cause is believed to be economic or demographic, or global, national or individual actions. Education can be used to mitigate specific environmental issues and respond to their impact, but also to address the behaviour that causes them.

For example, education, especially of girls and women, is the single most effective means of curtailing population growth, by increasing people's autonomy over fertility-related decisions and delaying pregnancy (see Chapter 3). And education not only improves livelihoods by increasing earnings, but also produces the literate and skilled workers who are essential to ensure the technological transformation of economies and food systems (see Chapter 2).

This section discusses the ways in which education can influence individual and collective environmental behaviour through contemporary, traditional and lifelong approaches to learning: formal education, learning within communities, media and public awareness campaigns, and leadership in a wide range of sectors. Also shown is the need to learn from traditional knowledge systems and local communities.

CONTEMPORARY APPROACH: LEARNING THROUGH SCHOOLING

The primary contemporary approach to addressing environmental challenges via education is through formal schooling. Education helps students understand an environmental problem, its consequences and the types of action required to address it. With improved environmental and ecological literacy, students are more inclined to change behaviour affecting environmental issues. Examples include school-led awareness-raising campaigns and programmes on recycling, minimizing litter, conserving energy and improving water, sanitation and public health. Environmentally literate students are better equipped to see the links between specific issues and global environmental change. Formal education supplies the knowledge, vocabulary and key concepts required for environmental literacy, as well as the historical and philosophical background.

Three main types of relevant education programmes have been identified since the 19th century – nature conservation education, environmental education, and education for sustainable development – each pointing to the connection between humans and the planet (Wals, 2012). Each type is associated with a distinct period and focal area – connecting and reconnecting people with nature, developing ecological literacy to change environmental behaviour and lifestyles, and now capacity-building for sustainable development and global citizenship (**Table 1.2**). The trend shows increased awareness of the direct links between the environment, lifestyle and livelihoods, and a shift towards incorporating environmental education into the formal school curricula through education for sustainable development.

TABLE 1.2:
Environmental education has evolved over the years

Three types of contemporary environmental education

	Nature conservation education	Environmental education	Sustainability education
Starting period	Late 19th century	Late 1960s, early 1970s	Early 1990s
Main focus	Connecting with nature, understanding web of life, protecting species, raising awareness, knowledge and understanding	Raising environmental awareness about pollution of water, soil and air	Increasing citizen engagement, participation in sustainable development issues and increasing understanding of connections between environment, economy, culture and ecology, and how today's actions affect future generations
Intended impact	Ecological literacy, societal support base for nature conservation through national parks	Changing individual environmental behaviour, developing agency and societal support for environmental legislation	A more holistic or integrated approach of dealing with issues around water, food, energy, poverty and biodiversity, in governance, education and business
Examples	Visitor centres in national parks, public awareness campaigns, nature programmes in schools, school gardening	Environmental education centres in cities, public awareness campaigns, school curricula, teacher training	Multistakeholder platforms focusing on sustainable development issues, whole school approaches to sustainability, corporate social responsibility

Source: Wals (2012).

A *Global Education Monitoring Report* (GEM Report) analysis of 78 national curricula shows that topics associated with sustainable development are widespread – although sometimes framed and defined differently depending on the country – and generally draw on similar types of content: 73% of countries mention 'sustainable development', 55% use the term 'ecology' and 47% 'environmental education' in their curricula. These concepts are embedded in various parts of the curricula.

Some countries have prioritized environmental education programmes. In India, for example, environmental education was mandated by the Supreme Court in 1991, and in 2003 the government directed the National Council of Educational Research and Training to produce extensive content on environmental education (Centre for Environmental Education, 2015). As a result, over 300 million school students in the 1.3 million schools currently receive some environmental education training (Gardiner, 2015).

Evidence shows that curricular design affects student knowledge. In the 2006 Organisation for Economic Co-operation and Development (OECD) Programme for International Student Assessment (PISA) test of 'science competencies for tomorrow's world', students in Estonia and Sweden – where sustainable development content is in the curricula – were more likely to answer questions about environmental science correctly than their peers in countries at similar development levels (see Chapter 16).

In 62% of 119 countries covered by the Gallup World Poll conducted in 2007 and 2008, education level and beliefs about the cause of climate change were often the top predictors of climate change awareness and risk perception (Lee et al., 2015). People with more schooling were better able to identify various environmental issues in 70 out of 119 countries. People with access to communication tools were also more aware, demonstrating the growing importance of information and communications technology in environmental education.

Schooling improves sustainability-related knowledge, skills and attitudes

Education not only increases knowledge and awareness but also improves skills and enables individuals to make better, more environmentally informed decisions.

> **In 31 countries, more education increases the chance that people will express concern for the environment**

Evidence from the 2010 International Social Survey Programme (ISSP) on 31 mostly high income countries shows that each step on the education ladder, from primary to lower secondary, upper secondary and tertiary education, increases the chance that people will express concern for the environment, even after taking into account factors such as wealth, individual characteristics and political affiliation (Franzen and Vogl, 2013).

People with more education are also more likely to follow up environmental concern with activism to promote and support political decisions that protect the environment. Analysis of the 2010 ISSP finds that in almost all participating countries, respondents with more education were more likely to have signed a petition, given more money or taken part in a protest or demonstration in relation to the environment over the previous five years. In the Republic of Korea, one of the countries with the highest emission levels, the influence of education is apparent: 19% of respondents with secondary education had taken such political action, but 30% of those with tertiary education had done so (Clery and Rhead, 2013).

Schooling also teaches values, helping students develop a sense of place, reconnect with nature and build agency and competencies. Place-based experiences such as school garden programmes can build an emotional connection with both the urban and the natural world (Anderson, 2013; Gruenewald and Smith, 2008; Theimer and Ernst, 2012). Direct contact with the land and the living environment, and tangible exposure to the relation between humanity and nature in terms of impact and interdependency, have been key to programmes' success (Mackenzie et al., 2014; Rickinson et al., 2004). In India the concept of "handprint" was developed to emphasize positive actions in support of sustainability, in contrast to traditional environmental discussions on global footprints. The Paryavaran Mitra programme, launched in 2010, builds on this concept by promoting the value of a learning by doing. It developed a network of young 'friends of the environment' and currently reaches over 220,000 schools as well as government and civil society partners (Centre for Environmental Education, 2015).

In younger age groups, overemphasis on awareness of global issues can overshadow teaching of knowledge and skills needed to respond to and engage with local environmental issues and to maximize personal impact. PISA 2006 found that while students in OECD countries had a high sense of personal and social responsibility on environmental issues, they were not optimistic – only 13% to 21% believed the overall situation would improve in the next 20 years (OECD, 2009). As environmental problems can easily lead to feelings of apathy and powerlessness, it is critical for education to develop students' agency, environmental problem-solving abilities and competencies to bring about real change in their own community and everyday lives (Anderson, 2013).

Finally, studies show that engagement in out-of-school environmental activities strengthens in-class performance. The 2009 International Civics and Citizen Survey reported that two-thirds of students in 38 countries had participated in out-of-school civic activities (Schulz et al., 2010). Environmental

organizations were the most common, involving about 30% of students – and more than 50% in Colombia, the Dominican Republic, Guatemala, Indonesia and Thailand. In the Republic of Korea, students who studied and tackled real-life environmental issues tended to perform well upon entering university. And as the place of learning was shifted out of school, beneficial partnerships were created between environmental organizations and school education (UNESCO, 2014).

Leading by example: whole schools

As students spend significant time in the classroom, schools and universities are increasingly called upon to act as role models for sustainable development. The education sector can set an example in environmental stewardship. The 'whole school' approach to environmental education incorporates all aspects of a school: curriculum, extracurricular activities, teacher training, human resources and infrastructure operations and processes (Mcmillin and Dyball, 2009). The UNESCO International Bureau of Education describes the 'whole school' approach as 'addressing the needs of learners, staff and the wider community, not only within the curriculum, but across the whole-school and learning environment' and says it 'implies collective and collaborative action in and by a school community to improve student learning, behaviour and wellbeing and the conditions that support these (UNESCO-IBE, 2013).'

Aiming to make schools safe, climate-compatible and sustainable, this approach encourages institutions to change buildings, grounds and school schedules accordingly, and to engage with the local community (Anderson, 2012). In addition to rethinking curricula (are emerging subjects and concepts covered and new competencies being taught?), the 'whole school' approach implies reconsidering and redesigning schools' operations and environmental management (does the school conserve water and energy, provide healthy food, minimize waste and provide green and healthy school grounds?), pedagogy and learning (are teaching, learning and participation in decision-making adequate and appropriate?) and

> " Whole school approaches in England have improved schools' ethos and students' health and learning, and reduced schools' ecological footprints "

community relationships (does the school connect with community issues and resources?).

Research on the impact of whole school approaches in England (United Kingdom) has shown improvements in schools' ethos and students' health and learning, and reductions in schools' ecological footprints (Hacking et al., 2010). Unfortunately, however, while the approach is growing in popularity, it remains the exception rather than the rule (Hargreaves, 2008).

At the university level, the International Association of Universities, through its Higher Education for Sustainable Development initiative, promotes sustainability on campuses, including in business and community outreach, student engagement, management, institutional development, research and curriculum. One member, Ryerson University in Toronto, Canada, has developed a Campus Facilities and Sustainability programme to refocus the campus's efforts on developing sustainable operating practices and capital investment strategies (IAU, 2015).

TRADITIONAL APPROACH: LEARNING THROUGH COMMUNITY

While schools are one of the main sources of knowledge on sustainability, formal education does not reach everyone. Thus, another approach is important: learning through community, as done traditionally for generations. Often the groups left behind have the least access to typical resources. Local communities and traditional knowledge hold the key to reaching such groups. Local communities are much more than towns or villages; they are living entities that involve interaction of people with their local environment (Noguchi et al., 2015).

Traditional – and specifically indigenous – knowledge plays an important role in environmental sustainability.

> **Passed from generation to generation, traditional indigenous knowledge has been the basis for activities that sustain societies in much of the world**

Indigenous knowledge is local knowledge that is unique to a culture or society (Magni, 2016).[1] Passed from generation to generation, usually by word of mouth and rituals, it has been the basis for agriculture, food preparation, health care, education, conservation and many other activities that sustain societies in much of the world.

Indigenous people are the 'first' or 'original' people belonging to land or territories to which they are historically and culturally tied. About 370 million indigenous people live in over 90 countries worldwide (United Nations, 2009). Indigenous communities are stewards of traditional environmental knowledge, which sees nature as a living being and describes a reciprocal, interdependent, balanced and complementary relationship between humanity, nature and the universe. Traditional knowledge is dynamic, representing generations of creativity, innovation, and scientific and logical validity (Battiste, 2002; Maurial, 2002).

Most indigenous peoples share norms and values that are central to sustainable livelihoods (**Box 1.1**). Fundamental

BOX 1.1

Governments have adopted local community practices of *buen vivir*

In Latin America, the idea of *buen vivir* (living well) has been considered by academics, indigenous leaders, communities and politicians as a guiding principle for a new development regimen, incorporating the vision of indigenous peoples as well as traditional knowledge, that must be carried out collectively. Indigenous leaders in the region say *buen vivir* can be considered 'a contribution from indigenous populations to the world'.

Among *buen vivir* principles common to indigenous groups across the region is a relationship between humans, nature and the universe in which nature is considered a living being and has an indissoluble, interdependent, balanced and complementary relationship with the universe and with humans. The ideas of community and communitarianism are also important. The community, rather than the individual, is the main reference for natural and cultural property. Harmony within indigenous communities is reached through a system of equality and respect for all members but particularly women and elders as the primary holders and transmitters of traditional knowledge.

There are unique national and local manifestations of *buen vivir*. Two of the best-known national approaches are those of the Plurinational State of Bolivia and Ecuador. The Kichwa concept *sumak kawsay*, adopted in the 2008 Ecuadorian Constitution, and the Aymara concept *suma qamaña*, adopted in the 2009 Bolivian Constitution, mean living well, in harmony with nature and the universe. The Aymara concept has more emphasis on communitarian life: living well together. In Panama, at the local level, the Ngobe people use the expression *ti nüle küin*, which means be happy, live well, with good health, free from concerns and in harmony with nature. In Chile, the Mapuche indigenous group uses the expression *küme mongen*, which refers to a good life resulting from a balanced relationship between a person, the environment and the supernatural.

Sources: Cunningham (2010), Gudynas (2011a).

to these values are notions such as community, equality and complementarity (Gudynas, 2011a; Ibañez, 2011), where the fundamental conditions of well-being are sufficient food; strong family and community values of caring, reciprocity and solidarity; freedom to express one's identity and practise one's culture; and a safe, unpolluted environment (Tauli-Corpuz, 2010).

Indigenous peoples live in some of the most vulnerable ecosystems. Ranging from the Arctic, high mountains, floodplains and tropical rainforests to desert margins, small islands and low coastal areas, indigenous territories are directly affected by the ecological crisis that has brought climate change and loss of biodiversity. Despite hostile conditions, many indigenous peoples thrive, finding ways to resist and adapt to environmental changes, mainly due to their deep knowledge of and relationship with the environment (Nakashima et al., 2012).

Numerous examples of indigenous communities' traditional land management practices are being recognized globally for conserving biodiversity and maintaining ecosystem processes. Conservationists and researchers acknowledge the huge scale of biodiversity-rich terrestrial and marine habitats that are successfully managed outside government-designated protected areas. Estimated to be roughly equal to the size of total protected areas, indigenous and community-conserved areas and sacred natural sites are often managed as well as or more effectively than comparable government-managed areas. For example, research shows that such sites have been more effective in tackling rainforest deforestation by reducing logging and forest fires, thus contributing to rainforests' critical functions as biodiversity hotspots and carbon sinks, places that absorb more carbon than they release (ICCA, 2015).

The practice of sustainable traditional livelihoods is a testimony to indigenous peoples' resilience and their contribution to mitigating the impact of climate change (UNPFII, 2008). It was pointed out at the 2009 Asia Summit on Climate Change and Indigenous Peoples that indigenous groups have applied traditional knowledge to agriculture, agroforestry, coastal and river management, medicinal plants, water management and harvesting, and disaster management, among other areas (Tauli-Corpuz et al., 2009).

Notions like *buen vivir* offer an important contribution to today's world in crucial aspects such as social organization and economic structure. Harmony between humanity, nature and the universe can be used as a key principle for activities related to resource production and management. However, the discourse remains philosophical in some countries, even the Plurinational State of Bolivia and Ecuador, despite inclusion in their constitutions. On the other hand, Colombia's Council of Sustainable Settlements of the Americas is putting the concept into practice, for example in urban eco-barrio projects, transition towns, traditional sustainable villages, eco-caravans and sustainability education centres (Cunningham, 2010; Gudynas, 2011b; Tauli-Corpuz, 2010).

Traditional, local and indigenous knowledge have proved valuable for the functioning of ecosystems, early warning systems related to disasters, climate change adaptation, and resilience (Sheil et al., 2015). Integrating place-based knowledge with scientific climate models is valuable, as place-based approaches to climate issues can 'bring another level of awareness to consumer societies', and make them more resilient against disasters (Leduc and Crate, 2013).

Lessons from culturally integrated schools

The world can learn from indigenous communities' best practices. The latest Assessment Report of the Intergovernmental Panel on Climate Change identifies indigenous and traditional knowledge as a major resource for adapting to climate change. It highlights the need to integrate such knowledge with existing practices to increase the effectiveness of adaptation (IPCC, 2014). The success of many programmes has rested on deep intercultural respect, along with openness to a plurality of knowledge systems and cultures based on shared fundamental values (Leduc and Crate, 2013; Marika et al., 2009).

Intergenerational learning is critical to integrating traditional knowledge into contemporary society. Traditionally, elders are the custodians of indigenous knowledge and consequently the most valuable source of transmission (Dweba and Mearns, 2011). Successful education initiatives, such as the Alaska Rural Systemic Initiative in the United States, foster interaction of students with indigenous elders. For example, elders play a central role in instructional planning, curriculum design and programme implementation in culturally responsive schools, and lead activities related to knowledge transmission in cultural camps (Barnhardt, 2008).

One crucial way to incorporate traditional knowledge into schools is using the local language as the language of instruction. In Botswana, the Bokamoso preschool

> **One crucial way to incorporate traditional knowledge into schools is using the local language as the language of instruction**

programme provides teacher trainees with a system of nature-based educational tools incorporating the traditional knowledge of the San, a major indigenous group in the region. The curriculum of Bokamoso Teacher Training Centre was developed collaboratively over two years by a team of parents, community members, curriculum experts and members of non-government organizations (NGOs). The project provides trainees with the tools they need to teach pre-school in the San language (Batibo, 2013). Using the mother tongue as the language of instruction has a positive impact on learning across the curriculum, not only in languages (UNESCO, 2016).

The strong Western focus of education systems and institutions around the world impedes meaningful inclusion of indigenous populations and their knowledge and practices within the formal schooling system. Factors involved include curricula that lack local relevance and devalue indigenous knowledge; use of the dominant language for instruction instead of the home language (Batibo, 2009); standardized assessment strategies (Barnhardt and Kawagley, 2005); and faculty attitudes about curricula (Radoll, 2015). These factors often clash with traditional teachings (Nakashima et al., 2012).

Research has documented how formal schooling systems have resulted in the loss of significant background knowledge about nature, culture and values that indigenous children previously acquired in their communities. Examples from countries including Australia, Canada and the United States show an unquantifiable loss of indigenous knowledge from the beginning of the 20th century, when indigenous children were sent to residential schools or put up for forced adoption in an attempt to assimilate them into the dominant society (Reyhner and Eder, 2015). Separating them from their families and consequently from their cultural roots caused 'irreparable harm to the survival of indigenous cultures and societies' (Stavenhagen, 2015, p. 255).

However, while education can cause loss of indigenous knowledge, it can also be a cure (UNESCO, 2009). It is essential to foster dialogue and create partnerships between indigenous populations, civil society, government, development partners and management agencies, as well as scholars from a range of disciplines, to promote conservation of indigenous knowledge and its integration in various initiatives (Gorjestani, 2004).

LIFELONG LEARNING APPROACH: LEARNING THROUGH WORK AND DAILY LIFE

Environmental change requires other types of learning than formal schooling or traditional education in communities. People must act and contribute to environmental sustainability at all stages of their lives, so learning that takes place through work and daily life is crucial.

Lifelong learning comprises all learning activities undertaken throughout life with the aim of improving knowledge, skills and competencies within personal, civic, social and employment-related perspectives (UIL, 2015).

A lifelong learning approach focuses not only on curricula but also on intergenerational knowledge and values created by the community. It fosters synergy and connections between groups in society to tackle environmental challenges. Government agencies, faith-based organizations, non-profit and community groups, labour organizations and the private sector can all contribute to lifelong environmental education.

Governments and intergovernmental bodies

Governments have an important role to play in educating the public about environmental change. Government-backed campaigns raise awareness on an environmental problem, point to its underlying drivers and signal how stakeholders can address it and bring about meaningful change. Public awareness campaigns are most effective when they target groups with shared values and engage with community leaders to convey key messages (Stern, 2007). In 2015, for example, the Ethiopian Ministry of Water, Irrigation and Energy and other partners launched a two-year public awareness campaign aimed at encouraging solar lighting products. Targeting over 12 million Ethiopians, the campaign aimed to discourage households from using kerosene lamps and help them make informed decisions for purchasing off-grid lighting (World Bank, 2015).

A related initiative, Lighting Africa, has enabled more than 35 million people across Africa to have clean, affordable, safe lighting and energy. Currently operating in Burkina Faso, the Democratic Republic of the Congo,

Ethiopia, Kenya, Liberia, Mali, Nigeria, Senegal, South Sudan, the United Republic of Tanzania and Uganda, the programme addresses the lighting needs of rural, urban and suburban consumers without electricity access – predominantly low income households and businesses. It offers an alternative to kerosene lamps and candles, the most commonly used lighting sources among those without grid electricity. The programme has helped households reduce carbon dioxide emissions by about 700,000 tonnes, the equivalent of getting 147,000 cars off the road (World Bank, 2016).

The United Nations University Institute for the Advanced Study of Sustainability launched the first Regional Centres of Expertise (RCEs) on education for sustainable development in 2003 (Fadeeva et al., 2014). RCEs bring together regional and local institutions, build innovative platforms to share information and experiences, and promote dialogue among regional and local stakeholders through partnerships for sustainable development. By 2015, 138 RCEs around the globe were demonstrating the potential of multistakeholder learning and networking between schools, universities, local government, civil society groups and the private sector (IAU, 2016).

One example, RCE Minna, is located in Nigeria's North Central geopolitical zone, a largely rural and agrarian region with low population density and a variable climate. RCE Minna teaches educators, students, youths and community leaders to better manage their natural environment so as to ensure sustainable development in Niger state and its environs in a context of high unemployment and poverty rates, environmental degradation, poor sanitation and waste management systems, poor soil management, poor education, flooding, deforestation and declining freshwater resources (Fadeeva et al., 2014).

Religious and cultural leaders

Religious, cultural and social leaders can help spread environmentally sound values and behaviour (Zaval and Cornwell, 2015). Social incentives and peer pressure based on shared values and norms drive consumption choices and environmental behaviour. Leaders and role models can shape social aspirations and provide models for

> " Religious, cultural and social leaders can help spread environmentally sound values and behaviour "

sustainable behaviour. Faith-based examples include the environmental advocacy shown in Pope Francis's 2015 encyclical on environment, public statements by the Dalai Lama, and the founding documents of the Muslim Association for Climate Change Action.

Religious leaders are often skilled and insightful in using communication techniques to effect behaviour change, especially at the local level. In the United States, the Take Charge Challenge encouraged community members to reduce energy use by making homes more weather resistant and energy efficient. Rather than using conventional awareness-raising techniques, the initiative relied on religious leaders to appeal to community members' values. Local leaders successfully tied green initiatives into deeply held spiritual beliefs and encouraged households to make the right moral choice. It is estimated that communities saved 110.2 billion British thermal unit (Btu) of gas and electricity, about US$2.3 million in energy savings (Fuller et al., 2011).

Greener businesses and workplaces

People spend a great amount of time in the workplace, making it a useful location for informal and non-formal education. Over the past two to three decades, a series of corporate initiatives have been launched to reduce companies' ecological footprint and educate staff and the public about environmental protection. In addition to cutting costs and improving a company's reputation, initiatives in the realm of corporate social responsibility (CSR) help raise environmental awareness internally and externally.

In a 2008 Economist Intelligence Unit survey, over half of all the global executives who responded considered CSR a high or very high priority – up from 34.1% in 2005 (The Economist, 2008). Over 40% said it was important for their companies to align sustainability with their overall business goals, mission or values (McKinsey, 2014). Allianz Insurance, an international financial services group employing over 148,000 people, publicly committed to a 35% reduction of its 2006 carbon footprint by 2015. To reach its objective, it 'greened' its IT hardware purchasing policy, reduced unnecessary travel and imposed double-sided printing (TUC, 2014). Unilever developed a plan to improve environmental impacts throughout the entire supply chain; it reduced manufacturing carbon emissions by one third while increasing sustainable agricultural sources from 14% to 48% between 2010 and 2014 (The Economist, 2014). Initiatives such as these not only help reduce a company's carbon footprint but also encourage employees to adopt more sustainable practices outside the workplace.

In addition to preserving the environment, manufacturers' and retailers' decisions to market organic products, use environmentally sustainable packaging, ban plastic bags (**Box 1.2**) and inform consumers about how goods are produced contribute to consumer education and subsequent shifts in habits, allowing consumers to make decisions according to their values and preference (BIO Intelligence Service, 2012; Hertwich, 2003).

Labour organizations can play a key role in mainstreaming and transitioning towards more sustainable practices in the workplace. At the international level, the International Labour Organization (ILO) has an International Training Centre in Turin that delivers a course for worker representatives called 'Green jobs for a just transition to low-carbon and climate-resilient development' (ILO, 2016). Its purpose is to educate labour representatives from around the world about the links between environmental challenges and the world of work, distil lessons and good practices, and explore ways of promoting environmentally sustainable policies adapted to be nationally relevant and socially inclusive.

National and local trade unions also contribute to environmental education. In Argentina, the Construction Workers' Union provides environmental training courses to its members on topics such as solar panel installation, solar cooker construction, and waste management and recycling. A certificate is granted upon successful completion of a course (Fondación UOCRA, 2009).

Non-government organizations

NGOs can mobilize public support for environmental conservation. In countries with poorly resourced formal education sectors, they may be the main source of environmental education. Through public information campaigns, projects on the ground, partnerships and green alliances, NGOs substantially contribute to the shaping of public environment-related behaviour. Their strength, compared to other groups and the formal education sector, lies in their ability to deliver environmental education using more informal methods and channels.

> NGOs, such as Avaaz, can effectively mobilize public support for environmental conservation.

The internet is a crucial, efficient tool for many NGOs (Brulle, 2010). Web-based campaign groups like Avaaz help raise awareness and mobilize 'clicktivists' across the globe. With 44 million members in 194 countries, Avaaz is at the centre of many high profile environmental campaigns. In 2013, for instance, it launched a two-year campaign to ban bee-killing pesticides in the European Union. The campaign included a petition with over 2.6 million signatures, media-grabbing protests with beekeepers, the funding of opinion polls and the flooding of ministers with messages (Avaaz, 2013).

Senegal's Mekhe Solar Cooker Project, implemented by the Ndop Women's Association, is an example of NGOs' contribution to environmental education. From October 2004 to September 2006, it aimed to

---

BOX 1.2

Leading by example: nudging people to act green

'Nudging' is a way of influencing behaviour. In sustainability nudging, more sustainable behaviour is made the default option. The government and private sector can work together to make environment-friendly goods and services the 'green default' for consumers. Positive trends can rapidly be normalized, shifting responsibility to those who actively wish to behave unsustainably. Nudging can also help overcome cognitive bias such as a preference for the status quo, where any change from baseline is perceived as a loss. Nudging can be considered educational when there is transparency and when the desired change is supported by knowledge and information about why the change is deemed important. When there is no transparency, nudging can become manipulation, which may lead to desirable environmental outcomes but is not socially sustainable.

For sustainability nudging to work, the government, public and private sector have to work well together and share a vision of reducing emissions and improving energy efficiency. In Schönau, Germany, a utility provider made its green energy programme the default option, resulting in more than 90% enrolment. Residents could opt out, but few chose to do so. By contrast, participation in clean energy programmes in other German towns was low: Less than 1% of customers chose to participate through voluntary means in 2008, the time of the study.

Source: Zaval and Cornwell (2015).

> ## If education progress is stalled, it could lead to a 20% increase in disaster-related fatalities per decade

reduce environmental degradation by replacing wood-burning stoves with solar cookers. Various modes of education and training were used: Some villagers were trained to build the cookers, others to promote their use. A DVD movie and visits to nearby communities were used to engage households. Each family saved, on average, 3 metric tonnes of carbon dioxide equivalent. The project created 10 jobs and enhanced the capacity of 105 women and 22 men to use a renewable energy source (UNDP, 2015a).

Informal coalitions

Informal platforms and coalitions are characterized by interactive forms of learning. They have been described as participatory, collaborative, social, interactive, experiential and transformative. Examples include community groups in Detroit, United States, that have self-organized to develop urban farms that repurpose vacant property and strengthen community resilience (Greening of Detroit, 2015); participatory budgeting in Porto Alegre, Brazil (Touchton and Wampler, 2013); and urban farming in Hue, Viet Nam, where this practice by the local community has reduced the heat-island effect and has been promoted as an opportunity for ecotourism ventures and organic food production (van Dijk et al., 2012; Phuc et al., 2014).

Promoting sustainable behaviour can also be effective through one-to-one interactions. In community-based social marketing approaches, priority behaviour is selected and local solutions designed to overcome barriers to behaviour change. Programmes are rolled out more widely throughout community networks. Recognizing the power of social psychology, programmes – in areas ranging from promoting reusable mugs and water-efficient showerheads to carpooling and purchasing products with recycled contents – encourage getting public commitment from individuals during personal interactions, as this is known to increase the likelihood of following through on promises (McKinsey-Mohr, 2011).

REVERSING CLIMATE CHANGE REQUIRES AN INTEGRATED APPROACH TO LEARNING

The challenge of climate change demonstrates the complexity of, and urgent need for, using education to address environmental crises. All three approaches described in the sections above are required: learning at schools, in communities and through lifelong learning, along with integration between types of education and collaboration between education and other sectors. Thus deployed, education can contribute to actions to address climate change, including prevention, mitigation and disaster preparedness.

Climate change is by far the biggest environmental crisis facing humanity. Between 1995 and 2014, 15,000 extreme weather events caused more than 525,000 deaths worldwide and losses of nearly US$3 trillion (Kreft et al., 2015). Climate change poses a fundamental threat to livelihoods. It is directly responsible for the rise in global temperatures and increased frequency and scale of extreme weather and natural disasters such as droughts, floods, aggravated desertification and biodiversity loss. These in turn have a direct impact on global food stocks, human health and well-being, human security, economic growth and jobs. The effects of climate change also have serious implications for the functioning of education systems, and require adaptive strategies (**Box 1.3**).

At COP21 in Paris, the 2015 Convention of the Parties to the UN Framework Convention on Climate Change, a record 195 countries adopted the Paris Agreement, whose signatories agreed, among other things, to keep temperature rises well below 2 degrees Celsius and curb carbon emissions. Since the consequences of climate change are so severe, especially for those living in the areas most sensitive to changes in weather patterns, temperatures and sea levels, it is no surprise there are efforts worldwide to employ education at all levels to help citizens tackle the causes of climate change and to respond to its consequences.

BOX 1.3

Climate change and natural disasters severely affect education systems and outcomes

The growing frequency of natural disasters and extreme weather increases the vulnerability of many low income countries, and such events have multiple direct and indirect effects on education systems and outcomes.

Natural disasters interrupt education continuity by damaging or destroying school facilities, and they threaten communities' physical safety and psychological well-being. For example, the 2015 earthquakes in Nepal devastated the schooling infrastructure – in 11 of the most affected districts, 34,500 of 55,000 classrooms were assessed as unsafe for use, affecting education for over a million children. Natural disasters are a leading cause of internal and external migration globally, affecting both sending-country and receiving-country school systems as populations of young migrants change. In 2015, 19.2 million people worldwide were displaced internally due to natural disasters; twice as many as were displaced by conflict and violence. In addition, climate change is raising temperatures and sea levels, and causing loss of agricultural productivity, seriously affecting children's health, to the detriment of education outcomes.

Bangladesh is one of the world's poorest, most populous and most flood-prone countries. Climate experts project that by 2050, 27 million people there will be at risk from sea level rise. With increasing frequency of floods, many environmental migrants from rural areas become slum dwellers in Dhaka, the densely populated capital. Unsurprisingly, the school system is routinely affected by climate-related challenges. For instance, as a result of Cyclone Sidr in 2007, 849 schools were destroyed in 12 districts, affecting the education of over 140,000 students.

The Solar-Powered Floating Schools programme, developed by a Bangladesh NGO, Shidhulai Swanirvar Sangstha, is one example of a locally relevant education solution developed to adapt to severe weather effects. The "floating schools" (boats) help ensure year-round education and educational resources by collecting students from all over a locality, then docking in one location to provide classes.

Sources: Anderson (2013); Das (2010); Internal Displacement Monitoring Centre (2015); Internal Displacement Monitoring Centre (2016); Save the Children (2008); UNICEF (2015); Walsham (2010); Wheeler (2011); WISE Initiative (2012).

SCHOOLS, COMMUNITIES AND LIFELONG LEARNING WORK HAND IN HAND

Formal education has a particularly strong role in mitigating climate change and responding to its impact. In fact, education expansion is more effective in combating climate change than conventional investment in infrastructure such as sea walls and irrigation systems. Research on disaster vulnerability shows that female education, for instance, is negatively correlated with disaster fatalities. Projections indicate that universalizing upper secondary education by 2030 would prevent 200,000 disaster-related deaths in the 20 years that follow (Lutz et al., 2014).

In countries where access to education is weak, or education is not of good quality, integrated action is required to improve the education system as well as use of education for climate action. Reaching all youth, rich and poor, may require climate change education not only in classrooms but through additional government, NGO and private sector programmes.

The communities most at risk from climate-related events are generally situated in low and middle income countries. Of the 10 most affected countries between 1995 and 2014, 9 were in the low or lower middle income group: Bangladesh, Guatemala, Haiti, Honduras, Myanmar, Nicaragua, Pakistan, the Philippines and Viet Nam. The remaining one was Thailand, an upper middle income country (Kreft et al., 2015). Several of the poorer countries have low baseline educational attainment and wide disparity between the poorest and wealthiest students (**Figure 1.3**). In Guatemala, Haiti, Honduras and Pakistan, only about 10% of poor children complete lower secondary school, compared to 75% of rich children.

Education can be used to raise awareness of climate change, reduce vulnerability to it and mitigate its consequences. Schools can increase knowledge and awareness of the environment and climate change by incorporating environmental sustainability into classroom materials and curricula. In Bangladesh, after the National Curriculum and Textbook Board prepared and endorsed a school manual on climate change and health protection, 1,515 students in 30 schools received classroom training based on the manual while 1,778 students in 30 control schools received a leaflet on climate change and health

FIGURE 1.3:

Poor children in the countries most at risk for climate change disasters are less likely to complete secondary school
Lower secondary completion rate, by wealth

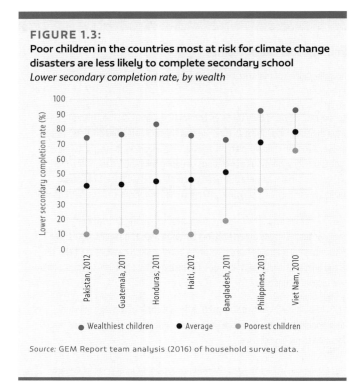

● Wealthiest children   ● Average   ● Poorest children

Source: GEM Report team analysis (2016) of household survey data.

issues instead. Six months later, results of a post-intervention test performed at both schools showed that the training led to dramatic increases in children's knowledge of the topic (Kabir et al., 2015).

Education can reduce vulnerability to climate change. A comparative study on Cuba, the Dominican Republic and Haiti focused on the role of formal education in reducing vulnerability, and explored education's potential impact on disaster management and prevention and on post-disaster management. It found that a lack of education and low literacy rates prevented people from understanding warnings. In Cuba, a country with high literacy and enrolment rates, the level of vulnerability to climate-related disasters was reduced (Pichler and Striessnig, 2013).

Education can also help people adapt to climate change effects. In Ethiopia, six years of education increases by 20% the chance that a farmer will adapt by using techniques such as soil conservation, varied planting dates and changes in crop varieties (Deressa et al., 2009). In Uganda, the likelihood that a family will adopt drought-resistant crop varieties increases when the father has basic education (Hisali et al., 2011). And a

survey of farmers in Burkina Faso, Cameroon, Egypt, Ethiopia, Ghana, Kenya, Niger, Senegal, South Africa and Zambia showed that those with education were more likely to make at least one adaptation: One year of education reduced the probability of no adaptation by 1.6% (Maddison, 2007).

To achieve all this requires attention to the quality of the education. Teacher training has been identified as critical in making education more responsive to climate change and related sustainability challenges. Short and circular modules for teacher training appear to hold significant benefits for teachers' understanding and confidence on climate change. In one study, the percentage of prospective teachers who felt climate change was a conceptually difficult subject to teach fell from over 21% to about 7% after less than four hours of training (Anderson, 2013).

As the previous sections showed, formal education is only one approach. Education can also take place within communities. A strong example was shown in disaster preparedness in the Philippines, where partnerships and diverse learning approaches were used effectively. Local communities worked with the Ministry of Education, Plan International and other partners to teach children and youth about climate change adaptation and preparation to reduce disaster vulnerability. Children learned to read rain gauges; undertook disaster simulation and drills; carried out risk mapping; and learned skills in first aid, swimming and water safety. Through theatre and music, children expressed what they had learned, thus delivering to their communities information on potential hazards and practical solutions. Evidence shows that these programmes were effective in building resilience in the community – potentially saving lives. In 2006, after three days of continuous rain, children and adults applied knowledge gained from the adaptation-focused risk reduction strategy to evacuate before landslides covered their homes (Plan International, 2008). Other work connecting formal schooling with community education is found in small island states (**Box 1.4**).

Lifelong learning programmes delivered by government, private industry and civil society are also critical. Effective responses to climate change include governance and legislation cooperation between the education sector and other sectors. National strategies that include awareness-raising and information dissemination on climate change will allow stakeholders to undertake adaptive and mitigating activities. For example, Namibia has produced Initial Communication Booklets on climate change

BOX 1.4

Small island states use the entire education system to prepare for climate change

The Pacific Island region will experience some of the most profound negative effects of climate change considerably sooner than other regions. Funded by the US National Science Foundation, the Pacific Islands Climate Education Partnership (PCEP) aims to educate the region's students and citizens in ways that exemplify modern science and indigenous environmental knowledge, address the urgency of climate change and honour indigenous culture. Students and citizens in the region will have the knowledge and skills to advance their understanding of climate change and adapt to its impact.

The PCEP Strategic Plan incorporates a range of interconnected strategic goals, including promotion of indigenous knowledge and practices, enhancement of learning and teaching about climate change from kindergarten to teacher training, a community-school partnership programme to connect school with community climate adaptation partners, and a focus on the content and skills necessary for students to understand the science of global and Pacific Islands climates, as well as adaptation to climate change effects.

Current activities include revising state and national science education standards to better incorporate climate change; adapting curricula to a wide variety of climate and education contexts; gathering local indigenous knowledge and practices related to climate education and adaptation; providing professional development; and supporting local professional learning communities.

Sources: Sussman et al. (2013); Vize (2012).

---

translated in local languages to empower citizens and allow them to make well-informed decisions (Mfune et al., 2009). The United Kingdom is putting more effort into communicating, informing and educating the public, such as by promoting energy conservation measures (DEFRA, 2006). The government is also promoting and funding renewable-based energy technology in all schools in England to reduce carbon emissions and use renewables technology as a learning resource for teaching science, geography, design, technology, citizenship and mathematics (DEFRA, 2006).

CONCLUSION

Education plays a major role in the transformation towards more environmentally sustainable societies and in addressing the impact of environmental crises such as climate change. The challenges are pressing. Human behaviour has led to environmental crises, with various kinds of problems contributing, including overpopulation, unsustainable lifestyles that consume more resources than are available and individual behaviour that harms the environment, such as using fossil fuels or landfilling waste.

Accordingly, solutions to environmental crises vary, and must address issues at all levels: individual, community, regional, national and, cumulatively, global. Approaches to learning will vary. Formal education can contribute at

the macro level, for example by reducing fertility rates, and at the individual level by building environmental literacy. Dynamic approaches are being used in primary, secondary and tertiary institutions to improve sustainable knowledge, skills and attitudes.

Yet, formal education does not reach everyone. Learning, creating awareness and building competencies to take action can take place in communities and through education that is based in the interaction between people and their local environments. Indigenous knowledge and belief systems can inspire better stewardship of the planet. Lifelong learning can help people live more sustainably all their lives. A multistakeholder, collaborative approach should involve government, civil society and the private sector inside and outside schools to shape values and perspectives, and contribute to the development of competencies to reduce or stop unsustainable practices and to adapt to consequences such as climate change due to the overstepping of planetary boundaries by humankind.

ENDNOTES

1. This section draws extensively on Magni (2016).

A man stands in a crop of cassava that is being cultivated using an improved technique in Boukoko, Central African Republic.

CREDIT: Riccardo Gangale/FAO

Prosperity: sustainable and inclusive economies

We are determined to ensure that all human beings can enjoy prosperous and fulfilling lives and that economic, social and technological progress occurs in harmony with nature.

– The 2030 Agenda for Sustainable Development

KEY MESSAGES

Education has a key role to play in moving towards environmentally sustainable and inclusive economic growth.

1 **Education and lifelong learning are needed to make production and consumption sustainable, to provide green skills for green industries and orient research and higher education towards green innovation.**

 a. Creating green industries relies on high-skill workers with specific training.
 b. Greening of industries will require continuing training and education for low- and medium-skill workers, often on the job.
 c. Research can be oriented towards green innovation and growth.

2 **Education can help food production and farming be more sustainable.**

 a. Agriculture urgently needs to transform to meet environmental and global needs: Agriculture contributes one-third of all greenhouse gas emissions.
 b. Primary and secondary education give future farmers foundation skills as well as critical knowledge about sustainability challenges in agriculture.
 c. Literacy and non-formal education in the form of extension programmes can increase farmer productivity.
 d. Yet many are halting investment in agricultural research at a time when it is urgently needed: In sub-Saharan Africa, the share in global expenditure on public agricultural research declined from 10% to 6% from 1960 to 2009.

3 **Education contributes to economic growth.**

 a. Educational attainment explains about half the difference in growth rates between East Asia and sub-Saharan Africa between 1965 and 2010.
 b. But education must keep up with the changing face of work and produce more high-skill workers. By 2020, there could be 40 million too few workers with tertiary education relative to demand.

4 **Education of good quality can help ensure economic growth does not leave anyone behind.**

 a. If 10 recent EU member states met 2020 targets to decrease early school-leaving and increase tertiary participation, they could reduce the numbers of those at risk of poverty by 3.7 million.
 b. Secondary and tertiary education is far more effective than just primary for helping people access decent work and earnings.

5 **Education reduces poverty and helps close wage gaps.**

 a. Education helps people find work: In South Africa, less than 45% of those with less than upper secondary education were employed in 2005 compared to roughly 60% who completed upper secondary.
 b. If workers from low socio-economic backgrounds had the same education as more advantaged counterparts, disparity in working poverty between the two groups would shrink by 39%.
 c. Education increases earnings by roughly 10% per year of schooling.
 d. Meanwhile, policies are needed to meet the increased global demand for skilled and qualified labour.

The world economy needs deep transformation in order to implement the Agenda for Sustainable Development by 2030, to prevent the collapse of the Earth's biosphere on which human civilization depends for survival, and to eradicate poverty – the central goal of the Millennium Development Goals (MDGs) and now of the Sustainable Development Goals (SDGs). This chapter reflects on the roles of education in this transformation towards environmentally sustainable and economically inclusive development.

The statement above from the Agenda for Sustainable Development makes a commitment to human beings enjoying prosperous and fulfilling lives. But as this chapter will explain, economic growth and both national and individual prosperity must occur 'in harmony with nature'. This requires fundamental changes in the world economy to create clean new industries and ensure that existing ones become greener.

Education and lifelong learning are needed to make production and consumption sustainable, supply skills for the creation of green activities and orient higher education and research towards green innovation. They also have a role to play in transforming key economic sectors, such as agriculture, upon which both rich and poor countries and households rely.

Education of good quality has been proved to contribute to long-term economic growth. Curricular contents, and the ways they are embedded in the everyday life of schools, need to be transformed to sustain a greener world economy. Investment in education and lifelong learning are also required for countries to adapt to the rapidly changing world of work, with polarization between high- and low-skill jobs, and further shifts to green industry and the service sector.

Just as the economy must become sustainable, so too must it become inclusive. With widespread poverty and inequality, economic growth has not benefited all people. Prosperity must be conceived in ways that leave no one behind. Education of good quality can contribute to this change as well. A better-educated labour force is essential to inclusive economic growth focused

> **A better-educated labour force is essential to inclusive economic growth**

on human welfare. Education helps reduce poverty by increasing chances of finding decent work and improved earnings, reducing job insecurity.

CURRENT MODELS OF ECONOMIC GROWTH CAUSE ENVIRONMENTAL DESTRUCTION

The type of economic growth experienced thus far could prove unsustainable over 2015–2030 and beyond. Models of economic growth in the 20th century emphasized aspects such as intensive production, industrial advances and exploitation of natural resources. These models legitimized practices and policies that thwart achievement of the environmental SDGs, causing damage to the Earth's biosphere and hence threatening civilization in the longer term.

As Chapter 1: Planet notes, all countries that are ranked very high on the Human Development Index (above 0.8) and have a high per capita income consume more resources per capita than the Earth can renew (Global Footprint Network, 2016). This creates a contradiction. Economic growth is the most powerful instrument for reducing poverty in developing countries (DFID, 2008), but if that growth depletes resources at an unsupportable rate, will it start to increase poverty? For example, poor people suffer the most from environmental degradation as they often live in the most vulnerable areas and their livelihoods tend to be linked more directly to access to natural resources.

Climate change is an example of the effects of economic growth, and the reason a transformation of economic models is necessary. The increased frequency and intensity of extreme climate events, reduced productivity of agriculture and natural ecosystems due to changing temperature and rainfall patterns, and resulting health shocks and reduced labour productivity may slow, stall or even reverse the trend towards eradication of extreme income poverty observed over 2000–2015.

Overall, climate change could cast as many as 122 million people into poverty by 2030, depending on how ecosystems, the economy and geographical features such as coastal areas and glaciers adapt. Climate change could reduce crop yields by 5% by 2030 and 30% by 2080 – even if agriculture adapts by changing crops and culture practices, extending irrigation and developing higher yield crops (Hallegatte et al., 2016).

SUSTAINABLE TRANSFORMATION WILL REQUIRE CLEAN NEW INDUSTRIES AND GREENER EXISTING ONES

The concepts of sustainable development and green growth are similar, having in common the ideas of using less resources more efficiently and limiting the harmful impact of economic activity on the environment by creating green industries and 'greening' existing ones (UNIDO, 2011b). They also mean dismantling the activities that contribute most to environmental degradation, such as coal-intensive industries, and converting them and their employees to greener work.

Green industry is defined by the United Nations Industrial Development Organisations as 'industrial production and development that does not come at the expense of the health of natural systems or lead to adverse human health outcomes' (UNIDO, 2011b). However, green industries are difficult to classify statistically, and there is no universally accepted definition.

Estimates suggest that sectors that fall under the green industry umbrella already employ large numbers of workers – 3.5 million in Bangladesh, 1.4 million in Brazil, 2 million in Germany and, in the United States, 2.5 million in the private sector and almost 900,000 in the public sector. The net impact of green growth on employment is usually forecast as positive, though some industries stand to lose jobs. Sectors such as alternative fuels, building technologies, wind power, alternative fuel vehicles, geothermal energy, water supply and wastewater treatment are expected to drive sustained expansion in green industries globally in coming decades (Hinojosa and Pickles, 2015). Renewable sources may account for almost half the total increase in global electricity generation between 2015 and 2040, with especially large increases predicted in China, India, Latin America and Africa (Hinojosa and Pickles, 2015).

The current concentration of green industries in high income countries, especially in Western Europe, is expected to wane. In 2009, the European Union accounted for 50% of recycling worldwide and 40% of the use of renewable energy sources (Hinojosa and Pickles, 2015). However, between 2005 and 2015, the share of developing countries in global renewable energy investment rose from 27% to 55%, reaching US$156 billion in 2015 to overtake developed economies (REN21, 2016). Key green businesses, such as producers of solar photovoltaic panels, have been moving from high to middle income countries. Green industries in developing countries may receive more than US$6.4 trillion in investment between 2015 and 2025, with China and Latin America each receiving nearly one-quarter of the total (InfoDev, 2014).

Existing industries need to be restructured for efficiency gains. This greening of industries, by the UNIDO definition, includes reducing the environmental impact of processes and products by using resources more efficiently, phasing out toxic substances, replacing fossil fuels with renewables, improving occupational health and safety, increasing producer responsibility and reducing overall risk (UNIDO, 2011). There could be significant benefits in terms of savings: by 2030, an estimated US$3.7 trillion could be saved annually worldwide from implementation of 130 resource productivity measures and adapted legislation (MGI Global, 2011).

GREEN SKILLS POLICIES CAN FOSTER JOB CREATION

Green growth will greatly affect employment. Jobs will be created in green industries; jobs will be shifted as industries are greened (e.g. with production-based renewables instead of fossil fuels); some will be destroyed; and many will be redefined as skills, work methods and job profiles are greened. The hardship caused by job destruction and redefinition should not be underestimated, as the industries affected – including fishing, forestry, extractive industries, fossil fuel generation and emission-intensive manufacturing (such as the cement and automotive industries) – employ large numbers (Hinojosa and Pickles, 2015).

However, forecasts indicate the net result should be positive. A review of cross country and national studies[1] by the International Labour Organization (ILO) indicates that the adoption of environmental reforms leads to net job gains of 0.5% to 2% of the workforce, translating to 15 million to 60 million additional jobs globally (ILO, 2012). In South Africa, the potential for new green jobs was estimated in 2011 at 98,000 in the short term, 255,000 in the medium term and 462,000 in the long term, especially in natural resource management such as biodiversity conservation, ecosystem restoration, and soil and land management (Maia et al., 2011).

One reason for the positive impact on employment is that green industries tend to be more labour-intensive. For instance, sustainable farming requires more labour than conventional farming, with more diverse crop rotation, integration of crops and livestock to recycle organic waste as soil nutrients, and reliance on biological processes for pest and weed management. Similarly, to improve energy efficiency the construction sector has employed large numbers of workers (Hinojosa and Pickles, 2015; Maia et al., 2011).

The changes in employment and job definitions accompanying green growth will create huge demand for skills development. The creation of green industries will rely on high skill workers with technical training; the greening of existing industries will require continuing education and training for low and medium skill workers, often on the job (ILO, 2013a; UNIDO, 2011b). The balance of skills required will vary across countries and industries – but in every context, skills policies can facilitate this transition.

 The creation of green industries will rely on high skill workers with technical training

It is difficult to define which skills would be specifically 'green' or 'non-green', as both green and greening industries use a mix of both. There is therefore very little evidence quantifying what the 'green skill gap' might be at the global level, although it is possible to identify skills which green and greening industries demand (**Box 2.1**).

The implications of green growth for education and training policies are complex and often industry-specific. Policy-makers and educators face the challenge of defining which skills to teach, even as the economy is undergoing rapid change. They must also balance current and long-term priorities, deciding, for example, how much focus to give to redefining initial education and training as opposed to up-skilling and retraining the current labour force. They need to develop flexible education and training frameworks in line with the capabilities and aspirations of students and trainees. Specific policy recommendations in this area are found in Chapter 8.

BOX 2.1

Green industries demand particular skills

Green industries demand particular skills, including basic, technical, and transferable and managerial skills.

- Basic skills, including literacy and numeracy, are indispensable. Green growth reinforces the need for good quality basic and remedial education, both in countries which have not yet reached universal enrolment at the primary and lower secondary levels, and in countries with low levels of basic skills in the adult population.

- Technical skills can be specific to green industries (e.g. diagnostic skills to measure a carbon footprint) or added to existing skills (e.g. up-to-date training in energy efficiency for construction workers with standard skills).

- Transferable and managerial skills include leadership, risk management, design, communication and commercial skills that are necessary to enable firms to make the transition towards green production. For example, those with entrepreneurial skills can seize the opportunities presented by low-carbon technology, and consulting skills can be used to advise consumers about green solutions and spread the use of green technology.

Source: GEM Report team analysis based on Hinojosa and Pickles (2015).

INNOVATION DEPENDS ON COOPERATION IN HIGHER EDUCATION AND R&D BACKED WITH PUBLIC FUNDING

The transition towards sustainable economies can be seen as being on a par with the paradigm shifts brought about by the industrial revolution and the advent of information and communication technology (ICT) (Stern, 2015). Sustainability and green growth require investment in research and development (R&D) to transform production in vast swaths of the economy. They involve refining existing technology to save energy, using renewables and, above all, introducing technology that is only just being developed (Aghion et al., 2009a).

In Cuba, the Centre for Research and Development of Structures and Construction Materials (CIDEM) developed alternative ways to solve a building and energy crisis. Researchers developed low-energy, low-carbon building materials and worked with communities, municipalities and manufacturers to get them into use building houses. In addition to environmental benefits, the project generated significant socio-economic benefits. In 2010 and 2011, 5,300 houses were built using such materials made by 138 manufacturers, providing livelihoods to many people. Three training centres have been established at universities and this model of developing sustainable building materials has been adopted by other countries in Latin America as well as Africa, Asia and the Middle East (Sarabhai and Vyas, 2015).

While examples of green innovation practices can be found around the world, more is needed to turn practices into a system – that is, an ensemble of actors and conditions that enable the creation and flow of knowledge and technology into the economy. For this, other conditions must be present, such as collaboration between researchers, funders, manufacturers, government and consumers, in a context of change in broader macroeconomic, investment and policy environments (Botta et al., 2015).

The role of education in innovation primarily concerns R&D in new technologies, as well as their dissemination. For higher education systems to provide enough researchers and developers with specialist knowledge and skills in a wide range of fields, diverse and specific curricula are needed along with cooperative study programmes across fields. Major emerging economies such as Brazil and China are expanding their tertiary education systems with that approach in mind. The European Commission estimates that at least 1 million new research jobs will be needed to meet a target of increasing EU R&D expenditure to 3% of gross domestic product (GDP) (European Commission, 2011).

Once developed, innovative knowledge and technology need to be introduced into the economy. Scaling up technology, building capacity and developing markets may require adaptation to local contexts, particularly in poorer countries, where technological transfer presents a hosts of challenges. A rigorous review of research reveals little evidence of the impact of technological transfer in developing countries, although two cases stand out (Oketch et al., 2014). Large state-run corporations in Viet Nam are more likely than small and medium-sized enterprises to demonstrate high levels of technological transfer, probably because of their contact with foreign firms. However, one of the studies reviewed indicated that university-generated research had improved productivity in local agriculture and aquaculture

(Ca, 2006). The small amount of empirical evidence available related to tech transfer and scaling up highlights the need to better understand the relationships between innovation, technology and economic development in poor countries.

Green innovation systems depend on public funding of R&D, as the private sector may be unable or unwilling to invest sufficiently in green technology in the early stages of development, when costs are high, returns are uncertain and the benefits are social rather than private (Aghion, 2009a; OECD, 2011). Unfortunately, total public and private R&D expenditure as a share of GDP has not grown discernibly in the OECD or major emerging countries since 2007. In 2013, it represented slightly less than 2.5% of GDP in OECD countries, ranging from less than 0.5% in Chile to almost 4.5% in the Republic of Korea (OECD, 2014c).

Moreover, public R&D spending in energy and the environment is only a small fraction of total public R&D budgets, averaging less than 12% in OECD economies, and less than 6% in the EU. Moreover, public R&D budgets for energy and the environment have stalled across the OECD in recent years. OECD military public R&D was more than double that of energy and environment in 2012, and approximately 30 times as large in the United States (OECD, 2014c). The International Energy Agency estimates that governments would need to increase annual energy R&D up to fivefold to significantly reduce carbon emissions by 2050 (IEA, 2010). Corresponding data on private R&D expenditure are not available, but the fact that over 2000–2006 only 2.15% of total patents applied for worldwide were environment-related indicates that it is low (Aghion et al., 2009b).

LIFELONG LEARNING ENABLES CONSUMERS AND PRODUCERS TO CONTRIBUTE TO SUSTAINABILITY

While green skills and green innovation can reduce environmental destruction caused by economic activity, the leap towards fully sustainable consumption and production requires a deeper transformation of the economy. The whole life cycle of products needs to be designed to minimize resource use, waste and pollution. Examples include certification of the entire production and consumption chain, and 'cradle-to-cradle' design where all products and waste can be used in making other products. Another approach is the service-based economy where consumers no longer own products but lease the services they provide.

Developing, understanding and working with such approaches requires learning by both consumers and producers, which education policies can best address in a lifelong learning perspective. The United Nations Environment Programme has identified learning-related priorities for sustainable consumption and production. These include new forms of (a) education for industry employees, including sustainability-oriented technical and vocational education and training (TVET) and ongoing training within companies; (b) learning at all levels of supply chains, with attention to empowerment of suppliers and customers, rather than compliance inspections; (c) interdisciplinary scholarship focusing on altering consumer habits; and (d) social learning at the community level (UNEP, 2015).

Relevant international agreements and programmes include the United Nations Decade for Education for Sustainable Development, with topics such as Education for Sustainable Consumption, TVET for Sustainable Development and Higher Education for Sustainable Development. The multistakeholder Marrakesh Process (2003–2011) led to the adoption of a framework at the United Nations Conference on Sustainable Development in 2012 (Rio+20). National sustainable consumption and production initiatives have been launched in countries including Finland, Germany and the United Kingdom (Geels et al., 2015).

Business owners, managers and financiers can be leaders in sustainability. Large and small corporations can develop strategies and analyse their business culture and work systems to make them more sustainable (see Chapter 1: Planet). Studies have shown that business courses increasingly teach the 'business case' for sustainability, and that professional networks of business leaders increasingly accept the importance, relevance and willingness of action (Sidiropoulos, 2014), although many of the findings are limited in geographical coverage and trends appear patchy across industries and locations.

Shareholder activism has resulted in movements to divest from fossil fuels and to invest so as to generate a positive social impact along with financial returns. Progress in corporate sustainability has seen the expansion of sustainable finance, with mainstream banks increasingly integrating environmental and social impact considerations and risk management strategies into loan and investment assessment (UNEP, 2012; OECD, 2016b).

AGRICULTURAL PRACTICES NEED TRANSFORMATION

Focusing on agriculture shows not only the scale of problems to be tackled but also how an economic sector can change and how education can address the changes. Globally, some 70% of people in extreme poverty live in rural areas (IFAD, 2011b) where agriculture is the main source of income and employment, and access to land serves as a tangible source of security despite natural disasters and weak economic opportunity. Solutions for global poverty must address the needs of agrarian societies and ensure the sustainability and productivity of agriculture. Agriculture provides the world's food supply, and major factors affecting it also affect the world's economy and ecosphere.

Agricultural production is the main emitter of carbon dioxide in the global food system (Vermeulen et al., 2012). Increases in carbon dioxide contribute to climate change, which in turn has a negative effect on crops. Yields of wheat, rice and corn are expected to fall in coming years, even as growing populations will need more to eat. By emitting high levels of greenhouse gases, conventional agricultural practices present a barrier to the main challenge they seek to address, potentially leading to food shortages instead of food security.

Education, both formal and non-formal, has a clear role in this context: It is necessary for sustainable food production and vital for the systemic changes required. Agricultural extension services, training and education, and research contribute to sustainable agricultural production through appropriate and affordable technology (such as efficient irrigation, water harvesting and water storage), increased efficiency of land management and reductions to food waste throughout the food supply chain. Research also helps preserve sustainable practices such as traditional seed supply systems and best practices of indigenous peoples and local communities.

> " Agricultural extension services, training and education, and research contribute to sustainable agricultural production "

Agriculture worldwide faces an unprecedented challenge over 2015–2030. Of all economic sectors, it is the most directly affected by environmental degradation. Cultivated and arable land is being lost to desertification, soil erosion and salinization, and urbanization. Climate change is altering temperature and rainfall patterns. Extreme weather is causing ever more frequent and intense damage to crops and cattle (Godfray et al., 2010). Groundwater depletion, from China and India to Saudi Arabia and the United States, is affecting harvests and could contribute to significant food scarcity (Wada et al., 2010). These phenomena will intensify, threatening agricultural productivity.

At the same time, population growth requires a huge but sustainable increase in food production to 'end hunger [and] achieve food security and improved nutrition' (SDG 2). The global population, as Chapter 1: Planet noted, is expected to reach 8.5 billion in 2030, with nearly four-fifths of the increase taking place in low and lower middle income countries, especially in sub-Saharan Africa and Southern Asia, where the food supply is the most fragile. According to various sources, the productivity of existing crop and pasture land would need to increase by 70% to 100% to feed over 9 billion people by 2050 (Godfray et al., 2010).

Conventional agriculture – the manufacture and distribution of seed, feed, fertilizer and pesticides; the growth and harvesting of crops, livestock, fish and wild foods; and along with primary and secondary processing, distribution and waste disposal – cannot respond to these challenges, as it causes environmental destruction and its future productivity is uncertain. The problem is threefold:

■ Along with energy and transport, agriculture is one of the sectors that contribute most to environmental degradation. It occupies 40% of the Earth's terrestrial surface, accounts for 33% of greenhouse gas emissions and causes loss of genetic biodiversity and functional ecosystems. The 'green revolution' that took place mainly in Asia in the 1960s and 1970s was 'green' only in the sense that it concerned agriculture, not in the sense of environmental preservation. Future increases in food production must not entail unsustainable use of land, water, energy, fertilizer and chemicals (Alston and Pardey, 2014; Dobermann and Nelson, 2013; Pretty et al., 2010).

- Conventional agriculture may be reaching a productivity limit. According to the Food and Agriculture Organization (FAO), the index of per capita net production for agriculture as a whole increased less rapidly over 2008–2013 than over 2003–2008 in the Americas (4.1% vs 10.3%), Asia (7.9% vs 15.3%) and Europe (3.4% vs 5.5%) (FAO, 2016). Increases in agricultural productivity were concentrated in developed countries and Asia. In sub-Saharan Africa and in low income countries in other regions, most growth in production since 2000 was due to use of new land rather than higher factor productivity (Dobermann and Nelson, 2013). Food prices, which had mostly declined steadily since the 1960s, started to increase in the 2000s, and have become more volatile due to speculation on financial markets. Major price increases in 2007 and 2008 especially hit the poor (IFAD, 2011a).

- Food distribution and consumption patterns are compounding the negative impact of food production on the environment. In developing countries, rising per capita income has led to tastes shifting away from cereals, pulses and vegetables and towards meat and dairy products, whose production is much more intensive in use of water, fodder and chemicals (Pretty and Bharucha, 2014). The major concern, however, is food waste, which represents 30% to 40% of food produced globally. In developing countries, most food waste arises on farms and in transport and processing due to deficient food-chain infrastructure. In India, for example, 35% to 40% of fresh produce is lost. This waste could be reduced through improved small storage facilities (Godfray et al., 2010). In developed countries, food waste takes place mostly in retail, food services and homes due to consumer preferences for 'foods of the highest cosmetic standard' and inflexible adherence to 'use by' dates (Godfray et al., 2010).

EDUCATION CAN SUPPORT SUSTAINABLE FOOD PRODUCTION

Enough food can be produced for the growing world population over 2015–2030 and beyond in an environmentally sustainable and socially inclusive way, but this will require significant changes in agricultural production (Godfrey et al., 2010; Pretty and Bharucha, 2014). With current food production reaching its limits, alternatives to conventional farming must be found. They will involve sustainable intensification of food production through a combination of innovative farming methods – including agroforestry, conservation agriculture, integrated farming, mixed crop and livestock systems and organic farming – accompanied by reduction of food waste and more equitable food distribution.

Growth in demand for agricultural products will mainly occur in emerging economies, particularly the most populous countries of Eastern and South-eastern Asia, Southern Asia and sub-Saharan Africa. The ways in which these countries, including Bangladesh, China, Ethiopia, India, Indonesia, Nigeria and South Africa, respond to this growth will be major determinants of environmental change at a global scale (Sayer and Cassman, 2013).

Not only is sustainable farming possible, but education plays a key role in the transition. Primary and secondary education can provide future farmers foundation skills as well as critical knowledge about sustainability challenges in agriculture. Vocational training and skills policies can bridge the gap between farmers and new technology. Literacy and non-formal education in the form of agricultural extension can help farmers increase crop yields. Agricultural research connected with tertiary education helps produce innovation leading to more sustainable systems.

> " Vocational training and skills policies bridge the gap between farmers and new technology "

The number of people relying on farming is considerable. In the early 2010s, half the world's population lived in rural areas and three-quarters of rural people belonged to agriculture-based households: 2.6 billion depended on agriculture for their livelihoods and 1.3 billion directly engaged in farming. However, value added in agriculture accounts for just 2.8% of global GDP (Alston and Pardey, 2014). A majority of farmers depend on farms of less than 2 hectares, of which there are more than 500 million (Dobermann and Nelson, 2013).

Rural development policies which improve agricultural productivity can have strong effects on poverty reduction. In China, for example, agricultural growth is estimated to have been three times more effective in reducing poverty between 1980 and 2011 compared to growth in other sectors of the economy. Similar magnitudes are found in studies examining other developing regions (de Janvry and Sadoulet, 2010). Among several sub-Saharan African countries, estimates suggest that GDP growth driven by agriculture would be similarly effective in reducing poverty - three to four times more than non-agricultural sectors in Rwanda and Kenya, for example (IFPRI, 2012).

AGRICULTURAL EXTENSION AND RESEARCH ARE VITAL FOR TRANSFORMING PRODUCTION

Agricultural extension programmes aim to educate farmers to apply improved technologies and farming practices, helping improve crop yields, increase food security and reduce poverty. They can take the form of non-formal education and advisory services provided by government, multinational agencies and other institutions, such as research institutes and universities. International agricultural research centres, in collaboration with national public organisations, were instrumental in the widescale introduction of new crop varieties which fuelled the agricultural 'green revolution' of the 20th century (Evenson and Gollin, 2003). Bringing new sustainable technologies to farmers over 2015-2030 calls for similar international and national efforts.

> " Literacy and non-formal education in the form of agricultural extension can help farmers increase crop yields "

Agricultural extension programmes can significantly increase farmer productivity. If not designed carefully, however, they can exacerbate inequality. Research in Mozambique and Ethiopia shows that extension services tend to target wealthier farms that are more likely to adopt existing technology, while extension services that target poor farmers can have a larger impact on productivity (Cunguara and Moder, 2011; Elias et al., 2013).

Like other development policies, extension programmes need to be strategically designed in order to be sustainable. This requires improved links between agricultural research, extension organisations, business development services, farmers and local communities. Programmes which are aware and responsive to the needs of resource-poor households are more likely to result in faster diffusion of innovations (World Bank, 2012).

At the farm level, knowledge and skill requirements are significant. Farming is complex and risky. It depends on the extent and quality of the land, as well as weather, markets, inputs, support services, capital and infrastructure (Dobermann and Nelson, 2013). Innovative farming is even more challenging. Extension programmes thus need to be participatory and incorporate local knowledge. They also need to address their frequent bias towards male farmers (Pretty et al., 2010). Women form a significant share of farmers and agricultural workers, and increasing their productivity could have a large positive impact on family and child nutrition (FAO, 2011).

Farmer field schools are particularly relevant to sustainable agricultural intensification. They have spread since the late 1980s as part of a broader shift away from top-down agricultural extension (Waddington et al., 2014). They now reach over 12 million farmers in some 90 countries with a participatory approach to adult education and learning. Their aims are to provide skills in areas such as cultivation practices and pest management so as to increase yield and revenue while reducing environmental impact (FAO, 2016).

A recent systematic review based on 92 evaluations found that farmer field schools increased farmers' knowledge by 0.21 standard deviation on average, leading to average increases in yield by 13% and net revenue by 19%. They also reduced environmental impact (an aggregate index decrease by 39% on average) and pesticide use (by 17%). Education quality is vital to this model: Facilitators with strong literacy and numeracy skills, experience with farming, and willingness to use bottom-up training methods, follow a locally relevant curriculum and use the local language obtain the best results (Waddington et al., 2014).

Critical questions about how to move agricultural extension forward remain. For example, how can extension services reach and engage the widest number of farmers to facilitate institutional change and technical innovation, and what are the most effective extension strategies (Pretty et al., 2010)? Increasing productivity is necessary but not sufficient to ensure food security, reduce poverty, improve nutrition and maintain the natural resource base for sustainable development (Sayer and Cassman, 2013). Innovation is needed across a broad spectrum of policies and technologies to confront the complex array of challenges at the agriculture–environment nexus.

In many regions, climate change will result in more frequent drought and low rainfall, making current farming practices less viable. Such conditions call for the introduction of new methods and technologies. This could include the application of sustainable organic farming methods, which have been shown to produce higher yields than conventional agriculture under drought conditions, as well as reduce negative environmental impacts (Reganold and Wachter, 2016).

Agricultural research can help answer some of the dilemmas extension services face. Through a cross-disciplinary lens vital to the systemic change needed, it can bring about more sustainable practices. Generally based at universities and technical institutes, agricultural research includes collaboration by a wide variety of scientists, industrial partners and government agencies. An analysis of more than 1,000 scientific publications by France's National Institute for Agricultural Research provides insight into the types of research taking place: methods and techniques to improve productivity and the environmental, health and socio-economic impact of agriculture, ways to improve coordination between public research and industry, and scientific advice to inform policy-making (Gaunand et al., 2015).

Such research highlights a shift from isolated campus research centres towards active engagement with farming communities and industry partners, and public programmes to encourage experimentation and innovation. New research provides insights from many areas, including innovation studies, socio-technical transition studies, rural and political geography, resilience thinking and climate risk management literature (Rickards and Howden, 2012).

The Integrated Agricultural Research for Development (IAR4D) concept is an example of this interdisciplinary approach. IAR4D is based on a systems science approach which includes many of the underlying principles of sustainability science. These include economic growth by linking farmers to markets, conservation of natural resources, biodiversity, limited carbon dioxide production, food security, and social inclusion and equity. This integrated approach to farming facilitates research on rural services and policies in order to understand farmers' access to markets, credit and other key rural services. Empirical evidence for the integrated approach is positive, although still sparse and weak. Impact analyses of household surveys in the Democratic

Republic of the Congo, Nigeria, Rwanda and Uganda show that the IAR4D approach has some benefits for farmer income compared with conventional research approaches (Ayanwale et al., 2013; Nkonya et al., 2013).

Climate change and associated food security concerns are prompting growing calls to reverse reductions in government investment in agricultural research, development and extension. Many countries have halted or reduced investment in agricultural research, whether directly or as donors. The key challenge is in sub-Saharan Africa, whose share in global expenditure on public agricultural research declined from 10% in 1960 to 6% in 2009. By comparison, Brazil, China and India together accounted for 31% in 2009. In 2010, public agricultural and food research worldwide received about US$35 billion, while private research totalled between US$20 billion and US$22 billion, which was heavily concentrated in high income countries and focused on innovations in off-farm sectors such as food processing (Alston and Pardey, 2014; Mellor, 2014). Much more investment is justified – the FAO estimates the returns to public spending on agricultural R&D in Uganda at more than 12% (Dobermann and Nelson, 2013).

EDUCATION AND LIFELONG LEARNING CONTRIBUTE TO LONG-TERM ECONOMIC GROWTH

Mainstream economic analysis has highlighted increased levels of primary and secondary education as a key driver of long-term economic growth. Data show that initial levels of educational attainment explain about half the difference in growth rates between East Asia and sub-Saharan Africa between 1965 and 2010 (UNESCO, 2014).

At the individual level, the knowledge and skills workers acquire through education and training make them more productive. Provision of good quality education can improve the knowledge and skills of a whole population beyond what traditional or informal systems can achieve. For business, educated and highly skilled workers foster productivity gains and technological change, through either innovation or imitation of processes developed elsewhere. At the societal level, education expansion helps build social and institutional capital, which has a strong impact on the investment climate and growth; it also helps in building social trust, developing participatory societies, strengthening the rule of law and supporting good governance (Acemoglu et al., 2014; Bjørnskov, 2012; Knack and Zak, 2003).

For countries to prosper in their participation in the world economy, investment in education is a must. Low and lower middle income countries need to invest in secondary and tertiary education and expand lifelong learning opportunities to increase high-value added activities in the industrial and service sectors. This is particularly true of sub-Saharan Africa. By 2014, the region's gross enrolment ratio in tertiary education was 8%, far below the second-lowest regional average, that of Southern Asia (23%), and the global average (34%).

> **Increasing tertiary attainment by one year on average would increase sub-Saharan Africa's long-term GDP level by 16%**

Historically, as the estimated benefits to investment in education were lower for higher education than for primary and secondary education, the World Bank and others discouraged investment in the tertiary level (Basset and Salmi, 2014). But recent evidence on the impact of higher educational attainment on growth, pertaining to 108 countries over 1975–2010, suggests that increasing tertiary attainment by one year on average would increase sub-Saharan Africa's long-term GDP level by 16% and increase growth through technological catch-up by 0.06 percentage points a year (Bloom et al., 2014).

... BUT THE QUALITY OF EDUCATION IS CRUCIAL

The provision of good quality education is central: Increasing enrolment rates will not have as much positive impact on national economic growth if students do not reach sufficient learning outcomes (Pritchett, 2006). Years of schooling is a problematic indicator of workers' actual skills because of differences in school quality within and between countries, in achievement between students of the same social class and in acquisition of skills through other sources.

While results of the Survey of Adult Skills in the OECD Programme for the International Assessment of Adult Competencies (PIAAC) are too recent to correlate with long-term growth, surveys of student achievement conducted since the 1960s by the International Association for the Evaluation of Educational

Achievement (IEA), along with results of the OECD Programme for International Student Assessment (PISA), have been used as a proxy for the quality of education that adults received (Barro, 2013).

This strand of research has provided evidence of a substantive link between skills developed through education and economic growth. It has clearly been shown in relation to skills in mathematics and science. Across 50 countries, the average of mathematics and science test scores available between 1964 and 2003 had a significant and positive impact on economic growth over 1960–2000. A standard deviation increase in test scores was associated with a two percentage point annual increase in GDP growth (OECD, 2015d).

Research also shows that basic and advanced skills have complementary effects on growth. Both the share of students achieving at least basic skills (ranging from 42% in low income countries to 80% in high income countries) and the share achieving advanced skills have a positive impact on growth. However, the impact of the share of advanced skills is comparatively larger in countries with more scope to catch up with the most advanced economies, reflecting the importance of advanced skills for technological diffusion (OECD, 2015d).

The provision or relative lack of good quality education helps explain the East Asian 'miracle' and Latin America's 'lost decades'. Despite relatively high average years of schooling and per capita income around 1960, most Latin American countries have had low test scores in the decades since, whether measured in international surveys or in regional assessments conducted by the Latin American Laboratory for Assessment of the Quality of Education. By contrast, many East Asian countries have had higher test scores than could be predicted based on the same variables. Differences in test scores between the two regions can explain their different growth records. Within the regions, countries with higher scores had more rapid growth, e.g. Brazil and Chile compared with the Plurinational State of Bolivia, Honduras and the Bolivarian Republic of Venezuela, and the Republic of Korea and Singapore compared with Indonesia and the Philippines (Hanushek and Woessmann, 2012).

Analysis of a sample of lower middle income countries found that if all children were to acquire basic skills by 2030, GDP would be 28% higher over the following 40 years compared with what would be expected with current skills levels. The increase in GDP for upper middle income countries would be 16% and that for non-OECD high income countries 10%, reflecting higher enrolment and skills levels. Even high income OECD countries would gain significantly from bringing all students up to basic skills by 2030, with GDP 3.5% higher than otherwise (OECD, 2015d).

EDUCATION POLICIES WILL HELP COUNTRIES ADAPT TO A FAST-CHANGING WORLD OF WORK

The world of work has undergone rapid change in recent decades. ICT has dramatically changed how we live and work and how economies are structured. This change is especially apparent in more developed regions and in urban areas. In poorer countries, there has been substantial movement from agricultural to non-farm employment. Moreover, greater integration of the global economy has opened up economic and trade opportunities across the world, enabling rapid growth in the now major economies of Brazil, China and India, while displacing industries and occupations in advanced economies through off shoring, particularly among less educated workers (Autor et al., 2014).

Two trends with profound implications can be expected to shape labour markets in many countries in the foreseeable future. First, polarization between low and high skill work and reduced demand for medium skilled employment has been widely documented in industrialized economies, but can also be observed on the global level. Second, stagnation in manufacturing employment makes it uncertain that poor countries can follow the developmental paths which historically have greatly improved working conditions among the poor. These interrelated trends can be expected to significantly shape the scope for decent employment across countries, challenging policy-makers to increase the supply of highly skilled and appropriately skilled workers, while creating conditions in which an educated workforce can be employed and adequately utilized.

Education systems must adapt to job polarization

Recent evidence from high income countries has led to increasing awareness of polarization between high and low skill work. A resulting proposition is that technological changes underpin the large relative drops in medium skill employment and corresponding increases in high and low skill employment across Europe and Northern America. Increasingly sophisticated technology has not only raised demand for high skill workers by complementing their creative and problem-solving abilities, but has also displaced workers in medium skill jobs whose relatively repetitive and procedural tasks are more easily replicated in computer hardware and code, and overseas (Autor and Dorn, 2013; Autor et al., 2006; Goos et al., 2014; Jaimovich and Siu, 2012).

Evidence suggests that similar processes may also be under way in other regions, although it is premature to draw conclusions. The global employment share of high skill workers has increased by almost 40% since 1990, and is projected to have accounted for almost 20% of the workforce in 2015 (**Figure 2.1**). Over the same period, the employment share of medium skill work decreased by almost 10%, while the share of low skilled work rose correspondingly. These trends are projected to continue in coming years.

> " The global employment share of high skill workers has increased by almost 40% since 1990 "

Globally, as in industrialized countries, the majority of employment remains in medium skill occupations, which are projected to have made up slightly less than two-thirds of total employment in 2015 (ILO, 2015c). However, their share may decline significantly in coming decades as increasingly cheap and capable computer programs replace clerical workers and robots displace garment makers and machine operators[2]. In China, for example, automation has had a substantial impact on factory employment, and this trend could accelerate as wages rise and automation technology becomes cheaper. In the context of rising manufacturing wages, President Xi Jinping in 2014 called for a 'robot revolution' (Chan, 2015), which already appears to be under way. The consumer electronics manufacturer Foxconn, one of the largest employers in China (and the world), plans to automate about 70% of its factory work by 2018, and already has a fully robotic factory in Chengdu (Lin, 2015).

Education systems face the dual challenge of ensuring that those who enter medium skill work have the skill sets to avoid obsolescence and of meeting the economy's increased demand for skilled workers, demand that is likely to continue in the foreseeable future given that computer code is no substitute for the creativity and cognitive abilities of high skill workers. Yet evidence suggests that most education systems are not keeping up.

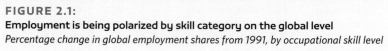

FIGURE 2.1:

Employment is being polarized by skill category on the global level

Percentage change in global employment shares from 1991, by occupational skill level

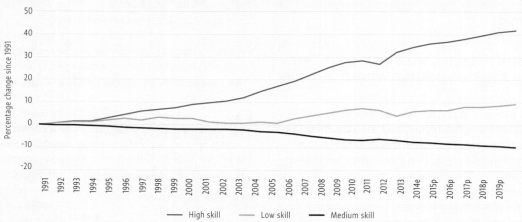

Notes: Skilled occupations are classified according to one digit ISCO-08 codes, following the ILO Global Employment Trends (GET) Model Extension (GME) methodology. High skill occupations are those of managers, professionals, technicians and associate professionals. Medium skill workers are clerical support workers, service and sales workers, skilled agricultural, forestry and fishery workers, craft and related trades workers, plant and machine operators, and assemblers. Low skill workers are those in elementary occupations. Data for 2014 are estimates (e). Data for 2015-2019 are projections (p).
Source: GEM Report team calculations based on ILO (2015c).

In high income countries such as the United States, an insufficient supply of tertiary graduates is well documented, as evidenced by the rising 'college premium' in wages and growing inequality (Goldin and Katz, 2010). On the global scale, by 2020 the world could have 40 million too few workers with tertiary degrees, relative to demand, and up to 95 million too many low and medium educated workers. Advanced economies could have up to 35 million excess workers without post-secondary education. In poorer countries the surplus of workers without secondary education could be as large as 58 million, combined with 45 million too few workers with secondary education (MGI Global, 2012).

Beyond the need for greater tertiary enrolment, what forms of skills development should governments promote? There is a case for expanding TVET at the post-secondary level in middle skill occupations that are less prone to automation (Autor, 2015). Investing in job-specific skills is risky given the uncertainty as to the effects of technological change. Still, capacities promoted by general and comprehensive education – for example, critical thinking, problem solving, team and project work, and solid literacy, communication and presentation skills – are likely to

remain valued in the labour market, including in green jobs, and throughout life.

In addition, education systems could do more to promote high value skills not easily replicated by machines or software. Studies based on analysis of job tasks in the UK and US labour markets show that two attributes in particular are the least likely to be replaced by machines: originality and social intelligence. The former – and most important – attribute refers to creative problem-solving and the generation of unusual or clever ideas about a given topic or situation. The latter entails tacit knowledge of social and cultural contexts enabling one to perform tasks such as negotiation, coordination, teaching and mentoring (Citi GPS, 2016; Frey and Osborne, 2013). Acquiring a wide range of transferable and foundation skills is therefore extremely important for future employment. The challenge for education systems is to discover how to most effectively impart them to students.

Countries need to make the leap to the high skill service sector

The decline of medium skill work, particularly manufacturing employment, has strong implications for lower income economies. In almost every country

> "
> By 2020, the world could have 40 million too few
> workers with tertiary degrees, relative to demand
> "

that has moved from low to high income status, manufacturing jobs provided the route by which poor agrarian workers moved into comparatively stable and better paid work. However, automation and technological developments are reducing demand for manufacturing workers, a trend expected to continue. Without growing manufacturing employment, the challenge of 'leapfrogging' from low skill agrarian to high skill service-sector economies is daunting for poorer countries and regions in which the majority of employment is still agricultural, such as sub-Saharan Africa and Southern Asia (World Bank, 2015).

Over the course of the 20th century, peak manufacturing employment in emerging economies has declined, relative to the historical experience of more advanced economies. Manufacturing employment in the United Kingdom peaked at 45% of total employment, while emerging economies such as Brazil and India saw manufacturing employment peak at no more than 15%. In sub-Saharan Africa, manufacturing employment has stagnated at around 6% for three decades (Citi GPS, 2016).

Countries which have not already developed a strong manufacturing sector face significant barriers. The decreasing cost of automation technology means that the abundance of cheap labour in, for example, sub-Saharan Africa is unlikely to provide sufficient incentive for manufacturing firms to invest (Citi GPS, 2016). So, as a form of 'premature deindustrialization', such nations are transforming into service economies without prior development of an industrial sector (Felipe et al., 2014; Rodrik, 2015).

This is already evident on a global scale: Employment in the service sector has grown substantially (ILO, 2015b). However, many of these jobs are characterized by low productivity and poor working conditions. In Latin America, work in the informal sector[3] has grown; in sub-Saharan Africa, urban migrants are crowding into subsistence employment in the informal service sector as well (Rodrik, 2015).

High productivity tradable service industries such as ICT and finance could provide an alternative means of growth in the absence of a manufacturing sector (Rodrik, 2015). So could jobs in growing green industries. But the highly educated and skilled workers upon which these sectors rely are typically in short supply in lower income countries. Nor is the shift to high value services such as ICT automatically positive, as it can have negative effects such as social exclusion and job insecurity (see Chapter 5: Place).

Policy-makers need to extend provision of education and skills beyond the basic literacy and numeracy that were valued in 20th century industry. The extent to which countries create conditions in which services and green industries can productively employ large numbers of workers will largely determine whether governments meet commitments to provide work for all. Countries hoping to emulate the export-led manufacturing growth of 'Asian miracle' economies may need to accept that this model now offers limited guidance.

ECONOMIC GROWTH DOES NOT MEAN PROSPERITY FOR ALL

Achieving a higher level of development has historically been linked with industrialization. But as the Agenda for Sustainable Development was being defined for 2015–2030 and the evidence of prior decades was considered, fundamental flaws became visible in the logic of economic growth reliant on the 20th century model of industrialization. These flaws concerned not only the impact on the environment but also the fact that such models of economic growth have failed to produce development that is inclusive of all (Sachs, 2015).

The previous sections presented evidence that investing in education and lifelong learning contributes to long-term economic growth and that education (and policies on education and skills development) can facilitate countries' ability to expand the higher skill service sector and provide decent work for all. But economic growth does not necessarily mean prosperity for all, in spite of the great strides made to improve the quality of life around the globe and reduce extreme poverty. The benefits of growth have been unevenly spread. The effects on the environment have meant a poorer quality of life for many, and thus a lack of prosperity. In addition, poverty remains prevalent in many countries.

While the incidence of extreme poverty declined rapidly over 2000–2015, the challenge is far from over. Almost 900 million people lived in extreme poverty in 2012. The share of people living on less than US$1.90 a day declined globally from 29% in 1999 to 13% in 2012, partly because of rapid economic development in China. Extreme poverty is now concentrated in Southern Asia (19% of the population) and sub-Saharan Africa (43%) (World Bank, 2016).

For those who are in work, earnings are often not sufficient to escape either extreme poverty or more moderate levels. In low income countries, largely in sub-Saharan Africa, 37% of workers are extremely poor and a further 32% moderately poor. More broadly, almost 90% of workers are either poor or close to poverty in low income countries, and nearly 70% in lower middle income countries. Among all developing regions, almost half of workers are poor or near poverty (**Figure 2.2**).

Inequality, as measured by the Gini coefficient, has persisted at an extremely high level globally, and has increased markedly in most countries and regions.

The Gini index measures per capita income equality: The closer the coefficient is to zero, the less the inequality, and the closer it is to one, the greater. The global Gini coefficient was 0.715 in 1998 and had not changed significantly by 2008, at 0.705 (Lakner and Milanovic, 2015).

Between 1993 and 2008, the poor did not benefit from growth as much as the rest of the population: The average per capita income of the world's poorest decile increased by 25%, but the income of the middle deciles grew roughly twice as fast, by over 50%, while the income of the richest 1% grew by 62% (Lakner and Milanovic, 2015).

Within countries, increases in inequality were more pronounced. By income group, average inequality increased significantly between the early 1990s and late 2000s: by 9% for high income countries and 11% for low and middle income countries (**Figure 2.3**). Over 1988–2008, inequality increased rapidly in China (Lakner and Milanovic, 2015).

The evidence on poverty and inequality shows that economic growth has not been equally shared and that the conventional development paradigm needs rethinking. The growth model of the past century is not suited for 21st century sustainability, even if it does include the aim of reducing extreme income poverty by raising GDP. A new concept of prosperity must include social inclusiveness of economic institutions and overall

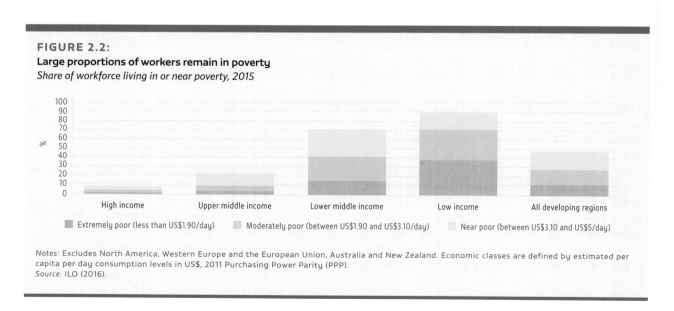

FIGURE 2.2:

Large proportions of workers remain in poverty
Share of workforce living in or near poverty, 2015

Legend:
- Extremely poor (less than US$1.90/day)
- Moderately poor (between US$1.90 and US$3.10/day)
- Near poor (between US$3.10 and US$5/day)

Notes: Excludes North America, Western Europe and the European Union, Australia and New Zealand. Economic classes are defined by estimated per capita per day consumption levels in US$, 2011 Purchasing Power Parity (PPP).
Source: ILO (2016).

well-being, along with environmental sustainability of production and consumption. A strong economy does not just grow but is also inclusive and sustainable.

In the past, growth has been tracked through gross measures such as increases in domestic product, without careful examination of its impact on the environment or the extent to which the vital economic activities of marginalized groups, such the poor and women, are included. Looking beyond a nation's averages is critical to understand how all citizens contribute to and are affected by economic growth; doing so helps keep poverty and inequality from persisting at levels that undermine social cohesion (Ravallion, 2015).

In fact, high and rising inequality has stalled progress in much of the world. Drawing on data from OECD countries over the past 30 years, analysis suggests that in relatively rich countries, the single biggest negative impact on economic growth was made by the widening gap in income between the lower middle class and poor households, on one hand, and the rest of society on the other (Cingano, 2014).

EDUCATION CAN HELP INCREASE INCLUSION

Education has an important role in creating a stronger relationship between expanding valued economic activities and promoting social inclusion as part of the process of transition to a sustainable and inclusive economy.

Education drives growth, increases the incomes of the poorest and, if equitably distributed, mitigates inequality. Making primary and secondary education of good quality widely accessible can enable large numbers of individuals and their families to increase their incomes above the poverty line. In lower income countries, achievement of basic education is associated with increased earnings and consumption among rural and informal sector workers. Calculations for the 2013/14 *EFA Global Monitoring Report* showed that if all students in low income countries left school with basic reading skills, 171 million people could be lifted out of extreme poverty, equivalent to a 12% reduction in the world total (UNESCO, 2014).

Higher levels of education reduce the likelihood of households experiencing long periods of chronic poverty or transmitting poverty between generations. If 10

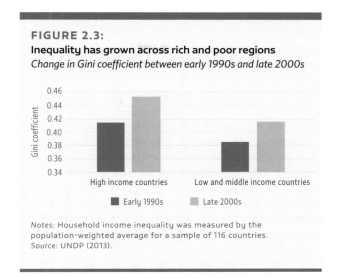

FIGURE 2.3:

Inequality has grown across rich and poor regions
Change in Gini coefficient between early 1990s and late 2000s

Notes: Household income inequality was measured by the population-weighted average for a sample of 116 countries.
Source: UNDP (2013).

recent EU member states[4] met 2020 targets to decrease early school leaving and increase tertiary participation, they could reduce the numbers of those at risk of poverty by 3.7 million (Ajwad et al., 2015). Education can also help make the labour market more inclusive by facilitating labour force participation and employment, and reduce working poverty as well.

However, assumptions on the role of education in economic development can often be overly reductive. The term 'education' encompasses a wide range of programmes, with differing levels of quality and objectives. The effects of a particular education investment in terms of desirable outcomes will accordingly vary in magnitude. Moreover, these effects will in turn vary across countries, depending on broader economic and labour market contexts. Looking more closely at the effects of levels and types of education across a range of outcomes can therefore be instructive in helping promote more participation in the economy, and more inclusion in its benefits.

EDUCATION'S IMPACT ON INEQUALITY MAY BE MIXED

While expanding education is indispensable to the fight against poverty, its impact on inequality is mixed. Increases in training and skills have not translated evenly into improved prospects for long-term economic growth or reduced social inequality. The impact of education varies by country context. Secondary or tertiary education is becoming key to obtaining decent jobs and decent earnings, even in low and middle income countries This trend is reinforced by job polarization and by the rise of the service sector in the context of rapid technological change and continued globalization.

Equitable education expansion over 2015–2030, especially at the secondary and post-secondary levels could help reverse the trend of widening income inequality within countries. Educated people, at all levels of education, receive a substantial payoff in individual earnings (Montenegro and Patrinos, 2014), meaning education reforms can be important in reducing income inequality and earnings disparities between groups. Furthermore, improving education outcomes among disadvantaged groups can improve intergenerational social and income mobility (OECD, 2012).

Generally, to tackle income inequality, education should be expanded and its provision equally distributed. Historical evidence suggests unequal distribution in educational attainment contributes to unequal income distribution (Birdsall and Londoño, 1997; Gregorio and Lee, 2002; Lundberg and Squire, 2003), while higher levels of education, in terms of both quality and quantity, positively affect growth in the income share of the poor (Gundlach et al., 2004). A meta-analysis of 64 empirical studies found that education – based on measures such as years of schooling and education expenditure – is significantly associated with an increased income share of the poor and a reduced income share of the rich. Effects were particularly strong for secondary school expansion, and for education expansion generally in Africa (Abdullah et al., 2015).

While reporting an overall positive effect, the meta-analysis cited above found that education was associated with increased inequality in a large number of studies (Abdullah et al., 2015). In the United States, it is estimated that moving 10% of non-college-educated males to a degree-level education would have little impact on overall inequality[5], mainly because many benefits would shift to the upper end of the income distribution (Hershbein et al., 2015).

> " Where education is unequally distributed and not effectively aligned with labour market designs, it can reinforce inequality "

The overall effect of education expansion on income inequality (before taxes and transfers) is ultimately determined by changes in the education distribution between levels of education; differences in labour market returns between (and within) these levels;[6] and whether the education expansion reduces differences in wages between education levels.

The dynamics of education expansion are commonly understood in terms of two sometimes contradictory processes – the *composition* effect and the *compression* effect (Gregorio and Lee, 2002; Knight and Sabot, 1983). The former, through increases in the incomes of beneficiaries, changes income distribution, and in theory can either increase or decrease inequality. For example, on this basis, education expansion in which beneficiaries increase their incomes significantly above average wages (e.g. expanding tertiary education in a country in which only a small proportion of the population has tertiary education) can be expected to increase inequality, all else being equal. On the other hand, education expansion in which a disadvantaged group increases its income to closer to the national average (e.g. moving to universal secondary attainment where attainment is relatively widespread) can be expected to lower inequality. Hence, the composition effect of education expansion at a given level of education tends to increase inequality initially, as more people attain higher income, then lower it over time, as fewer low income people remain.

At the same time, a *compression* effect takes place when the increased supply of workers with a given level of education exceeds the demand for them. This pushes wages down relative to the less educated. So while the composition effect can work to either increase or decrease inequality, the compression effect works to lower inequality. All else being equal, the effect of education expansion on earnings inequality depends on the net composition and compression effect. If, for example, a higher education expansion led to a compositional change – which would in theory widen the income distribution – this would have to be outweighed by a subsequent compression effect across higher education graduates in order to decrease inequality.

Given uncertainty of the future returns between and within various levels of education and labour market demand, accurately estimating the net composition and compression effects of an education reform in advance is challenging.

Education should therefore be viewed as a potential equalizing mechanism, but not as the sole solution to inequality. The degree to which education can decrease income inequality within countries over 2015–2030 will vary by countries, depending on context. Opportunities for large expansion of secondary education that could equalize income exist in many low income countries. Yet many countries, including in poor regions, will likely experience ever-increasing demand for tertiary education, both as a result of larger numbers graduating from secondary school and from employers wanting skilled workers (Altbach et al., 2011). If changes in the economy raise the pay-off to tertiary education, while tertiary graduation increases alongside, income inequality could widen in many countries.

Governments have an obligation to provide universal primary and secondary education and basic skills to all. But whether increased access to tertiary education improves income distribution over the short and medium term should not ultimately determine its desirability. Education is not the only tool available to policy-makers wishing to tackle inequality. Counteracting inequality with taxes and transfers between those on high and low incomes remains a necessary and often more effective method than education reform alone (Hershbein et al., 2015). Better access to education (leading to declining education inequality), combined with improved health outcomes and redistributive social policies, have been cited as three interventions that help raise the income share of the poor and middle class regardless of the level of economic development (Dabla-Norris et al., 2015).

EDUCATION IMPROVES LABOUR MARKET AND DECENT WORK OUTCOMES

The primary way education promotes economic inclusion is by expanding people's ability to participate productively in the economy on favourable terms. This objective, implicitly including poverty reduction and greater income equality, is encapsulated in SDG 8: promoting inclusive and sustainable economic growth, employment and decent work for all.

Decent work is both an aspiration and an expectation for the vast majority of working age adults, who depend on a decent wage for their labour (**Box 2.2**). However, widely available measures make clear that decent work remains out of reach for much of the global working population.

Education is widely considered one of the best investments to expand prospects of skilled and

---

BOX 2.2

What is decent work?

The ILO concept of decent work describes it as work that is 'productive and delivers a fair income, security in the workplace and social protection for families. Decent work means better prospects for personal development and social integration, and freedom for people to express their concerns, organize and participate in the decisions that affect their lives. It entails equality of opportunity and treatment for all women and men'.

Education primarily promotes decent work by enabling individuals with skills and knowledge to become more productive.[7] More specifically, it enables individuals to acquire a stock of capabilities (knowledge and skills) necessary to perform certain tasks effectively. Workers apply their skills to bundles of tasks (occupations) in order to produce output. Skilled workers can perform a variety of complex tasks more effectively, thereby producing more value and receiving higher earnings. Due to their relative scarcity, higher skill workers are more employable and demand not only higher earnings in the labour market, but also better working conditions. Higher skill work is often intrinsically more rewarding because of the freedom and creativity often inherent to higher skill occupations.

Sources: Acemoglu and Autor (2011); ILO (2007).

---

adequately paid employment. But while most policy-makers are aware of the importance of education for productive and decent work, it is less clear what forms of education expansion should be promoted to maximize better job opportunities. In addition, following the earlier discussion, it will be important for education to equip workers with green skills, for the new green economy.

EDUCATION CAN FACILITATE LABOUR FORCE PARTICIPATION AND ACCESS TO EMPLOYMENT

Globally, many individuals remain unable to secure work, or do not participate in the labour market. The share of the population in employment varies significantly across regions. It is systematically lower among women than men, particularly in Northern Africa and Western Asia and Southern Asia (ILO, 2015b).

In 2014, 201 million people globally were considered unemployed: that is, without work, though available for and seeking employment. Youth continue to be disproportionately affected, accounting for over one-third of the unemployed globally (ILO, 2015b). Some regions display considerable gender disparity, including Latin America and the Caribbean, sub-Saharan Africa and, in particular, Northern Africa and Western Asia, where 21% of women are unemployed – almost double the share of men. Underemployment is also significant. In the European Union, 10 million are underemployed, two-thirds of them women (Eurostat, 2015). Unemployment figures exclude those who have stopped actively seeking work, often because they cannot find employment or have given up. In 2013, the number of these 'discouraged workers' was estimated at 23 million globally (ILO, 2014).

Education can have a significant role in facilitating employment, as reflected in lower unemployment rates among the comparatively educated, particularly in richer countries. However, in poorer countries this relationship often breaks down, suggesting both that demand for skilled labour is limited and that education systems are not enabling students to acquire relevant skills (ILO, 2015a; Sparreboom and Staneva, 2014).

In richer countries, low educational attainment has a strong association with unemployment and inactivity. In the OECD, only 55% of adults aged 25 to 64 with less than an upper secondary education were employed in 2013, compared with 73% of those with an upper secondary or non-tertiary education and 83% with a tertiary qualification (OECD, 2015c).[8] The corresponding rates among those aged 15 to 29 who were not in education were 49%, 73% and 83% (OECD, 2015b).

Evidence across 11 EU countries shows that the probability of long-term unemployment decreases with higher educational attainment (Garrouste et al., 2010). In emerging economies such as South Africa and Turkey, there are large differences in employment rates by educational attainment. In South Africa, less than 45% of the adult population with less than upper secondary education were employed in 2005, compared to over 60% who completed upper secondary, and over 80% with a tertiary qualification (Quintini and Martin, 2013). In the United States, high

> ❝
> Evidence across 11 EU countries shows that long-term unemployment decreases with higher educational attainment
> ❞

school and university completion significantly increases the chance of unemployed workers finding work within a year (Riddell and Song, 2011).

By contrast, unemployment in non-OECD countries is often associated with higher levels of education. In Asia and the Pacific, North Africa and Western Asia, and sub-Saharan Africa the youth unemployment rate increases with the level of education. Youth with tertiary education in these regions are two to three times more likely to be unemployed than youth with primary education or less (ILO, 2015a). In several sub-Saharan African countries, differences are especially large among young adults aged 25-34. In the United Republic of Tanzania, for example, unemployment is almost negligible among those with primary education or less, but almost 17% for those with tertiary education (UCW, 2013). Such outcomes are partly due to the more educated coming from wealthier backgrounds and thus able to sustain periods of unemployment, whereas employment is necessary for survival among the poorer and less educated (UCW, 2013).

High unemployment rates among the relatively educated – particularly among youth – also reflect low education quality, weak skills acquisition and limited labour demand. In Northern Africa and Western Asia, where youth unemployment is pervasive, education quality is low, as indicated by the fact that some 75% of eighth grade students scored poorly on international mathematics tests. Tertiary enrolment is also weighted towards subjects with relatively low labour market demand (particularly law, the humanities and business/commerce). These factors may explain why almost 40% of firms in Northern Africa and Western Asia – the highest share of any region – identified an inadequately educated workforce as a major constraint to growth (Gatti et al., 2013).

TVET is often promoted as a potential solution to youth unemployment, facilitating school-to-work transition by providing skills more relevant to the labour market. However, the evidence is mixed: While some studies indicate that vocational education increases youth employment, the consistency of the finding in different settings and over the life course varies (Hanushek et al., 2011; OECD, 2015b).

There is a limit to the extent countries can educate themselves out of unemployment. In poorer countries, high unemployment rates among the educated likely reflects limited demand for skilled labour, amplified by large and growing youth populations (ILO, 2015a). In advanced economies, unemployment has always been a feature to various degrees; all else being equal, it is questionable whether educating the unemployed to minimum standards would lead to full employment. So it is important for education interventions to be accompanied by economic policies that aim to increase demand for skilled labour.

EDUCATION, ESPECIALLY SECONDARY AND TERTIARY, CAN ADDRESS PERVASIVE WORKING POVERTY AND JOB INSTABILITY

This chapter has already described how working people's earnings often do not allow them to escape poverty. Almost half of workers in developing regions are in or near poverty, with considerably higher proportions in low and lower middle income countries (Figure 2.2).

Even higher shares of workers are in 'vulnerable employment': they work on their own account or with one or more partners, or they are unpaid family workers. Beyond low income, vulnerable employment is associated with a lack of social protection and unstable working conditions. It was estimated to account for

45% of global employment in 2014 (ILO, 2015c), and 75% of workers in sub-Saharan Africa and Southern Asia. Women tend to be over-represented in vulnerable employment in most regions. Even higher proportions of workers are estimated to work informally, operating outside legislative frameworks and lacking employment protection. Evidence suggests that in many low and middle income countries, over half of non-agricultural employment is informal, particularly in sub-Saharan Africa and Southern Asia, as well as many Latin American countries (ILO, 2013b).

Increasing levels of education are progressively associated with lower working poverty rates, as illustrated by analysis of twelve low and lower middle income countries surveyed in the Skills Towards Employment and Productivity (STEP) programme (**Figure 2.4**)[9]. Attainment of upper secondary education[10] considerably reduces the likelihood of working in poverty compared to lower levels of education. Indeed, this advantage appears clear in comparison to lower-secondary attainment in most countries sampled. Those with tertiary education are least likely to be working in poverty, by a substantial margin.

FIGURE 2.4:

Increasing levels of education are associated with lower working poverty

Working poverty (below 50% of median weekly earnings) by education level in 12 low and middle income countries

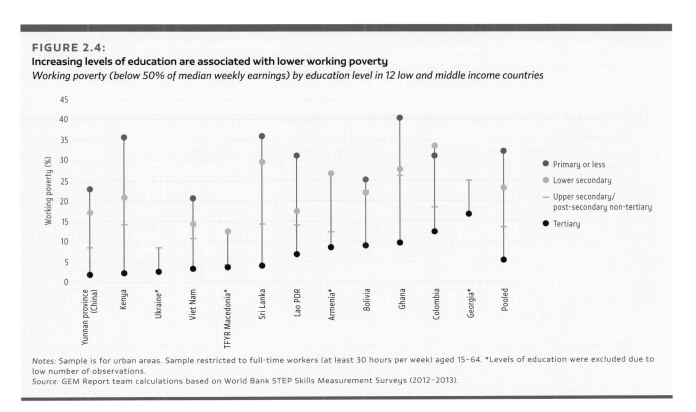

Notes: Sample is for urban areas. Sample restricted to full-time workers (at least 30 hours per week) aged 15–64. *Levels of education were excluded due to low number of observations.
Source: GEM Report team calculations based on World Bank STEP Skills Measurement Surveys (2012–2013).

> ## Globally, earnings increase by approximately 10% for each additional year of schooling

The benefits of upper secondary attainment and the equivalent are even more apparent when examining other measures of poor working conditions in low and middle income countries (**Figure 2.5**). Those with upper secondary education are significantly less likely than workers with lower secondary to be in vulnerable employment or to work informally without a contract or social benefits. This would suggest that upper secondary education can increase access to more productive occupations with decent working conditions. For this to hold true, any future increases in upper secondary attainment should be accompanied by growing opportunities in the labour market to productively utilize these skills.

However, vulnerable and informal employment remains sizeable in the low income countries of the sample, even among workers with upper secondary education. In the Plurinational State of Bolivia and Colombia, informality and own-account employment remain relatively widespread even among workers with tertiary education. Informality is partly driven by efforts to avoid

taxes and regulations. But widespread employment in low productivity small and micro-enterprises, largely reflects limited employment opportunities in larger formal sector firms (La Porta and Shleifer, 2014). Unless measures are taken to promote the growth of larger, higher productivity firms (which in addition to offering better working conditions are more likely to comply with regulations), the effects of education expansion may be muted in some countries (Herrera-Idárraga et al., 2015). However, since vulnerable employment has been growing in recent years, including in OECD countries (ILO, 2015b; Jütting and Laiglesia, 2009), it is questionable whether employment can be significantly 'formalised' by 2030.

EDUCATION SIGNIFICANTLY INCREASES EARNINGS AND EMPLOYMENT

Beyond reducing poverty, education has a well-established effect on earnings across the income distribution. Globally, in 139 countries, the private return[11] per additional year of schooling is 10%. Rates of return are highest in poorer regions such as sub-Saharan Africa,

---

FIGURE 2.5:
Upper secondary attainment can substantially lower the risk of vulnerable and informal employment
Vulnerable and informal employment in urban areas by educational attainment

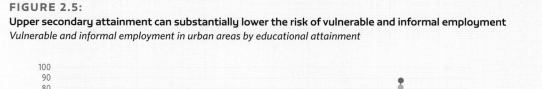
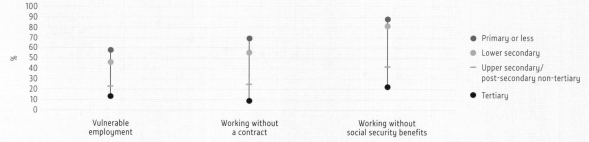

Notes: For urban areas of Armenia, the Plurinational State of Bolivia, Colombia, Georgia, Ghana, Kenya, the Lao People's Democratic Republic, Sri Lanka, the former Yugoslav Republic of Macedonia, Ukraine, Viet Nam and China (Yunnan province). Vulnerable employment is defined as the sum of own-account workers and contributing family workers. Data are for 2012–2013, weighted by population.
Source: GEM Report team calculations based on World Bank STEP Skills Measurement Surveys (2012–2013).

reflecting the scarcity of skilled workers (Montenegro and Patrinos, 2014).

In recent years, international surveys directly measuring skills among youth and adults have shown that literacy, numeracy and problem-solving abilities have a significant impact on earnings. For example, in 22 OECD countries, a standard deviation increase in literacy and numeracy skills is associated with an average increase in hourly wages of 17% and 18%, respectively[12] (Hanushek et al., 2013). Among urban populations in eight low and middle income countries, the increase in hourly earnings associated with a standard deviation increase in literacy scores ranges from 9 percentage points in Ukraine to about 25 percentage points in Ghana and Kenya (Valerio et al., 2015).[13] In both OECD and lower income countries, returns are highest among prime-age workers (35 to 54), who presumably are more able to apply their skills in employment (Chua, 2015; Hanushek et al., 2013).

Differences in returns to literacy skills on earnings between richer and poorer countries suggest their relative scarcity in the latter. For example, in the Plurinational State of Bolivia, Ghana and Kenya, the returns to literacy are the highest in the World Bank

STEP Skills Measurement Survey sample, but the literacy scores are the lowest, with the majority of adults possessing not even basic literacy skills of at least level 2 (Valerio et al., 2015). Nevertheless, there is considerable scope to improve literacy even in OECD countries, where large proportions of adults do not possess more developed skills above level 2 (OECD, 2015a).

Facilitating employment in higher skill occupations is an important route through which education increases earnings. It enables workers to perform a range of complex tasks inherent to higher skill work. In OECD economies, workers in managerial, professional and technical occupations have, unsurprisingly, the highest earnings by some margin compared to those in lesser skilled occupations (De La Rica and Gortazar, 2016). Analysis of STEP survey data shows similar patterns for the low and middle income countries sampled.

However, upper secondary education on its own does not appear to facilitate access to high skill occupations; instead tertiary education is likely a necessity. The education profiles between those in high skill and lower skill work are strikingly different (**Figure 2.6**). High skill employment largely remains the preserve of those

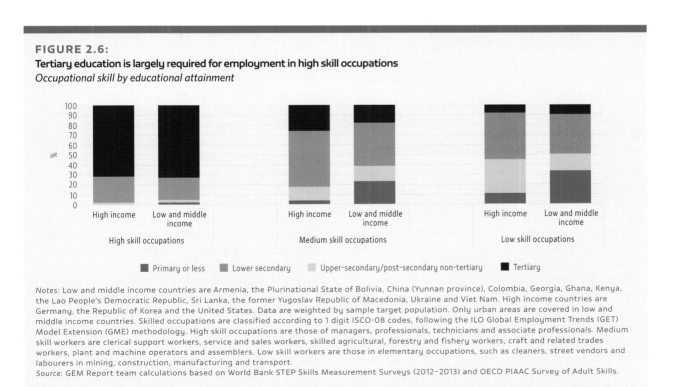

FIGURE 2.6:
Tertiary education is largely required for employment in high skill occupations
Occupational skill by educational attainment

Legend: ■ Primary or less ■ Lower secondary ■ Upper-secondary/post-secondary non-tertiary ■ Tertiary

Notes: Low and middle income countries are Armenia, the Plurinational State of Bolivia, China (Yunnan province), Colombia, Georgia, Ghana, Kenya, the Lao People's Democratic Republic, Sri Lanka, the former Yugoslav Republic of Macedonia, Ukraine and Viet Nam. High income countries are Germany, the Republic of Korea and the United States. Data are weighted by sample target population. Only urban areas are covered in low and middle income countries. Skilled occupations are classified according to 1 digit ISCO-08 codes, following the ILO Global Employment Trends (GET) Model Extension (GME) methodology. High skill occupations are those of managers, professionals, technicians and associate professionals. Medium skill workers are clerical support workers, service and sales workers, skilled agricultural, forestry and fishery workers, craft and related trades workers, plant and machine operators and assemblers. Low skill workers are those in elementary occupations, such as cleaners, street vendors and labourers in mining, construction, manufacturing and transport.
Source: GEM Report team calculations based on World Bank STEP Skills Measurement Surveys (2012–2013) and OECD PIAAC Survey of Adult Skills.

with tertiary education, while those in medium and low skill jobs are largely educated to the secondary level or below.[15] These patterns are more or less replicated across the sample of poorer and richer countries, suggesting that the education segmentation of high and medium/low skill work may be a general feature of economies regardless of income.

Educational attainment is associated with higher earnings within occupational categories, however. Analysis of prime-aged workers in full-time employment in the STEP countries shows that hourly earnings for low skill work increase with educational attainment. Among medium skill workers, educational attainment is associated with an even greater increase in earnings. High skill workers with tertiary education also earn substantially more than those with upper secondary attainment. On this basis, education expansion should lead to increases in earnings across all occupational groups regardless, but to a greater degree if it facilitates access to higher skill occupations.

The case for expanding tertiary education in developing countries is supported by recent evidence on labour market returns to education. In contrast to earlier research which found that the return to earnings was highest for a year of primary schooling, more recent global estimates show that the private returns to tertiary education exceed those to both primary and secondary education (Montenegro and Patrinos, 2014). This finding is confirmed in a smaller sample of 25 low and middle income countries (Fink and Peet, 2014).

EDUCATION CLOSES GENDER AND SOCIO-ECONOMIC EMPLOYMENT DISPARITY

In many countries, labour market outcomes are generally, and often significantly, worse among women and those with disadvantaged socio-economic backgrounds. Among the urban population of STEP countries, working poverty among women is on average double that of men, and in most countries is significantly higher for those of low-socio-economic background compared to more advantaged counterparts. Large disparities are also found in many OECD countries, such as Austria, Finland, the Republic of Korea and Switzerland, where the incidence of low pay among women is more than double that of men (OECD, 2016b). Wages among those with low socio-economic background are significantly below more advantaged counterparts in a majority of OECD countries (OECD, 2015c).

Gender disparity in vulnerable employment and informality, however, tends to differ by country and region. Among Eastern European and Central Asian countries of the STEP survey, informality is highest among men, but is higher among women in Latin American and sub-Saharan African countries.[16] In the majority of countries, workers from disadvantaged socio-economic backgrounds are more likely to work informally (Chua, 2015).

Differences in education and skills can be a significant source of disparity among disadvantaged groups. In STEP countries, workers of low socio-economic background on average have two years fewer of education than those from a middle socio-economic background, and three years less than those from a high background. Literacy skills are also significantly lower than advantaged socio-economic groups in most countries (Chua, 2015).

Gender disparity in educational attainment and literacy tends to vary by country. Among urban areas in the STEP sample, female workers in Eastern Europe and Central Asia tend to have both higher educational attainment and literacy levels than their male counterparts, while the opposite is true in Latin America and sub-Saharan Africa.[17] In Ghana, for example, men have over two more years of education than women, and score over 40 points higher on a 500 point literacy scale. More broadly, disparities in advanced economies across the world are lower, with men averaging 0.25 years more of education, compared to one year more among developing countries (Barro and Lee, 2013). Among the 22 PIAAC countries, differences in literacy between the genders are marginal, although men have slightly higher numeracy scores (OECD, 2013).

Given the influence of education and skills on labour market outcomes, closing education disparities can increase access to decent work among disadvantaged groups. For the STEP countries, analysis conducted for this report suggests that if workers from low socio-economic backgrounds had the same education as more advantaged counterparts, disparity in informal employment between the two groups could shrink by 37% and that in working poverty by 39%.[18] Within countries where group differences in employment outcomes are statistically significant, the effect of equalizing education outcomes is even stronger. In Colombia, Ghana, Kenya and Viet Nam, educational attainment explains nearly all the disparity in informal

> **"** If workers from poor and rich backgrounds received the same education, disparity between the two in working poverty could shrink by 39% **"**

employment between workers from low and high socio-economic backgrounds (Chua, 2015).

In the 22 PIAAC countries, skills account for 83% of the wage gap between low and high socio-economic status groups,[19] and 72% of the gap between foreign and native-born workers (OECD, 2015c). This analysis does not, however, control for educational attainment.

In STEP countries, analysis indicates that literacy does not have a strong effect on some indicators of decent work, independent of educational attainment. Here, differences in literacy explain 16% of the disparity in informal employment by socioeconomic status, reduced to 6% when controlling for educational attainment, while there is no statistically significant impact on disparity in working poverty (Chua, 2015).[20]

Regarding gender, marked differences in labour market outcomes, such as employment rates and wages, tend to decrease among more highly and similarly educated men and women (Ñopo et al., 2012; UNESCO, 2014). In the OECD, differences in cognitive skills account for 23% of the gender gap in wages (OECD, 2015c). However, differences in education and skills between men and women have comparatively limited explanatory power regarding labour market inequality in the low and middle income STEP countries, where closing gaps in either educational attainment or literacy would not have a statistically significant effect on gender disparity in informal employment and working poverty across the pooled sample (Chua, 2015).

Nevertheless, differences in educational attainment account for a significant proportion of employment disparity in the STEP countries where women are most educationally disadvantaged. Analysis suggests that equalizing educational attainment would reduce disparity in informal employment by 50% for Ghana and 35% for Kenya, with working poverty dropping by 14% and 7%, respectively (Chua, 2015).

Other factors affecting labour market outcomes are thus likely to have a far larger effect on gender disparity in many countries. For example, women are more likely to work in part-time employment due to child care responsibilities, or enter industries and occupations which are less well remunerated. Cultural norms and discrimination also limit the extent to which well-qualified women can get access to better-paid occupations and rise within work hierarchies (World Bank, 2011). It is telling that women in high skill occupations in STEP countries commonly have equivalent or higher literacy skills than their male counterparts, yet on average earn substantially less.

While education and skills policies can help reduce differences in wages between men and women, other policy interventions are required. For example, as noted above, the poor are often disproportionally employed in less secure jobs, often in the informal sector. Hence, they tend to benefit more from labour market regulations such as minimum wages and firing restrictions. Labour market deregulation and technological progress thus dampen the income share of the poor. In this context, while policy has a role in making education more accessible, it must also ensure that changes in labour market institutions do not excessively penalize lower income individuals (Dabla-Norris et al., 2015).

EDUCATION POLICIES CAN HELP ENSURE A SOCIALLY INCLUSIVE TRANSITION TO GREENER ECONOMIES

While green growth offers many opportunities for expanding employment, a degree of displacement is inevitable in environmentally unsustainable industries (Bowen and Kuralbayeva, 2015). Expanded lifelong learning policies are needed to promote education and training programmes that enable displaced workers to shift into new jobs without long spells of unemployment or inactivity.

In many countries, green growth may result in increased demand for low skill work. While in some contexts such employment may provide a route out of poverty, it will not necessarily be decent work. For example, some waste disposal and recycling work is precarious and hazardous, often taking place in the informal sector (ILO, 2013a). In such cases, national legislation and industrial policies have an important role in enforcing acceptable working conditions. At the same time, education policies should equip individuals with the skills to move into more favourable occupations considered of higher value to society.

The transition to more environmentally sustainable economies will also likely increase the demand for high skill technical, managerial and scientific occupations, potentially increasing wage inequality and job polarization.[21] An analysis of the US labour market indicates that occupations in green industries are biased towards higher skills levels than 'brown' industries such as coal and other mining, with work disproportionally made up of higher skill tasks (Vona et al., 2015). Thus, a concerted effort towards green growth may substantially increase demand for high skill workers. Unless education systems adapt to provide the required technical, analytic and managerial skills, wage inequality could increase.

CONCLUSION

Implementing the SDG agenda to 2030 means reorienting education vis-à-vis a fast-changing world economy. It means expanding, interrogating and exploiting education's complex relationship with the economy. For education to contribute most effectively to reductions in poverty and inequality and to better jobs, investments should be made with careful consideration of national contexts, and in combination with wider economic and social policies.

Education and lifelong learning will also play a central part in the creation of a green and inclusive economy with sustainable models of production and consumption, and new and retooled sectors, industries and jobs. It is difficult to predict precisely what education can achieve over the next 15 years, given the uncertainties in the transition towards sustainable economies and major shifts in the world of work. Yet it is clear that education will play a critical dual role of addressing poverty and inequality while supporting the transition to a new model of sustainable development.

For this to occur, all stakeholders, from civil society and non-government organizations – often at the forefront of the fight for sustainability and inclusion – to multilateral organizations, bilateral aid agencies and all levels of government, will need to make concerted efforts to reorient systems of education, skills development, and research and innovation.

Education will remain a central component of prosperous societies. Yet its reorientation and transformation will be necessary to create green industries, to match the massive changes expected in the labour market and to ensure social inclusion. Whether defined as knowledge transmission and skills formation, as research and innovation, or as social and institutional capital, education will largely determine the ability of countries, firms and citizens to transform the economy.

ENDNOTES

1. The countries and regional groupings covered included Australia, Brazil, China, Germany, Indonesia, Norway, Mauritius, the Republic of Korea, South Africa and the United States, as well as the European Union.

2. It is predicted that the decline in medium skill employment will level off at some point, as many of these jobs depend on uniquely human interaction. Displaced medium skill workers can also move into similar level jobs in the same industry. The impact of automatic teller machines (ATMs) in US banking is illustrative: While ATM numbers grew substantially, the number of tellers actually increased slightly as reduced branch costs allowed branches to proliferate and tellers moved into sales and 'relationship banking' roles (Autor, 2015).

3. The World Bank describes the informal economy as activities and income that are completely or partly outside of government regulation and taxation.

4. Bulgaria, the Czech Republic, Estonia, Hungary, Latvia, Lithuania, Poland, Romania, Slovakia and Slovenia.

5. However, the bottom quartile of income distribution would receive an increased share of income.

6. For example, a society which hypothetically shifted from universal secondary education (but no more) to universal tertiary education would likely be more unequal due to the larger variance of wages among those with tertiary education.

7. Education attainment also acts as a signal of ability to employers, opening the door to more productive (and decent) work irrespective of the actual knowledge acquired during study.

8. The corresponding unemployment rates were 13.7%, 8.1% and 5.3%.

9. Poverty is defined relative to the median as a more comparable measure of economic contexts.

10. In GEM Report analysis of STEP/PIAAC data, upper secondary and post-secondary non-tertiary programmes are merged into a single category, and referred to as 'upper secondary' for brevity.

11. Latest available year, including foregone earnings and excluding income taxes.

12. The effect of problem-solving abilities is slightly lower at 14.3%.

13. This may underestimate the returns relative to PIAAC countries given that STEP data for waged workers are after tax and transfers, while in PIAAC countries they are before.

14. Across the STEP sample, relative to full-time, low skill workers, hourly earnings are 50% higher among medium skill employees on average, and over twice as high among high skill workers. These figures underestimate productivity, as earnings from self-employment, which tends to be higher in lower skill occupations, are reported before tax, whereas earnings from employees are after tax.

15. The value of tertiary education is reinforced by the observation that 65% of those with tertiary education in the low/middle income countries and 74% in the high income countries had high skill employment, compared with 18% and 25%, respectively, of those with upper secondary education.

16. Informal sector workers are defined here as either wage workers without social benefits, unpaid family workers or self-employed workers in an establishment with only one employee.

17. Note that in the developing world, men have on average over a year more of educational attainment (Barro and Lee, 2013).

18. Controlling for experience, gender, literacy and country effects.

19. Parental educational attainment is used here as a proxy for socio-economic status.

20. Relative to educational attainment, skills generally have less (although often significant) power to explain wages among STEP countries, while in PIAAC countries the opposite is true (Hanushek et al., 2013; Valerio et al., 2015).

21. Evidence suggests that the onset of a new wave of technological change initially creates a surge in demand for new skills, which later dissipates as codification and standardization facilitate diffusion of new best practices.

Selina Akter, second year midwifery student, plays the role of a mother as students practise postnatal care at the Dinajpur nursing institute in Bangladesh.

People: inclusive social development

We are determined to end poverty and hunger, in all their forms and dimensions, and to ensure that all human beings can fulfil their potential in dignity and equality and in a healthy environment.

– The 2030 Agenda for Sustainable Development

KEY MESSAGES

Progress in health, nutrition and gender equality is inextricably linked with progress in education.

1 **Substantive gender equality is far from being achieved.**

   a. Gender gaps still exist in pay, work conditions and leadership roles, even among similarly qualified men and women.

   b. Gender-based violence continues to be a major issue.

2 **Millions of people – particularly the marginalized – are still denied their right to education.**

   a. Poverty, gender, location, disability and immigrant status all pose barriers to the completion of basic education of good quality.

3 **Education improves health by giving people relevant knowledge and skills.**

   a. There is huge potential for delivering health and nutrition interventions through schools, which subsequently also increase school attendance and learning.

   b. Innovative education programmes can improve sanitation practices.

4 **Educating women is at the heart of social development.**

   a. Gender gaps in education and health are key drivers of income inequality in low and middle income countries.

   b. Learning to read and write helps women challenge practices that perpetuate their low social status, including by making their participation in politics more likely.

   c. Female literacy helps reduce child and maternal mortality and reduce high fertility levels.

5 **Children need to be healthy and well-nourished in order to attend school and learn.**

   a. Health and nutrition infrastructure can be used to deliver education.

   b. Disease causes teacher absenteeism and attrition.

   c. Access to water, sanitation, hygiene and energy have an impact on education outcomes.

5 **Education on its own is not enough to achieve equality in society; the health, gender and education sectors must work together.**

   a. Equal numbers of boys and girls in school has not yet resulted in gender-equal societies because of persistent discrimination.

   b. Education needs to work with other sectors to change daily and community behaviours.

   c. Men and women need to be engaged through comprehensive education and empowerment approaches to improve gendered attitudes and behaviours.

A broad concept of social development is expressed in the 2030 Agenda for Sustainable Development, as cited above. Social development has also been described as 'a process of change that leads to improvements in human well-being and social relations that are equitable and compatible with principles of democratic governance and justice' (UNRISD, 2015 p. 4).

Achieving sustainable development implies that all women and men, girls and boys have access to essential basic services required for decent, dignified living. It also implies that people can participate in their daily lives and relationships free of discrimination and disadvantage. Social development has been achieved for some, but not for all. Social development needs to be inclusive.

Social development should be not only inclusive, but also transformative, which means it 'must involve changes in social structures, institutions and relations, including patterns of stratification' (UNRISD, 2015, p. 4). So, besides improving specific measurable outcomes, society needs to change legislation, political processes, and social and economic policies.

This chapter suggests why inclusive social development is important and assesses progress. It views education as a key dimension of social development that also enables other social objectives and can transform societies. Education can equip people with knowledge, skills and values that help improve social outcomes and change social norms. Moreover, the education sector can improve how other sectors function. As examples, the chapter looks at education's effects on health and gender issues.

At the same time, social development has various effects on education. What is needed, therefore, is integrating social and education interventions, which requires understanding how other institutions and sectors affect education, recognizing the limits of education's role and ensuring integrated commitments and actions. The chapter concludes by examining how participatory, inclusive approaches can sustain transformation.

INCLUSIVE SOCIAL DEVELOPMENT IS CRITICAL FOR SUSTAINABLE FUTURES FOR ALL

To examine whether social development is inclusive globally, this section analyses service provision, gender inequality and other marginalization.

> Ending poverty is not only about income, but also concerns critical services such as education, health, water, sanitation, energy, housing and transport

Inclusive social development requires universal provision of services. Ending poverty is not only about income, but also concerns critical services such as education, health, water, sanitation, energy, housing and transport. In addition, assessing if social development is inclusive requires statistics disaggregated by gender, ethnicity, location, immigrant and refugee status and other context-relevant types of marginality to understand whether these services are available to all.

At the same time, inclusive social development requires more than providing services. Social structures must be changed to ensure that all women and girls, men and boys have a measure of equality between them, and that one's gender does not adversely affect opportunities in life and work. Gender equality remains elusive but is a key requirement.

Inequality must be addressed. To achieve inclusive social development, entrenched marginalization and discriminatory attitudes towards women, people with disabilities, indigenous populations, ethnic and linguistic minorities, refugees and displaced people, among other vulnerable groups, have to be challenged. Changing discriminatory norms and empowering women and men requires improving knowledge and influencing values and attitudes.

THE WORLD IS FAR FROM UNIVERSAL PROVISION OF MOST ESSENTIAL SERVICES

The essential services for a dignified life and healthy environment can be defined widely. Income is not the only necessity to escape poverty. *World Development Report 2004: Making Services Work for Poor People* viewed 'freedom from illiteracy' and 'freedom from illness' as key to escaping poverty, with water, sanitation, transport and energy as important services for achieving good education and health outcomes (World Bank, 2003).

Others have argued for water and sanitation, waste collection and management, transport and energy as fundamental needs; as one report notes, 'Everyone needs water, a toilet, energy, a way to dispose of household waste and the ability to get from place to place' (United Cities and Local Governments, 2014 p. 13).

The Sustainable Development Goals (SDGs) contain ambitious goals and targets for universal access to lifelong learning, health care, good nutrition, water and sanitation, and energy (United Nations, 2015a). It is important to make progress on all these complementary outcomes at once, as they are interconnected and neglecting any of them has compound negative effects.

Lack of clean water, sanitation and energy can have a long-term impact on health. Water-related ailments, such as diarrhoea, worm infestations and dehydration, result from poor water, sanitation and hygiene, and are well documented as key causes of under-5 mortality. They also have long-term effects on neurological development, lowering IQ and learning performance (Joshi and Amadi, 2013). Extreme consequences of malnutrition, such as stunting (low height for age), which also severely affects brain development, are not just a result of nutrition deficiency but also poor sanitation and hygiene (Chambers and Von Medeazza, 2013). High use of biomass, coal and kerosene has dramatic negative health effects, especially for women and children; lower respiratory infections are a leading cause of under-5 mortality (WHO, 2014).

The Millennium Development Goals (MDGs) emphasized poverty reduction in poorer countries, so indicators on education, health, water and sanitation, and energy access have been systematically monitored. Data show progress, with major improvements over 2000–2015 in primary education enrolment, basic health delivery and under-5 mortality rates.

However, below the global level, basic service provision varies tremendously. Problems remain particularly acute in low income countries (**Figure 3.1**), and there is substantial inequality within countries. For instance, water and energy scarcity, conservation and management have become pressing global environmental, social and economic problems, but lack of access to clean energy and sanitation services is particularly dire in low income countries in Southern Asia and sub-Saharan Africa, in rural areas and among the urban poor (International Energy Agency and World Bank, 2015; WHO and UN Water, 2014).

The SDGs on service provision are more ambitious than those of the MDGs and intend to be universally relevant, not only focused on poorer countries. The vast majority of the world's people lack access to the kinds of services implicit in SDG targets. For example, while access to primary education has increased tremendously, the world is far from providing all girls and boys free, high quality

> " The vast majority of the world's people lack access to the kinds of basic services implicit in SDG targets "

FIGURE 3.1:
There has been progress in improving basic education and health outcomes and providing essential basic services, but major challenges remain
Access to basic services, and health and education outcome improvements, 2000 and latest year

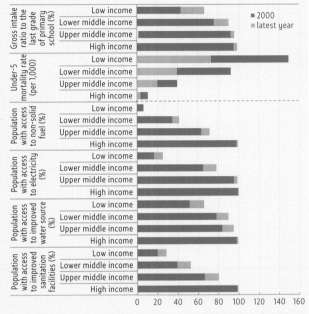

Notes: The 'latest year' is 2012 for access to non-solid fuels and access to electricity, 2014 for gross intake ratio to the last grade of primary education, and 2015 for under-5 mortality rate and access to water and sanitation facilities.
Sources: UIS database and World Bank (2016).

relationships of well-being they value, without penalties associated with their gender (Robeyns, 2007; Sen, 1999, 2011).

While the concept of equality between women and men was set out in the Universal Declaration of Human Rights in 1948, SDG 5 still aims to 'Achieve gender equality and empower all women and girls' by 2030. Clearly, gender inequality has persisted in all countries, in a variety of forms, despite the long-standing recognition that resolving gender inequality is important for all other human and social development indicators (Aguirre et al., 2012; Amin et al., 2015; Klasen and Lamanna, 2009).

There has been progress. In the past 70 years, myriad efforts have focused on improving women's access to social and legal institutions and services through international agreements, such as the Convention on the Elimination of All Forms of Discrimination Against Women (CEDAW) in 1979, and national reforms, such as the 2016 ruling in India by the High Court of Delhi that the eldest woman in a Hindu family can be the head of the family (Garg, 2016). With more women in the workforce, an increasing number of countries have introduced laws and policies to equalize women's status at work and provide maternity leave and child care services (UN Women, 2015). National and global commitment and advocacy have led to improvement in girls' access to education and in reduced gender gaps (UNESCO, 2015).

secondary education, which is part of just one of the seven targets under SDG 4 on education (Chapter 10). Similarly, while health outcomes have improved, most of the world's people lack access to universal health coverage and to sexual and reproductive health services, which are some of the targets under SDG 3 on health (WHO, 2016). Nor is the availability of services the only issue; access to them and who benefits from them are equally important, and affected by diverse factors.

SUBSTANTIVE GENDER EQUALITY REMAINS ELUSIVE

Inclusive social development means access not only to services, but also to participation in processes, along with freedom from discrimination.[1] For gender equality, individuals and groups should have equal opportunity to choose and realize the actions, attributes and

Nevertheless, participation in key economic, political and social activities remains highly gendered. Men and women work in different sectors, with unequal pay and work conditions. Significant pay gaps exist between men and women doing the same job in virtually all occupations (UN Women, 2015). Within institutions, women face difficulty in moving to more senior positions (the 'glass ceiling') and are over-represented in low paid, insecure and low status positions (ILO, 2012). Women in many countries do at least twice as much unpaid work as men, and work longer hours than men if paid and unpaid work is combined (UN Women, 2015). Women disproportionately work in the informal economy in countries with high informality, and in the agricultural workforce without land and asset ownership (UN Women, 2015) (**Figure 3.2**).

Analysis of occupation and education trends shows that men and women continue to be concentrated in

FIGURE 3.2:

Women do more unpaid work than men, and often are more likely to be employed in the informal sector

a. Time spent on unpaid work by men and women

b. Men's and women's share of informal work in total employment

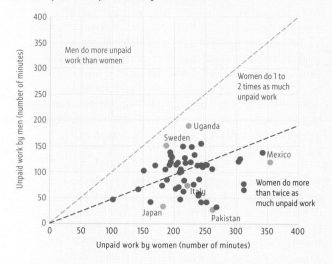

Notes: Data for Figure 3.2a range from 1999 to 2013. Data for Figure 3.2b range from 2004 to 2010.
Sources: ILO and WIEGO (2014); United Nations (2015b).

FIGURE 3.3:

Men and women work in different formal occupations

Female share of total professionals in information and communication technology (ICT) and in teaching

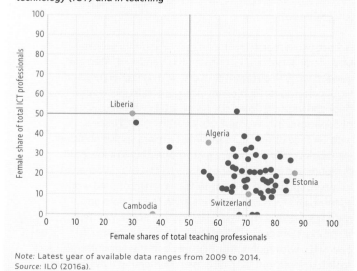

Note: Latest year of available data ranges from 2009 to 2014.
Source: ILO (2016a).

different labour market sectors, often with different levels of status, pay and security (**Figure 3.3**). Figures from the International Labour Organization (ILO) show such occupational segregation decreasing until the 1990s, but rising since then (ILO, 2012, 2016c). Even in the Organisation for Economic Co-operation and Development (OECD) countries, where gender parity in education was achieved decades ago, only 14% of women entering higher education for the first time in 2012 chose science-related fields, compared to 39% of men. Girls are much less likely than boys to consider a career in computing or engineering, which are key sectors in the knowledge economy (OECD, 2015).

Relatively few women are in political and other leadership positions (**Figure 3.4**). Only 20% of members of lower or single legislative bodies, 19% of heads of state or government and 18% of ministers are women (in the last case, usually assigned to social issues). The gender balance of private company executive boards is even further from parity. Among 43 countries with data, women hold over 25% of the seats on executive boards nowhere but in Finland, Norway and Sweden; the share is below 2% in 8 countries from Western Asia and Eastern Asia (United Nations, 2015b). Women are often absent from decision-making in cultural and

FIGURE 3.4:

Relatively fewer women hold leadership positions in corporations and governments in middle and high income countries
Percentage of women on executive boards and legislative bodies

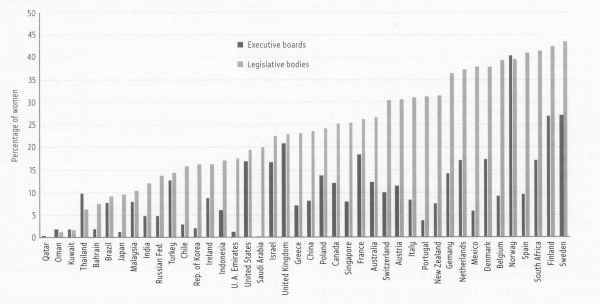

Note: Data for female share in parliament are from 2015. Data for female share in executive boards comes from sources between 2010 and 2014.
Source: United Nations (2015b).

social organizations, including those of major religions (Domingo et al., 2015). Formal requirements for women's representation in local government, such as reservation schemes in India and municipal representation in South Africa, may increase women's visibility and some economic outcomes (Deininger et al., 2011), but their impact on underlying power dynamics is unclear (Beall, 2010).

Gender-based violence is a significant global issue. Recent conflict, instability and migration have been associated with particularly high levels of sexual and gender-based violence. In many countries, social media are creating new spaces for sexual harassment (Parkes and Unterhalter, 2015). Around one-third of women worldwide have experienced physical and/or sexual violence from an intimate partner, or sexual violence by a non-partner, at some point in their lives; in most countries less than 40% of them sought help at any point (United Nations, 2015b).

Due to a combination of biological and social factors, many health challenges have a gendered dimension.

In low income countries, a woman living in a rural area is 38% less likely to give birth with a skilled health professional than her urban counterpart (UN Women, 2015). In some countries, limited reproductive rights mean that maternal conditions and AIDS are the leading causes of death for young women; the right to abortion is selectively available and frequently challenged, including in the United States. More than 200 million girls and women alive today have been subject to female genital mutilation (UNICEF, 2016). Men, meanwhile, experience a higher burden of disease and have higher risk behaviour and lower life expectancy than women (Hawkes and Buse, 2013).

Legal rights for women have not translated into gender equality. Therefore, to clarify the issue and motivate responses, UN Women has defined 'substantive equality for women' as encompassing 'three interconnected dimensions along which actions need to be taken' to develop real equality: redressing women's socio-economic disadvantage, addressing stereotyping, stigma and violence, and strengthening agency, voice and participation (UN Women, 2015). A holistic approach is called for. Women's empowerment and overall economic development are strongly interrelated (Duflo, 2012). Legal reforms complemented by economic and social policies are needed to undo past inequality and create conditions in which women's rights are respected and much more equitable conditions supported.

Finally, to address gender inequality, critics advocate a more nuanced, holistic understanding of the concept of gender in which, for example, 'gender' is not equivalent to 'girls and women' but it is understood that unequal gender relations and gendered preconceptions also harm men and boys, and that the involvement of men and boys is integral to improving gender-related power relations (Edström et al., 2015). At the same time, efforts to remedy gender imbalances need to recognize how societies create and enforce notions of gender, and how power relations and conceptions of feminine and masculine roles translate to institutional practices and norms (Connell, 2009).

VULNERABLE POPULATIONS REMAIN ON THE MARGINS OF SOCIETY AND LACK EQUAL ACCESS TO SOCIO-ECONOMIC OPPORTUNITY

Inequality is the result of both income disparity (see Chapter 2: Prosperity) and the marginalization of groups that experience intersecting disadvantages relating to factors such as poverty, ethnicity, gender, disability and location.

For instance, people with disabilities are significantly more likely to be poor and less likely to be employed.

> **People with disabilities are significantly more likely to be poor and less likely to be employed**

An analysis of 15 lower income countries in Asia, Latin America and Africa using 2002–2003 data found that in a majority of the countries, disability was significantly associated with lack of primary school completion and employment, and higher health expenditure (Mitra et al., 2013). Also with regards to health, for example, a qualitative analysis of the experience of pregnancy among disabled women in Nepal suggested a need to improve health worker training; health workers felt unprepared to meet the needs of disabled married women who were pregnant or considering pregnancy (Morrison et al., 2014).

Indigenous populations are often among the most disadvantaged groups. A global analysis of key education, health and poverty indicators of populations who met literature-based ethnic or linguistic definitions of indigeneity found that for nomadic or semi-nomadic pastoralists in Africa, education indicators were much worse than the national average, and the education gap was much higher than gaps in health and other indicators. In Latin America, stunting, water deprivation and primary enrolment rates were worse among indigenous populations. In some countries in Asia, the well-being of some indigenous groups was found to lag behind national averages, while others performed just as well on multiple indicators (Macdonald, 2012). Yet despite vulnerability based on socio-economic status and health outcomes, many indigenous communities maintain lifestyles and engage in practices that contribute to the sustainability aspirations of the new SDG agenda (see Chapter 1: Planet).

Caste and religious minority status continue to determine disadvantage on various indicators of health, inequality, poverty, education, employment, wages, gender empowerment and access to public goods. For example, in India higher caste Hindu households hold distinct advantages in these areas over scheduled caste, scheduled tribe and Muslim households (Borooah et al., 2015).

Many other large subgroups remain at the fringe of society and legality, such as child labourers and orphans, and the growing numbers of refugees and forcibly displaced populations affected by conflict and climate change (see Chapters 4: Peace and 5: Place). Moreover, the extent of marginalization may be underestimated: some recent studies suggest that 250 million to 350 million people may be missing from global estimates because they are undercounted or omitted from household surveys (Carr-Hill, 2013; Villegas and Samman, 2015).

The extent of persistent discrimination by race, religion and ethnicity is confirmed by a growing body of field experiments. In some studies, real or fictitious individuals are matched on all relevant characteristics except those presumed to lead to discrimination, such as race, ethnicity and gender. How they fare in job or housing applications or purchases of goods is then compared. A seminal field experiment in the United States found that white candidates were called back far more than black candidates with otherwise identical CVs, and that the better the CVs, the more the race gap widened (Bertrand and Mullainathan, 2004). Evidence from India suggests that formal education for Dalit populations has not led to commensurate increases in life chances, due to severe economic discrimination (Thorat and Neuman, 2007). In a range of countries in Eastern and South-eastern Asia, Europe, Latin America and the Caribbean, the Pacific and Southern Asia, there is consistent evidence of discrimination based on race or ethnicity affecting people's labour market outcomes (Bertrand and Duflo, 2016).

WHO ARE THE MOST MARGINALIZED IN EDUCATION?

The discussion above outlines the scale of the challenge to provide universal services, achieve gender equality and address discrimination against marginalized groups. This section describes marginalization in education, identifies the most marginalized groups, defines barriers to inclusive social development and shows who must be reached to achieve it.

Access to education is a powerful means of mitigating disadvantage, ending poverty and reducing inequality, which are core goals of the SDG agenda. However, many overlapping disadvantages limit education outcomes as a result of serious marginalization and inequality (UNESCO, 2010). As the *Education for All Global Monitoring Reports* (GMRs) point out, the groups most marginalized in terms of education access and quality vary substantially; they include racial, ethnic and linguistic minorities, people with disabilities, pastoralists, slum dwellers, children with HIV, 'unregistered' children, and orphans (UNESCO, 2010, 2015). Improved data and monitoring efforts are needed to better identify marginalized children, youth and adults and to develop policy solutions to combat marginalization (see Chapter 14: Equity).

Universal access to primary and secondary education implies leaving no one behind, including members of marginalized groups (see Chapter 10). In the school year ending in 2014, nearly 61 million children of primary school age and 202 million adolescents of secondary school age were out of school. In addition, country commitments to halve adult illiteracy levels by 2015 remain unfulfilled despite much progress.

> " In 2014, nearly 61 million children of primary school age and 202 million adolescents of secondary school age were out of school "

Worldwide, some 758 million adults, 63% of them women, have not attained even minimal literacy skills.

Within countries and at all levels of development, education marginalization is most acute among disadvantaged subpopulations – distinguished typically by wealth, gender, ethnicity and migration status – who face persistently low educational opportunities and poor quality provision. Even as countries make overall progress on various education outcomes, such groups are much more likely to be left behind.

Poverty continues to be the largest determinant of education deprivation and inequality. For example, based on GEM Report team calculations, among youth aged 20 to 24 in 101 low and middle income countries, those in the poorest quintile average 5 fewer years of schooling than those in the richest quintile, compared with a 2.6 year difference between those from rural and urban locations, and a 1.1 year difference between females and males.

However, different characteristics tend to overlap and compound deprivation. For example, females from poor, ethnically or spatially marginalized backgrounds often fare substantially worse than their male counterparts, and gender gaps in disadvantaged groups may be larger than in more advantaged groups. In all aspects of lifelong learning – access and completion of formal education, post-school training and adult education – gender compounds disadvantages related to socio-economic status, ethnicity, location, religion, sexuality, disability, age and race (Kabeer, 2015). For example, the UN has identified poverty and location as the factors most likely to determine whether girls participate in school (UN Women, 2014). And in Latin America, illiteracy rates among indigenous women are often more than double those of non-indigenous women (Vinding and Kampbel, 2012).

Wide disparity in educational attainment is clearly evident where wealth and gender intersect. GEM Report team calculations show that in almost every country, but particularly those with low average educational attainment, youth in the richest quintile have substantially more years of education than those in the poorest quintile. Extreme disparity in attainment is found in countries including Nigeria and Pakistan, where the wealthiest quintiles have more than 8 years more than the poorest. Education disparity between rich and poor tends to decrease in richer countries, but often remains significant. In Argentina, an example of a high income country, the wealthiest have three more years

FIGURE 3.5:

There are large disparities within countries in educational attainment by wealth and gender

Years of schooling attained in low and middle income countries by 20- to 24-year-olds, selected countries

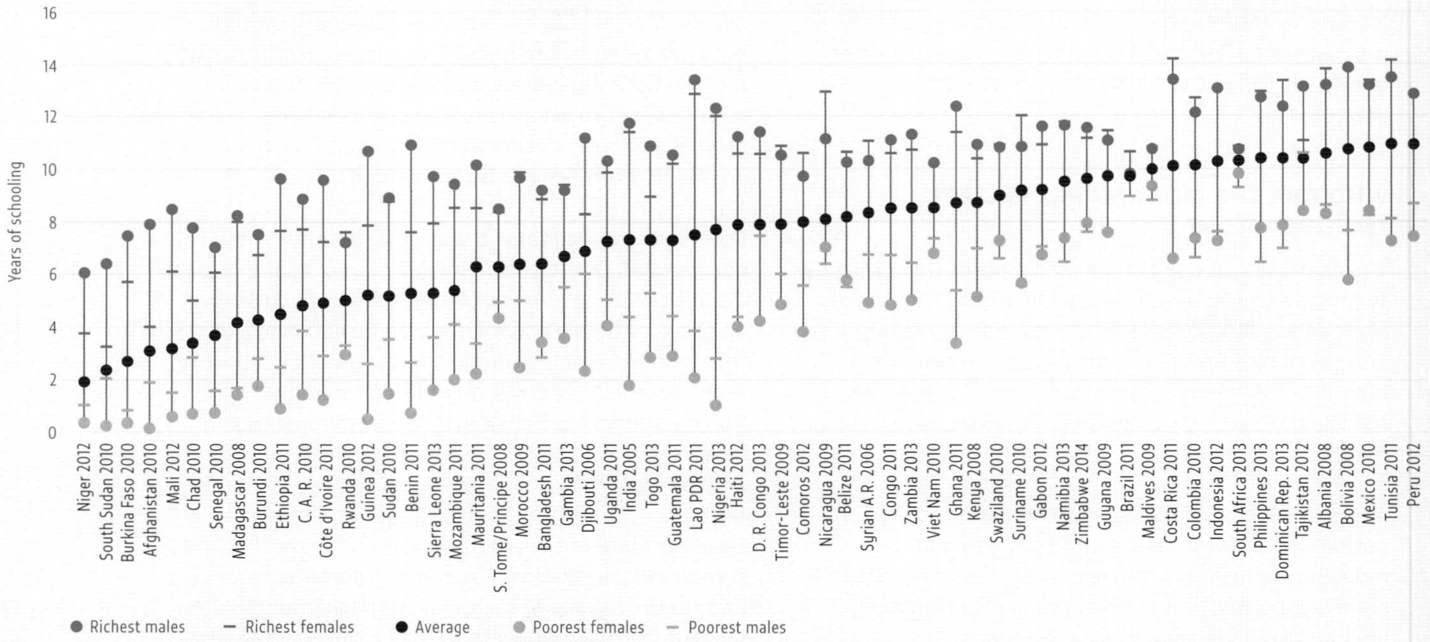

● Richest males   — Richest females   ● Average   ● Poorest females   — Poorest males

Note: Data range from 2005 to 2014.
Source: GEM Report team analysis (2016) based on Demographic and Health Survey, Multiple Indicator Cluster Survey and national household survey data.

of education than the poorest, on average. Large gaps in other education outcomes exist in OECD countries. In a sample of 24 countries, the average difference in adult literacy skills between low and high socio-economic backgrounds is 15.7%, and in the United States it is 24.5% (OECD, 2014a).

Disparities in wealth are often magnified by gender (**Figure 3.5**). The poorest females are the worst off in the majority of countries, often substantially so in comparison to the poorest males. In countries including Afghanistan, Benin, Chad, Ethiopia, Guinea, and South Sudan, the poorest female youth have attained less than a single year of schooling, on average, compared to about two years or more for the poorest males.

Disadvantage, however, is not uniformly against girls and women. Males attain fewer years of education on average than females in many countries in the Caribbean and in Europe and Northern America, where average years of schooling are relatively high. The poorest boys have less schooling than the poorest girls in almost two-

thirds of the countries where average attainment is at least 9 years, compared to just 6 out of the 57 countries with an average of less than 9 years.

Overlapping disparity in youth literacy between and within urban and rural populations is also evident. Youth in rural areas generally have significantly lower levels of literacy than urban youth (**Figure 3.6**). Poor rural female youth tend to have significantly lower literacy rates in relation not only to the rural average, but also to their male counterparts. In the majority of countries with available data, less than half of poor rural females have basic literacy skills. In some countries, including Burkina Faso, Guinea, Mali and Nigeria, less than 10% can read; in Niger, the rate is 2%. Literacy rates of the poorest rural males, by contrast, are much closer to the rural average. In Pakistan, for example, the literacy rate of poor rural males is 64%, compared to 14% for their female counterparts. Very large gaps can also be observed in Cameroon, Congo, the Democratic Republic of the Congo, Liberia, Sierra Leone and Togo.

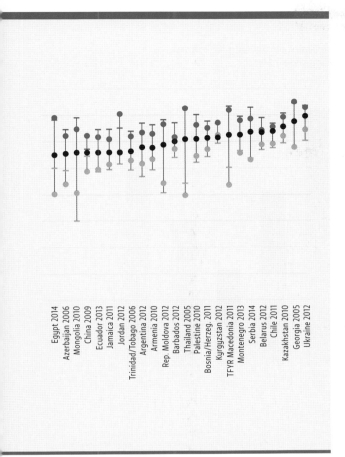

Egypt 2014
Azerbaijan 2006
Mongolia 2010
China 2009
Ecuador 2013
Jamaica 2011
Jordan 2012
Trinidad/Tobago 2006
Argentina 2012
Armenia 2010
Rep. Moldova 2012
Barbados 2012
Thailand 2005
Palestine 2010
Bosnia/Herzeg. 2011
Kyrgyzstan 2012
TFYR Macedonia 2011
Montenegro 2013
Serbia 2014
Belarus 2012
Chile 2011
Kazakhstan 2010
Georgia 2005
Ukraine 2012

FIGURE 3.6:

Many rural areas have low levels of literacy, particularly among poor females
Youth literacy (ages 15 to 24) by location, gender and wealth

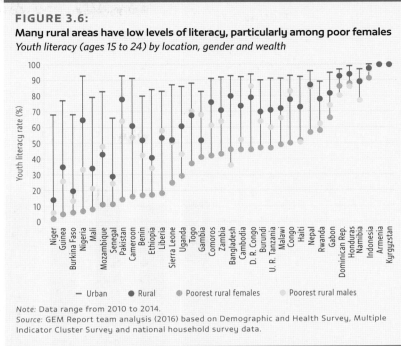

Note: Data range from 2010 to 2014.
Source: GEM Report team analysis (2016) based on Demographic and Health Survey, Multiple Indicator Cluster Survey and national household survey data.

In many countries, particular regions or ethnic groups may face significant education disadvantage relative to the population as a whole. Young adults in the Extreme North region of Cameroon and Karamoja region of Uganda have less than half the national average for educational attainment. In the Alibori department of Benin, they have 1.5 years of schooling, on average – less than one-third of the national average (**Figure 3.7**). Gaps are also often evident according to ethnicity. In Serbia, the Roma population has less than half the national average, as do the Hausa in the Central African Republic.

Within disadvantaged regions and ethnic groups, male-female disparity also tends to be comparatively greater. In Cameroon, where young adults in the Extreme North average 3.2 years of education, young women have less than half the attainment of young men, compared to a gender parity ratio of 0.8 at the national level. In Serbia, young Roma women have two-thirds the educational attainment of their male counterparts, while at the national level, young women on average

have more education than men. But gender disparity against women among marginalized regional and ethnic populations is not always found. In Brazil, for example, indigenous young men have less attainment than their female counterparts, reflecting national patterns.

Disparities in educational attainment and performance by income, race, ethnicity and immigrant status are also prevalent in higher income countries. For instance, in a sample of 24 OECD countries, literacy skills of foreign-born adults were 10% lower, on average, than those of the native born, and as much as 18% lower in Finland and Sweden (OECD, 2014a).

An extensive analysis of low performing students from the 2012 Programme for International Student Assessment (PISA) in OECD countries finds that 'a socio-economically disadvantaged girl who lives in a single-parent family in a rural area, has an immigrant background, speaks a different language at home from the language of instruction, had not attended pre-primary school, had repeated a grade, and is enrolled in a vocational track has an 83% probability of being a low performer' (OECD, 2016a, pp. 13-14). Boys were found to be more likely to be less engaged, repeat classes and get lower grades while girls were found to be less likely to believe that they will do well on mathematics and science tasks.

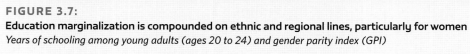

FIGURE 3.7:

Education marginalization is compounded on ethnic and regional lines, particularly for women

Years of schooling among young adults (ages 20 to 24) and gender parity index (GPI)

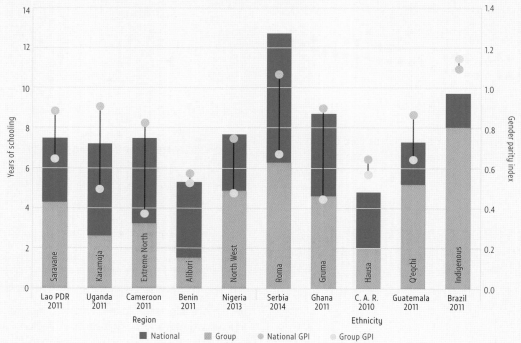

Note: A GPI below 0.97 denotes disparity at the expense of females while one above 1.03 denotes disparity at the expense of males.
Source: GEM Report team analysis (2016) based on Demographic and Health Survey, Multiple Indicator Cluster Survey and national household survey data.

The proportion of students who come from immigrant backgrounds varies considerably across OECD countries, but in 32 of 57 countries and economies, low performers in mathematics are a higher share of immigrant students than of non-immigrants. In other countries, including Qatar and the United Arab Emirates, immigrant students are far less likely than non-immigrants to be low performers. In 14 countries and Hong Kong (China), Shanghai (China) and Taiwan Province of China, not speaking the dominant language at home increased the probability of low performance, even after controlling for other factors (OECD, 2016a).

In addition, wide disparity is evident in dimensions not captured by conventional demographic disaggregation. Disability is one such factor. Although measuring disability precisely is challenging due to wide differences in various forms of disability and their magnitudes, available evidence suggests disability is a significant barrier to participation in education. For example, an estimated one-third of all out-of-school children at the primary level have a disability (Sæbønes et al., 2015).

Overall, evidence shows that the demographic markers of income, location, ethnicity and gender reliably account for major patterns of education marginalization within countries. These factors often overlap, so certain subgroups often have substantially lower education outcomes than more advantaged groups or the national average, sometimes by an order of magnitude. The extent of disparity can vary dramatically between countries. In poorer countries, where average educational attainment is low, inequality is comparatively larger. In richer countries, variance in education outcomes is generally lower, but may also differ in other aspects; for example, boys and young men are often at a disadvantage compared to females on various education outcomes, while the reverse is true in poorer countries. Policies responding to such inequity, therefore, have to account for specific contextual factors – political, cultural and economic – underlying disadvantage not only in a given country, but also in the subpopulation in question.

FORMAL EDUCATION SYSTEMS MAY NOT BE RELEVANT FOR SOME VULNERABLE POPULATIONS

Marginalization in education is not an issue simply of access and attainment, but also of content. Officially sanctioned content, conveyed through curricula, syllabuses, textbooks and assessment, may privilege the language, knowledge, history and culture of some groups and not others. This is especially true for indigenous groups, for whom education is seen as both the reason indigenous knowledge is lost and a potential way to restore it (UNESCO, 2009).

Formal education systems, conceptualized under Western or national norms, have often promoted homogenization rather than plurality, which has led to denial and destruction of indigenous knowledge (Mato, 2015; Stavenhagen, 2015). They can be disempowering and run counter to a lifestyle and culture. For example, there is evidence that formal education initiatives that lack an understanding of pastoralists'

> Formal education systems, conceptualized under Western or national norms, have often led to denial and destruction of indigenous knowledge

traditional way of living have been used to transform pastoralists into settled farmers and wage labourers (Kratli and Dyer, 2006).

Besides issues related to language of instruction, barriers to meaningful inclusion of indigenous populations include lack of contextual relevance, devaluing of indigenous knowledge and reduction of the time spent with indigenous communities gaining traditional knowledge (Magni, 2016). Processes through which education disadvantage is created or sustained need to be examined, as do ways in which classroom and school life may contribute to further marginalization.

Attempts to include indigenous knowledge and practices in formal schooling have had mixed success. One project aimed to address issues of school attendance, achievement and well-being of Yolngu youth in Australia while maintaining their cultural integrity. It was never implemented because the indigenous community was not involved in decision-making. School staff were to be imposed by the territory government without consulting Yolngu elders, who wanted the right to choose staff with good attitudes towards their people (Marika et al., 2009).

EDUCATION IMPROVES SOCIAL DEVELOPMENT OUTCOMES

Having established ways in which social development is not inclusive, this chapter points to a solution: education can improve social development outcomes across a range of areas. The following section focuses on how education interventions, at school and in the home, can facilitate better health, improve the status of women and contribute to other social development outcomes. Examples will be also shown of the interaction between good health and better gender equality.

EDUCATION HELPS PEOPLE AND THEIR FAMILIES MAINTAIN OR IMPROVE THEIR HEALTH

Education can help people and their families keep in good health, or improve their health, in terms of nutrition, disease prevention, better relations with healthcare professionals and improved provider accountability, and making choices in the home that affect health, such as reducing pollution or contaminants. General knowledge and skills acquired through education facilitate access to specific knowledge on health and nutrition issues, helping people process information on prevention and treatment, and change their behaviour in healthful ways.

Education is closely associated with health and nutrition. Individuals who receive more education are more likely to be in good health and well fed. Among women aged 15 to 49, household survey data in 61 low, middle or high income countries between 2004 and 2009 found that, within each country, educational attainment was significantly correlated with indicators of height, weight, haemoglobin levels, sexually transmitted infections and smoking (Cutler and Lleras-Muney, 2014).

More educated individuals are likelier to know about disease, seek medical advice and follow treatment. They are the first to adopt medical innovations (Lleras-Muney and Lichtenberg, 2002). In low and middle income countries, where morbidity in general and from disease is high, information campaigns have proved effective in fostering adoption of simple measures such as sleeping under insecticide-treated nets to prevent malaria, purifying water against waterborne diseases and using oral rehydration to treat diarrhoea. There is growing evidence that more educated heads of families are more responsive to such campaigns (Dupas, 2011b).

Education can lead to a better-functioning health sector in terms of patient relationships with healthcare providers and improved accountability. Observations in India, Indonesia, Paraguay and the United Republic of

Tanzania revealed that many doctors had insufficient medical knowledge and provided low standards of care to their patients. Poor patients had access to less competent doctors who exerted even less effort with them than with other patients (Das et al., 2008). A review of 122 studies on informal healthcare providers in low and middle income countries found they accounted for a highly variable share of health interactions (ranging from 9% to 90%) and followed poor practices (Sudhinaraset et al., 2013).

But patients with higher education engage differently with doctors. Owing to their better mastery of health knowledge and ability to locate medical information, educated patients often seek to become 'co-producers' of their health. They perceive themselves as sharing decision-making and responsibility, which can lead to better treatment adherence and reduced costs (Crisp and Chen, 2014).

As regards accountability, a synthesis of 71 articles on doctor–patient relationships in low and middle income countries confirmed that many healthcare providers did not listen carefully to their patients' preferences, facilitate their access to care, offer them detailed information or treat them with respect. But education can help facilitate measures to enforce accountability by, for instance, 'creating official community participation mechanisms in the context of health service decentralization; enhancing the quality of health information that consumers receive; [and] establishing community groups that empower consumers to take action' (Berlan and Shiffman, 2012, p. 272).

Education levels also matter in adopting healthier and more environment-friendly energy options. Female education is strongly associated with choosing modern energy sources and technology (Ekouevi and Tuntivate, 2011). Meta-analytic reviews confirm that education levels matter in improving take-up of cleaner cook stoves and fuels (Lewis and Pattanayak, 2012; Malla and Timilsina, 2014). In Ethiopia, households with higher levels of education were more likely to use non-solid fuels (Mekonnen and Köhlin, 2009). In rural China, several studies have linked education levels with the adoption of cleaner fuels, such as biogas. A study by Zhang and colleagues of nine Chinese provinces found that the probability of adopting cleaner fuels increased by 0.66% for every year of education (Shen et al., 2014). Analysis of the household energy mix in Uganda indicates that education is critical in increasing consumption of cleaner fuels (Lee, 2013).

SCHOOLS CAN DELIVER KEY HEALTH INTERVENTIONS THAT MAY INFLUENCE OUTCOMES AND BEHAVIOUR

Health and nutrition interventions

As access to education continues to expand, and school systems reach an unprecedented global share of the child and adolescent population, the potential for delivering health and nutrition interventions through the education sector has never been so great.

School-based interventions, such as meals and health campaigns, can have an immediate impact on students' health and nutrition status. School meals provided at the primary and secondary levels may increase attendance, alleviate short-term hunger and improve nutrition status, and are a key multisector intervention (see Chapter 6: Partnerships). Programmes often target locations with high poverty or schools with low attendance. Meals may be served at breakfast or lunch, and be pre-cooked or cooked in the school. Take-home rations, such as a monthly portion of cereals and oil, are sometimes made conditional on attendance. A study in northern rural Burkina Faso showed that daily school lunches and a monthly take-home ration of 10 kilograms of flour (conditional on girls attending at least 90% of class hours) increased female enrolment by 5 to 6 percentage points after one year. Take-home rations also improved the nutritional status of beneficiaries' younger siblings (aged 1 to 5) (Kazianga et al., 2012).

> " School feeding programmes in Burkina Faso increased female enrolment by 5 to 6 percentage points after one year "

A systematic review of 26 studies conducted mostly in countries of sub-Saharan Africa, South-eastern Asia, Southern Asia, and Latin America and the Caribbean found that school meals consistently improved health and nutrition outcomes, including anaemia, nutrient levels and morbidity. Some of the programmes also improved students' growth, but many did not reduce the prevalence of stunting or wasting, as meals served in primary and secondary school are too late to compensate for these results of chronic early childhood malnutrition (Lawson, 2012).

In higher income countries, school meal policies are

varied and often used to achieve multiple policy goals. Alongside measures to prevent the rising challenge of childhood obesity, discussed later, school feeding programmes have been used to foster lifelong nutrition and well-being and to compensate for household poverty. Finland was the first country to serve free school meals to all, viewing them as an investment in learning. The goals of the Finnish system are not only to improve nutrition but also to teach long-lasting eating habits and promote awareness of the importance of food choices (Tikkanen and Urho, 2009). In Japan, school meals and dieticians are used to inculcate healthy nutrition practices and combat lifestyle-related ailments such as eating disorders and obesity (Tanaka and Miyoshi, 2012). In the United States, free or reduced-price school meals are provided to lower income students using income eligibility criteria. In the 2012/13 school year, the National School Lunch Program provided daily meals to nearly 31 million children in nearly 100,000 schools, with over 21 million receiving free or reduced-price lunches (Food Research and Action Center, 2015). Analysis of the programme's impact found shorter-term health effects but a major positive impact on adult educational attainment (Hinrichs, 2010).

School-based deworming campaigns could address some of the most prevalent neglected tropical diseases: infection with soil-transmitted helminths and schistosomiasis. These diseases, which particularly affect children in sub-Saharan Africa, can be easily treated with safe, low cost drugs. Free provision through schools could reach a large share of children, with benefits extending to out-of-school children through reduced risk of transmission. This could also be used as part of the response to World Health Organization (WHO) recommendations of mass treatment once a year in regions with infection prevalence above 20%, and twice a year in regions with prevalence above 50% (Ahuja et al., 2015).

Curricular interventions

School-based interventions can also provide information on health and improve knowledge and behaviour in the long term. The effectiveness of such interventions depends on the quality and relevance of the information.

Sexual and reproductive health education needs to acknowledge that some students are sexually active and rely on a risk reduction strategy. Many sub-Saharan African countries have introduced HIV education in their curricula, but promote abstinence until marriage instead of providing information on how to reduce the risk of HIV transmission during sex. In Kenya, an experiment showed that the official curriculum made no difference to the sexual behaviour of adolescent girls. Yet information on the fact that HIV prevalence was much higher among adult men than among boys of their age led girls to switch from unprotected sex with older partners to condom-protected sex with partners of their age (Dupas, 2011a).

Childhood obesity is a rising concern. While its prevalence is much more common in higher income countries (**Figure 3.8**), it is also a rapidly increasing challenge in lower income ones (Bhurosy and Jeewon, 2014; Popkin et al., 2012). A systematic review of 24 studies pertaining to students aged 5 to 18 in countries of North America and Western Europe as well as Brazil, China and New Zealand found that obesity prevention – mostly using a mix of classroom activities, provision of fruit and vegetables in school meals, and parental involvement – could reduce students' body mass index and increase their consumption of fruit and vegetables. A larger impact was found for interventions that lasted at least one year and were integrated into the regular curriculum and school activities (Silveira et al., 2011). Yet, the potential of school-based prevention, especially through early childhood interventions, has not been fully exploited (World Obesity Foundation, 2014). A systematic review of 26 early childhood studies revealed a paucity of properly designed and evaluated interventions, especially in low and middle income countries (Mikkelsen et al., 2014).

Water, sanitation and hygiene in schools

In the past 40 years, water, sanitation and hygiene programmes have evolved from purely infrastructural interventions, such as building latrines and handwashing facilities, towards more comprehensive interventions incorporating elements of hygiene education, awareness and promotion. Hygiene promotion in schools became increasingly common after 2000, based on the belief that children can be influenced to not only improve their health, but also be agents of change in their communities (UNICEF, 2006).

School-based interventions have a demonstrated impact on health, education, economic and gender-equity outcomes. For instance, a comprehensive, integrated programme to improve school water, sanitation and hygiene in Kenya resulted in a nearly 50% reduction in girls' absence (Freeman et al., 2012), and was especially important for schools that had had poor water

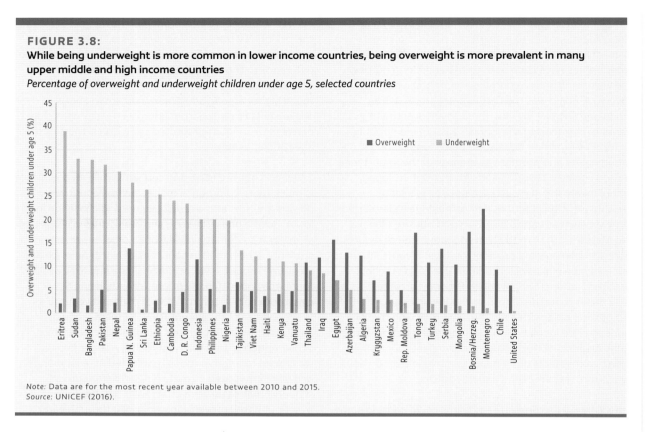

FIGURE 3.8:

While being underweight is more common in lower income countries, being overweight is more prevalent in many upper middle and high income countries

Percentage of overweight and underweight children under age 5, selected countries

Note: Data are for the most recent year available between 2010 and 2015.
Source: UNICEF (2016).

availability (Garn et al., 2013).

But policy-makers need to show more leadership. In a 2014 survey of 94 countries, just over one-fifth of water, sanitation and hygiene measures in national plans had been fully implemented, funded and regularly reviewed; just over one-third of countries included specific targets to reach universal access to water and sanitation in schools, and less than 30% of countries aspired to universal coverage for hygiene promotion in schools in the next decade (WHO and UN Water, 2014).

Similarly, leadership is needed to promote school-based interventions and facilities for better menstrual hygiene management. A recent systematic review of three studies, conducted in urban schools in Egypt, India and Saudi Arabia, showed that providing multiple hour sessions led to stronger knowledge of menstrual hygiene and better practices (such as using, changing, washing and drying sanitary pads) (Sumpter and Torondel, 2013). In Uttar Pradesh, India, an intervention begun in 2011 targeted men and boys to support menstrual hygiene through focus group discussions, games, media tools

and regular meetings. Better management can be complemented by needed infrastructure. As the 2015 GMR confirmed, access to better facilities for girls is likely to have positive effects on their dignity and the quality of their schooling experience (UNESCO, 2015).

EDUCATION OPENS OPPORTUNITIES FOR WOMEN

A wealth of studies and global and national reports have documented the variety of ways in which individuals and societies benefit from providing better education to women and girls (UNESCO, 2014), although content and processes determine how they derive the benefits.

The link between education and earning prospects is well documented. Education helps widen women's employment opportunities beyond low skill work (see Chapter 2: Prosperity). The socio-economic benefits of educating women, both for individual and family outcomes and for national and global economic growth, have long been used to advocate for more investment in girls' education (Miranda, 2015; Murphy et al., 2009; Wils and Bonnet, 2015). Gender disparity also affects overall income inequality, not just employment prospects, for women and girls; education and health disparity are key drivers of overall income inequality in low and middle income countries, and lower female labour force participation is associated with higher income inequality in higher income countries (Gonzales et al., 2015).

By imparting core skills such as literacy, education facilitates women's access to information about social and legal rights and welfare services. Learning to read and write can bring greater confidence and agency to identify and challenge inequality, unjust traditions, and norms and practices that perpetuate women's low status. For instance, low levels of education are a significant risk factor in perpetuating and experiencing intimate partner violence (Capaldi et al., 2012; United Nations, 2015b; WHO and London School of Hygiene and Tropical Medicine, 2010). Data from recent Demographic and Health Surveys (DHS) show that in most countries with data, women with secondary and tertiary education are less likely to report having experienced physical or sexual violence from their spouses (**Figure 3.9**), and less likely to have undergone female genital mutilation (**Figure 3.10**).

Gender-based violence is not just an issue in low income countries. Over 23% of women were found to have experienced physical or sexual intimate partner violence in high income countries (WHO, 2013). In England (United Kingdom), economically deprived and less educated women were more likely to have experienced such violence (Khalifeh et al., 2013).

Gender-based power relations can have complex links with education. For instance, in Norway, women in relationships

FIGURE 3.9:

In most countries, women with secondary and higher levels of education are less likely to report having experienced spousal violence

Percentage of ever-married women who have ever experienced physical or sexual violence committed by their husband or partner, selected countries

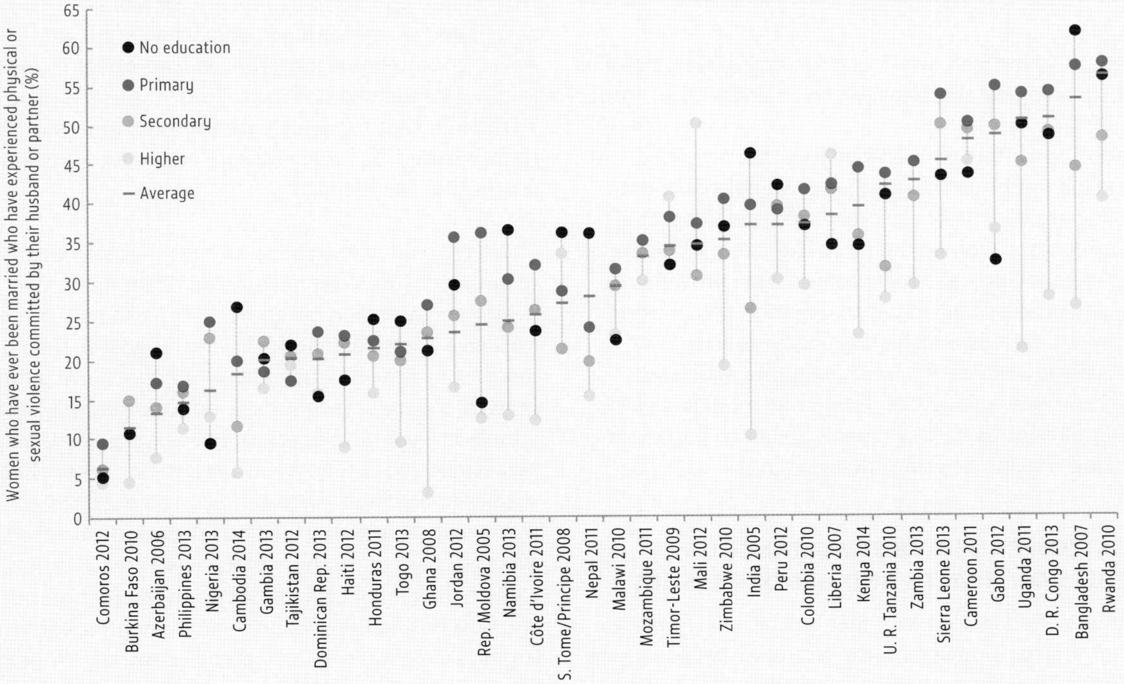

Source: The DHS Program (2016).

FIGURE 3.10:

In most countries, women with higher levels of education are less likely to have undergone female genital mutilation

Percentage of women who have experienced female genital cutting (FGC), selected countries

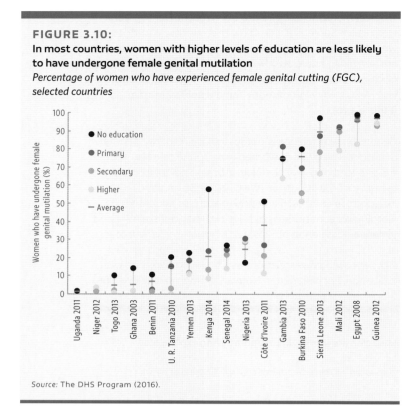

Source: The DHS Program (2016).

intergenerational effects which can transform societies. Second, because gender is often erroneously associated only with women, examples will be given of the effects of education on the health of men and boys.

Education has large intergenerational benefits in many areas of children's lives, and these payoffs persist over time (UNESCO, 2014). Educated parents – mothers in particular – are better able to feed their children well (from exclusive breastfeeding in the first few months of life to a good quality, diversified diet later) and to keep them in good health.

Maternal education has long been identified as a major determinant of child mortality, independently of income (Smith-Greenaway, 2013). Mothers with more education are more likely to seek prenatal care, birth attendance by trained medical personnel, immunization and modern medical care for their young children. They are also more likely to protect their young children from health risks, for instance by boiling water and avoiding unsafe food. Evidence from Guatemala, Mexico, Nepal, the Bolivarian Republic of Venezuela and Zambia showed that literacy predicted mothers' ability to read printed health messages, understand radio messages and explain their child's condition to a health professional, and was associated with health-seeking behaviour (LeVine and Rowe, 2009). Higher maternal education was found to improve infant health in the United States, a finding linked to the fact that more educated women were more likely to be married, use prenatal care and reduce smoking (Currie and Moretti, 2003).

Short-term education programmes that support mothers of young children can have a significant impact on health and nutrition outcomes. They can help promote exclusive breastfeeding for infants aged less than 6 months, as recommended by WHO to achieve optimum growth; the most recent data indicate that only 47% of infants in least developed countries were exclusively breastfed (UNICEF, 2016). A systematic review of 66 studies (including 27 in lower income countries) showed that short-term breastfeeding education increased the average share of mothers exclusively breastfeeding by 43% on the day of birth, 30% during the first month and 90% during the second to sixth months, with the largest increases in lower income countries. Programmes combining individual and group counselling appeared to be most effective, whether facility- or community-based (Haroon et al., 2013). Short-term programmes also can reduce the prevalence of stunting in lower income

with less educated men were found to be more likely to suffer from psychological and physical violence (Bjelland, 2014).

Education can affect women's political participation and engagement by imparting skills which enable them to participate in democratic processes (see Chapter 4: Peace). Educated women are more likely to participate in civic life and advocate for community improvements. Numeracy enables individuals to question and critique government data, strengthening accountability. Conversely, low education levels, negative attitudes and stereotypes, and lack of strong role models, as in Ethiopia, all contribute to women's ability to participate in decision-making positions (Kassa, 2015).

EDUCATION CAN HAVE SIMULTANEOUS BENEFITS ON HEALTH AND GENDER ISSUES

The effects of education, whether formal, non-formal or informal, are not simple or linear. Not only can education have powerful outcomes for health and gender equality separately, but as this section shows, education can support gendered areas of health, and health aspects of gender. First, maternal education can have powerful countries. According to a systematic review of 17 articles, the provision of complimentary food (either coupled with nutritional counselling or not) to mothers of babies aged 6 to 24 months led to significant gains in their weight and height (Imdad et al., 2011).

A positive long-term relationship has been shown between maternal education and child health and basic education. The extension of compulsory education from 5 to 8 years in Turkey in 1997 increased by 32 percentage points the likelihood that mothers of young children in 2008 had completed at least 8 years of education, and improved child health as measured by the share with very low birth weight, height for age and weight for age (Güneş, 2015). As a result, at the country level, simple indicators of education development among women, such as literacy, are strong predictors of key infant health outcomes (**Figure 3.11**).

The spread of education transforms societies by changing family preferences, social norms and cultural practices. This is central to the demographic transition towards low fertility levels that facilitate investment in children's health, nutrition and education. EFA policies implemented to 2015 accelerated fertility decline. For instance, Nigeria's universal primary education policy was estimated to have reduced early fertility by 0.26

births per year of increase in female attainment (Osili and Long, 2008). Over 2015–2030, continued efforts towards universal basic education of good quality will be decisive in countries that still have very high fertility, increasingly concentrated in sub-Saharan Africa.

Education can lead to reductions in fertility in various ways. Educated women may feel confident their children will survive to adulthood and so have fewer. They may have greater bargaining power as well as improved access to and use of contraceptive methods to achieve a desired number of births and to space consecutive births, with benefits for their own and their children's health. At the family and community levels, educated young adults and their parents – who remain key decision-makers in many societal contexts – may have a preference for those who marry to be educated, delay marriage and first birth, and have spaced births and smaller families (Basu, 2002).

In Ethiopia, Malawi and Uganda, the transition to universal primary education from the mid-1990s led to a decline in women's ideal family size and their desire for very high fertility (Behrman, 2015). In Bangladesh, the rise in female educational attainment may have accelerated the country's remarkable fertility decline, including by lengthening the interval between births. The median interval increased by 26% between 1991 and

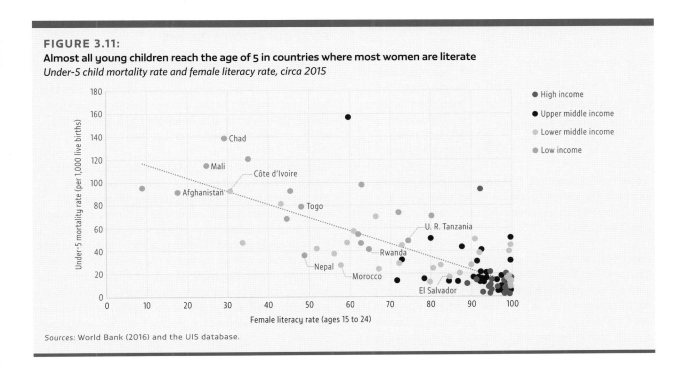

FIGURE 3.11:
Almost all young children reach the age of 5 in countries where most women are literate
Under-5 child mortality rate and female literacy rate, circa 2015

Sources: World Bank (2016) and the UIS database.

2007, to 44 months. By 2007, birth intervals were about 40% longer among women with secondary or higher education than among illiterate women (Rabbi et al., 2013). In Madagascar, 1 year of additional attainment among women aged 12 to 25 delayed marriage by 1.5 years, and delaying marriage by 1 year delayed age at first birth by 0.5 years (Glick et al., 2015).

In the short term, targeted, specific non-formal education programmes may be effective in helping women plan childbirth. Counselling women who had recently given birth about family planning led to better contraceptive use and fewer unplanned pregnancies, especially among adolescents, in countries as diverse as Australia, Nepal, Pakistan and the United States (Lopez et al., 2010).

Education can reduce maternal mortality, which is caused by pregnancy complications such as pre-eclampsia, bleeding and infections, and by unsafe abortion. Despite a global 44% decrease in maternal mortality between 1990 and 2015, it remains a significant threat, especially in sub-Saharan Africa (546 deaths per 100,000 births in 2013) and Southern Asia (182 deaths) (UNICEF, 2016). Education helps women understand information about hygiene and early symptoms of pregnancy complications, gain access to treatment and birth attendance, and avoid unsafe abortion. Analysis of data on 108 countries over 1990–2010 finds that an initial increase in female attainment from 0 to 1 year of education would reduce maternal mortality by 174 deaths per 100,000 births, and an increase from 7 to 8 years would bring a reduction by 15 deaths. The impact of expanding women's education might be as large as that of broadening access to skilled birth attendants (Bhalotra and Clarke, 2013).

> The impact of expanding women's education might be as large as that of broadening access to skilled birth attendants

Education can also have positive outcomes for men's health, as behaviour relating to health and mortality can be highly gendered, and is often linked to gender socialization norms. In a number of countries, men have been shown to be more at risk of poor mental health and suicide, traffic injuries and hazardous work, and violence and homicide as both victims and perpetrators (Barker,

2005; Hawkes and Buse, 2013; Kato-Wallace et al., 2016). In Brazil, rates of violence and violent death are especially high for young men, particularly in urban areas, where lack of education and employment opportunities may lead them to adopt risky lifestyles associated with gangs and work in the drug trade (Imbusch et al., 2011). Harmful stereotypes of masculinity and manhood can lead men to tend to be worse at seeking help on mental health, consume excessive amounts of drugs and alcohol, and be more prone to aggressive and risky behaviour. Education can address the perpetuation of such stereotypes. A study of mortality data by education level in 16 European countries found higher mortality among less educated populations, especially for preventable deaths (Mackenbach et al., 2015). A study of road traffic injuries in Europe found education inequality among men over age 30, but not among women (Borrell et al., 2005).

SOCIAL DEVELOPMENT INFLUENCES EDUCATION

Education helps make social development more inclusive by supporting health outcomes, gender equality and areas where health and gender intersect. Social development, in turn, has an impact on education, both positive and, if lacking in inclusivity, negative.

HEALTH AND NUTRITION FORM A FOUNDATION FOR EDUCATION SYSTEMS

The causal impact of education on health and nutrition is mirrored by the causal impact of health and nutrition on education. A large body of literature documents the latter, arguing that health and nutrition condition the ability of children to attend school and learn, and the ability of their families to support them.

Living conditions in early childhood set the stage for learning. Shocks suffered in utero by babies whose mothers contracted diseases such as influenza or malaria, or were malnourished due to famine or drought, were found to cause lower attainment in a variety of country contexts from the early 20th century to recent years. Chronic malnutrition in early childhood is known to impair the development of cognitive, socio-emotional and physical skills. Public health policies such as malaria eradication can thus accelerate education expansion, and nutrition interventions for pregnant women and young children should also be viewed as an education policy priority (Cutler and Lleras-Muney, 2014).

Improvements in child health and nutrition can boost attendance and achievement. Short-term hunger and intestinal worm infection weaken children, making it more difficult for them to travel to school and to concentrate on learning. The benefits of school meals and deworming thus extend to education outcomes. In experiments in areas of Kenya and Uganda with high rates of worm infection, deworming had a dramatic impact on school attendance in the short term, and on test scores and employment in the long term. In Kenya, girls who received the treatment were 25% more likely to pass the national primary school exit exam, and as adults were more likely to grow cash crops and reallocate time from agriculture to entrepreneurship (Ahuja et al., 2015).

Parental health has a critical impact on children's education. Disease weakens parents' ability to educate their children and support them through schooling.

> " In Kenya, girls who received deworming treatment were 25% more likely to pass the national primary school exit exam "

Children suffer emotional distress and may need to take on parental roles at home, such as taking care of younger siblings, to the detriment of learning. In countries without effective social welfare systems, the loss of income caused by parental disease and the cost of medical care may impoverish families, making schooling unaffordable. Parental death is particularly devastating. Evidence from the AIDS epidemic in sub-Saharan Africa and from Indonesia shows that the timing of parental death is associated with the timing of school dropout, and orphans are less likely to attend school than the children of their caretakers (Vogl, 2014).

Health and nutrition infrastructure can be used to deliver education interventions. Care programmes for infants and toddlers up to age 3 can complement medical care and food supplementation with child stimulation and parenting education. Home visits by community health workers can include sessions in which mothers learn how to stimulate their children by playing with them, using positive feedback and avoiding physical punishment. Longitudinal evidence from a series of experiments targeting stunted children, run in Jamaica since the 1980s, shows long-term benefits including higher cognitive skills at ages 7 and 11; improved reading achievement, attention, behaviour and self-esteem at

age 17; and higher earnings at age 22. More recent trials in Bangladesh, Brazil, India, Pakistan, Saint Lucia and South Africa tend to confirm these results, which depend on the quality of the training received by community health workers (Leclercq, 2015). Short-term health education programmes, such as nutritional counselling and contraceptive education, are usually delivered by health professionals or community health workers.

Access to quality health care for teachers and students is indispensable to the functioning of the education sector. Disease is a cause of teacher absenteeism and attrition (Ejere, 2010; Herrmann and Rockoff, 2010). Teachers in rural areas, in particular, face shortages of qualified health professionals, and when unwell may be absent for longer than if medical care were readily available. The impact of disease and treatment availability on the education sector has been particularly strong in the case of the AIDS epidemic in the worst affected countries of sub-Saharan Africa. Without antiretroviral therapy, infected teachers are increasingly absent and eventually die. Other teachers may be absent to take care of infected family members. Teachers who are infected or suspected of being infected may face discrimination and stigma from colleagues, parents or the community (World Bank, 2009). In that respect, the advent and spread of antiretroviral therapy has contributed to the sustainability of education systems.

ACCESS TO WATER, SANITATION AND ENERGY AFFECTS EDUCATION OUTCOMES

Just as health services and interventions can support education, so can access to water, sanitation and energy. For example, reducing the time it takes to collect water and firewood can improve education outcomes by freeing time for educational activities, especially for women and girls (UNESCO, 2015). In Ghana, research using four rounds of DHS (1993/94 to 2008) found that halving water fetching time increased school attendance by 2.4 percentage points, on average, among girls aged 5 to 15, and the impact was stronger in rural areas (Nauges and Strand, 2013). In 2001, female literacy rates were found to be almost 5% higher for women in villages with better water access in Uttar Pradesh, India (Sekhri, 2013).

Similarly, electricity availability can improve study time and education outcomes via means such as night-time studying, access to technology and, when demand is great, use of double shifts. Access to electricity has been shown to have a positive impact on education outcomes in many countries, including Bangladesh, India, Ethiopia, Kenya and South Sudan (UNESCO, 2015). A comprehensive review of studies discussing pro-poor electricity provision in 74 developing countries, mostly from sub-Saharan Africa, and South and East Asia, found consistent positive impacts of electrification on education in terms of improvements in study time, enrolment and years of schooling (Pueyo et al., 2013).

A variety of examples across world regions demonstrate this effect. An analysis of the impact of rural hydro-electrification between 1960 and 2000 in Brazil showed large positive effects on literacy and enrolment rates. Counties that went from no electricity to full electrification saw drops of 8% in illiteracy and 21% in the population with less than four years of education, and a two-year increase in school completion (Lipscomb et al., 2013). In rural Peru, the number of households with access to electricity increased from 7.7% in 1993 to 70% in 2013, with much of the expansion happening after 2006. Providing access to electricity led to children studying an extra 93 minutes a day (Aguirre, 2014). In another study on rural Peru's electrification, conducted using household survey panel data from 2007 to 2010, girls living in districts that received electricity access were found more likely to be enrolled in school, though increased access to electricity did not lead to improved attendance and was associated with a short-term reduction in learning outcomes (Dasso et al., 2015).

The source of electricity does not seem to matter. Children in households with solar home systems in Bangladesh and community micro hydro in Nepal were shown to spend more time studying than households without any electricity (Banerjee et al., 2011; Samad et al., 2013).

Electrification can improve indoor air quality and reduce health challenges (Torero, 2014), which can in turn positively affect education. In a causal analysis of a grid extension and intensification programme in El Salvador, household electrification was shown to reduce indoor air pollution by reducing use of traditional light sources. School-age children from households that received discount vouchers increased their time studying at home in less polluted environments, and saw improvements in math skills (Barron and Torero, 2014).

While home electrification does not seem to have a consistently greater impact on girls' education, it can have other education benefits which may especially benefit women. In six states in India, analysis using 1996 survey data found that in households with electricity, even poor women read more than women in wealthier households without electricity (World Bank, 2002). Furthermore, since electricity greatly increases access to modern media, it may provide the opportunity to gain and practice literacy and expose women to non-traditional lifestyles, which can in turn affect women's standing and education (Köhlin et al., 2011).

Basic access to electricity alone is not sufficient to improve education. Electricity access can also increase opportunities for child employment or free time for other pursuits, such as television watching and digital game playing. Access to electrification in Honduras between 1992 and 2005 was found to reduce educational attainment and attendance, and increase childhood employment. To curb perverse effects of electricity on education, awareness of them needs to be raised (Squires, 2015).

Other electricity-related challenges can disproportionately affect the poor and their education outcomes. Despite huge investments and the development of grid infrastructure in Kenya, a lack of mass connection and credit access has prevented significant progress in electrification rates for the poor (Lee et al., 2014). Quality of electrification is as important as connection. Kinshasa, Democratic Republic of the Congo, reported a 90% access rate to electricity, but received only 30 points out of 100 on a newer metric that factored in reliability, quality, affordability, legality and other aspects (International Energy Agency and World Bank, 2015). Research is needed on the relationship between access and quality of electrification and education outcomes, as well as a more nuanced definition of electricity access.

DISCRIMINATORY INSTITUTIONS AND SOCIAL STRUCTURES AFFECT EDUCATION OUTCOMES

The impact of social development on education is not always positive. It is well known that social institutions have gendered dimensions with implications for education outcomes. This is the backdrop of much programming to support girls' education in recent decades, including raising awareness of the need to educate girls and providing stipends as encouragement (UNESCO, 2015).

Among countries with relevant data, there was a negative association between discriminatory legal institutions and the gap between girls and boys in lower secondary completion rates in 2014. Girls were often found to attend school longer in countries with less discriminatory social institutions, and the reverse was true in countries with more discriminatory institutions. But the relationship was not always straightforward: in more economically advanced countries such as Kuwait, more women than men completed lower secondary education despite discriminatory legal and social practices (**Figure 3.12**).

But the removal of discriminatory legislation does not eliminate discrimination. People continue to be oppressed because of race, caste and ethnicity, including in education systems (Krieger, 2014; Siddique, 2011). For instance, in the United States, racial discrimination continues through unequal distribution of education financing, strong residential segregation and a 'school to prison' pipeline affecting African Americans (see Chapter 5: Place).

INTEGRATED SOCIAL AND EDUCATION INTERVENTIONS ARE NEEDED

Inclusive social development will not be achieved by interventions only in one sector. There is a lack of evidence on sustained health-related behaviour change through education. Similarly, the fact that progress in gender parity in education has not systematically translated to gender equality points to a need for broader interventions and policies that integrate education with actions such as legislative change and workforce policies. More is needed to remedy social challenges than single sector-focused interventions.

What are some possible solutions? Social protection programmes can influence multiple outcomes at once, including education. Gender-balanced lives can be facilitated through integrated, comprehensive measures. Education can contribute to innovation in the delivery of essential services. Water, sanitation and hygiene can be improved in communities, combining training with community-building and improvements in governance.

EVIDENCE OF SUSTAINED HEALTH-RELATED BEHAVIOUR CHANGE THROUGH EDUCATION IS LACKING

While education helps people acquire knowledge, it does not always lead to substantive long-term behavioural change. People with education may know more about the health risks they take but without developing

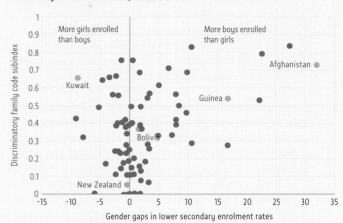

FIGURE 3.12:

Many countries with discriminatory social institutions have worse gender gaps in lower secondary completion rates

Discriminatory family code subindex, 2014; and gender gap in lower secondary enrolment rates, circa 2014

Notes: The discriminatory family code subindex of the 2014 Social Institutions and Gender Index (SIGI) is composed of formal and informal laws, social norms and practices such as legal age of marriage, early marriage, parental authority and inheritance laws. The SIGI and subindex values are between 0 and 1, with 0 indicating no inequality and 1 indicating complete inequality.
Sources: OECD (2014b) and UIS database.

critical thinking and decision-making skills may engage in risky behaviour. In a survey in Zimbabwe, persons with secondary education were 30% more likely to have comprehensive knowledge of HIV, yet there was no evidence that they were more likely to get tested for HIV or be HIV negative (Agüero and Bharadwaj, 2014). In fact, the quality of the information provided is a critical factor in ensuring education can play a positive role in influencing behaviours, since educated people are better able to critically process information. For instance, early in the HIV pandemic in sub-Saharan Africa more educated, wealthier individuals were more likely to have multiple partners and unprotected sex. As information on HIV transmission improved over time, the more educated were better able to interpret the information and change their behaviour. In recent years, more education is associated with a lower likelihood of HIV prevalence in many countries in sub-Saharan Africa, including Cameroon, Ghana, Kenya and Tanzania (Smith et al., 2012).

Similarly, systematic reviews of hygiene-focused interventions, which include school-based, household and community-level interventions, have often concluded that most behaviour changes are not sustained. A review of 27 handwashing studies yielded no single instance of definitive, long-term behavioural change (Vindigni et al., 2011). Part of the problem has been providing resources to sustain the behaviour. The state of Lagos, Nigeria, included in its curriculum programmes promoting hygiene knowledge and practices. They appeared to improve student knowledge of the importance of such practices, but primary and secondary school pupils were found to lack adequate access to facilities to practise their knowledge (Babalobi, 2013; Olukanni, 2013).

Education and sensitization campaigns can encourage the adoption of cleaner fuel. Household energy programmes involve awareness-raising, education and information on inefficient and unhealthy cooking stoves and fuels. Education and media campaigns are critical to ensure that families understand the challenges and make the transition (Halff et al., 2014). But there has been limited analysis on whether improved cooking stoves translates into sustained use over time or leads to full adoption of clean fuel (Lewis and Pattanayak, 2012). Households may switch back to traditional fuel due to factors such as fuel prices, reliability and availability of fuel supply, and lifestyles and tastes (Malla and Timilsina, 2014).

PROGRESS IN GENDER PARITY IN EDUCATION

FIGURE 3.13:

Women consistently earn less than men in OECD countries, even though gender gaps in secondary attainment vary

Gender gaps in upper secondary attainment and formal employment wages, circa 2014

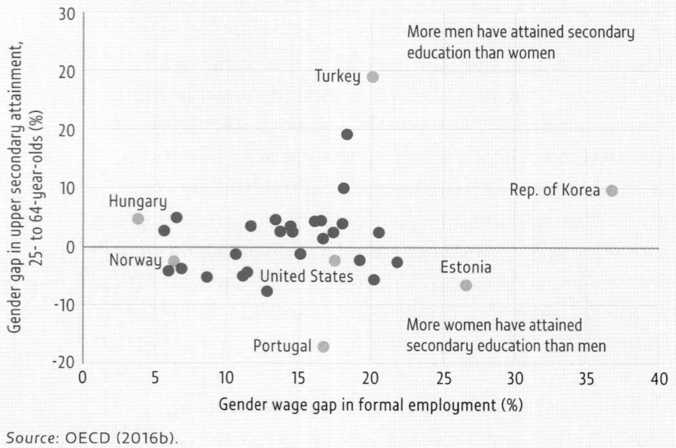

Source: OECD (2016b).

HAS NOT SYSTEMATICALLY TRANSLATED TO GENDER EQUALITY

Just as knowledge acquisition does not always lead to behavioural change, ensuring gender parity in school does not necessarily result in longer-term equality between the sexes. EFA and the MDGs promoted gender parity, and in recent decades the overall numbers of girls and women enrolling in all levels of education have increased substantially (UNESCO, 2015). But there are many indications that improving education access and gender parity are not sufficient to empower women in society. Ensuring greater equality in outcomes such as literacy, numeracy, soft skills and entering work-related training or higher education does not clearly translate to greater equality in economic activity or employment on equal terms with men. For instance, women's secondary attainment is now higher than men's in many OECD countries, yet the gender pay gap favouring men remains substantial (**Figure 3.13**).

Female labour force participation is determined by many policy, family and individual factors (Mincer, 1962), and by levels of national economic development (Elborgh-Woytek et al., 2013). Factors influencing women's entry into the market include wages, types of available jobs, access to resources and bias in markets and institutions (ILO, 2016c; World Bank, 2012).

Perhaps not surprisingly, then, the links between women's education and employment are not straightforward (**Figure 3.14**). For instance, while girls' education at all levels has been a significant factor in rising labour market involvement in Latin America and the Caribbean, only tertiary education has had a significant employment effect in the Middle East and North Africa (ILO, 2012).

Countries that have seen rapid growth in education attainment among girls have not seen a commensurate increase in decent work or changes in gendered social norms. In India, the female employment rates have decreased while female education increased, partly due to how labour force participation is measured (Bhalla and Kaur, 2011). Furthermore, while the levels of girls' and women's enrolment in all levels of education is rising in the country, the female-to-male infant ratio is simultaneously dropping, especially among more urban populations, with gender-discriminatory views leading to sex-selective abortion and gender-discriminatory child-rearing practices (Jha et al., 2011; Patel, 2007). In Sri Lanka, significant improvement in female enrolment

FIGURE 3.14:

Growth in female lower secondary completion rates is not always linked to higher female labour force participation

Change in the female labour force participation rates and female lower secondary completion rates, circa 2000 and 2014

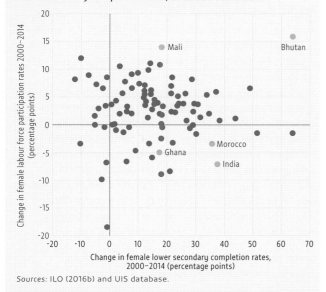

Sources: ILO (2016b) and UIS database.

and completion has not translated into workforce advantages, and instead has been accompanied by low and stagnant female labour force participation (Gunewardena, 2015).

Rising levels of women's education have also seemed to have little impact on patterns of unpaid domestic and care work. A study examining rising school enrolments for girls in Bangladesh and Malawi found no impact on the imbalance in girls' and boys' domestic work (Chisamya et al., 2012). In Ghana, despite increases in women's education and female labour force participation overall, women's wage employment stagnated. Unemployment for women rose, as did informal economic activity and self-employment, although more years of education increased chances of wage employment (Sackey, 2005). One study argues that education increases labour force participation when decent work in the public sector is available. However, in recent decades, public sector employment in Ghana has declined while education levels have risen. As a result, women above 50 in the formal sector worked in public sector jobs that provide more pay, but half of women aged 18 to 29 worked in the private informal sector with insecure incomes. This suggests that to empower women, education reforms must be matched with better access to public sector jobs or laws ensuring that private formal and informal sector employers provide decent work (Darkwah, 2010).

Analysis for this report using World Bank STEP data (see Chapter 2: Prosperity) found that women were more likely to work in the informal sector in countries including the Plurinational State of Bolivia, Colombia, Ghana and Kenya, while the reverse was true in Armenia, Georgia and Ukraine. Across all low and middle income countries, women were more likely than men to be classified as working and poor. However, as analysis showed the gap in educational attainment was not a strong explanatory factor, other reasons for women not having equitable access to stable, decent work should be examined (Chua, 2016).

The lack of a clear positive link between education and employment is also an issue for countries that have had persistently high levels of girls' education attainment. For instance, in the United States, there continue to be low political participation, highly segregated labour markets and human rights concerns such as gender-based violence and the right to reproductive health services (Goetz, 2003; McBride and Parry, 2014). Similarly, high income Asian countries such as Japan and the Republic of Korea are famous for limited female labour force participation despite high levels of education and the acknowledged need for more female labour force participation as the population ages. A simulation-based analysis comparing the experiences of Finland and Norway to Japan and the Republic of Korea showed that family-friendly policies and flexible work arrangements could enable more women and men to balance their work and family lives, promote fertility and encourage continued female labour force participation (Kinoshita and Guo, 2015).

As Chapter 4: Peace shows education can improve women's political participation. However, higher levels of women's education do not necessarily translate to greater participation. Malaysia has seen increasing female enrolment, particularly in tertiary education, but women's political participation has remained steady in the last 10 years (Salleh, 2012; World Bank, 2015b). Some countries with historically high levels of girls' and women's education, such as the United Kingdom and United States, have fewer women in senior political posts than some countries with fewer girls in school. Where women reach higher levels, they are often responsible for social, education and health portfolios – in 2010, they were twice as likely to hold a social portfolio as an economic one (World Bank, 2011).

Similarly, gender-based violence can continue in spite of high levels of education. Kerala state, India, has a high level of women's education and literacy, yet rates of domestic violence and dowry-related crimes have been increasing. Furthermore, women's levels of mental ill-health, and changes in marriage, inheritance and succession practices have weakened women's access to and control over inherited resources (Eapen and Kodoth, 2003).[2]

Attitudes towards normative gender roles persist. One reason is they are transmitted across generations. Using data from the 1970 British Cohort Study, a study found that mothers' and children's gender role attitudes, measured 25 years apart, were strongly correlated, for both sons and daughters. Daughters and sons' wives had greater levels of education and labour force participation if their mothers had non-traditional gender attitudes (Johnston et al., 2014). Analysis from high income countries including Australia and the United States found that parents' gender attitudes and behaviour had a significant impact on children's fertility choices, household division of labour and women's labour market participation (Fernández and Fogli, 2006; Grosjean and Khattar, 2015).

> 66
> A study in the United States found that women's attitudes have a significant effect on their children's views towards working women, which influences female labour market decisions
> 99

A survey-based analysis of intergenerational transmission of gender attitudes in India finds strong positive correlations between parent and child attitudes, with mothers having greater influence than fathers. On average, when a parent holds a discriminatory gender attitude, their child is 15 percentage points more likely to hold that attitude; the effect is 50% larger for mothers than for fathers. Girls with more gender-discriminatory parents tend to drop out of school earlier than those with more gender-progressive parents (Dhar et al., 2015). A longitudinal analysis based on linked mother-child pairs in the United States finds that women's attitudes have a statistically significant effect on their children's views

towards working women, which influences female labour market decisions (Farré and Vella, 2013).

INTERVENTIONS WITH MULTIPLE PERSPECTIVES ARE NEEDED TO CREATE MORE EQUAL SOCIETIES

Multiple stakeholders from multiple sectors can work together to create innovative interventions that integrate education in a central role, achieve more equitable delivery of services to society and build more equitable power structures. Both processes and outcomes require multiple perspectives and understandings. Integrating complex approaches and viewpoints, with education at the centre, is needed for overall social inclusion and participation. Examples discussed below include social protection and rural sanitation programmes. They show the need to tackle gender inequality and ways to do it. They show how education can encourage innovative service delivery, with positive results for participation and inclusion.

Social protection programmes can have multiple, simultaneous outcomes, including on education

Social protection programmes that seek to reduce risk and vulnerability – such as pensions, employment initiatives, social security and programmes targeting the poor, such as cash transfers and microfinance – can have outcomes in multiple areas, from lessening income poverty to improving educational access (UNESCO, 2015).

Traditional social protection regimes such as pensions, social security and other employment insurance represent large shares of government spending and can have remarkable impact. For instance, in South Africa, the pension programme was expanded to the black population in the early 1990s, leading to a sudden large increase for many in household income. Evidence suggests pensions received by women had a systematic positive impact on young girls living with them: girls' height for age and weight for height improved (Duflo, 2003), and girls were significantly more likely to be in school (Case and Menendez, 2007). Studies found no effects when pensions were received by men; women were evidently more likely to use additional resources productively.

Microfinance is an example of why more research is needed on the multiple effects of social interventions. Often taking the form of small loans and savings plans, it has been used as a key tool to empower poor women, aiming to improve decision-making power and overall socio-economic status, and better risk management. But despite anecdotal evidence on multiple benefits, few analyses exist (Duvendack et al., 2011). What evidence does exist is mixed. For instance, providing savings to AIDS-orphaned young people in Uganda helped increase their aspirations for secondary schooling and primary examination results (Curley et al., 2010). But data from Malawi showed that microcredit decreased primary school attendance among borrowers' female children (Shimamura and Lastarria-Cornhiel, 2010).

A key challenge in assessing the impact of social protection programmes is to look at the collective impact of integrated efforts, not isolating the impact of separate outcomes (see Chapter 6: Partnerships). For example, evidence suggests that cash transfer programmes in low and middle income countries, especially in Latin America, have had an impact on education access, especially for primary schooling, but more understanding is needed of their impact on education persistence and learning outcomes (UNESCO, 2015).

Gender bias can be addressed by working together

As gender equality in education cannot work in isolation, and achieving gender parity in education will not necessarily have direct consequences for women's empowerment and economic freedom, more holistic engagement is needed at the community level, recognizing institutionalized and cultural biases and ensuring that men are included in the process.

Reducing gender bias by using behavioural insights in policy-making. Since behaviour is often deeply embedded, recognizing subconscious, automatic biases can help in designing more effective strategies at the institutional level to help reduce the negative consequences of gender bias (see Chapter 1: Planet) (Bohnet, 2016). The introduction of cable television in rural India, which led to increased information on alternative ways of living, led to improvement in gender attitudes and behaviour between 2001 and 2003 (Jensen and Oster, 2009). Analysis of the US Scholastic Aptitude Test found that women were less likely to take risks and guess in these tests (Baldiga, 2014); and led to the test being redesigned

> " The presence of female leaders in India was found to narrow the gender gap in girls' aspirations and advancement in education "

to remove the penalty for wrong answers in order to reduce gender bias (Bohnet, 2016).

Studies confirm the importance of female role models. The presence of female leaders in India was found to narrow the gender gap in girls' aspirations and advancement in education (Beaman et al., 2012). Female students were found to perform better in introductory math and science courses if taught by female faculty, and more likely to pursue careers in science, technology, engineering and mathematics (STEM) (Carrell et al., 2009). Observing and interacting with female experts in STEM fields improved female students' attitudes about the fields (Stout et al., 2011).

Men and women working together. Focusing on women's initiatives is not enough. Men and women have to work together to achieve gender-balanced lives. Analysis of results of the International Men and Gender Equality Survey from 10,490 men aged 18 to 59 in 8 countries (Bosnia and Herzegovina, Brazil, Chile, Croatia, the Democratic Republic of the Congo, India, Mexico and Rwanda) found that men's education and income, and equitable practices in men's childhood homes, were associated with their attitudes to equity. Men's equitable attitudes were reflected in practices such as more participation in the home, reduced use of violence and higher relationship and sexual satisfaction; men's education and their mother's education were found to be positively associated with progress towards gender equality, except in India. An argument can be made for the importance of intergenerational learning in the childhood home, where fathers who participate more equally can help encourage less stereotypical role models (Levtov et al., 2014).

Using survey-based research on gender-equitable attitudes, Instituto Promundo developed Program H/M in Brazil. Program H included group education sessions, youth-led campaigns and activism to transform gender stereotypes among young men. Program M aided young women to challenge deeply held stereotypes. Now adopted in over 20 countries, it has been lauded as best practice in promoting gender equality. Evaluations of Instituto Promundo educational workshops with young men to prevent gender-based violence and promote gender equality in Brazil, Chile, India and Rwanda found they led to significant changes in gender-equitable attitudes, and significant decreases in self-reported violence against female partners (Instituto Promundo, 2012). Promundo's MenCare campaign in

Brazil, Indonesia, Rwanda and South Africa aims to conduct group education sessions and focus on men's roles in active fatherhood and caregiving, since fathers' involvement supports children's development, fosters positive gender role models for the next generation, and benefits men and women's health and economic outcomes (Levtov et al., 2015).

Many community-based projects with integrated interventions target men and women working together for more equitable gender relations. In South Africa, Stepping Stones involved young men and women in a combined sexual health and gender and economic empowerment intervention, and demonstrated positive results in increasing women's and men's earnings, reducing intimate partner violence and creating more equitable gender attitudes (Jewkes et al., 2014). Senegal's Tostan project encourages women and men to discuss human rights together and to develop new social norms around equality for men and women (Gillespie and Melching, 2010). An adult literacy programme in rural Nepal employed a participatory and social empowerment approach to increase family and community recognition of women's unpaid work by engaging marginalized women and some men in collecting data on their time use. The programme achieved a more equitable distribution of women's unpaid care work in rural Nepal, and helped make women more active agents in public spaces (Marphatia and Moussié, 2013).

Education can facilitate efforts to innovate in service delivery

Various studies suggest that education and information can be combined with other strategies for improved service delivery. For instance, low income citizens who applied for food ration cards were often ignored in India, but those who filed official information requests about the status of their application and district-level processing times, bolstered by the 2010 Right to Information Act, were successful in obtaining the cards (Peisakhin and Pinto, 2010). Awareness-raising (of official information requests) was combined with capacity-building (to make the requests) and an enabling legal environment to improve access to services.

ICT can be used for innovative interventions and initiatives that equip citizens to improve the delivery of public services and enhance democratic participation. For example, relying more on technology such as mobile phones and e-governance platforms can help address a lack of administrative capacity (United Nations, 2014).

Success depends on how well public and private sector providers develop the systems, and how and which citizens access the tools.

Social accountability initiatives can improve service provision, increasing transparency and accountability, as well as the voice of citizens in decision-making (Fox, 2015). For example, participatory budgeting is now used in over 1,500 cities worldwide, where citizens participate in decisions on how a portion of the municipal or local budget is spent (Dias et al., 2014).

Low education levels, however, will impede effective use of innovative technology or interventions. In low income countries, low adult literacy rates and levels of educational attainment limit access to ICT-based government initiatives and services (United Nations, 2014). The digital divide is linked to availability of infrastructure and tools, but also disparity in the education and skills to use the technology (OECD, 2001). Citizens need to be trained and educated to use ICT services, and computer literacy is pivotal in ensuring citizens' acceptance and usage. In sub-Saharan Africa, the most common challenges to implementation of e-government initiatives include issues of language, literacy and human capacity, alongside infrastructure, legal frameworks and internet access (Nkohkwo and Islam, 2013).

Similarly, participatory budgeting was found in Peru to be less effective and susceptible to takeover by elites when populations were less literate and lacked access to information in local languages (Dias et al., 2014). Participants with higher levels of education are shown to have higher influence on participatory meetings (Ganuza and Francés, 2012). Participatory budgeting in La Serena, Chile, was considered successful because the mayor emphasized education for civil society (Cabannes, 2014).

> " Training and development of facilitators, called 'natural leaders', is the key way education has helped influence community members and facilitate sanitation improvements "

Community ownership and training achieved sustained changes in rural sanitation

While it is hard to change ingrained behaviour such as sanitation practices, community-level ownership, through committed community facilitators, has led to significant, sustained success in rural sanitation. Changing sanitation practices, such as open defecation, has been difficult; their link with cultural norms and mindsets requires community-wide systematic changes. The most significant success in changing rural sanitation practices in recent decades is the community-led total sanitation (CLTS) programme, which has been implemented in over 60 countries and incorporated into national plans in over 20 (World Bank, 2015a).

What makes this programme different from other interventions is using the community to shape norms. The intervention's goal is to change community norms by triggering shame and disgust for open defecation. It relies strongly on key community facilitators, and culminates in a celebration of a village free from open defecation. Community members with minimal specialized training have been exceptionally important in educating and influencing sanitation-related change. Training and development of facilitators, called 'natural leaders', is the key way education has helped influence community members and facilitate sanitation improvements. The natural leaders and community consultants have been institutionalized into local government in many countries. Experts have argued that this mainstreaming has been a significant innovation in helping scale up CLTS. The programme has led to profound change in sanitation practice and policy, though experts warn not to link success to specific tools and indicators rather than the empowerment and education of community members (Cavill et al., 2015; Kar, 2014).

CONCLUSION

If social development is viewed as the right to healthy, empowered lives, then it is clear that education is a powerful enabler, and a key aspect, of social development. Whether understood as knowledge and skills which young people acquire at school or as an infrastructure that can be used to deliver interventions, education is central to ensuring that people can live healthy lives and improve their children's lives. Education can also have powerful transformative effects in enhancing gender equality in society and improving agency, voice and participation for vulnerable populations, a majority of whom are adolescent girls

and women.

The evidence also makes it clear that education systems and outcomes are interlinked with other sectors. The availability of health systems and adequate nutrition, water and energy sources are central to education: the health status of infants and children determines their ability to learn, health infrastructure can be used to deliver education interventions, and access of teachers to good health care is indispensable to the functioning of the education sector. Ultimately, convergence between education policy planning and that concerning health, nutrition, water and sanitation, and energy is required to promote a holistic approach to human development and address multidimensional poverty challenges.

At the same time, education progress is not enough to combat social development challenges. There is a strong persistence of marginalization, discrimination and disadvantage of various vulnerable groups in most societies. Nor has major progress in increasing girls' educational attainment had a straightforward effect on their economic and life chances. Achieving substantive gender equality, reducing inequality and influencing behaviour related to health and well-being requires multifaceted strategies that involve and engage sectors beyond education.

ENDNOTES

1. The gender equality related discussion in this section and the rest of the chapter draws extensively on Peppin Vaughan (2016).

2. It is important to note that higher levels of education may also encourage a higher level of reporting violence.

Children look through a destroyed classroom window at Yerwa Primary School, Maiduguri, Borno state, damaged by Boko Haram during attacks in 2010 and 2013. The school, established in 1915, was the first primary school in northeast Nigeria.

Peace: political participation, peace and access to justice

We are determined to foster peaceful, just and inclusive societies which are free from fear and violence. There can be no sustainable development without peace and no peace without sustainable development.

– The 2030 Agenda for Sustainable Development

KEY MESSAGES

Getting children into school doesn't result in more peace, but the right type of education can help.

Conflict and violence are meanwhile destroying education systems.

---

1 **Education makes people more likely to participate in political processes constructively and non-violently.**
   a. Education and communication campaigns can teach people how to participate in politics and access political information.
   b. The right type of education and teaching promotes the transition to more participatory political systems.
   c. Democratic regimes tend to result in more and better quality education.

---

2 **Better education is clearly linked to more women in political leadership.**
   a. Gender equality in politics is far from being achieved.
   b. Women with more education possess more skills to take up leadership roles.
   c. When there are more women in politics, gender gaps in education shrink.

---

3 **An education that is provided equally, with inclusive teaching and learning materials, is a powerful preventive tool and antidote for conflict.**

---

4 **Conflict is taking an increasingly large toll on education systems.**
   a. Children, teachers and schools are frequently under attack.
   b. Forcibly displaced people, especially children and youth, are in dire need of access to education.
   c. Other forms of violence, including school-based bullying and sexual violence, are of concern.

---

5 **Education should be better recognized in peacebuilding agendas for its role in helping with conflict resolution.**

---

6 **Education can reduce crime and violence against children and youth.**

---

7 **Educational programmes help marginalized people access justice and legal protection.**

Violence can be prevented and stable peace is more likely in societies where institutions are democratic and representative – of women as well as minorities, of the poorest as well as the most affluent. Marginalized groups may resort to conflict and violence if there are no peaceful alternatives for resolving their grievances. It is projected that by 2030 up to 62% of people living in extreme poverty will be in countries at risk of high levels of violence (OECD, 2015).

Education has a key role in contributing to the political participation and inclusion vital to ensure social cohesion, and to prevent and mitigate tensions in societies that are – as described in the statement above from the preamble to the 2030 Sustainable Development Goals (SDGs) – 'peaceful, just and inclusive' and 'free from fear and violence'.

Sustainable peace also requires a well-functioning justice system that offers citizens, regardless of social status, a more attractive alternative to violence to resolve personal and political disputes. If people feel they have no access to justice to address their legal needs and to assert and protect their rights, they are more likely to resort to violent means, undermining the establishment and consolidation of peace.

This chapter is divided into three sections. It starts by documenting links between education and politics, showing that education offers transformative possibilities for participation, inclusion, advocacy and democracy. It then examines the multifaceted relationship between education and conflict and

> Education is a key ingredient for acquiring political knowledge

violence, especially in contexts where education is lacking, unequal or biased. It shows that education can contribute to conflict, but can also reduce or eliminate it. The chapter also shows how education can play a crucial role in peacebuilding and help address the alarming consequences of its neglect. It examines education and violence unrelated to conflict and war. The final section provides evidence of how education initiatives, in particular driven by civil society organizations, can help marginalized populations gain access to justice.

EDUCATION AND LITERACY CONTRIBUTE TO MORE PARTICIPATORY POLITICS

Political inclusion is about facilitating participation throughout the political cycle, not just at elections. Active participation in political processes enables people to understand and engage with the underlying causes of social problems at the local and global levels. It also makes the electorate and polity more representative of society, holds governments more effectively to account and helps enforce constitutionally guaranteed rights. Education is a key ingredient for acquiring political knowledge, though opportunities to learn are determined by the availability of information, free from restrictions or censorship.

EDUCATION MATTERS IN INCREASING POLITICAL KNOWLEDGE

Political participation requires knowledge and understanding. Educated people are more likely to know facts related to the key players and workings of their political system. In the county of Busia in the former Western Province of Kenya, a scholarship programme targeting girls from politically marginalized ethnic groups led to their increased participation in secondary schooling and boosted their political knowledge. Girls who benefited from the programme were 14% more likely to read newspapers that reported extensively on national politics. Political knowledge also went up – for instance, those who received scholarships were much more likely to be able to name the president and the health minister of Uganda (Friedman et al., 2011).

In countries where the predominant administrative language is spoken by a minority of the population, understanding this language gives individuals access to a wider range of political knowledge. In Mali, secondary or tertiary education attainment was the factor with the greatest effect on respondents' ability to name the heads of the assembly and of the majority party (Bleck, 2015).

Beyond formal schooling, civic education can instil specific political knowledge. In the Democratic Republic of the Congo, the Voter Opinion and Involvement through Civic Education programme, implemented in 2010/11, increased participation in the political decentralization process mandated by a 2007 law. Adult literacy was low, so a key strategy was to organize community education sessions using simple drawings and other images, resulting in significant gains in knowledge – by a full three correct answers out of the six questions asked about decentralization. The greatest impact was among the participants who had the least information before the programme began (Finkel and Rojo-Mendoza, 2013).

EDUCATION HELPS SHAPE ELECTORAL PARTICIPATION

Voting is generally considered one of the less demanding forms of political participation, and can provide equal opportunities for all to participate. But individuals need knowledge and skills to register to vote, understand the stakes and take an interest in the outcomes of an election.

In many North American and Western European democracies, formal education has been shown to have an impact on the probability that an individual will vote.[1] In the United States, for instance, studies showed that students receiving more educational interventions, such as being taught in smaller classes, getting extra mentoring and taking part in pre-school activities, participated in elections at higher rates (Sondheimer and Green, 2010).

In some developing countries, providing citizens with specific information affected voter turnout. In Mozambique, right before the 2009 elections, a voter education campaign was conducted with support and collaboration by a newspaper and a consortium of eight non-government organizations (NGOs). Three interventions provided information to voters and called for electoral participation – an SMS-based information campaign conveying neutral information about the elections, an SMS hotline receiving and disseminating information about electoral misconduct, and a free newspaper focusing on civic education. The three together increased official voter turnout by close to five percentage points (Aker et al., 2013).

In several young democracies, women are less likely to vote than men and, when they do vote, are more likely to follow the preferences of household males. In Pakistan, just before the 2008 national elections, a non-partisan, door-to-door voter awareness campaign provided information to women on the importance of voting and the secrecy of the ballot. Women who received this information were found to be 12 percentage points more likely to vote than those who did not, and significantly more likely to choose a candidate independently (Giné and Mansuri, 2011).

Yet, whether better-educated citizens decide to use their capabilities or deliberately disengage may depend on the political context. When electoral participation does not provide genuine input into a political process – because opposition parties are harassed, for example, or judicial institutions are biased – voters can express displeasure by withdrawing from politics. In Zimbabwe, the 2002 and 2005 elections were marked by severe repression of the opposition; better-educated individuals deliberately chose to reduce their electoral participation, possibly believing that voting

> In Pakistan, a voter-awareness campaign before the 2008 elections made women 12 percentage points more likely to vote

would legitimize the regime in power. This negative effect of education on electoral participation dissipated following 2008's relatively more competitive election, which initiated a power-sharing arrangement. Better-educated people re-engaged with politics when political conditions allowed them to reflect their political preferences more meaningfully (Croke et al., 2015).

Voter education campaigns can respond to electoral misconduct

In newly democratic low income countries, elections sometimes increase the propensity for civil conflict. Kenya, Nigeria and Zimbabwe provide examples of election cycles marked by thousands of deaths. Politicians may secure votes by stirring up greed, rivalry and fear. Well-designed voter education campaigns can reduce such behaviour. In Nigeria, an anti-violence campaign, conducted in the run-up to the national and state elections in 2007, involved town meetings, popular theatre and door-to-door distribution of materials. It reduced intimidation, voter turnout was nearly 10% higher where the campaign was implemented, and independent journalists reported a decrease in the intensity of violence (Collier and Vicente, 2014).

In New Delhi slums, in India, during the run-up to the 2008 state legislature elections, door-to-door distribution of newspapers provided information about the performance and qualifications of the incumbent and the two other candidates. The campaign not only increased the average voter turnout by 4% but also decreased by almost 20% the use of vote-buying as an electoral strategy (Banerjee et al., 2011).

EDUCATION CAN HELP PEOPLE MAKE THEIR VOICES HEARD

While voting is a pivotal form of political participation, elections are not the only type of political or civic participation in which citizens can exercise regular control and influence on government actors and hold them accountable. A wide array of political activities can convey more precise demands and generate more pressure than a single vote. Better education can help people be more critically minded and politically engaged in such activities. It can also increase representation by marginalized groups, such as women (**Box 4.1**).

BOX 4.1

Better education and women's involvement in national and local decision-making bodies are closely linked

Recent years have seen a rising tide of women's political representation. For example, more women than ever before are being elected to national assemblies, including in Argentina, Portugal and Rwanda. The global average has been climbing and in 2014 was close to 22% – far from equality but an improvement over 14% in 2000. The adoption of affirmative action measures – such as quotas on party electoral lists or reserved seats – has been critical in facilitating women's entry into national assemblies.

Yet, in local governance, women remain under-represented. According to one estimate, just 16% of mayors of capital cities across the world were women in 2015. In executive positions in governments, too, women continue to be very much in a minority and confined mainly to gender-stereotyped portfolios.

Structural barriers to women's involvement and advancement in formal representative politics include their relative lack of material resources to support their move into politics; their additional work burden, which denies them the time necessary to engage in politics; the prevalence of masculine models of political life and elected government bodies; and cultural values such as those barring women from the public sphere.

But girls' education helps give women the skills they need to take on leadership roles in public life – on community councils, in national office and on international bodies. In many countries, such as Sierra Leone, women who consider entering politics often feel disadvantaged by a lack of education and of the experience of campaigning and public speaking. A study drawing on the life histories of women leaders at various levels of government in eight countries, including Brazil, Egypt and Ghana, found that those with higher educational levels held office in higher tiers of government.

Greater representation of women in politics and public office can also reduce gender disparities in education and provide positive role models for other women, increasing their educational aspirations and achievements, and thereby improving female educational attainment levels. Across the 16 biggest states in India, a 10% increase in the number of women involved in district politics would lead to an increase of nearly 6% in primary school completion, with a larger impact on girls' education. Similarly, in villages assigned a female leader for two election cycles, the gender gap in career aspirations shrank by 25% in parents and 32% in adolescents.

Sources: Beaman et al. (2012); Burchi (2013); Castillejo (2009); Domingo et al. (2015); Monteiro (2012); Powley (2005); Tadros (2014); UCLG (2015); UN Women (2011, 2015).

One direct form of political participation is contacting a public representative to request information or express an opinion. Across 102 countries, adults with a tertiary education were 60% more likely to request information from the government than those with a primary education or less – and 84% more likely in developing countries (World Justice Project, 2015). In Côte d'Ivoire and Ghana, higher levels of formal education were associated with a greater likelihood of contacting an elected official (MacLean, 2011).

Better-educated people are also more likely to make their voices heard by participating in political and community meetings and processes. An analysis drawing on recent data from over 27,000 respondents in 20 emerging sub-Saharan African democracies found that people with primary schooling were three percentage points more likely to attend community meetings than those with no education. For people with secondary or post-secondary education, the impact was about twice that (Isaksson, 2014). In Benin, adults who had attended the first elementary schools established by the French were 32% more likely to be party members and 34% more likely to campaign for parties, and made up the majority of the few people who stood for election to political office (Wantchekon et al., 2015).

Schools are not the only locus for political socialization. Civil society plays an important role in educating adults and increasing their political participation, especially at the local level. In rural Senegal, a study of 1,484 voting-age individuals found that beneficiaries of NGO-run, non-formal education programmes were more likely to contact a political official or influential person to obtain help resolving community and personal problems. Furthermore, such programmes increased political participation even more than formal education did, a finding partly attributed to their being conducted in local languages (Kuenzi, 2006, 2011).

Well-designed civic education programmes can increase political participation

In many countries, youth involvement in political processes is low. Across 38 countries taking part in the 2009 International Civic and Citizenship Education Study (ICCS), only a small minority of 14-year-old students reported participating in organizations such as party youth groups, unions, environmental groups and human rights organizations (Schulz et al., 2010).

Students who attend schools that provide well-designed civics education are more likely to be actively involved in politics. Most teachers from the European countries participating in the 1999 International Association for the Evaluation of Educational Achievement (IEA) Civic Education Study agreed that teaching civic education could make a difference for students' political and civic development: the percentages agreeing ranged from 53% in the Czech Republic and 65% in Cyprus to over 80% elsewhere (Torney-Purta, 2002). Moreover, civic education can have long-lasting effects. A study drawing on data from eight European countries, including Denmark, Poland and Slovenia, showed that some civic skills and political values acquired in school were retained into adulthood (Hooghe and Wilkenfeld, 2008).

> 66 **Student-centred activities such as mock elections and discussion boards result in more political participation** 99

In many countries, citizenship education is part of the compulsory curriculum, whether delivered in discrete lessons, integrated into other disciplines or taught in a cross-curricular approach (Eurydice, 2012). Yet, the impact of civic education critically depends on how programmes are designed, the kinds of teaching methods employed and the quality of facilitators or trainers. In the United States, the Student Voices in the Campaign curriculum educated high school students on national and local elections during the 2002/03 school year. The curriculum included student-centred activities such as mock elections, meetings with those campaigning for local political office, letter-writing, and online polls and discussion boards. A follow-up evaluation with students after the 2004 elections found the curriculum led to increased and sustained interest in formal types of political engagement such as volunteering for a campaign (Pasek et al., 2008; Syvertsen et al., 2009).

In the Dominican Republic, Poland and South Africa, adults who were exposed to civic education programmes conducted by NGOs were significantly more active in local politics, for example attending municipal meetings or participating in community problem-solving activities. The impact was greater when individuals received more frequent exposure to civic education; when messages were taught through active and participatory methods;

and when individuals had sufficient prior political resources to act on messages received through training (Finkel, 2002, 2003).

EDUCATION CAN CHANNEL DISCONTENT INTO NON-VIOLENT CIVIL MOVEMENTS

From the Occupy movement to the Arab Spring and mass protests on the streets of Brazil and Turkey, people around the world are increasingly using unarmed tactics to challenge oppressive, corrupt and unfair political and economic systems. Education makes it more likely that discontented citizens will channel their concerns through non-violent civil movements, such as protests, boycotts, strikes, rallies, political demonstrations and social non-cooperation and resistance. In China, citizens with a college degree not only agreed on the need to improve democracy, but supported various types of political participation, such as mass demonstrations and political rallies, and resisted the official government petitioning system (Wang et al., 2015).

Such non-violent actions take place outside traditional political channels, making them distinct from other non-violent political processes such as lobbying, electioneering and legislating. For those who fail to get what they need from the political system through the electoral system or by direct communication or negotiations, non-violent civil actions offer the potential for issues to be heard and possibly addressed. Using data on 238 ethnic groups in 106 states from 1945 to 2000, a study found that ethnic groups with higher levels of educational attainment were more likely to engage in non-violent protests than those with lower levels of education (Shaykhutdinov, 2011).

> 66
> Studies from 106 states show that groups with higher education are less likely to engage in violent protests
> 99

Not all non-violent actions succeed, but such activities are effective means of achieving significant social and political change. An analysis of 323 non-violent and violent resistance campaigns for regime change, anti-occupation and secession from 1900 to 2006 showed that non-violent resistance was nearly twice as effective as violent resistance in removing incumbent governments from power. Moreover, countries where authoritarian regimes fall to non-violent uprisings are much more likely to transition to democracy and experience civil peace than if regimes fall to armed uprisings (Chenoweth and Stephan, 2011). Non-violent action was a central component of 50 out of 67 democratic transitions from 1973 to 2005 (Johnstad, 2010; Karatnycky and Ackerman, 2005).

In some countries, protest has arisen from higher educated individuals lacking suitable jobs. In the years leading up to the Arab Spring, the expansion of schooling in the Arab world increased the pool of individuals who had completed primary school and attained some secondary schooling (and beyond) but had not seen that education rewarded in the labour market. According to one study drawing on the World Values Survey from 2005–2007, in many countries in the Middle East marked by the Arab Spring, more educated individuals were more likely to engage in demonstrations, boycotts and strikes; the link between education and political protest was stronger among individuals who had poor outcomes in the labour market (Campante and Chor, 2012).

INVESTMENTS IN EDUCATION AND DEMOCRACY CAN BE MUTUALLY SUPPORTIVE

Broad and equitable access to good quality education plays an important role in sustaining democratic practices and institutions. Higher literacy levels, induced by the expansion of mass primary schooling, accounted for half the regime transitions towards higher levels of democracy over 1870–2000 (Murtin and Wacziarg, 2014). The likelihood of a country establishing and maintaining a democratic regime is higher the more educated its population. Oligarchic societies that started with a more equal distribution of education would be expected to democratize sooner (Bourguignon and Verdier, 2000). A study of 104 countries over 1965–2000 found that, even after controlling for country-specific effects, a more equal distribution of education was the main determinant for the transition to democracy (Castelló-Climent, 2008).

In many countries, greater access to tertiary education has played a critical role in promoting the transition to democracy and sustaining democratic regimes. University students were a driving force behind the popular protests that brought down many authoritarian regimes in sub-Saharan Africa in the early 1990s (Bratton and Walle, 1997). A study on Benin, Ghana, Kenya and Senegal showed that elected representatives with tertiary education formed the core of cross-party coalitions that initiated recent reforms (Barkan et al., 2004).

Just as equal education opportunities for all can facilitate democratic regimes, democratic governance tends to result in more and better education. The success of the Universal Primary Education programme in Uganda was heavily influenced by Uganda's return to multicandidate – if not multiparty – political competition in 1996. It increased the incentive for the government to successfully implement the programme because of perceptions that the government's performance would be judged accordingly. Ugandan voters indeed evaluated their president's overall performance highly, and the Universal Primary Education programme was one of the major reasons (Stasavage, 2005).

HOW TEACHING IS DONE MATTERS FOR THE POLITICAL OUTCOMES OF EDUCATION

An open learning environment that supports discussion of controversial political and social issues, and allows students to hear and express differing opinions, has been shown to lead to better political outcomes (Davies, 2009). Through interactions with peers, teachers and political leaders, students gain knowledge about the political process, engage in careful reasoning about policy issues and practise how to argue and debate. Similarly, active and participatory teaching methods, such as role playing, dramatizations and group decision-making, have a greater effect on individual political orientation than more traditional rote learning does (Harber and Mncube, 2012).

Drawing on data from 35 countries participating in the 2009 ICCS, a recent study showed that openness in classroom discussions, with students having the opportunity to discuss and give their opinion on political and social issues, was positively associated with individuals' future intention to participate in civic and political engagement (Quintelier and Hooghe, 2013). In Israel and Italy, an open and democratic classroom climate has been shown to help students become civically and politically involved by fostering citizenship self-efficacy (Ichilov, 2007; Manganelli et al., 2015). More specifically, an open classroom climate can foster political participation by students from disadvantaged socio-economic backgrounds, as a study in the United States showed (Campbell, 2008).

In South Africa, since the early 1990s, Street Law's Democracy for All programme has provided civic education in grades 11 and 12, including participatory activities such as case studies, role playing and mock trials. Students exposed to this programme at least weekly were found far more likely to correctly identify names of key South African political leaders and possess basic knowledge of the constitutional structure than students who received civics instruction less often or not at all (Finkel and Ernst, 2005).

In Guatemala, the Nueva Escuela Unitaria model's active participatory learning approach in rural and indigenous schools included self-instructional workbooks and teacher guides, an integrated active pedagogy, the development of pedagogical materials, and extensive community involvement. First and second graders attending these schools showed significantly more democratic behaviours (including turn-taking, expressing opinions, assisting others and leading) than their counterparts in traditional schools (De Baessa et al., 2002; Mogollón and Solano, 2011).

Implementing learner-centred pedagogy is not without challenges

The implementation of learner-centred pedagogy in classrooms can admittedly be difficult, especially in contexts with few textbooks and teaching materials, large class sizes and inappropriate furniture (Schweisfurth, 2011). It can also be challenging because pedagogy ultimately relates to power relations within classrooms and beyond (Altinyelken, 2015). In Ethiopia and Namibia, the basic tenets of student-centred pedagogy sometimes conflicted with local understandings of authority structures, obedience and teacher–student relationships (O'Sullivan, 2004; Serbessa, 2006). In some East Asian countries, teacher-dominated pedagogy prevails; it is considered more compatible with societies that value high stakes testing and show deference to teachers (Nguyen et al., 2006).

The external political environment can also shape the internal characteristics of classrooms. Interviews with teachers and school management in Ankara, Turkey, found that the authoritarian nature of political and social environments, combined with increasing limitations on freedom of speech, gave children a strong message that dissenting voices were not welcome and, worse, not tolerated (Altinyelken, 2015).

THE RELATIONSHIP BETWEEN EDUCATION AND CONFLICT IS MULTIFACETED

It is estimated that well over 100,000 people were killed in armed conflict in 2014 – the highest annual fatality count in 20 years. There were important regional variations. The Middle East was the most violence-prone region, with developments in Iraq and the Syrian Arab Republic mainly responsible for driving up the death toll (Melander, 2015). The underlying causes of armed conflict are multiple and complex; lack of good quality education is seldom, if ever, the primary precipitating factor. But under certain conditions, it can exacerbate the wider grievances, social tensions and inequalities that drive societies towards armed conflict.

TOO LITTLE EDUCATION OR UNEQUAL EDUCATIONAL OPPORTUNITIES CAN MAKE SOCIETIES MORE PRONE TO CONFLICT

When large numbers of young people are denied access to a good quality education, the resulting poverty, unemployment and hopelessness can act as recruiting agents for armed militia. An analysis of 120 countries over 30 years found that countries with large numbers of young men were less likely to experience violent conflict if their populations had higher levels of education (Barakat and Urdal, 2009). In Sierra Leone, young people who had no education were nine times as likely to join rebel groups as those with at least secondary education (Humphreys and Weinstein, 2008).

Yet, more education is not automatically a panacea for the threat posed by the combination of mass unemployment and a high proportion of youth to adults. As was noted above, when education levels rise but labour markets are stagnant, the result can be a rapid increase in the number of better-educated unemployed young people resentful over their lack of prospects.

In Uttar Pradesh state, India, the disillusionment of educated youth (usually young men) who were unable to secure jobs was seen as undermining social cohesion and political stability (Jeffrey et al., 2007). In Peru, large-scale qualitative research identified dissatisfaction with public education, corruption in the education sector and a lack of mobility associated with education (particularly outside the capital) as key causes for the growth of armed factions, as these grievances were used to recruit both students and teachers (Comisión de la Verdad y Reconciliación de Peru, 2003).

> **An analysis of 120 countries over 30 years found that conflict was less likely when education inequality is lower**

Inequality in education, interacting with wider disparity, heightens the risk of conflict. A recent study drawing on data from 100 countries over 50 years found that countries with higher levels of inequality in schooling due to ethnic and religious differences were much more likely to experience conflict (FHI 360 Education Policy and Data Center, 2015). Across 22 countries in sub-Saharan Africa, sub-national regions with very low average education had a 50% probability of experiencing the onset of conflict within 21 years, while the corresponding interval for regions with very high average education was 346 years (Østby et al., 2009).

A striking body of evidence suggests that people willing to use violence to pursue political ends are more likely to come from higher educated sections of society. Drawing on public opinion polls, a study found that, among Palestinians in Gaza and the West Bank in the 1980s, higher levels of education did not necessarily decrease support for violent attacks. In Lebanon, Hezbollah combatants who were killed during paramilitary operations had more education than non-combatants of the same age group and regional background (Krueger and Maleckova, 2003).

CONTENT AND PEDAGOGY CAN MAKE SOCIETIES MORE OR LESS PRONE TO VIOLENT CONFLICT

Why does access to formal education not always keep people from participating in violence, particularly in the context of violent extremism? Part of the answer lies not in the amount of education but in what and how students are taught. When sites of learning are used not to nurture minds, by teaching learners to think critically, but to inculcate prejudice, intolerance and a distorted view of history, they can become breeding grounds for violence.

In many countries, curricula and learning materials have been shown to reinforce stereotypes and exacerbate political and social grievances. In Rwanda,

> 35% of out-of-school children live in conflict-affected countries

a review of major education policies and programmes implemented between 1962 and 1994 argued that the content of education reflected and amplified ethnic inequality in society and contributed to categorizing, collectivizing and stigmatizing Hutu and Tutsi into exclusive groups (King, 2014). In India and Pakistan, textbooks and curricula have perpetuated images of the rival nation to suit their adversarial relationship and political goals (Lall, 2008).

Disputes over curricular contents have sometimes directly spilled over into violent conflict. In 2000, when overtly Sunni textbooks were introduced in Pakistan's Federally Administered Northern Areas, the local Shia population began to agitate for equal representation in textbook discussions of Islam. The conflict became acute in 2004–2005 as violent confrontations took place between Shia and Sunni communities, with the resulting curfews closing down schools for almost a year (Ali, 2008).

Language in education policies can be a source of wider grievances. In multi-ethnic countries, the imposition of a single dominant language as the language of instruction in schools, while sometimes a necessity, has been a frequent source of grievance linked to wider issues of social and cultural inequality (UNESCO, 2016). By one estimate, over half the countries affected by armed conflict were highly diverse linguistically, making decisions over the language of instruction a potentially divisive political issue (Pinnock, 2009).

Violent conflict has often followed group-based inequality exacerbated by language policies in education. In Nepal, the imposition of Nepali as the language of instruction fed into broader grievances among non-Nepali-speaking groups that drove the civil war (Murshed and Gates, 2005). Guatemala's imposition of Spanish in schools was seen by indigenous people as part of a broader pattern of social discrimination. Armed groups representing indigenous people demanded bilingual and intercultural education during negotiations on a peace agreement, leading to a constitutional commitment (Marques and Bannon, 2003).

ARMED CONFLICT PLACES A HEAVY BURDEN ON EDUCATION SYSTEMS

Armed conflict is one of the greatest obstacles to progress in education. In conflict-affected countries, almost 21.5 million children of primary school age and almost 15 million adolescents of lower secondary school age are out of school. Over the last decade, the problem of out-of-school children has been increasingly concentrated in conflict-affected countries, where the proportion increased from 29% in 1999 to 35% in 2014. This trend is especially marked in Northern Africa and Western Asia where the share increased from 63% to 91% (UNESCO, 2016). Recent estimates indicated that surging conflict and political upheaval across the Middle East and North Africa prevent more than 13 million children from going to school (UNICEF, 2015).

The experience of the Syrian Arab Republic provides a stark example of how conflict can reverse achievements in education. According to data from the UNESCO Institute for Statistics (UIS), by 2001 the country had achieved universal primary enrolment and relatively high secondary enrolment. Yet, as the civil war spread, the primary net enrolment ratio, which was still at 98.9% in 2009, declined to under 71% in 2013, with the number of primary school-age children out of school increasing from 21,000 to 563,000.

Armed conflict also interrupts progress in education. Two decades of conflict in Afghanistan up to 2001 resulted in a loss of 5.5 years on the total average years of national schooling; Burundi's civil war cost the country over 3 years (UIS, 2010). Similarly, the 1992–1998 civil conflict in Tajikistan resulted in a decrease in school attainment for girls. Girls exposed to conflict were 12% less likely to complete compulsory schooling than older cohorts who completed their schooling before the conflict (Shemyakina, 2011).

In addition, armed conflict exacerbates inequality. Conflict-affected areas are often marked by extreme disadvantage in education, with the poor typically faring worst.[2] Young adults in the Autonomous Region in Muslim Mindanao in the Philippines are four times more likely than the national average to have fewer than four years of education – and six times more likely for poor males (**Figure 4.1**).

When Guatemala's civil war started in 1965, indigenous people averaged three years fewer in school than the average. By the start of the 1991 peace talks, indigenous people in areas not affected by the conflict had gained 3.1 years in education while for those in conflict-affected areas, the education gap with the rest of the indigenous population had increased from 0.4 to 1.7 years (UIS, 2010).

CHILDREN, TEACHERS AND SCHOOLS ARE INCREASINGLY ON THE FRONT LINE OF CONFLICT

Children, teachers and schools are on the front line of conflict and many have been deliberately targeted. State and non-state actors alike often blur the line between combatants and civilians. In the majority of countries with armed conflicts – including at least 26 between 2005 and 2015 – government armed forces and non-state armed groups have used schools and other education institutions for military purposes. In addition to risking students' and teachers' lives and safety, the military use of education institutions impinges upon access to education, decreases the quality of education and compromises efforts to create safe learning spaces (Global Coalition to Protect Education from Attack, 2015).

Deliberate destruction of education facilities is a long-standing practice in armed conflicts (UNESCO, 2011). Most of Timor-Leste's education infrastructure was destroyed in the 1998–1999 war, and 95% of schools required rehabilitation. In Iraq, 85% of schools were damaged or destroyed by fighting during the conflict of 2003–2004 (Buckland, 2005). Between 2009 and 2015, attacks in north-eastern Nigeria destroyed more than 910 schools and forced at least 1,500 to close. By early 2016, an estimated 952,029 school-age children had fled the violence (HRW, 2016). By 2016, the Syrian Arab Republic had lost more than one-quarter of its schools – more than 6,000 damaged by the violence, forced to close, or used for fighting or sheltering hundreds of displaced families (UNICEF, 2016).

Teachers are at risk. During the Rwandan genocide, more than two-thirds of the teaching force in primary and secondary schools was killed or fled (Buckland, 2005). In Colombia, 140 teachers were killed over 2009–2013, around 1,100 received death threats and 305 were forced to leave their homes because their lives were at risk (Global Coalition to Protect Education from Attack, 2015). As of 2015, in Nigeria, where Boko Haram has targeted education workers and students, at least 611 teachers had been deliberately killed and 19,000 forced to flee since 2009 (HRW, 2016).

The forced recruitment of children into armed forces, often through abduction, is widespread. It is an immense barrier to education, not just because child soldiers receive no formal education, but also because abductions and trauma have far wider effects on the children themselves and their home communities. Reliable and recent data on the global number of child soldiers are not available.

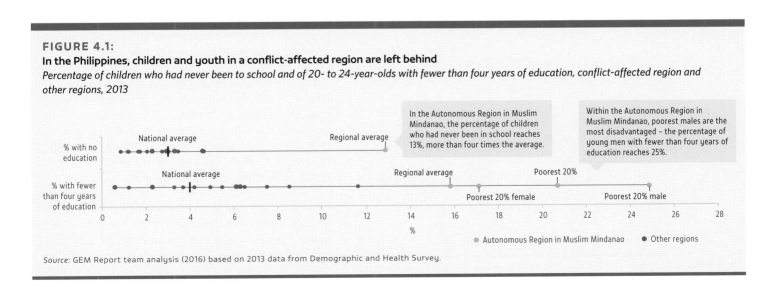

FIGURE 4.1:

In the Philippines, children and youth in a conflict-affected region are left behind
Percentage of children who had never been to school and of 20- to 24-year-olds with fewer than four years of education, conflict-affected region and other regions, 2013

Source: GEM Report team analysis (2016) based on 2013 data from Demographic and Health Survey.

> "
> Refugee children and adolescents are five times more likely to be out of school than others
> "

Refugees are a huge challenge for education systems

Almost 60 million people were in forced displacement in 2015, the highest number since 1945 (UNHCR, 2015). They include internally displaced people (IDPs), asylum seekers and refugees, a small percentage of whom are resettled. Moreover, people are spending longer and longer time in displacement and refuge, compromising prospects of durable solutions and reinforcing the urgency of a sustainable, comprehensive response by the international community.

Data remain limited for many refugee situations, but the most recent data from the United Nations High Commissioner for Refugees estimate that, worldwide, 50% of primary school-age refugee children are out of school and 75% of adolescent refugees at secondary level are out

of school. Refugee children and adolescents are five times more likely to be out of school than their non-refugee peers. However, this average obscures significant differences across countries. Primary enrolment rates among the displaced are 80% in Egypt and Yemen but 40% at refugee sites in Pakistan. Enrolment rates are substantially lower at the secondary level: only 4% of 12- to 17-year-old refugees were enrolled in school in Kenya and Pakistan (**Figure 4.2**).

The provision and quality of education in some refugee settings are limited, with shortages of qualified teachers proficient in an appropriate language, pupil/teacher ratios as high as 70:1 and high proportions of unqualified teachers. Official learning validation and certification, which are important for the effective education of refugee children, are often ignored (UNESCO and UNHCR, 2016).

EDUCATION CAN HELP BUILD SOCIETIES AFTER CONFLICT

Segregation is a common legacy of conflict. Institutional environments play an important role in reintegrating post-conflict communities and can address differences between ethnic and religious groups (Alexander and Christia, 2011). On the other hand, where schools maintain the status quo, they can predispose young people towards segregation and engrain discriminatory attitudes, leading them to believe intolerance is socially acceptable (Ramirez-Barat and Duthie, 2015).

Integrated schools have been found to positively influence minority group identity, prevailing attitudes towards inclusion and exclusion, and a sense of forgiveness, with the potential to heal division and promote less sectarian perspectives (McGlynn, 2004). Members of communities educated together may develop more tolerance (Hansson et al., 2013).

In Bosnia and Herzegovina, schools have been segregated along linguistic and ethnic lines since the end of the war in 1996. In some cases, students from different ethnic groups attend the same school but are

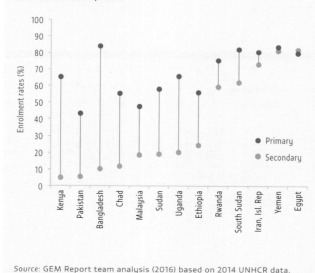

FIGURE 4.2:
Education conditions for refugee children vary widely
Primary and secondary enrolment rates, selected refugee sites in selected countries, 2014

Source: GEM Report team analysis (2016) based on 2014 UNHCR data.

physically separated, are taught in different languages and follow specific ethnic curricula. An interim measure meant to facilitate the return of refugees immediately after the war became an entrenched practice that impedes younger generations' learning to live together (Ramirez-Barat and Duthie, 2015).

In Northern Ireland in 2013, 15 years after the Belfast Agreement, 93% of children and youth attended schools segregated by religion. A bottom-up movement for integrated cross-community schools began in the late 1970s, largely because of a campaigning group of parents known as All Children Together. As of 2008, 61 integrated schools had been created, where children from both communities are brought together daily to interact in the classroom and during extracurricular activities. The schools include training programmes to prepare teachers for cross-community settings, as well as a curriculum that includes opportunities to discuss potentially contentious aspects of the country's cultural traditions and sectarian conflict (Aiken, 2013).

In Israel, there are six Arab-Jewish bilingual schools, where mixed classrooms are a central aspect, reflecting the schools' commitment to strengthening group identity while encouraging tolerance and respect for pluralism (Bekerman, 2016). These schools have had some success in mediating conflicting national narratives, creating opportunities to talk about the conflict and recognizing ethnic, religious and other differences (Bekerman, 2012).

Curricular content can help or harm inter-group relations after conflict. Developing curricula about the recent past is difficult and may be contested. In Bosnia and Herzegovina three parallel education systems, each with distinct historical narratives, were created; in Rwanda the teaching of history was postponed for 10 years following the genocide (Freedman et al., 2008; Jones, 2012). In Guatemala, Peru and South Africa, while history education teaches about recent conflicts, it does not engage substantively with the causes of conflict and past injustices. Conflict is presented as exceptional, an aberration overcome by what is believed to be the present's democracy, active citizenship and a culture of peace (Paulson, 2015).

Education's contribution to peacebuilding also depends on the sensitivity of reforms and programmes to the legacies of past injustice. Transitional justice promotes accountability and the redressing of major violations

of human rights. It is increasingly recognized as a fundamental part of peacebuilding efforts, helping to strengthen the rule of law, address grievances among affected communities and prevent the recurrence of violations. Adding a dimension of transitional justice to the reconstruction of education after conflict is challenging, yet measures can be designed to establish links with and catalyse change in education (Ramirez-Barat and Duthie, 2015).

The success of any curricular reform or innovation in learning materials depends on the availability of motivated, engaged and trained teachers. Teaching in ways that encourage critical thinking and embrace complexity is difficult, all the more so in conflict-ridden countries, such as Bosnia and Herzegovina and Rwanda, where teachers may be reluctant or ill-prepared to discuss contentious issues, fear engaging with political issues or have been socialized to accept one-sided narratives. In Lebanon, teachers chose to avoid contentious historical issues in lessons, partly because their training had failed to equip them with skills to manage, contain or solve classroom conflicts (van Ommering, 2015). In Guatemala, teachers believed it was important to teach about the civil war but often felt unprepared to facilitate discussions for lack of appropriate training and learning materials (Bellino, 2014).

> 66 To ensure the best results from peace education, we need to train teachers how to discuss contentious history 99

In Kenya, a review of peace education programmes in refugee camps and nationwide highlighted challenges for teachers in embracing learner-centred pedagogy such as participatory and interactive approaches. For example, classroom observations in Dadaab and Kakuma refugee camps showed that most teachers had poor questioning skills (Mendenhall and Chopra, 2016; Obura, 2002).

Peace education can offer a response to direct violence and help prevent further violence

In many countries, thousands of children are being taught by educators using peace education curricula involving methods and learning processes that include inquiry, critical thinking, and dialogue towards greater equity and social justice. The scope of peace education has expanded in recent years to become more inclusive of areas such as human rights education, citizenship education, multicultural education, environmental education and social justice education (Bajaj, 2008; Bajaj and Hantzopoulos, 2016).

Although well-designed peace education interventions are rarely subjected to rigorous scrutiny, studies show they can reduce student aggression, bullying and participation in violent conflict, and increase the chances that students will work to prevent conflict (Barakat et al., 2008; Barakat et al., 2013; Davies, 2005).

Many NGOs have contributed to peace education. In Gujarat state, India, the NGO Navsarjan focuses on the rights of Dalits (formerly called 'untouchables'), who make up around 16% of India's population (HRW, 2014). To address widespread caste discrimination in schools and the high dropout rate of Dalit students, Navsarjan set up several schools that specially cater to Dalit children living in the surrounding communities. Classes and assemblies reiterate messages about caste equality to eradicate the notion that Dalit children are less worthy than their higher caste peers. Students are also encouraged to critically analyse their society and become active in their communities by spreading awareness, joining campaigns for equality and fighting for justice (Bajaj, 2012, 2014).

EDUCATION NEEDS MORE EMPHASIS ON INTERNATIONAL PEACEBUILDING AGENDAS

Building sustainable peace is a major challenge. A 2009 study estimated that 40% of all conflicts reignited within the first decade of peace, highlighting the need for concerted international effort focused not just on ending conflict but on post-conflict peacebuilding (World Bank, 2009). Despite growing evidence of the role of education in peacebuilding, international actors have prioritized security issues - such as spending in military and securiy personnel - as in Lebanon, Nepal and Sierra Leone (Novelli et al., 2015). Of 37 publicly available full peace agreements signed between 1989 and 2005, 11 do not mention education at all. Even in those that do, education is addressed with great variation (Dupuy, 2008). Moreover, education stakeholders often lack skills and knowledge to integrate peacebuilding measures into education programmes or sector plans, or to lobby for education's role in peacebuilding frameworks (Novelli et al., 2015).

VIOLENCE IS A CHALLENGE FOR ALL, NOT ONLY FOR CONFLICT-AFFECTED COUNTRIES

The costs of interpersonal violence are far higher than those of armed conflict. The death toll of disputes between individuals, including domestic and family violence, is estimated at nine times that of war and other such conflict (Hoeffler and Fearon, 2014). Could education make a difference? Policies designed to increase educational attainment can significantly reduce crime rates. In Italy, more than 75% of convicted persons had not completed high school in 2001, while United Kingdom incarceration rates among men aged 21 to 25 were more than eight times higher for those with no qualifications than for those with some qualification (Buonanno and Leonida, 2006; Machin et al., 2011). In Sweden, each additional year of schooling decreased the likelihood of a conviction for a violent crime by 10%, for property crime by 14% and for other crimes by almost 6% (Hjalmarsson et al., 2015).

> " In Sweden, each additional year of schooling decreased the likelihood of a conviction for a violent crime by 10% "

Education can be used to reduce violence against children

A prominent share of violence against children occurs within their own households. Around 6 in 10 children between the ages of 2 and 14 are regularly subjected to physical punishment by their caregivers (UNICEF, 2014). Action from the education sector can make a difference. For instance, parental and family-based skill-building initiatives on child protection and early childhood development can lead to behavioural change. In Liberia, the Parents Make the Difference programme involved a ten week parenting intervention including training in positive parenting and non-violent behaviour. When asked later about the last time their child misbehaved, only 9% of those who had participated reported beating their child, compared with 45% of those who had not. Participants replaced harsh punishment with non-violent discipline strategies using newly acquired knowledge and skills (Sim et al., 2014).

Around 120 million girls under the age of 20 have been subjected to forced sexual acts, including intercourse, at some point in their lives (UNICEF, 2014). A Ugandan programme provided life skills to build knowledge and reduce risky behaviour, combined with vocational training to enable girls who had been forced into sexual acts to establish small enterprises. The programme reduced the incidence of girls who unwillingly had sex during the previous year by 83%, an impact largely attributed to life skills sessions and to discussion on negotiation, rape, legal rights and preventive measures (Bandiera et al., 2014).

All kinds of violence against children affect schooling, leading to lower educational attainment and poor employment prospects. Across 18 sub-Saharan African countries, gender-based violence – as measured by intimate partner violence, early marriage and female genital mutilation – had a negative impact on girls' schooling. In Comoros, Mozambique and Sierra Leone, the probability of attending school is, respectively, 42%, 25% and 15% lower for girls whose mothers justified intimate partner violence than for those whose mothers did not (Koissy-Kpein, 2015) – thus showing a cross-generational impact.

Schools are exposed to many forms of violence

To help sustain peaceful societies, schools must offer children a non-violent environment providing appropriate skills and practices for school and home.

Recent estimates from Plan International, based on the numbers of those affected by verbal bullying, a common form of violence in school, indicate that 246 million children suffer school-related violence every year (Greene et al., 2013). This violence and abuse can seriously harm children's health, well-being and ability to learn to their full potential, reducing school participation, learning levels and completion rates. In Brazil, Ghana and the United States, bullying has been shown to increase absenteeism (Abramovay and Rua, 2005; Dunne et al., 2006; Kosciw et al., 2013).

A study drawing on data from the 2011 Trends in International Mathematics and Science Study (TIMSS) from 48 countries showed that grade 4 students who reported being bullied weekly at school scored 32 points lower in mathematics than those who reported they had almost never been bullied (Mullis et al., 2012). New analysis of the same data shows that in many countries students in grade 8 who had reported being involved in physical fights in school scored lower in mathematics than those who had not. In Australia and Chile, the learning gap between students who were involved in physical fights in school and those who were not was almost 30 percentage points (**Figure 4.3**).

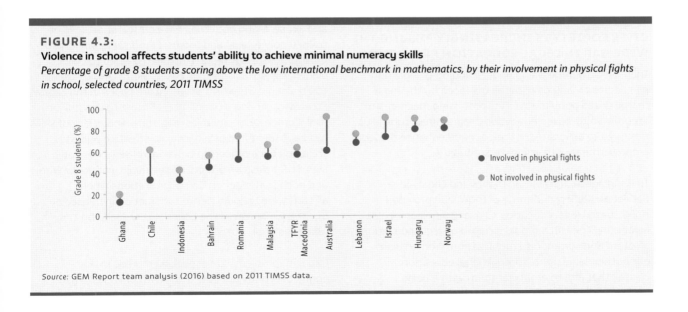

FIGURE 4.3:

Violence in school affects students' ability to achieve minimal numeracy skills

Percentage of grade 8 students scoring above the low international benchmark in mathematics, by their involvement in physical fights in school, selected countries, 2011 TIMSS

- Involved in physical fights
- Not involved in physical fights

Source: GEM Report team analysis (2016) based on 2011 TIMSS data.

> " Lack of knowledge and education severely hampers citizens' ability to interact with the justice system "

EDUCATION CAN PLAY A KEY ROLE IN BUILDING A FUNCTIONING JUSTICE SYSTEM

A functioning justice system that upholds the rule of law is considered critical for sustaining peaceful societies. Lack of knowledge and education, however, severely hampers citizens' ability to interact with the justice system. In 2011, according to court user survey results in the Former Yugoslav Republic of Macedonia, only 32% of individuals with primary education were 'well or partially informed' about the judicial system and its reforms, compared with 77% of those with higher education (World Bank, 2011). In Bangkok, many female victims of violence were unaware of the laws and legal procedures in place to protect them from, or redress, gender-based violence. Thus, even when financial resources were not a problem, they did not seek legal protection or justice (International Commission of Jurists, 2012).

CIVIL SOCIETY IS INCREASINGLY FILLING THE WIDE GAP IN LEGAL EDUCATION PROVISION

Increased awareness and understanding of legal rights can address many daily problems faced by the most marginalized populations. One promising mechanism is community-based education programmes, typically designed to advocate for the poor and enhance the legal empowerment of marginalized groups.

In Bangladesh, the Human Rights and Legal Aid Services (HRLS) programme of BRAC had provided rights-based legal education to over 3.8 million people as of 2013. The HRLS model is based on legal education, legal aid and community mobilization. Women learn about their legal rights through legal education classes that aim to empower them with a basic understanding of their rights and the laws, the first step in seeking justice. The programme also uses street theatre, a popular community outreach tool,

to promote behavioural change and create community acceptance of access to property rights for the poor (Kolisetty, 2014).

In Sierra Leone, over half of all people behind bars have not been convicted of any crime but are awaiting trial. Timap for Justice, an NGO, recruits and hires local community members, who receive basic legal training as paralegals. As a result of Timap's intervention, paralegals have succeeded in getting inappropriate charges dropped in 28% of cases, and secured bail for an additional 55% of suspects (Open Society Justice Initiative, 2015).

BUILDING THE CAPACITY OF JUDICIAL AND LAW ENFORCEMENT OFFICERS IS CRITICAL

Insufficient training and capacity-building for judicial and law enforcement officers hinders the carrying out of justice and can result in delays, flawed or insufficient evidence-gathering, lack of enforcement, and abuse. Many countries have critical shortages of trained police, legal and forensic staff. Only one doctor in Timor-Leste has reportedly been trained to collect evidence in sexual violence cases. Sierra Leone has just 100 trained lawyers, 90 of whom are based in the capital, Freetown, serving a population of more than 5 million (UN Women, 2011). In Rajasthan state, India, lack of skills has been identified as a barrier to effective policing. Training police officers in behavioural skills has had significant positive effects on the quality of police work and public satisfaction. In police stations where all staff were trained, victim satisfaction increased by 30%, while fear of the police was reduced by 17% (Banerjee et al., 2012).

Capacity problems are especially marked in post-conflict settings or in the aftermath of crises, when levels of violence are exceptionally high. In Haiti, the national police went from being the least to the most trusted institution of the state over five years through a training programme established by the United Nations Stabilization Mission in Haiti. The mission provided a seven month initial recruit training programme, rather than the typical two to three weeks often seen in post-conflict environments, alongside other specialized training programmes. When Haitian citizens were asked in 2009 whether they had seen a change in police work over the past year, 72% reported a positive change, and 83% reported that the security situation in the country was either a lot or at least a little better than in the previous year (UNDPKO, 2010).

CONCLUSION

What makes a peaceful and non-violent society? How can development be made sustainable in conditions of violent conflict and insecurity? The answers are complex, yet education's role, though multifaceted, is crucial, whether it involves encouraging people, particularly the young, to vote, or supports participation in political processes and becoming politically active. What students are taught and how teaching is conducted are cornerstones of the relationship between education, conflict and peacebuilding. Peace and non-violence are not promoted simply by the virtue of children and youth attending school, but by teachers enabling students to acquire useful skills when confronted with circumstances that may lead to conflict or violence.

Education reflects social tensions, including conflict-related ideologies and stereotypes, so the relationship between education, peace and conflict deserves far more attention to enable the promotion of positive contributions to peacebuilding, access to justice and protection from violence, whether large-scale or intimate.

ENDNOTES

1. The institutional contexts in which voting decisions are made also matter. In countries where voter registration is undertaken by local authorities and is compulsory (e.g. the United Kingdom), the impact of education on voting behaviour can be largely muted (Milligan et al., 2004).

2. Intra-country comparisons should be treated with caution. It cannot automatically be assumed that conflict is the main source of educational disparity. Inequality associated with wider social, economic and political factors in conflict zones also influences opportunities for education.

Favelas in Rio de Janeiro, which formed when lots of people moved from the Brazilian countryside to the city.

CREDIT: Anna Spysz/GEM Report

CHAPTER

5

Place: inclusive and sustainable cities

We recognize that sustainable urban development and management are crucial to the quality of life of our people.

– The 2030 Agenda for Sustainable Development

KEY MESSAGES

Education must be integrated into urban planning to create sustainable cities.

 Cities are growing fast, putting strain on education systems.
   a. There are significant education gaps within urban areas.
   b. There is a lack of access to public education in urban slums and peri-urban areas.
   c. Half of the world's refugees are children and youth, many of whom end up in cities.
   d. Ethnic and racial segregation in schools can exacerbate broader inequalities.
   e. Migrants to cities, and especially female migrants, urgently need skills for work.

 Until education is part of urban planning, urban challenges, such as unequal provision of services and discrimination, will never be fixed.
   a. By improving skills, education can foster more inclusive economies.
   b. Policies for urban education must reduce unequal access to quality public schools and teachers.
   c. Teacher training can reduce prejudice and discrimination.

 Education reduces crime in cities.
   a. Education increases job opportunities, and makes people more averse to risks, such as punishment for crimes.
   b. Early childhood interventions and a focus on high school graduation can reduce crime.

 Education can propel cities' competitiveness and productivity.
   a. Investing in research and innovation, and fostering ties between universities and industry, can transform a city into a prosperous knowledge-based economy.
   b. But attention is needed to ensure that knowledge-driven economic development does not increase inequality.

 Including education in urban planning makes environmental sustainability more likely.
   a. Communication strategies and school-based interventions teach people the importance of environmental approaches to planning, and encourage sustainable transportation.

 Education efforts alone will not lead to inclusive and safe cities.
   a. Urban planners need training in integrating education into urban planning and strategies.
   b. Communities affected by urban development must be included in renewal initiatives and plans for change.

 Urban governance must include education in its approach.
   a. Informed city leaders can use education and lifelong learning to transform their cities.
   b. Strengthened global networks of leaders of cities can solve urban challenges, including education gaps.

In addition to the areas highlighted in the preamble to the Sustainable Development Goals (SDGs) – people, planet, prosperity, peace and partnership – the *GEM Report 2016* also looks at 'place' with a focus on cities.

Urbanization is one of today's defining trends – more than half the global population lives in cities and urban areas. The concentration of productive activity, the availability of large markets and the promise of better living standards all draw people and commerce to cities. Global projections of urbanization indicate the majority of future urban population growth will take place in lower income countries (**Figure 5.1**).

This chapter presents evidence of how cities and urbanization affect education, and how education affects urban issues. Population growth, migration and the refugee crisis all have particular consequences for education. Cities – with their concentration of universities, research institutions, high skill industries and informal knowledge – are engines of knowledge-based innovation and growth. The scale and speed of urban change will require good governance, including flexibility and innovation, with multiple stakeholders and an adaptive approach (Jones et al., 2014; Wild et al., 2015), all of which will benefit from citizens engaging in lifelong learning.

Education and lifelong learning also influence cities and are key to taking advantage of cities' physical and social capital. They can have positive effects, such as reducing crime, and be used in good urban planning, for example to encourage sustainable transport. Education can also help address urban challenges. Cities are the sites of massive inequality. Vulnerable populations in cities in both low and high income countries suffer from poor access to basic services – such as education, housing and transport – which fosters disillusion, discontent and sometimes violence. Education can play a crucial role in tackling inequality and discrimination in urban areas.

> " Education and lifelong learning are key to taking advantage of cities' physical and social capital "

Improvements in planning are crucial for ensuring that the opportunities of urbanization outweigh the challenges and result in more inclusive, environmentally sustainable and prosperous cities. And education can play a crucial role in urban planning at the local level as well as in tackling related regional and global policy issues.

While most of the SDG agenda is driven by action at the level of member states, integrated policy-making is also required at the subnational level. Cities are both incubators and locations of change, and their importance to the world means the relationships between space and sectors such as the economy and education must be better understood. Such understanding would facilitate a comprehensive, contemporary perception of

FIGURE 5.1A:
We live in an increasingly urban world ...
Population in urban areas, projections to 2050 (%)

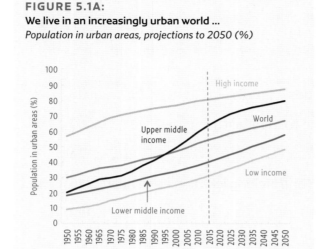

FIGURE 5.1B:
... and much future urban growth is expected to happen in lower income countries
Projected annual city population growth rates (%), 2015–2030

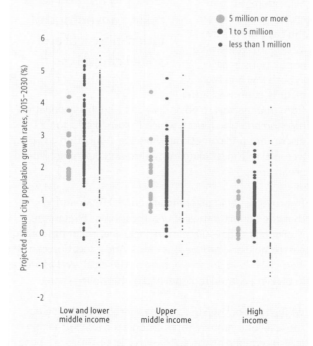

Notes: For Figure 5.1b, the size of the bubble represents the size of the cities in 2014.
Source: UNDESA (2014).

how humanity can tackle poverty, create inclusive and sustainable economic growth, protect the planet from degradation and destruction, and fulfil SDG 4 by ensuring inclusive and equitable education and promoting lifelong learning opportunities for all.

CITIES AFFECT EDUCATION PLANNING

Education must be integrated in urban planning to address the consequences on education of characteristics and processes related to urbanization, for example the need for education for refugee, migrant and slum-dwelling populations.

POPULATION CHANGE AFFECTS EDUCATION PLANNING

The continued growth of urban areas has implications for education system planning. While urbanization is a global trend, considerable variation exists in how urban populations grow, whether through natural population increases, migration or the reclassification of rural settlements. Globally, about half of urban growth is due to natural population growth and half to migration from rural areas (McGranahan and Satterthwaite, 2014). In China, 56% of urban population growth between 2000 and 2010 was a result of rural-to-urban migration despite strong disincentives such as rural residents being prevented access to education and health benefits once in cities (Bosker et al., 2015; World Bank and China Development Research Center of the State Council, 2014). In India, the reclassification of rural settlements into towns was responsible for 30% of urban population growth between 2001 and 2011; 44% of the growth was due to natural population increases (Ellis and Roberts, 2016).

Growth in cities, mostly unplanned, not only is the primary challenge for urban education systems but also has effects in rural areas (**Box 5.1**). The flow of migrants within and between countries, combined with continued growth in local populations, can raise demand for basic education access, skills development and more teachers, and increase the need to foster social cohesion and tolerance of cultural diversity through education.

BOX 5.1

Dealing with declining populations with rural school consolidation

Population increases in cities as a result of rural–urban migration has the converse effect of a declining population in rural and remote areas, with implications for rural education planning. Rural consolidation policies have been implemented in China and the United States to address the loss of students in rural schools. However, such policies need to be carefully planned and crafted. Recent reviews of the policy in China have deemed it to be largely unsuccessful, leading to increased dropouts, overcrowding in town schools, more teacher burden and higher financial pressures on the rural poor. The policy was suspended by the Ministry of Education in 2012. In the United States, there has been long-standing resistance to rural school consolidation, which historically was part of the Progressive movement's effort to make school districts more efficient. However, studies showed that school consolidation without adequate community involvement increased student absenteeism, led to community disintegration and hardships for families, and did little to improve fiscal efficiency.

Sources: Bard et al. (2006); Howley et al. (2011); Mei et al. (2015); Strang (1987); Tyack and Hansot (1982).

Urban refugees and displaced populations need access to education

The refugee crisis is deepening. The crisis is also more prevalent in and around cities. Analysis based on 12.2 million refugees finds that by late 2014, 6 out of 10 lived in urban areas. Globally, the number of forcibly displaced people increased by over 40% between 2011 and 2014, to 59.5 million (UNHCR, 2015). Refugees may not be formally registered in camps, which can limit their access to basic services and to employment authorization and access (UNESCO and UNHCR, 2016). It can also make it hard to get accurate counts of the number of refugees and internally displaced people in urban areas.

Globally, education systems are substantially affected by this crisis, since more than half the world's refugees are under 18. Given the long-term nature of displacement and the magnitude of the challenge in some countries, national and urban education systems that receive forcibly displaced children and youth need to adapt to support their long-term integration.

Turkey is host to almost 3 million registered Syrian refugees. As of late 2015, almost 700,000 Syrian refugee children and adolescents aged 6 to 17 needed access to education (3RP, 2016). Around 85% were scattered outside camps in towns and cities. The percentage of refugee children enrolled in formal education was over 85% in camp settings but only 30% in urban areas. Overall, enrolment rates were 7% in pre-primary education, 52% in primary education, 31% in lower secondary education, and 10% in upper secondary education (UNESCO and UNHCR, 2016).

Along with economic constraints, a major barrier to education is the language of instruction. The acquisition of a second language can be especially challenging for children who have fallen behind academically due to school interruptions, which is the case for many Syrian refugee children. In addition to the language barrier, teachers are not trained to address the emotional trauma experienced by many refugee children (Sirin and Rogers-Sirin, 2015).

The skills of migrant workers must be retained and improved

Migrants to cities face a number of challenges while trying to gain employment, such as discrimination, language barriers, unemployment, and exploitation in the informal economy. Addressing these requires, among other interventions, a focus on skills development (International Organization for Migration, 2015).

For example, China's unprecedented economic growth was accompanied by a tremendous wave of internal migration. In 2004, there were 120 million migrants, of whom 18% had primary education or less and 65% had completed lower secondary education (nine years of schooling). Migrant workers have very limited job security: a survey of 40 Chinese cities found that only 12.5% of workers had written contracts (Shi, 2008). An integrated skills development and employment training project conducted between 2007 and 2014 focused on improving training available to rural migrants, enhancing access to employment services and raising awareness of worker protections (World Bank, 2015).

A parallel problem is the deskilling of migrants, which has a gendered dimension. Women from the Philippines who hold university degrees travel to the Middle East to work as housemaids, and Eastern European women work in low skill jobs in wealthier EU countries (Kofman and Raghuram, 2009). Global research also indicates that a longer period in the host country did not significantly improve migrants' opportunities. Some highly skilled women could not continue in their professions despite adequate knowledge of the local language (International Organization for Migration, 2013).

Education for slum dwellers is a challenge

More than one-third of all urban residents in many developing countries live in slums or shanty towns in city centres or urban peripheries. Slums' conditions vary greatly within and between countries, but many are characterized by poor and crowded housing conditions, insecurity of land and housing, and poor access to basic services, including education (UN Habitat, 2009a). There has been increased recognition of the need to improve their liveability since the Millennium Development Goals, culminating in a strong focus on the issue in SDG 11.

> There is a distinct lack of access to public education in urban slums and peri-urban areas

Major collective efforts, such as by the Shack/Slum Dwellers International (SDI) network, have involved documenting inequality in services and advocating for change in government policy by empowering communities to participate in data collection and decision-making processes (Patel et al., 2012). However, the focus is on basic services, such as housing, water and sanitation, with the situation of education often unclear (Kielland, 2015). Yet, education remains a priority for communities. For instance, new data compiled for the GEM Report 2016 collected from 130 slum settlement profiles in 12 cities and towns of Uganda to identify community needs indicated that, while most settlement respondents agreed that students had access to pre-primary, primary and secondary schooling, in their qualitative responses they still highlighted the need to increase the number of schools, especially public schools (Shack/Slum Dwellers International et al., 2016).

Private school growth is an urban planning issue

The prevalence of private schools, especially in major cities, is often underestimated or disregarded in discussions of public education systems. In India, studies of two major cities, Mumbai and Patna, suggest that private schools serve over 75% of the children there (Ernst and Young LLP, 2014). The 2010/11 private school census of Lagos state, Nigeria revealed that over 85% of pre-primary and 60% of primary students were enrolled in private schools. Overall, the survey identified 12,098 private schools while there were only 1,606 government schools (Härmä, 2011, 2013).

Private schools play a crucial role in education in peri-urban areas (on the periphery of cities). Growth in such areas is mostly informal, often not captured in official statistics, and critically neglected (Ellis and Roberts, 2016). For example, satellite imagery shows that for many of the 12 largest Indian cities, the proportion of population outside the official boundaries exceeds that within (Ellis and Roberts, 2016). Evidence on peri-urban schooling suggests that private schools dominate provision, as in informal urban settlements and slums. A study of peri-urban areas in four sub-Saharan African countries found the majority of pre-primary schools were private. Given the strong demand for pre-primary education, the growth of private schools is likely the result of a lack of good quality public schools (Bidwell and Watine, 2014).

EDUCATION HAS A POSITIVE INFLUENCE ON CITIES

Education and lifelong learning need to be integrated in urban planning to take advantage of their positive effects on cities in economic and social terms. Education encourages productivity and innovation in cities, and can transform them into knowledge economies. It can also support a more prosperous city that accurately reflects its economic activities, for example by including the dynamic informal economy. Education can have positive social effects, such as crime reduction. It can be a primary tool for environmental initiatives, such as sustainable transport.

HIGHLY SKILLED WORKERS ARE CRITICAL FOR INNOVATION AND GROWTH

Economic growth is highly concentrated in urban areas – half of the world's population lives in cities, which generate more than 80% of global gross domestic product (GDP). Only 600 urban centres, with one-fifth of the world's population, generate 60% of global gross domestic product (GDP). By 2025, new smaller cities, mostly in China and India, are expected to replace many developed country cities in the list of top 600 cities (Dobbs et al., 2011). Urban economic growth is strongly linked to the extent of agglomeration, where firms and people are located closer together in cities and clusters, attracting higher investment, skilled workers and talented graduates.

> ## Education can propel cities' competitiveness and productivity

Education propels innovation and productivity-led economic growth, and provides and improves human capital (Mankiw et al., 1992). Good quality primary and secondary education and high enrolment rates in tertiary education are fundamental for fostering innovation and increasing productivity in knowledge economies (World Economic Forum, 2014). Talent and creativity are decisive factors in shaping economic opportunity and knowledge-based urban development (Carillo et al., 2014; Yigitcanlar et al., 2007).

City's authorities recognize this and seek to attract talent as a way to be competitive in the global economy and to develop a knowledge economy. A city's competitiveness is determined by its ability to retain graduates of local higher education institutions and attract highly qualified graduates from the rest of the country (A.T. Kearney, 2015; The Economist Intelligence Unit, 2012).

Cities attract talent in different ways. Because of their scale, larger cities, such as megacities with populations of over 10 million people, have an advantage over smaller ones in attracting human capital. Shanghai, a megacity in China, is located within a network of smaller cities and attracts a wide range of talent, including from overseas. It has access to over 100,000 graduates from 60 higher education institutions every year. More than one-quarter of the labour force is college-educated, double the proportion of a decade ago (Dobbs et al., 2011). Some secondary cities have tried to promote themselves as alternatives to larger cities by touting their clean air, good public services and health benefits.

The development of technology clusters has invigorated some smaller cities. Recent data indicate that the Indian state of Karnataka, which includes the elite Bangalore technology innovation cluster, attracts a higher proportion of highly educated internal migrants than the states that include the megacities of Delhi and Mumbai (Chandrashekhar and Sharma, 2014). Hyderabad, hailed as India's most competitive city in 2013, developed services related to information and communication technologies (ICT) and a special enclave for ICT firms, research institutions and similar services called the Cyberabad Development Authority (Das, 2015). Such new investments and city–industry links have facilitated a brain gain or reverse migration in India (Chacko, 2007).

CITIES INCREASE COMPETITIVENESS WITH A FOCUS ON EDUCATION AND RESEARCH

Countries (or cities or zones) aim to attract human capital and foreign direct investment by positioning themselves as global hubs for higher education, skills, talent, knowledge and innovation. Qatar has focused on becoming a regional hub to reduce its dependence on natural resources and move towards a knowledge economy. Singapore aimed to become the 'Boston of the East' with its Global Schoolhouse strategy to attract students and executives, and become a 21st century knowledge hub (Knight, 2014).

In analyses of urban competitiveness, the San Francisco Bay Area in the United States and Tokyo are regularly near the top (A.T. Kearney, 2015), with synergistic collaborations between higher education, government and industry, referred to as the Triple Helix model of innovation (Etzkowitz, 2003). Stanford University has served as an anchor for talent and innovation – the university has reportedly had significant global economic impact, and 18,000 firms created by its alumni are based in California (Eesley and Miller, 2012).

Governments can also take the lead. Tsukuba Science City in Japan was established near Tokyo in the 1970s. Its cluster of universities, publicly funded scientific research laboratories and national research institutes has received about half of Japan's public research and development budget and become an important global site for government–industry research collaborations (Mega, 2013).

THE EDUCATION SECTOR CAN PROMOTE BETTER INCLUSION OF INFORMAL SECTOR ACTIVITY

The informal sector is well recognized as a major, heterogeneous source of employment and income in developing countries, and as an important stop gap employer or buffer in higher income economies during recessions or economic crises. Recognizing and including it in urban economies is important for a city's prosperity, an accurate understanding of its economy and the social inclusion of those involved in the sector.

Targeted analyses of informal employment by type of occupation show that in 2013, domestic workers, home-based workers and street vendors accounted for about one-third of urban employment in India, and that street vendors alone accounted for 15% of the urban workforce in South Africa. In China, analysis of an urban labour survey of six cities found informal employment fairly high at 33%, especially for women (ILO and WIEGO, 2014).

> " Improving basic education levels and skills development fosters more inclusive economies "

Since education is inextricably tied to employment prospects, continuous improvement in basic education levels and skills development is needed to foster more inclusive economies (UNESCO, 2012). For example, based on data on Mumbai, India, from the 2011 Indian Census, the GEM Report team calculated that adult women who were not fully employed had a higher level of illiteracy (19.2%) compared to fully employed women (13.5%).

Education institutions can play an important role in improving working conditions in the informal sector. For instance, in a project in Chicago, the Institute for Justice and the University of Chicago Law School partnered with informal sector workers to improve their legal standing, helping around 2,000 street food vendors sell their products legally. They set up a legal clinic to empower the vendors and provide them with legal services, education, outreach and advocacy. An ordinance drafted in the project was used to change local regulation (Carrera et al., 2016).

EDUCATION HAS A POSITIVE SOCIAL IMPACT, PARTICULARLY IN REDUCING CRIME

Education is well documented to have a positive social impact, particularly in reducing crime. It does this by increasing the potential for certain types of employment opportunities, thus creating less incentive for crime, which is often more prevalent in urban areas. Education may also teach individuals to be more patient and to be more averse to risks such as punishment for crimes, and increase their interactions with more educated persons. Going to school in and of itself reduces the incidence of crime (Lochner, 2011).

Global empirical evidence confirms that educational attainment is strongly negatively associated with crime indicators, especially when contrasting populations with and without high school diplomas (Lochner, 2011). Using 2007/08 data, a study calculated that a 5 percentage point increase in male high school graduation rates would have nearly US$20 billion in total benefit to the US economy via reduced crime and higher earnings (DeBaun and Roc, 2013).

Similar crime-reducing effects are shown in Europe. In Norway, people who complete upper secondary education enjoy better labour market prospects and are less apt to use public welfare benefits and less likely to be charged with a crime (Falch et al., 2010). In England and Wales (United Kingdom), prolonging compulsory schooling led to a major reduction in crime and violence (Machin et al., 2011).

A similar trend is found in middle income countries. A city-level analysis of seven Colombian cities found that a higher level of human capital in a city (education levels, primary and secondary education coverage) was associated with a lower homicide rate (Poveda, 2012). Being educated to grade 12 or higher in South Africa decreases the likelihood of being incarcerated (Jonck et al., 2015).

In the United States, strong evidence has been found of the long-term effects of early childhood education on crime in adulthood. An analysis of Chicago's government-funded Child-Parent Centers found that children who did not go to the pre-school programme at age 3 to 4 were 70% more likely to be arrested for a violent crime by age 18 (Lochner, 2011).

EDUCATION IS KEY FOR WIDESPREAD ADOPTION OF MORE SUSTAINABLE TRANSPORT

Education should be integrated into urban planning as a tool to achieve social and environmental aims. One example is the widespread adoption of more sustainable transport.

Current trends show that cities consume the vast majority of natural resources and are responsible for most greenhouse gas emissions. Education can improve awareness of environmental challenges and individual and communal responsibilities to address them (see Chapter 1: Planet). For example, it can support more sustainable transport within cities. Many rapidly growing cities will become unsustainable in relation to space and transport (Pucher et al., 2007). Increased acceptability of public transport is clearly needed (UN Habitat, 2013), as is a re-envisioning of urban space and promotion of nonmotorized transport (Clean Air Asia, 2013). Educational tools have been important in the mass adoption of two forms of more sustainable transport: bus rapid transit (**Box 5.2**) and cycling (**Box 5.3**).

EDUCATION AND KNOWLEDGE CAN CONTRIBUTE TO INEQUALITY IN CITIES

Education is not invariably a positive influence in urban areas. It can both embody and reflect existing inequity, and can contribute to or cause inequality. Knowledge-driven economic development has been a factor in rising inequality and vanishing middle skill jobs (see Chapter 2: Prosperity). To ensure that education does not exacerbate unequal patterns of social stratification, governments need to acknowledge the relationship between education and inequality, and balance education-related activities that can improve the competitiveness of a city with those that can improve social inclusion.

INEQUALITY IN EDUCATION IS RELATED TO LOCATION, WEALTH AND OTHER FACTORS

Location and wealth

There is substantial inequality in education between rural and urban areas (see Chapter 3: People). In-depth data also suggest strong intra-urban inequality. According to GEM Report team calculations, while urban areas often provide greater access to education, the urban poor have worse primary completion rates than the average rural household in 26 out of the 35 countries with available data. In the case of lower secondary completion rates, which entail a more select group of households and students, the urban poor disadvantage is even more pronounced: Outcomes among the urban poor are much worse than those of the rural poor in many lower income countries. This is likely attributable to factors such as the opportunity cost of forgoing paid employment and difficulty affording education (**Figure 5.2**).

Thus, the potential positive benefits of being located in an urban area can be undermined by a lack of policies that address inequity.

Various spatial and social patterns in most major cities – gentrification, slums, urban sprawl, housing discrimination, immigrant enclaves – separate residents in terms of wealth, access and privilege (UN Habitat, 2009a). These

---

BOX 5.2

Education for awareness and consensus-building has been important for smooth adoption of bus rapid transit systems

Bus rapid transit (BRT) is a high capacity mass transit system with features such as dedicated bus lanes and off-board fare collection, which improve efficiency and reduce traffic congestion. The BRT model is a key component of the concept of global sustainable urban mobility. Two hundred and three cities around the world have BRT systems, partly due to advocacy by mayors.

Experience with BRT systems shows that information and communication strategies are especially important to engage stakeholders who may be adversely affected by introduction of the system, such as other transit operators and private vehicle users. In Johannesburg, South Africa, inadequate communication among stakeholders (local government and two private taxi organizations) at an early stage of the discussion led to lack of trust among parties, severely delaying implementation of the system. By contrast, in Lagos, Nigeria, local government engaged stakeholders in a communication programme from the beginning, including in planning and implementation. This helped Lagos avoid deadlock with stakeholders and the project was implemented relatively quickly.

Sources: Allen (2013); EMBARQ (2015); Kumar et al. (2012).

BOX 5.3

Education is a critical component of making cycling the norm in urban transport

In countries with best-practice cities, such as Denmark, Germany and the Netherlands, cycling became the norm for transport as a result of both urban planning and education, with right of way for cyclists, bike parking, comprehensive traffic education and training for cyclists and motorists, and a range of promotional events to generate support. Education is woven into an integrated approach in which Danish, Dutch and German children from an early age receive extensive training in safe and effective cycling – in classrooms and on the road – as part of their curriculum by the fourth grade. Police officers test children, who receive official certificates and stickers for their bikes once they pass the test.

Starting early ensures that children begin cycling when they are young. A comprehensive approach provides greater impact than individual, uncoordinated measures. Policies also de-incentivized driving through taxes and restrictions on car ownership and use, while education shifted public opinion in favour of walking, cycling and public transport in reaction to the negative impact of car use.

Paris's bike-sharing or 'public bicycle' system, Vélib, has reduced traffic in private vehicles and increased daily bicycle trips enormously. Similar systems have been adopted in over 50 countries and over 700 cities. Education is important to promote public understanding and frequent use of such systems. Bike-sharing programmes are being widely adopted in Latin American cities, including Buenos Aires, Mexico City and Rio de Janeiro.

Sources: Ferreiro (2015); Godefrooij et al. (2009); Pucher et al. (2010); Pucher and Buehler (2008).

> ## Education gaps are often wider within urban areas, than between urban and rural

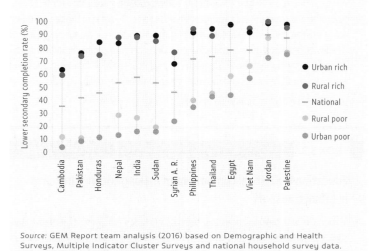

FIGURE 5.2:
Developing countries have rural–urban disparity but also very high intra-urban disparity
Disparity based on location (rural–urban) and wealth (bottom and top quintile) in lower secondary completion rates

- ● Urban rich
- ● Rural rich
- – National
- ● Rural poor
- ● Urban poor

Source: GEM Report team analysis (2016) based on Demographic and Health Surveys, Multiple Indicator Cluster Surveys and national household survey data.

region, especially with regard to access to good quality schooling (De la Fuente et al., 2013). Similarly, district-level analysis in São Paulo, Brazil, found that public services and utilities, including education, were more intensively allocated to districts with higher levels of human development (Haddad and Nedovic-Budic, 2006). In the province of Free State, South Africa, high crime rates were associated with a bifurcated society and with high levels of social exclusion and marginalization, including through segregated, marginalized schools (Jonck et al., 2015).

Within cities, the distribution of amenities can vary. Important amenities are usually concentrated in city centres. For instance, 2007 data from Kisumu, Kenya, showed the city centre had far more primary schools than the rest of the city, schools with lower pupil/teacher ratios, and a high number of primary school toilets, as well as most of the private schools (**Figure 5.3**). The more populated central district, Kibuye, had 31 primary schools while the remaining districts averaged 7 primary schools each.

Inequitable distribution of good teachers can exacerbate educational inequality. It is well documented that qualified teachers, especially women, are less likely to transfer to and stay in rural areas or low income schools in inner cities (Chudgar and Luschei, 2015; UNESCO, 2014, 2015). Countries have used payment- and accountability-based teacher recruitment and retention policies to counter this bias (Chudgar and Luschei, 2015). However, policies to redistribute teachers to rural areas or low performing schools can be difficult to implement due to teacher preferences, as well as the role of political influence in teacher placement. For instance, research on teachers in India revealed a clear patronage-based relationship between teachers and politicians; the teacher transfer system was not based on objective criteria such as the needs of schools or regions (Beteille, 2009).

Private schools can both alleviate and cause inequality. In many countries, private schools address the needs of increased urban populations and serve the entire socio-economic spectrum to provide a perceived or actual higher quality of education than the public system,

types of inequality are linked to income levels, the location of employers, transport options and spending policies (Kilroy, 2007), as well as current and historical legislation that institutionalizes ethnic and racial discrimination and segregation (Rothstein and Santow, 2012). Pockets of poverty in cities can evolve into persistent disadvantage as their populations become isolated from job opportunities, experience crime and violence more frequently and are physically separated from other income groups. In recent years, growing fears for personal safety from crime and violence have led to a proliferation of gated communities, some of which have even expanded to become gated cities (Borsdorf and Hidalgo, 2008; UN Habitat, 2009a).

Policy
Discriminatory policies and practices exacerbate inequality in education. An in-depth analysis of Chile's second-largest urban region, the Concepción metropolitan area, found major differences in the distribution of schools in the

and deliver education services when the public system has not expanded to meet the population's needs (Day Ashley et al., 2014).

School choice – allowing parents to choose between the public system and private, charter or other non-state institutions, usually in search of better quality education – is often both a cause and consequence of demographic stratification. National education plans have facilitated school choice in contexts as diverse as Chile (Hsieh and Urquiola, 2006), Nepal (Joshi, 2016) and Sweden (Bunar, 2010). The empirical literature has shown that a consistent result is greater stratification. The evidence on the benefits of school choice in terms of quality has been mixed and heavily debated (Day Ashley et al., 2014; Härmä, 2015).

Attitude and school environment

Inequality in education can also be perpetuated by attitude. Teachers routinely exhibit discriminatory attitudes towards children of migrants and minorities, which can contribute to their social marginalization. A recent study using the 2014 China Child Well-Being Survey found that teachers of first-graders in Shanghai were likely to report that migrant students performed further below their grade level in language than local peers, even after controlling for background characteristics (Cherng and Han, 2016). Similarly, a randomized evaluation which assigned children's characteristics to examination cover sheets in India found that teachers gave worse scores to lower caste than higher caste children, suggesting that 20% of the performance gap between higher and lower caste students was attributable to caste-based discrimination (Hanna and Linden, 2012).

Education can also perpetuate social exclusion where schools that serve the disadvantaged are violent. In 2011/12, 10% of US public school teachers reported being threatened with injury (Robers et al., 2015). In Latin America, where crime and violence are the number one concern of the public (Corbacho et al., 2015), crime has been shown to deter participation in formal schooling (Leeds, 2006). In addition, without appropriate targeted interventions schools can become spaces where gender-based violence is perpetuated (see the discussion on gender in Chapter 17: Target 4.a).

Racial and ethnic segregation

Segregation by ethnicity, social class or race has been well documented. It is a near-permanent feature of the socio-economic and education landscape in cities in the United States, much of Europe, and countries with legacies of troubled race relations, such as South Africa (Iceland, 2014; Massey and Denton, 1993).

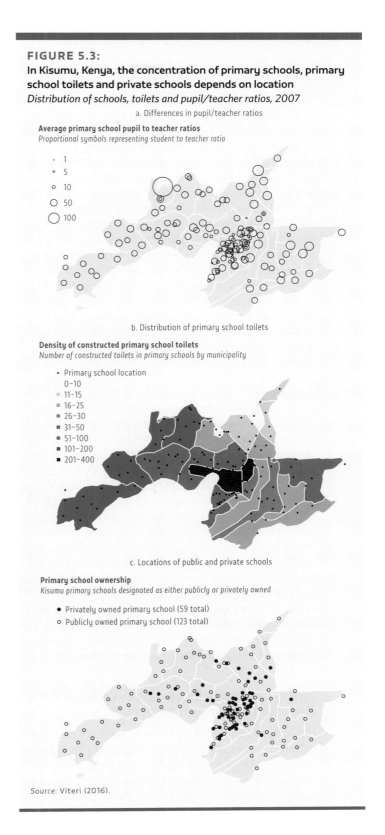

FIGURE 5.3:

In Kisumu, Kenya, the concentration of primary schools, primary school toilets and private schools depends on location
Distribution of schools, toilets and pupil/teacher ratios, 2007

a. Differences in pupil/teacher ratios

Average primary school pupil to teacher ratios
Proportional symbols representing student to teacher ratio

· 1
· 5
○ 10
○ 50
○ 100

b. Distribution of primary school toilets

Density of constructed primary school toilets
Number of constructed toilets in primary schools by municipality

· Primary school location
0–10
11–15
16–25
26–30
31–50
51–100
101–200
201–400

c. Locations of public and private schools

Primary school ownership
Kisumu primary schools designated as either publicly or privately owned

● Privately owned primary school (59 total)
○ Publicly owned primary school (123 total)

Source: Viteri (2016).

In the United States, the 1954 Supreme Court decision *Brown v. Board of Education of Topeka* was meant to desegregate 'separate and unequal' schools. A study of the lives of children born between 1945 and 1968, following them up to 2013, found that the desegregation effort had a significant long-term impact. For African-Americans, attending a desegregated school improved educational and occupational attainment, college quality and earnings; lowered the probability of incarceration; and improved adult health status. In these schools, students benefited from improved access to school resources, reduced class size and increased per-pupil spending (Johnson, 2011).

However, recent data suggest that racial segregation in education has persisted, with white Americans fleeing city schools to suburban and private ones (Rothstein, 2015). Legislation in the early 2000s released hundreds of US school districts from court-enforced integration. As a result, by 2011, in districts released from the desegregation order, 53% of black students attended so-called 'apartheid schools' where less than 1% of the student body was white (Hannah-Jones, 2014).

In developed countries, especially in Europe and North America, ethnic immigrant enclaves in cities are prevalent (International Organization for Migration, 2015) and can have detrimental effects on educational outcomes and employment (Heath et al., 2008; Musterd, 2005). Analysis of ethnic segregation in Sweden from 1998 and 1999 showed that attending schools with very high concentrations of immigrants (over 40%) was associated with lower test scores, a result that affected relatively few schools but 14% of immigrant children (Szulkin and Jonsson, 2007). But evidence also suggests that living in some ethnic enclaves can have positive effects on education. In the United States, analysis of 2005–2012 community surveys shows that nearly 35% of all foreign-born residents live in ethnic enclaves; while South American and sub-Saharan African immigrants living in enclaves performed worse than their counterparts outside them, the situation was reversed for Korean and South Asian immigrants (Foad, 2014).

THE KNOWLEDGE ECONOMY IS LINKED WITH INCOME INEQUALITY IN CITIES

Not only education but also knowledge more broadly can be linked to inequality. Chapter 2: Prosperity notes that, as economic growth from manufacturing becomes limited or stagnates, some countries will shift to high skill economies based on services, including ICT. Knowledge-based urban development is reputed to balance all dimensions of development – economic, social, environmental and institutional (Yigitcanlar, 2014). Yet, evidence suggests that cities with a strong focus on knowledge industries have experienced rising income inequality.

The gap between rich and poor has been growing in the United States, and is reflected in geographical divisions – 27 of the country's 30 largest metropolitan areas show an increase in the segregation between upper and lower income households (Florida and Mellander, 2015).

Education-based segregation is greater in high tech, knowledge-based metropolitan areas. Populations where college graduates dominate are more segregated than those of people without high school degrees (Florida and Mellander, 2015). Recent research from 13 major European cities similarly indicates that socio-economic and spatial segregation is rising as more educated populations fuel the growth of knowledge-intensive industries (Marcinczak et al., 2016).

While knowledge workers appear to value and favour diversity and openness, they have been found to favour only particular types of diversity (Florida, 2002). And knowledge workers in highly competitive cities were found to be interested in, and more likely to use, private health and education services, thus fostering social inequality (Yigitcanlar et al., 2007).

EDUCATION CAN INFLUENCE URBAN PLANNING

While urban development influences education planning, education also has the potential to influence urban planning. However, realizing this potential will require change: more integration in interventions, better training for urban planners, and deeper involvement from the education sector in providing leadership for city initiatives and urban planning.

SUSTAINED IMPROVEMENT IN INCLUSION REQUIRES INTEGRATED EFFORTS

Education and lifelong learning can contribute to urban planning, including for better social inclusion, but they need to be part of integrated efforts. Education alone cannot lead to enhanced social inclusion (see Chapter 3: People) but must be integrated with economic and social initiatives related to urban planning and sustainable development.

Urban planners need training in integrating education and lifelong learning into urban development

For example, integration of migrants requires a broad range of policies relating to community-building and public participation. Higher income cities sometimes focus on language acquisition for migrant workers. Due to a growing influx of foreign migrant workers in key manufacturing-based municipalities in Japan, a committee was formed in 2001 to develop policies and programmes to facilitate their integration, including a focus on job security and special language classes (International Organization for Migration, 2015).

Another approach to social inclusion is found in Berlin's attempt to create a 'socially integrative city' through activities, education and employment opportunities. Neighbourhood management projects are launched in communities that require special attention. The approach has reached 34 neighbourhoods in Berlin, and seeks active participation from key partners in local businesses, schools, housing companies and neighbourhood centres to curb social disintegration (Berlin Senate Department for Urban Development and the Environment, 2010). Another example of an integrated intervention is the Harlem Children's Zone (**Box 5.4**).

BETTER URBAN PLANNING REQUIRES A MULTIDISCIPLINARY APPROACH

For urban planning to achieve sustainable and inclusive cities, better training is needed, particularly in developing countries, to ensure that planners adopt approaches that integrate education and learning. Key examples from around the world show that education and knowledge generation incorporated into urban planning can engage and build consensus among diverse stakeholders and improve the lives of the disadvantaged, particularly through participatory approaches (**Box 5.5**).

A global overview finds education on urban planning has evolved significantly from its initial focus on architectural design to better incorporation of social and scientific approaches (UN Habitat, 2009a). Especially in Europe, urban planning is part of a sound policy environment

---

BOX 5.4

A cradle-to-career approach can integrate education with community development

The socio-economic situation of the Harlem district in New York City in the United States is dire. In 2014, 65% of children were born into poverty and 54% to single mothers; 30% of middle-schoolers and high-schoolers had lost a family member to violence.

The Harlem Children's Zone is a community-based initiative that seeks to break cycles of intergenerational poverty, primarily through education. Since 1997, it has provided children with comprehensive educational assistance at each development stage, culminating in college graduation. Acting on a belief that children's success requires community strengthening, the project complements educational assistance with programmes addressing drug use, violent crime and chronic health problems. Research suggests that its Promise Academy charter schools and support services have reversed the gap in achievement between white Americans and African-Americans in mathematics and reduced it in English language arts.

Educational programmes are administered in collaboration with other institutions, including schools, universities, other non-profit organizations, foundations, businesses and government. Government funders from the city, state and federal levels and departments of education and other social protection services contribute about 8% of the budget. The initiative has inspired a national programme that currently reaches 48 communities. For holistic change, the long-term impact will need to be evaluated more robustly, not only through specific education measures such as test scores or college acceptance rates, but also through broader indicators.

This example raises important questions. How can the determination and leadership needed for the initiative's success be sustained? How can these capacities be constrained or supported in other contexts?

Sources: Dobbie and Fryer Jr. (2009); Hanson (2013); Harlem Children's Zone (2015).

---

that synergizes research, knowledge and capacity. For instance, city planning in Maastricht, the Netherlands, uses a tool that combines information systems, allowing systematic analysis of interactions among sociocultural, economic and environmental developments (Rotmans et al., 2000). However, most urban planning schools and local governments need to greatly improve their capacity to plan and implement, engage with professional and

Better urban planning can foster inclusion of slum dwellers

Slum rehabilitation is a main point of action for the SDG urban agenda. Yet, decades of experience have shown that major urban planning experiences, including 'master plans', have resulted in exclusion, not inclusion. Delhi's efforts to become a 'world-class city' in advance of the 2010 Commonwealth Games included the demolition and rehabilitation of many slums. Investigation of the 'clean-up' drive showed that, of the 56 demolished sites, 16 had been rebuilt or were under construction, but only one of the new sites had a school.

Sustainable development requires the involvement of communities affected by urban planning. Participatory processes, such as participatory budgeting, decentralized planning and systematic community development of the types initiated by the anti-poverty Cities Alliance partnership can empower communities and build social capital, especially for women.

The approach of SDI is another example. The project that led to its establishment was linked to the World Bank-funded Mumbai Urban Transport Project, which aimed to upgrade the city's rail infrastructure. A large-scale enumeration process in 1986 documented residents living close to the proposed railway lines. This led to a community-based strategy for planning the upgraded lines and relocating residents. The community mapping made informal, illegal settlements 'visible'. After the map was validated by the local government, it paved the way for legal recognition of land tenure and post-relocation compensation. Community involvement has remained a key part of SDI's methodology and philosophy.

The Association of African Planning Schools (AAPS) was established in 1999 in Dar es Salaam, in the United Republic of Tanzania, as a peer-to-peer network of planning schools. Since 2008, with funding from donors and non-government organizations (NGOs), AAPS has identified a disconnect between technocratic, conservative, colonial-era planning education and the issues planners face upon graduation. It has therefore assessed and developed more relevant curricula. In 2008, at its first all-school meeting, AAPS identified five key issues for urban planning in Africa: actor collaboration, climate change, spatial planning and infrastructure, informality, and access to land. A 2010 initiative between SDI and AAPS recognized the need for urban planning to address informal settlements. It fostered learning approaches that give students direct experience of projects in informal settlements and enable them to apply this to advocacy, for example to change national planning legislation.

Sources: Dupont (2008); UN Habitat (2009b); Watson (2011); Watson and Odendaal (2012); Patel et al. (2012); Patel and Mitlin (2010).

academic networks, and educate professionals, elected officials and citizens (UN Habitat, 2009a).

More planning schools are needed, particularly in lower income countries. Of 550 planning schools documented worldwide, only 69 are in sub-Saharan Africa. Of these, 39 are in Nigeria (UN Habitat, 2009a). In India, some 3,000 planners are registered with the Institute of Town Planners, 1 planner for every 100,000 urban residents, far less than the average of 1 planner for every 5,000 residents in Canada and the United States (Ramanathan, 2013).

Planning for sustainability requires working across disciplines and sectors, but many urban planners lack the training and the collaboration mechanisms to do so (Corburn, 2004; Martino, 2016). A review of nine visions for urban sustainability from Australia, Canada, Germany, Ireland, Sweden and the United States found they were not aligned with robust sustainability principles and instead focused narrowly on the built environment (John et al., 2015). In Peru, analysis from a management education programme indicated architects in charge of urban planning often lacked adequate education and overemphasized physical interventions instead of considering the integrated social, political and economic needs of urban management (Steinberg and Miranda Sara, 2000).

A CITY CAN TRANSFORM BY PLACING EDUCATION AND LIFELONG LEARNING AT ITS HEART

More and more cities have been putting education and lifelong learning at the heart of their development. To promote sustainable economic, social and environmental development, cities from Amman (Jordan) and Balange (the Philippines) to Bahir Dar (Ethiopia) and Ybycuí (Paraguay) are turning themselves into learning cities (Valdes-Cotera et al., 2015).

The UNESCO Global Network of Learning Cities (GNLC) connects cities with global actors to promote education and lifelong learning at the local level. The GNLC defines 'learning cities' as those that promote inclusive learning, from basic to higher education; revitalize learning in families and communities; facilitate learning for and in the workplace; extend the use of modern learning technology; enhance quality and excellence in learning; and nurture a culture of learning throughout life. All this creates and reinforces individual empowerment and social cohesion, economic and cultural prosperity, and sustainable development (UNESCO Institute for Lifelong Learning, 2015). Learning cities contribute to SDG 4, promoting 'inclusive and equitable quality education', and SDG 11 on improving urban life by making 'cities and human settlements inclusive, safe, resilient and sustainable' (United Nations, 2015).

This section describes two initiatives, both from Latin America, where cities integrated education into urban planning with successful results. The transformation of Curitiba, Brazil (**Box 5.6**), and Medellín, Colombia, demonstrated dramatic improvement in the environmental, economic and social dimensions of sustainable development. Both had strategies that valued education's role in the transformation and viewed education holistically as an integral part of cities that were both educating and learning. They exemplify the concept of learning cities.

The success of such initiatives is often attributed to visionary mayoral leadership. But also particularly important was an enabling environment in which successive mayors had the political autonomy and authority to envision and carry out major transformations.

In the 1980s, Medellín was the headquarters of Pablo Escobar's drug cartel and a hub of trafficking, narcoterrorism and corruption. After Escobar's death in 1993, the city established a progressive agenda, which included involving communities in the expansion of public spaces and services such as schools and libraries. As a result it became one of the most innovative and equity-oriented cities in the world, leading international rankings in health and public investment (Bomberg, 2014).

Medellín's transformation from one of the world's most violent cities to one of its most innovative was explicitly based on education-led social change. Mayor Sergio Fajardo's 2004 strategy *Medellín, la más educada* (the most educated) involved the community in planning and designing investment and allocating funds. The Medellín public utilities company has been a key source of sustainable financing (Cadena et al., 2011; The Lauder Institute, 2014), used to build schools, public plazas, parks and a metro (Kimmelman, 2012) and has continued to fund the city's reforms under successive mayors.

The investment programme targeted crime and violence in the poorest and most violent areas via integrated urban planning, which included transport systems, innovative buildings as learning spaces and, significantly, the construction of 120 new public schools and 9 library parks (Nolen, 2014). The incidence of crime and violence has fallen dramatically over the past two decades as a result of city reforms (Cerdá et al., 2012) (**Figure 5.4**).

To reduce inequality, Fajardo focused on improving public education, rather than supporting private education, believing that 'public education must be the motor of social transformation'. The government mobilized businesses, universities and private schools to improve the public education system, and allocated up to 40% of its municipal budget to education (Kurtz-Phelan, 2007).

BOX 5.6

Curitiba used both explicit and implicit education initiatives to become a green city

Curitiba is renowned as a highly planned city, and its decades-old planning institute has always invested in interdisciplinary teams to develop urban solutions. Curitiba's urban transformation was started in the mid-1960s by a visionary architect, Jaime Lerner, who argued for cities as people-centric spaces where all systems and initiatives work together cohesively. The city and its mayor are lauded for their BRT system, development of green spaces and recycling strategy, which transformed the city economically, socially and environmentally. As a result of decades of improvement, Curitiba is considered one of the most environment-friendly cities in the world and is a leader in green technology innovation.

The Curitiba education system was one of the key systems that Lerner holistically transformed and used in the process of urban transformation. A central characteristic of the strategy was synergy, the idea that comprehensive planning could cope with several problems simultaneously. The city was turned into a learning institution, promoting educational processes and environmental awareness using formal and informal frameworks.

Noteworthy interventions included:

- Construction of lighthouse towers that both provided lookout facilities for security guards and incorporated new libraries, thus reinforcing civic identity by providing beacons of knowledge and security.

- Use of schools as a starting point for urban change through a citywide recycling campaign involving elementary schools. Children learned about garbage separation, and as they became enthusiastic about recycling in schools, they convinced parents to sort garbage at home. The 'garbage that is not garbage' programme gave marginalized citizens food in return for trash collection, leading to income opportunities in the recycling sector and changing the perception of garbage in the city.

- Use of retired buses as mobile training centres and free transport to parks and open spaces. Buses were also sent on certain days to slums to teach adults basic literacy skills, combining literacy studies with health education.

- Establishment of the Open University, in the ruins of an old mine, to facilitate formal learning for citizens on sustainability. It also offered in-service training for professionals who wanted to learn about the environmental aspects of their jobs.

Sources: Arbel (2014), Carvalho et al. (2012); Graham and Booth (2010); Macedo (2013).

The city developed a library network to promote social interaction and inclusion and bring education to marginalized communities. Libraries became beautiful, symbolic community centres to raise the self-esteem of poor children and curb violence (Castro and Echeverri, 2011). The Spain Library, strategically located atop a hill, became a landmark, conveying a message of public domain and presence in a place once belonging to crime gangs (Kimmelman, 2012).

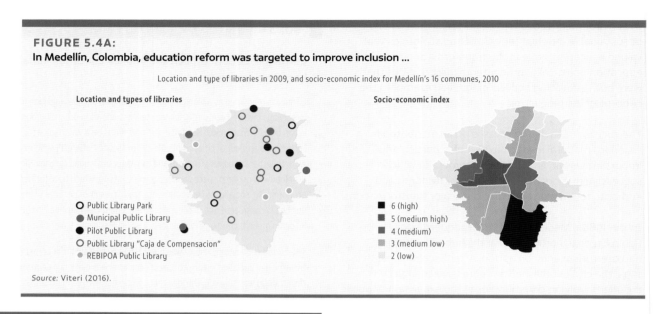

FIGURE 5.4A:

In Medellín, Colombia, education reform was targeted to improve inclusion ...

Location and type of libraries in 2009, and socio-economic index for Medellín's 16 communes, 2010

Location and types of libraries

○ Public Library Park
● Municipal Public Library
● Pilot Public Library
○ Public Library "Caja de Compensacion"
• REBIPOA Public Library

Socio-economic index

■ 6 (high)
■ 5 (medium high)
■ 4 (medium)
■ 3 (medium low)
□ 2 (low)

Source: Viteri (2016).

FIGURE 5.4B:

... and linked to crime reduction

Homicide rate per 100,000 inhabitants, 1998–2014, Medellín, Colombia

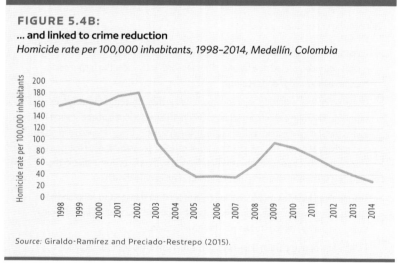

Source: Giraldo-Ramírez and Preciado-Restrepo (2015).

Since 2012, the public utilities company has been required to assign 7% of its annual profits to support the city's science, technology and innovation plan (OECD, 2015). Medellín is the only Latin American city with such a plan, and has a strong foundation to develop health, energy, and ICT clusters (Bomberg, 2014).

URBAN PLANNING BENEFITS FROM CITY-LEVEL LEADERSHIP

The role of city-level leadership is important both for urban planning in general and for integrated urban planning that addresses education. As the previous section shows, a degree of autonomy is an important condition for strong city-level ownership of urban reform.

City-level leadership can also have a positive impact at the global and regional levels. As cities have grown in size and political importance, their role in local and global governance has grown. Global networks of city governance can provide urban solutions. Mayors are linked through long-term global–local ('glocal') initiatives such as Local Governments for Sustainability (ICLEI), United Cities and Local Governments (UCLG), and the GNLC.

Efforts to address climate change benefit from city-level leadership. The climate leadership group C40 involves many major cities working with international actors, such as the World Bank, the Organisation for Economic Co-operation and Development (OECD) and the Clinton Foundation. It promotes the leadership of mayors in global governance (Acuto, 2013; Barber, 2013). Transnational municipal networks have also been instrumental in advancing knowledge and methods for addressing climate change at the local level (Bouteligier, 2012; Fünfgeld, 2015).

To solve pressing urban challenges, however, many governance challenges in these networks of knowledge exchange and generation need to be addressed to realize their potential. Even as expectations of city governments are growing, action at the city level in service delivery and collaboration can be hampered by poor data, lack of technical capacity, unclear jurisdiction and lack of fiscal

> "Education is largely absent in discussions of implementing SDG 11 on cities and human settlements"

decentralization. In a survey of 50 cities in 30 primarily middle income and high income countries, many city representatives said lack of local government capacity and public funding, and unpredictability of resources, were key governance constraints (LSE, 2014).

Meanwhile, education as a sector is largely absent in discussions of implementing SDG 11 on cities and human settlements. For instance, it is rarely mentioned when considering how urban areas should respond to climate change, disaster preparedness or urban sprawl. The role of schools is mostly missing from debates on urban priorities such as slum upgrading (Minnery et al., 2013).

A relative lack of local government jurisdiction in education provision also limits education's inclusion in an integrated urban planning agenda. City governments in many high and middle income countries are far less engaged in the provision of education services than in other sectors (**Figure 5.5**).

While local autonomy does not guarantee positive changes, greater city-level autonomy is a prerequisite for strong city level ownership of urban reforms that incorporate education strategies, as was shown in the case of Curitiba and Medellín. Similarly, a recent investigation of five cities (Dubai in the United Arab Emirates, Ho Chi Minh City in Viet Nam, London, New York City and Rio de Janeiro in Brazil), which were assessed because their learning outcomes were improving or high, argued that effective leadership at all levels, but particularly inspirational education leadership at the city level, was key to the effectiveness of education reform (Elwick and McAleavy, 2015).

CONCLUSION

Given the complex and holistic nature of urban challenges, education and lifelong learning need to be embedded and integrated in urban planning. They form a critical instrument for sustainable urban development. In turn, urbanization and other processes related to cities

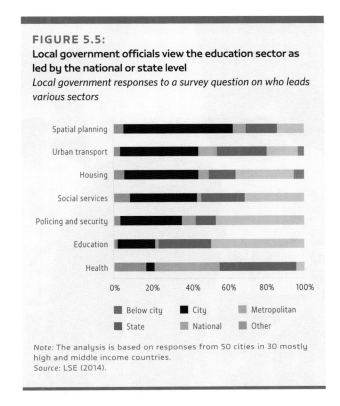

FIGURE 5.5:
Local government officials view the education sector as led by the national or state level
Local government responses to a survey question on who leads various sectors

Note: The analysis is based on responses from 50 cities in 30 mostly high and middle income countries.
Source: LSE (2014).

create a need for education system planning. Education is pivotal to ensure economic growth, innovation, and improvement in economic inclusion; formal and non-formal education must also be monitored to ensure that they help reduce inequality, not exacerbate it.

The broad education sector is largely missing from key urban development discussions on social inclusion and environmental sustainability. These aims will very likely not be achieved unless education is integrated in their planning. At the same time, stronger advocacy and leadership by education stakeholders and urban leaders, such as mayors, are needed if education is to gain a seat in discussions on the future of cities. Moreover, there needs to be far more appreciation of education's role in transformative urban development, regarding both formal schooling and beyond.

Young people in
El Savador take part
in an activity with the
Asociación SERES.

CREDIT: Ben Rosenzweig on behalf of
SERES/Play for Peace

Partnerships: enabling conditions to achieve SDG 4 and the other SDGs

We are determined to mobilize the means required to implement this Agenda through a revitalized Global Partnership for Sustainable Development, based on a spirit of strengthened global solidarity, focused in particular on the needs of the poorest and most vulnerable and with the participation of all countries, all stakeholders and all people.

The interlinkages and integrated nature of the Sustainable Development Goals are of crucial importance in ensuring that the purpose of the new Agenda is realized. If we realize our ambitions across the full extent of the Agenda, the lives of all will be profoundly improved and our world will be transformed for the better.

– The 2030 Agenda for Sustainable Development

KEY MESSAGES

The world must pull together to overcome barriers to achieving the 2030 Agenda for Sustainable Development

1 **More domestic resources are needed to achieve the Sustainable Development Goals (SDGs).**

a. Many poorer countries still collect less than 15% of their national income in tax (compared with 26% in richer countries).

b. Domestic and international efforts on tax evasion and avoidance are needed for countries to get the tax revenues they are owed.

c. Resources can be channelled to education spending by reducing fossil fuel subsidies and earmarking funds for education expenditure.

d. Aid can play a catalytic role in increasing domestic resources.

e. Education can improve taxpayer behaviour and increase tax compliance.

2 **Aid must increase to achieve the Education 2030 targets, but is declining.**

a. Even with substantial increases in domestic resources, there will be an annual finance gap of US$21 billion in low income countries to achieve the Education 2030 targets.

b. The education finance gap could be filled if select donors allocated 0.7% of GNI to aid, and 10% of that to education.

c. But overall aid to education is on the decline: It fell by US$1.2 billion in 2014 relative to its peak in 2010.

3 **Aid to education is not effectively targeted to those most in need.**

a. Poor and conflict-affected countries are not adequately prioritized in aid allocations.

b. Early childhood care and education can significantly benefit disadvantaged children but received less than 3% of the aid that goes to post-secondary education.

4 **Governments and international agencies must work together to achieve the sustainable development agenda.**

a. The broad SDG agenda requires multisector approaches.

b. Successful national efforts to improve multisector planning, while rare, usually have strong political commitment, institutional and financial support, and strong capacity.

c. Aid agencies often lack a coherent vision of development and do not always prioritize poverty reduction.

5 **The ambition of the SDGs requires partnerships if it is to be achieved.**

a. Civil society and the private sector have to play important roles in financing, implementing and ensuring mutual accountability of the new agenda.

b. International coordination and financing bodies are critical to support countries, review progress, encourage coordination of partner activities, and leverage funds.

The 2030 Agenda for Sustainable Development views the social, economic and environmental challenges of our time as indivisible, meaning that responses must be integrated. Sustainable Development Goal (SDG) 17, which articulates the 'means of implementation' for achieving the goals, calls for a revitalized global partnership. The targets under SDG 17 highlight the need for cooperation – to ensure adequate financing, develop and diffuse technological innovation, and build capacity to implement national plans; systemic improvements – to enhance policy coherence, build multistakeholder partnerships, and improve data, monitoring and accountability; and favourable macroeconomic conditions – including inclusive trade, debt sustainability and healthy investment (United Nations, 2015c).

Fulfilling the SDGs requires integrated plans and actions where diverse sectors, levels of government and types of actors have to work together. Adequate financing as well as other enabling conditions – particularly, human capacity, effective institutions and political will – are critical if the new agenda is to succeed (**Figure 6.1**). This chapter examines what changes to current financing, policy and partnership arrangements are needed within education and in its interactions with other sectors for progress to be realized.

FINANCE

No plan or strategy can be implemented without adequate financial resources. Major financing shortfalls were a key reason for the lack of sufficient progress towards the Education for All (EFA) goals between 2000 and 2015 (UNESCO, 2015a). The focus of this section is primarily on financing to achieve SDG 4 in lower income countries.

There have been several approaches to understanding what it will cost to achieve the SDGs and who should provide financing. A recent estimate suggests that an additional 1.5% to 2.5% of global gross domestic product (GDP) will need to be invested each year from the public and private sectors to achieve the SDGs by 2030. Low and lower middle income countries will need to increase expenditure by about 4% of their projected GDP (Schmidt-Traub, 2015). The Addis Ababa Action Agenda that came out of the 2015 Third International Conference on Financing for Development acknowledges that all

The 2030 Agenda for Sustainable Development views the social, economic and environmental challenges of our time as indivisible

> **There is an annual finance gap of at least US$39 billion per year for providing quality education from pre-primary through to upper secondary education**

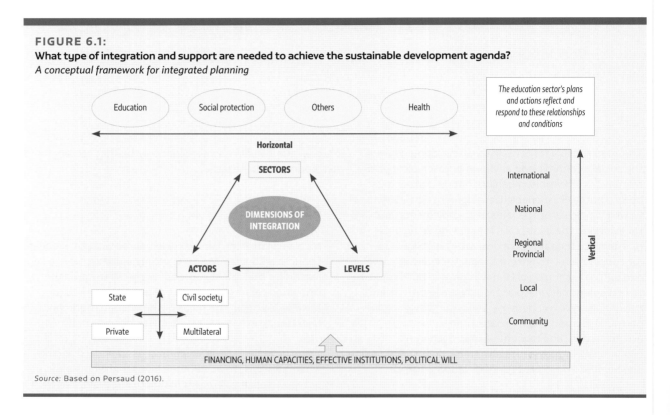

FIGURE 6.1:
What type of integration and support are needed to achieve the sustainable development agenda?
A conceptual framework for integrated planning

Source: Based on Persaud (2016).

sources of finance (public and private, domestic and international) and a long-term investment perspective will be needed (United Nations, 2015a). This is in contrast to the emphasis given to official development assistance (ODA) during the Millennium Development Goal (MDG) era (Fehling et al., 2013).

In the education sector, the 2015 *EFA Global Monitoring Report* estimated the cost of ensuring that every child and adolescent in low and lower middle income countries accessed good quality education from the pre-primary to upper secondary level. The total annual cost is projected to increase from US$149 billion, based on 2012 estimates, to US$340 billion over the next 15 years. Even after improvements in domestic revenue mobilization are taken into account this leaves an annual US$39 billion financing gap (UNESCO, 2015b).

To identify measures to address this funding gap, the high level International Commission on the Financing of Global Education Opportunities was announced at the Oslo Summit in July 2015 (Oslo Summit on Education for Development, 2015). Co-convened by the prime minister of Norway; the presidents of Chile, Indonesia and Malawi; and the Director-General of UNESCO, it is chaired by the UN Special Envoy for Global Education, with political leaders, policy-makers and researchers making up the members.

Its purpose is to make a strong case for investment in education and provide recommendations for deploying resources in more effective, accountable and coordinated ways, especially in determining budget allocations. It will look at a wide range of financing sources, including increased domestic resource mobilization through more strategic aid, non-traditional partnerships, innovative finance and the private sector.

The commission is expected to submit its report to the UN Secretary-General in September 2016. In view of its highly anticipated recommendations, which will also draw on an expert panel on education financing, this section focuses on a more select set of domestic and international financing issues.

DOMESTIC RESOURCES

Mobilizing more domestic resources will be critical for fulfilling the SDGs. Domestic resources funded 71% of public expenditure on MDG-related sectors in 66 low and lower middle income countries in 2014 (Development Finance International and Oxfam, 2015). For education, the share was 86% (Action Aid, 2016).

The Education 2030 Framework for Action set two benchmarks on domestic financing for education: 4% to 6% of GDP and 15% to 20% of public expenditure. As the 2015 *EFA Global Monitoring Report* showed, poorer countries have made considerable efforts to prioritize education in their budgets but are more likely to miss spending targets because their overall budgets are small due to lack of domestic revenue (UNESCO, 2015a). The key question, then, is how to mobilize revenue.

Raising more domestic resources

In about half of all developing countries, tax ratios are below 15% of GDP, compared with 18% in emerging economies and 26% in advanced economies (Lagarde, 2016). Raising the ratio in poorer countries requires global and domestic efforts.

> " In about half of all developing countries, tax ratios are below 15% of GDP "

Addressing tax evasion and avoidance is a global responsibility. Many challenges in tax collection faced by poorer countries are global in nature. The pervasiveness of secret offshore companies that hide wealth and the use of taxes as a competitive advantage in global competition for investment are among the significant factors limiting countries' ability to raise domestic resources through taxation (Sachs and Schmidt-Traub, 2014). Tax incentives to attract multinational companies have often disadvantaged developing countries. Corporate income

tax exemptions have led to estimated losses of US$139 billion a year in developing countries (Action Aid, 2013). Similarly, tax treaties often put poorer countries at a disadvantage; it is estimated that non-Organisation for Economic Co-operation and Development (OECD) countries lost US$1.6 billion in 2010 as a result of US treaty provisions (IMF, 2014).

Recent estimates suggest that developing countries lose about US$100 billion annually in revenue from multinational tax avoidance through offshore investments (UNCTAD, 2015). Illicit financial flows, defined as illegal movements of money or capital between countries, are symptoms of governance failures, weak institutions and corruption (OECD, 2015f). Lower income countries lost over US$1 trillion in such flows in 2013 – over 10 times the amount of ODA received that year (Kar and Spanjers, 2015). Coordinated domestic and international action on tax incentives, treaties and harmful corporate decisions is needed for countries to get tax revenue they are owed (Action Aid, 2016).

Education can influence taxpayer behaviour and increase compliance. While important taxation-related challenges are global, the fact that in many poorer countries taxes account for less than 15% of the national income also reflects on an inability to broaden the tax base and collect income, property and other progressive taxes (IMF, 2013a).

Taxpayer behaviour is influenced by factors outside the tax system, such as how tax revenue is spent and the extent to which taxation mobilizes citizens' political engagement (Fjeldstad and Heggstad, 2012; OECD, 2015a). Those who avoid paying taxes are often highly educated elites within countries and within multinational corporations. But it is also true that educational attainment and tax knowledge are positively associated with tax-related attitudes. Data from the 2005 World Values Survey on 55 countries indicate that more educated individuals had more positive attitudes towards paying taxes (OECD, 2013b). Data from the same survey in India over 1990–2006 showed that university education was associated with decreasing tolerance for tax evasion and bribery (Shafiq, 2015).

Education also has an effect on tax-related behaviour. Income and sales taxes in 100 countries increased with educational attainment, which allowed the use of newer types of taxes that rely on widespread literacy (Kenny and Winer, 2006). An analysis of 123 countries over 1996–2010 associated very low literacy levels with reduced tax revenue (Mutascu and Danuletiu, 2013). Nevertheless, the effect has been found to be stronger in some regions, such as Latin America, than in others, such as Asia (Profeta and Scabrosetti, 2010).

Some countries have used taxpayer education programmes to improve compliance and instil a culture of paying taxes, thus increasing revenue and strengthening the compact between citizens and government, while others have incorporated tax education in their school curriculum. In Latin America, nine countries have included tax education in their curricula and developed materials jointly between education ministries and tax authorities. The government of Jamaica extended the Schools Tax Education Programme down to primary schools. Studies indicate that influencing tax culture requires education from an early age (OECD, 2015a).

Channelling more resources towards education spending

Collecting more revenue is an important starting point for ensuring that education receives adequate funding. But there is also scope in many countries to reallocate expenditure for the benefit of education.

Countries at similar levels of economic development have had very different trajectories in terms of prioritizing education. Among low income countries, Ethiopia almost doubled the share of its budget allocated to education, from 15% in 2000 to 27% in 2013, while Guinea, from the same starting point, slightly reduced its commitment to education. Among lower middle income countries in 2014, Kyrgyzstan and the Lao People's Democratic Republic reached the recommended minimum benchmark of 15%, while Pakistan only allocated 11.3% (**Figure 6.2**).

Two ways to prioritize spending for education are to remove fossil fuel subsidies and to earmark education funds.

Redirecting fossil fuel subsidies can boost education spending. A major source of potential revenue for education is the reform of fossil fuel subsidy regimes, which keep prices for certain energy goods lower than market prices (IMF, 2013b). Fossil fuel subsidies are well documented to be inefficient and inequitable because mostly richer families benefit while funds that could be used for pro-poor expenditure are limited (Anand et al., 2013; Arze del Granado et al., 2012; Clements et al., 2013).

The most recent International Monetary Fund (IMF) analysis suggests that global energy subsidies could

reach $US5.3 trillion in 2015, or 6.5% of global GDP (Coady et al., 2015). This estimate incorporates the high environmental and health costs of fuel consumption to calculate other subsidies implicit in existing fuel prices. Redirecting explicit and implicit fuel subsidies would be a useful way to fund the SDGs (Merrill and Chung, 2014), including education (Steer and Smith, 2015). In Indonesia, public expenditure on education increased by over 60% between 2005 and 2009, largely due to fuel subsidy reform (Tobias et al., 2014).

Governments have earmarked funds to increase education expenditure. Some governments have earmarked taxes for education expenditure. Knowledge that a tax will be used for social purposes can reduce resistance to paying it. Taxpayers may also like the accountability they believe earmarking provides regarding how their tax money is spent (Prichard, 2010). Earmarked taxes have been used to support primary and secondary education in Brazil and India, and tertiary education in Ghana and Nigeria (Action Aid, 2016).

Some fear that earmarking may dissuade other sources of funding and leave total revenue unchanged, lead to misallocation of resources within a sector and between

---

FIGURE 6.2:

Increased allocation to education spending can happen at every level of economic development

Education as a share of total government expenditure, selected countries, 2000 and 2014 or most recent year

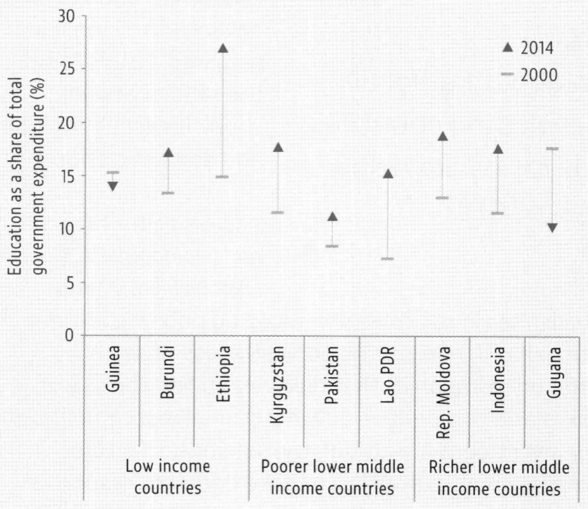

Source: UIS database.

> **Even with substantial increases in domestic resources, there is still an annual finance gap of US$21 billion that external aid must fill**

sectors, and reduce flexibility in managing fiscal policy (Welham et al., 2015). However, such concerns are minor compared to the size of the need for financing to ensure education and lifelong learning opportunities for all.

EXTERNAL RESOURCES

Even if low income countries intensify domestic resource mobilization, the annual financing gap is estimated at US$21 billion, the equivalent of 42% of the projected total annual cost of achieving universal pre-primary, primary and secondary education by 2030 (UNESCO, 2015b). Aid will therefore continue to be a necessity for many low income countries. Among low income countries with data, three-quarters received direct aid to education that exceeded 10% of their total public expenditure on education (UNESCO, 2015a).

Total aid averages 0.31% of gross national income among member countries of the OECD Development Assistance Committee (DAC), having been more or less constant for 10 years. This is well below the 2005 pledge by 15 EU countries to allocate 0.7% to aid; in 2014, only Denmark, Luxembourg, Sweden and the United Kingdom did so. If DAC members and selected non-DAC donors reached the 0.7% pledge and committed to spend 10% of that on basic and secondary education, that alone would raise enough funds to close the entire US$39 billion financing gap of low and lower middle income countries (OECD-DAC, 2016).

Instead, the volume of aid to education fell by about US$600 million from 2013 to 2014 and by US$1.2 billion relative to its peak in 2010 (see Chapter 20). In the context of a negative outlook for aid to education, this section discusses three options: the potential for earmarking more funds for education through multilateral mechanisms; the prospect of using more aid to build national authorities' capacity to raise domestic resources; and the gains that could be made by targeting aid to the countries and education levels most in need.

Multilateral mechanisms can help mobilize additional funds

Donors can provide aid through bilateral mechanisms, directly engaging with governments or non-government organizations (NGOs), or through multilateral mechanisms, channelling funds through international institutions. Multilateral channels appear less politicized, more responsive to recipient countries, more likely to target countries based on poverty, less fragmented, more flexible and better for delivery of global public goods in areas such as health and climate change. On the other hand, there is no clear consensus as to whether multilateral channels are more efficient than bilateral channels (Gulrajani, 2016).

It has become more common for donors to earmark the funds they provide to multilateral agencies through trust funds specific to sectors or issues. A survey of DAC members attributed this trend to donors' desire for visibility and influence (Reinsberg et al., 2015). However, more multilateral earmarking can create challenges if earmarking increases fragmentation within multilateral organizations (Gulrajani, 2016; Killen and Rogerson, 2010).

Still, earmarking has been used extensively to increase funding to the health sector. Between 2006 and 2014, aid disbursed to health by multilateral organizations increased by US$2.6 billion due to issue-specific funds such as the GAVI, the Vaccine Alliance. In education the corresponding increase was only US$952 million. It is vital for the education sector to improve its use of such mechanisms to raise additional funds (OECD-DAC, 2016).

Aid can play a catalytic role in increasing domestic resources

Given limited political will to expand aid resources, how can existing aid be better used to support domestic resource mobilization? In 2013, only US$96 million, less than 0.07% of total development assistance, was allocated to projects supporting domestic revenue mobilization in low income countries. Afghanistan,

Mozambique and the United Republic of Tanzania collectively received one-third of the total.

In Mozambique, a revenue authority was created in 2006. A pool of donors provides direct support in a partnership arrangement with the authority. As a result, tax collection doubled between 2008 and 2013, and the contribution of more progressive direct taxes tripled (Strawson and Ifan, 2016).

The role of aid in catalysing domestic resources was endorsed as a key aspect of international cooperation under the Addis Tax Initiative at the Third International Conference on Financing for Development in July 2015. Donors committed to double technical cooperation for domestic resource mobilization by 2020 (Strawson and Ifan, 2016). In recent years, more funds are being channelled to international initiatives such as the IMF Tax Policy and Administration Topical Trust Fund (Strawson and Ifan, 2016).

In the case of health, the United States has announced that US$63.5 million previously allocated to the President's Emergency Plan for AIDS Relief (PEPFAR) would be retargeted to domestic resource mobilization initiatives in Kenya, Nigeria, the United Republic of Tanzania, Viet Nam and Zambia, with the express

intention of raising US$1 billion for public health-related activities (Runde et al., 2014).

Aid to education is not effectively targeted where it is most needed

One of the main aims of development assistance is to benefit those in need. Mapping the mandates of 50 aid agencies indicates that 6 include a legal act requiring them to make poverty reduction a goal of development cooperation, 21 view poverty reduction as a primary goal, 10 view it as a joint goal and 13 have no specific goal for poverty reduction. Among agencies with a legal mandate to end poverty, over 80% of their development assistance is allocated to countries with a higher than average poverty rate. Agencies with no explicit poverty reduction goal allocate only 31% of their development assistance to such countries (Strawson et al., 2015).

Economic and political interests are key aspects of donors' funding decisions (Alesina and Dollar, 2000; Claessens et al., 2009). An analysis of 170 recipient countries found that aid allocation to basic education since 2003 reflected donor trade-related interests more than receiving country needs as measured by enrolment or completion rates (Sumida, 2016).

The percentage of children completing primary school is a potential measure of country need. The average child in Mongolia received US$45 in aid to basic education in 2014 even though the primary completion rate was 97% in 2010 (UNESCO, 2016a). By contrast, Chad, where the primary completion rate was 28% in 2010, received US$3 per primary school age child in 2014 (**Figure 6.3**). In Liberia and Mauritania, about half the children complete primary school, but Liberia receives 10 times the amount of aid to basic education per school-age child.

While per capita allocations of aid to basic education to Afghanistan and Liberia have generally increased in recent years, they have remained essentially flat in Chad and have been decreasing in Mauritania (**Figure 6.4**). Donors need to address such disparities if they are to help to achieve ambitious targets and ensure equity.

Aid to education should also be spent where it has the highest potential to improve equity. Public spending for higher education benefits the wealthy most (Lustig, 2015) while early investment in education has strong benefits for disadvantaged children (UNESCO, 2015a). Yet, early childhood care and education received only US$106 million in 2014, less than 3% of disbursements for post-secondary

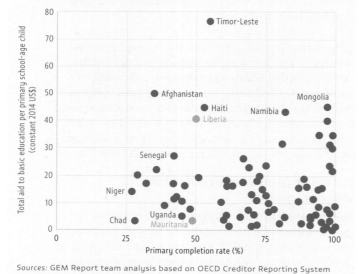

FIGURE 6.3:

Aid to basic education is not related to need

Total aid to basic education per primary school-age child (2014) and primary completion rate (2008–2014)

Sources: GEM Report team analysis based on OECD Creditor Reporting System data (OECD-DAC, 2016); World Inequality Database on Education.

FIGURE 6.4:
Inequities in aid to basic education persist
Total aid to basic education per primary school-age child, selected countries, 2002–2014

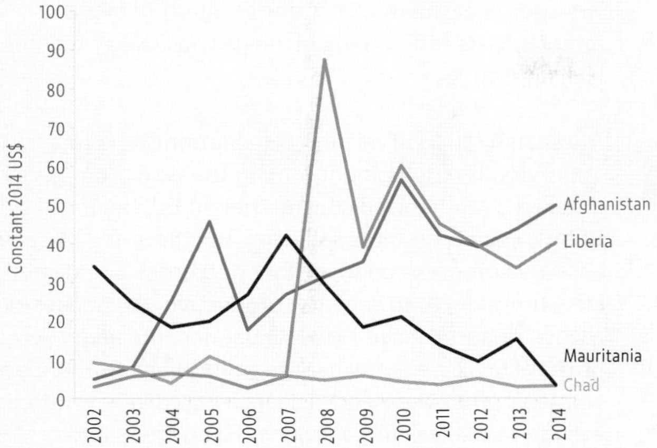

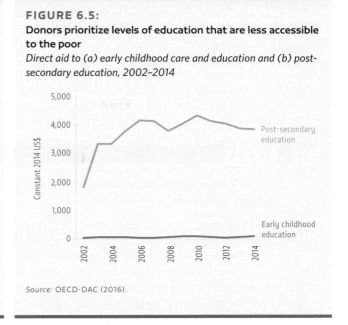

Source: OECD-DAC (2016).

FIGURE 6.5:
Donors prioritize levels of education that are less accessible to the poor
Direct aid to (a) early childhood care and education and (b) post-secondary education, 2002–2014

Source: OECD-DAC (2016).

education (**Figure 6.5**). Most aid to post-secondary education, moreover, largely supports students coming to study in the donor countries. Thus, a substantial portion of it does not even reach developing countries (UNESCO, 2015a).

POLICY COHERENCE

In the SDG era, sector-specific approaches are insufficient to meet the cross-cutting, interdependent challenges of sustainable development (Le Blanc, 2015). Instead, the context is more favourable to concepts such as 'collective impact' (Kania and Kramer, 2011), which suggests intentional, structural coordination of efforts to meet broader outcomes; 'systems thinking' (Chapman, 2004), or viewing the integrated whole as greater than the sum of its parts; and 'whole-of-government' approaches (United Nations, 2014), which require ministries to work together.

From a policy perspective, multisector approaches can prevent competition for scarce resources and help use existing resources more efficiently. Integrated service provision can be a means of reaching the most vulnerable, addressing their multiple needs simultaneously and reducing the cost of service duplication (OECD, 2015d).

Since diverse perspectives are needed for improved integration and problem solving (Hong and Page, 2004),

education planning may also benefit from a range of expertise beyond education ministries (Jacobs, 1964). For instance, an education ministry that aims to mitigate gender disparity in school enrolment and attainment would need to be aware of the non-education structural barriers to girls' and boys' schooling, which require a greater understanding of social development and the labour sector. SDG-related development efforts require such horizontally integrated action (Le Blanc, 2015). There is also a strong need for vertical integration, i.e. coordination and collaboration between levels of government, with clarity in their roles and responsibilities (OECD, 2013a). Figure 6.1 illustrates these horizontal and vertical relationships.

The broad SDG agenda with its multisector demands requires good local planning linked with coherent, nationally relevant vision and support (Antonio et al., 2014; Urama et al., 2014). This section looks at examples of national efforts to improve coherence, effective multisector planning, and challenges in integrated planning.

POLICY COHERENCE IN GOVERNMENTS

Integrated planning has gained prominence in post-2015 development discussions. However, multisector planning initiatives, especially those that focus on integrated basic service delivery for the poor, are not new. Integrated approaches to development have been carried out since the 1970s and 1980s, such as strategies that couple loans for rural economic development with those to address basic needs in health, sanitation and education, to jointly address rural poverty (Belgian Survival Fund and IFAD, 2009; Bovill, 2009).

A meta-analysis of literature on interventions that combined health with other sectors (education, economic development, nutrition, environment) found that 13

of the 25 interventions assessed produced mostly positive findings, 9 produced mostly mixed findings and 3 had a neutral or unknown effect. School feeding and deworming programmes, obesity interventions in schools and integrated early childhood development initiatives were some of the multisector education-relevant interventions found to yield mostly positive outcomes (FHI 360, 2015).

A research study of an integrated programme to improve self-employment among the very poor entailed 6 randomized control trials in Ethiopia, Ghana, Honduras, India, Pakistan and Peru, and assessed progress on 10 welfare outcomes or indices (consumption, food security, productive and household assets, financial inclusion, time use, income and revenue, physical health, mental health, political involvement and women's empowerment). The integrated interventions included skills training on running a business and choosing livelihoods, and health, nutrition and hygiene training. The evaluation found a significant impact on all 10 outcomes, with gains sustained in 8 of the 10, a year after programme completion. The evaluation also conducted a cost–benefit analysis, and estimated that benefits were higher than costs in all countries except Honduras (Banerjee et al., 2015).

Multisector interventions can also provide arguments for investment in interventions that do not appear cost-effective if evaluated from the perspective of only one sector. In Senegal, it was estimated that addressing literacy, health and nutrition challenges simultaneously would be more likely to break the intergenerational cycle of poverty (Nordtveit, 2008). While a cost-effectiveness analysis of a cash transfer programme in Zomba, Malawi, found that the cost per prevented HIV infection was prohibitive at US$5,000 to US$12,500 (Baird et al., 2012), a co-financing, cross-sector approach could help secure funding because of the multiple benefits of such programmes (Remme et al., 2012). School feeding and school health interventions are important examples indicating that addressing child health and nutrition through the school system is cost-effective (**Box 6.1**).

There are good examples of integrated planning …

While there is a robust rationale for integrated planning and some credible evidence in its favour, successful implementation requires political commitment, an appropriate institutional environment, financial and technical know-how, and an appreciation of power dynamics (Persaud, 2016). This section discusses three

---

BOX 6.1

School feeding and school health as integrated delivery mechanisms

School feeding programmes are among the most widespread social protection programmes. Providing food in schools can improve some of the education, health and nutrition outcomes of school-age children while supporting the agricultural sector and benefiting the community. As a result, these programmes are often jointly coordinated by ministries of health, agriculture and education. It is estimated that every dollar spent on school feeding brings three dollars in economic returns.

International cross-institutional collaboration includes the Nourishing Bodies, Nourishing Minds initiative, established in 2013 by the World Food Programme, UNICEF and UNESCO to work with governments and the private sector in Haiti, Mozambique, Niger and Pakistan, taking advantage of the synergy inherent in nutrition and education. Additionally, funding from the Bill and Melinda Gates Foundation for local agriculture has focused on connections between smallholder farm production and school feeding.

School provision of health services such as deworming and sexual and reproductive health education is also efficient. FRESH (Focusing Resources on Effective School Health), an initiative of UNESCO, UNICEF, the World Health Organization and the World Bank, argues that multiple strategies, including health-related school policies, safe water and sanitation, skills-based health education and school-based health and nutrition services, should be used in schools.

School feeding and health interventions appear to be cost-effective compared to other means of delivery, though evidence is limited. In low income countries, there are typically more teachers than nurses and more schools than clinics. Employing teachers to deliver simple interventions, such as pills or micronutrient supplements, may cost one-tenth as much as delivery through traditional mobile health teams, even after considering additional teacher training costs.

Sources: Guyatt (2003); Krishnaratne et al. (2013); UNESCO (2002); UNESCO (2015a); UNESCO et al. (2013); World Food Programme (2009); World Food Programme (2013).

instructive examples of national efforts to improve multisector planning. They reflect the importance of political will, institutional support, adequate capacity and available data to support the integration process.

Nigeria: large-scale, local implementation to meet the MDGs. Nigeria used US$18 billion from debt relief in the 2005 Heavily Indebted Poor Countries initiative to launch its Office of the Senior Special Assistant to the President on the Millennium Development Goals. Between 2007 and 2009, it provided conditional grants at the state level targeting health, water and sanitation, electricity, and poverty alleviation (Phillips, 2009; Zamba and Oboh, 2013). In 2010, the office established the Conditional Grants Scheme to Local Government Areas (CGS-LGA) Track to more effectively reach local governments, strengthen primary health and education systems, and help them provide priority services through a strong emphasis on local, data-driven planning (Iyengar et al., 2015).

> " Nigeria established a grants scheme integrating responses for health, education, and water and sanitation "

The CGS-LGA Track had significant political support, including a high powered steering committee and a special MDG adviser from an associated presidential office. Since the funds were provided under a debt relief initiative, the Ministry of Finance was able to tag funds for pro-poor investment (Persaud, 2016).

The design and implementation of the CGS-LGA Track demonstrated strong horizontal and vertical integration, prioritizing health, education, and water and sanitation. Local project priorities were discussed in joint meetings of the planning unit and the other sectors. A joint federal, state and local financing arrangement motivated commitment at all levels (Persaud, 2016). Local officials had to develop proposals that identified priority local needs using the Nigeria MDG system of indicators and inputs, which was developed for this project (Iyengar et al., 2014; Iyengar et al., 2015). This use of data-driven decision-making eventually led to the first common database on health and education facilities, which eventually became available to all government programmes, development partners and civil society groups.

The focus was on filling financial gaps where sector-specific funding was inadequate and avoiding duplication of line ministries' projects. In some cases, such as drilling boreholes at schools or in communities, water and education officials had to agree on detailed joint plans (Persaud, 2016).

According to a report, by 2014, the project had disbursed more than US$300 million towards strengthening MDG-focused health and education interventions in one-third of the country, and efforts were being made to scale up nationwide. Over 90% of the funds were used for infrastructure projects in the three sectors. An independent assessment of progress from the first round of grants found that over 80% of the more than 5,000 projects could be sustained through community efforts (Earth Institute, 2015).

Colombia: a pioneer of SDG implementation. Colombia's government has been instrumental in developing the post-2015 agenda and proposing an integrated approach to development (Development Finance International, 2016; OECD, 2015f). It is also active in global efforts to understand how to incorporate the SDG agenda into national development plans.

In February 2015, even before the SDGs were agreed, the government established an inter-agency commission on preparation and implementation of the post-2015 development agenda and SDGs (Lucci et al., 2015). It is composed of ministers and vice-ministers, signalling strong political commitment to cross-sector implementation (Persaud, 2016).

There is clear vertical integration of the national development plan. Once consensus was reached at the national level, the government encouraged governors and mayors to include the SDGs in their development plans, which define the main local development priorities for 2014–2018 (Development Finance International, 2016).

The three core pillars are education, peace and equity, and are considered to be presidential priorities. The new agenda also aims at a lifelong learning perspective that defines targets for all education levels and ages. The national development plan aims to make Colombia the most educated country in Latin America by 2025 (Development Finance International, 2016).

Colombia was one of the first countries in Latin America to decentralize its education system to tackle inequitable spending across regions. The Ministry of Education formulates policy and objectives, and monitors the system, while municipalities manage and plan the use of physical, human and financial resources and are responsible for education outcomes. The ministry introduced a project in 2004 to provide technical assistance to local governments based on their needs, recognizing that effective service provision depends on local financial and human capacity (Development Finance International, 2016).

While the national education plan is developed at the national level, there are also regional development plans and municipal education plans. Multilevel planning is accompanied by a decentralized budget system, with a mechanism to redistribute national funds to the main social sectors: education receives 58.5%. There is also an equity-based formula to distribute funding across territorial entities (Development Finance International, 2016).

Malaysia: integrating the technical and vocational education strategy. Technical and vocational education can be key for workforce development. The sectors typically involved are education, labour, youth and economic development. In Malaysia, there is political support to improve workforce development in the interest of national economic development. The Tenth Malaysia Plan 2011–2015 and accompanying Education Blueprint 2013–2025 project are being used to overhaul educational and training systems. A primary objective is to raise the workforce's skills and employability so Malaysia can compete with more advanced economies in the region and become a high income nation by 2020 (Malaysia Economic Planning Unit, 2009; Sander et al., 2013).

> " Malaysia works across education, labour, youth and economic development in order to help with workforce development "

A key emphasis has been on ensuring that technical and vocational education, delivered by multiple ministries, is better harmonized and in line with industry requirements. The establishment of a national qualifications framework helped significantly broaden, unify and streamline the qualifications system. Between 2000 and 2010, the number of occupations covered by the national occupational skills standards increased from 500 to 1,585 (World Bank, 2013).

The development of competency standards is participatory and includes representation from women's organizations and private industry. A common set of standards and testing has effectively unified the substance of training, despite the fact that it is spread across ministries. Since 2000, several government-sponsored incentive programmes have aimed to foster links between education institutions and industry to improve employability and enhance workforce qualifications with on-the-job training (World Bank, 2013).

... but planning and financing processes remain fragmented

Despite such positive examples, governments typically define mandates, priorities, budgets, administrative and planning processes, and monitoring and evaluation in ways that are at odds with integration (Persaud, 2016). Government agencies tend to focus on policy formulation and implementation in their respective sectors, hampering coordination and collaboration, within the context of a myriad of bureaucratic and political structures that influence decision-making.

An analysis of 76 low and middle income countries for the GEM Report indicates that well-developed national plans that are linked to good education financing plans and decentralized planning and financing systems, and that lead to good cross-sector integration, are the exception rather than the rule in most poorer countries (Development Finance International, 2016).

National plans need to coordinate sectors horizontally. Yet, out of 27 countries with survey-based information on coordination mechanisms for early childhood development, for instance, while 17 had a national-level, explicitly stated multisector strategy, only 8 had established processes to coordinate budget-setting across ministries (World Bank, 2016).

Similarly, the lack of a unified, coordinated approach has been identified as a major challenge in technical and vocational education policy (Marope et al., 2015). In Ghana, institutional training, employment opportunities and industry needs are reportedly mismatched. Parliament established a council for technical and vocational education in 2006 to reform the sector, with representation from nine ministries and state partners. However, the council was placed under Ministry of Education control, which led to rivalries and hindered collaboration (Ansah and Ernest, 2013).

National plans need to be well coordinated vertically with local implementation strategies. Where local planning is done well, sector silos can be broken down. Success in vertical integration is often contingent on subnational governments having the capacity to plan, budget, coordinate, implement and oversee processes between sectors – and the authority to do so. At the same time, good central planning that provides the flexibility for local adaptation is also important (OECD, 2013a).

Ethiopia has a sophisticated set of horizontal and vertical planning strategies. A robust federal and regional process is in place for planning, coordination and integrated budgeting in education. Regional education ministries are responsible for some oversight and spending but most decisions are taken at the local (*woreda*) level. Local plans take a multisector approach, e.g. health clinics and centres being planned alongside schools. However, there have been some challenges. Local education offices reportedly feel more accountable to local councils, which provided their budget, than to regional education bureaus. This hampered regional-level monitoring (Development Finance International, 2016).

> " In Ethiopia, local education plans take a multisector approach "

In South Africa, the 1996 Constitution pertained to the national and provincial levels of government. Financing decentralization was the key measure used to address historical spatial inequality. Education had high political priority. In provincial budgets, education received the largest portion of the funding reserved to enhance equity. There were also grant programmes available for education infrastructure and other projects.

However, the system hindered cross-sector planning. More than 20 agencies and structures provided education, contributing to very slow delivery and even litigation against the government. When provinces could not deliver school infrastructure, some of the management was reinstated at the national level. A review of a national integrated plan for early childhood development between 2005 and 2010 showed that it was extremely difficult to coordinate and integrate the services offered by the several departments involved (Development Finance International, 2016).

Nevertheless, some improvement has been seen. With the adoption in 2012 of the National Development Plan 2030, which sets forth outcomes and roles for various sectors, and a dedicated monitoring and evaluation department, South Africa has created a chain of education accountability with lines of responsibility from state to classroom (South Africa National Planning Commission, 2012).

POLICY COHERENCE IN AID AGENCIES

Agencies that provide overseas development assistance, like all government agencies, face two challenges in delivering programmes that are consistent with the integrated planning needs of the SDGs: they may lack a coherent vision of their approach to development, and they face difficulties in coordinating programmes that span different sectors.

Achieving policy coherence for development

The concept of policy coherence for development aid emerged in the 1990s with growing concern over aid effectiveness. At that time, donors committed to increase coherence between aid and other policies affecting lower income countries (OECD, 2015c). For instance, Policy Coherence for Development was a tool intended to ensure that EU policies supported lower income countries' needs and the MDGs, and at the very least did not contradict aims of poverty eradication. All EU countries are legally obliged to follow this approach (Latek, 2015; Trocaire, 2013).

Many donors recognize the importance of addressing development challenges more holistically. For instance, EU allocation of at least 20% of the development budget to social protection, health, education and jobs suggests recognition of the need for integrated planning across SDG sectors, including education (Mercer, 2014). The most effective education-aided activities are those that target issues beyond schools, such as community participation and costs for families, and engage with actors beyond education ministries (Samoff et al., 2016).

Germany has long advocated policy coherence in development. Its Coalition Treaty committed to improve coordination to make policy more development oriented. This support of policy coherence for development has translated into a holistic approach to the SDG agenda (OECD, 2015e). Its education aid strategy emphasizes that it addresses every level of education from early childhood to tertiary education; the transition phases between levels; and formal, non-formal and informal education with a view to encourage lifelong learning (Mercer, 2014).

The United States, which issued a Global Directive on Development Policy in 2010, has historically lacked a coherent set of policies. Efforts to promote a whole-of-government approach have also largely failed in recent years, since the administration promoted development to the level of diplomacy and defence but did not give the US Agency for International Development the tools necessary to act at this level (Gavas et al., 2015).

Implementing multisector aid programmes

Even if an agency has a coherent vision of development, implementing multisector programmes is a major task.

UNICEF's social protection strategy takes a multipronged, systematic and coordinated approach to reduce social and economic vulnerability faced by children and their families. It tries to address multiple factors and maximize effectiveness and impact across sectors (UNICEF, 2012). In Ghana, UNICEF has supported a cross-sector integrated approach through the Livelihood Empowerment Against Poverty programme. While overall coordination is the responsibility of the Department of Social Welfare, participation by other line ministries, such as Education, Health and Labour, is facilitated by an interministerial committee (UNICEF, 2012). Similarly, with regard to education outcomes, UNICEF highlights the value and impact of other sectors' actions on education, including water and sanitation, public works, health, child protection, social development, welfare and protection, and employment (UNICEF, 2012).

Other examples of multisector aid programmes, such as the Millennium Development Goals Achievement Fund and its successor, the Sustainable Development Goals Fund, suggest growing acceptance of the integrated planning discourse within the United Nations (**Box 6.2**).

The World Bank has adopted sector-wide approaches across multiple sectors to facilitate an integrated approach to development (Independent Evaluation Group, 2010). In 2005, its Ceará Multi-Sector Social Inclusion Development Project in Brazil integrated education, health, water and sanitation, water source management, and environment. It promoted multisector policy coordination and applied a result-based management approach: failure to meet performance indicators affected the release of resources from the Treasury. For instance, when a target on hospital admissions was missed, a multisector study was required to determine the reason; it led to a strong demonstration of the need for intersector coordination, since failure to meet the target resulted from issues beyond the health sector (Batley et al., 2007; Persaud, 2016).

Experience from other World Bank programmes, however, indicates that despite the logic of multisector projects,

---

BOX 6.2

The MDG Achievement Fund and the SDG Fund

The Millennium Development Goals Achievement Fund was the first significant UN initiative to support inter-agency work and integrated, multidimensional joint programmes on the MDGs. The fund also aimed to promote system-wide coherence across UN agencies. Established in 2006 through an over US$840 million deal between Spain and the UN system, it has financed 130 joint programmes in 50 countries on 8 thematic areas, such as youth employment and migration. Country-specific evaluations have found that the multisector approach helped avoid or reduce overlap between development programmes, and increased coordination and collaboration within and between governments and development partners.

Its successor, the Sustainable Development Goals Fund (SDG Fund), was created in 2014 and has programmes in 21 countries on 3 thematic areas – inclusive growth for poverty eradication, food security and nutrition, and water and sanitation – and 3 cross-cutting issues: sustainability, gender equality and public–private partnerships. At least three UN agencies, on average, are engaged in each joint programme. The thematic areas were those identified as key areas requiring integrated action to improve outcomes. The SDG Fund has established an advisory group to engage more proactively with the private sector.

Sources: Capra International Inc. (2014); ILO (2013); UNDP (2013); Sustainable Development Goals Fund (2016).

---

it is often difficult to execute them. In an evaluation of World Bank health, nutrition and population sector activities, three-quarters of the country assistance strategies acknowledged the importance of other sectors for health, nutrition and population outcomes. Education was the second most cited sector, after water and sanitation, in regard to its impact on health, nutrition and population. Two multisector lending strategies were implemented to improve health outcomes: one on projects in complementary sectors to health and the other on multisector projects linking actions in many sectors through a single loan (Independent Evaluation Group, 2009).

An evaluation of the two strategies concluded that multisector projects, which mostly took place in low income countries and focused on HIV and AIDS, were demanding to implement due to the number of agencies involved. Countries often had limited capacity to deal with this complexity. As a result, while about two-thirds of single-sector projects were deemed to have performed satisfactorily, less than half the multisector projects had satisfactory outcomes (Independent Evaluation Group, 2009).

PARTNERSHIPS

Local and national government authorities, civil society, academics, the scientific community, the private sector and global multistakeholder partnerships are some of the important partners that have helped implement global agendas such as the MDGs (United Nations, 2015b). A recent analysis highlights 10 factors in making development partnerships effective. They include securing high level leadership, ensuring context-specific and country-led partnerships, clarifying roles and responsibilities, and focusing on financing, results and accountability (OECD, 2015b).

> **The ambition of the SDGs calls for partnerships between civil society, the private sector and multistakeholder partnerships, such as GPE**

The ambition of the SDGs points to potential roles for civil society, the private sector and multistakeholder partnerships in financing, implementing and ensuring mutual accountability of a new agenda that is expected to be driven by national governments (Hazlewood, 2015; UNIDO and UN Global Compact, 2014; World Economic Forum, 2014). This section examines some of the global discussions of the roles of civil society, the private sector and multistakeholder partnerships in the SDG agenda.

CIVIL SOCIETY IS A KEY PARTNER WITH DIVERSE INTERESTS

In 1996, the UN Economic and Social Council established consultative status for NGOs and civil society organizations (CSOs). The 2030 Agenda for Sustainable Development has provided a new platform for them to participate in the global follow-up and review process for the SDGs (United Nations, 2015b).

In the education sector, increased civil society activity was a key achievement of the EFA agenda and Dakar Framework after 2000 (UNESCO, 2015a). CSOs became more active in tracking budgets to increase transparency, advocating for more funding for marginalized groups,

and raising awareness and empowering communities to reform corrupt practices.

National civil society activity has been supported by global efforts, such as the Global Campaign for Education and the Civil Society Education Fund, which have helped build networks and national capacity to improve advocacy and monitor progress (UNESCO, 2015a). Some large international NGOs are significant funders of education in lower income countries, and their financing and programming support better prioritizes basic education and humanitarian aid to education than do donor countries (Naylor and Ndarhutse, 2015).

But there are challenges in designing civil society partnerships more productively in relation to the SDG agenda. How can organizations heavily dependent on donor funding maintain an independent voice (UNESCO, 2015a)? Another challenge is the enormous variety of disparate actors with differing priorities and influence under the civil society umbrella (Moksnes and Melin, 2012). Whose voices are being captured at the global and national levels? These questions need careful consideration.

THE ROLE OF THE PRIVATE SECTOR IS VIEWED WITH AMBIVALENCE

While the MDGs made only limited reference to the private sector, the 2030 Agenda more explicitly recognizes its importance, particularly regarding involvement in mobilizing the funds required to meet the SDGs. The dynamism and funding the private sector can bring to the SDGs is reason for optimism (UNIDO and UN Global Compact, 2014). But there are also strong concerns about the role of corporate practices in fostering unsustainable behaviour (Pingeot, 2014).

Within the education sector, views are divided on public–private arrangements to finance and manage education delivery, which are becoming more common in much of the world (Ginsburg, 2012). In richer countries, governments have entered into elaborate funding and monitoring arrangements with private actors. But in poorer countries, the private sector is loosely regulated. While some hail the growth of private involvement as bringing financing, flexibility, innovation and improved learning outcomes (Patrinos et al., 2009), sceptics, who view the private sector's growing role as a result of the public sector retreating from its responsibility to provide education, see a potential for undue market influences in schooling and widening inequality (Robertson and Verger, 2012).

Perhaps as a result of this debate, the Education 2030 Framework for Action, while calling for private involvement in mobilizing additional resources and aiding school-to-work transition, also stresses respecting education as a human right and ensuring that private efforts do not increase inequality (UNESCO, 2016b).

GLOBAL MULTISTAKEHOLDER PARTNERSHIPS IN EDUCATION

If global aspirations for SDG 4 are to be fulfilled, the role of coordination and financing bodies is critical. The formation of a steering committee, led by UNESCO, is expected to bring coherence in Education 2030 activities. The Global Partnership for Education (GPE) is the main multistakeholder financing partnership in education, and better leveraging it will be key to meeting financing requirements. A new fund for education in crises is being added to the global architecture to improve links between development and humanitarian aid.

Education 2030 coordination structures

The Education 2030 Framework for Action specifies that the global coordination mechanism includes the SDG-Education 2030 Steering Committee, Global Education Meetings, regional meetings and the Collective Consultation of NGOs on Education for All. Preparation for the mechanism is informed by the results of the internal evaluation of UNESCO's role in global EFA coordination, which recognized that its task was made more difficult by the varying level of engagement of the other four convening partners. The evaluation also called for UNESCO to strengthen coordination through a strategic approach that is results-oriented and closely monitored (UNESCO, 2016c).

The SDG-Education 2030 Steering Committee, which met for the first time in May 2016, is expected to be the main mechanism to support countries, review progress (drawing on the GEM Report) and encourage harmonization and coordination of partner activities. The committee is made up of representatives of member states from six regions, the E9 forum (nine countries committed to achieving EFA), the three key convening agencies (UNESCO, UNICEF and the World Bank), and representation from another agency (rotating between United Nations Development Programme, United Nations High Commissioner for Refugees, United Nations Fund for Population Activities, UN Women and the International Labour Office), the GPE and the OECD, as well as from NGOs, teacher organizations and regional organizations (UNESCO, 2016b).

The steering committee is to act as the voice of the international education community in SDG agenda implementation. An important consideration, therefore, is what it will say in global SDG 'follow-up and review' structures, especially the High-Level Political Forum for Sustainable Development and its thematic reviews (see Chapter 9).

Global Partnership for Education

Global financing partnerships target particular sectors, as in the case of GAVI and the Global Fund for Tuberculosis, AIDS and Malaria, or have cross-sector mandates, such as those of the Urban Poor Fund International and the Global Alliance for Improved Nutrition. They can serve a variety of purposes, from improving collaboration among stakeholders in a given sector to catalysing new investment, raising national and local funds, and fostering public–private collaboration. Pooled mechanisms such as these can reduce fragmentation as well as transaction costs for donors and receiving countries. Since the SDG agenda is more integrated and universal than that of the MDGs, more significant cross-sector collaboration and learning are needed to achieve system-wide impact (Hazlewood, 2015).

The GPE, established in 2002 as the EFA Fast Track Initiative, is the education sector's principal multistakeholder partnership. Its broad mission, according to its 2016–2020 Strategic Plan, is 'to mobilize global and national efforts to contribute to the achievement of equitable, quality education and learning for all, through inclusive partnership, a focus on effective and efficient education systems and increased financing' (GPE, 2016).

Since its first external evaluation in 2010, the GPE has made many strategic and operational changes, such as better targeting fragile contexts, helping build national capacity for education planning and revamping its board of directors. Its second evaluation stressed that the GPE needed to improve its approach for evaluating success, as it had not introduced a theory of change or a result framework, features that have been added in its new strategic plan. The evaluation also noted the GPE's limited ability to raise additional education financing, despite an increasingly ambitious mission. About US$2.1 billion in aid was pledged to the GPE Fund in the 2015–2018 replenishment round, the equivalent of US$525 million disbursed per year (Results for Development and Universalia, 2015).

By contrast, the health sector's multistakeholder partnerships are believed to have leveraged substantial funds; mobilized civil society and business partners; improved the allocation, predictability and transparency of funds; and facilitated knowledge transfers (Sachs and Schmidt-Traub, 2014). While health and education are fundamentally different sectors in terms of their objectives and functioning (Chabbott, 2014; de Moura Castro and Musgrove, 2007), learning from health partnerships could be especially important for education.

Education Cannot Wait fund for education in crises

Education Cannot Wait, a new fund for education in crises, was launched at the World Humanitarian S ummit in May 2016. It aims, by 2020, to raise up to US$3.85 billion and reach 18% of children and youth whose education is affected by conflict, natural disasters and disease outbreaks. It will work to address the challenges of the field and raise the profile of education in crises (see Chapter 20) (ODI, 2016).

Its main component, the Breakthrough Fund, will serve three functions. First, it will channel immediate support in a crisis through existing agencies. Grants will be given to consolidated appeals, which already meet a certain

> **"** The Education Cannot Wait fund aims, by 2020, to reach 18% of children and youth whose education is affected by conflict, natural disasters and disease outbreaks **"**

benchmark of funding. This rapid response mechanism could finance temporary access, essential supplies or back-to-school campaigns.

Second, it will facilitate engagement at the country level for up to five years, based on a country plan to be devised within three months of the onset of a crisis to bridge and consolidate existing plans. The plan is to be informed by a joint comprehensive need assessment and integrated into existing national planning processes and aid flows, such as those provided by the GPE.

Third, it will aim to attract non-traditional donors, philanthropists and the private sector, which may not be able to provide contributions directly to a general purpose fund.

In addition, to improve education response capacities, the fund's Acceleration Facility will invest in existing initiatives such as the Education Cluster, the UN Refugee Agency and the Inter-Agency Network for Education in Emergencies.

CONCLUSION

There is growing recognition that stakeholders need to plan together, act together and commit to equity and sustainability. Some countries have made significant strides in increasing financing and engaging in more integrated planning across sectors and levels of government. Calls for multistakeholder partnerships firmly recognize the importance of non-state actors.

However, the status of financing, planning and implementation arrangements shows that the current environment is very far from what is needed to achieve the aspirational goals of the 2030 Agenda for Sustainable Development. From the perspective of the education sector, the vast majority of government action still takes place in sector or subsector silos constrained by a narrowly focused administrative structure. It is difficult to identify instances in which planning and financing is well coordinated across levels of government. Education funding from the private sector and multilateral institutions is limited. Moreover, from the broader perspective of all sectors involved in the SDG agenda, integration is also lacking. And incentives and administrative tools to link activities across sectors are underdeveloped.

This state of affairs provides a useful reference point for assessing future progress as well as anticipating challenges in achieving the global education goal. There is a clear need to keep correcting inefficiency in financing and advocating for more funds for education. Political commitment and administrative capacity are key to ensure successful multisector, multilevel government arrangements. Finally, it is necessary to keep pressuring donors to fulfil their most relevant role for education funding: ensuring that the holistic agenda of SDG 4 and the other SDGs is achieved.

A young Chinese boy examines the nature around him.

7

Projections: forecasting the effects of education expansion on sustainable development outcomes

KEY MESSAGES

The world will be 50 years late in achieving its global education commitments: On current trends, universal primary completion will be achieved in 2042; universal lower secondary completion in 2059; and universal upper secondary completion in 2084.

The poorest countries will achieve universal primary education over 100 years later than the richest.

The poorest countries will not achieve universal lower secondary completion until the end of the century.

The richest countries are also not on track to achieve global education commitments: Even at the fastest rate of progress ever seen in the region, 1 in 10 countries in Europe and Northern America would still not achieve universal upper secondary completion by 2030.

The projections show that universal secondary completion requires an unprecedented and immediate break with past trends.

And yet even if key provisions of the global education goal will not be met in time, modest progress can make a big difference to other development outcomes.

Achieving universal lower secondary education for women by 2030 in sub-Saharan Africa would prevent up to 3.5 million child deaths from 2050-2060.

Universalising upper secondary education in low income countries could increase per capita earnings by 75% and lift 60 million people out of poverty.

Universal upper secondary completion by 2030 would prevent up to 50,000 disaster-related deaths per decade by 2040-2050.

Previous chapters of the Global Education Monitoring (GEM) Report have introduced ways in which education can unlock the global potential for sustainable development. They have also examined how the 2030 Agenda for Sustainable Development requires reconsidering how education of good quality can address pressing social, economic and environmental challenges. This chapter looks at ways in which likely scenarios of education progress might shift development outcomes in the next 15 years.

The GEM Report commissioned the Wittgenstein Centre for Demography and Global Human Capital, a specialized, multidisciplinary research centre, to analyse the impact of education dynamics on selected social, economic and environmental outcomes (Barakat et al., 2016). On the basis of this analysis, the chapter discusses two questions.

First, what do past rates of education expansion indicate about the prospects of achieving the ambitious new education goal? The news is not good. Unless there is rapid acceleration unlike any observed to date, there is no chance of achieving the target of universal secondary completion by 2030. Instead, it is projected that 69% of those aged 15 to 19 in 2030 will complete upper secondary education and 84% will complete lower secondary education. Not even the Education for All (EFA)

> **It is projected that less than 70% of children will complete primary school in 2030 in low income countries**

goal of universal primary completion will be achieved; in low income countries, less than 70% of children will complete primary school in 2030.

Second, what would different rates of progress in education mean for development in other sectors such as health, the economy and the environment? This chapter's analysis considers the impact

of education improving at the speed of past trends, as well as three more optimistic pathways, on three sets of outcomes: social (health, including child mortality and life expectancy), economic (poverty and economic growth) and environmental (disaster-related deaths). As the effects of any social change, and especially education, take a long time to reach fruition – sometimes generations – the impact on these outcomes is explored at both 2030 and 2050.

PROJECTING GLOBAL EDUCATIONAL ATTAINMENT TO 2030 AND BEYOND

For the World Education Forum in May 2015, the GEM Report team published projections of whether the goal of universal secondary completion, set in the Education 2030 Framework for Action, would be achieved by 2030 (UNESCO, 2015). The conclusion was stark: progressing at past expansion rates, not even the EFA goal of universal primary completion will be achieved by 2030 in low and middle income countries.

The new projections for this report have been updated in two ways. First, a larger set of data is used, covering 163 countries that account for the vast majority of the global population. A potential disadvantage of this wider coverage is that data sometimes draw on censuses, which are conducted every 10 years, so the impact of recent changes in enrolment and attainment may be missed.

Second, a more sophisticated methodology is applied to project the share of the population that will attain a given level of education, by country and gender. Yet, the approach shares some of the limitations of other global projections (**Box 7.1**).

By calling for universal secondary education, the Sustainable Development Goals (SDGs) agenda entered uncharted territory. It is unknown whether the future

BOX 7.1

Key considerations in projecting educational attainment

Attainment histories, reconstructed from the most recent censuses or household surveys, are the basis for the new projections. Data were projected backwards. For example, the share of 40- to 44-year-olds with at least upper secondary education in 2000 indicates the likely share of 30- to 34-year-olds with that level of education in 1990.

These backwards projections account for differences in mortality between education groups. Where possible, they have been validated using contemporary data sources. They are disaggregated by country, gender, five-year periods between 1970 and 2010, five-year age groups, and six education levels: none, incomplete primary, primary, lower secondary, upper secondary and post-secondary.

Using these attainment rates, the new projections aim to predict the probability that, in a given country, a particular share of the population will have attained at least a specified education level.

To make these predictions more realistic, several assumptions are made. When a country's attainment rate slows or even reverses in one period, because of economic recession or political conflict, it is not expected to bounce back in the following period. This makes it necessary to limit, to some extent, the degree of deviation from the long-term trend.

Another issue in extrapolating past trends is that short-term declines may lead one to project that a country's education system will collapse. Many countries experience setbacks in their history of education development – one recent example being the Syrian Arab Republic – but no precedent exists for a country moving along a long-term reverse trajectory. The model therefore assumes that such countries' attainment rate will move towards the regional average after a setback, albeit more slowly.

Given the continuing large gaps between male and female attainment levels in some countries, and the differences in how fast countries converge to parity, additional assumptions are needed to project attainment by gender. In particular, it is assumed that in each period, gender-specific attainment rates converge towards the average for both males and females at a rate that differs across education levels and countries but is constant over time.

The scenarios also make explicit assumptions about how accelerating expansion at one level of the education system affects higher levels. When more members of a cohort complete a given education level, demand for access to the next level increases too. This is particularly noticeable in the transition to post-secondary education: increases in the pool of upper secondary graduates will raise participation rates in post-secondary education.

Finally, it is assumed, as in the 2015 projections, that the attainment level for considering a target achieved is 97%. While this is unavoidable, because of the requirements of the statistical model, it should by no means be interpreted as meaning that the hardest to reach do not count.

Sources: Barakat et al. (2016); Lutz et al. (2014).

trajectory of upper secondary (and higher) education will resemble the historical trajectory of basic education, which has become universal in many countries. As of 2010, nearly 80% of 20- to 24-year-olds in the European Union had completed upper secondary school. Even the countries with the highest attainment rates, such as the Republic of Korea, stood at 95%. With no country having yet achieved universal upper secondary attainment, it is difficult to assume all countries will converge to universal completion. Thus, assumptions for secondary education growth are driven more by statistics than by experience.

The projections reported here focus on the cohort that will be aged 15 to 19 in 2030. The aspiration of countries and others in the international community is that this group will ultimately achieve universal secondary completion.

ATTAINMENT RATE PROJECTIONS FOR FOUR SCENARIOS

In this chapter, results for the attainment rates, or the highest level of education completed, of 15- to 19-year-olds by 2030 are presented for four scenarios (**Table 7.1**).

The analysis confirms the earlier GEM Report projection that, on past trends, not even the Millennium Development Goal (MDG) and EFA goal of universal primary completion is likely to be achieved by 2030. The target of universal secondary completion is clearly beyond reach. Under the scenario that past growth rates will continue, 84% of 15- to 19-year-olds in 2030 are projected to complete lower secondary education, and only 69% upper secondary. On these trends, universal lower secondary completion would be achieved in 2059, and universal upper secondary completion only in 2084 (**Table 7.2**).

The challenge for low income countries is particularly salient. At past rates, half of 15- to 19-year-olds in 2030 will complete lower secondary education and less than 30% will complete upper secondary. Low

TABLE 7.1:
Projection scenarios

Scenarios	Description
Trend	Past progress rates will continue into the future ('business as usual') ...
... or the cohort of those aged 15 to 19 in 2030 will attain:	
Low	Universal lower secondary by 2030
Slow	Universal upper secondary by 2040
	(i.e. all transitions up to upper secondary will be universal by 2030; universal upper secondary will be completed for the cohort entering school in 2030)
SDG 4.1	Universal upper secondary by 2030 (= target 4.1)

TABLE 7.2:
Projected attainment rates in 2030 and year of achieving universal attainment in the trend scenario, by education level

	Primary attainment rate (%) (2030)	Projected year of universal primary attainment	Lower secondary attainment rate (%) (2030)	Projected year of universal lower secondary attainment	Upper secondary attainment rate (%) (2030)	Projected year of universal upper secondary attainment
World	91.5	2042	84.4	2059	68.6	2084
Low income	69.6	2088	50.0	2096	29.0	After 2100
Lower middle income	93.2	2054	86.8	2066	71.8	2088
Upper middle income	99.1	2020	96.1	2045	75.2	2087
High income	99.6	Achieved	98.7	2017	94.9	2048
Caucasus and Central Asia	99.8	Achieved	99.4	Achieved	96.4	2044
Eastern and South-eastern Asia	99.3	2015	96.9	2040	76.5	2080
Europe and Northern America	99.7	Achieved	99.5	Achieved	96.8	2044
Latin America and the Caribbean	96.6	2042	90.0	2066	72.7	2095
Northern Africa and Western Asia	92.3	2048	87.0	2062	77.1	2082
Pacific	99.7	Achieved	99.3	2020	96.8	2045
Southern Asia	95.1	2051	89.0	2062	73.5	2087
Sub-Saharan Africa	77.1	2080	62.1	2089	42.4	After 2100

Source: Barakat et al. (2016).

income countries, in this scenario, would only achieve Target 4.1 at the end of the century. Middle income countries would meet the target in the late 2080s. Thus, achieving universal secondary completion requires an unprecedented and immediate break with past trends (**Figure 7.1**).

Among world regions, only Europe and Northern America and Caucasus and Central Asia have achieved universal lower secondary completion. They will be very close to universal upper secondary education in 2030 but are not expected to reach it. The region of Eastern and South-eastern Asia is likely to come close to universal lower secondary completion by 2030, but not achieve universal upper secondary for at least another 30 years.

The new projections indicate that three regions will not even achieve universal primary completion by 2030. Northern Africa and Western Asia is expected to come very close, as is Southern Asia. Sub-Saharan Africa will likely lag behind considerably and is expected to have a completion rate of 77% in primary education, 62% in lower secondary and 42% in upper secondary (**Figure 7.2**).

How much progress is required? It is useful to look at whether a country would achieve universal secondary

Universal secondary completion requires an unprecedented and immediate break with past trends

completion by 2030 if it expanded at the fastest rate ever observed in its region. For the vast majority of countries, this would still not be sufficient – even for 1 in 10 countries in Europe and Northern America, and for every country in Southern Asia and sub-Saharan Africa (**Table 7.3**).

This scenario shows that the speed in education progress required to meet the SDG target would be unprecedented. Even disregarding differences in income, institutions, tradition, governance and policy between countries, and the fact that what works in one country may not be successfully replicated elsewhere, analysis shows the ambition of SDG target 4.1 to be unrealistic.

PREDICTING EFFECTS OF EDUCATION ON DEVELOPMENT OUTCOMES

While projections suggest that target 4.1 is not likely to be met, even modest acceleration of education progress could make a big difference to other SDGs. However, there are limitations to understanding the complex relationships between education and sustainable development outcomes. In many instances, insufficiencies of data and research mean some relationships cannot be analysed. Standardized cross-country information permits examination only of the effects of educational attainment. Even then, most studies have looked at relationships for particular populations, which cannot necessarily be projected to a global scale.

As this report maintains, while educational attainment matters for development, so do education quality and learning outcomes. Yet, widely shared definitions of quality

FIGURE 7.1:

Not even universal primary completion will be achieved by 2030 in low and lower middle income countries, on past trends

Projected attainment rates of 15- to 19-year-olds by education level and country income group, 2010–2080

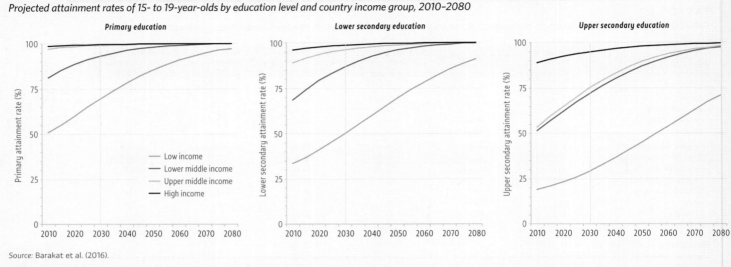

Source: Barakat et al. (2016).

FIGURE 7.2:

Achieving universal secondary completion by 2030 will require unprecedented acceleration

Projected attainment rates of 15- to 19-year-olds by education level and region, based on past trends and SDG 4.1 scenario for universal upper secondary completion by 2030, 2000–2080

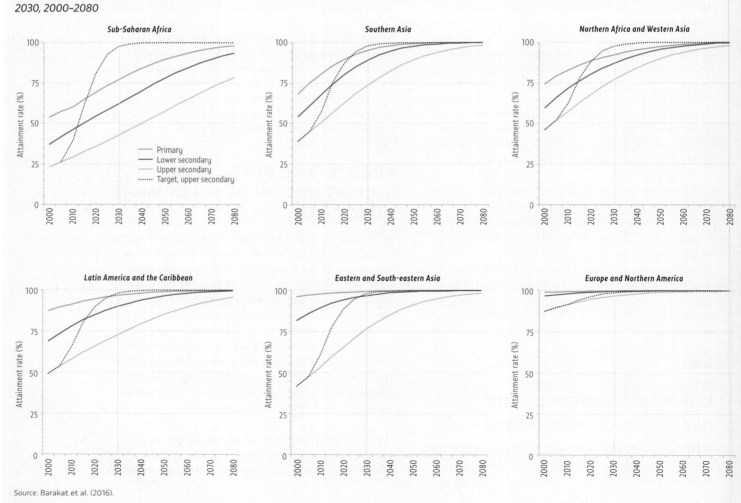

Source: Barakat et al. (2016).

TABLE 7.3:
Percentage of countries that would achieve selected targets at the highest rate of improvement in education previously achieved in their region

	Universal lower secondary by 2030	Universal upper secondary by 2040	Universal upper secondary by 2030
Caucasus and Central Asia	100	100	86
Eastern and South-eastern Asia	76	35	35
Europe and Northern America	100	95	90
Latin America and the Caribbean	62	10	3
Northern Africa and Western Asia	81	69	19
Southern Asia	71	0	0
Sub-Saharan Africa	8	0	0

Source: Barakat et al. (2016).

and learning outcomes are lacking, and data coverage across countries and over time is limited. Some research has used learning outcome data from international assessments. But the conclusions so far are tentative and only relevant for a limited set of outcomes, such as economic growth. If, for example, education helps people live longer, then better education is likely to have an even larger effect on life expectancy. However, there is insufficient evidence to quantify the effect of improved education quality on other outcomes. The results presented below should therefore be seen as representing a lower limit of the potential effects, which assumes that current education quality levels will continue. If quality improves, as the 2030 Agenda intends, the effects could be stronger.

This section examines the effects of education in three sets of relationships: with infant and child mortality (SDG 3.2) and adult life expectancy (related to SDG 3.3 and SDG 3.4); with aggregate national economic growth (related to SDG 8.1 and SDG 8.2) and extreme poverty (SDG 1.1); and with disaster vulnerability (related to SDG 1.5, SDG 11.5 and SDG 13.1). Yet, it is clear these analyses form a small part of a larger sustainability picture.

EDUCATION CAN HELP SAVE MILLIONS OF CHILDREN'S LIVES

Health targets are prominent among the SDGs. Their relationship with education is known to be robust and is relatively well studied (e.g. UNESCO, 2014, and, especially, Lutz et al., 2014, on which the following model is based).

To understand how increased education could reduce infant and child mortality, this analysis looks at the education of women of child-bearing age in 2030 with progress continuing on past trends ('trend scenario') and with SDG target 4.1 being met ('SDG 4.1 scenario') (Table 7.1). To isolate the potential additional contribution of

education, the analysis assumes that current fertility and mortality trends continue.

In the SDG 4.1 scenario, very few women of child-bearing age with low education would be left at the end of the next 15 years. The effects are studied for 2030 and 2050, since women who complete their schooling in about 2030 will have most of their children in the following two decades. Indeed, the education effect will continue to grow between 2030 and 2050, even in absolute terms, despite the fact that overall mortality levels will be significantly lower towards the end of this period.

Achieving universal secondary schooling would make a meaningful contribution to reducing infant and child mortality. In particular, achieving universal lower secondary education by 2030 would reduce the under-5 mortality rate in sub-Saharan Africa from 68 to 62 deaths per 1,000 live births by 2030 and from 51 to 44 by 2050. Achieving universal upper secondary education by 2030 would lower the under-5 mortality rate further to 54 deaths by 2030 and to 38 deaths by 2050 (**Figure 7.3**). With an estimated 25 million children expected to be born in the region in 2050 under the SDG scenario, this would be equivalent to 300,000–350,000 fewer child deaths per year in 2050. Without additional education expansion, as according to the trend scenario, however, the decline in child mortality in sub-Saharan Africa may well begin to slow.

Some evidence shows that children's health can benefit from community-level effects and the general diffusion of healthy practices and behaviour, which in turn suggests that improvements in child mortality would be greater than those suggested by simply improving women's education.

While these effects appear moderate, it should not be forgotten that the trend scenario, which assumes education attainment continues to grow at past rates, already entails significant education expansion. Moreover, much of the additional expansion implied by the SDG target scenario occurs at the upper secondary and post-secondary levels, while the largest gains in terms of child health come with increases in the primary and lower secondary attainment rates, which are already high in most regions. Therefore, much of the global benefit of education with relation to child mortality has already taken effect, with most of the remaining benefit expected in sub-Saharan Africa.

Another potential health contribution of achieving target 4.1 is to raise the average life expectancy at age 15 between 2030 and 2050. Yet, despite significant variance in life expectancy at different education levels, even in high income countries, the change to overall life expectancy would be marginal in most regions due to the short time horizon and modest increases in a population with a given level of educational attainment. Even in sub-Saharan Africa, the cohort that would benefit from universal secondary education will not have reached ages of high mortality even by 2050. Indeed, robust studies highlighting the strong impact of education on life expectancy have used cohorts in high income countries born in the 1940s (Lager and Torssander, 2012), underlining the long time-frame needed to demonstrate an education effect on life expectancy.

EDUCATION CAN CHANGE THE COURSE OF ECONOMIC DEVELOPMENT IN POOR COUNTRIES

The economic effects of education have been among the most widely studied (Krueger and Lindahl, 2001). Of particular interest in connection with the SDGs is the role of education in increasing aggregate economic growth and reducing extreme poverty.

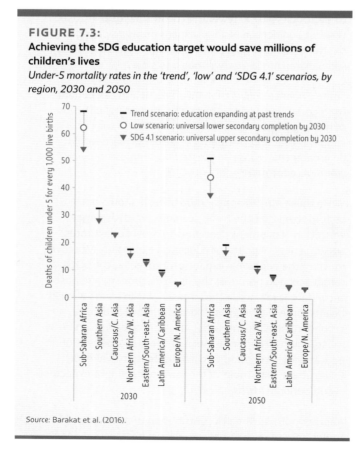

FIGURE 7.3:
Achieving the SDG education target would save millions of children's lives
Under-5 mortality rates in the 'trend', 'low' and 'SDG 4.1' scenarios, by region, 2030 and 2050

Source: Barakat et al. (2016).

Economic growth gains can be enormous in low income countries

Improvement in human capital is assumed to have two distinct effects on income per capita. First, it increases labour productivity. Second, it spurs technological development and adoption, which in turn increases the productivity of all factors of production.

Yet, as with health effects, the effects of education on the economy take time to materialize. Young people who benefit from education expansion in the next 15 years need to enter the labour force in significant numbers before their additional human capital can make an impact. This will occur long after 2030. In middle income countries, the additional growth from achieving universal secondary education by 2030 would likely be small, because many of these countries already have relatively high and increasing levels of participation in secondary education – even under the trend scenario.

In low income countries, though, universalizing upper secondary completion would lead to an increase in per capita income of 75% by 2050. Universal lower secondary completion would account for about half of the gain. However, this again understates the contribution of education expansion, as significant education growth is expected in the baseline trend scenario.

Expanding education can have a drastic effect on poverty reduction

To estimate the impact of increased educational attainment on poverty reduction as achieved through national economic growth, assumptions are necessary on how sensitive poverty rates are to growth rates (Ravallion, 2012).

While accelerated education expansion can make a sizeable contribution to overall growth, meeting target 4.1 might not contribute much to eliminating extreme poverty. In the poorest countries, however, achieving universal secondary education by 2030 could bring poverty elimination forward by 10 years, even if it is insufficient to eliminate extreme poverty altogether by 2030. In particular, the poverty headcount rate in low income countries – the proportion of the population living below the poverty line of US$1.25 at 2005 purchasing power parity – would be 24% in the SDG 4.1 scenario instead of 28% in the trend scenario by 2030, and 2% instead of 9% by 2050 (**Figure 7.4**). With 875 million people expected to be living in low income countries in 2050 under the SDG scenario this would correspond to more than 60 million fewer million

FIGURE 7.4:
Universal upper secondary completion by 2030 could lift millions out of poverty by 2050 in low income countries

Poverty headcount rate in low income countries under four education expansion scenarios, 2030 and 2050

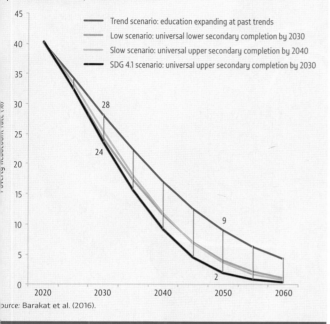

Trend scenario: education expanding at past trends
Low scenario: universal lower secondary completion by 2030
Slow scenario: universal upper secondary completion by 2040
SDG 4.1 scenario: universal upper secondary completion by 2030

Source: Barakat et al. (2016).

the more educated tend to exhibit greater awareness of risks, a higher degree of preparation and appropriate responses, and smaller average losses when disaster does strike. Although it is argued that natural disasters strike indiscriminately, disaster risk reduction assumes that information and preparedness can make a difference to the survival and livelihoods of individuals and communities.

Human-induced climate change is likely to increase the frequency, intensity and severity of extreme climate events such as heat waves and heavy precipitation, and cause rising sea levels (IPCC, 2014). Analyses carried out for the GEM Report examine how different rates of progress in education affect the numbers of deaths from extreme climate events and other natural catastrophes, including storms, floods, droughts and landslides (Lutz et al., 2014) The model uses past information on the relationship between education and disaster deaths (from the Emergency Events Database EM 2010) as a basis for forecasts of changes in disaster deaths in coming decades.

The findings show, for example, about 250,000 disaster-related deaths over 2000–2010. If trends in education continue at the current pace (which will reduce disaster deaths), but the frequency of natural disasters increases by 20%, the number of disaster-related deaths will remain at this high level to mid-century and beyond. If, however, the pace of education expansion quickens, and universal secondary education is achieved by 2030, then by 2040–2050 there will be 10,000 to 20,000 fewer disaster-related deaths per decade at constant disaster frequency, and 30,000 to 50,000 fewer deaths in a scenario of increased disaster frequency. Increased secondary education in Asia would have an especially strong impact on the predicted global pattern, as the continent is home to some of the largest populations, many of whom reside in coastal areas where most disasters occur. In short, meeting the SDG 4.1 challenge to achieve universal primary and secondary education could significantly help countries combat climate change and its impact (SDG 13).

people in poverty. Most of the difference is accounted for by increases in secondary rather than post-secondary attainment.

EDUCATION'S EFFECTS ON CLIMATE CHANGE ADAPTATION CAN REDUCE DISASTER-RELATED DEATHS

There are various links between education and climate change. On the one hand, while the more educated may be more supportive of institutional reforms and interventions aimed at climate change mitigation, educated people tend to have higher incomes and consume more resources, which is likely to increase emissions and global warming. Estimating these relationships using current models is not possible.

On the other hand, evidence shows that those with higher education levels are less vulnerable and more resilient to natural disasters. While comprehensive data on people's education levels in disaster-prone situations are rare, current information suggests that

Girls wash their hands outside their classroom in the government-run United Methodist School in Freetown, Sierra Leone. Schools throughout Sierra Leone, including this one, were closed for eight months at the height of the Ebola crisis.

CREDIT: Kate Holt/GEM Report

8

Education and sustainable development: conclusions and policy recommendations

KEY MESSAGES

For education to be transformative in support of the new sustainable development agenda, 'education as usual' will not suffice.

Collaborate across sectors: Include ministries, civil society, the private sector, at the local and national level.

Use education as a capacity-building tool in all sectors. Invest in integrated interventions that will have multiplier effects for several development outcomes.

Education cannot fight inequality on its own. Labour markets and governments must not excessively penalize lower income individuals. Cross sectoral cooperation can reduce barriers to gender equality.

Education funding needs to be both adequate and predictable to ensure the provision of good quality education, especially to marginalized groups.

PLANET: A whole-school approach is needed to build green skills and awareness. Campaigns, companies, as well as community and religious leaders must advocate for sustainability practices. Non-formal education and research and development should also help solve global environmental challenges.

PROSPERITY: Invest in teaching green and transferable skills in school and the workplace. Incentivize universities and agricultural extension to focus on green economic growth and sustainable agricultural production. Promote cooperation across all sectors to encourage full economic participation by women or minority groups.

PEOPLE: Ensure universal access to basic services. , Support the integration of marginalized groups by investing in early childhood care and education, social protection programmes and awareness campaigns. Fund integrated delivery of basic services in schools.

PEACE: Expand education on global citizenship, peace, inclusion and resilience to conflict. Emphasize participatory teaching and learning especially in civic education. Invest in qualified teachers for refugees and displaced people, and teach children in their mother language. Incorporate education into the peacebuilding agenda.

PLACE: Distribute public resources equitably in urban areas, involving the community in education planning. Include education in all discussions on urban development. Improve and fund urban planning programmes and curricula to include cross-sector engagement and develop locally-relevant solutions.

PARTNERSHIPS: Develop equitable funding mechanisms. Use progressive public finance policies to fund lower levels of education; combine grants and loans to finance upper levels of education. Increase multilateral aid mechanisms and engagement with the private sector. Mobilize domestic resources by improving knowledge about tax systems, halting tax evasion, and eliminating fossil fuel subsidies.

The 2030 Agenda for Sustainable Development grew out of intensifying concerns over the health of the planet and the prosperity of all its inhabitants. Clearly, education matters for people and planet. It transforms the lives of children, youth and adults. The fact that education is a positive force for social, economic and environmental change – that it can significantly influence how we think, perceive and act – is neither new nor revolutionary. And yet important questions remain: How does education function to create societal change? In what contexts does it matter more or less? Which types of education have lasting impact on sustainability issues? Answers to these questions are critical as concrete proposals for improving economic, social and environmental sustainability are being considered.

> "
> **There are concerns that evolving global conditions may weaken the impact of education**
> "

They are particularly salient in places where widespread access to schooling is a recent achievement or remains an ambition.

The preceding chapters – *Planet, Prosperity, People, Peace and Place* – have showcased evidence about the many and varied effects of education. The benefits of completing primary and secondary education are substantial, not only for the individuals involved but also for their families, communities and workplaces. Adult men and women who have completed some secondary education tend to be more environmentally aware, more resilient to the impact of climate change, more productive and able to generate income, and more likely to live healthier lives, be politically engaged and exercise greater control over their lives. The effects of broadening access to girls and women, in particular, are numerous and intergenerational.

The *Projections* chapter goes one step further and underscores the stakes involved in universalizing primary and secondary education by 2030. Enabling every child in the world to complete 12 years of schooling would not only catalyse education progress more broadly (e.g. in many targets of the education goal, Sustainable Development Goal 4), but would also help save millions of lives among children who might not otherwise reach age 5 and among those residing in disaster-prone areas. It would also improve overall worker productivity and economic growth.

Concern exists, however, that evolving global conditions – social, economic, political and environmental – may weaken the impact of education. Over the past two centuries, the world economy has been massively transformed through industrialization, mechanization, computerization, innovation and globalization, the latest iteration resulting in today's 'knowledge economies'. These transformations have created enormous wealth for some and, in many instances, helped expand sizeable middle classes. At the same time, huge populations throughout the world have been left behind, their lives and livelihoods remaining vulnerable to economic dislocation or persistent poverty or both. The vicissitudes of economic cycles, which often exacerbate political insecurity and violent conflict, have forced millions of families and even whole communities to relocate under difficult circumstances.

Despite challenges, the worldwide movement to universalize a long cycle of education and improve learning levels gathers steam. These aspirations are deeply embedded in the aims, policies and plans of almost all countries, regardless of population, location and degree of development. Education, which historically served elite interests, has been made more accessible, expanded into national systems that seek to provide all students, even those in hard-to-reach locations and marginalized groups, with the opportunity to become educated and skilled. The aim of good quality education for all has become the norm, driving national commitments and the activities of international agencies and external donors, bolstered by human rights conventions.

If it were to be achieved, the new global education goal would mean that each and every child, regardless of birth circumstances, would have a chance to acquire valuable knowledge, skills and attitudes that could improve the quality of their lives from personal, civic, social and employment-related perspectives. But the scale of the challenge is pronounced: 263 million children and adolescents are currently excluded from primary and secondary education and unable to acquire relevant skills and competencies for life and work. Education's many benefits now go disproportionately to some individuals at the expense of others. The ones who are far less likely to reap them include people who face discrimination, are unhealthy, lack access to basic services and live in remote or sparsely populated areas.

The *Global Education Monitoring Report* (GEM Report) emphasizes the inequity and unsustainability of global and national economies, and the various roles education plays in this respect. Modern economic systems have increased the value of and demand for educated labour, especially as a source of innovation-led economic growth. Economic benefits and social status accrue to those with credentialed knowledge and skills, leaving behind huge numbers of people who may never have had access to school or to lifelong learning opportunities and who therefore face persistent obstacles in obtaining decent work or escaping from working poverty.

From a sustainability perspective, the world's wealthy, with their high levels of education and standards of living, leave large ecological footprints and make the planet less sustainable. Educated people may have considerable knowledge about environmental and other progressive issues, but do not always act on it. Education and qualifications do not necessarily translate into desirable outcomes, such as greater tolerance for diversity, respect for women and men, less risky health behaviour, waste prevention, more balanced diets and a commitment to social justice. At the same time, the least educated and most vulnerable contribute little to the planet's burdens. And yet they are most exposed to the impact of climate change and increasingly frequent and severe natural disasters. Inequality in opportunity and living conditions, including in access to education of good quality, are especially visible in our growing cities and urban areas, which has often led to civil unrest and discontent.

Education cannot serve as a cure-all for society's problems. Global social and economic challenges are interdependent, involving sectors beyond education, and education is provided within the context of entrenched social and political institutions that are resistant to change. Radical transformation of how and what we consume and produce, and of the basis for sharing economic rewards, requires commitments that must cross economic sectors and political boundaries. At the same time, education reforms are no quick fix if not reinforced by changes in the home, workplace and community that result in altering, for example, stereotypical gender roles or attitudes towards people who face discrimination on any grounds, from ethnicity to disability.

Politics, economics, health, water, sanitation, energy, migration, conflict and climate have direct effects on education systems. Poor air quality or extreme weather can destroy schools, force them to close or make learning nearly impossible. Groups such as people displaced by climate change or conflict, economic migrants and poor slum dwellers can place enormous pressure on education systems. Education is much affected by the context in which it operates.

Yet formal, non-formal and informal education can lay the groundwork for transforming institutions and norms to address today's pressing challenges in tangible ways. Schools can deliver knowledge on sustainability issues and promote good environmental, health and sanitation practices. When designed smartly, and conveyed by well-prepared teachers, school-based programmes can inculcate values of tolerance and equality.

Evidence gathered for this report suggests that education systems do not change quickly, despite well-articulated intentions, since content and pedagogy often reflect deeply set social, economic and environmental norms. And in many instances, schools lack adequate financing for transformation, even if school leaders are committed to this aim.

Several of the GEM Report chapters document a wide range of non-formal and informal learning initiatives, especially targeting girls and women, that fill gaps in useful knowledge – such as how to demand local services or fight for justice – and equip learners for stronger economic and political participation. The report also highlights learning-focused actions by national and local governments, civil society organizations and private companies, recognizing the ways in which education and lifelong learning matter for reducing inequality, encouraging sustainable transport and waste prevention, and both preventing conflict and natural disasters and recuperating from them.

The GEM Report also pays special attention to the importance of developing integrated approaches to solve complex, collective problems. Such strategies align well with key points made in the 2030 Agenda for Sustainable Development. However, the Partnerships chapter finds that the notion of integrated planning, though part of the post-2015 development discourse, still exists mostly on paper and there is limited evidence of its benefits, partly because there is little appetite for difficult collaborative arrangements. Few countries have genuinely pushed for integrated actions to provide, for instance, early childhood development or joint basic services. Without strong political incentives and adequate financial backing, planning and implementation in most contexts will remain in silos. We know the many ways education matters for shaping knowledge, values and attitudes; education and lifelong learning policies targeting all learners of all ages must be given their rightful priority and embedded in integrated national and local planning efforts.

For education to truly be transformative, 'education as usual' will not suffice. Schools need to become exemplary places that breathe sustainability, finding ways to be more inclusive, participatory and healthy, as well as carbon-neutral and producing no waste and pollution. Formal and non-formal learning needs to foster thinking that is more relational, integrative, empathic, anticipatory and systemic.

POLICY RECOMMENDATIONS

Keeping all of the above discussion in mind, the GEM Report presents general and specific policy recommendations for how education systems can more effectively contribute to sustainable development:

■ Support collaborations and synergies across all sectors and partners. Since systemic problems require multiple actors and diverse perspectives, stronger efforts are needed to involve all partners at the local and national level and across sectors. Finance and planning ministries need to engage in more systemic planning. Education ministries should be better linked with ministries of health, gender, environment and labour. Education experts need to learn from and work with civil society and communities, which already carry out an impressive array of education and training. Stronger focus is required on cross-sector collaboration and integrated perspectives in the activities of civil society and the private sector, as well as in urban planning and research and development strategies. The private sector, civil society, multiple sectors of government activity and international actors should work together to fund various facets of education, since education matters for all aspects of sustainable development.

■ Integrate formal and non-formal education and training into government efforts to tackle complex problems. Education can be an important tool for capacity-building in all public sectors. Many of the Sustainable Development Goal targets will require the specialized skills and expertise education can provide, for instance in water management or addressing global health and climate risks. The case for education interventions should focus on both immediate and longer-term cross-sector benefits that education solutions can provide, so that funds additional to those traditionally targeted for education can be used. Governments and other stakeholders also need to better investigate and invest in combinations of integrated interventions that are likely to have multiplier effects for several development outcomes, including education. Investment is particularly needed

> " For education to truly be transformative, 'education as usual' will not suffice "

in low income countries so they can build their own expertise by improving higher education and vocational institutions, as well as informal adult learning initiatives.

■ Education can be an important means of reducing inequality but cannot be seen as the sole solution. Making primary and secondary education of good quality widely accessible can enable large numbers of individuals and their families to raise their incomes above the poverty line. Expanding educational opportunities to marginalized groups and further reducing gender inequality in the school system are crucial to reduce disparity in labour market outcomes, much of which is accounted for by lower levels of attainment. Policy-makers must ensure that changes in labour market institutions, such as technological progress and easing of labour market restrictions, do not excessively penalize lower income individuals, who are disproportionally employed in lower paying and less secure jobs, often in the informal sector. At the same time, cooperation across all sectors of society and the economy is needed to reduce prejudice and any policy-related obstacles to full economic participation by women and minority groups.

■ Increase the level and predictability of education system financing. Education funding needs to be both adequate and predictable to ensure the provision of good quality primary and secondary education, especially to marginalized groups. This would entail ensuring appropriate inputs and teachers, and transforming school systems to better inculcate values of social and environmental sustainability in addition to a specific set of cognitive skills. Improved financing is also critical to support non-formal and informal learning initiatives instead of waiting for the longer-term effects of formal systems. Such initiatives are often innovative, localized, targeted to adults and capable of helping address pressing issues such as disaster risk resilience and conflict prevention.

> 66
> Education can be an important means of reducing inequality but cannot be seen as the sole solution
> 99

More specifically, stakeholders working to promote the sustainable development agenda should consider the following actions to expand education's focus and create more equitable opportunities for all:

PLANET

In order to lessen environmental degradation and the impact of climate change:

■ Develop whole-school approaches that promote environmental teaching, learning, planning and operations by drawing attention to the ties between the environment, economy and culture.

■ Provide disaster risk-resilience training in schools and equip learners with the means to support communities in times of disasters.

■ Fund efforts to ensure that education infrastructure is resilient to climate change.

■ Engage community elders in curricular development and school governance, produce appropriate learning materials and prepare teachers to teach in mother languages.

■ Promote the value of indigenous livelihoods, traditional knowledge and community-managed or -owned land through actions such as land conservation and locally relevant research.

■ Initiate large-scale awareness campaigns that 'nudge' people to engage in sustainability practices and behaviour.

■ Work with community and religious leaders to spread ideas about environmental stewardship, and incentivize companies that incorporate sustainability into workplace practices.

■ Scale up non-formal education initiatives promoting family planning and maternal well-being.

■ Increase funding of research and development that promote technological innovations in energy, agriculture and food systems.

PROSPERITY

In order to reduce poverty and stimulate green and inclusive economies:

- Invest in teaching green skills in formal and non-formal programmes. Coordinate green-focused curricula through cooperation between education and training systems, policy-makers and industry.

- Train and support teachers and instructors at all education levels and in the workplace to enable learners to acquire green skills.

- Ensure universal access to good quality education that emphasizes skills and competencies for entry into economically productive, environmentally sustainable industries.

- Develop short-term strategies focused on workforce retraining and upskilling, together with longer-term strategies to improve or revise curricula in secondary education, initial higher education and vocational training.

- Incentivize universities to produce graduates and researchers who address large-scale systemic challenges through creative thinking and problem-solving.

- Promote cooperation across all sectors to reduce policy-related obstacles to full economic participation by women or minority groups, as well as discrimination and prejudice that also act as barriers.

PEOPLE

In order to ensure that all human beings can fulfil their potential in dignity and equality and in a healthy environment:

- Target marginalized groups consistently left behind by adequately redistributing existing resources and ramping up funds to improve access to good quality education.

- Support strong investment in early childhood care and education, especially for infants and toddlers, who gain lifelong benefits from participation in integrated interventions combining stimulation with health care and nutrition supplementation.

- Promote partnerships between education ministries and ministries responsible for health, water and sanitation, and gender issues, to help simultaneously improve multiple, linked and connected outcomes.

> **All schools should provide meals, access to water and sanitation, adequate gender-specific toilets and child-friendly spaces**

- Fund integrated delivery of basic services in schools. Ensure that all schools provide meals, access to water and sanitation, adequate gender-specific toilets and child-friendly spaces, and can deliver curricular interventions focused on behavioural change, such as hygiene education, sexual and reproductive health education, and obesity prevention education.

- Provide awareness campaigns and training to boost innovation in service delivery, such as e-government and participatory budgeting.

- Fund community-oriented education and training programmes in relation to health and sanitation.

- Ensure all girls complete primary and secondary education to promote their autonomy and decision-making abilities.

- Invest in programmes that address gender stereotypes and roles by engaging men and women in group education sessions, youth-led campaigns and multipronged empowerment approaches.

- Support media-based awareness campaigns, the development of positive role models and other initiatives to change gender norms inside and outside the education system.

- Support efforts to improve participation of girls and women in science, technology, arts and design, and mathematics so as to improve employment prospects.

- Support social protection programmes, health policies and child-care support that improve maternal education and facilitate men's and women's employment-related decision-making.

PEACE

In order to foster peaceful, just and inclusive societies that are free from fear and violence:

- Expand the emphasis on global citizenship and peace education in curricula.

- Invest in civic education programmes that contribute to a functioning justice system, including participation and access for marginalized communities.

- Promote learning emphasizing the values of tolerance and peace education to help build less violent and more constructive societies.

- Teach in children's mother languages. Countries with high proportions of minorities should consider training teachers in methods for teaching second-language learners, in both initial teacher training and professional development.

- For refugees and internally displaced persons, implement policies that expand the pool of qualified teachers proficient in their languages, and address the issue of official validation and certification of learning by refugees. Refugees who were teachers in their home countries could be an important resource.

- Incorporate education into official foreign policy, transitional justice efforts and the peacebuilding agenda when trying to prevent and recover from conflict situations.

- Ensure curricula and learning materials are not biased or prejudiced against ethnic and minority groups. Engender resilience in students and communities in post-conflict societies through curricula, teacher training, transitional justice programmes and supporting integrated schools.

- Fund civil society organizations and other institutions that provide legal and political education in communities.

PLACE

In order to foster sustainable, inclusive and prosperous cities and other human settlements:

- Ensure urban areas distribute public resources equitably, including amenities and good quality teachers, so as to promote social inclusion and reduce inequality resulting from education disparity.

- Take steps to halt segregation stemming from increased opportunities to choose between public and private schools.

- Work to reduce school-based violence, including gender violence, and discriminatory attitudes among teachers.

- Develop local autonomy and localized system-wide education planning, especially in populous African and Asian cities, considering education as a local as well as national issue.

- Better incorporate education into local, national and global agendas focused on improving cities and other human settlements.

- Educate and engage with those who are disenfranchised, include them in planning, and collaborate with civil society actors who work with them.

- Fund schools and training programmes for slum dwellers and other disadvantaged groups who live in absolute poverty, so that assistance for them is not limited to basic services such as housing and water and sanitation.

- Fund urban planning education to increase the numbers of planners, and promote integration of education as well as multidisciplinary approaches.

- Improve urban planning curricula to include cross-sector engagement, community engagement, learning by doing and the development of locally relevant solutions.

- Involve communities in any processes to consolidate and improve schools in rural and other areas affected by population declines due to migration.

- Monitor and address any unintended consequences of the growth of knowledge economies, such as gentrification and middle class flight, with strong economic and housing policies to limit social segregation and societal discontent.

> We should educate and engage with those who are disenfranchised, and include them in urban planning

PARTNERSHIPS

In order to ensure adequate financing, policy coherence and multisector capacity:

- Make links with tax authorities and others to improve tax-related knowledge through formal education.

- Develop equitable funding mechanisms to address in-country disparities in education funding.

- Use progressive public finance policies to ensure adequate funding of lower levels of education, and combine public allocations and a well-designed system of student grants and loans to finance upper levels of technical, vocational and tertiary education.

- Increase multilateral aid mechanisms and engagement with the private sector, learning from health sector efforts to increase and diversify funding.

- Mobilize domestic resources, stop corporate tax evasion and eliminate fossil fuel subsidies to generate government revenue for fundamental needs such as education and health.

- Provide political and financial support for planning and implementation of education and other activities to be carried out with an integrated approach to policy and development at the national and local levels. Develop knowledge exchange programmes to learn from successful integrated policies involving education.

- Support multistakeholder governance for the sustainable management of natural resources and of public and semi-public rural, urban and peri-urban spaces.

Vang Seo Phu, a
9-year-old Hmong,
during a math
class at PS La Pan
Tẩn, Viet Nam.

CREDIT: Nguyen Thanh Tuan/UNESCO

9

The challenges of monitoring education in the Sustainable Development Goals

Ensure inclusive and equitable quality education and promote lifelong learning opportunities for all

KEY MESSAGES

Sustainable Development Goal 4 (SDG 4) and its 10 targets represent the vision and aspirations of the global education community for 2030. Their ambition goes beyond any previous global education agreement.

Monitoring progress towards SDG 4 is critical to show what needs to be done, by when and by whom.

The *Global Education Monitoring Report* has a mandate outlined in the Incheon Declaration and the Education 2030 Framework for Action to monitor and report on SDG 4 and on education in the other SDGs.

Many important concepts in the 10 SDG 4 targets are not yet covered by any proposed indicator. Among those that are covered, several details remain to be fixed in the indicators, and this report aims to inform the debate.

The ambition of SDG 4 is reflected in its focus on improvements in education *outcomes*, such as learning achievement; *access* at post-basic education levels, including upper secondary and tertiary education; its *lifelong learning* perspective, including adult education; the reduction of *disparity* in education based on factors such as wealth, gender and location; and changes in the *content* of education to better align it with the challenges of sustainable development.

There is a huge task ahead for national statistical systems to monitor progress towards SDG 4 and for education ministries to make effective use of the new information.

The 17 Sustainable Development Goals (SDGs) reflect the heart of the 2030 Agenda for Sustainable Development. Goal 4, which focuses on education within a lifelong learning perspective, represents the vision and aspirations of the global education community for 2030. With its seven targets and three means of implementation, the fourth SDG represents a level of ambition for the next 15 years that goes beyond any previous global education agreement. Education is also part of all the other SDGs to some extent.

Developing a solid platform for reviewing and monitoring progress on the SDGs is crucial to their success. It will help inform national governments where headway has been made and where more attention is needed. It will also help intergovernmental and non-government organizations (NGOs) understand what actions should be taken at the global, regional and national levels. It is worth noting, however, that the very concept of monitoring the SDGs is more strongly contested than was the case for the Millennium Development Goals (MDGs), which were perceived to be more top-down. Finalizing the overall architecture for monitoring all 17 goals and 169 targets with measurable indicators will take time.

This part of the 2016 *Global Education Monitoring Report* presents the challenges of monitoring progress on education in the 2030 agenda with a particular focus on SDG 4 and its targets. It critically analyses each target and the respective indicators. What concepts are to be monitored in each target? What indicators are best suited to the task? Are the indicators already being measured? If so, what baselines can be determined? If indicators are not yet measured or defined, what are the technical challenges and steps needed to develop measurement tools? The discussion also provides critical analysis of both the broad technical challenges of monitoring 10 sometimes poorly formulated, targets, and the specific demands of developing valid, reliable and comparable measurement tools for new indicators. It also examines the policy implications of choosing particular measurement tools.

> 66
>
> The monitoring part of this Report presents the challenges of tracking progress on education in the 2030 Agenda
>
> 99

Against this background, the following chapters ask what the priorities are for global education monitoring, and where countries and organizations need to focus resources. They examine the institutional, political and technical context within which indicators will be measured. They also analyse the tools and mechanisms necessary to monitor the components of the agenda, both looking at existing ones to ask whether they can be made more efficient or used more effectively, and identifying the scope for new ones. These chapters aim to facilitate the discussions needed to reach consensus, as a broader agenda means more issues to resolve and stakeholders to involve.

REACHING CONSENSUS ON THE POST-2015 EDUCATION TARGETS

In the years and months leading up to the UN General Assembly decision on the post-2015 development agenda, it was not known that a standalone global education goal would be proposed and adopted. Some countries and development experts preferred to see education combined with or subsumed under other goals in the interest of a more concise agenda.

Yet, the *EFA Global Monitoring Report* had shown that education is necessary for the achievement of other development outcomes (UNESCO, 2014a). And education had considerable popular support around the world. It emerged as the top priority among the more than 7 million people who contributed to the United Nations' MY World survey of 2015.

Since 2000, the international education agenda had been split into two processes: the Education for All (EFA) goals and the MDG agenda. The EFA goals were broader in scope, covered most education levels and had participatory mechanisms. The narrower MDG agenda focused on universal primary completion and gender parity in education, and was characterized by relatively top-down governance arrangements. It was not clear whether these approaches would merge after 2015 or remain distinct.

Initially, there were concerns that the SDG education agenda would be as narrow as its MDG predecessor. In November 2012, the Global EFA Meeting in Paris emphasized the importance of 'ensuring that EFA and the international development goals are coherent and mutually reinforcing' (UNESCO, 2012a; p.4). This assumed that two parallel agendas would continue to exist; it was not then evident that EFA would be subsumed under the SDGs. The main EFA coordination body, the EFA Steering Committee, therefore worked towards a set of targets, which education ministries of a large number of countries endorsed through the Muscat Declaration at the Global EFA Meeting in Muscat in May 2014 (UNESCO, 2014b).

Concurrently, the intergovernmental Open Working Group (OWG) process in New York, which member states had established in January 2013 to propose the SDGs, was advancing (see Introduction). UNESCO and its EFA partners had to draw member states' attention to the targets in the Muscat Declaration, which eventually was just one input (albeit timely and influential) into the OWG process that helped determine the formulation of targets in the OWG outcome document (United Nations, 2014a).

This cumbersome process meant the OWG outcome document, a product of delicate political negotiations, was written in language that was sometimes unclear and ambiguous. Member states did not want to disrupt the balance, so at the World Education Forum in Incheon, Republic of Korea, in May 2015, they simply approved the OWG targets.

> 66
> The Open Working Group outcome document was written in a language that was sometimes unclear and ambiguous
> 99

The forum opened the discussion on the Education 2030 Framework for Action, the document that elaborates key concepts and outlines implementation strategies for SDG 4. The framework was officially endorsed in November 2015 in Paris. Its extended commentary on issues ranging from teachers and finance to monitoring indicators and mechanisms is the basis upon which much of this report is built (UNESCO, 2015b).

DIFFERENCES BETWEEN THE EFA GOALS, THE MDGS AND THE SDGS

The SDGs, unlike the MDGs, bring the four pillars of sustainable development (economic, social, environmental and institutional) under an integrated framework. The process that resulted in the SDGs was more transparent and open. Countries, rather than UN agencies, led the negotiations. The consensus meant the final product was less elegant and concise, having to accommodate many interests. But there is a stronger sense that the SDGs apply to all countries and are not being dictated by rich countries to poor countries. The MDGs were focused on developing countries exclusively, whereas the SDGs are universally applicable.

The SDG education targets are stronger than the MDGs in various ways. They draw upon the comprehensive and holistic vision of the EFA movement. They recognize that different levels of education cannot be addressed in isolation from one another. While the EFA goals sought to ensure equal access to good quality basic education, the SDG targets shift attention to higher levels (e.g. universal secondary completion, equal access to tertiary education) and broader content, such as

> The SDG education targets are stronger than the Millennium Development Goals in various ways

skills in information and communication technology and education for sustainable development and global citizenship. There is also a separate target on ensuring teachers are well qualified, a key condition for quality education and learning outcomes. The SDG education targets are also more oriented to outcomes and more closely aligned with a lifelong learning framework.

On the other hand, they are more ambitious, some would say too much so. For example, it was generally expected that target 4.1 would focus on universal lower secondary education, but instead it extended to upper secondary. While there are strong reasons to raise aspirations, this report shows that the expanded target is unattainable. At past rates of progress, even universal primary completion is not guaranteed by 2030.

REACHING CONSENSUS ON EDUCATION MONITORING INDICATORS AND MECHANISMS

Monitoring progress towards achievement of the targets is critical to provide guidance for what needs to be done, by when and by whom. However, the SDG process for determining monitoring indicators and mechanisms is complex and political. This is unsurprising given the large number of targets, the ambiguities in their formulation and the diversity of stakeholders. To better understand the proposed education monitoring indicators and mechanisms, the process through which the overall SDG monitoring indicators and mechanisms were adopted is described below.

Indicators

The Synthesis Report of the UN Secretary-General on the Post-2015 Agenda, released in December 2014, offers a useful framework to understand the layers of monitoring required (United Nations, 2014b). The report identified four levels, each of which has distinct implications for indicator selection:

■ **Global:** To monitor the 17 goals and 169 targets, globally comparable indicators are needed. Countries would commit to report on them and the results would appear in an annual SDG Report that would succeed the MDG Report.

■ **Thematic:** The scope of a set of global indicators that aims to capture the entire development agenda will be unlikely to fully satisfy the needs of communities interested in specific goals and themes. An additional set of globally comparable indicators is therefore needed for individual targets within goals such as education.

■ **Regional:** Some indicators may not be globally relevant but are essential for regional constituencies to respond to specific contexts and policy priorities.

■ **National:** Every country has its own context and priorities, which call for tailored monitoring and reporting mechanisms.

The UN Statistical Commission established the Inter-agency and Expert Group on SDG Indicators (IAEG-SDGs) in March 2015 to develop global indicators for monitoring the new goals and targets. The commission agreed a list of indicators in March 2016 as a first step before endorsement by the Economic and Social Council in July 2016 and adoption by the General Assembly in September.

However, it is widely recognized that further methodological work is needed. The expert group has classified the proposed indicators into three tiers, depending on whether established methodology and sufficient data coverage exist. It will work until March 2017 on a plan for further development of indicators without established methodology. It will also agree on a global reporting mechanism and identify the entities to be responsible for compiling data for reporting on individual indicators.

For the education goal, 11 global indicators have been agreed, based on an original submission by UNESCO and UNICEF, co-chairs of the Technical Support Team for SDG 4. There is one indicator per target except in the case of Target 4.2, for which two are proposed. Four are identified as tier I indicators ('established methodology … and data regularly produced by countries'), three as tier II indicators ('established methodology … but data are not regularly produced by countries'), two as tier III indicators ('no established methodology') and two have been classified at multiple levels (IAEG-SDGs, 2016).

The 11 global indicators do not by any means capture the full scope of the agenda. Hence UNESCO set up a Technical Advisory Group on post-2015 education indicators to prepare consolidated recommendations on measurement of an education goal, targets and indicators. Its proposed 43 thematic indicators, which include the 11 global indicators, were incorporated in the Education 2030 Framework for Action as an annex.

In order to implement and develop the thematic monitoring framework, the Technical Advisory Group has become the Technical Cooperation Group (TCG) on the Indicators for SDG4-Education 2030, co-convened by the UNESCO Institute for Statistics (UIS) and the UNESCO Division of Education 2030 Support and Coordination. Its objective is to promote the production of necessary data at the country level to enable the reporting of cross-nationally comparable measures.

The TCG mimics some of the features of the IAEG-SDGs. For example, it includes the 28 countries of the IAEG-SDGs as members. In addition, at its first meeting in May 2016, the TCG discussed a classification of indicators like the one used by the IAEG-SDGs. As part of this process, it identified eight tier III indicators that need further work, either because they are not sufficiently aligned with the concept or because implementation challenges are envisaged (UIS, 2016d).

Mechanisms

Transforming Our World: The 2030 Agenda for Sustainable Development, the foundation document of the post-2015 era, expresses member states' clear intention to take a stronger role in monitoring mechanisms. This accountability for achievement of international goals is built on a commitment to a 'robust, voluntary, effective, participatory, transparent and integrated follow-up and review framework' to 'track progress in implementing this Agenda' (United Nations, 2015c; §72). Details of these mechanisms were spelled out in the UN Secretary-General's report on 'critical milestones' in January 2016 (United Nations, 2016) and are expected to be adopted through a General Assembly resolution.

At the global level, the High-Level Political Forum (HLPF) on Sustainable Development is the UN platform for follow-up and review of the 2030 agenda. It will be held every four years under the auspices of the General Assembly and in the intervening years under the auspices of the Economic and Social Council. Its mandate is to provide political leadership, guidance and recommendations on implementation and follow-up, keep track of progress and encourage coherent policies informed by evidence, science and country experiences, as well as address new and emerging issues.

Two documents will support the HLPF global follow-up and review process. First, the annual SDG Report will be prepared by the Secretary-General, in cooperation with the UN system and based on the global indicator framework. A glossy variant for the wider public follows the model of the MDG Report prepared by the UN Department of Economic and Social Affairs since 2005. UNESCO is the reporting agency for SDG 4.

Second, a *Global Sustainable Development Report* will provide 'a strong evidence-based instrument to support policymakers in promoting poverty eradication and sustainable development' (United Nations, 2015c; §83). A first edition was published in July 2015. Originally conceived as an annual document, it is now expected to be published every four years, when the HLPF is held under General Assembly auspices.

Each year, the HLPF is expected to carry out at least two sets of reviews. First, there will be voluntary national reviews of countries' contributions to the agenda, and for the first time a platform will be offered to other stakeholders, such as NGOs, to do the same. Second, there will be thematic reviews of progress. In the July 2016 HLPF, the selected cross-cutting theme was 'Ensuring that no one is left behind'. In each of the next three years, the theme will be linked to a set of goals, ensuring that all goals are reviewed over the course of a four-year cycle. Education is scheduled for review in 2019 under the theme 'Empowering people and ensuring inclusiveness'; health, gender, inequality, and peaceful and inclusive societies will also be covered then.

At the thematic level, it is envisaged that global follow-up and review mechanisms will 'build on existing platforms and processes, where these exist' (United Nations, 2015c; §74f). The HLPF is the apex of a network of follow-up and review processes and its thematic reviews should be supported by intergovernmental bodies and forums, 'where much of the real discussion, analysis and eventual follow-up must take place' (Halle and Wolfe, 2016, p.3).

In the case of education, the Secretary-General's January 2016 report identified the World Education Forum as one intergovernmental mechanism upon which the global follow-up and review process should build. The forum, in its Incheon Declaration, requested 'an independent *Global Education Monitoring Report* (GEMR), hosted and published by UNESCO, as the mechanism for monitoring and reporting on the proposed SDG 4 and on education

> ## "
> The Incheon Declaration requested an independent Global Education Monitoring Report, hosted and published by UNESCO, for monitoring SDG 4
> "

in the other proposed SDGs, within the mechanism to be established to monitor and review the implementation of the proposed SDGs' (UNESCO, 2015b; §18). The report had already been identified as a follow up and review mechanism in a United Nations Technical Support Team inventory (United Nations, 2015b).

As the World Education Forum was convened only three times between 1990 and 2015, the Education 2030 Framework for Action identified the SDG4–Education 2030 Steering Committee as the main global coordination body supporting member states and partners in achieving Education 2030. The committee will 'provide strategic guidance, review progress drawing on the GEMR, and make recommendations to the education community on key priorities and catalytic actions to achieve the new agenda; monitor and advocate for adequate financing; and encourage harmonization and coordination of partner activities' (UNESCO, 2015b; §94). The framework also reiterates the mandate of the report, including as a mechanism for monitoring 'the implementation of national and international strategies to help hold all relevant partners to account for their commitments' (UNESCO, 2015b; §101).

OPPORTUNITIES AND CHALLENGES IN GLOBAL EDUCATION MONITORING AND THE ROLE OF THE GEM REPORT

The global follow-up and review, together with the thematic, education-specific monitoring and reporting mechanisms, are an elaborate set of new processes that will be developed in coming years. The *Global Education Monitoring Report* (GEM Report) has a recognized mandate to help the international community, through established structures and channels, to understand whether and how the world

is making progress in education. But while the report is seen as having fulfilled its mandate during the EFA period, the more complex new agenda will require adjustments (UNESCO, 2016c).

The global education monitoring landscape is rapidly changing with the expanded scope of the sustainable development agenda. While a set of monitoring indicators has been formulated, the methodology for measuring many of them is yet to be developed. In addition, many indicators only partly cover the concepts that feature in each target. Alternative ways to measure and monitor at the national and regional levels can, and should, also be explored. There is a need for open discussion and debate to help stakeholders move to consensus on establishing a monitoring approach.

The role of the GEM Report is crucial in that respect. Between 2002 and 2015, as the *EFA Global Monitoring Report*, it took a critical look at global progress in education and lifelong learning, using available indicators, questioning their usefulness, reflecting on the quality of sources and introducing new ways of looking at evidence and advocating for improvement. These are functions the new series will continue to carry out in coming years.

The GEM Report recognizes the strengths of measurement and the demand for it – as well as its limits – but also the need for transparency. Indeed, the report team is aware that indicators are not merely technical constructions but also reflect overlapping interests, often of a political nature. Given their potential influence on country efforts, donor assessments and civil society advocacy, the report will carefully scrutinize what indicators are reported and how they are interpreted.

Finally, the monitoring part of this report has acknowledged limitations. While it tries to address the full spectrum of education provision from a global perspective, many, if not most, major issues in education are context-specific and difficult to generalize or compare. Nor is it known to what extent the results of monitoring exercises will help schools facilitate learning environments and teachers improve teaching and learning processes in classrooms. These and related issues cannot be addressed through statistical tables, however well aligned with SDG 4 targets. The GEM Report is intended to provide readers with ways to frame and interpret quantitative evidence supplemented with policy analysis and in-depth exploration of annual themes.

THE LEVEL OF AMBITION IS HIGH, BUT CAUTION IS NEEDED

Overall, the SDG 4 global indicators match the ambition of the agenda and greatly expand the scope of education monitoring. The MDG indicators were narrower, measuring the primary enrolment rate, the survival rate to the last grade of primary school, the adult literacy rate and gender parity.

There is a distinct emphasis in the SDG indicators on outcomes – in other words, the consequences of the experience of education on children, youth and adults. These outcomes include minimum proficiency levels in reading and mathematics, readiness for school and digital literacy skills.

Another change is the clear shift to disaggregation: analysing education participation and outcome indicators by individual demographic and socio-economic characteristics. The only equivalent MDG indicator was the gender parity index in enrolment rates by level of education. The inclusion of other characteristics, notably location and wealth, is a consequence of increasing availability of information sources from school and household surveys in the last two decades, which now permit comparison across countries.

The third change from the MDG indicators is interest in the content of education – in particular, the mainstreaming of education for sustainable development and global citizenship through curricula, textbooks and teacher preparation.

The complementary Education 2030 thematic indicators are better aligned with the concepts in the SDG 4 targets. However, this higher ambition has consequences. It will require major investment of resources and building of capacity at the national level. Many issues

need resolution, from defining the 'participation rate in technical-vocational education programmes' to demonstrating what are 'relevant and effective learning outcomes' in primary and secondary education and an 'adequate understanding of issues relating to global citizenship and sustainability'. Organizational mechanisms need to be established to address such questions and develop tools for measurement. Even as countries begin to agree on definitions and methods, and invest in monitoring capacity, there will be a gap of quite a few years during which there may be no reporting on several global indicators, or limited reporting in terms of country coverage.

> " There will be a gap of quite a few years during which there may be no or limited reporting on several global indicators "

The tasks for national statistical systems in the area of education could be enormous. While some are hopeful that a data revolution will allow poorer countries to leapfrog costly traditional data collection mechanisms, improved coordination and capacity-building will still be needed. Tough decisions will have to be made to prioritize actions and focus on what is most important. Moreover, the proposed indicators, however ambitious, still do not cover the full range of concepts in SDG 4 targets, as the following chapters will show.

A different concern is related to potential unintended consequences of quantitative indicators and international comparisons. Critics believe unchecked use of indicators misleads by oversimplifying reality, discouraging discussion about data quality and distorting priorities. Much of the criticism concerns excessive use of composite indices, which carry particular ideas or theories about what countries should do. The content of such indices is often not openly debated and yet they exert undue influence on policies (Kelley and Simmons, 2015).

Within and beyond the international education community, the generalized use of rankings of schools, higher education institutions and countries is often seen as reducing education to the lowest common denominator. Critics say rankings remove education from its context, ignore content and do not necessarily offer policy-makers sufficient information to work towards improving learning (Goldstein and Moss, 2014). There is also the problem of deriving relevant and informative policy information for a particular case or country from cross-national statistics and patterns.

The challenge is how to make effective use of the kind of information cross-national and comparative education monitoring can provide. For example, an indicator on how many children achieve a minimum level of proficiency in mathematics based on a nationally representative sample should highlight the plight of millions of disadvantaged children, especially in poorer countries. Such is the traditional use of statistics as tools for proof and coordination (Desrosieres, 2010), and it is a far cry from the generalized use of standardized tests that assess each student and evaluate each teacher, as in some high income countries. This report stands ready to bring the best in comparative education measurement while cautioning against the misuse of such information.

OUTLINE OF THE MONITORING PART

The monitoring part of the 2016 GEM Report presents the wide-ranging challenges and debates involving monitoring for the Education 2030 agenda and how countries and the international community can move forward. It is organized into 15 chapters.

The next 10 (Chapters 10–19) look separately at each of the 7 education targets and 3 means of implementation. They identify the concepts that are explicitly or implicitly embedded in the target formulation. Each chapter discusses how the concepts are articulated within the proposed global and thematic indicators. They focus primarily on the extent to which the methodology of the indicators is established, and on identifying tools currently available to collect relevant data.

To the extent that methodology is established and information available for a sufficient number of countries, indicative baseline information is presented. Approaches for monitoring areas not yet covered by the proposed indicators are also discussed. At the same time, it is also too early to provide definitive data for 2015 at the end of the EFA period.

Chapters 20 to 22 address cross-cutting issues. Chapter 20 discusses education finance, for which

there is no dedicated SDG target, though the Education 2030 Framework for Action gives a clear set of recommendations. Using a framework provided by national education accounts, the chapter discusses prospects for better data on public spending, aid and household expenditure. Chapter 21 reflects on the fact that some proposed indicators are about neither inputs nor outcomes but instead relate to growing interest in the role of education systems. It provides an overview of available mechanisms and the scope for better coordination, especially at the regional level. Chapter 22 looks at all targets under other SDG goals, as well as the corresponding global indicators, to identify those where education is mentioned directly or indirectly.

The monitoring part of the GEM Report tries not to be prescriptive but rather to make a timely contribution to the debate on what should be monitored and how. The state of global education monitoring is in flux. Many initiatives are under way to respond to the challenges of the proposed indicator frameworks.

This comprehensive overview of the global education monitoring challenges offers insights, brings together disparate pieces of information and identifies stakeholders whose work needs recognition and coordination. Given that implementing such an agenda may be daunting and confusing, especially for countries, the GEM Report's monitoring part is meant to support countries and partners as they discuss and determine the best steps forward in achieving SDG 4. To conclude, Chapter 23 draws attention to common themes and missing pieces in this discussion – and identifies building blocks and potential synergies for a more effective and efficient global education monitoring agenda over the next 15 years at the national, regional and international levels.

Children peek through a primary school window in Indonesia.

CREDIT: Alland Dharmawan/UNESCO

KEY MESSAGES

Progress towards this target will be a key measure of commitment to the SDGs.

Universal *access* to primary education is far from achieved. As of 2014, about 25 million children worldwide were not expected ever to attend school.

In 2014, 263 million children, adolescents and youth were out of school around the world.

Universal secondary *completion* seems unattainable by 2030: Over 2008–2014, the upper secondary completion rate was 84% in high income, 43% in upper middle income, 38% in lower middle income and 14% in low income countries.

There is a long way to go to ensure that every child completes 12 years of primary and secondary education. Out of 90 low and middle income countries, youth had attained at least 12 years of education, on average, in only 10.

In 23% of countries, the law requires fewer than nine years of *compulsory* education. To know whether education is also really *free* requires knowing how much households contribute to the total cost.

Global indicators capture *quality* only through learning outcomes, which is not sufficient. Better data are needed on inputs such as textbook availability, and processes through tools to monitor what is happening in the classroom.

There is no common definition yet of what are 'relevant and effective' *learning outcomes* that would enable a global learning measure to be calculated from different international, regional and national assessments.

Decisions on such definitions need to be taken in a way that is open and collaborative and puts the priorities of countries first by helping build national learning assessment systems.

CHAPTER 10

TARGET 4.1

Primary and secondary education

By 2030, ensure that all girls and boys complete free, equitable and quality primary and secondary education leading to relevant and effective learning outcomes

GLOBAL INDICATOR 4.1.1 – *Percentage of children and young people: (a) in grades 2/3; (b) at the end of primary; and (c) at the end of lower secondary achieving at least a minimum proficiency level in (i) reading and (ii) mathematics, by sex*

THEMATIC INDICATOR 2 – *Administration of a nationally representative learning assessment (i) during primary, (ii) at the end of primary and (iii) at the end of lower secondary education*

THEMATIC INDICATOR 3 – *Gross intake ratio to the last grade (primary, lower secondary)*

THEMATIC INDICATOR 4 – *Completion rate (primary, lower secondary, upper secondary)*

THEMATIC INDICATOR 5 – *Out-of-school rate (primary, lower secondary, upper secondary)*

THEMATIC INDICATOR 6 – *Percentage of children over-age for grade (primary, lower secondary)*

THEMATIC INDICATOR 7 – *Number of years of (i) free and (ii) compulsory primary and secondary education guaranteed in legal frameworks*

arget 4.1 envisages the attainment of universal primary and secondary completion as a means of improving learning. These two education levels attract the largest share of education resources by governments. Progress towards the target will be a key way to demonstrate commitment to achieving Sustainable Development Goal (SDG) 4.

 Progress towards this target will be a key measure of commitment to SDG 4 "

Target 4.1 combines, modifies and extends the corresponding formulations of Education for All (EFA) goals 2, on universal primary education, and 6, on quality. The characterization of the learning outcomes to be achieved has been changed from 'recognized and measurable', as found in the EFA formulation, to 'relevant and effective'. Overall expectations of the target have been raised considerably because of the new formulation's scope, the proposed monitoring indicators and the recommendation that these indicators be disaggregated by individual characteristics.

Detractors argue that a push for universal upper secondary completion will (a) distract from the priority of ensuring at least 10 years of basic education for all, including one year of pre-primary education; the Global Education Monitoring Report (GEM Report) reaffirms that even universal primary completion will not be attained by 2030 if recent trends continue (see Chapter 7); and (b) reduce the offering of diversified and more relevant programmes at this level, especially opportunities for technical and vocational education and training.

This chapter reviews existing and potential indicators for each concept included in target 4.1. Issues of equity are briefly touched upon but are covered in greater detail in other chapters, especially Chapters 14 (on equity) and 20 (on finance).

ACCESS, PARTICIPATION AND COMPLETION

SDG 4, the education goal of the 2030 Agenda for Sustainable Development, brings universal primary and secondary education under a single target. This allows a coherent approach on all indicators that track the progress of children, adolescents and youth through about 12 years of formal education, from entry in the first grade of primary to the end of secondary education.

ACCESS

As the new international education agenda opens, it should not be forgotten that millions of children in low and lower middle income countries do not even begin school. The issue of children being denied access to education remains unresolved and needs to be monitored closely.

The UNESCO Institute for Statistics (UIS) breaks down the total estimated number of out-of-school children into those who will never go, those who will eventually go and those who were enrolled but left. The first step is identifying the age at which the highest school participation rate is observed. The proportion of children not participating at that age is used as a proxy for the rate of children who will never participate across all ages (UIS and UNICEF, 2005). As of 2014, about 41% or 25 million children of the current primary school-age cohort will never enrol in school. Two-thirds of them are girls.

FIGURE 10.1:

More than 4 in 10 children not in school will never enrol

Distribution of out-of-school children by school exposure, world and selected regions, 2014

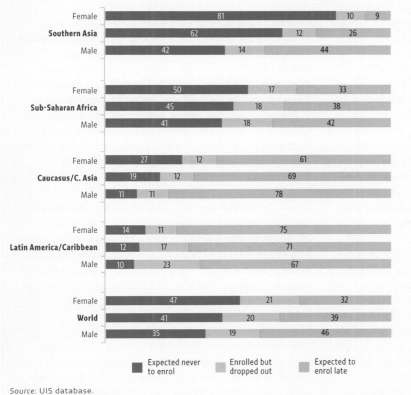

Expected never to enrol | Enrolled but dropped out | Expected to enrol late

Source: UIS database.

FIGURE 10.2:

Almost 30% of the poorest children in low income countries have never been to school

Distribution of out-of-school children by school exposure, world and selected regions, 2014

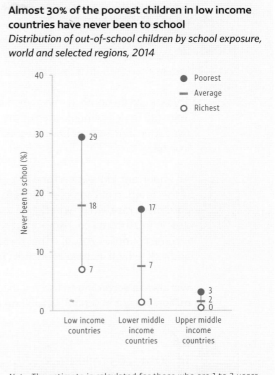

Note: The estimate is calculated for those who are 1 to 3 years above primary school graduation age, which approximately corresponds to adolescents aged 12 to 14.
Source: GEM Report team analysis (2016) using household surveys.

In low and middle income countries, where 10% of children of primary school age were out of school in 2014, 4% of the current cohort of children will never go to school. The magnitude of the challenge is highest in Southern Asia, where 62% of children not in school are expected never to enrol; the proportion rises to 81% among girls (**Figure 10.1**).

Household surveys provide complementary information on access to education. Parents and guardians are directly asked whether each child has ever attended school. But survey data are available only with a time lag and therefore overestimate the percentage of those who have never been to school. What survey-based estimates may lack in timeliness and precision, however, they make up with information on disparity in access to school. For example, in lower middle income countries, while just 1% of children from the richest households have never been to school, the corresponding share from the poorest households is 17%, and in low income countries almost 30% of children from the poorest households have never been to school (**Figure 10.2**).

PARTICIPATION

Target 4.1 draws attention to participation not only in primary and lower secondary but also in upper secondary education. In doing so, it extends the scope of monitoring into an education level that in most countries is not compulsory and consists of diverse tracks and programmes.

The key indicator for monitoring participation, and the basis for calculating the number of those out of school, is the adjusted net enrolment rate. At the primary education level, it is the percentage of children in the official primary age group who are in primary school or above; enrolment in pre-primary education, the level below, is not included. But at the lower secondary education level, the rate is the percentage of those in the age group who are in school regardless of level, including primary education, the level immediately below. This asymmetry is unjustified. Consideration should be given to amending the definition of the primary adjusted net enrolment rate to include children in pre-primary school, if only because the likelihood these children will continue into primary school is very high.

This should be borne in mind when interpreting the adjusted net enrolment rates of 91% for primary education and 84% for lower secondary education in 2014.

An important innovation for participation indicators is the addition of the upper secondary adjusted net enrolment rate, which was 63% in 2014. It ranged from 40% in low income countries to 52% in lower middle income countries, 77% in upper middle income countries and 92% in high income countries (**Table 10.1**).

Worldwide, according to these indicators, some 263 million are not in school – including 61 million children

> **"**
>
> In 2014, 263 million children, adolescents and youth were out of school around the world
>
> **"**

of primary school age, 60 million adolescents of lower secondary school age and 142 million youth of upper secondary school age. Sub-Saharan Africa is the region with the most children out of school

(31 million, 52% of the total) and adolescents out of school (24 million, 39%). Southern Asia is the region with the most out-of-school youth of upper secondary age (69 million, 48%).

Gender disparity exists between primary school-age children: 9.7% of girls, but 8.1% of boys, are out of school. The gap is largest in Western Asia (5.6 percentage points). While there is no gender gap overall among adolescents of lower secondary school age and youth of upper secondary school age, disparity in participation in individual regions exists. Among youth of upper secondary school age, there is a 7 percentage point gap at the expense of females in sub-Saharan Africa, but an 8 percentage point gap at the expense of males in Eastern Asia.

Due to large differences in population size, the countries with the highest numbers of out-of-school children, adolescents and youth are rarely those with the highest out-of-school rates (**Table 10.2**). For example, India has achieved universal primary enrolment with an adjusted net enrolment rate of 98%, but has the second-highest number of children out of school among countries with data.

For many countries, data are missing and have been imputed to allow the estimation of regional and global numbers. Examples in the case of out-of-school children of primary school age include Afghanistan, the Democratic Republic of the Congo and Nigeria, which might otherwise have been near the top of the list.

TABLE 10.1:
Primary and secondary education participation indicators, 2014

	Adjusted net enrolment rate (%)			Out of school (millions)		
	Primary	Lower secondary	Upper secondary	Children of primary school age	Adolescents of lower secondary school age	Youth of upper secondary school age
World	91	84	63	60.9	60.2	141.8
Low income	81	65	40	18.9	16.8	23.2
Lower middle income	90	80	52	30.9	34.9	91.7
Upper middle income	95	93	77	8.3	7.2	22.9
High income	97	98	92	2.8	1.3	4.0
Caucasus and Central Asia	94	96	84	0.3	0.3	0.6
Eastern and South-eastern Asia	96	91	77	6.2	8.2	19.5
Europe and Northern America	97	98	92	2.2	1.0	3.2
Latin America and the Caribbean	94	92	76	3.6	2.8	7.5
Northern Africa and Western Asia	89	86	67	5.5	3.6	8.5
Pacific	94	98	66	0.2	0.0	0.5
Southern Asia	94	80	50	11.4	20.7	68.7
Sub-Saharan Africa	80	66	43	31.4	23.6	33.1

Source: UIS database.

TABLE 10.2:
Countries with the largest out-of-school numbers and rates, 2014 or latest available year

Out-of-school rate (%)			Out of school (millions)		
Primary school age	Lower secondary school age	Upper secondary school age	Children of primary school age	Adolescents of lower secondary school age	Youth of upper secondary school age
Liberia 62	Niger 70	Niger 89	Pakistan 5.6	India 11.1	India 46.8
Eritrea 59	Eritrea 62	C. A. R. 84	India 2.9	Pakistan 5.5	Pakistan 10.4
Sudan 45	C. A. R. 55	Burkina Faso 77	Sudan 2.7	Ethiopia 3.6	Indonesia 4.0
Djibouti 43	Guinea 52	Mauritania 73	Ethiopia 2.1	Indonesia 1.9	Mexico 3.0
Equat. Guinea 42	Pakistan 48	Mozambique 71	Indonesia 2.0	Myanmar 1.9	Brazil 1.8

Source: UIS database.

The percentage of out-of-school children who live in conflict-affected countries increased from 29% in 2000 to 35% in 2014 (21.5 million children); among girls, it was 37%. In Northern Africa and Western Asia, the share increased from 63% in 2000 to 91% in 2014. Globally, the percentage of out-of-school adolescents who live in conflict-affected countries also increased from 21% to 25% over the same period.

As mentioned above, caution is needed in interpreting the percentage of adolescents and youth in school. In Mozambique, 71% of adolescents in school were enrolled at the primary level in 2014. High percentages of students at a lower education level than the one expected for their age are cause for concern. An important factor that is linked to leaving school, especially at the secondary education level, is over-age students – generally due to a combination of late entry to school and repetition.

The global share of repeaters in primary education was 3.8% in 2014, but regional figures ranged from 0.1% in Caucasus and Central Asia to 5.9% in Northern Africa and Western Asia and 8.3% in sub-Saharan Africa. The share of repeaters at the secondary level was 3.9%, with figures as high as 8.9% in Latin America and the Caribbean and 12.1% in sub-Saharan Africa.

Administrative data are available on the percentage of students who are over-age – that is, at least two years older than the official age for their grade. Globally, 4% of primary and 10% of lower secondary school students are over-age according to UIS data. But in the 10 countries where the problem is most severe, all of which are in sub-Saharan Africa, more than 35% of primary school students are over-age.

Analysis of household survey data for this report indicates that administrative data may underestimate

> " The countries with the 10 highest proportions of over-age primary school students are all in sub-Saharan Africa and have more than 35% over-age students "

the over-age pattern in primary education by an average difference of at least 7 percentage points in a sample of 22 low and middle income countries. In some countries, the gap is very large. In Sierra Leone, the percentage of over-age students was 36%, according to the 2013 Demographic and Health Survey (DHS), but only 14% according to the UIS.

Household survey data help illustrate why monitoring over-age attendance is important, especially among girls. The percentage of over-age students is already high from the first grade but generally increases as students repeat and fall further behind. However, in Ghana, the percentage of over-age girls was 57% among grade 5 students but 50% among grade 8 students. In Malawi, it was 51% in grade 6 but 34% in grade 8, while the percentage of over-age boys stayed the same. Since students rarely skip grades, this suggests that those over-age are more likely to drop out (**Figure 10.3a**).

Household surveys also indicate that late entry is more common among children from poor households. In Haiti, 36% of the poorest 60% of students, but 21% of the richest 40%, entered primary school at least two years later than the official entrance age in 2012. The gap almost doubled by grade 4, when 75% of the poorest students were over-age, suggesting they were more likely to repeat school and fall behind. In Haiti, as well as in Swaziland, the percentage of the over-age among the poorest stops rising after grade 5 suggesting that they are more likely to leave school (**Figure 10.3b**).

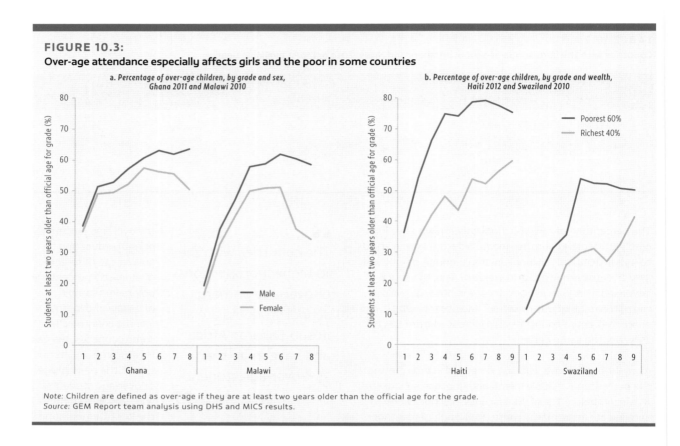

FIGURE 10.3:
Over-age attendance especially affects girls and the poor in some countries

a. Percentage of over-age children, by grade and sex, Ghana 2011 and Malawi 2010

b. Percentage of over-age children, by grade and wealth, Haiti 2012 and Swaziland 2010

Note: Children are defined as over-age if they are at least two years older than the official age for the grade.
Source: GEM Report team analysis using DHS and MICS results.

COMPLETION

Target 4.1 emphasizes completion of primary and secondary education. But consistent information across countries on graduation from the various education levels is lacking. Administrative data focus on the gross intake rate into last grade, i.e. the number of students enrolled in the final grade as a percentage of the number of people of graduation age for that education level.

Globally, the gross intake rate into the final grade of primary school was 90% in 2014. There was a low of 67% in low income countries, ranging up to 98% in high income countries. The rate exceeded 90% in all regions except sub-Saharan Africa, where it was 69%. The gross intake rate into the final grade of lower secondary school was 75% globally in 2014 and ranged from 38% in low income countries to 92% in high income countries. Again the lowest value, 42%, was in sub-Saharan Africa. No data are reported at the upper secondary level. It is important to note that the gross intake rate can exceed 100% because the numerator (students in final grade) and denominator (people of graduation age) come from different sources and may be inconsistent. Indeed, the

value exceeded 100% in 54 of the 157 countries with data in primary education.

Completion indicators based on household survey data can help address this issue. Parents and guardians are directly asked whether each child has completed a given education level. Comparing administrative and survey data from the same country suggests that intake rates tend to overestimate completion. For example, among 80 low and middle income countries, the median value of the gross intake rate into the final grade of lower secondary exceeded the completion rate at that level by 11 percentage points.

In 2008–2014, the primary completion rate was 51% in low income countries, 84% in lower middle income countries and 92% in upper middle income countries. There were major gaps between the poorest and richest: 28% of the poorest children but 77% of the richest completed primary school in low income countries. This disparity is exacerbated when comparing boys and girls. The primary completion rate among the poorest girls is 25% in low income countries (**Table 10.3**).

TABLE 10.3:
Completion rates by education level, income group, sex and wealth, 2008–2014 (%)

	Primary			Lower secondary			Upper secondary			
	Low income countries	Lower middle income countries	Upper middle income countries	Low income countries	Lower middle income countries	Upper middle income countries	Low income countries	Lower middle income countries	Upper middle income countries	High income countries
Total	51	84	92	27	68	79	14	38	43	84
Female	49	83	93	24	67	80	12	36	44	87
Male	53	84	90	31	70	77	18	40	43	82
Poorest 20%	28	69	86	10	50	63	2	20	27	76
Female	25	67	87	7	47	65	1	17	29	79
Male	30	71	85	13	52	60	4	23	23	75
Richest 20%	77	95	96	52	88	87	34	66	60	93
Female	75	96	95	48	88	91	30	67	60	95
Male	79	95	96	58	88	84	39	65	60	91

Source: GEM Report team analysis using household surveys.

The lower secondary completion rate is 27% in low income, 68% in lower middle income and 79% in upper middle income countries. Only half of the poorest adolescents, but 88% of the richest, complete lower secondary education in lower middle income countries.

> In 2008–2014, the primary completion rate was 51% in low income countries, 84% in lower middle income countries and 92% in upper middle income countries

The upper secondary completion rate is 14% in low income, 38% in lower middle income, 43% in upper middle income and 84% in high income countries. Only 20% of the poorest youth, but 66% of the richest, complete upper secondary education in lower middle income countries. Not even the richest in high income countries (93%) achieve universal completion. Just 1% of the poorest girls in low income countries complete upper secondary school.

Given that the target is universal primary and secondary completion by 2030, current evidence suggests the scale of this ambition is unattainable. Out of 125 countries, in only 64 have at least half of young people completed upper secondary school. In 15 countries, fewer than half of children have completed primary school (**Figure 10.4**).

In short, there is a long way to go to ensure that every child completes 12 years of primary and secondary education. Out of 90 low and middle income countries, 20- to 24-year-olds had attained at least of 12 years of education, on average, in only 10. The richest had attained at least 12 years of education in 36 countries but the poorest only in Kazakhstan and Ukraine. In more than half the countries, the average attainment of the poorest was fewer than six years. In Nigeria, the richest youth attained 12.2 years, the poorest only 1.7 years, on average. In Burkina Faso, Mali, Niger and South Sudan, the poorest youth attained an average of less than one year of education (**Figure 10.5**).

COMPULSORY AND FREE EDUCATION

The Education 2030 Framework for Action, adopted by over 180 countries, committed countries to 'ensure the provision of 12 years of free, publicly funded, equitable quality primary and secondary education, of which at least nine years are compulsory'. Thus, one of the proposed thematic indicators is the number of years of (a) free and (b) compulsory primary and secondary education guaranteed in legal frameworks. The main source of information for this indicator is the UIS database, complemented where necessary with constitutional, legislative and policy documentation from the Eurydice network, the International Bureau of Education and national education ministries.

Out of the 191 countries with data on compulsory education, 44 (23%) require fewer than 9 years (**Figure 10.6**), ranging from 52% of low income countries to 7% of high income countries.

While the median number of years of compulsory education is 9, the median for free education is 11 years. However, even if fees are abolished, education is not free when related costs burden families. National education

FIGURE 10.4:

Universal secondary completion is a distant target for most countries

Completion rate, by level of education, selected countries, 2008–2014

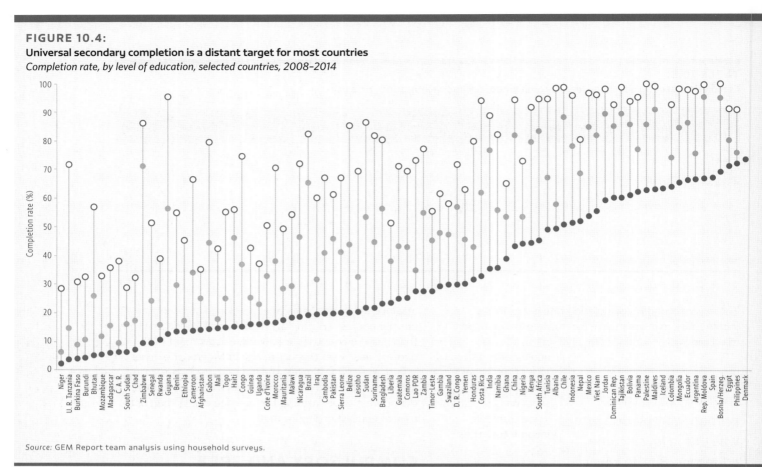

Source: GEM Report team analysis using household surveys.

FIGURE 10.5:

In just 2 out of 90 low and middle income countries have the poorest young people attained at least 12 years of education

Years of education attained among 20- to 24-year-olds, by wealth, selected countries, 2008–2014

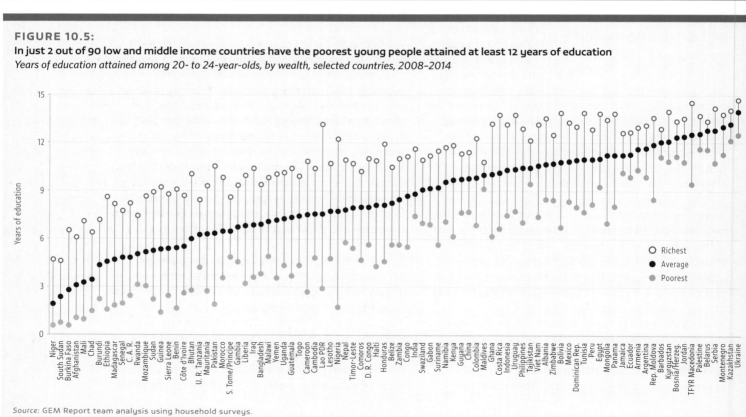

Source: GEM Report team analysis using household surveys.

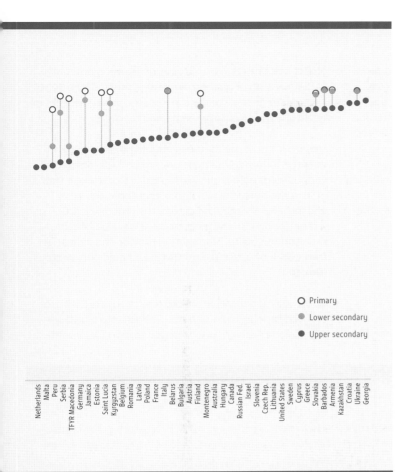

Primary

Lower secondary

Upper secondary

FIGURE 10.6:

In almost one-quarter of countries, education is compulsory for fewer than nine years

Number of countries by years of compulsory primary and secondary education, 2014

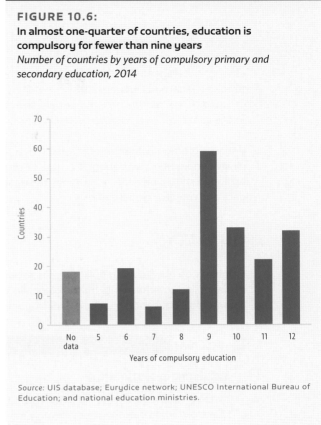

Source: UIS database; Eurydice network; UNESCO International Bureau of Education; and national education ministries.

accounts, which capture the share of total education expenditure borne by households, will be a strong indication of the extent to which education is free (see Chapter 20).

The growth in private schooling in education provision in some countries threatens national commitments to free education. The share of private institutions in total enrolment was 13% in primary education in 2014, up from 10% in 2000. Across regions, it ranged from 1% in Caucasus and Central Asia to 19% in Latin America and the Caribbean. At the secondary level, the share increased from 19% in 2000 to 25% in 2014, ranging from 3% in Caucasus and Central Asia to 28% in South-eastern Asia and 47% in Southern Asia. Differences are apparent within regions. In Latin America, the share of private primary enrolment doubled from 13% to 27% in Peru but was constant at about 8% in Mexico. Information is missing for many countries, while not all forms of private schooling are systematically captured. No regional average of the share of private institutions in primary education is available in Southern Asia, where privatization is known to be above the global average, as shown below.

Household surveys are a complementary data source. According to 2008–2011 surveys, about 27% of children of primary school age attended private schools in Southern Asia, driven by India where 26% of primary school-age children attended private schools in 2009/10. In Nepal, 18% of 6- to 10-year old students attended private school in 2009/10. The share ranged from 5% among the poorest quintile of the population to 56% among the richest (Dahal and Nguyen, 2014).

Similar analysis of 16 sub-Saharan African countries suggests that administrative data tend to underestimate the share of private school enrolment, especially in countries where the private sector is expanding and some schools operate without official recognition (Wodon, 2014). In Nigeria, private schools accounted for 5% of primary enrolment in 2005 and 8% in 2010, according to the UIS. Yet survey data indicate the share was already 13% in 2004 and reached 24% by 2015 (Nigeria NPC and ORC Macro, 2004; Nigeria NPC and RTI International, 2016).

That said, if the main objective is to monitor the extent to which the increase in private education threatens fulfilment of the right to education, not all private schools pose such a threat. For example, in Bangladesh, where the share of private schooling in 2010 was 55% among those aged 11 to 15 and 80% among those aged 16 to 18 (Dahal and Nguyen, 2014), the vast majority of private schools receive government aid and charge fees at the same low level as public schools.

While a common definition of private schools remains elusive, more questions about the type of school attended should be added to surveys to supply missing data and monitor global trends.

QUALITY

Emphasis on good quality builds on and expands earlier policy commitments by the global education community. Education quality is explicitly mentioned in

SDG 4 and targets 4.1–3. A focus on learning outcomes, a key dimension of quality, permeates much of the 2030 Agenda. Targets 4.a and 4.c are related to key aspects of quality: learning environments and teachers.

However, the scope for cross-country monitoring of quality is limited. Quality is understood and defined in various ways across the world. And with the exception of learning outcome indicators, and some equity- and inclusion-related indicators, the proposed SDG 4 monitoring framework provides a weak basis for monitoring quality. This section provides an indicative framework of quality to motivate and guide discussions (**Box 10.1**).

Good quality education should not be equated with, or reduced to, learning outcomes. To facilitate a broader discussion of quality under target 4.1, two classroom-

---

BOX 10.1

Monitoring quality in SDG 4

The concept of quality is explicitly mentioned in SDG 4 and the first three education targets, and is strongly implicit in the remaining seven targets – for example, striving towards equity; ensuring safe, non-violent, inclusive and effective learning environments; and deploying qualified teachers are all markers of good quality education.

The framework for understanding education quality proposed in the 2005 *EFA Global Monitoring Report* has been the standard reference over the past decade. With education systems added as a distinct dimension, separate from the general economic, political and social context, this new framework (**Table 10.4**) helps organize the presentation of the sections that discuss quality in this report.

TABLE 10.4:
A framework for education quality

LEARNERS	SCHOOL AND CLASSROOM SETTINGS	OUTCOMES
e.g. health and nutrition, parental engagement, stimulating home environments, emotionally supportive relationships, abilities, traits, barriers to learning, poverty, and language at home.	**Teachers and teaching process** e.g. motivated, well-prepared, attention to diversity, interactions, language, pedagogy, time on task, assessment for learning, and various teaching strategies.	**For learners** *In pre-primary education* e.g. school readiness, executive function, social-emotional and motor development, and pre-academic skills.
SYSTEMS e.g. finance, planning and monitoring, curriculum and language, standards and accountability, recruitment and incentives, professional development, links with other sectors, links across tiers of government, and inclusive policy development	**School leadership and governance** e.g. setting expectations, focusing on learning, and fostering collaboration. **Structures and material inputs** e.g. teaching and learning materials, technology, facilities, and water and hygiene.	*In primary, secondary and tertiary education* e.g. learning achievement, critical thinking skills, collaborative skills, values and attitudes (including a better understanding of the world). **For society** e.g. behaviours linked with sustainable economic, social and environmental development; culture of peace and non-violence; global citizenship; and cultural diversity.

CONTEXT
Economic, political and social conditions

Source: UNESCO (2004).

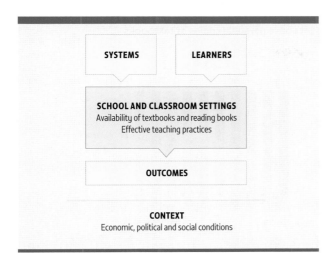

related inputs and processes have been selected. First, despite the importance of textbooks and reading books to learning, information on their availability is incomplete. Second, while monitoring pedagogy across countries is a major undertaking and cannot be served properly by quantitative studies, tools are available to observe teaching practices in classrooms and more use should be made of them.

INPUTS: AVAILABILITY OF TEXTBOOKS AND READING BOOKS

Access to textbooks, teacher guides and reading books is especially important for learning in low resource and print-poor settings. But comparative data on their availability is scant and unsystematic. Since 2008, the UIS has collected data on textbooks based on education ministry reports for 45 countries in Africa. These data can be used for indicators such as textbook/pupil ratios by grade level (1 to 7) and subject (mathematics and reading).

Some countries have sophisticated computerized management information systems for instructional materials, developed with donor support, which allow officials to receive real-time updates. Namibia and Rwanda introduced online supply chain management systems that enable schools to order the books they want from publishers, and the government to monitor whether the books have been delivered (Read, 2016).

Less sophisticated mechanisms can also be informative. As part of its primary school census, Bangladesh collects information on timeliness of delivery, one aspect of

availability. In 2013, nearly 100% of schools had received their textbooks within the first month of the school year. This was a substantial improvement over 2010, when only one-third of the schools had received their textbooks in that period (Bangladesh Directorate of Primary Education, 2014).

Even when governments have good data on schools and students and procure the correct number of books, local education authorities may not have storage and distribution facilities or, in some cases, the funds for delivery (Read, 2015). A survey of teaching and learning materials in Ghana found that 57% of the stock of grade 3 English textbooks to be delivered to districts could not be accounted for (Read, 2016).

> **A survey of teaching and learning materials in Ghana found that 57% of the stock of grade 3 English textbooks to be delivered to districts could not be accounted for**

In some countries, when textbooks reach schools, uncertainty over future supplies means they are kept in storage for fear of damage or loss. Loss and damage rates are underestimated. Ethiopia has increased print runs by 8% to compensate for that (Read, 2016). Corruption in public procurement and reselling of books for personal profit are believed to be common in many countries (Transparency International, 2013).

In this context, school visits and classroom observations have a distinct advantage. They can validate or call into question the accuracy of official data. For example, the UIS reported that the average number of mathematics textbooks per grade 2 student in Burundi was 1.5 in 2014. However, evidence from the 2014 PASEC learning achievement survey shows that this overestimates textbook availability, as only 18% of students had their own mathematics textbook while 31% had to share with another student and 51% with two or more students (**Figure 10.7**). In Chad, about 90% of students in grades 2 and 6 reading and mathematics classes had to share textbooks with at least two students.

An effective monitoring system would need to report textbook availability by grade, subject, school type and language, but that would be complex. Data on languages used in schools are scarce and data on textbooks scarcer

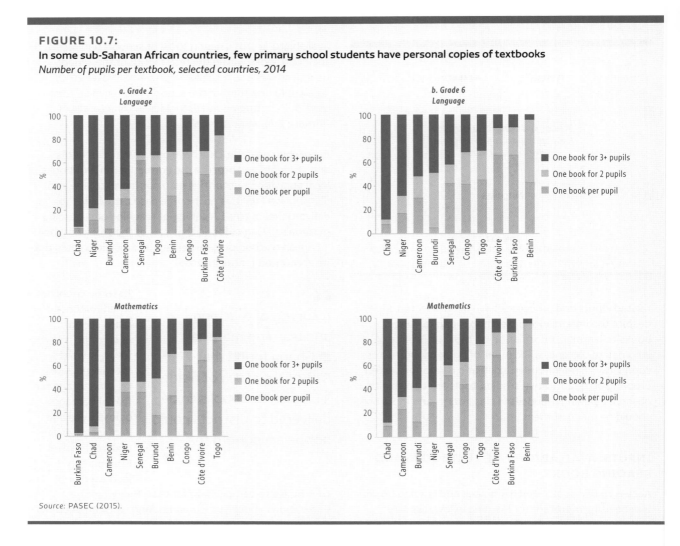

FIGURE 10.7:

In some sub-Saharan African countries, few primary school students have personal copies of textbooks

Number of pupils per textbook, selected countries, 2014

Source: PASEC (2015).

(Read, 2016) (see Chapter 14). Uganda has approved 12 languages for early primary grades.

In linguistically diverse Central Asia, countries have multiple languages of instruction in primary and secondary education. Uzbekistan has seven, Kyrgyzstan four. When these countries were part of the Soviet Union, they had a common curriculum and education structure. Uzbekistan could import Kyrgyz textbooks cheaply from Kyrgyzstan because they were identical in content, presentation and production to Uzbek textbooks. When country curricula diverged following independence, each country had to produce its own textbooks. Already struggling with costs, countries focus on their national language plus Russian. There are severe shortages of costlier minority language textbooks. In Kyrgyzstan, textbook availability in 2014 was less than 40% for Kyrgyz and Russian, and even less for Uzbek and Tajik textbooks – whose quality, a neglected dimension of availability, has been poor due to the lack of qualified translators (Read, 2016).

Beyond textbooks, the availability of reading books is vital for strengthening the literacy environment, especially for poor children without access to books at home (see Chapter 11). In Burera district, Rwanda, a baseline survey of primary schools found an average of 3.3 storybooks per school and none in almost half the schools (Save the Children, 2013).

In many multilingual countries, few, if any, reading books are available languages children speak. In conjunction with a USAID effort to establish a Global Book Fund, an inventory of reading materials from 11 sub-Saharan African countries was prepared, focusing on lesser-used languages. More than 5,900 titles in 262 languages were collected. Data show scarcity in all African languages and the near-absence of books in many key languages. In Nigeria, reading materials were found for 9 of the country's 520 languages, and in the United Republic of Tanzania, for 3 of 125 (IE Partners and R4D, 2015).

PROCESSES: CLASSROOM OBSERVATIONS OF EFFECTIVE TEACHING PRACTICES

Studies of the impact of good teaching practices on learning outcomes in high income countries indicate that teachers who improved learning 'built relationships with their students ... helped students to have different and better strategies or processes to learn the subject ... and demonstrated a willingness to explain material and help students with their work' (Hattie, 2009, p. 108). Teachers also improve learning when they set high expectations for students, do not discriminate among them, ask them to learn from one another and provide feedback.

Similar results are emerging from low and middle income countries. In rural India, teachers asking questions, using local examples to explain lessons and having children work in small groups were positively correlated with test scores in grades 2 and 4 (Banerji et al., 2013). Studies in South Africa identified a focus on reading and writing text and the adjustment of pace to pupil ability as critical for learning, though most classrooms were lacking in these factors (Hoadley, 2012).

A systematic review of 54 empirical studies highlighted group and pair work, student questioning, use of local languages, the planning and varying of lesson sequences and the use of a range of learning materials as effective pedagogic strategies. It argued that 'future research designs could fruitfully combine qualitative with quantitative studies, for example with both baseline and post-tests measuring student attainment as a result of an intervention or reform, and systematic, structured classroom observation' (Westbrook et al., 2013, p. 65).

Classroom observations are routinely conducted to inform teacher education and professional development and to evaluate interventions. Could they also be used for monitoring? If so, how much has been done and what methodological issues were raised? Such studies have so far served to measure availability of teaching and learning materials (see previous section), assess instructional time and its use in lessons, and confirm the use of effective teaching practices (**Box 10.2**).

A survey of 15,000 classrooms in Brazil, Colombia, Honduras, Jamaica and Peru showed that teachers spent between 60% and 65% of their time on academic instruction, well below the recommended 85%. Even during instruction, the entire class was engaged only one-third of the time. In the Federal District, Mexico, teachers spent almost 40% of their time managing the classroom (Bruns and Luque, 2014).

BOX 10.2

Collecting comparable classroom observation data in sub-Saharan Africa

The Service Delivery Indicators programme aims to develop a standardized approach to measure the quality of health and education services in sub-Saharan Africa. It was launched in 2010 as a partnership between the World Bank, the African Economic Research Consortium and the African Development Bank, with core funding from the Hewlett Foundation. Nationally representative surveys of primary schools, typically between 200 and 400 per country, have been done in Kenya, Mozambique, Nigeria, Senegal, Togo, Uganda and the United Republic of Tanzania (2 rounds), and are in process in the Democratic Republic of the Congo, Madagascar and Niger.

As in other studies, teacher absenteeism, which combines absence from school with absence from the classroom while at school, was typically between 40% and 50%. It was more than 55% in Mozambique, where if time lost within the lesson is also taken into account, the average child experienced just 1 hour and 40 minutes of actual daily teaching time. Such data call for attention to governance, management and oversight.

Classroom observation also captured the nature of interactions. Across countries, about 30% of teaching and learning time was spent interacting with students (either as one group, several small groups or individually); another 30% was spent either writing on the blackboard or reading and lecturing to students (an activity negatively associated with learning outcomes); 22% of classroom time was spent waiting for students to respond to a question or listening to student responses; and 6% was devoted to testing.

Observers were asked to identify whether certain types of teacher practices were deployed during the lesson. While 84% of teachers introduced the lesson, only 43% summarized it at the end of class. Most of the questions asked were related to memorized information. It was observed that only 61% of teachers had smiled at pupils and 29% had used negative reinforcement. Such information provide insights into how pedagogical teacher training could focus more strongly on practices associated with better learning.

Further analysis of data from Kenya, Mozambique, Nigeria, Togo and Uganda shows that classroom effects – a combination of teacher knowledge, time allocation and teaching practices – explained roughly 15% of the total variance of student achievement, three times more than in high income countries. Positive reinforcement and frequent formative assessment were most strongly associated with increased student achievement, while mistreating students had a negative effect.

Source: Filmer et al. (2015); Filmer (2016).

Multiple factors influence the time students spend learning in early grades. In Ethiopia, Guatemala, Honduras, Mozambique and Nepal, after combining time losses due to schools being closed, teachers being absent and students being either absent or, especially, off task, schools used less than 50% of the available time for instruction (Moore et al., 2012).

Other factors further reducing time on task include teacher strikes, late student registration, lack of supplies at the start of term or schools closing earlier than planned. Taking these into account, primary school students in Senegal were on task during 388 of the 1,090 intended annual instructional hours, or 36% of the time (Niang, 2015).

In Bauchi and Sokoto states, Nigeria, only one-quarter of grade 2 time is allocated to teaching, partly because what is supposed to be a 45-minute literacy lesson is actually much shorter, and because only half the teachers in the classrooms are teaching literacy skills during the lesson time (RTI International, 2016b) (**Figure 10.8**).

Classroom observations do not just record time allocation. They can also record teaching practices – and commonly show that teacher–student and student–student interactions are limited. In Cambodia, a tiny part of mathematics class time in lower secondary schools was spent doing applied individual or group work. There were limited opportunities for interaction or creative thinking. About 61% of class time was spent receiving various forms of instruction, of which one-third involved copying; and another one-fifth of the time was spent on recitation, mostly involving students responding to teacher queries (Benveniste et al., 2008).

In Uganda, a study of 742 lower secondary school classrooms showed teachers struggling to make connections to students' everyday life experiences and unlikely to provide specific feedback (Seidman et al., 2015). In Ethiopia, a study of 776 primary school mathematics classes assessed implementation of government policy to shift away from teacher-oriented learning methods. The target was 30% of class time spent on student-centred activity, but only 11% was reached, compared with 74% on teacher-oriented activities and 15% off task (Frost and Little, 2014).

Classroom observation tools expect observers to use varying levels of subjective judgement. Low inference tools gather information on environments, time use and interactions between the teacher and students without drawing immediate conclusions. They focus on directly observable actions that are easy to code using checklists. Tools are administered by experts for research, monitoring and evaluation purposes and by district supervisors or instructional coaches to provide feedback to teachers as part of a support mechanism (RTI International, 2016a).

High inference tools are more informal and open-ended. Observers must use their own judgement about what happens in the classroom and code teacher practices and student behaviour with more nuance. While these tools provide more insights, they are costly because they require extensive training to ensure reliability and consistency.

Whether classroom observation tools can be used for comparing classroom instruction across countries is debatable. Classroom behaviour depends on system-level factors, such as government education policies, and differences in the home, such as household living conditions. In addition, classroom practices vary according to cultural beliefs and expectations. No single tool can meet the needs of all countries (Jukes et al., 2006).

Yet, despite these limitations, the studies reviewed here often agree on what inhibits learning in classrooms around the world. The availability of broadly consistent monitoring tools can bring critical issues of pedagogy

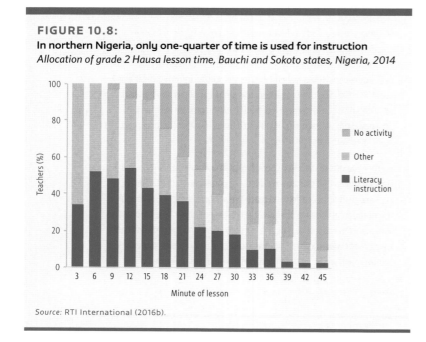

FIGURE 10.8:

In northern Nigeria, only one-quarter of time is used for instruction
Allocation of grade 2 Hausa lesson time, Bauchi and Sokoto states, Nigeria, 2014

Source: RTI International (2016b).

and classroom climate to policy-makers' attention. It is thus important to keep searching for tools that are adaptable yet reliable, valid, cost-efficient and easy to use at scale.

LEARNING OUTCOMES

Education systems have traditionally measured whether children go to school rather than whether learners benefit from their schooling experience, let alone what happens inside schools and classrooms. The focus has gradually shifted over the past 15 years, however, with the rapid increase in the use of national, regional and international learning assessments.

Target 4.1 echoes this shift. Its message is that the completion of primary and secondary education should lead to 'relevant and effective learning outcomes'. The GEM Report welcomes this change in focus. All education systems need to find ways to improve a wide range of learning outcomes. Benchmarks can help policy-makers understand where and with whom progress is not taking place, and what steps are needed to remedy the situation. However, questions arise as to which learning outcomes are 'relevant and effective', how they can be measured, and whether and how the information is used by those who enable learning.

Proponents of a swift move to learning measurements that are comparable across countries argue they are long overdue (Study Group on Measuring Learning Outcomes, 2013). The plight of millions of children, especially in poorer countries, who do not master basic skills and competencies in primary school is insufficiently recognized and threatens the chances of achieving the SDGs. These learning outcomes need to be monitored in an internationally comparable fashion to maintain interest and mobilize policy responses.

At the same time, focusing on a relatively limited set of skills that are more amenable to measurement risks marginalizing subjects and skills that are prioritized in each country's curriculum (Muskin, 2015). Moreover, 'relevant and effective' learning outcomes cannot be reduced to literacy and numeracy skills. They include much broader sets of knowledge, attitudes and skills, whose value is independent of their measurement status. Also, learning contexts are diverse; differences between countries can undermine the comparability of even a narrow set of skills like literacy and numeracy

(Goldstein and Thomas, 2008). Finally, while large-scale assessments are useful in tracking system-level performance, evidence is limited on how useful they are in guiding teacher training and classroom practices and improving learning outcomes over time (Best et al., 2013).

These vantage points – the need for comparison and the challenges and consequences of comparison – represent a key issue in the global debate on learning. This directly relates to the need to report on the global indicator for target 4.1, i.e. the percentage of those in early primary, late primary and late lower secondary education achieving at least a minimum proficiency level in reading and mathematics (IIEP, 2015).

> " The need for comparison and the challenges and consequences of comparison represent a key issue in the global debate on learning, and directly relate to country efforts to report on the global indicator for target 4.1 "

In some ways, these views can be bridged. The adage 'don't value what you measure, measure what you value' is instructive. Improved proficiency in the key foundation skills of reading and mathematics has value and clearly indicates a well-functioning education system. And data on reading and mathematics skills are often used to explore the effects of learning on other development outcomes. But measuring proficiency in these areas requires sensitivity to national needs and circumstances. The project should be 'open source' and developed collaboratively and transparently.

The next subsections describe three preconditions for the measurement of reading and mathematics skills: consensus on the content of the learning outcomes to be assessed, agreement on quality standards and a process to assure they are met, and a process to link information from various sources to produce a common measure.

Challenges include (a) ensuring that assessments also serve other purposes beyond the relatively narrow objective to support global monitoring, (b) resolving the political – and not just the technical – dimensions of agreeing what is to be measured and compared and (c) finding sustainable solutions with respect to finance and resources. This is a tall order; solutions will inevitably be imperfect. However, various options are possible and it is important to use open and inclusive approaches, taking into account country needs.

LEARNING OUTCOME MEASURES: DEFINING THE CONTENT

To define a minimum proficiency level in a domain such as reading or mathematics, a learning assessment needs to set basic parameters (Anderson and Morgan, 2008). First, what are the boundaries of the domain being assessed? In most countries, these are determined by curriculum contents. What happens when common ground must be found between differing national or subnational contents? Second, what is an expected progression of learning within these boundaries in primary and secondary education? Third, what questions and responses demonstrate that a learner has reached a particular level of proficiency, i.e. what evidence is used to determine whether specific skills have been acquired? How should test questions be allocated across content areas? How are proficiency levels defined and what criteria used to distinguish between them?

Agreement is possible, though it does not come easily. The 2013 Third Regional Comparative and Explanatory Study (TERCE) was coordinated by the Latin American Laboratory for Assessment of the Quality of Education, a network of national education quality assessment directors, with the support of the UNESCO Regional Bureau for Education in Latin America and the Caribbean. It was administered in 15 countries, in grades 3 and 6, in reading, mathematics, natural sciences and writing, with questions based on analysis of common cross-curricular elements.

Each domain was benchmarked to four proficiency levels jointly determined with experts. For example, at grade 3, students at level 2 of reading proficiency were expected to locate explicit information, infer information from connections made in the text, establish links that demonstrated understanding of the text's overall meaning, and recognize a non-literary text's communication purpose. Students at level 2 of mathematics proficiency were expected to read and write numbers, interpret simple fractions, extract information from tables and graphs, and identify measurement units, relative positions of objects on maps and elements on geometric shapes. Different descriptions applied to level 2 at grade 6.

The assessment found that, across the 15 countries, 60% of grade 3 and 82% of grade 6 students were at level 2 and above in reading, and 53% of both grade 3 and grade 6 students were at level 2 and above in mathematics. In the Dominican Republic, just 15% of grade 3 and 20% of grade 6 students were at level 2 and above in mathematics. In Chile, about 85% of grade 3 and grade 6 students achieved this proficiency level (UNESCO, 2015g) (**Figure 10.9**).

However, the 2013 TERCE used a different scale to report scores than its predecessor, the 2006 SERCE. To ensure results could be made comparable over time, a High Level Consultative Technical Council was established to advise national coordinators. Countries were closely involved in the process of reaching consensus and communicating the change. Even though Latin American countries' education systems share many features, negotiation was required.

A similar process will be needed at the global level to define what areas of existing national and cross-national assessments can be used, how learning progression in these areas is understood, and which questions in these assessments best capture this progression.

Achieving agreement for a global indicator of minimum proficiency is difficult. Curriculum experts, policy-makers and education managers should be involved. Two examples of challenges are discussed below: assessing learning outcomes in early grades and among out-of-school populations.

Assessing skills in early grades

A highly contested issue in developing global indicators for monitoring SDG 4 was whether early grades would be included as a distinct stage in assessing reading and mathematics learning outcomes. In a letter to the United Nations Statistical Commission, more than 200 civil society organizations (CSOs) and education professionals expressed deep concern about 'the last-minute inclusion of early grade assessment among the global indicators' (Global Campaign for Education, 2016). By contrast, the People's Action for Learning (PAL) Network, consisting of CSOs in nine countries that support citizen-led learning assessments, has advocated 'for the continued inclusion of an indicator that measures learning progress early [in primary education] … to support timely corrective measures' (PAL Network, 2016).

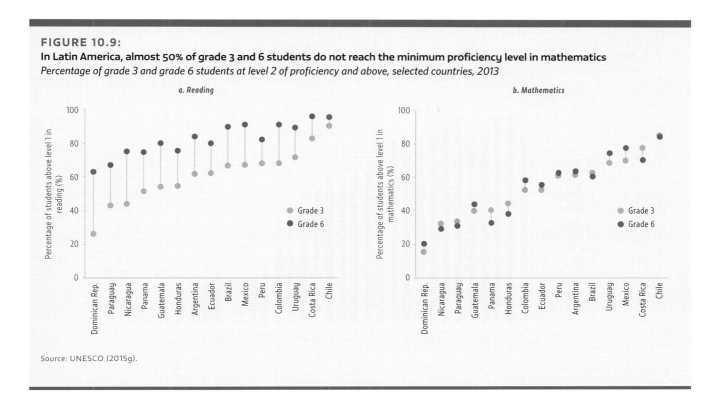

FIGURE 10.9:

In Latin America, almost 50% of grade 3 and 6 students do not reach the minimum proficiency level in mathematics

Percentage of grade 3 and grade 6 students at level 2 of proficiency and above, selected countries, 2013

Source: UNESCO (2015g).

Early grade learning achievement owes its inclusion in the global indicator for target 4.1 to the remarkable influence of two types of oral assessments that began in the mid-2000s: school-based assessments, notably the Early Grade Reading Assessment (EGRA) and Early Grade Math Assessment (EGMA), funded by USAID in low and middle income countries; and household-based assessments, notably the Annual Status of Education Report (ASER) in India, a citizen-led assessment, which generated an assessment approach since followed in nine countries and coordinated by the PAL Network. Both approaches revealed that millions of children in poorer countries were learning at a level well below what is expected (UIS, 2016e).

EGRA was developed as a reliable and valid measure of skills that contribute to reading acquisition in three domains: sensitivity to language at the level of its sound structure, understanding about the orthographic system and written language, and understanding about words in their written forms (Dubeck and Gove, 2015). Special attention was paid to oral reading fluency as an indicator linked to reading comprehension. About one in five grade 3 students could not read a single word from a grade 2 passage in middle income countries such as

Guyana, Jordan and Iraq. In a poorer country, Malawi, 90% of grade 2 students could not read a single word in Chichewa in 2012 (**Figure 10.10**). Almost 40% could still not do so by the time they were in grade 4 (RTI, 2015).

The percentage of those unable to read a single word or sentence is a basic indicator that could be used for cross-national monitoring. However, more nuanced measures are not suited for the purpose. Critics point out that while the cognitive processes involved in learning to read are universal, they are mediated through contexts, literacy environments and the availability of teaching and learning materials. The process varies by student motivation, student and teacher beliefs, and – especially – language and script (Bartlett et al., 2015). A large-scale review concluded that although 'most oral assessments measure the same reading constructs ... differences in language structure and complexity make direct comparison of the results impractical', especially in the case of a task such as oral reading fluency (UIS, 2016e, pp. 293-4).

Despite the debate on measuring learning outcomes in early grades, efforts continue to identify early skills that can be measured and compared. A prominent example

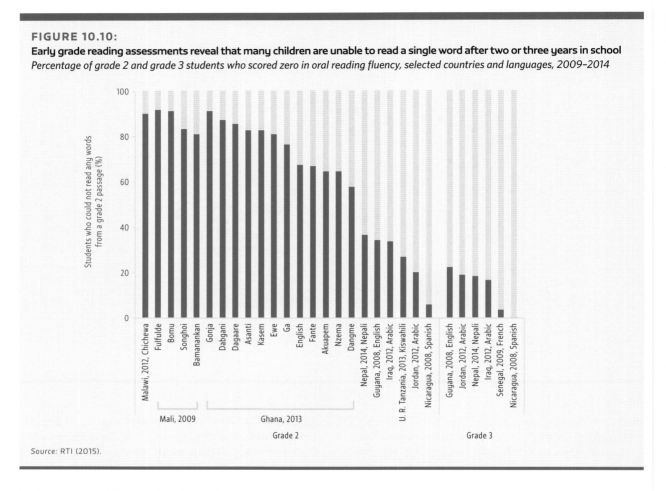

FIGURE 10.10:
Early grade reading assessments reveal that many children are unable to read a single word after two or three years in school
Percentage of grade 2 and grade 3 students who scored zero in oral reading fluency, selected countries and languages, 2009–2014

Source: RTI (2015).

is a learning module added to the forthcoming round of UNICEF's Multiple Indicator Cluster Surveys (MICS) (**Box 10.3**). It and other initiatives underscore the need to balance a sound theoretical approach with practical considerations, which will likely delay agreement on cross-nationally valid measures and benchmarks.

Assessing skills in out-of-school populations

One weakness of the global indicator is that it focuses on monitoring learning outcomes of those in school rather than all children; many consider the latter more appropriate for an agenda that aims to leave no one behind. Reporting learning outcomes only for those in school will overestimate the percentage of children who attain agreed reading and numeracy benchmarks.

Citizen-led assessments are preferable because they are administered to all children and youth in a given age group, regardless of whether they are or have been enrolled in school. In rural Pakistan, the 2014 ASER survey found the proportion of students in grade 6 who could read a grade 2 level story in Urdu, Sindhi or Pashto was 65% while among all children aged 10 (the theoretical grade 6 age) the share was 31%. Many 10-year-olds had never been to school, had already left (often because of not benefiting from the experience) or were in a lower grade and had not yet developed reading skills. While 89% of grade 10 students could read a very simple text, only 64% of sampled 14-year-olds could do so, a difference of 25 percentage points (**Figure 10.11a**). Similar results emerge from analysis of the 2013 Uwezo survey in the United Republic of Tanzania (**Figure 10.11b**). These comparisons illustrate that the global indicator is flawed in its current form.

That said, including out-of-school children and adolescents in learning assessments has its own challenges. As out-of-school populations have lower skills on average, levels of difficulty might have to be reconfigured. This could reduce the levels' relevance for those in school because they would give less information about higher skill levels.

A new module on learning outcomes in Multiple Indicator Cluster Surveys

Inspired by the need to create tools to measure the equity and learning dimensions of SDG 4, UNICEF is developing a new module in its MICS household survey programme to provide a snapshot of reading and mathematics learning outcomes. The module will be administered to 7- to 14-year-olds, including those who do not attend school. This information is expected to show whether children have basic reading and mathematics skills across a large sample of countries and their links to home environments and individual characteristics.

The mathematics skills to be assessed relate to number sense and operations, such as reading numbers, comparing numbers, doing addition and recognizing patterns. These are considered foundational and predictive of further skills development.

Two reading skills will be assessed: oral reading accuracy and reading comprehension. The ability to read accurately predicts reading comprehension reliably. The module will include a short text for children to read aloud. Accuracy will be assessed by specially trained interviewers.

Comprehension is the ultimate goal of reading and should be the focus of any assessment of reading skills, although a household survey imposes serious constraints. Two to three literal comprehension questions will ask readers to retrieve information directly from the text. One to two inferential comprehension questions will call for readers to understand relationships that may not be explicitly stated in the text. Research showed that just three questions can be used to assess reading comprehension almost as well as a larger number.

Indicators from the module will include the percentage of children who demonstrate early reading and number skills, based on the mastery of the tasks assessed in the module. Before the skills assessment, a set of questions will collect important background information while establishing rapport with the child. Questions will address parental involvement, such as how frequently parents read or tell oral stories to the children; language, including the home language; medium of instruction; and preferred language of the test (see Chapter 14).

Important logistical issues should be considered. A major task is establishing a mechanism to ensure texts and questions follow general guidelines. This will also require creating a repository of word lists (from textbooks), texts and questions. Interviewers will require special training. It will also be necessary to ensure children can answer the questions without intrusion. Finally, sample designs must allow disaggregation by grade, age and socio-economic status.

Sources: Cardoso and Dowd (2016); UNICEF (2015c).

FIGURE 10.11:
Whether indicators cover all students or all children can make a huge difference to global reporting

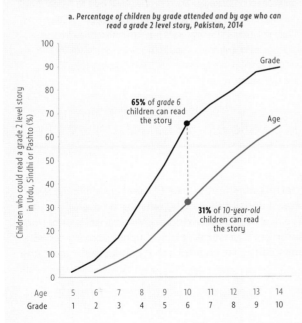

a. *Percentage of children by grade attended and by age who can read a grade 2 level story, Pakistan, 2014*

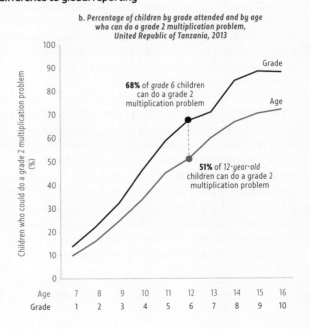

b. *Percentage of children by grade attended and by age who can do a grade 2 multiplication problem, United Republic of Tanzania, 2013*

Source: GEM Report team analysis using Pakistan ASER and United Republic of Tanzania Uwezo data.

Take PISA for Development, which aims to administer a learning assessment not just to those in school, as the main Programme for International Student Assessment survey does, but to all 14- to 16-year-olds found in sampled households. It will be administered in four Latin American and two sub-Saharan African countries in 2018. Due to the prospect of low skills in out-of-school populations, the conceptual framework for reading literacy has extended the main PISA framework to lower levels of reading proficiency for better coverage of basic processes such as literal reading comprehension (OECD, 2016c).

These examples highlight the contested nature of measuring learning outcomes. The choice of a learning assessment in Nigeria provides another example of potential trade-offs (**Box 10.4**). In short, the need to balance a sound theoretical approach with numerous practical considerations is likely to influence whether agreement on cross-national measures and benchmarks can be reached.

LEARNING OUTCOME MEASUREMENT TOOLS: ASSURING ASSESSMENT QUALITY

Agreeing what areas to assess is a critical first step, which needs to be followed by consensus on measurement tools. One thematic SDG indicator is whether a country has carried out nationally representative learning assessments during primary education, at the end of primary and at the end of lower secondary. Its objective is to raise awareness of the need for countries to monitor learning outcomes through regular, good quality assessments during primary and secondary education. The indicator could further encourage the development and use of national assessments to inform global learning measures, alongside existing and newly proposed regional and international assessments.

National assessments focus on system-level learning outcomes using criteria set by education authorities. They are generally low stakes and differ from high stakes public examinations, which are used for certification, institutional tracking or selection to higher levels of education. The UIS Catalogue of Learning Assessments collects information on their scope, purpose, funding and design and the dissemination of results (UIS, 2014b). Its first version included 65 examples of assessments from 29 countries; a second version is being designed.

BOX 10.4

Assessing learning outcomes in Nigeria

Nigeria's National Assessment of Learning Achievement in Basic Education (NALABE) has been administered four times since 2001 by the Universal Basic Education Commission, the federal agency that works with state education ministries in delivering primary and lower secondary education. In the most recent round, in 2011, students in primary grades 4, 5 and 6 and lower secondary grade 1 were assessed in English, mathematics and life skills in more than 1,500 schools. The results were published as percentage scores with no reference to proficiency level. There was also no indication whether results could be compared over time.

Unlike neighbouring countries, Nigeria is not involved in cross-national assessments. It participated in the UNESCO-UNICEF Monitoring Learning Achievement project in 1996 and 2003. To the extent that results were comparable across countries, they showed the performance of Nigerian students to be among the weakest in sub-Saharan Africa.

A citizen-led, household-based assessment, Let's Engage, Assess, and Report Nigeria (LEARNigeria), is to be launched in six states in 2017. The Lagos-based Education Partnership Centre is coordinating LEARNigeria in collaboration with over 30 private and public agencies. A pilot survey in Kano and Lagos states in late 2015 assessed about 2,000 children aged 5 to 15 for basic numeracy and English and Hausa literacy.

The new initiative followed publication of findings from the first review of the impact of citizen-led assessments. Key recommendations included reducing assessment frequency, broadening the set of assessed skills and developing communication strategies. The results led ASER India to decide not to carry out its 2015 survey so as to think through its future strategy. Citizen-led assessments mainly aim to raise awareness of actual learning outcomes and push government to act. Their success is now putting pressure on them to increase their scope and sophistication.

Sources: Nigeria UBEC (2013); PAL Network (2015); Results for Development (2015).

Global mapping for the 2015 *EFA Global Monitoring Report* (Benavot and Köseleci, 2015) provides an overall picture of the availability and external characteristics of national assessments. Most take place in upper primary school grades. Of the 135 countries that conducted at least one assessment between 2007 and 2013, 75 did so in grades 1 to 3, 123 in grades 4 to 6, 88 in grades 7 to 9 and 45 in grades 10 to 12. Almost all national assessments tested language (reading and writing) and mathematics; 53% of countries tested learning outcomes in natural/physical sciences, 34% in social sciences and 34% in foreign languages (**Figure 10.12**).

Carrying out national assessments regularly helps consolidate education systems, as it spurs demand for timely data, especially when education reforms are being implemented. Yet there are significant variations by country. About one-third of national assessments in the UIS catalogue, including those of the Dominican Republic, Mauritius and Zimbabwe, are administered annually (UIS, 2016d). Some countries that carry out annual assessments rotate subjects. In Chile, the tested grades and subjects alternate to make more time and resources available for substantive data analysis (Ferrer, 2006).

Apart from assessments' availability, it will be necessary to establish clear standards for them and to introduce a strong mechanism to assure their quality. Ultimately, only assessments of good quality should be used to inform a global indicator on learning outcomes.

Setting quality standards for national assessments

Two dimensions of assessment quality are relevant. First, an enabling institutional context needs to ensure sustainability and strong links with the education system. Second, assessments should be valid and reliable, providing relevant information to policy-makers and the public, without interference or compromising factors.

An enabling context is the key driver of long-term effectiveness of an assessment system. It requires supportive policies and institutions, and sufficient financial and human resources (Clarke, 2012). Broad political support is needed, since results could reveal serious challenges or inequality in learning. Over the last two decades in Brazil, committed and stable political leadership and support enabled the development of a strong, large-scale national assessment programme (Castro, 2012).

Among 24 countries reviewed in the World Bank Systems Approach for Better Education Results (SABER) programme on student assessment since 2009, only Samoa, Uganda, the United Arab Emirates and Zambia were considered to have established an enabling context, mostly as a result of external support. A legal document

FIGURE 10.12:

Most national assessments test learning outcomes in language and mathematics

Percentage of countries that tested a particular subject among those that carried out at least one national assessment during the period, 1990–1999, 2000–2006 and 2007–2013

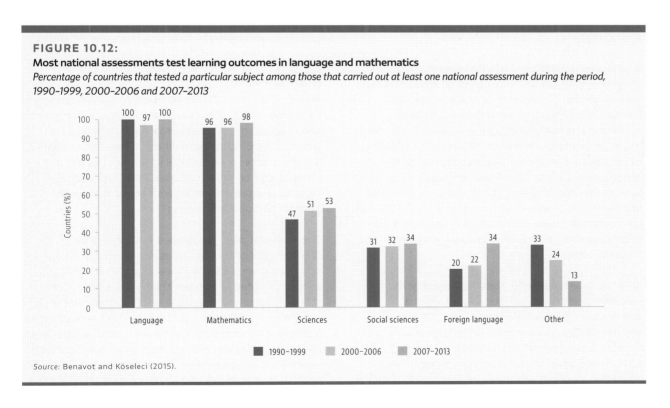

Source: Benavot and Köseleci (2015).

mandating a particular assessment activity can ensure continuity. There is a formal policy in place in more than half the countries reviewed by SABER, including Ghana, Kazakhstan and Sri Lanka (World Bank, 2016a).

Regular funding is also required. Yet only in one-third of the countries reviewed by SABER was a budget allocated to the national assessment programme. In Armenia, where a national assessment was carried out in 2010 to assess grade 8 students in language and history, regular funding is provided to the Assessment and Testing Centre (World Bank, 2011). In Zambia, the budget funds all national assessment activities while aid from development partners is used for supplementary support (OECD and World Bank, 2014). Public funding of national assessments can be weak; in Pakistan, the activities of the National Education Assessment System, financed by the World Bank, waned when responsibility was transferred to provincial governments (Dundar et al., 2014).

An assessment should be carried out by organizations whose work is recognized, respected and widely accepted. SABER reports indicate that 60% of countries had a stable national assessment body. In Uganda, putting the National Examinations Board in charge of assessments has clarified institutional structures and improved development and implementation (Kanjee and Acana, 2013).

A widely debated issue is whether assessment bodies should be attached to ministries of education. Many Latin American countries have made significant changes in institutional arrangements. Ecuador established its National Education Evaluation Institute in 2012, transferring responsibility from the Ministry of Education, in response to a mandate in the new constitution. In Brazil, Colombia and Mexico, bodies have seen their autonomy strengthen and responsibilities broaden through sheer practice or legal provisions. But some specialized education ministry units have also been successful, as in Guatemala and Peru (Ferrer and Fiszbein, 2015).

Another issue is capacity. National assessments require experts to act as national and regional coordinators, item writers, statisticians, data managers and translators. The pool of qualified professionals for such highly specialized positions is limited. Some tertiary education departments lack programmes in education statistics and measurement. Many qualified professionals move to other government posts or the private sector, or pursue graduate studies abroad.

Only six countries with SABER reports were considered adequately staffed (World Bank, 2016a). Of the two poorest, the Democratic Republic of the Congo relied heavily on an EGRA project; only Mauritania had a strong team, although staff were mainly temporary or part time (World Bank, 2013e, 2014a).

As to the second dimension of assessment quality, countries need to take steps to assure a valid and reliable national assessment programme. Many assessment units' technical reports are unavailable or not sufficiently detailed to establish whether these criteria are met. Only four SABER countries made comprehensive, high quality technical reports publicly available: Mauritania, Uganda, the United Arab Emirates and Viet Nam.

Concerns related to field operations may affect the perceived representativeness and legitimacy of assessment results. Almost half the countries with SABER reports, including Mozambique and Sudan, had no regular internal review mechanism (World Bank, 2016a). In Serbia, the quality of test items and instruments in the National Assessment of Fourth Grade Students was verified by external experts and psychometric analysis. A standardized administration manual is used (World Bank, 2012a). In Latin America, many technical reports do not indicate the criteria used to judge item validity, such as cultural biases, nor do they comment on curricular relevance or comparability across years (Ferrer, 2006).

Ensuring learning assessment quality standards and providing support

Providing a supportive enabling environment and clear standards that help ensure reliability, validity and transparency is no easy matter. But doing so is critical if national assessment results are to be counted as valid sources for the global indicator. How can the international community be assured that national, regional or international assessments are fit for the purpose of global monitoring?

This question raises two issues. First, if technical requirements of conducting assessments are overly stringent, then the institutional or organizational capacity needed to conduct them will be beyond the reach of many countries. As a result, a small pool of private service providers could dominate the business of learning assessments, undermining their relevance and use by countries. Assessing learning outcomes for global monitoring should be seen, first and foremost, as a public good that contributes to country progress in education and sustainable development. It should not become an opportunity to increase market share.

The second issue is that resources to bolster the capacity to conduct robust learning assessments are not allocated efficiently. Some long-standing regional programmes have not received consistent financial support. Individual countries have also struggled at times to obtain funding to participate in assessment programmes. Donor support of national assessments has too often followed short-term objectives, which only rarely result in countries developing sustained capacity to build effective and well-used assessment systems (**Box 10.5**). Coordination is needed to allocate financial resources efficiently. A new initiative by the Global Partnership for Education, Assessment for Learning, has been proposed as a platform, the main aim being to strengthen national learning assessment systems (GPE et al., 2016).

Ensuring the relevance of learning assessments for teaching and learning

Global measures of learning outcomes 'should and indeed must link deliberately and strategically to the supreme aim of improving the quality and relevance of teaching and, ultimately, of learning' (Muskin, 2016, p. 75). Critics say cross-national assessments often promise this direct link to improved learning but do not deliver it (Carnoy et al., 2015).

For an assessment framework to be relevant, it must be aligned with education goals, student learning, and in-service and pre-service teacher development objectives. Countries need to 'think purposefully and strategically about how best to choose and use student learning assessments' to ensure relevance and impact (Muskin, 2016, p. 57). The 2030 Agenda presents an opportunity for countries to strengthen national assessment systems while contributing to international efforts to compile comparable data on learning outcomes. External and domestic funding should provide sustained support for robust national assessment systems, aligned with country needs, rather than simply seeking results for global monitoring.

LEARNING OUTCOME MEASURES: REPORTING RESULTS FROM VARIOUS ASSESSMENTS

The third building block for a global measure of learning outcomes is agreement on reporting and defining benchmarks by level (or age) and subject (or domain). This entails developing a set of items from various assessments, which can be linked through analysis of their relative level of difficulty. Much technical knowledge on linking originates in the United States, where efforts were made to link state tests to the long-standing national

---

BOX 10.5

Multiple assessments but no national learning assessment system in the United Republic of Tanzania

The United Republic of Tanzania has a formal system of examinations which the National Examinations Council administers at the end of the primary and secondary cycles. As in many countries, such high stakes examinations attract the interest of media, parents and politicians. This was especially so in 2012, when there was a sudden drop in pass rates. In recent years, a growing number of donor-funded learning assessments have tried to shift attention from pass rates to literacy and numeracy skills.

Uwezo, the first citizen-led assessment in eastern Africa, showed that only 1 in 10 grade 3 students could read a grade 2 level story in English and only 3 in 10 in Kiswahili in 2011. The 2010 World Bank Service Delivery Indicator survey also showed that less than 10% of grade 4 students could read correctly all the words in a short sentence in English.

Learning assessments have been used to monitor and evaluate national or subnational donor programmes. For example, the government introduced an EGRA/EGMA survey of grade 2 students called 3Rs (Reading, Writing, Arithmetic) as part of the Big Results Now programme. It was also used for the results framework of the Literacy and Numeracy Education Support programme, a Global Partnership for Education initiative. And it was linked to a Programme for Results finance instrument of the World Bank, the United Kingdom Department for International Development and the Swedish International Development Cooperation Agency. Aid disbursements will be proportional to the increase in average Kiswahili reading speed, benchmarked at 18 words per minute in 2013.

Results are not comparable across these studies and, sometimes, even within a particular study over time. These learning assessments are not yet managed by a single government agency and, as they are not only funded but also largely run by donors, it is doubtful that capacity is being built. Meanwhile, donors have used progress in learning outcomes, with their uncertain results, as a condition for aid disbursement. Aid could be used instead to help develop a robust and sustainable national student learning assessment system.

The United Republic of Tanzania participated in the Southern Africa Consortium for Monitoring Educational Quality (SACMEQ) survey in 2000 and 2007; this robust regional assessment enabled tracking across countries and over time. However, the country did not participate in the latest round, in 2013, because of a lack of external funding. And despite the proliferation of learning assessments in recent years, the main measure of success for the Big Results Now programme is the end-of-cycle examination pass rate.

Sources: Rawle and Attfield (2015); Twaweza (2012); United Republic of Tanzania government (2013); World Bank (2012b).

assessment (Feuer et al., 1999). Still, linking items is not just a technical issue but a process fundamentally related to the intended purpose of the indicator (Mislevy, 1992).

In the context of global monitoring, two key issues are worth considering. First, given the 2030 Agenda's emphasis on leaving no one behind, accurate background information on the learners whose knowledge and skills are being assessed is essential. But the information is collected inconsistently by various assessments and cannot be compared, especially when primary school-age children are expected to provide accurate information about their family circumstances. This hampers tracking the global indicator by population characteristics.

Second is the need to collect pertinent information about cultural, linguistic and contextual elements to advance more valid interpretations of differences between countries. Take the 2014 CONFEMEN Programme for the Analysis of Education Systems (PASEC) survey, which

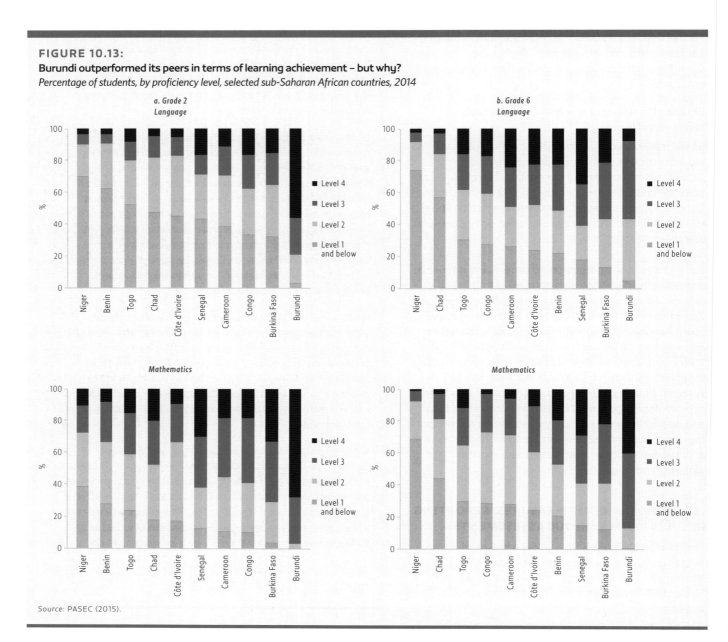

FIGURE 10.13:
Burundi outperformed its peers in terms of learning achievement – but why?
Percentage of students, by proficiency level, selected sub-Saharan African countries, 2014

Source: PASEC (2015).

> For global monitoring of learning, information about cultural and linguistic context is needed

was administered in 10 francophone sub-Saharan African countries at grades 2 and 6 in language and mathematics (PASEC, 2015).

The results showed Burundi outperforming all the other countries in each grade-subject combination. Only 3% of grade 2 students were in the two lowest levels in language, while the average was 43% for all 10 countries (**Figure 10.13**). While Burundi was the poorest of the 10, it was the only one where the assessment was in the national language and language of instruction, not in French. Such information is essential for interpreting the results.

CONCLUSION

A recent review of learning assessments concludes they are 'an effective and relevant way to judge that a population is acquiring the basic knowledge and competencies' (Muskin, 2016, p. 4). But can they provide useful and valid information for global monitoring purposes?

Numerous assessment sources demonstrate technical obstacles to reporting globally comparable learning indicators. Solutions will be imperfect and incomplete. When evaluating options, it is important to choose one that serves national needs as well as the aim of global monitoring.

This chapter emphasized the importance of applying the criteria of inclusivity, efficiency and feasibility. It underscored the principle that learning assessments should be considered a public good, delivered in the broad interest of the people. They should enhance prospects for improving a broad range of learning outcomes and reduce student disparity. The recently established Global Alliance to Monitor Learning, which aims to harmonize assessment frameworks and standards and help coordinate capacity-building efforts, is a welcome initiative. Clear governance mechanisms are needed to advance global collective action on these issues (UIS, 2016a).

Globally, the drive to test and assess learning outcomes has taken root. Most countries are committed to assessing learning; a surprisingly large percentage already conduct national assessments or have participated in cross-national assessments to compare learning levels with their neighbours or other systems. And yet most low income countries face enormous challenges to monitoring learning, in and out of school, and to committing to act on findings. In such contexts, many assessment systems are ineffective or of low quality and attention by government and school leaders to improve learning outcomes, especially among the marginalized, is low and unsustained.

One trap to avoid is focusing on a narrow range of assessed subjects. National curricular policies and assessment approaches should be well aligned to gain legitimacy and set the stage for reform. Support for initial assessments in certain subject domains should be contingent on sustained future efforts to develop valid, high quality assessments in other areas, such as sustainability issues and global citizenship, which are critical for the larger sustainable development agenda (see Chapter 16). Knowledge and skills in these and other areas can and should be assessed.

Countries should not see the need to report against a global measure as a constraint. They should not be required to participate in a cross-national assessment. This is an opportunity for countries to review their assessment strategies and invest in the approach that best serves their long-term interests. The next 15 years stand a good chance of driving improvement in the quality of national assessments, facilitated by the establishment of an international peer network and through efficient resource use.

Finally, once a global measure of learning is in place, it is important to set realistic expectations about the progress possible by 2030. Evidence from international assessments suggests that improvement in the percentage of students reaching minimum proficiency in reading and mathematics tests is likely to remain modest during such a short time span (Clarke, 2016).

Early learning in
Dublin, Ireland.

CREDIT: Jason Clarke Photography/
Department of Children and Youth Affairs,
Ireland

KEY MESSAGES

Comparing rates of *participation* in pre-primary education is difficult because age groups and starting ages differ a lot across countries. Pre-primary education is compulsory in 50 countries, and free and compulsory for at least one year in 38.

Globally, 67% of children of pre-primary school age are attending school. However, available data sources do not yet allow a reliable global estimate of how many children benefit from at least one year of pre-primary education.

Available data sources also do not fully capture the diversity of services providing learning opportunities for young children.

Among 3- to 4-year-olds, the richest children are almost 6 times more likely to attend an early childhood education programme than the poorest.

Quality standards of early childhood care and education need to be set, monitored and enforced.

Early childhood development can be assessed in four areas: executive function, social and emotional development, motor development, and early literacy and numeracy.

According to UNICEF, about 70% of 3-year-olds and 80% of 4-year-olds are developmentally on track in 56 low and middle income countries. However, this measure focuses strongly on literacy and numeracy. More research is needed on normative development of children in diverse cultures and contexts.

CHAPTER 11

TARGET 4.2

Early childhood

By 2030, ensure that all girls and boys have access to quality early childhood development, care and pre-primary education so that they are ready for primary education

GLOBAL INDICATOR 4.2.1 – *Proportion of children under 5 years of age who are developmentally on track in health, learning and psychosocial well-being, by sex*

GLOBAL INDICATOR 4.2.2 – *Participation rate in organized learning (one year before the official primary entry age), by sex*

THEMATIC INDICATOR 9 – *Percentage of children under 5 years of age experiencing positive and stimulating home learning environments*

THEMATIC INDICATOR 11 – *Gross pre-primary enrolment ratio*

THEMATIC INDICATOR 12 – *Number of years of (i) free and (ii) compulsory pre-primary education guaranteed in legal frameworks*

Target 4.2 reaffirms the focus of the international community on ensuring that all children receive a strong foundation through early childhood care and education. In fact, compared with the first Education for All (EFA) goal, the 2030 Agenda for Sustainable Development goes beyond care and education as a means of meeting children's learning needs, and includes early childhood development as an outcome. This is expressed in the concept of school readiness, which covers physical, social/emotional and language/cognitive domains.

This chapter identifies three monitoring challenges in relation to the concepts in target 4.2. The first, in regard to access and participation, is that no available source provides enough information on how many children benefit from pre-primary education – and organized learning programmes more generally – for at least one year. Two complementary participation-related indicators have been proposed, drawing on administrative and survey data, to address this.

Second, none of the proposed indicators capture the quality of provision. This chapter discusses proposed approaches for assessing the quality of early childhood education settings and systems.

Finally, the feasibility of introducing a monitoring mechanism for early childhood development is uncertain. That uncertainty is partly why this is the only target

under the education Sustainable Development Goal (SDG) for which the Inter-agency and Expert Group on Sustainable Development Goal Indicators put forward two global indicators, complementing the outcome measure with a participation measure.

ACCESS AND PARTICIPATION

Comparing pre-primary education participation rates across countries is more difficult than comparing participation measures in primary and secondary education, for several reasons. First, the age groups and starting ages are less standardized in pre-primary education than at other levels. Almost half the world's countries have a three-year pre-primary education age group, with children expected to first enrol at the age of 3. However, many other combinations of duration and starting age are common (**Table 11.1**). Calculating participation rates over such varied groups of children may lead to misleading conclusions.

Second, relatively few countries have free and/or compulsory pre-primary education. Among the 207 countries and territories, pre-primary education was compulsory in 50, and free and compulsory for at least one year in 38.

Third, pre-primary education takes diverse forms. Non-government provision is common (accounting for 42%

Of 207 countries and territories, pre-primary education was compulsory in 50, and free and compulsory for at least one year in 38

In 2014, 44% of children were enrolled in pre-primary education worldwide

globally in 2014 and 58% in South-eastern Asia) but more likely to not be registered. A variety of programmes have learning components, not all of which are purely educational. As a result, some countries struggle to capture the full scale of provision.

Fourth, the willingness and capacity of government to expand pre-primary education provision has been limited in some countries. In many poorer ones, the intake rate into the first grade of primary school has been consistently in excess of 100% of the relevant population. One explanation is an absence of pre-primary classes to absorb the demand (Crouch, 2015). Without pre-primary access, parents enrol their children in primary classes to improve their school readiness, but they are ill prepared for them.

These challenges affect the understanding of the real levels of participation in early childhood learning programmes, as a comparison of different indicators also shows.

The most common indicator with the widest country coverage is the pre-primary gross enrolment ratio, which is the number of children enrolled in pre-primary education as a percentage of the population of children in the relevant age group.

TABLE 11.1:

Distribution of countries by pre-primary education duration and starting age, and whether it is free and compulsory

	Duration (years)				Total
	1	2	3	4	
Starting age (years)					
3	-	25	103	20	148
4	5	34	6	-	45
5	5	8	-	-	13
6	1	-	-	-	1
Total	11	67	109	20	207
Free	14	27	30	8	79
Compulsory	30	15	5	0	50
Free and compulsory	22	12	4	0	38

Sources: UIS database; GEM Report team calculations.

In 2014, the global gross enrolment ratio was 44%, considerably lower than in 2012 as a result of a large downward adjustment to the estimate for India. Indeed, Southern Asia is the region with the lowest participation rate at 18.5%, followed by sub-Saharan Africa (21.5%) and Northern Africa and Western Asia (29%). Much higher rates are observed in Latin America and the Caribbean (73%), Eastern and South-eastern Asia (76%) and Europe and Northern America (85%).

A variant of the indicator considers enrolment not only in pre-primary but in all early childhood education programmes. Among the 148 countries with data for both indicators, the median value increases by 3 percentage points when accounting for these programmes. This includes 92 countries where there is no difference between the indicators but also 23 countries where the difference exceeds 20 percentage points: in Namibia, the enrolment ratio more than doubles, from 21% to 55%, while in Indonesia, it increases from 58% to 95%. This raises the question whether other early childhood education programmes are consistently being captured across all countries.

The Pacific is the region with the highest gross enrolment ratio, 98%. This is somewhat misleading, however, and gives a good example of the indicator's weakness. As the gross enrolment ratio value for Australia is not reported, the regional value is imputed. When all early childhood education programmes were taken into account, however, Australia reported a gross enrolment ratio of 216% because its pre-primary education age lasts only one year (4-year-olds), compared with two years for New Zealand (3- to 4-year-olds) and three years for Papua New Guinea (3- to 5-year-olds).

An alternative indicator is the net enrolment ratio: the number of children one year younger than the primary school entrance age who are enrolled in pre-primary education as a percentage of the population of that age group. This indicator is an improvement because it tries to control for the differences across countries by considering a comparable age group. Its median value does not differ from that of the gross enrolment ratio. Ideally, this would be true for all countries, in which case the pair of values for the two indicators would lie on the diagonal line (**Figure 11.1**).

But the values for individual countries can vary considerably, e.g. the pre-primary gross enrolment ratio for 4- to 5-year-olds in Costa Rica was 53% but the net enrolment ratio among 5-year-olds, the last year of pre-primary education, was 93%. This suggests that almost all 5-year-olds are enrolled in pre-primary education but many 4-year-olds are not.

Discrepancies are also observed in the opposite direction. The pre-primary gross enrolment ratio for Ireland was 108% but the net enrolment ratio among 4-year-olds, the last year of pre-primary education, was 58%. This is because a considerable proportion of 4-year-olds are already enrolled in primary school, which means the official pre-primary education age group does not capture actual national enrolment patterns (OECD, 2015b).

The UNESCO Institute for Statistics (UIS) recently developed an extension of this indicator. Called the adjusted net enrolment ratio, it captures the number

of children one year younger than the primary school entrance age who are enrolled in pre-primary or primary education as a percentage of the population of that age group. Globally, data from 135 countries show the adjusted net enrolment ratio to be equal to 67%. This indicator is being used as a proxy for global indicator 4.2.2.

Another indicator – the percentage of new entrants to the first grade of primary school who have participated in any early childhood education programmes – directly measures whether children have attended at least one year of pre-primary education. However, there are two approaches to getting the answer.

The first is based on school reporting. Overall, for the 67 countries with data on all three indicators, the average percentage of new primary school entrants who had apparently participated in an early childhood programme was 15 percentage points higher than the net enrolment ratio in the last year of pre-primary school. This could suggest that primary schools exaggerate the extent to which their students attended early childhood education, though more evidence is needed to substantiate that explanation.

The second approach is based on direct household reporting through, for instance, the UNICEF Multiple Indicator Cluster Survey (MICS), which collects systematic retrospective information on students in the first grade of primary school who had participated in pre-primary education the previous year. As this reflects direct responses from parents, it can serve as a standard against which to compare other potential proxy indicators for global indicator 4.2.2 based on administrative data, such as the net and adjusted net enrolment ratio.

Such a comparison is possible for 38 countries with data over 2010–2015. The median proportion of children in the first grade whose parents reported their attendance in pre-primary school the previous year was around 77%. This compares with a median net enrolment ratio for these countries of 59%, and a median adjusted net enrolment ratio of 80%. Thus it appears that the adjusted net enrolment ratio provides a more accurate picture of the percentage of children who participated in organized learning one year before the official primary entry age.

However, it is important to note there can be significant differences for individual countries; e.g. in Mali the net enrolment ratio was 1% and the adjusted net enrolment

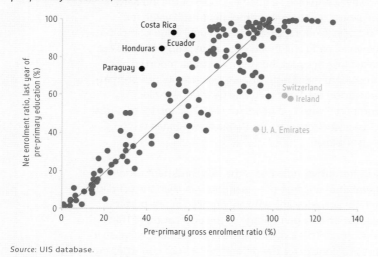

FIGURE 11.1:

Similar indicators of pre-primary education participation give different results in many countries

Pre-primary gross enrolment ratio and net enrolment ratio in the last year of pre-primary education, 2014

Source: UIS database.

ratio was 44%, while the percentage of those directly reported as having attended pre-primary school the previous year was 15% (**Figure 11.2**).

But the MICS does not just report the percentage of children in first grade of primary school who attended pre-primary school the previous year. It also collects information on attendance in early childhood education programmes for 3- to 4-year-olds. Among 42 mostly low and middle income countries with observations for all three age groups over 2009–2015, the median attendance rate was 24% among 3-year-olds, 45% among 4-year-olds and 72% among those in the last year of pre-primary education.

The MICS-based indicators also enable disaggregation by individual characteristics, which is necessary to report on disparity. The extent of wealth-based disparity is striking. Among 3- to 4-year-olds, children in the richest households are almost six times more likely to attend an early childhood education programme than children from the poorest. In Tunisia in 2011/12, 81% of the richest 3- to 4-year-olds but 13% of the poorest attended an early childhood education programme. The wealth disparity decreases among children in the first grade of primary school who had attended pre-primary school the previous year. Still, in the Lao People's Democratic Republic, 67% of the richest but 10% of the poorest had attended pre-primary education (**Figure 11.3**).

Pre-primary education-related questions in the MICS are split between two sections of the questionnaire. The first refers to children up to age 5 and the second to children age 5 and older, but the questions asked are not the same. Similar problems beset the Demographic and Health Survey, the other major household survey tool, which does not ask any education-related questions for children up to age 5, and only rarely includes pre-primary education as a possible response to questions for children age 5 and older.

Household surveys are better at capturing the diversity of available early childhood development programmes than administrative data, which are generally limited to formal pre-primary education. To enhance comparability, surveys should coordinate questions related to early childhood and pre-primary education so improved statistics for monitoring participation rates under target 4.2 can be calculated. They also need to compile more detailed information on pre-primary programmes and providers to better understand the extent to which children are exposed to organized learning opportunities.

FIGURE 11.2:

Accounts of participation in early childhood care and education programmes differ between households and schools

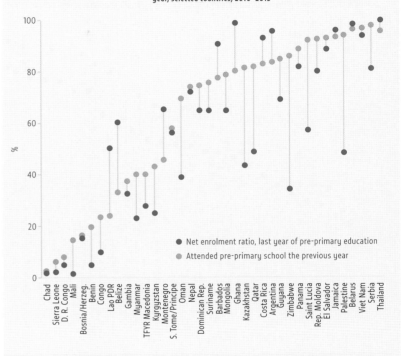

a. Pre-primary net enrolment ratio in the last year of pre-primary education, 2014; and percentage of students in the first grade of primary school who participated in pre-primary education the previous year, selected countries, 2010–2015

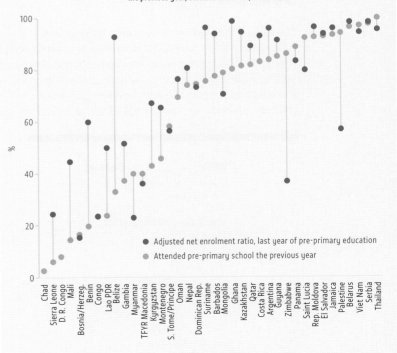

b. Pre-primary adjusted net enrolment ratio in the last year of pre-primary education, 2014; and percentage of students in the first grade of primary school who participated in pre-primary education the previous year, selected countries, 2010–2015

Sources: UIS database for the net and adjusted net enrolment ratio; MICS final and key findings reports for the percentage of students in the first grade of primary school who attended pre-school during the previous school year.

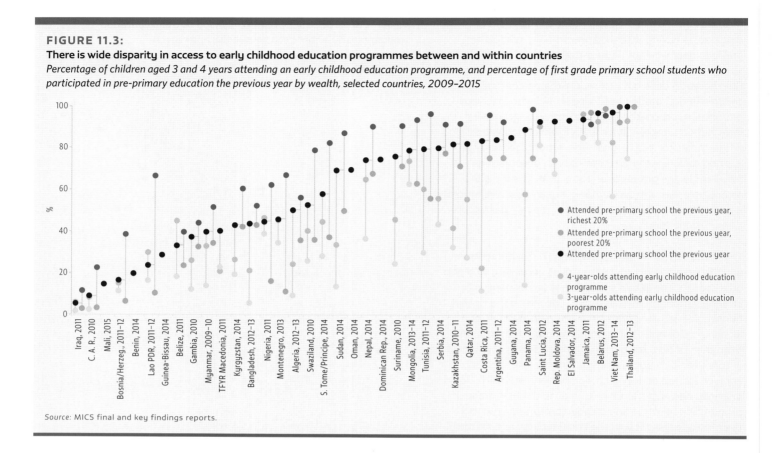

FIGURE 11.3:
There is wide disparity in access to early childhood education programmes between and within countries
Percentage of children aged 3 and 4 years attending an early childhood education programme, and percentage of first grade primary school students who participated in pre-primary education the previous year by wealth, selected countries, 2009–2015

Legend:
- Attended pre-primary school the previous year, richest 20%
- Attended pre-primary school the previous year, poorest 20%
- Attended pre-primary school the previous year
- 4-year-olds attending early childhood education programme
- 3-year-olds attending early childhood education programme

Source: MICS final and key findings reports.

QUALITY

The early childhood target explicitly emphasizes education of good quality. Quality may be understood in this context as the extent to which school and classroom settings (including structures and teaching processes) and systems support the holistic development of children, particularly those at risk of social exclusion.

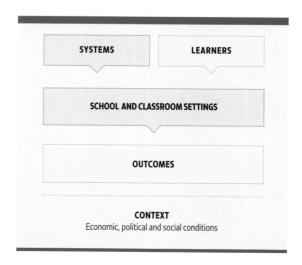

The effectiveness of early childhood education in terms of outcomes (in particular, executive function, social-emotional development, motor development, and pre-academic skills that improve the school readiness of children) is described in the next section. This section focuses on tools that assess quality in processes and structures, and – to a lesser extent – systems.

DEFINING QUALITY IN SETTINGS AND SYSTEMS

Much of the information on quality in early childhood education has been generated through observation of classrooms, surveys of teachers and directors, and examination of policies and regulations. This approach to defining and measuring quality relies on observable attributes of early childhood education services that research has linked to children's future school achievement and well-being. The approach has its critics, who argue that quality should be defined as context-based, subjective, relative and based on values (Dahlberg et al., 1999).

Because of the range and diversity of early childhood programmes, these two viewpoints need to be integrated. Many observable attributes have been shown to promote child development, yet they must be relevant and applicable to each setting in which they are applied. The absence of standards can result in toleration of poor quality provision and a lack of guidance on how professional development programmes might be structured (Siraj-Blatchford and Wong, 1999). A pathway that draws upon measurement expertise while allowing for adaptation, revision and alignment with cultural values and discourse is essential for accurately measuring and comparing the quality of early childhood education.

Consensus can be reached on many crucial dimensions of the process and structures of quality in early childhood settings. For example, the International Step by Step Association (ISSA), a non-government network of professionals especially active in Europe and Central Asia, has identified principles that underpin teaching practices of high quality (ISSA, 2009). They cover seven domains: interactions; family and community; inclusion, diversity, and values of democracy; assessment and planning; teaching strategies; learning environment; and professional development. Such frameworks can help form the basis for monitoring quality.

Perhaps the most critical element of process quality is the interaction between teachers and children, its nature and depth, and the extent to which interactions enable children to be autonomous and stimulated (Mashburn et al., 2008; Britto et al., 2011). ISSA highlights three principles when assessing interactions: whether educators interact with children in a friendly and respectful manner that supports the development of each child's construction of self/identity and learning; whether interactions help develop a learning community where all children are supported to reach their potential; and whether educators engage in purposeful, reciprocal interactions with other adults to support children's development and learning.

Early childhood education environments of high quality are also inclusive. Educators should provide opportunities for every child and family to learn and participate, identify children who are falling behind, and address individual differences in needs and skills. A key aspect of inclusiveness is that children have the opportunity to learn in their native language. In areas with linguistic

> " One of the most critical elements of a quality pre-primary education is the interaction between teachers and children, and whether children are enabled to be autonomous and stimulated "

diversity, teachers who are fluent in children's native tongues can have enormous benefits for language and literacy development (Ball, 2011).

Much of the attention on monitoring quality has focused on quantitative measures – such as child/teacher ratios, class sizes, teacher qualifications, access to water and good hygiene, or availability of materials – because the data are easier to collect. However, while improvement in these measures can increase process quality, it does not ensure it. Studies show modest correlations between the two dimensions at the classroom or programme level (Yoshikawa et al., 2013).

Finally, the quality of early childhood care and education systems is understood to play a major role in achieving desirable outcomes. Five elements of achieving quality have been identified for high income countries: setting quality goals and regulations; designing and implementing curriculum standards; improving qualifications, training and workforce conditions; engaging parents and communities; and advancing data collection, research and monitoring (OECD, 2012c). The applicability and relevance of these actions in low and middle income countries have not yet been addressed. In integrated and devolved systems, the quality of governance, both horizontal (across sectors) and vertical (across levels, from national to local), has also been considered critical (Britto et al., 2014).

MEASURING QUALITY OF SETTINGS

Several measures of early childhood education quality have been tested. They tend to involve trainees rating a setting using observation, documentation and interviews during a two- to four-hour visit. The most desirable characteristic of an effective measure of quality assessment is validity, i.e. the extent to which the element assessed is meaningful and has proven positive effects on child outcomes. Establishing validity becomes more complicated when aiming for a measure comparable across countries and various types of service provision (Ishimine and Tayler, 2014). Many measures have yet to be fully validated in all countries.

> **There are different tools for measuring early childhood education quality, which tend to involve class observation, documentation and interviews**

The most widely used tool, the Early Childhood Environment Rating Scale (ECERS), was developed at the University of North Carolina in 1980 and revised in 1998 (ECERS-R) and 2015 (ECERS3). Variants of it focus on infants/toddlers, family child care and school age care. As part of a 3-hour visit, the tool uses 43 items to measure process and structure aspects of quality in 7 key areas: space and furnishings; personal care routines; language and reasoning; activities; interaction; programme structure; and parents and staff. In the latest revision, the 'parents and staff' subscale, which relied on self-reporting, has been dropped (Harms et al., 2015).

ECERS-R forms the core of formal, observation-based quality assurance systems in much of the United States and has been translated and adapted for countries including Germany and Italy. Researchers in Bahrain (Hadeed, 2014), Bangladesh (Aboud, 2004), Brazil (Campos et al., 2011) and Cambodia (Rao and Pearson, 2007), and in the Caribbean (Lambert et al., 2008), have also used this tool. However, while it tries to be comprehensive, ECERS-R only uses a selected set of questions for each domain.

The Classroom Assessment Scoring System (CLASS), developed at the University of Virginia in 2008, focuses instead on just one domain, teacher-child interactions (Hamre et al., 2007). It relies on 4 cycles of 15-minute observations of teacher and child interactions, evaluating the degree of instructional and socio-emotional support and overall classroom organization.

CLASS was validated in the United States but has also been applied in research and policy-oriented studies in Europe (e.g. Finland, Pakarinen et al., 2010), Latin America (e.g. Ecuador, Araujo et al., 2015) and sub-Saharan Africa (e.g. United Republic of Tanzania, Shavega et al., 2014).

Neither ECERS-R nor CLASS was originally developed for international use. By contrast, the Global Guidelines Assessment (GGA) of the Association for Childhood Education International, developed in collaboration with the US national committee of the World Organization for Early Childhood, set out to measure progress on the 2002 Global Guidelines for Early Childhood Education and Care in the 21st Century (Barbour et al., 2004). The GGA is divided into five areas: environment and physical space; curriculum content and pedagogy; early childhood educators and caregivers; partnership with families and communities; and young children with special needs. It has been used in East Asia (e.g. the Republic of Korea, Wortham, 2012), Europe (e.g. Greece, Rentzou, 2010) and Latin America (e.g. Guatemala, Hardin et al., 2008). However, it has not been validated in relation to child outcomes.

Overall, several studies, mostly using ECERS-R, find positive associations between programme quality and measures of child development linked to pre-academic cognitive skills or social-behavioural development (Burchinal et al., 2008; Sylva et al., 2006). But the size of the effects tends to be small (Sabol and Pianta, 2014; Gordon et al., 2015).

The use of such tools is a helpful prompt for debating quality in target 4.2. It helps decision-makers address priorities, e.g. in China, where views are divided on the relative merits of whole classroom vs child-centred learning (Li et al., 2014; Hu, 2015). It also points out differences in quality between facilities or types of programmes within countries – e.g. in rural Indonesia, where differences in quality were shown between various types of provision (Brinkman et al., 2016) – and identify significant differences between countries (e.g. Vermeer et al., 2016).

Countries and the international community should consider using such tools to monitor the quality of early childhood education provision more systematically. The process of consensus building should begin with countries setting their own goals and standards – and using a mechanism to monitor them. They should use and adapt the tools that are most applicable to their context and that give useful feedback to educators for professional development (UNICEF, 2012a).

MEASURING QUALITY OF SYSTEMS

At the system level, a variety of tools have been developed. The World Bank Systems Approach for Better Education Results (SABER) has published

30 country reports in 3 areas, not limited to education: the enabling environment (legal framework, intersectoral coordination and finance); implementation (programme scope, coverage and equity); and monitoring and quality assurance (data availability, standards and compliance).

An important aspect of quality is the extent to which standards are set and enforced. Among 21 countries with data, 8 did not have standards on the pupil/teacher ratio in public early childhood education institutions. Of those that did, 5 enforced them, and 3 set and enforced a standard of no more than 15 children per teacher (**Table 11.2**).

In Europe, a monitoring mechanism helps countries exchange information on aspects of early childhood care and education systems, finding, for example, large differences between processes of evaluating whether settings meet standards. Evaluations are carried out at the central (e.g. Croatia), regional (e.g. Spain) or local (e.g. Lithuania) level or jointly at two (e.g. Denmark) or three levels (e.g. Finland). They are sometimes delegated to independent agencies (e.g. in Scotland [United Kingdom]) or to non-profit companies operating on behalf of central authorities (e.g. in Ireland). In Italy, there is no external evaluation process for institutions serving older children, but local authorities evaluate institutions for younger children (European Commission/EACEA/Eurydice/Eurostat, 2014).

The Organisation for Economic Co-operation and Development (OECD) undertakes voluntary reviews of the early childhood care and education systems of member and non-member countries every three years. The most recent round focused on national monitoring systems of quality. In Kazakhstan, there is a standardized national framework of quality and effective feedback mechanisms between central authorities and local public providers. Monitoring is relatively infrequent, once every five years, and tends to have limited information about private institutions. In Mexico, despite very diverse institutional provision, involving federal and other public home-based and centre-based care, monitoring occurs annually and in-service training for evaluators is provided (OECD, 2015g).

CHILD DEVELOPMENT OUTCOMES

Target 4.2 focuses on ensuring that children begin formal schooling developmentally on track and 'ready for primary education'. This holistic view linked to school-based

TABLE 11.2:

Setting and enforcing standards on the pupil/teacher ratio in public early childhood education institutions, selected countries, 2012–2015

No standards	Belize, D. R. Congo, Gambia, Kyrgyzstan, Mali, U. R. Tanzania, Uganda, Yemen
Yes >15 children/teacher; not enforced	Burkina Faso, Guinea, Malawi, Nigeria
Yes ≤15 children/teacher; not enforced	Tonga
Yes >15 children/teacher; enforced	Albania, Jamaica, Kiribati, Mauritius, Nepal
Yes ≤15 children/teacher; enforced	Bulgaria, Indonesia, Samoa

Source: World Bank SABER early childhood development country reports.

learning marks a shift from a view of child development based exclusively on health-related indicators.

Early childhood development, which refers to neurological and physical growth in the early years of life, has lasting implications for learning, health and well-being (Walker et al., 2007). Accurate, reliable measures of early childhood development can inform policy-making and investment alternatives, contribute to curricular reform and teacher training, and identify children at risk.

Promoting early childhood development, especially for the marginalized, is a pathway to reducing inequality by ensuring that all children begin formal schooling on an even plane. Tracking early childhood development will likely reveal disparities that begin very early in life, at birth or earlier, and grow larger over time.

Measuring young children's development and readiness to learn has long entailed debate on the reliability of tools and the ethics of involving very young children (e.g. Myers, 2006; Zill, 2005). Critics question whether measuring such aspects of early childhood at a population level is even possible.

Despite concerns, efforts to track progress towards target 4.2 should carefully consider recently developed measures of early childhood development. Efforts should focus on population-based measurement, or measures designed to inform policy at the national level, rather than diagnose individual children with delayed development. Population-based measures differ from measures designed for research or programme evaluation, as they are designed for use at scale, with an emphasis on feasible, cost-effective measurement.

This subsection reviews key issues on early childhood development and some of the most commonly used regional and global measures.[1]

WHAT DOES IT MEAN TO BE DEVELOPMENTALLY ON TRACK?

'Developmentally on track' means children are developing the skills and competencies that will allow them to participate successfully in their environments and reach their current and future developmental potential. Deciding how best to measure child development is complex. Four significant themes are outlined below.

First, development proceeds in trajectories. Young children's development at the start of school is the extension of a trajectory that began at conception and continues through infancy and toddlerhood. Disparities in children's cognitive and language development are apparent as early as 4 months of age, and tend to widen, not decrease, over time (Fernald et al., 2012). Interpretation of data on child development and learning at a given point in time, such as the start of school, should be based on a view of children's development as a trajectory that begins at birth.

> " Disparities in cognitive and language development are apparent as early as 4 months of age, and tend to widen, not decrease, over time "

Second, patterns of child development are similar in all settings, but environmental influences have a profound impact on development. Genetic information leads to common developmental patterns in all people, such as the acquisition of early language and communication and the first expression of cognitive problem-solving skills. But nearly all human traits, skills and competencies reflect a complex set of interactions between genetic information and environmental stimuli, with some traits more strongly influenced by environment or genes than others (van Izjendoorn et al., 2011).

The strongest, most reliable predictor of young children's development in both high and low income countries is the home environment, even when children attend high quality pre-schools (Bornstein et al., 2015). Stimulating, supportive home environments can be measured by asking about the frequency of activities or observing caregiver–child interactions (**Box 11.1**).

Children who are given more opportunities to communicate, room to explore and cognitive stimulation develop skills faster and more consistently. Children develop language faster when spoken to more frequently (Hart and Risley, 1995; Snow, 1997) regardless of whether the frequency of language interaction varies due to cultural preference (e.g. some cultures hold babies on the backs of adults, where they have less face-to-face interaction) or an inability to fully bond with a dedicated, emotionally available caregiver. It is not yet known whether children's failure to show competencies in certain cultures is due to lack of cultural relevance or inadequacy of stimulation. Measurement must accept this lack of clarity, and continue to test core assumptions on the universality of children's development.

Third, some areas of child development, such as the accumulation of vocabulary words and early literacy skills, proceed in a linear fashion and are straightforward to measure (Thompson, 2014). Other developments, such as understanding that people have diverse perspectives, emerge at about the same age in more than one culture, at the age of about 4 years (Sabbagh et al., 2006). In yet others, development at an early age does not seem to show much relation to learning and achievement over time in intermediate years, but emerges later as a strong influence (Vandell et al., 2010).

In addition, development in one area fuels development in others. Language development, for example, has a strong influence on social interactions because children with better language skills can communicate better with peers. This means that measuring early childhood development should include all domains of development, rather than focusing only on early academic skills. For some areas, the effects of early childhood development may take several years to become apparent.

Fourth, while the science underlying basic developmental processes is clear, defining 'on track' development has not yet been fully established for children in many cultures. Measurement is relativistic: standards for what children should be able to do are informed by knowing what is typical, or what children around them can do. What is normative is ideally established through the creation of normal distributions of children's development and skills acquisition in various parts of the world, with ages at which children are typically demonstrating specific skills.

It is difficult to define normative development in a globally comparable manner because culture influences development and, primarily, because the extent to

BOX 11.1

Defining positive and stimulating home learning environments

While rapid brain development takes place during the first three to four years, at this age most children lack access to organized learning opportunities outside the home. To draw attention to this issue, the proposed thematic monitoring framework includes an indicator on the 'percentage of children under 5 years of age experiencing positive and stimulating home learning environments'.

A stimulating home learning environment provides educational interactions and learning materials. UNICEF's MICS collects comparable information on both. In relation to interactions, the surveys estimate whether adult household members have engaged children aged 36 to 59 months in reading or looking at picture books; telling stories; singing songs; going outside the home; playing; and naming, counting and/or drawing things.

UNICEF reported the percentage of children with whom adult household members had engaged in at least four of these activities in the past three days over 2009–2012. While adults had engaged almost all children in at least four activities in Ukraine, that was true for only 40% of children in Ghana. The probability that the father had engaged in at least one activity was typically about 25 percentage points lower, although smaller gaps were observed in countries including Jordan, Iraq and Tunisia (**Figure 11.4a**). Comparisons are affected by considerable differences between countries in the extent to which children live with their biological father.

In 2013, UNICEF changed its reporting, and the new way of presenting results suggests that levels of parental engagement are actually considerably lower. In Zimbabwe, 43% of children had engaged in at least four activities in the past three days with an adult household member. About 75% of 3- to 4-year-olds lived with their biological mother but just 17% had engaged in at least four activities with her. And while about 50% of children lived with their biological father, only 3% had engaged in at least four activities with him.

With respect to learning materials, the MICS collects information on the presence of children's books at home. Across 54 mostly low and middle income countries over 2010–2015, 19% of households had at least 3 books and 7.5% had at least 10 books. Among the poorest 20%, less than 1% of households had at least 10 books at home (**Figure 11.4b**).

FIGURE 11.4:

Home learning environments differ substantially between countries

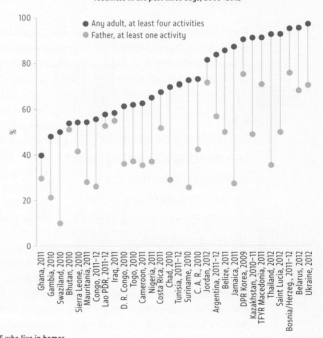

a. Percentage of children age 36 to 59 months with whom an adult household member and the father engaged in activities that promote learning and school readiness in the past three days, 2009–2012

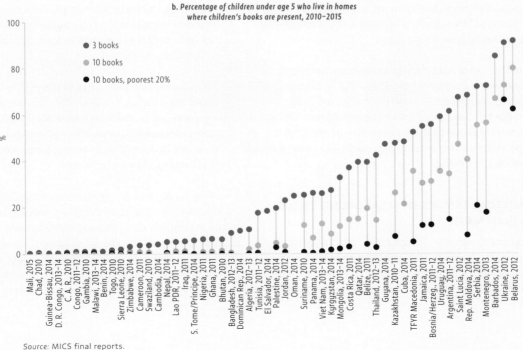

b. Percentage of children under age 5 who live in homes where children's books are present, 2010–2015

Source: MICS final reports.

Sources: Bradley and Caldwell (1995); Zimbabwe National Statistics Agency (2015).

which children achieve milestones or demonstrate skills is unknown in much of the world (Marfo et al., 2011). Parental or cultural concepts of child development vary. Policy may not match them. Measurement of culturally inappropriate expectations for children's development would mask the true competencies of a population. A priority for research for the new education agenda is which measures are relevant to all children and can be used to define global standards for a child to be 'developmentally on track'.

Three conclusions emerge. First, as child development and skill acquisition proceed in trajectories, their measurement should ideally begin earlier than entry to school. From a developmental standpoint, the start of formal schooling is not significant. Over time, measurement methodologies should be created to track progress over time rather than focusing on a single point in time.

> " A priority for research for the new education agenda is which measures can be used to define global standards for a child to be 'developmentally on track' "

Second, measures of context are needed as well as indicators of child development and readiness to learn. The lack of information on children's health, nutrition and family environment makes it hard to determine whether and why children's development is on track or not, and which policies and interventions could effectively support healthy development.

Third, the use of national-level measurement that allows careful consideration of cultural and contextual influences on the timing and expression of child competencies and skills should be considered, alongside a research agenda to track normative development across cultures and develop approaches to measurement based on the findings.

PRACTICAL ISSUES IN MEASURING CHILD DEVELOPMENT

The above conclusions must be weighed against the need for feasible, cost-effective approaches to measurement that can be used at scale and over time. This entails a technical challenge. Given the gap between an ideal system and countries' capacity in the near future, balance is needed between technical strength, the protection of children's rights and feasibility.

There is widespread agreement that children develop in four related domains that include a range of skills and competencies:

- Executive function: Self-regulation, approaches to learning and other skills drive learning across a number of areas. This domain includes some of the strongest drivers of academic performance over time, including sustained attention, working memory and the ability to inhibit impulses.

- Social-emotional development: Social and emotional skills facilitate children's successful interactions with others (including peers, teachers and family members) as well as children's inclusion and may help them engage in school over time.

- Motor development: Fine and gross motor skills include coordination in walking, balancing, jumping and throwing balls; and the ability to write, pick up small objects and otherwise use the fingers successfully. Fine motor development predicts cognition, presumably because it indicates to some degree whether neurological development is on track (Grissam et al., 2010).

- Pre-academic (early mathematics and literacy) skills: This is perhaps the most established domain in research and includes early skills such as letter/sound identification and counting that are considered fundamental to developing literacy and numeracy skills later in life.

Measurement of each domain is possible but requires varied approaches. For example, social-emotional development is measured more accurately through reports by parents or teachers who know children well, while pre-academic skills are best measured through direct interaction with children.

More agreement on measurement methodology exists in some domains than in others. There is agreement on measuring early literacy skills, but less on how to measure social-emotional development and executive function, because the constructs are less clearly defined and the related skills manifest less directly, and thus are more likely to vary by culture and context.

At the start of the process to develop or evaluate tools, it is essential to define measurement and its uses in a manner that protects children's rights. There are notable risks for children; for example, measuring their learning at the start of the school year could exclude them from school on the grounds that they are unready.

> **It is essential to define measurement of early literacy skills and its uses in a manner that protects children's rights**

For measurement to accurately address equity concerns, all children, including those at risk for disabilities, must be included in samples. Thus, even though measures are not intended to identify individual children, the range of items must be broad enough to capture all children's development, not just those that are typical. Measures based on nationally representative household surveys thus produce better data than those based on assessments only of children who are in pre-school.

As measuring child development and learning is complex, questions remain. How comprehensive can surveys be? No survey, especially not one that can be conducted in 20 minutes, will fully describe children's competencies or the quality of learning environments. For school readiness, many constructs may not be directly observable in their entirety. For example, social-emotional development refers to a group of behaviours or capacities, including those not easy to measure.

How can reliability be ensured, i.e. the degree to which an assessment tool produces stable and consistent results, even if applied at different times or by different administrators? Assessments require trained assessors who are skilled and practised in assessing children. This level of training and expertise may not be possible in all regions. Language of administration is also critical for accurate assessment of children's pre-academic skills.

How can validity be ensured, i.e. the extent to which the test measures what it says it measures? A valid measure of school readiness should indicate how well children will perform later in school. However, many tools have not yet been used in studies that give clear evidence of how scores relate to children's achievement over time.

SELECTED APPROACHES TO MEASURING CHILD DEVELOPMENT

Several population-based measures of early childhood development have been tested in recent years (**Table 11.3**). UNICEF developed the East Asia Pacific Child Development Scales (EAP-CDS). A validation study was conducted in 2013–2014 on a sample of over 7,000 children in Cambodia, China, Mongolia, Timor-Leste, Vanuatu and Viet Nam. Some patterns varied by country (e.g. children in China had significantly higher mathematics scores). The impact of age, gender and maternal education on child development also varied by country. The size of the effect of attendance in early childhood programmes on early child development varied as well, with the biggest impact, in Cambodia, nearly three times the size of the smallest, in Timor-Leste (Rao et al., 2015).

The International Development and Early Learning Assessment (IDELA), developed by Save the Children, was piloted in 11 countries and has since been used in more than 30, although not in representative samples (Pisani et al., 2015). A randomized trial in partnership with the World Bank in Mozambique demonstrated that children who attended pre-school had higher scores at the end of pre-school and more engagement in early years of school (Martinez et al., 2012).

The Regional Project on Child Development Indicators (PRIDI) project was developed by the Inter-American Development Bank. A study in four countries (Costa Rica, Nicaragua, Paraguay and Peru) indicated that the items showed expected sensitivity to age and cultural background, including maternal education (Verdisco et al., 2014)

The Early Childhood Development Index (ECDI) was developed by UNICEF for the MICS programme (Zill and Ziv, 2007). A child is considered developmentally on track in four domains if:

■ In the literacy-numeracy domain, a child can do at least 2 of 3 tasks: identify/name at least 10 letters of the alphabet, read at least 4 simple popular words and know the name and recognize the symbols of all numbers from 1 to 10.

■ In the physical domain, a child can pick up a small object, such as a stick or a rock, with two fingers from the ground, and the mother/caretaker does not indicate that the child is sometimes too sick to play.

TABLE 11.3:
Early childhood development tools

Tool • Organization Age group	History	Domains	Other information
East Asia Pacific Child Development Scales (EAP-CDS) • UNICEF and Asia Region Network for Early Childhood Ages 3 to 5	Based on the Early Learning Development Standards, which helped countries outline developmentally appropriate expectations for young children's development	85 items that cover approaches to learning; social-emotional development; cognitive development; cultural participation and knowledge; language and emergent literacy; motor development; health, hygiene and safety	Home environments, including maternal education and frequency of learning-related activities at home
International Development and Early Learning Assessment (IDELA) • Save the Children Ages 3 to 6	Originally a programme evaluation tool (based on items of other assessments) but now promoted as a measure for population-based monitoring	65 items that cover physical development, language, mathematics-cognitive development, social-emotional development	
Regional Project on Child Development Indicators (PRIDI) • Inter-American Development Bank Ages 2 to 4		Cognition, language and communication, social-emotional skills, motor skills	Child, family, community characteristics and child participation in early childhood development programmes Priority given to indigenous and marginalized populations
Early Childhood Development Index (ECDI) • UNICEF MICS Ages 3 to 4	Aimed at creating a global indicator of holistic early childhood development, drawing on the Early Development Index	10 items that cover numeracy and literacy (3), social-emotional development (3), approaches to learning (2), physical development (2)	Family environment module, with information on caregiver–child activities and access to playthings
Measuring Early Learning Quality and Outcomes (MELQO) • Brookings Institution, UNESCO, UNICEF and World Bank Ages 4 to 6	Initiated to promote feasible measurement of child development and learning and quality of learning environments in low and middle income countries	Social-emotional development, early literacy and mathematics, executive functioning and approaches to learning	Measurement of quality in formal, pre-primary learning environments

Source: Raikes (2016).

■ In the social-emotional domain, a child exhibits at least two of three behaviours: gets along well with other children; does not kick, bite or hit other children; and does not get distracted easily.

■ In the learning domain, a child can follow simple directions on how to do something correctly and, when given something to do, is able to do it independently.

The overall index is calculated as the percentage of children aged 3 to 4 who are developmentally on track in at least 3 of these 4 domains.

The ECDI has been estimated in more than 50 countries. Its strength is that the information it provides can be combined with information on home environments, children's health and nutrition, improving its policy relevance. It is considered to be the source of information on global indicator 4.2.1, even though it is only available for children under 5, which is before the start of formal schooling for most countries. There is also tension between trying to fully capture children's development over a span of 2 years and relying on 10 items to make collection at scale feasible.

ECDI-generated data from 56 mostly low and middle income countries over 2009–2015 indicated that about 70% of 3-year-olds and 80% of 4-year-olds were developmentally on track. However, results differed considerably by domain. More than 95% of children were on track in the physical domain, about 90% in the learning domain and almost 75% in the social-emotional domain. But in the literacy-numeracy domain, just 25% of children were on track. Results also showed predicted associations with family wealth, with only 12% of children from the poorest quintile of households on track in the literacy-numeracy domain (**Figure 11.5**); in Cameroon in 2011, 3% of children from the poorest households and 45% of children from the richest were on track in that domain.

Measuring Early Learning Quality and Outcomes (MELQO) was designed to help create and scale up workable open source tools, with joint leadership from the Brookings Institution, UNESCO, UNICEF and the World Bank in partnership with independent experts and non-profit organizations. The tools include a common core of questions from other assessments, which can be adapted by countries to align with their standards. The tools have been trialled in Bangladesh, Kenya, the Lao People's Democratic Republic, Madagascar, Mongolia, Sudan and the United Republic of Tanzania (Devercelli et al., 2015).

In high income countries, the OECD is to carry out an international survey of early child outcomes in 2017/18 to allow countries to monitor system-level progress (OECD, 2015g). Information on the domains the survey will cover is not yet available.

FIGURE 11.5:

About three-quarters of 3- to 4-year-olds are developmentally on track in 56 countries

Early Childhood Development Index, selected countries, 2009–2015

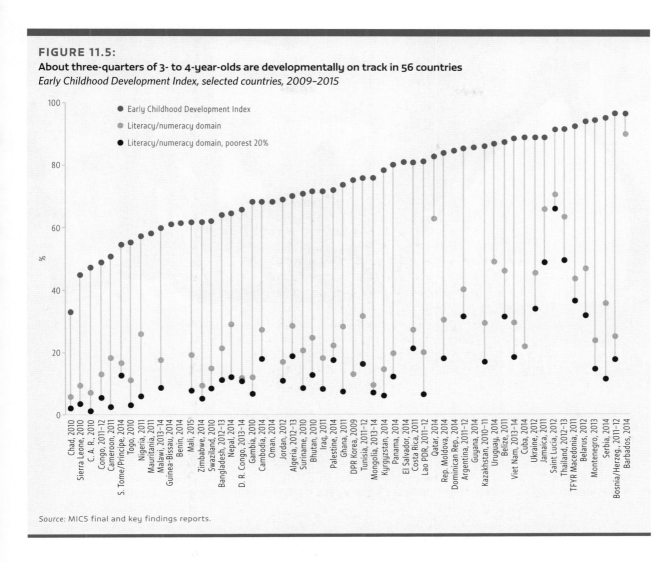

- Early Childhood Development Index
- Literacy/numeracy domain
- Literacy/numeracy domain, poorest 20%

Source: MICS final and key findings reports.

The case for measuring child development at the population level is strong. Among other reasons, it can identify sources of inequality that begin early in life and may persist through formal education and beyond. Equally important is the notion that development proceeds in patterns that are relevant across all groups of children, thus underscoring the efficiency of using a common set of constructs.

That said, evidence is lacking as to whether one set of items on children's development should be used everywhere, or if items should take into account culture and context (while keeping equivalent constructs) (e.g. Frongillo et al., 2014). The evidence clearly supports a more holistic set of measures of children's development and early childhood care and education, including those directly related to the target. Finally, to accurately monitor progress on this aspect of the education Sustainable Development Goal, more research is needed on normative development of children in diverse contexts.

ENDNOTES

1.   This section draws on Raikes (2016).

A young woman
studies chemistry
in the Russian
Federation.

CREDIT: V Makhorov/GEM Report

KEY MESSAGES

About 61 million of the world's secondary school students, or 11%, were enrolled in some formal **technical and vocational** education programme in 2014.

Relatively little is known about opportunities to learn skills in the workplace. New analysis from 12 countries shows about 20% of youth had participated in workplace-based programmes.

No one indicator can capture the *affordability* of technical and vocational and training (TVET). One approach is to contrast the amount students pay to institutions with the amount of financial support they receive from government.

One way to assess *quality* in TVET is whether a national qualification framework is in place. Such frameworks exist in 140 countries.

Access to **tertiary** education has expanded rapidly. Enrolment doubled from 2000 to 2014, but with huge disparity across and within countries. Across 76 countries, 20% of the richest 25- to 29-year-olds had completed at least 4 years of tertiary education, compared with less than 1% of the poorest.

The extent to which government financial assistance to households targets those most in need should be monitored to assess the *affordability* of tertiary education.

University rankings are easy to understand but give a partial and unreliable picture of the *quality* of student learning.

The diversity of provision makes monitoring *access* to and *participation* in **adult** education particularly difficult. Globally, adults made up 4% of those enrolled in formal primary education, and 5% and 10%, respectively, in lower and upper secondary education.

Less is known about participation in non-formal adult education. In European Union countries, 37% of adults participated in non-formal education in 2011.

Assessment of *affordability* in adult education is constrained by the greater role of private financing and the lack of information on public financing. Governments in fewer than one in six countries spent more than 0.3% of GDP on adult education.

CHAPTER 12

TARGET 4.3

Technical, vocational, tertiary and adult education

By 2030, ensure equal access for all women and men to affordable and quality technical, vocational and tertiary education, including university

GLOBAL INDICATOR 4.3.1 – *Participation rate of youth and adults in formal and non-formal education and training in the previous 12 months, by sex*

THEMATIC INDICATOR 13 – *Gross enrolment ratio for tertiary education*

THEMATIC INDICATOR 14 – *Participation rate in technical-vocational education programmes (15- to 24-year-olds)*

Target 4.3 introduces technical, vocational and tertiary education into the global development agenda. These areas were considered in the Dakar Framework for Action, but only indirectly, as a way to support alternate goals. Technical and vocational education was seen as a way for youth to acquire skills, and tertiary education as a way to prepare teachers. Tertiary education also appeared in the Millennium Development Goals (MDGs) but only in the context of gender parity.

> Target 4.3 introduces technical, vocational and tertiary education into the global development agenda

While targets 4.1 and 4.2 include both education participation and education outcomes, target 4.3 focuses only on participation. But it is closely linked to targets 4.4 and 4.6, which focus on outcomes that may be acquired through education participation at the technical, vocational and tertiary levels.

In its attempt to monitor the wide scope of target 4.3, the Inter-agency and Expert Group on SDG Indicators proposed as a global indicator the percentage of youth and adults participating in formal or non-formal education or training in the previous 12 months. This broad measure embraces education and training in all its forms, well beyond technical, vocational and tertiary education.

While the indicator may not match the exact formulation of the target, it helps redress an important omission. SDG 4 includes 'lifelong learning opportunities for all'. Lifelong learning comprises all activities undertaken throughout life with the aim of improving knowledge, skills and competencies from a personal, civic, social or employment-related perspective. However, the 10 targets fail to deal explicitly with adult education, though they capture all other aspects of lifelong learning. Hence, this report covers adult education participation under target 4.3 via global indicator 4.3.1.

This chapter examines three education levels – technical-vocational, tertiary and adult – from the angle of the three concepts in the target formulation: (equitable) access, affordability and quality. The proposed indicators do not capture affordability and quality.

Moreover, the target's reference to 'equal access for all women and men' generates ambiguity. The inclusion of 'all' shifts the emphasis from 'equal access' to 'access for all'. Does the target imply that everyone above age 15 should participate in technical, vocational and tertiary – or indeed also adult – education at least once in their life? Are the three levels interchangeable? Such questions could complicate monitoring, so this report avoids them and focuses on identifying measures of access, affordability and quality separately for each of the three levels.

TECHNICAL AND VOCATIONAL EDUCATION AND TRAINING

The thematic indicator proposed for technical and vocational education and training (TVET) is the participation rate in technical-vocational education programmes for youth. Traditionally, participation in TVET has been measured as a percentage of those enrolled at either the secondary or tertiary level. However, this indicator is expressed as a percentage of an age group (15- to 24-year-olds). Note that the indicator overlaps with global indicator 8.6.1, the percentage of youth not in education, employment or training, under the SDG 8 on employment. The following discussion addresses both education and training.

A typology of TVET recognizes three main means of provision: at an institution, at the workplace or through a combination of the two (**Table 12.1**).

Institution-based provision includes formal programmes, which provide students with an official diploma or certificate that is recognized by industry or corporations. Some of these programmes are not supervised by education ministries and enrolment in those may not be recorded in the data reported to the UNESCO Institute for Statistics (UIS). Institution-based provision also includes non-formal programmes, which are often not taken into account even when they result in certification.

TABLE 12.1:
A typology of technical and vocational education and training provision

Domain	Indicator
1. Institution-based	(i) In formal education • Supervised by the Ministry of Education • Not supervised by the Ministry of Education (ii) Outside formal education
2. Institution- and workplace-based	Multiple types (e.g. dual systems)
3. Workplace-based	(i) Training before employment (e.g. apprenticeships) (ii) Training during employment

Source: Adapted from IAG-TVET Working Group (2014).

Workplace-based provision can be prior to employment, as in apprenticeships, or during employment. The question is whether participation in workplace-based training should be included in a measure of TVET participation.

Given the variety of policy frameworks, institutional arrangements and organizational approaches, data collected through national statistical systems may only capture a partial picture, making TVET provision difficult to compare across countries.

ACCESS

About 62 million of all secondary school students, or 11%, were enrolled in some formal technical and vocational programme in 2014. There was a gender gap of two percentage points at the expense of females. On average, TVET students account for 1.5% of lower secondary and 23% of upper secondary enrolment. The highest share of technical and vocational education in secondary education is observed in Eastern and South-eastern Asia (17%) and the Pacific (26%), as a result of high enrolment levels in China and Australia, respectively. The lowest share is observed in Southern Asia (2%) (**Figure 12.1**).

FIGURE 12.1:
Only 2% of secondary school students were enrolled in technical and vocational programmes in Southern Asia
Technical and vocational programmes as a share of secondary education enrolment, 2014

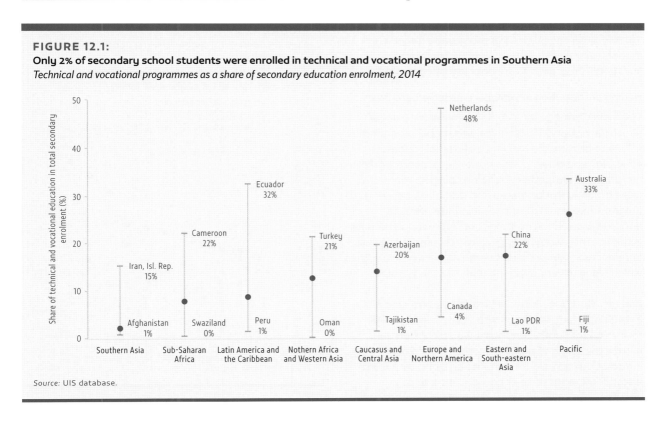

Source: UIS database.

Almost 19% of countries did not report this information in 2014, mostly because they reported no secondary enrolment data at all. A further 8% could not distinguish technical-vocational from general secondary enrolment, sometimes due to differences between national and international definitions. For example, national sources showed 19% of US secondary school graduates focusing on a technical-vocational course of study in 2009 (Dortch, 2014). As these studies may be offered as a single course or part of a career pathway, they do not map neatly onto the international definitions that separate general from vocational secondary school programmes. Hence UIS does not report technical-vocational enrolment data for the United States.

In 2014, 11 million students were in post-secondary non-tertiary education programmes, which may last from six months to several years. In the 54 countries that identified the type of programme, 95% of students were enrolled in technical and vocational programmes. Notable cases where the share of enrolment in technical-vocational programmes was lower were China (38%), Egypt (18%) and France (51%).

Many national systems offer technical and vocational programmes at the tertiary level, through either a short-cycle tertiary or a professional programme, but the UIS annual survey does not separate out this enrolment. Therefore, for the purpose of monitoring target 4.3, students enrolled in tertiary level technical and vocational programmes are not currently counted.

Adding participation in workplace-based programmes

The main challenge for a comprehensive measure of youth participation in technical-vocational programmes is how to capture the incidence of workplace-based education and training. One option is to ignore workplace programmes altogether. Combined participation rates from institution-based and workplace-based programmes would need to reflect differences in duration, instruction methods and, ultimately, the skills acquired. They would also need to account for the vast differences in labour market contexts between countries, which result in very different kinds of skills training.

And yet, workplace-based education and training is a very important source of technical-vocational skill formation for youth. Ignoring it would considerably narrow the scope of monitoring the target. Such information can only be captured by using data from labour force, enterprise or household surveys.

For this report, an analysis of 12 countries[1] drew upon administrative and survey data to explore the implications of a broader measure of participation in technical-vocational programmes. In keeping with the remit of the proposed indicator, the analysis pooled data for all youth aged 15 to 24.[2]

In the case of institution-based programmes, about 7% of youth participated in such technical and vocational programmes in lower, upper or post-secondary non-tertiary formal education, according to administrative data reported by UIS in the 12 countries. The estimate increased to 9% if ministry reports, agency databases and other sources of official information on institution-based programme enrolments, whether from education ministries or other recognized providers, were added (**Figure 12.2**). The data were validated with comparisons to the reported national qualifications frameworks.

Two factors account for the two percentage point difference. First, no data are reported in some cases. For example, no UIS data are available for technical-vocational participation in Jordan and Viet Nam, even though both countries have well-developed national programmes. In Viet Nam, 2.4 million students, or 14% of all youth, were enrolled in such programmes in 2010/11. The programmes

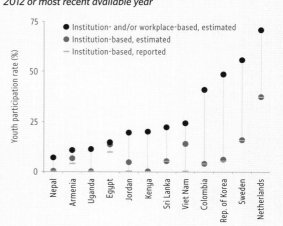

FIGURE 12.2:

A broader definition suggests wider youth access to technical-vocational programmes
Youth participation rate in technical-vocational institution-and/or workplace-based programmes, selected countries, 2012 or most recent available year

Source: GEM Report team analysis based on UIS data, official country reports and household surveys (World Bank Skills Toward Employment and Productivity, ILO School-to-Work Transition Survey, OECD Programme for the International Assessment of Adult Competencies).

are operated by the General Department of Vocational Training in the Ministry of Labour, Invalids and Social Affairs, which coordinates provision (ADB, 2014).

Second, enrolment in formal education programmes not supervised by education ministries may be under-reported. For example, Egypt reported to UIS in 2009/10 only the 1.5 million students enrolled in Ministry of Education technical-vocational programmes, but an additional 440,000 were enrolled in short and long programmes offered at public and private vocational training centres by 16 other ministries (Amin, 2014).

Capturing the considerable amount of education and training that happens outside institutions requires

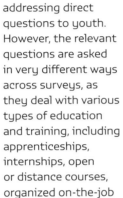

Capturing the considerable amount of education and training that happens outside institutions requires addressing direct questions to youth

addressing direct questions to youth. However, the relevant questions are asked in very different ways across surveys, as they deal with various types of education and training, including apprenticeships, internships, open or distance courses, organized on-the-job

training, seminars and workshops. The surveys usually do not reveal the programmes' duration and other characteristics. That said, on average, about 20% of youth appear to have participated in workplace-based programmes in the 12 countries (Figure 12.2).

Sri Lanka took part in the World Bank Skills Toward Employment and Productivity survey. About 18% of youth had either been on a training course lasting at least 30 hours in the past 12 months or completed an apprenticeship. Uganda participated in the International Labour Organization (ILO) School-to-Work Transition Survey. It showed 11% of youth had completed an apprenticeship, internship or other kind of training.

These sources provide snapshots of young people at specific times; they do not track the education and training of particular young people over time. More educated youth are more likely to participate in additional training than those with less education, which means they may be double-counted in technical-vocational programmes, especially in countries with high rates of provision.

Improved measurement of workplace-based programmes requires the use of comparable definitions in cross-country household surveys. It also calls for collecting more details on programme characteristics and retrospective information from individuals to better understand who benefits from multiple programmes. In recent years, one-third of all countries have participated in one of the major household surveys that report on some dimension of TVET. These surveys, which are necessary for monitoring equity, should coordinate their definitions and questionnaires. The ILO, responsible for monitoring global indicator 8.6.1, should lead in ensuring this coordination.

AFFORDABILITY

The funding of TVET is shared by governments, employers and learners. Questions of affordability need to focus on the extent to which government policy helps address inequality in TVET access. Governments have a range of policy tools at their disposal, including grants, fee exemptions, loans, allowances and subsidies. However, the context differs widely between richer and poorer countries.

In *richer countries*, the average student in technical and vocational education is more likely to come from a relatively disadvantaged background. For example, in Australia, the poor are almost four times as likely (22%) to enrol in vocational training as the wealthy (6%) (Lamb, 2011). Yet, fees are often charged. Australia introduced fees for publicly funded programmes in the 1990s. Student fees and charges accounted for about 5% of total institution revenues in 2014, ranging from 2% in the Northern Territories to 9% in Western Australia (NCVER, 2015a).

For students in both public and private programmes, the Australian government introduced VET FEE-HELP, an income-contingent loan programme that assists eligible students attending certain courses with an approved provider by paying all or part of their tuition. In 2014, 87% of eligible students benefited, or 203,000 out of 3.9 million students at all levels (Australia DoET, 2015; NCVER, 2015b). The average loan was AUD 12,300 per student; poor students borrowed almost AUD 3,300 more than rich students (Australia DoET, 2014). The programme has not yet been evaluated.

A qualitative evaluation of 35 loan programmes in European countries found that while they supported participation, they did not target the learners in greatest need. Many did not provide sufficient guidance and

"

Attempts to support technical and vocational participation are less likely to benefit the poorest

"

information to reach target groups averse to debt. Programmes with long repayment periods were more equity-oriented. Public programmes focusing on technical and vocational education in Finland, the Netherlands and Sweden were among the more successful. In Finland, support consists of a study grant, a housing allowance and a student loan guarantee. To qualify for a loan guarantee, the learner must receive a study grant. Once the guarantee has been approved, learners contact banks and agree the interest rate, repayment conditions and other features of the loan (CEDEFOP, 2012).

In *poorer countries*, youth from disadvantaged backgrounds are far less likely to enrol in post-basic education. Those who make it to technical and vocational programmes tend to come from relatively more advantaged backgrounds than in richer countries. An analysis of 22 countries that took part in the 2009 the Programme for International Student Assessment (PISA) of the Organisation for Economic Co-operation and Development (OECD) showed that 4 of the 5 countries with the lowest proportion of vocational secondary school students from the bottom socio-economic group were middle income countries, such as Colombia and Indonesia (Altinok, 2012).

This means attempts to support technical and vocational participation are less likely to benefit the poorest. In Kenya, the Technical and Vocational Vouchers Programme offered a voucher worth US$460, enough to fully or almost fully cover tuition for both government and private vocational programmes – but also twice the participants' average annual salary level (Hicks et al., 2011).

A study of seven countries in the Pacific found that the share of income from student fees in institution-based technical and vocational programmes was 35%, although it varied significantly from 1% at the Kiribati Institute of Technology to 64% at the five Technical and Business Colleges in Papua New Guinea (Schofield, 2015). Fees can be very high relative to household budgets. Those charged at the School of Engineering in Samoa equal half the income of the poorest 10% of households.

Financial aid programmes to offset student costs differ widely even within countries. In Samoa, there are two such arrangements. The aid-funded Australia-Pacific Technical College receives none of its income from students, as the cost of fees is covered through scholarships. The public National University of Samoa receives one-third of its income from fees but awards a full or partial scholarship to one in six students in technical-vocational programmes. Students enrolled in other institutions do not receive aid (Maglen et al., 2013).

The extreme diversity of providers, cost structures, public policies and national contexts makes it unlikely that a single indicator can describe the affordability of a TVET system. As the section below on affordability of higher education notes, however, a possible approach might be to contrast the amount of institution income that is covered by students with the amount of financial support the government provides to students. This would require consensus on common guidelines and major investment in information systems.

QUALITY

There is a very broad range of issues related to quality in technical and vocational education. One approach to assessing quality is to focus on systems.

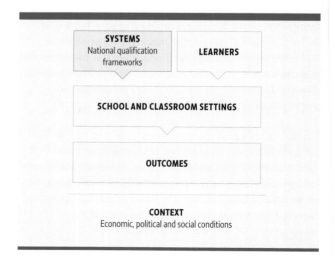

Within its Systems Approach for Better Education Results (SABER) programme, the World Bank has developed a tool to assess national policies for skills development (World Bank, 2013c). One dimension of system quality is whether there are relevant and reliable standards codified in a national qualification framework, which helps in recognizing, certifying and accrediting skills.

At least 140 countries have implemented a national qualification framework (Keevy and Chakroun, 2015). The frameworks vary in effectiveness and do not ensure education quality in and of themselves (Blackmur, 2015). But they can help learners, training providers and employers focus on outcomes, rather than on the precise way qualifications were acquired (Tuck, 2007; Veal, 2009).

Simple frameworks classify formal learning programmes and associated qualifications and certificates. More advanced frameworks facilitate stakeholder interactions, support wider quality assurance, recognize learning gained outside formal education and training, and make national qualification systems more transparent to the international community (Coles et al., 2014). In fact, regional groupings, such as Association of Southeast Asian Nations (ASEAN), Caribbean Community (CARICOM), the Commonwealth, the European Union, the Pacific Community and the Southern African Development Community, have helped coordinate recognition of national qualifications in regional frameworks (ETF, 2012; UIL et al., 2016).

Among 18 countries analysed over 2012–2014 with the SABER tool, there was quick progress towards establishing national qualification frameworks. In Malaysia, the 2006 National Skills Development Act and 2007 Malaysian Qualifications Agency Act helped establish such a framework. Coverage of occupations under the National Occupational Skills Standards tripled over the 2000s, and there was greater certification of skills testing. All publicly funded programmes had to be accredited, which strengthened coordination among training providers (World Bank, 2013a).

Overall, two of three countries demonstrated considerable room for improvement. For example, Sri Lanka launched a national vocational qualification framework in 2004. Competency standards were developed for 114 occupations at the certificate level. Most institutions under the Ministry of Youth Affairs and Skills Development based their training on these

standards. But by 2011, less than 10% of all graduates had received certificates. The government has recognized the national vocational qualification certificate for recruitment to specific grades in the public service but the certificate has not yet gained the same level of recognition among private employers (World Bank, 2014c).

By focusing efforts on understanding the relevance and reliability of their qualifications frameworks, countries can then target efforts to improve quality throughout their TVET systems. An approach based on expert and peer reviews with the support of regional bodies will be necessary to achieve these synergies.

TERTIARY EDUCATION

Tertiary education is very diverse, ranging from short courses, often with career or vocational focus, to bachelor's, master's and doctoral programmes. Tertiary education institutions vary widely within each country in terms of size, cost, course offerings, procedures, tradition, governance and quality. Differences between countries are far more visible than they are for primary and secondary education systems.

The proposed thematic indicator – the tertiary education gross enrolment ratio – captures only a small part of the diversity in access – and does not touch upon the two other concepts of the target: affordability and quality. Examining the target in its entirety is the objective of this section.

ACCESS

Pre-entry, entry, progression and graduation in tertiary education systems are distinct phases (Orr, 2016). Ideally, different indicators should capture each of these key transitions to better understand who is eligible to apply for tertiary education, who is selected, who enrols and who graduates (Belyakov et al., 2009) (**Table 12.2**). Participation in higher education reflects national policies on secondary education, admissions norms, standardized entrance exams, costs and financial aid, private provision, and university curricular design (Clancey and Goastellec, 2007).

Pre-entry indicators. In some countries, secondary school graduates sit a central tertiary education entrance examination. In others, all young people who graduate from upper secondary school have the right to enrol in tertiary education but have to perform well during their first year to continue (Orr and Hovdhaugen, 2014). According to the UIS, among 53 countries with relevant data, 92% of secondary school graduates, on average, have direct access to tertiary education – but the rates range as low as 61% in Mali, 43% in Mongolia and 71% in Poland.

Entry indicators. Two examples can be considered. First, the transition rate from upper secondary to tertiary

education, i.e. the number of students enrolled in the first year of tertiary education expressed as a percentage of the number of students who were enrolled in the last year of secondary education. Among 42 countries with data, the average was 78%. Second, the entry ratio, i.e. the number of students enrolled in the first year of tertiary education expressed as a percentage of the population of that age group. Among 53 countries with data, the intake ranged from 5% in Eritrea to 90% in Belarus (**Figure 12.3**).

Participation indicators. Enrolment in tertiary education has grown steadily, doubling from 100 million students worldwide in 2000 to 207 million in 2014 (**Table 12.3**). The tertiary education gross enrolment ratio, which expresses enrolment as a percentage of the population of the five-year age group following secondary school graduation (typically ages 19 to 23) increased from 19% to 34% over the period. The ratio ranges from 8% in sub-Saharan Africa to 75% in Europe and Northern America.

These figures may hide important differences between countries. In countries where part-time and older students are more likely to enrol, participation rates will be inflated. Likewise, countries with more credit requirements spread out over more years will have higher participation rates than countries where shorter-cycle bachelor's programmes are more common.

Graduation indicators. Two sources can be used. Administrative data provide information on the number of degrees awarded. Surveys and censuses ask individuals directly what is their highest level of education attained.

TABLE 12.2:
Indicators of tertiary education

Phase	Process	Indicator
1. Pre-entry	Qualification	Share of people of secondary school graduation age (e.g. 18 years) who leave secondary education with a qualification that enables them to apply to enter tertiary education (*secondary gross graduation rate with direct access to tertiary*)
	Application	Share of people of secondary school graduation age (e.g. 18 years) who complete the central entrance examination (where relevant)
2. Entry	Offer	Share of people who qualified or applied and received an offer of a tertiary education study place
	Transition	Share of people who enrolled in the final grade of secondary education the previous year who were admitted into tertiary education this year (*transition rate*)
	Entry	Share of people of tertiary education entry age (e.g. 19 years) who enrol in first year of tertiary education (*entry ratio*)
3. Participation	Enrolment	Share of people who enrol in tertiary education among those of tertiary education age (usually a five-year age group, e.g. 19 to 23) (*gross enrolment ratio*)
	Dropout	Share of students who entered tertiary education who drop out
4. Graduation		Share of people who completed tertiary education among those of tertiary education graduation age (usually a five-year age group, e.g. 25 to 29) (*attainment rate*)

Source: Adapted from Orr (2016).

FIGURE 12.3:
There are huge disparities across countries in terms of access to tertiary education
Gross entry ratio to first tertiary programmes, selected countries, 2014 or most recent available year

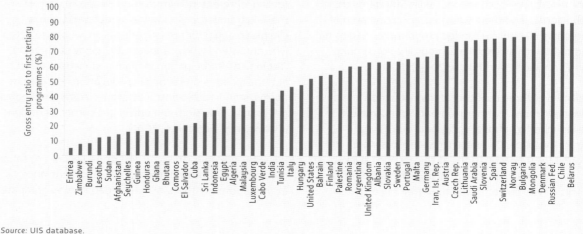

Source: UIS database.

Administrative sources provide evidence on the gross graduation ratio, i.e. the number of graduates from first degree programmes, expressed as a percentage of the population of graduation age. This is available for almost 100 countries. In Madagascar, less than 3% of the population of graduation age completed tertiary education at least at the bachelor level in 2013. By contrast, 65% did so in Lithuania (**Figure 12.4**).

This definition considers only bachelor- and master-level diplomas to be first degrees. Across 94 countries with

data in 2014, an average of 79% of tertiary education graduates obtained a bachelor- or master-level degree. In countries where a larger share of tertiary education graduates obtain a short-cycle degree, such as Colombia (30%), the Republic of Korea (33%) and the United States (28%), there are wider discrepancies between the gross graduation and enrolment ratios.

A comparison between the two ratios also provides insights into gender disparity in tertiary education. In general, in the relatively few countries where there is

TABLE 12.3:
Tertiary education participation indicators

	Enrolment (000)		Gross enrolment ratio (%)		Gender parity index	
	2000	2014	2000	2014	2000	2014
World	99 516	207 272	19	34	0.99	1.11
Low income	1 237	4 460	3	8	0.43	0.53
Lower middle income	24 996	58 642	11	22	0.79	0.97
Upper middle income	24 798	78 729	14	41	0.94	1.16
High income	48 485	65 441	55	74	1.17	1.25
Caucasus and Central Asia	1 427	1 956	22	24	0.95	1.04
Eastern and South-eastern Asia	24 213	67 351	15	39	0.83	1.11
Europe and Northern America	39 940	51 870	56	75	1.25	1.28
Latin America and the Caribbean	11 318	23 845	22	44	1.17	1.29
Northern Africa and Western Asia	6 854	15 261	20	37	0.83	0.99
Pacific	1 044	1 748	46	62	1.26	1.39
Southern Asia	12 162	38 097	9	23	0.66	0.93
Sub-Saharan Africa	2 557	7 145	4	8	0.66	0.70

Source: UIS database.

FIGURE 12.4:
The share of young people who graduate with a bachelor's or master's degree differs widely between countries

Tertiary education gross enrolment and gross graduation ratios for first degree programmes in tertiary education, selected countries, 2013 or most recent available year

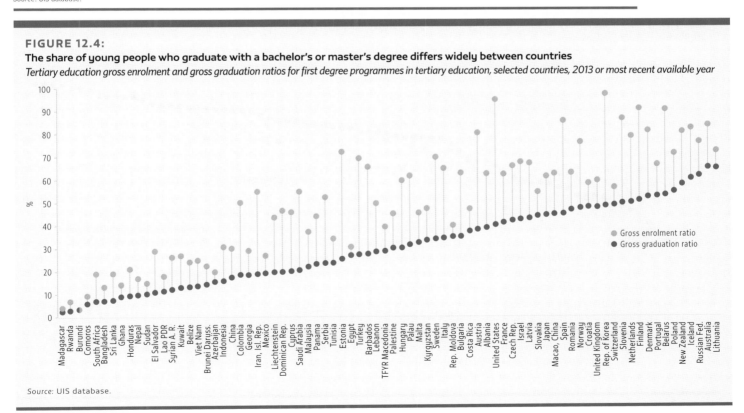

Source: UIS database.

disparity at the expense of women in enrolment, disparity in graduation is smaller. For example, in Egypt in 2013, there were 89 women for every 100 men enrolled in tertiary education, but there was gender parity in the graduation rate. It is less common for disparity to be exacerbated between enrolment and graduation. In Rwanda, 79 women enrolled but only 51 graduated for every 100 men in 2013.

Globally, however, it is more common for disparity at the expense of men at the enrolment level to be exacerbated by the time of graduation. For example, in Costa Rica, 80 men enrolled but 53 graduated for every 100 women in 2011. In Caribbean countries, such as Barbados, and in Arab countries, such as Kuwait, more than twice as many women as men graduated from tertiary education (**Figure 12.5**).

Survey and census sources can provide complementary information in several contexts, e.g. when there are many private providers that do not report regularly to the authorities on graduates. The main indicator is the tertiary education attainment rate – the percentage of a population group that has obtained a tertiary education degree or qualification. There is no

consensus on which age group to use for reference. While the average age of students in Georgia and Ukraine was up to 21 years, in Norway and Sweden it was 29 years (Eurostudent, 2015). Eurostat reports the tertiary education attainment rate among 30- to 34-year-olds, based on the European Labour Force Survey, was 38% in 2014 across the 28 European Union countries; among women, attainment rates were on average nine percentage points higher than among men (Eurostat, 2016).

The main advantage of survey sources is that they help in analysing inequality. New analysis for the GEM Report shows a very large disparity between the poorest and richest 25- to 29-year-olds in terms of those who have completed at least four years of tertiary education. Across 76 countries, 20% of the richest 25–29 year olds completed at least four years of tertiary education compared with less than 1% of the poorest. In the Philippines, 21% of 25- to 29-year-olds had completed at least four years of tertiary education in 2013, but the corresponding levels were 52% for the richest and 1% for the poorest. In Mongolia, 72% of the richest completed at least four years of tertiary education, compared with 3% of the poorest, in 2010.

FIGURE 12.5:
Disparity for men worsens between tertiary education entry and completion
Gender parity index of the tertiary education gross enrolment ratio and gross graduation ratio from first degree programmes, selected countries, 2013 or most recent available year

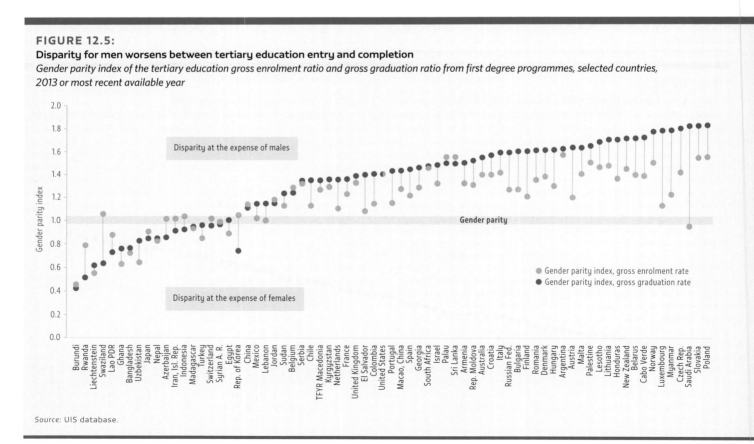

Source: UIS database.

FIGURE 12.6:
There are vast differences in tertiary attainment between the poor and the rich
Percentage of 25- to 29-year-olds who have completed at least four years of tertiary education, by wealth, selected countries, 2008–2014

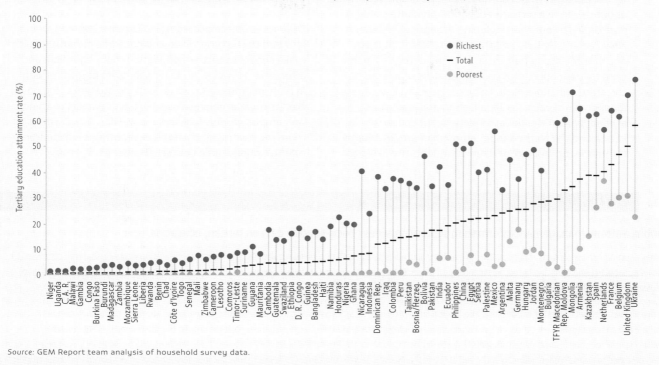

Source: GEM Report team analysis of household survey data.

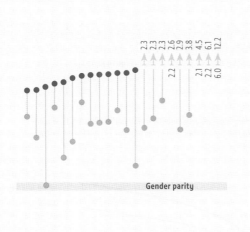

Wide disparity is also present in some countries in Eastern Europe, such as Bulgaria, the Republic of Moldova and the former Yugoslav Republic of Macedonia (**Figure 12.6**).

However, surveys have certain disadvantages for analysing tertiary education patterns, especially at the level of participation indicators. Standard surveys do not collect sufficiently detailed information on, for example, course duration or the actual award of a degree. In addition, questions capture the current conditions in which individuals live and not the conditions in which they grew up.

While much can be gained from comparable indicators of tertiary education, robust management information systems inevitably are better at capturing the nuances of national contexts and are more useful for policy-makers, as was found in Colombia (**Box 12.1**). But both national and international reporting need to adjust to enable monitoring of the growing diversity in student attendance, programme delivery and private provision patterns, which have implications on inequality in access.

Part-time vs full-time enrolment. Data from the UNESCO/OECD/Eurostat (UOE) database on education show that about one in five tertiary education students study part time. In countries including Argentina, Finland, New Zealand, Poland and the United States, at least one in three study part time. In many countries, part-time tertiary education courses are less regulated by the state and more likely to be provided by the private independent sector. In Japan, almost all part-time students are in the private independent sector; in Latvia and the Netherlands, almost half are. In Albania, Denmark and Ireland, part-time students are likely to pay higher tuition fees than students in full-time studies (European Commission/EACEA/Eurydice, 2015b).

Distance vs on-campus learning. Distance learning, being less tied to the time, place and pace of a campus, could make access to tertiary education more equitable and affordable. However, so far, it seems its biggest effect in high income countries is enabling students to gain credits for learning modules before or parallel to their on-campus studies (Lokken and Mullins, 2014). This is a more modest result than the expectations surrounding massive online open courses (Barber et al., 2013).

BOX 12.1

In Colombia, a strong management information system provides policy-specific data on tertiary education

Colombia has a comprehensive system of publicly available tertiary education data based on detailed regulations. The Ministry of Education works closely with campuses to communicate updates to definitions and to resolve technological issues. In turn, campuses invest in staff professional development to ensure timely submission and meet the latest data quality standards.

There are five distinct data sets. The Higher Education Information System (SNIES) includes base indicators on academic programmes, students, professors, campus administration, research, continuing education, internationalization and infrastructure. SPADIES tracks enrolment patterns in order to monitor and prevent university dropout, with a special focus on disadvantaged students. The Colombian Institute for the Promotion of Higher Education (ICFES) records data on Saber Pro, a national examination designed to assess student learning at the end of the first university degree. The Labor Observatory for Education (OLE) tracks students into the labour market, providing information on graduate work status, salaries, and shifts in workforce demands linked to student history. The International Network of Information and Knowledge Sources for Science, Technology and Innovation Management (SCIENTI) monitors detailed information about academic research and development, doctoral research programmes and research institutes.

Tertiary education enrolment increased rapidly between 2000 and 2015. However, the expansion affected the student intake. The percentage of newly admitted students who had scored at the lowest level in the secondary school exit examination increased from 25% in 2000 to 37% in 2010 (**Figure 12.7a**). The low scoring students are more likely to drop out before finishing a degree. After eight semesters, 55% had dropped out, compared with 35% of the high scoring students (**Figure 12.7b**).

FIGURE 12.7:
In Colombia, students with lower admission scores are less likely to graduate

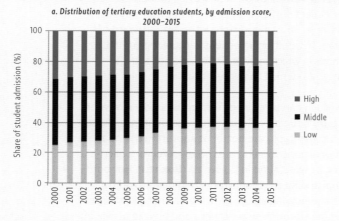

a. Distribution of tertiary education students, by admission score, 2000–2015

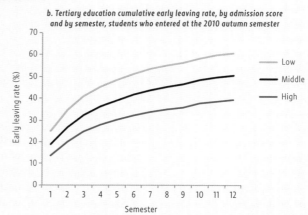

b. Tertiary education cumulative early leaving rate, by admission score and by semester, students who entered at the 2010 autumn semester

Source: Colombia Ministry of Education (2016a, 2016b).

But data in this area are still patchy. An international monitoring effort on the provision and use of online and particularly open educational resources, the Global Online Higher Education Report, collected data in the second half of 2015 (ICDE, 2015).

Public vs private higher education provision. According to UOE data, 17.5% of students were studying in private, independently funded institutions in 2012. Most countries have a very small share of students in this sector. Prominent exceptions are Brazil, Chile, Colombia, Indonesia, Japan, Mexico and the Republic of Korea, where the share is 80%. In Brazil, where 70% of students are in private universities, the Prouni University for All programme was implemented in the private sector to widen access to tertiary education (Somers et al., 2013).

AFFORDABILITY

The affordability of tertiary education depends on the relationship between costs and income – current, forgone or future. Students pay direct education costs but also general living costs, such as transport, food and accommodation. Total costs can be compared with average household income levels based on household surveys. For example, the total cost of tertiary education in Mexico is 1.75 times the level of the average national household income, while it is only half that level in Canada and New Zealand (Higher Education Strategic Associates, 2014). While this is a useful guide, it does not show how many young people cannot afford higher education.

Collating information on direct costs of tertiary education is not straightforward. Tuition, registration and examination fees often differ by subject area and by institution, especially between public and private. Detailed national data on costs are more likely to exist when there is a government policy to provide financial assistance to make tertiary education participation more affordable. For example, governments and tertiary education institutions may provide grants, repayable loans and discounted accommodation (halls of residence), food (canteens) or transport (travel cards).

Comparing financial burden on households with financial assistance to households can help highlight differences between countries (Orr, 2016). Across 26 countries in Europe, households contributed an average of 15% of

FIGURE 12.8:

There are diverse ways of making tertiary education affordable

Household expenditure as a share of total expenditure for higher education institutions and support to students enrolled in tertiary education as a percentage of public expenditure on tertiary education, selected countries, 2011

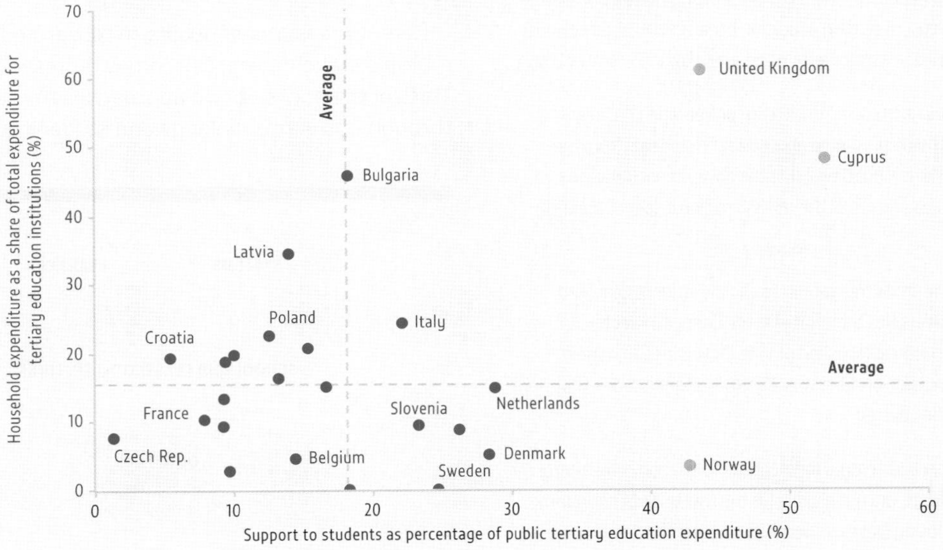

Source: European Commission/EACEA/Eurydice (2015a).

> In Chile, about 165,000 students began attending university for free when the new academic year began in March 2016. They represented about half the students from the poorest 50% of Chilean households

total expenditure for tertiary education institutions in 2011, and student aid made up 18% of public tertiary education expenditure (**Figure 12.8**).

There was substantial variation between countries. Cyprus, Norway and the United Kingdom provided well over 40% of public tertiary education expenditure in the form of student aid. In Norway, there are almost no fees and aid was used to compensate for differences in students' ability to afford living costs during their studies. In Cyprus and the United Kingdom, aid was used to offset the impact of high tertiary education fees (European Commission/EACEA/Eurydice, 2015b).

Using a national education accounts approach (Chapter 20) shows the share of households in total

tertiary education expenditure to have been even higher in 2012 in non-European high income countries: for example, 40% in Australia, 42% in the Republic of Korea, 46% in the United States, 52% in Japan and 55% in Chile, where recent reforms came in response to strong political protests (**Box 12.2**) (OECD, 2015b).

Large household contributions are not necessarily related to lack of equity and affordability. For example, Australia has more than twice the entry rate into bachelor's programmes as Austria (76% vs. 34%), even though households contribute several times more to total tertiary education expenditure (40% vs. 2%) (OECD, 2015b). Australia has combined loans with income-contingent repayments and means-tested grants, encouraging disadvantaged students to enter tertiary education and reducing the risk of indebtedness (OECD, 2016b). The precise mix of policy tools and their success in targeting those most in need are clearly critical, and should be monitored to understand how to facilitate affordability (see Chapters 20 and 21).

QUALITY

Different measures of quality in tertiary education serve multiple stakeholders. Outcomes represent one measure. This section looks at two approaches to measuring them: through university rankings and student outcomes.

BOX 12.2

In Chile, persistent student demands for affordable higher education triggered reform

High fees made Chile one of the most expensive countries in the world to be a university student. Student protests against the cost of tertiary education began in 2011 and became a central political issue, which eventually led to a major reform and a new law in December 2015.

As a result, about 165,000 students began attending university for free when the new academic year began in March 2016. They represented about half the students from the poorest 50% of Chilean households. The new policy will cost the government between US$300 million and US$400 million a year, on top of the US$858 million it spends annually on scholarships and student loans.

As currently designed, the programme limits free tuition to eligible students enrolled in 25 public and traditional private universities that make up the Council of Rectors of Chilean Universities and in 5 more recently established private universities that meet certain criteria on accreditation and not-for-profit status. By 2018, all institutions that meet the government criteria are to be covered.

Critics note that professional institutes and centres for technical formation, which enrol a high proportion of low income students, are not eligible for the free tuition programme and that offering a flat rate tuition subsidy leaves universities to cover the gap in more expensive disciplines.

Sources: Hurtado (2012, 2015, 2016); Guzmán-Valenzuela (2016).

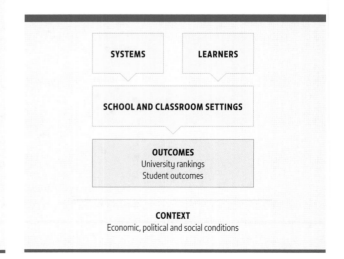

University rankings

Ever since first appearing in the 1980s, university rankings have continued to grow in number and popularity as basic reference points of performance by tertiary education institutions. The first global ranking system, the Academic Ranking of World Universities, based in Shanghai, was created so that Chinese university leaders could better understand how their institutions compared to those in the rest of the world and how to improve them.

In 2015, 11 global ranking systems produced updated lists. Of these, 5 are commercially based, generally published through existing news outlets; 3 are funded by governments; 2 are located at universities; and 1 is run by an independent non-profit organization. The systems use 118 indicators in all, half of which are related to faculty publications or research citation indices. In 7 systems, research measures make up at least 50% of all information. By contrast, teaching and learning account for less than 10% of all indicators and are found in only 4 ranking systems (**Figure 12.9**).

One of the systems, U-Multirank, does not actually stack universities up against each other but has designed a tool that allows users to create their own tables based on 29 indicators in 6 categories – teaching, research, innovation, internationalization, finance and employment.

Rankings attract attention because they are simple to understand. However, they have major flaws.

They exclude the vast majority of universities around the world and collect information only on those whose faculties have produced at least a few hundred publications in the prior year. Only the Spanish groups Scimago and Webometrics evaluate more than 1,500 universities. Both use information on web presence to establish the pool of universities to rank. Webometrics focuses its analysis on principles of open access, providing information on over 22,000 institutions.

Despite some methodological improvements, university rankings are primarily marketing tools that rely heavily on institutional reputation and faculty publications. As currently designed, rankings are not based on indicators of teaching quality or student learning that are reliable, valid, standardized and internationally comparable.

Student outcomes

While a typical student outcome measure would be the graduation rate, an increasingly broad range of student cognitive, affective, behavioural and psychological skills are being evaluated to assess the quality of tertiary education. Assessments of skills include engagement and satisfaction surveys, professional licensing exams and direct assessments of learning (Nusche, 2008).

Direct assessments of student learning in higher education measure a combination of cognitive skills, such as verbal and quantitative reasoning, analytic

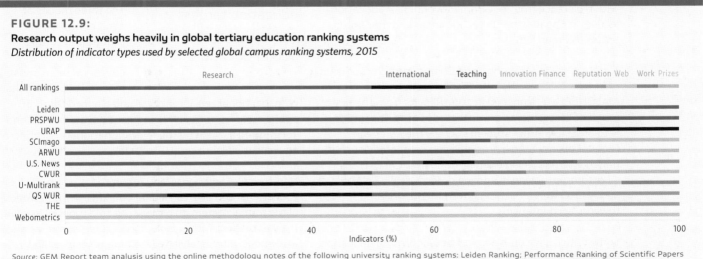

FIGURE 12.9:

Research output weighs heavily in global tertiary education ranking systems
Distribution of indicator types used by selected global campus ranking systems, 2015

Source: GEM Report team analysis using the online methodology notes of the following university ranking systems: Leiden Ranking; Performance Ranking of Scientific Papers for World Universities; University Ranking by Academic Performance; SCImago Institutions Ranking; Academic Ranking of World Universities; Global Universities Ranking U.S. News; Center for World University Rankings; U-Multirank; QS World University Rankings; THE World University Rankings; and Ranking Web of World Universities.

operations, critical thinking and problem solving. Assessments are designed to measure either generic skills or those that reflect a body of knowledge within a given field.

Few countries deliver national assessments of student cognitive skills. Brazil initiated the Exame Nacional de Desempenho dos Estudantes (ENADE) through legislation in 1996 and has administered it nationally since 2004. About 80% of students in public and private institutions take the exam as they enter and exit bachelor studies. Results across 19 fields of study show that students display more improvement in subject-specific areas than in the general knowledge component of the test (Melguizo and Wainer, 2015).

These findings suggest that the curriculum significantly influences learning, since the general skills portion of the test is not aligned with the curricula of the study programmes. Another reason for the difference is the knowledge level associated with generic skills assessment. For example, students in medicine show almost no general skills gains over four years but substantial content area gains, most likely because they enter university with high general academic abilities.

Cross-national comparisons of higher education learning outcomes have also been attempted. OECD completed a feasibility study on Assessment of Higher Education Learning Outcomes (AHELO) in 2013 with participation from 17 countries and jurisdictions. China, Finland and Norway supported a full assessment, but the project met with resistance from governments or higher education leaders in Canada, the United Kingdom and the United States (Morgan, 2015).

A project called Measuring and Comparing Achievements of Learning Outcomes in Higher Education in Europe (CALOHEE) was launched in 2015. Results from the first round of assessments are expected in 2017. The intent is to assess whether students across the European Higher Education Area are achieving competencies that match internationally defined standards. CALOHEE is a bottom-up, university-driven process, while ENADE and AHELO were driven by governments oriented towards accountability.

Some critics have questioned whether tertiary education learning assessments in general are measuring what they claim to measure (Primi et al., 2010; 2011). Universities also question their purpose. Assessments of student outcomes have largely been developed to promote accountability and are designed by external bodies – government agencies, private testing companies and non-profit groups (Nusche, 2008). Critics note the absence of faculty in design and implementation, a crucial weakness considering that tertiary faculty have a relatively high degree of autonomy as stewards of academic content (Possin, 2013).

The methodological limitations and costs of student outcome assessments are cause for reflection. Differences in national policy structures and resources, and in university missions in the education system, pose considerable barriers to a meaningful global measure of quality in tertiary education.

ADULT EDUCATION

While SDG 4 calls for ensuring lifelong learning opportunities for all, none of the education targets explicitly mentions adult education. However, the proposed global indicator for target 4.3 incorporates the concept of adult education, and adult learning, education and training opportunities form a strategy for achieving target 4.3, according to the Education 2030 Framework for Action.

> " While SDG 4 calls for ensuring lifelong learning opportunities for all, none of the education targets explicitly mentions adult education "

The three modes of adult education are formal, non-formal and informal. Formal education refers mostly to initial education that is 'institutionalized, intentional and planned through public organizations and recognized private bodies' and 'recognized as such by the relevant national education or equivalent authorities' (UIS, 2012b).

Non-formal education is 'any organized, systematic, educational activity, carried on outside the framework of the formal system, to provide selected types of learning'. It takes distinct forms, including lectures, seminars and workshops with established learning objectives and content, tutoring and private lessons, on-the-job training, and open and distance learning. While the dominant reason for participation is job related, it is difficult in practice to neatly determine precisely why people engage in non-formal adult learning (Rubenson, 1999).

Informal education, in the widest sense, is arguably the most prevalent mode. It is defined as intentional or deliberate, but not institutionalized. Activities include learning 'in the family, workplace, local community and daily life, on a self-directed, family-directed, or socially directed basis' (UIS, 2012b). Because it is less organized and structured than the other two modes, it falls outside the scope of measuring participation in education.

ACCESS

The diversity of formal and, especially, non-formal provision makes the task of monitoring participation in adult education particularly difficult.

The UIS collects information on learners aged 15 and over in formal education. For example, among 49 countries with data, adults made up 4% of those enrolled at the primary education level; the rate exceeded 5% in six countries, including Thailand (5.2%), Brazil (5.3%), and India (6.5%), where more than 9 million adults were enrolled. Among 55 countries with data, adults accounted for 5% of those enrolled at the lower secondary and 10% of those enrolled at the upper secondary level.

In Latin America and the Caribbean, one-quarter of adults have not completed primary school and half have not completed secondary school. A regional survey on adult learners (UIS, 2013) found that in Mexico, 3.5% of adults with less than primary education participated in primary school completion programmes, such as Education Model for Life and Work, which combines primary learning with employment skills and active citizenship training. In the Plurinational State of Bolivia, where 13% of adults with less than secondary school participated in secondary school completion programmes, lessons are often combined with vocational training and adults can obtain a qualification certificate from a professional school (**Figure 12.10**).

Currently, however, there is no measure of adult formal and non-formal education participation. Useful lessons can be drawn from the experience of Europe. Ever since the European Union set a target of reaching an adult education participation rate of 15% by 2020, major efforts have been made to develop relevant data-collection tools.

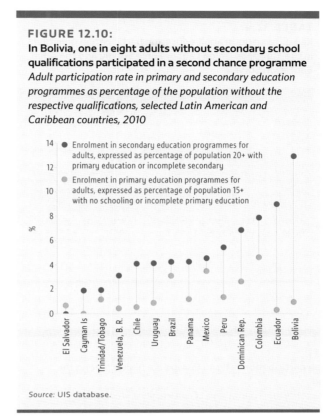

FIGURE 12.10:

In Bolivia, one in eight adults without secondary school qualifications participated in a second chance programme
Adult participation rate in primary and secondary education programmes as percentage of the population without the respective qualifications, selected Latin American and Caribbean countries, 2010

- Enrolment in secondary education programmes for adults, expressed as percentage of population 20+ with primary education or incomplete secondary
- Enrolment in primary education programmes for adults, expressed as percentage of population 15+ with no schooling or incomplete primary education

Source: UIS database.

Two household surveys collect information on adult education participation in Europe. The European Union Labour Force Survey (LFS) has been carried out quarterly since 1983 in 33 countries and is the official source of information on the adult education participation target. The Adult Education Survey (AES) was carried out in 2007 and 2011 in 30 countries, with a third round scheduled for 2016. There are important differences between the two, e.g. in terms of reference periods or education and training definitions (Eurostat, 2011) (**Table 12.4**). In addition, there are differences within the LFS across countries (Holford and Mleczko, 2011).

The 2011 AES indicated that the average adult education participation rate in both formal and non-formal activities during the 12 months prior to the survey was 40% in the 28 European Union countries. The average non-formal education participation rate was 37% and the formal rate 6% (with some crossover). The formal adult education participation rate varied widely across countries, from 1% in Romania to 15% in the United Kingdom.

TABLE 12.4:
Key differences in adult education participation questions in the European Union Labour Force Survey and the Adult Education Survey

Issue	European Union Labour Force Survey	Adult Education Survey
Reference period	4 weeks	12 months
Definition of education and training	Excludes some activities, such as guided on-the-job training Captures only formal education courses lasting at least one semester	All types of non-formal activities Captures all formal courses of short duration
Sequence of questions and prompts	Uses simple questionnaire and emphasizes work-related training	Uses terms capturing slightly wider variety of activities, such as 'private lessons, courses, conferences, talks, workshops, seminars and activities designed to train you for a job'
Rationale for education	Narrow range of outcomes: related to current/prospective job – or not	A slightly broader range of outcomes outside work such as meeting other people or other personal reasons, or updating knowledge in the field

Source: ICF (2015).

FIGURE 12.11:
Adult education participation rates in Europe are higher among the more educated
Adult education participation rate by type of opportunity and education attainment, European Union countries, 2011

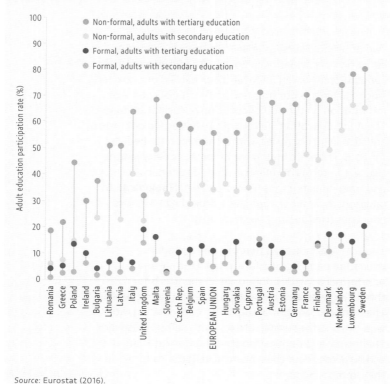

Source: Eurostat (2016).

Participation rates in adult education differ considerably by the level of education already attained. In general, adults who have attained tertiary education have more access to formal adult education opportunities than adults who have attained only secondary education (**Figure 12.11**). Large gaps in formal education participation rates between the more and less educated are found in Poland, Slovakia and Sweden. The smallest gaps are observed in Finland and Slovenia, while in Portugal those with secondary education have a higher chance of formal education (**Box 12.3**).

By contrast, the LFS indicated the average adult education participation rate during the four weeks prior to the survey was closer to 10%. In Germany and Italy, the rate remained more or less constant over 2005–2013,

BOX 12.3

The adult education system in Portugal supports the more disadvantaged

Portugal was the only country in Europe where the participation rate in formal education was higher for adults with secondary education (15%) than for adults with tertiary education (13%). This is exceptional: those who are more educated usually have access to a higher number of formal adult education opportunities.

Portugal has by far the European Union's highest rate of adults with less than lower secondary education (39% in 2013, well above second-highest Greece with 19%) and less than upper secondary education (60% in 2013, compared with number two Spain at 44%). The adult education system is oriented towards helping these adults catch up. More than 5% of all Portuguese adults aged 25 to 64 acquired an upper secondary education certificate in adulthood, the highest rate in southern Europe in 2013. Provision comes under the umbrella Programa de Formação em Competências Básicas, a basic skills training programme introduced in 2010.

In addition, Portuguese adults with secondary education are more likely to enter non-formal education (55%) than their counterparts in France (48%), Italy (40%) and Spain (36%).

Under the New Opportunities Initiative, the largest public programme in recent decades, qualification and vocational training centres were established as 'one-stop shops' to deliver three lifelong learning services in an integrated way through guidance, validation of non-formal and informal learning, and provision of training programmes. There are also strong incentives to participate in adult education, such as income tax deductions and employer-funded training leave.

Sources: CEDEFOP (2011); European Commission/EACEA/Eurydice (2015a); Nico and Nico (2011); OECD (2005a); UNEVOC (2014).

while in Latvia it declined until 2011. Adults in Slovenia were more likely to enrol in some kind of training than in the other countries (**Figure 12.12**).

The LFS and AES diverged not only in their estimates of average adult education participation rates but also in their estimates of participation rate trends over time. For example, between 2007 and 2011, a negative trend was observed for 10 countries in the AES and for 8 countries in the LFS – but with only three countries in common (ICF, 2015), underlining how differing definitions lead to very different conclusions.

To summarize, the proposed global indicator of adult participation in education during the previous 12 months presents several challenges. Consensus will be needed on the equivalency of diverse types of education experience. The tools to collect this information will need to be standardized accordingly to improve cross-country comparability of results. The experience of attempts to standardize related questions in Europe offers a basis for discussion.

AFFORDABILITY

Even more than in technical-vocational and tertiary education, assessment of affordability in adult education is constrained by the lack of information on participation and public expenditure.

The 2009 Belém Framework for Action on adult learning and education called on countries to work towards 'increased investment in adult learning and education' but set no financing targets. The *Global Report on Adult Learning and Education* (GRALE), published every three years, requests countries to report the share of adult education in government spending. One-quarter of the over 90 countries that provided information (but 41% of high income countries) reported spending more than 4% on adult education. This, combined with information on public expenditure on education as a share of the gross domestic product (GDP), indicates that fewer than one in six countries spent more than 0.3% of GDP on adult education, all of them high income countries except for Kyrgyzstan and the United Republic of Tanzania. Future editions of GRALE will need to collect more precise information, but it is clear that adult education remains a low priority in budgets.

Government expenditure is critical because it is more likely to cater for disadvantaged groups. For example, adult professional education and training in France accounted for 1.52% of GDP in 2012. This was shared

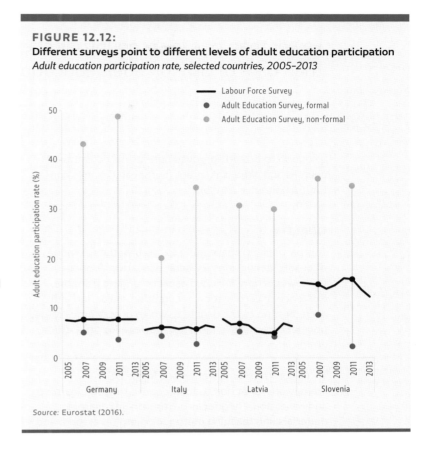

FIGURE 12.12:
Different surveys point to different levels of adult education participation
Adult education participation rate, selected countries, 2005–2013

Source: Eurostat (2016).

between the state (53%), firms (43%) and households (4%). But the share of the state was 76% for apprentices and 84% for the unemployed (DARES, 2015).

Overall, more information on public expenditure is needed to understand how it is targeted at the groups most in need. Government funding may take the form of direct provision of adult education courses or subsidies to accredited providers so that participants pay no fees. It can also take the form of support to individual adults to pay for education (through grants, vouchers and loans) or support to firms to encourage them to provide more education and training opportunities.

A review of relevant policies in Europe found examples of co-funding arrangements that were successfully targeted at groups in need. For example, in Sweden, which has a system of grants and loans to encourage adults to return to education, the grant component of total support was higher for those with up to upper secondary education (73%) than for other learners (31%). In Latvia, unemployed adults participating in a training programme received

> **Fewer than one in six countries spent more than 0.3% of GDP on adult education**

a coupon to attend approved non-formal education courses and a monthly grant (European Commission/EACEA/Eurydice, 2015b).

QUALITY

It is particularly challenging to monitor the full range of quality dimensions for adult education. Proposed frameworks have included aspects ranging from the existence of certification, recognition, validation and accreditation to the degree to which programmes target population groups in need (e.g. Borkowsky, 2013; ICF, 2015).

Three commitments were made in the Belém Framework for Action to foster quality in adult learning and education. They focus on (a) curricula, learning materials and teaching methodologies, (b) research and knowledge management systems, and (c) training and capacity-building for adult educators. Adult educator preparation and professional development are used here as an example of a system-related quality dimension.

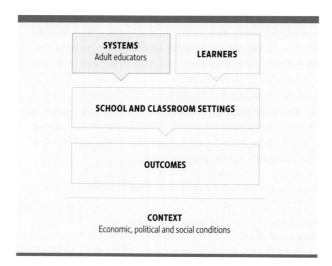

As part of GRALE III, three questions focused on adult educators. Among the two-thirds of countries that responded, 80% claimed they had pre-service education and training for adult teachers and facilitators. However, only 39% required pre-service qualifications to teach in all adult education programmes. And only 29% claimed they had sufficient capacity in their continuing, in-service education and training programmes for adult education teachers (UIL, 2016).

These averages provide a useful overview but are short on detail and difficult to validate. A series of country case studies was commissioned for the 2016 GEM Report to provide further insights. Cambodia has established 348 Community Learning Centres to deliver multiple programmes, including vocational skills acquisition and income-generation initiatives, particularly in rural areas. Community teachers receive 16 days of in-service training provided by the provincial Department of Early Childhood Education (Vanna, 2016).

The Jamaican Foundation for Lifelong Learning maintains a network of 29 adult education centres with 129 adult facilitators, 65% of whom are qualified; a few have received specialized training in areas needed to provide relevant instruction and address learning deficits (Cross, 2016).

In Mexico, adult education counsellors receive initial and continuous training, including on issues such as digital culture, written culture, worker education, competencies in indigenous languages and updates to National Institute of Adult Education guidelines. Certified courses are available for further study at various levels, while educators with a good record in terms of enrolment or student learning are provided with incentives, including training allowances (Hernández Flores, 2016).

Since the 1990s, Mozambique has established the National Institute of Adult Education, bachelor's and master's degrees in adult education and three adult education associations. However, more than half the facilitators lack initial pedagogical training (Ussene, 2016).

Except in high income countries, the knowledge base on adult education remains limited. The common EU target for adult education has provided impetus for investment in collecting system-related information on adult education. It was concluded from GRALE III that efforts to improve data 'need to set careful priorities and ensure that their ambitions are in line with available resources in different countries and contexts' (UIL, 2016), and that there is a need to promote peer review and peer learning. Groups of countries with comparable profiles should establish networks within existing organizations to generate and exchange information on the quality of adult education.

ENDNOTES

1. Armenia, Colombia, Egypt, Jordan, Kenya, Nepal, the Netherlands, the Republic of Korea, Sri Lanka, Sweden, Uganda and Viet Nam.

2. See technical note on *GEM Report* website for further information.

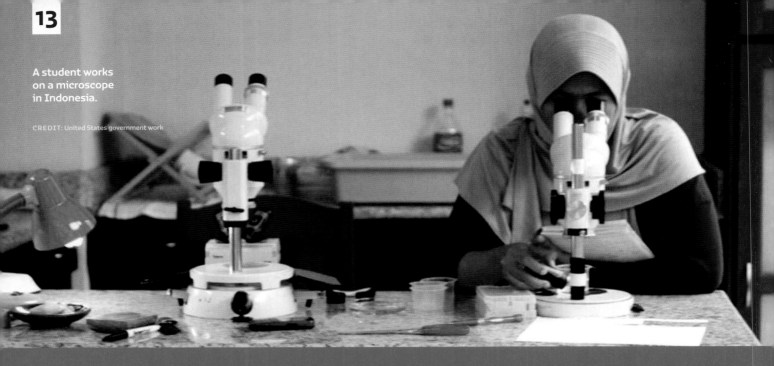

A student works
on a microscope
in Indonesia.

CREDIT: United States government work

KEY MESSAGES

The probability of having a decent job is almost double among those with high, rather than low, reading skills. However, other than literacy and numeracy, it is difficult to identify skills that both help with access to decent work in various contexts and can be measured.

Information and communication technology (ICT) skills have become essential to daily life and work. In the European Union in 2014, 65% of adults could send an email with an attachment, 44% could use basic arithmetic formulas in a spreadsheet and 28% could download and configure software.

Digital literacy skills are a better marker for this target than ICT skills. However, monitoring them globally requires keeping up with rapid technological change and keeping diverse contexts in mind.

Many of the most valued skills in the workplace, such as creativity, critical thinking, problem-solving and collaboration, are not easy to define and are hard to monitor.

Non-cognitive skills, such as perseverance, self-control and social skills, improve employment outcomes. How much they are valued varies by employment context and position. It is not recommended to try monitoring these skills at the global level.

Financial literacy and entrepreneurship skills are relevant for the world of work. According to one definition, 33% of adults worldwide are financially literate. Assessments of entrepreneurship skills are still at the research stage.

CHAPTER 13

TARGET 4.4

Skills for work

By 2030, substantially increase the number of youth and adults who have relevant skills, including technical and vocational skills, for employment, decent jobs and entrepreneurship

GLOBAL INDICATOR 4.4.1 – *Percentage of youth and adults with information and communications technology (ICT) skills by type of skill*

THEMATIC INDICATOR 16 – *Percentage of youth and adults who have achieved at least a minimum level of proficiency in digital literacy skills*

THEMATIC INDICATOR 17 – *Youth/adult educational attainment rates by age group, economic activity status, levels of education and programme orientation*

Target 4.4 focuses on one of education's outcomes: skills for work. It is similar to target 4.6, on literacy and numeracy, in two respects: both refer to work-related skills and neither refers to the means by which these skills are to be acquired.

With its explicit reference to technical and vocational skills, target 4.4 appears closely linked to target 4.3, which refers to technical and vocational education. However, skills for work are acquired in almost all education programmes and, critically, can be acquired outside education systems – for example, within families, communities and workplaces. Indeed, unlike hereditary traits, work-related skills originate in deliberate and intentional experiences: they are dynamic and can be developed throughout the course of a lifetime.

A central concept for this target is decent work, which is enshrined within Articles 6 and 7 of the 1966 International Covenant on Economic, Social and Cultural Rights. According to the United Nations (UN) Committee on Economic, Social and Cultural Rights, decent work respects fundamental human rights as well as worker rights in terms of work safety, remuneration and the physical and mental integrity of the worker.

> **Other than literacy and numeracy, it is difficult to envisage any skills that are relevant and easy to measure**

It is less clear what skills are needed for decent work. Moreover, skill requirements are specific to job opportunities, which differ enormously across countries. Other than the foundation skills of literacy and numeracy, in fact, it is difficult to envisage any skills for work that can satisfy all the criteria: measurable along a common scale at low cost; able to be acquired through education; and relevant in various labour market contexts. Faced with this challenge, the Inter-agency and Expert Group on Sustainable Development Goal Indicators (IAEG-SDGs) proposed measuring ICT skills, opting for relative ease of measurement at the cost of narrowing the scope of the target.

This chapter reviews the skills that matter most for work and asks whether they can be monitored. It focuses on general skills, which are applicable in a range of work contexts, and not on technical and vocational skills, which are specific and not suitable for global comparisons. It skips one of the proposed thematic indicators, the attainment rate – not only because it was covered under target 4.1 but also because it has relatively little relation to the possession of actual skills.

The chapter discusses cognitive and non-cognitive skills, a somewhat arbitrary distinction as non-cognitive skills – known by several other labels, such as soft or socio-emotional skills – involve cognition. In practice, depending on the context, a combination of skills is usually relevant. The chapter closes with a discussion of financial literacy and entrepreneurship skills as examples of work skills that develop at the nexus of intellectual, social and emotional abilities.

COGNITIVE SKILLS

Basic cognitive skills include literacy and numeracy. They are essential for getting work that pays enough to meet daily needs, pursuing further education and training opportunities, leading a healthy life and engaging actively in the social and political life of the community (UIL, 2016). Depending on the structure of the labour market, other cognitive skills, such as the ability to operate a computer, can also lead to improved employment opportunities.

LINKING BASIC COGNITIVE SKILLS WITH DECENT WORK

A higher level of basic cognitive skills, as captured through an internationally comparable measure of literacy proficiency, is associated with a higher chance of access to decent work opportunities. New analysis for this report shows that the average probability of holding a decent job almost doubles between those whose reading skills only allow them to locate a single piece of information in a short text (19%) and those who can interpret information from complex texts (35%).

The analysis used data on adults from urban areas of seven middle income countries, drawing on the World Bank Skills Towards Employability and Productivity (STEP) survey, which was conducted in 2011–2013. For the purpose of the analysis, a job was defined as decent if it satisfied three criteria: it offered an adequate number of working hours per week, provided employees with a written contract to protect their rights, and guaranteed social benefits. On average across the seven countries, one in four employees held a decent job according to these criteria. Nationally the figure ranged from one in eight in Ghana to one in two in Armenia as a result of variations in the sector composition of employment (between agriculture, manufacturing and services) and labour policies.

Measurement of literacy skills is covered in depth in Chapter 15 on target 4.6. Across the seven countries in the present sample, literacy proficiency varied greatly. In Ghana, 61% of adults read below even the lowest level of proficiency, compared with 1% in Armenia. Completing secondary school makes a big difference: in Colombia and Viet Nam, adults who had not done so were more than twice as likely not to reach level 2 of literacy proficiency.

ICT AND DIGITAL LITERACY SKILLS

ICT has quickly become essential to daily life and work in most countries. A survey of 32 mostly middle income countries found that, on average in 2014, 38% of households had a computer at home and 44% used the internet at least occasionally (or had a smartphone). The latter measure ranged from 8% in Pakistan and 11%

in Bangladesh to 62% in Lebanon and 63% in China (Pew Research Center, 2015).

Demographic shifts and increasing access to education mean ICT use will continue to rise in the next 15 years. Already, the internet is used by 66% of people aged 18 to 34, compared with 27% of those over 35, and by 75% of those with at least secondary education, compared with 19% of those with less (Pew Research Centre, 2015). It is essential for education systems to help everybody acquire ICT and digital literacy skills, especially where a considerable proportion of the population is at risk of being excluded from society and work opportunities because of a 'digital divide'.

ICT skills

Defining, measuring and monitoring ICT skills presents several challenges for making comparisons over time and across countries. Technology – and the skills needed to use it – develops so rapidly that what is relevant today may be less so tomorrow. And wide disparities between countries in technology availability mean the context in which such skills are exercised differs considerably.

The proposed global indicator for target 4.4 is the percentage of individuals with ICT skills according to the definition of the International Telecommunication Union (ITU), formulated in the framework of the Partnership on Measuring ICT for Development (ITU, 2014). 'ICT skills' refers to nine computer-related activities that individuals have undertaken in the previous three months (**Table 13.1**). The information is to be collected by national statistical offices as part of standard household surveys or censuses.

The ITU maintains globally comparable indicators in the World Telecommunication/ICT Indicators database.

TABLE 13.1:
Computer-related activities included in the definition of ICT skills

Copy or move a file or folder
Use copy and paste tools to duplicate or move information within a document
Send emails with attached files (e.g. a document, picture or video)
Use basic arithmetic formulas in a spreadsheet
Connect and install new devices (e.g. a modem, camera or printer)
Find, download, install and configure software
Create electronic presentations with presentation software (including text, images, sound and video)
Transfer files between a computer and other devices
Write a computer program using a specialized programming language

Source: ITU (2014).

As the indicator of ICT skills (HH15) was defined only recently, data were available for just eight countries by 2016. But European countries have been collecting similar information since the early 2000s (Eurostat, 2014), and it is possible to combine information from these two comparable sources. In the European Union, among adults in 2014, 65% could send an e-mail with an attachment, 44% used basic arithmetic formulas in a spreadsheet, and 28% could download and configure software. The percentage of adults outside the European Union (EU) who had carried out this task was 3% in the Islamic Republic of Iran and 15% in Brazil (**Figure 13.1**).

While the ITU has not synthesized activities into an easily communicated index of ICT skills, the European Union has proposed ways of adding up the number of activities carried out and assigning individuals to skill levels (European Commission, 2014). However, there is no consensus on how to aggregate the information. Moreover, in coming years further ICT skills are likely to be considered highly relevant for work. For example, the Organisation for Economic Co-operation and Development (OECD) countries are collecting information related to security and privacy, such as the ability to protect personal data (OECD, 2015h).

Digital literacy skills

The ICT skills indicator has the advantage of being straightforward to interpret and collect. However, it reflects only the prevalence of certain computer-related activities and not the skill level at which they are performed. Such skills cannot be self-reported but need to be assessed directly.

A measure of these skills should capture how individuals use technology in a critical and creative way to manage and create information, solve problems and communicate (JRC, 2013). Accordingly, ICT (or digital) literacy was first defined as the cognitive ability to use 'digital technology, communications tools, and/or networks to access, manage, integrate, evaluate, and create information in order to function in a knowledge society' (International ICT Literacy Panel, 2002). The definition drew on an earlier concept of information literacy as changed by the advent of digital technology (Catts and Lau 2008; Erstad, 2010).

The International Computer and Information Literacy Study (ICILS), which was administered to grade 8 students in 21 education systems in 2013, defined computer and information literacy as 'an individual's ability to use computers to investigate, create, and communicate in order to participate effectively at home, at school, in the workplace, and in society' (Fraillon et al., 2014).

Students completed a computer-based test that consisted of two modules randomly selected out of four. Each 30-minute module was based on a theme and consisted of a set of small discrete tasks followed

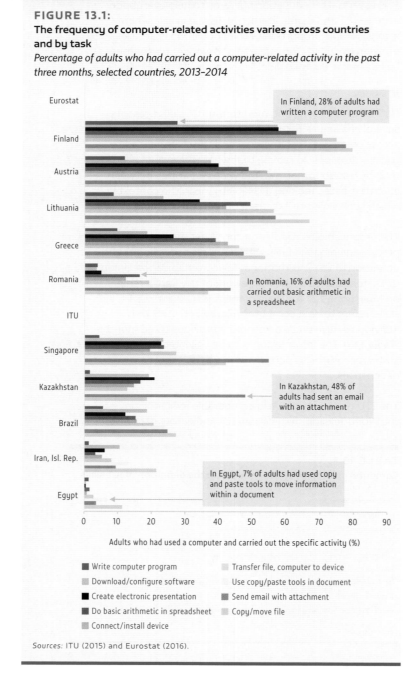

FIGURE 13.1:

The frequency of computer-related activities varies across countries and by task

Percentage of adults who had carried out a computer-related activity in the past three months, selected countries, 2013–2014

In Finland, 28% of adults had written a computer program

In Romania, 16% of adults had carried out basic arithmetic in a spreadsheet

In Kazakhstan, 48% of adults had sent an email with an attachment

In Egypt, 7% of adults had used copy and paste tools to move information within a document

Adults who had used a computer and carried out the specific activity (%)

- Write computer program
- Download/configure software
- Create electronic presentation
- Do basic arithmetic in spreadsheet
- Connect/install device
- Transfer file, computer to device
- Use copy/paste tools in document
- Send email with attachment
- Copy/move file

Sources: ITU (2015) and Eurostat (2016).

by a large task. The four themes involved creating an advertising poster for an after-school exercise programme, a web page on a school band competition, a presentation to explain breathing to students and an information sheet about a trip for their peers.

Four proficiency levels were developed. Students at level 1 demonstrated a functional working knowledge of computers as tools and a basic understanding of the consequences of a computer having multiple users. They applied conventional commands to perform basic communication tasks and add simple content to information products. They demonstrated familiarity with the basic layout conventions of electronic documents. In the Czech Republic, 85% of students performed above this level, compared with 9% in Turkey and 13% in Thailand (**Figure 13.2**).

The apparent large gap in digital literacy between richer and poorer countries may reflect the degree of access to computers at home and school. Even within countries, ICILS results showed large differences according to socio-economic status. For example, in Chile students with parents of low occupational status scored on average at level 1, while those with parents of high status scored on average at level 2 (Fraillon et al., 2014).

However, the choice of themes in the assessment appears vulnerable to the criticism of cultural bias. To extend coverage to low and lower middle income countries, it is essential to develop context-appropriate material for surveys of this kind.

ICILS is not the only attempt to assess and compare digital literacy skills across countries. The OECD has included a module on digital reading in the Programme for International Student Assessment (PISA) and one on problem-solving in technology-rich environments in the Programme for the International Assessment of Adult Competencies (PIAAC) (OECD, 2011b; 2014d). In addition, the University of Melbourne has launched the research-oriented Assessment and Teaching of 21st Century Skills project with the support of three ICT corporations (Griffin and Care, 2015).

Looking ahead, a global tool to assess progress in digital literacy will need to address rapid technological changes over time and incorporate changes in patterns of ICT use. For example, the introduction of tablets and smartphones has resulted in new ICT applications and ways of working digitally. Assessment of ICT and digital literacy skills needs to be designed to incorporate such developments without losing comparability over time (Ainley et al., 2016).

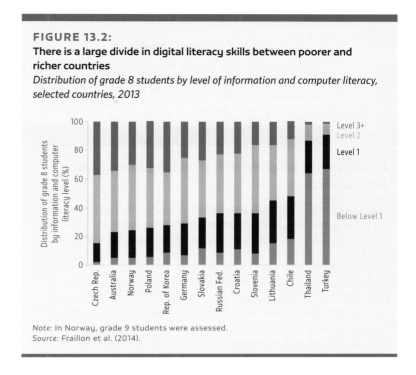

FIGURE 13.2:
There is a large divide in digital literacy skills between poorer and richer countries
Distribution of grade 8 students by level of information and computer literacy, selected countries, 2013

Note: In Norway, grade 9 students were assessed.
Source: Fraillon et al. (2014).

One possibility is choosing a design where some test modules are replaced with new ones that reflect newer aspects of ICT. The Australian national assessment programme of ICT literacy, which has been conducted every three years since 2005, has taken such an approach. This has provided comparable test results over nine years during which numerous changes have occurred in relation to ICT and the use of digital devices (ACARA, 2015).

NON-COGNITIVE SKILLS

Well-developed cognitive skills are necessary, but not sufficient for desirable employment-related outcomes. Their effect may be best realized in specific contexts or in combination with other individual characteristics. In particular, there has been growing interest in the role of non-cognitive skills, distinguished from cognitive skills in that they are less related to raw cognitive processing (Kautz et al, 2014; OECD, 2015f).

This review, which is not meant to be comprehensive, examines three non-cognitive skills that have been shown to have a positive effect on employment outcomes, can improve through education and training, and can be meaningfully measured and compared between countries (Zhou, 2016).

Despite decades of research, instruments to assess non-cognitive skills are still at an early stage of development. Measurements mostly rely on self-reporting, which is sensitive to response bias. Importantly for cross-cultural measurement, different non-cognitive skills might be desirable in different cultures. For example, some

cultures place higher value on empathy, sociability and cooperation (Triandis and Gelfand, 1998). Accordingly, some skills are emphasized in the labour market in one country but may have negative consequences in another (Miyamoto et al., 2015).

Possessing more of a skill is usually considered an asset. However, evidence is lacking to show the level at which non-cognitive skills are most likely to predict employment outcomes. The optimal skill level likely depends on the employment context, as different jobs require different sets of skills (Borghans et al., 2006).. For instance, caring attitudes are highly relevant for positions in medical and therapeutic professions, but may not be rewarded in sales jobs that consider more direct and persistent behaviour an asset. The right mix of skills also depends on perspective. For instance, is a person carrying out monotonous work tasks better off with more or fewer coping skills (Green, 2011)?

The development of measures to allow cross-country comparisons of non-cognitive skills, therefore, is challenging. While this report does not recommend large-scale measurement for global comparisons, the growing research on measuring non-cognitive skills acquisition deserves attention. Finally, distinguishing between cognitive and non-cognitive skills is complicated because many of the most valued skills in the workplace are combinations that are not easily categorized (Gutman and Schoon, 2013) (**Box 13.1**).

PERSEVERANCE

Perseverance involves 'steadfastness on mastering a skill or completing a task' (Gutman and Schoon, 2013). It can take the form of 'grit', which has been defined as 'perseverance to accomplish long-term or higher-order goals in the face of challenges and setbacks, engaging the student's psychological resources' (Shechtman et al., 2013). Experiments have shown that perseverance is malleable. For example, individuals who reflect on failures or obstacles tend to have more grit and perform better on tasks involving sustained attention (Duckworth et al., 2011; Dimenichi and Richmond, 2015).

A commonly adopted measurement tool is the Grit Scale, which contains 12 self-reported items on consistency of interest and perseverance of effort (Duckworth and Quinn, 2009). The World Bank STEP survey, which was carried out in middle income countries, included three items from the Grit Scale and

---

| BOX 13.1 |

The fundamental but elusive skills of creativity, critical thinking and collaboration

The Education 2030 Framework for Action states that all individuals should acquire a solid foundation of knowledge, develop creative and critical thinking and collaborative skills, and build curiosity, courage and resilience. Yet, such skills are not easy to define, assess or teach.

Creativity involves producing novel and useful content through divergent thinking, i.e. exploring various possible solutions. The Torrance Tests of Creative Thinking are considered a valid and reliable predictor of creative achievement. However, they focus on identifying specific cognitive processes. In practice, creativity is much broader. It involves motivation, perseverance, focus, flexibility, independence and the ability to overcome problems. Moreover, standardized tests tend to be incompatible with the type of divergent thinking that is the focus of creativity assessment.

Critical thinking is a concept with several layers and means different things to different people. The most widely recognized definition includes six cognitive dimensions: the abilities to interpret, analyse, evaluate, infer, explain and self-regulate. These abilities are amenable to assessment, but experts involved in the definition could not reach consensus on whether non-cognitive elements such as honesty in evaluating one's own biases or understanding of others' opinions are a necessary part of the definition. More generally, a technical view of critical thinking is challenged by those who believe there is no such thing as objective truth because knowledge is socially constructed.

Collaboration skills include coordination, communication, conflict resolution, decision-making and negotiation. The 2015 PISA included collaborative problem-solving, which the framework defines as the 'capacity of an individual to effectively engage in a process whereby two or more agents attempt to solve a problem by sharing the understanding and effort required to come to a solution and pooling their knowledge, skills and efforts to reach that solution'. A student with a low level of these skills 'pursues random or irrelevant actions, operates individually, and makes little contribution to resolve potential obstacles'.

Understanding of these skills is still in exploratory stages. Designing an assessment of collaboration skills involves innovative thinking in identifying tasks through which shared understanding is developed, a team is organized and common actions are taken. It also requires finding approaches to assessing the collaboration skills of an individual when the responsibility for the failure of teamwork is hard to observe and the available time is limited. One solution has been the use of computer-simulated participants, but this raises the question whether the interactions are valid.

Sources: Facione (1990); Kaufman and Sternberg (2010); Lai (2011); OECD (2013e); Plucker and Makem (2010); Sternberg (2012).

found that workers who scored better had spent less time finding their first job after graduation (World Bank, 2014d). But the items of the Grit Scale have also been criticized as being subject to social desirability bias (Dimenichi and Richmond, 2015).

The 2012 PISA assessed perseverance of 15-year-old students in more than 60 countries. It was defined via five components: the extent to which students (a) felt they gave up easily when confronted with a problem, (b) put off difficult problems, (c) remained interested in the tasks they started, (d) continued to work on a task until everything was perfect and (e) did more than was expected of them when confronted with a problem (OECD, 2013d). The study showed that 56% of the students indicated that they do not give up easily when confronted with a problem, and that there was a 14 percentage point gap in perseverance levels at the expense of socio-economically disadvantaged students (**Figure 13.3**).

SELF-CONTROL

Self-control has been defined as 'the capacity for altering one's own responses, especially to bring them into line with standards such as ideals, values, morals, and social expectations, and to support the pursuit of long-term goals' (Baumeister at al., 2007). Other terms used to describe it include self-regulation, self-discipline and willpower (Duckworth and Kern, 2011).

Self-control positively influences personal initiative and proactive coping. A survey of about 400 prospective vocational training graduates in the Netherlands suggested that self-control predicted student preparation for a job search before they entered the labour market (Baay et al., 2014). Low self-control of emotions in children has been directly linked to long-term unemployment in adulthood (Kokko et al., 2000).

Early childhood experiences help develop brain regions related to self-control and are important to developing

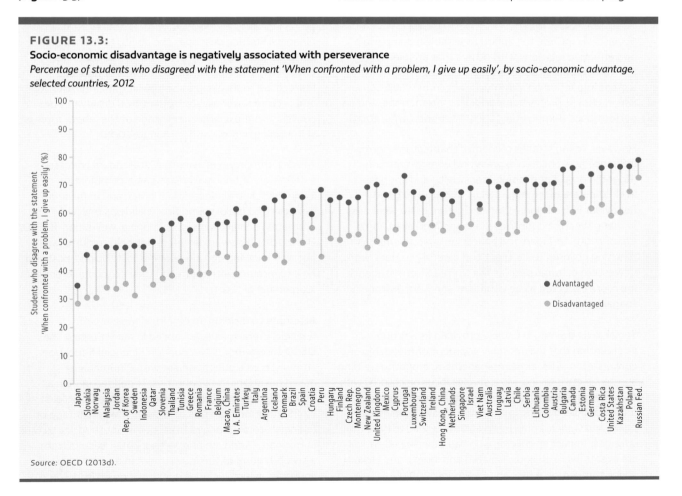

FIGURE 13.3:

Socio-economic disadvantage is negatively associated with perseverance

Percentage of students who disagreed with the statement 'When confronted with a problem, I give up easily', by socio-economic advantage, selected countries, 2012

Source: OECD (2013d).

self-discipline (Tarullo et al., 2009). Difficult circumstances in childhood, such as poverty and chronically depressed parents, can negatively affect children's self-control skills (Evans and Rosenbaum, 2008; Sektnan et al., 2010). Schooling can be an important corrective to help children develop or regain these skills. Education interventions can promote self-regulation and lower the impact of early childhood risk factors (McClelland and Tominey, 2014). Emotional support from teachers and targeted curricula can increase attention control, cognition and the ability to suppress impulses (Diamond et al., 2007).

Several approaches have been used to measure self-control, including clinical experiments on the executive function (the cognitive processes that control behaviour). The most common tools are self-reported personality questionnaires such as the Eysenck I7 Impulsiveness Scale, the Self-Control Scale and the Barratt Impulsiveness Scale (Eysenck et al., 1984; Tangney et al., 2004; Barratt, 1985).

SOCIAL SKILLS

Social skills include the ability to establish compatible and effective relations with others that are pleasing in interpersonal situations (Segrin, 2001). They have a great impact on an individual's academic success, career choice, professional and peer interactions, and job performance (Riggio et al., 2003; Witt and Ferris, 2003).

However, many studies recognize that cultural norms influence how children express and control emotions (Rogoff, 2003). For example, sensitivity and shyness in children are often regarded as mature and good behaviour in traditional Chinese culture but a weakness in many Western countries (Katz and McClellan, 1997; Chen, 2009). In Japan, the education system emphasizes teaching children to be silent and careful listeners, while in Western cultures such as the United States students are more expected to be confident speakers (Hatano and Inagaki, 1998).

Social skills training is usually provided as a group intervention that includes development of friendship and conversation skills, anger management, empathy training and perspective-taking. Most studies focus on children with social communication problems. But the results of research on social skills training interventions have been mixed (Kjøbli and Ogden, 2014). Interventions tended to have the strongest impact on children who had experienced critical life events, were anxious, isolated and lonely, and lacked social stimulation (Lösel and Beelmann, 2003).

Two measurement tools are frequently used to assess social skills. The Social Skills Inventory measures seven dimensions, including emotional/social expressiveness, sensitivity and control (Riggio, 1986). The Interpersonal Competence Questionnaire examines five interpersonal skill domains: initiation, self-disclosure, conflict management, emotional support and negative assertion (Muralidharan et al., 2011).

COMBINATIONS OF COGNITIVE AND NON-COGNITIVE SKILLS FOR WORK

It is often not possible to disentangle particular skills. Two examples of blended cognitive and non-cognitive skills are financial literacy and entrepreneurship skills. Both are relevant for the world of work but present challenges for measurement and monitoring.

FINANCIAL LITERACY

Financial literacy describes the ability to manage personal finances and allocate business resources effectively. Individuals with low levels of financial literacy are more likely to borrow at high interest rates and acquire fewer assets, both critical disadvantages in contexts where a large percentage of the labour force is self-employed (Cole and Fernando, 2008).

In 2012, the Group of Twenty (G20) leaders endorsed a definition of financial literacy as 'a combination of awareness, knowledge, skill, attitude and behaviour necessary to make sound financial decisions and ultimately achieve individual financial well-being' (OECD/INFE, 2011). 'Knowledge' refers not only to numeracy but also knowing certain financial institutions exist and how to interact with them and their products effectively (Carpena et al., 2011).

Attempts to develop an empirical measure of financial literacy have advanced in recent years. The OECD International Network on Financial Education administered a questionnaire with 8 numeracy-based questions in 14 countries. It defined people as financially literate if they correctly answered at least 6 of 8 questions. On this definition, the percentage of financial literacy ranged from 33% in South Africa to 69% in Hungary (Atkinson and Messy, 2012). Results from a second round of the assessment in a wider range of countries, which includes questions on attitudes and behaviour, will be released in 2016 (OECD, 2015i).

A Standard & Poor's module with numeracy-based questions related to interest, compound interest, inflation and risk diversification was attached to the Gallup World Poll and administered in more than 140 countries in 2014. The survey defined people as financially literate if they correctly answered questions on at least three of these four financial concepts. It found that 33% of adults worldwide were financially literate, from a low of 13% in Yemen to a high of 71% in Norway (Klapper et al., 2015).

There is wide variation in the level of financial development around the world. For example, the percentage of people with a bank account varied from 89% in high income countries to 24% in low income countries, and just 7% among the poorest fifth of the population in Northern Africa and Western Asia (Demirguc-Kunt and Klapper, 2012). However, the survey showed no evidence that income was associated with financial literacy for countries with the gross domestic product (GDP) per capita below US$12,000. This suggests the limited relevance of some knowledge in poorer countries.

More critically, knowledge does not lead directly to particular behaviour; other factors play a role, including traits such as decisiveness and the social contexts in which decisions are made. The World Bank, accordingly, differentiated between a knowledge-based measure of financial literacy and a measure of financial capability, which looked at how knowledge interacted with skills and attitudes to generate behaviour that led to positive outcomes. In a study of five countries, knowledge was not always positively correlated with capability. A notable example was that, in some cases, women had lower levels of financial literacy but higher levels of financial capability (Holzmann et al., 2013).

Unlike assessments that targeted the entire adult population, the 2012 PISA measured financial literacy among 15-year-olds. It referred to 'knowledge and understanding of financial concepts and risks, and the skills, motivation and confidence to apply such knowledge and understanding in order to make effective decisions across a range of financial contexts, to improve the financial well-being of individuals and society, and to enable participation in economic life' (OECD, 2014a).

At level 2, the minimum proficiency level, students would be able to apply their knowledge of common financial products and commonly used financial terms and concepts, and use information to make financial decisions in relevant contexts. They would recognize the value of a simple budget and interpret features of everyday financial documents. By this definition, 15% of students in participating countries fell below level 2, ranging from 5% in Estonia to 23% in Israel. But in Colombia, 56% of 15-year-olds fell below level 2 (OECD, 2014a) (**Figure 13.4**).

Other factors influencing financial literacy include whether it is part of the intended curriculum, the prevalence of appropriate teaching and learning materials, and teacher knowledge. In general, evaluations demonstrate that education programmes can improve financial literacy. A meta-analysis of 21 experimental studies found that interventions led to modest improvements in financial knowledge and smaller effects on financial attitudes and behaviours (O'Prey and Shepherd, 2014).

Few financial literacy programmes targeted at adults have undergone rigorous evaluation. Results are mixed, although this may be the result of the diversity of content, training, medium of instruction and outcomes studied. One study among urban households in India found that traditional financial education alone did not affect long-term financial behaviour (Carpena et al., 2015).

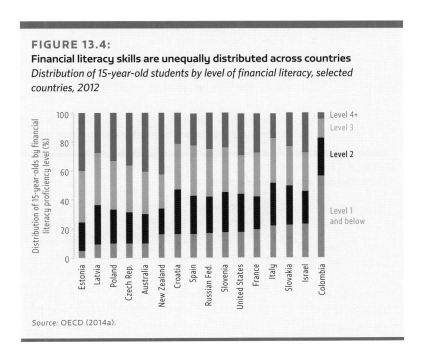

FIGURE 13.4:

Financial literacy skills are unequally distributed across countries
Distribution of 15-year-old students by level of financial literacy, selected countries, 2012

Source: OECD (2014a).

ENTREPRENEURSHIP SKILLS

Entrepreneurship, also a focus of target 4.4, requires a mix of skills. The European Commission defined entrepreneurship as 'the mindset and process needed to create and develop economic activity by blending risk-taking, creativity and/or innovation with sound management, within a new or existing organisation' (European Commission, 2003). Accordingly, entrepreneurship skills encompass 'creativity, initiative, tenacity, teamwork, understanding of risk, and a sense of responsibility' (European Commission, 2014).

It helps to group these skills into three categories. Technical skills are specific to the industry in which the business is active. Management skills include planning, finance, accounting, marketing and quality control. Personal skills include self-control and discipline, creativity, persistence, leadership and the ability to manage risk (OECD, 2014d). A need for achievement and autonomy, self-efficacy, innovativeness, stress tolerance and a proactive personality have been identified as relevant characteristics (Rauch and Frese, 2007). Inevitably, there is no straightforward approach to measuring such a diverse set of cognitive and non-cognitive attributes.

The Global Entrepreneurship Monitor included indicators on self-perceived capabilities in a survey of entrepreneurial activity across 60 countries in 2015. These perceptions were lowest in Europe at 43% and highest in sub-Saharan Africa, where more than 70% of adults in four of five participating countries were not only confident but also saw the most opportunities for entrepreneurial activity (GEM, 2016; OECD, 2015i). These results raise the question of comparability, as neither business characteristics nor risks are comparable between poor and rich countries.

The research project on Assessment Tools and Indicators for Entrepreneurship Education went a step further to validate self-reported measures of entrepreneurship skills using a sample of students across 13 European countries and 3 age groups: 10 to 11, 16 to 17 and 20 or older (Moberg et al., 2014). The tools covered five dimensions (**Table 13.2**). They have not yet been applied to monitor differences between countries.

Research-based studies of entrepreneurship within countries offer interesting insights. In Sri Lanka, a survey collected background data on a sample of wage workers, micro-firm owners, and larger firm owners with more than five employees to identify differences between them in terms of measures including cognitive ability, entrepreneurial personality, financial literacy and risk attitudes. Larger firm owners had significantly higher cognitive abilities and were more competitive and better organized than micro-firm owners. Moreover, over two and a half years, the few own-account workers who were more similar in skills to larger firm owners were more likely to expand by hiring more employees (de Mel et al., 2010).

In Peru, as part of a village microfinance programme, a training session of 30 to 60 minutes per week was added over a period of 1 to 2 years. The training focused on basic business practices, such as how to treat clients, where to sell, the use of special discounts and selling on credit. Participants demonstrated greater business knowledge and some better business practices, such as reinvesting profit in their business and maintaining sales records (Karlan and Valdivia, 2011).

For entrepreneurship skills to be gained and to be effective, relevant topics and exercises should be explicitly integrated in school curricula and assessed as an education outcome. In Europe, the most common concrete learning outcomes at the upper secondary education level were attitudes such as initiative, risk-taking and problem-solving, which were specified in 19 of 36 education systems (European Commission/EACEA/Eurydice, 2012a). Spain specified the broadest range of entrepreneurship-related outcomes in its secondary education curricula, including assessment criteria. Overall, though, assessment guidance remains limited not just in Europe but around the world despite the variety of programmes on offer, as in the case of Palestine (**Box 13.2**).

In general, there is little clarity to guide this aspect of target 4.4 because of the wide diversity of possible outcomes, targeted groups and modes of delivery; the tenuous links between programmes and outcomes; and the complexity of measuring some key outcomes.

TABLE 13.2:
Dimensions of entrepreneurial skills

Entrepreneurial skills	Exploration: creativity
	Evaluation: planning and financial literacy
	Exploitation: marshalling resources, managing ambiguity, teamwork
Entrepreneurial mindset	Self-efficacy, locus of control, self-esteem
Entrepreneurial knowledge	Perceived knowledge about how to assess business opportunities; role and function entrepreneurs have in society; and knowledge about different types of entrepreneurial career options
Connectedness to education	(=student-teacher relationship)
Connectedness to future career	(=student enterprising activities, work experience, and intention to start a company)

Source: Moberg et al. (2014).

CONCLUSION

This chapter has reviewed a select set of skills 'for employment, decent jobs and entrepreneurship' with three important questions in mind.

First, what skills are particularly relevant for global monitoring across diverse economic, social and cultural contexts? Popular accounts of '21st century skills' are criticized for cultural specificity. Some critics caution against overemphasizing skills that reflect norms of powerful social groups or countries. An additional challenge relates to the mix of skills: while higher levels of cognitive skills may be better in most contexts, this is less the case for non-cognitive skills. Nevertheless, different skills in different combinations are relevant for different formal and informal jobs in poor and rich countries alike. For that reason, they should be explored within the scope of target 4.4.

Second, once identified, are skills mainly acquired in education and training systems, or elsewhere? Views differ on the extent to which some skills are stable or malleable, whether they have a genetic element or are learned – at home or in school classrooms – or are indelibly affected by workplace expectations and training. Target 4.4 offers an excellent opportunity to explore these questions. Considerable education resources are spent on programmes that aim to develop skills of future workers, but there is often insufficient comparative evidence of what skills are most important for which employment sectors and why.

Third, are available measures valid and feasible at low cost? Several skills have been measured for decades, although mostly from a research angle, in high income countries and without cross-country comparability. There are limitations in using self-reporting tools to measure employment-related skills, given the temptation for respondents to provide socially desirable responses. Socially constructed skills are especially difficult to measure reliably across cultures. Nevertheless, innovative approaches are being developed to measure important complex skills such as communication and collaboration. These approaches involve simulating interactions in laboratory conditions, which makes them less realistic and quite expensive, and hence, not suitable for global monitoring. Yet, they merit closer attention to guide future education interventions.

The debates around these questions are reflected in the proposed indicators for target 4.4. One is the education attainment rate in the adult population, which is not a measure of skill and whose use is an approach the international education community seeks to distance itself from. As the target formulation specifies technical and vocational skills, a more reasonable approach would be to capture acquisition of certified skills, although the cost of developing and maintaining a related administrative system in all countries would be high. The new agenda makes a tentative step instead to directly monitor a particular skill: ICT and digital literacy. While this risks narrowing the agenda, it should be seen as a call to begin focusing on acquisition of concrete, measurable skills.

BOX 13.2

Nurturing entrepreneurship skills in Palestine

In Palestine, a variety of interventions exists to improve entrepreneurship skills, encourage youth to launch their own businesses and help them work productively in small and medium-sized enterprises. However, a review has concluded that none of the programmes have made attempts to assess their effectiveness in increasing their target population's capacities.

The Know About Business programme, initiated by the International Labour Office and the United Nations Development Programme (UNDP) in 2009, mainstreamed entrepreneurship courses in the curricula of vocational training centres under the Ministry of Labour and vocational schools under the Ministry of Education and Higher Education in 2011. A spin-off project introduced entrepreneurship courses into the curricula of the United Nations Relief and Works Agency (UNRWA) training centres.

In addition, the Food and Agriculture Organization implemented its worldwide Junior Farmer Field and Life Schools programme in 16 rural schools, providing disadvantaged youth with agricultural and life skills. The programme provided technical entrepreneurship skills – including agricultural business management, marketing strategy and cost–benefit analysis – and raised awareness on crops as a source of income.

Non-government organisations are also active. INJAZ Palestine helps students set up businesses in laboratory conditions to solve real business problems. The Youth Entrepreneurship Development programme, funded by the US Agency for International Development and implemented by the International Youth Foundation, has trained 9,000 young people aged 14 to 29. The Palestine Education for Employment initiative delivers a certified course on business plan formulation.

Overall, these programmes focus mostly on technical and management skills. However, personal skills may be more critical to overcoming gaps, notably by gender, in entrepreneurial activity. Data from the Global Entrepreneurship Monitor show that fear of failure, which was more common among women, was negatively associated with the probability of becoming an entrepreneur. The factor most associated with this fear was a negative perception of one's own skills, suggesting a needed area of focus for future programmes.

Sources: Daoud et al. (2015); Education for Employment (2015); FAO (2010); Hashweh (2012); ILO (2012); Intel (2015); Youth Entrepreneurship Development (2015).

Jaspreet, a girl at
the Patiala School
for Deaf and Blind,
Punjab, India.

CREDIT: Shivam Kapoor/UNESCO

KEY MESSAGES

The SDG agenda requires a major shift in monitoring, reporting and policy-making on inequality.

Measurement focuses on disparity in results, such as how many girls are in school compared to boys, but tends to ignore the contributing causes, such as textbook bias, discriminatory classroom practices or social norms, and the policies that could address them.

There are two challenges with inequality measures. First, as they can be used for any education indicator and broken down by any characteristic, such as gender, location or wealth, there is too much information to absorb. Second, different measures can give very different, even contradictory, results.

Disparity by wealth is the most extreme. In low income countries, for every 100 among the richest youth who complete primary education, only 36 do so among the poorest; in lower and upper secondary education the corresponding figures are 19 and 7.

Global or regional averages mask substantial **gender** gaps in education. While parity was achieved globally in 2014, only 63% of countries achieved parity in primary education, 46% in lower secondary and 23% in upper secondary.

More comprehensive monitoring of gender equality in education is needed, which requires evaluating curricula, textbooks, assessments and teacher education.

People with **disabilities** are routinely denied their right to education. Across 30 education systems in Europe, 4.6% of pupils were identified as having a special educational need in 2010. Yet monitoring is difficult because disability takes different forms and degrees.

About 40% of people around the world are not taught in a **language** they speak or understand. Monitoring should assess whether policies help students gain *access* to education in their home language, whether these policies are implemented and whether teachers are prepared.

Migrants have specific education needs. In high income countries, first-generation immigrant students scored well below their peers in reading and mathematics. **Forcibly displaced** populations are among the most neglected. According to the UN refugee agency, 50% of primary school-age refugees and 75% of secondary school-age refugees are out of school worldwide.

CHAPTER 14

TARGET 4.5

Equity

By 2030, eliminate gender disparities in education and ensure equal access to all levels of education and vocational training for the vulnerable, including persons with disabilities, indigenous peoples and children in vulnerable situations

GLOBAL INDICATOR 4.5.1 – *Parity indices (female/male, rural/urban, bottom/top wealth quintile and others such as disability status, indigenous people and conflict-affected as data become available) for all indicators on this list that can be disaggregated*

THEMATIC INDICATOR 18 – *Percentage of students in primary education whose first or home language is the language of instruction*

(reviewed in the Finance chapter)

THEMATIC INDICATOR 19 – *Extent to which explicit formula-based policies reallocate education resources to disadvantaged populations*

THEMATIC INDICATOR 20 – *Education expenditure per student by level of education and source of funding*

THEMATIC INDICATOR 21 – *Percentage of total aid to education allocated to low-income countries*

The desire to leave no one behind permeates the entire 2030 Agenda for Sustainable Development. For example, two Sustainable Development Goals (SDGs) are dedicated to addressing gender inequality (SDG 5) and reducing income inequality (SDG 10). There is also an unprecedented global commitment to monitor progress using data disaggregated 'by income, gender, age, race, ethnicity, migratory status, disability, geographic location, and other characteristics relevant to national contexts' (United Nations, 2015a, p. 27). This is expected to spur demand for global monitoring and reporting of inequality.

> "The desire to leave no one behind permeates the entire 2030 Agenda for Sustainable Development"

In the case of education, target 4.5 focuses exclusively on the need to 'ensure equal access to all levels'. The cross-cutting nature of this target is reflected in the selection of global indicator 4.5.1, which aims to measure disparities in access to education from early childhood to adult education.

This chapter addresses three main issues. First, what are appropriate ways to measure inequality and its evolution over time? Gender disparity in primary, secondary and tertiary education was monitored as part of the third Millennium Development Goal (MDG), contributing to greater awareness of challenges in many countries. The new agenda extends the scope to other population groups, notably those defined by location and wealth. The accumulation of large data sets in recent years makes the global measurement of inequality in education possible. But the question of how best to measure disparity remains to be addressed.

Second, how can information be collected that identifies individuals as members of other vulnerable groups, such as people with disabilities and those who are forcibly displaced or speak a language other than the language of instruction?

Third, what are broader aspects of equity in education beyond parity? Target 4.5 is limited to disparity and, in this respect, does not capture aspects of equity unrelated to access. In practice, education remains a social institution that reflects and reproduces socio-economic and cultural disadvantages that prevail in the rest of society. For instance, even if they are in school, students from weaker socio-economic or marginalized backgrounds are more likely to attend schools characterized by substandard infrastructure, fewer qualified teachers, less ambitious peers and less effective pedagogical practices. These factors have a negative influence on their achievement in school and overall attainment.

While the target formulation makes no reference to the means for tackling disadvantage in education, three relevant thematic indicators have been proposed on policies, expenditure and aid; they are discussed in Chapter 20 on education financing.

INEQUALITY MEASURES

Measuring inequality in education is critical, but is challenging because of three main factors. First, inequality can be examined with reference to any education indicator, such as the primary completion rate or the number of years of education attained (Morrisson and Murtin, 2013; Meschi and Scervini, 2014). The increasing availability of national and international learning achievement surveys further enables the measurement of inequality in learning outcome indicators (OECD, 2010; Fereira and Gignoux, 2014). An important difference is between education indicators that are delimited between 0% and 100% and those that are not. For example, inequality would be zero if 100% of all students pass a minimum learning proficiency level but high in terms of the score in the same assessment.

Second, different inequality measures can be used to see how an education indicator is distributed in the population, each with advantages and disadvantages. Some measures have solid conceptual foundations and can be linked better to social perceptions of justice and equity. Others are less rigorous but can be easily communicated. Different inequality measures can also lead to different conclusions about the degree of inequality and the extent to which it changes over time (**Box 14.1**).

Third, policy-makers need to know how an education indicator varies by learner characteristics. The usual comparable markers of potential disadvantage are gender, location, and income or wealth. There is insufficient information for comparisons to be made for other important characteristics, such as disability. On other critical markers, comparisons can be made within but not between countries. For example, being a member of an ethnic, linguistic or religious group can be a marker of education advantage or disadvantage, depending on the country.

> **There is insufficient information on important markers of disadvantage, such as disability**

Issues arise even among more comparable characteristics. For example, regarding location, national definitions of rural and urban areas vary across countries. Some surveys, moreover, may not use the national definitions. In addition, the definitions have different implications depending on whether a country is small or large, or whether it is sparsely or densely populated.

Household wealth levels are also difficult to compare. Household surveys such as the Demographic and Health Surveys (DHS) and Multiple Indicator Cluster Surveys (MICS) have popularized asset indices (based, for example, on house construction materials or ownership of consumer durables) as a proxy measure of household socio-economic status in low and middle income countries. However, asset indices are not comparable between countries and over time (Rutstein and Staveteig, 2014). Television ownership does not have the same implication in a European country as an African one, or in 2000 vs 2010. Each asset index is specific to the country and the year. Its value is in comparing relative rather than absolute wealth levels.

PARITY INDEX

The Inter-agency and Expert Group on SDG Indicators has proposed the parity index as the global measure of inequality in education. This is the ratio between the values of two groups and ranges from 0 (extreme inequality at the expense of one group) to 1 (parity) to infinity (extreme inequality at the expense of the other group). For example, if 30% of the poorest and 60% of the richest have completed primary school, then the value of the wealth parity index of the primary completion rate is 0.5. This measure has been proposed because it is the easiest to communicate to a broad audience and has been effective for describing gender disparity over the past two decades.

New analysis for this report estimates average parity index values by region and country income group for several education indicators and three individual-level characteristics. The data refer to 2008–2014 and cover 82 low and middle income countries, which represent over 90% of the population in the two combined groups. Information is also provided on disparity in completion rates in high income countries.

In the case of children who have ever been to school, there is gender parity for middle income countries, but disparity at the expense of girls in low income countries, where 93 girls for every 100 boys have ever been to school (**Figure 14.2a**). Disparity in having been to school is exacerbated when location and wealth are used as markers. In low income countries, disparity is at the expense of children in rural areas, with the location parity

BOX 14.1

Different measures can lead to different conclusions on inequality

A hypothetical country example is used to explain how different inequality measures can lead to opposite conclusions. It shows the distribution of the school attendance rate in two years. In 2000, only 5% of the poorest 20% of children attended school, compared with 40% of the richest 20%. In 2010, 20% of the poorest 20% of children attended school, compared with 82% of the richest 20%.

Four indicative inequality measures are calculated:

- The *range*, i.e. the absolute difference in the value of the attendance rate between the poorest and richest 20%. By this measure, inequality increased from 2000 (35 percentage points) to 2010 (62 percentage points) (**Figure 14.1a**).

- The *ratio*, i.e. the attendance rate for the poorest over that for the richest, more commonly known as the parity index, in which a higher value means lower inequality. This measure would have inequality decreasing from 2000 (0.12) to 2010 (0.24) (**Figure 14.1b**).

- The *odds ratio* – the odds of attending school (i.e. the chance of attendance instead of non-attendance) among the richest over the odds of attending school among the poorest. It would indicate that inequality increased from 2000 (14) to 2010 (18) (**Figure 14.1c**).

- The *concentration index*, which takes into account the value of the attendance rate not only among the poorest and the richest 20% but for all five quintiles. It is based on the cumulative distribution of the attendance rate (on the vertical axis) against the cumulative proportion of individuals ranked from poorest to richest (on the horizontal axis). For example, the poorest 20% were 5% of those attending school in 2000 and 10% in 2010. If there were perfect equality, the latter share would be 20%. The index measures the distance from the line of perfect equality. It would show inequality decreasing from 2000 (0.40) to 2010 (0.28) (**Figure 14.1d**).

Selecting a measure needs to be based on careful weighing of the options' advantages and disadvantages.

FIGURE 14.1:
For the same population, different measures can yield opposite conclusions on education inequality
Trends in inequality of school attendance rate, by inequality measure, hypothetical example

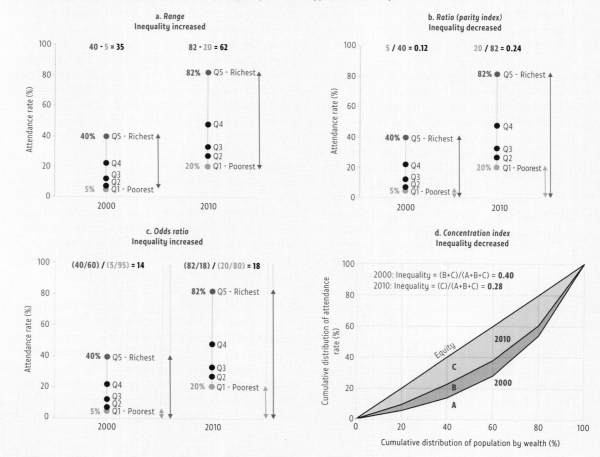

Sources: Cowell, 2010; Vallet and Montjourides (2015); O'Donnell et al. (2007).

index equal to 0.86, and at the expense of children from the poorest households, with the wealth parity index equal to 0.75 (**Figures 14.2b and 14.2c**).

Disparity can also move in the opposite direction. Among adolescents of lower secondary school age, 75 females for every 100 males complete lower secondary school in low income countries, but there are 96 males for every 100 females in upper middle income countries (Figure 14.2a).

Disparity by wealth is the most extreme. In upper middle income countries, the wealth parity index of the completion rate equals 0.90 in primary education, 0.71 in lower secondary and 0.44 in upper secondary. In low income countries, the wealth parity index equals 0.36 in primary education, 0.19 in lower secondary and just 0.07 in upper secondary (Figure 14.2c).

Disparities are much higher for completion than for attendance. For example, in lower middle income countries, the wealth parity index is 0.82 for the attendance rate of adolescents of lower secondary school age but 0.57 for the lower secondary completion rate. This suggests that many poorer adolescents still attend primary school.

Overall, gender disparity appears less severe than disparity by location or wealth. However, this average can mask important differences when gender interacts with either of the other two characteristics. In sub-Saharan Africa, there is gender parity in the percentage of those who have ever been to school and those who have completed primary education among the richest 20%. However, among the poorest 20% there were 89 females for every 100 males who had ever been to school and 83 females for every 100 males who had completed primary education. The disparity widens to 73 females for lower secondary completion and 40 females for upper secondary completion. By contrast, there is considerable disparity at the expense of the poorest males in Eastern and South-eastern Asia in lower and upper secondary completion (**Figure 14.3**).

Changes in the parity index over time can also be monitored. Between 2000 and 2010, across a wide range of education indicators, Southern Asia made considerable progress in reducing wealth disparity but sub-Saharan Africa hardly any; in fact, in upper secondary education, disparity in the latter region increased, with the value of the wealth parity index falling from 0.11 in 2000 to 0.09 in 2010 (**Figure 14.4**).

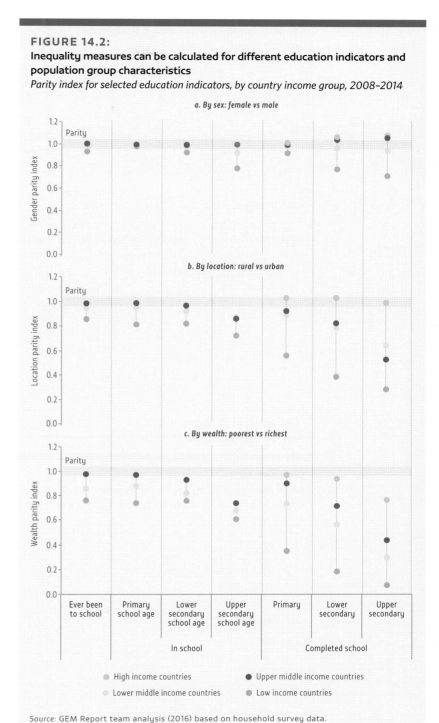

FIGURE 14.2:
Inequality measures can be calculated for different education indicators and population group characteristics
Parity index for selected education indicators, by country income group, 2008–2014

Source: GEM Report team analysis (2016) based on household survey data.

FIGURE 14.3:

Gender disparity is higher among the poorest

Gender parity index for selected education indicators, interaction with wealth, by region, 2008–2014

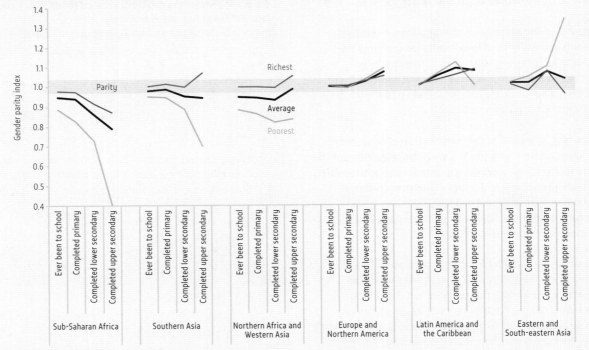

Note: Values for Eastern and South-eastern Asia and for Northern Africa and Western Asia refer only to low and middle income countries.
Source: GEM Report team analysis (2016) based on household survey data.

FIGURE 14.4:

Education disparity by wealth declined faster in Southern Asia than in sub-Saharan Africa

Wealth parity index for selected education indicators, Southern Asia and sub-Saharan Africa, circa 2000 and 2010

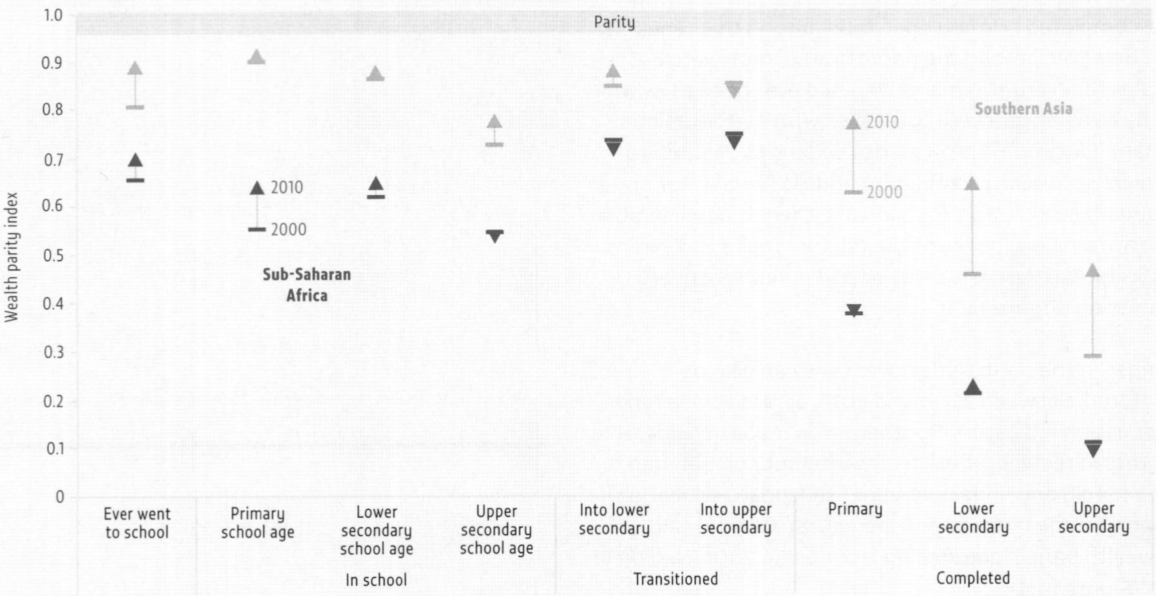

Source: GEM Report team analysis (2016) based on household survey data.

The parity index must be interpreted cautiously, for various reasons. For education indicators ranging from 0% to 100%, its value tends to depend on the level of the indicator, with low inequality being recorded when the level is high, approaching the 'ceiling' (Mingat and Ndem, 2014). Thus it risks offering limited information, as knowing the level of education development (e.g. the level of the primary completion rate) can predict, to a large extent, the level of inequality.

Plotting the primary completion rate against the wealth parity index illustrates this (**Figure 14.5**). It would be misleading to compare the value of the index of two countries, such as Honduras and Mauritania, at different completion rate levels and conclude that the latter country is more unequal. However, the index is useful to analyse inequality between countries at similar levels of education development: for example, the wealth parity index of the primary school completion rate was only 0.27 in Pakistan, compared with 0.56 in the Gambia.

Also, the parity index, by comparing two groups, only uses a small part of available information. To show how an education indicator is distributed in a population ranked by a characteristic such as wealth (from poorest to richest), the concentration index can be used (Figure 14.1d). Its calculation is based on the area between the concentration curve (which shows the actual distribution) and the diagonal line (which shows perfect equality): the farther a line is to the right of the diagonal, the higher the inequality.

For example, with respect to the distribution of the lower secondary education completion rate in sub-Saharan Africa by wealth in 2000 and 2010, the poorest 40% of young people represented less than 20% of lower secondary school completers. According to this measure, inequality fell overall between 2000 and 2010, as the curve moved closer towards the diagonal. However, the two concentration curves intersect, showing that the middle classes benefited most, while the poorest did worse (**Figure 14.6**).

Many governments have insufficient understanding of the need to monitor, report and act on education inequality. However, it is expected that the 2030 Agenda's focus on leaving no one behind will lead to a

FIGURE 14.5:

The parity index as a measure of education inequality needs to be interpreted cautiously

Primary education completion rate and wealth parity index, selected low and middle income countries, 2008–2014

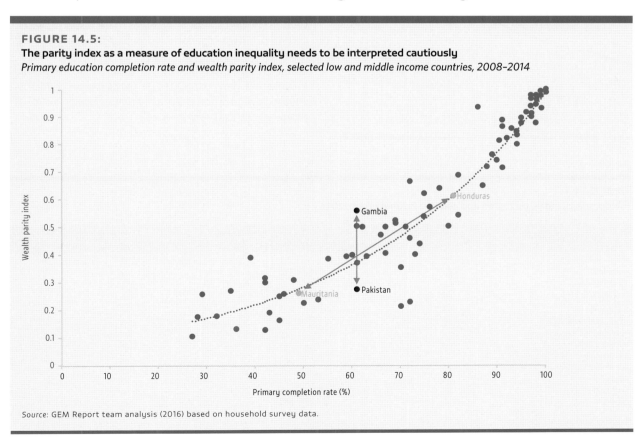

Source: GEM Report team analysis (2016) based on household survey data.

major shift. The increasing availability of household and school-based surveys makes it possible to carry out in-depth analyses both within and between countries.

Nevertheless, distinct challenges remain for monitoring equal access to all education levels. The multiplicity of education indicators, inequality measures, individual characteristics and their combinations means hundreds of estimates could be reported, too many to be useful. It is therefore necessary to agree on a limited number of key inequality measures. Consensus by the international community is also needed to generate consistent estimates from household surveys. Some important steps have been taken in that direction (**Box 14.2**).

GENDER

Ensuring that boys and girls participate in education at equivalent rates featured prominently in the MDG and Education for All (EFA) agendas. Genuine progress was achieved in gender parity in primary and secondary education, although global or regional averages have masked continuing disparity in two respects.

First, while parity was achieved globally, on average, in 2014 in primary, lower secondary and upper secondary education, only 63% of individual countries achieved parity in primary, 46% in lower secondary and 23% in upper secondary (**Table 14.1**). Second, as the previous section showed, national averages mask disparity within countries between particular groups. Poor females (and males as well), particularly from rural areas or minority ethnic groups, often face big obstacles. Third, and most importantly, despite progress towards parity, gender equality in education is a much broader issue. This is where attention is now needed.

FIGURE 14.6:

Much nuance in education inequality is lost using simple measures
Concentration curve of the lower secondary education completion rate, sub-Saharan Africa, 2000 and 2010

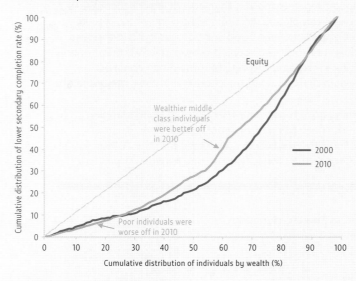

Source: GEM Report team analysis (2016) based on household survey data.

TABLE 14.1:

Gender parity index, by region and country income group, 2014

	Primary education		Lower secondary education		Upper secondary educaation	
	Gender parity index	Countries with parity (%)	Gender parity index	Countries with parity (%)	Gender parity index	Countries with parity (%)
World	0.99	63	0.99	46	0.98	23
Low income	0.93	31	0.86	9	0.74	5
Lower middle income	1.02	52	1.02	33	0.93	17
Upper middle income	0.97	71	1.00	60	1.06	22
High income	1.00	81	0.99	59	1.01	37
Caucasus and Central Asia	0.99	100	0.99	83	0.98	29
Eastern and South-eastern Asia	0.99	86	1.01	57	1.01	37
Europe and Northern America	1.00	93	0.99	67	1.01	31
Latin America and the Caribbean	0.98	48	1.03	39	1.13	19
Northern Africa and Western Asia	0.95	56	0.93	46	0.96	33
Pacific	0.97	64	0.95	44	0.94	0
Southern Asia	1.06	29	1.04	25	0.94	38
Sub-Saharan Africa	0.93	38	0.88	19	0.82	6

Note: All values shown are medians.
Source: UIS database.

BOX 14.2

The Inter-Agency Group on Education Inequality Indicators

The increasing availability of household surveys has made it possible to analyse disparity within and between countries. The 2012 launch of the World Inequality Database on Education (WIDE) by the *EFA Global Monitoring Report* (GMR) marked an innovative development for visualizing the stark differences in education between advantaged and disadvantaged groups. Using WIDE, this year's *Global Education Monitoring Report* (GEM Report) shows averages for regions and country income groups that cover more than 90% of the global population.

At the same time, the GEM Report team observed that this rich information is being used inefficiently at the global level. In the absence of common methodology, agencies are producing different estimates of the same indicators from the same data sources. Consensus remains elusive on definitions of key survey-based indicators – and too few of the available household survey data sources are being used.

This contrasts with other sectors, where agencies collaborate to reach consensus on estimates of key socio-economic variables. For example, the Roll Back Malaria Partnership, the inter-agency team on joint child malnutrition estimates and the Joint Monitoring Programme for Water Supply and Sanitation have been generating global reference statistics, in the last case for more than 25 years.

Accordingly, the GEM Report team presented a proposal at the World Education Forum in Incheon, Republic of Korea, in May 2015, within the framework of the Technical Advisory Group on post-2015 education indicators. It called on key institutions to agree on a harmonized set of definitions and methods to enable the international community to report official estimates on education inequality, in line with SDG objectives.

The Inter-Agency Group on Education Inequality Indicators first convened in April 2016, led by the UNESCO Institute for Statistics (UIS), UNICEF and the World Bank. Its goal is to 'promote and coordinate the use of household survey data for education monitoring purposes at the global, regional and national level, ensuring standardized analysis and reporting in order to complement evidence available through administrative data'. It has committed to producing a first report by the end of 2017, with results covering three indicators related to target 4.1: completion rate, out-of-school rate and over-age rate at the primary, lower secondary and upper secondary education levels.

This is a modest but promising start. The group's success will rest on partners' ability to pool resources, including currently underused data sources. An agreement between UIS and the World Bank to tap the latter's rich databases is a step in the right direction. It is also essential to gradually target activities to build countries' capacity to contribute to, and learn from, the estimation of survey-based education indicators.

Finally, the group needs to make effective use of existing information. For example, in Nigeria, there have been four DHS rounds and two MICS rounds in less than 15 years, on top of national household surveys that collect education information. However, surveys do not always produce consistent results on levels and trends, even on basic indicators such as the primary completion rate (**Figure 14.7**). The experience of other groups could be useful. The Inter-Agency Group for Child Mortality Estimation uses several sources to produce a single estimate for each country and year, assigning weights to each data source depending on their quality and reliability.

Sources: Alkema et al. (2014); UIS (2016); UNICEF et al. (2012); UNICEF and WHO (2015).

FIGURE 14.7:

What is the primary completion rate in Nigeria?

Primary education completion rate, Nigeria, 1980–2013

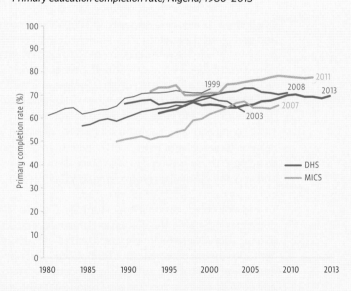

Notes: The analysis is based on six household surveys carried out in 1999–2013. The primary completion rate estimates are based on a retrospective cohort analysis over 20 years prior to the year of the survey. For example, for a survey carried out in 2000, the estimated completion rate for 1999 refers to 15-year-olds while the estimated completion rate for 1980 refers to 35-year-olds.
Source: GEM Report team analysis (2016) based on household survey data.

BEYOND PARITY: MEASURING SUBSTANTIVE GENDER EQUALITY IN EDUCATION

The formulation of target 4.5 does not refer to gender equality in education unlike the fifth EFA goal. The formulation of SDG 5 and its targets on gender equality is much stronger. Moreover, the Education 2030 Framework for Action explicitly recognizes gender equality as a guiding principle, linked to the realization of the right to education and referring to the need for girls and boys, women and men, to be equally empowered 'in and through education' (UNESCO, 2015b).

Equalizing education access for all girls and boys is a crucial first step towards realizing gender equality in education and the intrinsic right to education for all. Yet, schools, as concrete institutions in education, can reproduce existing gender inequality rather than challenge it (Murphy-Graham, 2009). This can manifest through teacher behaviour, expectations and interactions with male and female students; peer group norms; the curriculum (whether gender is explicitly addressed or not); the distribution of education resources; and school structure, organization and management.

In addition to reducing disparity in education attendance and completion, education for gender equality entails building knowledge and skills to empower disadvantaged girls or boys, depending on context. Students and teachers need to reflect on existing norms and traditions and be encouraged to challenge them. Gender-based discrimination and violence need to be addressed. Healthy life choices should be supported, including with regards to sexual and reproductive health. Interventions to achieve these results can take place through teacher training and curricular reform, among other means.

In addition to educational opportunities, five other domains help frame the discussion of gender equality in education. These include gender norms, values and attitudes (many of which can be influenced through education); institutions outside the education system; laws and policies in education systems; resource distribution; and teaching and learning practices (Unterhalter, 2015).

The adoption of the parity index by the Inter-agency and Expert Group on SDG Indicators to monitor the gender aspects of target 4.5 extends its use beyond enrolment ratios to all education indicators, including learning outcomes. While this is positive, there are indicators that could track equality across all six domains using available and often globally comparable data (**Table 14.2**).

Well-established indicators exist on norms, highlighting contextual factors with a direct impact on gender equality in and outside education (UNICEF, 2014c; Loaiza and Liang, 2013). For example, 45% of women aged 20 to 24 in South Asia were married before age 18 (UNICEF, 2015e). The World Values Survey suggests that women in countries with great gender inequality are more likely to agree that a university education is more important for boys than girls, and that men have more right to jobs when they are scarce (Bhatkal, 2014). Among adult men, 20% in Croatia, 43% in Brazil, 66% in Rwanda and 81% in India believed a man should have the final word about decisions in the home (ICRW and Instituto Promundo, 2011). The global lifetime prevalence of intimate partner violence among women who have ever had a partner is 30% (WHO, 2013). The share of women aged 15 to 49 who say a husband is justified in hitting or beating his wife

TABLE 14.2:
Potential indicators of gender inequality in education, by domain

Domain	Indicator
Educational opportunities	• Gender parity index on enrolment, transition and completion rates, and learning outcomes (alone or gender interacting with location and wealth)
Gender norms, values and attitudes e.g. sexual and reproductive health decisions; women's autonomy and empowerment: domestic violence; household expenditure decisions	• Percentage of population aged 20 to 24 married before age 18 • Percentage of women aged 20 to 24 who had a live birth before age 15 to 18 • Percentage who agree with statement 'A university education is more important for a boy than for a girl' (e.g. World Values Survey) • Percentage who agree with statement 'If a wife burns the food, a husband is justified in hitting her' (e.g. DHS and MICS) • Degree of decision-making on family planning • Degree of decision-making on earnings and household expenditure • Labour force participation rate or employment rate • Percentage of women in leadership positions in political and economic life
Institutions outside education e.g. legislation forbidding gender-based discrimination	• Whether the constitution contains at least one approach to gender equality • Whether the country is a signatory of the Convention on the Elimination of All Forms of Discrimination Against Women (CEDAW) • Social Institutions and Gender Index (SIGI) results
Laws and policies in education systems e.g. guarantees of the right to education for girls and women	• Whether the constitution protects the right to education regardless of gender • Whether the country has a policy on gender equality in education
Resource distribution e.g. gender parity in teacher pay, water and sanitation, training, learning materials	• Percentage of women in school leadership and management positions • Gender parity in teacher education graduates by sector and level • Gender parity in teacher employment by sector and level • Gender parity in teacher pay by sector and level • Percentage of single-sex toilets • Percentage of poor girls (or boys) who receive incentives to attend school (cash transfers, stipends, scholarships)
Teaching and learning practices e.g. teacher and student gender-related attitudes and interactions	• Percentage of teachers who received training in gender sensitivity • Percentage of countries that include gender equality topics in their curricula (gender discrimination, gender roles, violence, sexual and reproductive health)

Source: Based on Peppin Vaughan et al. (2016).

for at least one of five reasons (e.g. burning the food) was 75% in the Democratic Republic of the Congo, 60% in Tajikistan and 49% in Yemen (UNICEF, 2016a).

Regarding institutions outside education, annual national implementation reports on the Convention on the Elimination of All Forms of Discrimination against Women (CEDAW) provide information on legislation forbidding gender-based discrimination. The Social Institutions and Gender Index (SIGI) is based on formal and informal laws, attitudes and practices that restrict women's and girls' access to rights, justice and empowerment opportunities across 160 countries. Focusing on discriminatory family codes, restricted physical integrity, son bias, restricted resources and assets, and restricted civil liberties, it collects information on laws, attitudes and practices. It finds that 17 of 108 countries have very high levels of discrimination against women (OECD, 2014b).

An important basis for understanding gender equality in education is analysis of aspects of teaching and learning practices. The extent of gender equality in curricula and textbooks can be captured as part of research studies based on expert reviews (see Chapter 16). In the case of teaching practice, classroom observations are necessary but are costly and not easy to generalize. In Malawi, as part of an early grade reading project, almost 5,000 grade 1–3 teachers were observed in 11 districts in 2014; of those, 28% were found not to use appropriate and gender-sensitive language. In the northern Nigerian states of Bauchi and Sokoto, 25% of teachers did not provide equal opportunities to boys and girls to speak in class (RTI International, 2016).

> " In Malawi, 28% of 5,000 teachers observed in 11 districts were found not to use appropriate and gender-sensitive language "

From the learner's point of view, evidence from surveys in the Programme for International Student Assessment (PISA) suggests that girls tend to have a much lower belief in their ability to solve specific mathematics tasks than boys, as well as in their mathematics abilities. Across OECD countries, boys were 11 percentage points more likely than girls to agree or strongly agree that school advanced science topics were easy for them (OECD, 2015a).

Priorities for monitoring substantive gender equality

There are two priorities for improving monitoring of gender equality in education. First, efforts need to focus on collecting more comprehensive data on gender aspects of curricula, textbooks, assessments and teacher education. In addition, consensus is needed on what aspects of gender sensitivity in teaching practice could be included in classroom observation tools (see Chapter 10). Such efforts would benefit by being embedded within the framework of gender-responsive sector planning, as in the case of the recent collaboration between the Global Partnership on Education and the United Nations Girls' Education Initiative (GPE and UNGEI, 2013).

Second, closer links are needed between those working on indicators on gender equality in education and those focusing on broader indicators of gender equality (UN Women, 2015). Wider dissemination of findings and discussion with international bodies concerned with women's rights are needed. The Commission on the Status of Women would be an appropriate forum for discussion of how to enhance links between SDG 5 and education reforms.

To reach consensus on how best to measure substantive gender equality in education, and to establish a process for collaborating and sharing practice, it is important to form a working group on measurement methodology – it could include UIS, UNGEI and UN Women – as well as build a transnational network for groups concerned with gender equality in education to share strategies related to global progress on measurement.

DISABILITY

People with disabilities are among the most marginalized and excluded groups and are routinely denied their right to education of good quality. The 2006 Convention on the Rights of Persons with Disabilities commits governments to ensure an inclusive education system at all levels (United Nations, 2006). The SDG agenda also focuses on disability and target 4.5 specifically commits all countries to ensure equal access to all levels of education and vocational training, regardless of disability status. However, determining progress depends on an operational and internationally comparable measure of disability, which has remained elusive, because disability has diverse forms and there are important ethical and cost considerations. Still, progress has been made.

Cross-country comparisons are complicated by differences in classification systems. In education, the concept of special educational needs is commonly used, which is broader than the concept of disability: in some countries, it includes children from other socially marginalized groups. Across 30 education systems in Europe, 3.7% of compulsory education pupils were identified as having a special educational need in 2010. It was less than 2% in Sweden and almost 12% in Lithuania. Considerable variation can be observed even within one country – in the United Kingdom, it ranged from 2.8% in England to 7% in Scotland – and over time, with Estonia, for instance, reporting 19% of children having special educational needs in 2008 but 9% in 2010 when a different definition was used. Policies vary considerably. More than 40% of students with special educational needs overall were in special schools, but the share was more than 80% in Belgium and Germany and almost zero in Italy and Norway (NESSE, 2012) (**Figure 14.8**).

Two approaches have sought to develop a common classification framework. In the first, the OECD asked countries to reorganize their national classification systems into three categories: (a) 'disabilities', which have organic origins and for which there is substantial agreement about categories (e.g. sensory, motor, severe, profound intellectual disabilities); (b) 'difficulties', which do not appear to have organic origins or to be directly linked to socio-economic, cultural or linguistic factors (e.g. behavioural difficulties, mild learning difficulties, dyslexia); and (c) 'disadvantages', which arise from socio-economic, cultural and/or linguistic factors (OECD, 2005b).

This approach resulted in unexpected variation. For example, under the tightly defined 'disabilities' category, the average percentage of primary education students who received additional resources in 2001 was 2.5%, but the range was from 0.5% in the Republic of Korea and Turkey to 6.1% in the United States. The range under the other two categories was much broader (e.g. an average of 2.1% of students with 'difficulties', ranging from zero in Italy to 19% in England, United Kingdom), revealing very different applications of the terms (OECD, 2005b).

The second approach is the International Classification of Functioning, Disability and Health (ICF), adopted by the World Health Assembly in 2001. Based on the bio-psychosocial model, which defines disability as a result of the interaction between the features of a person and those of the environment in which that person lives, ICF assesses disability in terms of: body functions and structures; activities (execution of tasks or actions) and participation (involvement in a life situation); and contextual factors.

The ICF covers a detailed framework of thousands of subdomains, which in practice are difficult to measure. A set of principles is recommended for an operational measure of disability in large-scale population surveys. Questions are to focus on functional limitations (instead of disability) and responses should be scaled, instead of a yes-no choice (Mont, 2007). The Washington Group on Disability Statistics, under the auspices of the United Nations Statistical Division, has tried to adapt the ICF framework into a module that assesses six adult functioning domains: seeing, hearing, walking, remembering/concentrating, self-caring, and communicating (Washington Group, 2006).

The Washington Group also recognized that assessing disability among children required different methodologies, so they developed the Module on Child Functioning in collaboration with UNICEF. It is made up of questions to be answered by mothers or by primary caregivers of children aged 2 to 4 and 5 to 17 (Washington Group and UNICEF, 2014). Assessed domains included seeing, hearing, mobility/walking, attention, learning, communicating, self-care, motor skills, emotions,

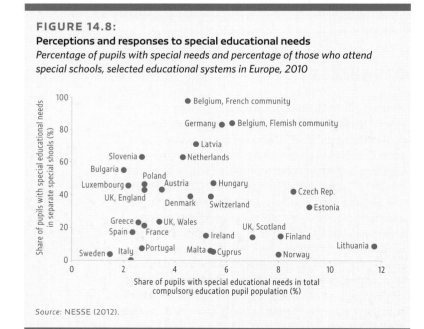

FIGURE 14.8:

Perceptions and responses to special educational needs

Percentage of pupils with special needs and percentage of those who attend special schools, selected educational systems in Europe, 2010

Source: NESSE (2012).

behaviour, play, development of relationships and coping with change. Where appropriate, respondents are asked to compare the functional difficulties of their child with those of a child of similar age (**Table 14.3**).

The module underwent extensive cognitive and field testing between 2012 and 2016. For example, it was field tested with questions on 12 domains in Samoa as part of the 2014 DHS. It showed that 2.7% of 5- to 9-year-olds were unable to function at all in at least one domain, while 5.3% faced a lot of difficulty in at least one domain (Loeb, 2015). A parallel validation process is incorporating the module into the next round of UNICEF's MICS. In 2016, the development of guidelines for producing statistics on children with disabilities and a user manual with technical information for implementation are due to be completed.

An operational measure of disability is important to keep the education challenges of individuals with disabilities high on the global agenda. But other steps are needed. To ensure that education is inclusive, educators must be better prepared and school infrastructures properly adapted to address the needs of individuals with disabilities (see Chapter 17). Monitoring these aspects is important to ensure that schools and teachers do not leave any learners behind.

TABLE 14.3:
Selected questions from the Washington Group/UNICEF Survey Module on Child Functioning

Seeing domain	
1a. Does (name) wear glasses?	(If no, skip to question 1c)
1b. When wearing his/her glasses, does (name) have difficulty seeing?	Would you say (name) has: no difficulty, some difficulty, a lot of difficulty or cannot do at all?
1c. Does (name) have difficulty seeing?	Would you say (name) has: no difficulty, some difficulty, a lot of difficulty or cannot do at all?
Mobility domain	
2a. Does (name) use any equipment or receive assistance for walking?	(If no, skip to question 2d)
2b. Without using his/her equipment or assistance, does (name) have difficulty walking 100/500 meters on level ground?	Would you say (name) has: no difficulty, some difficulty, a lot of difficulty or cannot do at all?
2c. When using his/her equipment or assistance, does (name) have difficulty walking 100/500 meters on level ground?	Would you say (name) has: no difficulty, some difficulty, a lot of difficulty or cannot do at all?
2d. Compared with children of the same age, does (name) have difficulty walking 100/500 meters on level ground?	Would you say (name) has: no difficulty, some difficulty, a lot of difficulty or cannot do at all?
Coping with change domain	
3. Does (name) have difficulty accepting changes in his/her routine?	Would you say (name) has: no difficulty, some difficulty, a lot of difficulty or cannot do at all?

Source: UNICEF (2016b).

LANGUAGE

In most multilingual countries, many children are taught and tested in languages they do not speak at home, hindering their early acquisition of reading and writing proficiency. Their parents may lack literacy skills or familiarity with the language of instruction,[1] reinforcing learning opportunity gaps between linguistic groups (UNESCO, 2016d).

Evidence suggests the most effective language education policy involves the use of a child's first[2] or home language in the early years of schooling, alongside the introduction of a second one,[3] both as subject and, later, as a parallel medium of instruction. Implementation of such a policy has been found to improve performance in the second language as well as in other subjects (Benson, 2016). Recent studies also highlight the importance of sustained use of the first or home language as a medium of instruction for at least six years of schooling – increasing to eight years in resource-poor contexts (Heugh et al., 2007; Ouane and Glanz, 2011).

One proposed thematic indicator under target 4.5 is the percentage of primary education students whose first or home language is used as language of instruction. Collecting reliable information on this is not easy or straightforward. By combining population statistics, language demographics and language in education policies, the *Human Development Report* estimated that 35% of people did not have access to primary education in their mother tongue in 2000 (UNDP, 2004). A more recent study concluded that about 40% of people around the world do not have access to instruction in a language they speak or understand (Walter and Benson, 2012). This could be expected; populations are growing faster in parts of the world where fewer people are taught in their mother tongue.

In linguistically diverse countries and regions, language in education issues are especially salient. Of the 25 countries with the highest index of linguistic diversity, 20 were in sub-Saharan Africa and the remainder in South-eastern Asia, the Pacific and Southern Asia (**Figure 14.9**). These issues are also vocally debated in many countries in Europe and Northern America, where a large share of students from immigrant families have particular educational needs.

A starting point for monitoring language policies in primary and secondary education is the systematic

FIGURE 14.9:

Linguistic diversity is greatest in countries in sub-Saharan Africa
Index of linguistic diversity

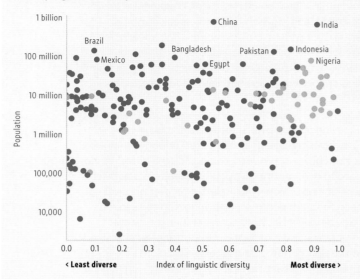

Notes: The index of linguistic diversity is the probability that two people selected from the population at random will have different mother tongues; it ranges from 0 (everyone has the same mother tongue) to 1 (no two people have the same mother tongue). Sub-Saharan African countries are marked in orange. The population axis is in the logarithmic scale.
Source: Lewis et al. (2016).

FIGURE 14.10:

Use of local languages is rising in sub-Saharan Africa, but most countries are far from nationwide mother tongue instruction
Scale of language of instruction use in primary education, anglophone and francophone countries in sub-Saharan Africa, 1960–2010

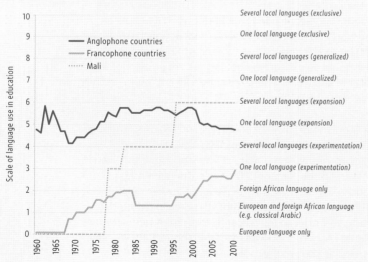

Notes: 'Experimentation' (levels 3 and 4) refers to government-authorized pilot programmes to promote one or more local languages in a handful of schools. 'Expansion' refers to a significant increase in the number of schools participating (levels 5 and 6). 'Generalized' refers to nationwide implementation of such programmes, usually in the early years before transition to an international language. 'Exclusive' refers to situations where one or more local language is used as the medium of education throughout the primary cycle, and the foreign language is taught only as a subject.
Source: Albaugh (2012).

and regular mapping of official policy documents, the national constitution and laws related to linguistic and cultural groups. A recent study of policy changes in sub-Saharan Africa over 1960–2010 showed that at the time of countries' independence, 20 (or 43%) out of 43 sub-Saharan African countries used local languages in primary education, compared with 38 (80%) now (Albaugh, 2012, 2015). This study suggests convergence towards high levels of local language use across the region. But it also points to the different routes followed by francophone and anglophone countries in this region. Though progress in anglophone countries has slowed, they are ahead of francophone countries; local languages are gaining strength in the latter, influenced by advocacy by local actors, but not enough to catch up (**Figure 14.10**).

Information for many countries can be found in the online catalogue L'aménagement linguistique dans le monde (Language planning around the world), which shows the status of language in national education policies, legislation and constitutions (Leclerc, 2016). Until 2011, the International Bureau of Education's World Data on Education compiled information from weekly lesson timetables on which language(s) curricula were delivered in. Combining information from these two data sources would provide a global snapshot of national language in education policies by grade or education level.

But monitoring the proposed thematic indicator based on national policy documents has its limits. Such documents rarely provide information on student access to teaching and learning materials in their home language. And it is difficult to determine whether official policies on language in education are implemented at the local level, and if not, whether this reflects a lack of initial teacher preparation or in-service professional development opportunities.

Take Mali, for example, a country that has moved quickly to adopt the use of local languages in education (Figure 14.10). Starting with innovations in the early 1980s, the government set forth a multilingual curriculum in 2002, introducing 11 national languages as media of instruction in addition to French (Traore, 2009). Yet, even a decade after this reform, school-level implementation problems were considerable. In 2010, in the Mopti region, for instance, a census of teachers and principals in 949 primary schools found that only 24% of schools followed the curriculum and, of those, only 1 in 3 offered bilingual education for the entire 6-year primary cycle. Even in these schools, only 11% of teachers had been trained in the bilingual curriculum, which means only 1% of schools were providing bilingual instruction in the appropriate language and by a trained teacher throughout primary school (MEALN, 2011).

Other countries face challenges in scaling up effective use of a child's first or home language as a medium of instruction. In Viet Nam, as part of a pilot project, three languages (Hmong, Jarai and Khmer) have been used as a medium of instruction (UNESCO, 2012b). A survey of pre-primary and primary schools in Lao Cai province of student and teacher language proficiencies found Vietnamese was the first language of 70% of teachers but it was the strongest language for only 1 in 5 students (**Figure 14.11**).

Classroom observation can help countries identify challenges in implementing policies on language in education that build on home language proficiency. In the Philippines, the multilingual education policy involved using local mother tongues to instruct during early years of schooling, with Filipino and English introduced as the language of instruction after grade 3. Despite this policy's overall success, some regions lagged behind. In Maguindanao province, while 93% of grade 2 students spoke Maguindanaoan at home, only 73% of teachers were reported to use it in the classroom. And of those, 41% never used the multilingual education textbook (RTI International, 2015).

In Kenya and Uganda, countries with similar policies of teaching in the language of the school catchment area, a study recorded the language used by teachers and students in more than 1,500 primary schools, by grade, subject and activity. In Kenya's Central and Nyanza provinces, English continued to be the medium of instruction. While hardly spoken in any of the children's homes, it was used for about 60% of classroom time, increasing to 80% in mathematics and social studies. By contrast, in the Central region and Lango subregion of Uganda, mother tongue instruction was provided about 75% of the time in grades 1 to 3 and 90% of the time in mathematics and social studies. However, the transition to English in grade 4 was more abrupt (Piper and Miksic, 2011) (**Figure 14.12**).

Cross-national and national learning assessments can be employed to capture language policy implementation in schools. In the Trends in International Mathematics and Science Study (TIMSS) and the Progress in International Reading Literacy Study (PIRLS), parents of fourth-

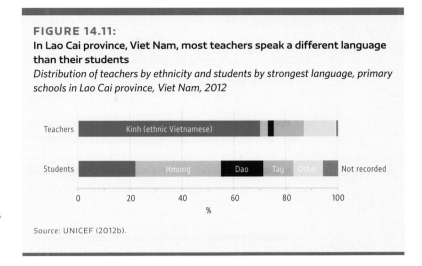

FIGURE 14.11:

In Lao Cai province, Viet Nam, most teachers speak a different language than their students

Distribution of teachers by ethnicity and students by strongest language, primary schools in Lao Cai province, Viet Nam, 2012

Source: UNICEF (2012b).

graders were asked to report the language spoken by the child before starting school. In the 2011 round of PIRLS, 92% of fourth-graders spoke the test language before starting schooling. But there were differences among countries: 1 in 3 students in Indonesia and 1 in 5 in the Islamic Republic of Iran did not speak the language of instruction before starting school, compared with less than 1 in 20 in Denmark, Hungary and Norway (Mullis et al., 2012b).

TIMSS and PIRLS also collect data from eighth-graders themselves about how frequently they speak the test language at home. In 2011, on average, across countries participating in TIMSS, 79% of eighth-graders always or almost always spoke the language of the test at home, with 17% sometimes speaking it and 4% never speaking it (Mullis et al., 2012a).

Similarly, in PISA surveys, 15-year-old students are asked whether the language spoken at home most of the time is the language of assessment (which in PISA is the language of instruction). Findings indicated that in 2012, on average, nearly 15% of students did not speak the language of instruction at home. The proportion varied considerably among countries: in Malaysia and Thailand, nearly half the students did not speak the assessment language at home, compared with less than 1% in Chile and Poland (OECD, 2013c). Not surprisingly, students from immigrant families were disadvantaged: 63% of first-generation immigrant 15-year-old students, on average (and more than 80% in the Czech Republic, Israel and Sweden), spoke a different language at home than the assessment language; 38% of second-generation

FIGURE 14.12:
Kenya and Uganda followed different routes in implementing their language of instruction policy
Selected indicators of language use in primary education, selected regions of Kenya and Uganda, 2009

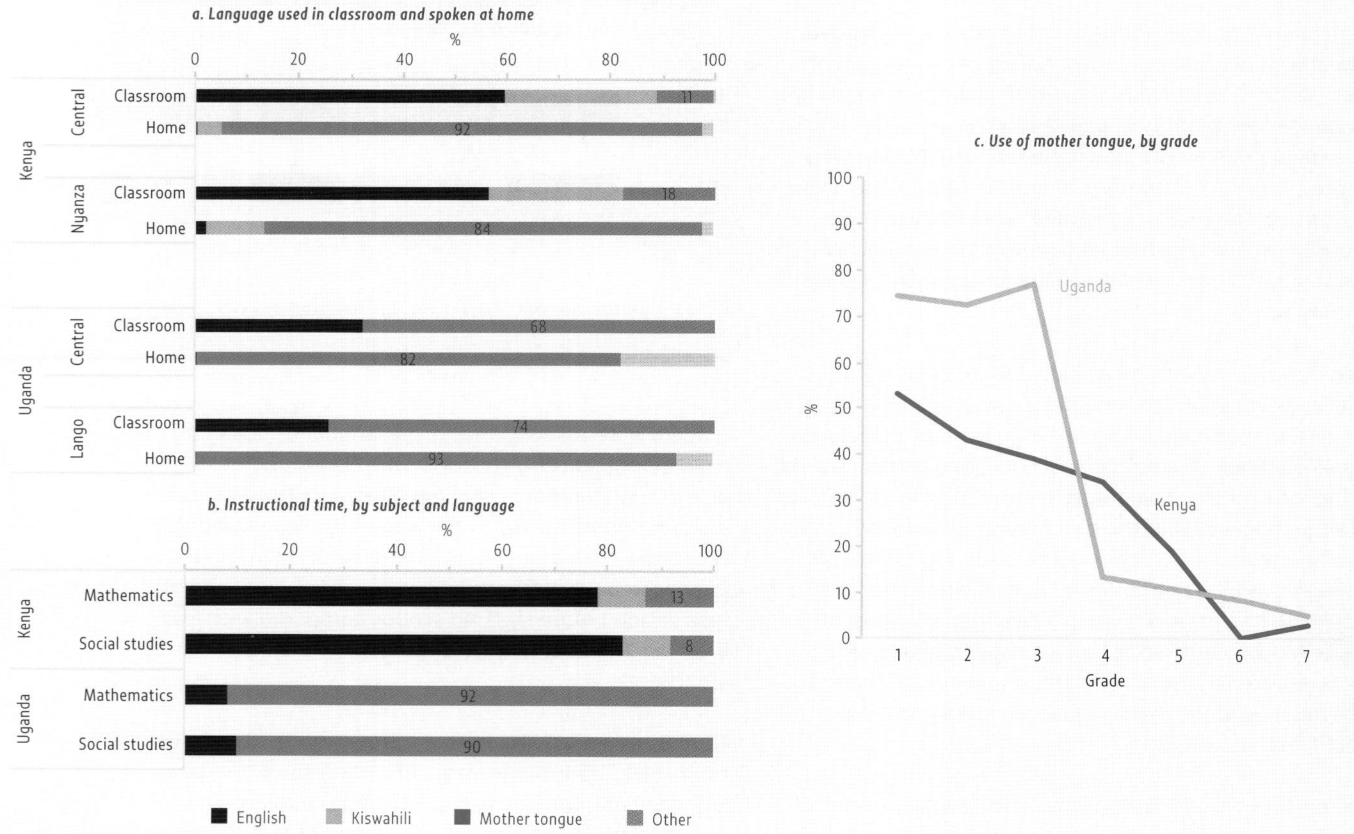

a. Language used in classroom and spoken at home

b. Instructional time, by subject and language

c. Use of mother tongue, by grade

Legend: ■ English ▨ Kiswahili ▨ Mother tongue ▨ Other

Source: Piper and Miksic (2011).

immigrant students still spoke a different language at home (OECD, 2015d).

For Latin America and sub-Saharan Africa, information on language use at home and school can be compiled from three regional assessment programmes: the Analysis Programme of the CONFEMEN Education Systems (PASEC), the Southern and Eastern Africa Consortium for Monitoring Educational Quality (SACMEQ) and the Second Regional Comparative and Explanatory Study (SERCE). Analysis of PASEC countries by the GEM Report team shows the percentage of grade 5 students who did not speak the language of assessment at home to be very high, ranging from nearly 70% in Cameroon and Gabon to over 90% in Senegal and Togo. Among

countries taking part in SACMEQ, 90% of sixth-graders did not speak the language of assessment at home in Malawi and Swaziland. Across Latin America, the largest shares of grade 6 students who did not speak the test language at home were found in Guatemala (16%) and Paraguay (45%).

The continuing neglect of mother tongue-based multilingual education in linguistically diverse countries helps explain large disparities in education outcomes. While tracking language of instruction is fraught with technical and possibly political challenges, it is a key issue that countries and regions need to tackle head-on if no one is to be left behind.

MIGRATION AND FORCED DISPLACEMENT

Voluntary and forced population movement affects the education opportunities and needs of hundreds of millions of children, young people and adults around the world. It also increases challenges for host governments. Four groups are discussed in this section: internal migrants, international migrants, internally displaced people and refugees.

The largest population movement is internal migration, usually rural to urban. Migration statistics rely on censuses, carried out every 10 years. As a result, regional and global estimates are available only with considerable delay. The latest estimates, from 2005, suggest that globally 763 million were living outside their region of birth (UNDESA, 2013). It is more important for education planners to know the intensity of internal migration flows; over the past five years, it has been above average in countries including Chile, the Republic of Korea and Senegal (Bell et al., 2015).

China has experienced what is considered the largest migration in human history (Chan, 2013). A household registration system restricted access to public schools for children of rural migrants in order to discourage them from moving to cities. Substandard private schools were created to serve rural migrant children, attended by 60% of those in Shanghai and 75% in Guangzhou in the early 2000s. The government then abolished fees for rural migrant children in urban public schools and provided additional funding to the schools to help absorb these students. By 2010, the proportion of migrant students attending public schools had increased to 74% (Hao and Yu, 2015).

Despite problems in accommodating the influx of rural migrants, who often move into slum or peri-urban areas where public school access is limited, migration to urban areas generally facilitates access to public services. Analysis for the 2015 GMR showed that even if primary completion rates had remained constant in urban and rural areas in sub-Saharan Africa, the increase in the share of people living in urban areas would have been enough to raise the average primary completion rate by 1.5 percentage points between 2000 and 2010 (UNESCO, 2015d).

Although much smaller in magnitude, international migration attracts far more attention. In 2015, 244 million people were living outside their country of birth and the proportion of international migrants in the total population was 3.3%, compared with 2.8% in 2000. South–South migration exceeded South–North migration for the first time in 2015, though immigrants remain a significant share of the population in high income countries in Europe (10%), Northern America (e.g. 15% in the United States) and the Pacific (e.g. 28% in Australia) (GMDAC, 2016).

> In high income countries, first-generation immigrant students scored about 50 points below students without an immigrant background in reading and mathematics

In high income countries, the education-related experiences of immigrant students are of concern. First-generation immigrant students scored about 50 points below students without an immigrant background in reading and mathematics in the 2012 PISA in OECD countries, while second-generation immigrant students scored about 20 points below. Still, the difference in mathematics performance between students with and without an immigrant background shrank by around 10 points between 2003 and 2012 (OECD, 2015d).

The challenge for policy-makers is that students with an immigrant background tend to be concentrated in schools in socio-economically disadvantaged areas. If the socio-economic status of students and schools is taken into account, the average difference in mathematics performance in OECD countries between students who attend schools where more than 25% of students are immigrants compared to students who attend schools with no immigrant students drops by almost 75% (OECD, 2015d).

Voluntary migration can disrupt education but can also have benefits. Both domestic migrants in China and international migrants in OECD countries may not do as well in school as their peers in host communities, but tend to do much better than if they had stayed in their communities of origin. In contrast, forced displacement tends to lead to gross violations of the right to education.

The number of internally displaced people (IDPs) has been growing. At the end of 2014, 38 million IDPs were estimated to live in 60 countries. The Democratic Republic of the Congo, Iraq, Nigeria, South Sudan and the Syrian Arab Republic accounted for 60% of new IDPs (IDMC, 2015b). Internal displacement is predominantly urban, with IDPs often having fled conflict-affected areas to the relative safety of towns and cities, as in Colombia and Uganda.

IDPs are nationals of their country and hence the responsibility of their government. However, education management information systems seldom collect data on children of IDPs and when they do, it is annually – too infrequent for such transient populations. One exception is Ukraine, which collects monthly education status information on children displaced by conflicts in Crimea, Donetsk and Lugansk. As of March 2016, 51,000 displaced children (1.4% of the total student population) were enrolled in schools in other areas (Ukraine Ministry of Education and Science, 2016).

IDPs are relatively invisible and their education needs neglected. In Nigeria, as a result of violent attacks on civilians by Boko Haram since 2009, 1 million school-age children were estimated to have fled violence by early 2016 (HRW, 2016). The Displacement Tracking Matrix of the International Organization for Migration reported that in 19 of 42 displacement camps in 6 states in June 2015, children had no access to formal or non-formal education facilities (IOM, 2015).

> In Iraq, only 45% of internally displaced children and adolescents living in camps were enrolled in schools

In Iraq, conflict between armed groups and government forces has escalated rapidly, resulting in around 3.3 million IDPs as of end of 2014 (IDMC, 2015b). In July 2015, out of 78,000 IDP children and adolescents aged 6 to 17 living in camps, only 45% were enrolled in schools, and only 30% of the 730,000 IDP children and adolescents not in camps had access to education (OCHA, 2015a).

Refugees are the most vulnerable group, numbering, by mid-2015, 15 million under the global mandate of the Office of the United Nations High Commissioner for Refugees (UNHCR) (UNHCR, 2015b). There are also 5.1 million Palestinian refugees registered with the United

Nations Relief and Works Agency for Palestine Refugees in the Near East. Despite the visibility of the refugee influx in Europe, 86% of all refugees are hosted in lower income countries, some of which have weak education system capacity (UNHCR, 2015b).

According to UNHCR, 50% of primary school-age refugees and 75% of secondary school-age refugees are out of school worldwide. Access to secondary education is particularly limited. In Bangladesh, Kenya and Pakistan, less than 5% of adolescent refugees aged 12 to 17 were enrolled in secondary education (UNESCO and UNHCR, 2016).

Data on refugee education come largely from camps and camp-like settings. Yet, more than half the world's refugees reside in urban areas (UNHCR, 2015c). While the right to choose where to live increases livelihood opportunities for refugees, monitoring and evaluation of their education becomes problematic, as they are frequently not identified as refugees in schools.

Some countries have taken steps to better monitor refugee children's education status. Chad developed an integrated system to improve refugee education data management so as to eventually integrate the data in the national education management information system (UNHCR, 2016). However, refugee children and adolescents are usually not identified in information systems. This omission may help limit the risk of discrimination, but some information is needed to protect refugees and address their vulnerability.

Information may need to come from other sources. In Jordan, 83% of the approximately 630,000 Syrian refugees live outside camps (Jordan Ministry of Planning and International Cooperation, 2015). Since 2012, interviews have been conducted with more than 170,000 Syrian refugee households in non-camp settings under UNHCR's Home Visits Programme. In 2014, 53% of school-age children were enrolled in formal education, up from 44% in 2013 (UNHCR, 2015a).

Adding to the four groups discussed above are the average 26 million people per year who were displaced from their homes by natural disasters between 2008 and 2014 (IDMC, 2015a). As this report shows, the probability is high that this trend, already increasing in 1970, will continue rising in coming decades.

There are important, sometimes intractable, challenges in monitoring the education status of migrant and forcibly displaced populations. However, coordinated efforts need to be stepped up to improve systems so as to better understand the reasons for the observed disparity in their access to education in general, and education of good quality in particular.

ENDNOTES

1. Language of instruction refers to the language used for teaching the basic curriculum (Ball, 2011).

2. The first language is defined as the language an individual (a) learned first, (b) identifies with, (c) knows best, (d) uses most, and/or (e) speaks and understands well enough to learn age-appropriate academic content (Benson, 2016).

3. Second language refers to a language used in school and the community, learned after the first language and drawing on learners' experiences outside the classroom (Benson, 2016).

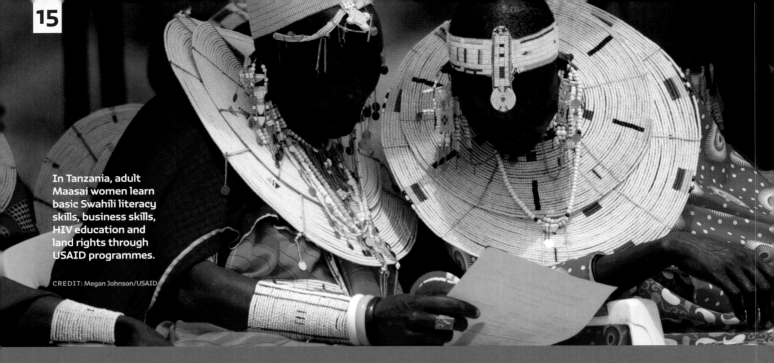

In Tanzania, adult Maasai women learn basic Swahili literacy skills, business skills, HIV education and land rights through USAID programmes.

CREDIT: Megan Johnson/USAID

KEY MESSAGES

There are challenges in monitoring adult *participation* in literacy programmes because of the diversity of providers. Surveys of adults can be a more reliable source of information than governments.

New analysis shows that over 2004–2011, 6% of adults aged 15 to 49 in 29 poorer countries had ever participated in a literacy programme. Most of those were male and from richer households, even though the majority of illiterate adults were female and poor.

The SDG agenda shifts attention from a concept of literacy in which someone is literate or not to a more nuanced concept of how proficient they are in literacy skills along a continuum.

In the absence of data on literacy proficiency levels, reporting based on traditional rates continues. Over 2005–2014, some 758 million adults, almost two-thirds of them women, lacked any literacy skills.

A better picture of literacy challenges can be found by directly assessing skills, as is the case in many high income countries. Among adults who participated in an OECD assessment, 15% did not have basic literacy skills.

International collaboration is needed to help conduct more international literacy and numeracy assessments by 2030. A successful approach should balance the ability of a country to proceed on its own against the need for its assessment to meet global quality standards.

CHAPTER 15

TARGET 4.6

Literacy and numeracy

By 2030, ensure that all youth and a substantial proportion of adults, both men and women, achieve literacy and numeracy

GLOBAL INDICATOR 4.6.1 – *Percentage of population in a given age group achieving at least a fixed level of proficiency in functional (a) literacy and (b) numeracy skills, by sex*

THEMATIC INDICATOR 23 – *Youth/adult literacy rate*

THEMATIC INDICATOR 24 – *Participation rate of youth/adults in literacy programmes*

In the words of the 2006 *Education for All Global Monitoring Report* (GMR), understanding of literacy has expanded from 'a simple process of acquiring basic cognitive skills, to using these skills in ways that contribute to socio-economic development, to developing the capacity for social awareness and critical reflection as a basis for personal and social change' (UNESCO, 2005b).

Accordingly, that GMR presented four discrete concepts of literacy, which can be summarized as:

- A set of cognitive skills (reading and writing) that are independent of context.

- A set of skills that are determined by the context in which they are applied, practised and situated; this is underpinned by the widely used definition of functional literacy referring to a person 'who can engage in all those activities in which literacy is required for effective functioning of his group and community and also for enabling him to continue to use reading, writing and calculation for his own and the community's development' (UNESCO, 1978).

- An active and broad-based learning process, rather than a product of a more limited and focused educational intervention, referring to its potential to transform not only individuals but also societies.

- The texts people produce and consume, which vary in terms of language complexity and their explicit or hidden content.

Target 4.6 maintains the international focus on adult literacy that was part of the fourth Education for All

> " The global indicator on literacy and numeracy is expressed in terms of skills proficiency "

goal. While that goal for 2000–2015 was halving the adult illiteracy rate, the corresponding target for 2015–2030 has been left vague. Member states agreed that universal adult literacy would be unattainable over the next 15 years, but not what level should be reached. Universal youth literacy, which was not included previously, has been added to the target.

The Sustainable Development Goals (SDGs) and agenda bring two important innovations. First, the global indicator on literacy and numeracy is formulated explicitly in terms of skills proficiency. This decision considerably improves on the weak target formulation, which views literacy as something to be 'achieved'. The indicator comes closer to the view of literacy as not just a set of skills but also their application. And it tacitly recognizes recent advances in direct assessments that show literacy is not a skill people either do or do not possess. Rather, different levels and types of literacy empower adults to achieve different functions in life. Because of the constraints of global monitoring requirements, not all approaches to the concept of literacy are captured. However, the SDG agenda's treatment of literacy represents a considerable advance.

Second, the target specifies numeracy as a skill to be acquired. Some definitions of literacy have always encompassed numeracy, whether under 'functional literacy', as above, or under 'operational literacy', i.e. the ability 'to identify, understand, interpret, create, communicate

> **Literacy is a basic cognitive skill that is fundamental for access to decent work**

and compute' (UNESCO, 2005a). However, explicitly referring to numeracy calls attention to its specific properties.

Target 4.6 complements target 4.3, which implicitly focuses on adult education participation, and target 4.4, which focuses on youth and adult skills relevant for work. The separation of literacy and numeracy from other skills is artificial and unfortunate. As the review of selected skills under target 4.4 suggested, literacy is a basic cognitive skill that is fundamental for access to decent work. Literacy and numeracy are essential components of other specialized skills, such as digital and financial literacy, and blended skill sets, such as entrepreneurship.

Nevertheless, maintaining a separate target on literacy and numeracy helps keep it from being seen as a skill solely tied to economic benefits. And it reminds the world of literacy's distinctive role in community advancement and social inclusion. This chapter discusses the challenges of monitoring the participation rate in literacy programmes, which is one of the proposed thematic indicators. It then explores global indicator 4.6.1 on literacy and numeracy proficiency skills.

PARTICIPATION IN ADULT LITERACY PROGRAMMES

Measuring participation in formal and non-formal adult literacy programmes has proved surprisingly difficult. It has been hard to compile information from diverse providers in the absence of more detailed information about their programmes' characteristics. This section builds on the discussion of the related challenge of measuring participation in adult education programmes, covered under target 4.3 (see Chapter 12).

While it should be possible to estimate participation rates in the large share of literacy programmes provided or sponsored by government, this elementary information has so far proved difficult to collect. The main source of information on literacy programmes should in principle be the *Global Report on Adult Learning and Education* (GRALE), published about every three years. However, the first three editions did not report participation rates, focusing simply on whether

enrolment, attendance and completion information was collected. For example, in 2012, GRALE reported that literacy programmes were provided in 119 countries by the government, in 67 countries by the private sector and in 97 countries by civil society.

Because comparing literacy programmes is difficult, information on participation rates is lacking. Courses differ in aims, content, relative intensity and duration. It may be difficult to differentiate between literacy programmes and those on other basic skills. It is also unclear whether participation rates should be defined relative to all adults, adults without literacy skills or another group.

Regardless of the fragmented provision of literacy programmes and often weak oversight by governments, GRALE, as the key reference on adult literacy, needs to help develop a standardized reporting template that, at the very least, captures adult participation in publicly provided or sponsored literacy programmes.

Given the diversity of provision, surveys of individuals are likely to be a more reliable source of information than governments. However, as levels of adult participation in literacy programmes tend to be low, estimates of participation rates may be less precise and general household survey programmes give little priority to questions capturing relevant details.

Nevertheless, the information household surveys can provide has not yet been fully exploited. New analysis for this report uses a question once regularly included in the Demographic and Health Surveys (DHS) administered to all 15- to 49-year-olds, but unfortunately discontinued in recent rounds: whether respondents had 'ever participated in a literacy programme or any other programme that involves learning to read or write (not including primary school)'.

The question has clear disadvantages – it is retrospective and provides neither information on when respondents attended the programme nor background on the type of programme attended – but is the sole source of comparative information. Among 29 low and middle income countries with relevant information over 2004–2011, about 6% of adults aged 15 to 49 had ever participated in a literacy programme. In all the countries except Ethiopia, Honduras, Nepal and Senegal, these retrospective participation rates were below 15%.

From an equity perspective, literacy programmes should target those who need them most: adults with low literacy skills, the majority of whom are women and/or from poor households. However, background information shows the average disparity in participation rates was slightly in favour of men. Across the 29 countries, 6.7% of men had attended a literacy programme, compared with 5.7% of women. A similar disparity favoured richer adults: 5.4% of the poorest had ever attended a literacy programme, compared with 7.1% of the richest. This may reflect the relative ease of access to such programmes in urban areas. But since the question is retrospective, it may also be that some individuals who were identified as rich were poor in the past but benefited from their literacy skills to earn a higher income.

While the surveys did not ask when these adults participated in a programme, their ages indicate the prevalence of participation over time: 3.6% of 15- to 19-year-olds, 6% of 30- to 34-year-olds and 9.2% of 45- to 49-year-olds had attended a literacy programme.

The lower participation rates among younger adults may reflect increasing overall literacy levels, which means younger adults are less likely to need literacy programmes. However, it may also reflect decreasing prevalence of mass literacy campaigns as access to formal education has increased in recent years.

As important as knowing whether adults participated in literacy programmes is whether, and to what extent, they acquired functional literacy skills. The surveys provided information on whether respondents could read a simple sentence from a card, which could indicate indirectly whether the programmes had been effective. Across the 29 countries, an average of 8.7% of adults who could read a sentence had attended a literacy programme, compared with 5.2% of adults who could not (**Figure 15.1**). In countries including Mali, Niger and Sierra Leone, the literacy skills of a large percentage of adults could be traced to their participation in a literacy programme (**Box 15.1**).

At the same time, a considerable share of adults had not learned to read despite taking part in a literacy programme. Hence, Action Research on Measuring Literacy Programme Participants' Learning Outcomes, an initiative of the UNESCO Institute for Lifelong Learning (UIL), is focusing on better understanding the effectiveness of such programmes (UIL, 2016).

LITERACY RATES

The SDG agenda rightly shifts attention away from the conventional dichotomy of literacy/illiteracy to measures of proficiency in literacy skills. For policy-makers, the rigid distinction between adults who do or do not possess literacy skills is less informative than the range of proficiency levels found among adults in various contexts and the kinds of policy interventions that can effectively improve literacy levels among particular groups.

For the time being, however, the needed measurement tools are not widely available, so reporting on youth and adult literacy based on traditional literacy rates continues. According to the most recent estimates, the global adult literacy rate was 85%, which means 758 million adults lacked any literacy skills. There were 91 literate women for every 100 literate men – and as few as 74 literate women for every 100 literate men in low income countries. The youth literacy rate was 91%, meaning 114 million youth lacked any literacy skills. The

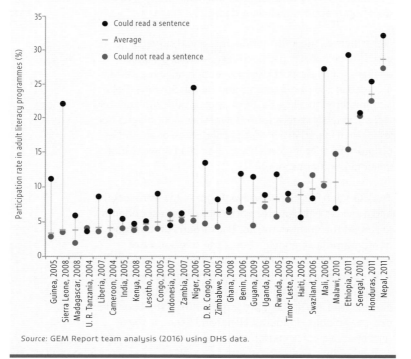

FIGURE 15.1:

In poorer countries, less than 1 in 10 adults has ever participated in an adult literacy programme

Percentage of adults who had ever participated in a literacy programme, 15- to 49-year-olds, by literacy status, selected countries, 2004–2011

Source: GEM Report team analysis (2016) using DHS data.

BOX 15.1

Measuring participation in literacy programmes in Niger

Niger is burdened with one of the world's lowest adult literacy rates as well as one of the largest gender disparities in this indicator: according to the UNESCO Institute for Statistics (UIS), the adult literacy rate was 15% in 2012 and there were 38 literate women for every 100 literate men. The situation was also dire among youth, who had a literacy rate of 24% in 2012. A direct assessment approach, based on the ability to read a simple sentence from a card administered as part of the 2012 DHS, confirmed these findings and highlighted extreme inequality: just 4% of youth in the poorest 20% of households could read, compared with 65% in the richest 20%.

Only a small percentage of the population had ever participated in an adult literacy programme. The 2011 National Survey on Household Living Conditions and Agriculture found that 1.5% of adults aged 25 to 49 had ever attended a literacy programme; the rate for men was twice that for women. However, participation may have been underestimated. Literacy programmes were considered a separate category from formal and Islamic education, but some adults may have attended both a literacy programme and formal or Islamic schooling.

The 2006 DHS asked a separate question on adult literacy. It found that 5.7% of adults aged 15 to 49 had ever attended a literacy programme. While a retrospective measure cannot establish where people lived at the time they attended literacy classes, evidence suggests more common participation in urban areas (**Figure 15.2a**). However, literacy programmes made a bigger difference in rural areas: 31% of literate adults in rural areas had participated in a programme, compared with 18% in urban areas (**Figure 15.2b**).

FIGURE 15.2:

Fewer adults in rural areas had participated in an adult literacy programme in Niger, but more adults with literacy skills in rural areas had done so

Percentage of adults who had ever participated in a literacy programme, by location, Niger, 2006

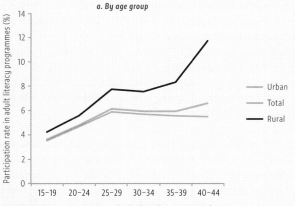

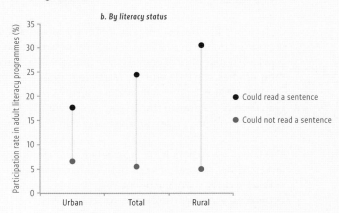

Source: GEM Report team analysis (2016) using DHS data.

The Functional Literacy Programme for Women and Girls of the Directorate of Literacy and Adult Education Programmes, which was launched in 1987 and had been rolled out across the country by 1997, is the main national literacy intervention; it received an honourable mention in the 2012 UNESCO international literacy prizes. Its objective is to help participants acquire not only literacy but also life skills, including knowledge on health, environment, women's rights and income-generating activities. Income from these activities also helps sustain the programme. To strengthen solidarity, facilitators are recruited from among former students or newly literate adults. Programme coverage is limited; about 57,000 women and girls from 1,284 centres participated between 1987 and 2012, while the estimated population of adult women who could not read was 4 million.

A more recent programme, Basic Literacy Teaching by Mobile Phone (Alphabétisation de Base par Cellulaire or ABC), was implemented between 2009 and 2011 in 113 villages of the Dosso and Zinder regions, with about 5,500 adults following literacy and numeracy courses in their mother tongues. Classes were three hours a day, five days a week, during two four-month periods. In half the classes, mobile phones were introduced, one phone for five learners, as a way for them to practise previous lessons by using text messages. Assessments conducted before, during and after the programme found significant outcomes for both groups. The group provided with phones improved more, and its gains were larger by the last assessment. The mobile phone intervention was also found to be cost-effective. However, there was high attrition between the first and second sessions as a result of a drought.

Sources: Aker et al. (2012); UNESCO (2016a).

TABLE 15.1:
Youth and adult literacy

	Youth literacy rate%	Gender parity index	Illiterate youth (000)	Adult literacy rate %	Gender parity index	Illiterate adults (000)
	2005–2014	2005–2014	2005–2014	2005–2014	2005–2014	2005–2014
World	91	0.96	114 127	85	0.91	757 920
Low income	68	0.85	35 078	57	0.74	134 811
Lower middle income	86	0.93	72 405	74	0.83	493 776
Upper middle income	99	1.00	5 854	94	0.95	114 350
High income						
Caucasus and Central Asia	100	1.00	15	100	1.00	120
Eastern and South-eastern Asia	99	1.00	3 217	95	0.96	84 135
Europe and Northern America						
Latin America and the Caribbean	98	1.00	2 266	93	0.99	33 373
Northern Africa and Western Asia	93	0.96	6 073	82	0.86	52 878
Pacific						
Southern Asia	84	0.91	52 848	68	0.76	389 408
Sub-Saharan Africa	71	0.86	48 765	60	0.76	188 315

Source: UIS database.

youth literacy rate was as low as 71% in sub-Saharan Africa (**Table 15.1**).

In recent years, the estimation of literacy rates has been supported by the availability of direct assessments in two large international comparative household survey programmes, the DHS and the Multiple Indicator Cluster Surveys (MICS). Both ask individuals aged 15 to 49 to read a simple sentence from a card. In recent MICS rounds, the literacy questions are asked only of women.

The UIS began using direct assessments in countries lacking other sources of information, then gradually extended them more systematically to improve literacy estimates, especially in low income countries.

Increased use of direct assessments has reduced discrepancies between official literacy rates and those obtained from direct assessments in household surveys. For example, among 19 low income countries, the median female youth literacy rate reported in the 2010 GMR was nine percentage points above the corresponding estimate based on DHS and MICS; the gap had been reduced to four percentage points for the literacy rates reported in the 2015 GMR.

However, there are still discrepancies in both directions. For example, the estimated female youth literacy rate based on the 2010 MICS in Chad is 27 percentage points below the official rate, while the 2013 DHS in Zambia estimates the female youth literacy rate to be 21 percentage points higher than the official rate (**Figure 15.3**).

The use of direct assessments to more accurately estimate literacy rates needs to be done carefully to ensure that the literacy rate trend is consistent. For example, according to the DHS, the primary education attainment rate of young women increased from 12% in 2001 to 29% in 2012 in Mali and from 14% in 1999 to 33% in 2012 in Guinea. But while the official female youth literacy rate increased from 24% in 2003 to 39% in 2011 in Mali, it appears to have fallen from 34% in 2003 to 22% in 2010 in Guinea.

Overall, official literacy rates have improved considerably. Yet, this should not distract from a key shortcoming: even direct assessments measure only the most rudimentary of literacy skills. Effectively determining proficiency levels requires more nuanced and intensive efforts to assess the abilities of youth and adults 'to identify, understand, interpret, create, communicate and compute'.

LITERACY AND NUMERACY PROFICIENCY LEVELS

In the past 20 years, international interest in in-depth assessments of literacy and numeracy skills has increased (UNESCO, 2015d). For many high income countries, information on adult literacy and numeracy proficiency is available from the Organisation for Economic Co-operation and Development (OECD) Programme for the International Assessment of Adult Competencies (PIAAC) and its predecessors, the International Adult Literacy Survey (IALS) and the

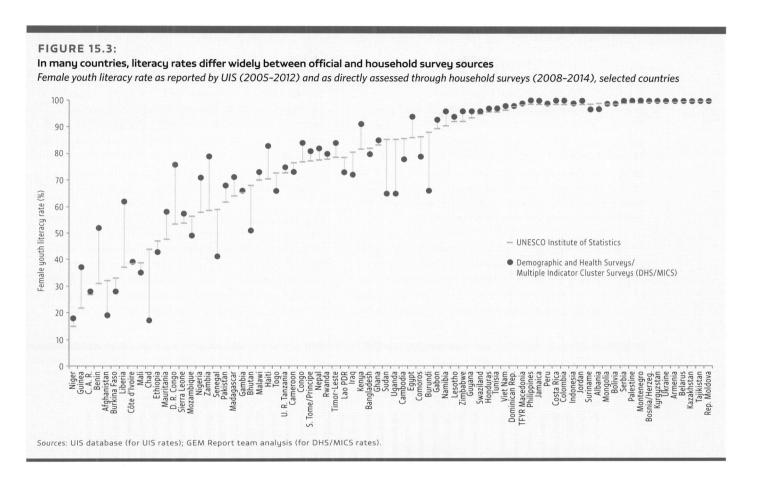

FIGURE 15.3:

In many countries, literacy rates differ widely between official and household survey sources

Female youth literacy rate as reported by UIS (2005–2012) and as directly assessed through household surveys (2008–2014), selected countries

Sources: UIS database (for UIS rates); GEM Report team analysis (for DHS/MICS rates).

Adult Literacy and Lifeskills Survey (ALL). However, such assessments are lacking for most low and middle income countries. Exceptions include the World Bank Skills Toward Employment and Productivity (STEP) survey, the UIS Literacy Assessment Monitoring Programme (LAMP) and a few nationally administered surveys.

International collaboration is needed to facilitate the conducting of comparative literacy and numeracy assessments. Three challenges need to be overcome. First, operational definitions of literacy and numeracy need to be agreed and validated. Second, a reporting framework is needed that captures levels of proficiency and what tasks survey participants can perform with their literacy and numeracy skills. Third, implementation issues, including costs, sampling demands and technical capacity, need to be resolved. The cost of assessments in high income countries and urban areas of some middle income countries is beyond reach for poorer countries. Cost-effective yet meaningful literacy and numeracy assessment modules need to be developed.

The number of countries carrying out direct assessments of literacy and numeracy skills needs to increase. This would enable the true skills of adults in a range of contexts to be captured and global indicator 4.6.1 to be monitored. However, coordinating such efforts across countries remains an issue. This section looks at challenges for literacy and numeracy assessment, placing more emphasis on numeracy, which has received less attention so far.

LITERACY

Experience in conducting assessments using different definitions to describe adult literacy has grown over the years. For PIAAC, which is conducted in 40 countries, literacy is defined as 'the ability to understand, evaluate, use and engage with written texts to participate in society, to achieve one's goals and to develop one's knowledge and potential' (OECD, 2013a). Literacy is conceived as an activity with a purpose and social function.

PIAAC goes beyond the false dichotomy of literate vs non-literate and establishes a reporting framework of six proficiency levels describing tasks individuals can typically undertake within a relevant score range. For example, individuals at level 2 'can integrate two or more pieces of information based on criteria, compare and contrast or reason about information and make low-level inferences'; this could be considered a basic proficiency standard. In the first round of PIAAC, 15% of adults fell below this level, ranging from less than 5% in Japan to almost 28% in Italy. Yet, all the participating countries were presumed to have achieved universal literacy, in the most rudimentary sense of being able to read.

The STEP survey, administered in urban areas of middle income countries, was designed to record results using PIAAC's literacy scale. In Colombia, where 75% of people live in urban areas, STEP showed that 36% of the population in 13 major metropolitan areas scored below

level 2 (**Figure 15.4**). This stands in sharp contrast with Colombia's official literacy rate of 94%.

Extending this approach to additional countries would require addressing several implementation issues, starting with developing tools that are robust but relatively inexpensive. The OECD, UIL and UIS recently agreed to develop a literacy assessment framework to underpin a short standardized adult literacy assessment that will be linked to the PIAAC scale, while being adapted to the context of each country (OECD, 2016d).

The aim is to create a cost-effective module to collect data on literacy proficiency: adults would respond to a series of literacy-related questions as well as a background questionnaire within 30 minutes as part of a household visit. The assessment could stand alone but also be administered as a supplement to existing national studies such as the labour force survey.

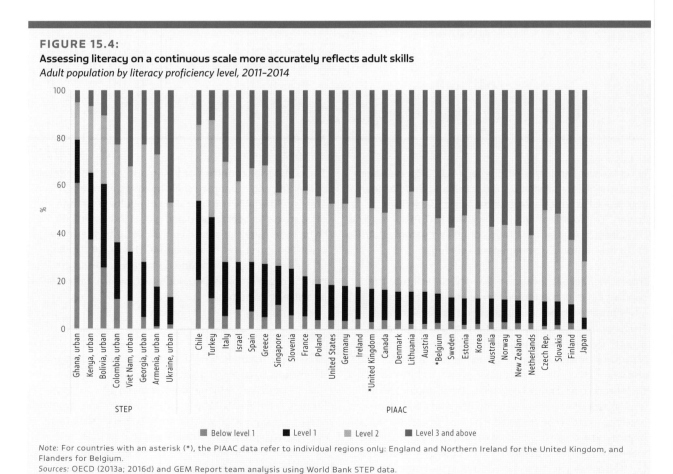

FIGURE 15.4:
Assessing literacy on a continuous scale more accurately reflects adult skills
Adult population by literacy proficiency level, 2011–2014

Note: For countries with an asterisk (*), the PIAAC data refer to individual regions only: England and Northern Ireland for the United Kingdom, and Flanders for Belgium.
Sources: OECD (2013a; 2016d) and GEM Report team analysis using World Bank STEP data.

The assessment would need to have enough test items to accurately locate assessed individuals on a particular level of the scale. It should also be possible to identify whether individuals with very low literacy have problems mastering the basic components of reading. One option would be to assess the basic building blocks for reading comprehension, including knowledge of vocabulary, understanding of sentence logic and fluency in reading text passages. Considerable research would be required to ensure cross-cultural validity. As the section below on numeracy points out, care should be taken to adopt a model that is both relevant and feasible for countries with few resources.

NUMERACY

While the concept of numeracy connotes different things to different people, common themes are found in the definitions used in international assessments. First, they capture a continuum of skills. Second, they focus on competencies to effectively engage with quantitative tasks in everyday life, rather than on what people should have learned in school. Third, they refer to a broader set of knowledge and skills than just the ability to count, estimate and measure.

In PIAAC, numeracy is defined as 'the ability to access, use, interpret, and communicate mathematical information and ideas, in order to engage in and manage the mathematical demands of a range of situations in adult life' (PIAAC Numeracy Expert Group, 2009; Gal and Tout, 2014; Tout and Gal, 2015). National and international assessments share aspects of this definition and other operational aspects to a lesser or greater extent (**Box 15.2**).

Numeracy assessment is feasible in low and middle income countries, though issues of validity, comparability and policy relevance need to be addressed given the diverse needs and technical capacities of stakeholders. One assessment system is unlikely to address the information needs of all stakeholders even in a single high income country, let alone in a large number of countries. To provide useful monitoring data by 2030, a successful approach has to balance the ability of a country to proceed on its own against the need for its assessment to meet global quality standards. For poorer countries, a model is needed that demands modest resources and time, and fits local technical capacity and policy needs (Gal, 2016).

BOX 15.2

Differences between national and international numeracy assessments

A review of three waves of OECD numeracy surveys (IALS, ALL and PIAAC), LAMP (which carried out surveys in Jordan, Mongolia, Palestine and Paraguay) and four national surveys (Bangladesh, Brazil, France and Kenya) suggests several areas for comparison.

Brazil, Kenya and the LAMP countries adopted a broad definition of adult numeracy that is similar to that of PIAAC. Bangladesh and France focused on a narrower set of arithmetic operations and basic functional numeracy skills; for both countries, the assessment was designed to identify low ability adults who could benefit from public programmes.

The LAMP countries and France measured and reported numeracy results separately from those for literacy. In contrast, Bangladesh, Brazil and Kenya considered numeracy an integral part of literacy and did not report separate results, instead providing a combined result on functional literacy.

The potential influence of literacy skills on performance of numeracy tasks was acknowledged. In LAMP and PIAAC, the design of items was changed to reduce literacy demands or text density. In France, an oral assessment was used. There were also differing levels of text usage. For example, in Bangladesh more items looked like school arithmetic exercises, using symbols and no text.

Survey sessions per household ranged on average from 60 to 90 minutes and numeracy was only one of several domains assessed alongside literacy, with additional items in a background questionnaire. Given the time constraint, it is not surprising that the numeracy tests were short: 12 items in Bangladesh, 18 in France and Kenya, and 25 (out of a pool of 57) in PIAAC.

Other differences in key aspects of the assessment framework included the difficulty of items (how they were spread across a continuum of levels from 'easy' to 'difficult'), their contextualization (context-free computational items or items embedded in a particular cultural and functional context) and an estimation of proficiency (a simple total score or psychometric modelling).

The levels of reporting used further complicate comparisons. LAMP reports on three numeracy levels, some countries used four levels ranging from non-literate to advanced literacy, and PIAAC used a five-level system plus the additional category 'below level 1'. Consequently, it is not possible to benchmark results from one country against another.

Source: Gal (2016).

With respect to definitions, numeracy should receive separate attention from literacy in the monitoring of adult basic skills. The PIAAC definition of numeracy could be adopted, with some extension to assess the most rudimentary skills (for example, the ability to sort objects) that are necessary for adults to carry out even the simplest numeracy tasks. This would provide more information at the low end of the numeracy reporting scale to drive policy interventions.

The choice of a reporting framework – the number of reporting levels, the knowledge and skills they represent and the labels used – will depend on different considerations. The names given to levels of performance carry value judgement, such as 'semi-literate' in Bangladesh or 'minimum mastery level' in Kenya. What is 'low' or 'high' is relative to the social and economic progress of each country. These considerations must be taken into account. Finally, when more reporting levels are desired, more items are needed to cover each level reliably.

> " The names given to levels of performance in literacy and numeracy can carry value judgement, such as 'semi-literate' in Bangladesh or 'minimum mastery level' in Kenya "

A reporting framework of at least four levels may be preferable. LAMP and most of the countries reviewed included in the lowest level both those who have no skills and those with low skills. Yet, there is a fundamental difference between literacy and numeracy in this regard. Persons who are deemed 'illiterate' (i.e. who cannot read and write at all) cannot automatically be considered 'innumerate'; several mathematical practices are believed to be universal even in non-literate cultures. In other words, people may still have selected functional computational or context-specific mathematical skills.

It is therefore necessary to distinguish between people with no formal skills (those who have relatively few mental calculation skills beyond counting simple quantities and who cannot understand the meaning of written digits) and with low formal skills (those who can engage in some mental calculations using indigenous number systems or measurement techniques but know few print-based or formal numeracy symbols and systems, even if they may be able to complete very simply written math problems).

A basic level of numeracy would describe individuals with mental and written numeracy skills, including mathematical operations typically learned in school, as well as everyday mathematics, such as estimates and graphs, that might be used in newspapers. This level could vary widely in different societies, depending on economic development and urbanization or other country-specific factors, and would need to be standardized.

Finally, an advanced level would describe individuals who can, with little difficulty or few errors, perform various arithmetic functions in formal school and everyday settings, locate and use quantitative information in assorted displays, solve multistep calculations and use measuring devices.

Implementation issues include the number, types and range of items in terms of content areas, difficulty levels, amount of text and other parameters (e.g. how authentic the settings are or whether open-ended responses should be used instead of multiple choice items). However, the starting point should be based on conducting the survey. Realistically, for instance, how many items can be administered? Assuming the survey can take up to 90 minutes per respondent, countries and the international education community face a choice between two options in assessing numeracy skills.

The first is to use a testing model that adapts to respondents' ability, as was done in Brazil and France and by LAMP and PIAAC. This includes an initial test that screens out those with very low skills. Often, it covers a broader range of skills and difficulty levels and requires a larger number of items to choose from. But such designs are much costlier due to the need to train personnel and use computer technology adapted to multiple scripts and indigenous languages. Further, they require sophisticated modelling and a high capacity for statistical analysis.

The second option is to use a simpler design in which all respondents receive the same assessment items, as Bangladesh and Kenya have done. This enables a country to do its own analysis. However, the number of usable items is lower and it may not be possible to cover all desired reporting levels with enough items, which may reduce the assessment's validity and reliability. Nevertheless, this option may be more realistic and able to be implemented regularly.

A critical issue for both options is cross-country comparability. How can countries make comparisons of numeracy skills if they use different types of items, scale them in different ways and use different formulas to assign items to reporting levels?

In the first option, countries would use statistical analysis to equate their skills distribution in terms of a common scale. In the second, an international expert group could create a common pool of 40 to 50 assessment items that would fit the reporting (i.e. difficulty) levels in terms of the demands of tasks. All countries would draw items from the same international item pool and be permitted to translate and adapt them to local systems and circumstances (e.g. numbers and measurement units). But they would retain the underlying intent of mathematical and statistical demands.

The latter approach would be somewhat less reliable and valid than the proficiency estimates created, for example, by PIAAC, which uses a longer test and more sophisticated statistical procedures. However, it would arguably create the first ever way for many countries to report the percentage of their citizens at multiple levels of numeracy proficiency, using a common item pool and common reporting terminology, thus offering in effect a measure consistent with the requirements of global indicator 4.6.1. It would also be compatible with current practices in many countries and therefore have the potential to be understood by policy-makers and launched quickly.

This approach also uses many of the actual working processes of comparative large-scale assessments. In all of them, joint expert groups agree a conceptual framework, solicit items from participating countries, create a common item pool and try to gauge difficulty levels, using a variety of consensus-building or standard-setting procedures (Tannenbaum and Katz, 2013). A key step is to identify a focal institution to facilitate coordination. All countries engage in a process of localization and adaptation. This preparatory stage could take two to three years, assuming partner countries contribute items to the pool. Afterwards, countries should be able to carry out surveys within a year or two.

CONCLUSION

The new international agenda promises to improve our understanding of population literacy and numeracy skills. These skills are important for poverty reduction, employability, healthier lives, and social inclusion. This section has provided a brief overview of the opportunities and challenges that accompany the monitoring of this new agenda.

The global indicator draws attention of policy makers to the importance of different levels of these skills and the need to stop thinking about 'eradicating' illiteracy and innumeracy. But this will require coordinated action and choices to be made between competing options for assessing skills.

ENDNOTES

1. This section draws on Gal (2016).

In Cairo, the Recycling School, created with the support of UNESCO, gives children from the Zabbaleen community basic education, as well as health recommendations and practical training to turn recycling into a true profession.

CREDIT: Anne-Laure Cahen/Sipa Press/ GEM Report

KEY MESSAGES

Target 4.7 is closely aligned with the vision of the 2030 SDG agenda. But the proposed ways of measuring progress towards it do not reflect its full ambition.

Curricula are the main way countries promote knowledge and skills on sustainable development and global citizenship to students. Most countries report that human rights education is included in their curricula and education standards. Comprehensive sexuality education, however, is not widely included.

Three-quarters of countries had some emphasis on sustainable development in their curricula over 2005–2015, but far fewer referred to terms related to global citizenship. Only 15% of countries included key terms related to gender equality.

Textbooks are a valuable source of information about national commitment to sustainable development. Close to 50% of secondary school textbooks mentioned human rights over 2000–2013, compared with around 5% over 1890–1913. A regular monitoring mechanism on textbooks is needed.

Teachers need to be trained to teach sustainable development and global citizenship, yet more than two-thirds of European countries do not include these topics in teacher training. The share of countries completely integrating sustainable development in teacher education rose from 2% in 2005 to 8% in 2013.

Monitoring knowledge and skills relevant to target 4.7 is not easy. Few assessments examine understanding of history, politics, geography, science and their interdependence. An assessment of grade 8 students in 38 countries showed that only two-thirds were familiar with the Universal Declaration of Human Rights.

Initiatives to monitor this target must address the tension between national values and commitment to a global agenda. Equally important is the need to evaluate knowledge and skills about sustainable development among adults as well as children and adolescents.

CHAPTER 16

TARGET 4.7

Sustainable development and global citizenship

By 2030, ensure that all learners acquire the knowledge and skills needed to promote sustainable development, including, among others, through education for sustainable development and sustainable lifestyles, human rights, gender equality, promotion of a culture of peace and non-violence, global citizenship and appreciation of cultural diversity and of culture's contribution to sustainable development

---

GLOBAL INDICATOR 4.7.1 – *Extent to which (i) global citizenship education and (ii) education for sustainable development, including gender equality and human rights, are mainstreamed at all levels in (a) national education policies, (b) curricula, (c) teacher education and (d) student assessment*

THEMATIC INDICATOR 26 – *Percentage of students by age group (or education level) showing adequate understanding of issues relating to global citizenship and sustainability*

THEMATIC INDICATOR 27 – *Percentage of 15-year-old students showing proficiency in knowledge of environmental science and geoscience*

THEMATIC INDICATOR 28 – *Percentage of schools that provide life skills-based HIV and sexuality education*

THEMATIC INDICATOR 29 – *Extent to which the framework on the World Programme on Human Rights Education is implemented nationally (as per UNGA Resolution 59/113)*

Target 4.7 introduces education for global citizenship and sustainable development, and several related topics, explicitly linking education to other Sustainable Development Goals (SDGs) and capturing the transformative aspirations of the new global development agenda. More than any other education target, it touches on the social, humanistic and moral purposes of education, and their impact on policies, curricular contents and teacher preparation. It also acknowledges the important role of culture and the cultural dimensions of education.

The Inter-agency and Expert Group on SDG Indicators proposed a broad global indicator to capture the wide scope of target 4.7: 'the extent to which global citizenship education and education for sustainable development are mainstreamed in national education policies, curricula content, teacher education and student assessment'. This measure embraces indicators relating to inputs and processes, but sidesteps the target's aspirational intent of ensuring that all learners, young and old, acquire knowledge and skills aligned with the transformative 2030 Agenda for Sustainable Development.

This chapter focuses on the proposed global indicator and examines how global citizenship and sustainable development are included in system-wide interventions, curricular materials such as national curriculum frameworks and textbooks, and teacher education programmes. It addresses themes underpinning target 4.7, including human rights, gender equality, climate change, sustainable livelihoods, sexual and reproductive rights, health and well-being, and responsible and engaged citizenship.

Target 4.7 is closely aligned with a lifelong learning framework, and does not specify the education levels or age groups to which its themes apply. Yet, the proposed global and thematic indicators mainly focus on children and adolescents in formal education. None of the proposed thematic indicators explicitly capture adult learners in non-formal and informal education settings. Data gaps for monitoring national and global progress towards target 4.7 outside the formal education system are particularly wide. Hence, this chapter discusses recent initiatives to collect data more closely aligned with the concepts in target 4.7. Given the fluidity of country initiatives to address the many issues involved, it is important to use existing data sources to provide initial benchmarks for national and regional authorities.

> " Data gaps for monitoring national and global progress towards target 4.7 outside the formal education system are particularly wide "

Identifying indicators to monitor knowledge and skills that are needed to promote sustainable development – and that have meaning across a wide spectrum of socio-economic levels, political systems and cultural contexts – remains arduous (Fricke et al., 2015). This chapter examines several initiatives that could be used to monitor acquisition of relevant knowledge and skills.

Individuals may acquire knowledge, understanding and skills but lack the disposition to use them. While target 4.7 does not explicitly say as much, the development of the right attitudes is an important dimension of global citizenship education (GCED) and education for sustainable development (ESD). This chapter thus briefly reviews several approaches to monitoring adolescents, youth and adult attitudes, and highlights challenges in establishing a global monitoring mechanism.

INTERNATIONAL STANDARD-SETTING INSTRUMENTS

Almost all the concepts mentioned in target 4.7 that promote sustainable development are found in international frameworks and conventions, notably the International Recommendation concerning Education for International Understanding, Co-operation and Peace and Education relating to Human Rights and Fundamental Freedoms, adopted by member states at UNESCO's 18th session in 1974. This recommendation lays out a normative framework for countries on issues related to peace and human rights in the goals, policies, contents and teacher training materials of national education systems (Arora et al., 1994; Savolainen, 2010; UNESCO, 2008).

Although compliance is voluntary, UNESCO has monitored member states' implementation on five occasions since 1974 (UNESCO, 2013). These monitoring exercises aimed to track the extent to which human rights materials and principles had been incorporated into the legal, administrative, educational and teaching tools that guide everyday practices in education (Prada, 2011). Response rates were low, however, though they increased from 18% of countries in 2009 to 28% in 2013 (UNESCO, 2009; 2013).

> "
> The percentage of countries that responded to monitoring exercises of human rights in education, legal and administrative systems rose from 18% in 2009 to 28% in 2013
> "

The adoption of the SDGs highlighted strong alignment between the 1974 recommendation and target 4.7 concepts. As a result, the significance of effective monitoring of country implementation of the recommendation became clearer. In 2016, UNESCO initiated a sixth consultation, asking member states to assess implementation of the recommendation over 2013–2016. The terms are relevant to the monitoring of target 4.7. Member states are asked to report whether the following topics are included in their curricula and, if so, at which levels of education and in which subjects: peace and non-violence, human rights and fundamental freedoms, cultural diversity and tolerance, and human survival and well-being. Additional questions monitor the inclusion of these topics in textbooks, teacher education, student assessments/examinations, and programmes outside the school system, including non-formal education, informal education, adult education and media-based education (UNESCO, 2016e). To increase response rates, the 2016 questionnaire includes many more multiple choice questions than before.

Nevertheless, as past low response rates showed, many national ministries are limited in the capacity to respond to such surveys and the resources to prepare high quality national reports. Gathering the information to be included is hampered by the need to coordinate responses across relevant ministries and departments (Yusuf, 2007). It is difficult to assure the objectivity and validity of self-reported information, which can lower its monitoring value. Therefore, more systematic and rigorous approaches to monitoring country progress towards target 4.7 are needed to supplement country reports.

CURRICULA

Curricula are the main way in which knowledge and skills to promote sustainable development and global citizenship are typically conveyed to students. This section reviews mechanisms to monitor the adoption of topics relevant to sustainable development and global citizenship into official curricula. It then discusses a comparative approach for monitoring curricula at the global level.

HUMAN RIGHTS EDUCATION

One thematic indicator proposes measuring the extent of national implementation of the framework on the World Programme on Human Rights Education, in which the Office of the United Nations High Commissioner for

Human Rights (OHCHR), in cooperation with UNESCO, has developed programmes and curricula to teach human rights. This indicator captures elements of target 4.7 as regards human rights, fundamental freedoms and tolerance, among others.

The first phase of the World Programme for Human Rights Education, 2005–2009, focused on integrating human rights education in primary and secondary schools. An evaluation in 2010 analysed implementation of this aspect, relying primarily on responses to an OHCHR questionnaire distributed to 192 member states (UNIACC, 2010).

Most countries, including Australia, Barbados, Chile, Côte d'Ivoire, Indonesia, Namibia and Zambia, reported human rights education as being integrated into national curriculum and educational standards. A few countries teach human rights as a stand-alone subject but many integrate it as a cross-cutting issue, most often in subjects such as citizenship, civic education and social studies, but also in disciplines such as law, religion, life skills, ethical and moral education, and environment (UNIACC, 2010).

> **Most countries report human rights education as being integrated into national curriculum and educational standards**

The second phase of the programme, 2010–2014, focused on human rights in higher education and for teachers and educators, civil servants, law enforcement officials and military personnel.[1] Responses from 28 countries showed that the topic was most often addressed as a core curricular element in university undergraduate and graduate faculties or departments of law, political science, social science and/or international relations, as well as in general humanities and socio-economic courses (OHCHR, 2015).

At the global level, in addition to this programme, the Universal Periodic Review process and the work of Special Rapporteurs help in monitoring human rights education, but response rates are low and responses insufficiently systematic for a clear global picture.

To ensure that governments meet their obligations to report to the international community, review and monitoring activities initiated by local actors are very important. HRE 2020, a civil society coalition to support and strengthen compliance with international human rights education commitments, recently provided an indicator framework to systematically document national commitments to carry out a comprehensive and coordinated effort for human rights education and training (HRE 2020, 2015).

Other monitoring efforts have been undertaken on specific elements tied to universal human rights frameworks, such as education about the Holocaust (**Box 16.1**).

■ **BOX 16.1**

Monitoring Holocaust education in curricular content

Education about the Holocaust is expected to provide learners with knowledge and skills to help them become responsible and active global citizens who think critically, value human dignity and respect, reject prejudice that leads to violence and genocide, and contribute to a more peaceful, tolerant, inclusive and secure world.

Analyses of textbooks worldwide show that Holocaust education is increasingly taught in the context of universal human rights frameworks rather than as an isolated European historical event, thereby reflecting growing expectations about the humanistic and universal significance of learning about the Holocaust.

A recent study by UNESCO and the Georg Eckert Institute for International Textbook Research analysed Holocaust education in 272 national secondary-level curricula in 135 countries. It showed the Holocaust was part of the curriculum in about half of the countries, with varying contexts and terminologies. National curricula tend to 'domesticate' Holocaust history by explaining it in relation to local histories of mass atrocities. The Holocaust is most frequently mentioned in history in the context of the Second World War, but also in relation to human rights and human rights violations. In a comparatively high proportion of curricula in countries in Europe and Northern America, the Holocaust is a compulsory topic.

One-quarter of curricula contain no references to the Holocaust. Yet, while they do not prescribe specific content, they discuss the purpose of the subject and methods to be used in its teaching. About one-third of the curricula do not mention the Holocaust explicitly but refer to its context. For example, in Zimbabwe the curriculum refers to injustices practised by Nazis and atrocities against minorities, and that of the Democratic Republic of the Congo discusses the harmful effects of Nazism.

Sources: Bromley, (2013); Bromley and Russell, (2010); UNESCO (2014c); Carrier et al. (2015).

COMPREHENSIVE SEXUALITY EDUCATION

One proposed thematic indicator for tracking progress towards target 4.7 is the percentage of schools providing life skills-based education on HIV and on sexuality.

> **Out of 28 countries in Asia and the Pacific, 22 included comprehensive sexuality education in secondary school curricula; 12 did at the primary level**

Comprehensive sexuality education is one of the most pressing and universal priorities for the health, well-being and development of young people. Recent evidence indicates that such education not only plays an important role in preventing negative sexual and reproductive health outcomes, but also offers a platform to discuss gender issues and human rights, and promote respectful, non-violent relationships (UN Trust Fund and Instituto Promundo, 2012; UNFPA, 2007).

Sexual health, gender equality and human rights are interrelated. The 1994 International Conference on Population and Development's Programme of Action and other international agreements, such as the Ottawa Charter for Health Promotion, reflect this relationship and make clear that sexuality education must integrate these domains (Haberland and Rogow, 2015). The proposed thematic indicator thus responds to five elements of target 4.7: human rights, gender equality, culture of peace, non-violence, and knowledge and skills to promote sustainable development and lifestyles (e.g. by helping reduce early pregnancy and family size and instill values and skills for responsible parenthood).

Several multicountry reviews of comprehensive sexuality education have been conducted. A review of 335 national laws, policies, strategies, curricula and training materials in 28 countries in Asia and the Pacific showed considerable variation in addressing sexual and reproductive health issues. Some countries, including Cambodia, Indonesia, Malaysia, Thailand and Viet Nam, integrated comprehensive sexuality education across primary and secondary education, while there was no or very limited integration in Brunei Darussalam, the Islamic Republic of Iran and Pakistan. Comprehensive sexuality education was included in secondary school curricula in 22 of the 28 countries; 12 did so at the primary level. Information on curriculum integration at tertiary level was scarce (UNESCO, 2012c).

Providing comprehensive sexuality education mainly at the secondary level misses the many adolescents in much of the world who are not in secondary school. It is thus important to track the extent to which children and adolescents benefit from such content in non-formal education. In 17 of the 28 countries, sexuality issues were included in non-formal education, targeting out-of-school youth and others, though the scope and nature of these activities were unclear (UNESCO, 2012c).

In 10 countries of sub-Saharan Africa, an in-depth review of curricula found that most included at least some information on gender, but the messages were sometimes contradictory and reinforced gender inequality. Gender-based and intimate-partner violence were sometimes overlooked, including in South Africa, which has one of the world's highest rates of sexual violence. The inclusion of human rights varied but mostly did not address sexual rights. None of the curricula addressed sexual diversity. The issue of child marriage was omitted or poorly addressed in many of the countries where it is highly prevalent, including Kenya, Lesotho and Malawi (UNESCO and UNFPA, 2012).

The Sexuality Education Review and Assessment Tool provides a framework for assessing the scope, content and delivery of comprehensive sexuality education. Used to assess national sexual education programmes in 13 countries of sub-Saharan Africa, it showed that less than half met global standards for required content across all age groups. The weakest content was related to the coverage of gender and social norms (Herat et al., 2014; UNFPA, 2015b).

In Latin America and the Caribbean, the International Planned Parenthood Federation used a standardized questionnaire to collect data from 19 countries' health and education ministries. Only half of the countries reported comprehensive sexuality education curricula that adequately included lessons on topics including gender equality, sexuality, HIV and AIDS, violence prevention and interpersonal relationships (Hunt et al., 2014).

Where sexuality education has been integrated into curricula, its implementation can vary substantially. The Joint United Nations Programme on HIV/AIDS (UNAIDS) Inter-Agency Task Team on Education has developed 15 core indicators on the education response to HIV. One relates to the percentage of schools that provided life skills-based HIV and sexuality education in the previous academic year at either primary or secondary level. Until 2011, this indicator was gathered through the United Nations General Assembly Special

FIGURE 16.1:

In 32 countries, fewer than half of schools provide life skills-based HIV education

Percentage of schools that provided life skills-based HIV education at either the primary or secondary level in the previous academic year, selected countries, 2009-2010

Source: UNAIDS (2011).

Session country reporting system (Clarke and Aggleton, 2012). However, there were no standard guidelines for what constituted life skills-based education in response to HIV, and the information was self-reported, making its quality difficult to establish.

Despite such drawbacks, the indicators suggested how life skills-based HIV education was being carried out (**Figure 16.1**). In 2009, in sub-Saharan Africa, it had been provided in Burkina Faso, Côte d'Ivoire, Liberia and Togo in less than 10% of schools in the past academic year, compared with over 85% in some countries including Botswana, Swaziland and Zimbabwe (UNAIDS, 2011).

The inclusion of this indicator in education management information systems and school-based surveys has been field-tested in some countries, including the United Republic of Tanzania and Zambia, and will allow for better future monitoring (UNESCO, 2015h).

TOWARDS A GLOBAL MECHANISM TO MONITOR CURRICULUM CONTENT

These brief reviews of mechanisms that monitor the integration of human rights and comprehensive sexuality education into curricula show scope for improvement, particularly the need to include additional concepts and improve country coverage in monitoring.

Analysis for this Report reviewed over 110 national curriculum framework documents for primary and secondary education in 78 countries[2] for 2005–2015, focusing on five topics in target 4.7: human rights; gender equality; peace, non-violence and human security; sustainable development; and global citizenship/ interconnectedness. The documents were coded using a standard protocol with a set number of key terms on each topic (IBE, 2016a).

This analysis highlights which topics and themes countries emphasize in their curricula. Elements pertaining to human rights are the most prevalent. Among the 78 countries, key terms such as rights (88%) and democracy (79%) were the most common. There was also some emphasis on sustainable development issues in about three-quarters of the countries, though key terms such as social and economic sustainability were present in less than one-third of the curricula.

Countries make less reference in curricula to key terms related to global citizenship, with only about 10% including concepts such as 'global inequality' and 'global thinking', and half mentioning globalization, multiculturalism and interculturalism. Gender equality is also less prevalent: less than 15% of the countries integrate key terms such as gender empowerment, gender parity or gender-sensitive, while half mention gender equality (**Figure 16.2**).

In Latin America and the Caribbean, key terms related to sustainable development are common in Guatemala and Nicaragua, but much less so in Argentina, Belize, Dominica and Haiti. In sub-Saharan Africa, almost all key words related to sustainable development are found in Mauritius, but none in the United Republic of Tanzania and 10% in the Democratic Republic of the Congo and Niger. Terms related to global citizenship are much less prevalent. In Europe and Northern America, none are found in the United Kingdom, and only 30% were included in Croatia, France and Hungary (**Figure 16.3**).

The limited availability of curricular data poses a challenge for monitoring the intended content of education. While data for this new analysis cover many more countries than any other previous study, much less than half of the world's countries were included.

Further research into subject curricula would aid in understanding progress on target 4.7. Systematic lists of national curriculum frameworks and related materials are needed, which would require close collaboration between national education ministries and a leading international coordinating body such as the UNESCO International Bureau of Education (IBE). As national curricula are usually updated every five to seven years, on average, such global monitoring could be carried out in a similar time-frame (IBE, 2016a).

Whole-school approach

Education for global citizenship and sustainable development is not necessarily an additional subject to the curriculum. It is best adopted in a whole-school approach, with these themes explicitly expressed in school-wide priorities and school ethos, involving everyone from learners to the wider community. Whole-school approaches require more participatory and democratic decision-making that engages all stakeholders, including community members, school management, principals, teachers, parents and students (Bourn et al., 2016; UNESCO, 2015f).

The 2016 International Civic and Citizenship Education Study (ICCS) includes items that reflect components of the whole-school approach. Principals are asked about

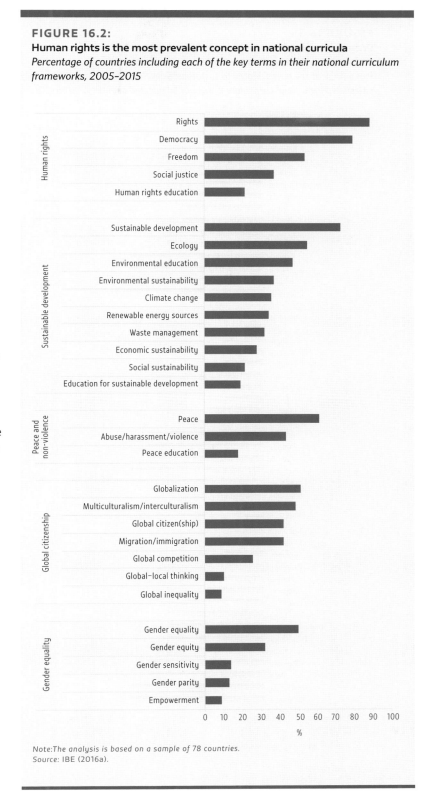

FIGURE 16.2:

Human rights is the most prevalent concept in national curricula

Percentage of countries including each of the key terms in their national curriculum frameworks, 2005–2015

Note: The analysis is based on a sample of 78 countries.
Source: IBE (2016a).

FIGURE 16.3:
Prevalence of key terms relating to global citizenship and sustainable development varies across countries
Percentage of key terms related to sustainable development and global citizenship in national curriculum frameworks, selected countries, 2005–2015

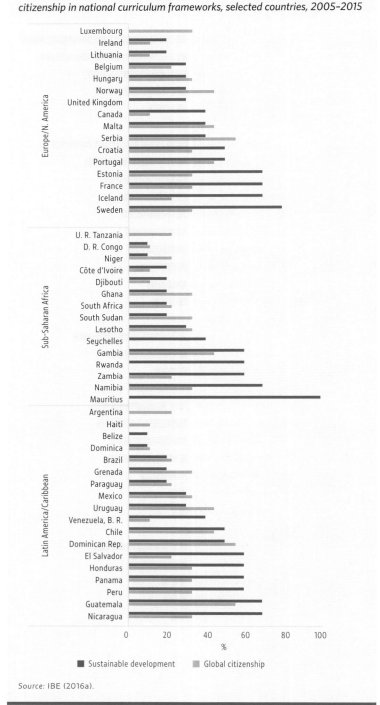

■ Sustainable development   ■ Global citizenship

Source: IBE (2016a).

initiatives to create environments in which sustainable development principles are respected and students experience them by, for example, saving energy, reducing and separating waste, purchasing environment-friendly items and, more generally, having environment-friendly behaviour encouraged. Teachers are asked about their involvement in initiatives and programmes related to environmental sustainability (Schulz et al., 2016). Evaluating implementation of this approach will be challenging, as data will mainly draw on self-reporting and address only some aspects.

Some progress has been made in evaluating participation and decision-making. The 2012 Programme for International Student Assessment (PISA) asked principals the proportion of parents participating in activities including school governance. The results showed less than 5% involved in countries such as Belgium, the Netherlands, New Zealand and the United Kingdom and over 50% in Colombia, Indonesia and Kazakhstan (OECD, 2013b).

International standard-setting instruments are also used to monitor democratic school governance. In 2010, 50 countries adopted the Council of Europe Charter on Education for Democratic Citizenship and Human Rights Education. In 2012, the first monitoring of its implementation involved responses from 40 of the 50 countries, with over 90% reporting that they promoted democratic governance through student participation and parental involvement in decision-making. A follow-up questionnaire will be sent to governments in 2017 (Kerr, 2012).

TEXTBOOKS

Textbooks are a valuable source of information about national commitment to sustainable development. They tend to reflect classroom reality more closely (in terms of both contents and pedagogy) than official curricular policy statements (Torney-Porta et al., 2001). Recent advances in textbook content analysis are promising for gauging curricular content, especially if applied to large samples of textbooks from many countries.

An analysis of over 500 secondary education history, social science and geography textbooks, spanning 1970 to 2008, found that specific mentions of international events increased from 30% in the early 1970s to over 40% in 2005. While almost none of the textbooks mentioned

> Close to 50% of secondary school textbooks mention human rights over 2000–2013, compared with around 5% over 1890–1913

globalization in 1970, nearly 40% did in 2005 (Buckner and Russell, 2013). Between 1975-1994 and 1995-2010, depictions of children as victims of mistreatment more than tripled, and descriptions of discrimination against women more than doubled (Terra and Bromley, 2012).

In the Republic of Korea, a study documented the rapid rise of global citizenship education by describing trends in civic education textbooks, based on the average number of mentions of major national and global themes by page. National citizenship topics and themes remain core elements but emphasis on them has weakened over time, while global citizenship topics and themes have increased, especially in the 1990s and 2000s. In addition, textbook content and presentation have become more 'progressive' and increasingly learner centred, encouraging students to become self-directed, empowered individuals in a global society (Moon and Koo, 2011).

Analysis for this Report took a similar approach. Three data sets on secondary school textbooks in history, civics, social studies and geography were compiled. The vast majority of textbooks were drawn from the most extensive collection of textbooks from around the world, at the Georg Eckert Institute for International Textbook Research in Germany. Textbooks were coded using standardized protocols developed after much piloting and intercoder reliability testing (Bromley et al., 2016).

Analysis showed close to 50% of the textbooks mentioning human rights over 2000–2013, compared with around 5% over 1890–1913. The proportion of textbooks mentioning international human rights documents rose from 12% in the 1950s to 28% in the 2000s. The proportion mentioning women's rights has increased since 1980 (**Figure 16.4**), but with considerable regional variation, from just above 10% in Northern Africa and Western Asia to 40% in Europe and Northern America and in sub-Saharan Africa (Bromley et al., 2016).

Five indicators were used to measure the extent to which textbooks explicitly emphasized environmental issues,

FIGURE 16.4:

Some progress has been achieved in the extent to which textbooks include gender equality

Percentage of textbooks that include an explicit statement on women's rights

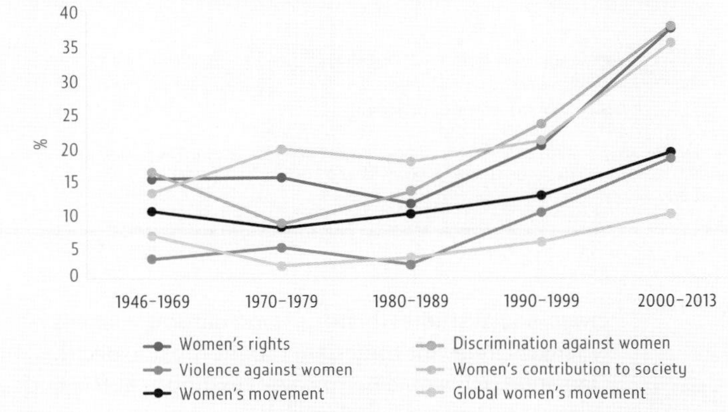

Notes: Sample sizes for each period: 54 textbooks over 1950–1959, 88 over 1960–1969, 108 over 1970–1979, 103 over 1980–1989, 131 over 1990–1999 and 219 over 2000–2011 and 2000–2013. The latest data sets on women's rights and discrimination are for 2000–2013; for the other statements, the data sets are for 2000–2011.
Source: Bromley et al. (2016).

including if environmental protection or damage was discussed in at least one paragraph, if this issue was linked to rights, and if it was discussed as a global issue. Coverage of issues related to environmental protection or damage has increased: in the 1950s, just under 5% of textbooks discussed the issue in at least one paragraph, while 50% did in 2000–2011 (**Figure 16.5**).

This analysis shows it is possible to develop valid and reliable measures using textbooks. A regular monitoring mechanism should be established to provide globally comparable data on textbook contents across countries and systems and over time (Bromley et al., 2016).

Data collection needs to take into account subject and grade. There will be trade-offs between breadth and depth. Instead of analysing all textbooks in each subject and grade, the focus should be on the social sciences –

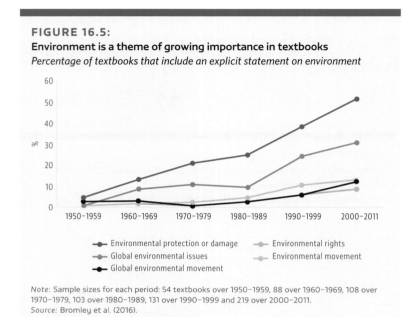

FIGURE 16.5:
Environment is a theme of growing importance in textbooks
Percentage of textbooks that include an explicit statement on environment

Environmental protection or damage ● Environmental rights
Global environmental issues ● Environmental movement
Global environmental movement

Note: Sample sizes for each period: 54 textbooks over 1950–1959, 88 over 1960–1969, 108 over 1970–1979, 103 over 1980–1989, 131 over 1990–1999 and 219 over 2000–2011.
Source: Bromley et al. (2016).

civics, social studies, history – and natural sciences, where the relevant topics are taught most explicitly. One approach would be to cover textbooks at the end of primary, lower secondary and upper secondary education. As textbooks rarely change dramatically from year to year, gathering data every five years would be sufficient. It would also be possible to examine past trends.

Ensuring that questions are valid across countries with different languages and cultures will be a challenge, but asking multiple questions on each theme would reduce errors associated with any single question. Questions need to be factual to minimize interpretation by coders. For instance, asking whether textbooks 'discuss human rights' would lead to responses varying with the coder's understanding of this concept. But asking whether textbooks explicitly use the exact phrase 'human rights' would provide more consistent responses.

Cooperation between governments and international organizations is necessary for a global monitoring system to work. National governments should give researchers open access to curricular content and information on how textbooks are developed and approved. An international coordinating body such as the IBE will be critical to the success of local data collection efforts.

TEACHER EDUCATION

The mainstreaming of sustainable development and global citizenship knowledge and skills in national curricula and textbooks is a prerequisite to monitoring country efforts to meet target 4.7. But it is not enough. Teachers who are prepared to teach in areas related to sustainable development and global citizenship are needed. Are global citizenship, human rights, sustainable development and comprehensive sexuality education included in teacher education? The content of teacher training programmes is seldom readily available, but some information, mostly regional, has been collected.

In teacher training programmes in 10 countries in Asia and the Pacific, information is very limited on how teachers are trained in areas related to global citizenship, including empathy, understanding discrimination, cultural sensitivity, tolerance, acceptance and communication skills. Yet, there are some national examples. After Sri Lanka established a Unit for Social Cohesion and Peace Education in 2008, head teachers, teachers and teacher trainers attended orientation and training in peace and values education. The Republic of Korea reported that policy guidelines on Major Directions for Training of Teacher Personnel encourage local education offices to provide in-service training on human rights (UNESCO, 2014d).

Various forms of in-service teacher education on citizenship education have a component on issues related to global citizenship and sustainable development. Nearly one-third of 36 European countries have programmes to help teachers develop professional knowledge and competencies on citizenship. In Latvia, national in-service training for secondary school teachers includes programmes to develop citizenship education competencies, including values and diversity in society and quality of life and sustainability. Italy's Puntoedu Europa programme offers teachers online courses and regional workshops on topics such as human rights, intercultural dialogue and sustainable development and environment (Eurydice, 2012).

National reports to the OHCHR on the second phase of the World Programme on Human Rights Education can help monitor the extent to which countries include human rights in pre-service or in-service teacher education, although the response rate was has been typically low. Of the 28 countries that submitted information in 2015, 7 reported integrating human rights training in pre-service teacher education. In Togo, such training is necessary to obtain the professional qualification to teach in schools. In Honduras, a course helps teachers detect human rights violations, identify people in vulnerable situations and use appropriate methods to teach human rights in public schools. For in-service teacher education, 13 countries, including Estonia, the Gambia and Seychelles, reported that human rights training was an essential element of their programmes (OHCHR, 2015).

In some countries, civil society organizations have been involved in monitoring teachers' preparedness to teach human rights. In 2012, the Danish Institute for Human Rights conducted a mapping study of human rights education in primary and lower secondary schools and teacher training programmes. It found that human rights were not incorporated adequately in teacher training at universities and colleges. In focus groups, teachers and teacher trainers reported lacking theoretical knowledge on adapting human rights education for different grades. International and regional instruments on human rights education were also largely unknown (Danish Institute for Human Rights, 2014).

The quality of comprehensive sexuality education also depends ultimately on teachers' knowledge of the subject matter and their confidence and skill in its delivery. A review of policy documents and mapping of teacher training institutions in 21 countries in sub-Saharan Africa found that more than half the countries integrated comprehensive sexuality education in pre-service teacher education curricula. In Ethiopia, it was included in cross-cutting subjects that all trainees studied. In seven countries, including the United Republic of Tanzania, it was a specialization option. Only eight countries, including Lesotho, Malawi and Namibia, made comprehensive sexuality education a compulsory module (UNESCO, 2015a).

> " In sub-Saharan Africa, more than half of countries integrated comprehensive sexuality education in pre-service teacher education curricula "

Information on teacher preparation in life skills-based HIV education comes from the 2011–2012 Education Sector HIV and AIDS Global Progress Survey, commissioned by the UNAIDS Inter-Agency Task Team. Of the 39 countries surveyed, 74% reported providing pre-service teacher education on generic life skills and 62% on HIV education at the primary level. At the secondary level, the respective percentages increased to 79% and 72%. This survey is, however, relatively limited in scope, mainly reflecting self-reported data from national education ministries and civil society (UNESCO and UNAIDS, 2013).

In sub-Saharan Africa, 6 of 13 countries that used the Sexuality Education Review and Assessment Tool had strong ratings for more than 40% of elements of their teacher training programmes. The other 7 did not explicitly prepare teachers in areas such as addressing embarrassment when talking about sexuality, avoiding bias caused by personal norms and beliefs, and not pressuring learners to talk about sensitive topics (UNESCO, 2015b).

A recent analysis of teacher education programmes for primary and secondary school found changes over the past decade in attitudes, acceptance and discourse on education for sustainable development in teacher education. The analysis, based on 66 survey responses as part of a UNESCO assessment of the UN Decade of Education for Sustainable Development (2005–2014), found the share of countries completely integrating sustainable development in teacher education rose from 2% in 2005 to 8% in 2013. In pre-service teacher education, climate change, environment and human rights were the prevalent themes. They often integrated local issues, such as illegal logging and deforestation in Indonesia and disaster risk management in Japan, Pakistan and Viet Nam (McKeown and Hopkins, 2014).

More work is needed to develop system-level indicators that accurately capture teacher training needs for teaching knowledge and skills to promote sustainable development. One example is the UN Economic Commission for Europe framework for integrating ESD in teacher training curricula. It identifies key competencies for teachers and educators, including integrative thinking, inclusivity, dealing with complexity, critical analysis, active engagement in contemporary issues, creative thinking about alternative futures, and transformative pedagogy (UNECE, 2012).

The data collection tools presented above, which all serve different purposes and respond to different needs, are too infrequently applied to fill the data gaps. Nor do they follow a systematic format that would ensure country comparability. Monitoring in this area, whether for teacher competencies or classroom interactions, will be challenging (**Box 16.2**). Therefore, stronger efforts are urgently needed to assess concepts in target 4.7 for teacher preparation and training. The application of a standard coding protocol – as for curricula and textbooks – to teacher training institutions' curricula or to the possible inclusion of global competence as a theme in future rounds of the Teaching and Learning International Survey (TALIS), for instance, would make it possible to analyse the effectiveness of professional development in preparing teachers to respond to various

---

BOX 16.2

Monitoring classroom interactions on sustainable development is challenging

In GCED and ESD, participatory, learner-centred and inclusive teaching and learning practices are central. Qualitative tools have been used to track progress in adopting such practices. A study in 10 countries in Asia and the Pacific used qualitative techniques, such as classroom observations, to examine if teaching methods were conducive to a participatory and interactive learning environment. As part of this project, a study of 18 classes in 6 schools across 3 districts observed that in about half the classes, teachers relied on teacher-dominant and teacher-centred methods, while in the remaining half, teachers tried to make classes more interactive.

Methodological limitations and implementation costs make it unrealistic to look for global measures of classroom interactions. Yet, some cross-national assessments have looked at classroom practices in relation to GCED and ESD.

The 2009 ICCS, for instance, measured the climate for classroom discussion, within the limitations of self-reporting. Students were asked whether they expressed opinions in class even when their opinions differed from those of most other students, for example, and whether teachers presented several sides of an issue when explaining it in class.

Across the participating countries, 52% of students, on average, often observed that teachers encouraged them to express their opinions, and 11% reported that students often brought up current events in the classroom. Students were more likely to report an open classroom climate in some countries, including Denmark, Indonesia and Italy, than in others, including Malta and the Republic of Korea. ICCS 2016 will continue to ask questions about classroom interaction.

Sources: Schulz et al. (2010); UNESCO (2014d).

---

groups of students, potentially through a range of teaching strategies (OECD, 2016a).

ACTIVITIES OUTSIDE THE CLASSROOM

While classrooms may be effective places to introduce students to sustainability and global citizenship issues, they are not the only ones, or necessarily the most potent. Extracurricular activities can strengthen and complement classroom interventions and textbook contents. Such activities outside the classroom that complement core academic content include academic clubs and competitions, student government associations, sports activities and teams, debate clubs, theatre productions, music groups and volunteer work.

An analysis for this Report has reviewed the impact of various extracurricular activities around the world. It finds that well-designed, inclusive activities that are accessible to all population groups improve conflict resolution and relationships for social cohesion, increase awareness of legal frameworks and concepts related to human rights as well as the personal capacity to claim and advocate for them, and promote a sense of global citizenship that transcends national boundaries and allows for greater communication and collaboration with people from other countries (Akar, 2016).

Such activities can empower young people to be confident and active agents of positive change to advance various elements of target 4.7, including equality and inclusion, peace, human rights and improved health, particularly as related to HIV prevention.

Some surveys monitor access to extracurricular activities, mostly organized by schools. The 2006 PISA, for instance, asked principals what kinds of extracurricular science activities their schools offered. On average, across OECD countries, 89% of students attended schools whose principals reported commonly offering science-related field trips. Other extracurricular science activities were less prevalent: 56% of students were in schools holding science competitions, 48% in schools encouraging extracurricular science projects, 42% in schools organizing science fairs and 41% in schools with science clubs (OECD, 2012b).

The 2009 ICCS asked teachers if they and their students participated in school-organized activities in the local community, including activities related to environment, human rights, underprivileged people or groups, local multicultural/intercultural events, and awareness-raising campaigns such as World AIDS Day. Principals were asked how many students had the opportunity to take part in such activities. Across the countries surveyed, participation in environment-related awareness-raising campaigns and activities appeared to be widespread. Support of underprivileged people or groups was less common, except in Indonesia and Thailand, where around 70% of teachers said they had participated in such activities (Schulz et al., 2010).

Less information is available about extracurricular activities not organized by schools. Providers of such activities may not give information to or participate in any monitoring and reporting systems. It is hard to imagine global-scale monitoring of this area.

Some opinion surveys have collected data on involvement in extracurricular and similar activities. In 2014, Flash Eurobarometer telephone interviews, collected data on participation in society, in particular involvement in voluntary and cultural activities, from people aged 15 to 30 in the 28 European Union (EU) countries. Around 30% of respondents reported being active in a sports club in the past 12 months, while 16% were involved in a youth club, leisure-time club or other youth organization. On average, 5% participated in an organization promoting human rights or global development, and 3% in one involved in climate change and other environmental issues (European Commission, 2015).

In some countries, national surveys can help track progress. In England (United Kingdom), the National Foundation for Education Research carried out a nine-year evaluation of citizenship education. The Citizenship Education Longitudinal Study began in 2001 and tracked a cohort of young people from age 11 to age 18; the group entered secondary school in 2002. The eighth and final report found a clear, steady decline in the share taking part in extracurricular activities (sports, arts, drama and hobbies), from 80% in grade 7 to 66% in grade 13 (Keating et al., 2010).

In the United States, the 2008 panel of the nationally representative Survey of Income and Programme Participation included a topical module on child well-being in the 10th wave of interviews conducted in 2011. The survey collected information on a variety of child well-being indicators to illustrate children's daily experiences, including participation in extracurricular

activities. Data were limited to children aged 6 to 17 and based on parents' responses about children's involvement in three extracurricular activities: sports, clubs and lessons. It was found that 35% of children participated in sport and 29% in clubs or lessons including music, dance and language (Laughlin, 2014).

A major shortcoming of all these data collection tools is a lack of attention to the quality of experiences or development processes within extracurricular activities. And the absence of common or shared standards for publicly reporting information on extracurricular activities limits the chance of obtaining consistent and reliable data.

OUTCOMES

Monitoring the core aspiration of target 4.7 – acquisition of knowledge and skills needed for sustainable development – is not easy. Challenges include the scarcity of relevant student assessments or specially developed opinion or values surveys, the difficulty of developing test items that are context-relevant but not culturally biased, the broad scope of the target's topics and the relative lack of research on adult learning. One strategy would be to develop a pool of materials from which countries could select components that were both culturally and age appropriate and could be linked to a comparative or international scale.

> " It is hard to test knowledge and skills for sustainable development in a way that is context-relevant but not culturally biased "

ASSESSING GLOBAL KNOWLEDGE AND UNDERSTANDING

Knowledge and understanding of global themes and issues (e.g. peace and conflict, poverty, migration, globalization, climate change), events and institutions are essential to an ability to contribute to sustainable development (Davies, 2006). A basic, interdependent understanding of world history, geography, international institutions and global processes could serve as a starting point to monitor knowledge regarding the concepts in target 4.7. Yet, few cognitive assessments exist in this area.

One example of student cognitive assessments comes from the 2009 ICCS, which drew on the 1999 Civic

> **Very few cognitive assessments exist for the understanding of world history, geography, international institutions and global processes**

Education Study. With the aim of reporting on students' conceptual knowledge and understanding in civic and citizenship education, it used a 79 item test administered to grade 8 students in 38 countries of Europe, Asia and Latin America (Schulz et al., 2010).

The 2009 assessment included an item on knowledge of the Universal Declaration of Human Rights, which can provide a set of universal values as a basis for judgements about global issues (Osler and Starkey, 2000).[3] An average of 68% of students responded correctly to this item. In Finland, Poland and the Republic of Korea, over 80% recognized that the declaration was intended to apply to all people; around 40% did so in the Dominican Republic and Thailand (**Figure 16.6**).

Regional modules for Asia, Europe and Latin America

were added to the 2009 ICCS. In Europe, students were asked about basic facts on the EU and its policies, institutions, practices and processes to gauge their knowledge of supra-national political governance structures (UNESCO, 2015f). Only 57% knew how many countries were EU member states; national averages ranged from 35% in England (United Kingdom) to 75% in Slovakia (Kerr et al., 2010).

National assessments with a civics component can also gauge knowledge relating to global issues. In the United States, the 2014 National Assessment of Educational Progress assessed grade 8 students' knowledge of the benefits of international interactions such as trade, treaties and humanitarian aid. While 62% of students described benefits of two or three types of interactions, 11% could not describe a benefit of any type of interaction (Institute of Education Sciences, 2016).

Preparing learners for a future of climatic and environmental instability begins by helping them understand issues such as why and how climate change takes place, and its likely effects on habitats and ecosystems (Mansilla and Jackson, 2011). The 2006

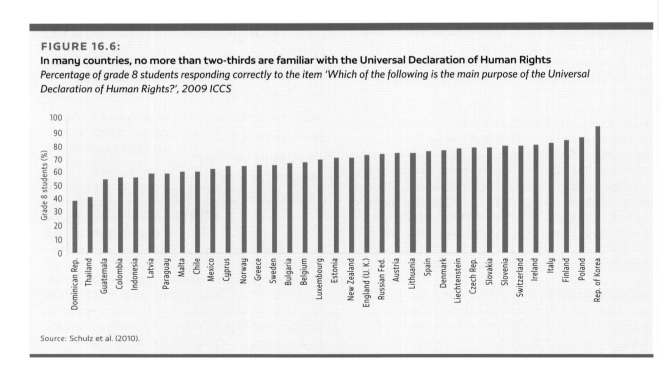

FIGURE 16.6:

In many countries, no more than two-thirds are familiar with the Universal Declaration of Human Rights

Percentage of grade 8 students responding correctly to the item 'Which of the following is the main purpose of the Universal Declaration of Human Rights?', 2009 ICCS

Source: Schulz et al. (2010).

PISA included questions designed to assess knowledge, skill and dispositions on environmental and geoscience among more than 400,000 15-year-olds from 57 countries. The study provided the first internationally comparable data on students' knowledge of the environment and related problems, the sources of this knowledge, their attitudes on environmental issues and the relationship between their results in environmental science and their environmental attitudes (OECD, 2009a).

Of the 108 questions in the PISA 2006 science assessment, 24 were related to environmental science; of these, 14 focused on geoscience. Each subset was the basis for a performance index. At the lower end of the index distribution, students were unable to interpret a graph or figure when given appropriate cues, or show basic knowledge of common environmental processes (OECD, 2009a). The environmental science performance index highlighted wide differences between countries. In Azerbaijan, Indonesia, Kyrgyzstan and Qatar, more than 70% of students were at level D or below, compared with around 25% in Canada, Estonia, Finland and Japan (**Figure 16.7**). These results from PISA 2006 could be taken as a baseline for the level of environmental science knowledge among 15-year olds.

Since 2000, some national cognitive assessments have measured understanding of environmental issues and the ability to use critical thinking in decisions about individual and collective action strategies.

A national assessment of grade 6 and 12 students conducted in Israel over 2004–2006 included nearly 20 questions on general environmental principles and national and global issues. Some 80% of sixth graders correctly answered questions about bottle-deposit laws and recycling, but only 25% were successful on questions about global warming and bird migration. Older students had higher scores: only 25% of sixth graders knew about waste management and the most polluting mode of transport, compared with 55% of 12th graders (Negev et al., 2008).

In Turkey, as part of a nationally representative survey of 2,412 grade 5 students, cognitive skills on environmental protection were assessed in terms of identifying, evaluating and solving problems. About 5% could correctly order the scientific processes given to solve water pollution. About 50% knew that identifying and assessing a problem starts with searching for relevant information from various sources, but only 27% knew

FIGURE 16.7:

Environmental knowledge varies widely between countries
Percentage of 15-year-olds at level D or below on environmental science performance index, PISA 2006

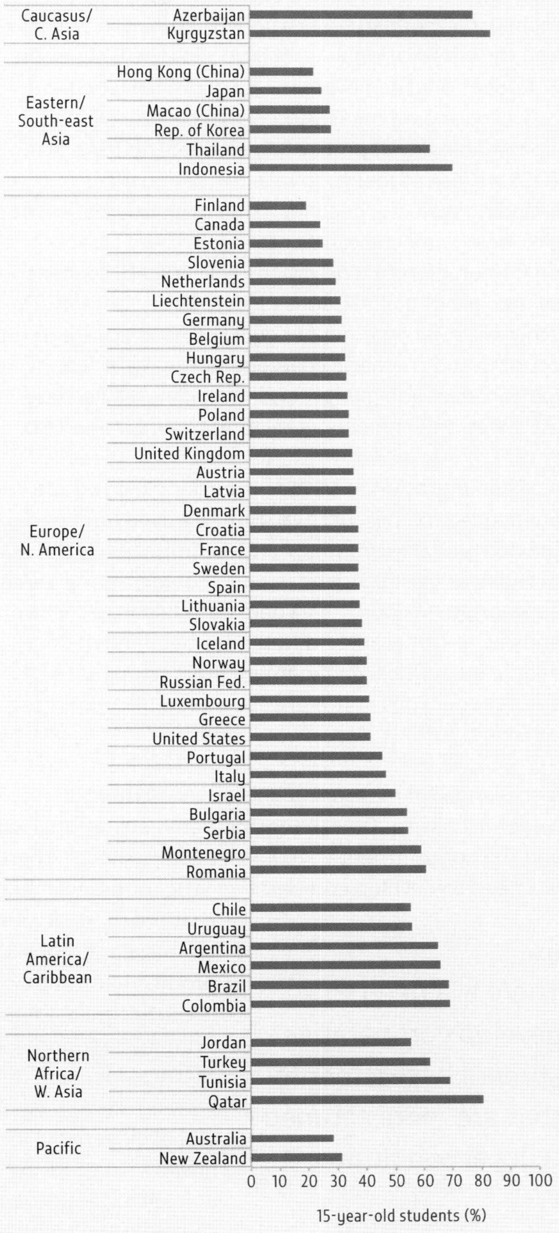

Note: At the lower end (level D or below) of the index distribution, students cannot interpret a graph or figure when given appropriate cues, or show basic knowledge of common environmental processes.
Source: OECD (2009a).

that the last step was reporting and presenting the data collected (Erdogan and Ok, 2011).

Improving on current assessments

Recent initiatives seek to improve monitoring mechanisms for target 4.7 regarding adolescents, mainly in secondary education. In 2016, UNESCO and the International Association for the Evaluation of Educational Achievement (IEA) officially began collaborating on measuring global citizenship and sustainable development knowledge. The IEA's 2016 ICCS will ask students to rate the seriousness of threats including poverty; declines in living standards, economic well-being and environmental health; and attacks on human dignity. The ratings will indicate student awareness of global issues (Schulz et al., 2016). ICCS 2019 will build on the main cycle of ICCS 2016, extending country and thematic coverage. Critically, it will include indicators of knowledge, understanding, skills, beliefs, attitudes and behaviours relating to GCED and ESD.

A major limitation of ICCS is the country coverage. More are needed for this instrument to be used effectively to provide global estimates. Another limitation is the age of those assessed. Ages 13 and 14 could be considered appropriate in countries where compulsory education ends at 14, but marked differences between young people on political engagement start to appear at age 15 to 16. These differences need to be recognized (Hoskins, 2016).

A challenge for measuring outcomes related to target 4.7 has to do with tension between national values and the commitment to a global agenda. Hence, there is a need to develop comparative student assessments that are more attuned to local conditions. One promising example is the Southeast Asia Primary Learning Metrics, focusing on literacy, numeracy and global citizenship in grade 5. In 2016–2017, at least six countries in the region will pilot the assessment tools. By 2020, all countries of the Southeast Asian Ministers of Education Organization and the Association of Southeast Asian Nations are expected to join (SEAMEO and UNICEF, 2015).

> " There is a need to develop comparative student assessments that are more attuned to local conditions "

Another recent development is the OECD decision to include global competence as a field for testing in PISA 2018 (see **Box 16.3**).

Data sources on adult global knowledge and understanding are even more limited

Existing data on knowledge and skills related to global citizenship and sustainable development tend to be limited to children and adolescents. Yet, it is equally important to evaluate similar knowledge and skills in the adult population. There have been very few cognitive assessments, however.

One example was an early survey of global understanding in the United States that included measures of cognitive dimensions of global awareness and was not limited to knowledge of a particular culture or area. This nationally representative survey of some 3,000 undergraduates featured 101 items testing knowledge in 13 areas, including environment, international monetary and trade arrangements, human rights, and race and ethnicity. Only 31% of students identified crop cultivation as the human activity that has contributed most directly to environmental alteration of the greatest area of earth's surface (Barrows et al., 1981).

A more recent assessment of sustainability knowledge is the UN Sustainability Literacy Test (SULITEST). It is administered by higher education institutions to assess and verify sustainability literacy upon graduation. This online multiple-choice test measures the level of knowledge on social, environmental and economic issues and a basic understanding of the earth system. Of the 50 questions, two-thirds are related to international issues such as global warming, the rest being on national and regional issues such as legislation and culture. Between January and October 2014, almost 20,000 students in higher education took the SULITEST; the average score was 54% (Sustainability Literacy Test, 2014).[4]

Building on the idea that broad, integrated geographic knowledge is critical to becoming a global citizen, the National Geographic–Roper 2002 Global Geographic Literacy Survey assessed the geographic knowledge of 3,250 people aged 18 to 24 in nine countries.[5] The survey contained multiple-choice questions on country identification from maps and on factual knowledge of world issues and current events, including population, natural resources, religion, politics and nuclear weapons. Results showed young adults were uninformed about global population issues, which affect, among other things, food and energy consumption. Only 40% or less of young adults in all surveyed countries except Sweden (61%) correctly named China and India as the countries with more than 1 billion people (RoperASW, 2002).

The follow-up National Geographic–Roper Public Affairs 2006 Geographic Literacy Study was conducted in the United States. As in 2002, factual questions were addressed to a representative sample of young adults. Only 35% correctly chose Pakistan from four possible choices as the country hit by a catastrophic earthquake in October 2005. Seven in ten young Americans could find China on a map but less than two in ten knew that Mandarin Chinese was was the world's most widely spoken native language (GfK Roper Public Affairs, 2006).

International opinion surveys, such as the regional barometer surveys (Afro, Arab, Asian, Eurasia and Latino) and the World Values Survey (WVS), include questions on self-reported knowledge and understanding of global and intercultural issues. The 2005–2009 WVS asked about awareness of the Millennium Development Goals (MDGs); only 5% of people surveyed in the United States and 11% in Japan had heard about them, compared with 27% in Germany and 31% in Sweden. Sub-Saharan African countries registered the highest awareness of the MDGs, with 66% in Ethiopia, 47% in Mali and 44% in Zambia. This result indicated that people in countries that received aid were more likely to be aware of the MDGs than people in donor countries (Freschi, 2010). The potential of using international opinion surveys to measure adult global knowledge and understanding needs to be further explored.

SKILLS AND ATTITUDES

Critical skills for promoting sustainable development include communicating appropriately and effectively with people from other cultures or countries; comprehending other people's thoughts, beliefs and feelings and seeing the world from their perspective; adjusting one's thoughts, feelings or behaviours to fit new contexts and situations; and analysing and thinking critically in order to scrutinize and appraise information and meanings.

PISA 2018 will be an important step to assess such skills on a broader scale (OECD, 2016a). The cognitive assessment will be designed to test knowledge, understanding, and analytical and critical thinking in

---

BOX 16.3

Assessment of global competence in the 2018 PISA assessment

Countries participating in PISA are collaborating to develop an assessment of global competence to be conducted in 2018. It will involve testing 15-year-olds, who also take separate tests in reading, mathematics and science.

Global competence is a multidimensional learning domain encompassing three dimensions needed to engage in productive and respectful relationships with people from different cultures: knowledge and understanding, skills, and attitudes. It is defined as the capacity to analyse global and intercultural issues critically and from multiple perspectives; to understand how differences affect perceptions, judgements and ideas of self and others; and to engage in open, appropriate and effective interactions with others from different backgrounds on the basis of a shared respect for human dignity.

The cognitive assessment in the 2018 PISA currently proposed by the OECD aims to build a single scale to test knowledge, understanding, and analytical and critical thinking in a problem-solving context concerning a global or intercultural issue. It would include tasks that draw on numerous types of knowledge and thinking processes and would be designed to be appropriate to the context and learning of 15-year-olds.

The questionnaire would also include self-reported components on the dimension of knowledge and understanding – for instance, how familiar students are with global issues such as climate change and global warming, global health and population growth – and on linguistic, communication and behavioural skills required to interact respectfully, appropriately and effectively with others. Students' flexibility, empathy, openness to and respect for cultural otherness, global mindedness and responsibility will also be assessed.

Sources: OECD (2015e); OECD (2016a); Reimers (2010).

---

an authentic problem-solving context. Self-reported items will be incorporated to measure skills such as communication, flexibility and empathy (Box 16.3).

A number of cross-national assessments examine attitudes, including openness towards people from other cultures or countries, respect for cultural otherness and responsibility for one's own actions.

ICCS 2009 contained scales for monitoring supportive attitudes, e.g. on gender equality and towards migrants. Supportive attitudes on gender equality were captured by how students responded to positive and negative statements on ideas such as equal opportunity to take part in government and equal pay for the same jobs. Large majorities agreed with positive and disagreed with negative statements about gender equality, with girls expressing more support for gender equality than boys (Schulz et al., 2010).

Regional ICCS modules reflect local, national and regional differences. The 2009 Latin American questionnaire included items measuring acceptance and respect of social minority groups as neighbours. While most students in the participating countries (Chile, Colombia, the Dominican Republic, Guatemala, Mexico and Paraguay) were tolerant of people of a different nationality, from other regions of the country or with a different skin colour, fewer approved of people with a different sexual orientation or with HIV (Schulz et al., 2011).

In the 2010 Australian National Assessment, student attitudes on indigenous cultures were measured in grades 6 and 10. In both grades, 9 out of 10 students agreed that Australia should support cultural traditions and languages of Indigenous Australians. A similar proportion agreed on the importance of recognizing traditional land ownership and giving everyone the chance to learn about promoting reconciliation between Indigenous and non-Indigenous Australians (Australian Curriculum Assessment and Reporting Authority, 2011).

The annual International Social Survey Programme (ISSP) is a cross-national collaborative project on attitudes concerning social issues, conducted in multiyear modules.[6] Its third module on environment, in 2010, mainly dealt with attitudes on issues such as environmental protection, and respondents' behaviour and preferences regarding government measures on environmental protection.

An ISSP summary index on environmental attitudes shows Canada, Denmark and Switzerland leading the ranks in environmental concern, with Bulgaria, the Philippines and South Africa at the lower end. Longitudinal analysis of successive ISSP waves shows environmental concern decreasing in almost all countries over the past two decades. In the United States, for instance, about 46% of the population was very willing or fairly willing to pay much higher prices to protect the environment in 2000 and 2010, down by six percentage points from 1993 (Franzen and Vogl, 2013).

> ❝
> The International Social Survey Programme shows that environmental concern is decreasing in almost all countries over the past two decades
> ❞

The European Social Survey, conducted every two years, consists of a core questionnaire and rotating questions. In 2014, the rotating questions were related to immigration. An active willingness to seek out and take up opportunities to engage with people from other cultures can be measured by, for instance, having close friends of another cultural group. In France, Sweden and Switzerland, 35% of respondents reported not having close friends of a different race or ethnic group (ESS, 2014).

In 2015, the Pew Research Centre conducted a survey in 40 countries to measure perceptions of global challenges. The survey of representative samples of adults over age 18 showed that climate change was cited as the biggest challenge in 19 countries, making it the most widespread concern. In Latin America and sub-Saharan Africa, 50% of adults reported high concern about climate change. Global economic instability was the biggest concern in several countries and the second biggest in half the countries surveyed (Pew Research Centre, 2015).

Cross-national opinion surveys have their limits, however. Attempts to measure and analyse self-reported data on attitudes often confront the social desirability problem: adults are rarely willing to admit prejudices in relation to gender, race and religion in opinion surveys but may be more likely to give a socially acceptable or desirable response.

Overall, target 4.7 makes explicit the need for 'all learners [to] acquire the knowledge and skills to promote sustainable development'. Currently proposed indicators refer only to school-age children and adolescents. An appropriate monitoring framework would find ways to better capture the target's intent. Future data collection efforts should strengthen the knowledge base on out-of-school youth and all adults.

Furthermore, coordinated efforts are needed in developing a shared monitoring framework and conducting assessments of learners' knowledge and skills. Establishing common understandings at the regional level, such as the Southeast Asia Primary Learning Metrics, is likely to prove more feasible in coming years.

ENDNOTES

1. The third phase, 2015–2019, focuses on strengthening the work of the first two phases and promoting human rights training for media professionals (OHCHR, 2014).

2. 18 countries in Latin America and the Caribbean, 16 in Europe and Northern America, 15 in sub-Saharan Africa, 11 in the Pacific, 7 in Eastern and South-eastern Asia, 6 in Southern Asia, 3 in Northern Africa and Western Asia, and 2 in the Caucasus and Central Asia.

3. Understanding the importance of human rights helps understand the rights and responsibilities of individuals and groups, examine the multiple ways in which intolerance violates human rights, and recognize human rights violations such as racism, sexism and xenophobia (Reimers, 2010).

4. The SULITEST will also be available for companies and organizations in 2016.

5. Canada, France, Germany, Italy, Japan, Mexico, Sweden, the United Kingdom and the United States.

6. Module topics have included environment; the role of government; social inequality; social support; family and gender issues; work orientation; the impact of religious background, behaviour, and beliefs on social and political preferences; and national identity.

Somali children wash their hands before eating lunch at Shabelle boarding school in Mogadishu. "We learn about hygiene at school – we learn that it is important to wash our hands after going to the toilet – we learn that it is important to wash our hands before eating too. I feel better now that I am washing my hands – I don't get sick as often.".

CREDIT: Kate Holt/GEM Report

KEY MESSAGES

While the target recognizes the principles of a child-friendly school – child-centredness, democratic participation and inclusiveness – not all these are amenable to global monitoring.

A lot of work remains to be done on improving data, but existing sources show that 3 in 10 primary schools still lack adequate **water** supply, increasing to 5 in 10 in the 49 least developed countries.

Some countries inspect school **structural safety** closely, but not in detail. Participatory methods have been developed to help students and the community provide information on school conditions.

Due to lack of consensus on a definition and often limited monitoring capacity, it is hard to know how many school facilities are **accessible to children with disabilities**.

ICT in education is commonly considered an essential element of an effective learning environment. But in some of the poorest countries most primary schools do not even have electricity. Even if they do, other factors may prevent schools from being connected to the internet. And in many developing countries, there are far too many learners per computer to make the activity beneficial.

School-related violence is a global phenomenon. About 40% of 13- to 15-year-old students in 37 countries reported having been involved in physical fights. Overall, better coordination is needed between various international surveys to reveal more about where and how often violence occurs.

A high number of **attacks** on schools, teachers and students by state security forces or non-state armed groups are recorded every year. Military use of schools took place in 26 countries between 2005 and 2015. Between 2009 and 2012, 1,000 or more education-related attacks took place in 6 countries.

CHAPTER 17

TARGET 4.A

Education facilities and learning environments

Build and upgrade education facilities that are child, disability and gender sensitive and provide safe, non-violent, inclusive and effective learning environments for all

GLOBAL INDICATOR 4.A.1 – *Percentage of schools with access to: (a) electricity, (b) the Internet for pedagogical purposes, (c) computers for pedagogical purposes, (d) adapted infrastructure and materials for students with disabilities, (e) basic drinking water, (f) single-sex basic sanitation facilities, and (g) basic handwashing facilities (as per the water, sanitation and hygiene (WASH) indicator definitions)*

THEMATIC INDICATOR 33 – *Percentage of students experiencing bullying, corporal punishment, harassment, violence, sexual discrimination and abuse*

THEMATIC INDICATOR 34 – *Number of attacks on students, personnel and institutions*

This target is built on the concept of child-friendly schools, which is promoted by UNICEF and based on the 1990 Convention on the Rights of the Child. The target recognizes the principles of a child-friendly school – child-centredness, democratic participation and inclusiveness – which have been measured in cross-country research studies (Godfrey et al., 2012). However, it is hard to imagine them monitored on a global scale. Hence this chapter focuses on three aspects of child-friendly schools with potential for global monitoring: school infrastructure, information and communication technology (ICT), and violence and attacks in schools.

BOX 17.1

A school infrastructure index in Paraguay

Good school infrastructure is an element of an effective learning environment and can contribute to improved learning outcomes. The challenge is to collect up-to-date information on various aspects of school facilities, assess priorities and act upon the evidence.

In 2008, with funding from the Inter-American Development Bank, the government of Paraguay carried out an infrastructure census, which generated a wealth of data on classrooms, ancillary rooms, libraries, laboratories, electricity, technology, water and sanitation. A basic school infrastructure index was developed to synthesize the information. The index ranged from zero to one, with one representing the best infrastructure level a school could achieve. The mean value by district ranged from 0.08 to 0.37 for primary schools and from 0.12 to 0.44 for secondary schools, with the lowest values in rural districts, such as Caazapá and Canindeyú, which are inhabited by Guarani-speaking communities, and the highest values in the district of the capital city, Asunción.

The infrastructure in indigenous areas was particularly poor. Only 6% of schools had access to running water in indigenous schools, compared with 37% in other rural areas and 67% in urban areas. In indigenous schools, 47% of classrooms were in good condition, compared with 69% in other rural areas and 88% in urban areas.

Despite a more than tenfold increase of the construction and equipment investment budget between 2008 and 2012, from US$1.4 million to US$13.4 million, the amount allocated for primary and secondary schools stagnated. The bulk of the increase went to tertiary education, improvements in the offices of the Ministry of Education and Culture, and repairs for the Higher Institute of Fine Arts. Short-term infrastructure plans focused on new headquarters for the ministry, leaving the updating of the infrastructure census for the medium term and the development of early childhood facilities for the long term.

Sources: Juntos por el Educación (2013); UNICEF (2013a); Wodon (2016).

SCHOOL INFRASTRUCTURE

Adequate education facilities and learning environments are necessary not only to safeguard learners' health and well-being but also to fulfil their right to education. School infrastructure refers to a wide range of elements, including light and ventilation, insulation, furniture, blackboards and laboratories. The formulation of infrastructure standards and introduction of monitoring mechanisms at the national and sometimes international level have progressed (**Box 17.1**) but need to be further built upon so that comparable information is available for every school.

Three aspects of school infrastructure that are explicit or implicit in the target formulation are reviewed in this section: water, sanitation and hygiene ('build and upgrade education facilities'); structural safety ('safe'); and accessibility for people with disabilities ('disability … sensitive').

Water, sanitation and hygiene

Improving water, sanitation and hygiene facilities in education institutions can have significant positive effects on health and education outcomes. These facilities include potable drinking water; clean, safe toilets; and handwashing facilities. Inadequate facilities increase the risk of disease transmission. Improved facilities, coupled with hygiene education, can reduce absenteeism. They can also increase demand for education, particularly among adolescent girls, who may drop out due to a lack of girls-only toilet facilities (UNICEF, 2010).

> In the least developed countries, only half of primary schools had an adequate water supply in 2013

The main mechanism of global monitoring in this area is the WHO/UNICEF Joint Monitoring Programme, established in 1990, which has provided regular national, regional and global estimates of progress towards the Millennium Development Goal (MDG) targets. In recent years, it has expanded its focus to include water, sanitation and hygiene in schools.

The existing Joint Monitoring Programme global data set is composed of data from national education census reports, the UNESCO Institute for Statistics (UIS) sub-Saharan Africa regional module, the Latin American Laboratory for Assessment of the Quality of Education (LLECE) and the 2011 UN-Water Global Analysis and Assessment of Sanitation and Drinking Water. Where primary data sources were unavailable or inaccessible, UNICEF country office annual reports were used. For 2013, data are available from 149 countries representing 83% of the global population and 96% of the population of developing countries (UNICEF, 2015a).

These data show that school water and sanitation provision has improved since 2008 but remains low. The average share of primary schools with adequate water supply in 2013 was 71% worldwide, but 52% in the 49 least developed countries. The respective estimates for adequate sanitation were 69% and 51% (**Figure 17.1**). The data are insufficient for global figures on school hygiene, but availability of handwashing facilities in the 11 countries with data is very low.

Caution is needed in interpreting the estimates, as underlying definitions are inconsistent across data sources or countries. For example, the definition of an adequate sanitation facility may cover the mere existence of toilets, improved toilets (e.g. flush, ventilated, improved pit latrine, pit latrine with slab or composting), functional toilets, or toilets meeting national standards. Precise definitions are unavailable for 60% of countries.

In other words, while several dimensions are inherent in the definition of adequate water supply and sanitation (including quantity, quality, proximity, functionality, gender segregation and accessibility to children with disabilities), many are often not captured. A review of

54 school census questionnaires found that 48 included items on water and sanitation, but only Myanmar collected information on all parameters for water, and only Belize and Iraq for sanitation. Only 30 countries gave information on gender-segregated toilets (UNICEF, 2015a).

There are guidelines on how to formulate relevant questions on school census forms and household surveys to improve information quality (UNICEF, 2011). The Joint Monitoring Programme is working with partners to recommend a core and expanded set of questions to support the harmonization of indicators across national monitoring systems (WHO and UNICEF, 2015). It will also establish a systematic data quality review process to weight national coverage figures for more accurate regional and global estimates. It seeks to expand the data set to include both primary and secondary schools.

FIGURE 17.1:
Three in 10 primary schools still lack adequate water supply and sanitation
Proportion of primary schools with adequate water supply and sanitation, average and country groups, 2008 and 2013

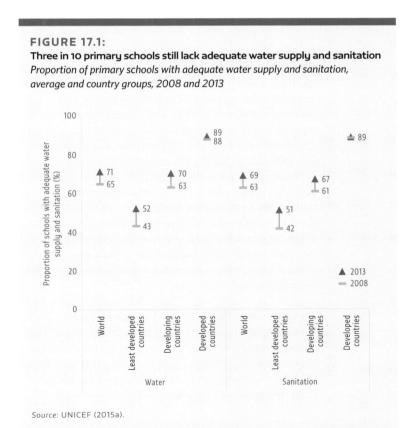

Source: UNICEF (2015a).

Structural safety of schools

Disasters often damage or destroy school infrastructure, claim lives of students and teachers, and disrupt education provision. In the last 10 years, earthquakes in China, Haiti and Nepal; cyclones in Bangladesh; and typhoons in the Philippines have destroyed thousands of schools. The effects of such events extend beyond the short term. In Nicaragua, Hurricane Mitch resulted in a 45% increase in child labour among the most affected households, while increases in repetition and poor education performance rates followed Typhoon Mike in the Philippines (World Bank, 2015b).

While the occurrence of natural hazards is mostly beyond human control, the impact is magnified when schools are unsafe and communities are vulnerable. This issue is even greater with the increasing likelihood of extreme weather events associated with climate change.

The Global Alliance for Disaster Risk Reduction and Resilience in the Education Sector has drawn up a Comprehensive School Safety Framework. It includes a disaster-resilient infrastructure component with guidelines and regulations on specific local risks, and skilled personnel and inspection mechanisms to assess the risk profile of buildings and compliance with standards (GADRRRES/UNISDR, 2014).

Good examples of international guidelines include the guidance notes on safer school construction developed by the Inter-agency Network for Education in Emergencies and the Global Facility for Disaster Reduction and Recovery (INEE and GFDRR, 2009), since complemented by a manual on community-based approaches (GADRRRES, 2015). At the national level, Guatemala's School Buildings Safety Indicator and guidelines for assessment have been adopted by UNICEF and other countries in Latin America. In Indonesia, the Centre for Disaster Mitigation at the Institute of Technology Bandung published, with Save the Children, a handbook of typical school design and a manual on retrofitting vulnerable school buildings, following the experience of the Aceh and West Sumatra Earthquake Response programmes (UNISDR, 2011).

The risk profile of buildings and compliance with standards can be assessed. The Islamic Republic of Iran passed a school safety act in 2006; in the following five years some 25% of classrooms were rebuilt or retrofitted (Ghafory-Ashtiany, 2014). Before any work began, a comprehensive database was prepared on whether

> " After a school safety act was passed in the Islamic Republic of Iran, 25% of classrooms were rebuilt or retrofitted in the following five years "

school buildings met requirements for a technical certificate of school building safety, covering more than 100,000 schools. Data are updated and published annually. The certificate has been updated and incorporated into regular monitoring (Mahdizadeh, 2011).

However, not all countries can afford detailed inspection-based assessment. Tools that can help bridge these gaps are critical. The Global Alliance for Disaster Risk Reduction and Resilience in the Education Sector has developed three assessment tools for use on tablets and smartphones, as part of the Comprehensive Safe Schools Self-Assessment Suite. With these tools, students and community members can provide information on school conditions through crowd-sourcing; safety committees and education administrators can assess buildings; and trained surveyors can carry out on-site inspections. Under the Safe Schools Initiative of the Association of Southeast Asian Nations, the self-assessment and on-site inspection components have been applied in the Lao People's Democratic Republic (ASSI, 2015).

The Global Programme for Safer Schools of the Global Facility for Disaster Reduction and Recovery also advocates community auditing of school buildings as a valuable alternative monitoring tool. Community mapping initiatives have been undertaken in Haiti, Indonesia, Nepal and Sri Lanka (GFDRR, 2015).

Accessibility for people with disabilities

To gain access to education facilities and learning environments, people with disabilities need to overcome obstacles such as lack of mobility equipment, poor transport infrastructure and road conditions, inappropriately designed buildings, negative social attitudes, absence of teaching aids and unsuitable curricula.

UNICEF has designed an Inclusive Education Rating System tool, which includes the physical environment as a key dimension, to enable specialists to assess national policy and the school system. UNICEF has also developed criteria on which to base assessments at the school level, including detailed guidance on getting to, entering and moving through the school; using water, sanitation and recreational facilities; and developing school evacuation safeguards (UNICEF, 2014a; 2014f).

Even if accessibility is defined to narrowly focus on physical barriers in school buildings, it is difficult to know if facilities in a given country are suitable for children with disabilities, due to the lack of a definition of accessible schools and, more often, limited monitoring capacity.

Article 9 of the 2006 Convention on the Rights of Persons with Disabilities calls on countries to '[d]evelop, promulgate and monitor the implementation of minimum standards and guidelines for the accessibility of facilities and services open or provided to the public' and explicitly refers to schools (United Nations, 2006). Accessibility standards are a necessary basis for monitoring compliance. A review in Asia and the Pacific found that at least 25 of 36 countries had such standards for buildings, public transport or both (UNESCAP, 2010).

In South Africa, the Department of Basic Education issued a comprehensive set of legally binding norms and standards for all public schools in 2013. They include universal design principles on minimum space, toilets and parking spots for children with disabilities and are to be followed in all future construction work (South Africa Government, 2013). However, the presence of standards is not sufficient. While South Africa has a National Education Infrastructure Management System, it does not appear to monitor implementation of the standards with respect to disability (South Africa Government, 2015). Civil society groups do, however, conduct social audits and point to cases where schools do not meet the norms and standards (Equal Education, 2015).

In India, the Sarva Shiksha Abhiyan programme, promoting education for all, supports ramps, railings and modification in toilets and provides manuals to village education committees. Data in the District Information System for Education led the government to declare 82% of schools 'barrier free' in 2015. However, this assessment only captured the availability of ramps and not all aspects that should be considered before a school can be declared compliant with accessibility standards (India Government, 2015; NUEPA, 2014).

Education management information systems are ill-prepared to collect relevant information. A review of 40 school census forms showed that only one mentioned physical infrastructure provisions for children with disabilities in each room; similarly, only one asked whether toilets were accessible to children with disabilities (UNICEF, 2014b).

INFORMATION AND COMMUNICATION TECHNOLOGY IN SCHOOLS

ICT is commonly considered an essential element of an effective learning environment. Available evidence has not established a direct link between ICT in schools and learning outcomes, but school computers (desktop, laptop or notebook) and mobile phones may be the only way for students to gain access to digital content and the digital world in many countries.[1]

The 2015 Qingdao Declaration on ICT and post-2015 education called upon the *Global Education Monitoring Report* to report on ICT in education but did not set specific targets. The basis for monitoring ICT in education has been the 2003 Geneva Plan of Action of the World Summit on the Information Society. Two of its 10 targets, which were to be achieved by 2015, were related to education: to 'connect universities, colleges, secondary schools and primary schools with ICTs' and to 'adapt all primary and secondary school curricula to meet the challenges of the Information Society, taking into account national circumstances' (ITU, 2011).

The UIS focuses on eight core indicators to monitor these targets (**Table 17.1**). It has conducted regional data collection in Latin America and the Caribbean (UIS, 2012), the Arab States (UIS, 2013), Asia (UIS, 2014a) and sub-Saharan Africa (UIS, 2015). In some sub-Saharan African

TABLE 17.1:
UIS core indicators on ICT in education

Domain	Indicator
Infrastructure	EDR1: Proportion of schools with electricity
	ED1. Proportion of schools with a radio used for educational purposes
	ED2. Proportion of schools with a television used for educational purposes
	ED3. Proportion of schools with a telephone communication facility
	ED4. Learner-to-computer ratio in schools with computer-assisted instruction
	ED4bis. Learner-to-computer ratio
	ED5. Proportion of schools with internet access, by type of access
Usage	ED6. Proportion of learners who have access to the internet at school
Participation	ED7. Proportion of learners enrolled at the post-secondary non-tertiary and tertiary level in ICT fields
Teaching staff	ED8. Proportion of ICT-qualified teachers in primary and secondary schools

Source: UIS (2009).

countries, such as Burkina Faso, Comoros, Guinea, Madagascar and Niger, ICT is not a relevant curricular objective and courses related to basic computer skills or computing may not even be available in primary or secondary education.

Using ICT in schools requires readily and regularly available electricity. Secondary schools, which are more likely to be in urban areas, are better connected. But in many sub-Saharan African countries, the lack of mains electricity hampers the use of ICT, despite the increasing availability of solar panels and other solutions. In the Central African Republic, practically no primary or secondary school was connected to an electrical grid (**Figure 17.2**). Even if schools are connected to a power source, power surges and brownouts are common, further impeding the reliable usage of ICT (Mudenda et al., 2014; Practical Action, 2013).

Electricity is a poor predictor of access to the internet in many countries. Despite full electrification, internet access was 56% in Trinidad and Tobago, 30% in Palestine, 27% in Azerbaijan and 6% in Kyrgyzstan (**Figure 17.3**). Internet connectivity depends on the national telecommunications infrastructure, geography

> " Internet connectivity depends on the national telecommunications infrastructure, geography and schools' ability to pay "

and schools' ability to pay. In Mongolia, 91% of primary and secondary schools had internet connection in 2012. When some schools began disconnecting due to high costs, the Ministry of Education, Culture and Science provided central funds to ensure connectivity (ADB, 2012).

Measuring internet connectivity requires information on the type and speed of connection as well as distinguishing between its use for administrative and pedagogical purposes. The Broadband Commission's target of Broadband for All by 2020 commits the international community to monitor school connectivity (Broadband Commission, 2013). Private sector internet service providers should contribute relevant data..

To ensure that computer- and internet-assisted instruction meets all pupils' needs, enough computers must be available. Pupil/computer ratios around 2:1 or

FIGURE 17.2:
Most primary schools do not have electricity in some of the poorest countries
Proportion of primary and secondary schools with electricity, 2009–2014

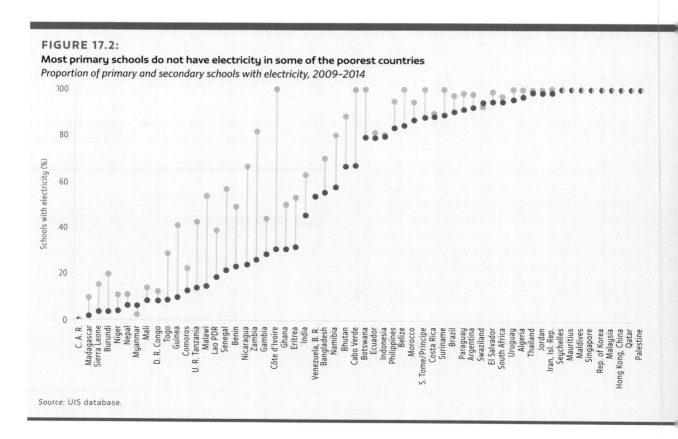

Source: UIS database.

FIGURE 17.3:
Electricity access does not automatically translate to internet access in schools
Proportion of schools with electricity and internet, primary and secondary schools, selected countries, 2009–2014

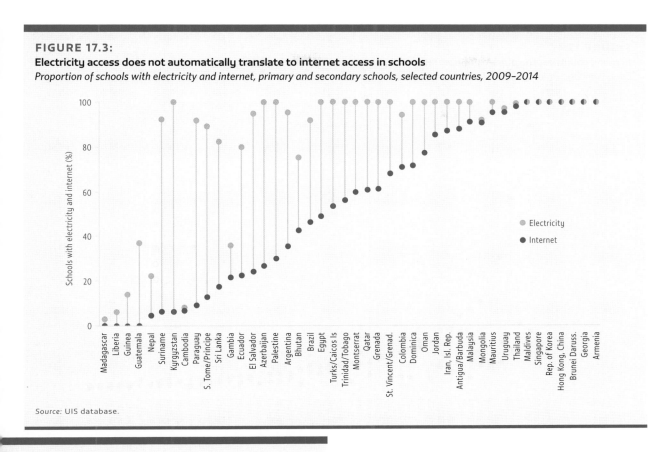

Source: UIS database.

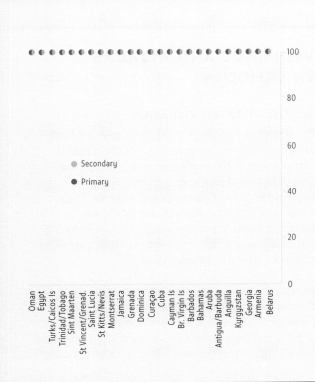

3:1 promote collaborative learning. In many developing countries, however, the number of learners per computer may be so high that time on task per pupil is too limited. In Guinea and Madagascar, the pupil/computer ratio was at least 500:1. In most countries, pupil/computer ratios decrease from primary to secondary education. For example, in the Islamic Republic of Iran, the pupil/computer ratio was 83:1 in primary education, 28:1 in lower secondary education and 17:1 in upper secondary education in 2012 (**Figure 17.4**).

Several countries have invested in well-publicized projects to increase computer availability. Rwanda has reduced its pupil/computer ratio in primary and secondary schools as part of the One Laptop per Child project, which manufactures low cost, durable computers for schools in developing countries. Georgia reduced its ratio from more than 200:1 in 2004 to 7:1 in 2012 as a result of spearheading the ambitious Deer Leap programme to ensure computers were placed in all schools (UIS, 2014b).

However, national averages mask differences within countries. In China, computer availability is twice as high in

FIGURE 17.4:

In many countries, the pupil/computer ratio is too high to enable meaningful learning
Pupil/computer ratio in primary, lower and upper secondary education, 2009–2014

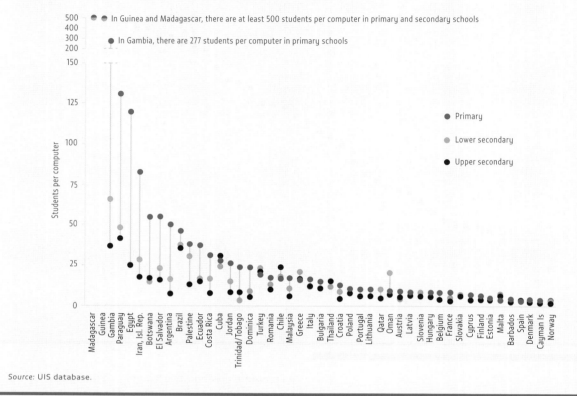

Source: UIS database.

urban primary schools (14:1) as in rural schools (29:1) (Zeng et al., 2012). In contrast, computers are more available in rural areas in Tajikistan due to a policy to provide all schools with a laboratory with the same fixed number of devices, regardless of enrolment; this has the effect of favouring pupils in small rural schools (ADB, 2012).

The UIS will be collecting global data on ICT in education every two years, including on device type and deployment patterns. However, understanding the impact of ICT on outcomes will require better data on how, when and how much teachers and pupils use ICT. For internet use, such data will be far easier to collect through internet traffic statistics than through physical surveys. Finally, to the extent that mobile phones become more commonly used for teaching and learning in the future, provision should be made to monitor their use.

VIOLENCE AND ATTACKS IN SCHOOLS

SCHOOL-RELATED VIOLENCE

The UN World Report on Violence against Children identified violence in schools and other education settings as a global phenomenon (Pinheiro, 2006). School-related violent acts or threats comprise psychological, physical and sexual violence. They occur on school premises but also on the way to school, at home or in cyberspace. They are enforced by unequal power dynamics and are often the result of gender norms and stereotypes.

In schools, manifestations of violence include bullying, corporal punishment, verbal and emotional abuse, intimidation, sexual harassment and assault, gang activity and the presence of weapons. While attention usually focuses on extreme events, such as shootings, it is the more common and often unnoticed forms of violence that have the largest negative impact on the education experience of children and adolescents. These tend to be under-reported, as they often involve taboos (UNICEF, 2014d).

Large-scale, cross-country school-based surveys are increasingly used to collect data on aspects of violence in schools; some countries also have well-established monitoring mechanisms. Yet, overall, consistent evidence on the global prevalence of school-related violence is lacking. A recent report by the Technical Working Group on Data Collection on Violence against Children identified a surge of interest but also fragmented approaches. Studies use different definitions of violence and record different behaviours. Their methods are not consistent in terms of time frames, sequencing of questions, response options, privacy arrangements or ethical protocols (UNICEF, 2014e). Better coordination is needed to enable the monitoring of global trends.

Bullying is the most widely documented form of violence in schools

Bullying is repeated exposure to aggressive behaviour from peers with the intent to inflict injury or discomfort. It can include physical violence, verbal abuse and the intent to cause psychological harm through humiliation or exclusion.

The 2011 Trends in International Mathematics and Science Study (TIMSS) collected data on grade 8 students' experience of six bullying behaviours, such as whether someone 'spread lies' about them or made them 'do things' they did not want to do (Mullis et al., 2012). About 41% reported having been bullied at least once in the past month. In Ghana, almost four-fifths did so. Boys were more likely to report being victims of bullying in almost every country, a trend particularly notable in Japan and the Republic of Korea, as well as in Arab States, such as Bahrain and Qatar.

> " In the 2011 TIMSS, about 41% of grade 8 students reported having been bullied at least once in the past month "

The 2013 Third Regional Comparative and Explanatory Study (TERCE), administered to grade 6 students in 15 Latin American countries, distinguished between two forms of bullying,

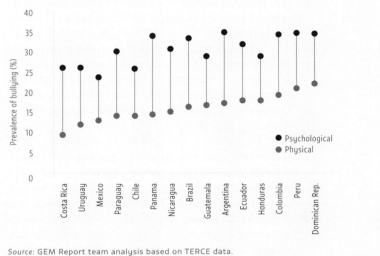

FIGURE 17.5:

In Latin America, psychological bullying is twice as prevalent as physical bullying
Percentage of grade 6 students who reported being bullied when in school, by type, 2013

Source: GEM Report team analysis based on TERCE data.

showing that psychological bullying was twice as prevalent as physical bullying. The prevalence of physical bullying varied from 9% in Costa Rica to 22% in the Dominican Republic, while rates of psychological bullying varied from 24% in Mexico to 35% in Peru (**Figure 17.5**).

The Health Behaviour in School-Aged Children Survey collects data every four years on health and well-being, social environments and health behaviours of boys and girls in more than 40 countries in Europe and North America. Results of the 2009/10 round show that those who reported having been bullied at least two or three times at school in the previous two months decreased from 13% among 11-year-olds to 9% among 15-year-olds. By contrast, the proportion who reported having bullied others increased from 8% among 11-year-olds to 12% among 15-year-olds (Currie et al., 2012). In the United States, 7% of students aged 12 to 18 reported having been cyberbullied during the previous year (Robers et al., 2015).

Physical violence is very common

Physical violence in schools manifests differently across countries. The Global School-based Student Health Survey (GSHS) asked adolescents whether they had been involved in physical fights at school in the past year. About 40% of 13- to 15-year-olds in 37 countries reported having been involved in physical fights between 2009 and 2012, and the prevalence reached almost 70% in Samoa (**Figure 17.6**).

In the United States, a large group of surveys administered over two decades allows the Departments of Justice and Education to monitor levels of physical violence. The rate of violent victimization at school of students ages 12-18 declined from 9% in 1993 to 4% in 2013. The percentage of grade 9-12 students carrying a weapon such as a gun, knife or club on school property declined from 12% to 5% during that period. But the percentage of those threatened or injured with such a weapon on school property remained constant at 7% (Robers et al., 2015).

In the Caribbean, school violence is a major problem. According to the Citizen Security Survey carried out in seven Caribbean countries, 16% of youth carried weapons during the day (UNDP, 2012). The Trinidad and Tobago Youth Survey, which was administered in about 25% of the country's secondary schools, albeit mostly in high risk urban areas, found that 6% of students were gang members and 8% were gang associates (Katz and Fox, 2010). The Community Safety and Security Branch of the Jamaica Constabulary Force regularly collects statistics on fights, stabbings and weapons found and seized in school (Jamaica Observer, 2015).

In the Caribbean, school violence is a major problem

A culture of physical violence is often embedded in teacher–pupil relations. In rural Uganda, in a baseline survey of 42 primary schools using the child institutional version of a screening tool developed by the International Society for the Prevention of Child Abuse and Neglect, 54% of students reported physical violence by a staff member (Devries et al., 2015). Such behaviour is sometimes condoned by communities and even tolerated by the state. According to the Global Initiative to End All Corporal Punishment of Children, corporal punishment of children in schools is not fully prohibited by law in 73 states (Global Initiative, 2015).

Much of the scale and scope of sexual violence in schools remains hidden

Sexual violence, a highly destructive form of violence in schools, is a global concern, yet knowledge of its extent is limited. It manifests as verbal and psychological harassment, sexual assault, rape, coercion, exploitation and discrimination in and around schools.

The 2007 Southern and Eastern Africa Consortium for Monitoring Educational Quality (SACMEQ) survey provides comparable data on sexual harassment in primary schools across 15 education systems in sub-Saharan Africa. In six countries, including Kenya and Zambia, over 40% of school principals reported that pupil–pupil sexual harassment had occurred either 'sometimes' or 'often'. Teachers were also reported to be perpetrators, with an average of 39% of school principals stating that teacher–pupil harassment had occurred in their schools, with the range varying from one-fifth of surveyed schools in Mozambique to over three-quarters in Seychelles (UNESCO, 2015j).

But the way school principals perceive the problem provides an incomplete picture. Violence against Children Surveys of youth aged 13 to 17 have collected information about the location and circumstances of incidences of sexual violence in eight countries. In Malawi, one in five females and one in eight males had experienced at least one incident of sexual abuse in the year prior to the survey in 2013. Among victims of abuse, 21% of boys and 10% of girls reported that their most recent experience of sexual abuse happened in schools (Malawi Ministry of Gender, Children, Disability, and Social Welfare, 2014).

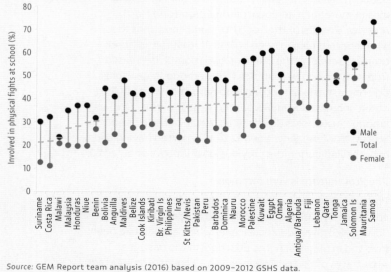

FIGURE 17.6:

Many adolescents across the world are involved in physical fights

Percentage of 13- to 15-year-olds who reported having been involved in physical fights over the past 12 months, 2009–2012

Source: GEM Report team analysis (2016) based on 2009–2012 GSHS data.

> " Violence and attacks against civilian populations in north-eastern Nigeria and neighbouring countries have forced more than 1 million children out of school "

School violence cannot be addressed unless it is better monitored

Wide-ranging information is becoming available on various facets of school-related violence around the world. But all three principal types of sources – self-reports, citizen perceptions and police statistics – have their weaknesses. A monitoring framework with standardized indicators would be a first step to improve reporting. The Technical Working Group on Data Collection on Violence against Children can help draw attention to good practice and methodological challenges. Core indicators should be integrated into national systems and international surveys, which currently approach school violence from a variety of perspectives. A higher degree of coordination is required to ensure that international surveys are carried out with sufficient regularity in the next 15 years to measure global school-based violence trends.

ATTACKS

Attacks related to education come in various forms. They are any intentional threat or use of force, including those directed at students and educators, at education institutions, including recruitment into armed groups. They can occur on the way to or from an education institution because of someone's status as a student or educator. They can be directed at activists, including teacher union members, as well as education personnel and education aid workers. Schools, teachers and students are often directly attacked, whether by state security forces or non-state armed groups, for political, military, ideological or sectarian reasons.

Such direct attacks have a disastrous effect on the affected individuals, but the wider effects of a climate of fear and instability can paralyse whole education systems. The risk of attack can force schools to close and discourage attendance and teacher recruitment. Violence and attacks against civilian populations in north-eastern Nigeria and neighbouring countries have forced more than 1 million children out of school, putting them at risk of dropping out altogether. In Nigeria alone, around

600 teachers have been killed during the Boko Haram insurgency (UNICEF, 2015d).

Monitoring such attacks is necessary to respond effectively and hold perpetrators accountable. However, obtaining accurate information is particularly challenging since incidents may often take place in remote areas with poor security and infrastructure, where governments may have little authority. More broadly, systems enabling schools, teachers, students and citizens to report incidents are often lacking.

One way to acquire first-hand, detailed data is to improve schools' capacity for reporting incidents to the government. Human rights monitoring groups such as the Committee on Economic, Social and Cultural Rights, the Human Rights Committee, the Committee on the Rights of the Child and the Human Rights Council could then use the data to bring greater attention to monitoring and reporting of attacks on education.

An open platform enabling teachers, students and citizens to report incidents anonymously holds promise, as those with information may lack skills, resources or motivation to make reports, and may face serious threats to their safety. The potential to receive such real-time information is expanding with the growing availability of mobile phone technology.

Following two reports published by UNESCO in 2007 and 2010, the Global Coalition to Protect Education from Attack (GCPEA) launched the third Education under Attack report in 2014. Based on analysis of interviews and secondary sources, the report documented pervasive violence against education institutions, teachers and students. The majority of the incidents were concentrated in certain countries. Between 2009 and 2012, 1,000 or more education-related attacks per country took place in Afghanistan, Colombia, Pakistan, Somalia, Sudan and the Syrian Arab Republic, and between 500 and 999 attacks in Côte d'Ivoire, the Democratic Republic of the Congo, Iraq, Israel, Libya, Mexico, Palestine and Yemen (GCPEA, 2014). Military use of schools took place in 26 countries between 2005 and 2015 (GCPEA, 2015). A fourth report is scheduled for release in 2018.

ENDNOTES

1. This section draws on Wallet (2016).

KEY MESSAGES

The target on scholarships could exacerbate inequality, because beneficiaries tend to come from more advantaged backgrounds.

The target's formulation is lacking in several respects. For example, it does not specify whether a degree should be completed or whether students should return to their home countries.

Scholarships should be counted as contributing to the target only if they are at least partly publicly funded, because it is not possible to hold non-government providers to account.

There is no single source of information on scholarship numbers, let alone on recipients' nationality or fields of study. Information collected for this report from 54 government scholarship programmes indicates that some 22,500 scholarships were offered in 2015, corresponding to 1% of the 2.5 million mobile students from developing countries.

Aid data can give partial information on scholarship programmes. In 2014, US$2.8 billion in aid was allocated to scholarships and imputed student costs. But only US$386 million of that was directed to least developed countries and small island developing states.

CHAPTER 18

TARGET 4.B

Scholarships

By 2020, substantially expand globally the number of scholarships available to developing countries, in particular least developed countries, small island developing States and African countries, for enrolment in higher education, including vocational training and information and communications technology, technical, engineering and scientific programmes, in developed countries and other developing countries

GLOBAL INDICATOR 4.B.1 – *Volume of official development assistance flows for scholarships, by sector and type of study*

THEMATIC INDICATOR 35 – *Number of higher education scholarships awarded, by beneficiary country*

Scholarship programmes are a means of providing higher education opportunities for suitably prepared youth and adults from developing countries who would otherwise not be able to afford them. Target 4.b reflects one of the commitments of the Istanbul Programme of Action for the Least Developed Countries for the Decade 2011–2020, which pledged to '[c]ontinue providing, and encourage, as appropriate, higher education institutes to allocate, places and scholarships for students and trainees from least developed countries, in particular in the fields of science, technology, business management and economics' (United Nations, 2011).

As the 2015 *Education for All Global Monitoring Report* noted, the formulation of target 4.b came as a surprise. Because it targets specific countries, it does not appear consistent with a universal agenda. While it nominally aspires to reduce inequality in access between countries, it could instead exacerbate it because beneficiaries tend to have advantaged backgrounds and easier access to information about scholarship programmes. In addition, there is some evidence that a considerable share of scholarship recipients do not return to their countries after ending their studies (Hein and Plesch, 2009). This would suggest that scholarships tend to support the higher education institutions of developed countries instead of benefiting developing countries. This chapter reviews available sources of information and finds several obstacles to achieving this target.

NUMBER OF SCHOLARSHIPS

CHALLENGES IN DEFINING SCHOLARSHIPS

A close analysis of target 4.b raises many questions and finds its formulation to be lacking in several respects.[1] The target refers to scholarships being 'available' rather than 'awarded'. An agency in a developed country may advertise a scholarship to everyone in the world but award it to a student from a developed country, or target a scholarship to candidates from developing countries but not award it. Target 4.b should therefore be interpreted to mean that scholarships are available to students from developing countries, these scholarships are awarded, and the offers are accepted.

> 66 **The target should be interpreted to mean the number of scholarships 'awarded', rather than 'available'** 99

The target states that scholarships must be 'available to developing countries'. This wording suggests that they do not originate in developing countries and thus would exclude cases where developing countries fund scholarships out of their own resources for their citizens to study abroad. That in turn raises questions beyond the traditional concept of aid flows from one country to another. For example, should the government of Indonesia or Tajikistan or Zimbabwe expand the number of scholarships for its citizens to study abroad or instead invest these resources in its own universities?

Even if we limit attention to scholarships made 'available to developing countries' from external sources, should all scholarship programmes based in developed countries be counted equally? Government and public higher education institutions are not the only providers; corporations, foundations, non-government organisations, philanthropists and other individuals also donate scholarship funds.

For example in 2013, the MasterCard Foundation announced a US$500 million programme of scholarship support for students from sub-Saharan Africa. Other private corporations run their own scholarship programmes. The Tullow Group Scholarship Scheme funds a programme managed by the British Council that makes scholarships available in selected sub-Saharan African and Latin American countries where Tullow Oil operates. The Graça Machel SASOL Scholarships are available to women from Mozambique. Yet, making non-state scholarship providers accountable for achievement of the target does not appear to make much sense. These are not public funds and there is no obligation to make, let alone to 'substantially expand', such contributions.

Note that even government scholarship programmes can have a mix of funding sources. For example, the two main UK government scholarship programmes that are open to students from developing countries are the Chevening Scholarships, funded through the Foreign and Commonwealth Office, and the Commonwealth Scholarships, funded mostly through the Department for International Development. Both actively solicit co-funding from private and philanthropic interests.

The target also states that scholarships must be tenable 'in developed countries and other developing countries'. 'Other' is the keyword here. The target refers to scholarships for students who cross a border to study at a higher education institution in a country other than their own. Just as the target does not mean scholars who are supported by their own government to study abroad, it would also exclude programmes that sponsor nationals of developing countries to study in their own country, such as USAID scholarships in Pakistan. Thus the Fulbright programme, which offers scholarships for post-graduate study in the United States, would qualify under this target, while a larger programme that in 2015 offered 3,000 university scholarships for study in Pakistan, half to women, would not.

Even if non-government scholarship programmes funded by developed countries were to be counted for this target, issues would remain unresolved. The MasterCard Foundation scholarships are applicable at a range of schools and universities, in developed and developing countries, including a recipient's home country. Under this programme, a Ghanaian student could study in Ghana, Nigeria or the United States. In the second and third cases, these scholarships would qualify under target 4.b, because the recipients are studying 'in developed countries' (United States) or 'other developing countries' (Nigeria). But the student studying in Ghana would not qualify.

It is also unclear whether the target includes scholarships for study by distance learning, which is increasingly popular. 'Split site' arrangements allow developing country students to be registered at a home university but have their research supervised by staff at a university in a developed country. How would these scholarships be considered?

> **The target does not refer to the completion of a degree, or whether students return to their home countries**

Scholarships must be 'for enrolment in higher education'. However, enrolment is not equivalent to graduation. Although many scholarship programmes track success rates as far as graduation, few go beyond that. The number of scholarships awarded does not indicate the completion of a degree, or whether students return to their home countries.

A related question is whether a scholarship should have particular characteristics in terms of duration and size. For comparability purposes, scholarships would also have to be specified in terms of year-equivalents to ensure that short-term placements are not counted as equal to longer ones, and to prevent incentives against scholarships for longer programmes. In addition, the amount awarded may cover full or partial tuition as well as living expenses. It is not clear how such options would count in terms of their contribution towards the target.

Finally, methods of support besides scholarships do not count toward the target, even though they may serve the same objective. For example, the Partnership for Higher Education in Africa, a consortium of funding bodies from the United States, dedicated US$440 million towards higher education initiatives in nine African countries between 2000 and 2010 (PHEA, 2010). While it did not provide scholarships directly to individuals, it did include grants, usually to universities, through which scholarships were awarded. But as a subsidiary part of the programme, these scholarships may not have been reported as such, and would have been difficult to track.

Therefore, it is recommended that scholarships be counted as eligible under target 4.b to the extent that they are taken up by (not just made available to) students from developing countries (available to 'students', not just 'countries'). The scholarships should refer to study at higher education institutions in countries other than the students' home country, including those by distance learning. They should require no further contribution from the student to meet study, travel and living costs. Finally, they should be, at least partly, publicly funded and accounted for as a scholarship in the public accounts of the donor countries (including scholarships co-funded by private interests).

This will exclude many scholarships, especially from private and philanthropic sources, since they are under no obligation to sponsor scholarships in the first place. It is still necessary to monitor these scholarships since their availability can influence the policies and actions of donor countries, which might spend less on scholarships in response.

It is further recommended that a set of indicators include the number of scholarships awarded; the number of scholarship years awarded; the number of scholarship recipients who complete their studies; and the number of scholarship recipients who return to their country. All indicators would be disaggregated by country origin of beneficiary, sex, field of study, level of study, mode of study (e.g. on site vs distance) and country of study.

DATA CHALLENGES AND NEXT STEPS

Even this more precise definition of scholarships presents a major challenge because providers have not designed monitoring and reporting systems to respond to such a global target. Hardly any studies have tried to assess scholarship trends. The few that have tried to look at scholarships across countries have stumbled; there are insufficient measures to evaluate policies and programmes (CSC, 2014). The absence of common or shared standards for publicly reporting scholarship programme data limits the chances of obtaining consistent and reliable data on levels of government funding and on numbers of applicants and recipients (Perna et al., 2014).

What is known is the size of the total target population for scholarship programmes, which is the number of internationally mobile students in higher education. In 2013, out of a global population of 199 million students in post-secondary institutions, 3.5 million were studying outside their country, of which 2.5 million were from developing countries. With respect to the country groups

identified in the target, there were 235,000 students from least developed countries, 271,000 from sub-Saharan Africa and 106,000 from small island developing states. Among the 90 countries belonging to these three groups (some belong to two or even all three of them), there were 451,000 mobile students.

The outbound mobility ratio, i.e. the number of students from a country studying abroad, expressed as a percentage of total tertiary enrolment in that country, was 1.8% for developing countries. However, in some countries, notably among small island developing states, the ratio is considerably higher. For example, in Saint Lucia, there are 5 nationals studying abroad for every 10 students in the country. In Seychelles, there are twice as many tertiary students abroad than at home (**Figure 18.1**).

Establishing a baseline against which to measure progress towards target 4.b is challenging due to the limited data on recipients' characteristics. Many programmes are reluctant to share detailed information. Funders might consider recipient data confidential and proprietary, just as how some higher education institutions do not disclose how admission decisions are made. Also, disclosing recipient data might reveal that some programmes are not meeting their declared targets

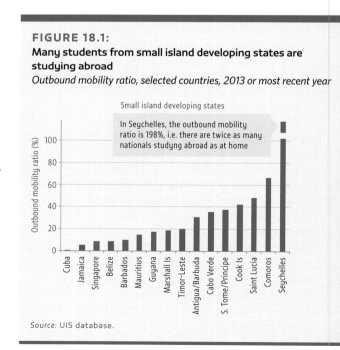

FIGURE 18.1:

Many students from small island developing states are studying abroad

Outbound mobility ratio, selected countries, 2013 or most recent year

Small island developing states

In Seychelles, the outbound mobility ratio is 198%, i.e. there are twice as many nationals studying abroad as at home

Source: UIS database.

> **Around 22,500 scholarships were offered in 2015, corresponding to 1% of the number of internationally mobile students from developing countries**

for some populations. Many large programmes do not assign quotas by country so this information is not even monitored. The absence of data is not limited to the nationality of scholarship recipients but extends to all other characteristics of interest listed in the target, such as destination countries and fields of study ('information and communications technology, technical, engineering and scientific programmes').

Information collected for this report from 54 government scholarship programmes, of which 9 were based in developing countries, indicates that some 22,500 scholarships were offered in 2014/15, corresponding to 1% of the number of mobile students from developing countries (IIE, 2016a). While this is likely to be an underestimate, it is the best baseline available.

Scholarship programmes need to more openly share information that can lead to better understanding of how they contribute to the target 4.b. Programmes should be encouraged to collect and report disaggregated data on intended recipients, actual recipients and their country of origin. To move forward, three options can be considered.

First, governments of developing countries could monitor and report the number of their tertiary-level students receiving scholarships from domestic or external sources. This approach would miss individuals not enrolled in their home country who receive scholarships to pursue full degrees overseas.

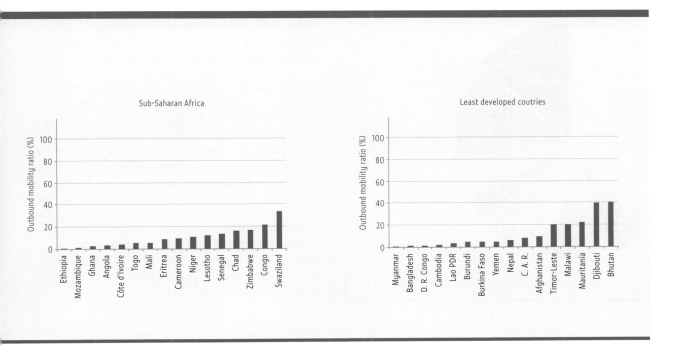

Second, higher education institutions could be engaged by their supervising authority to gather and report data on foreign students as to whether they use scholarship funds. For example, in the United States, the Department of Education Integrated Postsecondary Education Data System could require all accredited institutions to report the number of students from other countries pursuing studies on scholarship.

Third, an independent, non-government entity could be appointed to incorporate scholarship information into existing student mobility data collection efforts, especially since many scholarship recipients are already captured in such data. For example, the Institute of International Education operates Project Atlas, bringing together 25 national-level mobility data collection agencies from around the world that annually share data on the number of foreign students they receive and the number of their domestic students that study overseas. Project Atlas includes all major host countries of globally mobile students, including Australia, Canada, China, France, Germany, the United Kingdom and the United States (IIE, 2016b).

AID DATA ON SCHOLARSHIPS

An alternative way to get information on scholarship programmes is through examining aid to education. Much debate has occurred as to whether scholarships should be counted as official development assistance. The definition of the Organisation for Economic Co-operation and Development (OECD) of 'core' aid, otherwise referred to as country programmable aid, excludes scholarships.

Data from the OECD Development Assistance Committee (DAC) provide some evidence on aid from OECD DAC member states that is directed at scholarships and imputed student costs. The latter are the costs incurred for students from developing countries studying at higher education institutions of host countries. However, OECD DAC member states vary a lot in how they report this expenditure.

For France and Germany, scholarships and imputed student costs (i.e. indirect costs of tuition in donor countries) account for more than half of their total direct aid to education. These two donors provide more aid as scholarships and imputed student costs than all donors together do for basic education in low income countries.

By contrast, the United Kingdom and the United States are major providers of scholarships but only a very small proportion of these are registered as aid. An aid-based measure of scholarships does not therefore provide a comprehensive picture of expenditure on scholarships and is not appropriate as a global indicator.

Nevertheless, this indicator is still informative. In 2014, an average of US$2.8 billion of aid was allocated to scholarships and imputed student costs. Most of this funding goes to middle income countries (81%). China is the single largest recipient (13%) and its share is almost equal to that received by all least developed countries and small island developing states together. Scholarships and imputed student costs for Algeria, China, India, Morocco, Tunisia and Turkey in 2014 came almost to the equivalent of the total amount of direct aid to basic education in low income countries that year (**Figure 18.2**). At the same time, China provides thousands of scholarships every year, notably through the Forum on China-Africa Cooperation (Reilly, 2015).

FIGURE 18.2:
Half of all aid for scholarships and imputed student costs is concentrated in 13 middle income countries
Distribution of scholarships and imputed student costs by recipient country, 2014

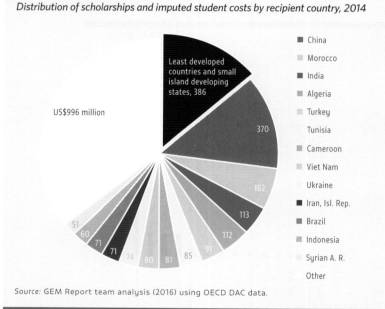

Source: GEM Report team analysis (2016) using OECD DAC data.

About 70% of aid to higher education in 2013/14 was disbursed for scholarships and imputed student costs rather than strengthening higher education institutions in developing countries. The share varied from 57% in low income countries to 83% in upper middle income countries (**Figure 18.3**).

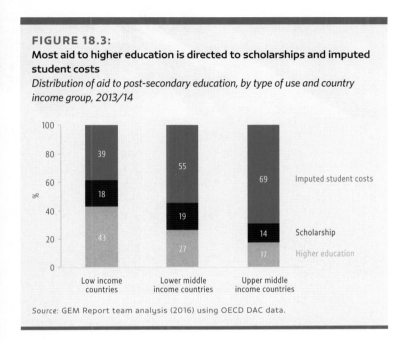

FIGURE 18.3:

Most aid to higher education is directed to scholarships and imputed student costs

Distribution of aid to post-secondary education, by type of use and country income group, 2013/14

Source: GEM Report team analysis (2016) using OECD DAC data.

ENDNOTES

1. This section draws on Balfour (2016).

Ednam Boyle,
a teacher, teaches
a class with her baby
on her back in the
Temple of Faith Primary
School, Western Area of
Freetown, Sierra Leone.

CREDIT: Kate Holt/GEM Report

KEY MESSAGES

There are two major challenges in defining a teacher shortage. First, showing how many teachers are available in a country does not show how many there are per school. Second, the quantity of teachers cannot be isolated from quality.

Data are scarce on the number of **qualified teachers** classified by academic qualification. In 2014, on average, 82% of teachers had the minimum qualifications required to teach in pre-primary education, 93% in primary education and 91% in secondary education.

Comparing how many teachers are trained in each country is difficult because national standards are not comparable.

Many teachers have not received minimum training. In the Caribbean, 85% of primary school teachers are trained. In Northern Africa and Western Asia, 73% of pre-primary school teachers are trained. In sub-Saharan Africa, less than half of pre-primary and less than three quarters of secondary school teachers are trained.

Aid to teacher training tripled between 2002 and 2014 to reach US$251 million. Least developed countries received 41% of the total.

The target is very narrowly defined. It is also necessary to monitor whether teachers are **motivated and supported**. This includes monitoring induction and mentoring programmes, on-the-job training, working conditions and contracts, pay and teacher attrition.

CHAPTER 19

TARGET 4.C

Teachers

By 2030, substantially increase the supply of qualified teachers, including through international cooperation for teacher training in developing countries, especially least developed countries and small island developing States

GLOBAL INDICATOR 4.C.1 – *Proportion of teachers in: (a) pre-primary; (b) primary; (c) lower secondary; and (d) upper secondary education who have received at least the minimum organized teacher training (e.g. pedagogical) pre-service or in-service required for teaching at the relevant level in a given country*

THEMATIC INDICATOR 37 – *Percentage of teachers qualified according to national standards, by education level and type of institution*

THEMATIC INDICATOR 38 – *Pupil/qualified teacher ratio, by education level*

THEMATIC INDICATOR 40 – *Pupil/trained teacher ratio, by education level*

THEMATIC INDICATOR 41 – *Average teacher salary relative to other professions requiring a comparable level of education qualification*

THEMATIC INDICATOR 42 – *Teacher attrition rate, by education level*

THEMATIC INDICATOR 43 – *Percentage of teachers who received in-service training in the last 12 months, by type of training*

The formulation of a target on teachers has been both applauded and criticized. The international community recognizes the importance of a distinct target relating to the teaching profession, which had been missing from the Education for All and Millennium Development Goals agendas. However, there has been dissatisfaction that in the Sustainable Development Goals (SDGs), teachers are considered a means of implementation, which risks underestimating the profession's fundamental contribution to the provision of good quality education and an enabling learning environment. The actual formulation of the target is also weak, referring only to the 'supply of qualified teachers' and including a limited conception of how to enhance teachers' qualifications.

This chapter will go beyond these relatively narrow confines to address the monitoring implications of the more general commitment, expressed in the Education 2030 Framework for Action, to 'ensure that teachers and educators are empowered, adequately recruited, well-trained, professionally qualified, motivated and supported'.

ADEQUATE SUPPLY OF QUALIFIED TEACHERS

Overcrowded classrooms are still common in many of the poorest countries, pointing to an inadequate supply of teachers. The 'teacher gap' is the number of teachers at each education level needing to be recruited to achieve universal enrolment while ensuring that the average pupil/teacher ratio does not exceed a set target level. In richer countries, teacher shortages are reflected in hard-to-fill vacancies in specialized subjects, resulting in teachers teaching subjects for which they are not qualified (Santiago, 2002).

There are two major challenges in defining a teacher shortage. First, statistics on average teacher availability hide substantial inequality within countries. Second, the quantity of teachers cannot be isolated from quality. Policy-makers have often responded to the challenge of expanding enrolment and increasing class size by lowering hiring standards.

TEACHER AVAILABILITY AND DEPLOYMENT

The traditional indicator of teacher availability is the pupil/teacher ratio. Globally, there are 17 pupils per teacher in pre-primary education, 24 in primary education, and 18 in lower and upper secondary education.

> " Globally, there are 17 pupils per teacher in pre-primary education, 24 in primary education, and 18 in lower and upper secondary education "

Yet, there is no global consensus on the recommended pupil/teacher ratio by level of education. Moreover, while a higher pupil/teacher ratio is linked with a larger average class size, the relationship is not one-to-one and varies considerably between countries. Class size depends on how teachers are allocated to classes. This, in turn, is linked to factors such as the proportion of time teachers spend teaching and the relationship between the length of the teacher working day and student instruction time.

In a group of about 30 mostly high income countries, a pupil/teacher ratio of 10 was linked with an average class size of 20 in primary and lower secondary education. For a pupil/teacher ratio of 17 in primary education, the average class size was 18 in Slovakia but 27 in Japan in 2013. Likewise, for an average class size of 27 in lower secondary education, the pupil/teacher ratio was 15 in the United States but 32 in Mexico (**Figure 19.1**).

FIGURE 19.1:

The pupil/teacher ratio is not the same as the number of students in a classroom

Pupil/teacher ratio and average class size, selected middle and high income countries, 2013

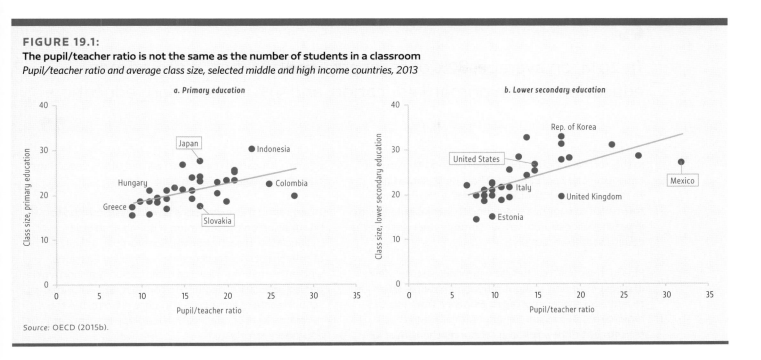

Source: OECD (2015b).

In richer countries, there is no solid evidence that a smaller class size has a positive effect on learning outcomes, or, where such an effect has been established, that it is sizeable (Hanushek, 2006). In poorer countries, evidence from the SACMEQ learning achievement survey in southern and eastern Africa suggested negative effects once a class size exceeded 60 (Fehrler et al., 2009).

But recent examples have raised doubt about the direct effect on learning of lowering class size from even these high levels unless accompanied by interventions to improve teacher quality. For example, data from the Uwezo citizen-led assessment survey in Uganda in 2010–2013 showed that average class size in government primary schools was 68 but even halving it would have a negligible effect on learning (Jones, 2016). Similarly, in a randomized control trial among 210 primary schools in the former Western Province of Kenya, the effect of nearly halving the first grade class size from 82 to 44 had no effect on learning (Duflo et al., 2015).

The pupil/teacher ratio indicator has further weaknesses, as it does not reflect real availability of teachers in classrooms. While the UNESCO Institute for Statistics (UIS) tries to collect data on teachers working full time, many countries still report on total teacher headcount regardless of working hours (UIS, 2006).

Nor does the pupil/teacher ratio account for teacher absenteeism. Views vary as to whether teachers are at fault for not turning up at work or whether governments poorly manage teacher time, for example by requiring them to travel to be paid or to fulfil non-school duties. Regardless, absenteeism remains high in some countries. In Indonesia, the percentage of primary school teachers not in classrooms during two unannounced visits fell from 19% in 2003 but was still 10% in 2013 (ACDP, 2014).

The problem of absenteeism is multilayered. A survey of 100 primary schools in 17 disadvantaged districts in the United Republic of Tanzania found that 12% of teachers were absent from school on the day of an unannounced visit in 2014. Of the teachers present, 63% had arrived late, and 67% of the teachers present at school and scheduled to teach were not in the classroom (Pettersson and Rawle, 2015). Service Delivery Indicator surveys of primary schools in seven countries of sub-Saharan Africa in 2011–2014 estimated that, out of average scheduled daily teaching time of 5 hours and 31 minutes, teachers spent 2 hours and 53 minutes teaching, or 52% (Filmer, 2016).

Teachers may be deployed unequally among schools. In Uganda, where there were as many as 57 pupils per teacher on average in primary schools in 2010, 20 out of 112 districts had more than 70 pupils per teacher. While only 13% of schools had a teacher deficit in the district of the capital, Kampala, 100% of schools had a deficit

> 66
>
> In 2014, on average, 82% of teachers were qualified in pre-primary education, 93% in primary education, and 91% in secondary education
>
> 99

in the northern district of Kotido (Uganda Ministry of Education and Sport and IIEP Pôle de Dakar, 2014). In rural China, a shift of deployment authority from townships to counties was found to increase inequality in teacher allocation to favour communities close to the county seat (Han, 2013).

Finally, the pupil/teacher ratio provides a static view of a past situation without reflecting national efforts to address teacher shortages. Evidence from the UIS regional module in sub-Saharan Africa shows that recruitment of new primary school teachers, relative to teacher stocks, was higher on average in countries with higher pupil/teacher ratios, as would be expected of lagging countries trying to catch up. But among them there were wide variations. For example, Niger had a pupil/teacher ratio of 39 in 2012 but recruited new teachers in 2010–2013 at a rate three times faster than Madagascar, which had a pupil/teacher ratio of 43.

DEFINING QUALIFIED TEACHERS

In addition to these weaknesses, the simple pupil/ teacher ratio assumes that all those teaching are fully qualified and prepared to teach. This is why the target refers to the supply of 'qualified' teachers, to ensure that quality is not compromised. However, the definition of 'qualified' is ambiguous. It is understood in terms of both academic qualifications (the level of education a teacher has completed, regardless of domain of study) and training qualifications (successful completion of a training course that represents the minimum condition to enter teaching). A teacher may possess one but not the other. The proposed global indicator focuses on training rather than academic qualifications.

Academic qualifications

The percentage of teachers with the minimum academic qualifications required to teach at each level of education is the indicator that captures the intention of target 4.c, although it was not proposed as the global indicator. Overall, the median share of qualified teachers was 82% in pre-primary education (based on 59 countries), 93% in

primary education (84 countries), and 91% in secondary education (60 countries) in 2014.

Interpreting these statistics is not possible without information on the minimum required academic qualification in each country. For example, only 47% of primary school teachers are qualified in Palestine, where the minimum level of qualification is a short-cycle tertiary education degree. By contrast, 88% of primary school teachers are qualified in Côte d'Ivoire, but the minimum level of qualification is an upper secondary education certificate.

The new UIS global module on teachers collects information on the minimum academic qualifications required to teach at each level of education; thus far the information is available for 37 countries. It shows, for example, that to teach in pre-primary education, a primary school diploma is required in Mauritania but a bachelor's or equivalent degree in Algeria. To teach primary school, an upper secondary diploma is enough in China but a bachelor's or equivalent degree is needed in Indonesia. Such information clearly is needed for all countries.

Training qualifications

According to the UIS, a trained teacher has 'at least the minimum organized teacher training requirements (pre-service or in-service) to teach a specific level of education according to the relevant national policy or law'. The requirements usually include pedagogical knowledge (approaches, methods and techniques of teaching) and professional knowledge (instruments and legal frameworks governing the teaching profession). Some programmes may also cover content knowledge (curriculum, subject matter and use of relevant materials).

The entry requirements for such training differ by country, however, and no information is available on the level of training required. In that sense, the global indicator for target 4.c – the percentage of teachers with minimum training – is even weaker than the percentage of teachers with minimum academic qualifications, as there is no benchmark with which to compare the data.

The coverage of both indicators remains low. In 2014, the percentage of countries with data for the global indicator of trained teachers varied from 22% in upper secondary education to 46% in primary. Coverage has increased little over time: it was 34% for primary education in 1999. For the qualified teacher indicator, coverage is about seven percentage points lower than for the trained teacher indicator.

There are several reasons for data gaps. In some cases, data simply do not exist – for example, countries with a large private education sector often cannot report accurately on personnel in the sector. More commonly, data exist but require coordination of several databases. New UIS initiatives to collect global teacher data, as well as subnational teacher data in Asia, will help countries better integrate education information systems.

Despite the limitations, there is clear evidence that a large share of teachers appears not to have received the minimum training. For example, in the Caribbean only 85% of primary school teachers are trained. In Northern Africa and Western Asia, only 73% of pre-primary school teachers are trained. In sub-Saharan Africa, fewer than half of pre-primary and three quarters of secondary school teachers are trained (**Figure 19.2**).

If countries are ranked in terms of the percentage of trained teachers, from lowest to highest, fewer countries are seen to have a very low percentage of untrained teachers in primary than in pre-primary education. For example, in the bottom quarter of countries, at least one in four primary teachers are not trained. This compares with one in two at the pre-primary level. In the bottom half of countries, at least one in four pre-primary teachers are not trained (**Figure 19.3**).

Higher country coverage would not be enough to indicate all the trained teacher gaps. For example, the percentage of trained staff may be lowest in pre-primary education but the situation is likely to be worse for early childhood care and education as a whole, as teachers tend to have higher initial education requirements than carers. Thus, carers may remain without sufficient education or training. However, there are exceptions. For example, in some high income countries, such as Japan and Portugal, both types of staff must have initial education at the tertiary level. Some countries, including the Czech Republic, Israel and Italy, provide integrated initial education to care workers and pre-primary teachers (OECD, 2012a).

FIGURE 19.2:

More than half of pre-primary and one-quarter of secondary school teachers in sub-Saharan Africa are not trained

Percentage of trained teachers, by education level and region, 2014

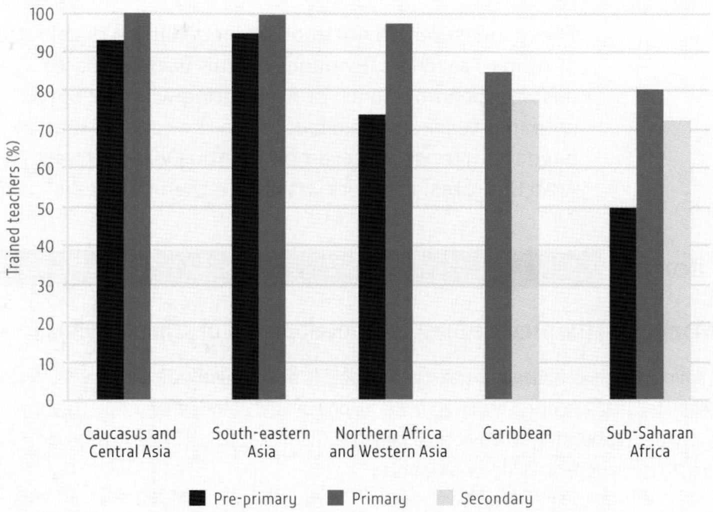

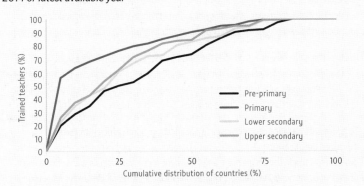

Source: UIS database.

FIGURE 19.3:

In half of countries, more than one in four pre-primary teachers are not trained

Cumulative distribution of percentage of trained teachers, by level of education, 2014 or latest available year

Note: Distributions were calculated over 76 countries in pre-primary education, 96 in primary, 56 in lower secondary and 50 in upper secondary.
Source: UIS database.

In secondary education, in addition to training qualifications, many countries face teacher gaps in particular specializations. In Germany in 2009, 28% of secondary school principals said they faced a shortage of mathematics teachers and 42% a shortage of science teachers (European Commission/EACEA/Eurydice, 2012b). Almost half of all principals in countries that participated in the 2013 Teaching and Learning International Survey (TALIS) reported a shortage of teachers with competence in teaching students with special needs (OECD, 2014c).

These measures do not capture inequality in distribution of trained teachers. Evidence on this issue is scarce despite the importance of monitoring whether better-prepared teachers are allocated to the schools that need them most. For example, in Abu Dhabi, United Arab Emirates, teachers with more than five years

of teaching experience are 60% less likely to work in schools with higher proportions of students from diverse language backgrounds. In Sweden, teachers with more experience are half as likely to work in schools with larger proportions of students from socio-economically disadvantaged homes (OECD, 2014c). This is the result of both allocation decisions and higher teacher turnover rates in challenging schools.

Finally, some categories of educators require specialized training but are not covered by general measurements. Notably, school principals are engaged in an increasingly complex set of activities and their qualifications need to be monitored (**Box 19.1**).

As was shown above, minimum training requirements are difficult to compare across countries. In particular, initial teacher education courses differ in terms of duration, length of induction period and modality – whether they are provided alongside general education or after the completion of subject-based study. In the case of subject teachers, courses also differ with respect to the degree of specialization (European Commission/EACEA/Eurydice, 2012b).

Structural aspects also make comparing qualifications difficult, for a number of reasons (Tatto et al., 2012). For example, countries may apply more or less strict criteria for admission to teacher education programmes. Botswana requires candidates for primary and lower secondary mathematics teacher training to prove proficiency in mathematics before enrolling.

Country policies of teacher education programme quality assurance differ. In Thailand, the Office for National Education Standards and Quality Assessment is an external evaluation body with the power to rescind programmes' accreditation. Chile encourages alternative teacher education provision, which inflates the supply of trainee posts and lowers admission criteria, but the system is not regulated.

Some countries add a layer of quality assurance by not allowing all graduates of teacher education programmes into the profession. In Oman and the Philippines, those with a teaching qualification must also take a test set by external agencies (Tatto et al., 2012).

The profile of teacher educators differs as well, particularly in poorer countries where they may have had very little training themselves. Analysis in six sub-Saharan African countries found that early reading teacher

---

BOX 19.1

Monitoring the preparedness and development of school leaders

Committed school leaders can transform schools. In richer countries, it has been estimated that school leadership accounts for one-quarter of the difference in student outcomes explained by school-related variables. This makes school leadership second only to teachers as an influence on learning.

However, cross-country information on school leader qualifications is fragmented. In Europe, headship training is required in 21 countries or regions; the duration varies from one week in Romania to a master's programme in Malta. Specific training programmes also exist in countries where it is not an official requirement for appointment.

In countries that participated in the 2013 TALIS, 92% of lower secondary principals had tertiary education qualifications but many lacked preparation for specific tasks. For example, only 14% of principals in Denmark had participated in school administration or principal training programmes prior to their appointment, and 45% had still not done so by the time of the survey. The latter share was as high as 51% in Serbia and 58% in Croatia. In addition, 41% of principals in Spain and 57% in Poland had never received training in instructional leadership.

In Chile, the government introduced the Good School Leadership Framework, a competitive process for selecting principals, and in 2011 the Programme for the Training of Excellent Principals, which in its first two years trained more than one-third of principals in leadership skills through graduate degrees.

To address its absence of a professional qualification, South Africa introduced an Advanced Certificate in Education: School Leadership. Following positive evaluation, the government made the programme a requirement for new principals within three years of their appointment. Jamaica recently established the National Centre for Educational Leadership to train and certify aspiring and existing principals.

In poorer countries, it is rare for school heads or principals to have preparation or in-service training; they get little support from local education authorities. Among 12 mostly low income sub-Saharan African and South Asian countries, only Bangladesh made an effort to train all school leaders.

Sources: Bennell and Akyeampong (2007), Bruns and Luque (2014), Bush (2008), Bush and Glover (2012), European Commission/EACEA/Eurydice (2013), Leithwood et al. (2008), OECD (2014c), Vaillant (2015).

educators were rarely experts in the field (Pryor et al., 2012). In Eritrea, Gambia and Zambia, instructors in many primary school teacher preparation courses tended to be former secondary school teachers with little experience of teaching at the primary level (Mulkeen, 2010).

The introduction of a global indicator defined in terms of professional qualifications is expected to increase the pool of information on trained teachers. However, more work needs to be done to develop system-level indicators that capture more accurately the nuances in minimum requirements for entering the profession. Even so, the extent to which teachers meet the requirements is not a predictor of their skills (**Box 19.2**).

INTERNATIONAL COOPERATION IN TEACHER TRAINING

The target formulation explicitly refers to 'international cooperation for teacher training in developing countries, especially least developed countries and small island developing States' as a means of increasing the supply of qualified teachers. However, this addition to the target seems out of proportion to the role that international cooperation can play in teacher education.

The OECD Development Assistance Committee, which is the international platform on aid finance, has a special code for teacher training. It does not capture the total amount of external support to teacher training, though, as part of it may be subsumed under general purpose codes. Between 2002 and 2014, donors tripled their disbursements from US$77 million to US$251 million, which is equivalent to 2% of total direct aid to education. Least developed countries received 41% of total aid to teacher training and small island developing states 7%. The three donors that prioritized teacher training the most in their education aid portfolio in 2014 were Canada (9.5%), Portugal (8.5%) and Australia (6.2%).

TEACHER MOTIVATION AND SUPPORT

How to motivate and support teachers does not feature in the formulation of target 4.c but is a major policy concern reflected in the Education 2030 Framework for Action, which asserts that strongly supported and motivated teachers are more likely to ensure that learners benefit from their classroom experience. Models have been proposed to explain how personalities, values and skills interact with external factors and circumstances to shape

---

BOX 19.2

Directly assessing teacher skills

Improving data on teacher qualifications will yield better information on how school systems comply with minimum standards, but will not address the need for evidence on teacher knowledge and skills. Given the diversity of competencies teachers bring to the classroom, it is unrealistic to look for global measures of teacher skills. But some aspects of teacher competencies can be assessed. The initiatives discussed below should be followed closely. While they may not lead to global indicators, they are likely to answer policy questions at the regional and national levels and could provide useful benchmarks.

On general knowledge, data from 23 countries that participated in 2011 in the OECD Programme for the International Assessment of Adult Competencies (PIAAC) showed that teachers' numeracy skills relative to those of the average employed adult with a university degree varied substantially. For example, the numeracy skills of teachers in France and Spain were at the top 75% to 80% of the average adult skill distribution, whereas teachers in Denmark and the Russian Federation were close to the middle of the distribution.

On subject-specific skills, as part of SACMEQ in 2007, grade 6 teachers took the same assessment as their students. Analysis for this report shows that results varied strongly among the 15 countries. While only 2% of teachers in Kenya scored below the concrete problem-solving level in mathematics, the share was 35% in South Africa, 39% in Mozambique and 43% in Zambia. The next round of the CONFEMEN Programme for Analysis of Education Systems (PASEC) in francophone African countries in 2019 will include a similar assessment of teacher skills.

On professional skills, the Teacher Education and Development Study in Mathematics (TEDS-M), conducted by the International Association for the Evaluation of Educational Achievement, assessed teacher trainees in terms of pedagogical content knowledge. It included three subdomains: curricular knowledge, knowledge of planning for teaching and learning, and enacting mathematics for teaching and learning. A proficiency level was developed which corresponded to the ability to 'recognize whether or not a teaching strategy was correct for a particular concrete example, and to evaluate students' work when the content was conventional or typical of the primary grades'. Less than 1% of teachers who were being trained for the lower primary grades in Georgia achieved the level, compared with 44% in Germany.

In the OECD, the Teacher Knowledge Survey, a pilot survey in six countries in 2016, will assess the general pedagogical knowledge of lower secondary school teachers, trainee teachers and teacher educators. The survey will assess teachers' performance in three key areas of pedagogy required for effective teaching: instruction, learning and assessment.

Sources: Hanushek et al. (2014); König (2014); Tatto et al. (2012).

---

teachers' thoughts, feelings and beliefs (Neves de Jesus and Lens, 2005; Richardson et al., 2014) (**Figure 19.4**).

Recent comparative studies have provided valuable insights. For example, the 2013 TALIS showed that teachers' levels of job satisfaction were higher when they had opportunities to participate in decision-making

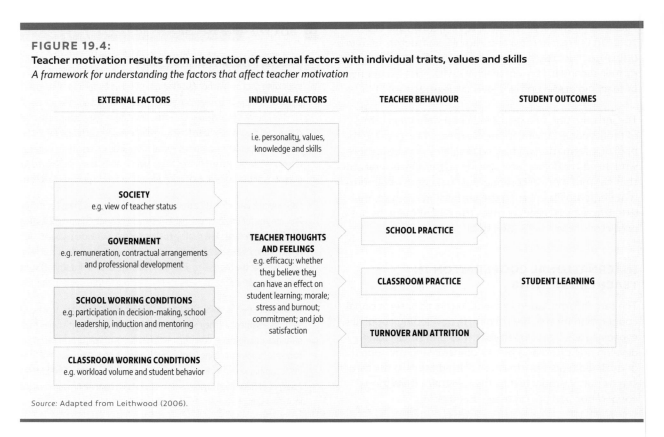

FIGURE 19.4:
Teacher motivation results from interaction of external factors with individual traits, values and skills
A framework for understanding the factors that affect teacher motivation

Source: Adapted from Leithwood (2006).

in schools, collaborate with colleagues and receive meaningful feedback from their supervisors (OECD, 2014c).

A diagnostic tool on teacher motivation in poorer countries was developed by two international non-governmental organizations (NGOs) on behalf of the Teacher Motivation Working Group and piloted in Bangladesh, India, Uganda and Viet Nam. It includes asking teachers to describe whether they feel they can influence decisions at the school and how to deal with students who lag behind (Save the Children and World Vision, 2015).

However, the collection of direct information across countries on motivation and job satisfaction would entail considerable challenges for the purposes of international monitoring, which requires consistent definitions to capture long-term trends.

This chapter covers selected aspects of teacher motivation and support. It looks at external factors, primarily related to government policy: induction and mentoring mechanisms for new teachers; continuous professional development opportunities; working conditions, notably in terms of contractual arrangements; and remuneration. It then reviews evidence on one potential manifestation of low motivation: the rate at

which teachers leave the profession. Overall, it suggests there is a long way to go before reliable data on salaries, working conditions and attrition can be captured.

INDUCTION

Teachers face their biggest challenges as they make the transition from being learners to being leaders in the classroom. Induction and mentoring programmes, which cover a range of activities and take different forms, are aimed at supporting teachers who are new to the profession as well as those new to a school. They can be structured and organized along a set of formally specified rules, as in formal induction, or done informally.

In 34 countries and subregional entities participating in the 2013 TALIS, 44% of lower secondary school teachers who were new to the school had access to formal induction programmes, according to their head teachers; this support mechanism was available to 66% of teachers at all levels who were new to the profession. However, according to the teachers themselves, only 49% had participated in an induction programme. The share ranged from more than four in five in East Asian countries, such as Japan, Malaysia and Singapore, to less than one in five in Estonia, Finland, Norway and Sweden.

The survey also asked lower secondary school teachers whether they were participating at a mentoring programme at the time. About 13% said they had been assigned a mentor; the rate increased to 25% among those with fewer than five years of experience. Within this latter group, the range varied from 6% in Chile and 9% in Italy to 52% in Abu Dhabi, United Arab Emirates. In Mexico, the share of teachers assigned a mentor was 22% in primary education, 17% in lower secondary education and 13% in upper secondary education (OECD, 2014c).

The effectiveness of induction and mentoring programmes depends on the quality of interaction with mentors. It can be bolstered if teachers have been exposed to classrooms in their initial education. As part of the teacher module of the World Bank Systems Approach for Better Education Results (SABER), information was collected on formal policies related to the incidence and duration of prior classroom experience for primary school teachers in conjunction with induction or mentoring programmes (**Table 19.1**).

Some patterns emerge. In Cambodia, teacher trainees are required to have up to three months of prior classroom experience, with no formal systems to facilitate the transition of new teachers into schools. By contrast, teacher trainees in Lebanon are required, among other, to do at least one year of classroom teaching to get their certification, and to take part in an induction programme when joining a school (World Bank, 2016b).

Differences between induction and mentoring programmes can make it hard to compare results. A study of six countries in Eastern Europe and the Caucasus found that only Azerbaijan had a formal induction programme for new teachers, lasting one year. Yet, fewer systematic support measures may exist at the school level, as for example in Ukraine. Georgia introduced a pilot teacher induction and mentoring programme in 2009/10, as part of which mentors received training and a special allowance, but called it off subsequently due to problems in implementation (GHK, 2011; World Bank, 2016b).

Teachers in western Balkan countries tend to have an extended probation period of up to one year under the guidance of appointed mentors. In the Sarajevo canton of Bosnia and Herzegovina, mentors receive an allowance equal to 5% to 10% of their salary, but no training, and may not come from the same institutions as their mentees, which can reduce their contact hours (ICF GHK, 2013).

IN-SERVICE TRAINING

One of the proposed thematic indicators aims to explore the availability of in-service training as a way to support teachers. The indicator presents more challenges than those on teacher qualifications, as continuous professional development programmes are even more diverse than pre-service programmes and less easy to classify into clear categories.

As the information is not collected in a systematic and comparable way from administrative data, the UIS does not currently report on it. In any case, in-service training is rarely delivered in a centralized way, with significant variation even at the school level. It also depends on institutional requirements and the willingness of teachers to participate, as well as whatever obstacles they face, such as cost, time and schedule conflicts. A global approach to gathering data would have to solicit information directly from a sample of teachers.

The 2013 TALIS provides good insights into the possibilities and challenges posed by this indicator. Among lower secondary school teachers in 34 countries and subregional entities, about 88% reported participation in at least one professional development activity in the 12 months prior to the survey, with the lowest rates observed in Chile (72%) and Slovakia (73%). Participation rates remained constant on average across countries in the two TALIS rounds, although they fell from 100% to 84% in Spain and from 85% to 75% in Italy between 2008 and 2013. Teachers sometimes paid for training themselves, but this should be excluded from the indicator to capture the degree of support teachers receive.

TABLE 19.1:

Support opportunities for new primary school teachers, selected countries, 2010–2014

Induction, mentoring or student experience programme opportunities	Prior classroom experience needed			
	3 months or less	Less than 12 months	12 to 24 months	More than 24 months
Classroom experience during initial teacher education or participation in induction or mentoring programmes	Cambodia, Republic of Moldova	Côte d'Ivoire, Djibouti, Kenya, Mali, Russian Federation (St Petersburg and Tomsk regions)	Bulgaria, Serbia	
Both classroom experience in initial teacher education and through induction or mentoring programmes		Guinea-Bissau, Jordan, Kazakhstan, Nigeria (Anambra and Bauchi), Palestine, TFYR Macedonia	Benin, Guyana, Nigeria (Ekiti), Uganda	Lebanon, Tunisia

Source: World Bank (2016b).

Information on participation rates needs to be complemented with information on the type and duration of training. Activities range from organized and structured to informal and self-directed learning. Among the structured approaches, 71% of teachers reported attending courses or workshops for an average of eight days during the previous year, making these the most common form of activity in participating countries.

Among informal approaches, 37% of teachers reported participating in a professional development-oriented network, with the prevalence ranging from less than 20% in the Czech Republic, France and Portugal to 63% in Croatia. In addition, 30% of teachers reported involvement in mentoring and peer observation as part of a formal school arrangement, ranging from 5% in Finland to 65% in Singapore (OECD, 2014c).

Institutional frameworks of continuous professional development

While it is preferable to estimate actual levels of participation in continuous professional development by asking teachers directly, an alternative is to assess national policy as an indicator of a country's commitment to provide such development opportunities.

In Europe, government expectations for professional development differ. From pre-primary to upper secondary education, continuous professional development is considered a duty in Belgium and Hungary, necessary only for promotion in France and Poland, and simply optional in Greece and Ireland. Countries also differ in the range of incentives offered to teachers. In Spain, professional development plans at the school level are compulsory; monetary incentives are provided, time is compensated and professional development is applied as a criterion for mobility. In Sweden, where professional development plans at the school level are not compulsory, none of these incentives are used (European Commission/EACEA/Eurydice, 2013).

Similar information has been collected as part of the SABER module on teachers. For example, primary school teachers are not required to participate in professional development in Benin, Cambodia and Palestine, while in Djibouti, Egypt and Kazakhstan they must participate for at least 10 days but do not have to share the cost (World Bank, 2016b).

WORKING CONDITIONS

While the majority of teachers globally are employed on a permanent basis, the use of short-term contracts is growing. Alternative routes to teaching have been used to fill temporary needs and overcome particular recruitment challenges. They have also been used to control the cost of teacher salaries.

Frequent use of short-term contracts can damage the status of teaching as a career (ILO and UNESCO, 2015). They have been associated with high teacher turnover, which disrupts school management and reduces the quality of student learning experiences (Burns and Darling-Hammond, 2014). They also create unequal opportunities in teacher careers, as in the case of Cameroon (**Box 19.3**).

The UIS distinguishes between civil servants, teachers on fixed or short-term contracts, community teachers and volunteers. While data from the global module on teachers have not yet been made available, according to the regional module on teachers in Asia the percentage of teachers on civil service contracts varies between and within countries. For example, in both the Lao People's Democratic Republic and Malaysia, the share of private schools is below 5%. And yet only 69% of primary school teachers in the Lao People's Democratic Republic and 82% in Malaysia had public sector permanent contracts. Only about 4 in 10 primary school teachers in the capital city districts of Delhi and Jakarta were on such contracts (**Figure 19.5**).

In India, the state with the lowest percentage of civil servant teachers was Jharkand, at just 24%. The hiring of contract teachers began during the District Primary Education Programme in the late 1990s. These teachers do not have the same career opportunities as those on civil service contracts. Even though the Right to Education Act states that teachers should only be recruited as civil servants, the government had planned to fill half the vacant posts in Jharkand with contract teachers as recently as 2012 (Rao et al., 2015).

In Brazil, according to the National Household Sample Survey, 54% of teachers from the pre-primary through to the secondary levels are public servants, 23% are on regular contracts and a further 23% lack a formal contract, with this share rising to 31% in the North-East region (Alves and Pinto, 2011).

Short-term contracts are far more common for beginning teachers than for experienced ones. For example, in the Czech Republic, 61% of beginning teachers are on short-term contracts, compared with less than 10% of experienced teachers (Burns and Darling-Hammond, 2014).

Comparing definitions of employment status across countries is complicated. In Europe, teachers may be

Upgrading 'parents' teachers' in Cameroon

The three types of employment status for primary school teachers in Cameroon are civil servants, contract teachers and parents' teachers. The minimum qualification for primary school teachers is a certificate for basic aptitude in pedagogy for early childhood and primary education (CAPIEMP), although a bachelor's degree may also be accepted under certain circumstances. To obtain the CAPIEMP, trainee teachers need to study at an Ecole Normale d'Instituteurs for three years if they have a diploma of the first secondary education cycle or one year if they have a diploma of the second secondary education cycle (baccalauréat). The CAPIEMP conveys the right to become a category B permanent civil servant, though not all holders are hired by the state.

Fixed-term contract teachers have been hired in Cameroon since 2003. As of 2013, contract teachers were paid at a rate 55% below that of civil servant teachers. They are not entitled to the bonuses civil servant teachers receive, nor do they have a career path, even though they tend to have the required qualifications.

Parent associations have been hiring so-called parents' teachers, especially in rural areas. They are paid even less than contract teachers. As of 2014, out of 94,000 primary school teachers, about 18% were parents' teachers.

To address inequality in working conditions, the government decided to hire about 3,000 contract teachers each year over three years. In 2014 and 2015, only parents' teachers were hired, while in 2016, both parents' teachers and young CAPIEMP graduates were to be hired on contract. The government set criteria including that those hired through this arrangement must have obtained the CAPIEMP before 2013, be younger than age 40 and be currently working in a public primary school that faces a teacher gap.

Sources: Cameroon Tribune (2014); Nkengne (2010); WDE (2011).

FIGURE 19.5:

The percentage of contract teachers varies between and within countries

Percentage of primary school teachers with public sector permanent contracts, by province/region, selected countries, 2014

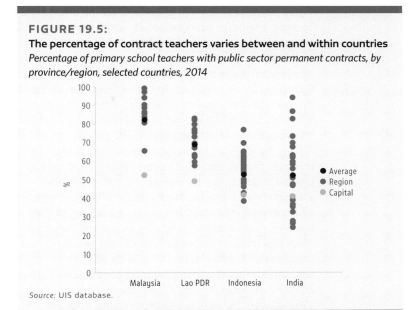

Source: UIS database.

civil servants or, especially those employed at the local or school level, may have a contract subject to general labour law, but the two may be similar in practice. In the Netherlands, teachers in public schools are career civil servants while those in grant-aided private schools are on contract, yet they have the same working conditions, and collective agreements cover the whole education sector (European Commission/EACEA/Eurydice, 2013).

SALARIES

While many people choose to become teachers because they derive an intrinsic benefit from teaching, the profession also needs to be socially valued as a viable

and attractive career choice. A competitive remuneration package is an essential component of recruiting and retaining the best people to the profession.

In general, it is difficult to estimate the average teacher salary, even within a particular education level. Statutory salaries differ among countries in many aspects, including maximum and minimum levels, the number of years after which a teacher can reach the maximum level and the distribution of teachers within salary scales. Evidence on hours of work or overtime pay is often scarce. There are major differences in what allowances are included and excluded and how social security contributions are calculated.

Detailed analysis for comparable countries can be insightful and identify national differences. For example, salary progression varies enormously in Europe. In Denmark, primary and lower secondary school teachers with 12 years of experience can reach the maximum statutory salary, which is less than 20% above the minimum level. By contrast, in Hungary, primary and secondary school teachers need 42 years of experience to reach the maximum statutory salary, which is more than twice the minimum level (European Commission/ EACEA/Eurydice, 2015c). In OECD countries, teacher salaries increase with the level of education taught, with an average gap of 26% between pre-primary and upper secondary teachers (OECD, 2015b).

These indicators are internal to the teaching profession. To know a remuneration package's worth, it must be compared with an external benchmark. The most common approach has been to express average annual salaries as a percentage of per capita income. For example, the Education for All Fast Track Initiative recommended that the average annual salary of primary school teachers in low income countries, inclusive of benefits, should be 3.5 times the GDP per capita (EFA-FTI, 2004).

However, the relationship between salaries and per capita income largely reflects the level of a country's socio-economic development, the structure of labour markets and income distribution. In poor countries, people with teaching qualifications tend to be scarce and therefore more expensive, on average. For example, among countries with data on teacher salaries, as used to estimate the costs of the Education 2030 targets in the 2015 *EFA Global Monitoring Report*, primary school teacher salaries were 2.4 times the GDP per capita in lower middle income countries but 3.3 times in low income countries. Comparing salary levels between countries at similar levels of development may be meaningful but direct comparisons between richer and poorer countries are likely to mislead.

An alternative approach, which the proposed thematic indicator favours, is to focus on the average teacher salary as a percentage of the salary of similarly educated adult full-time workers. For example, administrative data of OECD countries indicate that primary school teachers earn 78% and lower secondary school teachers 80% of the salary of similarly educated adults. Within the latter group, the range varies from 57% in Slovakia and 60% in Chile to about 100% in Denmark and France (OECD, 2015b).

In practice, establishing the relative attractiveness of teacher salaries using administrative data can be challenging in many countries. For example, instead of being determined centrally, salaries are often set at lower tiers of government or the school level. Nor are administrative sources always well placed to capture data on the pay of teachers in the private sector or those on contracts.

For this reason, one approach is to look at labour force survey data. The advantage of this approach is that a single source provides comparable information on salaries as well as other individual background characteristics for both teachers and other workers. This makes it possible to estimate the earnings gap while accounting for explanatory factors.

Analysis of labour force surveys from 13 Latin American countries showed results quite similar to those in OECD countries. Pre-primary and primary school teachers earned 76% of what other professionals and technicians did, while secondary school teachers earned 88%, after accounting for differences in sex, age and education (**Figure 19.6**). However, there were large differences within the group. In the Dominican Republic, the average teacher earned about 70%, while in Uruguay, teachers enjoyed a slight advantage over other professionals and technicians (Mizala and Ñopo, 2012).

While this approach provides a solid basis to discuss the relative pay of teachers across countries, it also has considerable disadvantages. Labour force surveys are not sufficiently frequent for monitoring purposes, nor are their data sets easily available in all parts of the world. Their sample sizes need to be large enough to accommodate the fact that teachers tend to be only about 3% of the labour force. Even if samples are large, they are unlikely to distinguish between levels and sectors of education or between teachers and head teachers.

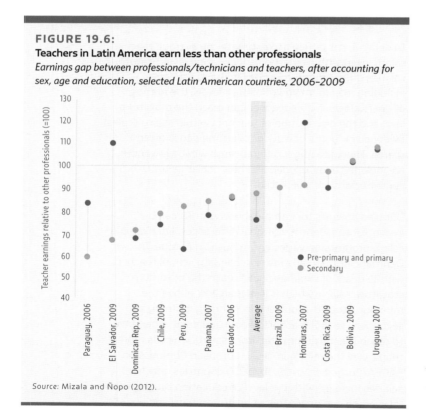

FIGURE 19.6:

Teachers in Latin America earn less than other professionals

Earnings gap between professionals/technicians and teachers, after accounting for sex, age and education, selected Latin American countries, 2006–2009

Pre-primary and primary
Secondary

Source: Mizala and Ñopo (2012).

As information on occupations is not collected in the same way everywhere, it may not be possible to establish a consistent definition of a comparison group of 'other professionals' across countries. In addition, self-employed professionals often do not declare all their income, resulting in underestimation of the earnings gap between them and teachers, who are more likely to be on civil service contracts.

Nevertheless, such an approach is likely to give a more consistent view of the relative pay of teachers and its evolution over time than what is currently available. Adopting this approach will require improved coordination and the establishment of an inter-agency mechanism with the support of the International Labour Organization.

ATTRITION

Teachers may leave the profession for many reasons, from retirement or dismissal to illness or death, as well as voluntarily. While some level of voluntary attrition in the first years is desirable (when teachers discover they have no vocation for teaching), excessive attrition represents a waste of resources on teacher training and recruitment. Higher turnover and attrition may disrupt students' classroom and learning experiences, especially in disadvantaged areas where teaching is viewed as a less attractive profession and where replacing teachers may be difficult and time-consuming.

The degree to which teachers quit the profession voluntarily to search for other work can serve as a potential indicator of low motivation among teaching professionals.

While few countries regularly report overall annual teacher attrition rates, what rates are available vary widely between and within countries. In sub-Saharan Africa, the most recent annual attrition rates among public primary teachers range from 1% in Mauritania to 15% in Togo. Among 14 OECD countries with comparable data, attrition rates for public school teachers were below 3% in three countries, between 3% and 6% in six and above 6% in five (OECD, 2005c). Attrition rates also change within countries over time. In the United States, attrition rose by 41% between 1988/89 and 2008/09, from 6.4% to 9% (Ingersoll et al., 2014).

Where surveys capture the reasons for attrition, resignation, rather than retirement, is often the most significant cause. Voluntary resignation was top of

the list in a survey of anglophone sub-Saharan African countries (Mulkeen, 2010). In high income countries, attrition rates are highest among new teachers for reasons such as lack of support and broader disillusionment with working conditions and pay. Higher rates of teacher attrition are observed in disadvantaged areas and schools for children with special education needs. Teachers in such schools are also more likely to transfer to more affluent schools (Borman and Dowling, 2008; Boe et al., 2008; Ingersoll et al., 2014; OECD, 2005c).

Working conditions can play a major role in influencing turnover. In Punjab province, Pakistan, 24% of public schools reported that a teacher had left in the previous year, compared with 71% of private ones (Andrabi et al., 2008), which had lower pay and less job protection. In Mexico, the attrition rate of community teachers in remote areas was higher than in other schools but fell from 22% to 17% after the introduction of a monthly stipend incentive (IADB, 2014). In Uganda, teacher attrition fell by 24% from 2005 to 2006 following a 33% pay rise (Mulkeen, 2010).

Data collection methods are inconsistent. They may not clearly distinguish between teaching and non-teaching staff, or whether attrition refers only to teachers leaving the profession altogether or includes teachers moving between schools. Commonly, attrition rates are gathered through an annual survey conducted at school level. But this leaves considerable margin for error. More appropriate data collection would be through a centralized human resources database that records both attrition and transfers between schools. An alternative approach would be a survey that collects information directly from teachers. For example, in the United States, the National Center for Education Statistics carries out the Schools and Staffing Survey about every four years and then revisits a sample of teachers a year later as part of the Teacher Follow-up Survey (NCES, 2014).

A young girl stands and writes on the blackboard in Germany.

CREDIT: Fotolia

KEY MESSAGES

A lack of adequate and equitable finance was a key reason why the world fell short of achieving the Education for All goals between 2000 and 2015. Yet no SDG 4 target specifically relates to education finance.

Reporting on education spending rarely combines funds from governments, external donors and households. **National education accounts** look at all three sources simultaneously and give a more accurate picture.

On average worldwide, **public expenditure** on education passes the two minimum thresholds proposed in the Education 2030 Framework for Action, but at least 35 countries spent less than the recommended 4% of GDP on education and less than 15% of total public expenditure.

Data are incomplete, as only 60% of countries report total education expenditure as a percentage of GDP for any given year; they are also out of date, as they become available with a three-year reporting lag.

Monitoring of government spending must track whether funds go to those most in need. Countries should establish regional peer review mechanisms to learn from each other in promoting equity.

Aid needs to increase at least sixfold to fill the US$39 billion annual gap to reach the new targets. But in 2014, aid levels were 8% lower than at their peak in 2010. The gap could be filled if donors dedicated 0.7% of gross national income to aid and allocated 10% of their aid to basic and secondary education.

Poorer countries should be prioritized in aid, yet low income countries received 28% of total aid to basic education in 2014 while accounting for 36% of all out-of-school children.

Levels of humanitarian aid need to be tracked as well. In 2015, education received US$198 million, or less than 1.9% of total humanitarian aid.

Households still pick up a lot of the cost of education. In the poorest countries, their share of total education spending was almost triple that in the richest countries. New analysis shows that information on household spending is available in most countries but rarely used.

CHAPTER 20

Finance

(selected finance-related indicators from target 4.5)

THEMATIC INDICATOR 19 – *Extent to which explicit formula-based policies reallocate education resources to disadvantaged populations*

THEMATIC INDICATOR 20 – *Education expenditure per student by level of education and source of funding*

THEMATIC INDICATOR 21 – *Percentage of total aid to education allocated to low-income countries*

While the 2030 Agenda for Sustainable Development includes three targets related to means of implementation, remarkably, none of these refers to education financing. This partly reflects a perceived lack of an education expenditure target that would be appropriate for all countries. But it also reflects concerns that spending volume is unrelated to effectiveness and efficiency: Critics point out that countries with similar levels of spending in terms of income per capita produce widely different educational outcomes.

However, the 2015 *EFA Global Monitoring Report* (GMR) argued that the lack of equitable and adequate financing was a key reason why the world fell short of achieving the EFA goals in 2015 – and that where progress accelerated, there was clear evidence of increased allocations to education, usually from a very low starting point.

Regardless of the absence of a financing target, comprehensive and regular education financing data are a prerequisite both for effective education sector planning and for monitoring the commitment of all partners to the global education agenda. This section focuses on the need for better information on the volume and composition of education financing. Gaps in data are so wide that simple national, regional and global trends cannot be ascertained. This may also be one reason why stronger links between education financing and outcomes have not yet been established.

The section begins by proposing an overall framework for capturing all education financing flows. It then discusses gaps in data on public expenditure, aid and household spending, along with recent initiatives to address these gaps.

NATIONAL EDUCATION ACCOUNTS

National and global debates on education financing are incomplete. For example, in poor countries they tend to focus either on what the government spends or on what the country receives from external sources – but they rarely consider how the two flows combine and affect each other. In some countries, education ministry expenditure is only part of what a government may spend on education, with other ministries, lower tiers of government and autonomous agencies also channelling funding. Even if information on the other sources exists, it may be compiled using different classifications.

Another problem is the lack of evidence on the share of total education spending funded by households. For example, the 2015 GMR showed that if government and household expenditure were added up, households contributed a much larger share of total expenditure on education in poorer countries than in richer countries. This finding has major implications for equity, yet does not receive the attention it deserves.

The lack of equitable and adequate finance was a key reason why the world fell short of achieving the EFA goals in 2015

”

Faced with similar challenges, the health sector developed the concept of national health accounts as a common framework to collect and process health expenditure data. Efforts began in the 1960s, although not until the 1990s was the approach systematically adopted worldwide. By 2010, 130 countries had used national health accounts at least once, while around 41 countries were doing so more or less regularly (World Bank, 2010). In several countries, national health accounts are institutionalized with a specific unit, often in the health ministry.

In education, there have been fragmented efforts to introduce a similar approach in individual countries; a recent project aims to establish and systematically apply common national education account (NEA) standards. This section presents emerging lessons from the project and future priorities for this approach.

MAPPING EDUCATION FINANCING FLOWS

Generally, NEAs are designed to collect education expenditure data from public, private and external sources coherently and comprehensively. The methodology tracks all education financial flows from education funders – financing units such as governments, households or external sources – to their use by providers of education services – producing units such as education institutions or administrative offices (**Figure 20.1**). All data are processed and sorted into common categories around five dimensions: financing units, education levels, producing units, activities and economic transactions.

Over 2013–2016, with support from the Global Partnership for Education, the UNESCO Institute for Statistics (UIS), the UNESCO International Institute for Educational Planning (IIEP) and the IIEP-Pôle de Dakar implemented a project that supported eight countries in using a common NEA methodology. All the countries collected government expenditure data. In addition:

- Guinea and Zimbabwe focused on public resource allocation within the system

- Côte d'Ivoire and Viet Nam focused on household expenditure

- The Lao People's Democratic Republic and Senegal focused on external funding

- Nepal and Uganda carried out full NEAs, covering all funding sources.

The development of NEAs requires several steps. The first is to establish a national technical team with representatives from the education and finance ministries and the national statistical office. A steering committee made up of senior staff from these organizations ensures that the process is anchored in their respective institutions and responds

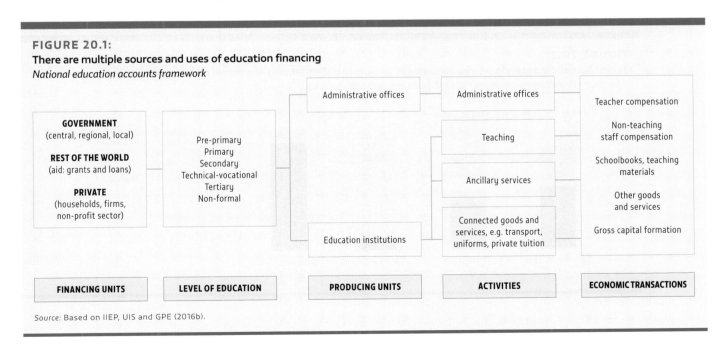

FIGURE 20.1:
There are multiple sources and uses of education financing
National education accounts framework

| FINANCING UNITS | LEVEL OF EDUCATION | PRODUCING UNITS | ACTIVITIES | ECONOMIC TRANSACTIONS |

GOVERNMENT (central, regional, local)
REST OF THE WORLD (aid: grants and loans)
PRIVATE (households, firms, non-profit sector)

Pre-primary / Primary / Secondary / Technical-vocational / Tertiary / Non-formal

Administrative offices / Education institutions

Administrative offices / Teaching / Ancillary services / Connected goods and services, e.g. transport, uniforms, private tuition

Teacher compensation / Non-teaching staff compensation / Schoolbooks, teaching materials / Other goods and services / Gross capital formation

Source: Based on IIEP, UIS and GPE (2016b).

to policy planning and decision-making needs. Then all financial flows are mapped, along with the mechanisms through which funds are made available to education providers. After identifying data sources and collecting the data, a series of financing tables (for financing units) and income and expenditure tables (for producing units) is developed to consolidate total education expenditure from all sources. The final step is to generate indicators and communicate evidence to help planners, researchers and policy-makers make sense of them.

The lessons that emerge from NEAs can be startling. For example, large parts of public education expenditure can be missed, depending on the accounting classifications used. In Zimbabwe, the civil service commission pays the pensions of education sector staff, but they do not appear in formal reporting of education expenditure. Yet, such payments make up about 10% of total government spending on education. In Côte d'Ivoire, three main ministries fund education. But, in addition, the President's Emergency Programme and 12 other ministries also fund education expenditure. These additional sources add about 9% to the total government spending on education.

The main surprises emerge when household education expenditure is added. For example, the government of Nepal spends 3.5% of GDP on education, 2.6 percentage points less than Viet Nam. But when households and other sources are taken into account, the order is reversed: Nepal allocates 1.5 percentage points more on education than Viet Nam (**Figure 20.2**).

The use of NEAs in more countries would not only provide a more accurate picture of national education funding, but would also allow publication of some interesting indicators. Among them is one of the thematic indicators of the Education 2030 Framework for Action: expenditure per student by level of education and source of funding. For example, the government of Nepal spends about US$326 (in purchasing power parity terms) per primary student annually, but the country as a whole spends significantly more when funding from all sources is considered (**Table 20.1**).

Other indicators include the degree of decentralization of education expenditure, and the distribution of education expenditure between remuneration and other uses, such as textbooks and teaching materials. Although the UIS already reports on these indicators, the number of countries able to provide good quality information on them is low and will continue to be so until an NEA approach is more widely used.

A key output of the project is a methodological guide on NEAs (IIEP et al., 2016b). It aims to help countries produce education financing data that are systematic, comprehensive and comparable to those of other countries, but flexible enough to describe specific national contexts. The methodology draws heavily on international standards such as the UN System of National Accounts (SNA), the Government Finance Statistics Manuals of the International Monetary

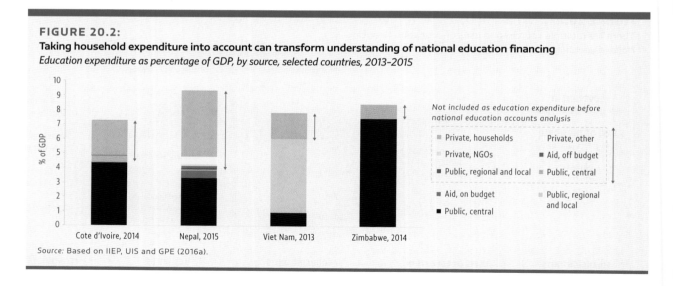

FIGURE 20.2:
Taking household expenditure into account can transform understanding of national education financing
Education expenditure as percentage of GDP, by source, selected countries, 2013–2015

Source: Based on IIEP, UIS and GPE (2016a).

TABLE 20.1:

Selected education financing indicators based on national education accounts

Indicator	Côte d'Ivoire, 2014	Nepal, 2015	Viet Nam, 2013	Zimbabwe, 2014
Total expenditure per primary student (PPP US$)	594	535	1 256	-
Government expenditure per primary student (PPP US$)	419	326	1 098	202
Share of education expenditure (%) funded by:				
• governments	66	38	77	-
• households	33	55	23	-
• external sources	1	7		-
Share of government education expenditure spent by local and/or regional governments (%)	0	1	65	0
• teacher (%)	81	79	63	99
• non-teacher (%)	64	74	-	98
Expenditure on non-teacher compensation as a share of government expenditure on primary education (%)	17	5	-	1
Expenditure on schoolbooks and teaching materials as a share of total government expenditure on primary education (%)	4	5	-	0

Notes: Some indicators are missing - because not all countries carried out the full set of analyses. In Nepal, the share of education expenditure funded by households (55%) includes a part funded by other private sources (7%).
Source: UIS, IIEP and GPE (2016a).

Fund (IMF) and the International Standard Classification of Education.

Ensuring consistency with the SNA and the Classification of the Functions of Government, which is the basis for the IMF Government Finance Statistics, is not only necessary for developing countries. A comparison of total government education expenditure estimates as a percentage of GDP found discrepancies between a national accounts approach and the UIS-OECD-Eurostat data collection tool amounting to at least 0.5% of GDP in half of 28 European countries (Mejer, 2006).

CHALLENGES AND PRIORITIES

Experience from the recently completed project shows that carrying out a full NEA is intensive, with challenges linked to data collection, capacity, resources, institutionalization and sustainability. Required data are not always available, easily accessible or usable. Most education management information systems do not cover income and expenditure of schools. Data on regional and local governments are not always consolidated at a central level or, when they are, often lack details, such as how much is specifically spent on education. Development partners provide a large part of their contributions to the education sector outside of the recipient government's budget. Non-government, community-based and faith-based organizations often do not put their education expenditure and financial reporting information in the public domain.

In addition to obtaining data from these sources, national teams have to complement this with other data collection, which may require significant unbudgeted resources. Ministries may not have the required capacity in statistical and economic analysis, which would make it difficult to use the NEA approach on a regular basis.

The experience of the health sector could be beneficial. At the national level, in countries where national health accounts are used, the education ministry could learn from obstacles faced by health ministries, especially in terms of institutionalizing the process and mobilizing resources. At the international level, national health accounts have become a widely used tool with the backing of the World Health Organization (WHO) and several donors. Dialogue with WHO could help the education sector learn how to achieve similar commitment for NEAs from key actors.

Countries seeking to adopt NEAs should embed them into national planning processes to ensure sufficient institutional and political support. More awareness is needed of the utility of education financing data for policy, planning and management. It is important for countries to follow the NEA methodology from the start, even if the actual exercise is done in stages, e.g. by starting in the first phase with government sources. In this way, a full set of accounts can eventually be published.

The publication of the first international methodological guide and the experience built by the few countries

In 2014, 51 out of 138 countries spent less than 4% of GDP on education

that have taken the NEA approach have created momentum on which the international education community should build. It is often said that 'the perfect is the enemy of the good'; not all implementation challenges can be resolved, especially in countries with weaker capacity. The key lesson that the NEA project brings to the Education 2030 agenda is its perspective. Planners need to look at education financing flows comprehensively. This approach holds the key for understanding who benefits from different funding sources, and for addressing equity and quality issues in education.

IMPROVING FINANCIAL DATA

To build strong NEAs, information on expenditure flows from the three main financing pillars – government, aid partners and households – needs to improve. This section covers key challenges.

PUBLIC EXPENDITURE

The two key indicators on public financing of education appear in the Education 2030 Framework for Action,

which proposed two benchmarks as 'crucial reference points' (§105):

■ allocate at least 4% to 6% of GDP to education, and/or

■ allocate at least 15% to 20% of public expenditure to education.

In 2014, the median global public education expenditure was 4.6% of GDP, i.e. within the range proposed by the framework. Expenditure varied from 2.8% in Caucasus and Central Asia to 5% in Europe and Northern America. In terms of country income group, low income countries spent 3.9% of GDP on education, at the low end of the range. If countries are taken as the unit, 51 of the 138 countries with data spent less than 4% of GDP on education. Among them were 13 low income countries and 16 high income countries.

Public education expenditure was 14.2% of total public expenditure in 2014, which was below the range proposed by the Framework for Action. Expenditure varied from 12.1% in Europe and Northern America to 16.6% in sub-Saharan Africa. Low income countries as a group were at 16.7%. Overall, 70 of the 132 countries with data allocated less than 15% of public expenditure to education, including 9 low income countries and 37 high income countries (**Table 20.2**).

The formulation of the Framework for Action is not entirely clear. It is first of all inconsistent. On one hand, it refers to ranges ('4% to 6%') but at the same time it

TABLE 20.2:
Public education expenditure, by region and country income group, 2014

	Public education expenditure as % of GDP	Number of countries that spent <4% of GDP	Public education expenditure as % of public expenditure	Number of countries that spent <15% of public expenditure	Number of countries that spent <4% of GDP and <15% of public expenditure
World	4.6	51	14.2	70	35
Low income	3.9	13	16.7	9	9
Lower middle income	4.1	13	15.6	13	10
Upper middle income	4.6	9	15.7	11	7
High income	4.9	16	11.9	37	9
Caucasus and Central Asia	2.8	4	12.9	3	3
Eastern and South-eastern Asia	3.9	7	15.4	6	4
Europe and Northern America	5.0	7	12.1	31	5
Latin America and the Caribbean	4.9	7	16.1	6	3
Northern Africa and Western Asia	...	3	...	5	3
Pacific	...	2	...	2	1
Southern Asia	3.8	5	15.3	4	4
Sub-Saharan Africa	4.3	16	16.6	13	12

Note: All values shown are medians.
Source: UIS database.

suggests the lower limit of the range as a minimum requirement ('at least 4%'). Even if this inconsistency is ignored, the benchmark is open to two different interpretations ('and/or'). Countries may meet one target while not meeting the other.

Of the two options, the achievement of either of the two targets as a minimum condition is a more relevant requirement because it recognizes differing national contexts. For example, poorer countries may have low capacity for mobilizing domestic resources but high commitment to spend a larger share of their budget on education. Conversely, richer countries tend to raise more domestic resources but spend a lower share of the budget on education because the cohorts of school-age children are smaller.

Among 132 of the 209 countries with data on both indicators, 35 spent less than 4% of GDP on education and allocated less than 15% of their total public expenditure on education. For example, Sri Lanka spent 1.6% of GDP and 9.8% of total public expenditure on education (**Figure 20.3**).

If spending is inefficient, more of it will not be the way to reach education targets. Yet it is equally the case that no country can achieve the international education targets if expenditure is kept very low. The purpose of this Framework for Action target is to highlight countries that clearly spend considerably below international norms – including countries not regularly reporting to the UIS, such as Myanmar (**Box 20.1**).

Understanding the data gap

Analysis of the key public education financing indicators not only draws attention to countries where expenditure is so low it compromises their chance to achieve 2030 targets, but also reveals an erratic supply of information. For example, no more than 60% of countries have data on total education expenditure as a percentage of GDP for any given year since 2000. Coverage rates increase to about 70% for countries having data at least once in a three-year period. Moreover, data become available with a considerable lag: only 45% of countries had reported 2012 data by 2016.

On the positive side, the percentage of countries with expenditure data by level increased steadily over

FIGURE 20.3:
One in four countries falls below both international education financing benchmarks
Public education expenditure as a share of GDP and as a share of total public expenditure, 2014

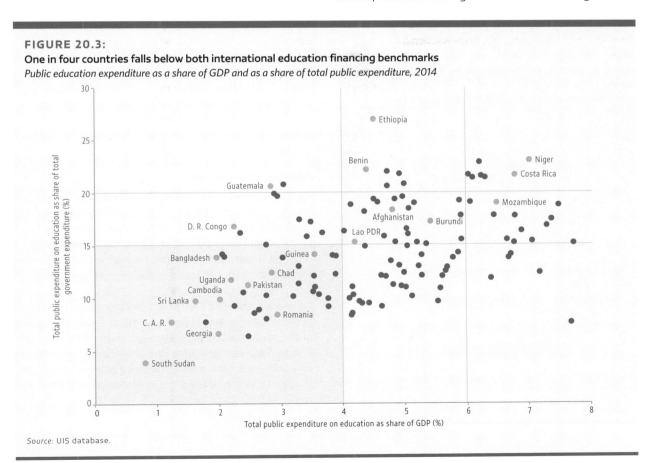

Source: UIS database.

BOX 20.1

Ending a legacy of very low public spending on education in Myanmar

Myanmar has historically allocated a very low share of its national resources to education. The scarce data that exist suggest that education spending hardly ever exceeded 1% of GDP throughout the 1990s and 2000s, a level that set Myanmar apart not only from its regional neighbours but also globally. About 70% of total education expenditure was borne by households.

Part of the reason for Myanmar's situation was a very low rate of domestic resource mobilization. This began to change in recent years. Tax revenue increased from 3.9% of GDP in 2011/12 to 7.1% in 2012/13, partly because a managed float exchange rate system was introduced, but also because tax administration improved. Natural resource revenue from gas sales and income from the sale of state property led to a further increase of tax revenue to over 8% in 2014/15. However, some of the gains were not sustainable, and revenue from income tax remains very low at about 3% of GDP.

The government has more than doubled the share of public expenditure allocated to education, from less than 5% to 13% – and in 2015/16, the combined share of education, health and other social services is expected for the first time to be greater than that of defence.

In 2015, the share of public education expenditure exceeded 2% of GDP for the first time in at least two decades (Figure 20.4), though it has a long way to go to breach the recommended international threshold at 4%. In the 1970s, the country spent at times 3% of GDP on education.

FIGURE 20.4:
Myanmar is making an effort to reach minimum benchmarks in education financing
Public education expenditure as a share of GDP and of public expenditure, Myanmar, 2000–2014

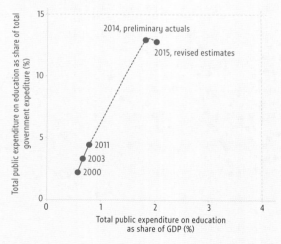

Sources: IMF (2015); Myanmar Government (2015); Myanmar Ministry of Education (2014); OECD (2013f); UIS database; UNICEF (2013b); World Bank (2013b, 2015d); World Bank and AusAid (2013).

2000–2010, from 20% to 40% for at least primary and secondary education (**Figure 20.5**). But values for all levels frequently do not add up to 100%, which hampers data interpretation.

To estimate an indicator's average at the level of a region or country income group, at least half the countries in the group need to have the data. Low coverage makes it difficult to estimate averages in regions, such as Northern Africa and Western Asia, and the Pacific.

If it is difficult to establish the validity of average levels of education expenditure for the most recent year, it is even more difficult to show trends because fewer countries will have observations on two points in time. However, the evidence suggests an overall increase in both indicators of public education expenditure over the period, from 4% to 4.6% of GDP and from 13.8% to 15% of total public expenditure (**Figure 20.6**).

It should also be noted that averages treat countries equally regardless of size. For example, the Eastern and South-eastern Asia regional average is reported because 14 of the 18 countries had data – but China was not among them. Conversely, if each observation is weighted by national GDP, then public education expenditure in Latin America and the Caribbean exceeded the global average at 5.5% of GDP.

Beyond these two indicators, even less information is available. For example, data on teacher salaries in primary education as a share of current public education expenditure is available for only 80 countries, or 38% of the total.

Addressing the data gap

The key factor in ensuring availability of good quality data on education expenditure is good public expenditure management at the national level. The national education budget and expenditure reporting must be transparent. Education ministries cannot ensure this alone; it requires interventions across government.

An overall attitude of openness regarding reporting of public education expenditure is critical. Fewer than 3 in 10 of the countries scoring the lowest on the International Budget Partnership's Open Budget Index reported data on public education expenditure as a percentage of GDP in 2012/13; at the two highest levels, however, almost 8 in 10 did so (IBP, 2015).

FIGURE 20.5:

Information on even the most basic education financing indicators is often missing

Percentage of countries with data on public education expenditure as a share of GDP, by education level, 2000–2014

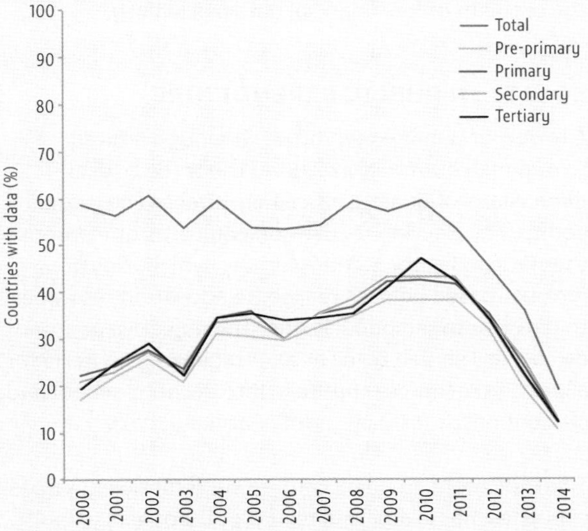

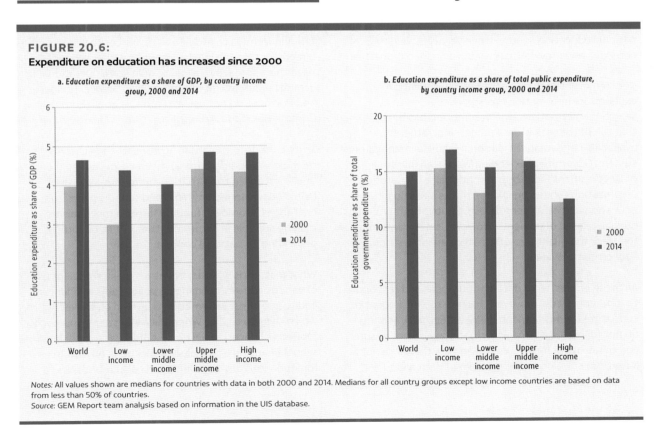

Source: GEM Report team analysis based on information in the UIS database.

The Public Expenditure and Financial Accountability (PEFA) programme, a multi-agency partnership, outlined 7 pillars and 31 performance indicators of an 'open and orderly' public financial management system to guide country assessments (PEFA, 2016). Areas of interest are captured in indicators related to the transparency pillar, such as budget classification, resources received by service delivery units and public access to key fiscal information.

Inevitably, the national context affects the quality of public financial management. An analysis of PEFA assessments in 93 countries carried out over 2006–2010 found that the public financial management system score was negatively associated with state fragility, while quality was positively associated with per capita income and economic growth as well as external capacity-building support (de Renzio et al., 2010).

One example of external support in many developing countries is the introduction of financial management information systems to increase budget credibility through comprehensive reporting and information transparency. The United Republic of Tanzania has been commended for having established the most successful

FIGURE 20.6:

Expenditure on education has increased since 2000

a. Education expenditure as a share of GDP, by country income group, 2000 and 2014

b. Education expenditure as a share of total public expenditure, by country income group, 2000 and 2014

Notes: All values shown are medians for countries with data in both 2000 and 2014. Medians for all country groups except low income countries are based on data from less than 50% of countries.
Source: GEM Report team analysis based on information in the UIS database.

information system in sub-Saharan Africa since 1994, and upgrades have further strengthened its budget preparation (Diamond and Khemani, 2005; World Bank, 2015c). Information on public expenditure data for education started being reported regularly in 2004.

> ## Open public financial management systems are associated with economic growth

Support by international agencies can facilitate reporting of existing data. For example, since the 1990s, World Bank-led public expenditure reviews, in partnership with finance ministries, often analyse the level and pattern of public education expenditure and assess effectiveness and equity.

Since 2009 another World Bank initiative, BOOST, has compiled public expenditure data from treasury systems using national budget classification codes in 16 countries, divided by government level, administrative unit, economic and functional classification.

Similarly, since 2003, the IIEP, often jointly with the World Bank, has led country status reports in 22 sub-Saharan African countries. These in-depth diagnostic tools for national education systems involve intensive data collection and provide capacity-building for national teams.

Concern over the timeliness of public education expenditure information has sometimes led to a search for alternatives. The assumption has been that the bottleneck is data processing, rather than availability of data in the national financial management system. Government Spending Watch, an initiative of Development Finance International, a non-profit organization funded by Oxfam, tracks spending in education and other sectors using public and semi-public budget-related documents. However, this information may lack the quality assurance that an international agency can provide.

All these efforts serve different purposes and respond to different needs. However, they are too infrequent to substitute for missing data (UIS, 2016c). And, as they do not follow a systematic format, they do not ensure comparability across countries and are therefore not a long-term solution to the problem of data gaps.

Following the example of WHO in the health sector, greater engagement with the IMF and its Government Finance Statistics could be helpful (Seiferling, 2013). However, the IMF does not prioritize data collection in individual sectors. Reform of public financial management systems thus remains the main answer to the problem of low financial data availability.

EQUITY IN PUBLIC EXPENDITURE

A review of public expenditure cannot be limited to quantity but must extend to the three critical dimensions of quality: efficiency, effectiveness and equity. This section focuses on equity, as one proposed thematic indicator is the 'extent to which explicit formula-based policies reallocate education resources to disadvantaged populations'. The objective of equity can be well served by clear and transparent criteria for allocating resources that take into account school and student needs (Levacic, 2008; Fazekas, 2012).

This indicator can be monitored systematically across countries. For example, a review of European school financing systems identified differences in the extent to which formula funding was used, alone or in combination with other rules, to allocate resources to schools. Five countries, including Bulgaria, Norway and Spain, used a funding formula to allocate all resources to schools either directly or through local authorities. Other countries used this approach to allocate only staff, operational or capital resources. Yet others, such as Greece, Hungary and Portugal, do not use any formula at all (European Commission/EACEA/Eurydice, 2014).

In its current formulation, however, the indicator is restrictive. Funding formula mechanisms are only one of several policy tools that governments can use to help disadvantaged students and schools overcome challenges. Moreover, funding formula mechanisms may be suitable in some countries but not in others, depending on national context.

What matters is whether countries make sufficient use of various education financing policy tools to address equity concerns. Information is limited on the extent to which they do so. The World Bank's Systems Approach for Better Education Results (SABER) has a module on school financing that includes questions on resources for students from disadvantaged backgrounds, and a new module on equity and inclusion (World Bank, 2013c; 2016c). But neither has been tested extensively at the country level. Benchmarking and other mechanisms are needed to assess and compare efforts between countries.

For the purpose of this report, a framework with five main questions was used as a basis for assessing the extent to which education financing policies in 10 countries[1] compensated for disadvantage in education (**Table 20.3**). The answers were based on analysis of secondary data on laws, policies and programmes relating to coverage, targeting and other areas (Makarova, 2016).

A common finding was that provision of policies and programmes addressing disadvantage in education was not integrated. Although some countries had made an effort to link social and education support programmes, none had an integrated policy document providing information on all available mechanisms targeting disadvantage in education.

While all countries in the sample had made an explicit general commitment in laws and strategies to address disadvantage in education, fewer had detailed policies and regulations, such as the decree on the normative

cost per student and the standard voucher in Georgia, and the regulation on calculation of the education subvention in Poland.

All 10 countries had adopted at least one policy or programme to provide special funding to disadvantaged students and schools. Diverse interventions aimed to improve demand for education, including social protection programmes, such as conditional cash transfers (e.g. PKH in Indonesia, PATH in Jamaica, Juntos in Peru), school meals, scholarships (e.g. the BSM Scholarship programme in Indonesia and the National Scholarship Program in Poland), disability benefits (e.g. in Sri Lanka), universal and targeted child benefit programmes (e.g. in the Netherlands) and full or partial subsidies for school supplies, transport and boarding (e.g. in Morocco) (**Box 20.2**).

To improve the supply of education, formula funding was used to provide additional resources for students with special education needs (e.g. in Jamaica and the Netherlands) and to cover higher operating costs of small and remote schools (e.g. in Georgia and Sri Lanka). There are inclusive education programmes, special training for teachers in disadvantaged schools, school rehabilitation, and education programmes targeting specific groups

TABLE 20.3:
A framework to assess country commitment to equity through financing

	Question	Elaboration
1	Is the legal framework explicit on the obligation of the government to address disadvantage in education?	The commitment would be considered strong if the needs of several disadvantaged groups were addressed through laws, as well as specific regulations on school funding.
2	a. Is the provision of universal and free pre-primary, primary and secondary education a directive principle of state policy?	The commitment would range from minimum when fees exist in pre-primary, primary and secondary education to maximum if there is free universal education at each level.
	b. In the case of payments that can have a detrimental impact on the education opportunity of disadvantaged children, does the government offer waivers?	The commitment would be highest if there were waivers or other mechanisms to compensate for costs such as textbooks, school transport or uniforms.
3	a. Are there policies to provide more resources to students from disadvantaged households?	The commitment would be strong if there were policies that provided resources to students from disadvantaged households, such as cash transfers, grants, scholarships and in-kind incentives such as school meals.
	b. ...and if so what share of total public education and/or social protection spending is being reallocated...	i.e. what is the depth of the intervention
	c. ...and what percentage of the student population does it reach?	i.e. what is the coverage of the intervention
	d. How are targeting decisions made...	i.e. is there any targeting, are criteria clear and can records be checked
	e. ...and is the success of targeting monitored and evaluated?	i.e. does the country have a well-developed M&E system analysing beneficiaries and feeding into policy
4	a. Are there policies to provide more resources to disadvantaged schools?	The commitment would be strong if schools that are disadvantaged due to their student intake, size or location get extra resources to compensate for their higher costs, through weighted per-pupil funding rules.
	b. ...and if so what share of total public education spending is being reallocated	i.e. what is the depth of the intervention
	c. ...and what percentage of schools does it reach?	i.e. what is the coverage of the intervention
	d. How are targeting decisions made...	i.e. is there any targeting, are criteria clear and can records be checked
	e. ...and is the success of targeting monitored and evaluated?	i.e. does the country have a well-developed M&E system analysing beneficiaries and feeding into policy
5	Are there policies to provide more resources to disadvantaged regions?	The commitment would be strong if decentralization of education responsibilities to lower tiers of government were accompanied by additional financial support to regions whose relatively fewer resources put them at a disadvantage.

Source: Makarova (2016).

(e.g. intercultural bilingual education policies for indigenous people in Peru and the Programme for the Roma community in Poland).

Three countries provide useful examples in examining overall how countries address equity through financing. The policy of the Netherlands on disadvantage in education is not only integrated, comprehensive and systemic, but also strongly focused on prevention, early detection and early support mechanisms for vulnerable children, with emphases on measurement and better cooperation between professionals (Hilverdink, 2013). Between 2003 and 2012, the socio-economic status of 15-year-olds became a weaker predictor of performance in mathematics (OECD, 2013b).

BOX 20.2

Promoting equity through education financing policies in Morocco

In Morocco, free universal education to age 15 is a principle of state policy. Equity is enshrined in the foundation education policy texts: the 1999 National Education and Training Charter and the 2011 Constitution. Yet, households were still bearing significant costs that impeded their children's schooling. The 2009–2012 National Education Emergency Plan and the 2013–2016 Education Action Plan tried to improve equity through financing policies. The former included subsidies for transport and boarding and free school lunches.

In addition, the Tayssir cash transfer programme provides direct financial support to poor rural families to reduce dropout and improve school attendance. Labelling the transfers as education support without making them strictly conditional has led to large gains in school participation. In 2013/14, 825,000 students (13% of the total population of primary and secondary school age) benefited from the Tayssir programme. By contrast, the cash transfer programme for education in Tunisia covered fewer than 80,000 children in 2013. Close to 4 million students have also benefited from the One Million Schoolbags initiative, which targets poorer first grade students. Over half the total budget for social support to education was directed at these two programmes in 2014–2015.

Despite improvement towards gender parity in primary education since 2000 in Morocco, girls' enrolment in secondary education is lagging due to cultural obstacles as well as access and quality issues in rural areas. In response, the government developed a strategy to construct dedicated schools and boarding facilities. The Ministry of National Education and Vocational Training also identified criteria for targeting the most disadvantaged schools, including areas with high levels of dropout and low income populations. An evaluation of the Emergency Plan in 2012 showed impressive progress in developing education services and ensuring more equitable access, particularly in rural and disadvantaged areas. A development that will facilitate further evaluations is the establishment of a monitoring programme through the longitudinal survey of the National Observatory of Human Development.

Source: Benhassine et al. (2015), UNESCO (2015c), UNICEF (2014g), and World Bank (2014b).

Samoa has made an effort to address the needs of disadvantaged students through the Samoa School Fees Grant Scheme, which removed primary and secondary education fees and covered all schools' operating costs with grants to help them meet minimum service standards (SSFGS, 2010). However, the programme's long-term prospects need to be secured, as it is mainly funded by international donors. In addition, the country lacks direct social protection programmes for disadvantaged households and children (Amosa, 2012).

In the Democratic Republic of Congo, the government developed a mechanism for equalizing fiscal transfers between provinces. It also abolished fees for grades 1–5 in 2011. However, only 68% of teachers were registered on the payroll in 2013, with the remaining teachers still being paid by households through so-called motivation fees (World Bank, 2015e). Household out-of-pocket payments accounted for 64% of total expenditure in primary education in 2012 (UNICEF, 2015b). In response to these challenges, the government produced its Education and Training Sector Strategy 2016–2025 with equity as one of three strategic axes (D. R. Congo Government, 2015). Key actions include the expansion of classroom construction in remote areas, the abolition of fees at grade 6 and for the end of primary cycle examination, and improvements in salary payments (GPE, 2016).

Comparing the equity focus of national education financing policies across countries is feasible. However, considerable effort will be required in introducing a process, agreeing on a framework and actually carrying out an assessment. To get countries on board, the emphasis should be on establishing a peer review mechanism through which they can learn from each other. This is discussed in more detail in the next chapter, on system indicators.

AID EXPENDITURE

Government is the main source of education expenditure. However, as cost projections in the 2015 GMR showed, external financing remains vital for low income countries. The financing gap was estimated at 42% of the total cost of reaching the new targets, assuming the countries could increase domestic resource mobilization and ensure that 20% of public expenditure was allocated to education (UNESCO, 2015i).

It is not surprising that countries look to external financing to fill this gap. Aid to basic and secondary education in low income countries would have to

> "There is a 42% financing gap for reaching the new targets in low income countries"

rise least sixfold but the gap could be filled if countries on the OECD Development Assistance Committee (DAC) and selected non-DAC donors (Brazil, China, India, Kuwait, Qatar, the Russian Federation, Saudi Arabia, South Africa and the United Arab Emirates) dedicated 0.7% of their gross national income (GNI) to aid – a longstanding target for international aid levels – and allocated 10% of their aid to basic and secondary education.

However, data from the OECD-DAC Creditor Reporting System (CRS), the main global platform for reporting aid to education, suggest that the outlook for aid is unfavourable. Since 2005, total aid flows have fluctuated at around 0.3% of donor countries' GNI. With developed countries growing slower than developing countries

since 2000, aid is declining in relative importance in the latter. In addition, the share of aid to education in total aid fell from 10% in 2010 to 8% in 2014.

Overall, since peaking in 2010, total aid to education declined by 8% to US$13.1 billion in 2014 (**Figure 20.7**). Aid to basic education is 14% below its 2010 levels; in sub-Saharan Africa it is down by 22%. However, aid to secondary education increased by 14% (**Table 20.4**).

Targeting aid to countries in need

The share of total aid to education allocated to low income countries has been identified as a thematic indicator for the equity-focused target 4.5. Various options can be considered for monitoring this indicator. One is to use the 2015 World Bank income classification and

FIGURE 20.7:
Aid to education has yet to return to 2010 levels
Total aid to education disbursements, 2002–2014

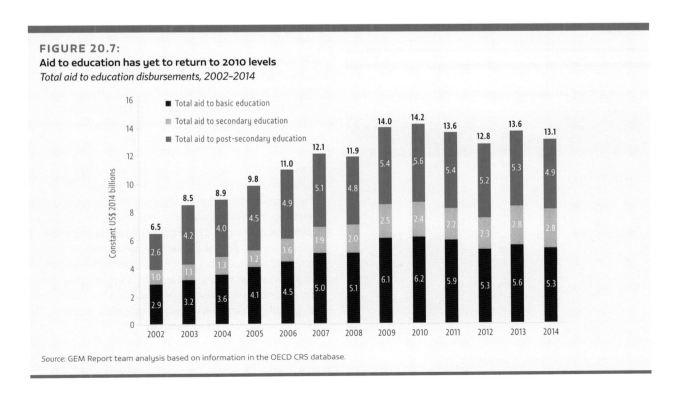

Source: GEM Report team analysis based on information in the OECD CRS database.

focus on its 32 low income countries, all but 6 of which are in sub-Saharan Africa. By this measure, low income countries received 22% of total aid and 28% of total aid to basic education in 2014, and the shares have remained constant for 10 years (**Figure 20.8**). The percentages are slightly higher if aid unallocated by income group is excluded. Note that the definition

of aid to education used by the GEM Report includes 20% of direct budget support, which is assumed to be allocated to education.

One challenge with this approach is that the definition of low income countries is changing. The number of low income countries according to the World Bank classification fell from 63 in 2000 (when the threshold income level was US$755 per capita) to 32 in 2015 (by which time the threshold income level had risen to US$1,035). Between 2014 and 2015, four more countries 'graduated' into lower middle income status (Bangladesh, Kenya, Myanmar and Tajikistan), while one slipped back into low income status (South Sudan).

An alternative option is to focus on least developed countries, a group whose membership changes less frequently. In December 2015, it consisted of 48 countries, of which only Equatorial Guinea and Vanuatu are expected to exit by 2020. Least developed countries received 30% of total aid and 37% of total aid to basic education in 2014.

Neither of these measures indicates need. One measure of need is the percentage of those who do not complete primary school. For example, low income countries received 28% of total aid to basic education while accounting for 43% of children who do not complete primary school.

An important question is which donors prioritize aid to low income countries. One way to establish this is to compare the donor's share of aid to education to low income countries with its share of aid to education to all countries. If the former is higher than the latter, the donor prioritizes low income countries.

For example, the United Kingdom has prioritized low income countries for the past few years and has in fact increased its relative focus. In 2012–2014, it accounted for 17% of total aid to education for low income countries but 10% of total aid to education for all countries. By contrast, Australia accounted for 0.3% of total aid to education for low income countries but as much as 4% of total aid to education to all countries, as its aid programme focuses on Asia and the Pacific and not sub-Saharan Africa, where most low income countries are located (**Figure 20.9**).

One weakness in estimating the extent to which aid to education (or an individual donor) targets low income

FIGURE 20.8:

The share of aid to education to low income and least developed countries has remained constant

Share of low income and least developed countries in total aid to education and to basic education disbursements, 2002–2014

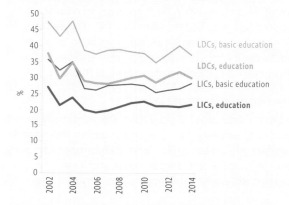

Note: LDCs = least developed countires; LICs = low income countries
Source: GEM Report team analysis based on information in the OECD CRS database.

TABLE 20.4:

Aid disbursements to education, by region and income level, 2010 and 2014

	Total aid to education Constant 2014 US$ millions		Total aid to basic education Constant 2014 US$ millions		Total aid to secondary education Constant 2014 US$ millions	
	2010	**2014**	**2010**	**2014**	**2010**	**2014**
World	14 218	13 055	6 210	5 330	2 444	2 782
Low income	3 213	2 810	1 701	1 509	682	646
Lower middle income	5 482	5 504	2 631	2 267	1 032	1 400
Upper middle income	2 935	2 655	700	694	338	350
High income	664	158	281	41	240	60
Unallocated by income	1 925	1 927	898	818	152	326
Caucasus and Central Asia	284	213	86	47	67	37
Eastern and South-eastern Asia	1 957	503	556	110	269	271
Europe and Northern America	497	1,601	94	420	68	75
Latin America and the Caribbean	1 180	882	476	306	237	175
Northern Africa and Western Asia	2 014	2 108	810	889	238	292
Pacific	242	228	125	105	59	37
Southern Asia	2 278	2 687	1 300	1 234	362	800
Sub-Saharan Africa	3 978	3 233	1 913	1 489	856	788
Overseas territories	510	72	237	24	217	41
Unallocated by region or country	1 277	1 528	613	705	72	265

Source: GEM Report team analysis based on information in the OECD CRS database.

countries is that estimates exclude about 15% of total aid to education, which is not assigned to any particular country. Much of this corresponds to disbursements by the Global Partnership for Education (GPE), a growing source of funding for education in low income countries.

Donors' contributions to the GPE are subsumed within their aid reporting to the CRS, and GPE disbursements are estimated through GPE records, not CRS records. Donors differ in how they report to the GPE: some report aid as going to recipient countries, others as aid through the World Bank as the implementing agency, and others through undisclosed channels, of which some are specified by region or country.

The GPE disbursed US$524 million in 2014, of which two-thirds, or US$349 million, was directed at low income countries (GPE, 2015). For example, Australia appears to have disbursed only US$7 million in aid to basic education to low income countries in 2012–2014. However, it also disbursed US$88 million on average per year to the GPE over that period, of which two-thirds was likely to have gone to low income countries (GPE, 2016). Omitting this growing financing flow risks biasing conclusions about aid targeting. Hence, it is important for the CRS to include the GPE as a reporting entity.

Monitoring other trends in aid to education

When figures for official development assistance (ODA) are reported, the impression is often given that aid is a single transfer of resources to developing countries. In practice, it is diverse, using a range of forms, modes, instruments and channels. One trend worth monitoring relates to types of aid: loans are growing in relation to grants. Another involves aid channels, namely the extent to which aid passes through governments.

Type of aid: grants and loans. Grants made up 83% of total aid to education in 2014, a larger share than that of all aid across sectors (74%). Low income countries receive 84% of their total aid, as well as their total aid to education, in the form of grants, with the largest recipients being Ethiopia, Mozambique and Nepal (**Figure 20.10**). By contrast, lower middle income countries traditionally receive a larger proportion of their education aid in the form of loans.

Between 2007 and 2014, within total ODA flows from OECD-DAC members, loans increased by 122% while grants grew by 21%. It will be important to

FIGURE 20.9:

There are differences in the focus on low income countries across donors and over time

Ratio of donor share of total aid to education to low income countries over donor share of total aid to education to all countries, top ten donors, 2002–2004, 2008–2010 and 2012–2014

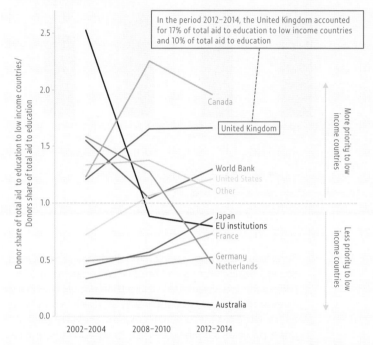

In the period 2012–2014, the United Kingdom accounted for 17% of total aid to education to low income countries and 10% of total aid to education

Note: The top ten donors are defined on the basis of their total aid to education disbursements in 2002–2014.

Source: GEM Report team analysis based on information in the OECD CRS database.

track loan agreements per country and lender, including by non-OECD donors, to monitor implications of this trend. There is a risk that increasing borrowing could begin to crowd out spending on education and other social sectors.

Channels of aid: through or bypassing government. In low income, fragile and conflict-affected countries, donors often bypass government aid disbursement systems, partly as a result of concerns over capacity. Out of total aid, 66% was delivered through government in lower middle income countries in 2014, compared with 52% in low income countries, where NGOs, civil society organizations and multilateral agencies are a more common delivery channel (36%).

FIGURE 20.10:

Loans are a considerable part of official development assistance, even in education

Share of official development assistance (ODA) disbursements and other official flows, by type of aid, 2014

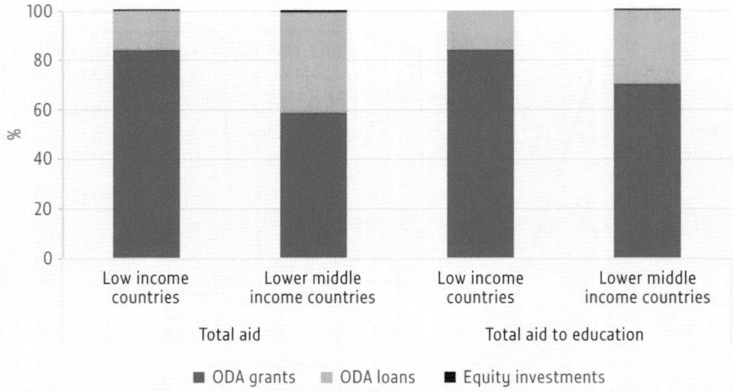

Total aid:
- Low income countries
- Lower middle income countries

Total aid to education:
- Low income countries
- Lower middle income countries

Legend: ■ ODA grants ▨ ODA loans ■ Equity investments

Source: GEM Report team analysis based on OECD CRS data.

Similarly, aid to education channelled through NGOs, civil society organizations and multilateral agencies is 26% for low income countries – more than double the share in lower middle income countries (12%). It will be important to track the extent to which governments increase in importance as a channel of aid in the poorest countries.

Humanitarian aid

Humanitarian aid makes up only a small share of the external financing countries receive for education. In 2014, the education sector received US$188 million in humanitarian aid, less than 1.5% of the amount of development aid disbursed for education that year.

In 2015, out of a total of US$10.6 billion in humanitarian aid, the education sector received US$198 million (**Figure 20.11a**). This is less than 1.9% of total funding, despite a target set by the UN Secretary-General's Global Education First Initiative for education to receive at least 4% of humanitarian aid (**Figure 20.11b**) (United Nations, 2012). Education is at a double disadvantage because it not only receives the smallest share in humanitarian appeals, but what it does receive is consistently less than the average compared with requests: in 2015 the sector received 31% of its requests for humanitarian aid, compared with an average of 55% across all sectors (**Figure 20.11c**).

HOUSEHOLD EXPENDITURE

The share of households in total education expenditure tends to be much higher in poorer than in richer countries. Reducing that share is key to achieving the new education targets. As an analysis of 50 countries in the 2015 GMR showed, households' share of total education expenditure was 18% in high income countries, 34% in middle income countries and 49% in low income countries.

While public expenditure as a share of GDP equals 4.4% in low income countries and 4.8% in high income countries, the addition of household expenditure would reduce and could even reverse the gap in total education expenditure between the two groups. This highlights a key challenge: not only to improve the level of national support to education but also to distribute this cost between households and government. That is why an NEA approach could challenge established views about the relative efforts countries make to support education.

Information on household expenditure is available in most countries. Using the online catalogue of the International Household Survey Network and information available on websites of national statistical agencies, analysis for this report of all 142 low and

FIGURE 20.11:

Education remains an underprioritized and underfunded sector of humanitarian aid

Selected statistics on consolidated and flash appeal requests and funding for the education sector, 2000–2015

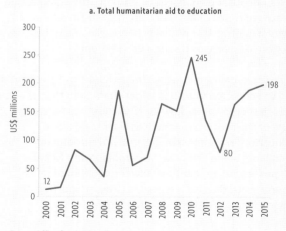

a. Total humanitarian aid to education

Source: Office for the Coordination of Humanitarian Affairs (2016).

middle income countries suggests that the vast majority collect information on household education expenditure. However, it is rarely used: either policy-makers are unaware of its existence and importance or their capacity to analyse it and draw relevant conclusions is often limited.

At least 99 of the 142 countries included questions in a national expenditure survey between 2008 and 2014 on items related to education; deeper analysis was possible for data from 82 countries. Of these 82 countries' questionnaires, all but 15 included questions on individual expenditure items. While the most common question concerned school fees, 59 countries collected information on textbooks, 49 countries on stationery and 33 countries on private tuition. At least 29 countries make survey data publicly available to the broader research community.

Household surveys could be improved. It is possible for information to be recorded for individual children and easily linked to their education level and, in some cases, the grade, school (with an EMIS number) or sector (i.e. public or private). However, two-thirds of the countries only collected aggregate information for education-related expenditure incurred by the household. While there are statistical methods to use this information to estimate education expenditure per child and level of education (Tiyab and Ndabananiye, 2013), it would be preferable if household expenditure surveys were designed to collect information separately for each child.

In coming years, coordinated national action is needed on two fronts. First, education ministries need to work with national statistical agencies to build capacity, analyse existing data and use them as part of an effort to develop and improve NEAs. Second, survey questions must be formulated in a way that would make them more relevant for education policy. The establishment of the Task Force on Standards for Education Spending Estimates based on Household Survey Data under the auspices of the UN Statistical Commission's Inter-Secretariat Working Group on Household Surveys is a step in that direction.

ENDNOTES

1. The Democratic Republic of the Congo, Georgia, Indonesia, Jamaica, Morocco, the Netherlands, Peru, Poland, Samoa and Sri Lanka.

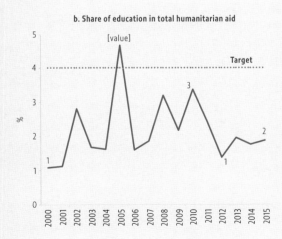

b. Share of education in total humanitarian aid

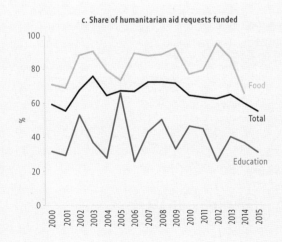

c. Share of humanitarian aid requests funded

Hmong girls line up after their exercise during break time at a primary school in Lao Cai, Viet Nam.

CREDIT: Nguyen Thanh Tuan/UNESCO

KEY MESSAGES

The quality of education systems and policies cannot be monitored through statistics alone.

There are many global tools for monitoring education systems and policies, such as on free and compulsory education or teachers. However, in order for such tools to serve monitoring purposes, agreement on their scope, coverage and regularity as well as country ownership are necessary.

While a global framework for reviewing education systems and policies might be desirable, in practice a regional approach is more practical. Regional partners have shared contexts, and a genuine interest in each other's performance.

Better coordination is needed between existing global and regional monitoring bodies on education system diagnostic tools to address gaps and reduce overlaps.

CHAPTER

Education systems

(selected system-related indicators from different targets)

THEMATIC INDICATOR 2 – *Administration of a nationally representative learning assessment (i) during primary (ii) at the end of primary and (iii) at the end of lower secondary education*

THEMATIC INDICATOR 19 – *Extent to which explicit formula-based policies reallocate education resources to disadvantaged populations*

GLOBAL INDICATOR 4.7.1. – *Extent to which (i) global citizenship education and (ii) education for sustainable development are mainstreamed in (a) national education policies, (b) curricula, (c) teacher education, and (d) student assessment*

This report has reviewed a wide range of proposed and potential indicators that are aimed at supporting efforts – by countries, regions and other stakeholders – to monitor progress towards all Sustainable Development Goals (SDG) targets that explicitly include education.

To inform and guide education decision-making, and to understand whether and why progress is being made, it is necessary to analyse factors at the level of national education systems, such as major legislation; policies on teachers, curriculum and assessment; finance and governance practices; non-formal education programmes; and recent reforms.

Certain aspects of systems and policies can be represented with straightforward quantitative indicators. For example, information on the existence and duration of free and compulsory education can be gleaned from official documents. In other instances – for example, in relation to the indicators above – measures are more complex and qualitative. They require both an examination of pertinent sources and the use of expertise and proper judgement.

Take national learning assessments: for an indicator of them to be relevant, it is necessary to determine whether they are nationally representative and sufficiently robust in design to provide valid and reliable data that can be compared over time. Such information cannot be self-reported. In another example, the indicator on financing to promote equity is meant to determine, in part, how education policies address the needs of disadvantaged and marginalized groups. And the indicator on country efforts to mainstream sustainable development and global citizenship topics in curricula or teacher education requires careful judgement related to the contents of education.

Several concepts in the SDG 4 targets, such as gender equality and education quality, merit monitoring but are not covered by any of the proposed thematic indicators. Yet, systematic information related to such concepts can be compiled from various sources using a more qualitative approach.

> **Several concepts in the education targets, such as gender equality, merit monitoring but are not covered by any of the proposed thematic indicators**

This chapter looks at selected approaches to monitoring aspects of education systems and policies. Many organizations provide descriptive information and conduct diagnostic assessments of education systems and policies. The assessments vary in scope, purpose, frequency, methodology and use, depending on organizations' priorities. This can result in duplication of effort and gaps in country coverage. Improved coordination is needed, therefore, to strengthen the evidence base for monitoring at the regional and global levels.

Note that monitoring education systems does not in any way suggest that governments should be held to account for their policies and institutional arrangements. Rather, it is necessary to help explain why progress toward different aspects of the SDG agenda is, or is not, being achieved.

The chapter also discusses circumstances in which countries more willingly share information on their education systems and policies. This is especially important at the regional level, where countries that may share traditions based on history, tradition and culture can build useful frameworks for comparisons and learn from each other.

DIAGNOSTIC TOOLS FOR MONITORING EDUCATION SYSTEMS

A review of work by various international and regional agencies highlights a variety of approaches used to map education systems and provide useful comparative information for policy-makers.

GLOBAL TOOLS

In 1996, the UNESCO International Bureau of Education (IBE) established the World Data on Education (WDE) series. Originally, the WDE reproduced the National Reports on the Development of Education that member states submitted to IBE before each International Conference on Education. Later, national profiles were organized using a common structure to cover principles and general objectives; laws and other basic regulations; administration and management; structure and organization by level; education processes, including learning achievement assessments; and teaching staff. The seventh edition in 2011 covered about 160 countries (IBE, 2016b).

The WDE has been a valuable source of information on education systems at the global level. However, resource constraints plagued its development. Initially, national governments verified the profiles before publication. However, by the third edition this process ceased. Country networks or digital platforms to regularly update profiles never emerged, so profiles quickly went out of date. In addition, the depth of coverage narrowed and eight areas were dropped, including current educational priorities, financing of education, and higher education.

UNESCO has no current plan to update the series, although regional initiatives have been developed. For example, the Education Policy and Reform Unit at the Asia and Pacific Regional Bureau for Education in Bangkok recently began publishing system profiles as part of the National Education Systems and Policies in Asia-Pacific platform.

UNESCO does provide at least three other examples of global databases that are regularly maintained. The UNESCO Institute for Statistics (UIS), as part of its annual education survey, collects data on the availability of compulsory and free education in every country. The UIS carries out quality assurance on these data, which are used in the statistical tables in the GEM Report annex. Information is collected by age or grade on whether countries legislate for compulsory and free education.

> **The UNESCO Institute for Statistics (UIS) collects data on the availability of compulsory and free education in every country**

A second example, initiated in 2014, is the Global Database on the Right to Education. Country data on fulfilment of the right to education are organized into five categories: ratification of normative instruments; observations from UN bodies such as the Universal Periodic Review under the Human Rights Council; constitutional frameworks; legislative and administrative frameworks; and education policies. The information is regularly updated with reports which countries submit to the UN, together with official national documents they are encouraged to share (UNESCO, 2016b). Within the framework of its strategy on standard-setting instruments in the field of education, UNESCO intends to upgrade this database to an Observatory on the Right to Education as a research tool.

A third example of a standardized – albeit more specialized – resource is the World Technical and Vocational Education and Training (TVET) Database, an online repository developed by UNESCO-UNEVOC. It provides concise, reliable and up-to-date information on TVET systems worldwide to help officials, experts, stakeholders and researchers learn about trends and challenges. The database comprises over 70 country profiles containing key descriptive information about national TVET systems, including national policies, strategies, structure, qualification frameworks and reforms. They are compiled from various national and international sources and validated by UNEVOC centres or other national authorities (UNESCO-UNEVOC, 2016).

These system-level profiles cover a wide selection of countries but a narrow range of education policy issues. In general, they emphasize factual information communicated by countries, but omit important areas of education policy-making.

One initiative aiming to create a global platform of system-level information is the World Bank's Systems

Approach for Better Education Results (SABER), launched in 2011 to increase knowledge on education policies and institutions so as to improve understanding of the link between resources and outcomes. SABER collects 'comparable data on policies and institutions of education systems around the world and benchmarks them against good practice' (World Bank, 2013d; p. 5).

To do this, it examines 13 domains of national education systems in a format that facilitates comparisons across countries. The domains are organized into four groups related to particular levels of education (such as early childhood and tertiary education), resources and support mechanisms (such as teachers and learning assessments), governance and finance (such as school finance and autonomy), and cross-cutting areas (such as equity and inclusion) (**Figure 21.1**).

An analytical framework underpins each domain and draws attention to policy choices. It informs the development of a questionnaire, which is administered with the support of a contracted expert. Data on policies and institutions are then evaluated and rated on a four-level scale of system development (from 'latent' to 'advanced') and aggregated into a national score. Once governments agree on the outcome, the results are published in a report and an online database. While over 100 countries have been reviewed in at least one domain, the coverage for any individual domain is relatively limited. The highest coverage is for student assessment,

with 36 countries participating. No country has been studied more than once in a particular domain.

The World Bank plans to extend the project's scope so that it captures not only policy intentions but also evidence of implementation. In addition, information from all the domains is being repackaged under six themes: standards, governance, resources, information, delivery and accountability. This new structure reflects the fact that it is not the disparate elements that constitute a system but the interactions and synergies between them (Abdul Hamid, 2016).

SABER follows a tradition of diagnostic tools that the World Bank has deployed in several policy areas. The most notable is the Country Policy and Institutional Assessment, which assesses several policies, including education, and informs the Bank's loan allocation decisions. In principle, SABER not only provides a rating but also engages countries in a process to improve their policies, notably by comparing policies of peers. That said, World Bank analytical and policy-rating frameworks tend to reflect Bank priorities. Moreover, education policies do not progress in a clear and unambiguous way; many studies have shown that different policies can be combined to achieve similar outcomes, depending on context. Thus, identifying universal education policies that can be prescribed in other contexts can be problematic.

FIGURE 21.1:

The SABER programme covers a wide range of aspects of education systems

Policy domains covered in the World Bank Systems Approach for Better Education Results

EDUCATION LEVELS	QUALITY RESOURCES AND SYSTEMS SUPPORT	GOVERNANCE AND FINANCE
Early childhood development (32)	Student assessment (36)	Finance (4)
Workforce development (25)	Teachers (28)	School autonomy and accountability (13)
Tertiary education (0)	Information and communication technology (0)	Education management information systems (4)
	School health and school feeding (8)	Private sector (1)

CROSS-CUTTING ISSUES	RESILIENCE (7)	EQUITY AND INCLUSION (0)

Note: The number in brackets indicates the number of reviews carried out, according to the SABER website, as of May 2016.
Source: World Bank (2016a).

While SABER has extended the evidence base on education systems in many areas, it is not meant to serve as a global monitoring tool. For that, at least two issues need to be addressed: agreement on the scope, coverage and regularity of the reviews; and greater country ownership. Both require partnerships with other organizations that are interested in developing and applying system-level tools. For example, the International Teacher Task Force, based at UNESCO, recently collaborated with the World Bank to apply the SABER teacher module, which had been previously administered to 28 countries, to a further 27. The objective is to produce country reports in 2016 that will follow the SABER format. An additional report will provide an international synthesis of what countries consider key requirements of teaching as a profession in their policies and practices (World Bank, 2015a). However, as the next section argues, monitoring may be best served at a regional rather than a global level.

REGIONAL TOOLS

For countries to contribute information to a mechanism that assesses the strengths and weaknesses of their education systems, consensus is needed on how best to identify, develop and validate system-level indicators. Achieving a shared understanding around these issues may prove difficult. Yet, members of a regional entity or broad transnational organization (e.g. the Commonwealth, the Organisation for Economic Co-operation and Development (OECD) or the International Organisation of La Francophonie) are more likely to voluntarily exchange information on their education systems – and a consensus about purpose, policy priorities and mechanisms is more easily reached, facilitated by deeper country commitment and engagement.

Two examples stand out. The Eurydice Network on Education Systems and Policies in Europe was established in 1980. The primary treaties of the European Union (EU) respect the 'responsibility of the Member States for the content of teaching and the organization of education systems'. In the 1970s, the countries were concerned that joint activities

> " The Eurydice Network in Europe has an online database of education systems in 36 countries "

on education would exert pressure on their systems to become more similar and thus impinge on national sovereignty. Nevertheless, they agreed on the value of exchanging information and documentation on education systems (Eurydice, 2000).

Since 1992, education has been increasingly recognized as an area of EU competency, and this exchange has increased, gaining particular momentum with the adoption of Europe 2020, an overarching strategy on growth and jobs. It includes investment in education as a priority and sets two relevant core targets for 2020: that no more than 10% of adolescents should leave school before completing upper secondary education, and that at least 40% of 30- to 34-year-olds should have attained tertiary education (European Union, 2015). As part of the related Education and Training 2020 programme, member states receive guidance on priority reforms in the form of annual country-specific recommendations. These generate more awareness of the importance of education and strengthen incentives to share examples of good policy practice.

From its tentative initial steps, Eurydice has grown into a network of 40 national units in 36 countries, including 8 that are not EU members. Its work is relevant to the global debate on education system-level information. It produces an online database of national education systems that covers a broad range of issues and is continuously updated by national authorities (Eurydice, 2016a). It also prepares comparative thematic studies on topics decided jointly by the European Commission and member states. The 2015 topics, for instance, were higher education, adult education, school evaluation and teachers (Eurydice, 2016b). The studies visualize complex information on policy choices in a transparent way to facilitate cross-country comparisons.

Another example of a cross-country framework of education system indicators is the OECD's Indicators of Education Systems (INES) programme, introduced in 1992. One of its three networks focused on 'learning environment and the organization of schools' and collected information on issues such as curricular content and decision-making responsibilities in education systems. In 2009, this network evolved into the INES Network for System-Level Indicators (NESLI), which collects system-level data. 'As mutual confidence and understanding is a prerequisite for establishing internationally comparable data', the data collection process 'requires considerable specialized expertise that depends on stable international working arrangements' (OECD, 2009b). The INES oversight and coordination bodies determine the NESLI work plan following strategic direction by the OECD Education Policy Committee, which is responsible for the organization's work on education.

NESLI collects information such as indicators on teacher remuneration and instruction time, using annual, cyclical or ad hoc surveys. Much of the information is published in the annual OECD *Education at a Glance* reports. Extensive annexes to the reports describe sources of information by country. In recent years, information on non-member countries has been included (**Box 21.1**).

BOX 21.1

Engaging in multiple initiatives to diagnose education systems – the case of Brazil

In recent years, the OECD has increasingly extended its diagnostic assessments of education systems to cover non-member countries. For example, it has carried out reviews of national education policies in the Dominican Republic, Indonesia and Tajikistan. For some reviews, such as in Malaysia and Thailand, it has collaborated with UNESCO. NESLI has also sought to engage OECD candidate countries, such as Colombia and Lithuania, and non-member countries, such as Brazil and the Russian Federation.

Brazil joined the network after participating in the World Education Indicators project, a joint effort of the OECD, UIS and World Bank. Brazil has benefited from exchanging information with other countries through NESLI but also from improved domestic coordination between government departments, which was necessary to collect the information. But since it is not an OECD member, Brazil cannot influence NESLI's agenda toward its areas of interest. And as a federal country with a large degree of decentralization, it has also found it difficult to report national-level information.

Brazil is also a member of two regional groupings that promote exchange of information on education systems: the Organization of Ibero-American States (OEI), which has a common education agenda that increasingly looks at qualitative aspects of education systems; and Mercosur, a customs union and trading bloc, which considers education as one factor promoting regional integration and has carried out comparative reviews of member countries' education systems.

Sources: Mercosur (2008); OEI (2010).

The OECD has carried out systematic country education policy reviews since the 1970s; INES and NESLI follow in a long tradition of diagnostic tools developed by the organization. Policy reviews are becoming more diversified, focusing on selected areas or levels of education, such as early childhood or post-secondary skills acquisition. At the same time, there are attempts to unify different strands of work, for example through the Education GPS database, which links information on system indicators with other sources, and the Education Policy Outlook series (OECD, 2015c).

An excellent example of such efforts, albeit in a different context, is the OEI education strategy known as Metas Educativas 2021 ('Education Goals 2021'), agreed by Latin American education ministers in 2008. A specialized body, the Institute of Monitoring and Evaluation, was established to review progress on 11 targets and 39 indicators, at least one of which explicitly refers to the functioning of education systems (OEI, 2014). At the 2015 meeting of the OEI Governing Council, vice-ministers requested the development of more qualitative indicators to capture aspects of targets on equity and teacher professional development (OEI, 2015).

Other regional organizations have analysed systems and policies, although usually in relation to particular aspects of education. For example, the Association of Southeast Asian Nations and the South-east Asian Ministers of Education Organization are taking steps to harmonize regional higher education systems to facilitate mobility of students, faculty and researchers for better regional economic integration. This analysis has led to work that compares, links and coordinates higher education systems in areas such as quality assurance (Niedermeier and Pohlenz, 2016; Ratanawijitrasin, 2015).

A final example of high quality education system diagnostic assessment is the long-standing Country Status Report series of the UNESCO International Institute for Educational Planning (IIEP) in sub-Saharan Africa (IIEP et al., 2014). This initiative seeks to build national decision-makers' capacity for sector analysis and facilitate domestic policy dialogue. Attempts to compare countries – for example through the IIEP Pôle de Dakar database – focus almost exclusively on quantitative indicators. A coordinated effort would be needed to improve the basis for comparing systems and policies, which would generate sustained regional dialogue.

LOOKING AHEAD

In essence, policies are about transforming resources (the main focus of education monitoring in the past) into effective processes (rarely monitored), resulting in measurable outcomes (the focus of the SDG agenda). Determining which systems and policies are effective relies considerably on the nature of the evidence collected and analysed. Linking policies to measurable results through a system-oriented approach in education reflects a similar trend in the global health field (WHO, 2009). The focus on systems in education also affects the research agenda. One example is the Research on Improving Systems of Education project funded by the UK Department for International Development and the Australian Department of Foreign Affairs and Trade (Hanson, 2015).

A broad range of validated indicators of education systems and policies is needed to support the monitoring of the Education 2030 agenda. However, as this chapter has shown, education system diagnoses differ widely in their objectives (e.g. referring to different agendas and targets), scope (e.g. general vs specific), methodology (e.g. country driven vs externally imposed or conducted by experts) and use (e.g. whether they lead to policy changes). Much could be done to address gaps and reduce overlap among diagnostic instruments.

Sharing experiences between countries and promoting policy dialogue, based on broadly comparable qualitative information on education systems, will facilitate effective decision-making. While a global framework for reviewing education systems and policies might be desirable, in practice a regional or subregional approach is more feasible. Many regions have common education contexts and can structure reviews to better reflect their shared values, objectives and challenges. Members of regional entities are more likely to express deeper political commitment and national ownership for such an undertaking – critical conditions for creating valid, up-to-date system-level indicators of education. And the results of regional monitoring are much more likely

> " A regional or subregional approach is more feasible than a global framework for reviewing education systems "

to be used in policy-making and be sustained over time, not least because governments have an interest in neighbouring countries' performance.

The key to successfully exchanging information on education systems between countries is strong coordination mechanisms from regional intergovernmental organizations that include education development among their objectives. Countries can draw on the experience of the EU, OEI or OECD to initiate policy dialogue through system-level indicators that are relevant to their regions as well as to the Education 2030 agenda. The African Union (with the Association for the Development of Education in Africa), the Arab League Educational, Cultural and Scientific Organization, the South Asian Association for Regional Cooperation, the Caribbean Community, the Commonwealth and the International Organisation of La Francophonie are examples of potential mechanisms for peer learning.

Women farmers from Zambia take part in a planting day of new trees.
CREDIT: Sydelle Willow Smith/GEM Report

KEY MESSAGES

Education is explicitly mentioned in global indicators for five SDGs other than SDG 4, pertaining to poverty, employment and the environment.

Education should be monitored in at least three ways: how it affects development outcomes, such as fertility; how it increases the number of skilled professionals working in all sectors; and how it can change adult attitudes and behaviour.

Many other SDGs should break down their indicators by education level to understand underlying inequality holding back progress. For instance, across 54 countries, there would be over 100 fewer births for every 1,000 adolescent women if they had secondary education rather than no education. The prevalence of malaria among children aged 6 months to 59 months in 15 sub-Saharan African countries over 2009–2015 would have been halved if their mothers had had secondary rather than primary education.

CHAPTER

Education in the other SDGs

(global indicators from goals other than SDG 4 that are education-related)

GLOBAL INDICATOR 1.A.2 – *Proportion of total government spending on essential services (education, health and social protection)*

GLOBAL INDICATOR 5.6.2 – *Number of countries with laws and regulations that guarantee women aged 15–49 years access to sexual and reproductive health care, information and education*

GLOBAL INDICATOR 8.6.1 – *Proportion of youth (aged 15–24 years) not in education, employment or training*

GLOBAL INDICATOR 12.8.1 – *Extent to which (i) global citizenship education and (ii) education for sustainable development (including climate change education) are mainstreamed in (a) national education policies; (b) curricula; (c) teacher education; and (d) student assessment*

GLOBAL INDICATOR 13.3.1 – *Number of countries that have integrated mitigation, adaptation, impact reduction and early warning into primary, secondary and tertiary curricula*

The *Global Education Monitoring Report* (GEM Report) demonstrates the importance of education as both a human right and as tool for the advancement of all Sustainable Development Goals (SDGs). The 2030 Agenda for Sustainable Development recognizes the importance of a separate education goal as well as the need to achieve other goals through education. Accordingly, the Incheon Declaration of the World Education Forum nominated the GEM Report 'as the mechanism for monitoring and reporting on ... SDG 4 and on education in the other ... SDGs' (§18).

This chapter addresses SDGs other than SDG 4 through their global indicators that are relevant for education. It begins with a discussion of indicators that directly refer to education, as listed above. It then addresses indicators that can be indirectly linked to education: those linked to development outcomes, which can be disaggregated by education; and those linked to means of implementation, which refer to the national capacity necessary for achieving the SDGs, for example, as found in trained professionals and researchers. Finally, it offers a perspective on the underestimated role of lifelong learning for the achievement of the goals by 2030.

DIRECT REFERENCES TO EDUCATION IN GLOBAL SDG INDICATORS

> **Education is directly mentioned in five global indicators outside SDG 4**

Education is directly mentioned in five global indicators outside SDG 4, under poverty, gender equality, economic growth, sustainable consumption and production, and climate change. Each of the indicators suggests that education plays a key role for achieving broader development outcomes.

Global indicator 1.a.2 calls for monitoring government spending on education, health and social protection under a target that focuses on 'mobilization of resources ... to implement programmes and policies to end poverty in all its dimensions'. Attention to government education expenditure is justified by the fact that public expenditure in social sectors, aided by a fair taxation system, can play a major role in reducing poverty. For example, across 27 Organisation for Economic Co-operation and Development (OECD) countries, adding the value of public services to household income reduced the poverty rate by 46% because such services were targeted to households most in need (OECD, 2011a). And a review showed that public education and health expenditure reduced inequality in six Latin American countries more than cash transfers to households (Lustig et al., 2013).

There is a well-recognized methodology for reporting such expenditure (see Chapter 20). Nevertheless, the Inter-agency and Expert Group on Sustainable Development Goal Indicators (IAEG-SDGs) has classified it as a Tier III indicator, implying that 'there are no established methodology and standards' and referring to the need for a reporting mechanism (with the International Labour Organization, World Health Organization and UNESCO responsible for the respective sectors of economy, health and education and the World Bank as a potential custodian agency).

Global indicator 5.6.2 is the only indicator under SDG 5, which explicitly refers to education as a means to gender equality, although other indicators also closely relate to educational development, such as the proportion of time spent on unpaid domestic and care work or the seats held by women in national parliaments and local governments. It measures the number of countries with laws and regulations that guarantee access to sexual and reproductive health care, information and education, in accordance with the Programme of Action of the International Conference on Population and Development and the Beijing Platform for Action.

One component of the indicator will therefore focus on the number of countries with such laws and regulations in education, noting if they are age-appropriate, gender-focused and human rights-based. The methodology, currently under development, consists of initial self-reporting by governments. Data collection is expected to start in July 2017 (UNFPA, 2016). As the approach has not yet been tested, the indicator has been classified as Tier III. This qualitative systems indicator approach (see Chapter 21) is very similar to that used for issues raised under target 4.7 (see Chapter 16).

Global indicator 8.6.1 monitors the proportion of youth not in education, employment or training (NEET). It complements global indicator 4.3.1, the youth participation rate in formal and non-formal education and training. The difference between them is that the SDG 8 global indicator also includes employment. The indicator captures youth who are either discouraged from or not interested in participating in the labour force. A methodology has been established, so the indicator has been classified as Tier I (ILO, 2013).

However, this indicator cannot easily be compared across countries. For example, a comparison of 28 countries that participated in the School-to-Work Transition Survey shows that Cambodia and Madagascar had NEET rates below 10% among 15- to 29-year-olds, while Bangladesh and Samoa exceeded 40%. The European Union average was 15% in 2012/13, similar to the low income countries average (18%) but well below that of middle income countries (26%). It is unclear what the target should be. It is important to look at the parts that constitute the indicator to understand whether the challenge in a country is, for example, access to education and training or constraints to labour force participation for women (ILO, 2015).

Finally, global indicators 12.8.1 and 13.3.1 focus on global citizenship education and education for sustainable development as means to support the transition to sustainable production and consumption patterns as well as addressing the causes and impact of climate change. In that respect, they are essentially identical to global indicator 4.7.1 (see Chapter 16). Accordingly, the proposed sources of information are the quadrennial national

reports on the implementation of the Recommendation concerning Education for International Understanding, Co-operation and Peace and Education relating to Human Rights and Fundamental Freedoms, adopted at the 1974 UNESCO General Conference. Nevertheless, this has been classified as a Tier III indicator.

Alternative sources and approaches may be necessary. This report has argued for more specificity than these reports allow and to increase country coverage in the monitoring process. A global process to code national curriculum framework documents using a standard protocol could be established. This would require close collaboration with ministries and a leading international coordinating body (see Chapter 16).

INDIRECT REFERENCES TO EDUCATION IN GLOBAL SDG INDICATORS

Apart from monitoring indicators that explicitly refer to education, future GEM Reports will also pay attention to indirect references to education in the other SDGs. Two examples are highlighted in this section: education as a factor associated with other development outcomes and therefore as a characteristic by which particular global indicators can be disaggregated; and indicators that refer to human resource capacity, which are related to professional and higher education.

EDUCATION AS A FACTOR ASSOCIATED WITH DEVELOPMENT OUTCOMES

The GEM Report has presented strong examples of the relationship between education and other development outcomes. In many cases, research has clearly shown that education attainment has a causal effect over and above other related influences such as wealth. In other cases, this causal relationship has not yet been established.

Observing the correlation of education attainment with other development outcomes and how this relationship varies by country and evolves over time is interesting. It can indicate whether the relationship is consistent and how it may contribute to reaching the targets. It can also point at cases where the relationship is weak to give useful feedback to education planners. Taking the education level into account can also show the intergenerational effects of education on other outcomes.

> "
>
> On average across 54 countries, there would be over 100 fewer births for every 1,000 women if they had secondary education compared to no education at all
>
> "

But caution is needed. A population with particular levels of education attainment changes over time as education systems expand. For example, the characteristics of women who had never been to school in low income countries in 1990, when this circumstance was relatively common, are very different from those in 2015, when this situation has become rarer.

Three examples from the health SDG show disparity in development outcomes by level of education. The adolescent birth rate – the number of births per 1,000 women aged 15 to 19 (global indicator 3.7.2) – varies considerably by education level. Across 54 low and middle countries with data over 2008–2015, the unweighted average number of births per 1,000 women was 176 if they had no education, 142 if they had primary, 61 if they had secondary and 13 if they had tertiary. In sub-Saharan Africa, the negative association of adolescent birth rate with secondary education appears to have become stronger over time (**Figure 22.1a**).

Since 2000, the under-5 mortality rate (global indicator 3.2.1) has rapidly declined in Southern and Eastern Africa. In countries including Rwanda and Zambia, the mortality rate of children whose mothers had secondary education was 20% to 30% lower than children with primary-educated mothers. It was about 50% lower in countries such as the Plurinational State of Bolivia, Guinea and the

FIGURE 22.1:

Education is positively associated with desirable development outcomes

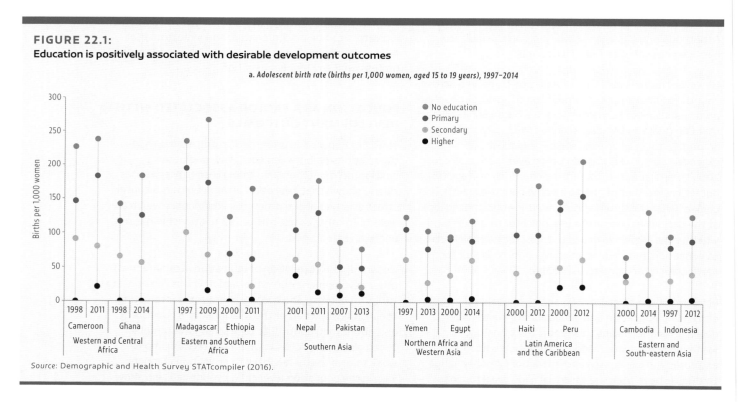

a. Adolescent birth rate (births per 1,000 women, aged 15 to 19 years), 1997–2014

Source: Demographic and Health Survey STATcompiler (2016).

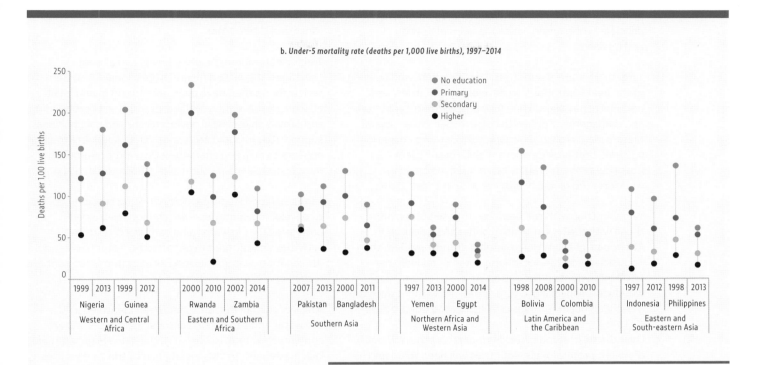

b. *Under-5 mortality rate (deaths per 1,000 live births), 1997–2014*

- ● No education
- ● Primary
- ● Secondary
- ● Higher

1999	2013	1999	2012		2000	2010	2002	2014		2007	2013	2000	2011		1997	2013	2000	2014		1998	2008	2000	2010		1997	2012	1998	2013
Nigeria		Guinea			Rwanda		Zambia			Pakistan		Bangladesh			Yemen		Egypt			Bolivia		Colombia			Indonesia		Philippines	
Western and Central Africa					Eastern and Southern Africa					Southern Asia					Northern Africa and Western Asia					Latin America and the Caribbean					Eastern and South-eastern Asia			

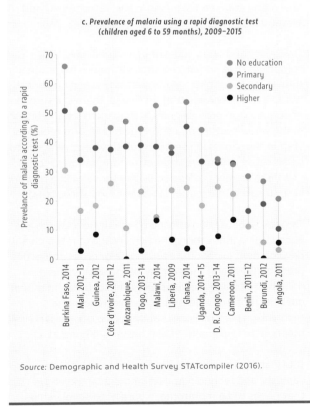

c. *Prevalence of malaria using a rapid diagnostic test (children aged 6 to 59 months), 2009–2015*

- ● No education
- ● Primary
- ● Secondary
- ● Higher

Burkina Faso, 2014; Mali, 2012–13; Guinea, 2012; Côte d'Ivoire, 2011–12; Mozambique, 2011; Togo, 2013–14; Malawi, 2014; Liberia, 2009; Ghana, 2014; Uganda, 2014–15; D. R. Congo, 2013–14; Cameroon, 2011; Benin, 2011–12; Burundi, 2012; Angola, 2011

Source: Demographic and Health Survey STATcompiler (2016).

Philippines (**Figure 22.1b**). The prevalence of malaria was also half among children aged 6 to 59 months whose mothers had secondary rather than primary education in 15 sub-Saharan African countries over 2009–2015 (**Figure 22.1c**).

In brief, disaggregating relevant global indicators by education levels would shed more light on their relationship and on the underlying inequality that obstructs the achievement of the SDG targets. Global indicators that could be monitored this way include, for example, those related to poverty (1.1.1; by the level of education of the household head), malnutrition (2.2.2), child marriage (5.3.1), access to improved sanitation (6.2.1), access to electricity (7.1.1), unemployment (8.5.2), urban slum population (11.1.1), recycling (12.5.1), disaster deaths (13.1.2), violence (16.1.3) and birth registration (16.9.1).

EDUCATION AS A FACTOR RELATED TO NATIONAL CAPACITY FOR SDG IMPLEMENTATION

A number of other targets and indicators across the SDGs are indirectly linked to the potential of education to build capacity. Education systems can prepare professionals and researchers to implement sustainable development plans in academia, administration and business.

Targets 3.c and 3.d refer to the development and training of the health workforce in developing countries, and national capacity-building for early warning, reduction and management of health risks, respectively. Several factors play a role but, among them, strong education systems that provide relevant skills in sufficient quantities are a prerequisite. In brief, 'no health workforce, no global health security' (Lancet, 2016).

Yet, countries with the heaviest disease burden are those with the lowest density of health professionals. About 44% of the WHO's member states have less than 1 physician and 28% less than 1 nurse or midwife per 1,000 inhabitants (WHO, 2015). At least 1 billion people worldwide, especially in rural areas, are without access to a qualified health professional (Crisp and Chen, 2014).

Over the next decade, besides increasing the number of health professionals, countries will need to adapt the curricula of medical education: new diagnostics, vaccines and drugs are being developed; medical technology is progressing; and patient conditions are changing owing to ageing populations, urbanization and the increasing

number of deaths due to non-communicable diseases (Crisp and Chen, 2014).

Trained community health workers can alleviate shortages of qualified health professionals. A systematic review found they have been effective in giving health education, preventing malaria, promoting breastfeeding and providing essential newborn care and psychosocial support (Gilmore and McAuliffe, 2013). Adequate training appears to be a key characteristic of programmes that have been scaled up successfully (Pallas et al., 2013).

Target 6.a focuses on capacity-building support to developing countries – which requires trained professionals – in water- and sanitation-related activities and programmes, including water harvesting, desalination, water efficiency, wastewater treatment and recycling and reuse technologies.

A lack of human resources has been identified in the water and sanitation sector since the UN Water conference in 1991. However, surveys reveal governments lack awareness. In 2011, nearly half of the 74 countries surveyed for a global status update were unable to state how many staff were working in the sector (WHO and UN Water, 2012).

Only one-third of 94 countries surveyed have comprehensive human resource strategies for urban and rural areas for drinking water, sanitation and hygiene (WHO and UN Water, 2014). In Ghana, there is a surplus of about 3,000 professionals in management and finance in the water sector but a shortage of 280,000 technical staff in the sanitation sector if full service coverage is to be achieved. The more stigmatized sanitation sector is unable to attract professionals and those willing to work in rural areas (International Water Association, 2014).

Target 9.5 focuses on enhancing scientific research and encouraging innovation. The percentage of research and development expenditure as a share of gross domestic product (GDP) and the number of researchers per 1 million inhabitants serve as global indicators of national capacity. For example, at just 21 researchers and 5 technicians per 1 million inhabitants in 2011, Lesotho is ill prepared to implement SDG strategies (**Figure 22.2**).

International cooperation is needed to develop research capacity and technology development, an objective that needs to be monitored in parallel to scholarships. This is the intention, among others, of targets related to medical research (3.b), environmentally sound technologies (12.a) and marine technology (14.a).

FIGURE 22.2:
There is vast disparity in the availability of scientific and technical personnel
Researchers and technicians (in full-time equivalent) per million inhabitants, 2011–2013

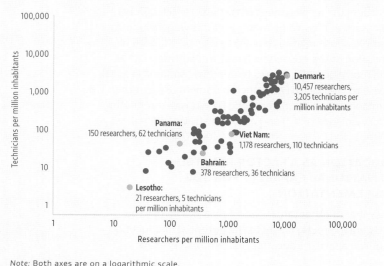

Note: Both axes are on a logarithmic scale.
Source: UIS database.

LIFELONG LEARNING AS A FACTOR CONTRIBUTING ACROSS THE SDGS

Fulfilling the SDG agenda will require a massive and rapid transformation. As formal schooling systems receive most of the attention, behaviour change – crucial for achieving SDGs – appears to be neglected. Thus, despite the reference in the SDG 4 goal formulation, the critical role of adult education and learning has been overlooked in the other targets.

> **As formal schooling receives most of the attention for achieving the SDGs, behaviour change and the critical role of adult education and learning have been overlooked**

How can mortality from non-communicable diseases be reduced by one-third in 15 years unless adults drastically change behaviours related to the consumption of food, alcohol and tobacco? How will the number of deaths and injuries from traffic accidents be halved without dramatic changes in road behaviour? How will equal opportunities for leadership at all levels of decision-making in political, economic and public life be enhanced unless stereotypical attitudes are challenged? And how will food and general waste be substantially reduced in the context of today's consumerism?

For such changes to take place in such a short period of time, campaigns with an active education component will be necessary. This is where the intersectoral nature of the new agenda will come to full force but also where various facets of adult education and learning opportunities will need to be explored and monitored.

For some people, the learning programmes expressed or implied in the other SDGs tend not to be seen as 'education' but as 'extension' programmes in health, agriculture, skills development, environmental management, citizenship or community development. While they are not regarded as the responsibility of ministries of education, this by no means suggests they should be neglected.

Young Nepalese students study their textbooks.

CREDIT: Anup Vaswani/GEM Report

KEY MESSAGES

Global monitoring of SDG 4 requires sufficient comparable information to foster a global dialogue over progress. Such monitoring does not undermine country reviews of its own progress in education, which focuses on national context and specific needs.

Countries should be encouraged to contribute to discussions on the monitoring of SDG 4 in an informed and meaningful way. The Technical Cooperation Group should set up a decision-making mechanism to foster consensus and strengthen its legitimacy.

AT THE NATIONAL LEVEL: BUILD CAPACITY IN SIX KEY AREAS

Equity. Cooperation between education ministries and national statistical agencies is needed to shed light on basic disparities. Education ministries should help create questions concerning education for household surveys.

Learning outcomes. Countries need to ensure that a robust, sample-based national learning assessment is in place, which can be used to monitor progress in learning over time.

Quality. Countries need to monitor curricula, textbooks and teacher education programmes closely.

Lifelong learning. Countries need to monitor education needs, opportunities and accomplishments of their adult populations who are actively involved in critical decisions on sustainable development.

Systems. Regional organizations offer countries appropriate forums for exchanging information on the aims and characteristics of their education and learning systems.

Finance. Countries are encouraged to adopt the national education accounts approach to understand better how education expenditure is shared between governments, donors and households.

AT THE REGIONAL LEVEL: SUPPORT PEER LEARNING

Using regional networks as peer learning mechanisms, countries can exchange information on policy successes and challenges, including on addressing disadvantages and improving education for global citizenship and sustainable development.

AT THE GLOBAL LEVEL: FOSTER CONSENSUS AND COORDINATION

An international household survey programme dedicated to education is needed to fill several major gaps.

A consistent approach to monitor learning outcomes is also required, including a code of conduct among donors to avoid overlap.

The establishment of a research hub related to global education measurement issues is strongly recommended.

CHAPTER

Priorities for monitoring education in the Sustainable Development Goals

The *Global Education Monitoring Report 2016* (GEM Report) makes a strong case that education is a catalyst for achieving the ambitious 2030 Agenda for Sustainable Development, with its 17 Sustainable Development Goals (SDGs), including SDG 4 on education. It provides evidence on the extent to which achieving the SDG 4 targets by 2030 would accelerate the achievement of the key economic, health and environment-related SDGs.

The monitoring part of the GEM Report reviewed the scope for monitoring education in the SDGs, especially SDG 4, carefully examining concepts in target formulations, analysing proposed as well as missing indicators, discussing the latest developments in measurement tools and identifying the main gaps in conceptualization and measurement.

Viewed in one way, the Education 2030 monitoring agenda, when presented by individual target is daunting in its breadth. Responding to each target would pose significant challenges to education ministries and national statistical agencies, not only in poor countries but also in rich ones.

At the same time, the proposed monitoring agenda is underwhelming. Given the severity of sustainable development challenges, it barely scratches the surface of the fundamental questions facing education and lifelong learning. How do education systems help learners of all ages acquire relevant knowledge, practice critical thinking, manage uncertainty, act responsibly regarding the environmental crisis, understand their shared humanity and behave as global citizens? The monitoring framework does not go far enough to answer these questions.

Yet, overall, important steps have been taken. The agenda is instilling a new sense of purpose in education monitoring activities, compared with the emphasis of past decades on counting heads in schools. The

> The new Education 2030 agenda is instilling a new sense of purpose in education monitoring, compared with the emphasis of past decades on counting heads in schools

expanded approach to reviewing progress should be celebrated and safeguarded. It offers a starting point for advancing the sustainable development agenda, with education at its heart.

The challenge is for governments and the international community to take concrete steps to achieve the new education targets while acting swiftly and purposefully to enable their monitoring, based on agreed indicators, even those with identified weaknesses.

This concluding chapter has two objectives. First, it aims to distil the detailed discussions by target to provide a summary of emerging priorities for monitoring the new agenda. Second, using these conclusions as a basis, the chapter describes key implications in terms of the necessary steps forward at the national, regional and global levels. In doing so, it points to potential links between approaches that can support an efficient and feasible monitoring strategy for countries and the international community.

The driving consideration in forming these recommendations is not monitoring per se, let alone global monitoring, but whether monitoring can significantly help catalyse improvements in education systems and the quality of learning environments serving all learners, regardless of background and age.

All countries are now committed to global monitoring. While global monitoring is not the main objective of the Education 2030 agenda, its contribution should not be underestimated. The GEM Report's mandate is to facilitate well-informed and meaningful comparisons between countries and regions so as to spur debates, especially between governments, civil society and engaged citizens, on what, how and how well education systems deliver. Comparative monitoring should not be seen as an attempt to impose particular global norms, but rather as an invitation to dialogue, engagement and commitment.

SYNTHESIS OF MONITORING CHALLENGES AND OPPORTUNITIES

As the first in the new series of GEM Reports, the 2016 edition has looked in depth at the monitoring issues related to each individual SDG 4 target. This is timely: while the basic parameters of the global and thematic monitoring framework have been agreed, in many cases important details are still being decided. These issues need to be presented openly to the international community as a contribution to technical and political debate.

The scope of the monitoring agenda is wide, and the issues involved are often complex. This section aims to provide the bigger picture by drawing together conclusions, summarizing key messages and indicating common themes in challenges across targets.

Target 4.1: Following several decades of focus on participation measures based on enrolment, the new agenda marks an important advance with its shift to completion rates, an approach the GEM Report team has advocated in recent years.

After this positive step, the main outstanding question is how the international community will monitor 'relevant and effective learning outcomes'. This involves the content of learning (what is 'relevant') as well as whether it is achieving various aims (what is 'effective'). Monitoring learning outcomes effectively will require making processes open and collaborative, and building national learning assessment systems that take country priorities into account. While the urge to report on the global indicator is understandable, the process should respect these two principles.

As important as reporting on learning outcomes is for monitoring, equally valuable is reporting on key, yet neglected, background characteristics that will help explain these outcomes. For example, governments need to be sensitized to monitor the languages students speak at home as compared with those in which they are taught and assessed. Another issue is ensuring

that children who are out of school are not left behind: reporting needs to include all children or adolescents in a given age group and not just those who attend school.

Target 4.2: Two issues emerge in relation to the target on early childhood care, education and development. First, the diversity of services needs to be better understood. Current approaches to measurement are highly fragmented and do not capture many characteristics of provision, especially the strength of education and learning components in early childhood programmes outside pre-primary education. This calls for stronger coordination between national and international surveys to measure participation across a wider spectrum of programmes.

Second, the search for a measure of early childhood development must continue. The current measure, based on the UNICEF Early Childhood Development Index, has four components but is strongly influenced by the literacy and numeracy component. These questions have been criticized as being too advanced and reflecting norms on early education rather than young children's cognitive capacity (McCoy et al., 2016). To understand whether children are reaching their development potential, more research is needed on measures that are valid across a wide range of countries.

Target 4.3: Two clear issues arise in relation to monitoring technical-vocational, tertiary and adult education. First, as with early childhood education, the available monitoring tools are not even close to capturing the increasingly large diversity of education and learning opportunities. For example, monitoring systems tend to focus on formal technical and vocational education. They do not capture new forms of tertiary education. Nor do they include adult education, except in a few high income countries. Similar problems beset household survey approaches.

Second, the proposed indicator framework entirely ignores affordability – but progress towards this target in the next 15 years relies on it. Although debates on this issue are complex, it is important to agree on basic parameters that will help ensure government policies on these types of education and learning opportunities are better targeted to those most in need.

Target 4.4: This target covers a broad range of skills for the world of work. However, while education systems need to help learners acquire several transferrable skills for decent work, such skills may not be suitable for large-scale monitoring, especially at the global level.

By contrast, the focus of the global indicator on information and communications technology (ICT) skills is much narrower. Based on self-reported competencies related to computer use, it is in fact inadequate. Instead, an emphasis on digital literacy skills would represent an advance. While still narrow, it is broader than ICT skills and has two concrete advantages: it would focus on direct measurement of an actual skill, which should be a priority for this agenda, and it would focus on a skill likely to become very relevant as a marker of disadvantage in the world of work for most, if not all, people. Therefore, the international community should learn how to better measure digital literacy skills. Current school-based measures are culturally biased and need to be further developed to be suitable for monitoring beyond a select group of high income countries.

Target 4.5: In recent years, the World Inequality Database on Education has helped bring disparity in education opportunities between and within countries to the attention of the wider public. The launch of the Inter-Agency Group on Education Inequality Indicators will now advance this agenda by making effective use of a very large number of data sets.

Three major challenges remain. First, the choice of a suitable inequality measure is still open. The parity index, proposed as the global indicator, is easy to communicate but has notable weaknesses. Second, despite progress in global coordination, many education ministries do not yet monitor disparity. Third, global comparisons are currently possible only by sex, location and wealth. The search for measures of other markers – notably disability, language, migration and displacement – needs to continue.

Leaving no one behind, the rallying cry of the new agenda, will not be answered solely by a proliferation of disparity measures. It also calls for a concerted effort to monitor the policies pursued by countries to address education disadvantage, including policies outside education. A mechanism is needed to allow countries to collect and compare this qualitative information.

> A new mechanism is needed to help countries collect and compare information about policies successfully addressing disadvantages in education

Target 4.6: One example of the gaps in monitoring adult education opportunities is the continuing absence of information on participation in adult literacy programmes. After years of advocacy, the new agenda has embraced a shift to a nuanced direct assessment of a range of literacy and numeracy proficiency levels instead of relying on dubious self-reported skills. However, as with assessments of learning outcomes in basic education, it is essential to help build national systems to monitor these skills. In addition, diversity in literate environment contexts and variations in national capacity for collecting and analysing data must be accounted for.

Target 4.7: In response to explicit reference in the target to knowledge and skills related to sustainable development and global citizenship, the international community has prioritized progress assessments based on the content of education. This is positive, as it will encourage countries to reflect on what is taught in classrooms. However, it has not been clarified how such information is to be collected and communicated at the global level.

UNESCO member states' reports on implementation of the 1974 Recommendation concerning Education for International Understanding, Co-operation and Peace and Education relating to Human Rights and Fundamental Freedoms are proposed as the mechanism to monitor progress towards the target. But low response rates and submission quality mean the process is weak and needs to be complemented by a more systematic and rigorous approach.

The GEM Report has proposed an approach that would require a systematic listing of national curriculum frameworks and a coding protocol to analyse curricular materials. Such a mechanism would also require close collaboration between education ministries and regional or international organizations to ensure that the quality of the information is good and that the process is country-led. The mechanism could also cover other aspects of national policies, including teacher education programmes, learning assessments and textbooks.

Target 4.a: Interest in the concept of child-friendly schools drove the formulation of this target. The most meaningful measures of such environments are observation-based, making this a particularly difficult target for global monitoring. One potential entry point is the growing interest in measures of school violence, though further progress will require collaboration to ensure that definitions in student surveys, currently fragmented, are aligned. School infrastructure indicators may be the easiest to measure but also the least likely to capture the spirit of an effective learning environment.

Target 4.b: There is a surprising gap in information on scholarships. Providers need to collaborate to develop an entirely new global mechanism for reporting on government and non-government scholarships. Collected information must cover the basic characteristics not only of scholarships, but also of their recipients, notably their origin, destination and field of study. This process needs to start as soon as possible, since the target is to be achieved by 2020 and the currently proposed global indicator, based on scholarships funded from aid programmes, provides a very incomplete picture.

Target 4.c: The formulation of the teacher target also put the spotlight on a weak evidence base. Current measures of qualified and trained teachers are hard to compare because standards are not comparable. The fact that personnel databases are often not linked to overall education management information systems makes it difficult to monitor equity in staff distribution across schools, teachers' working conditions and the rate at which they to leave the profession. Not enough use is made of labour force surveys that could show how teacher remuneration compares with other professions.

Considerable insights could be gained from a tool that collects information directly from teachers, along the lines of the Organisation for Economic Co-operation and Development (OECD) Teaching and Learning International Survey, whose contribution has been acknowledged by all stakeholders. Given the dual potential for allowing cross-country comparison with high quality data but also for informing policy, it is worth considering the expansion of such a tool to cover low and middle income countries.

Finance: The coverage of basic data on government expenditure is remarkably low and there is a considerable time lag. But the main challenge is providing a comprehensive picture of all financing sources. Therefore the priority is to support the institutionalization of national education accounts, similar to national health accounts. This key step would bring all financing sources into a common measure and clarify who benefits from public education services.

Civil society organizations have advocated the use of normative instruments for monitoring whether governments guarantee free education. While understanding whether education is free is important, the GEM Report argues that this is less likely to come from official policy documents than from monitoring the share of total education expenditure that households bear. Civil society organizations should therefore rally behind national education accounts and ensure that household income and expenditure survey data are available to facilitate analysis.

Systems: A strong case has been made for education system indicators to be monitored. This is not to suggest that governments should be held to account for their institutional arrangements. Rather, the purpose is to facilitate dialogue and encourage governments to learn from each other.

This idea has two implications. First, it would require agencies involved in collecting such information to collaborate to reduce overlaps in their diagnostic tools and make more effective use of resources. Second, regional organizations, which may include education as one of their areas of cooperation, would have to play a larger role in developing their vision vis-à-vis the Education 2030 agenda and use this as a first step to collect in-depth information on comparable aspects of education systems.

Education in the other SDGs: The scope for monitoring education in goals other than SDG 4 cannot be limited to the small number of global indicators in which education is explicitly mentioned. It also needs to consider education's role in achieving particular development outcomes, building national capacity for SDG implementation and supporting adults in contributing to the broader transformation needed in economic and political structures and in relation to the environment, all of which are key to the sustainable development agenda.

RECOMMENDATIONS ON MONITORING THE EDUCATION AGENDA

The above review of the monitoring of each target points to several priorities for action at the national, regional and global levels, the most important being to produce sufficient comparable information that allows global dialogue on progress towards SDG 4. This aim does not contradict the message that every country should be empowered to monitor its own progress towards SDG 4, focusing on its own national context and needs.

The international education community has agreed on the monitoring framework, which consists of two complementary sets of indicators. First, there are 11 global indicators that were developed as part of the Inter-agency and Expert Group on Sustainable Development Goal Indicators process; countries are expected to sign these during the United Nations General Assembly in September 2016. These indicators will be mandatory for monitoring SDG 4.

Second, there are 43 thematic indicators, of which 11 constitute the set of global indicators. The need for this expanded list arose because the global indicators could not capture the full range of global education priorities. Countries are not required to report on the additional thematic indicators, unlike the global indicators. Instead, the additional indicators are meant to provide guidance as countries consider more in-depth ways to track their progress.

The original list of thematic indicators was based on an initial expert proposal. UNESCO and the UNESCO Institute for Statistics (UIS) then set up the Technical Cooperation Group (TCG) on the Indicators for SDG4-Education 2030 to support their further development and implementation. The TCG includes 28 countries as members and 14 as observers, in addition to 5 international bodies (including the GEM Report) and 2 international representatives of civil society. It is meant to be an umbrella group, incorporating bodies dedicated to specialized areas of the agenda, such as the Global Alliance for Monitoring Learning and the Inter-Agency Group on Education Inequality Indicators. The UIS serves as its secretariat.

For every thematic indicator in the framework, the secretariat has provided detailed information on the definition and sources and a preliminary classification according to the availability of methodology and actual data. One of the TCG's first tasks is to address 8 of the 43 thematic indicators that have already been identified as poorly aligned with the target or difficult to implement. Initial decisions are expected when the TCG next meets in October 2016.

The establishment of a permanent group for technical cooperation, representing a large number of countries, is a considerable advance in the international dialogue on education monitoring, and fills a notable gap experienced during the Education for All period. At least two challenges lie ahead. First, countries must be assured an opportunity to contribute to discussions in an informed and meaningful way. Their active role in the TCG is critical. Indeed, one objective of the monitoring part of the 2016 GEM Report is to serve as a reference document for such discussions. Second, a mechanism is needed for future decision-making within the TCG, to help reach consensus and strengthen the group's legitimacy.

> **Countries must be given a chance to contribute to discussions in the Technical Cooperation Group in an informed and meaningful way**

AT THE NATIONAL LEVEL: BUILD CAPACITY IN SIX KEY AREAS

Where do countries stand in relation to the emerging monitoring challenges? It is essential for education ministries and national statistical agencies not to lose track of the big picture with so many competing requests for their time and resources. This section focuses on six key steps countries need to take to strengthen national monitoring of education in the next three to five years while concurrently contributing to the development of a global monitoring framework.

Work is needed to address *equity*. Education management information systems produce data usually based on school censuses that fail to shed light on basic disparity – in access, participation, completion and learning – by student characteristics. But the rest of the national statistical system can often produce highly relevant information on education inequality through household or labour force surveys. Unfortunately, these two systems are disconnected in many countries so education ministries lack the capacity to recognize the complementary and critical nature of the evidence produced by national statistical agencies. A classic example is that education ministries are not sufficiently involved in the design of national household surveys and hence education questions are poorly formulated, undermining analysis and cross-country comparisons.

This situation needs to change. Dialogue and cooperation are needed between education ministries and national statistical agencies. Target 4.5 requires reporting on disparity through a series of education indicators. Countries need to agree on a new mechanism for this reporting. The work of the Inter-Agency Group on Education Inequality Indicators can help initiate a process for continued dialogue.

Definitions of *learning outcomes* need to be broadened. Countries need to ensure the establishment of sample-based national learning assessments that can be used to monitor progress on a range of learning outcomes over time. Such assessment frameworks need to be of good quality and meet standards that the international community can help define, regarding not only technical aspects of reliability and validity but also openness and transparency in the publication of results.

Countries will need good guidance to build assessment frameworks to ensure they produce information to improve teaching and learning processes. Reporting for a global indicator would be a helpful by-product, though not the main concern. Countries also need to take responsibility for monitoring the skills of those who have never been to school or who left school early. A first step would be to assess the skills of youth and adults.

A new strategy for assessing learning, and communicating its purpose, is essential to shift the nature of national education debates. In many countries, learning outcomes are still often mistakenly equated with pass rates in national high stakes examinations, such as those at the end of the basic education cycle or for transition into higher education. In contexts with high stakes testing, change is likely to be slow.

In terms of *quality*, learning outcomes are not the only key element. A focus on learning is essential to generate debate that has often been lacking. But such a focus can also create high expectations that learning outcomes will improve rapidly; experience over the last two decades suggests this is not likely (Clarke, 2016). If there is too much focus on learning outcomes, other urgent questions on education quality risk being neglected.

For example, target 4.7, on sustainable development and global citizenship, is a linchpin of the new global education agenda. To ensure commitment to its objectives, countries need to closely monitor policies, curricula, textbooks and teacher education programmes, as well as learning outcomes.

Another important aspect of quality is to identify the topics and concepts which should be conveyed through education, then define the desired results of education systems in relation to them. One way to start would be mapping how these concepts are promoted at different levels of the education system in policies, textbooks and classroom practices. It would also be useful for countries to engage in frank dialogue with each other on how effectively they address issues of tolerance, respect for diversity, group identity, collaboration, human rights and sustainability in their education systems. Such openness is not easy and requires political courage.

It is essential not to lose track of *lifelong learning* and its monitoring and expansion. Achievement of the SDGs calls for massive social and economic transformation. Schooling alone cannot deliver all the desired outcomes. Even if the entire cohort of 15- to 19-year-olds were to complete secondary education by 2030, this would be insufficient; the vast majority of the adults who will be called upon to make critical decisions relating to sustainable development

will have already completed their schooling and not been exposed to the relevant content.

In most of countries, the education needs, opportunities and accomplishments of the adult population are not being monitored. Countries need mechanisms that track adult education and learning opportunities, including those geared to the sustainable development agenda. This report has provided the example of the systematic approach followed in Europe, yet even that was only from the perspective of what is relevant for work. The world needs to move beyond this to capture a fuller range of lifelong learning opportunities that is fit for the purpose of the SDGs.

Analysing education *systems* requires finding the right forums and prioritizing the right issues. It is relatively easy for countries to engage in debate on key education challenges through their membership in organizations of regional cooperation, which can offer the best channels for exchanging information on education structures and system characteristics. Countries need to champion such collaboration. This is not a call for increased homogenization of education systems, but rather for openness in comparing how countries deal with similar problems.

Equity and inclusion are examples of issues to prioritize. Much can be gained by comparing how countries approach them. The GEM Report advocates for countries to answer a set of basic questions on how they try to offset disadvantage among students and schools, so as to better understand which countries have the most effective results.

Finally, countries are encouraged to adopt the national education accounts approach to improve monitoring of *finance*. Education finance has often focused on government spending or on how much poorer countries receive in aid. What is needed is to shift the debate to better understand who contributes what resources to what activities.

This outlook provides a completely different picture, showing how education expenditure is shared between governments and households. What emerges is the realization that while there may be a policy of free education, households often bear a very large share of the total cost. This undermines equity, a fact that remains underappreciated by policy-makers.

Shifting to the new approach will be tricky. The international community must encourage countries to adopt national education accounts, but not overburden them with procedures that pose excessively technical demands.

These recommendations in six key areas are relevant to all countries, reflecting the universal character of the SDG agenda, even if low and middle income countries need to do more work. The recommendations assume that countries take seriously their responsibility for monitoring the SDGs and are prepared to do what it takes, receiving technical and financial support where needed.

Countries have already engaged at the regional level with the UIS in important mapping exercises assessing where they stand vis-à-vis the global and thematic indicators (UIS, 2016). This rapid appraisal exercise served an important purpose of familiarizing countries with the monitoring framework as well as giving an early indication of data availability. But this exchange may also have overwhelmed countries with details and technical issues.

The recommendations above try to address the big picture. Numerous key changes are needed, which are a condition for reforms in education monitoring systems that will allow them to cope with the challenges of the Education 2030 agenda. Getting these changes right first will make it easier for countries to then take ownership of their monitoring agenda and make decisions on where to allocate resources and from where to seek technical and financial support.

AT THE REGIONAL LEVEL: SUPPORT PEER LEARNING

While the Education 2030 agenda is global, progress in many areas is more likely to happen at the regional level, particularly where qualitative, system-related information is needed. Countries are increasingly collecting better and more systematic information through quantitative indicators. This is insufficient, however; comparative information is needed to understand how countries in similar situations have responded and to help guide governments in the next steps.

The role of regional organizations is critical. Where such organizations include education among their concerns, this can help make the global education agenda more specific to members' contexts. The GEM Report highlights the experience of bodies such as the European

Union and the Organization of Ibero-American States. The European Union's education strategy is supported by a network that regularly provides policy information on key issues to member states, which exchange information voluntarily, and take part in forums to learn from their peers.

Countries in a given region tend to have common education contexts. Their comparative reviews often reflect shared values, objectives and challenges. Members of regional entities are therefore more likely to express deeper political commitment to, and national ownership of, undertaking peer reviews. And the results of regional monitoring are much more likely to be used in policy-making and sustained over time, not least because governments have an interest in neighbouring countries' performance.

> " Regional organizations should help make the global education agenda more specific and relevant to the contexts of their members "

AT THE GLOBAL LEVEL: FOSTER CONSENSUS AND COORDINATION

With the basic parameters of the monitoring framework and a global consultation mechanism in place, the GEM Report has three recommendations on how to improve the global coordination of monitoring approaches.

First, an international household survey programme, dedicated to education, is needed to cover many of the information gaps in the new agenda. There have been attempts to establish such a programme. Beginning in the early 2000s, alongside the Demographic and Health Survey (DHS) programme, USAID funded education-specific EdData surveys in a few countries. However, this initiative was limited to only a few countries and did not become generalized. Since then, funders have shown a lack of willingness to finance an education-specific survey. Few questions are dedicated to education in the questionnaires of major cross-country multipurpose surveys such as the DHS, the UNICEF Multiple Indicator Cluster Surveys and the World Bank Living Standards Measurement Study. And these surveys are reluctant to add more questions on education, given the many demands on their resources.

In light of the expanded scope of the Education 2030 monitoring agenda and its many gaps, the question of an education-specific survey needs to be revisited. Such a tool could address issues such as participation in early childhood, technical-vocational, tertiary and adult education; the use of language at home and in school; the collection of detailed information on school attendance; and the direct assessment of literacy and numeracy skills. Potential donors need to discuss the cost-effectiveness of a new tool of this kind.

The second recommendation is for a consistent approach to support the monitoring of learning outcomes. Countries need support to build national assessment systems that have solid foundations and are in their best interests. Some countries face a multitude of options from development partners that stretch their capacity. A code of conduct among donors and a common pool of resources are needed, with priorities including the building of national capacity, the provision of long-term support and the avoidance of overlap. Coordinated support would also help countries gain access to shared resources and knowledge networks.

Third, analysis of several measurement challenges in the GEM Report highlights the fact that, with the expanded scope of the Education 2030 agenda, many targets have not yet been measured on a global scale. Indicators, especially those related to learning outcomes, have not yet been fully developed. A common challenge is that large differences in culture and other contextual factors hamper clear, comparable definitions of such concepts as early childhood development, relevant learning outcomes in basic education, digital literacy and skills for global citizenship.

Therefore, this report recommends that institutions like the UIS, with the support of the TCG, set a research agenda related to the challenges of comparative measurement in education. To be valid, proposed measures need to be tested on the ground and at scale. In key areas of global education, research on measurement is fragmented. While there is much national expertise, there is little pooling of resources to address questions in a cross-country, cross-cultural context. In the absence of a coordinating institution, it is strongly recommended that a research hub be established to focus on issues related to the major gaps in the global monitoring of education. Education could draw lessons from partnerships or networks in health or agriculture that have pooled research resources to similar effect.

Framing the debate: what data revolution for education?

Much of the discussion about global monitoring of the SDGs has been cast in terms of a 'data revolution'. The term can be defined in many ways, but one of the most widely used descriptions is found in the final document of the United Nations Secretary-General's Independent Expert Advisory Group on the Data Revolution for Sustainable Development: 'New technologies are leading to an exponential increase in the volume and types of data available, creating unprecedented possibilities for informing and transforming society and protecting the environment. Governments, companies, researchers and citizen groups are in a ferment of experimentation, innovation and adaptation to the new world of data, a world in which data are bigger, faster and more detailed than ever before' (United Nations, 2014c).

> " The GEM Report believes that the concept of a 'data revolution' associated with technology and 'big data' is likely to be irrelevant in education, if not misleading "

The GEM Report takes the view that the concept of a 'data revolution' associated with technology and 'big data' is likely to be irrelevant in education, if not misleading. Most countries are still grappling with compiling basic education data and understanding their purposes and uses. And most of the issues confronting countries are about basic concepts, such as what is meant by literacy proficiency skills or early childhood development. In addition, there is a need to invest in robust monitoring systems. In both these areas, the international community is called upon to provide assistance. Rather than overhauling ways of collecting data and bringing about a 'revolution' through technological means, better coordination between agencies and more resources to implement plans would bring about the changes needed to monitor Education 2030.

Moreover, accessibility, openness and accountability of data in education remain constrained. Many countries carry out household, school or learning achievement surveys but do not make the results or the data public. Countries need to do much more to promote the availability of data and encourage their use. This must be a key part of any 'revolution' if it is to be in the service of all.

Rotan, who lives in the Korail slum, Dhaka, Bangladesh prepares to leave for classes at the BRAC primary school.

CREDIT: Conor Ashleigh/Australian Department of Foreign Affairs and Trade

CHAPTER

24

Epilogue

One year has passed since 193 member states of the United Nations unanimously adopted the 2030 Agenda for Sustainable Development. As efforts to implement the ambitious 17 Sustainable Development Goals (SDGs) gather steam, member states and the international community can build on the experience gained from the agenda's two predecessors, Agenda 21 and the Millennium Development Goals (MDGs).

One vital lesson learned from these earlier global development agendas was that systematic follow-up and review are critically important. A crucial challenge has been the tension between global commitment and national implementation. The 2030 Agenda is not legally binding and cannot be legally enforced. Instead, it sets out a collective vision for people and planet that requires political will, resources and collaboration.

> Systematic follow-up and review is critical for global development agendas; a crucial challenge is the tension between global commitment and national implementation

Legitimate issues have been raised about past agendas such as the MDGs. Did the international goals and targets establish an agenda that was truly global, or mainly applied to 'developing countries'? Were the targets to be monitored in global terms without reference to national boundaries, or were they meant to influence national policies and strategies and be monitored as such? If success is defined in all-or-nothing terms, does this not ignore countries' progress, which may have been significant even without reaching the actual goal? Branding struggling countries with a mark of failure while disregarding their accomplishments is not constructive. Moreover, successful national strategies may look quite different, reflecting the diversity of context between and even within countries (Vandemoortele, 2014).

Hindsight has not solved these issues. They are still valid one year into the 2030 Agenda's implementation and certainly relevant for SDG 4 on education. What does the universal sustainable development agenda mean in practice? Are all targets appropriate for all countries, in equal measure? What about wealthy countries that in the past have participated solely in terms of official development assistance? How can progress be measured in a way that reflects the diversity of country implementation? If a country decides to prioritize some targets over others, for whatever reasons, should this be considered a failure?

The international community has taken the first steps to build a global architecture for follow-up and review. A rough sketch was originally outlined in the UN Secretary-General's report on 'critical milestones', which are expected to be adopted through a General Assembly resolution (United Nations, 2016c).

The High-Level Political Forum (HLPF) has served as the main international platform to provide political leadership and guidance on development issues. Participants included UN member states and commissions, intergovernmental bodies, major groups – such as business, non-government organizations, partnerships and alliances – and large cities. When it convened in

> When the High-Level Political Forum first convened in July 2016, it emphasized that assessment of SDG success must be based on the well-being of the most vulnerable groups

July 2016, under the theme 'Leaving no one behind', it emphasized that assessment of SDG success must be based on the well-being of the most vulnerable groups, both nationally and globally.

The HLPF's work has been informed by the first edition of the SDG Report, an annual progress report following in the footsteps of the MDG Report, which summarizes regional and global patterns and trends for each goal, based on a subset of the SDG indicator framework expected to be approved by the UN General Assembly in September 2016 (United Nations, 2016b). The SDG data repository, on which the report is based, is an achievement in its own right. However, there are concerns that certain indicators covered by the SDG Report are not relevant to many countries.

The HLPF was also informed by the first set of national reviews, submitted voluntarily by 22 member states (United Nations, 2016a).[1] These reviews are the backbone of the new follow-up and review architecture. They suggest that several obstacles common to many SDGs circumscribe progress on them: financing, capacity, governance and the immediate day-to-day concerns of national governments. The national reviews also show wide gaps in how countries perceive their role. For some wealthier countries, the 2030 Agenda may still be seen as a development strategy that pertains to other countries.

Experience from this first year highlights a standing dilemma in international agreements: what are effective means and instruments to promote implementation of global statements of intent at the national level?

THE GEM REPORT AS AN INFORMED AND HONEST BROKER ON ISSUES OF EDUCATION AND SUSTAINABLE DEVELOPMENT

Experience has shown that regional associations (in which countries typically share values, objectives and challenges) and thematic groups (within which particular themes and concerns come to be shared and seen as appropriate) can serve as bridges between global dialogue and national initiatives. The proposed follow-up and review architecture has opened space for thematic reviews and regional indicators – a welcome development, as high level global discussions can be difficult to link to the concerns of individual countries as well as specialized groups such as the international education community.

In the Education for All (EFA) agenda, the *EFA Global Monitoring Report* series begun in 2002 became accepted by governments and civil society as a major thematic follow-up and review mechanism. It provided in-depth information and analysis and acted as an international reference point. It sharpened the focus and gave voice to important emerging issues in education, helping prioritize and clarify what is at stake. It facilitated dialogue among global, regional and national actors and, to a lesser extent, among sectors including health, gender and social protection.

At the World Education Forum in May 2015, representatives of the international education community renewed the report's mandate to continue as the *Global Education Monitoring Report* (GEM Report). The fundamental aim of the new series is to address how education at all stages of life – in school, at the workplace, at home and in the community – can be made more inclusive, equitable and of higher quality.

> **❝**
> The aim of the new GEM Report series is to address how education at all stages of life – in school, at the workplace, at home and in the community – can be made more inclusive, equitable and of higher quality **❞**

The 2016 GEM Report focuses attention on two overarching issues. First, it carefully addresses an integral feature of the SDG agenda – the interdependent nature of the goals – by exploring the close links between education and other sustainable development outcomes. The challenges facing people and planet are enormous and urgent. The broad role that education and lifelong learning can and must play is not always fully appreciated. The report draws attention to the interconnectedness of natural and social systems and interlinkage between sectors, with education as a powerful catalyst. The need to integrate equitable education of good quality into the SDG agenda should be a primary aspiration of the education and development communities.

Second, the broadening of the education agenda's scope requires reflection. How will the world monitor progress on so many ambitious targets? A monitoring framework has been devised that attempts to capture many of the new areas. However, the framework for SDG 4 is underwhelming in its ability to capture core concerns and challenges of sustainable development. By drawing attention to gaps and needed actions, the 2016 GEM Report seeks to become a critical reference document as the international community discusses the existing monitoring framework and seeks to improve it.

There is much to be learned. The 2019 HLPF will be the first high level gathering of the SDG period to discuss the state of education. Given what is known about the strengths and weaknesses of the SDG process, it is not too early to ask what key issues should be discussed at this gathering, what decisions should be taken, what information is needed to facilitate the decisions and how this information should be presented and communicated.

For example, a key to accelerating progress is sustained financing. Investing in education is fundamental for global well-being. The 2019 HLPF could be an important occasion to take stock of implementation of the September 2016 recommendations of the International Commission on the Financing of Global Education Opportunity. Another key is the ability to disaggregate data to enable rapid and appropriate response to the needs of diverse groups and ensure that no one is left behind.

The GEM Report's role in this process is understood to be that of an honest broker, an impartial but visionary mediator of information, working towards the delivery of global public goods for the elimination of poverty, for healthy lives, for the sustainable use of natural resources and for a better future for the planet and coming generations. The education of children, youth and adults has a critical role in each of these scenarios.

STRENGTHENING ACCOUNTABILITY IN THE SDG FOLLOW-UP AND REVIEW ARCHITECTURE – AND IN EDUCATION

For the follow-up and review process to work towards achievement of the SDGs, information will need to spur action and action must be turned into results. But will this happen? It is expected that highlighting inequality in education will result in larger financial allocations that are better targeted to schools or countries in need, and that evidence on poor learning outcomes will translate into better efforts to understand where teaching needs to improve. In other words, it is believed that identifying problems will spur the right action to make a difference by those who are responsible at various levels – global, national, local, community and individual.

However, it has been shown time and again that such positive action does not always occur. There are donors that continue to allocate much less than 0.7% of their gross national income to aid, governments that spend well under 4% of their gross domestic product on education, systems that assign resources unequally between schools, budgets that favour the advantaged, and teachers who are unsupported or do not respect their code of conduct – all of which combine to result in millions of children achieving well below their potential. How to encourage responsible behaviour is still a burning question.

As part of the SDG process, accountability for achieving international goals is built on a commitment to a 'robust, voluntary, effective, participatory, transparent and integrated follow-up and review framework' to 'track progress in implementing this Agenda' (United Nations, 2015).

> **The 2017 GEM Report will explore the role of accountability in education at all levels**

How will this be achieved? The 2017 GEM Report will explore the role of accountability in education at all levels, recognizing that multiple, diverse actors working within and across countries are responsible for the future of the SDGs. For each of these actors to be successful, there must be a strong enabling environment in which they understand their responsibilities and have the capacity and resources to act accordingly, along with the will and motivation to make an honest effort.

These actors need to buy into the process, accept its worth, and then take on their responsibility. But creating a genuine buy-in that motivates actors to do what is necessary to fulfil their obligations often involves a shift in culture. Mutual accountability can help with this shift by combining top-down and bottom-up approaches, as well as internal and external mechanisms. This motivates actors by creating a more just and fair system that assists in the development and realization of collective aims, which carry enormous value in education.

ENDNOTES

1. The 22 countries are China, Colombia, Egypt, Estonia, Finland, France, Georgia, Germany, Madagascar, Mexico, Montenegro, Morocco, Norway, the Philippines, the Republic of Korea, Samoa, Sierra Leone, Switzerland, Togo, Turkey, Uganda and the Bolivarian Republic of Venezuela.

Children use the
blackboard to lean
on in the Dan Saa
school, Niger.

CREDIT: Tagaza Djibo/UNESCO

Annex

Statistical Tables

A shoe rack in a school in the Chittagong, Bangladesh, showing the number of children attending class that day.

CREDIT: Ripon Barua/UNESCO

Statistical tables[1]

INTRODUCTION

FROM EDUCATION FOR ALL TO THE EDUCATION SUSTAINABLE DEVELOPMENT GOAL: NEW AGENDA, NEW STATISTICAL TABLES

With the adoption in September 2015 of the 2030 Agenda for Sustainable Development – which sets new development priorities, including for education through the fourth Sustainable Development Goal (SDG 4) – and, in November 2015, of the Education 2030 Framework for Action at the 38th session of the UNESCO General Conference, the Education for All (EFA) cycle came to an end. With this edition of the *Global Education Monitoring Report* (GEM Report), the statistical tables are evolving to reflect the new education agenda.

The tables have been reorganized to reflect and align with (a) the aspirational nature and great ambition of the Education 2030 agenda, which has at its core equity and inclusion and embraces a lifelong perspective; (b) the seven SDG 4 targets and three means of implementation, which are not only about access to, participation in and completion of education, but also have education quality at their core in terms of inputs, outputs, processes, learning outcomes and environments, and the skills youth and adults must be equipped with for decent work; and (c) a broad set of 43 internationally comparable thematic indicators, of which 11 are global indicators.[2]

Consequently, the statistical tables of the GEM Report aim to be more comprehensive than in earlier reports, while reflecting significant limitations in terms of data availability and country coverage, particularly regarding some indicators that still need to be defined and developed. Accordingly, placeholders or proxy indicators

are occasionally used. These statistical tables contain more indicators than in earlier reports, particularly on education quality, learning outcomes, youth and adult skills (including not only literacy and numeracy but also information and communications technology skills) and tertiary education. While aligned with the proposed thematic and global indicators, the statistical tables include additional indicators – such as repetition, dropout, and transition from primary to secondary education and from secondary to tertiary – which remain critical but were left out of the new indicator set.

In addition to administrative data provided to the UIS by education ministries worldwide, the statistical tables rely on data from other sources, including national, regional and international learning assessments; national and international household surveys, such as the Demographic and Health Surveys and UNICEF's Multiple Indicator Cluster Surveys; and bodies including the Joint United Nations Programme on HIV/AIDS (UNAIDS), the Organisation for Economic Co-operation and Development (OECD), UNICEF, the United Nations Population Division (UNPD), the World Bank and the World Health Organization (WHO).

The new statistical tables are organized by targets and means of implementation instead of by education level (from pre-primary to tertiary) as was formerly the case; this results in some seeming anomalies, such as early childhood care and education coming after primary and secondary education. As in the past, the tables include domestic education finance, which, though absent from the SDG 4 targets, is a key means of implementation and an enabling factor to achieve the targets. Because of the comprehensiveness of the new statistical tables and the size constraints of the GEM Report, they continue to be presented in two versions: a shorter version in the printed report and a more complete version, containing all indicators to date, published on the GEM Report website (see footnote 1).

METHODOLOGICAL NOTES

While the statistical tables present data from multiple sources, most of the education data included are still provided by the UIS. The most recent data on pupils, students, teachers and education expenditure presented in the tables are for the school year or financial year ending in 2014.[3] They are based on survey results reported to and processed by the UIS before the end of March 2016. A small number of countries[4] submitted data for the school year ending in 2015, presented in bold in the tables. These statistics refer to all formal education, both public and private, by level of education.

The statistical tables list 209 countries and territories, all of which are UNESCO member states or associate members. Most of them report their data to the UIS using standard questionnaires issued by the institute itself. For some countries, however, education data are collected by the UIS via surveys carried out jointly by the UIS, OECD and the statistical office of the European Union through the UIS/OECD/Eurostat (UOE) questionnaires.[5]

POPULATION DATA USED AND ISCED CLASSIFICATION

The population-related indicators used in the statistical tables, including enrolment ratios, number of out-of-school children, adolescents and youth, and number of youth and adults, are based on the 2015 revision of population estimates produced by the UNPD. Because of possible differences between national population estimates and those of the United Nations, these indicators may differ from those published by individual countries or by other organizations.[6]

In the 2015 revision, the UNPD does not provide population data by single years of age for countries with total population of less than 90,000, including Andorra, Anguilla, Cayman Islands, Dominica, Monaco, Montserrat, Saint Martin, Sint Maarten and Turks and Caicos Islands. For Bermuda, Dominica, Marshall Islands and Turks and Caicos Islands, the UIS decided to use population data from the previous UNPD revision (2012). Where no UNPD population estimates exist, national population figures, when available, or UIS estimates were used to calculate enrolment ratios. In the case of Brazil, due to inconsistencies between UNPD estimates and national enrolment data, the UIS has agreed with the country to temporarily use its national population estimates, derived from the PNAD household survey, until a solution is found.

Education data reported to the UIS are in conformity with the International Standard Classification of Education (ISCED), revised in 2011. Countries may have their own definitions of education levels that do not correspond to ISCED 2011. Differences between nationally and internationally reported education statistics may be due to the use of nationally defined education levels rather than the ISCED standard, in addition to the population issue raised above.

LITERACY DATA

The literacy statistics presented in the statistical tables are often based on a definition of literacy as the ability to read and write, with understanding, a short simple statement related to one's daily life[7] and are largely based on data sources that use self-declaration or third party declaration methods, in which respondents are asked whether they and the members of their household are literate, as opposed to being asked a more comprehensive question or to demonstrate the skill.[8] Some countries assume that anyone who completes a certain level of education is literate.[9] As definitions and methodologies used for data collection differ by country, data need to be used with caution.

Literacy data presented in the statistical tables cover adults aged 15 and over as well as youth aged 15 to 24. They are for the 2005–2014 reference period, and include both national observed data from censuses and household surveys, indicated with an asterisk (*) and UIS estimates (**). The latter are for 2014 and are based on the most recent national observed data. They were produced using the Global Age-specific Literacy Projections (GALP) model.[10] The reference years and literacy definitions for each country are presented in the table of metadata for literacy statistics posted on the GEM Report website (see footnote 1).

ESTIMATES AND MISSING DATA

Regarding UIS statistics provided by the UIS itself, both observed and estimated education data are presented throughout the statistical tables. Wherever possible, the

UIS encourages countries to make their own estimates, which are presented as national estimates and marked with one asterisk (*). Where this does not happen, the UIS may make its own estimates if sufficient supplementary information is available. These estimates are marked with two asterisks (**). Gaps in the tables may arise where data submitted by a country are found to be inconsistent. The UIS makes every attempt to resolve such problems with the countries concerned, but reserves the final decision on omitting data it regards as problematic.

If information for the year ending in 2014 are not available, data for earlier or later years are used. Such cases are indicated by footnotes.

REGIONAL AND OTHER COUNTRY GROUPING AVERAGES

Regional figures for literacy and education rates and ratios (gross intakes rates, gross, net and adjusted net enrolment ratios, dropout rates, etc.) are weighted averages, taking into account the relative size of the relevant population of each country in each region. The figures for countries with larger populations have a proportionately greater influence on the regional aggregates. The averages are derived from both published data and imputed values, for countries for which no recent data or reliable publishable data are

available. Weighted averages marked with two asterisks (**) in the tables are UIS partial imputations due to incomplete country coverage (between 33% and 60% of the population of a given region or country grouping). Where insufficient reliable data are available to produce an overall weighted mean, a median figure is calculated based only on countries with available data – at least half in a given region or country grouping.

INDICATORS PRESENTED IN THE STATISTICAL TABLES

In the longer version of the annex on the website, the GEM Report presents 16 statistical tables covering 283 distinct indicators (not counting gender breakdowns). Among these are the 43 thematic indicators, including the 11 global indicators and 32 others yet to be finalized at time of publication. In the meantime, some placeholders or proxy measures are presented to help keep attention on issues to be monitored and policy priorities across the SDG 4 targets, while highlighting areas for further work and indicator development.

Table 1 focuses on the thematic and global indicators included in the statistical tables. A number of them are new indicators. This table gives some assessment of data availability and country coverage, shows what is missing and indicates the placeholders used.

TABLE:
Proposed thematic and global indicators presented in the statistical tables

	SDG 4 targets and related indicators	Included in tables	Global indicators	Placeholders	Missing aspects	Sources of data
4.1 – By 2030, ensure that all girls and boys complete free, equitable and quality primary and secondary education leading to relevant and effective learning outcomes[1]						
1	Proportion of children and young people: (a) in grades 2/3; (b) at the end of primary; and (c) at the end of lower secondary achieving at least a minimum proficiency level in (i) reading and (ii) mathematics, by sex	Yes	4.1.1		Comparable only across countries that took part in the same survey	Altinok (2013); Cheng and Omoeva (2014); education ministry national reports and websites; EGMA/EGRA; PASEC; PILNA; PIRLS; PISA; SACMEQ; TERCE; TIMSS; ASER; Uwezo
2	Administration of a nationally representative learning assessment (a) during primary (b) at the end of primary and (c) at the end of lower secondary education	Yes				Altinok (2013); Cheng and Omoeva (2014); education ministry national reports and websites; EGMA/EGRA; PASEC; PILNA; PIRLS; PISA; SACMEQ; TERCE; TIMSS; ASER; Uwezo
3	Gross intake ratio to the last grade (primary, lower secondary)	Yes				UIS database
4	Completion rate (primary, lower secondary, upper secondary)	Yes				GEM Report team calculations based on national and international household surveys (e.g. DHS, MICS)
5	Out-of-school rate (primary, lower secondary, upper secondary)	Yes				UIS database
6	Percentage of pupils over-age for grade (primary, lower secondary)	Yes				UIS database
7	Number of years of (a) free and (b) compulsory primary and secondary education guaranteed in legal frameworks	Yes				Eurydice (2014, 2015, 2016); UNESCO-IBE (2012); national education ministry websites; UIS database

	SDG 4 targets and related indicators	Included in tables	Global indicators	Placeholders	Missing aspects	Sources of data
4.2 – By 2030, ensure that all girls and boys have access to quality early childhood development, care and pre-primary education so that they are ready for primary education						
8	Proportion of children under 5 years of age who are developmentally on track in health, learning and psychosocial well-being, by sex	Yes	4.2.1	UNICEF MICS Early Childhood Development Index		UNICEF MICS 4/5 country reports
9	Percentage of children under 5 years of age experiencing positive and stimulating home learning environments	Yes				UNICEF MICS 4/5 country reports
10	Participation rate in organized learning (one year before the official primary entry age), by sex	Yes	4.2.2	Adjusted net enrolment ratio, one year before the official primary school entry age		UIS database
11	Pre-primary gross enrolment ratio	Yes				UIS database
12	Number of years of (a) free and (b) compulsory pre-primary education guaranteed in legal frameworks	Yes				Eurydice (2014, 2015, 2016); UNESCO-IBE (2012); national education ministry websites; UIS database
4.3 – By 2030, ensure equal access for all women and men to affordable and quality technical, vocational and tertiary education, including university						
13	Gross enrolment ratio for tertiary education	Yes				UIS database
14	Participation rate in technical-vocational education programmes (15- to 24-year-olds)	No		Percentage of youth (15-24) enrolled in secondary technical and vocational education	Programmes at tertiary education level and outside education (work-based and other settings)	UIS database
15	Participation rate of youth and adults in formal and non-formal education and training in the previous 12 months, by sex	Yes	4.3.1	Adults enrolled in formal education as a share of total enrolment by level	Youth participation rate	Eurostat Adult Education Survey 2011
4.4 – By 2030, substantially increase the number of youth and adults who have relevant skills, including technical and vocational skills, for employment, decent jobs and entrepreneurship						
16.1	Percentage of youth and adults who have achieved at least a minimum level of proficiency in digital literacy skills	No		Percentage of students at each proficiency level in digital literacy skills		IEA International Computer and Information Literacy Study
16.2	Proportion of youth and adults with information and communications technology (ICT) skills, by type of skill	Yes	4.4.1			Eurostat database; ITU World Telecommunication / ICT Indicators database
17	Youth/adult educational attainment rates by age group, economic activity status, levels of education and programme orientation	No, but placeholder presented		Percentage of adults aged 25 and over by minimum level of education attained	Educational attainment rate of youth (15-24)	UIS database
4.5 – By 2030, eliminate gender disparities in education and ensure equal access at all levels of education and vocational training for the vulnerable, including persons with disabilities, indigenous peoples and children in vulnerable situations						
	Parity indices (female/male, rural/urban, bottom/top wealth quintile and others such as disability status, indigenous peoples and conflict-affected, as data become available) for all education indicators on this list that can be disaggregated	Yes	4.5.1		Data on people with disabilities, indigenous people	UIS database; GEM Report team calculations based on national and international household surveys (e.g. DHS, MICS)
18	Percentage of students in primary education whose first or home language is the language of instruction	No				
19	Extent to which explicit formula-based policies reallocate education resources to disadvantaged populations	No				
20	Education expenditure per student by level of education and source of funding	No, but placeholder presented		Government expenditure per pupil/student by level of education in constant 2013 US$; in constant 2013 PPP$; as % of GDP; as % of GDP per capita		UIS database
21	Percentage of total aid to education allocated to low income countries	Yes (aid tables)				OECD DAC
4.6 – By 2030, ensure that all youth and a substantial proportion of adults, both men and women, achieve literacy and numeracy						
22	Percentage of population in a given age group achieving at least a fixed level of proficiency in functional (a) literacy and (b) numeracy skills, by sex	No, but placeholder presented	4.6.1	Percentage of youth and adults achieving at least a fixed level of proficiency in functional literacy skills and numeracy skills		OECD PIAAC
23	Youth/adult literacy rate	Yes				UIS database
24	Participation rate of youth/adults in literacy programmes	No, but placeholder presented		Participants in literacy programmes, expressed as percentage of the illiterate population		UIS database, regional survey for Latin Amercia and the Caribbean

	SDG 4 targets and related indicators	Included in tables	Global indicators	Placeholders	Missing aspects	Sources of data
4.7 – By 2030, ensure that all learners acquire the knowledge and skills needed to promote sustainable development, including, among others, through education for sustainable development and sustainable life-styles, human rights, gender equality, promotion of a culture of peace and non-violence, global citizenship and appreciation of cultural diversity and of culture's contribution to sustainable development						
25	Extent to which (i) global citizenship education and (ii) education for sustainable development, including gender equality and human rights, are mainstreamed at all levels in (a) national education policies; (b) curricula; (c) teacher education and (d) student assessment	Yes	4.7.1	Inclusion in national curricula frameworks of issues relating to global citizenship and sustainable development: gender equality; human rights; sustainable development; and global citizenship	Inclusion of the given issues in national education policies, teacher education and student assessments	UNESCO IBE (2016)
26	Percentage of students by age group (or education level) showing adequate understanding of issues relating to global citizenship and sustainability	No, but placeholder presented		Percentage of youth with adequate understanding of issues relating to HIV/AIDS and sexuality education	Gender equality, human rights and global citizenship	UNAIDS (2011), 2015 UNAIDS AIDSInfo Online Database and DHS StatCompiler
27	Percentage of 15-year-old students showing proficiency in knowledge of environmental science and geoscience	No, but placeholder presented		Percentage of 15-year-old students performing at or above proficiency level 2 in science literacy as a proxy measure of environmental science and geoscience		GEM Report team calculations based on PISA 2012 data (OECD, 2013)
28	Percentage of schools that provide life skills-based HIV and sexuality education	Yes			Sexuality education	UNAIDS (2011), 2015 UNAIDS AIDSInfo Online Database and DHS StatCompiler
29	Extent to which the framework on the World Programme on Human Rights Education is implemented nationally (as per UNGA Resolution 59/113)	No				
4.a – Build and upgrade education facilities that are child, disability and gender sensitive and provide safe, non-violent, inclusive and effective learning environments for all						
30–32	Proportion of schools with access to (a) electricity; (b) the Internet for pedagogical purposes; (c) computers for pedagogical purposes; (d) adapted infrastructure and materials for students with disabilities; (e) basic drinking water; (f) single-sex basic sanitation facilities; and (g) basic handwashing facilities (as per the water, sanitation and hygiene indicator definitions)	Yes	4.a.1			UNICEF (2015); UIS database
33	Percentage of students experiencing bullying, corporal punishment, harassment, violence, sexual discrimination and abuse	Yes			Corporal punishment, harassment, sexual discrimination and abuse	Global School-based Student Health Survey
34	Number of attacks on students, personnel and institutions	No				
4.b – By 2030, substantially expand globally the number of scholarships available to developing countries, in particular least developed countries, small island developing States and African countries, for enrolment in higher education, including vocational training and information and communications technology, technical, engineering and scientific programmes, in developed countries and other developing countries						
35	Number of higher education scholarships awarded, by beneficiary country	No				
36	Volume of official development assistance flows for scholarships by sector and type of study	No	4.b.1			
4.c – By 2030, substantially increase the supply of qualified teachers, including through international cooperation for teacher training in developing countries, especially least developed countries and small islands developing States						
37	Percentage of teachers qualified according to national standards, by education level and type of institution	Yes			Information by type of institution	UIS database
38	Pupil/qualified teacher ratio, by education level	Yes				UIS database
39	Proportion of teachers in: (a) pre-primary, (b) primary, (c) lower secondary; and (d) upper secondary education who have received at least the minimum organized teacher training (e.g. pedagogical training) pre-service or in-service required for teaching at the relevant level in a given country	Yes	4.c.1			UIS database
40	Pupil/trained teacher ratio by education level	Yes				UIS database
41	Average teacher salary relative to other professions requiring a comparable level of education qualification	No				
42	Teacher attrition rate, by education level	Yes (long)				UIS database
43	Percentage of teachers who received in-service training in the last 12 months, by type of training	No				

Source: GEM Report team.

SYMBOLS USED IN THE STATISTICAL TABLES (PRINTED AND WEB VERSIONS)

*   National estimate
**   UIS partial estimate
...   No data available
-     Magnitude nil or negligible
.   Category not applicable or does not exist

Footnotes to the tables, along with the glossary following the statistical tables, provide additional help in interpreting the data and information.

COMPOSITION OF REGIONS AND OTHER COUNTRY GROUPS

With the adoption of a new education agenda in the 2030 Agenda for Sustainable Development, the country classification in the statistical tables has shifted from the EFA regions to those used by the United Nations Statistical Division (UNSD) as of May 2015, with some adjustments. The UNSD classification includes all territories, whether independent national entities or parts of bigger entities; however, the list of countries presented in the statistical tables includes only full UNESCO member states and associate members, as well as Bermuda and Turks and Caicos Islands, non-member states that were included in the EFA statistical tables. To this list, a territory and a country, Hong Kong (China) and Liechtenstein, previously excluded, have been added. Other territories contained in the UNSD regional classification but not covered by UNESCO are still excluded: American Samoa, the Channel Islands, the Falkland Islands (Malvinas), French Guiana, French Polynesia, Greenland, Guadeloupe, Guam, the Isle of Man, Martinique, Mayotte, New Caledonia, the Northern Mariana Islands, Réunion, Puerto Rico, the US Virgin Islands and Western Sahara. The UIS does not collect data for most of these territories. Nor does it collect data for the Faroe Islands, so this territory is not included in the GEM Report despite its status as UNESCO associate member.

World classification[11]

- **Countries in transition (17):**
  Albania, Armenia, Azerbaijan, Belarus, Bosnia and Herzegovina, Croatia, Kazakhstan, Kyrgyzstan, Montenegro, Republic of Moldova, Russian Federation, Serbia, Tajikistan, The former Yugoslav Republic of Macedonia, Turkmenistan, Ukraine, Uzbekistan.

- **Developed countries (41):**
  Andorra, Australia, Austria, Belgium, Bermuda, Bulgaria, Canada, Cyprus, Czech Republic, Denmark, Estonia, Finland, France, Germany, Greece, Hungary, Iceland, Ireland, Israel, Italy, Japan, Latvia, Liechtenstein, Lithuania, Luxembourg, Malta, Monaco, Netherlands, New Zealand, Norway, Poland, Portugal, Romania, San Marino, Slovakia, Slovenia, Spain, Sweden, Switzerland, United Kingdom, United States.

- **Developing countries (151):**
  Eastern and South-eastern Asia (except Japan); Latin America and the Caribbean (except Bermuda); Northern Africa and Western Asia (except Israel); Pacific (except Australia and New Zealand); Southern Asia; sub-Saharan Africa.

GEM Report regions

- **Caucasus and Central Asia (8 countries)**
  Armenia, Azerbaijan, Georgia, Kazakhstan, Kyrgyzstan, Tajikistan, Turkmenistan, Uzbekistan.

- **Eastern and South-eastern Asia (18 countries/ territories)**
  Brunei Darussalam, Cambodia, China, Democratic People's Republic of Korea, Hong Kong (China), Indonesia, Japan, Lao People's Democratic Republic, Macao (China), Malaysia, Mongolia, Myanmar, Philippines, Republic of Korea, Singapore, Thailand, Timor-Leste, Viet Nam.

  - *Eastern Asia (7 countries/territories)*
    China, Democratic People's Republic of Korea, Hong Kong (China), Japan, Macao (China), Mongolia, Republic of Korea.

  - *South-eastern Asia (11 countries)*
    Brunei Darussalam, Cambodia, Indonesia, Lao People's Democratic Republic, Malaysia, Myanmar, Philippines, Singapore, Thailand, Timor-Leste, Viet Nam.

- **Europe and Northern America (46 countries)**
  Albania, Andorra, Austria, Belarus, Belgium, Bosnia and Herzegovina, Bulgaria, Canada, Croatia, Cyprus, Czech Republic, Denmark, Estonia, Finland, France, Germany, Greece, Hungary, Iceland, Ireland, Italy, Latvia, Liechtenstein, Lithuania, Luxembourg, Malta, Monaco, Montenegro, Netherlands, Norway, Poland, Portugal, Republic of Moldova, Romania, Russian Federation, San Marino, Serbia, Slovakia, Slovenia, Spain, Sweden,

Switzerland, The former Yugoslav Republic of Macedonia, Ukraine, United Kingdom, United States.

- **Latin America and the Caribbean (43 countries/ territories)**
  Anguilla, Antigua and Barbuda, Argentina, Aruba, Bahamas, Barbados, Belize, Bermuda, Plurinational State of Bolivia, Brazil, British Virgin Islands, Cayman Islands, Chile, Colombia, Costa Rica, Cuba, Curaçao, Dominica, Dominican Republic, Ecuador, El Salvador, Grenada, Guatemala, Guyana, Haiti, Honduras, Jamaica, Mexico, Montserrat, Nicaragua, Panama, Paraguay, Peru, Saint Kitts and Nevis, Saint Lucia, Saint Martin, Saint Vincent and the Grenadines, Sint Maarten, Suriname, Trinidad and Tobago, Turks and Caicos Islands, Uruguay, Bolivarian Republic of Venezuela.

  - *Caribbean (24 countries/territories)*
    Anguilla, Antigua and Barbuda, Aruba, Bahamas, Barbados, Belize, Bermuda, British Virgin Islands, Cayman Islands, Curaçao, Dominica, Grenada, Guyana, Haiti, Jamaica, Montserrat, Saint Kitts and Nevis, Saint Lucia, Saint Martin, Saint Vincent and the Grenadines, Sint Maarten, Suriname, Trinidad and Tobago, Turks and Caicos Islands.

  - *Latin America (19 countries)*
    Argentina, Plurinational State of Bolivia, Brazil, Chile, Colombia, Costa Rica, Cuba, Dominican Republic, Ecuador, El Salvador, Guatemala, Honduras, Mexico, Nicaragua, Panama, Paraguay, Peru, Uruguay, Bolivarian Republic of Venezuela.

- **Northern Africa and Western Asia (20 countries/ territories)**
  Algeria, Bahrain, Egypt, Iraq, Israel, Jordan, Kuwait, Lebanon, Libya, Morocco, Oman, Palestine, Qatar, Saudi Arabia, Sudan, Syrian Arab Republic, Tunisia, Turkey, United Arab Emirates, Yemen.

  - *Northern Africa (6 countries)*
    Algeria, Egypt, Libya, Morocco, Sudan, Tunisia.

  - *Western Asia (14 countries and territories)*
    Bahrain, Iraq, Israel, Jordan, Kuwait, Lebanon, Oman, Palestine, Qatar, Saudi Arabia, Syrian Arab Republic, Turkey, United Arab Emirates, Yemen.

- **Pacific (17 countries/territories)**
  Australia, Cook Islands, Fiji, Kiribati, Marshall Islands, Micronesia (Federated States of), Nauru, New Zealand, Niue, Palau, Papua New Guinea, Samoa, Solomon Islands, Tokelau, Tonga, Tuvalu, Vanuatu.

- **Southern Asia (9 countries)**
  Afghanistan, Bangladesh, Bhutan, India, Islamic Republic of Iran, Maldives, Nepal, Pakistan, Sri Lanka.

- **Sub-Saharan Africa (48 countries)**
  Angola, Benin, Botswana, Burkina Faso, Burundi, Cabo Verde, Cameroon, Central African Republic, Chad, Comoros, Congo, Côte d'Ivoire, Democratic Republic of the Congo, Djibouti, Equatorial Guinea, Eritrea, Ethiopia, Gabon, Gambia, Ghana, Guinea, Guinea-Bissau, Kenya, Lesotho, Liberia, Madagascar, Malawi, Mali, Mauritania, Mauritius, Mozambique, Namibia, Niger, Nigeria, Rwanda, Sao Tome and Principe, Senegal, Seychelles, Sierra Leone, Somalia, South Africa, South Sudan, Swaziland, Togo, Uganda, United Republic of Tanzania, Zambia, Zimbabwe.

Conflict-affected countries (31 as of 2013)

Afghanistan, Algeria, Burundi, Central African Republic, Chad, Colombia, Democratic Republic of the Congo, Ethiopia, India, Indonesia, Islamic Republic of Iran, Iraq, Libya, Mali, Myanmar, Nepal, Nigeria, Pakistan, Palestine, Philippines, Russian Federation, Rwanda, Somalia, South Sudan, Sri Lanka, Sudan, Syrian Arab Republic, Thailand, Turkey, Uganda and Yemen.

Income groups[12]

- **Low income (32 countries)**
  Afghanistan, Benin, Burkina Faso, Burundi, Cambodia, Central African Republic, Chad, Comoros, Democratic People's Republic of Korea, Democratic Republic of the Congo, Eritrea, Ethiopia, Gambia, Guinea, Guinea-Bissau, Haiti, Liberia, Madagascar, Malawi, Mali, Mozambique, Nepal, Niger, Rwanda, Sierra Leone, Somalia, South Sudan, Togo, Tokelau, Uganda, United Republic of Tanzania, Zimbabwe.

- **Lower middle income (50 countries)**
  Armenia, Bangladesh, Bhutan, Plurinational State of Bolivia, Cameroon, Cabo Verde, Congo, Côte d'Ivoire, Djibouti, Egypt, El Salvador, Georgia, Ghana, Guatemala, Guyana, Honduras, India, Indonesia, Kenya, Kiribati, Kyrgyzstan, Lao People's Democratic Republic, Lesotho, Mauritania, Micronesia (Federated States of), Morocco, Myanmar, Nicaragua, Nigeria, Pakistan, Palestine, Papua New Guinea, Philippines, Republic of Moldova, Samoa, Sao Tome and Principe,

Senegal, Solomon Islands, Sri Lanka, Sudan, Swaziland, Syrian Arab Republic, Tajikistan, Timor-Leste, Ukraine, Uzbekistan, Vanuatu, Viet Nam, Yemen, Zambia.

- **Upper middle income (54 countries)**
Albania, Algeria, Angola, Azerbaijan, Belarus, Belize, Bosnia and Herzegovina, Botswana, Brazil, Bulgaria, China, Colombia, Costa Rica, Cuba, Dominica, Dominican Republic, Ecuador, Fiji, Gabon, Grenada, Islamic Republic of Iran, Iraq, Jamaica, Jordan, Kazakhstan, Lebanon, Libya, Malaysia, Maldives, Marshall Islands, Mauritius, Mexico, Mongolia, Montenegro, Montserrat, Namibia, Nauru, Palau, Panama, Paraguay, Peru, Romania, Saint Lucia, Saint Vincent and the Grenadines, Serbia, South Africa, Suriname, Thailand, The former Yugoslav Republic of Macedonia, Tonga, Tunisia, Turkey, Turkmenistan, Tuvalu.

- **High income (73 countries/territories)**
Andorra, Anguilla, Antigua and Barbuda, Argentina, Aruba, Australia, Austria, Bahamas, Bahrain, Barbados, Belgium, Bermuda, British Virgin Islands, Brunei Darussalam, Canada, Cayman Islands, Chile, Cook Islands, Croatia, Curaçao, Cyprus, Czech Republic, Denmark, Equatorial Guinea, Estonia, Finland, France, Germany, Greece, Hong Kong (China), Hungary, Iceland, Ireland, Israel, Italy, Japan, Kuwait, Latvia, Liechtenstein, Lithuania, Luxembourg, Macao (China), Malta, Monaco, Netherlands, New Zealand, Niue, Norway, Oman, Poland, Portugal, Qatar, Republic of Korea, Russian Federation, Saint Kitts and Nevis, Saint Martin, San Marino, Saudi Arabia, Seychelles, Singapore, Sint Maarten, Slovakia, Slovenia, Spain, Sweden, Switzerland, Trinidad and Tobago, Turks and Caicos Islands, United Arab Emirates, United Kingdom, United States, Uruguay, Bolivarian Republic of Venezuela.

ENDNOTES

1. A full set of statistics and indicators related to this introduction is found in Excel tables on the GEM Report website at http://en.unesco.org/gem-report.

2. The thematic indicators were proposed by the Technical Advisory Group on post-2015 education indicators – now the Technical Cooperation Group, whose secretariat is based at the UNESCO Institute for Statistics (UIS) – to monitor progress towards the targets at the global, regional and national levels. The global indicators were approved at the 47th session of the UN Statistical Commission in March 2016. At time of publication, consultations were still under way on the other thematic indicators, which were to be officially adopted in October 2016.

3. This means 2013/14 for countries with a school year that overlaps two calendar years, and 2014 for those with a calendar school year. The most recent reference year for education finance for the UOE countries (see below) is the year ending in 2013.

4. Djibouti, Ghana, Kazakhstan, Mauritania, Montenegro, Nepal, the Republic of Korea, Sao Tome and Principe, Tajikistan and Turks and Caicos Islands.

5. The countries concerned are most European countries as well as Australia, Brazil, Canada, Chile, China, India, Indonesia, Israel, Japan, Jordan, Mexico, New Zealand, Republic of Korea, Turkey and United States.

6. Where obvious inconsistencies exist between enrolment reported by countries and the United Nations population data, the UIS may decide not to calculate or publish enrolment ratios. This is the case, for instance, with Armenia, Australia, Bahrain, the Plurinational State of Bolivia, Hong Kong (China), Jamaica, Kuwait, Macao (China), Malaysia, Maldives, Oman, Qatar, Saint Lucia, Singapore and the United Arab Emirates.

7. That is the definition long used by UNESCO, but a parallel definition arose with the introduction in 1978 of the notion of functional literacy, which emphasizes the use of literacy skills. That year the UNESCO General Conference approved defining as functionally literate those who can engage in all activities in which literacy is required for the effective functioning of their group and community and also for enabling them to continue to use reading, writing and calculation for their own and the community's development.

8. In the data released by the UIS, some literacy rates are based on direct tests rather than individuals' declarations. This is the case for Benin, Central African Republic, Congo, Côte d'Ivoire, the Democratic Republic of the Congo, Egypt, Gabon, Guyana, Haiti, Jordan, Kenya, Lesotho, Liberia, Madagascar, Malawi, Mauritania, Niger, Nigeria, Rwanda, Swaziland and Zimbabwe. Care should therefore be taken when analysing trends over time and when interpreting these results.

9. For reliability and consistency reasons, the UIS does not publish literacy data based on educational attainment proxies. Only data reported by countries based on self-declaration or household declaration are included in the statistical tables. However, in the absence of such data, educational attainment proxies for some countries, particularly developed ones, are used to compute regional weighted averages.

10. For a description of the GALP methodology, see UNESCO (2005, p. 261) and UIS (2006).

11. This is a UNSD classification in three main country groupings as per the May 2015 version published online at http://unstats.un.org/unsd/methods/m49/m49regin.htm.

TABLE 1

Background demographic statistics, legal guarantee of compulsory and free education and structure of national education system – part 1

	DEMOGRAPHY[1]		GDP AND POVERTY[2]			LEGAL GUARANTEE OF COMPULSORY AND FREE EDUCATION[4]				
						PRE-PRIMARY EDUCATION		PRIMARY AND SECONDARY EDUCATION		
									Free education (years)	
	Total population (000)	Average annual growth rate (%)	GDP per capita		Population living on less than PPP US$1.90 a day (%)	Compulsory education (age group)	Free education (years)	Compulsory education (age group)	Primary	Secondary
			Current US$	Current PPP US$						
Country or territory	2016	2016	2014	2014	2003–2013[3]					
Caucasus and Central Asia										
Armenia[6]	3,026	0.1	3,874	8,070	2.4	.	.	6-16	4	7
Azerbaijan[7]	9,868	1.0	7,884	17,516	0.0	.	.	6-15	4	7
Georgia	3,980	-0.1	3,670	7,582	11.5	.	.	6-14	6	6
Kazakhstan	17,855	1.1	12,602	24,228	0.0	6-6	4	7-18	4	7
Kyrgyzstan	6,034	1.4	1,269	3,322	2.9	.	4	7-16	4	7
Tajikistan	8,669	2.1	1,114	2,691	4.7	.	.	7-16	4	5
Turkmenistan	5,439	1.1	9,032	15,474	…	.	3	6-18	4	8
Uzbekistan	30,300	1.2	2,037	5,573	66.8	.	.	7-18	4	7
Eastern and South-eastern Asia										
Brunei Darussalam	429	1.3	40,980	71,185	…	5-5	1	6-15	6	7
Cambodia	15,827	1.5	1,095	3,263	6.2	.	.	.	6	3
China	1,382,323	0.4	7,590	13,206	11.2	.	.	6-15	6	3
DPR Korea	25,281	0.5	…	…	…	6-6	1	7-16	5	5
Hong Kong, China[6]	7,346	0.7	40,170	55,084	…	.	.	6-15	6	6
Indonesia	260,581	1.1	3,492	10,517	15.9	.	.	7-15	6	3
Japan	126,324	-0.2	36,194	36,426	…	.	.	6-15	6	3
Lao People's Democratic Republic	6,918	1.7	1,793	5,321	30.0	.	.	6-14	5	.
Macao, China[6]	597	1.5	96,038	139,767	…	5-5	3	6-15	6	6
Malaysia	30,752	1.3	11,307	25,639	0.3	.	.	6-11	.	.
Mongolia	3,006	1.4	4,129	11,946	0.4	.	.	6-17	5	7
Myanmar	54,363	0.9	1,204	,,,	…	4-4	.	5-9	5	.
Philippines	102,250	1.5	2,873	6,969	13.1	5-5	1	6-18	6	6
Republic of Korea	50,504	0.4	27,970	34,356	…	.	.	6-15	6	3
Singapore[6]	5,697	1.4	56,285	82,763	…	.	.	6-14	6	.
Thailand	68,147	0.2	5,977	15,735	0.1	.	.	6-15	6	6
Timor-Leste	1,211	2.1	1,169	2,227	46.8	.	.	6-15	6	3
Viet Nam	94,444	1.0	2,052	5,629	3.2	5-5	.	6-14	5	.
Europe and Northern America										
Albania	2,904	0.3	4,564	10,305	1.1	.	.	6-16	.	.
Andorra[8]	69	-0.2	…	…	…	.	.	6-16	6	4
Austria	8,570	0.3	51,191	46,222	…	.	3	6-15	4	8
Belarus	9,482	-0.3	8,040	18,185	0.0	.	.	6-15	4	7
Belgium[9]	11,372	0.6	47,353	42,578	…	.	3	6-18	6	6
Bosnia and Herzegovina	3,802	-0.3	4,790	9,891	0.1	5-5	.	6-15	5	4
Bulgaria	7,098	-0.8	7,851	16,617	2.0	6-6	4	7-16	4	8
Canada	36,286	0.9	50,235	44,057	…	.	2	6-16	6	6
Croatia	4,225	-0.4	13,475	21,210	0.9	.	.	7-15	4	4
Cyprus[7]	1,177	0.9	27,194	30,873	…	5-5	1	6-15	6	6
Czech Republic[9]	10,548	0.1	19,530	30,407	0.1	.	.	6-15	5	8
Denmark[9]	5,691	0.4	60,707	44,916	…	.	3	6-16	7	.
Estonia[9]	1,309	-0.3	20,162	26,946	1.0	.	.	7-17	6	3
Finland[9]	5,524	0.3	49,824	39,981	…	.	.	7-16	6	3
France[9]	64,668	0.4	42,733	38,847	…	.	3	6-16	5	7
Germany[9]	80,682	-0.1	47,822	45,802	…	.	3	6-18	4	9
Greece	10,919	-0.2	21,498	25,877	…	5-5	2	6-15	6	6
Hungary	9,821	-0.3	14,029	24,721	0.3	6-6	.	7-18	4	8
Iceland	332	0.8	52,004	43,304	…	.	.	6-16	7	3
Ireland[9]	4,714	0.8	54,374	48,755	…	.	.	6-16	8	5
Italy	59,801	0.0	34,909	34,706	…	.	.	6-16	5	3
Latvia	1,956	-0.5	15,719	22,873	1.4	5-6	4	7-16	6	6
Liechtenstein[7,9]	38	0.6	…	…	…	.	3	6-15	5	7
Lithuania	2,850	-0.6	16,507	26,742	1.0	4-6	4	7-16	4	8
Luxembourg	576	1.3	116,664	97,662	…	4-5	2	6-16	6	7
Malta[9]	420	0.2	…	…	…	.	2	5-16	6	7
Monaco[8,9]	38	0.4	…	…	…	.	3	6-16	5	7
Montenegro	626	0.0	7,378	14,338	1.7	.	.	6-15	5	4
Netherlands	16,980	0.3	52,172	47,663	…	5-5	.	6-18	6	6
Norway[9]	5,272	1.1	97,307	64,856	…	.	.	6-16	7	3
Poland	38,593	-0.1	14,343	24,744	0.0	6-6	.	7-18	6	6
Portugal[9]	10,304	-0.4	22,132	28,393	…	.	.	6-18	6	3
Republic of Moldova[7]	4,063	-0.2	2,239	4,983	0.1	6-6	4	7-16	4	7
Romania	19,373	-0.7	9,997	19,401	0.0	5-5	3	6-16	5	8
Russian Federation	143,440	-0.1	12,736	25,636	0.0	.	.	7-18	4	5
San Marino[7]	32	0.4	…	…	…	.	.	6-16	…	…
Serbia[7]	8,813	-0.4	6,153	12,660	0.1	6-6	.	7-15	4	8
Slovakia	5,429	0.0	18,501	27,711	0.2	.	.	6-16	4	9
Slovenia[9]	2,069	0.1	23,999	29,963	0.0	.	.	6-15	6	3
Spain[9]	46,065	0.0	29,767	33,211	…	.	.	6-16	6	4
Sweden[9]	9,852	0.7	58,939	45,183	…	.	.	7-16	6	6
Switzerland	8,379	0.8	85,594	57,235	…	5-6	2	7-16	6	3
TFYR Macedonia	2,081	0.1	5,456	13,142	1.3	5-5	1	6-18	5	8
Ukraine	44,624	-0.5	3,082	8,665	0.0	5-5	1	6-17	4	7
United Kingdom[9]	65,111	0.6	46,332	39,762	…	.	2	5-16	6	7
United States	324,119	0.7	54,629	54,629	…	.	1	5-18	6	6
Latin America and the Caribbean										
Anguilla[8]	15	0.9	…	…	…	.	.	5-17	7	5
Antigua and Barbuda	93	1.0	13,432	22,077	…	.	.	5-16	7	5

TABLE 1

Part 1 (Continued)

Country or territory	DEMOGRAPHY[1]		GDP AND POVERTY[2]			LEGAL GUARANTEE OF COMPULSORY AND FREE EDUCATION[4]				
						PRE-PRIMARY EDUCATION		PRIMARY AND SECONDARY EDUCATION		
			GDP per capita		Population living on less than PPP US$1.90 a day (%)	Compulsory education (age group)	Free education (years)	Compulsory education (age group)	Free education (years)	
	Total population (000)	Average annual growth rate (%)	Current US$	Current PPP US$					Primary	Secondary
	2016	2016	2014	2014	2003–2013[3]					
Argentina	43,847	0.9	12,510	...	1.8	5-5	3	6-18	6	6
Aruba	104	0.3	...	...	...	4-5	2	6-17	6	5
Bahamas	393	1.1	22,217	23,491	...	.	2	5-16	6	6
Barbados	285	0.2	15,366	16,058	...	.	2	5-16	6	5
Belize	367	2.0	4,831	8,417	...	.	.	5-14	6	.
Bermuda	62	-0.4	...	...	...	.	.	5-16	6	7
Bolivia, Plurinational States of[6]	10,888	1.5	3,124	6,630	7.7	5-5	2	6-16	6	6
Brazil[7]	209,568	0.8	11,384	15,838	4.9	4-5	2	6-17	5	7
British Virgin Islands[7]	31	1.6	...	...	...	.	.	5-16	7	5
Cayman Islands[8]	61	1.3	...	...	...	.	2	5-17	6	6
Chile	18,132	1.0	14,528	22,346	0.9	5-5	1	6-21	6	6
Colombia	48,654	0.8	7,904	13,357	6.1	5-5	3	6-15	5	6
Costa Rica	4,857	1.0	10,415	14,918	1.7	3-5	3	6-15	6	5
Cuba	11,393	0.0	...	...	...	.	3	6-15	6	6
Curaçao	159	0.8	...	...	...	4-5	...	6-18	...	...
Dominica	73	0.4	7,244	10,877	...	.	.	5-16	7	4
Dominican Republic	10,649	1.1	6,164	13,262	2.3	5-5	3	6-18	6	6
Ecuador	16,385	1.4	6,346	11,372	4.4	5-5	3	6-18	6	6
El Salvador	6,146	0.3	4,120	8,351	3.3	4-6	3	7-15	6	3
Grenada	107	0.5	8,574	12,425	...	.	2	5-16	7	5
Guatemala	16,673	1.9	3,673	7,454	11.5	5-6	2	7-15	6	5
Guyana	771	0.5	4,054	...	...	.	2	6-15	6	5
Haiti	10,848	1.2	824	1,732	53.9	.	.	6-11	6	.
Honduras	8,190	1.4	2,435	4,909	18.9	5-5	3	6-15	6	3
Jamaica[6]	2,803	0.3	5,105	8,875	1.7	.	.	6-14	6	.
Mexico	128,632	1.2	10,326	17,108	2.7	4-5	2	6-18	6	6
Montserrat[8]	5	0.5	...	...	...	.	.	5-16	7	5
Nicaragua	6,150	1.1	1,963	4,918	10.8	5-5	.	6-11	6	3
Panama	3,990	1.5	11,949	20,895	2.9	4-5	2	6-15	6	3
Paraguay	6,725	1.2	4,713	8,911	2.2	5-5	3	6-18	6	6
Peru	31,774	1.2	6,541	11,989	3.7	3-5	3	6-18	6	5
Saint Kitts and Nevis	56	1.0	15,510	23,239	...	.	.	5-16	7	4
Saint Lucia[6]	186	0.7	7,648	10,733	...	.	.	5-15	7	3
Saint-Martin[8]	...	...	...	...	...	.	...	...	...	...
Saint Vincent and the Grenadines	110	0.2	6,669	10,727	...	.	2	5-16	7	5
Sint-Maarten[8]	40	1.3	...	...	...	.	...	...	...	...
Suriname	548	0.8	9,680	16,638	...	.	.	6-11	6	.
Trinidad and Tobago	1,365	0.3	21,324	31,967	...	.	.	5-11	6	.
Turks and Caicos Islands[8]	35	1.5	...	...	...	4-5	.	6-17	...	...
Uruguay	3,444	0.4	16,807	20,884	0.3	4-5	2	6-17	6	6
Venezuela, Bolivarian Republic of	31,519	1.3	...	...	9.2	4-5	3	6-14	6	5
Northern Africa and Western Asia										
Algeria	40,376	1.6	5,484	14,193	...	.	1	6-16	5	7
Bahrain[6]	1,397	1.5	24,855	45,500	...	.	.	6-15	6	6
Egypt	93,384	1.9	3,199	10,530	...	.	.	6-14	6	6
Iraq	37,548	2.8	6,420	15,057	...	.	.	6-11	6	6
Israel	8,192	1.6	37,208	33,230	...	.	.	6-18	6	6
Jordan	7,748	1.5	5,423	12,050	0.1	.	.	6-16	6	6
Kuwait[6]	4,007	2.1	43,594	73,246	...	.	.	6-14	5	4
Lebanon	5,988	0.1	10,058	17,462	...	.	2	6-12	6	.
Libya	6,330	1.3	6,573	15,597	...	5-5	1	6-15	6	3
Morocco	34,817	1.2	3,190	7,491	3.1	.	.	6-15	6	3
Oman[6]	4,654	1.4	19,310	38,631	...	.	.	.	4	8
Palestine	4,797	2.7	...	...	0.3	.	.	6-16	4	8
Qatar[6]	2,291	1.9	96,732	140,649	...	.	.	6-18	6	3
Saudi Arabia	32,158	1.7	24,161	51,924	...	.	.	6-15	6	6
Sudan	41,176	2.4	1,876	4,069	14.9	.	.	6-13	6	2
Syrian Arab Republic	18,564	2.5	...	...	...	.	.	6-15	4	8
Tunisia	11,375	1.0	4,421	11,436	2.0	.	3	6-16	6	7
Turkey	79,622	0.9	10,515	19,199	0.3	.	3	6-18	4	8
United Arab Emirates[6]	9,267	1.4	43,963	67,674	...	.	2	6-12	5	7
Yemen	27,478	2.3	...	...	...	.	.	6-15	6	3
The Pacific										
Australia[6]	28,875	1.2	61,925	43,930	...	.	1	5-17	7	6
Cook Islands[7]	21	0.6	...	...	...	.	2	5-16	6	7
Fiji	898	0.5	5,112	8,792	3.6	.	.	6-18	6	6
Kiribati	114	1.7	1,510	1,809	14.1	.	.	6-15	6	3
Marshall Islands	53	0.1	3,530	3,803	...	5-5	1	6-14	6	2
Micronesia (Federated States of)	532	1.0	3,057	3,331	...	.	.	6-14	6	2
Nauru[7]	10	0.4	...	...	...	.	2	6-16	6	6
New Zealand	4,565	0.9	44,342	36,390	...	.	.	6-16	6	7
Niue[7]	2	0.1	...	...	...	.	1	5-16	6	6
Palau[7]	22	1.1	11,880	14,757	...	.	3	6-17	6	6
Papua New Guinea	7,776	2.0	2,268	2,855	39.3	.	.	.	.	.
Samoa	195	0.6	4,172	5,789	0.8	.	.	5-14	.	.
Solomon Islands	595	1.8	2,024	2,130	45.6	.	.	.	.	.
Tokelau[7]	1	1.6	...	...	...	.	.	5-16	...	...
Tonga	107	0.8	4,114	5,211	1.1	4-5	.	6-18	.	.

TABLE 1

Part 1 (Continued)

Country or territory	DEMOGRAPHY[1]		GDP AND POVERTY[2]			LEGAL GUARANTEE OF COMPULSORY AND FREE EDUCATION[4]				
						PRE-PRIMARY EDUCATION		PRIMARY AND SECONDARY EDUCATION		
	Total population (000)	Average annual growth rate (%)	GDP per capita		Population living on less than PPP US$1.90 a day (%)	Compulsory education (age group)	Free education (years)	Compulsory education (age group)	Free education (years)	
			Current US$	Current PPP US$					Primary	Secondary
	2016	2016	2014	2014	2003–2013[3]					
Tuvalu[7]	10	0.4	3,827	3,765	...	.	.	6-15	6	.
Vanuatu	270	2.1	3,148	3,031	15.4	.	.	.	.	.
Southern Asia										
Afghanistan	33,370	2.3	634	1,933	...	.	4	7-16	6	6
Bangladesh	162,911	1.1	1,087	3,123	43.7	.	.	6-10	5	.
Bhutan	784	1.1	2,561	7,816	2.2	.	.	.	7	3
India	1,326,802	1.2	1,582	5,701	21.3	.	.	6-14	5	3
Iran, Islamic Republic of	80,043	1.1	5,443	17,303	0.1	.	.	6-14	6	2
Maldives[6]	370	1.6	7,635	12,530	5.6	.	.	.	7	5
Nepal	28,851	1.1	702	2,374	15.0	.	.	.	5	.
Pakistan	192,827	2.0	1,317	4,811	8.3	.	.	5-16	5	7
Sri Lanka	20,811	0.4	3,819	11,181	1.7	.	1	5-14	5	8
Sub-Saharan Africa										
Angola	25,831	3.1	...	...	30.1	.	.	6-11	6	.
Benin	11,167	2.6	903	2,030	53.1	.	.	6-11	6	.
Botswana	2,304	1.7	7,123	16,099	18.2	.	.	.	.	.
Burkina Faso	18,634	2.8	713	1,620	55.3	.	.	6-16	6	4
Burundi	11,553	3.2	286	770	77.7	.	.	.	6	...
Cabo Verde	527	1.2	3,641	6,520	17.6	.	.	6-16	6	2
Cameroon	23,924	2.4	1,407	2,972	29.3	.	.	6-11	6	.
Central African Republic	4,998	2.0	359	594	66.3	.	3	6-15	6	7
Chad	14,497	3.1	1,025	2,182	38.4	.	3	6-16	6	7
Comoros	807	2.3	810	1,429	13.5	.	.	6-14	6	.
Congo	4,741	2.6	3,147	6,277	28.7	.	3	6-16	6	7
Côte d'Ivoire	23,254	2.4	1,546	3,258	29.0	.	.	.	.	.
Democratic Rep. of the Congo	79,723	3.1	442	746	77.2	.	.	6-15	6	.
Djibouti	900	1.3	1,814	3,270	18.3	.	2	6-16	5	7
Equatorial Guinea	870	2.8	18,918	34,739	...	.	.	7-12	6	.
Eritrea	5,352	2.4	...	...	...	.	.	6-13	.	.
Ethiopia	101,853	2.4	574	1,500	33.5	.	.	.	6	.
Gabon	1,763	2.1	10,772	19,430	8.0	.	.	6-16	5	5
Gambia	2,055	3.1	...	...	45.3	.	.	.	...	.
Ghana	28,033	2.2	1,442	4,082	25.2	4-5	2	6-15	6	3
Guinea	12,947	2.6	540	1,221	35.3	.	.	7-16	6	...
Guinea-Bissau	1,888	2.3	568	1,386	67.1	.	.	6-15	.	.
Kenya	47,251	2.5	1,358	2,954	33.6	.	3	6-18	6	6
Lesotho	2,160	1.1	1,034	2,638	59.7	.	.	6-12	7	.
Liberia	4,615	2.5	458	841	68.6	.	.	6-16	6	.
Madagascar	24,916	2.7	449	1,439	81.8	.	3	6-10	5	7
Malawi	17,750	3.0	255	822	70.9	.	...	.	6	...
Mali	18,135	3.0	705	1,599	49.3	.	4	7-15	6	6
Mauritania	4,166	2.3	1,275	3,912	10.9	.	.	6-14	.	.
Mauritius	1,277	0.3	10,017	18,585	0.5	.	...	5-16	6	7
Mozambique	28,751	2.7	586	1,129	68.7	.	.	6-12	.	.
Namibia	2,514	2.1	5,408	9,956	22.6	.	.	7-16	7	.
Niger	20,715	4.0	427	938	50.3	4-6	.	7-16	.	.
Nigeria	186,988	2.5	3,203	5,911	53.5	.	.	6-15	6	3
Rwanda	11,883	2.3	696	1,661	60.3	.	.	7-16	6	3
Sao Tome and Principe	194	2.1	1,811	3,176	33.9	.	.	6-11	6	.
Senegal	15,589	2.9	1,067	2,333	38.0	.	.	6-16	6	4
Seychelles	97	0.5	15,543	26,386	0.4	.	.	6-16	6	7
Sierra Leone	6,592	2.1	766	1,966	52.3	.	.	6-15	6	3
Somalia	11,079	2.8	543	...	...	.	3	.	6	6
South Africa	54,979	0.8	6,483	13,046	16.6	.	.	7-15	.	.
South Sudan	12,733	2.7	1,115	2,019	...	.	.	6-11	6	.
Swaziland	1,304	1.2	3,477	8,292	42.0	.	.	6-12	7	.
Togo	7,497	2.5	635	1,429	54.2	.	.	6-15	6	.
Uganda	40,323	3.2	715	1,771	33.2	.	.	6-12	7	.
United Republic of Tanzania	55,155	3.0	955	2,538	46.6	.	2	7-13	7	6
Zambia	16,717	3.1	1,722	3,904	64.4	.	.	.	7	...
Zimbabwe	15,967	2.3	931	1,792	...	4-5	2	6-14	7	2

TABLE 1
Part 1 (Continued)

Country or territory	DEMOGRAPHY[1]		GDP AND POVERTY[2]			LEGAL GUARANTEE OF COMPULSORY AND FREE EDUCATION[4]				
						PRE-PRIMARY EDUCATION		PRIMARY AND SECONDARY EDUCATION		
			GDP per capita		Population living on less than PPP US$1.90 a day (%)	Compulsory education (age group)	Free education (years)	Compulsory education (age group)	Free education (years)	
	Total population (000)	Average annual growth rate (%)	Current US$	Current PPP US$					Primary	Secondary
	2016	2016	2014	2014	2003–2013[3]					
	Sum	Weighted average	Median		Median					
World	7,406,355	1.1	5,484	11,989	8.3	...	...	...	...	...
Countries in transition	305,006	0.2	4,790	10,305	0.6	...	...	...	...	...
Developed countries	1,047,103	0.3	42,733	36,426	...	...	...	...	...	...
Developing countries	6,054,245	1.2	3,673	7,816	15.6	...	...	...	...	...
Caucasus and Central Asia	85,172	1.2	3,772	7,826	2.9	...	...	...	...	...
Eastern and South-eastern Asia	2,236,001	0.5	5,977	14,471	8.7	...	...	...	...	...
Eastern Asia	1,595,382	0.3	32,082	35,391	...	...	...	...	...	...
South-eastern Asia	640,619	1.0	2,873	8,743	9.6	...	...	...	...	...
Europe and Northern America	1,100,096	0.3	22,132	29,963	...	...	...	...	...	...
Latin America and the Caribbean	636,133	1.0	7,648	12,425	...	...	...	...	...	...
Caribbean	38,871	0.7	8,111	12,844	...	...	...	...	...	...
Latin America	597,262	1.0	6,541	11,989	3.7	...	...	...	...	...
Northern Africa and Western Asia	471,169	1.7	10,058	17,462	...	...	...	...	...	...
Northern Africa	227,458	1.8	3,810	10,983	3.1	...	...	...	...	...
Western Asia	243,711	1.7	24,161	38,631	...	...	...	...	...	...
Pacific	44,045	1.3	3,827	3,803	...	...	...	...	...	...
Southern Asia	1,846,768	1.2	1,582	5,701	6.9	...	...	...	...	...
Sub-Saharan Africa	986,971	2.6	1,025	2,258	38.4	...	...	...	...	...
Conflict-affected countries	3,109,793	1.4	1,449	5,256	15.4	...	...	...	...	...
Countries with low income	655,764	2.6	665	1,599	53.1	...	...	...	...	...
Countries with middle income	5,366,318	1.1	4,117	8,834	4.9	...	...	...	...	...
Lower middle	2,958,865	1.4	2,052	4,918	15.6	...	...	...	...	...
Upper middle	2,407,454	0.6	7,123	13,357	1.7	...	...	...	...	...
Countries with high income	1,384,272	0.4	29,767	36,408	...	...	...	...	...	...

TABLE 1

Background demographic statistics, legal guarantee of compulsory and free education and structure of national education system – part 2

	STRUCTURE OF NATIONAL EDUCATION SYSTEM AND OFFICIAL SCHOOL-AGE POPULATION								
	Age group					Official school-age population (000)			
	Pre-primary	Primary	Lower secondary	Upper secondary	Tertiary	Pre-primary	Primary	Total secondary	Tertiary
	School year ending in 2014		School year ending in 2014		School year ending in 2014	School year ending in 2014[5]			
Country or territory									
Caucasus and Central Asia									
Armenia[6]	3-5	6-9	10-13	14-16	17-21	124	...	...	256
Azerbaijan[7]	3-5	6-9	10-14	15-16	17-21	464*	488*	923*	844*
Georgia	3-5	6-11	12-14	15-17	18-22	154	244	283	309
Kazakhstan	3-6	7-10	11-15	16-17	18-22	1,334	1,008	1,575	1,501
Kyrgyzstan	3-6	7-10	11-15	16-17	18-22	497	404	717	583
Tajikistan	3-6	7-10	11-15	16-17	18-22	780	680	1,202	855
Turkmenistan	3-5	6-9	10-14	15-17	18-22	300	402	763	556
Uzbekistan	3-6	7-10	11-15	16-17	18-22	2,322	2,031	4,238	3,038
Eastern and South-eastern Asia									
Brunei Darussalam	3-5	6-11	12-13	14-18	19-23	18	38	49	36
Cambodia	3-5	6-11	12-14	15-17	18-22	1,032	1,829	1,885	1,652
China	3-5	6-11	12-14	15-17	18-22	47,723	91,520	94,021	106,433
Democratic People's Republic of Korea	5-6	7-11	12-14	15-17	18-22	691	1,843	2,339	2,015
Hong Kong, China[6]	3-5	6-11	12-14	15-17	18-22	...	292	413	443
Indonesia	5-6	7-12	13-15	16-18	19-23	9,198	28,218	27,389	20,781
Japan	3-5	6-11	12-14	15-17	18-22	3,228	6,633	7,103	6,096
Lao People's Democratic Republic	3-5	6-10	11-14	15-17	18-22	493	749	1,050	766
Macao, China[6]	3-5	6-11	12-14	15-17	18-22	...	...	33	43
Malaysia	4-5	6-11	12-14	15-18	19-23	904	2,974	3,845	2,896
Mongolia	4-5	6-10	11-14	15-17	18-22	115	235	315	273
Myanmar	3-4	5-9	10-13	14-15	16-20	1,933	5,195	6,221	4,784
Philippines	5-5	6-11	12-14	15-15	16-20	2,132	12,436	8,175	9,967
Republic of Korea	3-5	6-11	12-14	15-17	18-22	1,377	2,818	3,807	3,522
Singapore[6]	3-5	6-11	12-13	14-15	16-20	...	...	...	...
Thailand	3-5	6-11	12-14	15-17	18-22	2,386	4,998	5,317	4,634
Timor-Leste	3-5	6-11	12-14	15-17	18-22	95	180	163	111
Viet Nam	3-5	6-10	11-14	15-17	18-22	4,442	6,799	9,612	8,833
Europe and Northern America									
Albania	3-5	6-10	11-14	15-17	18-22	92	174	346	277
Andorra[8]	3-5	6-11	12-15	16-17	18-22	...	...	...	4
Austria	3-5	6-9	10-13	14-17	18-22	236	320	702	527
Belarus	3-5	6-9	10-14	15-16	17-21	311	373	606	582
Belgium[9]	3-5	6-11	12-13	14-17	18-22	393	738	734	676
Bosnia and Herzegovina	3-5	6-10	11-14	15-18	19-23	110	161	335	235
Bulgaria	3-6	7-10	11-14	15-18	19-23	290	261	514	400
Canada	4-5	6-11	12-14	15-17	18-22	775	2,209	2,422	2,390
Croatia	3-6	7-10	11-14	15-18	19-23	176	163	374	239
Cyprus[7]	3-5	6-11	12-14	15-17	18-22	30*	54*	59*	63*
Czech Republic[9]	3-5	6-10	11-14	15-18	19-23	350	516	743	634
Denmark[9]	3-5	6-12	13-15	16-18	19-23	198	461	426	370
Estonia[9]	3-6	7-12	13-15	16-18	19-23	63	78	71	84
Finland[9]	3-6	7-12	13-15	16-18	19-23	245	347	369	345
France[9]	3-5	6-10	11-14	15-17	18-22	2,375	3,976	5,375	3,710
Germany[9]	3-5	6-9	10-15	16-18	19-23	2,006	2,770	7,030	4,448
Greece	4-5	6-11	12-14	15-17	18-22	219	644	627	595
Hungary	3-6	7-10	11-14	15-18	19-23	393	387	802	619
Iceland	3-5	6-12	13-15	16-19	20-24	14	30	32	24
Ireland[9]	4-4	5-12	13-15	16-17	18-22	73	525	274	263
Italy	3-5	6-10	11-13	14-18	19-23	1,681	2,819	4,479	2,939
Latvia	3-6	7-12	13-15	16-18	19-23	87	114	105	134
Liechtenstein[7,9]	5-6	7-11	12-15	16-18	19-23	1*	2*	3*	2*
Lithuania	3-6	7-10	11-16	17-18	19-23	112	106	260	217
Luxembourg	3-5	6-11	12-14	15-18	19-23	18	36	46	34
Malta[9]	3-4	5-10	11-13	14-17	18-22	8	25	35	28
Monaco[8,9]	3-5	6-10	11-14	15-17	18-22	...	...	...	...
Montenegro	3-5	6-10	11-14	15-18	19-23	24	40	68	43
Netherlands	3-5	6-11	12-14	15-17	18-22	540	1,171	1,190	1,016
Norway[9]	3-5	6-12	13-15	16-18	19-23	190	425	390	344
Poland	3-6	7-12	13-15	16-18	19-23	1,638	2,140	2,443	2,588
Portugal[9]	3-5	6-11	12-14	15-17	18-22	289	621	660	552
Republic of Moldova[7]	3-6	7-10	11-15	16-17	18-22	155*	149*	281*	280*
Romania	3-5	6-10	11-14	15-18	19-23	629	1,051	1,698	1,087
Russian Federation	3-6	7-10[4]	11-15[5]	16-17[2]	18-22	6,440	5,809	9,009	8,894
San Marino[7]	3-5	6-10	11-13	14-18	19-23	1*	2*	3*	1*
Serbia[7]	3-6	7-10	11-14	15-18	19-23	266*	282*	581*	418*
Slovakia	3-5	6-9	10-14	15-18	19-23	172	212	506	374
Slovenia[9]	3-5	6-11	12-14	15-18	19-23	64	112	131	109
Spain[9]	3-5	6-11	12-15	16-17	18-22	1,472	2,828	2,526	2,225
Sweden[9]	3-6	7-12	13-15	16-18	19-23	461	626	622	689
Switzerland	5-6	7-12	13-15	16-19	20-24	158	469	618	506
The former Yugoslav Rep. of Macedonia	3-5	6-10	11-14	15-18	19-23	66	120	217	153
Ukraine	5-5	6-9	10-14	15-16	17-21	475	1,622	2,735	2,607
United Kingdom[9]	3-4	5-10	11-13	14-17	18-22	1,678	4,376	5,130	4,166
United States	3-5	6-11	12-14	15-17	18-22	12,257	24,654	24,835	22,732
Latin America and the Caribbean									
Anguilla[8]	3-4	5-11	12-14	15-16	17-21	...	...	...	...
Antigua and Barbuda	3-4	5-11	12-14	15-16	17-21	3	10	8	8

TABLE 1
Part 2 (Continued)

Country or territory	STRUCTURE OF NATIONAL EDUCATION SYSTEM AND OFFICIAL SCHOOL-AGE POPULATION								
	Age group					Official school-age population (000)			
	Pre-primary	Primary	Lower secondary	Upper secondary	Tertiary	Pre-primary	Primary	Total secondary	Tertiary
	School year ending in 2014		School year ending in 2014		School year ending in 2014	School year ending in 2014[5]			
Argentina	3-5	6-11	12-14	15-17	18-22	2,196	4,346	4,168	3,461
Aruba	4-5	6-11	12-13	14-16	17-21	3	8	7	7
Bahamas	3-4	5-10	11-13	14-16	17-21	12	30	34	33
Barbados	3-4	5-10	11-13	14-15	16-20	7	23	19	19
Belize	3-4	5-10	11-14	15-16	17-21	15	47	46	36
Bermuda	4-4	5-10	11-13	14-17	18-22	1	5	6	4
Bolivia, Plurinational States of[6]	4-5	6-11	12-13	14-17	18-22	469	...	1,325	1,011
Brazil[7]	4-5	6-10	11-14	15-17	18-22	5,579*	14,974*	23,761*	16,380*
British Virgin Islands[7]	3-4	5-11	12-14	15-16		1*	3*	2*	2*
Cayman Islands[8]	3-4	5-10	11-13	14-16	17-21	...	...	...	...
Chile	4-5	6-11	12-13	14-17	18-22	475	1,461	1,550	1,391
Colombia	3-5	6-10	11-14	15-16	17-21	2,299	3,994	4,888	4,168
Costa Rica	3-5	6-11	12-14	15-16	17-21	217	429	382	409
Cuba	3-5	6-11	12-14	15-17	18-22	364	778	833	736
Curaçao	4-5	6-11	12-13	14-17	18-22	4	12	12	11
Dominica	3-4	5-11	12-14	15-16	17-21	2	7	6	7
Dominican Republic	3-5	6-11	12-13	14-17	18-22	638	1,260	1,188	959
Ecuador	3-5	6-11	12-14	15-17	18-22	953	1,825	1,802	1,459
El Salvador	4-6	7-12	13-15	16-18	19-23	325	693	771	611
Grenada	3-4	5-11	12-14	15-16	17-21	4	13	10	10
Guatemala	5-6	7-12	13-15	16-17	18-22	792	2,334	1,835	1,641
Guyana	4-5	6-11	12-14	15-16	17-21	25	100	98	81
Haiti	3-5	6-11	12-14	15-18	19-23	743	1,425	1,583	1,044
Honduras	3-5	6-11	12-14	15-16	17-21	506	1,054	906	877
Jamaica[6]	3-5	6-11	12-14	15-16	17-21	132	...	325	269
Mexico	4-5	6-11	12-14	15-17	18-22	6,957	14,148	14,349	11,420
Montserrat[8]	3-4	5-11	12-14	15-16	17-21	...	...	...	...
Nicaragua	3-5	6-11	12-14	15-16	17-21	373	736	608	603
Panama	4-5	6-11	12-14	15-16	18-22	145	417	413	325
Paraguay	3-5	6-11	12-14	15-17	18-22	406	792	816	663
Peru	3-5	6-11	12-14	15-16	17-21	1,772	3,447	2,793	2,808
Saint Kitts and Nevis	3-4	5-11	12-14	15-16	17-21	2	7	5	4
Saint Lucia[6]	3-4	5-11	12-14	15-16	17-21	6	...	16	17
Saint-Martin[8]	...	...	...	...	...	...	...	...	...
Saint Vincent and the Grenadines	3-4	5-11	12-14	15-16	17-21	4	13	10	10
Sint-Maarten[8]	3-4	5-11	12-13	14-17	18-22	...	...	...	...
Suriname	4-5	6-11	12-15	16-18	19-23	20	59	67	43
Trinidad and Tobago	3-4	5-11	12-14	15-16	17-21	39	130	87	95
Turks and Caicos Islands[8]	4-5	6-11	12-14	15-16	17-21	...	...	...	...
Uruguay	3-5	6-11	12-14	15-17	18-22	146	296	307	263
Venezuela, Bolivarian Republic of	3-5	6-11	12-14	15-16	17-21	1,763	3,464	2,802	2,757
Northern Africa and Western Asia									
Algeria	5-5	6-10	11-14	15-17	18-22	761	3,171	4,140	3,600
Bahrain[6]	3-5	6-11	12-14	15-17	18-22	60	...	...	103
Egypt	4-5	6-11	12-14	15-17	18-22	3,880	10,707	9,533	8,031
Iraq	4-5	6-11	12-14	15-17	18-22	2,017	5,283	4,601	3,287
Israel	3-5	6-11	12-14	15-17	18-22	454	827	754	570
Jordan	4-5	6-11	12-15	16-17	18-22	360	1,007	909	680
Kuwait[6]	4-5	6-10	11-14	15-17	18-22	...	246	302	268
Lebanon	3-5	6-11	12-14	15-17	18-22	220	511	601	535
Libya	4-5	6-11	12-14	15-17	18-22	266	721	637	515
Morocco	4-5	6-11	12-14	15-17	18-22	1,251	3,470	3,570	3,151
Oman[6]	4-5	6-9	10-15	16-17	18-22	127	212	...	...
Palestine	4-5	6-9	10-15	16-17	18-22	252	466	862	486
Qatar[6]	3-5	6-11	12-14	15-17	Tertiary	65	...	...	160
Saudi Arabia	3-5	6-11	12-14	15-17	18-22	1,871	3,437	3,158	2,449
Sudan	4-5	6-11	12-13	14-16	17-21	2,219	6,184	4,479	3,783
Syrian Arab Republic	...	...	...	...	...	1,443	2,846	2,695	1,806
Tunisia	3-5	6-11	12-14	15-18	19-23	528	963	1,164	959
Turkey	3-5	6-9	10-13	14-17	18-22	3,950	5,268	10,628	6,341
United Arab Emirates[6]	4-5	6-10	11-14	15-17	18-22	180	384	...	649
Yemen	3-5	6-11	12-14	15-17	18-22	2.233	4.051	3.662	2.926
The Pacific									
Australia[6]	4-4	5-11	12-15	16-17	18-22	...	...	...	1,610
Cook Islands[7]	3-4	5-10	11-14	15-17	18-22	1*	2*	2*	1*
Fiji	3-5	6-11	12-15	16-18	19-23	54	101	108	78
Kiribati	3-5	6-11	12-14	15-18	19-23	9	14	16	11
Marshall Islands	4-5	6-11	12-13	14-17	18-22	3	9	7	3
Micronesia (Federated States of)	3-5	6-11	12-13	14-17	18-22	7	15	16	12
Nauru[7]	3-5	6-11	12-15	16-17	18-22	1*	2*	1*	1*
New Zealand	3-4	5-10	11-14	15-17	18-22	127	365	418	322
Niue[7]	4-4	5-10	11-14	15-16	17-21	0.03*	0.16*	0.16*	0.1*
Palau[7]	3-5	6-11	12-13	14-17	18-22	0.7*	1.4*	1.4*	1*
Papua New Guinea	3-5	6-12	13-14	15-18	19-23	584	1,278	986	694
Samoa	3-4	5-10	11-12	13-17	18-22	10	30	30	18
Solomon Islands	3-5	6-11	12-14	15-18	19-23	48	90	90	53
Tokelau[7]	3-4	5-10	11-13	14-15	16-20	0.1*	0.1*	0.2*	0.1*
Tonga	4-5	6-11	12-14	15-16	17-21	5	16	17	10

TABLE 1
Part 2 (Continued)

Country or territory	Age group Pre-primary	Primary	Lower secondary	Upper secondary	Tertiary	Official school-age population (000) Pre-primary	Primary	Total secondary	Tertiary
	School year ending in 2014		School year ending in 2014		School year ending in 2014	School year ending in 2014[5]			
Tuvalu[7]	3-5	6-11	12-15	16-18	19-23	0.8*	1.4*	1.5*	1*
Vanuatu	3-5	6-11	12-15	16-18	19-23	14	37	37	23
Southern Asia									
Afghanistan	3-6	7-12	13-15	16-18	19-23	3,996	5,564	4,676	3,035
Bangladesh	3-5	6-10	11-13	14-17	18-22	9,237	16,034	22,895	15,389
Bhutan	4-5	6-12	13-16	17-18	19-23	29	100	88	78
India	3-5	6-10	11-13	14-17	18-22	76,420	127,694	174,269	118,681
Iran, Islamic Republic of	5-5	6-11	12-13	14-17	18-22	1,280	6,815	6,554	7,104
Maldives[6]	3-5	6-12	13-15	16-17	18-22	...	...	32	38
Nepal	3-4	5-9	10-12	13-16	17-21	1,221	3,255	4,732	2,897
Pakistan	3-4	5-9	10-12	13-16	17-21	9,326	20,768	27,106	18,656
Sri Lanka	4-4	5-9	10-13	14-17	18-22	349	1,756	2,633	1,564
Sub-Saharan Africa									
Angola	5-5	6-11	12-14	15-17	18-22	826	4,341	3,431	2,286
Benin	4-5	6-11	12-15	16-18	19-23	625	1,699	1,650	976
Botswana	3-5	6-12	13-15	16-17	18-22	148	317	220	220
Burkina Faso	3-5	6-11	12-15	16-18	19-23	1,731	2,985	2,775	1,602
Burundi	5-6	7-12	13-16	17-19	20-24	1,005	1,604	1,540	1,032
Cabo Verde	3-5	6-11	12-14	15-17	18-22	31	59	65	58
Cameroon	4-5	6-11	12-15	16-18	19-23	1,357	3,648	3,544	2,185
Central African Republic	3-5	6-11	12-15	16-18	19-23	387	722	753	464
Chad	3-5	6-11	12-15	16-18	19-23	1,396	2,373	2,195	1,232
Comoros	3-5	6-11	12-15	16-18	19-23	66	117	116	73
Congo	3-5	6-11	12-15	16-18	19-23	412	705	658	387
Côte d'Ivoire	3-5	6-11	12-15	16-18	19-23	1,974	3,545	3,534	2,033
Democratic Rep. of the Congo	3-5	6-11	12-13	14-17	18-22	7,407	12,652	10,087	6,893
Djibouti	4-5	6-10	11-14	15-17	18-22	39	95	126	92
Equatorial Guinea	4-6	7-12	13-16	17-18	19-23	67	115	99	75
Eritrea	4-5	6-10	11-13	14-17	18-22	313	706	777	489
Ethiopia	4-6	7-12	13-16	17-18	19-23	8,231	15,714	13,924	9,318
Gabon	3-5	6-10	11-14	15-17	18-22	131	198	251	163
Gambia	3-6	7-12	13-15	16-18	19-23	257	321	259	171
Ghana	4-5	6-11	12-14	15-17	18-22	1,430	3,867	3,377	2,583
Guinea	4-6	7-12	13-16	17-19	20-24	1,074	1,895	1,843	1,087
Guinea-Bissau	3-5	6-11	12-14	15-17	18-22	156	273	236	174
Kenya	3-5	6-11	12-13	14-17	18-22	4,092	7,323	6,012	4,241
Lesotho	3-5	6-12	13-15	16-17	18-22	155	342	251	239
Liberia	3-5	6-11	12-14	15-17	18-22	396	715	588	395
Madagascar	3-5	6-10	11-14	15-17	18-22	2,054	3,142	3,887	2,367
Malawi	3-5	6-11	12-15	16-17	18-22	1,630	2,796	2,330	1,650
Mali	3-6	7-12	13-15	16-18	19-23	2,321	2,826	2,209	1,493
Mauritania	3-5	6-11	12-15	16-18	19-23	336	605	598	361
Mauritius	3-4	5-10	11-13	14-17	18-22	29	103	136	105
Mozambique	3-5	6-12	13-15	16-17	18-22	2,679	5,445	3,197	2,635
Namibia	5-6	7-13	14-16	17-18	19-23	118	385	266	252
Niger	4-6	7-12	13-16	17-19	20-24	1,987	3,225	2,737	1,393
Nigeria	3-5	6-11	12-14	15-17	18-22	16,707	28,768	23,212	16,040
Rwanda	4-6	7-12	13-15	16-18	19-23	1,015	1,796	1,501	1,017
Sao Tome and Principe	3-5	6-11	12-14	15-17	18-22	17	31	25	17
Senegal	3-5	6-11	12-15	16-18	19-23	1,352	2,335	2,229	1,365
Seychelles	4-5	6-11	12-14	15-18	19-23	3	8	9	7
Sierra Leone	3-5	6-11	12-14	15-18	19-23	577	1,023	987	585
Somalia	3-5	6-11	12-13	14-17	18-22	1,075	1,805	1,493	966
South Africa	6-6	7-13	14-15	16-18	19-23	2,236	7,215	5,283	5,257
South Sudan	3-5	6-11	12-13	14-17	18-22	1,085	1,925	1,672	1,139
Swaziland	3-5	6-12	13-15	16-17	18-22	100	213	147	151
Togo	3-5	6-11	12-15	16-18	19-23	645	1,130	1,070	658
Uganda	3-5	6-12	13-16	17-18	19-23	4,006	7,941	5,331	3,474
United Republic of Tanzania	5-6	7-13	14-17	18-19	20-24	3,268	9,822	6,563	4,462
Zambia	3-6	7-13	14-15	16-18	19-23	2,091	3,064	1,763	1,498
Zimbabwe	4-5	6-12	13-14	15-18	19-23	909	2,739	2,026	1,605

TABLE 1

Part 2 (Continued)

Country or territory	STRUCTURE OF NATIONAL EDUCATION SYSTEM AND OFFICIAL SCHOOL-AGE POPULATION								
	Age group					Official school-age population (000)			
	Pre-primary	Primary	Lower secondary	Upper secondary	Tertiary	Pre-primary	Primary	Total secondary	Tertiary
	School year ending in 2014		School year ending in 2014		School year ending in 2014	School year ending in 2014[5]			
						Sum			
World	...	...	...	...	...	351,952	687,228	756,430	602,031
Countries in transition	...	...	...	...	...	13,936	14,049	24,258	21,447
Developed countries	...	...	...	...	...	33,234	64,987	75,870	63,682
Developing countries	...	...	...	...	...	304,782	608,193	656,301	516,901
Caucasus and Central Asia	...	...	...	...	...	5,975	5,403	9,990	8,008
Eastern and South-eastern Asia	...	...	...	...	...	76,092	167,109	171,918	173,672
Eastern Asia	...	...	...	...	...	53,294	103,339	107,946	118,900
South-eastern Asia	...	...	...	...	...	22,798	63,770	63,971	54,772
Europe and Northern America	...	...	...	...	...	37,230	64,001	80,417	68,738
Latin America and the Caribbean	...	...	...	...	...	27,397	60,023	67,846	53,650
Caribbean	...	...	...	...	...	1,965	4,027	4,157	3,242
Latin America	...	...	...	...	...	25,432	55,996	63,689	50,408
Northern Africa and Western Asia	...	...	...	...	...	22,260	49,984	52,835	40,751
Northern Africa	...	...	...	...	...	8,905	25,217	23,523	20,131
Western Asia	...	...	...	...	...	13,355	24,767	29,312	20,620
Pacific	...	...	...	...	...	1,175	4,006**	3,456**	2,835**
Southern Asia	...	...	...	...	...	101,878	182,029	242,986	167,441
Sub-Saharan Africa	...	...	...	...	...	79,945	154,674	126,983	86,936
Conflict-affected countries	...	...	...	...	...	174,756	332,622	376,592	271,027
Countries with low income	...	...	...	...	...	53,977	101,309	86,962	57,909
Countries with middle income	...	...	...	...	...	250,174	498,346	568,226	456,231
Lower middle	...	...	...	...	...	162,693	315,291	366,407	264,781
Upper middle	...	...	...	...	...	87,481	183,055	201,819	191,450
Countries with high income	...	...	...	...	...	47,802	87,574	101,243	87,891

Source: UIS database, except where noted.

Note: The country groupings by level of income are as defined by the World Bank but include only countries listed in the table. They are based on the list of countries by income group as revised in July 2015.

1. United Nations Population Division (UNPD) estimates, revision 2015 (United Nations, 2015), based on the median variant.

2. World Bank (2015); World Bank WDI database, December 2015 release.

3. Data are for the most recent year available during the period specified. For more details see World Bank (2015).

4. Eurydice (2014, 2015, 2016); UNESCO-IBE (2012); national education ministry websites; UIS database.

5. Data are for 2014 except for countries with a split calendar school year, in which case data are for 2013.

6. School-age population data are not presented for some or all levels of education due to inconsistencies in population data.

7. National population data are presented instead of UNPD populations estimates due to inconsistencies in, or lack of, UNPD population data.

8. School-age population data are not presented due to lack of United Nations population data by age.

9. For pre-primary education there is legal entitlement but it is not compulsory. Legal entitlement to early childhood care and education (ECCE) means providers have a statutory duty to ensure that publicly subsidized ECCE provision is available for all children living in a given catchment area whose parents, regardless of employment, socio-economic or family status, require a place for them. Children are entitled, but not obliged, to participate (Eurydice, 2014).

(.) The category is not applicable or does not exist.

(...) No data are available.

TABLE 2

SDG 4, Target 4.1 – Universal access, participation and completion, primary education – part 1

By 2030, ensure that all girls and boys complete free, equitable and quality primary education leading to relevant and effective learning outcomes

	ACCESS TO AND PARTICIPATION IN PRIMARY EDUCATION											PROGRESSION AND COMPLETION				
	Percentage of pupils over-age for grade (%)[1]	Total enrolment in primary education		Gross enrolment ratio (GER) in primary education (%)			Primary adjusted net enrolment ratio (ANER) (%)			Out-of-school children[2]		Gross intake rate (GIR) to last grade (%)			Primary education completion rate[3]
	School year ending in 2014	School year ending in 2014		School year ending in 2014			School year ending in 2014			School year ending in 2014		School year ending in 2014			Most recent survey year 2009–2014[5]
	Total	Total	% F	Total	Male	Female	Total	Male	Female	Total	% F	Total	Male	Female	Total
Country or territory		(000)								(000)					
Caucasus and Central Asia															
Armenia[7,8]	0.7	143	47	…	…	…	…	…	…	…	…	…	…	…	100
Azerbaijan[8,9]	2.2	518	46	106*	107*	105*	95*	96*	94*	23	55	98*	99*	98*	…
Georgia[8]	1.0	285	47	117	116	118	…	…	…	…	…	116	116	117	…
Kazakhstan	0.2	1,196		111	111	111	100	100	100	1	32	113	113	113	100
Kyrgyzstan	0.4	435	49	108	108	107	98	98	98	8	60	105	106	104	100
Tajikistan	0.1	683	48	98	98	98	98	98	98	13	43	100	100	99	98
Turkmenistan	…	359	49	89	90	89	…	…	…	…	…	…	…	…	…
Uzbekistan	…	…	…	…	…	…	…	…	…	…	…	…	…	…	…
Eastern and South-eastern Asia															
Brunei Darussalam	1.5	41	49	107	107	108	…	…	…	…	…	101	101	100	…
Cambodia	22.9	2,129	48	116	120	113	95	96	94	97	59	96	96	96	67
China[8]	…	95,107	46	104	104	104	…	…	…	…	…	…	…	…	94
DPR Korea	…	…	…	…	…	…	…	…	…	…	…	…	…	…	…
Hong Kong, China[8]	1.0	324	48	111	112	110	99	100	99	2	69	99	100	99	…
Indonesia[8]	…	29,838	48	106	107	104	93	93	92	2.008	52	103	106	100	95
Japan[8]	-[z]	6,802[z]	49[z]	102[z]	102[z]	101[z]	100[z]	100[z]	100[z]	3[z]	49[z]	102[y]	102[y]	102[y]	…
Lao PDR	23.7	871	48	116	119	113	95	96	94	36	57	100	102	99	73
Macao, China[7]	4.1	23	48	…	…	…	…	…	…	…	…	…	…	…	…
Malaysia	-	3,178	49	107	…	…	95[y]	…	…	169[y]	…	102	…	…	98
Mongolia	2.0	239	49	102	103	101	96	96	95	10	57	110	111	108	…
Myanmar	3.1	5,177	49	100	101	98	95	…	…	284	…	85	103	67	…
Philippines	17.7[z]	14,460[z]	48[z]	117[z]	117[z]	117[z]	97[z]	95[z]	99[z]	402[z]	18[z]	101[z]	97[z]	105[z]	90
Republic of Korea[8]	0.3	2,791	48	99	99	99	96[z]	97[z]	96[z]	104[z]	52[z]	103	104	103	…
Singapore[8]	…	…	…	…	…	…	…	…	…	…	…	…	…	…	…
Thailand	3.1	5.182	49	104	103	104	92	93	92	380	52	94	94	93	…
Timor-Leste	30.8	246	49	137	138	136	98	96	99	4	13	98	97	100	55
Viet Nam	-	7.435	48	109	110	109	98[z]	…	…	127[z]	…	106	104	108	96
Europe and Northern America															
Albania	2.3	196	47	112	114	111	96	…	…	7	…	108	108	108	…
Andorra[7]	3.0	4	47	…	…	…	…	…	…	…	…	…	…	…	…
Austria	…	327	49	102	103	102	…	…	…	…	…	99	99	99	…
Belarus	1.2	369	49	99	99	99	94	94	94	22	48	98	98	98	100
Belgium	1.6	774	49	105	105	105	99	99	99	7	44	88	87	90	…
Bosnia and Herzegovina	0.6	161	49	100	100	100	99	98	99	2	24	97	97	97	99
Bulgaria	1.8	259	48	99	99	99	96	96	97	10	45	99	99	99	…
Canada[8]	…	2,206[z]	49[z]	101[z]	100[z]	101[z]	99[z]	…	…	12[z]	…	…	…	…	…
Croatia	0.3	161	49	99	99	99	98	97	100	3	10	96	96	95	…
Cyprus[9]	0.5	53	49	99*	99*	100	97*	97*	98*	2*	37*	100*	100*	100*	…
Czech Republic[8]	…	511	49	99	99	99	…	…	…	…	…	98	98	99	…
Denmark[8]	0.4	467	49	101	102	101	98	98	99	7	40	99	99	99	…
Estonia	0.3[z]	76[z]	49[z]	101[z]	101[z]	100[z]	100[z]	100[z]	99[z]	0.3[z]	62[z]	107[z]	107[z]	106[z]	…
Finland[8]	…	352	49	101	101	101	100	99	100	2	11	99	99	99	…
France[8]	…	4,189	49	105	106	105	99	99	100	22	30	…	…	…	…
Germany	…	2,863	49	103	104	103	100	…	…	4	…	100	101	100	…
Greece	…	634[z]	48[z]	99[z]	99[z]	98[z]	97[z]	98[z]	97[z]	18[z]	57[z]	97[z]	98[z]	96[z]	…
Hungary	1.5	393	48	102	102	101	96	96	96	16	49	97	97	96	…
Iceland[8]	…	29[y]	49[y]	99[y]	98[y]	99[y]	99[y]	98[y]	99[y]	0.4[y]	42[y]	97[y]	94[y]	101[y]	…
Ireland[8]	0.0[z]	528[z]	49[z]	103[z]	103[z]	103[z]	99[z]	99[z]	100[z]	4[z]	25[z]	…	…	…	…
Italy[8]	0.5[z]	2,861[z]	48[z]	102[z]	102[z]	101[z]	99[z]	100[z]	99[z]	15[z]	70[z]	100[z]	100[z]	100[z]	…
Latvia	1.8	115	49	100	101	100	97	97	97	3	44	105	104	106	…
Liechtenstein	0.2	2	49	103*	103*	102*	97*	97*	98*	0.05*	38*	92*	100*	84*	…
Lithuania	0.4	108	49	102	102	103	99	99	100	0.6	12	101	102	101	…
Luxembourg	1.8[z]	35[z]	49[z]	97[z]	96[z]	97[z]	95[z]	94[z]	96[z]	2[z]	39[z]	82[z]	79[z]	85[z]	…
Malta[8]	0.1	24	49	97	100	95	97	99	94	0.8	86	92	94	90	…
Monaco[7]	-[y]	2	49	…	…	…	…	…	…	…	…	…	…	…	…
Montenegro	0.9	38	48	94	95	93	94	94	93	3	52	93	92	93	99
Netherlands[8]	…	1,223	49	104	105	104	100[y]	…	…	2[y]	…	…	…	…	…
Norway[8]	-	426	49	100	100	100	100	100	100	0.5	59	98	98	99	…
Poland[8]	…	2,161[z]	49[z]	101[z]	101[z]	101[z]	97[z]	97[z]	97[z]	62[z]	48[z]	98[z]	98[z]	98[z]	…
Portugal[8]	…	674	48	109	111	106	99	99	99	8	54*	…	…	…	…
Republic of Moldova[9]	0.5	138	48	93*	93*	93*	90*	90	90*	15*	49	92*	92	92*	99
Romania	…	807[y]	48[y]	96[y]	96[y]	95[y]	91[y]	92[y]	91[y]	72[y]	51[y]	94[y]	95[y]	93[y]	…
Russian Federation	…	5,726	49	99	98	99	96	96	97	220	40	100	100	101	100
San Marino[9]	0.3[y]	2[y]	46[y]	93*[y]	94*[y]	93*[y]	93*[y]	93*[y]	93*[y]	0.1*[y]	47*[y]	95*[y]	98*[y]	93*[y]	…
Serbia[9]	0.4	285	49	101	101	101	99	98	99	4	39	102	102	102	98
Slovakia	…	214	49	101	102	100	…	…	…	…	…	98	98	98	…
Slovenia[8]	0.6	112	49	99	99	99	98	97	98	2	37	99	99	99	…
Spain	0.1	2,961	49	105	104	105	99	99	99	29	40	98	98	98	…
Sweden[8]	-	757	50	121	118	124	100	100	100	2	29	101	101	101	…
Switzerland	0.2	484	49	103	103	103	100	99	100	2	17	95	95	96	…
TFYR Macedonia	…	107[y]	48[y]	86[y]	86[y]	85[y]	88[y]	89[y]	88[y]	15[y]	52[y]	…	…	…	97
Ukraine	1.1	1,685	49	104	103	105	97	96	98	56	34	110	109	112	100
United Kingdom	…	4,737	49	108	108	108	100	…	…	6	…	…	…	…	…
United States[8]	2.9	24,538	49	100	100	99	94	94	94	1,471	46	…	…	…	…

TABLE 2
Part 1 (Continued)

Country or territory	Percentage of pupils over-age for grade (%)[1] School year ending in 2014 Total	Total enrolment in primary education School year ending in 2014 Total (000)	%F	Gross enrolment ratio (GER) in primary education (%) School year ending in 2014 Total	Male	Female	Primary adjusted net enrolment ratio (ANER) (%) School year ending in 2014 Total	Male	Female	Out-of-school children[2] School year ending in 2014 Total (000)	%F	Gross intake rate (GIR) to last grade (%) School year ending in 2014 Total	Male	Female	Primary education completion rate[5] Most recent survey year 2009–2014 Total
Latin America and the Caribbean															
Anguilla[8]	...	...	...	...	...	...	...	...	...	...	...	...	...	...	...
Antigua and Barbuda	7.1	10	48	97	101	93	86	87	85	1	54	102	112	93	...
Argentina	5.2[z]	4,792[z]	49[z]	111[z]	111[z]	110[z]	99[z]	100[z]	99[z]	28[z]	89[z]	101[z]	101[z]	100[z]	97
Aruba	9.0	10	48	117	119	115	99	99	99	0.1	40	101	101	101	...
Bahamas	...	...	...	...	...	...	...	...	...	...	...	...	...	...	...
Barbados	5.1	21	49	94	93	94	91	91	92	2	43	96	92	99	99
Belize	7.9	52	48	112	114	109	99	100	98	0.4	88	102	104	101	85
Bermuda	0.0[y]	4	48	87	89	86	83[y]	85[y]	82[y]	0.8[y]	55[y]	79	...	...	...
Bolivia, P.S.[7]	10.4[z]	1,349[z]	48[z]	...	...	...	...	...	...	...	...	...	...	...	...
Brazil[8,9]	10.6[z]	16,761[z]	48[z]	110[*,z]	112[*,z]	107[*,z]	94[*,z]	94[*,z]	94[*,z]	950[*,z]	48[*,z]	...	...	...	80
British Virgin Islands[9]	5.7	3	47	98[*]	...	...	...	...	...	...	...	78	...	...	...
Cayman Islands[7]	0.3[z]	4[z]	50[z]	...	...	...	...	...	...	...	...	...	...	...	...
Chile	5.8	1,469	48	101	102	99	93	93	93	101	50	96	96	96	98
Colombia[8]	15.5	4,543	48	114	116	112	92	92	92	309	48	101	101	100	92
Costa Rica	9.3	476	49	111	111	110	96	96	96	16	49	99	99	98	94
Cuba	0.4	763	47	98	100	96	93	93	94	53	46	98	96	100	...
Curaçao	...	21[z]	48[z]	175[z]	179[z]	171[z]	...	...	...	...	...	...	...	...	...
Dominica	3.9	8	49	118	118	118	...	...	...	...	...	107	104	110	...
Dominican Republic	20.1	1,268	47	101	105	96	86	86	85	179	51	91	91	90	92
Ecuador	9.8	2,068	49	113	113	113	97	96	98	63	34	113	112	113	97
El Salvador	17.8	777	48	112	115	110	94	94	94	41	46	105	104	105	...
Grenada	1.4	13	48	103	104	102	97	97	97	0.3	50	89	89	90	...
Guatemala	19.8	2,417	48	104	106	102	89	89	89	258	50	87	88	85	71
Guyana	0.4[y]	94[y]	49[y]	85[y]	87[y]	84[y]	85[y]	86[y]	84[y]	17[y]	55[y]	84[y]	87[y]	81[y]	95
Haiti	...	...	...	...	...	...	...	...	...	...	...	...	...	...	56
Honduras	17.4	1,150	49	109	110	108	95	95	95	54	46	91	89	93	79
Jamaica	1.1	266	48	...	...	...	...	...	...	...	...	...	...	...	99
Mexico	2.9	14,627	49	103	104	103	98	97	98	340	38	105	104	105	96
Montserrat[7]	-	0	49	...	...	...	...	...	...	...	...	...	...	...	...
Nicaragua	...	...	...	...	...	...	...	...	...	...	...	...	...	...	72
Panama	10.1[z]	436[z]	48[z]	105[z]	107[z]	104[z]	97[z]	97[z]	96[z]	14[z]	55[z]	102[z]	103[z]	101[z]	95
Paraguay	16.0[y]	838[y]	48[y]	106[y]	108[y]	104[y]	89[y]	89[y]	89[y]	85[y]	50[y]	89[y]	89[y]	90[y]	...
Peru	8.2	3,496	49	101	101	101	95	95	96	162	45	96	95	97	93
Saint Kitts and Nevis	0.3	6	50	84	83	84	81	80	83	1	46	82	78	86	...
Saint Lucia	1.0	17	48	...	...	...	...	...	...	...	...	...	...	...	99
Saint Martin	...	...	...	...	...	...	...	...	...	...	...	...	...	...	...
St. Vincent and the Grenadines	1.1	13	49	105	106	103	91	92	91	1	51	101	102	99	...
Sint-Maarten[7]	15.4	4	49	...	...	...	...	...	...	...	...	...	...	...	...
Suriname	21.5	70	49	120	122	118	91	91	92	5	47	94	87	100	81
Trinidad and Tobago[8]	...	...	...	...	...	...	...	...	...	...	...	...	...	...	...
Turks and Caicos Islands[7]	1.2	3	49	...	...	...	...	...	...	...	...	...	...	...	...
Uruguay	5.6[z]	327[z]	48[z]	110[z]	111[z]	108[z]	99[z]	100[z]	99[z]	2[z]	58[z]	103[z]	104[z]	102[z]	97
Venezuela, B.R.	7.8	3,493	48	101	102	100	93	93	93	243	48	96	96	97	...
Northern Africa and Western Asia															
Algeria	6.5	3,765	48	119	122	115	...	...	...	...	...	109	109	109	...
Bahrain[7,8]	2.1	104	49	...	...	...	...	...	...	...	...	...	...	...	...
Egypt	2.2	11,128	48	104	104	104	99	99	99	113	29	104[z]	103[z]	104[z]	91
Iraq	...	...	...	...	...	...	...	...	...	...	...	...	...	...	60
Israel[8]	0.5	862	49	104	104	104	97	97	97	24	44	102	102	103	100
Jordan[8]	...	849[y]	49[y]	89[y]	89[y]	88[y]	88[y]	88[y]	87[y]	119[y]	51[y]	...	...	...	98
Kuwait[8]	1.0	253	49	103	102	103	99	98	99	3	25	103[z]	100[z]	107[z]	...
Lebanon[8]	8.2[z]	472[z]	48[z]	97[z]	102[z]	93[z]	89[z]	92[z]	86[z]	54[z]	64[z]	78[z]	80[z]	76[z]	...
Libya	...	...	...	...	...	...	...	...	...	...	...	...	...	...	...
Morocco[8]	14.1	4,030	48	116	119	113	99	99	99	37	54	102	103	101	70
Oman	0.5	233	51	110	106	115	97	97	97	6	49	109	110	108	...
Palestine	0.8	442	49	95	95	95	93	93	93	33	49	97	99	95	99
Qatar[7,8]	1.4	117	49	...	...	...	...	...	...	...	...	...	...	...	...
Saudi Arabia[8]	8.2	3,737	49	109	109	108	96	98	95	121	70	111	113	109	...
Sudan	33.7[y]	4,292[z]	47[z]	70[z]	74[z]	67[z]	55[y]	53[y]	56[y]	2,713[y]	48[y]	57[z]	59[z]	54[z]	86
Syrian Arab Republic	4.9[z]	1,547[z]	48[z]	80[z]	81[z]	79[z]	71[z]	72[z]	70[z]	563[z]	50[z]	69[z]	69[z]	69[z]	...
Tunisia[8]	4.3	1,089	48	113	115	111	100[z]	...	...	4[z]	...	100	99	100	94
Turkey	...	5,594[z]	49[z]	107[z]	107[z]	107[z]	93[z]	94[z]	93[z]	357[z]	53[z]	100[y]	101[y]	99[y]	...
United Arab Emirates	1.4	410	49	107	106	107	96	96	96	15	46	103	102	104	...
Yemen[8]	17.1[z]	3,875[z]	45[z]	97[z]	106[z]	89[z]	85[z]	92[z]	78[z]	583[z]	73[z]	69[z]	77[z]	61[z]	63
The Pacific															
Australia[7]	0.2	2,169	49	...	...	...	97[z]	97[y]	98[z]	51[z]	45[z]	...	...	...	...
Cook Islands[9]	0.5	2	49	106[*]	108[*]	104[*]	98[*]	...	...	0.03[*]	...	103[*]	102[*]	105[*]	...
Fiji[8]	8[z]	105[z]	48[z]	106[z]	105[z]	106[z]	97[z]	96[z]	98[z]	3[z]	27[z]	103[z]	103[z]	103[z]	...
Kiribati[8]	4	16	49	113	111	115	98	...	...	0.3	...	112	106	120	...
Marshall Islands[8]	...	...	...	...	...	...	...	...	...	...	...	...	...	...	...
Micronesia F.S.[8]	10	14	48	98	98	98	87	86	88	2	44	...	...	...	...
Nauru[8,9]	0.2	2	48	105[*]	110[*]	100[*]	87[*]	89[*]	84	0.2[*]	58[*]	112[*]	128[*]	97[*]	...
New Zealand[8]	0.2	360	49	99	99	98	98	99	98	5	53	...	...	...	...
Niue[8,9]	...	0	54	126[*]	127[*]	125[*]	...	...	...	...	...	131[*]	91[*]	160[*]	...

TABLE 2

Part 1 (Continued)

	ACCESS TO AND PARTICIPATION IN PRIMARY EDUCATION											PROGRESSION AND COMPLETION			
	Percentage of pupils over-age for grade (%)[1]	Total enrolment in primary education		Gross enrolment ratio (GER) in primary education (%)			Primary adjusted net enrolment ratio (ANER) (%)			Out-of-school children[2]		Gross intake rate (GIR) to last grade (%)			Primary education completion rate[3]
	School year ending in 2014	School year ending in 2014		School year ending in 2014			School year ending in 2014			School year ending in 2014		School year ending in 2014			Most recent survey year 2009–2014[5]
	Total	Total	% F	Total	Male	Female	Total	Male	Female	Total	% F	Total	Male	Female	Total
Country or territory		(000)								(000)					
Palau[8,9]	14	2	46	114*	116*	112*	99	...	...	0.01*	...	96*	97*	94*	...
Papua New Guinea[8]	...	1,427[y]	46[y]	115[y]	120[y]	109[y]	87[y]	90[y]	84[y]	160[y]	61[y]	79[y]	84[y]	72[y]	...
Samoa[8]	8	31	48	106	106	106	97	97	98	0.8	34	100	103	98	...
Solomon Islands[8]	...	102	48	114	116	112	...	...	...	...	...	87	87	88	...
Tokelau[8]	...	...	...	...	...	...	...	...	...	...	...	...	...	...	...
Tonga	0.2	17	48	108	109	107	99	99	99	0.2	47	111*	115*	106*	...
Tuvalu[8,9]	-	1	47	101*	101*	102*	96*	95*	98*	0.06*	27*	93*	89*	98*	...
Vanuatu	...	44[z]	47[z]	124[z]	125[z]	122[z]	...	...	...	...	...	94[z]	90[z]	98[z]	...
Southern Asia															
Afghanistan	6	6,218	40	112	131	92	...	...	...	...	...	...	...	...	35
Bangladesh	...	...	...	...	...	...	...	...	...	...	...	...	...	...	80
Bhutan[8]	15	102	50	102	101	103	89	88	90	11	44	97	91	103	56
India	5[z]	141,155[z]	50[z]	111[z]	105[z]	117[z]	98[z]	97[z]	98[z]	2,886[z]	32[z]	96[z]	94[z]	99[z]	88
Iran, Islamic Republic of[8]	3[y]	7,441	50	109	107	112	99	...	...	45	...	102[y]	102[y]	102[y]	...
Maldives[7,8]	2	40	48	...	...	...	...	...	...	...	...	...	...	...	99
Nepal	34	4,335	51	135	130	141	97	98	96	92	62	106	101	111	77
Pakistan	-	19,432	44	94	101	86	73	79	67	5,612	59	74	80	67	61
Sri Lanka[8]	1[z]	1,778	49	101	102	100	97	98	96	47	66	98	99	97	...
Sub-Saharan Africa															
Angola	...	...	...	...	...	...	...	...	...	70	...	...	...	...	...
Benin	12	2,133	47	126	131	120	96	...	...	...	...	76	82	70	55
Botswana[8]	20[z]	340[z]	49[z]	109[z]	110[z]	107[z]	91[z]	91[z]	92[z]	27[z]	46[z]	100[z]	98[z]	101[z]	...
Burkina Faso	37	2,594	48	87	89	85	68	70	66	957	52	61	59	62	30
Burundi	38	2,047	51	128	127	128	96	95	97	69	39	67	63	70	32
Cabo Verde	11	67	48	113	116	110	98	98	98	1	44	100	101	98	...
Cameroon	16	4,143	47	114	120	107	95	100	90	193	96	72	77	68	66
Central African Republic	38[y]	662[y]	43[y]	93[y]	107[y]	80[y]	71[y]	79[y]	62[y]	207[y]	65[y]	44[y]	55[y]	34[y]	38
Chad	...	2,331[z]	43[z]	101[z]	115[z]	88[z]	84[z]	95[z]	74[z]	357[z]	83[z]	38[z]	46[z]	30[z]	32
Comoros[8]	23[z]	120[z]	48[z]	105[z]	108[z]	102[z]	85[z]	88[z]	83[z]	17[z]	57[z]	74[z]	72[z]	76[z]	69
Congo	23[y]	734[y]	52[y]	111[y]	107[y]	115[y]	93[y]	89[y]	97[y]	47[y]	23[y]	74[y]	70[y]	79[y]	74
Côte d'Ivoire	23	3,177	46	90	96	84	75	80	71	879	59	57	63	50	50
D.R. Congo	...	13,535	47	107	112	102	...	...	...	...	...	67[z]	73[z]	60[z]	71
Djibouti	10	63	46	66	70	62	57	61	54	40	53	64	68	59	...
Equatorial Guinea	46[y]	92[y]	49[y]	84[y]	85[y]	84[y]	58[y]	58[y]	58[y]	46[y]	50[y]	51[y]	51[y]	52[y]	...
Eritrea	33[z]	350[z]	45[z]	51[z]	55[z]	47[z]	41[z]	43[z]	38[z]	405[z]	51[z]	37[z]	40[z]	34[z]	...
Ethiopia	25	15,733	47	100	104	96	86	89	84	2,124	60	54	54	53	45
Gabon	...	...	...	...	...	...	...	...	...	...	...	...	...	...	79
Gambia[8]	27	275	51	86	84	88	69	66	72	99	45	67	66	69	61
Ghana	24	4,342	49	110	110	110	92	92	92	319	48	101	101	101	65
Guinea	15	1,730	45	91	99	84	78	84	72	417	63	62	68	56	42
Guinea-Bissau	...	...	...	...	...	...	...	...	...	...	...	...	...	...	...
Kenya	...	8,158	50	111	111	112	86[y]	84[y]	88[y]	956[y]	43[y]	104	103	104	91
Lesotho[8]	38	366	49	107	108	106	81	79	82	66	45	76	67	85	69
Liberia	86	684	47	96	100	92	38	39	37	442	50	59	63	54	51
Madagascar	...	4,611	50	147	147	147	...	...	...	...	...	69	67	71	...
Malawi	37	4,097	50	147	145	148	...	...	...	...	...	79	79	80	54
Mali	10	2,182	46	77	81	73	64	67	60	1.030	54	53	56	50	42
Mauritania	43	592	51	98	95	101	75	73	77	151	46	68	66	69	49
Mauritius	1	105	50	103	102	104	97	96	98	4	34	97	96	99	...
Mozambique	40	5,670	48	104	109	100	88	90	85	678	58	48	51	45	32
Namibia	27[z]	425[z]	49[z]	111[z]	113[z]	110[z]	91[z]	89[z]	92[z]	36[z]	42[z]	86[z]	84[z]	89[z]	82
Niger	6	2,277	45	71	76	65	62	66	57	1.233	55	59	65	52	28
Nigeria	...	...	...	...	...	...	...	...	...	...	...	...	...	...	72
Rwanda	30[y]	2,399	51	134	132	135	96[z]	95[z]	97[z]	68[z]	34[z]	67[z]	61[z]	72[z]	38
Sao Tome and Principe	18	36	49	114	116	111	96	97	95	1	62	92	84	101	...
Senegal	13	1,888	52	81	78	84	73	70	76	634	44	59	55	63	51
Seychelles	...	9	49	104	104	105	95	94	95	0.5	44	112	116	108	...
Sierra Leone	14[z]	1,300[z]	50[z]	130[z]	130[z]	130[z]	99[y]	100[y]	99[y]	7[y]	98[y]	70[z]	71[z]	68[z]	67
Somalia	...	...	...	...	...	...	...	...	...	...	...	...	...	...	...
South Africa[8]	...	7,195	49	100	102	97	...	...	...	...	...	...	...	...	94
South Sudan	...	...	...	...	...	...	...	...	...	...	...	...	...	...	28
Swaziland	50[z]	239[z]	47[z]	113[z]	118[z]	108[z]	79[z]	79[z]	78[z]	45[z]	50[z]	79[z]	78[z]	80[z]	58
Togo	...	1,413	48	125	129	121	93	96	90	79	73	85	91	79	55
Uganda[8]	32[z]	8,459[z]	50[z]	110[z]	109[z]	111[z]	94[z]	92[z]	95[z]	477[z]	38[z]	56[z]	56[z]	55[z]	37
U.R. Tanzania[8]	7[z]	8,232	51[z]	87[z]	86[z]	87[z]	82[z]	81[z]	82[z]	1,715[z]	49[z]	74[z]	70[z]	77[z]	71
Zambia	28	3,075[z]	50[z]	104[z]	103[z]	104[z]	89[z]	88[z]	90[z]	325[z]	45[z]	81[z]	82[z]	80[z]	77
Zimbabwe	23[z]	2,663[z]	50[z]	100[z]	101[z]	99[z]	86[z]	86[z]	87[z]	365[z]	47[z]	90[z]	90[z]	91[z]	86

TABLE 2
Part 1 (Continued)

	Percentage of pupils over-age for grade (%)[1]	Total enrolment in primary education		Gross enrolment ratio (GER) in primary education (%)			Primary adjusted net enrolment ratio (ANER) (%)			Out-of-school children[2]		Gross intake rate (GIR) to last grade (%)			Primary education completion rate
	School year ending in 2014	School year ending in 2014		School year ending in 2014			School year ending in 2014			School year ending in 2014		School year ending in 2014			Most recent survey year 2009–2014[5]
	Total	Total	% F	Total	Male	Female	Total	Male	Female	Total	% F	Total	Male	Female	Total
Country or territory		(000)								(000)					
	Median	Sum	% F	Weighted average			Weighted average			Sum	% F	Weighted average			Median
World	4	718,801	48	105	105	104	91	92	90	60,901	53	90	91	90	...
Countries in transition	0.8	14,066	49	100	100	100	95	95	96	654	46	102	101	102	99
Developed countries	0.3	66,284	49	102	102	102	97	97	97	1,979	46	98[z]	97[z]	98[z]	...
Developing countries	8	638,450	48	105	105	104	90	91	89	58,268	53	89	90	88	73
Caucasus and Central Asia	0.6	5,491	48	102	102	101	94	95	94	309	51	101	102	101	100
Eastern and South-eastern Asia	3	176,047	47	105	106	105	96	96	96	6,247	47	98	99	98	...
Eastern Asia	1.0	107,035	47	104	104	104	97	97	97	2,922	47	97	97	96	...
South-eastern Asia	3	69,011	48	108	109	107	95	95	95	3,325	48	100	100	100	82
Europe and Northern America	0.5	65,012	49	102	102	101	97	96	97	2,238	45	97	97	98	...
Latin America and the Caribbean	6	65,090	48	108	110	107	94	94	94	3,591	47	100	100	100	94
Caribbean	1	5,073	48	126	128	124	79	79	79	842	49	94	93	96	...
Latin America	10	60,017	48	107	108	106	95	95	95	2,749	47	100	100	101	93
Northern Africa and Western Asia	3	50,312	47	101	103	98	89	90	88	5,474	54	90	92	87	...
Northern Africa	7	25,192	48	100	102	98	89	88	89	2,897	47	93	93	92	94
Western Asia	1	25,119	47	101	105	98	90	92	87	2,577	62	87	90	83	...
Pacific	0.5	4,344	48	108	110	107	94	95	93	241	57	95[z]	94[z]	96[z]	...
Southern Asia	4	198,559	49	109	106	112	94	94	93	11,367	52	92	91	93	77
Sub-Saharan Africa	24	153,945	48	100	103	96	80	82	77	31,432	55	69	72	67	55
Conflict-affected countries	10	346,658	48	104	104	104	81**	84**	79**	21,549**	55**	88	88	87	67
Countries with low income	26	105,779	48	104	108	101	81	84	79	18,889	56	67	69	64	50
Countries with middle income	6	523,274	48	105	105	105	92	93	92	39,206	51	93	93	93	92
Lower middle	11	329,787	49	105	103	106	90	91	89	30,918	52	91	90	91	74
Upper middle	3	193,487	47	106	107	104	95	96	95	8,287	50	96	97	96	95
Countries with high income	0.8	89,748	49	102	103	102	97	97	97	2,807	48	98	98	99	...

TABLE 2

SDG 4, Target 4.1 – Universal access, participation and completion, primary education – part 2
By 2030, ensure that all girls and boys complete free, equitable and quality primary education leading to relevant and effective learning outcomes

	LEARNING ASSESSMENTS AND OUTCOMES[4]					
	Existence of nationally representative learning assessment		Percentage of pupils in early primary education grades (2 or 3) achieving at least a minimum proficiency level (%)[6] in:		Percentage of pupils at end of primary education achieving at least a minimum proficiency level (%)[6] in:	
	In early grades (2 or 3) of primary education	At the end of primary education	Reading	Mathematics	Reading	Mathematics
	Most recent survey year	Most recent survey year				
Country or territory	2009–2014[5]	2009–2014[5]	2009–2014[5] Total	2009–2014[5] Total	2009–2014[5] Total	2009–2014[5] Total
Caucasus and Central Asia						
Armenia[7,8]	No	Yes[I,N]	...	...	...	71[I]
Azerbaijan[8,9]	No	Yes[I,N]	...	...	82[I]	73[I]
Georgia[8]	Yes[I]	No	87[I]	73[I]	...	...
Kazakhstan	No	Yes[I,N]	...	...	...	88[I]
Kyrgyzstan	No	Yes[N]	...	...	...	...
Tajikistan	No	Yes[N]	...	...	...	...
Turkmenistan	...	...	...	...	...	...
Uzbekistan	No	Yes[N]	...	...	...	...
Eastern and South-eastern Asia						
Brunei Darussalam	...	...	...	...	...	...
Cambodia	Yes[I,N]	Yes[I,N]	88[I]	88[I]	85[I]	81[I]
China[8]	Yes[N]	No	...	...	...	...
DPR Korea	...	...	...	...	...	...
Hong Kong, China[8]	Yes[I]	...	99[I]	99[I]	...	...
Indonesia[8]	Yes[I]	No	66[I]	...	...	...
Japan[8]	Yes[I]	Yes[N]	...	99[I]	...	...
Lao PDR	Yes[I,N]	Yes[N]	86[I]	86[I]	75[I]	59[I]
Macao, China[7]	...	...	...	...	...	...
Malaysia	No	No	...	...	...	...
Mongolia	No	Yes[N]	...	...	...	...
Myanmar	Yes[N]	Yes[N]	...	...	...	...
Philippines	Yes[I,N]	Yes[N]	...	...	...	...
Republic of Korea[8]	Yes[I]	Yes[N]	...	100[I]	...	...
Singapore[8]	Yes[I]	No	97[I]	99[I]	...	...
Thailand[8]	Yes[I,N]	Yes[N]	...	78[I]	...	...
Timor-Leste	Yes[I]	No	...	...	...	...
Viet Nam	Yes[I]	Yes[I,N]	100[I]	100[I]	100[I]	100[I]
Europe and Northern America						
Albania	...	...	...	...	...	...
Andorra[7]	...	...	...	...	...	...
Austria	No	Yes[I,N]	...	...	98[I]	96[I]
Belarus	...	...	...	...	...	...
Belgium	Yes[N]	Yes[N]	...	...	...	...
Bosnia and Herzegovina	No	No	...	...	...	...
Bulgaria	No	Yes[I,N]	...	...	93[I]	...
Canada[8]	Yes[I]	No	98[I]	...	...	...
Croatia	No	Yes[I,N]	...	...	99[I]	92[I]
Cyprus[9]	Yes[N]	Yes[N]	...	...	...	...
Czech Republic[8]	No	Yes[I]	...	...	99[I]	94[I]
Denmark[8]	Yes[I,N]	Yes[N]	99[I]	97[I]	...	...
Estonia	Yes[N]	Yes[N]	...	...	...	...
Finland[8]	Yes[I,N]	Yes[N]	100[I]	98[I]	...	...
France[8]	Yes[N]	Yes[I,N]	...	...	96[I]	...
Germany	Yes[N]	Yes[I]	...	...	98[I]	98[I]
Greece	...	...	...	...	...	...
Hungary	No	Yes[I,N]	...	...	95[I]	90[I]
Iceland[8]	Yes[N]	Yes[N]	...	...	...	...
Ireland[8]	Yes[I,N]	No	97[I]	95[I]	...	...
Italy[8]	Yes[I,N]	Yes[N]	98[I]	94[I]	...	...
Latvia	Yes[N]	Yes[N]	...	...	...	...
Liechtenstein	...	...	...	...	...	...
Lithuania	No	Yes[I,N]	...	...	97[I]	96[I]
Luxembourg	Yes[N]	No	...	...	...	...
Malta[8]	Yes[I]	No	78[I]	89[I]	...	...
Monaco[7]	...	...	...	...	...	...
Montenegro	Yes[N]	No	...	...	...	...
Netherlands[8]	Yes[I,N]	Yes[N]	100[I]	100[I]	...	...
Norway[8]	Yes[I,N]	Yes[N]	96[I]	92[I]	...	...
Poland[8]	Yes[I]	Yes[N]	95[I]	87[I]	...	...
Portugal[8]	Yes[I]	Yes[N]	98	97	...	...
Republic of Moldova[9]	...	...	...	...	...	...
Romania[8]	No	Yes[I,N]	...	...	86[I]	79[I]
Russian Federation	No	Yes[I]	...	...	99[I]	98[I]
San Marino[9]	...	...	...	...	...	...
Serbia[9]	Yes[N]	Yes[I,N]	...	...	...	91[I]
Slovakia	No	Yes[I]	...	...	96[I]	91[I]
Slovenia[8]	Yes[I,N]	Yes[N]	96[I]	95[I]	...	...
Spain[8]	Yes[I]	Yes[N]	95	88	...	...
Sweden[8]	Yes[I,N]	Yes[N]	98[I]	94[I]	...	...

TABLE 2
Part 2 (Continued)

	LEARNING ASSESSMENTS AND OUTCOMES[4]					
	Existence of nationally representative learning assessment		Percentage of pupils in early primary education grades (2 or 3) achieving at least a minimum proficiency level (%)[6] in:		Percentage of pupils at end of primary education achieving at least a minimum proficiency level (%)[6] in:	
	In early grades (2 or 3) of primary education	At the end of primary education				
	Most recent survey year	Most recent survey year	Reading	Mathematics	Reading	Mathematics
Country or territory	2009–2014[5]	2009–2014[5]	2009–2014[5]	2009–2014[5]	2009–2014[5]	2009–2014[5]
			Total	Total	Total	Total
Switzerland	...	...	...	...	...	...
TFYR Macedonia	No	No	...	...	...	...
Ukraine	No	No	...	...	...	...
United Kingdom	Yes[N]	Yes[N]	...	...	...	...
United States[8]	Yes[I]	No	...	97[I]	...	...
Latin America and the Caribbean						
Anguilla[8]	Yes[N]	Yes[N]	...	...	...	...
Antigua and Barbuda	...	...	...	...	...	...
Argentina	Yes[R,N]	Yes[R,N]	62[R]	61[R]	83[R]	63[R]
Aruba	...	...	...	...	...	...
Bahamas	Yes[N]	Yes[N]	...	...	...	...
Barbados	Yes[N]	No	...	...	...	...
Belize	Yes[N]	Yes[N]	...	...	...	...
Bermuda	...	...	...	...	...	...
Bolivia, P.S.[7]	Yes[N]	Yes[N]	...	...	...	...
Brazil[8,9]	Yes[R,N]	Yes[N]	66[R]	63[R]	89[R]	60[R]
British Virgin Islands[9]	...	...	...	...	...	...
Cayman Islands[7]	...	...	...	...	...	...
Chile	Yes[R,N]	Yes[R,N]	90[R]	85[R]	95[R]	84[R]
Colombia[8]	Yes[R,N]	Yes[N]	68[R]	52[R]	90[R]	58[R]
Costa Rica	Yes[R,N]	Yes[R,N]	82[R]	77[R]	96[R]	70[R]
Cuba	Yes[N]	Yes[N]	...	...	...	...
Curaçao	...	...	...	...	...	...
Dominica	...	...	...	...	...	...
Dominican Republic	Yes[R,N]	Yes[R]	26[R]	15[R]	62[R]	20[R]
Ecuador	Yes[R,N]	Yes[R]	62[R]	52[R]	79[R]	55[R]
El Salvador	Yes[N]	Yes[N]	...	...	...	...
Grenada	...	...	...	...	...	...
Guatemala	Yes[R,N]	Yes[R,N]	54[R]	40[R]	80[R]	44[R]
Guyana	Yes[N]	Yes[N]	...	...	...	...
Haiti	...	...	...	...	...	...
Honduras	Yes[R,N]	Yes[R,N]	54[R]	44[R]	75[R]	38[R]
Jamaica	Yes[N]	Yes[N]	...	...	...	...
Mexico	Yes[R,N]	Yes[R,N]	67[R]	70[R]	90[R]	77[R]
Montserrat[7]	...	...	...	...	...	...
Nicaragua	Yes[R,N]	Yes[R,N]	44[R]	32[R]	74[R]	29[R]
Panama	Yes[R,N]	Yes[R,N]	51[R]	40[R]	74[R]	33[R]
Paraguay	Yes[R,N]	Yes[R,N]	43[R]	33[R]	66[R]	31[R]
Peru	Yes[R,N]	Yes[R,N]	68[R]	60[R]	82[R]	62[R]
Saint Kitts and Nevis	Yes[N]	Yes[N]	...	...	...	...
Saint Lucia	...	...	...	...	...	...
Saint Martin	...	...	...	...	...	...
St. Vincent and the Grenadines	...	...	...	...	...	...
Sint-Maarten[7]	...	...	...	...	...	...
Suriname	...	...	...	...	...	...
Trinidad and Tobago[8]	Yes[I,N]	Yes[I,N]	78[I]	...	...	...
Turks and Caicos Islands[7]	...	...	...	...	...	...
Uruguay	Yes[R,N]	Yes[R,N]	71[R]	68[R]	89[R]	74[R]
Venezuela, B.R.	Yes[N]	Yes[N]	...	...	...	...
Northern Africa and Western Asia						
Algeria	...	...	...	...	...	...
Bahrain[7,8]	Yes[I,N]	Yes[N]	...	67[I]	...	...
Egypt	Yes[I]	No	...	...	...	...
Iraq	...	...	...	...	...	...
Israel[8]	Yes[I,N]	Yes[N]	93[I]	...	...	...
Jordan[8]	Yes[I]	Yes[N]	...	...	...	...
Kuwait[8]	No	Yes[I]	...	...	58[I]	28[I]
Lebanon[8]	Yes[I]	Yes[I]	93[I]	88[I]	90[I]	91[I]
Libya	...	...	...	...	...	...
Morocco[8]	Yes[I,N]	Yes[N]	19[I]	24[I]	...	...
Oman	No	Yes[I,N]	...	...	46[I]	45[I]
Palestine	No	Yes[N]	...	...	...	...
Qatar[7,8]	Yes[I]	Yes[N]	58[I]	55[I]	...	...
Saudi Arabia[8]	Yes[I,N]	Yes[N]	65[I]	54[I]	...	...
Sudan	Yes[N]	No	...	...	...	...
Syrian Arab Republic	No	No	...	...	...	...
Tunisia[8]	Yes[I]	Yes[N]	...	33[I]	...	...
Turkey	No	Yes[I]	...	...	...	78[I]
United Arab Emirates	Yes[N]	Yes[I,N]	...	...	63[I]	64[I]
Yemen[8]	Yes[I]	No	...	8[I]	...	...
The Pacific						
Australia[7]	Yes[N]	Yes[N]	94[N]	95[N]	95[N]	95[N]

TABLE 2

TABLE 2
Part 2 (Continued)

Country or territory	Existence of nationally representative learning assessment — In early grades (2 or 3) of primary education — Most recent survey year 2009–2014[5]	At the end of primary education — Most recent survey year 2009–2014[5]	Percentage of pupils in early primary education grades (2 or 3) achieving at least a minimum proficiency level (%)[6] in: Reading 2009–2014[5] Total	Mathematics 2009–2014[5] Total	Percentage of pupils at end of primary education achieving at least a minimum proficiency level (%)[6] in: Reading 2009–2014[5] Total	Mathematics 2009–2014[5] Total
Cook Islands[9]	Yes[N]	Yes[R]	...	...	...	...
Fiji[8]	Yes[R,N]	Yes[R,N]	...	...	...	...
Kiribati[8]	Yes[R,N]	Yes[R,N]	...	...	...	...
Marshall Islands[8]	Yes[R]	Yes[R]	...	...	...	...
Micronesia F.S.[8]	Yes[R]	Yes[R]	...	...	...	...
Nauru[8,9]	Yes[R]	Yes[R]	...	...	...	...
New Zealand[8]	Yes[I]	No	92[I]	85[I]	...	...
Niue[8,9]	Yes[R]	Yes[R]	...	...	...	...
Palau[8,9]	Yes[R]	Yes[R]	...	...	...	...
Papua New Guinea[8]	Yes[R]	Yes[R]	...	...	...	...
Samoa[8]	Yes[R,N]	Yes[R]	...	...	...	...
Solomon Islands[8]	Yes[R,N]	Yes[R]	...	...	...	...
Tokelau[8]	Yes[R]	Yes[R]	...	...	...	...
Tonga	Yes[I]	Yes[N]	...	...	...	...
Tuvalu[8,9]	Yes[R,N]	Yes[R]	...	...	...	...
Vanuatu	Yes[I]	Yes[R]	...	...	...	...
Southern Asia						
Afghanistan	No	Yes[N]	...	...	...	...
Bangladesh	Yes[N]	Yes[N]	...	...	...	...
Bhutan[8]	No	Yes[N]	...	...	...	...
India	Yes[N]	Yes[N]	...	...	...	...
Iran, Islamic Republic of[8]	Yes[I]	No	76[I]	64[I]	...	...
Maldives[7,8]	Yes[N]	Yes[N]	...	...	...	...
Nepal	Yes[I,N]	Yes[N]	...	...	...	...
Pakistan	No	Yes[N]	...	...	...	...
Sri Lanka[8]	No	Yes[N]	...	...	...	...
Sub-Saharan Africa						
Angola	Yes[I]	No	...	...	...	...
Benin	Yes[I,N]	Yes[I]	85[I]	72[I]	95[I]	75[I]
Botswana[8]	Yes[I]	No	55[I]	59[I]	...	...
Burkina Faso	Yes[I,N]	Yes[I,N]	92[I]	90[I]	98[I]	87[I]
Burundi	Yes[I,N]	Yes[I]	100[I]	100[I]	100[I]	99[I]
Cabo Verde	Yes[N]	Yes[N]	...	...	...	...
Cameroon	Yes[I]	Yes[I]	91[I]	90[I]	94[I]	70[I]
Central African Republic	...	...	...	...	...	...
Chad	Yes[I]	Yes[I]	89[I]	82[I]	80[I]	56[I]
Comoros[8]	Yes[I]	Yes[I]	...	...	53[I]	58[I]
Congo	Yes[I]	Yes[I]	95[I]	97[I]	96[I]	72[I]
Côte d'Ivoire	Yes[I,N]	Yes[I,N]	92[I]	83[I]	95[I]	71[I]
D.R. Congo	No	No	...	...	...	...
Djibouti	...	...	...	...	...	...
Equatorial Guinea	...	...	...	...	...	...
Eritrea	Yes[N]	No	...	...	...	...
Ethiopia	Yes[I,N]	No	...	...	...	...
Gabon	No	No	...	...	...	...
Gambia[8]	Yes[I,N]	Yes[N]	...	...	...	...
Ghana	Yes[I,N]	Yes[I,N]	...	...	...	...
Guinea	Yes[N]	Yes[N]	...	...	...	...
Guinea-Bissau	Yes[N]	No	...	...	...	...
Kenya	Yes[R,N]	Yes[R]	32[R]	30[R]	83[R]	92[R]
Lesotho[8]	Yes[N]	Yes[N]	...	...	...	...
Liberia	Yes[I]	No	...	...	...	...
Madagascar	Yes[N]	Yes[N]	...	...	...	...
Malawi	Yes[I,N]	Yes[R]	...	...	...	...
Mali	Yes[I,N]	Yes[I]	78[I]	79[I]	84[I]	55[I]
Mauritania	No	Yes[N]	...	...	...	...
Mauritius	Yes[N]	No	...	...	...	...
Mozambique	Yes[N]	No	...	...	...	...
Namibia	No	Yes[N]	...	...	...	...
Niger	Yes[I,N]	Yes[I,N]	67[I]	61[I]	68[I]	32[I]
Nigeria	Yes[N]	Yes[N]	...	...	...	...
Rwanda	Yes[I,N]	Yes[I,N]	...	...	...	...
Sao Tome and Principe	...	...	...	...	...	...
Senegal	Yes[I,N]	Yes[I,N]	86[I]	87[I]	96[I]	85[I]
Seychelles	No	Yes[N]	...	...	...	...
Sierra Leone	...	...	...	...	...	...
Somalia	...	...	...	...	...	...
South Africa[8]	Yes[N]	Yes[N]	56[I]	...	...	...
South Sudan	No	Yes[R]	...	...	...	...
Swaziland	No	Yes[N]	...	...	...	...
Togo	Yes[I,N]	Yes[I]	79[I]	76[I]	94[I]	79[I]
Uganda[8]	Yes[R,N]	Yes[R,N]	27[R]	18[R]	73[R]	71[R]

TABLE 2

Part 2 (Continued)

	LEARNING ASSESSMENTS AND OUTCOMES[4]					
	Existence of nationally representative learning assessment		Percentage of pupils in early primary education grades (2 or 3) achieving at least a minimum proficiency level (%)[6] in:		Percentage of pupils at end of primary education achieving at least a minimum proficiency level (%)[6] in:	
	In early grades (2 or 3) of primary education	At the end of primary education	Reading	Mathematics	Reading	Mathematics
	Most recent survey year	Most recent survey year				
Country or territory	2009–2014[5]	2009–2014[5]	2009–2014[5]	2009–2014[5]	2009–2014[5]	2009–2014[5]
			Total	Total	Total	Total
U.R. Tanzania[8]	Yes[I,R,N]	Yes[R]	44[R]	12[R]	83[R]	43[R]
Zambia	No	Yes[N]	...	...	...	...
Zimbabwe	Yes[N]	No	...	...	...	...
World	...	...	...	...	...	...
Countries in transition	...	...	...	...	...	...
Developed countries	...	...	...	...	...	...
Developing countries	...	...	...	...	...	...
Caucasus and Central Asia	...	...	...	...	...	...
Eastern and South-eastern Asia	...	...	...	...	...	...
Eastern Asia	...	...	...	...	...	...
South-eastern Asia	...	...	...	...	...	...
Europe and Northern America	...	...	...	...	...	...
Latin America and the Caribbean	...	...	...	...	...	...
Caribbean	...	...	...	...	...	...
Latin America	...	...	...	...	...	...
Northern Africa and Western Asia	...	...	...	...	...	...
Northern Africa	...	...	...	...	...	...
Western Asia	...	...	...	...	...	...
Pacific	...	...	...	...	...	...
Southern Asia	...	...	...	...	...	...
Sub-Saharan Africa	...	...	...	...	...	...
Conflict-affected countries	...	...	...	...	...	...
Countries with low income	...	...	...	...	...	...
Countries with middle income	...	...	...	...	...	...
Lower middle	...	...	...	...	...	...
Upper middle	...	...	...	...	...	...
Countries with high income	...	...	...	...	...	...

Source: UIS database, except where noted. GER and GIR to last grade are based on the United Nations Population Division estimates, revision 2015 (United Nations, 2015), median variant.

Note: The country groupings by level of income are as defined by the World Bank but include only countries listed in the table. They are based on the list of countries by income group as revised in July 2015.

1. Over-age pupils are defined as those whose age is at least two years higher than the official age of entry in a given grade.

2. Data reflect the actual number of children not enrolled at all, derived from the age-specific or adjusted net enrolment ratio of primary school age children, which measures the proportion of those who are enrolled in either primary or secondary school.

3. GEM Report team calculations based on data from national and international household surveys.

4. Altinok (2013); Cheng and Omeova (2014); education ministry national reports and websites; EGMA/EGRA; PASEC; PILNA; PIRLS 2011; SACMEQ; TERCE; TIMSS 2011; Uwezo. 'Nationally representative learning assessment' refers to national (N), regional (R) and international (I) formative learning assessments. Information and data need to be used and interpreted with caution since the different types of assessments are not necessarily comparable.

5. Data are for the most recent year available in the period specified. For details see relevant sources.

6. Refers to the percentage of pupils performing at or above level 1 of proficiency in reading and or mathematics.

7. GIR, GER or NER were not calculated due to inconsistencies in the United Nations population data or lack of United Nations population by age.

8. In the absence of assessments conducted in the proposed indicator grade, surveys of student learning achievement in the grade below or above the proposed indicator grade are used as placeholders to report on learning assessments and/or learning outcomes in early grades and at the end of primary education.

9. National population data were used to calculate GIR, GER and NER due to inconsistencies in the United Nations population data or lack of United Nations population by age.

Data in bold are for the school year ending in 2015.

(z) Data are for the school year ending in 2013.

(y) Data are for the school year ending in 2012.

(x) Data are for the school year ending in 2011.

(*) National estimate.

(**) For country level data: UIS partial estimate; for regional and other country grouping sums and weighted averages: partial imputation due to incomplete country coverage (between 33% and 60% of population for the region or other country grouping).

(-) Magnitude nil or negligible

(.) The category is not applicable or does not exist.

(...) No data are available.

TABLE 3

SDG 4, Target 4.1 - Universal access, participation and completion, secondary education – part 1
By 2030, ensure that all girls and boys complete free, equitable and quality secondary education leading to relevant and effective learning outcomes

Country or territory	Effective transition from primary to lower secondary general education (%) School year ending in 2013			Percentage of students over-age for grade in lower secondary education (%)[1] School year ending in 2014			Total enrolment in secondary education School year ending in 2014		Gross enrolment ratio (GER) (%) Total secondary education School year ending in 2014			Lower secondary adjusted net enrolment ratio (ANER) (%) School year ending in 2014		
	Total	Male	Female	Total	Male	Female	Total (000)	% F	Total	Male	Female	Total	Male	Female
Caucasus and Central Asia														
Armenia[8]	97	97	97	...	...	...	245	48	...	...	...	...	...	...
Azerbaijan[9,10]	99	98	100	4	4	4	949	47	103*	103*	102*	87*	88*	86*
Georgia[10]	100	100	100	2	3	2	282	48	99	99	100	99	...	...
Kazakhstan	**100**	**99**	**100**	0.7	0.8	0.5	**1,679**	**50**	**109**	**107**	**111**	100z	...	...
Kyrgyzstan	100	99	100	0.7	0.8	0.6	651	49	91	90	91	92	92	92
Tajikistan	**99**	**100**	**98**	0.1	0.1	0.1	1,063z	46z	88z	92z	83z	...	...	...
Turkmenistan	...	...	...	...	...	...	651	48	85	87	84	...	...	...
Uzbekistan[10]	...	...	...	...	...	...	...	...	...	...	...	...	...	...
Eastern and South-eastern Asia														
Brunei Darussalam	100	99	100	4	4	3	49	48	99	99	99	98	...	...
Cambodia	80	76	84	27	30	24	...	...	...	...	...	83	84	81
China	...	...	...	...	...	...	88,692	47	94	93	95	...	...	...
DPR Korea	...	...	...	...	...	...	...	...	...	...	...	...	...	...
Hong Kong, China[10]	100	100	99	5	6	4	416	48	101	103	99	96**	97**	95**
Indonesia	89	88	90	11	11	11	22,587	49	82	83	82	86**	85**	88**
Japan[10]	...	...	...	-z	-z	-z	7,281z	49z	102z	102z	102z	100z	...	...
Lao PDR	90	92	89	37	42	31	601	47	57	60	55	79	81	77
Macao, China[10]	99	100	99	21	26	16	32	48	96	97	95	86	85	87
Malaysia[10]	89	89	89	-	-	-	3,038	50	79	...	...	90	...	...
Mongolia[10]	...	...	...	2	2	2	286	50	91	90	92	100	...	...
Myanmar	...	...	...	14	14	14	3,191	50	51	51	52	56	...	...
Philippines	...	...	...	23z	28z	18z	7,220z	51z	88z	84z	93z	96z	93z	98z
Republic of Korea[10]	100	100	100	0.4	0.5	0.4	3,720z	48z	98z	98z	97z	99z	...	...
Singapore	...	...	...	...	...	...	...	...	...	...	...	...	...	...
Thailand[10]	99	100	98	4	5	3	4,655z	51z	86z	83z	89z	...	...	...
Timor-Leste	91	90	92	50	55	45	119	51	73	70	76	90	90	90
Viet Nam[10]	87	85	89	-	-	-	...	...	...	...	...	...	...	...
Europe and Northern America														
Albania[10]	100	100	100	4	5	3	333	47	96	100	93	96	97	94
Andorra[8]	...	...	...	11	14	9	4	48	...	...	...	...	...	...
Austria[10]	100	100	100	...	...	...	697	48	99	102	97	...	...	...
Belarus	98	98	98	1	1	1	649	48	107	108	106	100	...	...
Belgium[10]	...	...	...	7	8	6	1,210	52	165	155	175	100	...	...
Bosnia and Herzegovina	...	...	...	0.4	0.5	0.4	297	49	89	87	90	...	...	...
Bulgaria[10]	100	100	99	5	5	5	519	48	101	103	99	98	98	98
Canada[10]	...	...	...	...	...	...	2,698z	49z	110z	110z	110z	...	...	...
Croatia[10]	100x	100x	100x	0.5	0.6	0.3	370	50	99	97	101	98	97	99
Cyprus[9,10]	99	99	100	2	2	1	59	49	99*	99*	99*	100*	...	...
Czech Republic[10]	100	99	100	...	...	...	781	49	105	105	105	...	...	...
Denmark	100	100	100	0.8	1.0	0.7	**554**	50	130	128	132	97	97	98
Estonia	100y	100y	99y	4z	5z	3z	81z	48z	109z	109z	108z	99z	...	...
Finland	100	100	100	...	...	...	537	51	145	139	152	99	99	98
France[10]	...	...	...	1	1	1	5,947	49	111	110	111	100	...	...
Germany	100	100	99	...	...	...	7,201	47	102	105	100	...	...	...
Greece[10]	99y	100y	98y	...	...	...	695z	48z	108z	110z	106z	99z	100z	98z
Hungary[10]	100	100	100	3	4	3	858	49	107	107	107	99	99	98
Iceland	100x	100x	99x	...	...	...	36y	49y	111y	112y	111y	98y	98y	97y
Ireland	...	...	...	...	...	...	341y	49y	126y	125y	127y	...	...	...
Italy[10]	100y	100y	100y	3z	4z	2z	4,594z	48z	102z	103z	101z	100z	...	...
Latvia	98	98	99	5	7	3	122	48	115	117	114	100z	...	...
Liechtenstein[9]	...	...	...	1	1	1	3	45	116*	128*	103*	97*	...	...
Lithuania[10]	99	99	100	3	4	2	277	48	107	109	105	100	...	...
Luxembourg[10]	...	...	...	9z	9z	8z	46z	49z	102z	101z	104z	95z	94z	95z
Malta	98	...	...	1	2	1	30	50	85	91	81	87	94	82
Monaco[8]	...	...	...	...	...	...	3	49	...	...	...	...	...	...
Montenegro[10]	...	...	...	0.5	0.6	0.4	**61**	**48**	**90**	**90**	**90**	...	...	...
Netherlands[10]	...	...	...	...	...	...	1,574**	...	132**	...	...	100y	...	...
Norway	100	100	100	-	-	-	439	48	113	114	111	100	99	100
Poland	...	...	...	...	...	...	2,778z	48z	109z	111z	107z	95z	95z	95z
Portugal[10]	...	...	...	...	...	...	769	49	116	118	115	99	...	...
Republic of Moldova[9]	98	99	98	0.9	1.0	0.7	246	49	87*	87*	88*	86*	86*	85*
Romania[10]	99x	100x	99x	5	6	4	1,609	48	95	95	94	94y	94y	93y
Russian Federation	100	100	100	...	...	...	9,061	48	101	102	100	...	...	...
San Marino[9]	99x	98x	100x	...	...	...	2y	48y	95*,y	93*,y	96*,y	...	...	...
Serbia[9,10]	100	100	100	0.5	0.6	0.4	548	49	94*	93*	95*	99*	99*	99*
Slovakia[10]	99	99	99	...	...	...	465	49	92	92	92	...	...	...
Slovenia[10]	100	99	100	0.8	1.0	0.6	145	48	111	111	111	99	99	99
Spain	100	100	100	10	11	8	3,288	49	130	130	130	100	...	...
Sweden	100	100	100	-	-	-	827	52	133	125	142	100	...	...
Switzerland	100	100	100	1	1	1	616	48	100	101	98	100	...	...

TABLE 3
Part 1 (Continued)

	ACCESS AND PARTICIPATION IN SECONDARY EDUCATION														
	Effective transition from primary to lower secondary general education (%)			Percentage of students over-age for grade in lower secondary education (%)[1]			Total enrolment in secondary education		Gross enrolment ratio (GER) (%) Total secondary education			Lower secondary adjusted net enrolment ratio (ANER) (%)		
	School year ending in 2013			School year ending in 2014			School year ending in 2014		School year ending in 2014			School year ending in 2014		
Country or territory	Total	Male	Female	Total	Male	Female	Total (000)	% F	Total	Male	Female	Total	Male	Female
TFYR Macedonia[10]	...	...	...	...	...	...	186ʸ	48ʸ	82ʸ	83ʸ	81ʸ	...	...	...
Ukraine[10]	100	100	100	2	2	2	2,714	48	99	100	98	100**	...	...
United Kingdom[10]	...	...	...	...	...	...	6,557	50	128	125	130	98	98	99
United States[10]	...	...	...	4	6	3	24,230	49	98	97	98	99	...	...
Latin America and the Caribbean														
Anguilla	...	...	...	...	...	...	...	...	...	...	...	...	...	...
Antigua and Barbuda	...	...	...	23	29	17	8	50	102	102	103	96	98	94
Argentina[10]	97ʸ	94ʸ	100ʸ	16ᶻ	16ᶻ	16ᶻ	4,406ᶻ	51ᶻ	106ᶻ	102ᶻ	110ᶻ	99ᶻ	...	...
Aruba	...	...	...	31	37	26	8ʸ	50ʸ	111ʸ	110ʸ	112ʸ	...	...	...
Bahamas	...	...	...	...	...	...	...	...	...	...	...	...	...	...
Barbados	...	97	99	11	13	10	21	50	109	108	111	99	...	...
Belize	98	97	99	16	21	12	37	51	80	78	82	90	91	90
Bermuda	93ˣ	87ˣ	100ˣ	...	...	...	4	52	73	68	77	...	...	...
Bolivia, P.S.	97ʸ	97ʸ	96ʸ	...	...	...	1,113ᶻ	49ᶻ	85ᶻ	85ᶻ	84ᶻ	97ᶻ	97ᶻ	96ᶻ
Brazil[9,10]	...	...	...	19ᶻ	23ᶻ	15ᶻ	24,881ᶻ	51ᶻ	102*,ᶻ	98*,ᶻ	106*,ᶻ	95*,ᶻ	94*,ᶻ	96*,ᶻ
British Virgin Islands[9]	95	100	90	21	27	16	2	52	98*	...	...	...	...	...
Cayman Islands[8]	97ʸ	93ʸ	100ʸ	...	...	...	3ᶻ	50ᶻ	...	...	...	...	...	...
Chile[10]	100	99	100	11	14	9	1,556	49	100	100	101	97	97	97
Colombia[10]	98	...	...	23	27	19	4,828	51	99	95	103	97	97	98
Costa Rica[10]	85	86	83	29	32	26	460	50	120	117	124	94	94	94
Cuba	99	99	99	0.8	1.2	0.5	830	49	100	98	101	99ᶻ	98ᶻ	100ᶻ
Curaçao	...	...	...	...	...	...	11ᶻ	51ᶻ	88ᶻ	86ᶻ	91ᶻ	...	...	...
Dominica	96	...	...	12	17	6	...	...	...	...	...	...	...	...
Dominican Republic	97	96	99	22	28	16	931	52	78	74	82	95	96	94
Ecuador	99	100	98	16	17	13	1,878	50	104	102	106	99ᶻ	...	...
El Salvador	93	93	93	22	26	18	625	50	81	81	81	99	...	...
Grenada	98	...	...	10	14	6	10	49	101	101	101	91	94	89
Guatemala	85	90	81	26	29	22	1,166	48	64	66	62	73	77	69
Guyana	...	...	...	...	...	...	86ʸ	50ʸ	89ʸ	90ʸ	89ʸ	...	...	...
Haiti	...	...	...	...	...	...	...	...	...	...	...	...	...	...
Honduras[10]	72	71	73	30	33	28	620	53	68	63	74	73	72	74
Jamaica	94	91	98	4	5	3	224	51	69	66	72	83	80	86
Mexico[10]	97	97	96	4	5	3	12,993	51	91	88	93	86ʸ	86ʸ	86ʸ
Montserrat[8]	...	...	...	...	...	...	0	48	...	...	...	...	...	...
Nicaragua	...	...	...	...	...	...	...	...	...	...	...	...	...	...
Panama[10]	99ˣ	100ˣ	97ˣ	...	...	...	310ᶻ	51ᶻ	75ᶻ	73ᶻ	78ᶻ	89ʸ	88ʸ	89ʸ
Paraguay	94ˣ	95ˣ	94ˣ	...	...	...	631ʸ	51ʸ	77ʸ	74ʸ	79ʸ	91ʸ	96ʸ	85ʸ
Peru[10]	94	95	94	13	15	12	2,671	49	96	96	96	92	91	92
Saint Kitts and Nevis	99	100	99	2	2	1	4	50	92	90	93	91	90	91
Saint Lucia	97	97	98	3	4	2	14	50	86	87	86	86ᶻ	87ᶻ	84ᶻ
Saint Martin	...	...	...	...	...	...	...	...	...	...	...	...	...	...
St. Vincent and the Grenadines	99	99	100	14	19	9	10	49	105	106	103	...	...	...
Sint-Maarten[8]	...	...	...	18	18	18	3	50	...	...	...	...	...	...
Suriname	70	61	78	33	35	32	52ᶻ	56ᶻ	78ᶻ	68ᶻ	89ᶻ	92ᶻ	91ᶻ	93ᶻ
Trinidad and Tobago[10]	...	...	...	...	...	...	...	...	...	...	...	...	...	...
Turks and Caicos Islands[8]	...	...	...	**3**	**5**	**1**	**2**	**52**	...	...	...	...	...	...
Uruguay[10]	...	...	...	27ᶻ	30ᶻ	25ᶻ	291ᶻ	52ᶻ	94ᶻ	88ᶻ	100ᶻ	86ᶻ	85ᶻ	86ᶻ
Venezuela, B.R.	100	100	99	...	...	...	2,567	51	92	88	95	92	91	93
Northern Africa and Western Asia														
Algeria	99	100	99	30	37	23	...	...	...	...	...	...	...	...
Bahrain[8,10]	100	100	100	5	6	5	90	49	...	...	...	...	...	...
Egypt[10]	...	...	...	5ᶻ	6ᶻ	5ᶻ	8,208	49	86	86	86	94	93	95
Iraq	...	...	...	...	...	...	...	...	...	...	...	...	...	...
Israel[10]	100	100	100	0.8	0.9	0.6	768	49	102	101	103	100	...	...
Jordan	...	...	...	...	...	...	724ʸ	50ʸ	84ʸ	82ʸ	86ʸ	...	...	...
Kuwait	98**,ʸ	97**,ʸ	100**,ʸ	4	5	3	283**	50**	94**	89**	99**	93ʸ	89ʸ	98ʸ
Lebanon[10]	98ʸ	97ʸ	99ʸ	...	...	...	389ᶻ	52ᶻ	68ᶻ	68ᶻ	68ᶻ	76**,ʸ	79**,ʸ	74**,ʸ
Libya	...	...	...	...	...	...	...	...	...	...	...	...	...	...
Morocco[10]	89	92	85	...	...	...	2,554ʸ	45ʸ	69ʸ	74ʸ	64ʸ	85**,ʸ	89**,ʸ	80**,ʸ
Oman[8,10]	100	100	100	4	5	4	391	49	...	...	...	98	...	...
Palestine[10]	99	100	99	2	3	2	709	51	82	78	86	86	84	88
Qatar[8,10]	100	100	100	4	4	4	88	48	...	...	...	...	...	...
Saudi Arabia[10]	96	100	92	14	14	14	3,419**	43**	108**	123**	94**	93**,ᶻ	96**,ᶻ	90**,ᶻ
Sudan	96ʸ	95ʸ	97ʸ	...	...	...	1,871ᶻ	48ᶻ	43ᶻ	44ᶻ	41ᶻ	63ʸ	76ʸ	49ʸ
Syrian Arab Republic[10]	57ʸ	57ʸ	57ʸ	...	...	...	1,857ᶻ	49ᶻ	50ᶻ	50ᶻ	51ᶻ	59ᶻ	60ᶻ	58ᶻ
Tunisia[10]	91	89	93	16	19	13	1,020	...	88	...	...	...	...	...
Turkey[10]	99ˣ	99ˣ	99ˣ	...	...	...	10,563ᶻ	48ᶻ	100ᶻ	102ᶻ	99ᶻ	97ᶻ	97ᶻ	96ᶻ
United Arab Emirates[8,10]	100	100	100	...	...	...	411	49	...	...	...	...	...	...
Yemen	90ʸ	91ʸ	89ʸ	...	...	...	1,768ᶻ	40ᶻ	49ᶻ	57ᶻ	40ᶻ	63**,ʸ	74**,ʸ	51**,ʸ
The Pacific														
Australia[8]	...	...	...	3	4	3	2,371	47	...	...	...	99ᶻ	...	...

TABLE 3

Part 1 (Continued)

Country or territory	ACCESS AND PARTICIPATION IN SECONDARY EDUCATION													
	Effective transition from primary to lower secondary general education (%)			Percentage of students over-age for grade in lower secondary education (%)[1]			Total enrolment in secondary education		Gross enrolment ratio (GER) (%) Total secondary education			Lower secondary adjusted net enrolment ratio (ANER) (%)		
	School year ending in 2013			School year ending in 2014			School year ending in 2014		School year ending in 2014			School year ending in 2014		
	Total	Male	Female	Total	Male	Female	Total (000)	% F	Total	Male	Female	Total	Male	Female
Cook Islands[9]	92	...	...	1	2	1	2	50	86*	83*	91*	90*·ʸ	89*·ʸ	90*·ʸ
Fiji	94ˣ	91ˣ	97ˣ	12ᶻ	13ᶻ	10ᶻ	97ʸ	51ʸ	89ʸ	84ʸ	93ʸ	96ʸ	...	...
Kiribati	...	...	...	7	9	6	...	...	...	...	...	...	...	...
Marshall Islands	...	...	...	...	...	...	...	...	...	...	...	...	...	...
Micronesia F.S.	...	...	...	16	18	13	...	...	...	...	...	...	...	...
Nauru[9]	...	...	...	...	...	...	1	49	83*	82*	83*	87*	87*	88*
New Zealand[10]	...	...	...	0.3	0.3	0.2	492	50	117	114	121	99	98	99
Niue	...	...	...	-	-	-	...	...	...	...	...	...	...	...
Palau[9]	97	98	95	15	21	8	2	50	114*	111*	117*	...	...	...
Papua New Guinea	...	...	...	...	...	...	378ʸ	41ʸ	40ʸ	46ʸ	35ʸ	...	...	...
Samoa	98ˣ	98ˣ	97ˣ	14	16	11	26	51	87	82	92	95	95	96
Solomon Islands	93	92	95	...	...	...	42ʸ	47ʸ	48ʸ	50ʸ	47ʸ	...	...	...
Tokelau	...	...	...	...	...	...	...	...	...	...	...	...	...	...
Tonga	...	...	...	...	...	...	15	50	90	86	94	89	85	93
Tuvalu[9]	...	...	...	4	3	5	1	53	81*	72*	90*	87*	81*	93*
Vanuatu	...	...	...	47ᶻ	51ᶻ	43ᶻ	...	...	...	...	...	...	...	...
Southern Asia														
Afghanistan	...	...	...	18	18	17	2,603	35	56	71	40	65	81	49
Bangladesh	...	...	...	4ᶻ	4ᶻ	4ᶻ	13,314ᶻ	51ᶻ	58ᶻ	56ᶻ	61ᶻ	...	...	...
Bhutan	99	98	100	35	37	33	74	51	84	81	87	84	80	88
India	...	...	...	7ᶻ	7ᶻ	7ᶻ	119,401ᶻ	48ᶻ	69ᶻ	69ᶻ	69ᶻ	85**·ᶻ	83**·ᶻ	88**·ᶻ
Iran, Islamic Republic of	97*·ˣ	97*·ˣ	97*·ˣ	3	4	2	5,795	48	88	89	88	98	99	98
Maldives	97ʸ	93ʸ	100ʸ	20	20	20	...	...	...	...	...	...	...	...
Nepal	**87**	**88**	**86**	**27**	**32**	**22**	3,176**	51**	67**	65**	70**	...	...	...
Pakistan	81	82	80	-	-	-	11,287	42	42	46	37	52	57	47
Sri Lanka	100**	99**	100**	1ᶻ	2ᶻ	1ᶻ	2,606ᶻ	51ᶻ	100ᶻ	97ᶻ	102ᶻ	95ᶻ	95ᶻ	95ᶻ
Sub-Saharan Africa														
Angola	...	...	...	...	...	...	...	...	...	...	...	...	...	...
Benin	85	85	86	28	30	25	897	40	54	65	44	63ᶻ	72ᶻ	55ᶻ
Botswana[10]	97ʸ	97ʸ	98ʸ	38ᶻ	45ᶻ	30ᶻ	184ᶻ	51ᶻ	84ᶻ	82ᶻ	86ᶻ	89ᶻ	88ᶻ	90ᶻ
Burkina Faso	69	71	67	58	58	58	842	46	30	32	28	53ᶻ	55ᶻ	52ᶻ
Burundi	77	80	75	78	80	75	583	47	38	41	35	69	68	70
Cabo Verde	96	95	97	35	40	30	60	53	93	87	99	91	91	91
Cameroon	65**·ˣ	62**·ˣ	69**·ˣ	28	31	25	2,000	46	56	61	52	63	67	58
Central African Republic	75ˣ	81ˣ	68ˣ	...	...	...	126ʸ	34ʸ	17ʸ	23ʸ	12ʸ	45ʸ	56ʸ	34ʸ
Chad	95ʸ	100ʸ	87ʸ	...	...	...	458ʸ	31ʸ	22ʸ	31ʸ	14ʸ	...	...	...
Comoros	...	...	...	...	...	...	68ᶻ	50ᶻ	59ᶻ	58ᶻ	60ᶻ	73ᶻ	72ᶻ	73ᶻ
Congo	76ˣ	78ˣ	75ˣ	...	...	...	339ʸ	46ʸ	55ʸ	58ʸ	51ʸ	...	...	...
Côte d'Ivoire	88	90	85	29	29	29	1,418	41	40	47	33	...	...	...
D.R. Congo	72ʸ	73ʸ	71ʸ	...	...	...	4,388	38	44	54	33	...	...	...
Djibouti	80	82	79	22	22	22	59	44	47	52	42	...	...	...
Equatorial Guinea	96ˣ	100ˣ	92ˣ	...	...	...	...	...	...	...	...	...	...	...
Eritrea	98ʸ	99ʸ	96ʸ	...	...	...	269ᶻ	44ᶻ	36ᶻ	39ᶻ	32ᶻ	38ᶻ	42ᶻ	35ᶻ
Ethiopia	98ˣ	100ˣ	97ˣ	27	30	24	4,736ʸ	47ʸ	36ʸ	38ʸ	35ʸ	60**·ʸ	61**·ʸ	58**·ʸ
Gabon	...	...	...	...	...	...	...	...	...	...	...	...	...	...
Gambia[10]	94	94	95	35	39	32	...	...	...	...	...	...	...	...
Ghana[10]	**98**	**98**	**99**	**40**	**41**	**39**	**2,440**	**48**	**71**	**73**	**69**	93**	93**	93**
Guinea	69	74	62	29	32	25	716	39	39	47	31	48	57	40
Guinea-Bissau	...	...	...	...	...	...	...	...	...	...	...	...	...	...
Kenya	...	...	...	...	...	...	3,833ʸ	48ʸ	68ʸ	70ʸ	65ʸ	...	...	...
Lesotho	85	83	86	55	63	48	131	57	52	44	60	77	73	82
Liberia	...	...	...	...	...	...	223	43	38	42	33	...	...	...
Madagascar	76	76	76	49	54	44	1,494	50	38	39	38	...	...	...
Malawi	86ˣ	88ˣ	84ˣ	...	...	...	920	47	39	41	38	80	80	79
Mali	85**	...	...	18	18	18	961	42	44	49	37	53	59	48
Mauritania	58	61	55	53	53	53	179	47	30	31	29	58	58	59
Mauritius	90	88	93	8	9	7	133	50	98	97	99	...	...	...
Mozambique	61	59	64	48	54	43	784	48	25	26	24	56	60	52
Namibia	96ʸ	95ʸ	97ʸ	48ᶻ	55ᶻ	42ᶻ	...	...	...	...	...	...	...	...
Niger	65	67	62	24	25	23	515	41	19	22	16	30	34	25
Nigeria	...	...	...	...	...	...	...	...	...	...	...	...	...	...
Rwanda	75ʸ	76ʸ	74ʸ	...	...	...	587	52	39	37	41	...	...	...
Sao Tome and Principe	**100**	**100**	**99**	**44**	**49**	**39**	**22**	**52**	**85**	**81**	**89**	...	...	...
Senegal	93ˣ	94ˣ	92ˣ	26	26	26	...	...	...	...	...	...	...	...
Seychelles	...	...	...	0.5	0.5	0.5	7	49	75	74	75	...	...	...
Sierra Leone	88ʸ	88ʸ	88ʸ	...	...	...	417ᶻ	47ᶻ	43ᶻ	47ᶻ	40ᶻ	69ʸ	71ʸ	67ʸ
Somalia	...	...	...	...	...	...	...	...	...	...	...	...	...	...
South Africa[10]	...	...	...	...	...	...	4,956**	51**	94**	85**	104**	...	...	...
South Sudan	...	...	...	...	...	...	...	...	...	...	...	...	...	...
Swaziland	99ʸ	100ʸ	98ʸ	70ᶻ	77ᶻ	64ᶻ	93ᶻ	49ᶻ	63ᶻ	64ᶻ	62ᶻ	88ᶻ	89ᶻ	87ᶻ
Togo	80	82	77	42	45	40	...	...	...	...	...	...	...	...
Uganda	...	...	...	...	...	...	1,421ᶻ	46ᶻ	28ᶻ	30ᶻ	26ᶻ	...	...	...

TABLE 3
Part 1 (Continued)

	ACCESS AND PARTICIPATION IN SECONDARY EDUCATION															
	Effective transition from primary to lower secondary general education (%)			Percentage of students over-age for grade in lower secondary education (%)[1]			Total enrolment in secondary education		Gross enrolment ratio (GER) (%) Total secondary education			Lower secondary adjusted net enrolment ratio (ANER) (%)		
	School year ending in 2013			School year ending in 2014			School year ending in 2014		School year ending in 2014			School year ending in 2014		
Country or territory	Total	Male	Female	Total	Male	Female	Total (000)	% F	Total	Male	Female	Total	Male	Female
U.R. Tanzania	56y	59y	54y	...	...	...	2,052z	48z	32z	34z	31z	...	...	...
Zambia	64y	66y	62y	...	...	...	...	...	...	...	...	...	...	...
Zimbabwe	78y	77y	79y	26z	31z	21z	957z	50z	48z	48z	47z	92z	94z	90z
	Median			Median			Sum	% F	Weighted average			Weighted average		
World	97	97	98	10	11	7	567,755	48	75	76	75	84	84	84
Countries in transition	100	99	100	0,9	1	0,7	23,716	48	98	99	97	96	...	...
Developed countries	100	100	100	3	4	2	81,283	49	107	107	107	98	99z	99z
Developing countries	95	100	89	17	19	15	462,755	48	71	71	70	82	82	82
Caucasus and Central Asia	99	99	100	0,7	0,8	0,6	9,539	48	95	96	95	96	...	...
Eastern and South-eastern Asia	91	90	92	5	6	4	150,710	48	88	87	88	91	90	91
Eastern Asia	...	...	...	2	2	2	102,689	48	95	94	96	94	94	94
South-eastern Asia	90	90	90	12	12	12	48,021	49	75	75	75	86	85	87
Europe and Northern America	100	100	100	2	2	1	84,867	49	106	105	106	98	98z	98z
Latin America and the Caribbean	97	96	98	16	18	14	63,883	51	94	91	97	92	92	93
Caribbean	...	...	...	12	16	7	2,906	51	70	68	72	88	88	89
Latin America	97	97	96	20	24	17	60,976	51	96	93	99	93	92	93
Northern Africa and Western Asia	99	98	99	5	5	4	41,982	47	79	82	77	86	89	83
Northern Africa	93	92	95	16	19	13	18,387	49	78	79	78	90	92	87
Western Asia	99	100	99	5	6	4	23,595	47	80	84	77	84	87	81
Pacific	...	...	...	7	9	6	3,504	47	101	104	98	98	97y	98y
Southern Asia	97	95	98	7	7	7	158,987	47	65	66	65	80	79	82
Sub-Saharan Africa	85	...	...	35	40	30	54,283	46	43	46	39	66	68	64
Conflict-affected countries	95	100	87	16	16	16	245,411	47	65	66	64	76**	79**	74**
Countries with low income	79	80	77	...	...	...	35,328	45	41	45	37	65	69	62
Countries with middle income	97	96	97	12	14	10	425,760	48	75	75	75	85	84	85
Lower middle	93	93	93	22	22	18	239,014	48	65	66	65	80	79	81
Upper middle	97	97	98	7	7	5	186,746	49	93	91	94	93	93	93
Countries with high income	100	100	99	4	4	3	106,667	49	105	105	105	98	98z	98z

TABLE 3

SDG 4, Target 4.1 - Universal access, participation and completion, secondary education – part 2
By 2030, ensure that all girls and boys complete free, equitable and quality secondary education leading to relevant and effective learning outcomes

Country or territory	ACCESS AND PARTICIPATION IN SECONDARY EDUCATION							COMPLETION IN SECONDARY EDUCATION					LEARNING ASSESSMENTS AND OUTCOMES[6]		
	Lower secondary out-of-school adolescents[2]		Upper secondary adjusted net enrolment ratio (ANER) (%)			Upper secondary out-of-school adolescents and youth[3]		Gross intake rate (GIR) to last grade of lower secondary education (%)			Lower secondary completion rate[4]	Upper secondary completion rate[4]	Existence of nationally representative learning assessment at the end of lower secondary education	Percentage of students at end of lower secondary education achieving at least a minimum proficiency level (%)[7] in:	
	School year ending in 2014		School year ending in 2014			School year ending in 2014		School year ending in 2014			2009–2014[5]	2009–2014[5]	2009–2014[5]	Reading 2009–2014[5]	Mathematics 2009–2014[5]
	Total (000)	% F	Total	Male	Female	Total (000)	% F	Total	Male	Female	Total	Total		Total	Total
Caucasus and Central Asia															
Armenia[8]	...	...	...	...	...	...	...	...	...	...	100	93	Yes[I]	...	77[I]
Azerbaijan[9,10]	82*	51*	99*,z	...	...	2*,z	...	87*	87*	86*	...	...	Yes[I]	90[I]	89[I]
Georgia[10]	1	...	88	87	89	19	45	101	103	100	99	96	Yes[N]	...[I]	61[I]
Kazakhstan	3z	...	95	...	...	21	...	108	107	109	99	93	Yes[I,N]	96[I]	85[I]
Kyrgyzstan	42	48	57	58	56	93	50	91	90	91	97	86	Yes[I]	70[I]	35[I]
Tajikistan	...	...	...	...	...	...	...	96	99	94	89	60	No	...	...
Turkmenistan	...	...	...	...	...	...	...	...	...	...	...	...	...	...	...
Uzbekistan[10]	...	...	...	...	...	...	...	...	...	...	...	...	Yes[N]	...	...
Eastern and South-eastern Asia															
Brunei Darussalam	0.3	...	86	85	86	5	46	106	107	105	...	...	...	...	...
Cambodia	160	54	...	...	...	...	...	45	45	45	41	19	Yes[N]	...	...
China	...	...	...	...	...	...	...	98	97	100	81	43	Yes[N]	...	...
DPR Korea	...	...	...	...	...	...	...	...	...	...	...	...	...	...	...
Hong Kong, China[10]	8**	60**	88**	88**	87**	27**	50**	93	94	92	...	...	Yes[I]	100[I]	97[I]
Indonesia	1,937**	43**	70**	73**	67**	4,032**	54**	86	83	90	78	51	Yes[I]	96[I]	58[I]
Japan[10]	2*	...	97z	96z	98z	105z	36z	...	...	...	...	...	Yes[I,N]	99[I]	97[I]
Lao PDR	123	53	50	53	46	231	53	54	56	52	35	27	No	...	...
Macao, China[10]	2	45	81	81	81	4	48	96	92	101	...	...	Yes[I]	100[I]	97[I]
Malaysia[10]	170	...	55	...	...	993	...	85	...	...	...	...	Yes[I]	94[I]	77[I]
Mongolia[10]	0.8	...	89	84	93	16	30	114	112	116	84	65	Yes[N]	...	...
Myanmar	1,857	...	39	...	...	1,217	49**	49	47	50	...	...	No	...	...
Philippines	272*	18z	80z	77z	85z	396z	38z	82z	77z	88z	75	72	No	...	...
Republic of Korea[10]	10z	...	94z	95z	94z	117z	52z	97z	98z	97z	...	...	Yes[I,N]	100[I]	97[I]
Singapore	...	...	...	...	...	...	...	...	...	...	...	...	Yes[I]	100[I]	98[I]
Thailand[10]	...	...	...	...	...	...	...	89	88	90	...	...	Yes[I,N]	99[I]	81[I]
Timor-Leste	8	49	73	71	74	21	46	72z	68z	76z	45	27	...	...	...
Viet Nam[10]	...	...	...	...	...	...	...	94	95	92	81	55	Yes[I,N]	100[I]	96[I]
Europe and Northern America															
Albania[10]	8	64	81	82	81	30	51	92	94	91	...	...	Yes[I]	88[I]	67[I]
Andorra[8]	...	...	...	...	...	...	...	...	...	...	...	...	...	...	...
Austria[10]	...	...	...	...	...	...	...	96	97	96	...	84	Yes[I,N]	99[I]	94[I]
Belarus	0.4	...	98	97	99	4	21	110	109	110	100	83	...	...	...
Belgium[10]	0.3	...	99	99	99	4	40	96	94	97	...	82	Yes[I,N]	98[I]	93[I]
Bosnia and Herzegovina	...	...	...	...	...	...	...	84	83	86	94	69	No	...	...
Bulgaria[10]	5	51	81	84	79	49	54	47	52	43	...	84	Yes[I,N]	92[I]	80[I]
Canada[10]	...	...	...	...	...	...	...	...	...	...	...	86	Yes[I,N]	100[I]	96[I]
Croatia[10]	3	18	91	89	94	17	36	95	94	97	...	95	Yes[I]	99[I]	91[I]
Cyprus[9,10]	0.1*	...	93*	92*	94*	2*	43*	101*	100*	101*	...	93	Yes[I]	94[I]	81[I]
Czech Republic[10]	...	...	...	...	...	...	...	98	98	99	...	90	Yes[I]	99[I]	93[I]
Denmark	5	39	89	88	89	24	47	96	96	97	...	73	Yes[I]	99[I]	96[I]
Estonia	0.3z	...	87z	85z	89z	5z	40z	106z	108z	104z	...	79	Yes[I]	100[I]	98[I]
Finland	3	64	92	92	92	15	50	97	98	97	...	85	Yes[I,N]	99[I]	97[I]
France[10]	2	...	100	...	...	5	...	103	103	104	...	83	Yes[I,N]	98[I]	91[I]
Germany	...	...	...	...	...	...	...	56	57	56	...	78	Yes[I]	99[I]	94[I]
Greece[10]	3z	97z	95z	95z	94z	17z	54z	98z	99z	97z	...	93	Yes[I]	97[I]	86[I]
Hungary[10]	5	56	92	92	93	31	49	94	94	94	...	85	Yes[I,N]	99[I]	90[I]
Iceland	0.3y	67y	82y	81y	84y	3y	45y	97y	98y	96y	...	63	Yes[I,N]	98[I]	93[I]
Ireland	...	...	99y	...	...	1y	...	...	...	...	...	...	Yes[I]	100[I]	95[I]
Italy[10]	8z	...	93z	93z	93z	200z	49z	103z	103z	103z	...	83	Yes[I,N]	98[I]	91[I]
Latvia	0.2z	...	89	89	89	6	48	106	105	107	...	82	Yes[I,N]	99[I]	95[I]
Liechtenstein[9]	0.1*	...	88*	...	...	0.2*	...	99*	114*	85*	...	...	Yes[I]	100[I]	97[I]
Lithuania[10]	0.0	...	91	90	92	7	42	99	100	99	...	91	Yes[I]	99[I]	91[I]
Luxembourg[10]	1z	41z	83z	82z	85z	4z	44z	99z	99z	98z	...	60	Yes[I,N]	98[I]	91[I]
Malta	2	76	79	84	75	4	63	90	94	87	...	73	No	...	...
Monaco[8]	...	...	...	...	...	...	...	...	...	...	...	...	...	...	...
Montenegro[10]	...	...	...	...	...	...	...	90	89	90	94	85	Yes[I,N]	96[I]	72[I]
Netherlands[10]	1y	...	97y	97y	97y	20y	50y	...	...	...	...	73	Yes[I,N]	99[I]	96[I]
Norway	1	33	91	91	91	18	47	97	97	98	...	68	Yes[I]	98[I]	93[I]
Poland	56z	49z	91z	91z	92z	118z	46z	95z	96z	95z	...	83	Yes[I]	100[I]	97[I]
Portugal[10]	3	...	99	...	...	4	...	...	...	...	...	60	Yes[I]	99[I]	91[I]
Republic of Moldova[9]	27*	50*	61*	60*	62*	35*	47*	85*	86*	84*	95	66	...	...	...
Romania[10]	54y	51y	...	...	...	...	...	89	88	89	...	82	Yes[I]	97[I]	86[I]
Russian Federation	...	...	...	...	...	...	...	99	98	100	99	87	Yes[I]	99[I]	93[I]
San Marino[9]	...	...	...	...	...	...	...	92*,y	91*,y	93*,y	...	...	...	...	...
Serbia[9,10]	3*	39*	88*	86*	89*	37*	42*	96*	96*	97*	92	75	Yes[I]	97[I]	85[I]
Slovakia[10]	...	...	...	...	...	...	...	88	88	88	...	93	Yes[I,N]	96[I]	89[I]
Slovenia[10]	1	48	95	95	96	4	45	94	93	95	...	89	Yes[I,N]	99[I]	95[I]
Spain	2	...	97	97	97	35	45	94	91	97	...	67	Yes[I,N]	99[I]	92[I]
Sweden	0.5	...	93	94	92	24	53	105	105	104	...	92	Yes[I,N]	97[I]	90[I]

TABLE 3
Part 2 (Continued)

	ACCESS AND PARTICIPATION IN SECONDARY EDUCATION							COMPLETION IN SECONDARY EDUCATION					LEARNING ASSESSMENTS AND OUTCOMES[6]		
	Lower secondary out-of-school adolescents[2]		Upper secondary adjusted net enrolment ratio (ANER) (%)			Upper secondary out-of-school adolescents and youth[3]		Gross intake rate (GIR) to last grade of lower secondary education (%)			Lower secondary completion rate[4]	Upper secondary completion rate[4]	Existence of nationally representative learning assessment at the end of lower secondary education	Percentage of students at end of lower secondary education achieving at least a minimum proficiency level (%)[7] in:	
	School year ending in 2014		School year ending in 2014			School year ending in 2014		School year ending in 2014			2009–2014[5]	2009–2014[5]	2009–2014[5]	Reading 2009–2014[5]	Mathematics 2009–2014[5]
Country or territory	Total (000)	% F	Total	Male	Female	Total (000)	% F	Total	Male	Female	Total	Total		Total	Total
Switzerland	0.1	...	80	81	79	73	51	95	93	98	...	72	Yes[i]	99[i]	96[i]
TFYR Macedonia[10]	...	...	...	...	...	...	...	...	...	...	81	75	Yes[i,N]	...[i]	60[i]
Ukraine[10]	8**	...	94**	92**	95**	53**	37**	96	96	95	99	95	Yes[i]	...[i]	82[i]
United Kingdom[10]	32	48	99	...	...	25	...	...	...	...	...	94	Yes[i,N]	99[i]	92[i]
United States[10]	115	...	92	92	93	944	42	...	...	...	...	92	Yes[i,N]	99[i]	92[i]
Latin America and the Caribbean															
Anguilla	...	...	85	84	...	...	...	...	...	...	...	...	No	...	...
Antigua and Barbuda	0.2	76	85	87	83	0.5	55	85	82	89	...	...		...	...
Argentina[10]	15[z]	...	89[z]	83[z]	94[z]	234[z]	26[z]	89[z]	88[z]	91[z]	75	66	Yes[L,N]	92[i]	65[i]
Aruba	...	...	...	...	...	...	...	99	95	103	...	...	No	...	...
Bahamas	...	...	...	...	...	...	...	...	...	...	...	...	No	...	...
Barbados	0.1	...	97	...	...	0.2	...	...	...	...	98	93	No	...	...
Belize	3	53	56	55	58	7	48	64	60	69	43	20	No	...	...
Bermuda	...	...	...	...	...	...	...	76[y]	69[y]	83[y]	...	...		...	...
Bolivia, P.S.	15[z]	61[z]	80[z]	81[z]	80[z]	170[z]	50[z]	90[z]	89[z]	90[z]	...	...	Yes[N]	...	...
Brazil[9,10]	669[*,z]	40[*,z]	83[*,z]	83[*,z]	84[*,z]	1,787[*,z]	47[*,z]	...	...	...	64	18	Yes[L,N]	96[i]	65[i]
British Virgin Islands[9]	...	...	...	...	...	...	...	84[*]	...	...	...	...		...	...
Cayman Islands[8]	...	...	...	...	...	...	...	...	...	...	...	...		...	...
Chile[10]	16	52	94	93	95	63	44	97	96	97	88	51	Yes[L,N]	99[i]	78[i]
Colombia[10]	90	40	81	80	83	303	46	78	73	84	73	63	Yes[L,N]	95[i]	58[i]
Costa Rica[10]	14	49	83	81	85	27	44	59	55	63	61	33	Yes[L,N]	99[i]	76[i]
Cuba	6[z]	9[z]	84[z]	83[z]	85[z]	70[z]	44[z]	96	93	99	...	...	Yes[N]	...	...
Curaçao	...	...	...	...	...	...	...	...	...	...	...	...		...	...
Dominica	...	...	...	...	...	...	...	93	90	96	...	...		...	...
Dominican Republic	20	60	75	75	76	193	48	76	71	80	85	60	Yes[i]	...	...
Ecuador	5[z]	...	83[z]	83[z]	84[z]	150[z]	48[z]	95	94	95	86	66	Yes[N]	...	...
El Salvador	2	...	73	74	72	105	52	85	84	87	...	...	Yes[N]	...	...
Grenada	0.5	63	78	76	80	0.9	45	96	92	100	...	...		...	...
Guatemala	297	57	47	50	44	381	52	59	61	57	43	25	Yes[N]	...	...
Guyana	...	...	...	...	...	...	...	...	...	...	56	12	Yes[N]	...	...
Haiti	...	...	...	...	...	...	...	...	...	...	46	15		...	...
Honduras[10]	148	47	53	49	56	172	46	54	49	59	43	31	Yes[L,N]	...	19[i]
Jamaica	27	40	64	62	67	60	45	86	84	89	96	79	No	...	...
Mexico[10]	1,005[y]	48[y]	58[y]	57[y]	59[y]	2,984[y]	48[y]	81	79	82	84	53	Yes[L,N]	97[i]	77[i]
Montserrat[8]	...	...	...	...	...	...	...	...	...	...	...	...		...	...
Nicaragua	...	...	...	...	...	...	...	...	...	...	46	18	Yes[N]	...	...
Panama[10]	23[y]	48[y]	86[y]	83[y]	88[y]	29[y]	40[y]	74[y]	70[y]	78[y]	76	62	Yes[L,N]	87[i]	49[i]
Paraguay	38[y]	78[y]	69[y]	68[y]	71[y]	125[y]	47[y]	74[y]	71[y]	77[y]	...	...	Yes[N]	...	...
Peru[10]	142	45	81	81	82	207	47	85	84	87	80	74	Yes[i]	90[i]	53[i]
Saint Kitts and Nevis	0.3	45	79	79	79	0.4	50	92	89	95	...	...	No	...	...
Saint Lucia	1[z]	55[z]	83[z]	81[z]	85[z]	1[z]	44[z]	87	86	87	92	79		...	...
Saint Martin	...	...	...	...	...	...	...	...	...	...	...	...		...	...
St. Vincent and the Grenadines	...	...	...	...	...	...	...	91	90	91	...	...		...	...
Sint-Maarten[8]	...	...	...	...	...	...	...	...	...	...	...	...		...	...
Suriname	3[z]	42[z]	70[z]	66[z]	74[z]	8[z]	43[z]	48	33	63	44	22		...	...
Trinidad and Tobago[10]	...	...	...	...	...	...	...	...	...	...	...	...	Yes[i]	90[i]	70[i]
Turks and Caicos Islands[8]	...	...	...	...	...	...	...	...	...	...	...	...		...	...
Uruguay[10]	22[z]	48[z]	82[z]	77[z]	86[z]	29[z]	37[z]	60[z]	53[z]	67[z]	66	33	Yes[L,N]	94[i]	71[i]
Venezuela, B.R.	135	41	72	68	76	311	42	76	72	81	...	...	Yes[N]	...	...
Northern Africa and Western Asia															
Algeria	...	...	...	...	...	...	...	79	72	87	...	...	No	...	...
Bahrain[8,10]	...	...	76	69	84	13	30	...	...	...	...	...	Yes[L,N]	...	53[i]
Egypt[10]	286	39	77	79	76	1,058	52	83**	81**	85**	80	71	Yes[N]	...	...
Iraq	...	...	...	...	...	...	...	...	...	...	31	19		...	...
Israel[10]	0.8	...	98	...	...	7	...	100	100	100	98	88	Yes[L,N]	96[i]	84[i]
Jordan	...	...	...	...	...	...	...	87[y]	86[y]	89[y]	89	59	Yes[L,N]	93[i]	64[i]
Kuwait	12[y]	15[y]	73[y]	74[y]	72[y]	35[y]	53[y]	89[**,z]	83[**,z]	96[**,z]	...	...	No	...	...
Lebanon[10]	63[**,y]	56[**,y]	66[**,y]	66[**,y]	66[**,y]	94[**,y]	51[**,y]	59	56	62	...	...	Yes[i]	...	73[i]
Libya	...	...	...	...	...	...	...	...	...	...	...	...		...	...
Morocco[10]	277[**,y]	65[**,y]	58[**,y]	64[**,y]	52[**,y]	787[**,y]	56[**,y]	68	70	66	38	16	Yes[L,N]	...	33[i]
Oman[8,10]	7	...	...	...	...	...	...	94	88	102	...	...	Yes[L,N]	...	37[i]
Palestine[10]	90	43	65	57	74	72	36	74	67	82	85	62	Yes[L,N]	...	51[i]
Qatar[8,10]	...	...	...	...	...	...	...	...	...	...	...	...	Yes[L,N]	86[i]	53[i]
Saudi Arabia[10]	114[**,z]	73[**,z]	91**	...	...	135**	...	98	104	91	...	...	Yes[L,N]	...	45[i]
Sudan	660[y]	68[y]	...	...	...	...	...	50[z]	53[z]	48[z]	53	21	No	...	...
Syrian Arab Republic[10]	979[z]	50[z]	33[z]	33[z]	33[z]	874[z]	48[z]	51[z]	51[z]	52[z]	...	...	Yes[i]	...	41[i]
Tunisia[10]	...	...	...	...	...	...	...	70	62	78	67	49	Yes[i]	94[i]	64[i]
Turkey[10]	176[z]	61[z]	83[z]	85[z]	81[z]	883[z]	55[z]	95[z]	97[z]	93[z]	...	...	Yes[L,N]	99[i]	85[i]
United Arab Emirates[8,10]	...	...	...	...	...	...	...	...	...	...	...	...	Yes[L,N]	97[i]	79[i]
Yemen	679[**,y]	64[**,y]	41[**,y]	49[**,y]	32[**,y]	1,070[**,y]	56[**,y]	48[z]	57[z]	40[z]	45	30	No	...	...
The Pacific															
Australia[8]	9[z]	...	91[z]	89[z]	93[z]	54[z]	38[z]	...	...	...	...	85	Yes[i]	99[i]	94[i]

TABLE 3
Part 2 (Continued)

	ACCESS AND PARTICIPATION IN SECONDARY EDUCATION							COMPLETION IN SECONDARY EDUCATION					LEARNING ASSESSMENTS AND OUTCOMES[6]		
	Lower secondary out-of-school adolescents[2]		Upper secondary adjusted net enrolment ratio (ANER) (%)			Upper secondary out-of-school adolescents and youth[3]		Gross intake rate (GIR) to last grade of lower secondary education (%)			Lower secondary completion rate[4]	Upper secondary completion rate[4]	Existence of nationally representative learning assessment at the end of lower secondary education	Percentage of students at end of lower secondary education achieving at least a minimum proficiency level (%)[7] in:	
	School year ending in 2014		School year ending in 2014			School year ending in 2014		School year ending in 2014			2009–2014[5]	2009–2014[5]	2009–2014[5]	Reading 2009–2014[5]	Mathematics 2009–2014[5]
Country or territory	Total (000)	% F	Total	Male	Female	Total (000)	% F	Total	Male	Female	Total	Total		Total	Total
Cook Islands[9]	0.1*,y	44*,y	86*,y	85*,y	87*,y	0.1*,y	42*,y	97*	95*	98*	...	...	No	...	...
Fiji	2y	...	74y	70y	77y	13y	42y	98ᶻ	94ᶻ	103ᶻ	...	...	No	...	...
Kiribati	...	...	...	...	...	...	...	101	92	110	...	...	No	...	...
Marshall Islands	...	...	...	...	...	...	...	...	...	...	...	...	...	...	...
Micronesia F.S.	...	...	...	...	...	...	...	...	...	...	...	...	...	...	...
Nauru[9]	0*	46*	47*	43*	50*	0.2*	44*	77*,y	85*,y	68*,y	...	...	...	...	...
New Zealand[10]	4	41	96	95	98	7	30	...	...	...	...	...	Yes[I]	99[I]	92[I]
Niue	...	...	...	...	...	...	...	104*	110*	100*	...	...	...	...	...
Palau[9]	...	...	98*,ᶻ	...	...	0.0*,ᶻ	...	105*	102*	107*	...	...	...	...	...
Papua New Guinea	...	...	...	...	...	...	...	63y	67y	58y	...	...	...	...	...
Samoa	0.4	45	86	80	92	3	27	101	104	98	...	...	No	...	...
Solomon Islands	...	...	...	...	...	...	...	66	67	65	...	...	No	...	...
Tokelau	...	...	...	...	...	...	...	...	...	...	...	...	No	...	...
Tonga	1	31	44	39	48	3	44	...	...	...	...	...	No	...	...
Tuvalu[9]	0.1*	26*	47*	37*	59*	0.3*	37*	100*	93*	108*	...	...	No	...	...
Vanuatu	...	...	...	...	...	...	...	53ᶻ	51ᶻ	55ᶻ	...	...	No	...	...
Southern Asia															
Afghanistan	852	72	48	61	34	1,148	62	...	...	...	25	14	No	...	...
Bangladesh	...	...	...	...	...	...	...	68ᶻ	62ᶻ	73ᶻ	56	23	Yes[N]	...	...
Bhutan	9	37	66	63	69	10	45	78	72	84	25	5	Yes[N]	...	...
India	11,123**,ᶻ	38**,ᶻ	52**,ᶻ	53**,ᶻ	51**,ᶻ	46,815**,ᶻ	48**,ᶻ	81ᶻ	79ᶻ	83ᶻ	76	35	Yes[N]	...	...
Iran, Islamic Republic of	33	57	77	77	77	1,012	48	96*,y	96*,y	97*,y	...	...	Yes[I]	...	54[I]
Maldives	...	...	...	...	...	...	...	93	92	95	90	63	Yes[N]	...	...
Nepal	...	...	**55**	**52**	**58**	**1,219**	**45**	84	80	89	61	42	Yes[N]	...	...
Pakistan	5,502	53	33	37	28	10,443	52	51	55	46	46	20	Yes[N]	...	...
Sri Lanka	68ᶻ	46ᶻ	...	...	...	...	...	96**	96**	97**	...	...	Yes[N]	...	...
Sub-Saharan Africa															
Angola	...	...	...	...	...	...	...	...	...	...	...	...	...	...	...
Benin	350ᶻ	61ᶻ	40ᶻ	51ᶻ	29ᶻ	389ᶻ	59ᶻ	42	50	34	29	13	No	...	...
Botswana[10]	15ᶻ	45ᶻ	81ᶻ	80ᶻ	81ᶻ	17ᶻ	49ᶻ	87ᶻ	86ᶻ	87ᶻ	...	...	Yes[I]	...	49[I]
Burkina Faso	758ᶻ	51ᶻ	23ᶻ	25ᶻ	21ᶻ	830ᶻ	50ᶻ	25	26	23	8	3	No	...	...
Burundi	275	49	34	36	31	425	53	26	29	23	10	4	No	...	...
Cabo Verde	3	49	70	66	74	10	44	76	67	85	...	...	No	...	...
Cameroon	788	55	43	48	39	814	54	36	36	35	34	13	Yes[N]	...	...
Central African Republic	239y	60y	16y	21y	10y	248y	54y	13y	17y	8y	9	6	...	...	...
Chad	...	...	...	...	...	...	...	18ᶻ	25ᶻ	10ᶻ	17	7	...	...	...
Comoros	19ᶻ	48ᶻ	44ᶻ	43ᶻ	45ᶻ	26ᶻ	49ᶻ	45ᶻ	42ᶻ	49ᶻ	43	25	...	...	...
Congo	...	...	...	...	...	...	...	52y	53y	51y	36	15	...	...	...
Côte d'Ivoire	...	...	...	...	...	...	...	33	38	27	32	16	No	...	...
D.R. Congo	...	...	...	...	...	...	...	48	62	34	57	30	...	...	...
Djibouti	...	...	...	...	...	...	...	45	49	41	...	...	...	...	...
Equatorial Guinea	...	...	...	...	...	...	...	32y	34y	30y	...	...	...	...	...
Eritrea	213ᶻ	52ᶻ	38ᶻ	43ᶻ	33ᶻ	254ᶻ	53ᶻ	55y	56y	54y	...	...	No	...	...
Ethiopia	3,635**,y	51**,y	...	...	...	...	...	29	31	28	17	13	Yes[N]	...	...
Gabon	...	...	...	...	...	...	...	...	...	...	44	14	...	...	...
Gambia[10]	...	...	...	...	...	...	...	62	61	62	48	29	Yes[N]	...	...
Ghana[10]	**121****	**49****	**62****	**63****	**60****	**633****	**51****	78	80	75	53	39	Yes[I]	...	19[I]
Guinea	567	58	32	40	24	507	55	35	42	28	25	16	No	...	...
Guinea-Bissau	...	...	...	...	...	...	...	...	...	...	...	...	No	...	...
Kenya	...	...	81**,y	85**,y	76**,y	709**,y	60**,y	83	83	84	79	44	No	...	...
Lesotho	34	40	56	52	60	45	45	43	36	50	32	20	No	...	...
Liberia	...	...	...	...	...	...	...	37	42	32	38	23	No	...	...
Madagascar	...	...	...	...	...	...	...	37	37	37	...	...	No	...	...
Malawi	327	50	41	44	38	432	53	21y	22y	20y	29	18	No	...	...
Mali	544	55	30	35	25	727	53	33	37	29	18	14	No	...	...
Mauritania	148	48	27	28	25	178	50	29	29	28	28	17	No	...	...
Mauritius	...	...	...	...	...	...	...	85	80	90	...	...	Yes[N]	...	...
Mozambique	882	54	29	32	25	864	53	22	22	21	11	5	Yes[N]	...	...
Namibia	...	...	...	...	...	...	...	59ᶻ	56ᶻ	63ᶻ	55	35	No	...	...
Niger	1,193	53	11	14	8	927	52	13	15	10	6	2	No	...	...
Nigeria	...	...	...	...	...	...	...	...	...	...	53	44	Yes[N]	...	...
Rwanda	...	...	...	...	...	...	...	36y	34y	38y	16	10	No	...	...
Sao Tome and Principe	...	...	...	...	...	...	...	**74**	**70**	**78**	...	...	No[N]	...	...
Senegal	...	...	...	...	...	...	...	40	41	40	24	9	No	...	...
Seychelles	...	...	89	87	91	1	41	109	103	116	...	...	Yes[N]	...	...
Sierra Leone	132y	54y	44y	47y	40y	219y	54y	52ᶻ	57ᶻ	48ᶻ	41	20	...	...	...
Somalia	...	...	...	...	...	...	...	...	...	...	...	...	...	...	...
South Africa[10]	...	...	...	...	...	...	...	...	...	...	83	45	Yes[I,N]	...	22[I]
South Sudan	...	...	...	...	...	...	...	...	...	...	16	6	...	...	...
Swaziland	10ᶻ	54ᶻ	69ᶻ	72ᶻ	67ᶻ	18ᶻ	54ᶻ	49ᶻ	49ᶻ	50ᶻ	47	30	Yes[N]	...	...
Togo	...	...	...	...	...	...	...	38	47	29	25	14	No	...	...
Uganda	...	...	...	...	...	...	...	29ᶻ	31ᶻ	28ᶻ	23	16	No	...	...

TABLE 3
Part 2 (Continued)

Country or territory	ACCESS AND PARTICIPATION IN SECONDARY EDUCATION							COMPLETION IN SECONDARY EDUCATION					LEARNING ASSESSMENTS AND OUTCOMES[6]		
	Lower secondary out-of-school adolescents[2]		Upper secondary adjusted net enrolment ratio (ANER) (%)			Upper secondary out-of-school adolescents and youth[3]		Gross intake rate (GIR) to last grade of lower secondary education (%)			Lower secondary completion rate[4]	Upper secondary completion rate[4]	Existence of nationally representative learning assessment at the end of lower secondary education	Percentage of students at end of lower secondary education achieving at least a minimum proficiency level (%)[7] in:	
														Reading	Mathematics
	School year ending in 2014		School year ending in 2014			School year ending in 2014		School year ending in 2014			2009–2014[5]	2009–2014[5]	2009–2014[5]	2009–2014[5]	2009–2014[5]
	Total (000)	% F	Total	Male	Female	Total (000)	% F	Total	Male	Female	Total	Total		Total	Total
U.R. Tanzania	...	...	...	...	...	...	...	35[z]	38[z]	32[z]	14	3	No	...	...
Zambia	...	...	...	...	...	...	...	55[z]	59[z]	51[z]	55	27	Yes[N]	...	...
Zimbabwe	56[z]	60[z]	47[z]	49[z]	45[z]	703[z]	52[z]	66[z]	64[z]	67[z]	71	9	No	...	...
	Sum	**% F**	**Weighted average**			**Sum**	**% F**	**Weighted average**			**Median**	**Median**		**Median**	
World	60,210	48	63	63	62	141,755	49	75	75	76	...	53		...	...
Countries in transition	681	...	85	84[z]	86[z]	1,271	45[z]	98	97	98	97	85		...	...
Developed countries	607	49[z]	93	92	93	2,717	45	92	92	92	...	83		...	...
Developing countries	58,923	48	59	59	58	137,767	49	73	72	73	46	25		...	...
Caucasus and Central Asia	284	...	84[y]	83[y]	85[y]	607[y]	47[y]	99	99	99	99	93		...	...
Eastern and South-eastern Asia	8,210	46	77	74	80	19,506	42	92	91	93	...	...		...	...
Eastern Asia	3,159	47	84	80	88	9,099	34	99	98	100	...	...		...	...
South-eastern Asia	5,050	45	63	63	63	10,407	49	81	79	84	60	39		...	...
Europe and Northern America	989	47[z]	92	91	92	3,199	45	92	91	92	...	83		...	...
Latin America and the Caribbean	2,769	46	76	75	77	7,545	47	77	74	79	73	51		...	...
Caribbean	212	47	76	76	75	575	50	71	68	74	...	...		...	...
Latin America	2,557	46	76	75	77	6,970	47	77	75	80	65	33		...	...
Northern Africa and Western Asia	3,647	60	67	69	66	8,459	51	73	74	72	...	...		...	...
Northern Africa	1,185	60	66	67	66	4,017	49	72	71	73	60	35		...	...
Western Asia	2,462	59	68	71	65	4,442	53	74	77	71	...	...		...	...
Pacific	43	38[y]	66	61	70	545	42	83[z]	84[z]	81[z]	...	...		...	...
Southern Asia	20,663	43	50	51	49	68,737	49	76	74	77	56	23		...	...
Sub-Saharan Africa	23,605	52	43	46	39	33,131	52	42	45	39	31	15		...	...
Conflict-affected countries	14,826[**]	55[**]	54[**]	56[**]	52[**]	25,515[**]	51[**]	70	70	70	45	20		...	...
Countries with low income	16,837	54	40	44	35	23,151	53	38	41	34	25	14		...	...
Countries with middle income	42,111	46	61	61	61	114,556	48	78	77	80	74	45		...	...
Lower middle	34,945	45	52	53	51	91,658	49	73	72	74	53	30		...	...
Upper middle	7,166	49	77	75	80	22,898	43	88	86	89	83	63		...	...
Countries with high income	1,262	47[z]	92	91	93	4,048	44	92	92	92	...	83		...	...

Source: UIS database, except where noted. Enrolment ratios and gross intake rates to last grade are based on the United Nations Population Division estimates, revision 2015 (United Nations, 2015), median variant.

Note: The country groupings by level of income are as defined by the World Bank but include only countries listed in the table. They are based on the list of countries by income group as revised in July 2015.

1. Over-age pupils are defined as those whose age is at least two years higher than the official age of entry in a given grade. The percentage is calculated as the sum of the numbers of pupils who are two or more years above the theoretical age of their grade divided by total enrolment in lower secondary education.

2. Data reflect the actual number of adolescents of lower secondary school age not enrolled at all, derived from the lower secondary ANER, which measures the proportion of lower secondary school age adolescents who are enrolled in primary, secondary, post-secondary or tertiary education.

3. Data reflect the actual number of adolescents and youth of upper secondary school age not enrolled at all, derived from the upper secondary ANER, which measures the proportion of upper secondary school age adolescents and youth who are enrolled in primary, secondary, post-secondary or tertiary education.

4. GEM Report team calculations based on data from national and international household surveys.

5. Data are for the most recent year available in the period specified. For details see relevant sources.

6. Altinok (2013); Cheng and Omeova (2014); Ministries of education national reports and websites; PISA 2012 (OECD, 2013), TIMSS 2011. 'Nationally representative learning assessment' refers to national (N) or international (I) formative learning assessments. Information and data need to be used and interpreted with caution since the different types of assessments are not necessarily comparable.

7. Refers to the percentage of pupils performing at or above level 1 of proficiency in in reading and or mathematics.

8. GER and GIR to last grade were not calculated due to inconsistencies in the United Nations population data or lack of United Nations population by age.

9. National population data were used to calculate GER and GIR to last grade due to inconsistencies in the United Nations population data or lack of United Nations population by age.

10. In the absence of assessments conducted in the proposed indicator grade, surveys of student learning achievement in the grade below or above the proposed indicator grade are used as placeholders to report on learning assessments and/or learning outcomes at the end of secondary education.

Data in bold are for the school year ending in 2015.

(z) Data are for the school year ending in 2013.

(y) Data are for the school year ending in 2012.

(*) National estimate.

(**) For country level data: UIS partial estimate; for regional and other country grouping sums and weighted averages: partial imputation due to incomplete country coverage (between 33% and 60% of population for the region or other country grouping).

(-) Magnitude nil or negligible

(.) The category is not applicable or does not exist.

(...) No data are available.

TABLE 4

SDG 4, Target 4.2 – Universal access to early childhood development, care and pre-primary education

By 2030, ensure that all girls and boys have access to quality early childhood development, care and pre-primary education so that they are ready for primary education

Country or territory	CHILD MORTALITY[1] AND MALNUTRITION[2]		PARTICIPATION IN PRE-PRIMARY EDUCATION								SCHOOL READINESS[5]		
	Under-5 mortality rate (deaths per 1,000 live births)	Under-5 moderate or severe stunting rate (%)	Total enrolment in pre-primary education		Gross enrolment ratio (GER) in pre-primary education (%)			Adjusted net enrolment ratio (ANER) one year before the official primary school entry age (%)[4]			Percentage of children under 5 experiencing positive and stimulating home learning environments (%)[6]	Percentage of children under 5 living in households with three or more children's books	Percentage of children under 5 who are developmentally on track in health, learning and psychosocial well-being (%)[7]
			School year ending in 2014		School year ending in 2014			School year ending in 2014			2009–2015[3]	2009–2015[3]	2009–2015[3]
	Total 2015	Total 2009–2014[3]	Total (000)	% F	Total	Male	Female	Total	Male	Female	Total	Total	Total
Caucasus and Central Asia													
Armenia	14	21	64[y]	49[y]	52[y]	46[y]	60[y]	...	...	...	...	...	...
Azerbaijan[8]	32	18	107	47	23[*]	23[*]	24[*]	21[*]	20[*]	21[*]	...	...	...
Georgia	12	11	...	...	...	...	...	...	...	...	...	...	...
Kazakhstan	14	13	852	51	60	57	64	95	90	100	92	48	86
Kyrgyzstan	21	13	126	49	25	25	25	67	66	69	72	27	78
Tajikistan	45	...	86	46	11	11	10	12	12	11	...	...	...
Turkmenistan	51	27	189	49	63	64	62	...	...	...	...	...	...
Uzbekistan	39	...	...	...	...	...	...	...	...	...	...	...	...
Eastern and South-eastern Asia													
Brunei Darussalam	10	20	13	49	74	73	74	100	99	100	...	...	...
Cambodia	29	32	182	48	18	18	18	33	34	32	59	4	68
China	11	9	38,947	46	82	82	82	...	...	...	...	...	...
DPR Korea	25	...	...	...	...	...	...	...	...	...	91	79	75
Hong Kong, China[9]	...	...	171	48	...	...	...	...	...	...	...	...	...
Indonesia	27	36	5,349	49	58	57	59	99[**]	100[**]	99[**]	...	...	...
Japan	3	7	2,910[z]	...	90[z]	...	...	96[z]	...	...	...	...	...
Lao PDR	67	44	150	50	30	30	31	50	50	51	57	5	81
Macao, China[9]	...	...	13	48	...	...	...	...	...	...	...	...	...
Malaysia	7	...	894	49	99	...	...	96	...	...	...	...	...
Mongolia	22	11	133[y]	50[y]	86[y]	85[y]	86[y]	71[y]	71[y]	71[y]	55	33	76
Myanmar	50	35	453	51	23	23	24	23	23	23	...	...	...
Philippines	28	30	...	...	...	...	...	...	...	...	...	...	...
Republic of Korea	3	...	1,262	49	92[z]	92[z]	92[z]	99[z]	99[z]	99[z]	...	...	...
Singapore	3	...	...	...	...	...	...	...	...	...	...	...	...
Thailand	12	16	1,737	48	73	73	73	96	96	96	93	43	92
Timor-Leste	53	58	16	50	17	17	17	64	59	68	...	...	...
Viet Nam	22	19	3,614	47	81	83	80	95[**,z]	...	...	96	26	89
Europe and Northern America													
Albania	14	23	81	48	89	90	87	98	99	97	...	...	...
Andorra[9]	3	...	2	51	...	...	...	...	...	...	...	...	...
Austria	4	...	240	48	102	102	101	...	...	...	...	...	...
Belarus	5	...	327	48	105	107	103	99	100	97	96	92	94
Belgium	4	...	463	49	118	118	118	100	100	99	...	...	...
Bosnia and Herzegovina	5	9	16	47	15	15	14	15[y]	16[y]	15[y]	95	56	96
Bulgaria	10	...	241	48	83	83	83	93	94	92	...	...	...
Canada	5	...	556[z]	49[z]	74[z]	74[z]	73[z]	97[z]	97[z]	96[z]	...	...	...
Croatia	4	...	108	48	61	62	61	95	96	95	...	...	...
Cyprus[8]	3	...	23	49	77[*]	77[*]	77[*]	92[*]	93[*]	92[*]	...	...	...
Czech Republic	3	...	367	48	105	106	104	...	...	...	...	...	...
Denmark	4	...	191	49	96	96	97	98	96	100	...	...	...
Estonia	3	...	52[y]	48[y]	88[y]	90[y]	87[y]	92[y]	94[y]	91[y]	...	...	...
Finland	2	...	196	49	80	80	79	98	99	98	...	...	...
France	4	...	2,584	49	109	109	109	100	100	100	...	...	...
Germany	4	...	2,225	48	111	111	110	...	...	...	...	...	...
Greece	5	...	167[z]	48[z]	76[z]	77[z]	76[z]	95[z]	96[z]	94[z]	...	...	...
Hungary	6	...	330	48	84	85	83	92	92	91	...	...	...
Iceland	2	...	13[y]	48[y]	97[y]	98[y]	97[y]	99[y]	99[y]	98[y]	...	...	...
Ireland	4	...	78[z]	49[z]	108[z]	107[z]	110[z]	96[z]	94[z]	98[z]	...	...	...
Italy	4	...	1,686[z]	48[z]	100[z]	101[z]	99[z]	99[z]	99[z]	98[z]	...	...	...
Latvia	8	...	79	49	91	91	90	99	98	100	...	...	...
Liechtenstein[8]	...	...	0,8	44	106[*]	109[*]	102[*]	100[*]	99[*]	100[*]	...	...	...
Lithuania	5	...	99	49	88	89	88	98	98	97	...	...	...
Luxembourg	2	...	16[z]	49[z]	93[z]	93[z]	94[z]	98[z]	96[z]	100[z]	...	...	...
Malta	6	...	9	49	115	112	119	100	100	100	...	...	...
Monaco[9]	4	...	0,9	47	...	...	...	...	...	...	...	...	...
Montenegro	5	9	13	47	55	57	54	66	68	63	98	73	94
Netherlands	4	...	512	49	95	95	95	100[**]	100[**]	100[**]	...	...	...
Norway	3	...	187	49	98	98	98	100	100	100	...	...	...
Poland	5	...	1,216[z]	49[z]	77[z]	78[z]	77[z]	89[z]	91[z]	88[z]	...	...	...
Portugal	4	...	265	48	92	93	90	98	100	96	...	...	...
Republic of Moldova[8]	16	6	130	48	84[*]	84[*]	83[*]	97[*]	96[*]	97[*]	89	68	84
Romania	11	...	569	49	90	90	91	90[**]	90[**]	90[**]	...	...	...
Russian Federation	10	...	5,397	48	84	84	83	89	90	89	...	...	...
San Marino[8]	3	...	1[y]	50[y]	107[*,y]	106[*,y]	108[*,y]	94[*,y]	94[*,y]	95[*,y]	...	...	...
Serbia[8]	7	6	157	49	59[*]	59[*]	59[*]	98[*]	98[*]	99[*]	96	72	95
Slovakia	7	...	158	48	92	93	91	...	...	...	...	...	...
Slovenia	3	...	60	48	93	95	92	98	98	97	...	...	...
Spain	4	...	1,443	48	98	98	98	100	100	100	...	...	...
Sweden	3	...	441	48	96	96	95	98	98	98	...	...	...
Switzerland	4	...	166	48	105	106	104	100	99	100	...	...	...
TFYR Macedonia	6	5	20[y]	49[y]	29[y]	28[y]	29[y]	36[y]	35[y]	38[y]	92	52	93

TABLE 4

(Continued)

Country or territory	Under-5 mortality rate (deaths per 1,000 live births) Total 2015	Under-5 moderate or severe stunting rate (%) Total 2009-2014[3]	Total enrolment in pre-primary education School year ending in 2014 Total (000)	% F	Gross enrolment ratio (GER) in pre-primary education (%) School year ending in 2014 Total	Male	Female	Adjusted net enrolment ratio (ANER) one year before the official primary school entry age (%)[4] School year ending in 2014 Total	Male	Female	Percentage of children under 5 experiencing positive and stimulating home learning environments (%)[6] 2009-2015[3] Total	Percentage of children under 5 living in households with three or more children's books 2009-2015[3] Total	Percentage of children under 5 who are developmentally on track in health, learning and psychosocial well-being (%)[7] 2009-2015[3] Total
Ukraine	9	...	1,354[y]	48[y]	104[y]	105[y]	103[y]	...	...	...	98	91	89
United Kingdom	4	...	1,480	49	88	88	88	100	100	99	...	...	...
United States	7	2	8,762	49	71	71	72	90	91	90	...	...	...
Latin America and the Caribbean													
Anguilla	...	...	...	...	...	...	...	...	...	...	...	...	...
Antigua and Barbuda	8	...	2	48	75	78	72	93	100	86	...	...	...
Argentina	13	...	1,567[z]	49[z]	72[z]	71[z]	72[z]	96[z]	96[z]	97[z]	84	61	85
Aruba	...	...	3	48	107	108	106	100	100	100	...	...	...
Bahamas	12	...	...	...	...	...	...	...	...	...	...	...	...
Barbados	13	8	6	50	84	83	86	94	93	95	...	85	97
Belize	17	19	8	49	50	50	51	93	92	93	86	40	88
Bermuda	...	...	0.4	50	54	54	55	61[y]	58[y]	63[y]	...	...	...
Bolivia, Plurinational States of	38	18	298[z]	49[z]	63[z]	64[z]	63[z]	81[z]	82[z]	80[z]	...	...	...
Brazil[8]	16	...	4,870[z]	49[z]	86[*,z]	86[*,z]	86[*,z]	88[*,z]	87[*,z]	89[*,z]	...	...	...
British Virgin Islands[8]	...	...	0,9	50	89[*]	...	...	98[*]	...	...	...	...	...
Cayman Islands[9]	...	...	1[z]	48[z]	...	...	...	...	...	...	...	...	...
Chile	8	2	609	49	128	130	126	99	99	99	...	...	...
Colombia	16	13	...	...	...	...	...	...	...	...	...	...	...
Costa Rica	10	...	115	49	53	53	53	93	93	94	68	37	81
Cuba	6	...	357	49	98	98	99	97	96	98	...	48	89
Curaçao	...	...	...	...	...	...	...	...	...	...	...	...	...
Dominica	21	...	2	48	85	88	82	...	...	...	...	...	...
Dominican Republic	31	7	278	50	44	43	45	74	72	75	...	10	84
Ecuador	22	25	587	49	62	61	62	99	100	97	...	...	...
El Salvador	17	14	233	50	72	71	73	94	92	95	...	18	81
Grenada	12	...	4	47	91	94	88	98[z]	97[z]	98[z]	...	...	...
Guatemala	29	48	521	50	66	65	66	76	76	76	...	...	...
Guyana	39	12	28[y]	49[y]	94[y]	95[y]	93[y]	91[y]	91[y]	92[y]	...	47	86
Haiti	69	22	...	...	...	...	...	...	...	...	...	...	...
Honduras	20	23	238	50	47	47	48	96	95	97	...	...	...
Jamaica	16	6	138	51	105	102	108	96	92	100	88	55	89
Mexico	13	14	4,798	49	69	68	70	99	98	100	...	...	...
Montserrat[9]	...	...	0,1	52	...	...	...	...	...	...	...	...	...
Nicaragua	22	...	...	...	...	...	...	...	...	...	...	...	...
Panama	17	...	102[z]	49[z]	71[z]	71[z]	72[z]	84[z]	83[z]	84[z]	...	26	80
Paraguay	21	11	152[z]	49[z]	38[y]	38[y]	38[y]	78[y]	78[y]	78[y]	...	...	...
Peru	17	18	1,551	49	88	87	88	99	98	99	...	...	...
Saint Kitts and Nevis	11	...	2	48	94	97	92	99	100	98	...	...	...
Saint Lucia	14	3	4	51	65	63	67	80	79	81	93	68	91
Saint Martin	...	...	...	...	...	...	...	...	...	...	...	...	...
Saint Vincent and the Grenadines	18	...	3	50	69	68	70	85	85	84	...	...	...
Sint-Maarten[9]	...	...	1	48	...	...	...	...	...	...	...	...	...
Suriname	21	9	18	49	94	92	96	96	95	98	73	25	71
Trinidad and Tobago	20	...	1	49	...	...	...	...	...	...	...	...	...
Turks and Caicos Islands[9]	...	...	1	49	...	...	...	...	...	...	...	...	...
Uruguay	10	11	103[z]	49[z]	70[z]	70[z]	70[z]	96[z]	96[z]	96[z]	93	59	87
Venezuela, B.R.	15	13	1,288	49	73	73	73	90	90	90	...	...	...
Northern Africa and Western Asia													
Algeria	26	12	...	...	...	...	...	...	...	...	78	11	70
Bahrain	6	...	33	49	55	55	55	41	41	41	...	...	...
Egypt	24	22	1,177	48	30	31	30	...	...	...	...	...	...
Iraq	32	23	...	...	...	...	...	72	77	67	58	5	72
Israel	4	...	502	49	111	111	111	...	...	...	...	...	...
Jordan	18	8	110[y]	48[y]	32[y]	33[y]	31[y]	...	...	...	82	23	69
Kuwait[5]	9	6	82	49	...	...	...	79	79	78	...	...	...
Lebanon	8	...	172[z]	48[z]	84[z]	87[z]	82[z]	...	...	...	...	...	...
Libya	13	...	...	...	...	...	...	99	99	100	...	...	...
Morocco	28	15	746	44	60	65	53	51[y]	52[y]	50[y]	...	...	...
Oman	12	10	69	50	54	53	55	...	...	...	...	25	68
Palestine	21	7	127	49	51	50	51	97[z]	100[z]	95[z]	78	20	72
Qatar	8	...	38	49	58	58	58	77	75	79	88	40	83
Saudi Arabia	15	...	306	55	16	14	18	57	56	57	...	...	...
Sudan	70	38	755[z]	51[z]	34[z]	33[z]	35[z]	89	88	91	...	...	...
Syrian Arab Republic	13	28	87[z]	48[z]	6[z]	6[z]	6[z]	14	13	15	...	...	...
Tunisia	14	10	226	49	43	42	43	41[z]	42[z]	40[z]	71	18	76
Turkey	14	10	1,078[z]	48[z]	28[z]	28[z]	27[z]	73[z]	73[z]	72[z]	...	...	...
United Arab Emirates	7	...	166	49	92	92	92	79	82	76	...	...	...
Yemen	42	47	29[z]	46[z]	1[z]	1[z]	1[z]	4[z]	5[z]	4[z]	...	...	...
The Pacific													
Australia[9]	4	...	357	48	...	...	...	80[z]	80[z]	80[z]	...	...	...
Cook Islands[8]	8	...	0.5	50	78[*]	75[*]	81[*]	94[*]	88[*]	100[*]	...	...	...
Fiji	22	...	...	...	...	...	...	...	...	...	...	...	...

TABLE 4
(Continued)

Country or territory	CHILD MORTALITY[1] AND MALNUTRITION[2] Under-5 mortality rate (deaths per 1,000 live births) Total 2015	Under-5 moderate or severe stunting rate (%) Total 2009–2014[3]	PARTICIPATION IN PRE-PRIMARY EDUCATION Total enrolment in pre-primary education, School year ending in 2014 Total (000)	% F	Gross enrolment ratio (GER) in pre-primary education (%), School year ending in 2014 Total	Male	Female	Adjusted net enrolment ratio (ANER) one year before the official primary school entry age (%)[4], School year ending in 2014 Total	Male	Female	SCHOOL READINESS[5] Percentage of children under 5 experiencing positive and stimulating home learning environments (%)[6] 2009–2015[3] Total	Percentage of children under 5 living in households with three or more children's books 2009–2015[3] Total	Percentage of children under 5 who are developmentally on track in health, learning and psychosocial well-being (%)[7] 2009–2015[3] Total
Kiribati	56	…	…	…	…	…	…	…	…	…	…	…	…
Marshall Islands	36	…	…	…	…	…	…	…	…	…	…	…	…
Micronesia F.S.	35	…	…	…	…	…	…	…	…	…	…	…	…
Nauru[8]	35	…	0.9	48	90*	85*	96*	71*	62*	82*	…	…	…
New Zealand	6	…	116	49	92	91	93	93	92	94	…	…	…
Niue[8]	23	…	0.0	47	119*	113*	125*	…	…	…	…	…	…
Palau[8]	16	…	0.5	52	74*	71*	77*	91*	100*	81*	…	…	…
Papua New Guinea	57	50	…	…	…	…	…	…	…	…	…	…	…
Samoa	18	…	4	51	37	35	39	30	27	32	…	…	…
Solomon Islands	28	…	47	49	98	98	98	…	…	…	…	…	…
Tokelau	…	…											
Tonga	17	8	2	48	39	39	38	…	…	…	…	…	…
Tuvalu[8]	27	…	0.7	48	93*	93*	93*	…	…	…	…	…	…
Vanuatu	28	29	13^z	48^z	97^z	98^z	97^z	…	…	…	…	…	…
Southern Asia													
Afghanistan	91	41	…	…	…	…	…	…	…	…	…	…	…
Bangladesh	38	36	2,961^z	49^z	32^z	32^z	32^z	…	…	…	78	9	64
Bhutan	33	34	5	51	17	16	18	…	…	…	54	6	72
India	48	39	7,376^z	45^z	10^z	10^z	9^z	…	…	…	…	…	…
Iran, Islamic Republic of	16	7	543	49	42	43	42	38	39	37	…	…	…
Maldives[9]	9	20	23	49	…	…	…	…	…	…	…	…	…
Nepal	36	37	1,014	48	85	87	84	81	81	81	67	5	64
Pakistan	81	45	6,550	45	70	74	66	94	100	89	…	…	…
Sri Lanka	10	15	335^z	49^z	95^z	95^z	95^z	…	…	…	…	…	…
Sub-Saharan Africa													
Angola	157	…	…	…	…	…	…	…	…	…	…	1	61
Benin	100	34	129	50	21	20	21	60^y	61^y	59^y	…	…	…
Botswana	44	…	27^z	49^z	18^z	18^z	18^z	28^z	27^z	28^z	…	…	…
Burkina Faso	89	33	72	51	4	4	4	9	9	9	…	…	…
Burundi	82	58	67	50	7	7	7	22	22	23	…	…	…
Cabo Verde	25	…	22	50	70	70	70	83	82	84	…	…	…
Cameroon	88	33	467	50	34	34	35	48	49	48	62	4	51
Central African Republic	130	41	…	…	…	…	…	…	…	…	74	1	47
Chad	139	39	11^z	47^z	1^z	1^z	1^z	…	…	…	70	1	33
Comoros	74	32	15^z	50^z	23^z	22^z	24^z	76^z	74^z	78^z	…	…	…
Congo	45	25	54^y	49^y	14^y	14^y	14^y	23^y	22^y	25^y	56	1	49
Côte d'Ivoire	93	30	129	50	7	7	7	19	21	18	…	…	…
Democratic Rep. of the Congo	98	43	309	51	4	4	4	…	…	…	61	1	66
Djibouti	65	34	2	46	5^{+1}	5^{+1}	4^{+1}	…	…	…	…	…	…
Equatorial Guinea	94	26	42^y	50^y	68^y	68^y	68^y	68^y	67^y	70^y	…	…	…
Eritrea	47	50	46^z	49^z	15^z	15^z	15^z	16^z	16^z	16^z	…	…	…
Ethiopia	59	40	2,496	48	30	31	30	25^**,y	24^**,y	26^**,y	…	…	…
Gabon	51	18	…	…	…	…	…	…	…	…	…	…	…
Gambia	69	25	87	51	34	33	35	52	51	53	48	1	68
Ghana	62	19	1,767	50	121	119	122	99^**	98^**	100^**	40	6	74
Guinea	94	31	…	…	…	…	…	…	…	…	…	…	…
Guinea-Bissau	93	28	…	…	…	…	…	…	…	…	…	1	61
Kenya	49	26	3,020	49	74	75	73	…	…	…	…	…	…
Lesotho	90	33	48	51	31	30	32	34	33	34	…	…	…
Liberia	70	32	…	…	…	…	…	…	…	…	…	…	…
Madagascar	50	49	285	51	14	13	14	…	…	…	…	…	…
Malawi	64	42	…	…	…	…	…	…	…	…	29	1	60
Mali	115	…	92	50	4	4	4	44	46	42	…	0	62
Mauritania	85	22	11	56	3	3	4	…	…	…	55	…	58
Mauritius	14	…	30	50	102	101	104	94	94	94	…	…	…
Mozambique	79	43	…	…	…	…	…	…	…	…	…	…	…
Namibia	45	23	25^z	51^z	21^z	21^z	22^z	48^z	46^z	50^z	…	…	…
Niger	96	43	142	50	7	7	7	17^z	17^z	16^z	…	…	…
Nigeria	109	33	…	…	…	…	…	…	…	…	65	6	57
Rwanda	42	38	142^z	51^z	14^z	14^z	15^z	47^z	46^z	47^z	…	…	…
Sao Tome and Principe	47	…	9^{+1}	52	51	49	54	57	56	58	63	6	55
Senegal	47	19	199	52	15	14	16	18	17	19	…	…	…
Seychelles	14	8	3	49	93	93	93	96	98	93	…	…	…
Sierra Leone	120	38	54^z	52^z	10^z	9^z	10^z	24^z	24^z	25^z	54	2	45
Somalia	137	26	…	…	…	…	…	…	…	…	…	…	…
South Africa	41	…	823^z	50^z	76^z	77^z	76^z	…	…	…	…	…	…
South Sudan	93	31	…	…	…	…	…	…	…	…	…	…	…
Swaziland	61	26	…	…	…	…	…	…	…	…	50	4	62
Togo	78	28	97	51	15	15	15	75	74	75	62	2	55
Uganda	55	34	430^z	50^z	11^z	11^z	11^z	…	…	…	…	…	…
United Republic of Tanzania	49	35	1,026^z	50^z	32^z	32^z	33^z	46^z	43^z	49^z	…	…	…
Zambia	64	40	…	…	…	…	…	…	…	…	…	…	…
Zimbabwe	71	28	374^z	50^z	42^z	42^z	43^z	37^z	36^z	37^z	43	3	62

TABLE 4
(Continued)

Country or territory	CHILD MORTALITY[1] AND MALNUTRITION[2]		PARTICIPATION IN PRE-PRIMARY EDUCATION								SCHOOL READINESS[5]		
	Under-5 mortality rate (deaths per 1,000 live births)	Under-5 moderate or severe stunting rate (%)	Total enrolment in pre-primary education		Gross enrolment ratio (GER) in pre-primary education (%)			Adjusted net enrolment ratio (ANER) one year before the official primary school entry age (%)[4]			Percentage of children under 5 experiencing positive and stimulating home learning environments (%)[6]	Percentage of children under 5 living in households with three or more children's books	Percentage of children under 5 who are developmentally on track in health, learning and psychosocial well-being (%)[7]
	Total 2015	Total 2009-2014[3]	School year ending in 2014		School year ending in 2014			School year ending in 2014			2009-2015[3]	2009-2015[3]	2009-2015[3]
			Total (000)	% F	Total	Male	Female	Total	Male	Female	Total	Total	Total
	Weighted average	Median	Sum	% F	Weighted average			Weighted average			Median	Median	Median
World	43	24	155,000**	48**	44**	44**	44**	67**	67**	66**	...	...	...
Countries in transition	19	12	8,661	48	62	62	62	73	73	73	...	...	...
Developed countries	5	...	28,820	49	87	87	87	94	95	94	...	...	...
Developing countries	48	26	117,519**	48**	39**	39**	38**	64**	62**,z	62**,z	...	...	...
Caucasus and Central Asia	32	16	2,008**	49**	34**	34**	34**	49**	49**	50**	...	...	...
Eastern and South-eastern Asia	17	25	57,653	47	76	76	76	79**	...	...	...	...	...
Eastern Asia	10	9	43,974	46	83	82	83	...	...	...	...	...	...
South-eastern Asia	27	32	13,679	49	60	60	60	78	78	78	...	...	...
Europe and Northern America	6	23	31,685	49	85	85	85	93	94	93	...	...	...
Latin America and the Caribbean	18	...	19,989**	49**	73**	73**	73**	90**	89**	91**	...	...	...
Caribbean	...	...	1,494**	50**	76**	75**	77**	81**	80**	83**	...	...	...
Latin America	17	14	18,495**	49**	73**	72**	73**	91**	90**	91**	...	...	...
Northern Africa and Western Asia	29	12	6,500**	48**	29**	29**	29**	51**	51**	50**	...	...	...
Northern Africa	35	15	3,538	48	40	40	39	59**	60**	58**	...	...	...
Western Asia	22	10	2,962**	49**	22**	22**	22**	43**	43**	42**	...	...	...
Pacific	24	...	1,148**	48**	98**	98**	97**	76**	76**	76**	...	...	...
Southern Asia	51	36	18,810**	46**	18**	19**	18**	...	...	...	...	...	...
Sub-Saharan Africa	84	33	17,207**	50**	22**	21**	22**	41**,z	40**,z	42**,z	...	...	...
Conflict-affected countries	57	35	39,512**	48**	23**	23**	22**	58**,y	59**,y	58**,y	...	...	...
Countries with low income	76	35	9,277**	49**	17**	17**	17**	41**	41**	41**	...	...	...
Countries with middle income	42	19	106,272**	47**	42**	43**	42**	67**	65**,z	65**,z	...	...	...
Lower middle	53	28	42,487**	48**	26**	26**	26**	60**,y	60**,y	59**,y	...	...	...
Upper middle	20	11	63,784	47	73	73	73	76**	75**,z	77**,z	...	...	...
Countries with high income	7	...	39,451	49	83	83	83	91	91	91	...	...	...

Source: UIS database, except where noted. Enrolment ratios are based on the United Nations Population Division estimates, revision 2015 (United Nations, 2015), median variant.

Note: The country groupings by level of income are as defined by the World Bank but include only countries listed in the table. They are based on the list of countries by income group as revised in July 2015.

1. Under-5 mortality rates are the updated estimates generated by the UN Inter-agency Group for Child Mortality Estimation in September 2015. They are based on the median variant.

2. UNICEF, WHO and World Bank (2015).

3. Data are for the most recent year available during the period specified.

4. ANER one year before the official primary school entry age is the percentage of children at the intended age a year before entry into primary education who are enrolled in either pre-primary or primary education.

5. UNICEF-MICS 4 and 5, country reports.

6. Data refer to the MICS indicator "Adult support for learning", which is the percentage of children 36 to 59 months old with whom an adult has engaged in four or more of the following activities to promote learning and school readiness in the previous 3 days: (a) reading books to the child, (b) telling stories to the child, (c) singing songs to the child, (d) taking the child outside the home, (e) playing with the child, and (f) spending time with the child naming, counting or drawing things.

7. Data refer to the MICS indicator "Early Child Development Index", which is the percentage of children who are developmentally on track in at least three of the following domains: (a) literacy-numeracy, (b) physical development, (c)

social-emotional development, and (d) learning (ability to follow simple instructions, ability to occupy herself/himself independently).

8. National population data were used to calculate enrolment ratios due to inconsistencies in the United Nations population data or lack of United Nations population by age.

9. Enrolment ratios was not calculated due to inconsistencies in the United Nations population data or lack of United Nations population by age.

Data in bold are for the school year ending in 2015.

(z) Data are for the school year ending in 2013.

(y) Data are for the school year ending in 2012.

(*) National estimate.

(**) For country level data: UIS partial estimate; for regional and other country grouping sums and weighted averages: partial imputation due to incomplete country coverage (between 33% and 60% of population for the region or other country grouping).

(-) Magnitude nil or negligible

(.) The category is not applicable or does not exist.

(...) No data are available.

TABLE 5

SDG 4, Target 4.3 – Universal access to technical, vocational and tertiary education
By 2030, ensure equal access for all women and men to affordable quality technical, vocational and tertiary education, including university – part 1

Country or territory	PARTICIPATION IN TECHNICAL AND VOCATIONAL EDUCATION PROGRAMMES								
	Share of technical and vocational education in total enrolment (%) by level						Percentage of youth (15–24) enrolled in secondary technical and vocational education (%)		
	Total secondary education			Post-secondary non-tertiary education					
	School year ending in 2014			School year ending in 2014			School year ending in 2014		
	Total	Male	Female	Total	Male	Female	Total	Male	Female
Caucasus and Central Asia									
Armenia	11	12	10	.	.	.	3[y]	4[y]	3[y]
Azerbaijan[2]	20	18	22	100	100	100	11[*]	10[*]	11[*]
Georgia	5	5	5	100	100	100	2	2	2
Kazakhstan	**11**	**12**	**11**	**100**	**100**	**100**	**7**	**7**	**7**
Kyrgyzstan	10	11	9	100[z]	100[z]	100[z]	6	6	5
Tajikistan	1[z]	2[z]	0.3[z]	...	...	...	...	...	...
Turkmenistan	8	9	6	.	.	.	...	...	...
Uzbekistan	...	...	...	...	...	...	...	...	...
Eastern and South-eastern Asia									
Brunei Darussalam	11	12	11	.	.	.	7	8	6
Cambodia	...	...	...				...	...	...
China	22	23	21	38	42	32	...	...	...
Democratic People's Republic of Korea	...	...	...				...	...	...
Hong Kong, China	2	3	0.5	68	79	53	1[*]	1[*]	0[*]
Indonesia	19	22	15	.	.	.	10	12	8
Japan	12[z]	13[z]	10[z]	100[y]	100[y]	100[y]	6[y]	7[y]	5[y]
Lao People's Democratic Republic	1	1	2	100	100	100	0	0	0
Macao, China	4	5	4	.	.	.	2	2	1
Malaysia	11	13	9	100	100	100	6		
Mongolia	10	12	8	100	100	100	5	6	4
Myanmar	-	-	-	...	...	...	-	-	-
Philippines	[z]	[z]	[z]	100[z]	100[z]	100[z]	[z]	[z]	[z]
Republic of Korea	9[z]	10[z]	8[z]	[z]	[z]	[z]	5[z]	5[z]	5[z]
Singapore[3]	...	...	...	...	...	...	...	...	...
Thailand	16[z]	19[z]	13[z]	.	.	.	8[y]	9[y]	7[y]
Timor-Leste	5	5	4	.	.	.	2	3	2
Viet Nam	...	...	...	100	100	100	...	...	...
Europe and Northern America									
Albania	8	12	4	100	100	100	4	7	2
Andorra[3]	8	9	8	100	100	100	...	...	...
Austria	36	39	34	100	100	100	...	...	...
Belarus	13	16	10	100	100	100	7	9	5
Belgium	46	47	45	93	95	90	22	24	20
Bosnia and Herzegovina	39	42	36	.[y]	.[y]	.[y]	...	...	...
Bulgaria	32	36	28	100	100	100	15	18	12
Canada	4[z]	5[z]	4[z]	...	...	...	...	...	...
Croatia	40	43	38	.	.	.	25	27	23
Cyprus[2]	8	12	3	100	100	100	4[*]	6[*]	2[*]
Czech Republic	39	42	36	16	24	12	...	...	...
Denmark	24	26	21	.	.	.	12	15	10
Estonia	19[z]	25[z]	13[z]	100[z]	100[z]	100[z]	9[z]	12[z]	6[z]
Finland	47	47	46	100	100	100	22	23	20
France	19	20	17	51	40	57	14	16	12
Germany	19	22	15	91	88	93	...	...	...
Greece	18[z]	21[z]	15[z]	...	...	...	10[y]	12[y]	8[y]
Hungary	14	16	12	100	100	100	9	11	7
Iceland	22[y]	25[y]	18[y]	100[y]	100[y]	100[y]	12[y]	15[y]	9[y]
Ireland	16[y]	15[y]	17[y]	100[z]	100[z]	100[z]	8[y]	7[y]	8[y]
Italy	36[z]	42[z]	30[z]	100[z]	100[z]	100[z]	23[z]	28[z]	19[z]
Latvia	22	26	18	100	100	100	11	13	9
Liechtenstein[2]	35	41	29	.	.	.	26[*]	33[*]	19[*]
Lithuania	10	12	7	100	100	100	6	8	4
Luxembourg	32[z]	33[z]	31[z]	100[z]	100[z]	100[z]	22[z]	22[z]	21[z]
Malta	8	9	7	96	97	96	4	5	4
Monaco	12	14	10	44	46	42	...	...	...
Montenegro	**33**	**35**	**30**	.[y]	.[y]	.[y]	...	...	...
Netherlands	48[y]	50[y]	46[y]	100	100	100	25[y]	27[y]	24[y]
Norway	29	34	24	100	100	100	17	21	14
Poland	28[z]	34[z]	22[z]	100[z]	100[z]	100[z]	15[z]	19[z]	12[z]
Portugal	28	31	24	100	100	100	17	20	14
Republic of Moldova[2]	13	15	11	100	100	100	6[*]	6[*]	5[*]
Romania	29	32	25	100	100	100	21[z]	24[z]	18[z]
Russian Federation	16	19	13	100	100	100	...	...	...
San Marino[2]	22[y]	30[y]	14[y]	.[y]	.[y]	.[y]	...	...	...
Serbia[2]	37	39	36	100	100	100	25[*]	26[*]	24[*]
Slovakia	32	34	30	100	100	100	...	...	...
Slovenia	42	46	37	.	.	.	26	29	22
Spain	17	18	16	.	.	.	9	11	7
Sweden	27	28	26	72	70	74	14	15	12
Switzerland	37	41	33	-	-	-	23	26	19
The former Yugoslav Rep. of Macedonia	30[y]	32[y]	27[y]	.[y]	.[y]	.[y]	...	...	...
Ukraine	9	11	7	100[y]	100[y]	100[y]	4	6	3
United Kingdom	32	32	32	...	...	...	18	19	17
United States	.	.	.	100	100	100	.	.	.

TABLE 5
Part 1 (Continued)

	PARTICIPATION IN TECHNICAL AND VOCATIONAL EDUCATION PROGRAMMES								
	Share of technical and vocational education in total enrolment (%) by level						Percentage of youth (15–24) enrolled in secondary technical and vocational education (%)		
	Total secondary education			Post-secondary non-tertiary education					
	School year ending in 2014			School year ending in 2014			School year ending in 2014		
Country or territory	Total	Male	Female	Total	Male	Female	Total	Male	Female
Latin America and the Caribbean									
Anguilla	...	...	...	...	...	...	...	...	...
Antigua and Barbuda	4	5	3	53[y]	53[y]	52[y]	2	2	1
Argentina	.[z]	.[z]	.[z]	.[z]	.[z]	.[z]	.[z]	.[z]	.[z]
Aruba	13[y]	16[y]	9[y]	.	.	.	...	...	...
Bahamas	...	...	...	...	...	...	...	...	...
Barbados	.	.	.	66	72	60	.	.	.
Belize	3	3	3	.[z]	.[z]	.[z]	2	2	2
Bermuda	.	.	.	.	.	.	.	.	.
Bolivia, Plurinational States of	-[z]	-[z]	-[z]	.[z]	.[z]	.[z]	-[z]	-[z]	-[z]
Brazil[2]	4[z]	3[z]	4[z]	100[z]	100[z]	100[z]	2[*,z]	2[*,z]	2[*,z]
British Virgin Islands	0,9	1	1	...	...	...	0[*]	...	...
Cayman Islands	.[z]	.[z]	.[z]	.[y]	.[y]	.[y]	...	...	...
Chile	21	22	20	.	.	.	10	10	10
Colombia	7	7	8	.	.	.	4	4	4
Costa Rica	22	21	23	.	.	.	7	7	7
Cuba	24	29	19	100	100	100	14[z]	17[z]	11[z]
Curaçao	72[z]	76[z]	69[z]	100[z]	100[z]	100[z]	...	...	...
Dominica	...	...	...	-	-	-	...	...	...
Dominican Republic	5	4	6	.	.	.	2	2	3
Ecuador	32[z]	33[z]	32[z]	...	...	...	19[z]	19[z]	18[z]
El Salvador	18	17	19	.	.	.	9	9	9
Grenada	.	.	.	100	100	100	.	.	.
Guatemala	27	25	29	.	.	.	9	9	9
Guyana	5[y]	6[y]	4[y]	21[y]	28[y]	15[y]	...	...	...
Haiti	...	...	...						
Honduras	32	33	31	.	.	.	7	7	8
Jamaica	.	.	.	84	86	82	.	.	.
Mexico	17[y]	15[y]	18[y]	.	.	.	3[y]	3[y]	3[y]
Montserrat	.	.	.	...	...	...	.	.	.
Nicaragua	...	...	...	...	...	...	...	...	...
Panama	14[y]	15[y]	13[y]	...	...	...	8[y]	8[y]	7[y]
Paraguay	16[y]	16[y]	15[y]	.[y]	.[y]	.[y]	5[y]	5[y]	5[y]
Peru	1	1	2	.	.	.	0	0	0
Saint Kitts and Nevis	.	.	.	100	100	100	.	.	.
Saint Lucia	1,0	1	0,4	66	67	66	-[z]	-[z]	-[z]
Saint-Martin	...	...	...	...	...	...	...	...	...
Saint Vincent and the Grenadines	...	...	...	40[y]	58[y]	31[y]	...	...	...
Sint-Maarten	59	67	51	.	.	.	...	...	...
Suriname	29[z]	43[z]	18[z]	...	...	...	15[z]	19[z]	11[z]
Trinidad and Tobago	...	...	...	...	...	...	...	...	...
Turks and Caicos Islands[3]	.	.	.	...	...	...	...	...	...
Uruguay	23[z]	28[z]	19[z]	.[z]	.[z]	.[z]	9[z]	10[z]	7[z]
Venezuela, Bolivarian Republic of	5	5	5	.	.	.	2	2	2
Northern Africa and Western Asia									
Algeria	...	...	...	.	.	.	...	...	...
Bahrain	8	14	2	99	99	98	3	5	1
Egypt	21	23	18	18	22	12	10	12	9
Iraq	...	...	...	...	...	...	...	...	...
Israel	20	20	19	.	.	.	13	13	13
Jordan	...	...	...	.[y]	.[y]	.[y]	...	...	...
Kuwait	2[**]	3[**]	2[**]	100[z]	100[z]	100[z]	-[y]	-[y]	-[y]
Lebanon	15[z]	18[z]	11[z]	.[z]	.[z]	.[z]	5[**,y]	6[**,y]	4[**,y]
Libya	...	...	...	...	...	...	...	...	...
Morocco	6[y]	7[y]	5[y]	100	100	100	2[**,y]	...	2[**,y]
Oman[3]	0,02	0,04	-	.	.	.	-	-	-
Palestine	0,4	0,7	0,1	100	100	100	0	0	0
Qatar	0,7	1	-	.	.	.	...	...	...
Saudi Arabia	5[**]	8[**]	2[**]	.	.	.	2[**]	2[**]	1[**]
Sudan	1[z]	2[z]	1[z]	.[z]	.[z]	.[z]	...	...	...
Syrian Arab Republic	5[z]	6[z]	4[z]	86[z]	92[z]	77[z]	2[z]	2[z]	2[z]
Tunisia	6	...	...	100	...	...	...	...	...
Turkey	21[z]	23[z]	20[z]	.[z]	.[z]	.[z]	13[z]	14[z]	12[z]
United Arab Emirates	2	2	1	.	.	.	...	...	...
Yemen	0,7[z]	1[z]	0[z]	.[z]	.[z]	.[z]	0[**,y]	...	...
The Pacific									
Australia	33	37	30	100	100	100	11[z]	14[z]	8[z]
Cook Islands[2]	4[y]	6[y]	2[y]	.	.	.	3[*,y]	5[*,y]	2[*,y]
Fiji	1[y]	2[y]	1[y]	100[z]	100[z]	100[z]	1[y]	1[y]	0[y]
Kiribati	...	...	...	...	...	...	...	...	...
Marshall Islands	...	...	...	...	...	...	...	...	...
Micronesia (Federated States of)	...	...	...	...	...	...	...	...	...
Nauru							.	.	.
New Zealand	17	16	19	100[z]	100[z]	100[z]	6	7	6
Niue	...	...	...	.	.	.	...	...	...
Palau[2]				...	...	...	.	.	.
Papua New Guinea	8[y]	10[y]	5[y]	...	...	...	...	...	...

TABLE 5

Part 1 (Continued)

Country or territory	PARTICIPATION IN TECHNICAL AND VOCATIONAL EDUCATION PROGRAMMES								
	Share of technical and vocational education in total enrolment (%) by level						Percentage of youth (15–24) enrolled in secondary technical and vocational education (%)		
	Total secondary education			Post-secondary non-tertiary education					
	School year ending in 2014			School year ending in 2014			School year ending in 2014		
	Total	Male	Female	Total	Male	Female	Total	Male	Female
Samoa	.	.	.	.	.	.	.	.	.
Solomon Islands	.[y]	.[y]	.[y]	.[y]	.[y]	.[y]	.[y]	.[y]	.[y]
Tokelau	...	...	...	...	...	...	...	...	...
Tonga	3	6	1	...	...	...	2	4	1
Tuvalu	-	-	-	.	.	.	-[*]	-[*]	-[*]
Vanuatu	...	...	...	...	...	...	...	...	...
Southern Asia									
Afghanistan	1,0	1	0,2	93	94	92	0	1	0
Bangladesh	3[z]	4[z]	2[z]	95[z]	96[z]	86[z]	1[**,z]	1[**,z]	1[**,z]
Bhutan	2	2	1	100[z]	100[z]	100[z]	-	-	-
India	1[z]	2[z]	0,5[z]	100[z]	100[z]	100[z]	...	...	...
Iran, Islamic Republic of	15	19	11	100[y]	100[y]	100[y]	6	7	4
Maldives	...	...	...	...	...	...	-	-	-
Nepal	...	...	...	.	.	.	...	...	...
Pakistan	3	3	3	100	100	100	1	1	1
Sri Lanka	6[z]	6[z]	5[z]	100[z]	100[z]	100[z]	...	...	...
Sub-Saharan Africa									
Angola	...	...	...	...	...	...	...	...	...
Benin	3	3	3	...	...	...	1[z]	1[z]	1[z]
Botswana	5[z]	6[z]	4[z]	...	...	...	-[z]	-[z]	-[z]
Burkina Faso	3	3	3	100[z]	100[z]	100[z]	1[z]	1[z]	1[z]
Burundi	6	7	6	.	.	.	2	2	1
Cabo Verde	3	4	2	100	100	100	1	2	1
Cameroon	22	26	18	16	18	14	7	9	5
Central African Republic	3[y]	3[y]	3[y]	.[y]	.[y]	.[y]	0[y]	0[y]	0[y]
Chad	1[y]	1[y]	2[y]	...	...	...	...	...	...
Comoros	0,5[z]	1[z]	0,1[z]	...	...	...	-[z]	-[z]	-[z]
Congo	10[y]	10[y]	10[y]	...	...	...	...	...	...
Côte d'Ivoire	7	6	8	...	...	...	...	...	...
Democratic Rep. of the Congo	19	20	17	.	.	.	...	...	...
Djibouti	7	8	6	.[z]	.[z]	.[z]	...	...	...
Equatorial Guinea	...	...	...	...	...	...	...	...	...
Eritrea	1[z]	1[z]	1[z]	100[z]	100[z]	100[z]	0[z]	0[z]	0[z]
Ethiopia	4[y]	4[y]	5[y]	...	...	...	...	...	...
Gabon	...	...	...	...	...	...	...	...	...
Gambia	...	...	...	100[y]	100[y]	100[y]	1[**]	1[**]	0[**]
Ghana	2	3	1	...	...	...	1	1	1
Guinea	4	3	4	.	.	.	1	1	1
Guinea-Bissau	...	...	...	...	...	...	...	...	...
Kenya	...	...	...	81[y]	84[y]	76[y]	-[y]	-[y]	-[y]
Lesotho	2	2	2	100	100	100	-	-	-
Liberia	...	...	...	...	...	...	...	...	...
Madagascar	2	2	1	100	100	100	1	1	0
Malawi	.	.	.	100[y]	100[y]	100[y]	.	.	.
Mali	13	15	12	100	100	100	4	5	3
Mauritania	1	1	1	.	.	.	0	0	0
Mauritius	14	18	10	32	45	20	...	...	...
Mozambique	5	6	4	.	.	.	1	1	0
Namibia	...	...	...	...	...	...	...	...	...
Niger	8	6	12	100	100	100	1	1	1
Nigeria	...	...	...	...	...	...	...	...	...
Rwanda	15	17	13	100	100	100	...	...	...
Sao Tome and Principe	7	8	7	.[y]	.[y]	.[y]	-[y]	-[y]	-[y]
Senegal	...	...	...	...	...	...	...	...	...
Seychelles	4	6	2	87	87	86	2	3	1
Sierra Leone	...	...	...	...	...	...	...	...	...
Somalia	...	...	...	...	...	...	...	...	...
South Africa	7[**]	8[**]	7[**]	100[**]	100[**]	100[**]	3[z]	3[z]	3[z]
South Sudan	...	...	...	...	...	...	...	...	...
Swaziland	0,4[z]	0,6[z]	0,3[z]	100[z]	100[z]	100[z]	-[z]	-[z]	-[z]
Togo	...	...	...	...	...	...	...	...	...
Uganda	4[z]	5[z]	4[z]	.[z]	.[z]	.[z]	...	...	...
United Republic of Tanzania	12[z]	12[z]	12[z]	84[y]	83[y]	85[y]	...	...	...
Zambia	...	...	...	.[z]	.[z]	.[z]	...	...	...
Zimbabwe	.[z]	.[z]	.[z]	...	...	...	.[z]	.[z]	.[z]

TABLE 5

Part 1 (Continued)

Country or territory	PARTICIPATION IN TECHNICAL AND VOCATIONAL EDUCATION PROGRAMMES								
	Share of technical and vocational education in total enrolment (%) by level						Percentage of youth (15–24) enrolled in secondary technical and vocational education (%)		
	Total secondary education			Post-secondary non-tertiary education					
	School year ending in 2014			School year ending in 2014			School year ending in 2014		
	Total	Male	Female	Total	Male	Female	Total	Male	Female
	Weighted Average			Median			Median		
World	10.7**	11.6**	9.7**	95	96	92	3	4	2
Countries in transition	15.8	17.5	13.9	100	100	100	6	7	5
Developed countries	17.0	18.6	15.2	100	100	100	14	15	12
Developing countries	9.3**	10.1**	8.5**	.	.	.	1	1	1
Caucasus and Central Asia	14.0**	14.3**	13.7**	100	100	100	6	6	5
Eastern and South-eastern Asia	17.3	18.6	15.9	53	60	42	5	5	5
Eastern Asia	19.9	20.8	18.9	53	60	42	5	5	4
South-eastern Asia	11.7	13.9	9.6	50	50	50	4	...	...
Europe and Northern America	16.9	18.7	15.0	100	100	100	14	16	12
Latin America and the Caribbean	8.9**	8.4**	9.4**	.	.	.	2	2	2
Caribbean	8.7**	10.0**	7.5**	46	56	42	.	.	.
Latin America	8.9**	8.3**	9.4**	.	.	.	6	6	6
Northern Africa and Western Asia	12.8**	14.1**	11.3**	.	.	.	2	4	2
Northern Africa	13.3**	15.2**	11.4**	18	22	12	...	...	...
Western Asia	12.3**	13.3**	11.1**	.	.	.	1.9	2.5	1.0
Pacific	26.1	28.3	23.6	.	.	.	0.4	0.7	0.2
Southern Asia	2.1**	2.9**	1.3**	100	100	100	0.7	0.9	0.3
Sub-Saharan Africa	6.5**	7.2**	5.7**	82	84	81	0.6	0.7	0.4
Conflict-affected countries	5.7**	6.8**	4.6**	.	.	.	1.2	...	...
Countries with low income	5.8**	6.3**	5.2**	93	94	92	...	...	...
Countries with middle income	10.0**	10.9**	9.1**	21	25	15	2	3	2
Lower middle	4.8**	5.7**	3.9**	19	25	15	1.0	1.2	0.9
Upper middle	16.7	17.6	15.7	32	45	20	5	5	4
Countries with high income	14.9	16.5	13.2	66	70	57	9	10	7

TABLE 5

SDG 4, Target 4.3 – Universal access to technical, vocational and tertiary education
By 2030, ensure equal access for all women and men to affordable quality technical, vocational and tertiary education, including university – part 2

Country or territory	Transition from upper secondary to tertiary education (ISCED levels 5, 6 and 7 combined) (%) School year ending in 2014			Gross intake rate (GIR) in tertiary education (%) School year ending in 2014			Total students enrolled in tertiary education School year ending in 2014		Gross enrolment ratio (GER) in tertiary education (%) School year ending in 2014			Participation rate of adults (25–64)[1] in formal or non-formal education and training in the last 12 months Most recent survey year 2011		
	Total	Male	Female	Total	Male	Female	Total (000)	F %	Total	Male	Female	Total	Male	Female
Caucasus and Central Asia														
Armenia	...	...	...	...	...	...	113	55	44	40	48	...	...	...
Azerbaijan[2]	...	...	...	...	...	...	195	52	23*	22*	25*	...	...	...
Georgia	...	...	...	...	...	...	121	55	39	35	44	...	...	...
Kazakhstan	...	...	...	...	...	...	**658**	**55**	**46**	**40**	**52**	...	...	...
Kyrgyzstan	...	...	...	...	...	...	268	56	46	40	52	...	...	...
Tajikistan	...	...	...	...	...	...	**225**	**39**	**26**	**32**	**21**	...	...	...
Turkmenistan	...	...	...	...	...	...	44	39	8	10	6	...	...	...
Uzbekistan	...	...	...	...	...	...	...	...	...	...	...	...	...	...
Eastern and South-eastern Asia														
Brunei Darussalam							11	61	32	24	40	...	...	...
Cambodia	...	...	...	...	...	...						...	...	...
China	...	...	...	...	...	...	41,924	51	39	37	43	...	...	...
DPR Korea	...	...	...				...	...				...	...	...
Hong Kong, China							305	52	69	64	74	...	...	...
Indonesia	44	39	49	30	29	32	6,463	52	31	29	33			
Japan	85	83	88				3,863ᶻ	47ᶻ	62ᶻ	65ᶻ	60ᶻ			
Lao People's Democratic Republic	...	...	...	...	...	...	132	48	17	18	17			
Macao, China	...	...	...				30	56	69	60	79			
Malaysia	41	37	43	35	...	...	860	57	30					
Mongolia				84	69	99	175	58	64	53	76	...	...	...
Myanmar	...	...	...				634ʸ	55ʸ	14ʸ	12ʸ	15ʸ	...	...	...
Philippines	...	...	...				3,563	55	36	31	40	...	...	...
Republic of Korea	...	...	...	...	...	...	3,342	40ᶻ	95ᶻ	108ᶻ	81ᶻ	...	...	...
Singapore[3]	...	...	...				255ᶻ	50ᶻ				...	...	...
Thailand	...	...	...	...	...	...	2,433	57	53	45	60	...	...	...
Timor-Leste	...	...	...				...	...	...	...	...			
Viet Nam	...	...	...				2,692	50	30	30	31			
Europe and Northern America														
Albania	99	96	102	64	55	72	174	57	63	52	74	...	...	...
Andorra[3]	29	24	33	...	...	...	0.5	57	...	...	...	...	...	...
Austria	75	67	82	75	68	82	421	53	80	73	88	48	49	48
Belarus	78ᶻ	63ᶻ	98ᶻ	90ᶻ	80ᶻ	101ᶻ	518	56	89	76	102	...	...	...
Belgium	94ᶻ	85ᶻ	103ᶻ	...	...	...	496	56	73	64	83	38	39	37
Bosnia and Herzegovina	...	...	...	...	...	...	112	56	48	41	55	...	...	...
Bulgaria	105	98	111	81	76	86	283	54	71	63	79	26	28	25
Canada	...	...	...	...	...	...	...	...	...	...	...	...	...	...
Croatia	...	...	...	...	...	...	166	57	70	59	81	...	...	...
Cyprus[2]	...	...	...	...	...	...	34	57	53*	44*	63*	42	43	42
Czech Republic	125	115	134	77	63	92	419	57	66	55	77	37	37	37
Denmark	92	89	94	87	78	97	301	57	82	68	95	59	55	62
Estonia	...	...	...	...	...	...	65ᶻ	58ᶻ	73ᶻ	59ᶻ	88ᶻ	50	46	53
Finland	40ᶻ	39ᶻ	40ᶻ	54ᶻ	48ᶻ	61ᶻ	306	54	89	81	97	56	49	63
France	...	...	...	...	...	...	2,389	55	64	58	71	51	50	51
Germany	78	75	82	67	66	69	2,912	47	65	68	63	50	53	51
Greece	...	...	...	...	...	...	659ᶻ	49ᶻ	110ᶻ	110ᶻ	110ᶻ	12	10	13
Hungary	65	62	68	48	41	55	329	55	53	47	60	41	43	39
Iceland	...	...	...	...	...	...	19ʸ	62ʸ	82ʸ	61ʸ	105ʸ	...	...	...
Ireland	...	...	...	...	...	...	199ᶻ	50ᶻ	73ᶻ	71ᶻ	75ᶻ	24	25	24
Italy	...	...	...	47ᶻ	40ᶻ	54ᶻ	1,873ᶻ	57ᶻ	63ᶻ	53ᶻ	74ᶻ	36	37	34
Latvia	...	...	...	...	...	...	90	58	67	55	79	32	27	37
Liechtenstein[2]	...	...	...	...	...	...	0.8	32	37*	51*	24*	...	...	...
Lithuania	...	...	...	78	70	87	148	58	69	56	82	29	23	33
Luxembourg	68ᶻ	72ᶻ	66ᶻ	37ᶻ	34ᶻ	41ᶻ	6ʸ	52ʸ	19ʸ	18ʸ	21ʸ	70	72	69
Malta	...	...	...	67	65	68	13	55	45	42	48	36	38	34
Monaco	...	...	...				...	...	...	...	...	...	...	...
Montenegro	...	...	...				...	...	...	...	...	...	...	...
Netherlands	...	...	...				794ʸ	51ʸ	79ʸ	75ʸ	82ʸ	59	63	56
Norway	133	144	125	81	72	90	264	58	77	63	91	60	59	61
Poland	102	99	104	...	...	...	1,903ᶻ	60ᶻ	71ᶻ	56ᶻ	87ᶻ	24	23	25
Portugal	67	59	75	66	57	75	362	54	66	61	70	44	44	45
Republic of Moldova[2]	...	...	...	...	...	...	122ᶻ	55ᶻ	41*·ᶻ	36*·ᶻ	47*·ᶻ	8	8	8
Romania	110ᶻ	121ᶻ	102ᶻ	60ᶻ	55ᶻ	66ᶻ	579	54	53	48	59	...	...	...
Russian Federation	...	...	...	90ᶻ	...	...	6,996	53	79	72	86	...	...	...
San Marino[3]	...	...	...				0.9ʸ	56ʸ	60*·ʸ	50*·ʸ	70*·ʸ	...	...	...
Serbia[2]	...	...	...				243	55	58*	51*	66*	17	17	16
Slovakia	91ᶻ	83ᶻ	97ᶻ	64	53	75	198	60	53	42	65	42	41	42
Slovenia	...	...	...	79ᶻ	72ᶻ	87ᶻ	91	58	83	68	98	36	35	38
Spain	99	100	98	79	74	85	1,982	53	89	82	97	38	39	37
Sweden	76ᶻ	64ᶻ	88ᶻ	64	53	76	429	59	62	49	76	72	69	74
Switzerland	76ᶻ	79ᶻ	74ᶻ	80ᶻ	80ᶻ	80ᶻ	290	50	57	57	58	66	65	66
TFYR Macedonia	...	...	...				61ᶻ	55ᶻ	39ᶻ	35ᶻ	44ᶻ	...	...	...
Ukraine	...	...	...				2,146	52	82	77	88	...	...	...
United Kingdom	...	...	...	64	56	72	2,353	56	56	49	64	36	34	38
United States	65	63	67	52	49	56	19,700	56	87	73	101	...	...	...

TABLE 5
Part 2 (Continued)

Country or territory	ACCESS, PARTICIPATION IN TERTIARY EDUCATION											PARTICIPATION IN EDUCATION AND TRAINING		
	Transition from upper secondary to tertiary education (ISCED levels 5, 6 and 7 combined) (%)			Gross intake rate (GIR) in tertiary education (%)			Total students enrolled in tertiary education		Gross enrolment ratio (GER) in tertiary education (%)			Participation rate of adults (25–64)[1] in formal or non-formal education and training in the last 12 months		
	School year ending in 2014			School year ending in 2014			School year ending in 2014		School year ending in 2014			Most recent survey year 2011		
	Total	Male	Female	Total	Male	Female	Total (000)	F %	Total	Male	Female	Total	Male	Female
Latin America and the Caribbean														
Anguilla	...	...	...	...	...	...	2[y]	69[y]	23[y]	15[y]	31[y]	...	...	...
Antigua and Barbuda	...	...	...	...	...	...	...	...	...	...	...	...	...	...
Argentina	103[z]	105[z]	101[z]	61[z]	52[z]	70[z]	2,768[z]	61[z]	80[z]	62[z]	99[z]	...	...	...
Aruba	...	...	...	...	...	...	1	68	17	10	24	...	...	...
Bahamas	...	...	...	...	...	...	...	...	...	...	...	...	...	...
Barbados	...	...	...	...	...	...	...	...	...	...	...	...	...	...
Belize	...	...	...	...	...	...	8[z]	62[z]	24[z]	18[z]	30[z]	...	...	...
Bermuda	...	...	...	...	...	...	1	65	27	19	36	...	...	...
Bolivia, Plurinational States of	...	...	...	...	...	...	...	...	...	...	...	...	...	...
Brazil[2]	...	...	...	...	...	...	7,541[z]	57[z]	46[*,z]	40[*,z]	53[*,z]	...	...	...
British Virgin Islands	...	...	...	...	...	...	...	...	...	...	...	...	...	...
Cayman Islands	...	...	...	...	...	...	...	...	...	...	...	...	...	...
Chile	101	98	103	90	84	96	1,205	52	87	81	92	...	...	...
Colombia	55	59	52	...	...	...	2,138	53	51	48	55	...	...	...
Costa Rica	...	...	...	...	...	...	217	54	53	48	59	...	...	...
Cuba	39	34	43	22	17	28	302	59	41	32	51	...	...	...
Curaçao	...	...	...	...	...	...	2[z]	70[z]	20[z]	12[z]	28[z]	...	...	...
Dominica	...	...	...	...	...	...	...	...	...	...	...	...	...	...
Dominican Republic	...	...	...	...	...	...	456	61	48	36	59	...	...	...
Ecuador	...	...	...	...	...	...	586[z]	...	40[z]			...	...	...
El Salvador	33	31	36	21	20	22	176	53	29	28	30	...	...	...
Grenada	...	...	...	...	...	...	...	...	...	...	...	...	...	...
Guatemala	...	...	...	...	...	...	294[z]	51[z]	18[z]	18[z]	19[z]	...	...	...
Guyana	...	...	...	...	...	...	9[y]	67[y]	12[y]	8[y]	17[y]	...	...	...
Haiti	...	...	...	...	...	...	...	...	...	...	...	...	...	...
Honduras	...	...	...	17[z]	15[z]	19[z]	186	57	21	18	24	...	...	...
Jamaica	...	...	...	...	...	...	74[z]	69[z]	28[z]	17[z]	39[z]	...	...	...
Mexico	...	...	...	...	...	...	3,419	49	30	30	30	...	...	...
Montserrat	...	...	...	...	...	...	...	...	...	...	...	...	...	...
Nicaragua	...	...	...	...	...	...	...	...	...	...	...	...	...	...
Panama	...	...	...	...	...	...	124[z]	59[z]	39[z]	31[z]	47[z]	...	...	...
Paraguay	...	...	...	...	...	...	...	...	...	...	...	...	...	...
Peru	...	...	...	...	...	...	...	...	...	...	...	...	...	...
Saint Kitts and Nevis	...	...	...	...	...	...	3	50	79	78	80	...	...	...
Saint Lucia	...	...	...	...	...	...	3	67	17	11	23	...	...	...
Saint-Martin	...	...	...	...	...	...	...	...	...	...	...	...	...	...
Saint Vincent and the Grenadines	...	...	...	...	...	...	...	...	...	...	...	...	...	...
Sint-Maarten	14	14	14	...	...	...	0.2	75	...	...	...	...	...	...
Suriname	...	...	...	...	...	...	...	...	...	...	...	...	...	...
Trinidad and Tobago	...	...	...	...	...	...	...	...	...	...	...	...	...	...
Turks and Caicos Islands[3]	...	...	...	...	...	...	0.3	...	...	...	...	...	...	...
Uruguay	...	...	...	...	...	...	...	...	...	...	...	...	...	...
Venezuela, Bolivarian Republic of	...	...	...	...	...	...	...	...	...	...	...	...	...	...
Northern Africa and Western Asia														
Algeria	109	131	98	34	26	42	1,245	60	35	27	42	...	...	...
Bahrain	...	...	...	54	41	70	38	60	37	24	57	...	...	...
Egypt	104	112	97	34	33	34	2,544	46	32	33	30	...	...	...
Iraq	...	...	...	...	...	...	...	...	...	...	...	...	...	...
Israel	...	...	...	...	...	...	377	56	66	57	76	...	...	...
Jordan	...	...	...	...	...	...	307[y]	53[y]	48[y]	44[y]	52[y]	...	...	...
Kuwait	...	...	...	...	...	...	72[z]	64[z]	27[z]	20[z]	33[z]	...	...	...
Lebanon	...	...	...	...	...	...	229	56	43	40	46	...	...	...
Libya	...	...	...	...	...	...	...	...	...	...	...	...	...	...
Morocco	...	...	...	...	...	...	774	48	25	25	24	...	...	...
Oman[3]	9	10	8	...	...	...	85	55	...	...	...	...	...	...
Palestine	91	87	95	58	48	69	214	60	44	35	54	...	...	...
Qatar	...	...	...	...	...	...	25	64	16	7	46	...	...	...
Saudi Arabia	110	110	111	78	85	72	1,497	49	61	62	60	...	...	...
Sudan	...	...	...	13[z]	12[z]	13[z]	640[z]	52[z]	17[z]	16[z]	18[z]	...	...	...
Syrian Arab Republic	...	...	...	...	...	...	630[z]	49[z]	33[z]	32[z]	34[z]	...	...	...
Tunisia	116	...	...	44	32	56	332	61	35	26	43	...	...	...
Turkey	138	147	130	...	...	...	4,976[z]	46[z]	79[z]	85[z]	73[z]	18	21	15
United Arab Emirates	87	87	87	...	...	...	143	55	22	15	35	...	...	...
Yemen	...	...	...	...	...	...	...	...	...	...	...	...	...	...
The Pacific														
Australia	...	...	...	...	...	...	1,390[z]	57[z]	87[z]	72[z]	102[z]	...	...	...
Cook Islands[2]	...	...	...	...	...	...	0.7	74	60[*]	29[*]	96[*]	...	...	...
Fiji	...	...	...	...	...	...	...	...	...	...	...	...	...	...
Kiribati	...	...	...	...	...	...	[y]	[y]	[y]	[y]	[y]	...	...	...
Marshall Islands	...	...	...	...	...	...	1[y]	49[y]	43[y]	45[y]	41[y]	...	...	...
Micronesia (Federated States of)	...	...	...	...	...	...	...	...	...	...	...	...	...	...
Nauru	...	...	...	...	...	...	...	...	...	...	...	...	...	...
New Zealand	...	...	...	...	...	...	261	57	81	68	94	...	...	...
Niue	...	...	...	...	...	...	...	...	...	...	...	...	...	...
Palau[2]	...	...	...	...	...	...	0.9[z]	58[z]	62[*,z]	49[*,z]	76[*,z]	...	...	...
Papua New Guinea	...	...	...	...	...	...	...	...	...	...	...	...	...	...

TABLE 5
Part 2 (Continued)

Country or territory	Transition from upper secondary to tertiary education (ISCED levels 5, 6 and 7 combined) (%) School year ending in 2014			Gross intake rate (GIR) in tertiary education (%) School year ending in 2014			Total students enrolled in tertiary education School year ending in 2014		Gross enrolment ratio (GER) in tertiary education (%) School year ending in 2014			Participation rate of adults (25–64)[1] in formal or non-formal education and training in the last 12 months Most recent survey year 2011		
	Total	Male	Female	Total	Male	Female	Total (000)	F %	Total	Male	Female	Total	Male	Female
Samoa	...	...	...	...	...	...	...	...	...	...	...	...	...	...
Solomon Islands	...	...	...	...	...	...	...	...	...	...	...	...	...	...
Tokelau	...	...	...	...	...	...	...	...	...	...	...	...	...	...
Tonga	...	...	...	...	...	...	...	...	...	...	...	...	...	...
Tuvalu	...	...	...	...	...	...	...	...	...	...	...	...	...	...
Vanuatu	...	...	...	...	...	...	...	...	...	...	...	...	...	...
Southern Asia														
Afghanistan	41	51	23	15	23	6	263	20	9	13	4	...	...	...
Bangladesh	...	...	...	...	...	...	2,068	42	13	15	11	...	...	...
Bhutan	32[z]	36[z]	28[z]	18[z]	20[z]	15[z]	9[z]	41[z]	11[z]	13[z]	9[z]	...	...	...
India	...	...	...	39[z]	40[z]	37[z]	28,175[z]	46[z]	24[z]	25[z]	23[z]	...	...	...
Iran, Islamic Republic of	...	...	...	69	73	65	4,685	47	66	68	64	...	...	...
Maldives	...	...	...	...	...	...	...	...	...	...	...	...	...	...
Nepal	...	...	...	...	...	...	459	...	16	...	...	...	...	...
Pakistan	...	...	...	...	...	...	1,932	50	10	10	11	...	...	...
Sri Lanka	57[z]	61[z]	54[z]	29	19	39	324	60	21	17	25	...	...	...
Sub-Saharan Africa														
Angola	...	...	...	...	...	...	219[z]	45[z]	10[z]	11[z]	9[z]	...	...	...
Benin	...	...	...	...	...	...	145[z]	27[z]	15[z]	22[z]	8[z]	...	...	...
Botswana	...	...	...	...	...	...	61	57	28	23	32	...	...	...
Burkina Faso	...	...	...	...	...	...	74[z]	32[z]	5[z]	6[z]	3[z]	...	...	...
Burundi	...	...	...	8[z]	13[z]	4[z]	45[z]	31[z]	4[z]	6[z]	3[z]	...	...	...
Cabo Verde	83	85	82	38	32	44	13	59	23	19	27	...	...	...
Cameroon	...	...	...	...	...	...	...	...	...	...	...	...	...	...
Central African Republic	...	...	...	...	...	...	13[y]	27[y]	3[y]	4[y]	1[y]	...	...	...
Chad	...	...	...	...	...	...	42**	16**	3**	6**	1**	...	...	...
Comoros	...	...	...	20[z]	...	...	6[z]	46[z]	9[z]	9[z]	8[z]	...	...	...
Congo	...	...	...	...	...	...	37[z]	43[z]	10[z]	11[z]	8[z]	...	...	...
Côte d'Ivoire	...	...	...	...	...	...	177	37	9	11	6	...	...	...
Democratic Rep. of the Congo	...	...	...	...	...	...	443[z]	31[z]	7[z]	9[z]	4[z]	...	...	...
Djibouti	...	...	...	...	...	...	...	...	...	...	...	...	...	...
Equatorial Guinea	...	...	...	...	...	...	...	...	...	...	...	...	...	...
Eritrea	...	...	...	5	5	4	13	33	3	3	2	...	...	...
Ethiopia	...	...	...	...	...	...	757	32	8	11	5	...	...	...
Gabon	...	...	...	...	...	...	...	...	...	...	...	...	...	...
Gambia	...	...	...	...	...	...	5[y]	41[y]	3[y]	4[y]	3[y]	...	...	...
Ghana	...	...	...	18	21	14	402	39	16	19	12	...	...	...
Guinea	...	...	...	17	23	11	118	30	11	15	7	...	...	...
Guinea-Bissau	...	...	...	...	...	...	...	...	...	...	...	...	...	...
Kenya	...	...	...	...	...	...	...	...	...	...	...	...	...	...
Lesotho	...	...	...	12	10	14	24	59	10	8	12	...	...	...
Liberia	...	...	...	...	...	...	44[y]	38[y]	12[y]	14[y]	9[y]	...	...	...
Madagascar	...	...	...	...	...	...	97[z]	49[z]	4[z]	4[z]	4[z]	...	...	...
Malawi	...	...	...	...	...	...	...	...	...	...	...	...	...	...
Mali	...	...	...	...	...	...	97[y]	29[y]	7[y]	10[y]	4[y]	...	...	...
Mauritania	...	...	...	**6**	**7**	**5**	**21**	**33**	**6**	**7**	**4**	...	...	...
Mauritius	...	...	...	...	...	...	40	55	39	35	43	...	...	...
Mozambique	...	...	...	...	...	...	157	42	6	7	5	...	...	...
Namibia	...	...	...	...	...	...	...	...	...	...	...	...	...	...
Niger	...	...	...	...	...	...	22[y]	28[y]	2[y]	3[y]	1[y]	...	...	...
Nigeria	...	...	...	...	...	...	...	...	...	...	...	...	...	...
Rwanda	...	...	...	...	...	...	77[z]	45[z]	8[z]	8[z]	7[z]	...	...	...
Sao Tome and Principe	...	...	...	...	...	...	2	50	13	13	14	...	...	...
Senegal	...	...	...	...	...	...	...	...	...	...	...	...	...	...
Seychelles	...	...	...	16	10	22	0.5	70	6	4	9	...	...	...
Sierra Leone	...	...	...	...	...	...	...	...	...	...	...	...	...	...
Somalia	...	...	...	...	...	...	...	...	...	...	...	...	...	...
South Africa	...	...	...	...	...	...	1,036[z]	58[z]	20[z]	16[z]	24[z]	...	...	...
South Sudan	...	...	...	...	...	...	...	...	...	...	...	...	...	...
Swaziland	...	...	...	...	...	...	8[z]	51[z]	5[z]	5[z]	5[z]	...	...	...
Togo	...	...	...	...	...	...	67	29	10	14	6	...	...	...
Uganda	...	...	...	...	...	...	...	...	...	...	...	...	...	...
United Republic of Tanzania	...	...	...	...	...	...	158[z]	35[z]	4[z]	5[z]	2[z]	...	...	...
Zambia	...	...	...	...	...	...	...	...	...	...	...	...	...	...
Zimbabwe	...	...	...	8[z]	9[z]	7[z]	94[z]	46[z]	6[z]	6[z]	5[z]	...	...	...

TABLE 5
Part 2 (Continued)

Country or territory	Transition from upper secondary to tertiary education (ISCED levels 5, 6 and 7 combined) (%) School year ending in 2014			Gross intake rate (GIR) in tertiary education (%) School year ending in 2014			Total students enrolled in tertiary education School year ending in 2014		Gross enrolment ratio (GER) in tertiary education (%) School year ending in 2014			Participation rate of adults (25–64)[1] in formal or non-formal education and training in the last 12 months Most recent survey year 2011		
	Total	Male	Female	Total	Male	Female	Total (000)	F %	Total	Male	Female	Total	Male	Female
	Median			Median			Sum	% F	Weighted Average			Median		
World	...	...	...	...	...	...	207,272**	51**	34**	33**	36**	...	...	...
Countries in transition	...	...	...	...	...	...	12,396	53	58	53	63	...	...	...
Developed countries	...	...	...	67	63	75	47,264	55	74	66	83	...	...	...
Developing countries	...	...	...	...	...	...	147,612**	50**	29**	28**	29**	...	...	...
Caucasus and Central Asia	...	...	...	...	...	...	1,956	50	24	24	25	...	...	...
Eastern and South-eastern Asia	...	...	...	20	18	25	67,351	51	39	37	41	...	...	...
Eastern Asia	...	...	...	...	...	...	50,250	50	42	40	44	...	...	...
South-eastern Asia	...	...	...	...	...	...	17,101	53	31	29	34	...	...	...
Europe and Northern America	...	...	...	67	...	...	51,870	55	75	66	85	39	40	39
Latin America and the Caribbean	...	...	...	...	...	...	23,845**	56**	44**	39**	50**	...	...	...
Caribbean	...	...	...	...	...	...	935**	59**	29**	23**	35**	...	...	...
Latin America	...	...	...	...	...	...	22,910**	56**	45**	40**	51**	...	...	...
Northern Africa and Western Asia	...	...	...	...	...	...	15,261**	49**	37**	38**	37**	...	...	...
Northern Africa	109	...	...	34	29	38	5,866	51	29	28	30	...	...	...
Western Asia	...	...	...	...	...	...	9,395**	47**	46**	47**	44**	...	...	...
Pacific	...	...	...	...	...	...	1,748	57	62**	52**	72**	...	...	...
Southern Asia	...	...	...	29	23	37	38,097**	46**	23**	24**	22**	...	...	...
Sub-Saharan Africa	...	...	...	...	...	...	7,145**	41**	8**	10**	7**	...	...	...
Conflict-affected countries	...	...	...	...	...	...	70,521**	48**	26**	26**	26**	...	...	...
Countries with low income	...	...	...	...	...	...	4,460**	35**	8**	10**	5**	...	...	...
Countries with middle income	...	...	...	...	...	...	137,371**	50**	30**	29**	31**	...	...	...
Lower middle	...	...	...	...	...	...	58,642**	48**	22**	22**	22**	...	...	...
Upper middle	...	...	...	...	...	...	78,729	52	41	38	44	...	...	...
Countries with high income	...	...	...	...	...	...	65,441	54	74	66	83	...	...	...

Source: UIS database, except where noted. GIR and GER are based on the United Nations Population Division estimates, revision 2015 (United Nations, 2015), median variant.

Note: The country groupings by level of income are as defined by the World Bank but include only countries listed in the table. They are based on the list of countries by income group as revised in July 2015.

1. Data are from 2011 Eurostat Adult Education Survey, which focuses on people aged 25 to 64 living in private households.

2. National population data were used to calculate GIR and GER due to inconsistencies in the United Nations population data or lack of United Nations population by age.

3. GIR and GER were not calculated due to inconsistencies in the United Nations population data or lack of United Nations population by age.

Data in bold are for the school year ending in 2015.

(z) Data are for the school year ending in 2013.

(y) Data are for the school year ending in 2012.

(*) National estimate.

(**) For country level data: UIS partial estimate; for regional and other country grouping sums and weighted averages: partial imputation due to incomplete country coverage (between 33% and 60% of population for the region or other country grouping).

(-) Magnitude nil or negligible

(.) The category is not applicable or does not exist.

(...) No data are available.

TABLE 6

SDG 4, Target 4.4 – Youth and adult skills for employment, decent jobs and entrepreneurship

By 2030, substantially increase the number of youth and adults who have relevant skills, including technical and vocational skills, for employment, decent jobs and entrepreneurship

Country or territory	ICT SKILLS ACQUISITION — Percentage of adults (15 and over) with ICT skills by type of skills (%)[1]			ADULT EDUCATIONAL ATTAINMENT — Percentage of adults (25 and over) (%) who have attained at least:											
	Sending email with attached files	Using basic arithmetic formulas in a spreadsheet	Finding, downloading, installing and configuring software	Primary education (ISCED level 1 to 8)			Lower secondary education (ISCED level 2 to 8)			Upper secondary education (ISCED level 3 to 8)			Short-cycle tertiary education (ISCED level 5 to 8)		
	2014	2014	2014	2009–2015[2]			2009–2015[2]			2009–2015[2]			2009–2015[2]		
	Total	Total	Total	Total	Male	Female	Total	Male	Female	Total	Male	Female	Total	Male	Female
Caucasus and Central Asia															
Armenia	...	...	...	99	100	99	97	97	96	90	90	90	44	42	45
Azerbaijan	...	...	...	99	99	98	96	98	94	89	92	85	25	27	24
Georgia	...	...	...	99	99	99	97	97	96	92	93	91	31	31	31
Kazakhstan	48	17	19	...	...	...	...	...	...	...	...	...	...	...	...
Kyrgyzstan	...	...	...	98	99	97	96	97	95	88	90	87	18	16	19
Tajikistan	...	...	...	...	...	...	...	...	...	...	...	...	...	...	...
Turkmenistan	...	...	...	...	...	...	...	...	...	...	...	...	...	...	...
Uzbekistan	...	...	...	100	100	100	100	100	100	92	93	90	.	.	.
Eastern and South-eastern Asia															
Brunei Darussalam	...	...	...	...	...	...	...	...	...	...	...	...	...	...	...
Cambodia	...	...	...	36	48	25	16	22	10	6	10	3	...	...	...
China	...	...	...	...	...	...	65	72	59	22	25	19	9	10	8
DPR Korea	...	...	...	...	...	...	...	...	...	...	...	...	...	...	...
Hong Kong, China	...	...	...	95	93	97	77	75	81	61	60	63	21	18	23
Indonesia	...	...	...	77	81	72	47	52	43	31	35	27	9	9	8
Japan	...	...	...	100	100	100	...	...	...	81	82	79	35	37	32
Lao PDR	...	...	...	...	...	...	...	...	...	...	...	...	...	...	...
Macao, China	...	...	...	88	90	85	69	71	66	45	47	43	17	18	17
Malaysia	...	...	...	91	94	88	68	71	65	51	52	50	...	...	...
Mongolia	...	...	...	95	95	96	85	84	85	68	64	71	24	20	27
Myanmar	...	...	...	...	...	...	...	...	...	...	...	...	...	...	...
Philippines	...	...	...	84	82	86	70	69	71	58	57	60	27	25	28
Republic of Korea	...	...	...	94	98	91	83	89	77	73	80	66	35	41	30
Singapore	55	24	23	85	88	82	79	82	76	70	72	67	42	46	39
Thailand	...	...	...	61	65	58	41	44	39	29	31	28	17	16	17
Timor-Leste	...	...	...	...	...	...	...	...	...	...	...	...	...	...	...
Viet Nam	...	...	...	...	...	...	65	71	59	26	30	21	7	8	6
Europe and Northern America															
Albania	...	...	...	96	97	94	87	89	85	45	46	44	13	13	12
Andorra	...	...	...	97	97	96	73	74	72	48	48	48	21	21	22
Austria	71	49	38	...	...	...	99	99	99	78	85	72	26	30	23
Belarus	...	...	...	99	100	99	92	95	89	85	88	82	52	48	54
Belgium	72	43	21	94	95	93	82	85	80	64	66	62	32	31	32
Bosnia and Herzegovina	...	...	...	78	87	69	...	...	...	60	73	48	11	13	10
Bulgaria	42	27	8	...	...	...	94	96	93	74	75	73	24	20	28
Canada	...	...	...	...	...	...	...	...	...	83	83	83	48	45	51
Croatia	45	37	...	97	99	95	89	94	85	71	79	63	18	18	18
Cyprus	49	37	15	94	96	92	79	81	77	69	71	68	35	34	36
Czech Republic	70	43	...	100	100	100	100	100	100	90	94	85	19	20	18
Denmark	83	58	38	100	100	100	91	91	92	77	77	76	33	37	29
Estonia	65	52	33	...	...	...	...	...	...	90	87	92	37	28	45
Finland	78	63	57	...	...	...	...	...	...	73	72	73	34	30	37
France	72	52	37	98	98	97	83	86	80	69	72	65	29	28	29
Germany	69	48	37	100	100	100	97	97	97	83	88	78	25	30	20
Greece	47	39	19	95	97	93	68	72	64	56	58	55	23	24	22
Hungary	69	34	12	100	100	99	97	98	96	74	79	70	21	20	22
Iceland	84	69	...	...	...	...	...	...	...	...	...	...	...	...	...
Ireland	64	41	...	...	...	...	83	82	85	66	64	69	32	29	34
Italy	55	36	17	94	96	93	76	81	71	47	48	46	13	12	13
Latvia	59	47	...	100	100	100	99	99	99	87	85	90	29	22	34
Liechtenstein	...	...	...	...	...	...	...	...	...	...	...	...	...	...	...
Lithuania	57	49	23	99	99	98	93	96	91	83	86	81	31	28	34
Luxembourg	79	63	43	...	...	...	...	...	...	79	83	76	43	46	40
Malta	55	43	17	98	99	98	77	81	73	36	37	34	16	17	16
Monaco	...	...	...	...	...	...	...	...	...	...	...	...	...	...	...
Montenegro	...	...	...	97	99	96	89	95	84	73	80	65	20	21	18
Netherlands	84	48	39	98	99	98	89	91	87	69	74	65	30	33	28
Norway	81	65	50	100	100	100	99	99	99	77	78	76	36	34	38
Poland	50	36	25	99	99	98	84	87	81	83	86	81	24	21	26
Portugal	53	47	...	90	94	87	51	52	51	34	32	36	.	.	.
Republic of Moldova	...	...	...	99	99	99	96	97	95	75	77	73	34	29	37
Romania	43	16	4	99	99	98	89	92	86	63	69	58	14	14	13
Russian Federation	...	20	3	99	100	99	94	95	92	85	86	83	62	60	64
San Marino	...	...	...	...	...	...	...	...	...	...	...	...	...	...	...
Serbia	...	...	...	94	97	91	87	92	82	69	75	62	19	19	19
Slovakia	73	50	11	100	100	100	99	100	99	85	90	81	18	18	19
Slovenia	58	48	26	100	100	100	97	98	96	80	85	75	25	23	28
Spain	60	42	28	90	92	88	74	77	71	47	48	47	29	29	29
Sweden	79	57	...	100	100	100	89	90	89	74	75	74	31	27	35
Switzerland	74	...	...	...	...	...	97	98	96	85	89	81	36	43	28
TFYR Macedonia	46	29	6	...	...	...	...	...	...	...	...	...	...	...	...

TABLE 6

(Continued)

	ICT SKILLS ACQUISITION			ADULT EDUCATIONAL ATTAINMENT											
	Percentage of adults (15 and over) with ICT skills by type of skills (%)[1]			Percentage of adults (25 and over) (%) who have attained at least:											
	Sending email with attached files	Using basic arithmetic formulas in a spreadsheet	Finding, downloading, installing and configuring software	Primary education (ISCED level 1 to 8)			Lower secondary education (ISCED level 2 to 8)			Upper secondary education (ISCED level 3 to 8)			Short-cycle tertiary education (ISCED level 5 to 8)		
	2014	2014	2014	2009–2015[2]			2009–2015[2]			2009–2015[2]			2009–2015[2]		
Country or territory	Total	Total	Total	Total	Male	Female	Total	Male	Female	Total	Male	Female	Total	Male	Female
Ukraine	...	...	...	...	...	...	...	...	...	...	...	...	...	...	...
United Kingdom	78	53	...	100	100	100	100	100	100	75	76	73	39	38	40
United States	...	...	...	99	99	99	95	95	95	88	88	89	42	41	43
Latin America and the Caribbean															
Anguilla	...	...	...	...	...	...	...	...	...	...	...	...	...	...	...
Antigua and Barbuda	...	...	...	...	...	...	...	...	...	...	...	...	...	...	...
Argentina	...	...	...	...	...	...	...	...	...	...	...	...	...	...	...
Aruba	...	...	...	...	...	...	...	...	...	...	...	...	...	...	...
Bahamas	...	...	...	95	95	95	89	89	89	82	81	82	23	18	27
Barbados	...	...	...	...	...	...	...	...	...	...	...	...	...	...	...
Belize	...	...	...	100	100	100	84	84	84	37	36	37	6	6	6
Bermuda	...	...	...	...	...	...	...	...	...	77	73	80	37	33	41
Bolivia, Plurinational States of	...	...	...	59	64	53	52	57	47	43	47	39	24	25	23
Brazil	25	15	19	76	75	77	56	54	57	42	40	44	13	11	14
British Virgin Islands	...	...	...	...	...	...	...	...	...	...	...	...	...	...	...
Cayman Islands	...	...	...	100	100	100	95	95	94	88	89	88	41	38	44
Chile	...	...	...	85	86	84	76	77	74	54	55	53	18	18	18
Colombia	...	...	...	75	75	76	49	49	50	45	44	45	...	...	...
Costa Rica	...	...	...	82	83	81	55	54	55	40	40	41	23	23	24
Cuba	...	...	...	91	92	90	81	83	79	57	58	57	15	13	17
Curaçao	...	...	...	...	...	...	...	...	...	...	...	...	...	...	...
Dominica	...	...	...	...	...	...	...	...	...	...	...	...	...	...	...
Dominican Republic	...	...	...	67	66	67	56	55	57	34	31	37	12	10	14
Ecuador	...	...	...	81	82	80	49	49	48	39	39	38	...	...	...
El Salvador	...	...	...	56	61	53	41	45	38	27	29	25	10	11	10
Grenada	...	...	...	...	...	...	...	...	...	...	...	...	...	...	...
Guatemala	...	...	...	62	62	61	37	36	37	27	26	27	9	10	7
Guyana	...	...	...	...	...	...	...	...	...	...	...	...	...	...	...
Haiti	...	...	...	...	...	...	...	...	...	...	...	...	...	...	...
Honduras	...	...	...	59	58	59	32	31	33	23	21	24	10	10	10
Jamaica	...	...	...	99	99	99	61	57	65	...	...	...	...	...	...
Mexico	...	...	...	79	80	78	57	59	56	32	33	31	14	16	13
Montserrat	...	...	...	...	...	...	...	...	...	...	...	...	...	...	...
Nicaragua	...	...	...	...	...	...	...	...	...	...	...	...	...	...	...
Panama	...	...	...	83	83	82	61	60	63	43	40	46	21	18	24
Paraguay	...	...	...	73	75	72	47	47	46	37	36	37	14	12	15
Peru	...	...	...	80	85	74	62	67	56	55	60	51	21	21	21
Saint Kitts and Nevis	...	...	...	...	...	...	...	...	...	...	...	...	...	...	...
Saint Lucia	...	...	...	...	...	...	46	43	49	40	38	43	10	8	12
Saint Martin	...	...	...	...	...	...	...	...	...	...	...	...	...	...	...
Saint Vincent/Grenadines	...	...	...	...	...	...	...	...	...	...	...	...	...	...	...
Sint Maarten	...	...	...	...	...	...	...	...	...	...	...	...	...	...	...
Suriname	...	...	...	90	93	88	62	63	61	25	23	26	.	...	...
Trinidad and Tobago	...	...	...	95	96	93	60	60	60	57	57	57	10	9	10
Turks and Caicos Islands	...	...	...	...	...	...	...	...	...	...	...	...	...	...	...
Uruguay	...	...	...	89	89	89	53	52	55	28	25	32	12	10	14
Venezuela, B.R.	...	...	...	...	...	...	65	63	68	...	...	...	25	21	29
Northern Africa and Western Asia															
Algeria	...	...	...	...	...	...	...	...	...	...	...	...	...	...	...
Bahrain	...	...	...	...	...	...	...	...	...	...	...	...	...	...	...
Egypt	4	2	1	...	...	...	...	...	...	...	...	...	...	...	...
Iraq	...	...	...	...	...	...	...	...	...	...	...	...	...	...	...
Israel	...	...	...	...	...	...	...	...	...	...	...	...	...	...	...
Jordan	...	...	...	...	...	...	40	47	33	...	...	...	...	...	...
Kuwait	...	...	...	68	70	64	55	54	57	42	41	45	19	18	22
Lebanon	...	...	...	...	...	...	...	...	...	...	...	...	...	...	...
Libya	...	...	...	96	97	94	89	90	87	81	81	81	47	43	50
Morocco	25	16	20	85	90	80	74	78	69	41	43	40	16	19	13
Oman	...	...	...	58	56	62	51	48	56	28	25	34	...	...	...
Palestine	...	...	...	...	...	...	...	...	...	...	...	...	...	...	...
Qatar	...	...	...	64	68	59	52	53	51	41	40	43	...	...	...
Saudi Arabia	...	...	...	93	96	89	59	61	56	38	39	37	23	24	22
Sudan	...	...	...	84	84	86	68	68	71	44	41	58	...	...	...
Syrian Arab Republic	...	...	...	81	86	74	67	70	60	49	51	46	21	21	21
Tunisia	...	...	...	67	76	58	34	39	29	22	25	19	6	8	4
Turkey	29	20	...	88	94	81	55	66	44	35	42	29	16	18	13
United Arab Emirates	...	...	...	...	...	...	...	...	...	...	...	...	...	...	...
Yemen	...	...	...	...	...	...	...	...	...	...	...	...	...	...	...
The Pacific															
Australia	...	...	...	...	...	...	91	92	91	71	73	70	35	32	38
Cook Islands	...	...	...	...	...	...	...	...	...	...	...	...	...	...	...
Fiji	...	...	...	...	...	...	...	...	...	...	...	...	...	...	...
Kiribati	...	...	...	...	...	...	...	...	...	...	...	...	...	...	...
Marshall Islands	...	...	...	96	96	96	92	92	92	70	72	68	.	.	.
Micronesia F.S.	...	...	...	...	...	...	...	...	...	...	...	...	...	...	...
Nauru	...	...	...	...	...	...	...	...	...	...	...	...	...	...	...

TABLE 6
(Continued)

	ICT SKILLS ACQUISITION			ADULT EDUCATIONAL ATTAINMENT											
	Percentage of adults (15 and over) with ICT skills by type of skills (%)[1]			Percentage of adults (25 and over) (%) who have attained at least:											
	Sending email with attached files	Using basic arithmetic formulas in a spreadsheet	Finding, downloading, installing and configuring software	Primary education (ISCED level 1 to 8)			Lower secondary education (ISCED level 2 to 8)			Upper secondary education (ISCED level 3 to 8)			Short-cycle tertiary education (ISCED level 5 to 8)		
	2014	2014	2014	2009–2015[2]			2009–2015[2]			2009–2015[2]			2009–2015[2]		
Country or territory	Total	Total	Total	Total	Male	Female	Total	Male	Female	Total	Male	Female	Total	Male	Female
New Zealand	...	...	...	...	...	...	100	100	100	69	72	67	31	29	33
Niue	...	...	...	...	...	...	...	...	...	...	...	...	...	...	...
Palau	...	...	...	...	...	...	...	...	...	...	...	...	...	...	...
Papua New Guinea	...	...	...	...	...	...	...	...	...	...	...	...	...	...	...
Samoa	...	...	...	99	99	99	...	...	...	72	70	75	...	...	...
Solomon Islands	...	...	...	...	...	...	...	...	...	...	...	...	...	...	...
Tokelau	...	...	...	...	...	...	...	...	...	...	...	...	...	...	...
Tonga	...	...	...	96	96	96	88	88	88	54	53	55	6	7	5
Tuvalu	...	...	...	...	...	...	...	...	...	...	...	...	...	...	...
Vanuatu	...	...	...	...	...	...	...	...	...	...	...	...	...	...	...
Southern Asia															
Afghanistan	...	...	...	...	...	...	...	...	...	...	...	...	...	...	...
Bangladesh	...	...	...	...	...	...	...	...	...	...	...	...	...	...	...
Bhutan	...	...	...	20	26	15	10	13	6	6	8	3	5	7	3
India	...	...	...	...	...	...	...	...	...	...	...	...	...	...	...
Iran, Islamic Republic of	9	3	11	...	...	...	68	70	65	46	47	46	21	22	21
Maldives	...	...	...	...	...	...	...	...	...	...	...	...	...	...	...
Nepal	...	...	...	...	...	...	...	...	...	...	...	...	...	...	...
Pakistan	...	...	...	49	61	35	35	45	25	26	33	19	8	11	5
Sri Lanka	...	...	...	...	...	...	74	76	73	...	...	...	14	13	15
Sub-Saharan Africa															
Angola	...	...	...	...	...	...	...	...	...	...	...	...	...	...	...
Benin	...	...	...	...	...	...	...	...	...	...	...	...	...	...	...
Botswana	...	...	...	...	...	...	...	...	...	...	...	...	...	...	...
Burkina Faso	...	...	...	...	...	...	8	12	6	3	4	2	-	-	-
Burundi	...	...	...	...	...	...	...	...	...	...	...	...	...	...	...
Cabo Verde	...	...	...	...	...	...	...	...	...	...	...	...	...	...	...
Cameroon	...	...	...	36	47	26	36	47	26	18	25	11	1	2	1
Central African Republic	...	...	...	...	...	...	...	...	...	...	...	...	...	...	...
Chad	...	...	...	...	...	...	...	...	...	...	...	...	...	...	...
Comoros	...	...	...	...	...	...	...	...	...	...	...	...	...	...	...
Congo	...	...	...	...	...	...	...	...	...	...	...	...	...	...	...
Côte d'Ivoire	...	...	...	...	...	...	...	...	...	...	...	...	...	...	...
Democratic Rep. of the Congo	...	...	...	57	74	41	42	59	28	20	31	10	5	9	3
Djibouti	...	...	...	...	...	...	...	...	...	...	...	...	...	...	...
Equatorial Guinea	...	...	...	...	...	...	...	...	...	...	...	...	...	...	...
Eritrea	...	...	...	...	...	...	...	...	...	...	...	...	...	...	...
Ethiopia	...	...	...	25	37	14	13	18	8	9	13	6	1	2	0
Gabon	...	...	...	...	...	...	...	...	...	...	...	...	...	...	...
Gambia	...	...	...	...	...	...	...	...	...	...	...	...	...	...	...
Ghana	...	...	...	65	73	57	54	65	45	21	27	15	3	5	2
Guinea	...	...	...	...	...	...	...	...	...	...	...	...	...	...	...
Guinea-Bissau	...	...	...	...	...	...	...	...	...	...	...	...	...	...	...
Kenya	...	...	...	51	55	47	29	32	25	22	26	18	-	-	-
Lesotho	...	...	...	...	...	...	...	...	...	...	...	...	...	...	...
Liberia	...	...	...	...	...	...	...	...	...	...	...	...	...	...	...
Madagascar	...	...	...	...	...	...	...	...	...	...	...	...	...	...	...
Malawi	...	...	...	...	...	...	...	...	...	...	...	...	...	...	...
Mali	...	...	...	22	29	16	12	16	7	6	9	3	2	3	1
Mauritania	...	...	...	...	...	...	...	...	...	...	...	...	...	...	...
Mauritius	...	...	...	67	71	63	54	59	50	44	48	40	5	7	4
Mozambique	...	...	...	23	28	17	16	19	12	5	7	4	2	3	2
Namibia	...	...	...	...	...	...	...	...	...	...	...	...	...	...	...
Niger	...	...	...	...	...	...	...	...	...	...	...	...	...	...	...
Nigeria	...	...	...	...	...	...	...	...	...	...	...	...	...	...	...
Rwanda	...	...	...	31	36	27	12	15	9	8	11	6	4	5	3
Sao Tome and Principe	...	...	...	...	...	...	39	46	32	...	...	...	.	.	.
Senegal	...	...	...	27	33	22	14	19	10	8	12	5	4	6	3
Seychelles	...	...	...	...	...	...	...	...	...	...	...	...	...	...	...
Sierra Leone	...	...	...	...	...	...	...	...	...	...	...	...	...	...	...
Somalia	...	...	...	...	...	...	...	...	...	...	...	...	...	...	...
South Africa	...	...	...	82	83	81	77	76	74	64	64	62	...	...	...
South Sudan	...	...	...	...	...	...	...	...	...	...	...	...	...	...	...
Swaziland	...	...	...	...	...	...	...	...	...	...	...	...	...	...	...
Togo	...	...	...	30	11	10	18	11	10	9	11	10	8	...	...
Uganda	...	...	...	33	11	10	24	11	10	10	11	10	8	11	10
United Republic of Tanzania	...	...	...	65	71	59	11	14	9	3	5	2	2	3	1
Zambia	...	...	...	...	...	...	52	60	43	32	39	23	15	18	11
Zimbabwe	...	...	...	81	11	10	61	11	10	6	11	10	.	.	.

TABLE 6

(Continued)

Country or territory	ICT SKILLS ACQUISITION Percentage of adults (15 and over) with ICT skills by type of skills (%)[1]			ADULT EDUCATIONAL ATTAINMENT Percentage of adults (25 and over) (%) who have attained at least:											
	Sending email with attached files	Using basic arithmetic formulas in a spreadsheet	Finding, downloading, installing and configuring software	Primary education (ISCED level 1 to 8)			Lower secondary education (ISCED level 2 to 8)			Upper secondary education (ISCED level 3 to 8)			Short-cycle tertiary education (ISCED level 5 to 8)		
	2014	2014	2014	2009–2015[2]			2009–2015[2]			2009–2015[2]			2009–2015[2]		
	Total	Total	Total	Total	Male	Female	Total	Male	Female	Total	Male	Female	Total	Male	Female
	Median	Median	Median	Median			Median			Median			Median		
World	...	...	...	91	93	89	69	72	69	54	54	52	21	20	21
Countries in transition	...	...	...	99	99	98	96	97	94	85	87	83	25	27	24
Developed countries	69	48	26	99	99	98	91	92	91	75	77	73	31	29	29
Developing countries	...	...	...	...	...	...	...	...	...	...	...	...	...	...	...
Caucasus and Central Asia	...	...	...	99	99	99	97	97	96	90	92	90	28	29	27
Eastern and South-eastern Asia	...	...	...	88	90	86	68	71	66	51	52	50	21	18	23
Eastern Asia	...	...	...	95	95	96	77	75	77	64	62	65	22	19	25
South-eastern Asia	...	...	...	80	82	77	65	69	59	31	35	28	...	...	...
Europe and Northern America	67	47	24	99	99	98	89	94	89	74	77	73	29	28	28
Latin America and the Caribbean	...	...	...	82	83	81	57	57	57	40	40	41	...	...	...
Caribbean	...	...	...	...	...	...	...	...	...	...	...	...	...	...	...
Latin America	...	...	...	79	81	77	55	54	55	38	38	38	14	14	15
Northern Africa and Western Asia	...	...	...	...	...	...	...	...	...	...	...	...	...	...	...
Northern Africa	...	...	...	...	...	...	...	...	...	...	...	...	...	...	...
Western Asia	...	...	...	83	85	77	57	64	56	41	41	41	19	19	21
Pacific	...	...	...	...	...	...	...	...	...	...	...	...	...	...	...
Southern Asia	...	...	...	...	...	...	...	...	...	...	...	...	...	...	...
Sub-Saharan Africa	...	...	...	...	...	...	...	...	...	...	...	...	...	...	...
Conflict-affected countries	...	...	...	...	...	...	45	50	41	...	...	...	...	...	...
Countries with low income	...	...	...	...	...	...	...	...	...	...	...	...	...	...	...
Countries with middle income	...	...	...	...	...	...	...	...	...	...	...	...	...	...	...
Lower middle	...	...	...	...	...	...	...	...	...	...	...	...	...	...	...
Upper middle	...	...	...	88	92	82	65	70	65	45	46	46	15	16	14
Countries with high income	...	...	...	97	98	96	84	88	83	73	74	70	30	29	29

Source: UIS database, except where noted.

Note: The country groupings by level of income are as defined by the World Bank but include only countries listed in the table. They are based on the list of countries by income group as revised in July 2015.

1. Eurostat database; ITU World Telecommunication/ICT Indicators database.

2. Data are for the most recent year available during the period specified.

(...) No data are available.

TABLE 7

SDG 4, Target 4.5 – Gender – Eliminating gender disparity in education

By 2030, eliminate gender disparities in education and ensure equal access at all levels of education and vocational training for the vulnerable, including persons with disabilities, indigenous peoples and children in vulnerable situations

Country or territory	GENDER DISPARITY IN PARTICIPATION IN EDUCATION — Gender parity index (GPI) of gross enrolment ratio (GER) in:				GENDER DISPARITY IN SCHOOL COMPLETION[1] — Gender disparity index (GPI) in completion rate in:			GENDER DISPARITY IN LEARNING OUTCOMES[2] — GPI in percentage of students with minimum level of proficiency in reading and mathematics				GENDER DISPARITY IN LITERACY — Gender disparity index (GPI) in youth and adult literacy rate		GENDER DISPARITY IN ADULT LITERACY AND NUMERACY SKILLS[3] — Disparity in percentage of adults achieving at least a fixed level of proficiency in:	
	Pre-primary	Primary	Secondary	Tertiary	Primary	Lower secondary	Upper secondary	Last grade of primary pupils — Reading	Last grade of primary pupils — Mathematics	Last grade of lower secondary — Reading	Last grade of lower secondary — Mathematics	Youth (15–24) literacy	Adult (15 and over) literacy	Functional literacy skills, Adults (16 and over)	Numeracy skills, Adults (16 and over)
	School year ending in 2014				School year ending in 2009–2014[4]			2009–2014[4]		2009–2014[4]		2005–2014[4]		2012–2015[4]	2012–2015[4]
	GPI (F/M)	GPI (F/M)	GPI (F/M)	GPI (F/M)	GPI (F/M)	GPI (F/M)	GPI (F/M)	GPI (F/M)	GPI (F/M)	GPI (F/M)	GPI (F/M)	GPI (F/M)	GPI (F/M)	GPI (F/M)	GPI (F/M)
Caucasus and Central Asia															
Armenia	1.30[y]	...	...	1.21	1.00	1.011	1.087	...	1.05[I]	...	1.07[I]	1.00*	1.00*	...	...
Azerbaijan⁵	1.04*	0.99*	0.99*	1.14*	...	...	...	1.06[I]	1.03[I]	1.07[I]	0.97[I]	1.00*	1.00*	...	...
Georgia	...	1.01	1.00	1.26	...	1.000	1.001	...	...	...[I]	1.02[I]	1.00**	1.00**	...	...
Kazakhstan	1.11	1.00	1.03	1.28	1.00	1.003	1.021	...	1.02[I]	1.06[I]	1.02[I]	1.00*	1.00*	...	...
Kyrgyzstan	1.00	0.99	1.01	1.30	1.00	1.018	1.040	...	...	1.37[I]	1.05[I]	1.00*	0.99*	...	...
Tajikistan	0.91	1.00	0.90[z]	0.67	0.99	0.903	0.637	...	...	...	...	1.00**	1.00**	...	...
Turkmenistan	0.97	0.98	0.96	0.64	...	...	...	...	...	...	...	1.00**	1.00**	...	...
Uzbekistan	...	...	...	...	...	...	...	...	...	...	...	1.00*	1.00*	...	...
Eastern and South-eastern Asia															
Brunei Darussalam	1.02	1.00	1.00	1.69	...	...	...	...	...	...	...	1.00*	0.97*	...	...
Cambodia	1.00	0.95	...	...	1.21	0.979	1.115	...	...	...	...	0.97*	0.80*	...	...
China	1.00	1.00	1.02	1.16	1.02	1.011	0.952	...	...	...	...	1.00*	0.95*	...	...
DPR Korea	...	...	...	...	...	...	...	...	...	...	...	1.00*	1.00*	...	...
Hong Kong, China	...	0.99	0.96	1.15	...	...	...	...	...	1.00[I]	1.00[I]	...	...	...	...
Indonesia	1.03	0.98	0.99	1.12	1.02	1.068	0.944	...	...	1.04[I]	0.97[I]	1.00*	0.97*	...	...
Japan	...	1.00[z]	1.00[z]	0.91[z]	...	...	...	...	...	1.01[I]	1.00[I]	...	...	1.00	1.00
Lao PDR	1.04	0.95	0.91	0.93	0.95	0.831	0.879	...	...	...	...	0.88*	0.77*	...	...
Macao, China	...	...	0.98	1.31	...	...	...	...	...	1.01[I]	1.01[I]	1.00*	0.96*	...	...
Malaysia	...	...	...	...	...	...	...	...	...	1.07[I]	1.06[I]	1.00*	0.95*	...	...
Mongolia	1.01[y]	0.98	1.03	1.44	1.02	1.115	1.366	...	...	...	...	1.01*	1.00*	...	...
Myanmar	1.04	0.97	1.03	1.23[y]	...	...	...	...	...	...	...	1.00	0.96**	...	...
Philippines	...	1.00[z]	1.10*	1.28	1.10	1.248	1.248	...	...	...	...	**	1.01*	...	...
Republic of Korea	1.00[z]	0.99[z]	0.99[z]	0.75[z]	...	...	...	...	...	1.01[I]	1.00[I]	1.01*	...	0.99	0.98
Singapore	...	...	...	...	...	...	...	...	...	1.01[I]	1.02[I]	...	0.96*	0.98	0.97
Thailand	0.99	1.01	1.07*	1.33	...	...	...	...	...	1.02[I]	1.06[I]	1.00*	0.97*	...	...
Timor-Leste	1.05	0.99	1.08	...	1.15	1.106	1.058	...	...	...	...	1.01*	0.83*	...	...
Viet Nam	0.97	0.99	...	1.05	1.01	1.096	1.172	...	...	1.00[I]	1.00[I]	0.98*	0.95*	...	...
Europe and Northern America															
Albania	0.98	0.98	0.93	1.41	...	...	...	...	...	1.02[I]	1.02[I]	1.00*	0.98*	...	...
Andorra	...	...	...	...	...	...	...	...	...	...	...	...	...	...	...
Austria	0.99	0.99	0.95	1.20	...	...	0.954	1.00[I]	0.99[I]	1.01[I]	0.98[I]	...	...	1.00	1.00
Belarus	0.96	1.00	0.98	1.33	0.99	1.004	1.079	...	...	...	...	1.00*	1.00*	...	...
Belgium	0.99	1.00	1.13	1.31	...	...	1.072	...	...	1.02[I]	1.00[I]	...	...	...	...
Bosnia and Herzegovina	0.94	1.00	1.03	1.34	1.00	1.007	1.246	...	...	1.10[I]	1.04[I]	1.00**	0.98**	...	...
Bulgaria	0.99	0.99	0.97	1.25	...	...	0.982	1.02[I]	...	1.10[I]	1.07[I]	1.00*	0.99*	1.00	0.98
Canada	0.99[z]	1.01[z]	1.00[z]	...	...	...	1.081	...	...	1.01[I]	1.00[I]	...	...	1.00	0.98
Croatia	0.98	1.00	1.04	1.37	...	...	0.974	1.01[I]	1.00[I]	1.01[I]	1.00[I]	1.00*	0.99*	...	...
Cyprus⁵	1.01*	1.01*	1.00*	1.42*	...	...	1.083	...	...	1.10[I]	1.07[I]	1.00*	0.99*	1.00	0.99
Czech Republic	0.98	1.00	1.00	1.40	...	...	1.012	1.00[I]	0.99[I]	1.01[I]	1.00[I]	...	...	0.99	0.99
Denmark	1.01	0.99	1.04	1.40	...	...	1.138	...	...	1.01[I]	0.99[I]	...	...	1.01	1.00
Estonia	0.97[y]	0.99[z]	0.99[z]	1.50[z]	...	...	1.063	...	...	1.00[I]	1.00[I]	1.00*	1.00*	1.01	1.01
Finland	0.99	1.00	1.09	1.21	...	...	1.042	...	...	1.01[I]	1.01[I]	...	...	1.01	1.00
France	1.00	0.99	1.01	1.23	...	...	1.061	1.00[I]	...	1.03[I]	1.00[I]	...	...	1.00	0.98
Germany	0.99	0.99	0.95	0.94	...	...	0.998	1.00[I]	0.99[I]	1.01[I]	0.99[I]	...	...	0.99	0.98
Greece	0.98[z]	0.99[z]	0.96[z]	1.00[z]	...	...	1.022	...	...	1.04[I]	1.03[I]	1.00**	0.98**	1.01	0.98
Hungary	0.98	0.99	1.00	1.29	...	...	1.004	1.03[I]	1.02[I]	1.01[I]	1.00[I]	...	...	...	...
Iceland	0.98[y]	1.00[y]	0.99[y]	1.72[y]	...	...	1.327	...	...	1.03[I]	1.03[I]	...	...	...	...
Ireland	1.03[z]	1.01[y]	1.02[y]	1.06[z]	...	...	1.110	...	...	1.02[I]	0.99[I]	1.00*	0.99*	1.01	0.99
Italy	0.98[z]	0.99[z]	0.98[z]	1.40[z]	...	...	1.163	...	...	1.01[I]	1.01[I]	1.00*	1.00*	1.01	0.98
Latvia	0.99	0.99	0.98	1.43	...	...	...	...	...	1.01[I]	1.01[I]	1.00*	1.00*	...	...
Liechtenstein⁵	0.94*	0.99*	0.81*	0.48*	...	...	...	...	...	1.01[I]	1.02[I]	...	...	1.01	1.00
Lithuania	0.99	1.00	0.96	1.47	...	...	1.088	1.02[I]	1.01[I]	1.01[I]	1.02[I]	1.00*	1.00*	1.01	1.00
Luxembourg	1.00[z]	1.01[z]	1.03*	1.14[y]	...	...	1.100	...	...	1.02[I]	0.96[I]	...	...	...	...
Malta	1.06	0.95	0.89	1.15	...	...	1.300	...	...	...	...	1.01*	1.03*	...	...
Monaco	...	...	...	...	...	...	...	...	...	...	...	...	...	...	...
Montenegro	0.94	0.98	1.00	...	1.01	0.979	1.037	...	...	1.07[I]	1.03[I]	1.00*	0.98*	...	...
Netherlands	1.01	0.99	...	1.10	...	...	1.228	...	...	1.01[I]	0.99[I]	...	...	1.00	0.99
Norway	1.00	1.00	0.97	[y]	...	...	1.018	...	...	1.01[I]	1.01[I]	...	...	1.00	1.00
Poland	0.99[z]	1.00[z]	0.96[z]	1.45	...	...	1.121	...	...	1.01[I]	1.01[I]	...	...	1.02	1.02
Portugal	0.97	0.96	0.98	1.55[z]	...	...	1.443	...	...	1.02[I]	1.01[I]	1.00*	0.96*	...	...
Republic of Moldova⁵	0.99*	1.00*	1.01*	1.16	1.00	1.040	1.168	...	...	1.03[I]	1.00[I]	1.00**	0.99**	...	...
Romania	1.00	0.98[y]	0.99	1.29*·[z]	...	...	1.063	1.04[I]	1.00[I]	1.03[I]	1.00[I]	...	0.99*	...	...
Russian Federation	0.99	1.01	0.98	1.24	1.00	1.005	0.996	1.01[I]	1.00[I]	1.01[I]	1.01[I]	...	...	1.01	1.02
San Marino⁵	1.02*·[y]	0.99*·[y]	1.03*·[y]	1.21	...	...	1.167	...	...	0.99[I]	0.98[I]	...	0.97*	...	...
Serbia⁵	1.01*	1.00*	1.02*	1.38*·[y]	1.00	1.028	1.167	1.01[I]	0.99[I]	1.02[I]	0.99[I]	...	...	1.00	1.00
Slovakia	0.98	0.99	1.01	1.31*	...	...	1.037	...	...	1.02[I]	0.99[I]	...	...	1.01	1.00
Slovenia	0.97	1.00	1.01	1.55	...	...	1.062	...	...	1.02[I]	1.00[I]	1.00**	1.00**	1.01	1.00

TABLE 7

(Continued)

Country or territory	GENDER DISPARITY IN PARTICIPATION IN EDUCATION — GPI (F/M) of GER, school year ending 2014				GENDER DISPARITY IN SCHOOL COMPLETION¹ — GPI (F/M) in completion rate, 2009–2014			GENDER DISPARITY IN LEARNING OUTCOMES² — GPI (F/M), 2009–2014				GENDER DISPARITY IN LITERACY — GPI (F/M), 2005–2014		GENDER DISPARITY IN ADULT LITERACY AND NUMERACY SKILLS³ — GPI (F/M), 2012–2015	
	Pre-primary	Primary	Secondary	Tertiary	Primary	Lower secondary	Upper secondary	Reading (last grade primary)	Mathematics (last grade primary)	Reading (last grade lower secondary)	Mathematics (last grade lower secondary)	Youth (15–24) literacy	Adult (15 and over) literacy	Functional literacy skills (Adults 16 and over)	Numeracy skills (Adults 16 and over)
Spain	1.00	1.01	1.00	1.44	...	...	1.239	...	...	1.02I	0.99I	1.00*	0.99*	1.00	0.97
Sweden	1.00	1.06	1.14	1.54	...	...	1.066	...	...	1.04I	1.03I	...	...	0.99	0.98
Switzerland	0.98	1.00	0.97	1.02	...	...	1.010	...	...	1.01I	1.00I	...	...	...	...
TFYR Macedonia	1.02y	0.98y	0.98y	1.26z	1.00	0.866	0.908	...	...	...I	1.06I	1.00**	0.98**	...	...
Ukraine	0.98y	1.02	0.98	1.16	0.99	1.001	1.007	...	...	...I	1.04I	1.00**	1.00**	...	...
United Kingdom	1.00	1.00	1.04	1.31	...	...	1.061	...	...	1.01I	0.99I	...	...	...	...
United States	1.00	0.99	1.02	1.37	...	...	1.032	...	...	1.01I	1.01I	...	...	1.00	0.97
Latin America and the Caribbean															
Anguilla	...	...	...	...	...	...	...	...	...	...	...	...	...	...	...
Antigua and Barbuda	0.93	0.92	1.01	2.07y	...	...	...	...	...	...	...	...	1.01**	...	...
Argentina	1.01z	0.99z	1.08z	1.61z	1.01	1.147	1.206	1.11R	0.93R	1.07I	0.91I	1.00**	1.00**	...	...
Aruba	0.98	0.97	1.02y	2.29	...	...	...	...	...	...	...	1.00*	1.00*	...	...
Bahamas	...	...	...	...	...	...	...	...	...	...	...	...	...	...	...
Barbados	1.03	1.01	1.03	...	1.01	0.995	1.102	...	...	...	...	...	...	...	...
Belize	1.02	0.95	1.05	1.64z	1.09	1.316	1.312	...	...	...	...	...	...	...	...
Bermuda	1.03	0.97	1.14	1.89	...	...	...	...	...	...	...	...	...	...	...
Bolivia, P.S.	0.98z	...	0.99z	...	...	...	...	...	...	...	...	1.00*	0.95*	...	...
Brazil§	1.01*,z	0.95*,z	1.09*,z	1.35*,z	1.12	1.240	1.428	1.07R	0.92R	1.04I	0.88I	1.01*	1.01*	...	...
British Virgin Islands	...	...	...	...	...	...	...	...	...	...	...	...	...	...	...
Cayman Islands	...	...	...	...	...	...	...	...	...	...	...	0.99*	1.00*	...	...
Chile	0.98	0.97	1.02	1.14	1.01	1.031	1.084	1.03R	1.01R	1.01I	0.90I	1.00*	1.00*	0.95	0.83
Colombia	...	0.97	1.08	1.15	0.98	1.011	1.078	1.02R	0.87R	1.04I	0.81I	1.01*	1.01*	...	...
Costa Rica	1.01	0.99	1.05	1.24	1.02	1.310	1.259	1.02R	0.96R	1.01I	0.89I	1.00*	1.00*	...	...
Cuba	1.01	0.96	1.03	1.59	...	...	...	...	...	...	...	1.00*	1.00*	...	...
Curaçao	...	0.96z	1.05z	2.33z	...	...	...	...	...	...	...	...	...	...	...
Dominica	0.93	1.00	...	...	...	...	...	...	...	...	...	...	...	...	...
Dominican Republic	1.05	0.91	1.11	1.62	1.07	1.098	1.353	1.14R	0.85R	...	...	1.01*	1.01*	...	...
Ecuador	1.02	1.00	1.04	...	1.00	1.030	1.063	1.00R	0.97R	...	...	1.00*	0.98*	...	...
El Salvador	1.03	0.96	1.01	1.09	...	...	...	...	...	...	...	1.01*	0.95*	...	...
Grenada	0.94	0.98	0.99	...	...	...	...	...	...	...	...	...	...	...	...
Guatemala	1.02	0.96	0.94	1.06z	0.94	0.906	0.964	1.00R	0.68R	...	...	0.98*	0.88*	...	...
Guyana	0.98y	0.97y	0.99y	2.03y	0.98	1.170	0.930	...	...	...	...	1.01**,a	1.06**,a	...	...
Haiti	...	...	...	...	1.20	0.957	0.730	...	...	...	...	0.95**,a	0.84**,a	...	...
Honduras	1.02	0.98	1.17	1.35	1.03	1.465	1.528	1.03R	0.89R	...	0.63I	1.01*	1.00*	...	...
Jamaica	1.06	...	1.08	2.28z	1.00	1.012	1.063	...	...	...	...	1.05**	1.11**	...	...
Mexico	1.02	1.00	1.07	1.01	1.02	1.019	1.037	1.00R	...	1.02I	0.95I	1.00*	0.98*	...	...
Montserrat	...	...	...	...	...	...	...	...	...	...	...	...	...	...	...
Nicaragua	...	...	...	...	1.16	1.321	1.275	1.03R	0.89R	...	...	1.04*	1.00*	...	...
Panama	1.01z	0.97z	1.06z	1.49z	1.01	1.034	1.222	1.08R	1.10R	1.07I	0.94I	0.99*	0.99*	...	...
Paraguay	1.00y	0.97y	1.07y	...	...	...	...	1.10R	0.96R	...	...	1.00*	0.98*	...	...
Peru	1.01	1.00	1.00	...	1.03	1.017	0.973	0.95R	0.85R	1.04I	0.85I	1.00*	0.93*	...	...
Saint Kitts and Nevis	0.95	1.02	1.03	1.02	...	...	...	...	...	...	...	...	...	...	...
Saint Lucia	1.07	...	0.99	2.09	1.00	1.122	1.158	...	...	...	...	...	...	...	...
Saint-Martin	...	...	...	...	...	...	...	...	...	...	...	...	...	...	...
St. Vincent and the Grenadines	1.02	0.97	0.97	...	...	...	...	...	...	...	...	...	...	...	...
Sint-Maarten	...	...	...	...	...	...	...	...	...	...	...	...	...	...	...
Suriname	1.04	0.97	1.31z	...	1.07	1.466	1.582	...	...	...	...	1.01*	0.99*	...	...
Trinidad and Tobago	...	...	...	...	...	...	...	...	...	1.11I	1.05I	1.00**	0.99**	...	...
Turks and Caicos Islands	...	...	...	...	...	...	...	...	...	...	...	...	...	...	...
Uruguay	1.01z	0.97z	1.13z	...	1.01	1.162	0.686	1.02R	0.93R	1.07I	0.97I	1.01*	1.01*	...	...
Venezuela, B.R.	1.01	0.98	1.08	...	...	...	...	...	...	...	...	1.01*	1.01*	...	...
Northern Africa and Western Asia															
Algeria	...	0.94	...	1.53	...	...	...	...	...	...	...	0.96	0.82*	...	...
Bahrain	1.00	...	...	2.33	...	...	...	...	...	...	1.48I	0.99	0.95*	...	...
Egypt	0.98	1.00	0.99	0.90	...	1.03	0.97	...	...	...	...	0.96*,a	0.81*,a	...	...
Iraq	...	...	...	...	...	0.92	0.98	...	...	...	...	0.97**	0.86**	...	...
Israel	1.00	1.00	1.02	1.34	...	1.03	1.11	...	...	1.05I	1.05I	...	...	1.00	0.97
Jordan	0.96y	0.99y	1.05y	1.18y	0.92	1.06	1.32	...	...	1.14I	1.24I	1.00*,a	0.99*,a	...	...
Kuwait	...	1.01	1.11**	1.62z	...	...	...	1.49I	1.48I	...	...	1.00*	0.98*	...	...
Lebanon	0.94z	0.91z	1.01z	1.16	1.00	...	...	...	...	...	0.96I	1.01*	0.92*	...	...
Libya	...	...	...	...	1.02	...	...	...	...	...	...	1.00**	0.88**	...	...
Morocco	0.82	0.95	0.85y	0.96	0.90	0.89	1.01	...	...	...	...	0.83*	0.76*	...	...
Oman	1.04	1.09	...	...	...	...	...	1.49I	1.27I	...	1.79I	1.00*	0.94*	...	...
Palestine	1.02	0.99	1.10	1.55	...	1.18	1.39	...	...	...	1.21I	1.00*	0.96*	...	...
Qatar	1.00	...	...	6.32	0.85	...	...	...	...	1.25I	1.17I	1.01*	1.00*	...	...
Saudi Arabia	1.29	0.99	0.76**	0.96	...	...	...	...	...	...	1.15I	1.00*	0.95*	...	...
Sudan	1.07z	0.90z	0.95z	1.12z	1.00	0.82	0.75	...	...	...	...	0.91*	0.78*	...	...
Syrian Arab Republic	0.97z	0.97z	1.00z	1.04z	1.02	...	...	...	...	...	0.91I	0.98**	0.88**	...	...
Tunisia	1.02	0.97	...	1.64	1.01	1.13	1.27	...	...	1.05I	0.88I	0.98*	0.82*	...	...
Turkey	0.96z	0.99z	0.97z	0.86z	...	...	...	...	...	1.02I	1.01I	0.99*	0.94*	0.93	0.82

TABLE 7
(Continued)

| Country or territory | GENDER DISPARITY IN PARTICIPATION IN EDUCATION — Gender parity index (GPI) of gross enrolment ratio (GER) in: School year ending in 2014 | | | | GENDER DISPARITY IN SCHOOL COMPLETION[1] — Gender disparity index (GPI) in completion rate in: 2009–2014[4] | | | GENDER DISPARITY IN LEARNING OUTCOMES[2] — Gender disparity index (GPI) in percentage of students with minimum level of proficiency in reading and mathematics | | | | GENDER DISPARITY IN LITERACY — Gender disparity index (GPI) in youth and adult literacy rate 2005–2014[4] | | GENDER DISPARITY IN ADULT LITERACY AND NUMERACY SKILLS[3] — Disparity in percentage of adults achieving at least a fixed level of proficiency in: | |
| | Pre-primary | Primary | Secondary | Tertiary | Primary | Lower secondary | Upper secondary | Last grade of primary pupils — Reading | Last grade of primary pupils — Mathematics | Last grade of lower secondary school students — Reading | Last grade of lower secondary school students — Mathematics | Youth (15–24) literacy | Adult (15 and over) literacy | Functional literacy skills Adults (16 and over) 2012–2015[4] | Numeracy skills Adults (16 and over) 2012–2015[4] |
	GPI (F/M)	GPI (F/M)	GPI (F/M)	GPI (F/M)	GPI (F/M)	GPI (F/M)	GPI (F/M)	GPI (F/M)	GPI (F/M)	GPI (F/M)	GPI (F/M)	GPI (F/M)	GPI (F/M)	GPI (F/M)	GPI (F/M)
United Arab Emirates	1.01	1.01	…	2.26	…	…	…	1.22¹	1.08¹	1.06¹	1.08¹	1.04*	1.02*	…	…
Yemen	0.88ᶻ	0.84ᶻ	0.69ᶻ	…	0.78	0.72	0.63	…	…	…	…	0.83**	0.63**	…	…
The Pacific															
Australia	…	…	…	…	…	1.007	1.089	1.03ᴺ	1.01ᴺ	1.01¹	1.00¹	…	…	1.00	0.99
Cook Islands⁵	1.08*	0.97*	1.10*	3.37*	…	…	…	…	…	…	…	…	…	…	…
Fiji	…	1.01ᶻ	1.11ʸ	…	…	…	…	…	…	…	…	…	…	…	…
Kiribati	…	1.04	…ʸ	…	…	…	…	…	…	…	…	…	…	…	…
Marshall Islands	…	…	…	0.92ʸ	…	…	…	…	…	…	…	1.01*	1.00*	…	…
Micronesia F.S.	…	0.99	…	…	…	…	…	…	…	…	…	…	…	…	…
Nauru⁵	1.13*	0.92*	1.02*	…	…	…	…	…	…	…	…	…	…	…	…
New Zealand	1.02	1.00	1.06	1.38	…	…	…	…	…	1.02¹	1.01¹	…	…	1.01	1.00
Niue⁵	1.10*	0.98*	…	…	…	…	…	…	…	…	…	…	…	…	…
Palau⁵	1.09*	0.96*	1.06*	1.55*,ᶻ	…	…	…	…	…	…	…	1.00*	1.00*	…	…
Papua New Guinea	…	0.91ʸ	0.76ʸ	…	…	…	…	…	…	…	…	0.93**	0.94**	…	…
Samoa	1.11	1.00	1.12	…	…	…	…	…	…	…	…	1.00*	1.00*	…	…
Solomon Islands	1.01	0.97	0.94ʸ	…	…	…	…	…	…	…	…	…	…	…	…
Tokelau	…	…	…	…	…	…	…	…	…	…	…	…	…	…	…
Tonga	0.98	0.99	1.09	…	…	…	…	…	…	…	…	1.00*	1.00*	…	…
Tuvalu⁵	1.00*	1.01*	1.25*	…	…	…	…	…	…	…	…	…	…	…	…
Vanuatu	0.99ᶻ	0.98ᶻ	…	…	…	…	…	…	…	…	…	…	…	…	…
Southern Asia															
Afghanistan	…	0.70	0.56	0.28	0.50	0.332	0.270	…	…	…	…	0.52*	0.39*	…	…
Bangladesh	1.00ᶻ	…	1.08ᶻ	0.74	1.13	1.029	0.799	…	…	…	…	1.06**	0.89**	…	…
Bhutan	1.08	1.01	1.07	0.74ᶻ	1.05	0.940	1.140	…	…	…	…	0.93*	0.73*	…	…
India	0.92ᶻ	1.12ᶻ	1.01ᶻ	0.94ᶻ	0.99	0.960	0.925	…	…	…	…	0.91*	0.75*	…	…
Iran, Islamic Republic of	0.97	1.04	0.99	0.93	…	…	…	…	…	…	0.98	0.99*	0.89*	…	…
Maldives	…	…	…	…	1.01	1.093	1.250	…	…	…	…	1.00*	1.00*	…	…
Nepal	**0.97**	**1.08**	**1.07****	0.82ᶻ	0.91	0.840	0.755	…	…	…	…	0.89*	0.68*	…	…
Pakistan	0.88	0.85	0.79	1.06	0.93	0.825	0.846	…	…	…	…	0.80*	0.61*	…	…
Sri Lanka	0.99ᶻ	0.98	1.05ᶻ	1.49	…	…	…	…	…	…	…	1.01*	0.97*	…	…
Sub-Saharan Africa															
Angola	…	…	…	0.80ᶻ	…	…	…	…	…	…	…	0.85**	0.73**	…	…
Benin	1.01	0.91	0.68	0.37ᶻ	0.89	0.584	0.428	1.01¹	1.05¹	…	…	0.56**,ᵃ	0.45**,ᵃ	…	…
Botswana	0.99ᶻ	0.97ᶻ	1.06ᶻ	1.37	…	…	…	1.01¹	0.99¹	…	1.18¹	1.04**	1.02**	…	…
Burkina Faso	1.04	0.96	0.87	0.49ᶻ	0.94	0.441	0.308	1.01¹	1.00¹	…	…	0.77*	0.59*	…	…
Burundi	1.01	1.01	0.85	0.42ᶻ	0.99	0.474	0.577	1.00¹	1.01¹	…	…	0.98*	0.95*	…	…
Cabo Verde	1.00	0.95	1.14	1.40	…	…	…	…	…	…	…	1.01*	0.89*	…	…
Cameroon	1.02	0.89	0.85	…	0.99	0.832	0.705	1.01¹	1.02¹	…	…	0.89*	0.83*	…	…
Central African Republic	…	0.74ʸ	0.51ʸ	0.36ʸ	0.68	0.584	0.531	…	…	…	…	0.55**,ᵃ	0.48**,ᵃ	…	…
Chad	0.90ᶻ	0.77ᶻ	0.46ʸ	0.20**	0.59	0.327	0.329	0.91¹	0.85¹	…	…	0.88**	0.63**	…	…
Comoros	1.05ᶻ	0.94ᶻ	1.04ᶻ	0.87ᶻ	1.07	1.073	1.432	..¹	..¹	…	…	1.01**	0.90**	…	…
Congo	0.99ʸ	1.07ᶻ	0.87ʸ	0.75ᶻ	0.97	0.915	0.915	1.02¹	0.86¹	…	…	0.90**,ᵃ	0.84**,ᵃ	…	…
Côte d'Ivoire	1.00	0.87	0.71	0.58	…	…	…	1.00¹	0.92¹	…	…	0.66**,ᵃ	0.59**,ᵃ	…	…
D.R. Congo	1.07	0.91	0.62	0.46ᶻ	0.91	0.746	0.694	…	…	…	…	0.84**,ᵃ	0.72**,ᵃ	…	…
Djibouti	**0.87**	**0.89**	**0.80**	…	…	…	…	…	…	…	…	…	…	…	…
Equatorial Guinea	1.01ʸ	0.98ʸ	…	…	…	…	…	…	…	…	…	1.01**	0.95**	…	…
Eritrea	1.00ᶻ	0.85ᶻ	0.80ᶻ	0.50	…	…	…	…	…	…	…	0.97**	0.79**	…	…
Ethiopia	0.95	0.92	0.91ʸ	0.48	0.95	0.954	0.850	…	…	…	…	0.75*	0.59*	…	…
Gabon	…	…	…	…	1.14	0.900	0.805	…	…	…	…	1.02**,ᵃ	0.94**,ᵃ	…	…
Gambia	1.06	1.05	…	0.68ʸ	0.95	0.954	0.843	…	…	…	…	0.92**	0.73**	…	…
Ghana	**1.03**	**1.00**	**0.95**	0.67	1.05	1.019	0.832	…	…	…	0.67¹	0.94*	0.83*	…	…
Guinea	…	0.85	0.66	0.45	0.72	0.565	0.443	…	…	…	…	0.58*	0.33*	…	…
Guinea-Bissau	…	…	…	…	…	…	…	…	…	…	…	0.89**	0.66**	…	…
Kenya	0.97	1.00	0.93ʸ	…	1.05	1.038	0.841	1.01ᴿ	1.02ᴿ	…	…	0.98**,ᵃ	0.86**,ᵃ	…	…
Lesotho	1.05	0.98	1.37	1.45	1.52	1.500	1.120	…	…	…	…	1.24**,ᵃ	1.30**,ᵃ	…	…
Liberia	…	0.92	0.78	0.63ʸ	0.88	0.669	0.459	…	…	…	…	0.59**,ᵃ	0.44**,ᵃ	…	…
Madagascar	1.06	1.00	0.98	0.94ᶻ	…	…	…	…	…	…	…	0.97**,ᵃ	0.91**,ᵃ	…	…
Malawi	…	1.02	0.91	…	1.21	0.955	0.774	…	…	…	…	0.94**,ᵃ	0.71**,ᵃ	…	…
Mali	1.05	0.90	0.76	0.43ʸ	0.82	0.500	0.423	…	…	…	…	0.69*	0.57*	…	…
Mauritania	1.30	1.06	0.91	0.50	0.83	0.696	0.525	…	…	…	…	0.72**,ᵃ	0.62**,ᵃ	…	…
Mauritius	1.03	1.02	1.02	1.23	…	…	…	…	…	…	…	1.01*	0.95*	…	…
Mozambique	…	0.92	0.92	0.71	0.74	0.448	0.279	…	…	…	…	0.71*	0.54*	…	…
Namibia	1.04ᶻ	0.97ᶻ	…	…	1.16	1.286	1.057	…	…	…	…	1.02**	0.99**	…	…
Niger	1.06	0.86	0.70	0.34ʸ	0.65	0.443	0.300	0.94¹	0.91¹	…	…	0.44**	0.38**,ᵃ	…	…
Nigeria	…	…	…	…	0.84	0.719	0.638	…	…	…	…	0.77**	0.68**,ᵃ	…	…
Rwanda	1.05ᶻ	1.02	1.10	0.79ᶻ	1.22	1.029	0.884	…	…	…	…	1.03*	0.89*	…	…
Sao Tome and Principe	**1.10**	**0.96**	**1.11**	**1.03**	…	…	…	…	…	…	…	0.99*	0.90*	…	…
Senegal	1.13	1.09	…	…	0.96	0.641	0.368	1.00¹	0.95¹	…	…	0.83*	0.64*	…	…
Seychelles	1.00	1.01	1.02	2.49	…	…	…	…	…	…	…	1.01*	1.01*	…	…
Sierra Leone	1.10ᶻ	1.00*	0.85ᶻ	…	1.06	0.653	0.737	…	…	…	…	0.77**	0.63**	…	…

TABLE 7

(Continued)

Country or territory	Pre-primary GPI (F/M)	Primary GPI (F/M)	Secondary GPI (F/M)	Tertiary GPI (F/M)	Primary completion GPI (F/M)	Lower secondary completion GPI (F/M)	Upper secondary completion GPI (F/M)	Reading (last grade primary) GPI (F/M)	Mathematics (last grade primary) GPI (F/M)	Reading (lower secondary) GPI (F/M)	Mathematics (lower secondary) GPI (F/M)	Youth (15–24) literacy GPI (F/M)	Adult (15 and over) literacy GPI (F/M)	Functional literacy skills Adults (16 and over) GPI (F/M)	Numeracy skills Adults (16 and over) GPI (F/M)
	School year ending in 2014				School year ending in 2009–2014[4]			2009–2014[4]		2009–2014[4]		2005–2014[4]		2012–2015	2012–2015
Somalia	...	...	...	...	...	...	...	...	...	...	...	...	...	...	...
South Africa	0.99[z]	0.95	1.22**	1.47[z]	1.05	1.119	1.220	...	...	...	1.07[l]	1.00*	0.98*	...	...
South Sudan	...	...	...	...	0.61	0.297	0.343					0.67*	0.55*	...	...
Swaziland	...	0.92[z]	0.98[z]	1.05[z]	1.24	1.226	1.022					1.03**ᵃ	0.98**ᵃ	...	...
Togo	1.03	0.94	...	0.42	0.90	0.554	0.491	1.00[l]	0.97[l]	...	...	0.84*	0.65*	...	...
Uganda	1.04[z]	1.02[z]	0.87[z]	...	1.29	0.843	0.594	0.99[R]	1.05[R]	...	...	0.95*	0.78*	...	...
U.R. Tanzania	1.01[z]	1.01[z]	0.91[z]	0.51[z]	1.03	0.796	0.732	0.99[R]	0.94[R]	...	...	0.97*	0.88*	...	...
Zambia	...	1.01[z]	...	...	0.99	0.834	0.648					0.95*	0.88*	...	...
Zimbabwe	1.02[z]	0.98[z]	0.98[z]	0.84[z]	1.10	1.128	0.728					1.03**ᵃ	0.91**ᵃ	...	...
	Weighted average				**Median**			**Median**				**Weighted average**		**Median**	
World	0.99**	0.99**	0.99**	1.11**	...	...	1.04					0.96**	0.91**	...	...
													1.00**		
Countries in transition	0.99	1.00	0.98	1.17	1.00	1.02	1.04					1.00**	0.88**	...	...
Developed countries	1.00	1.00	1.00	1.26	...	...	1.06					...**	1.00**	...	...
Developing countries	0.98**	0.99**	0.98**	1.05**	1.01	1.12	0.96					0.95**	0.96**	...	...
	1.01**												0.96**		
Caucasus and Central Asia	1.00	0.99	0.99**	1.04	1.00	1.00	1.06					1.00**	0.96**	...	...
Eastern and South-eastern Asia	1.00	0.99	1.01	1.11	...	...	...					1.00**		...	...
Eastern Asia	1.00	1.00	1.02	1.10	...	...	...					1.00**	0.99**	...	...
South-eastern Asia	0.99	0.98	1.00	1.17	1.06	1.16	0.97					1.00**	0.98**	...	...
Europe and Northern America	1.01**	1.00	1.00	1.28	...	...	1.07					...	0.99**	...	...
Latin America and the Caribbean	1.04**	0.98**	1.07**	1.29**	1.01	1.06	1.08					1.00**	0.86**	...	...
Caribbean	1.01**	0.97	1.06**	1.50**	...	...	...					0.99**	0.81**	...	...
Latin America	0.99**	0.98**	1.07**	1.28**	1.02	1.20	0.92					1.01**	0.90**	...	...
Northern Africa and Western Asia	0.97	0.95**	0.94**	0.99**	...	...	...					0.96**	...	...	...
Northern Africa	1.01**	0.96	0.99**	1.08	1.01	0.98	1.08					0.94**	0.76**	...	...
Western Asia	0.98**	0.93**	0.91**	0.95**	...	...	...					0.97**	0.76**	...	...
Pacific	0.94**	0.97**	0.95**	1.39**	...	...	...					...	0.83**	...	...
Southern Asia	1.01**	1.06**	0.99**	0.93**	0.99	1.02	0.80					0.91**	0.74	...	...
Sub-Saharan Africa	0.97**	0.93**	0.86**	0.70**	0.97	0.96	0.63					0.86**	0.90	...	...
	0.99**												0.83		
Conflict-affected countries	0.98**	1.00**	0.97**	0.99**	0.97	0.77	0.79					0.92**	0.95	...	...
	0.98**												...		
Countries with low income	1.00	0.93	0.82**	0.53**	1.01	0.44	0.35					0.85**		...	...
Countries with middle income	1.00	1.00**	1.00**	1.07**	1.01	1.05	1.01					0.96**		...	...
Lower middle	0.98	1.02**	0.98**	0.97**	1.00	1.01	0.96					0.93**		...	...
Upper middle	1.00	0.97	1.03	1.16	1.01	1.06	1.23					1.00**		...	...
Countries with high income	1.00	1.00	1.00	1.25	...	...	1.07					...		...	...

Source: UIS database, except where noted. Data presented in the present table come from previous and subsequent statistical tables in the longer and or the printed version where they are broken-down by gender (total, male, female). Gender parity indices in the table are based on those gender break-downs and are the ratio of female to male rates.

Note A: The country groupings by level of income are as defined by the World Bank but include only countries listed in the table. They are based on the list of countries by income group as revised in July 2015.

Note B: See previous and subsequent statistical tables for sources of data and detailed country notes.

1. Global Education Monitoring Report team calculations, based on data from national and international household surveys compiled in the World Inequality Database in Education (WIDE).

2. Altinok (2013); Cheng and Omeova (2014); ministries of education's national reports and websites; EGMA/EGRA; PASEC; PILNA; PIRLS 2011; PISA 2012; SACMEQ; TERCE; TIMSS 2011; Uwezo. Data on learning outcomes are from nationally representative national (N), regional (R) and international (I) formative learning assessments. Information and data need to be used and interpreted with caution since the different types of assessments are not necessary comparable.

3. PIACC 2012 (OECD, 2013).

4. Data are for the most recent year available in the period specified. For details see relevant sources.

5. National population data were used to calculate enrolment ratios due to inconsistencies in the United Nations population data or lack of United Nations population by age.

Data in bold are for the school year ending in 2015.

(z) Data are for the school year ending in 2013.

(y) Data are for the school year ending in 2012.

(*) National estimate.

(**) For country level data: UIS partial estimate; for regional and other country grouping sums and weighted averages: partial imputation due to incomplete country coverage (between 33% and 60% of population for the region or other country grouping).

(...) No data are available.

TABLE 8

SDG 4, Target 4.5 – Gender – Achieving gender equality in education
By 2030, ensure "substantive gender equality in education through gender-sensitive school and learning processes and environments, education content and teacher training, and challenging gender discrimination and unequal social norms in education"

	GENDER EQUALITY IN EDUCATION														
	Female presence in teaching staff				Gender-sensitive national curriculum frameworks and learning environments[1]							Gender discrimination and unequal social norms		Child domestic work[7]	
	Percentage of female teachers (%)				Inclusion of gender equality issues[2] in national curriculum frameworks[3]	Percentage of schools with basic sanitation facilities or toilets (%)		Percentage of students aged 13–15 experiencing school-related gender-based violence by type of violence (%)				Early marriage and pregnancies		Percentage of adolescents ages 12–14 involved in household chores during the previous week	
	Pre-primary	Primary	Total secondary	Tertiary		Total	Of which: single-sex toilets	Bullying		Physical violence		Early marriage	Early pregnancies		
												Percentage of the population aged 15–19 who are currently married (%)[5]	Age-specific fertility rate (births per 1,000 women aged 15–19)[6]	For 28 hours and more	
	School year ending in 2014				2005–2015[4]	2014	2014	2009–2015[4]		2009–2015[4]		2009–2014[4]	2016	2009–2014[4]	
Country or territory	% F	% F	% F	% F				Total (%)	GPI (F/M)	Total	GPI (F/M)	Female		Total	GPI (F/M)
Caucasus and Central Asia															
Armenia	100[y]	...	...	57	0	86	...	...	...	...	...	6.4	20	...	...
Azerbaijan	100	90	...	56	0	68	...	...	...	...	...	9.0	66	...	...
Georgia	...	90	80	50	...	70	...	...	...	...	...	10.6[a]	33	...	...
Kazakhstan	98	98	75	65	...	85	...	...	...	...	...	4.6[a]	24	...	...
Kyrgyzstan	...	98	78	59	...	53	15	...	...	...	...	9.8	38	1.4	1.80
Tajikistan	...	76	...	38	...	29	...	...	...	...	...	14.1	37	...	...
Turkmenistan	...	...	...	50	...	...	...	...	...	...	...	...	15	...	...
Uzbekistan	...	...	...	...	...	100	...	...	...	...	...	...	17	...	...
Eastern and South-eastern Asia															
Brunei Darussalam	96	77	67	47	0	...	...	23.4	0.9	24.4	0.5	...	20	...	...
Cambodia	93	51	...	...	...	81	...	22.4	1.0	13.8	0.8	9.9	54	...	...
China	97	61	51	...	...	62	...	...	...	...	...	2.1	7	...	...
DPR Korea	...	...	...	...	...	...	...	...	...	...	...	...	0,4	...	...
Hong Kong, China	...	78	57**	...	LOW	...	...	...	...	...	...	0.3	3	...	...
Indonesia	96	62	53	39	LOW	53	55	...	...	...	...	13.9	48	...	...
Japan	...	...	...	...	...	...	...	...	...	...	...	0.6	4	...	...
Lao PDR	98	51	50**	36	...	47	...	13.2	0.7	10.2	0.7	24.8[a]	62	...	...
Macao, China	99	87	59	36	...	...	...	...	...	...	...	0.3	3	...	...
Malaysia	96	70	65	52	...	100	...	20.9	0.7	30.1	0.6	6.0	14	...	...
Mongolia	98[y]	95	73	60	...	52	...	30.5	0.7	43.8	0.4	3.6[a]	12	11.8	1.17
Myanmar	99	84	87	80[y]	0	23	...	...	...	...	...	12.5	15	...	...
Philippines	...	87[z]	73[z]	...	0	53	...	47.7	1.0	37.7	0.7	10.0[a]	66	...	...
Republic of Korea	99[z]	79[z]	58[z]	35[z]	LOW	...	...	...	...	...	...	...	1	...	...
Singapore	...	...	...	35[z]	...	...	...	...	...	...	...	0.4	4	...	...
Thailand	...	...	...	61	LOW	45	...	33.2	0.7	29.0	0.6	11.3	45	...	...
Timor-Leste	...	...	...	...	...	64	...	...	...	...	...	8.3	41	...	...
Viet Nam	99	75	...	49	...	72	...	26.1	1.0	21.8	0.4	8.4	41	1.6	1.07
Europe and Northern America															
Albania	100	84	65	52	...	30	37	...	...	...	...	7.0	23	...	...
Andorra	89	80	64	45	...	...	...	...	...	...	...	...	...	...	...
Austria	99	91	65	43	...	...	...	...	...	...	...	2.7[a]	6	...	...
Belarus	99	100	81	61	...	100	...	...	...	...	...	7.5[a]	15	...	...
Belgium	97	82	63	48	0	...	...	...	...	...	...	2.2[a]	7	...	...
Bosnia and Herzegovina	98[y]	85	61	43	...	100	...	...	...	...	...	0.7[a]	6	...	...
Bulgaria	100	94	79	48	...	100	...	...	...	...	...	1.2	33	...	...
Canada	...	...	...	...	...	...	...	...	...	...	...	2.2[a]	8	...	...
Croatia	99	93	67	48	LOW	100	...	...	...	...	...	2.0[a]	8	...	...
Cyprus	99	84	66	39	...	...	...	...	...	...	...	3.1[a]	5	...	...
Czech Republic	...	...	...	...	...	...	...	...	...	...	...	0.2	9	...	...
Denmark	...	...	...	...	...	...	...	...	...	...	...	0.1	4	...	...
Estonia	...	92[z]	77[z]	...	LOW	...	...	...	...	...	...	0.4	10	...	...
Finland	97[z]	79[z]	65[z]	51[z]	...	...	...	...	...	...	...	0.4	6	...	...
France	83[z]	83[z]	59[z]	37[z]	LOW	...	...	...	...	...	...	2.7[a]	8	...	...
Germany	97	87	62	38	...	...	...	...	...	...	...	0.3	5	...	...
Greece	99	70	58	33	...	...	...	...	...	...	...	1.8[a]	6	...	...
Hungary	100	97	71	43	LOW	...	...	...	...	...	...	0.6[a]	17	...	...
Iceland	94[z]	82[z]	...	48[y]	LOW	...	...	...	...	...	...	0.6[a]	4	...	...
Ireland	...	85[y]	...	...	LOW	...	...	...	...	...	...	0.3	9	...	...
Italy	98[z]	96[z]	72[z]	37[z]	...	...	...	...	...	...	...	0.3	6	...	...
Latvia	100	93	83	56	...	...	...	...	...	...	...	0.8	12	...	...
Liechtenstein	100[y]	77[y]	...	30[y]	...	...	...	...	...	...	...	0.2[a]	...	...	...
Lithuania	99	97	82	56	LOW	...	...	...	...	...	...	0.0	8	...	...
Luxembourg	...	...	...	49[y]	HIGH	...	...	...	...	...	...	1.0[a]	5	...	...
Malta	97	86	64	34	0	...	...	...	...	...	...	0.5	15	...	...
Monaco	...	...	...	...	...	...	...	...	...	...	...	...	...	...	...
Montenegro	...	...	...	...	...	95	...	...	...	...	...	3.6	11	0	.
Netherlands	87	86	...	40[y]	...	...	...	...	...	...	...	0.2	3	...	...
Norway	...	75	62	45	0	...	...	...	...	...	...	0.1[a]	6	...	...
Poland	98[z]	85[z]	70[z]	44[z]	...	...	...	...	...	...	...	1.2[a]	12	...	...
Portugal	99	80	70	44[z]	0	...	...	...	...	...	...	0.6	8	...	...
Republic of Moldova	100[y]	98	78	56[z]	...	70	...	...	...	...	...	9.9[a]	20	...	...
Romania	100	89	70	49	...	90	...	...	...	...	...	6.7[a]	32	...	...
Russian Federation	...	99	82[y]	57[y]	...	100	...	...	...	...	...	7.5[a]	20	...	...
San Marino	96[y]	91[y]	...	...	...	...	...	...	...	...	...	0.0	...	...	...
Serbia	98	85	64	43	LOW	95	...	...	...	...	...	5.2[a]	17	1.5	1.07
Slovakia	100	90	75	45	...	...	...	...	...	...	...	1.2	19	...	...
Slovenia	98[z]	97[z]	73[z]	40[z]	...	...	...	...	...	...	...	0.3	3	...	...

TABLE 8

(Continued)

	GENDER EQUALITY IN EDUCATION														
	Female presence in teaching staff				Gender-sensitive national curriculum frameworks and learning environments[1]							Gender discrimination and unequal social norms		Child domestic w...	
	Percentage of female teachers (%)				Inclusion of gender equality issues[2] in national curriculum frameworks[3]	Percentage of schools with basic sanitation facilities or toilets (%)		Percentage of students aged 13–15 experiencing school-related gender-based violence by type of violence (%)				Early marriage and pregnancies		Percentage of adolescents ag... 12–14 involve... household cho... during the previous wee...	
	Pre-primary	Primary	Total secondary	Tertiary		Total	Of which: single-sex toilets	Bullying		Physical violence		Early marriage	Early pregnancies	For 28 hours and...	
	School year ending in 2014				2005–2015[4]	2014	2014	2009–2015[4]		2009–2015[4]		Percentage of the population aged 15–19 who are currently married (%)[5] 2009–2014[4]	Age-specific fertility rate (births per 1,000 women aged 15–19)[6] 2016	2009–2014[4]	
Country or territory	%F	%F	%F	%F				Total (%)	GPI (F/M)	Total	GPI (F/M)	Female		Total	GPI (
Spain	...	76ʸ	55ʸ	40ʸ	...	...	...	...	...	...	...	3.5ᵃ	8	...	
Sweden	...	82ʸ	58ʸ	43ʸ	LOW	...	...	...	...	...	...	0.4ᵃ	6	...	
Switzerland	97	82	48ʸ	34	...	...	...	...	...	...	...	0.4ᵃ	2	...	
TFYR Macedonia	99ʸ	81ᶻ	57ᶻ	48ᶻ	...	...	...	...	...	...	...	4.3ᵃ	16	0.3	
Ukraine	99ʸ	99	88	...	...	100	...	...	...	...	...	6.4ᵃ	20	0.5	3.
United Kingdom	...	...	61	44	0	...	...	...	...	...	...	2.9ᵃ	11	...	
United States	94	87	62	49	...	...	...	...	...	...	...		15	...	
Latin America and the Caribbean															
Anguilla	...	...	...	...	...	100	...	27.8	1.2	35.7	0.7	...	...	...	
Antigua and Barbuda	100ʸ	93	73	54ʸ	...	100	...	24.9	1.1	47.5	0.7	...	40	...	
Argentina	...	...	...	...	0	68	...	24.5	1.0	34.1	0.6	12.7ᵃ	64	...	
Aruba	98ʸ	85ʸ	59ʸ	54	...	...	...	...	...	...	...	0.8	18	0.5	2.
Bahamas	...	...	...	...	...	...	...	23.6	0.9	40.0	0.8	2.4ᵃ	25	...	
Barbados	94	84	...	...	...	100	...	13.3	0.7	38.4	0.6	2.4ᵃ	34	0	
Belize	99	74	63	51	LOW	21	32	30.7	1.0	36.0	0.7	3.3	62	1.5	0.
Bermuda	100	88	70	55	...	...	...	...	...	...	...	0.1	...	...	
Bolivia, P.S.	...	...	...	...	...	74	...	30.2	0.9	33.0	0.5	11.6ᵃ	69	...	
Brazil	95	90	65	45	0	98	...	...	...	...	...	3.9	66	...	
British Virgin Islands	...	89	69	...	...	100	...	17.2	0.9	35.0	0.6	...	...	...	
Cayman Islands[9]	90ʸ	88ʸ	67ʸ	...	...	...	...	...	...	...	...	1.1	...	...	
Chile	...	81ᶻ	59ᶻ	43ᶻ	LOW	90	...	15.1	0.9	28.5	0.5	5.7ᵃ	46	...	
Colombia	96	77	52	36	...	100	...	...	...	...	...	13.7ᵃ	43	...	
Costa Rica	93	80	57	...	...	53	...	19.0	1.1	22.1	0.4	9.0ᵃ	54	1.4	0.
Cuba	100ʸ	80	61	54	...	100	...	...	...	...	...	22.0ᵃ	43	...	
Curaçao	...	...	...	...	...	...	...	...	...	...	...	...	33	...	
Dominica	100	87	73	...	LOW	100	...	27.4	0.9	39.1	0.6	...	...	...	
Dominican Republic	94	79	67	43	LOW	60	...	...	...	...	...	18.7ᵃ	95	...	
Ecuador	81ᶻ	73	66	34ʸ	...	54	...	...	...	...	...	20.0ᵃ	74	...	
El Salvador	98ᶻ	71ᶻ	53ᶻ	37	LOW	67	...	...	...	...	...	...	64	...	
Grenada	100	79	63	...	LOW	100	...	...	...	...	...	...	26	...	
Guatemala	92ʸ	65	47	...	MEDIUM	49	50	...	...	...	...	19.8ᵃ	77	...	
Guyana	100ʸ	89ʸ	71ʸ	53ʸ	...	68	...	38.4	0.9	37.9	0.5	13.3	86	...	
Haiti	...	...	...	...	0	60	...	...	...	...	...	10.6	37	...	
Honduras	97	70	61	39	LOW	46	47	31.6	1.0	28.0	0.6	22.6ᵃ	61	...	
Jamaica	...	89	70	...	...	80	85	40.2	1.0	50.1	0.6	3.4ᵃ	55	0.2	1
Mexico	95	68	...	...	LOW	68	69	...	...	...	...	16.1ᵃ	60	...	
Montserrat	...	98	74	...	...	100	...	...	...	...	...	0.0	...	...	
Nicaragua	...	...	...	...	MEDIUM	26	...	...	...	...	...	...	85	...	
Panama	95ᶻ	73ʸ	59ʸ	47ᶻ	LOW	84	85	...	...	...	...	18.1ᵃ	71	...	
Paraguay	89ʸ	71ʸ	62ʸ	...	HIGH	70	...	...	...	...	...	...	55	...	
Peru	96ʸ	67	44	...	LOW	51	55	47.4	1.0	36.9	0.4	10.6ᵃ	46	...	
Saint Kitts and Nevis	100	90	69	...	...	100	...	22.7	0.8	37.8	0.7	...	...	...	
Saint Lucia	100	88	70	52	...	100	...	...	...	...	...	5.0ᵃ	52	0.2	
Saint Martin	...	...	...	...	...	...	...	...	...	...	...	...	...	...	
St. Vincent and the Grenadines	100ᶻ	80	66	...	...	100	...	...	...	...	...	...	48	...	
Sint Maarten	...	89	58	54	...	...	...	...	...	...	...	0.6	...	...	
Suriname	100	94	71ᶻ	...	...	65	68	26.3	1.0	20.5	0.4	2.3	44	0	
Trinidad and Tobago	...	...	...	...	...	100	...	15.4	0.7	35.9	0.6	2.1	28	...	
Turks and Caicos Islands	...	93	60	...	...	100	...	...	...	...	...	...	...	...	
Uruguay	...	...	...	...	LOW	100	...	...	...	...	...	11.1ᵃ	54	...	
Venezuela, B.R.	...	...	...	...	0	93	...	...	...	...	...	...	78	...	
Northern Africa and Western Asia															
Algeria	...	65	...	42	...	100	...	51.7	1.1	47.7	0.6	...	10	0.5	1
Bahrain	100	75	58	36	...	100	...	...	...	...	...	5.3	13	...	
Egypt	98	59	45	44	...	100	...	70.0	1.0	45.1	0.5	14.4	49	...	
Iraq	...	...	...	...	LOW	100	...	27.7	0.7	37.1	0.5	20.7	88	...	
Israel[10]	...	...	...	...	...	...	...	...	...	...	...	2.8	8	4	2
Jordan	100ʸ	...	...	...	...	50	68	...	...	...	...	5.9	20	0.2	
Kuwait	100	91	...	...	...	100	...	27.7	0.5	44.9	0.5	...	8	...	
Lebanon	98	87	66	48	...	...	...	25.1	0.5	48.5	0.4	...	11	1.7	7.
Libya	...	...	...	...	...	65	...	...	...	...	...	...	6	...	
Morocco	71	55	35ᶻ	...	...	73	...	19.0	1.2	42.6	0.4	11.0	30	...	
Oman	100	...	...	35	...	94	...	47.4	1.1	50.0	0.8	4.1	5	...	
Palestine	100	71	51	23	0	83	...	...	...	...	...	6.3	56	0.4	7
Qatar	100	86	55	37	LOW	100	...	42.1	0.7	50.6	0.6	...	10	...	
Saudi Arabia	100	52	51	40	...	...	...	...	...	...	...	...	7	...	
Sudan	97ᶻ	64ᶻ	54ᶻ	30ᶻ	...	44	...	...	...	...	...	23.5	64	...	
Syrian Arab Republic	98ᶻ	...	...	...	...	...	...	...	...	...	...	...	37	...	
Tunisia	...	59	...	48	...	99	60	...	...	...	...	1.2	7	...	
Turkey	94ᶻ	58ᶻ	48ᶻ	42ᶻ	...	99	...	...	...	...	...	6.6	24	...	
United Arab Emirates	99	91	61	32	...	100	...	22.8	0.8	46.6	0.6	...	32	...	
Yemen	...	...	...	...	...	53	...	...	...	...	...	16.7	58	...	

TABLE 8

(Continued)

	GENDER EQUALITY IN EDUCATION														
	Female presence in teaching staff				Gender-sensitive national curriculum frameworks and learning environments[1]							Gender discrimination and unequal social norms		Child domestic work[7]	
	Percentage of female teachers (%)				Inclusion of gender equality issues[2] in national curriculum frameworks[3]	Percentage of schools with basic sanitation facilities or toilets (%)		Percentage of students aged 13–15 experiencing school-related gender-based violence by type of violence (%)				Early marriage and pregnancies		Percentage of adolescents ages 12–14 involved in household chores during the previous week	
	Pre-primary	Primary	Total secondary	Tertiary		Total	Of which: single-sex toilets	Bullying		Physical violence		Early marriage	Early pregnancies	For 28 hours and more	
												Percentage of the population aged 15–19 who are currently married (%)[5]	Age-specific fertility rate (births per 1,000 women aged 15–19)[6]		
	School year ending in 2014				2005–2015[4]	2014	2014	2009–2015[4]		2009–2015[4]		2009–2014[4]	2016	2009–2014[4]	
Country or territory	% F	% F	% F	% F				Total (%)	GPI (F/M)	Total	GPI (F/M)	Female		Total	GPI (F/M)
The Pacific															
Australia	...	...	...	44z	LOW	...	...	...	...	...	...	0.5	13	...	...
Cook Islands	100	87	55	47	0	...	...	33.0	1.2	40.8	0.7	...	13	...	...
Fiji	...	59y	57y	...	0	95	...	42.0	0.9	47.3	0.6	...	47	...	...
Kiribati	...	82	...	.y	LOW	4	...	36.8	0.8	35.3	0.7	15.4	13	...	...
Marshall Islands	...	...	...	44y		10	...	...	...	...	...	...	...	...	...
Micronesia F.S.	...	...	...	...	0	...	...	...	...	...	...	...	11	...	...
Nauru	100	93	58	...	0	...	...	38.9	1.0	45.2	0.9	...	...	...	...
New Zealand	98	84	62	49	0	...	...	...	...	...	...	...	22	...	...
Niue	100	...	...	...	...	100	...	35.5	...	32.9	...	...	...	...	...
Palau	100	...	...	54z	...	100	...	...	...	...	...	...	...	...	...
Papua New Guinea	...	...	42y	...	LOW	...	...	...	...	...	...	...	53	...	...
Samoa	95	...	...	...	0	...	...	...	...	...	...	7.0a	22	...	...
Solomon Islands	87	47	30y	...	...	66	66	...	...	...	...	...	43	...	...
Tokelau	...	...	...	...	LOW	...	...	40.5	1.0	75.1	0.7	2.0	...	...	...
Tonga	100	72	66	...	...	...	...	50.3	1.1	49.1	1.0	4.6a	14	...	...
Tuvalu	100	...	...	...	MEDIUM	60	...	26.9	0.4	71.1	0.9	...	...	...	...
Vanuatu	95z	56z	...	...	...	69	70	67.3	1.0	50.5	0.7	11.5a	41	...	...
Southern Asia															
Afghanistan	...	31z	...	11	0	58	...	44.2	1.1	40.6	0.7	19.7a	60	3.6	5.64
Bangladesh	...	...	21z	18	...	60	...	23.6	0.6	21.1	0.4	44.7	81	...	...
Bhutan	99	41	39	27y	MEDIUM	74	73	...	...	...	...	15.2a	15	0.9	3.25
India	...	48z	45z	39z	LOW	53	78	...	...	...	...	21.1	19	...	...
Iran, Islamic Republic of	...	66	54	30	...	86	...	...	...	...	...	21.1	25	...	...
Maldives	100	75	...	...	0	73	...	30.1	1.0	31.7	0.6	5.0	4	...	...
Nepal	**90**	**42**	**22****	...	MEDIUM	68	...	...	...	...	...	23.1	69	7	3.22
Pakistan	...	50	...	37	LOW	63	...	...	...	...	...	13.1	37	...	...
Sri Lanka	...	...	...	...	...	82	...	...	...	...	...	...	12	...	...
Sub-Saharan Africa															
Angola	...	...	...	...	...	54	...	...	...	...	...	...	153	...	...
Benin	73	23	11	...	...	74	...	42.1	1.0	32.0	0.8	15.3	76	...	...
Botswana	98y	74z	53z	...	...	50	...	...	...	...	...	...	26	...	...
Burkina Faso	85z	42	16	8z	...	39	73	...	...	...	...	31.1	102	...	...
Burundi	84	52	23	12z	...	53	...	...	...	...	...	8.4	26	...	...
Cabo Verde	100	68	43	40	...	100	...	...	...	...	...	...	72	...	...
Cameroon	97	53	33	...	...	41	...	...	...	...	...	20.1	93	...	...
Central African Republic	...	20y	11y	...	...	44	...	...	...	...	...	54.9a	86	3.3	2.67
Chad	81z	...	...	...	...	36	40	...	...	...	...	47.8a	115	3.8	2.57
Comoros	...	43z	...	...	...	50	...	...	...	...	...	13.1	62	...	...
Congo	99y	54y	9y	...	...	15	...	...	...	...	...	18.3a	110	...	...
Côte d'Ivoire	96	26	15	15	LOW	45	...	...	...	...	...	21.9	136	...	...
Democratic Rep. of the Congo	95	28	12	8z	0	29	...	...	...	...	...	21.3	121	2	5.50
Djibouti	...	26	25	...	LOW	85	83	...	...	...	...	...	20	...	...
Equatorial Guinea	89y	39y	...	...	...	40	...	...	...	...	...	22.0a	103	...	...
Eritrea	98z	37z	18z	...	...	66	...	...	...	...	...	...	48	...	...
Ethiopia	...	42	24**,y	12	...	37	...	...	...	...	...	19.0a	50	...	...
Gabon	...	...	...	...	...	61	...	...	...	...	...	10.1	89	...	...
Gambia	50	31	14	8y	LOW	71	...	...	...	...	...	25.0	110	...	...
Ghana	**83**	**39**	**24**	19	LOW	62	...	54.4	...	27.1	0.8	7.6	63	...	...
Guinea	...	30	...	3	...	69	...	...	...	...	...	33.6	135	...	...
Guinea-Bissau	...	...	...	...	...	28	...	...	...	...	...	18.5a	80	1.4	4.40
Kenya	77	48**,y	41**,y	...	...	20	21	...	...	...	...	14.6	88	...	...
Lesotho	98	76	56**,z	50	MEDIUM	40	...	...	...	...	...	11.5a	95	...	...
Liberia	...	14	5	12y	...	82	...	...	...	...	...	14.5	100	...	...
Madagascar	89	56	44	32z	...	29	...	...	...	...	...	27.4	109	7.6	0.99
Malawi	...	41	20	...	...	25	...	...	...	...	...	23.9a	132	4.5	3.24
Mali	92	29	18	9y	...	24	...	...	...	...	...	42.2	170	...	...
Mauritania	96	36	12	7z	...	27	33	47.2	1.0	57.8	0.7	25.7	75	6.4	3.28
Mauritius	100	75	59	...	LOW	100	...	...	...	...	...	7.0a	28	...	...
Mozambique	...	42	21**,z	26	...	50	53	...	...	...	...	36.6	126	...	...
Namibia	...	...	...	...	LOW	80	...	46.6	0.9	35.8	0.7	4.1	74	...	...
Niger	90	48	20	13y	LOW	14	...	...	...	...	...	59.8a	196	...	...
Nigeria	...	...	...	...	...	32	59	...	...	...	...	29.6	104	1.1	1.44
Rwanda	85z	53	29z	17z	MEDIUM	95	...	...	...	...	...	3.4	23	...	...
Sao Tome and Principe	**94**	**56**	**34**	**28**	...	87	...	...	...	...	...	22.8	80	9.2	2.18
Senegal	75	32	...	...	...	66	...	...	...	...	...	24.7	70	...	...
Seychelles	100	88	62	39	LOW	100	...	...	...	...	...	...	55	...	...
Sierra Leone	82z	27z	13z	...	...	62	...	...	...	...	...	20.0	111	0.8	0.78
Somalia	...	...	...	...	...	45	...	...	...	...	...	...	97	13.8	2.83
South Africa	80**	78**	...	...	0	100	...	...	...	...	...	5.7a	40	...	...
South Sudan	...	...	...	...	MEDIUM	42	...	...	...	...	...	40.1a	54	...	...
Swaziland	...	70z	49z	38z	...	72	...	32.1	0.9	19.4	0.5	4.3a	54	0.1	...

TABLE 8
(Continued)

Country or territory	| GENDER EQUALITY IN EDUCATION														
	Female presence in teaching staff				Gender-sensitive national curriculum frameworks and learning environments[1]							Gender discrimination and unequal social norms		Child domestic w…	
	Percentage of female teachers (%)				Inclusion of gender equality issues[2] in national curriculum frame-works[3]	Percentage of schools with basic sanitation facilities or toilets (%)		Percentage of students aged 13–15 experiencing school-related gender-based violence by type of violence (%)				Early marriage and pregnancies		Percentage of adolescents ag… 12–14 involved … household chor… during the previous week…	
	Pre-primary	Primary	Total secondary	Tertiary		Total	Of which: single-sex toilets	Bullying		Physical violence		Early marriage	Early pregnancies		
												Percentage of the population aged 15–19 who are currently married (%)[5]	Age-specific fertility rate (births per 1,000 women aged 15–19)[6]	For 28 hours and …	
	School year ending in 2014				2005–2015[4]	2014	2014	2009–2015[4]		2009–2015[4]		2009–2014[4]	2016	2009–2014[4]	
	% F	% F	% F	% F		Total		Total (%)	GPI (F/M)	Total	GPI (F/M)	Female		Total	GPI …
Togo	94	16	…	6		22	…	…	…	…	…	13.2	92	1.8	3.0
Uganda	86ᶻ	42ᶻ	24ᶻ	…	…	75	…	…	…	…	…	18.2	97	…	…
United Republic of Tanzania	…	52ᶻ	28ʸ	30ʸ	LOW	11	47	26.9	1.1	30.9	0.8	20.6	114	…	…
Zambia	…	…	…	…	MEDIUM	45	40	…	…	…	…	16.7	78	…	…
Zimbabwe	93ᶻ	56ᶻ	46ᶻ	32ᶻ	…	43		…	…	…	…	22.1ᵃ	106	…	…
	Weighted Average					Median		Median		Median		Weighted Average		Median	
World	94**	64**	53**	42**	…	69	…	…	…	…	…	13.9	42	…	…
														…	…
Countries in transition	98**,ʸ	94	76**,ᶻ	54**,ᶻ	…	86	…	…	…	…	…	7.4	23	…	…
Developed countries	95**	83**	60**	41	…	…	…	…	…	…	…	1.5	11	…	…
Developing countries	93	59**	49**	40**	…	67	…	…	…	…	…	15.2	46	…	…
Caucasus and Central Asia	98**	90**	70**,ʸ	54**	…	70	…	…	…	…	…	8.5	28	…	…
Eastern and South-eastern Asia	97	64	52	40**,ʸ	…	53	…	…	…	…	…	5.2	22	…	…
Eastern Asia	98	62	50	38**,ʸ	…	…	…	…	…	…	…	2.0	7	…	…
South-eastern Asia	97	68	58	49	…	53	…	…	…	…	…	11.5	45	…	…
Europe and Northern America	95**	86	67**	47**	…	…	…	…	…	…	…	3.4	13	…	…
Latin America and the Caribbean	95**	77	58**	41**	…	87	…	…	…	…	…	…	62	…	…
Caribbean	95**,ᶻ	68**	54	51	…	100	…	…	…	…	…	…	57	…	…
Latin America	95	78	59**	40**	…	68	…	…	…	…	…	10.4	62	…	…
Northern Africa and Western Asia	93**	60**	48**	39**	…	99	…	…	…	…	…	…	40	…	…
Northern Africa	87**	60	44**	39	…	86	…	…	…	…	…	…	41	…	…
Western Asia	98**	61**	50**	39**	…	100	…	…	…	…	…	…	39	…	…
Pacific	…	…	…	44**	…	68	…	38.9	40.1	…	47.3	…	27	…	…
Southern Asia	…	49**	42**	36**	…	68	…	…	…	…	…	…	29	…	…
Sub-Saharan Africa	76**	44**	29**	21**	…	48	…	…	…	…	…	22.6	97	…	…
Conflict-affected countries	94**,ʸ	55**	49**	41**	…	53	…	…	…	…	…	19.5	44	…	…
Countries with low income	82**	40	23**	18**	…	48	…	…	…	…	…	23.2	91	…	…
Countries with middle income	94	61**	51**	42**	…	68	…	…	…	…	…	14.0	38	…	…
Lower middle	91**	56**	48**	40**	…	63	…	…	…	…	…	20.5	43	…	…
Upper middle	96	66	55	43**	…	85	…	…	…	…	…	5.4	30	…	…
Countries with high income	96**	82**	62**	42**	…	…	…	…	…	…	…	3.4	16	…	…

Source: UIS database, except where noted.

Note: The country groupings by level of income are as defined by the World Bank but include only countries listed in the table. They are based on the list of countries by income group as revised in July 2015.

1. UNESCO-IBE (2016); UNICEF-WASH-Report (2015); Global School-based Student Health Survey.

2. Key terms included are a) gender equality, b) gender equity, c) empowerment of girls/women, d) gender sensitive(ity) and e) gender parity. The degree of inclusion of the issue in curricula is assessed as LOW if 1 or 2 of the 5 items are covered, MEDIUM if 3 are covered and HIGH if 4 or 5 are covered; 0 indicates no inclusion of any items.

3. Curricula referred to are for primary education, lower secondary education or both.

4. Data are for the most recent year available in the period specified. For details see relevant sources.

5. United Nations, Department of Economic and Social Affairs, Population Division: World Marriage Data 2015 (POP/DB/Marr/Rev2015); GEM Report team calculations for total values and weighted averages.

6. The fertility indicators are from the United Nations Population Division estimates, revision 2015 (United Nations, 2015). They are based on the median variant.

7. UNICEF-MICS 4 and 5, country reports. Child domestic work refers to household chores such as cooking, cleaning and caring for children, as well as collecting firewood and fetching water.

a. Includes consensual unions

Data in bold are for the school year ending in 2015.

(z) Data are for the school year ending in 2013.

(y) Data are for the school year ending in 2012.

(*) National estimate.

(**) For country level data: UIS partial estimate; for regional and other country grouping sums and weighted averages: partial imputation due to incomplete country coverage (between 33% and 60% of population for the region or other country grouping).

(-) Magnitude nil or negligible

(.) The category is not applicable or does not exist.

(…) No data are available.

TABLE 9

SDG 4, Target 4.5 - Equity - Equal completion of school for vulnerable groups

By 2030, eliminate gender disparities in education and ensure equal access at all levels of education and vocational training for the vulnerable, including persons with disabilities, indigenous peoples and children in vulnerable situations

	DISPARITY IN SCHOOL COMPLETION[1]												
	Primary completion rate and disparity by location and wealth				Lower secondary completion rate and disparity by location and wealth				Upper secondary completion rate and disparity by location and wealth				
	Location	Wealth	Completion rate (%) of the poorest students		Location	Wealth	Completion rate (%) of the poorest students		Location	Wealth	Completion rate (%) of the poorest students		
	Location parity index[2]	Wealth parity index[3]	Poorest females	Poorest males	Location parity index[2]	Wealth parity index[3]	Poorest females	Poorest males	Location parity index[2]	Wealth parity index[3]	Poorest females	Poorest males	
Country or territory	2009–2014	2009–2014	2009–2014	2009–2014	2009–2014	2009–2014	2009–2014	2009–2014	2009–2014	2009–2014	2009–2014	2009–2014	Reference years and surveys
Caucasus and Central Asia													
Armenia	1.00	1.00	100	100	0.99	0.99	100	98	0.96	0.90	94	82	2010 DHS
Azerbaijan	...	...	...	...	...	...	...	...	...	...	...	...	
Georgia	...	...	...	...	0.99	0.99	96	100	0.98	0.89	92	85	2013 HIS
Kazakhstan	1.00	1.00	100	100	1.00	1.00	99	100	0.95	0.89	88	88	2010 MICS
Kyrgyzstan	1.00	1.00	100	99	0.99	1.01	98	99	0.90	0.92	89	86	2012 DHS
Tajikistan	0.99	0.98	97	98	0.95	0.88	77	90	0.77	0.66	38	66	2012 DHS
Turkmenistan	...	...	...	...	...	...	...	...	...	...	...	...	
Uzbekistan	...	...	...	...	...	...	...	...	...	...	...	...	
Eastern and South-eastern Asia													
Brunei Darussalam	...	...	...	...	...	...	...	...	...	...	...	...	
Cambodia	0.80	0.46	49	33	0.57	0.27	19	17	0.28	0.09	5	3	2014 DHS
China	0.93	0.91	89	88	0.81	0.71	66	60	0.47	0.49	32	21	2010 CFPS
DPR Korea	...	...	...	...	...	...	...	...	...	...	...	...	
Hong Kong, China	...	...	...	...	...	...	...	...	...	...	...	...	
Indonesia	0.95	0.88	88	86	0.78	0.55	50	53	0.54	0.26	20	24	2012 DHS
Japan	...	...	...	...	...	...	...	...	...	...	...	...	
Lao PDR	0.72	0.35	29	40	0.35	0.05	2	5	0.26	0.03	1	3	2011 MICS
Macao, China	...	...	...	...	...	...	...	...	...	...	...	...	
Malaysia	...	...	...	...	...	...	...	...	...	...	...	...	
Mongolia	0.97	0.94	97	92	0.72	0.54	62	46	0.47	0.29	45	14	2010 MICS
Myanmar	...	...	...	...	...	...	...	...	...	...	...	...	
Philippines	0.94	0.70	84	63	0.82	0.40	53	31	0.81	0.36	45	29	2013 DHS
Republic of Korea	...	...	...	...	...	...	...	...	...	...	...	...	
Singapore	...	...	...	...	...	...	...	...	...	...	...	...	
Thailand	...	...	...	...	...	...	...	...	...	...	...	...	
Timor-Leste	0.71	0.39	31	32	0.56	0.33	22	26	0.41	0.13	5	10	2009 DHS
Viet Nam	0.98	0.89	88	86	0.88	0.57	61	51	0.68	0.21	19	19	2013 MICS
Europe and Northern America													
Albania	...	...	...	...	...	...	...	...	...	...	...	...	
Andorra	...	...	...	...	...	...	...	...	...	...	...	...	
Austria	...	...	...	...	...	...	...	...	1.12	0.88	82	81	2013 EU-SILC
Belarus	1.00	1.00	100	100	1.01	1.00	99	100	0.93	0.74	59	75	2012 MICS
Belgium	...	...	...	...	...	...	...	...	0.65	71	49	2013 EU-SILC
Bosnia and Herzegovina	1.02	0.99	98	100	0.94	0.89	89	89	0.81	0.50	61	35	2011 MICS
Bulgaria	...	...	...	...	...	...	...	...	0.78	0.53	...	...	2013 EU-SILC
Canada	...	...	...	...	...	...	...	...	0.94	0.78	78	67	2010 SLID
Croatia	...	...	...	...	...	...	...	...	0.99	0.94	88	98	2013 EU-SILC
Cyprus	...	...	...	...	...	...	...	...	1.01	0.85	94	75	2013 EU-SILC
Czech Republic	...	...	...	...	...	...	...	...	1.02	0.78	79	74	2013 EU-SILC
Denmark	...	...	...	...	...	...	...	...	0.76	0.86	75	71	2013 EU-SILC
Estonia	...	...	...	...	...	...	...	...	0.89	0.85	75	73	2013 EU-SILC
Finland	...	...	...	...	...	...	...	...	0.95	1.01	82	83	2013 EU-SILC
France	...	...	...	...	...	...	...	...	0.98	0.84	79	74	2013 EU-SILC
Germany	...	...	...	...	...	...	...	...	1.04	0.77	69	73	2013 EU-SILC
Greece	...	...	...	...	...	...	...	...	0.90	0.89	92	83	2013 EU-SILC
Hungary	...	...	...	...	...	...	...	...	0.91	0.64	63	63	2013 EU-SILC
Iceland	...	...	...	...	...	...	...	...	0.79	1.04	71	55	2013 EU-SILC
Ireland	...	...	...	...	...	...	...	...	...	...	...	...	
Italy	...	...	...	...	...	...	...	...	0.99	0.73	80	64	2013 EU-SILC
Latvia	...	...	...	...	...	...	...	...	0.90	0.68	74	55	2013 EU-SILC
Liechtenstein	...	...	...	...	...	...	...	...	...	...	...	...	
Lithuania	...	...	...	...	...	...	...	...	0.88	0.89	96	83	2013 EU-SILC
Luxembourg	...	...	...	...	...	...	...	...	1.00	0.64	53	51	2013 EU-SILC
Malta	...	...	...	...	...	...	...	...	...	0.59	58	50	2013 EU-SILC
Monaco	...	...	...	...	...	...	...	...	...	...	...	...	
Montenegro	1.01	0.96	98	94	0.93	0.83	72	88	0.83	0.68	62	63	2013 MICS
Netherlands	...	...	...	...	...	...	...	...	...	1.00	90	67	2013 EU-SILC
Norway	...	...	...	...	...	...	...	...	0.79	0.96	67	68	2013 EU-SILC
Poland	...	...	...	...	...	...	...	...	0.99	0.81	82	69	2013 EU-SILC
Portugal	...	...	...	...	...	...	...	...	0.90	0.42	45	28	2013 EU-SILC
Republic of Moldova	0.99	0.98	97	98	0.97	0.79	...	...	0.59	0.14	16	10	2012 MICS
Romania	...	...	...	...	...	...	...	...	0.82	0.69	71	65	2013 EU-SILC
Russian Federation	0.99	1.00	100	100	1.01	1.01	100	100	0.89	0.92	80	90	2013 RLMS-HES
San Marino	...	...	...	...	...	...	...	...	...	...	...	...	
Serbia	1.01	0.89	86	91	0.96	0.73	76	70	0.84	0.49	50	42	2014 MICS
Slovakia	...	...	...	...	...	...	...	...	1.01	0.95	90	88	2013 EU-SILC
Slovenia	...	...	...	...	...	...	...	...	...	0.83	83	73	2013 EU-SILC
Spain	...	...	...	...	...	...	...	...	0.84	0.56	55	49	2013 EU-SILC
Sweden	...	...	...	...	...	...	...	...	0.99	0.93	93	82	2013 EU-SILC
Switzerland	...	...	...	...	...	...	...	...	1.04	0.85	69	64	2013 EU-SILC
TFYR Macedonia	1.02	0.93	94	93	0.76	0.49	30	63	0.71	0.38	26	43	2011 MICS

449

TABLE 9

Part 1 (Continued)

Country or territory	Primary completion rate and disparity by location and wealth				Lower secondary completion rate and disparity by location and wealth				Upper secondary completion rate and disparity by location and wealth				
	Location	Wealth	Completion rate (%) of the poorest students		Location	Wealth	Completion rate (%) of the poorest students		Location	Wealth	Completion rate (%) of the poorest students		
	Location parity index[2]	Wealth parity index[3]	Poorest females	Poorest males	Location parity index[2]	Wealth parity index[3]	Poorest females	Poorest males	Location parity index[2]	Wealth parity index[3]	Poorest females	Poorest males	Reference years and surveys
	2009–2014	2009–2014	2009–2014	2009–2014	2009–2014	2009–2014	2009–2014	2009–2014	2009–2014	2009–2014	2009–2014	2009–2014	
Ukraine	1.00	1.00	100	100	1.00	0.99	100	98	0.93	0.84	86	82	2012 MICS
United Kingdom	...	...	...	...	...	...	...	...	0.99	0.95	98	92	2013 EU-SILC
United States	...	...	98	98	...	...	98	98	...	0.88	87	84	2013 CPS-ASEC
Latin America and the Caribbean													
Anguilla	...	...	...	...	...	...	...	...	...	...	...	...	...
Antigua and Barbuda	...	...	...	...	...	...	...	...	...	...	...	...	...
Argentina	...	0.97	96	95	...	0.72	70	57	...	0.54	51	38	2012 EPH
Aruba	...	...	...	...	...	...	...	...	...	...	...	...	...
Bahamas	...	...	...	...	...	...	...	...	...	...	...	...	...
Barbados	1.00	0.98	...	...	1.01	0.97	...	...	1.05	0.92	...	...	2012 MICS
Belize	0.87	0.66	70	59	0.59	0.19	13	17	0.58	0.07	5	1	2011 MICS
Bermuda	...	...	...	...	...	...	...	...	...	...	...	...	...
Bolivia, P.S.	...	...	...	...	...	...	...	...	...	...	...	...	...
Brazil	0.94	0.92	83	71	0.91	0.90	67	53	0.76	0.84	21	12	2011 PNAD
British Virgin Islands	...	...	...	...	...	...	...	...	...	...	...	...	...
Cayman Islands	...	...	...	...	...	...	...	...	...	...	...	...	...
Chile	1.00	0.98	98	96	0.89	0.88	81	78	0.51	0.55	37	33	2011 CASEN
Colombia	0.90	0.83	84	81	0.62	0.46	47	42	0.49	0.31	32	27	2010 DHS
Costa Rica	0.91	0.84	84	81	0.74	0.40	46	29	0.64	0.05	1	6	2011 MICS
Cuba	...	...	...	...	...	...	...	...	...	...	...	...	...
Curaçao	...	...	...	...	...	...	...	...	...	...	...	...	...
Dominica	...	...	...	...	...	...	...	...	...	...	...	...	...
Dominican Republic	0.95	0.81	85	75	0.96	0.64	66	59	0.81	0.30	26	24	2013 DHS
Ecuador	0.98	0.98	98	95	0.86	0.87	80	81	0.63	0.60	50	47	2013 ENEMDU
El Salvador	...	...	...	...	...	...	...	...	...	...	...	...	...
Grenada	...	...	...	...	...	...	...	...	...	...	...	...	...
Guatemala	0.76	0.50	37	54	0.45	0.16	9	15	0.30	0.04	1	3	2011 ENCOVI
Guyana	0.95	0.84	79	90	0.68	0.33	29	19	0.30	0.09	3	3	2009 DHS
Haiti	0.55	0.26	27	17	0.49	0.17	11	13	0.26	0.02	0	1	2012 DHS
Honduras	0.82	0.62	66	58	0.48	0.15	19	11	0.33	0.07	11	3	2011 DHS
Jamaica	1.00	0.98	98	98	1.00	0.95	94	91	0.94	0.57	54	55	2011 MICS
Mexico	0.96	0.92	92	90	0.86	0.67	65	66	0.62	0.35	24	35	2012 ENIGH
Montserrat	...	...	...	...	...	...	...	...	...	...	...	...	...
Nicaragua	0.70	0.66	69	62	0.37	0.29	25	25	0.26	0.14	6	9	2009 ENMV
Panama	0.88	0.79	80	78	0.76	0.58	53	58	0.53	0.21	16	23	2013 MICS
Paraguay	...	...	...	...	...	...	...	...	...	...	...	...	...
Peru	0.92	0.86	86	84	0.73	0.57	55	56	0.57	0.38	32	40	2012 DHS
Saint Kitts and Nevis	...	...	...	...	...	...	...	...	...	...	...	...	...
Saint Lucia	0.99	...	...	...	1.01	...	...	...	1.11	...	...	...	2012 MICS
Saint-Martin	...	...	...	...	...	...	...	...	...	...	...	...	...
St. Vincent and the Grenadines	...	...	...	...	...	...	...	...	...	...	...	...	...
Sint-Maarten	...	...	...	...	...	...	...	...	...	...	...	...	...
Suriname	0.91	0.54	59	46	0.80	0.18	14	12	0.42	0.07	3	3	2010 MICS
Trinidad and Tobago	...	...	...	...	...	...	...	...	...	...	...	...	...
Turks and Caicos Islands	...	...	...	...	...	...	...	...	...	...	...	...	...
Uruguay	1.03	0.92	97	87	1.11	0.33	23	31	0.43	0.01	2	1	2012 MICS
Venezuela, B. R.	...	...	...	...	...	...	...	...	...	...	...	...	...
Northern Africa and Western Asia													
Algeria	...	...	...	...	...	...	...	...	...	...	...	...	...
Bahrain	...	...	...	...	...	...	...	...	...	...	...	...	...
Egypt	0.97	0.89	87	86	0.89	0.75	70	71	0.84	0.65	52	63	2014 DHS
Iraq	0.66	0.40	25	44	0.52	0.18	5	17	0.35	0.10	4	5	2011 MICS
Israel	1.00	1.00	100	100	1.02	0.95	100	92	1.04	0.85	89	71	2012 HES
Jordan	1.01	0.96	97	93	1.05	0.79	82	73	0.99	0.45	48	26	2012 DHS
Kuwait	...	...	...	...	...	...	...	...	...	...	...	...	...
Lebanon	...	...	...	...	...	...	...	...	...	...	...	...	...
Libya	...	...	...	...	...	...	...	...	...	...	...	...	...
Morocco	0.58	0.36	31	38	0.30	0.16	5	17	0.24	0.12	...	...	2009 HYS
Oman	...	...	...	...	...	...	...	...	...	...	...	...	...
Palestine	...	...	...	...	...	...	...	...	...	...	...	...	2014 MICS
Qatar	...	...	...	...	...	...	...	...	...	...	...	...	...
Saudi Arabia	...	...	...	...	...	...	...	...	...	...	...	...	...
Sudan	0.85	0.67	53	81	0.61	0.22	13	29	0.49	0.10	4	7	2010 MICS
Syrian Arab Republic	...	...	...	...	...	...	...	...	...	...	...	...	...
Tunisia	0.91	0.84	84	81	0.74	0.47	44	41	0.55	0.30	28	20	2011 MICS
Turkey	...	...	...	...	...	...	...	...	...	...	...	...	...
United Arab Emirates	...	...	...	...	...	...	...	...	...	...	...	...	...
Yemen	0.72	0.40	20	48	0.58	0.27	9	29	0.49	0.18	3	17	2013 DHS
The Pacific													
Australia	...	...	...	...	...	0.97	...	...	...	0.80	69	80	2010 HES/SIH
Cook Islands	...	...	...	...	...	...	...	...	...	...	...	...	...
Fiji	...	...	...	...	...	...	...	...	...	...	...	...	...
Kiribati	...	...	...	...	...	...	...	...	...	...	...	...	...
Marshall Islands	...	...	...	...	...	...	...	...	...	...	...	...	...

DISPARITY IN SCHOOL COMPLETION[1]

TABLE 9
Part 1 (Continued)

	DISPARITY IN SCHOOL COMPLETION[1]												
	Primary completion rate and disparity by location and wealth				Lower secondary completion rate and disparity by location and wealth				Upper secondary completion rate and disparity by location and wealth				
	Location	Wealth	Completion rate (%) of the poorest students		Location	Wealth	Completion rate (%) of the poorest students		Location	Wealth	Completion rate (%) of the poorest students		
	Location parity index[2]	Wealth parity index[3]	Poorest females	Poorest males	Location parity index[2]	Wealth parity index[3]	Poorest females	Poorest males	Location parity index[2]	Wealth parity index[3]	Poorest females	Poorest males	
Country or territory	2009–2014	2009–2014	2009–2014	2009–2014	2009–2014	2009–2014	2009–2014	2009–2014	2009–2014	2009–2014	2009–2014	2009–2014	Reference years and surveys
Micronesia, F.S.	…	…	…	…	…	…	…	…	…	…	…	…	…
Nauru	…	…	…	…	…	…	…	…	…	…	…	…	…
New Zealand	…	…	…	…	…	…	…	…	…	…	…	…	…
Niue	…	…	…	…	…	…	…	…	…	…	…	…	…
Palau	…	…	…	…	…	…	…	…	…	…	…	…	…
Papua New Guinea	…	…	…	…	…	…	…	…	…	…	…	…	…
Samoa	…	…	…	…	…	…	…	…	…	…	…	…	…
Solomon Islands	…	…	…	…	…	…	…	…	…	…	…	…	…
Tokelau	…	…	…	…	…	…	…	…	…	…	…	…	…
Tonga	…	…	…	…	…	…	…	…	…	…	…	…	…
Tuvalu	…	…	…	…	…	…	…	…	…	…	…	…	…
Vanuatu	…	…	…	…	…	…	…	…	…	…	…	…	…
Southern Asia													
Afghanistan	0.51	0.30	8	31	0.41	0.17	0	15	0.36	0.10	0.4	5	2010 MICS
Bangladesh	0.99	0.70	68	57	0.94	0.40	28	31	0.63	0.14	5	8	2014 DHS
Bhutan	0.58	0.32	26	28	0.40	0.14	3	13	0.27	0.05	0.8	1	2010 MICS
India	0.94	0.87	82	86	0.87	0.76	67	73	0.54	0.39	21	28	2011 HDS
Iran, Islamic Republic of	…	…	…	…	…	…	…	…	…	…	…	…	
Maldives	0.99	0.98	98	97	0.92	0.85	90	74	0.94	0.92	67	44	2009 DHS
Nepal	0.86	0.64	56	65	0.74	0.41	27	49	0.55	0.15	7	18	2011 DHS
Pakistan	0.71	0.27	16	30	0.62	0.14	5	18	0.42	0.07	1	6	2012 DHS
Sri Lanka	…	…	…	…	…	…	…	…	…	…	…	…	
Sub-Saharan Africa													
Angola	…	…	…	…	…	…	…	…	…	…	…	…	
Benin	0.71	0.34	20	31	0.47	0.13	2	11	0.25	0.02	0	1	2011 DHS
Botswana	…	…	…	…	…	…	…	…	…	…	…	…	
Burkina Faso	0.34	0.16	9	11	0.15	0.04	1	1	0.02	0.02	0	0	2010 DHS
Burundi	0.56	0.34	18	16	0.25	0.14	1	8	0.09	0.02	0	0	2010 DHS
Cabo Verde	…	…	…	…	…	…	…	…	…	…	…	…	
Cameroon	0.61	0.15	10	18	0.28	0.04	1	4	0.13	0.01	0	0	2011 DHS
Central African Republic	0.40	0.17	8	16	0.07	0.01	0	1	0.04	0.02	0	0.9	2010 MICS
Chad	0.45	0.24	10	18	0.19	0.07	1	5	0.07	0.05	0	3	2010 MICS
Comoros	0.80	0.53	52	40	0.66	0.31	18	20	0.55	0.21	9	8	2012 DHS
Congo	0.58	0.40	32	40	0.31	0.11	5	11	0.07	0.01	0	1	2011 DHS
Côte d'Ivoire	0.39	0.26	12	24	0.22	0.03	2	2	0.17	0.06	0	4	2011 DHS
DR Congo	0.67	0.50	39	53	0.54	0.35	22	41	0.33	0.14	3	14	2013 DHS
Djibouti	…	…	…	…	…	…	…	…	…	…	…	…	
Equatorial Guinea	…	…	…	…	…	…	…	…	…	…	…	…	
Eritrea	…	…	…	…	…	…	…	…	…	…	…	…	
Ethiopia	0.42	0.24	19	19	0.17	0.03	2	0.7	0.17	0.01	0	1	2011 DHS
Gabon	0.47	0.39	40	37	0.39	0.24	12	20	0.38	0.03	0	2	2012 DHS
Gambia	0.60	0.56	44	51	0.42	0.37	26	29	0.34	0.24	8	15	2013 DHS
Ghana	0.74	0.48	39	40	0.61	0.37	27	29	0.57	0.21	10	17	2014 DHS
Guinea	0.42	0.17	7	17	0.21	0.11	2	11	0.10	0.05	0.0	4	2012 DHS
Guinea-Bissau	…	…	…	…	…	…	…	…	…	…	…	…	
Kenya	0.94	0.78	79	75	0.80	0.55	52	51	0.55	0.17	8	16	2014 DHS
Lesotho	0.73	0.52	69	24	0.45	0.10	11	4	0.36	0.06	4	1	2009 DHS
Liberia	0.46	0.25	16	23	0.28	0.11	4	12	0.21	0.05	0.7	5	2013 DHS
Madagascar	…	…	…	…	…	…	…	…	…	…	…	…	
Malawi	0.67	0.44	43	28	0.34	0.11	7	7	0.28	0.07	3	3	2010 DHS
Mali	0.52	0.33	16	26	0.23	0.07	0.3	7	0.19	0.01	0	0.6	2012 DHS
Mauritania	0.60	0.24	14	23	0.36	0.08	2	7	0.34	0.05	2	2	2011 MICS
Mauritius	…	…	…	…	…	…	…	…	…	…	…	…	
Mozambique	0.44	0.15	6	16	0.22	0.02	0	2	0.10	0.00	0	Poorest	2011 DHS
Namibia	0.82	0.68	79	54	0.46	0.28	25	22	0.42	0.12	7	7	2013 DHS
Niger	0.31	0.15	6	10	0.05	0.05	0	3	0.02	0.06	0	1	2012 DHS
Nigeria	0.65	0.23	14	33	0.49	0.11	4	18	0.42	0.06	1	11	2013 DHS
Rwanda	0.64	0.26	11	13	0.38	0.15	4	4	0.27	0.03	0.3	2	2010 DHS
Sao Tome and Principe	…	…	…	…	…	…	…	…	…	…	…	…	
Senegal	0.54	0.39	28	33	0.36	0.13	3	8	0.19	0.03	0	2	2014 DHS
Seychelles	…	…	…	…	…	…	…	…	…	…	…	…	
Sierra Leone	0.66	0.50	47	41	0.38	0.21	10	22	0.13	0.04	1	2	2013 DHS
Somalia	…	…	…	…	…	…	…	…	…	…	…	…	
South Africa	…	0.90	93	85	…	0.75	79	62	…	0.29	23	19	2013 GHS
South Sudan	0.59	0.28	15	29	0.38	0.13	3	6	0.19	0.07	0	3	2010 MICS
Swaziland	0.68	0.42	41	27	0.67	0.38	29	23	0.55	0.18	9	9	2010 MICS
Togo	0.61	0.41	27	37	0.30	0.12	3	8	0.15	0.02	0.0	1	2013 DHS
Uganda	0.45	0.19	12	13	0.34	0.06	2	4	0.19	0.04	0.3	3	2011 DHS
U.R. Tanzania	0.75	0.55	46	55	0.29	0.03	2	1	0.18	0.00	0.1	0.0	2010 DHS
Zambia	0.71	0.48	44	49	0.49	0.24	14	31	0.26	0.02	0.4	2	2013 DHS
Zimbabwe	0.86	0.76	80	67	0.70	0.50	51	40	0.15	0.01	0.0	0.9	2014 MICS

TABLE 9

Part 1 (Continued)

	DISPARITY IN SCHOOL COMPLETION[1]												
	Primary completion rate and disparity by location and wealth				Lower secondary completion rate and disparity by location and wealth				Upper secondary completion rate and disparity by location and wealth				
	Location	Wealth	Completion rate (%) of the poorest students		Location	Wealth	Completion rate (%) of the poorest students		Location	Wealth	Completion rate (%) of the poorest students		
Country or territory	Location parity index[2]	Wealth parity index[3]	Poorest females	Poorest males	Location parity index[2]	Wealth parity index[3]	Poorest females	Poorest males	Location parity index[2]	Wealth parity index[3]	Poorest females	Poorest males	Reference year and survey
	2009–2014	2009–2014	2009–2014	2009–2014	2009–2014	2009–2014	2009–2014	2009–2014	2009–2014	2009–2014	2009–2014	2009–2014	
World[4]	...	...	...	...	...	...	...	...	0.55	0.30	23	21	
Countries in transition	1.00	0.99	99	99	0.99	0.99	97	98	0.89	0.74	62	75	
Developed countries	...	...	...	...	...	...	...	...	0.95	0.83	78	71	
Developing countries	0.74	0.52	47	49	0.56	0.27	18	22	0.39	0.10	4	6	
Caucasus and Central Asia	1.00	1.00	100	99	0.99	0.99	98	99	0.95	0.89	89	85	
Eastern and South-eastern Asia	...	...	...	...	...	...	...	...	...	...	...	...	
Eastern Asia	...	...	...	...	...	...	...	...	...	...	...	...	
South-eastern Asia	0.87	0.58	66	51	0.68	0.36	36	29	0.48	0.17	12	14	
Europe and Northern America	...	...	...	...	...	...	...	...	0.91	0.82	75	69	
Latin America and the Caribbean	...	...	...	...	...	...	...	...	...	...	...	...	
Caribbean	...	...	...	...	...	...	...	...	...	...	...	...	
Latin America	0.91	0.84	83	81	0.74	0.43	37	37	0.51	0.17	13	11	
Northern Africa and Western Asia	...	...	...	...	...	...	...	...	...	...	...	...	
Northern Africa	0.99	0.92	92	89	0.96	0.77	76	72	0.92	0.55	50	44	
Western Asia	...	...	...	...	...	...	...	...	...	...	...	...	
Pacific	...	...	...	...	...	...	...	...	...	...	...	...	
Southern Asia	0.86	0.64	56	57	0.74	0.40	27	31	0.54	0.14	5	8	
Sub-Saharan Africa	0.60	0.37	24	29	0.36	0.12	4	8	0.19	0.05	0	2	
Conflict-affected countries	0.69	0.37	20	40	0.56	0.22	7	24	0.42	0.12	2	12	
Countries with low income	0.58	0.32	19	27	0.34	0.12	2	8	0.19	0.04	0	2	
Countries with middle income	0.93	0.83	83	80	0.76	0.49	49	44	0.57	0.26	20	19	
Lower middle	0.74	0.52	66	54	0.61	0.33	25	26	0.46	0.14	6	10	
Upper middle	0.97	0.91	89	88	0.86	0.71	66	62	0.76	0.45	32	35	
Countries with high income	...	...	...	...	...	...	...	...	0.96	0.84	77	70	

Sources: GEM Report team calculations, based on data from national and international and household surveys compiled in the World Inequality Database in Education (WIDE).

Note: The country groupings by level of income are as defined by the World Bank but include only countries listed in the table. They are based on the list of countries by income group as revised in July 2015.

1. National averages of completion rates are presented in Statistical Tables 2 (primary) and 3 (lower and upper secondary)

2. Location parity index is the ratio of completion rate of students living in rural areas to that of their urban counterparts.

3. Wealth parity index is the ratio of completion rate of students living in the poorest households to that of their richest counterparts.

4. All regional values shown are medians.

(...) No data are available.

TABLE 10

SDG 4, Target 4.6 – Youth and adult literacy and numeracy
By 2030, ensure that all youth and a substantial proportion of adults, both men and women, achieve literacy and numeracy

	YOUTH AND ADULT LITERACY[1]						BASIC SKILLS ACQUISITION[3]				PARTICIPATION IN LITERACY PROGRAMMES		
	Youth literacy (15–24)			Adult literacy (15 and over)			Percentage of youth and adults achieving at least a fixed level of proficiency (%) in:				Participation rate of youth and adults in literacy programmes (%)		
	Youth literacy rate (%)	Number of youth illiterates		Adult literacy rate (%)	Number of adult illiterates		Functional literacy skills		Numeracy skills		Adults (15 and over)		
							Youth (16-24)	Adults (16 and over)	Youth (16-24)	Adults (16 and over)	School year ending in		
	2005–2014[2]	2005–2014[2]		2005–2014[2]	2005–2014[2]		2012-2015[2]		2012-2015[2]		2014		
Country or territory	Total	Total (000)	% F	Total	Total (000)	% F	Total	Total	Total	Total	Total	Male	Female
Caucasus and Central Asia													
Armenia	100*	0.8*	37*	100*	6**	62**	...	...	...	...	...	...	...
Azerbaijan	100*	0.7*	72*	100*	16*	68*	...	...	...	...	...	...	...
Georgia	100**	1**	35**	100**	8**	60**	...	...	...	...	...	...	...
Kazakhstan	100*	5*	41*	100*	33*	62*	...	...	...	...	...	...	...
Kyrgyzstan	100*	3*	40*	99*	29*	69*	...	...	...	...	...	...	...
Tajikistan	100**	2**	44**	100**	13**	61**	...	...	...	...	...	...	...
Turkmenistan	100**	2**	29**	100**	12**	63**	...	...	...	...	...	...	...
Uzbekistan	100*	-*	-*	100*	4*	63*	...	...	...	...	...	...	...
Eastern and South-eastern Asia													
Brunei Darussalam	99*	0.5*	35*	96*	12*	66*	...	...	...	...	...	...	...
Cambodia	87*	396*	54*	74*	2,438*	69*	...	...	...	...	...	...	...
China	100*	843*	54*	95*	53,767*	74*	...	...	...	...	...	...	...
DPR Korea	100*	0.0*	34*	100*	0.3*	71*	...	...	...	...	...	...	...
Hong Kong, China	...	...	...	...	...	...	...	...	...	...	...	...	...
Indonesia	100*	139*	49*	95*	8,942*	67*	...	...	...	...	...	...	...
Japan							...	99	99	99	...	...	...
Lao People's Democratic Republic	84*	198*	66*	73*	938*	69*	...	...	...	...	...	...	...
Macao, China	100*	0.3*	48*	96*	21*	76*	...	...	...	...	...	...	...
Malaysia	98*	90*	48*	93*	1,412*	67*	...	...	...	...	...	...	...
Mongolia	98*	9*	35*	98*	35*	48*	...	...	...	...	...	...	...
Myanmar	96**	357**	51**	93**	2,721**	67**	...	...	...	...	...	...	...
Philippines	98*	364*	31*	96*	2,371*	45*	...	...	...	...	...	...	...
Republic of Korea	...	...	...	...	...	...	...	98	99	96	...	...	...
Singapore	100*	0.7*	47*	97*	152*	79*	99	90	98	87	...	...	...
Thailand	98*	155*	40*	94*	3,465*	63*	...	...	...	...	...	...	...
Timor-Leste	80*	43*	52*	58*	259*	56*	...	...	...	...	...	...	...
Viet Nam	97*	515*	54*	94*	4,297*	68*	...	...	...	...	...	...	...
Europe and Northern America													
Albania	99*	4*	59*	97*	64*	70*	...	...	...	...	...	...	...
Andorra	...	...	...	...	...	...	...	...	...	...	...	...	...
Austria	...	...	...	...	...	...	98	98	98	97	...	...	...
Belarus	100*	3*	42*	100*	31*	72*	...	...	...	...	...	...	...
Belgium	...	...	...	...	...	...	...	...	...	...	...	...	...
Bosnia and Herzegovina	100**	2**	49**	98**	53**	86**	...	...	...	...	...	...	...
Bulgaria	98*	18*	53*	98*	105*	63*	...	...	...	...	...	...	...
Canada	...	...	...	...	...	...	97	96	96	94	...	...	...
Croatia	100*	1*	47*	99*	32*	80*	...	...	...	...	...	...	...
Cyprus	100*	0.3*	43*	99*	12*	72*	99	98	97	97	...	...	...
Czech Republic	...	...	...	...	...	...	99	98	98	98	...	...	...
Denmark	...	...	...	...	...	...	98	96	98	97	...	...	...
Estonia	100*	0.1*	39*	100*	1*	43*	99	98	99	98	...	...	...
Finland	...	...	...	...	...	...	99	97	98	97	...	...	...
France	...	...	...	...	...	...	98	95	95	91	...	...	...
Germany	...	...	...	...	...	...	99	97	97	95	...	...	...
Greece	99**	7**	56**	98**	232**	70**	95	95	94	94	...	...	...
Hungary	...	...	...	...	...	...	...	...	...	...	...	...	...
Iceland	...	...	...	...	...	...	...	...	...	...	...	...	...
Ireland	...	...	...	...	...	...	98	96	95	93	...	...	...
Italy	100*	8*	46*	99*	590*	64*	97	94	94	92	...	...	...
Latvia	100*	0.4*	39*	100*	2*	49*	...	...	...	...	...	...	...
Liechtenstein	...	...	...	...	...	...	...	...	...	...	...	...	...
Lithuania	100*	0.6*	45*	100*	5*	50*	...	98	99	97	...	...	...
Luxembourg	...	...	...	...	...	...	...	...	...	...	...	...	...
Malta	99*	0.6*	26*	93*	23*	39*	...	...	...	...	...	...	...
Monaco	...	...	...	...	...	...	...	...	...	...	...	...	...
Montenegro	99*	0.7*	58*	98*	8*	82*	...	...	...	...	...	...	...
Netherlands	...	...	...	...	...	...	99	97	98	97	...	...	...
Norway	...	...	...	...	...	...	98	97	96	96	...	...	...
Poland	...	...	...	...	...	...	99	96	97	94	...	...	...
Portugal	99*	6*	45*	94*	497*	68*	...	...	...	...	...	...	...
Republic of Moldova	100**	-**	-**	99**	23**	78**	...	...	...	...	...	...	...
Romania	99*	24*	49*	99*	236*	67*	...	...	...	...	...	...	...
Russian Federation	100*	62*	41*	100*	384*	61*	99	98	99	98	...	...	...
San Marino	...	...	...	...	...	...	...	...	...	...	...	...	...
Serbia	99*	8*	51*	98*	152*	83*	...	...	...	...	...	...	...
Slovakia	...	...	...	...	...	...	98	98	97	97	...	...	...
Slovenia	100**	0.3**	31**	100**	5**	54**	98	94	98	93	...	...	...
Spain	100*	12*	55*	98*	751*	68*	97	93	95	90	...	...	...
Sweden	...	...	...	...	...	...	98	96	97	96	...	...	...
Switzerland	...	...	...	...	...	...	...	...	...	...	...	...	...
TFYR Macedonia	99**	4**	54**	98**	39**	74**	...	...	...	...	...	...	...

TABLE 10
(Continued)

Country or territory	YOUTH AND ADULT LITERACY[1]						BASIC SKILLS ACQUISITION[3]				PARTICIPATION IN LITERACY PROGRAMMES		
	Youth literacy (15–24)			Adult literacy (15 and over)			Percentage of youth and adults achieving at least a fixed level of proficiency (%) in:				Participation rate of youth and adults in literacy programmes (%)		
	Youth literacy rate (%)	Number of youth illiterates		Adult literacy rate (%)	Number of adult illiterates		Functional literacy skills		Numeracy skills		Adults (15 and over)		
							Youth (16–24)	Adults (16 and over)	Youth (16–24)	Adults (16 and over)	School year ending in		
	2005–2014[2]	2005–2014[2]		2005–2014[2]	2005–2014[2]		2012-2015[2]		2012-2015[2]		2014		
	Total	Total (000)	% F	Total	Total (000)	% F	Total	Total	Total	Total	Total	Male	Female
Ukraine	100**	12**	40**	100**	95**	62**	…	…	…	…	…	…	…
United Kingdom	…	…	…	…	…	…	…	…	…	…	…	…	…
United States	…	…	…	…	…	…	98	96	93	91	…	…	…
Latin America and the Caribbean													
Anguilla	…	…	…	…	…	…	…	…	…	…	…	…	…
Antigua and Barbuda	…	…	…	99**	1**	29**	…	…	…	…	4ʸ	0ʸ	15
Argentina	99**	49**	37**	98**	631**	51**	…	…	…	…	…	…	…
Aruba	99*	0.1*	38*	97*	3*	55*	…	…	…	…	…	…	…
Bahamas	…	…	…	…	…	…	…	…	…	…	…	…	…
Barbados	…	…	…	…	…	…	…	…	…	…	…	…	…
Belize	…	…	…	…	…	…	…	…	…	…	…	…	…
Bermuda	…	…	…	…	…	…	…	…	…	…	…	…	…
Bolivia, Plurinational States of	99*	20*	58*	94*	374*	74*	…	…	…	…	…	…	…
Brazil	99*	431*	30*	91*	13,231*	50*	…	…	…	…	4	3	4
British Virgin Islands	…	…	…	…	…	…	…	…	…	…	…	…	…
Cayman Islands	99*	0.1*	62*	99*	0.5*	45*	…	…	…	…	…	…	…
Chile	99*	27*	47*	96*	518*	53*	89	80	80	69	3ʸ	…	…
Colombia	99*	123*	35*	94*	2,094*	49*	…	…	…	…	15	12	18
Costa Rica	99*	7*	42*	97*	91*	48*	…	…	…	…	6ʸ	4ʸ	7
Cuba	100*	2*	40*	100*	23*	41*	…	…	…	…	4ʸ	6ʸ	1
Curaçao	…	…	…	…	…	…	…	…	…	…	…	…	…
Dominica	…	…	…	…	…	…	…	…	…	…	…	…	…
Dominican Republic	98*	44*	42*	92*	598*	48*	…	…	…	…	9	…	…
Ecuador	99*	41*	48*	94*	647*	59*	…	…	…	…	12	9	14
El Salvador	97*	34*	46*	87*	579*	63*	…	…	…	…	17	18	16
Grenada	…	…	…	…	…	…	…	…	…	…	…	…	…
Guatemala	94*	186*	60*	81*	1,880*	66*	…	…	…	…	7	3	9
Guyana	93**,ᵃ	8**,ᵃ	45**,ᵃ	85**,ᵃ	75**,ᵃ	42**,ᵃ	…	…	…	…	…	…	…
Haiti	72**,ᵃ	561**,ᵃ	53**,ᵃ	49**,ᵃ	3,006**,ᵃ	56**,ᵃ	…	…	…	…	…	…	…
Honduras	96*	75*	42*	87*	687*	51*	…	…	…	…	…	…	…
Jamaica	96**	20**	16**	88**	251**	31**	…	…	…	…	3ʸ	2ʸ	3
Mexico	99*	231*	45*	95*	4,879*	60*	…	…	…	…	11	7	13
Montserrat	…	…	…	…	…	…	…	…	…	…	…	…	…
Nicaragua	87*	154*	42*	78*	758*	52*	…	…	…	…	16ʸ	15ʸ	16
Panama	98*	15*	56*	94*	152*	55*	…	…	…	…	…	…	…
Paraguay	99*	17*	57*	95*	243*	58*	…	…	…	…	4	2	5
Peru	99*	57*	58*	94*	1,409*	76*	…	…	…	…	10ʸ	9ʸ	11
Saint Kitts and Nevis	…	…	…	…	…	…	…	…	…	…	…	…	…
Saint Lucia	…	…	…	…	…	…	…	…	…	…	…	…	…
Saint-Martin	…	…	…	…	…	…	…	…	…	…	…	…	…
Saint Vincent and the Grenadines	…	…	…	…	…	…	…	…	…	…	…	…	…
Sint-Maarten	…	…	…	…	…	…	…	…	…	…	…	…	…
Suriname	98*	1*	37*	95*	20*	57*	…	…	…	…	…	…	…
Trinidad and Tobago	100**	0.8**	48**	99**	12**	65**	…	…	…	…	…	…	…
Turks and Caicos Islands	…	…	…	…	…	…	…	…	…	…	…	…	…
Uruguay	99*	6*	26*	98*	42*	40*	…	…	…	…	3	…	…
Venezuela, Bolivarian Republic of	98*	134*	36*	95*	1,088*	48*	…	…	…	…	…	…	…
Northern Africa and Western Asia													
Algeria	94	474	65	75*	6,279*	65*	…	…	…	…	…	…	…
Bahrain	98	3	57	95*	55*	54*	…	…	…	…	…	…	…
Egypt	92*,ᵃ	1,284*,ᵃ	59*,ᵃ	75*,ᵃ	14,804*,ᵃ	65*,ᵃ	…	…	…	…	…	…	…
Iraq	82**	1,264**	52**	80**	4,252**	65**	…	…	…	…	…	…	…
Israel	…	…	…	…	…	…	96	92	90	89	…	…	…
Jordan	99*,ᵃ	12*,ᵃ	43*,ᵃ	98*,ᵃ	92*,ᵃ	61*,ᵃ	…	…	…	…	…	…	…
Kuwait	99*	5*	56*	96*	125*	54*	…	…	…	…	…	…	…
Lebanon	99*	10*	38*	90*	307*	67*	…	…	…	…	…	…	…
Libya	100**	0.6**	67**	91*	394*	82**	…	…	…	…	…	…	…
Morocco	82*	1,153*	70*	67*	7,848*	65*	…	…	…	…	…	…	…
Oman	99*	7*	40*	92*	229*	49*	…	…	…	…	…	…	…
Palestine	99*	6*	52*	96*	97*	77*	…	…	…	…	…	…	…
Qatar	99*	4*	6*	98*	42*	25*	…	…	…	…	…	…	…
Saudi Arabia	99*	39*	54*	94*	1,198*	64*	…	…	…	…	…	…	…
Sudan	66*	2,309*	54*	54*	9,251*	57*	…	…	…	…	…	…	…
Syrian Arab Republic	96**	142**	59**	86**	1,671**	70**	…	…	…	…	…	…	…
Tunisia	97*	60*	67*	80*	1,658*	72*	…	…	…	…	…	…	…
Turkey	99*	84*	80*	95*	2,665*	84*	94	87	88	80	…	…	…
United Arab Emirates	95*	41*	20*	90*	368*	21*	…	…	…	…	…	…	…
Yemen	89**	623**	87**	69**	4,849**	75**	…	…	…	…	…	…	…
The Pacific													
Australia	…	…	…	…	…	…	98	97	96	94	…	…	…
Cook Islands	…	…	…	…	…	…	…	…	…	…	…	…	…
Fiji	…	…	…	…	…	…	…	…	…	…	…	…	…
Kiribati	…	…	…	…	…	…	…	…	…	…	…	…	…
Marshall Islands	98*	0.1*	41*	98*	1*	52*	…	…	…	…	…	…	…

TABLE 10

(Continued)

	YOUTH AND ADULT LITERACY[1]						BASIC SKILLS ACQUISITION[3]				PARTICIPATION IN LITERACY PROGRAMMES		
	Youth literacy (15–24)			Adult literacy (15 and over)			Percentage of youth and adults achieving at least a fixed level of proficiency (%) in:				Participation rate of youth and adults in literacy programmes (%)		
	Youth literacy rate (%)	Number of youth illiterates		Adult literacy rate (%)	Number of adult illiterates		Functional literacy skills		Numeracy skills		Adults (15 and over)		
							Youth (16–24)	Adults (16 and over)	Youth (16–24)	Adults (16 and over)	School year ending in		
	2005-2014[2]	2005-2014[2]		2005-2014[2]	2005-2014[2]		2012-2015[2]	2012-2015[2]	2012-2015[2]	2012-2015[2]	2014		
Country or territory	Total	Total (000)	% F	Total	Total (000)	% F	Total	Total	Total	Total	Total	Male	Female
Micronesia (Federated States of)	…	…	…	…	…	…	…	…	…	…	…	…	…
Nauru	…	…	…	…	…	…	…	…	…	…	…	…	…
New Zealand	…	…	…	…	…	…	98	97	96	95	…	…	…
Niue	…	…	…	…	…	…	…	…	…	…	…	…	…
Palau	100*	…*	…*	100*	0.1*	45*	…	…	…	…	…	…	…
Papua New Guinea	67**	488**	52**	63**	1,720**	52**	…	…	…	…	…	…	…
Samoa	99*	0.3*	34*	99*	1*	44*	…	…	…	…	…	…	…
Solomon Islands	…	…	…	…	…	…	…	…	…	…	…	…	…
Tokelau	…	…	…	…	…	…	…	…	…	…	…	…	…
Tonga	99*	0.1*	42*	99*	0.4*	47*	…	…	…	…	…	…	…
Tuvalu	…	…	…	…	…	…	…	…	…	…	…	…	…
Vanuatu	…	…	…	…	…	…	…	…	…	…	…	…	…
Southern Asia													
Afghanistan	47*	2,947*	62*	32*	10,373*	59*	…	…	…	…	…	…	…
Bangladesh	82**	5,558**	42**	61**	43,916**	54**	…	…	…	…	…	…	…
Bhutan	87*	19*	61*	57*	223*	56*	…	…	…	…	…	…	…
India	86*	32,620*	62*	69*	265,568*	65*	…	…	…	…	…	…	…
Iran, Islamic Republic of	98*	311*	57*	85*	9,058*	66*	…	…	…	…	…	…	…
Maldives	99*	0.5*	46*	98*	3*	49*	…	…	…	…	…	…	…
Nepal	85*	823*	69*	60*	6,989*	67*	…	…	…	…	…	…	…
Pakistan	72*	10,508*	63*	56*	51,956*	64*	…	…	…	…	…	…	…
Sri Lanka	98*	60*	38*	91*	1,323*	59*	…	…	…	…	…	…	…
Sub-Saharan Africa													
Angola	73**	1,270**	61**	71**	3,665**	70**	…	…	…	…	…	…	…
Benin	42**,a	945**,a	61**,a	29**,a	3,320**,a	59**,a	…	…	…	…	…	…	…
Botswana	98**	10**	12**	88**	185**	46**	…	…	…	…	…	…	…
Burkina Faso	50*	1,728*	56*	35*	6,189*	58*	…	…	…	…	…	…	…
Burundi	89*	215*	55*	87*	656*	59*	…	…	…	…	…	…	…
Cabo Verde	98*	2*	43*	85*	51*	68*	…	…	…	…	…	…	…
Cameroon	81*	812*	62*	71*	3,319*	62*	…	…	…	…	…	…	…
Central African Republic	36**,a	570**,a	59**,a	37**,a	1,659**,a	62**,a	…	…	…	…	…	…	…
Chad	52**	1,320**	53**	39**	4,308**	57**	…	…	…	…	…	…	…
Comoros	87**	20**	47**	78**	103**	59**	…	…	…	…	…	…	…
Congo	81**,a	147**,a	62**,a	79**,a	491**,a	67**,a	…	…	…	…	…	…	…
Côte d'Ivoire	48**,a	2,150**,a	59**,a	41**,a	7,029**,a	58**,a	…	…	…	…	…	…	…
Democratic Rep. of the Congo	84*,a	2,195*,a	72*,a	75*,a	9,325*,a	76*,a	…	…	…	…	…	…	…
Djibouti	…	…	…	…	…	…	…	…	…	…	…	…	…
Equatorial Guinea	98**	3**	36**	95**	25**	72**	…	…	…	…	…	…	…
Eritrea	93**	74**	60**	73**	796**	67**	…	…	…	…	…	…	…
Ethiopia	55*	7,176*	59*	39*	26,847*	59*	…	…	…	…	…	…	…
Gabon	89**,a	37**,a	45**,a	82**,a	177**,a	57**,a	…	…	…	…	…	…	…
Gambia	72**	105**	55**	54**	472**	61**	…	…	…	…	…	…	…
Ghana	86*	699*	59*	71*	4,203*	63*	…	…	…	…	…	…	…
Guinea	31*	1,524*	55*	25*	4,716*	58*	…	…	…	…	…	…	…
Guinea-Bissau	76**	85**	59**	59**	439**	65**	…	…	…	…	…	…	…
Kenya	82**,a	1,430**,a	52**,a	72**,a	5,878**,a	60**,a	…	…	…	…	…	…	…
Lesotho	83**,a	79**,a	23**,a	76**,a	301**,a	32**,a	…	…	…	…	…	…	…
Liberia	49**,a	338**,a	63**,a	43**,a	1,120**,a	65**,a	…	…	…	…	…	…	…
Madagascar	65**,a	1,419**,a	51**,a	64**,a	4,093**,a	55**,a	…	…	…	…	…	…	…
Malawi	72**,a	864**,a	54**,a	61**,a	3,055**,a	64**,a	…	…	…	…	…	…	…
Mali	47*	1,565*	57*	34*	5,444*	57*	…	…	…	…	…	…	…
Mauritania	56**,a	280**,a	60**,a	46**,a	1,045**,a	60**,a	…	…	…	…	…	…	…
Mauritius	98*	4*	38*	92*	76*	66*	…	…	…	…	…	…	…
Mozambique	67*	1,450*	69*	51*	6,261*	69*	…	…	…	…	…	…	…
Namibia	94*	27*	42*	89*	148*	55*	…	…	…	…	…	…	…
Niger	24**,a	2,332**,a	58**,a	15**,a	7,366**,a	55**,a	…	…	…	…	…	…	…
Nigeria	66**,a	9,675**,a	62**,a	51**,a	41,214**,a	60**,a	…	…	…	…	…	…	…
Rwanda	82*	384*	47*	68*	1,985*	60*	…	…	…	…	…	…	…
Sao Tome and Principe	97*	1*	56*	90*	10*	75*	…	…	…	…	…	…	…
Senegal	56*	1,246*	56*	43*	4,576*	61*	…	…	…	…	…	…	…
Seychelles	99*	0.2*	29*	94*	4*	45*	…	…	…	…	…	…	…
Sierra Leone	66**	432**	63**	47**	1,913**	61**	…	…	…	…	…	…	…
Somalia	…	…	…	…	…	…	…	…	…	…	…	…	…
South Africa	99*	119*	38*	94*	2,226*	61*	…	…	…	…	…	…	…
South Sudan	37*	1,143*	56*	27*	3,779*	56*	…	…	…	…	…	…	…
Swaziland	94**,a	19**,a	40**,a	83**,a	123**,a	54**,a	…	…	…	…	…	…	…
Togo	80*	265*	68*	60*	1,478*	68*	…	…	…	…	…	…	…
Uganda	84*	1,162*	56*	70*	5,362*	65*	…	…	…	…	…	…	…
United Republic of Tanzania	86*	1,318*	55*	78*	5,792*	62*	…	…	…	…	…	…	…
Zambia	89*	317*	60*	83*	1,251*	67*	…	…	…	…	…	…	…
Zimbabwe	91**,a	296**,a	44**,a	84**,a	1,349**,a	63**,a	…	…	…	…	…	…	…

TABLE 10
(Continued)

Country or territory	YOUTH AND ADULT LITERACY[1]						BASIC SKILLS ACQUISITION[3]				PARTICIPATION IN LITERACY PROGRAMMES		
	Youth literacy (15–24)			Adult literacy (15 and over)			Percentage of youth and adults achieving at least a fixed level of proficiency (%) in:				Participation rate of youth and adults in literacy programmes (%)		
	Youth literacy rate (%)	Number of youth illiterates		Adult literacy rate (%)	Number of adult illiterates		Functional literacy skills		Numeracy skills		Adults (15 and over)		
							Youth (16–24)	Adults (16 and over)	Youth (16–24)	Adults (16 and over)	School year ending in		
	2005–2014[2]	2005–2014[2]		2005–2014[2]	2005–2014[2]		2012–2015[2]		2012–2015[2]		2014		
	Total	Total (000)	% F	Total	Total (000)	% F	Total	Total	Total	Total	Total	Male	Female
	Weighted average	Sum	% F	Weighted average	Sum	% F	Median				Median		
World	91**	114,127**	59**	85**	757,920**	63**	...	...	...	...	...	...	...
Countries in transition	100**	110**	43**	100**	993**	69**	...	...	...	...	...	...	...
Developed countries	...	**	...	...	...	...	...	...	...	...	...	...	...
Developing countries	89**	113,577**	59**	82**	748,926**	63**	...	...	...	...	...	...	...
Caucasus and Central Asia	100**	15**	41**	100**	120**	65**	...	...	...	...	...	...	...
Eastern and South-eastern Asia	99**	3,217**	51**	95**	84,135**	71**	...	...	...	...	...	...	...
Eastern Asia	100**	960**	54**	96**	57,130**	73**	...	...	...	...	...	...	...
South-eastern Asia	98**	2,257**	49**	94**	27,006**	65**	...	...	...	...	...	...	...
Europe and Northern America	...	...	...	...	...	...	...	...	...	...	...	...	...
Latin America and the Caribbean	98**	2,266**	44**	93**	33,373**	54**	...	...	...	...	6	6	11
Caribbean	90**	638**	51**	85**	3,928**	53**	...	...	...	...	...	...	...
Latin America	98**	1,628**	41**	93**	29,445**	55**	...	...	...	...	...	...	...
Northern Africa and Western Asia	93**	6,073**	63**	82**	52,878**	67**	...	...	...	...	...	...	...
Northern Africa	91**	3,824**	63**	75**	36,784**	65**	...	...	...	...	...	...	...
Western Asia	95**	2,250**	62**	90**	16,094**	70**	...	...	...	...	...	...	...
Pacific	...	...	...	...	...	...	...	...	...	...	...	...	...
Southern Asia	84**	52,848**	60**	68**	389,408**	63**	...	...	...	...	...	...	...
Sub-Saharan Africa	71**	48,765**	59**	60**	188,315**	61**	...	...	...	...	...	...	...
							...	...	...	...			
Conflict-affected countries	85**	78,749**	61**	75**	496,010**	64**	...	...	...	...	...	...	...
							...						
Countries with low income	68**	35,078**	59**	57	134,811	61	...	...	...	...	...	...	...
Countries with middle income	92**	78,258**	60**	84	608,126	64	...	...	...	...	...	...	...
Lower middle	86**	72,405**	60**	74	493,776	63	...	...	...	...	...	...	...
Upper middle	99**	5,854**	53**	94	114,350	67	...	...	...	...	...	...	...
Countries with high income	...	...	...	...	...	...							

Sources: UIS database, except where noted.

Note A: The country groupings by level of income are as defined by the World Bank but include only countries listed in the table. They are based on the list of countries by income group as revised in July 2015.

Note B: For countries indicated with (*), national observed literacy data are used. For all others, UIS literacy estimates are used (**). The estimates were generated using the UIS Global Age-specific Literacy Projections model. Those in the most recent period are for 2014 and are based on the most recent observed data available for each country.

Note C: The population used to generate the number of illiterates is from the United Nations Population Division estimates, revision 2015 (United Nations, 2015). It is based on the median variant. For countries with national observed literacy data, the population corresponding to the year of the census or survey was used. For countries with UIS estimates, populations used are for 2014.

1. Literacy data presented in these columns are based on conventional assessment methods – either self- and third-party declarations or educational attainment proxies – and thus should be interpreted with caution; they are not based on any test and may overestimate actual literacy levels.

2. Data are for the most recent year available during the period specified. For literacy data, see the introduction to the statistical tables and the table of metadata on literacy statistics (published on the GEM Report Website) for a broader explanation of national literacy definitions, assessment methods, and sources and years of data.

3. Data on basic skills acquisition are from Survey of Adult Skills (PIAAC 2012-2015) (OECD, 2013, 2016).

(a) Literacy data are based on direct reading tests in national and international household surveys.

(*) For country level data: national estimate.

(**) For country level data: UIS estimate/projection; for regional and other country-grouping sums and weighted averages: partial imputation due to incomplete country coverage (between 33% and 60% of population for the region or other country grouping).

(...) No data are available.

TABLE 11

SDG 4, Target 4.7 – Education for sustainable development and global citizenship

By 2030, ensure all learners acquire knowledge and skills needed to promote sustainable development, including, among others, through education for sustainable development and sustainable lifestyles, human rights, gender equality, promotion of a culture of peace and non-violence, global citizenship and appreciation of cultural diversity and of culture's contribution to sustainable development

Country or territory	PROMOTING SUSTAINABLE DEVELOPMENT AND GLOBAL CITIZENSHIP IN CURRICULA — Gender equality[3] 2005-2015[8]	Human rights[4] 2005-2015[8]	Sustainable development[5] 2005-2015[8]	Global citizenship[6] 2005-2015[8]	Percentage of schools providing life skills-based HIV/AIDS education[7] 2009-2010[8]	Science literacy[9,10] 2012 Total	Male	Female	HIV/AIDS and sexuality education[7] 2009-2015[8] Total	Male	Female
Caucasus and Central Asia											
Armenia	0	MEDIUM	LOW	LOW	...	...	...	...	20	23	19
Azerbaijan	0	MEDIUM	0	LOW	100	...	...	...	15	...	15
Georgia	...	...	...	...	...	...	...	...	...	...	...
Kazakhstan	...	...	...	...	81	58	55	61	...	...	...
Kyrgyzstan	...	...	...	...	84	...	...	...	23	29	22
Tajikistan	...	...	...	...	5	...	...	...	54	59	48
Turkmenistan	...	...	...	...	...	...	...	...	...	...	...
Uzbekistan	...	...	...	...	100	...	...	...	13	14	11
Eastern and South-eastern Asia											
Brunei Darussalam	0	LOW	0	LOW	...	...	...	...	...	...	...
Cambodia	...	...	...	...	34	...	...	...	40	46	38
China	...	...	...	...	...	...	...	...	...	...	...
Democratic People's Republic of Korea	...	...	...	...	...	...	...	...	...	...	...
Hong Kong, China	LOW	MEDIUM	MEDIUM	LOW	...	94	94	95	...	...	...
Indonesia	LOW	LOW	0	0	...	33	33	34	...	10	11
Japan	...	...	...	...	100	92	91	92	...	...	...
Lao People's Democratic Republic	...	...	...	...	74	...	...	...	...	...	...
Macao, China	...	...	...	...	...	91	90	93	...	...	...
Malaysia	...	...	...	...	...	54	51	58	41	40	42
Mongolia	...	...	...	...	...	...	...	...	18	19	16
Myanmar	0	LOW	LOW	LOW	...	...	...	...	...	...	...
Philippines	0	0	0	0	...	...	...	...	...	...	15
Republic of Korea	LOW	LOW	LOW	LOW	...	93	92	94	...	...	...
Singapore	...	...	...	...	100	90	89	92	...	...	...
Thailand	LOW	MEDIUM	MEDIUM	LOW	...	66	60	71	...	...	...
Timor-Leste	...	...	...	...	0	...	...	...	14	20	12
Viet Nam	...	...	...	...	...	93	92	94	42	44	41
Europe and Northern America											
Albania	...	...	...	...	...	47	45	49	...	22	36
Andorra	...	...	...	...	...	...	...	...	...	...	...
Austria	...	...	...	...	...	84	84	85	...	...	...
Belarus	...	...	...	...	13	...	...	...	70	68	72
Belgium	0	MEDIUM	LOW	LOW	...	82	81	83	...	...	...
Bosnia and Herzegovina	...	...	...	...	...	...	...	...	...	...	...
Bulgaria	...	...	...	...	17	63	58	68	23	21	25
Canada	...	...	...	...	...	90	89	90	...	...	...
Croatia	LOW	MEDIUM	MEDIUM	LOW	5	83	81	85	...	...	...
Cyprus	...	...	...	...	...	62	58	66	...	...	...
Czech Republic	...	...	...	...	59	86	85	87	...	...	...
Denmark	...	...	...	...	...	83	84	83	...	...	...
Estonia	LOW	HIGH	MEDIUM	LOW	...	95	94	96	...	...	...
Finland	...	...	...	...	100	92	90	94	...	...	...
France	LOW	MEDIUM	MEDIUM	...	...	81	79	83	...	...	...
Germany	...	...	...	...	...	88	87	89	...	...	...
Greece	...	...	...	...	...	74	70	79	38	27	50
Hungary	LOW	LOW	LOW	LOW	...	82	81	83	...	...	...
Iceland	LOW	HIGH	MEDIUM	LOW	...	76	74	78	...	...	...
Ireland	LOW	LOW	LOW	LOW	...	89	88	89	...	...	...
Italy	...	...	...	...	...	81	80	82	...	...	...
Latvia	...	...	...	...	...	88	85	91	...	...	...
Liechtenstein	...	...	...	...	...	90	92	87	...	...	...
Lithuania	LOW	LOW	LOW	LOW	...	84	81	87	71	72	68
Luxembourg	HIGH	LOW	0	LOW	100	78	80	76	...	...	...
Malta	0	HIGH	LOW	LOW	...	...	...	...	...	...	...
Monaco	...	...	...	...	...	...	...	...	...	...	...
Montenegro	...	...	...	...	27	49	45	53	...	...	...
Netherlands	...	...	...	...	...	87	87	87	...	...	...
Norway	0	MEDIUM	LOW	LOW	...	80	79	82	...	...	...
Poland	...	...	...	...	...	91	90	92	...	...	...
Portugal	0	MEDIUM	MEDIUM	LOW	...	81	80	82	...	...	...
Republic of Moldova	...	...	...	...	0	...	...	...	...	...	...
Romania	...	...	...	...	67	63	61	65	...	...	...
Russian Federation	...	...	...	...	92	81	80	83	37	35	39
San Marino	...	...	...	...	...	...	...	...	...	...	...
Serbia	LOW	HIGH	LOW	MEDIUM	...	65	63	67	...	...	...
Slovakia	...	...	...	...	...	73	73	73	...	...	...
Slovenia	...	...	...	...	...	87	85	89	...	...	...
Spain	...	...	...	...	...	84	84	84	...	...	...
Sweden	LOW	HIGH	HIGH	LOW	100	78	75	80	60	59	61
Switzerland	...	...	...	...	...	87	87	87	...	...	...
The former Yugoslav Rep. of Macedonia	...	...	...	...	...	...	...	...	...	...	...

TABLE 11
(Continued)

Country or territory	PROMOTING SUSTAINABLE DEVELOPMENT AND GLOBAL CITIZENSHIP IN CURRICULA					KNOWLEDGE ACQUISITION ON SUSTAINABLE DEVELOPMENT AND GLOBAL CITIZENSHIP					
	Inclusion in national curricula frameworks of issues relating to global citizenship and sustainable development[1,2]				Percentage of schools providing life skills-based	Percentage of students and youth with adequate understanding of issues relating to global citizenship and sustainable development					
	Gender equality[3]	Human rights[4]	Sustainable development[5]	Global citizenship[6]	HIV/AIDS education[7]	Science literacy[9,10]			HIV/AIDS and sexuality education[7]		
	2005-2015[8]	2005-2015[8]	2005-2015[8]	2005-2015[8]	2009-2010[8]	2012			2009-2015[8]		
						Total	Male	Female	Total	Male	Female
Ukraine	...	...	...	...	59	...	...	...	23	25	21
United Kingdom	0	LOW	LOW	0	...	85	86	84	...	...	...
United States	...	...	...	...	...	82	80	84	...	...	...
Latin America and the Caribbean											
Anguilla	...	...	...	...	...	...	...	...	...	...	...
Antigua and Barbuda	...	...	...	...	100	...	...	...	...	...	...
Argentina	0	LOW	0	LOW	...	49	48	51	...	...	...
Aruba	...	...	...	...	...	...	...	...	...	...	...
Bahamas	...	...	...	...	78	...	...	...	4	6	3
Barbados	...	...	...	...	85	...	...	...	46	45	48
Belize	LOW	LOW	LOW	0	38	...	...	...	76	76	77
Bermuda	...	...	...	...	...	...	...	...	...	...	...
Bolivia, Plurinational States of	...	...	...	...	...	...	...	...	...	...	...
Brazil	0	HIGH	LOW	LOW	...	46	47	46	...	...	...
British Virgin Islands	...	...	...	...	...	...	...	...	...	...	...
Cayman Islands	...	...	...	...	...	...	...	...	...	...	...
Chile	LOW	HIGH	MEDIUM	LOW	...	66	67	64	82	78	85
Colombia	...	...	...	...	...	44	48	40	...	...	24
Costa Rica	...	...	...	...	...	61	64	58	...	...	...
Cuba	...	...	...	...	...	...	...	...	...	...	...
Curaçao	...	...	...	...	...	...	...	...	...	...	...
Dominica	LOW	MEDIUM	LOW	LOW	100	...	...	...	...	...	...
Dominican Republic	LOW	MEDIUM	MEDIUM	MEDIUM	8	...	...	...	43	41	45
Ecuador	...	...	...	...	63	...	...	...	...	...	...
El Salvador	LOW	HIGH	MEDIUM	LOW	100	...	...	...	37	34	40
Grenada	LOW	LOW	LOW	LOW	94	...	...	...	...	...	...
Guatemala	MEDIUM	HIGH	MEDIUM	MEDIUM	2	...	...	...	...	...	...
Guyana	...	...	...	...	...	...	...	...	51	47	54
Haiti	0	LOW	0	LOW	13	...	...	...	32	28	35
Honduras	LOW	HIGH	MEDIUM	LOW	11	...	...	...	33	35	33
Jamaica	...	...	...	...	44	...	...	...	...	...	...
Mexico	LOW	HIGH	LOW	LOW	...	53	55	51	...	...	...
Montserrat	...	...	...	...	...	...	...	...	...	...	...
Nicaragua	MEDIUM	HIGH	MEDIUM	LOW	88	...	...	...	...	...	...
Panama	LOW	MEDIUM	MEDIUM	LOW	...	...	...	...	14	12	15
Paraguay	HIGH	MEDIUM	LOW	LOW	...	...	...	...	...	...	...
Peru	LOW	HIGH	MEDIUM	LOW	...	32	32	31	...	...	27
Saint Kitts and Nevis	...	...	...	...	45	...	...	...	...	...	...
Saint Lucia	...	...	...	...	59	...	...	...	...	...	...
Saint-Martin	...	...	...	...	...	...	...	...	...	...	...
Saint Vincent and the Grenadines	...	...	...	...	100	...	...	...	...	...	...
Sint-Maarten	...	...	...	...	...	...	...	...	...	...	...
Suriname	...	...	...	...	0	...	...	...	...	...	...
Trinidad and Tobago	...	...	...	...	...	...	...	...	...	...	...
Turks and Caicos Islands	...	...	...	...	...	...	...	...	...	...	...
Uruguay	LOW	HIGH	LOW	LOW	90	53	53	53	...	...	...
Venezuela, Bolivarian Republic of	0	HIGH	LOW	LOW	100	...	...	...	...	...	...
Northern Africa and Western Asia											
Algeria	...	...	...	...	...	...	...	...	...	...	...
Bahrain	...	...	...	...	...	...	...	...	...	...	...
Egypt	...	...	...	...	...	...	...	...	...	...	3
Iraq	LOW	HIGH	MEDIUM	LOW	...	...	...	...	...	...	...
Israel	...	...	...	...	13	71	68	74	...	...	...
Jordan	...	...	...	...	...	50	39	61	...	...	9
Kuwait	...	...	...	...	...	...	...	...	...	...	...
Lebanon	...	...	...	...	...	...	...	...	...	...	...
Libya	...	...	...	...	...	...	...	...	...	...	...
Morocco	...	...	...	...	...	...	...	...	22	25	20
Oman	...	...	...	...	...	...	...	...	...	...	...
Palestine	0	LOW	LOW	LOW	...	...	...	...	...	...	...
Qatar	LOW	MEDIUM	MEDIUM	LOW	100	37	32	43	...	...	...
Saudi Arabia	...	...	...	...	...	...	...	...	...	...	...
Sudan	...	...	...	...	...	...	...	...	...	...	...
Syrian Arab Republic	...	...	...	...	...	...	...	...	...	...	...
Tunisia	...	...	...	...	...	45	45	45	8	5	11
Turkey	...	...	...	...	...	74	70	77	...	...	...
United Arab Emirates	...	...	...	...	...	65	57	72	...	...	...
Yemen	...	...	...	...	4	...	...	...	...	...	...
The Pacific											
Australia	LOW	HIGH	MEDIUM	MEDIUM	...	86	86	87	...	...	...
Cook Islands	0	LOW	LOW	LOW	...	...	...	...	...	...	...
Fiji	0	MEDIUM	MEDIUM	LOW	...	...	...	...	...	...	...
Kiribati	LOW	0	LOW	0	...	...	...	...	...	...	...
Marshall Islands	...	...	...	...	...	...	...	...	...	...	...
Micronesia (Federated States of)	0	LOW	LOW	LOW	...	...	...	...	...	...	...
Nauru	0	0	LOW	LOW	...	...	...	...	...	...	...

TABLE 11
(Continued)

Country or territory	PROMOTING SUSTAINABLE DEVELOPMENT AND GLOBAL CITIZENSHIP IN CURRICULA					KNOWLEDGE ACQUISITION ON SUSTAINABLE DEVELOPMENT AND GLOBAL CITIZENSHIP					
	Inclusion in national curricula frameworks of issues relating to global citizenship and sustainable development[1,2]				Percentage of schools providing life skills-based	Percentage of students and youth with adequate understanding of issues relating to global citizenship and sustainable development					
	Gender equality[3]	Human rights[4]	Sustainable development[5]	Global citizenship[6]	HIV/AIDS education[7]	Science literacy[9,10]			HIV/AIDS and sexuality education[7]		
	2005–2015[8]	2005–2015[8]	2005–2015[8]	2005–2015[8]	2009–2010[8]	2012			2009–2015[8]		
						Total	Male	Female	Total	Male	Female
New Zealand	0	LOW	MEDIUM	LOW	...	84	83	85	...	...	...
Niue	...	...	...	...	...	...	...	...	...	...	...
Palau	...	...	...	...	...	...	...	...	...	...	...
Papua New Guinea	LOW	MEDIUM	MEDIUM	LOW	100	...	...	...	...	...	...
Samoa	0	LOW	MEDIUM	0	...	...	...	...	5	6	5
Solomon Islands	...	...	...	...	...	...	...	...	...	...	...
Tokelau	LOW	LOW	MEDIUM	0	...	...	...	...	...	...	...
Tonga	...	...	...	...	...	...	...	...	...	...	...
Tuvalu	MEDIUM	MEDIUM	HIGH	MEDIUM	100	...	...	...	...	...	...
Vanuatu	...	...	...	...	8	...	...	...	...	...	...
Southern Asia											
Afghanistan	0	LOW	LOW	LOW	1	...	...	...	...	...	...
Bangladesh	...	...	...	...	...	...	...	...	...	...	13
Bhutan	MEDIUM	LOW	MEDIUM	MEDIUM	...	...	...	...	23	...	21
India	LOW	HIGH	HIGH	LOW	31	...	...	...	40	44	35
Iran, Islamic Republic of	...	...	...	...	...	...	...	...	18	21	16
Maldives	0	MEDIUM	MEDIUM	LOW	...	...	...	...	...	40	35
Nepal	MEDIUM	MEDIUM	LOW	MEDIUM	8	...	...	...	28	34	26
Pakistan	LOW	HIGH	LOW	LOW	...	...	...	...	4	5	4
Sri Lanka	...	...	...	...	...	...	...	...	...	...	...
Sub-Saharan Africa											
Angola	...	...	...	...	...	...	...	...	28	32	25
Benin	...	...	...	...	...	...	...	...	26	31	25
Botswana	...	...	...	...	100	...	...	...	...	...	...
Burkina Faso	...	...	...	...	10	...	...	...	32	36	31
Burundi	...	...	...	...	66	...	...	...	45	47	44
Cabo Verde	...	...	...	...	100	...	...	...	67	65	68
Cameroon	...	...	...	...	...	...	...	...	63	67	60
Central African Republic	...	...	...	...	27	...	...	...	...	...	...
Chad	...	...	...	...	75	...	...	...	...	...	...
Comoros	...	...	...	...	27	...	...	...	22	27	21
Congo	...	...	...	...	...	...	...	...	18	28	14
Côte d'Ivoire	LOW	HIGH	LOW	LOW	2	...	...	...	18	25	16
Democratic Rep. of the Congo	0	LOW	LOW	LOW	68	...	...	...	20	25	19
Djibouti	LOW	0	LOW	LOW	38	...	...	...	11	13	9
Equatorial Guinea	...	...	...	...	...	...	...	...	...	...	...
Eritrea	...	...	...	...	31	...	...	...	...	...	...
Ethiopia	...	...	...	...	38	...	...	...	28	34	24
Gabon	...	...	...	...	...	...	...	...	32	36	30
Gambia	LOW	HIGH	MEDIUM	LOW	...	...	...	...	29	30	28
Ghana	LOW	LOW	LOW	LOW	79	...	...	...	22	27	20
Guinea	...	...	...	...	82	...	...	...	26	34	23
Guinea-Bissau	...	...	...	...	...	...	...	...	22	22	23
Kenya	...	...	...	...	100	...	...	...	...	64	54
Lesotho	MEDIUM	HIGH	LOW	LOW	88	...	...	...	36	31	38
Liberia	...	...	...	...	2	...	...	...	34	29	36
Madagascar	...	...	...	...	...	...	...	...	34	26	23
Malawi	...	...	...	...	...	...	...	...	42	45	41
Mali	...	...	...	...	49	...	...	...	26	33	24
Mauritania	...	...	...	...	...	...	...	...	...	...	...
Mauritius	LOW	HIGH	HIGH	LOW	...	...	...	...	32	30	4
Mozambique	...	...	...	...	...	...	...	...	35	52	30
Namibia	LOW	MEDIUM	MEDIUM	LOW	...	...	...	...	58	51	62
Niger	LOW	0	LOW	0	82	...	...	...	17	25	14
Nigeria	...	...	...	...	23	...	...	...	24	27	22
Rwanda	MEDIUM	0	MEDIUM	LOW	...	...	...	...	51	47	53
Sao Tome and Principe	...	...	...	...	...	...	...	...	...	43	43
Senegal	...	...	...	...	...	...	...	...	30	31	29
Seychelles	LOW	HIGH	LOW	LOW	...	...	...	...	...	...	...
Sierra Leone	...	...	...	...	...	...	...	...	29	30	29
Somalia	...	...	...	...	...	...	...	...	...	...	...
South Africa	0	HIGH	LOW	0	100	...	...	...	...	...	...
South Sudan	MEDIUM	HIGH	LOW	0	...	...	...	...	...	...	...
Swaziland	...	...	...	...	85	...	...	...	56	54	58
Togo	...	...	...	...	0	...	...	...	26	32	23
Uganda	...	...	...	...	...	...	...	...	38	40	38
United Republic of Tanzania	LOW	LOW	0	LOW	...	...	...	...	43	47	40
Zambia	MEDIUM	LOW	MEDIUM	LOW	...	...	...	...	44	47	42
Zimbabwe	...	...	...	...	100	...	...	...	55	52	56

TABLE 11

(Continued)

Country or territory	PROMOTING SUSTAINABLE DEVELOPMENT AND GLOBAL CITIZENSHIP IN CURRICULA					KNOWLEDGE ACQUISITION ON SUSTAINABLE DEVELOPMENT AND GLOBAL CITIZENSHIP					
	Inclusion in national curricula frameworks of issues relating to global citizenship and sustainable development[1,2]				Percentage of schools providing life skills-based	Percentage of students and youth with adequate understanding of issues relating to global citizenship and sustainable development					
	Gender equality[3]	Human rights[4]	Sustainable development[5]	Global citizenship[6]	HIV/AIDS education[7]	Science literacy[9,10]			HIV/AIDS and sexuality education[7]		
	2005–2015[8]	2005–2015[8]	2005–2015[8]	2005–2015[8]	2009–2010[8]	2012			2009–2015[8]		
						Total	Male	Female	Total	Male	Female
	Median				Median	Median			Median		
World	...	...	...	...	...	...	...	...	...	...	...
Countries in transition	...	...	...	...	...	...	...	...	...	...	...
Developed countries	...	...	...	...	...	84	83	85	...	...	...
Developing countries	...	...	...	...	...	...	...	...	...	...	...
Caucasus and Central Asia	...	...	...	...	84	...	...	...	...	...	...
Eastern and South-eastern Asia	...	...	...	...	...	...	...	...	...	...	...
Eastern Asia	...	...	...	...	...	...	...	...	...	...	...
South-eastern Asia	...	...	...	...	...	...	...	...	...	...	...
Europe and Northern America	...	...	...	...	...	82	81	83	...	...	...
Latin America and the Caribbean	...	...	...	...	...	...	...	...	...	...	...
Caribbean	...	...	...	...	...	...	...	...	...	...	...
Latin America	...	...	...	...	...	...	...	...	...	...	...
Northern Africa and Western Asia	...	...	...	...	...	...	...	...	...	...	...
Northern Africa	...	...	...	...	...	...	...	...	...	...	...
Western Asia	...	...	...	...	...	...	...	...	...	...	...
Pacific	...	...	...	...	...	...	...	...	...	...	...
Southern Asia	...	...	...	...	...	...	...	...	23	...	...
Sub-Saharan Africa	...	...	...	...	67	...	...	...	31	...	...
Conflict-affected countries	...	...	...	...	...	...	...	...	...	...	...
Countries with low income	...	...	...	...	...	...	...	...	31	...	...
Countries with middle income	...	...	...	...	...	...	...	...	...	...	...
Lower middle	...	...	...	...	...	...	...	...	24	...	...
Upper middle	...	...	...	...	...	...	...	...	...	...	...
Countries with high income	...	...	...	...	...	84	83	84	...	...	...

Note: The country groupings by level of income are as defined by the World Bank but include only countries listed in the table. They are based on the list of countries by income group as revised in July 2015.

1. Source: UNESCO-IBE (2016).

2. Curricula referred to are for primary education, lower secondary education or both.

3. Key terms included are a) gender equality, b) gender equity, c) empowerment of girls/women, d) gender sensitive(ity) and e) gender parity. The degree of inclusion of the issue in curricula is assessed as LOW if 1 or 2 of the 5 items are covered, MEDIUM if 3 are covered and HIGH if 4 or 5 are covered; 0 indicates no inclusion of any items.

4. Key terms included are a) human rights, rights and responsibilities (children's rights, cultural rights, indigenous rights, women's rights, disability rights); b) freedom (of expression, of speech, of press, of association or organization) and civil liberties; c) social justice; d) democracy/democratic rule, democratic values/principles; e) human rights education. The degree of inclusion of the issue in curricula is assessed as LOW if 1 or 2 of the 5 items are covered, MEDIUM if 3 are covered and HIGH if 4 or 5 are covered; 0 indicates no inclusion of any items.

5. Key terms included are a) sustainable, sustainability, sustainable development; b) economic sustainability, sustainable growth, sustainable production/consumption, green economy; c) social sustainability (social cohesion and sustainability); d) environmental sustainability/environmentally sustainable; e) climate change/variability (global warming, carbon emissions/footprint); f) renewable energy/fuels, alternative energy sources (solar, tidal, wind, wave, geothermal, biomass); g) ecosystems, ecology (biodiversity, biosphere, biomes, loss of diversity); h) waste management, recycling; i) education for sustainable development, sustainability education, education for sustainability; j) environmental education/ studies, education for the environment, education for environmental sustainability. The degree of inclusion of the issue in curricula is assessed as LOW if 1 to 4 of the 10 items are covered, MEDIUM if 5 to 7 items are covered and HIGH if 8 to 10 items are covered; 0 indicates no inclusion of any items.

6. Key terms are a) globalization; b) global citizen(ship)/culture/identity/community; c) global-local thinking, local-global (think global[ly] act local[ly], glocal); d) multicultural(ism)/intercultural(ism) (and hyphenated forms); e) migration, immigration, mobility, movement of people; f) global competition/competitiveness, globally competitive, international competitiveness; g) global inequality(ies)/disparity(ies); h) national/local citizenship/culture/identity(ies)/culture(s)/ heritage, global citizenship education; i) education for global citizenship. The degree of inclusion of the issue in curricula is assessed as LOW if 1 to 4 of these items are covered, MEDIUM if 5 to 7 are covered and HIGH if 8 or 9 are covered; 0 indicates no inclusion of any items.

7. Data are from UNAIDS (2011), 2015 UNAIDS AIDSInfo Online Database and DHS StatCompiler. For more detailed country notes see these sources.

8. Data are for the most recent year available in the period specified. For details see relevant sources.

9. Source: GEM Report team calculations (2016) based on PISA 2012 data (OECD, 2013). PISA defines scientific literacy as a) scientific knowledge and its use to identify questions, acquire new knowledge, explain scientific phenomena and draw evidence-based conclusions about science-related issues; b) understanding of the characteristic features of science as a form of human knowledge and enquiry; c) awareness of how science and technology shape the material, intellectual and cultural environments; and d) willingness to engage in science-related issues, and with the ideas of science, as a reflective citizen. Science literacy is used in this table as a proxy measure of knowledge of environmental science, and geoscience and of sustainable development/sustainability more broadly, given the correlation between the two.

(...) No data are available.

TABLE 12

SDG 4, Means of implementation 4.a and 4.b – Education facilities, learning environments and internationally inbound and outbound tertiary students
by 2030, build and upgrade education facilities that are child, disability and gender sensitive and provide effective learning environments; enhance student international mobility

	EDUCATION FACILITIES AND INTERNATIONALLY INBOUND AND OUTBOUND TERTIARY STUDENTS										
	SAFE, NON-VIOLENT, INCLUSIVE AND EFFECTIVE LEARNING ENVIRONMENTS							INTERNATIONALLY MOBILE STUDENTS IN TERTIARY EDUCATION			
	Education facilities							Student international mobility			
	Water, sanitation and hygiene in schools[1]				Information, communication and technology			Internationally mobile students (inbound)		Internationally mobile students (outbound)	
	Percentage of schools (%) with:				Percentage of schools (%) with:						
Country or territory	Basic drinking water 2014	Basic sanitation or toilets 2014	Of which: single-sex toilets 2014	Basic handwashing facilities School year ending in 2014	Electricity School year ending in 2014	Internet used for pedagogical purposes School year ending in 2014	Computers used for pedagogical purposes School year ending in 2014	Number enrolled in tertiary education (000) School year ending in 2014 Total	Inbound mobility rate (%)[2] School year ending in 2014 Total	Number enrolled in tertiary education (000) School year ending in 2014 Total	Outbound mobility rate (%)[3] School year ending in 2014 Total
Caucasus and Central Asia											
Armenia	92	86	...	...	100ʸ	...	100ʸ	4	3.9	6.5**,ᶻ	5.6ᶻ
Azerbaijan[3,4]	5	68	...	...	100ʸ	27ʸ	84ʸ	4	2.3	22.0**,ᶻ	11.7ᶻ
Georgia	75	70	...	...	100ʸ	100ʸ	100ʸ	3	2.8	9.9**,ᶻ	8.8ᶻ
Kazakhstan[4]	85	85	...	...	...	...	100*,ʸ	**10**	**1.5**	48.9**,ᶻ	6.3ᶻ
Kyrgyzstan[4]	30	53	15	...	100ʸ	6ʸ	86ʸ	12	4.5	5.9**,ᶻ	2.1ᶻ
Tajikistan	51	29	...	...	...	...	...	**1.9**	**0.8**	9.7**,ᶻ	5.0ᶻ
Turkmenistan	...	...	...	...	...	...	...	0.1	0.2	35.9**,ᶻ	...
Uzbekistan	100	100	...	...	...	...	...	...	...	18.8**,ᶻ	...
Eastern and South-eastern Asia											
Brunei Darussalam	...	...	...	...	100**,ʸ	100**,ʸ	0.4	3.2	3.4*,ᶻ	38.3ᶻ	
Cambodia	58	81	...	...	...	...	3*,ʸ	...	...	4.2*,ᶻ	...
China	99	62	...	...	...	...	...	108	0.3	712.2**,ᶻ	2.1ᶻ
Democratic People's Republic of Korea	...	...	...	...	...	...	...	...	...	1.9**,ᶻ	...
Hong Kong, China[3,4]	...	...	...	...	100ʸ	100ʸ	100ʸ	30	9.8	31.8**,ᶻ	10.6ᶻ
Indonesia	83	53	55	...	...	...	...	7ʸ	0.1ʸ	39.1**,ᶻ	0.6ᶻ
Japan	...	...	...	...	...	...	...	136ᶻ	3.5ᶻ	32.3**,ᶻ	0.8ᶻ
Lao People's Democratic Republic	54	47	...	...	...	...	...	0.5	0.4	5.0**,ᶻ	3.6ᶻ
Macao, China	...	...	...	...	...	...	...	11	36.8	2.1*,ᶻ	7.6ᶻ
Malaysia[3,4]	100	100	...	...	100ˣ	91ˣ	100ˣ	36	4.1	56.3**,ᶻ	5.0ᶻ
Mongolia	48	52	...	...	91ʸ	...	100ʸ	1.1	0.6	8.0**,ᶻ	4.5ᶻ
Myanmar	57	23	...	...	...	...	5ʸ	0.1ʸ	0.0ʸ	6.4**,ᶻ	...
Philippines	91	53	...	...	...	...	...	...	...	11.5**,ᶻ	0.3ᶻ
Republic of Korea	...	...	...	...	100**,ʸ	100**,ʸ	100**,ʸ	56ᶻ	1.7ᶻ	116.9**,ᶻ	3.5ᶻ
Singapore[3,4,5]	...	...	...	...	100ˣ	100ˣ	100ˣ	49ᶻ	19.2ᶻ	22.6**,ᶻ	8.8ᶻ
Thailand	60	45	...	...	...	98*,ʸ	98*,ʸ	12	0.5	25.5**,ᶻ	1.1ᶻ
Timor-Leste	52	64	...	...	...	...	...	...	...	3.5**,ᶻ	...
Viet Nam	72	72	...	...	...	...	...	3	0.1	53.5**,ᶻ	2.4ᶻ
Europe and Northern America											
Albania	51	30	37	...	...	...	...	4	2.1	24.1**,ᶻ	14.0ᶻ
Andorra	...	...	...	...	...	...	...	-		1.2**,ᶻ	218.8ᶻ
Austria	...	...	...	...	...	...	...	65	15.5	15.6**,ᶻ	3.7ᶻ
Belarus[5]	100	100	...	...	100ʷ	...	...	15	2.9	35.9**,ᶻ	6.4ᶻ
Belgium	...	...	...	...	...	...	...	56	11.2	16.3**,ᶻ	3.3ᶻ
Bosnia and Herzegovina	100	100	...	...	...	...	...	8	7.3	10.9**,ᶻ	9.6ᶻ
Bulgaria	100	100	...	...	...	...	...	11	4.0	24.6**,ᶻ	8.7ᶻ
Canada	...	...	...	...	...	...	...	151ᶻ	...	45.8**,ᶻ	...
Croatia	100	100	...	...	...	...	...	0.6	0.4	8.6**,ᶻ	...
Cyprus	...	...	...	...	...	...	...	5	14.3	26.2**,ᶻ	82.1ᶻ
Czech Republic	...	...	...	...	...	...	...	41	9.8	12.5**,ᶻ	2.9ᶻ
Denmark	...	...	...	...	...	...	...	30	9.9	5.3**,ᶻ	1.8ᶻ
Estonia	...	...	...	...	...	...	...	2ᶻ	2.9ᶻ	4.2**,ᶻ	6.4ᶻ
Finland	...	...	...	...	...	...	...	23	7.4	8.3**,ᶻ	2.7ᶻ
France	...	...	...	...	...	...	...	235	9.8	84.1**,ᶻ	3.6ᶻ
Germany	...	...	...	...	...	...	...	211	7.2	119.1**,ᶻ	4.3ᶻ
Greece	...	...	...	...	...	...	...	28ᶻ	4.2ᶻ	34.0**,ᶻ	5.2ᶻ
Hungary	...	...	...	...	...	...	...	23	7.0	8.5**,ᶻ	2.4ᶻ
Iceland	...	...	...	...	...	...	...	1.2ʸ	6.2	2.8**,ᶻ	...
Ireland	...	...	...	...	...	...	...	13ᶻ	6.4ᶻ	16.3**,ᶻ	8.2ᶻ
Italy	...	...	...	...	...	...	...	82ᶻ	4.4ᶻ	48.0**,ᶻ	2.6ᶻ
Latvia	...	...	...	...	...	...	...	4	5.0	6.3**,ᶻ	6.7ᶻ
Liechtenstein	...	...	...	...	...	...	...	0.7	85.3	1.0**,ᶻ	...
Lithuania	...	...	...	...	...	...	...	4ᶻ	2.5ᶻ	11.9**,ᶻ	7.5ᶻ
Luxembourg	...	...	...	...	...	...	...	3ᶻ	...	9.0**,ᶻ	...
Malta	...	...	...	...	...	...	...	0.7	5.9	1.9**,ᶻ	15.4ᶻ
Monaco	...	...	...	...	...	...	...	...	...	0.3**,ᶻ	...
Montenegro	95	95	...	...	...	...	...	...	...	4.8**,ᶻ	...
Netherlands	...	...	...	...	...	...	...	69ᶻ	...	13.0**,ᶻ	...
Norway	...	...	...	...	100ʷ	...	...	9	3.5	17.9**,ᶻ	7.0ᶻ
Poland	...	...	...	...	...	...	...	28ᶻ	1.5ᶻ	23.0**,ᶻ	1.2ᶻ
Portugal	...	...	...	...	...	...	...	15	4.1	9.5**,ᶻ	2.6ᶻ
Republic of Moldova	51	70	...	...	...	...	...	2ᶻ	1.9ᶻ	17.4**,ᶻ	14.2ᶻ
Romania	90	90	...	...	...	...	...	24	4.1	31.1**,ᶻ	5.0ᶻ
Russian Federation	100	100	...	...	...	...	...	213	3.0	50.6**,ᶻ	0.7ᶻ
San Marino	...	...	...	...	...	...	...	...	...	3.7**,ᶻ	...
Serbia	95	95	...	...	...	...	...	9	3.7	11.9**,ᶻ	5.0ᶻ
Slovakia	...	...	...	...	...	...	...	11	5.6	33.1**,ᶻ	15.8ᶻ
Slovenia	...	...	...	...	...	...	...	2	2.7	2.7**,ᶻ	2.8ᶻ

TABLE 12

(Continued)

Country or territory	EDUCATION FACILITIES AND INTERNATIONALLY INBOUND AND OUTBOUND TERTIARY STUDENTS										
	SAFE, NON-VIOLENT, INCLUSIVE AND EFFECTIVE LEARNING ENVIRONMENTS							INTERNATIONALLY MOBILE STUDENTS IN TERTIARY EDUCATION			
	Education facilities							Student international mobility			
	Water, sanitation and hygiene in schools[1]				Information, communication and technology			Internationally mobile students (inbound)		Internationally mobile students (outbound)	
	Percentage of schools (%) with:				Percentage of schools (%) with:						
	Basic drinking water	Basic sanitation or toilets	Of which: single-sex toilets	Basic handwashing facilities	Electricity	Internet used for pedagogical purposes	Computers used for pedagogical purposes	Number enrolled in tertiary education (000)	Inbound mobility rate (%)[2]	Number enrolled in tertiary education (000)	Outbound mobility rate (%)[3]
	2014	2014	2014	School year ending in 2014	School year ending in 2014	School year ending in 2014	School year ending in 2014	School year ending in 2014	School year ending in 2014	School year ending in 2014	School year ending in 2014
								Total	Total	Total	Total
Spain	...	...	...	...	...	...	...	56ᶻ	2.9ᶻ	28.6**,ᶻ	1.5ᶻ
Sweden	...	...	...	...	...	...	...	25	5.9	17.7**,ᶻ	4.1ᶻ
Switzerland	...	...	...	...	...	...	...	50	17.1	11.9**,ᶻ	4.2ᶻ
TFYR Macedonia	...	...	...	...	...	...	...	1.3ᶻ	2.2ᶻ	4.3ᶻ	7.1ᶻ
Ukraine	100	100	...	...	...	...	...	60	2.8	39.7**,ᶻ	1.8ᶻ
United Kingdom	...	...	...	...	...	...	...	429	18.2	27.4**,ᶻ	1.1ᶻ
United States	...	...	...	...	...	...	...	842	4.3	60.3**,ᶻ	0.3ᶻ
Latin America and the Caribbean											
Anguilla[3,4]	100	100	...	...	100ʷ	100ʷ	100ʷ	...	...	0.4**,ᶻ	...
Antigua and Barbuda	100	100	...	...	100ʷ	...	...	0.2ʸ	12.0ʸ	0.6**,ᶻ	...
Argentina	70	68	...	...	...	23ᵛ	45ᵛ	...	...	7.2**,ᶻ	0.3ᶻ
Aruba	...	...	...	...	100ʷ	...	100ʷ	0.3	22.0	0.1**,ᶻ	10.8ᶻ
Bahamas	...	...	...	...	100ᵛ	...	...	...	...	2.4**,ᶻ	...
Barbados[3,4]	100	100	...	...	100ᵛ	100ᵛ	100ᵛ	...	...	1.2**,ᶻ	...
Belize	64	21	32	...	...	...	...	...	...	0.8**,ᶻ	8.9ᶻ
Bermuda	...	...	...	...	...	...	...	0.2	20.8	1.6**,ᶻ	131.9ᶻ
Bolivia, Plurinational States of	87	74	...	...	...	...	...	...	...	9.1**,ᶻ	...
Brazil	93	98	...	...	...	38ʷ	46ʷ	15ʸ	0.2ʸ	32.1**,ᶻ	0.4ᶻ
British Virgin Islands	100	100	...	...	100ʷ	100ʷ	100ʷ	...	...	0.4**,ᶻ	...
Cayman Islands[3,4]	...	...	...	...	100ʷ	100ʷ	100ʷ	...	...	0.4**,ᶻ	...
Chile[3,4]	90	90	...	...	...	70*,ᶻ	82*,ᶻ	3	0.3	8.9**,ᶻ	0.8ᶻ
Colombia[4,5]	73	100	...	...	94ˣ	...	88ˣ	0.9	0.0	25.5**,ᶻ	1.2ᶻ
Costa Rica	75	53	64	...	...	...	...	...	...	2.1**,ᶻ	1.0ᶻ
Cuba[4]	100	100	...	...	100ʷ	...	100ʷ	23ʸ	4.5ʸ	1.8**,ᶻ	0.5ᶻ
Curaçao	...	...	...	...	100ʷ	...	...	...	...	...	...
Dominica	100	100	...	...	100ʷ	...	75ʷ	...	...	0.7**,ᶻ	...
Dominican Republic	47	60	...	...	...	...	...	11	2.3	4.4**,ᶻ	...
Ecuador	58	54	...	...	...	18ʷ	54ʷ	3ʸ	0.6ʸ	11.1**,ᶻ	1.9ᶻ
El Salvador	100	67	...	...	...	...	61ᵛ	0.7	0.4	3.1**,ᶻ	1.7ᶻ
Grenada	100	100	...	...	100ʷ	...	...	...	...	0.5**,ᶻ	...
Guatemala[4]	70	49	50	...	37ᵛ	...	3ᵛ	...	...	2.8**,ᶻ	1.0ᶻ
Guyana	68	68	...	...	...	...	...	0.0ʸ	0.4ʸ	1.4**,ᶻ	...
Haiti	60	60	...	...	...	...	...	...	...	10.1**,ᶻ	...
Honduras	66	46	47	...	...	...	...	1.3	0.7	3.3**,ᶻ	1.8ᶻ
Jamaica	88	80	85	...	100ʷ	...	...	...	...	4.0**,ᶻ	5.4ᶻ
Mexico	95	68	69	...	...	...	...	8ᶻ	0.2ᶻ	27.1**,ᶻ	0.8ᶻ
Montserrat	100	100	...	...	100ʷ	60ʷ	60ʷ	...	...	0.0**,ᶻ	...
Nicaragua	50	26	...	...	...	...	...	...	...	2.5**,ᶻ	...
Panama	90	84	85	...	...	...	...	...	...	2.6**,ᶻ	2.1ᶻ
Paraguay	64	70	...	...	...	...	16*,ʷ	...	...	2.9**,ᶻ	...
Peru	60	51	55	...	...	...	...	...	...	14.2**,ᶻ	...
Saint Kitts and Nevis	100	100	...	...	100ʷ	100ʷ	100ʷ	2	73.2	0.4**,ᶻ	...
Saint Lucia	100	100	...	...	100ʷ	58ʷ	61ʷ	0.6	22.8	1.1**,ᶻ	48.1ᶻ
Saint-Martin	...	...	...	...	...	...	...	...	...	...	...
Saint Vincent and the Grenadines	100	100	...	...	100ʷ	68ʷ	...	...	...	0.8**,ᶻ	...
Sint-Maarten	...	...	...	...	100ʷ	...	100ʷ	0.1	43.3	...	...
Suriname	80	65	68	...	100ᵛ	...	...	...	...	0.8**,ᶻ	...
Trinidad and Tobago[4]	100	100	...	...	100ᵛ	...	77ᵛ	...	...	4.6**,ᶻ	...
Turks and Caicos Islands	100	100	...	...	100ʷ	7ʷ	100ʷ	...	...	0.1**,ᶻ	...
Uruguay	100	100	...	...	100ᵛ	96*,ᵛ	100*,ᵛ	...	...	2.4**,ᶻ	...
Venezuela, Bolivarian Republic of	96	93	...	...	...	...	49ᵛ	...	...	11.9**,ᶻ	...
Northern Africa and Western Asia											
Algeria	95	100	...	...	...	...	...	8	0.6	20.7**,ᶻ	1.7ᶻ
Bahrain	100	100	...	...	...	...	...	5	13.2	4.5**,ᶻ	12.1ᶻ
Egypt	100	100	...	...	...	...	98ʷ	48	1.9	19.7**,ᶻ	0.8ᶻ
Iraq	97	100	...	...	...	...	...	...	...	16.0**,ᶻ	...
Israel	...	...	...	...	...	...	...	5ʸ	1.2ʸ	14.7**,ᶻ	3.9ᶻ
Jordan	100	50	68	...	...	73ˣ	89ˣ	28ʸ	9.1ʸ	19.4**,ᶻ	...
Kuwait	100	100	...	...	...	...	...	...	...	16.8**,ᶻ	23.4ᶻ
Lebanon	...	...	...	...	...	...	...	17	7.6	12.0**,ᶻ	5.2ᶻ
Libya	25	65	...	...	...	...	...	...	...	6.4**,ᶻ	...
Morocco	86	73	...	...	...	...	...	...	...	38.6**,ᶻ	5.5ᶻ
Oman	96	94	...	...	100ʷ	77ˣ	100ˣ	3	3.0	11.3**,ᶻ	14.5ᶻ
Palestine[6]	89	83	...	...	100ʸ	21ʸ	64ʸ	.	.	20.9**,ᶻ	9.8ᶻ
Qatar[4]	100	100	...	...	100ʷ	61ʷ	100ʷ	10	39.9	5.0**,ᶻ	24.1ᶻ
Saudi Arabia	...	...	...	...	...	...	...	72	4.8	73.5**,ᶻ	5.4ᶻ
Sudan	55	44	...	...	...	...	...	...	...	...	...
Syrian Arab Republic	70	...	...	...	...	...	...	...	...	22.6**,ᶻ	3.6ᶻ

TABLE 12
(Continued)

	EDUCATION FACILITIES AND INTERNATIONALLY INBOUND AND OUTBOUND TERTIARY STUDENTS										
	SAFE, NON-VIOLENT, INCLUSIVE AND EFFECTIVE LEARNING ENVIRONMENTS							INTERNATIONALLY MOBILE STUDENTS IN TERTIARY EDUCATION			
	Education facilities							Student international mobility			
	Water, sanitation and hygiene in schools[1]				Information, communication and technology			Internationally mobile students (inbound)		Internationally mobile students (outbound)	
	Percentage of schools (%) with:				Percentage of schools (%) with:						
	Basic drinking water	Basic sanitation or toilets	Of which: single-sex toilets	Basic handwashing facilities	Electricity	Internet used for pedagogical purposes	Computers used for pedagogical purposes	Number enrolled in tertiary education (000)	Inbound mobility rate (%)[2]	Number enrolled in tertiary education (000)	Outbound mobility rate (%)[3]
	2014	2014	2014	School year ending in 2014	School year ending in 2014	School year ending in 2014	School year ending in 2014	School year ending in 2014	School year ending in 2014	School year ending in 2014	School year ending in 2014
Country or territory								Total	Total	Total	Total
Tunisia	66	99	60	...	...	...	...	6[z]	1.8[z]	16.9[**,z]	5.0[z]
Turkey	99	99	...	...	...	...	...	54[z]	1.1[z]	45.0[**,z]	0.9[z]
United Arab Emirates	100	100	...	...	...	...	...	64	44.8	8.5[**,z]	6.4[z]
Yemen	53	53	...	...	...	...	...	...	...	16.9[**,z]	...
The Pacific											
Australia	...	...	...	...	...	...	...	266	11.7[**,z]	...	0.8[z]
Cook Islands	...	...	...	...	...	...	...	...	...	0.2[**,z]	...
Fiji	100	95	...	...	...	...	...	...	...	1.2[**,z]	...
Kiribati	3	4	...	...	...	...	...	.[y]	.[y]	1.1[**,z]	...
Marshall Islands	20	10	...	...	...	...	...	0.0[y]	1.0[y]	0.2[**,z]	...
Micronesia (Federated States of)	...	...	...	...	...	...	...	...	...	...	...
Nauru	...	...	...	...	...	...	...	...	...	0.1[**,z]	...
New Zealand	...	...	...	...	100[x]	...	...	49	18.7	5.4[**,z]	2.1[z]
Niue	100	100	...	...	...	...	...	...	...	0.0[**,z]	...
Palau	100	100	...	...	...	...	...	0.2	22.8	...	...
Papua New Guinea	...	...	...	...	...	...	...	...	...	1.3[**,z]	...
Samoa	95	...	...	...	...	...	...	...	...	0.8[**,z]	...
Solomon Islands	50	66	66	...	...	...	...	...	...	3.2[**,z]	...
Tokelau	...	...	...	...	...	...	...	...	...	0.1[**,z]	...
Tonga	...	...	...	...	...	...	...	...	...	1.2[**,z]	...
Tuvalu	65	60	...	...	...	...	...	...	...	0.4[**,z]	...
Vanuatu	82	69	70	...	...	...	...	...	...	1.9[**,z]	...
Southern Asia											
Afghanistan	53	58	...	12	...	...	...	-	-	12.0[**,z]	...
Bangladesh	83	60	...	...	...	...	...	...	...	24.1[**,z]	...
Bhutan[3]	81	74	73	...	...	66[y]	...	...	...	3.5[**,z]	40.5[z]
India	75	53	78	42	...	...	...	34[z]	0.1[z]	181.9[**,z]	0.6[z]
Iran, Islamic Republic of	89	86	...	...	...	32[y]	72[y]	11	0.2	50.1[**,z]	1.1[z]
Maldives[3,4]	97	73	...	...	100[y]	40[**,y]	40[**,y]	...	...	4.1[**,z]	...
Nepal	81	68	...	...	...	...	3[x]	...	...	30.2[**,z]	6.3[z]
Pakistan	63	63	...	...	...	...	...	...	...	37.6[**,z]	2.0[z]
Sri Lanka	85	82	...	...	82[x]	18[x]	60[x]	0.9	0.3	16.0[**,z]	5.4[z]
Sub-Saharan Africa											
Angola	7	54	...	0	...	...	...	...	...	6.9[**,z]	3.2[z]
Benin	33	74	...	...	...	...	...	...	...	4.1[**,z]	2.8[z]
Botswana[4]	50	50	...	13	...	...	83[y]	1.0	1.6	4.4[**,z]	8.0[z]
Burkina Faso	48	39	73	...	...	...	...	2[z]	2.9[z]	3.7[**,z]	4.9[z]
Burundi	36	53	...	10	...	...	...	0.4[z]	1.0[z]	2.0[**,z]	4.5[z]
Cabo Verde	95	100	...	...	...	...	...	0.2	1.4	4.6[**,z]	35.4[z]
Cameroon[4]	31	41	...	...	...	...	6[**,z]	3[y]	...	19.5[**,z]	...
Central African Republic	25	44	...	...	...	...	...	1.8[y]	14.4[y]	0.9[**,z]	...
Chad	15	36	40	...	...	...	...	...	...	4.0[**,z]	...
Comoros	42	50	...	...	...	...	...	-	...	4.2[**,z]	66.6[z]
Congo	33	15	...	...	...	...	...	0.3[z]	0.9[z]	8.1[**,z]	21.8[z]
Côte d'Ivoire	70	45	...	...	...	...	...	3	1.7	7.0[**,z]	4.2[z]
Democratic Rep. of the Congo	20	29	...	...	...	...	...	5[z]	1.2[z]	5.8[**,z]	1.3[z]
Djibouti	86	85	83	...	...	...	...	...	...	1.8[**,z]	...
Equatorial Guinea	59	40	...	...	...	...	...	...	...	1.0[**,z]	...
Eritrea	59	66	...	...	...	...	...	...	...	1.6[**,z]	...
Ethiopia	39	37	...	7	...	...	...	...	...	5.6[**,z]	...
Gabon	66	61	...	...	...	...	...	...	...	5.9[**,z]	...
Gambia	91	71	...	...	...	...	22[**]	...	...	1.3[**,z]	...
Ghana	59	62	...	...	...	...	...	16	3.9	8.9[**,z]	2.5[z]
Guinea	20	69	...	...	...	...	...	0.9[y]	0.9[y]	5.7[**,z]	5.2[z]
Guinea-Bissau	25	28	...	...	...	...	...	...	...	1.5[**,z]	...
Kenya	42	20	21	...	...	...	...	0.1	0.4	12.1[**,z]	...
Lesotho	30	40	...	...	...	...	...	...	...	2.9[**,z]	12.1[z]
Liberia	57	82	...	...	6	...	...	...	...	0.7[**,z]	...
Madagascar[4]	25	29	...	...	...	...	-[z]	1.7[z]	1.7[z]	4.2[**,z]	4.4[z]
Malawi	88	25	...	4	...	...	...	...	...	1.9[**,z]	...
Mali	48	24	...	...	...	...	...	...	...	5.7[**,z]	...
Mauritania	18	27	33	...	...	...	...	**0.3**	**1.4**	4.3[**,z]	22.4[z]
Mauritius	100	100	...	...	100	...	99	1.5	3.8	6.0[**,z]	14.5[z]
Mozambique	68	50	53	...	...	...	...	0.6	0.4	1.8[**,z]	1.4[z]
Namibia	81	80	...	...	...	...	...	...	...	3.5[**,z]	...
Niger	14	14	...	...	...	...	...	1.2[y]	5.4[y]	2.4[**,z]	...
Nigeria	67	32	59	...	...	...	...	...	...	52.1[**,z]	...
Rwanda	89	95	...	37	...	...	...	0.7[z]	1.0[z]	5.2[**,z]	6.7[z]

TABLE 12
(Continued)

	EDUCATION FACILITIES AND INTERNATIONALLY INBOUND AND OUTBOUND TERTIARY STUDENTS										
	SAFE, NON-VIOLENT, INCLUSIVE AND EFFECTIVE LEARNING ENVIRONMENTS							INTERNATIONALLY MOBILE STUDENTS IN TERTIARY EDUCATION			
	Education facilities							Student international mobility			
	Water, sanitation and hygiene in schools[1]				Information, communication and technology			Internationally mobile students (inbound)		Internationally mobile students (outbound)	
	Percentage of schools (%) with:				Percentage of schools (%) with:						
	Basic drinking water	Basic sanitation or toilets	Of which: single-sex toilets	Basic handwashing facilities	Electricity	Internet used for pedagogical purposes	Computers used for pedagogical purposes	Number enrolled in tertiary education (000)	Inbound mobility rate (%)[2]	Number enrolled in tertiary education (000)	Outbound mobility rate (%)[3]
	2014	2014	2014	School year ending in 2014	School year ending in 2014	School year ending in 2014	School year ending in 2014	School year ending in 2014	School year ending in 2014	School year ending in 2014	School year ending in 2014
Country or territory								Total	Total	Total	Total
Sao Tome and Principe	86	87	…	…	…	…	…	…	…	0.5**,z	…
Senegal	55	66	…	…	…	…	…	…	…	11.3**,z	…
Seychelles[5]	100	100	…	…	100y	…	…	-	-	0.5**,z	198.3z
Sierra Leone	23	62	…	…	…	…	…	…	…	0.9**,z	…
Somalia	58	45	…	…	…	…	…	…	…	4.1**,z	…
South Africa	94	100	…	…	…	…	…	42z	4.1z	6.7**,z	0.6z
South Sudan	45	42	…	…	…	…	…	…	…	…	…
Swaziland	65	72	…	…	…	…	…	0.0z	0.5z	2.7**,z	33.3z
Togo	42	22	…	…	…	…	…	…	…	3.3**,z	5.2z
Uganda	74	75	…	37	…	…	…	…	…	4.7**,z	…
United Republic of Tanzania	59	11	47	1	…	…	…	…	…	5.0**,z	3.1z
Zambia	84	45	40	…	…	…	11y	…	…	4.0**,z	…
Zimbabwe	52	43	…	…	…	…	…	0.4y	0.4y	15.9**,z	16.9z
	Median				Median			Sum	Weighted average	Sum	Weighted average
World	75	69						4,056**,z	2.0**,z	3,545**,z	1.8z
Countries in transition	92	86	…	…	…	…	…	238**,z	1.8z	249**,z	1.9z
Developed countries	…	…	…	…	…	…	…	2,878z	6.1z	807z	1.7z
Developing countries	72.5	67	…	…	…	…	…	940**,z	0.7**,z	2,490z	1.8z
Caucasus and Central Asia	75	70	…	…	…	…	…	35z	1.7z	166z	8.3z
Eastern and South Eastern Asia	60	53	…	…	…	…	…	591**,z	1.0z	1,264**,z	2.1z
Eastern Asia	…	…	…	…	…	…	…	451z	1.1z	1,033**,z	2.4z
South-eastern Asia	60	53	…	…	…	…	…	140**,z	0.8z	231z	1.4z
Europe and Northern America	…	…	…	…	…	…	…	2,606z	4.9z	910z	1.7z
Latin America and the Caribbean	91.5	87	…	…	…	…	…	90**,z	0.4**,z	208z	0.9z
Caribbean	100	100	…	…	…	…	…	**		…	…
Latin America	74	68	…	…	…	…	…	…	…	…	…
Northern Africa and Western Asia	96	99	…	…	…	…	…	285z	1.9z	334z	2.2z
Northern Africa	76	86	…	…	…	…	…	…	…	…	…
Western Asia	99	100	…	…	…	…	…	…	…	…	…
Pacific	82	68	…	…	…	…	…	299z	17.8z	33z	1.9z
Southern Asia	81	68	…	…	…	…	…	38**,z	0.1**,z	359z	1.0z
Sub-Saharan Africa	53.5	48	…	…	…	…	…	112**,z	1.6**,z	271z	3.9z
Conflict-affected countries	67	53	…	…	…	…	…	314**,z	0.4**,z	733z	1.0z
Countries with low income	48	48	…	…	…	…	…	47**,z	1.1**,z	207z	4.8z
Countries with middle income	81	68	…	…	…	…	…	742**,z	0.6**,z	2,175z	1.7z
Lower middle	70	63	…	…	…	…	…	207**,z	0.4**,z	740z	1.3z
Upper middle	90	85	…	…	…	…	…	536z	0.8z	1,435z	2.0
Countries with high income	…	…	…	…	…	…	…	3,267z	5.0z	1,164z	1.8

Sources: UIS database; GEM Report team calculations for inbound and outbound mobility rates.

Note: The country groupings by level of income are as defined by the World Bank but include only countries listed in the table. They are based on the list of countries by income group as revised in July (2015).

1. UNICEF-WASH Report (2015).

2. Number of students from abroad studying in a given country, expressed as a percentage of total tertiary enrolment in that country.

3. Number of students from a given country abroad studying abroad, expressed as a percentage of total tertiary enrolment in that country.

4. The percentage of schools with internet refer to public institutions only.

5. The percentage of schools with computers refer to public institutions only.

6. The percentage of schools with electricity refer to public institutions only.

7. The percentages of schools with internet and computer refer to West Bank schools only.

Data in bold are for the school year ending in 2015.

(z) Data are for the school year ending in 2013.

(y) Data are for the school year ending in 2012.

(x) Data are for the school year ending in 2011.

(w) Data are for the school year ending in 2010.

(v) Data are for the school year ending in 2009.

(…) No data available.

(-) Magnitude nil or negligible

TABLE 13

SDG 4, Means of implementation 4.c – Teaching staff, teacher qualifications and training in pre-primary, primary, secondary and tertiary education – part 1

By 2030, substantially increase the supply of qualified teachers, including through international cooperation for teacher training in developing countries, especially least developed countries and small island developing States

	PRE-PRIMARY EDUCATION											PRIMARY EDUCATION			
	Teaching staff	Teacher qualifications			Teacher training			Pupil/ teacher ratio[3]	Pupil/ qualified teacher ratio[3]	Pupil/ trained teacher ratio[3]		Teaching staff	Teacher qualification		
	Number of classroom teachers	Qualified classroom teachers (%)[1]			Trained classroom teachers (%)[2]							Number of classroom teachers	Qualified classroom teachers (%)[1]		
	School year ending in 2014	School year ending in 2014			School year ending in 2014			School year ending in 2014	School year ending in 2014	School year ending in 2014		School year ending in 2014	School year ending in 2014		
Country or territory	Total (000)	Total	Male	Female	Total	Male	Female					Total (000)	Total	Male	Female
Caucasus and Central Asia															
Armenia	7[y]				80[y]			9[y]	...	12[y]		...	...	...	...
Azerbaijan	10	64	100	64	85	100	85	11	17	13		41	...	...	...
Georgia	...	...	...	...	...	...	...	...	...	...		31	...	...	...
Kazakhstan	82	100	100	100	100	100	100	9	9	9		74	100	100	100
Kyrgyzstan	...	...	...	...	...	...	...	...	33[z]	94[z]		17	74	74	74
Tajikistan	**6**	**89**	...	...	**100**			**14**	**16**	**14**		31	95	96	95
Turkmenistan	...	...	...	...	...	...	...	...	...	...		...	...	...	...
Uzbekistan	...	...	...	...	...	...	...	...	...	...		...	...	...	...
Eastern and South-eastern Asia															
Brunei Darussalam	0,8	30	66	28	64	75	64	17	58	26		4	48	49	48
Cambodia	6	100	100	100	100	100	100	31	31	31		48	100	100	100
China	1,851	...	...	...	...	...	...	21	...	...		5,860	...	...	...
DPR Korea	...	...	...	...	...	...	...	...	...	...		...	...	...	...
Hong Kong, China	...	...	...	...	...	...	...	...	...	...		23	100	100	100
Indonesia	428	...	...	...	...	...	...	13	...	...		1,802	...	...	...
Japan	112[z]	...	...	...	...	...	...	26[z]	...	...		407[z]	...	...	...
Lao People's Democratic Republic	8	48	31	48	91	93	91	19	40	21		35	83	80	86
Macao, China	0.8	100	100	100	92	82	92	16	16	17		2	100	100	100
Malaysia	50	100	100	100	100	100	100	18	18	18		278	100	100	100
Mongolia	5[y]	...	...	...	94[y]	85[y]	94[y]	27[y]	...	29[y]		9	98	95	98
Myanmar	16	...	...	...	48	...	...	28	...	58		188	...	...	...
Philippines	...	...	...	...	...	...	...	...	...	...		461[z]	99[z]	98[z]	100[z]
Republic of Korea	88[z]	...	...	...	...	...	...	14[z]	...	...		166[z]	...	...	...
Singapore	...	...	...	...	...	...	...	...	...	...		...	...	...	...
Thailand	...	...	...	...	...	...	...	...	...	...		337	100	...	...
Timor-Leste	...	...	...	...	...	...	...	...	...	...		...	...	...	...
Viet Nam	205	98	85	98	98	85	98	18	18	18		387	100	99	100
Europe and Northern America															
Albania	4	71	.	71	...	...	...	18	26	...		10	72	51	77
Andorra	0.2	100	100	100	100	100	100	14	14	14		0.4	100	100	100
Austria	20	...	...	...	...	...	...	12	...	...		31	...	...	...
Belarus	42	45	5	45	92	84	92	8	17	8		22	99	99	99
Belgium	34	...	...	...	...	...	...	13	...	...		69	...	...	...
Bosnia and Herzegovina	1[y]	...	...	...	...	...	...	14[y]	...	...		10	...	...	...
Bulgaria	19	...	...	...	...	...	...	13	...	...		15	...	...	...
Canada	...	...	...	...	...	...	...	...	...	...		...	...	...	...
Croatia	8	...	...	...	...	...	...	13	...	...		12	...	...	...
Cyprus	1	...	...	...	...	...	...	16	...	...		4	...	...	...
Czech Republic	26[z]	...	...	...	...	...	...	14[z]	...	...		26[z]	...	...	...
Denmark	...	...	...	...	...	...	...	...	...	...		...	...	...	...
Estonia	8[y]	...	...	...	...	...	...	7[y]	...	...		7[z]	...	...	...
Finland	16[z]	...	...	...	...	...	...	12[z]	...	...		26[z]	...	...	...
France	126[z]	...	...	...	...	...	...	20[z]	...	...		229[z]	...	...	...
Germany	272	...	...	...	...	...	...	8	...	...		233	...	...	...
Greece	14	...	...	...	...	...	...	...	...	...		67	...	...	...
Hungary	26	...	...	...	...	...	...	13	...	...		35	...	...	...
Iceland	3[z]	...	...	...	...	...	...	...	...	...		3[z]	...	...	...
Ireland	...	...	...	...	...	...	...	...	...	...		32[y]	...	...	...
Italy	133[z]	...	...	...	...	...	...	13[z]	...	...		238[z]	...	...	...
Latvia	7	...	...	...	...	...	...	11	...	...		10	...	...	...
Liechtenstein	0,1[y]	...	...	...	...	...	...	11[y]	...	...		0.3[y]	...	...	...
Lithuania	13	...	...	...	...	...	...	8	...	...		8	...	...	...
Luxembourg	2[y]	...	...	...	...	...	...	10[y]	...	...		4[y]	...	...	...
Malta	0,9	...	...	...	...	...	...	10	...	...		2	...	...	...
Monaco	...	...	...	...	...	...	...	...	...	...		...	...	...	...
Montenegro	...	...	...	...	...	...	...	...	...	...		...	...	...	...
Netherlands	33	...	...	...	...	...	...	15	...	...		105	...	...	...
Norway	...	...	...	...	...	...	...	...	...	...		48	...	...	...
Poland	81[z]	...	...	...	...	...	...	15[z]	...	...		211[z]	...	...	...
Portugal	16	...	...	...	...	...	...	17	...	...		50	...	...	...
Republic of Moldova	12[y]	...	...	...	92[y]	[y]	92[y]	10[y]	...	11[y]		8	...	...	...
Romania	35	...	...	...	...	...	...	16	...	...		51	...	...	...
Russian Federation	...	...	...	...	...	...	...	...	...	...		289	...	...	...
San Marino	0.1[y]	...	...	...	...	...	...	8[y]	...	...		0.3[y]	...	...	...
Serbia	12	100	100	100	69[y]	...	...	13	13	19[y]		18	100	100	100
Slovakia	13	...	...	...	...	...	...	13	...	...		14	...	...	...
Slovenia	6[z]	...	...	...	...	...	...	9[z]	...	...		6[z]	...	...	...
Spain	...	...	...	...	...	...	...	...	...	...		224[y]	...	...	...
Sweden	...	...	...	...	...	...	...	...	...	...		62[y]	...	...	...
Switzerland	14	...	...	...	...	...	...	12	...	...		48	...	...	...
TFYR Macedonia	2[y]	...	...	...	...	...	...	8[y]	...	...		7[z]	...	...	...

TABLE 13

Part 1 (Continued)

Country or territory	PRE-PRIMARY EDUCATION										PRIMARY EDUCATION			
	Teaching staff	Teacher qualifications			Teacher training			Pupil/ teacher ratio[3]	Pupil/ qualified teacher ratio[3]	Pupil/ trained teacher ratio[3]	Teaching staff	Teacher qualification		
	Number of classroom teachers	Qualified classroom teachers (%)[1]			Trained classroom teachers (%)[2]						Number of classroom teachers	Qualified classroom teachers (%)[1]		
	School year ending in 2014	School year ending in 2014			School year ending in 2014			School year ending in 2014	School year ending in 2014	School year ending in 2014	School year ending in 2014	School year ending in 2014		
	Total (000)	Total	Male	Female	Total	Male	Female				Total (000)	Total	Male	Female
Ukraine	145ʸ	...	...	...	...	...	...	9ʸ	...	...	100	85	82	85
United Kingdom	74	...	...	...	...	...	...	20	...	...	272	...	...	...
United States	634	...	...	...	...	...	...	14	...	...	1,688	...	...	...
Latin America and the Caribbean														
Anguilla	...	...	...	...	...	...	...	...	...	...	...	...	...	...
Antigua and Barbuda	0.1ʸ	...	...	...	71ʸ	.ʸ	71ʸ	21ʸ	...	30ʸ	0.7	...	...	...
Argentina	...							...						
Aruba	0.1ʸ	...	...	...	100ʸ	100ʸ	100ʸ	20ʸ	...	20ʸ	0.6ʸ	...	...	...
Bahamas	...							...						
Barbados	0.3	100	100	100	...	...	...	17	17	...	1	100	100	100
Belize	0.5	57	33	57	30	67	30	17	29	55	2	29	29	29
Bermuda	0.0	100	.	100	100	.	100	9	9	9	0.6	100	100	100
Bolivia, Plurinational States of	...							...			...			
Brazil	292	...	...	...	...	...	...	...	...	...	795	...	...	...
British Virgin Islands	...	...	...	...	...	...	...	...	...	...	0.3	94	90	94
Cayman Islands	0.1ʸ	...	...	...	77ʸ	100ʸ	75ʸ	8ʸ	...	11ʸ	0.3ᶻ	88ᶻ	94ᶻ	87ᶻ
Chile	...										75ᶻ			
Colombia	51	94	88	94	97	92	97	...	...	...	187	94	91	95
Costa Rica	9	...	...	...	87	87	87	13	...	15	36	...	...	...
Cuba	31ʸ	...	...	...	100ʸ	.ʸ	100ʸ	13ʸ	...	13ʸ	84	81	...	...
Curaçao	...													
Dominica	0.1	...	...	...	...	...	...	13	...	...	0.5	65	56	66
Dominican Republic	13	75	78	75	85ʸ	79ʸ	85ʸ	21	28	30ʸ	62	81	84	81
Ecuador	30ᶻ	...	...	...	81ᶻ	72ᶻ	83ᶻ	18ᶻ	...	22ᶻ	88	...	...	...
El Salvador	7ᶻ	...	...	...	...	...	...	34ᶻ	...	...	33ᶻ	...	...	...
Grenada	0.3	40	.	40	52	.	52	12	30	24	0.9	49	38	51
Guatemala	26ʸ	...	...	...	...	...	...	19ʸ	...	...	105	...	...	...
Guyana	2ʸ	...	...	...	65ʸ	60ʸ	65ʸ	16ʸ	...	24ʸ	4ʸ	...	...	...
Haiti	...													
Honduras	10	51ᶻ	41ᶻ	52ᶻ	51ᶻ	41ᶻ	52ᶻ	24	28ᶻ	28ᶻ	84	...	...	...
Jamaica	...							...			12	96	90	96
Mexico	191	...	...	...	...	...	...	25	...	...	534	...	...	...
Montserrat	...										0.04			
Nicaragua	...													
Panama	5ᶻ	...	...	...	21ᶻ	28ᶻ	21ᶻ	19ᶻ	...	87ᶻ	17ᶻ	100ᶻ	100ᶻ	100ᶻ
Paraguay	6ʸ	53ʸ	32ʸ	56ʸ	92ʸ	84ʸ	93ʸ	24ʸ	46ʸ	26ʸ	35ʸ	87ʸ	83ʸ	88ʸ
Peru	76ʸ	...	...	...	...	...	...	18ʸ	...	...	198	84	90	82
Saint Kitts and Nevis	0.1	100ᶻ	.ᶻ	100ᶻ	8	.	8	12	15*,ᶻ	151	0.4	100	100	100
Saint Lucia	0.4	...	...	...	70	.	70	10	...	15	1	...	...	...
Saint-Martin	...													
Saint Vincent and the Grenadines	0.4ᶻ	...	...	...	14ᶻ	-ᶻ	14ᶻ	7**,ᶻ	...	50**,ᶻ	0.9	16	9	18
Sint-Maarten	...										0.3	69		
Suriname	0.8	93	100	93	7	-	7	24	26	339	5	94	89	94
Trinidad and Tobago	...													
Turks and Caicos Islands	...										**0.3**	**90**	...	...
Uruguay	...													
Venezuela, Bolivarian Republic of	...										...			
Northern Africa and Western Asia														
Algeria	...										159			
Bahrain	2	53	100	53	50	100	50	15	29	31	9	96	98	96
Egypt	42	90	24	91	73	13	74	28	31	38	481	85	81	88
Iraq	...	...	...	...	...	...	...							
Israel	...													
Jordan	7ʸ	...	...	...	...	...	...	17ʸ	...	...	...	...	...	...
Kuwait	8	74	-	74	75	-	75	10	13	13	29	77	51	80
Lebanon	13	...	...	...	93ᶻ	93ᶻ	93ᶻ	...	...	15ᶻ	39	...	...	...
Libya	...													
Morocco	40	100	100	100	100	100	100	19	19	19	157	100	100	100
Oman	3	100	100	100	100	100	100	27	27	27	...	...	...	...
Palestine	7	...	...	...	100	.	100	19	...	19	19	47	40	50
Qatar	3	100	100	100	...	...	...	14	14	...	10	100	100	100
Saudi Arabia	28	100	.	100	100	.	100	11	11	11	347	100	100	100
Sudan	29ᶻ	...	...	...	...	...	...	26ᶻ	...	...	169ᶻ	...	...	...
Syrian Arab Republic	5ᶻ	47ᶻ	92ᶻ	46ᶻ	35ᶻ	-ᶻ	35ᶻ	16ᶻ	34ᶻ	46ᶻ	...	...	...	...
Tunisia	13	27	...	...	49	...	...	17	63	34	66	100	100	100
Turkey	63ᶻ	...	...	...	...	...	...	17ᶻ	...	...	282ᶻ	...	...	...
United Arab Emirates	9	100	100	100	100	100	100	19	19	19	22	100	100	100
Yemen	...	...			...			...			...	...		
The Pacific														
Australia	...	...									...	...		
Cook Islands	0.03	70	.	70	70	.	70	14	20	20	0.1	95	100	95
Fiji	...										4ʸ			
Kiribati	...										0.6	97	95	97
Marshall Islands	...										...			
Micronesia (Federated States of)														
Nauru	0.03	93	.	93	...	...	...	33	35	...	0.04	50	100	46

466

TABLE 13
Part 1 (Continued)

Country or territory	PRE-PRIMARY EDUCATION										PRIMARY EDUCATION			
	Teaching staff	Teacher qualifications			Teacher training			Pupil/ teacher ratio[3]	Pupil/ qualified teacher ratio[3]	Pupil/ trained teacher ratio[3]	Teaching staff	Teacher qualification		
	Number of classroom teachers	Qualified classroom teachers (%)[1]			Trained classroom teachers (%)[2]						Number of classroom teachers	Qualified classroom teachers (%)[1]		
	School year ending in 2014	School year ending in 2014			School year ending in 2014			School year ending in 2014	School year ending in 2014	School year ending in 2014	School year ending in 2014	School year ending in 2014		
	Total (000)	Total	Male	Female	Total	Male	Female				Total (000)	Total	Male	Female
New Zealand	13	...	...	...	...	...	...	9	...	...	25	...	...	...
Niue	0.0	...	...	...	...	...	...	5	...	...	0.02	...	...	...
Palau	0.03	100	.	100	...	...	...	18	18	...	...	...	...	...
Papua New Guinea	...	...	...	...	...	...	...	...	...	...	...	...	...	...
Samoa	0.3	100	100	100	100	100	100	11	11	11	...	...	...	...
Solomon Islands	1	68z	68z	68z	59	59	60	33	50z	56	5	69	71	67
Tokelau	...	...	...	...	...	...	...	...	...	...	...	...	...	...
Tonga	0.2	...	...	...	100y	.y	100y	12	...	11y	0.8	100z	99z	100z
Tuvalu	0.1	100	.	100	75	.	75	13	13	17	...	...	...	...
Vanuatu	0.9z	51z	56z	50z	...	...	...	15z	30z	...	2z	70z	72z	69z
Southern Asia														
Afghanistan	...	...	...	...	...	...	...	...	...	...	131z	...	...	...
Bangladesh	...	...	...	...	...	...	...	...	...	...	...	...	...	...
Bhutan	0.4	...	...	...	...	...	...	11	...	...	4	...	...	...
India	...	...	...	...	...	...	...	...	...	...	4,368z	...	...	...
Iran, Islamic Republic of	...	...	...	...	...	...	...	...	...	...	287	100	100	100
Maldives	1	73	-	73	73	-	73	17	23	23	3	86	88	85
Nepal	**46**	**82**	**36**	**87**	**88**	**38**	**93**	**22**	**27**	**25**	**188**	**94**	**94**	**94**
Pakistan	...	...	...	...	...	...	...	...	...	...	418	...	...	...
Sri Lanka	...	...	...	...	...	...	...	...	...	...	75**	93**,z	...	...
Sub-Saharan Africa														
Angola	...	...	...	...	...	...	...	...	...	...	...	...	...	...
Benin	5	32z	44z	27z	28y	42y	22y	27	83z	90y	46	100	100	100
Botswana	2y	55y	55y	55y	55y	55y	55y	11y	21y	21y	15z	99z	98z	99z
Burkina Faso	3z	...	...	...	20y	76y	8y	25z	...	120y	58	86z	83z	90z
Burundi	2	69	37	75	72	39	79	35	51	49	47	91	88	94
Cabo Verde	1	49	.	49	49	.	49	18	36	36	3	91	91	91
Cameroon	22	...	...	...	57y	55y	57y	21	...	39y	94	58	59	56
Central African Republic	...	...	...	...	...	...	...	...	...	...	8y	...	...	...
Chad	0.4z	...	...	...	52z	49z	53z	29z	...	56z	37z	...	...	...
Comoros	...	...	...	...	...	...	...	...	...	...	4z	75z	73z	77z
Congo	2y	...	...	...	92y	100y	91y	26y	...	28y	17y	...	...	...
Côte d'Ivoire	6	89	84	89	89	84	89	22	25	25	75	88	87	93
Democratic Rep. of the Congo	13	100	100	100	20	8	21	25	25	121	383	100	100	100
Djibouti	...	...	...	...	...	...	...	...	...	...	2	100	100	100
Equatorial Guinea	2y	...	...	...	...	...	...	17y	...	...	4y	...	...	...
Eritrea	1z	50z	35z	51z	50z	35z	51z	34z	67z	67z	9z	100z	100z	100z
Ethiopia	...	...	...	...	...	...	...	...	...	...	245	54	48	63
Gabon	...	...	...	...	...	...	...	...	...	...	...	...	...	...
Gambia	3	70	73	66	70	73	66	34	49	49	7	84	83	87
Ghana	**52**	**46**	**43**	**46**	**46**	**43**	**46**	**34**	**75**	**75**	**139**	**55**	**48**	**65**
Guinea	...	...	...	...	...	...	...	...	...	...	38	71	75	61
Guinea-Bissau	...	...	...	...	...	...	...	...	...	...	...	...	...	...
Kenya	115	...	...	...	82	90	80	26	...	32	142**,y	...	...	...
Lesotho	4	100	100	100	...	...	...	13	13	...	11	76	67	79
Liberia	...	...	...	...	...	...	...	...	...	...	26	...	...	...
Madagascar	15	83	69	84	16	25	15	19	23	120	111	99	99	99
Malawi	...	...	...	...	...	...	...	...	...	...	67	...	...	...
Mali	5	...	...	...	...	...	...	20	...	...	51	...	...	...
Mauritania	2	...	...	...	100	100	100	7	...	7	17	...	...	...
Mauritius	2	...	...	...	100	100	100	13	...	13	6	100	100	100
Mozambique	...	...	...	...	...	...	...	...	...	...	104	90	88	92
Namibia	...	...	...	...	...	...	...	...	...	...	...	...	...	...
Niger	5	100	100	100	90y	81y	91y	28	28	35y	64	100	100	100
Nigeria	...	...	...	...	...	...	...	...	...	...	41	...	...	...
Rwanda	3z	...	...	...	...	...	...	41z	...	...	41	...	...	...
Sao Tome and Principe	1	-	-	-	**28**	**24**	**29**	**13**	...	**46**	**0.9**	...	...	...
Senegal	12	100	100	100	26	32	24	17	17	67	60	100	100	100
Seychelles	0.2	68	.	68	36y	.y	33y	14	20	27y	0.7	76	68	78
Sierra Leone	3z	38z	26z	41z	45z	34z	47z	19z	49z	42z	37z	52z	47z	64z
Somalia	...	...	...	...	...	...	...	...	...	...	...	...	...	...
South Africa	26**	...	...	...	...	...	...	...	...	...	223**	...	...	...
South Sudan	...	...	...	...	...	...	...	...	...	...	9z	66z	60z	68z
Swaziland	...	...	...	...	...	...	...	...	...	...	9z	66z	60z	68z
Togo	3	61z	49z	62z	37z	33z	37z	30	48z	79z	34	66z	67z	60z
Uganda	15z	...	...	...	...	...	...	29 z	...	...	186z	...	...	...
United Republic of Tanzania	...	...	...	...	...	...	...	...	211z	211z	189z	99z	99z	99z
Zambia	...	...	...	...	...	...	...	...	...	...	64**,z	66**,z	...	...
Zimbabwe	10z	25z	41z	24z	27z	46z	26z	37z	150z	138z	73z	74z	71z	77z

TABLE 13

Part 1 (Continued)

	PRE-PRIMARY EDUCATION										PRIMARY EDUCATION			
	Teaching staff	Teacher qualifications			Teacher training			Pupil/ teacher ratio[3]	Pupil/ qualified teacher ratio[3]	Pupil/ trained teacher ratio[3]	Teaching staff	Teacher qualification		
	Number of classroom teachers	Qualified classroom teachers (%)[1]			Trained classroom teachers (%)[2]						Number of classroom teachers	Qualified classroom teachers (%)[1]		
	School year ending in 2014	School year ending in 2014			School year ending in 2014			School year ending in 2014	School year ending in 2014	School year ending in 2014	School year ending in 2014	School year ending in 2014		
Country or territory	Total (000)	Total	Male	Female	Total	Male	Female				Total (000)	Total	Male	Female
	Sum	Median			Median			Weighted average	Median	Median	Sum	Sum		
World	9,356**	...	...	...	...	...	...	17**	...	...	30,251**	...	...	...
Countries in transition	937**,ʸ	...	...	...	...	...	...	9**,ʸ	...	...	785			
Developed countries	2,017**	...	...	...	...	...	...	14**	...	...	4,644**	...	...	...
Developing countries	6,405	...	...	...	...	...	...	18**	...	...	24,821**	...	...	...
Caucasus and Central Asia	193**	...	...	...	93	...	...	10**	17	13	338**	100	100	100
Eastern and South-eastern Asia	2,932	...	...	...	...	...	...	20	...	...	10,115	100	99	100
Eastern Asia	2,094	...	...	...	...	...	...	21	...	...	6,544			
South-eastern Asia	838	...	...	...	94	...	...	16	...	24	3,572	100	99	100
Europe and Northern America	2,606**	...	...	...	...	...	...	12**	...	...	4,504	...	...	...
Latin America and the Caribbean	1,023**	...	...	...	...	...	...	20**	...	...	3,025	...	...	...
Caribbean	73**,ᶻ	...	...	...	...	...	...	20**,ᶻ	...	...	258**	88	...	...
Latin America	946	...	...	...	...	...	...	20**	...	...	2,767	...	...	...
Northern Africa and Western Asia	324**	95	...	...	93	53	96	20**	23	19	2,525**	...	...	...
Northern Africa	149	90	...	...	73	...	...	24	31	34	1,084	100	100	100
Western Asia	175**	100	100	100	96	47	96	17**	19	19	1,441**	...	...	...
Pacific	...							...	...	...	...			
Southern Asia	...	...	...	...	...	...	...	...	...	...	5,922**			
Sub-Saharan Africa	576**	...	...	...	49	45	50	30**	...	49	3,627**	87	87	91
Conflict-affected countries	2,645**,ʸ	...	...	...	...	...	...	14**,ʸ	...	...	11,677**	...	...	...
Countries with low income	335**	...	...	...	...	...	...	28**	...	...	2,469	91	88	93
Countries with middle income	6,072	...	...	...	...	...	...	18**	...	...	21,725**	...	...	...
Lower middle	2,927**	...	...	...	...	...	...	15**	...	...	11,246**	...	...	...
Upper middle	3,144	...	...	...	...	...	...	20	...	...	10,479	...	...	...
Countries with high income	2,950**	...	...	...	...	...	...	13**	...	...	6,057**	...	...	...

TABLE 13

SDG 4, Means of implementation 4.c – Teaching staff, teacher qualifications and training in pre-primary, primary, secondary and tertiary education – part 2

By 2030, substantially increase the supply of qualified teachers, including through international cooperation for teacher training in developing countries, especially least developed countries and small island developing States

Country or territory	PRIMARY EDUCATION Teacher training — Trained classroom teachers (%)[2] School year ending in 2014 Total	Male	Female	Pupil/ teacher ratio[3] 2014	Pupil/ qualified teacher ratio[3] 2014	Pupil/ trained teacher ratio[3] 2014	SECONDARY EDUCATION Teaching staff Number of classroom teachers 2014 Total (000)	Teacher qualification — Qualified classroom teachers (%)[1] 2014 Total	Male	Female	Teacher training — Trained classroom teachers (%)[2] 2014 Total	Male	Female	Pupil/ teacher ratio[3] 2014	Pupil/ qualified teacher ratio[3] 2014	Pupil/ trained teacher ratio[3] 2014
Caucasus and Central Asia																
Armenia	...	...	...	...	...	...	...	...	...	...	...	...	...	...	...	...
Azerbaijan	100	100	100	13	...	13	...	...	...	...	...	...	...	...	...	...
Georgia	...	...	...	9	...	...	39	...	...	...	...	...	...	7	...	...
Kazakhstan	**100**	**100**	**100**	**16**	**16**	**16**	**224**	**100**	**100**	**100**	**100**	**100**	**100**	**8**	**8**	**8**
Kyrgyzstan	72[y]	73[y]	72[y]	25	34	33[y]	57	...	...	...	...	...	...	11	...	...
Tajikistan	**100**	**100**	**100**	**22**	**23**	**22**	...	...	...	...	...	...	...	...	...	...
Turkmenistan	...	...	...	...	...	...	...	...	...	...	...	...	...	...	...	...
Uzbekistan	...	...	...	...	...	...	...	...	...	...	...	...	...	...	...	...
Eastern and South-eastern Asia																
Brunei Darussalam	87	92	86	10	21	12	5	87	84	88	91	90	92	9	11	10
Cambodia	100	100	100	45	45	45	...	...	...	...	...	...	...	...	...	...
China	...	...	...	16	...	...	6,211	...	...	...	...	...	...	14	...	...
DPR Korea	...	...	...	...	...	...	...	...	...	...	...	...	...	...	...	...
Hong Kong, China	96	95	97	14	14	14	31[**]	...	...	...	96[**]	96[**]	96[**]	14[**]	...	14[**]
Indonesia	...	...	...	17	...	...	1,460	...	...	...	...	...	...	15	...	...
Japan	...	...	...	17[z]	...	...	624[y]	...	...	...	...	...	...	12[y]	...	...
Lao PDR	98	98	98	25	30	26	33[**]	79[**]	...	...	100[**]	...	...	18[**]	23[**]	18[**]
Macao, China	88	74	90	14	14	16	3	100	100	100	82	77	85	12	12	15
Malaysia	99	99	99	11	11	12	260	100	100	100	98	100	98	12	12	12
Mongolia	100	100	100	27	28	27	21	98	93	100	100	100	100	14	14	14
Myanmar	100	...	...	28	...	28	100	...	...	...	94	...	...	32	...	34
Philippines	100[z]	100[z]	100[z]	31[z]	32[z]	31[z]	268[z]	100[z]	100[z]	100[z]	100[z]	100[z]	100[z]	27[z]	27[z]	27[z]
Republic of Korea	...	...	...	17[z]	...	...	238[z]	...	...	...	...	...	...	16[z]	...	...
Singapore	...	...	...	...	...	...	...	...	...	...	...	...	...	...	...	...
Thailand	100	...	...	15	15	15	...	...	...	...	...	...	...	...	...	...
Viet Nam	100	100	100	19	19	19	...	...	...	...	...	...	...	...	...	...
Europe and Northern America																
Albania	...	...	...	19	26	...	23	94	91	96	...	...	...	14	15	...
Andorra	100	100	100	10	10	10	0	100	100	100	100	100	100	9	9	9
Austria	...	...	...	11	...	...	73	...	...	...	...	...	...	10	...	...
Belarus	99	99	99	16	17	17	81	98	98	98	96	95	96	8	8	8
Belgium	...	...	...	11	...	...	128	...	...	...	...	...	...	9	...	...
Bosnia and Herzegovina	...	...	...	17	...	...	28	...	...	...	...	...	...	11	...	...
Bulgaria	...	...	...	18	...	...	39	...	...	...	...	...	...	13	...	...
Canada	...	...	...	...	...	...	...	...	...	...	...	...	...	...	...	...
Croatia	...	...	...	14	...	...	46	...	...	...	...	...	...	8	...	...
Cyprus	...	...	...	13	...	...	6	...	...	...	...	...	...	10	...	...
Czech Republic	...	...	...	19[z]	...	...	69[z]	...	...	...	...	...	...	12[z]	...	...
Denmark	...	...	...	...	...	...	10[z]	...	...	...	...	...	...	8[z]	...	...
Estonia	...	...	...	11[z]	...	...	43[z]	...	...	...	...	...	...	13[z]	...	...
Finland	...	...	...	13[z]	...	...	457[z]	...	...	...	...	...	...	13[z]	...	...
France	...	...	...	18[z]	...	...	590	...	...	...	...	...	...	12	...	...
Germany	...	...	...	12	...	...	80	...	...	...	...	...	...	...	...	...
Greece	...	...	...	...	...	...	79	...	...	...	...	...	...	11	...	...
Hungary	...	...	...	11	...	...	...	...	...	...	...	...	...	...	...	...
Iceland	...	...	...	...	...	...	...	...	...	...	...	...	...	...	...	...
Ireland	...	...	...	16[y]	...	...	404[z]	...	...	...	...	...	...	11[z]	...	...
Italy	...	...	...	12[z]	...	...	15	...	...	...	...	...	...	8	...	...
Latvia	...	...	...	11	...	...	34	...	...	...	...	...	...	8	...	...
Liechtenstein	...	...	...	7[y]	...	...	6[y]	...	...	...	...	...	...	8[y]	...	...
Lithuania	...	...	...	13	...	...	4	...	...	...	...	...	...	8	...	...
Luxembourg	...	...	...	8[y]	...	...	...	...	...	...	...	...	...	...	...	...
Malta	...	...	...	11	...	...	108[**]	...	...	...	...	...	...	15[**]	...	...
Monaco	...	...	...	...	...	...	51	...	...	...	...	...	...	9	...	...
Montenegro	...	...	...	12	...	...	291[z]	...	...	...	...	...	...	10[z]	...	...
Netherlands	...	...	...	9	...	...	78	...	...	...	...	...	...	10	...	...
Norway	...	...	...	10[z]	...	...	26	...	...	...	...	...	...	9	...	...
Poland	...	...	...	13	...	...	131	...	...	...	...	...	...	12	...	...
Portugal	94	100	94	17	...	18	1,046[y]	...	...	...	...	...	...	9[y]	...	...
Republic of Moldova	...	...	...	6[y]	...	...	63	100	100	100	40[y]	30[y]	46[y]	9	9	...
Romania	56[y]	35[y]	60[y]	16	16	28[y]	42	...	...	...	...	...	...	11	...	...
Russian Federation	...	...	...	15	...	...	15[z]	...	...	...	...	...	...	10[z]	...	...
San Marino	...	...	...	13[y]	...	...	290[y]	...	...	...	...	...	...	11[y]	...	...
Serbia	...	...	...	10[y]	...	...	71[y]	...	...	...	...	...	...	10[y]	...	...
Slovakia	...	...	...	10	...	...	65[y]	...	...	...	...	...	...	9[y]	...	...
Slovenia	...	...	...	...	...	...	18[z]	...	...	...	...	...	...	...	...	...

469

TABLE 13

Part 2 (Continued)

Country or territory	PRIMARY EDUCATION						SECONDARY EDUCATION									
	Teacher training			Pupil/ teacher ratio[3]	Pupil/ qualified teacher ratio[3]	Pupil/ trained teacher ratio[3]	Teaching staff	Teacher qualification			Teacher training			Pupil/ teacher ratio[3]	Pupil/ qualified teacher ratio[3]	Pupil/ trained teacher ratio[3]
	Trained classroom teachers (%)[2]						Number of classroom teachers	Qualified classroom teachers (%)[1]			Trained classroom teachers (%)[2]					
	School year ending in 2014			School year ending in 2014	School year ending in 2014	School year ending in 2014	School year ending in 2014	School year ending in 2014			School year ending in 2014			School year ending in 2014	School year ending in 2014	School year ending in 2014
	Total	Male	Female				Total (000)	Total	Male	Female	Total	Male	Female			
Ukraine	100^y	...	...	17	20	16^y	230	98	98	98	...	...	...	12	12	...
United Kingdom	...	...	...	17	...	...	414	...	...	...	...	...	...	16	...	...
United States	...	...	...	15	...	...	1,639	...	...	...	...	...	...	15	...	...
Latin America and the Caribbean																
Anguilla	...	...	...	...	...	...	...	...	...	...	...	...	...	...	...	...
Antigua and Barbuda	70	81	69	14	...	20	1	53	48	55	55	60	53	12	23	22
Argentina	...	...	...	...	...	...	...	...	...	...	...	...	...	...	...	...
Aruba	100^y	98^y	100^y	15^y	...	15^y	1^y	...	...	...	96^y	93^y	98^y	15^y	...	16^y
Bahamas	...	...	...	...	...	...	...	...	...	...	...	...	...	...	...	...
Barbados	100	100	100	18	18	18	...	...	...	...	...	...	...	...	...	...
Belize	61	56	62	22	78	37	2	50	58	45	45	35	50	18	35	40
Bermuda	100	100	100	7	7	7	1	100	100	100	100	100	100	5	5	5
Bolivia, P.S.	...	...	...	...	...	...	...	...	...	...	...	...	...	...	...	...
Brazil	...	...	...	...	...	...	1,451	...	...	...	...	...	...	...	...	...
British Virgin Islands	80	67	82	12	13	15	0	94	92	94	70	62	73	8	8	11
Cayman Islands	88^z	94^z	87^z	13^z	15^z	15^z	1^y	...	...	...	99^y	99^y	99^y	5^y	...	5^y
Chile	...	...	...	20^z	...	...	75^z	...	...	...	...	...	...	21^z	...	...
Colombia	98	97	99	24	26	25	194	98	98	99	99	99	99	25	25	25
Costa Rica	94	94	94	13	...	14	32	...	...	...	96	96	95	14	...	15
Cuba	100	100	100	9	11	9	94	79	...	...	100	100	100	9	11	9
Curaçao	...	...	...	...	...	...	...	...	...	...	...	...	...	...	...	...
Dominica	65	56	66	14	22	22	1	46	42	48	46	42	48	...	...	...
Dominican Republic	85^y	79^y	87^y	21	25	28^y	44	75	75	75	90^y	89^y	90^y	21	28	...
Ecuador	82	82	82	24	...	29	101	...	...	...	81	81	82	19	...	23
El Salvador	...	...	...	24^z	...	...	16^z	...	...	...	...	...	...	38^z	...	...
Grenada	63	70	61	14	30	23	1	33	29	35	40	40	40	13	38	31
Guatemala	...	...	...	23	...	...	92	...	...	...	...	...	...	13	...	...
Guyana	70^y	63^y	71^y	23^y	...	33^y	4^y	...	...	...	...	...	...	20^y	...	...
Haiti	...	...	...	...	...	...	...	...	...	...	...	...	...	...	...	...
Honduras	...	...	...	14	...	...	72	...	...	...	...	...	...	9	...	...
Jamaica	96	90	96	22	23	23	14	84	77	87	84	77	87	16	20	20
Mexico	...	...	...	27	...	...	806	...	...	...	...	...	...	16	...	...
Montserrat	...	...	...	11	...	...	0.03	...	...	...	...	...	...	13	...	...
Nicaragua	...	...	...	...	...	...	...	...	...	...	...	...	...	...	...	...
Panama	90^y	93^y	90^y	25^z	25^z	25^y	20^z	100^y	100^z	100^z	88^y	87^y	89^y	16^z	16^z	...
Paraguay	92^y	90^y	93^y	24^y	28^y	26^y	34^y	...	...	...	81^y	78^y	83^y	18^y	...	23^y
Peru	...	...	...	18	21	...	188	85	85	86	81	80	83	14	17	17
Saint Kitts and Nevis	68	60	69	14	14	20	1	100	100	100	51	46	53	8	8	17
Saint Lucia	79	73	80	14	...	18	1	...	...	...	71	61	76	13	...	18
Saint-Martin	...	...	...	...	...	...	...	...	...	...	...	...	...	...	...	...
Saint Vincent/Grenadines	76	68	78	16	97	21	1	37	34	38	50	47	52	15	42	31
Sint-Maarten	...	...	...	11	16	...	0	93	97	90	...	...	...	8	8	...
Suriname	6	11	6	14	15	236	5^z	...	...	...	19^z	21^z	18^z	11^z	...	61^z
Trinidad and Tobago	...	...	...	...	...	...	...	...	...	...	...	...	...	...	...	...
Turks and Caicos Islands	**90**			**9**	**10**	**10**	**0.2**	**98**			**98**			**10**	**10**	**10**
Uruguay	...	...	...	...	...	...	...	...	...	...	...	...	...	...	...	...
Venezuela, B.R.	...	...	...	...	...	...	...	...	...	...	...	...	...	...	...	...
Northern Africa and Western Asia																
Algeria	95	97	93	24	...	25	...	...	...	...	...	...	...	...	...	...
Bahrain	83	81	83	12	12	14	9	97	99	96	83	81	85	10	10	12
Egypt	73	69	75	23	27	32	572	85	83	88	63	59	68	14	17	23
Iraq	...	...	...	...	...	...	...	...	...	...	...	...	...	...	...	...
Israel	...	...	...	...	...	...	...	...	...	...	...	...	...	...	...	...
Jordan	...	...	...	...	...	...	...	...	...	...	...	...	...	...	...	...
Kuwait	79	52	82	9	11	11	...	...	...	...	...	...	...	...	...	...
Lebanon	97	96	97	...	...	13^z	48	...	...	...	99	98	99	...	...	...
Libya	...	...	...	...	...	...	...	...	...	...	...	...	...	...	...	...
Morocco	100	100	100	26	26	26	135^z	...	...	...	...	...	...	...	...	...
Oman	...	...	...	...	...	...	...	...	...	...	...	...	...	...	...	...
Palestine	100	100	100	24	51	24	36	28	24	31	100	100	100	20	71	20
Qatar	...	...	...	11	11	...	9	100	100	100	...	...	...	10	10	...
Saudi Arabia	100	100	100	11	11	11	312	100	100	...	100	100	100	11^**	11^**	11^**
Sudan	...	...	...	25^z	...	...	51^z	...	...	...	66^y	65^y	67^y	37^z	...	13^z
Syrian Arab Republic	...	...	...	...	...	...	...	...	...	...	...	...	...	...	...	...
Tunisia	100	100	100	17	17	17	...	...	...	...	...	...	...	...	...	...
Turkey	...	...	...	20^z	...	...	525^z	...	...	...	...	...	...	20^z	...	...
United Arab Emirates	100	100	100	19	19	19	31	100	100	100	100	100	100	13	13	13
Yemen	...	...	...	...	...	...	...	...	...	...	...	...	...	...	...	...
The Pacific																
Australia	...	...	...	...	...	...	...	...	...	...	...	...	...	...	...	...
Cook Islands	89	93	89	17	17	19	0	89	89	88	94	89	97	14	16	15
Fiji	100^y	100^y	100^y	28^y	...	28^y	5^y	...	...	...	100^y	100^y	100^y	19^y	...	19^y
Kiribati	...	...	...	26	27	...	...	...	...	...	...	...	...	...	...	...
Marshall Islands	...	...	...	...	...	...	...	...	...	...	...	...	...	...	...	...

TABLE 13
Part 2 (Continued)

	PRIMARY EDUCATION						SECONDARY EDUCATION									
	Teacher training Trained classroom teachers (%)[2]			Pupil/ teacher ratio[3]	Pupil/ qualified teacher ratio[3]	Pupil/ trained teacher ratio[3]	Teaching staff Number of classroom teachers	Teacher qualification Qualified classroom teachers (%)[1]			Teacher training Trained classroom teachers (%)[2]			Pupil/ teacher ratio[3]	Pupil/ qualified teacher ratio[3]	Pupil/ trained teacher ratio[3]
	School year ending in 2014			School year ending in 2014	School year ending in 2014	School year ending in 2014	School year ending in 2014	School year ending in 2014			School year ending in 2014			School year ending in 2014	School year ending in 2014	School year ending in 2014
Country or territory	Total	Male	Female				Total (000)	Total	Male	Female	Total	Male	Female			
Micronesia F.S.	…	…	…	…	…	…	…	…	…	…	…	…	…	…	…	…
Nauru	…	…	…	39	79	…	0	89	100	81	…	…	…	23	26	…
New Zealand	…	…	…	14	…	…	35	…	…	…	…	…	…	14	…	…
Niue	…	…	…	13	…	…	0	…	…	…	…	…	…	…	…	…
Palau	…	…	…	…	…	…	…	…	…	…	…	…	…	…	…	…
Papua New Guinea	…	…	…	…	…	…	14ʸ	…	…	…	100ʸ	100ʸ	100ʸ	27ʸ	…	27ʸ
Samoa	…	…	…	…	…	…	…	…	…	…	…	…	…	…	…	…
Solomon Islands	65	66	63	20	30	31	2ʸ	…	…	…	70ʸ	69ʸ	72ʸ	26ʸ	…	37ʸ
Tokelau	…	…	…	…	…	…	…	…	…	…	…	…	…	…	…	…
Tonga	97	98	97	22	26	23	1	85	100	77	48	54	45	11	13	24
Tuvalu	…	…	…	…	…	…	…	…	…	…	…	…	…	…	…	…
Vanuatu	…	…	…	23ᶻ	33ᶻ	…	…	…	…	…	…	…	…	…	…	…
Southern Asia																
Afghanistan	…	…	…	46ᶻ	…	…	…	…	…	…	…	…	…	…	…	…
Bangladesh	…	…	…	…	…	…	378ᶻ	98ᶻ	99ᶻ	97ᶻ	58ᶻ	56ᶻ	67ᶻ	35ᶻ	36ᶻ	61ᶻ
Bhutan	…	…	…	27	…	…	5	…	…	…	…	…	…	14	…	…
India	…	…	…	32ᶻ	…	…	3,879ᶻ	…	…	…	…	…	…	31ᶻ	…	…
Iran, Islamic Republic of	100	100	100	26	26	26	331	95	95	95	100	100	100	18	18	18
Maldives	86	88	85	12	14	14	…	…	…	…	…	…	…	…	…	…
Nepal	**94**	**95**	**94**	**23**	**25**	**24**	**111****	78**	78**	77**	82**	82**	80**	29**	…	**35****
Pakistan	84	93	74	47	…	55	…	…	…	…	…	…	…	…	…	…
Sri Lanka	80**,ᶻ	…	…	24**	26ᶻ	30ᶻ	150ʸ	…	…	…	…	…	…	17ʸ	…	…
Sub-Saharan Africa																
Angola	…	…	…	…	…	…	…	…	…	…	…	…	…	…	…	…
Benin	68	68	64	46	46	68	90	59	58	65	9	9	9	10	17	114
Botswana	99ᶻ	98ᶻ	99ᶻ	23ᶻ	23ᶻ	23ᶻ	17ᶻ	97ᶻ	97ᶻ	96ᶻ	100ᶻ	100ᶻ	100ᶻ	11ᶻ	12ᶻ	11ᶻ
Burkina Faso	86ᶻ	83ᶻ	90ᶻ	44	54ᶻ	54ᶻ	31	47	46	50	47	46	50	27	58	58
Burundi	92	89	95	44	48	47	16	72	75	63	72	75	63	37	51	51
Cabo Verde	96	95	96	23	25	24	4	71	67	76	87	84	91	16	23	18
Cameroon	79ʸ	79ʸ	78ʸ	44	77	58ʸ	98	54	49	63	54	49	63	20	38	38
Central African Republic	58ʸ	51ʸ	86ʸ	80ʸ	…	138ʸ	2ʸ	…	…	…	53ᶻ	…	…	68ʸ	…	…
Chad	65ᶻ	…	…	62ᶻ	…	96ᶻ	15ᶻ	…	…	…	…	…	…	9ᶻ	…	…
Comoros	75ᶻ	73ᶻ	77ᶻ	28ᶻ	37ᶻ	37ᶻ	8ᶻ	…	…	…	…	…	…	9ᶻ	…	…
Congo	80ʸ	72ʸ	88ʸ	44ʸ	…	55ʸ	18ʸ	…	…	…	59ʸ	55ʸ	96ʸ	19ʸ	…	32ʸ
Côte d'Ivoire	85	84	87	43	48	50	64	100	100	100	100	100	100	22	22	22
D.R. Congo	95	94	95	35	35	37	301	100	100	100	24	24	22	15	15	62
Djibouti	**100**	**100**	**100**	33	33	33	3	**100**	**100**	**100**	**100**	**100**	**100**	23	23	23
Equatorial Guinea	…	…	…	26ʸ	…	…	…	…	…	…	…	…	…	…	…	…
Eritrea	80ᶻ	…	…	40ᶻ	40ᶻ	50ᶻ	7ᶻ	83ᶻ	82ᶻ	87ᶻ	83ᶻ	82ᶻ	87ᶻ	38ᶻ	46ᶻ	46ᶻ
Ethiopia	95	95	95	64	118	68	122**,ʸ	…	…	…	75**,ʸ	79**,ʸ	65**,ʸ	39**,ʸ	…	52**,ʸ
Gabon	…	…	…	…	…	…	…	…	…	…	…	…	…	…	…	…
Gambia	84	83	87	37	44	44	5	92	92	90	92	92	90	…	…	…
Ghana	**55**	**48**	**65**	**31**	**57**	**57**	147	**73**	**70**	**82**	**74**	**71**	**83**	17	23	23
Guinea	75	73	80	46	64	61	…	…	…	…	…	…	…	…	…	…
Guinea-Bissau	…	…	…	…	…	…	93**,ʸ	…	…	…	…	…	…	41**,ʸ	…	…
Kenya	…	…	…	57**,ʸ	…	…	5**,ᶻ	…	…	…	…	…	…	25**,ᶻ	…	…
Lesotho	76	67	79	33	43	43	15	…	…	…	55	54	57	15	…	27
Liberia	56	55	63	26	…	47	15	…	…	…	…	…	…	15	…	…
Madagascar	17	13	20	42	42	250	65	91	90	92	21	19	22	23	25	112
Malawi	91**,ᶻ	90**,ᶻ	91**,ᶻ	61	…	76**,ᶻ	13	…	…	…	66**,ᶻ	61**,ᶻ	78**,ᶻ	70	…	…
Mali	…	…	…	42	…	…	51	…	…	…	…	…	…	19	…	…
Mauritania	91	91	92	34	…	38	5	…	…	…	87	86	91	33	…	38
Mauritius	100	100	100	19	19	19	9	…	…	…	44ʸ	…	…	15	…	…
Mozambique	90	88	92	54	61	61	24**,ᶻ	76**,ᶻ	75**,ᶻ	80**,ᶻ	87**,ᶻ	86**,ᶻ	89**,ᶻ	31**,ᶻ	41**,ᶻ	36ᶻ
Namibia	…	…	…	…	…	…	…	…	…	…	…	…	…	…	…	…
Niger	50	47	54	36	36	71	21	100	100	100	16	13	26	25	25	160
Nigeria	…	…	…	…	…	…	…	…	…	…	…	…	…	…	…	…
Rwanda	95ᶻ	95ᶻ	95ᶻ	58	…	63ᶻ	26ᶻ	…	…	…	89ᶻ	93ᶻ	81ᶻ	23ᶻ	…	26ᶻ
Sao Tome and Principe	34	33	36	39	…	113	1	**26**	**27**	**23**	**36**	**26**	**57**	21	80	57
Senegal	70	72	66	32	32	45	…	92	92	92	…	…	…	12	14	…
Seychelles	…	…	…	13	16	…	1	…	…	…	64ᶻ	63ᶻ	75ᶻ	21ᶻ	36ᶻ	32ᶻ
Sierra Leone	57ᶻ	53ᶻ	69ᶻ	35ᶻ	67ᶻ	61ᶻ	20ᶻ	57ᶻ	56ᶻ	67ᶻ	…	…	…	…	…	…
Somalia	…	…	…	…	…	…	…	…	…	…	…	…	…	…	…	…
South Africa	…	…	…	32**	…	…	…	…	…	…	…	…	…	…	…	…
South Sudan	…	…	…	…	…	…	…	…	…	…	…	…	…	…	…	…
Swaziland	79ᶻ	77ᶻ	80ᶻ	28ᶻ	43ᶻ	35ᶻ	6ᶻ	76ᶻ	77ᶻ	74ᶻ	76ᶻ	78ᶻ	75ᶻ	16ᶻ	21ᶻ	21ᶻ
Togo	76ᶻ	77ᶻ	69ᶻ	41	62ᶻ	54ᶻ	…	…	…	…	…	…	…	21ᶻ	…	…
Uganda	…	…	…	46ᶻ	…	…	67ᶻ	…	…	…	…	…	…	26ʸ	…	…
United Republic of Tanzania	99ᶻ	99ᶻ	99ᶻ	43ᶻ	44ᶻ	44ᶻ	80ʸ	…	…	…	…	…	…	…	…	…
Zambia	93**,ʸ	89**,ʸ	96**,ʸ	48**,ᶻ	73	53**,ʸ	…	…	…	…	…	…	…	…	…	…
Zimbabwe	86ᶻ	84ᶻ	88ᶻ	36ᶻ	49ᶻ	42ᶻ	43ᶻ	49ᶻ	45ᶻ	54ᶻ	73ᶻ	71ᶻ	75ᶻ	22ᶻ	46ᶻ	31ᶻ

TABLE 13

Part 2 (Continued)

Country or territory	PRIMARY EDUCATION						SECONDARY EDUCATION									
	Teacher training			Pupil/ teacher ratio³	Pupil/ qualified teacher ratio³	Pupil/ trained teacher ratio³	Teaching staff	Teacher qualification			Teacher training			Pupil/ teacher ratio³	Pupil/ qualified teacher ratio³	Pupil/ trained teacher ratio³
	Trained classroom teachers (%)²						Number of classroom teachers	Qualified classroom teachers (%)¹			Trained classroom teachers (%)²					
	School year ending in 2014			School year ending in 2014	School year ending in 2014	School year ending in 2014	School year ending in 2014	School year ending in 2014			School year ending in 2014			School year ending in 2014	School year ending in 2014	School year ending in 2014
	Total	Male	Female	Weighted Average	Median	Median	Total (000)	Total	Male	Female	Total	Male	Female	Weighted Average	Median	Median
	Median						Sum	Median			Median					
World	...	...	...	24**	...	...	32,094**	...	...	...	...	...	...	18**	...	...
Countries in transition				18			2,424**,ᶻ	...	...	...	...	...	...	10**,ᶻ	...	...
Developed countries	...	...	...	14**	...	...	6,344**	...	...	...	...	...	...	13**	...	...
Developing countries	97	96	97	26**	...	28	23,407**	...	...	...	...	...	...	20**	...	...
Caucasus and Central Asia	100	100	100	16**	23	19	829**,ʸ	...	...	...	...	...	...	12**,ʸ	...	...
Eastern and South-eastern Asia	100	...	...	17	20	19	9,861	...	...	...	...	...	...	15	...	...
Eastern Asia	...	...	...	16	...	...	7,238	...	...	...	...	...	...	14	...	...
South-eastern Asia	100	99	99	19	21	22	2,623	...	...	...	...	...	...	18	...	...
Europe and Northern America	...	...	...	14	...	...	7,022	...	...	...	...	...	...	12	...	...
Latin America and the Caribbean	85	79	87	22**	...	21	3,887	...	...	...	81	...	...	16**	...	...
Caribbean	85	79	87	20**	16	18	200	81	...	...	78	62	76	15**	...	16
Latin America	...	...	...	22**	...	...	3,687	...	...	...	...	...	...	17**	...	...
Northern Africa and Western Asia	98	98	99	20**	...	18	2,600**	...	...	...	...	...	...	16**	...	...
Northern Africa	97	99	97	23	26	25	1,090**	...	...	...	...	...	...	17**	...	...
Western Asia	...	...	...	17**	...	...	1,509**	...	...	...	...	...	...	16**	...	...
Pacific	...	...	...	...	...	...	...	...	...	...	...	...	...	...	...	...
Southern Asia	86	...	...	34**	...	...	5,498**	...	...	...	...	...	...	29**	...	...
Sub-Saharan Africa	80	72	88	42**	44	53	2,195**	...	...	...	72	71	75	25**	...	...
Conflict-affected countries	95			30**	...	30	10,587**	...	...	...	...	...	...	23**	...	...
Countries with low income	84	83	88	43	45	54	1,496**	...	...	...	66	61	78	24**	...	...
Countries with middle income	94	97	94	24**	...	26	22,022**	...	...	...	...	...	...	19**	...	...
Lower middle	85	...	...	29**	...	33	9,847**	...	...	...	...	...	...	24**	...	...
Upper middle	97	96	97	18	...	23	12,175	...	...	...	...	...	...	15	...	...
Countries with high income	...	...	...	15**	...	...	8,576**	...	...	...	...	...	...	12**	...	...

Sources: UIS database; Global Education Monitoring Report team calculations for pupil/qualified and pupil/trained teacher ratios.

Note: The country groupings by level of income are as defined by the World Bank but include only countries listed in the table. They are based on the list of countries by income group as revised in July 2015.

1. Qualified teachers are defined according to national standards.

2. Trained teachers are defined as those who have received at least the minimum organized and recognized pre-service and in-service pedagogical training required to teach at a given level of education. Data on trained classroom teachers are not collected for countries whose education statistics are gathered through the OECD, Eurostat or the World Education Indicators questionnaires.

3. Based on headcounts of pupils and teachers.

Data in bold are for the school year ending in 2015.

(z) Data are for the school year ending in 2013.

(y) Data are for the school year ending in 2012.

(*) National estimate.

(**) For country level data: UIS partial estimate; for regional and other country grouping sums and weighted averages: partial imputation due to incomplete country coverage (between 33% and 60% of the population of the region or other country grouping).

(-) Magnitude nil or negligible

(.) The category is not applicable or does not exist.

(...) No data are available.

TABLE 14

Domestic financial commitment to education: public spending

Country or territory	Government expenditure on education as % of GDP — 2014	Expenditure on education as % of total government expenditure — 2014	Government expenditure on pre-primary education per pupil in constant 2013 PPP$ — 2014	Government expenditure on pre-primary education per pupil as % of GDP per capita — 2014	Government expenditure on primary education per pupil in constant 2013 PPP$ — 2014	Government expenditure on primary education per pupil as % of GDP per capita — 2014	Government expenditure on secondary education per student in constant 2013 PPP$ — 2014	Government expenditure on secondary education per student as % of GDP per capita — 2014	Government expenditure on tertiary education per student in constant 2013 PPP$ — 2014	Government expenditure on tertiary education per student as % of GDP per capita — 2014	Primary education expenditure on textbooks and teaching materials as % of current expenditure on primary education in public institutions — 2014	Primary education teaching staff compensation as % of current expenditure on primary education in public institutions — 2014
Caucasus and Central Asia												
Armenia	2.2	9.4	989[y]	13.2[y]	875[z]	11.3[z]	1.193	15.0	645	8.1	0.2[y]	...
Azerbaijan	2.5[z]	6.5[z]	2,594[x]	15.9[x]	...	...	...	...	2,938[x]	18.0[x]	...	...
Georgia	2.0[y]	6.7[y]	...	...	737[y]	10.6[y]	...	...	1,190[y]	17.2[y]	...	...
Kazakhstan	...	...	1,531	6.4	...	...	4.743	19.9	2,240	9.4	2.3	...
Kyrgyzstan	6.8[y]	17.8[z]	1,088[z]	33.7[z]	...	...	1.070[z]	33.2[z]	561[z]	17.4[z]	...	...
Tajikistan	4.0[y]	16.4[y]	560[x]	24.3[x]	...	...	...	...	486[z]	19.1[z]	...	...
Turkmenistan	3.0[y]	20.8[y]	...	...	...	...	...	...	...	...	...	...
Uzbekistan	...	...	...	...	...	...	...	...	...	...	...	...
Eastern and South-eastern Asia												
Brunei Darussalam	3.8	10.0	...	...	...	...	8.320	11.6	40.376	56.2	...	...
Cambodia	2.0[y]	9.9[z]	170[z]	5.6[z]	208[z]	6.8[z]	...	...	...	...	10.1[y]	47.5[y]
China	...	...	...	...	...	...	...	...	...	...	...	...
DPR Korea	...	...	...	...	...	...	...	...	...	...	...	...
Hong Kong, China	3.6	17.6	3,319	6.3	7,852	14.9	10,162	19.3	12,944	24.6	...	...
Indonesia	3.3	17.5	285	2.8	1,273	12.3	1,032	10.0	2,025	19.5	...	...
Japan	3.8	9.3	1,611[z]	4.5[z]	8,514[z]	23.9[z]	9,137[z]	25.7[z]	8,977[z]	25.2[z]	...	...
Lao PDR	4.2	15.4	...	...	...	...	...	...	...	...	...	...
Macao, China	2.1[z]	14.3[z]	...	...	...	...	26,708[z]	19.0[z]	26,619[z]	18.9[z]	...	...
Malaysia	6.1[z]	21.5[z]	779[z]	3.2[z]	4,055[z]	16.8[z]	5,391[z]	22.3[z]	13,231[z]	54.7[z]	...	76.0[z]
Mongolia	4.6	12.2[z]	2,272[x]	24.7[x]	1,439[x]	15.7[x]	...	...	261[x]	2.8[x]	2.3[x]	40.9[x]
Myanmar	...	...	...	...	...	...	...	...	...	...	...	...
Philippines	...	...	...	...	...	...	...	...	...	...	...	...
Republic of Korea	4.6[y]	...	2,261[z]	7.1[z]	7,963[z]	24.9[z]	7,609[z]	23.8[z]	4,140[z]	12.9[z]	...	56.7[z]
Singapore	2.9[z]	19.9[y]	-[y]	-[y]	...	...	...	...	17,213[z]	22.4[z]	...	...
Thailand	4.1[y]	18.9[y]	...	...	3,564[z]	23.1[z]	2,751[z]	17.8[z]	2,778[z]	18.0[z]	...	...
Timor-Leste	7.7	7.7	149	6.8	539	24.6	512	23.3	...	...	8.5	47.3
Viet Nam	6.3[y]	21.4[y]	844[y]	16.6[y]	1,207[y]	23.8[y]	...	...	2,093[y]	41.2[y]	12.0[x]	68.0[x]
Europe and Northern America												
Albania	3.5[y]	12.1[y]	...	...	2,882[z]	29.3[z]	576[z]	5.9[z]	1,276[z]	13.0[z]	...	...
Andorra	3.1	...	...	13.8	...	13.5	...	11.7	...	30.0	0.1	53.4
Austria	5.6[z]	11.0[z]	7,532[z]	16.7[z]	10,608[z]	23.5[z]	12,418[z]	27.5[z]	16,285[z]	36.1[z]	...	61.9[z]
Belarus	5.0	12.4	5,581[x]	32.5[x]	...	...	...	...	2,763	15.4	...	...
Belgium	6.4[x]	11.9[x]	6,838[y]	16.5[y]	9,598[y]	23.1[y]	16,031[y]	38.6[y]	13,862[y]	33.4[y]	...	65.8[y]
Bosnia and Herzegovina	...	...	...	...	...	...	...	...	...	...	...	...
Bulgaria	3.5[y]	10.7[y]	4,331[y]	27.5[y]	2,997[y]	19.0[y]	3,156[y]	20.0[y]	2,536[y]	16.1[y]	...	60.2[y]
Canada	5.3[x]	12.2[x]	...	...	...	...	7,545[x]	18.3[x]	...	...	...	64.5[x]
Croatia	4.2[y]	8.6[x]	5,409[x]	24.7[x]	...	...	...	...	5,609[x]	25.6[x]	...	...
Cyprus	6.6[x]	15.5[x]	5,057[x]	14.8[x]	11,142[x]	32.6[x]	13,101[x]	38.3[x]	12,313[x]	36.0[x]	...	81.1[x]
Czech Republic	4.3[y]	9.7[y]	4,566[y]	15.7[y]	4,592[y]	15.8[y]	7,393[y]	25.4[y]	6,952[y]	23.9[y]	...	43.9[y]
Denmark	8.5[y]	15.0[y]	17,235[y]	38.6[y]	9,751[y]	21.8[y]	13,143[x]	29.4[x]	22,905[x]	51.3[x]	...	64.2[x]
Estonia	4.7[y]	12.1[y]	2,784[y]	10.8[y]	5,807[y]	22.6[y]	6,821[y]	26.5[y]	5,152[y]	20.0[y]	...	...
Finland	7.2[z]	12.5[z]	8,642[z]	21.6[z]	8,349[z]	20.9[z]	4,337[z]	10.8[z]	14,180[z]	35.4[z]	...	54.0[z]
France	5.5[y]	9.7[y]	6,545[y]	17.4[y]	6,929[y]	18.5[y]	10,084[y]	26.9[y]	13,256[y]	35.3[y]	...	56.3[y]
Germany	4.9[y]	11.2[y]	6,405[y]	14.5[y]	7,634[y]	17.3[y]	10,217[y]	23.2[y]	...	...	...	...
Greece	...	...	...	...	...	...	...	...	...	...	...	...
Hungary	4.6[y]	9.3[y]	4,254[y]	18.5[y]	4,338[y]	18.9[y]	4,526[y]	19.7[y]	4,801[y]	20.9[y]	...	...
Iceland	7.0[y]	15.4[y]	7,069[y]	17.4[y]	10,425[x]	25.7[x]	8,215[x]	20.3[x]	9,392[x]	23.2[x]	...	...
Ireland	5.8[y]	13.8[y]	3,144[y]	6.8[y]	8,740[y]	18.9[y]	12,040[y]	26.0[y]	13,632[y]	29.4[y]	...	71.6[y]
Italy	4.1[x]	8.4[x]	5,665[y]	15.7[y]	7,452[y]	20.7[y]	8,232[y]	22.8[y]	8,998[x]	24.2[x]	...	62.0[y]
Latvia	4.9[z]	13.1[z]	4,598[z]	20.9[z]	5,738[z]	26.0[z]	5,623[z]	25.5[z]	4,491[z]	20.4[z]	...	72.9[z]
Liechtenstein	2.6[x]	...	...	9.2[x]	...	17.9[x]	...	13.4[x]	...	...	...	62.3[x]
Lithuania	4.8[y]	13.5[y]	5,139[y]	20.9[y]	4,801[y]	19.5[y]	4,559[y]	18.5[y]	5,800[y]	23.6[y]	...	65.8[y]
Luxembourg	...	...	23,613[x]	24.9[x]	23,795[x]	25.1[x]	17,159[x]	18.1[x]	...	...	...	79.6[x]
Malta	6.8[y]	15.3[y]	6,270[y]	21.9[y]	7,812[y]	27.3[y]	11,874[y]	41.6[y]	14,719[y]	51.5[y]	...	73.8[y]
Monaco	1.0	5.0	...	1.8[x]	...	4.0[x]	...	9.9[x]	.	.	...	...
Montenegro	...	...	...	...	...	...	...	...	...	...	...	...
Netherlands	5.6[y]	12.1[y]	5,798[y]	12.4[y]	8,242[**,z]	17.6[**,z]	11,403[**,z]	24.4[**,z]	15,676[y]	33.3[y]	...	...
Norway	7.4[y]	17.5[y]	13,111[y]	19.9[y]	12,697[y]	19.3[y]	16,769[y]	25.8[y]	27,058[y]	41.6[y]	...	79.8[y]
Poland	4.8[y]	11.3[y]	4,262[y]	18.1[y]	6,021[y]	25.5[y]	5,620[y]	23.8[y]	5,036[y]	21.3[y]	...	...
Portugal	5.1[x]	10.2[x]	4,180[x]	14.5[x]	5,994[x]	20.8[x]	9,399[x]	32.6[x]	7,758[x]	26.9[x]	...	80.0[x]
Republic of Moldova	7.5	18.8	2,118	43.1	2,143	43.6	1,901	38.7	1,794[y]	41.8[y]	0.4	34.1
Romania	2.9[y]	8.4[y]	1,962[y]	10.2[y]	2,145[y]	11.6[y]	2,573[z]	13.4[z]	4,433[z]	23.1[z]	...	76.4[y]
Russian Federation	4.2[y]	11.1[y]	...	...	...	...	...	...	3,902[y]	15.8[y]	...	...
San Marino	2.4[x]	10.6[x]	...	15.2[x]	...	17.0[x]	...	12.0[x]	...	9.2[x]	...	...
Serbia	4.4[y]	9.6[y]	299[x]	2.4[x]	6,471[x]	51.0[x]	1,658[x]	13.1[x]	5,061[y]	40.1[y]	...	...
Slovakia	4.1[z]	10.0[z]	4,125[z]	15.5[z]	5,493[z]	20.7[z]	5,240[z]	19.7[z]	6,673[z]	25.1[z]	...	52.4[z]
Slovenia	5.7[y]	12.6[y]	7,044[y]	24.3[y]	8,695[y]	30.0[y]	9,206[x]	30.8[x]	6,901[y]	23.8[y]	...	...
Spain	4.3[y]	9.6[y]	4,988[y]	15.3[y]	5,810[y]	17.9[y]	7,309[y]	22.5[y]	7,437[y]	22.9[y]	...	68.7[y]
Sweden	7.7[z]	15.2[z]	12,865[z]	28.9[z]	10,081[z]	22.6[z]	10,987[z]	24.6[z]	19,186[z]	43.0[z]	...	52.6[z]
Switzerland	5.1[y]	16.1[y]	5,460[y]	9.7[y]	13,866[y]	24.5[y]	14,750[y]	26.1[y]	22,304[y]	39.4[y]	...	66.0[y]
TFYR Macedonia	...	...	...	...	...	...	...	...	...	...	...	...
Ukraine	6.7[z]	13.9[z]	3,013[y]	35.1[y]	2,787[y]	32.3[y]	2,623[y]	30.4[y]	3,777[z]	43.9[z]	...	...
United Kingdom	5.7[z]	13.0[z]	5,858[z]	15.6[z]	8,779[z]	23.3[z]	8,416[z]	22.4[z]	13,677[z]	36.4[z]	...	68.8[z]

TABLE 14

(Continued)

Country or territory	Government expenditure on education as % of GDP	Expenditure on education as % of total government expenditure	Government expenditure on pre-primary education per pupil in constant 2013 PPP$	Government expenditure on pre-primary education per pupil as % of GDP per capita	Government expenditure on primary education per pupil in constant 2013 PPP$	Government expenditure on primary education per pupil as % of GDP per capita	Government expenditure on secondary education per student in constant 2013 PPP$	Government expenditure on secondary education per student as % of GDP per capita	Government expenditure on tertiary education per student in constant 2013 PPP$	Government expenditure on tertiary education per student as % of GDP per capita	Primary education expenditure on textbooks and teaching materials as % of current expenditure on primary education in public institutions	Primary education teaching staff compensation as % of current expenditure on primary education in public institutions
	2014	2014	2014	2014	2014	2014	2014	2014	2014	2014	2014	2014
United States	5.2ˣ	13.1ˣ	5,902ʸ	11.6ʸ	10,421ʸ	20.6ʸ	11,561ʸ	22.8ʸ	10,092ˣ	20.1ˣ	...	54.6ʸ
Latin America and the Caribbean												
Anguilla	...	...	...	...	...	...	...	...	...	...	...	...
Antigua and Barbuda	...	...	...	...	...	...	2,022ˣ	9.8ˣ	...	...	...	...
Argentina	5.3ᶻ	15.1ᶻ	...	11.9ᶻ	...	14.2ᶻ	...	21.4ᶻ	...	16.6ᶻ	...	71.3ᶻ
Aruba	6.0ˣ	21.8ˣ	...	...	...	...	...	...	...	...	...	...
Bahamas	...	...	...	...	...	...	...	...	...	...	...	...
Barbados	6.7	14.2	...	...	...	...	3,230	20.7	...	...	ᶻ	...
Belize	6.2ᶻ	22.9ᶻ	330ᶻ	4.1ᶻ	1,295ᶻ	15.9ᶻ	1,762ᶻ	21.7ᶻ	2,723ᶻ	33.5ᶻ	...	...
Bermuda	1.8	7.8	11,345	22.0	4,364	8.5	6,474	12.6	9,837	19.1	...	...
Bolivia, P.S.	7.3	16.9	608ᶻ	9.7ᶻ	1,070ᶻ	17.0ᶻ	1,226ᶻ	19.5ᶻ	...	...	...	90.3
Brazil	5.9ʸ	15.6ʸ	3,927ʸ	25.4ʸ	3,311ʸ	21.4ʸ	3,566ʸ	23.1ʸ	4,179ʸ	27.1ʸ	...	72.0ˣ
British Virgin Islands	...	...	...	...	...	...	...	...	...	...	...	...
Cayman Islands	...	...	...	...	...	...	...	...	...	...	...	...
Chile	4.6ᶻ	19.1ᶻ	4,658ᶻ	21.2ᶻ	3,490ᶻ	15.9ᶻ	3,320ᶻ	15.1ᶻ	3,839ᶻ	17.5ᶻ	...	...
Colombia	4.7	15.9	1,138ˣ	9.6ˣ	2,303	17.5	2,282	17.3	2,853	21.7	4.2	83.7
Costa Rica	7.0	23.1	2,595	17.7	3,744	25.5	3,564	24.2	4,906	33.4	...	72.9
Cuba	...	...	...	...	...	...	...	...	...	...	...	...
Curaçao	4.9ᶻ	...	...	...	...	10.0ᶻ	...	23.0ᶻ	...	18.2ᶻ	6.0ᶻ	81.0ᶻ
Dominica	...	...	262ʸ	2.5ʸ	1,409ʸ	13.6ʸ	...	...	...	...	...	100.0ʸ
Dominican Republic	...	...	1,266	9.7	2,041	15.6	1,886	14.4	...	...	1.9	56.1
Ecuador	4.2ʸ	10.3ʸ	1,702	15.2	1,604	14.3	703	6.3	3,116ʸ	29.2ʸ	10.3	81.0
El Salvador	3.4ˣ	15.9ˣ	549ᶻ	7.0ˣ	...	...	...	...	849ˣ	10.8ˣ	...	...
Grenada	...	...	...	...	...	...	...	...	...	...	...	...
Guatemala	2.8ᶻ	20.6ᶻ	666ᶻ	9.3ᶻ	677ᶻ	9.4ᶻ	396ᶻ	5.5ᶻ	1,343ᶻ	18.7ᶻ	3.9	...
Guyana	3.2ʸ	10.3ʸ	659ʸ	10.1ʸ	514ʸ	7.8ʸ	615ʸ	9.4ʸ	908ʸ	13.8ʸ	...	84.6ʸ
Haiti	...	...	...	...	...	...	...	...	...	...	...	...
Honduras	5.9ᶻ	19.2ᶻ	672ᶻ	14.1ᶻ	910ᶻ	19.1ᶻ	864ᶻ	18.1ᶻ	2,042	42.2	ᶻ	81.2ᶻ
Jamaica	6.0	21.8	343	4.0	1,920	22.4	1,972	23.0	3,432ᶻ	40.1ᶻ	1.8	78.1
Mexico	5.2ˣ	19.0ˣ	2,179ˣ	13.8ˣ	2,322ˣ	14.7ˣ	2,530ˣ	16.1ˣ	5,938ˣ	37.7ˣ	...	86.4ˣ
Montserrat	...	...	...	...	...	...	...	...	...	...	...	...
Nicaragua	...	...	...	...	...	...	...	...	...	...	...	...
Panama	3.3ˣ	13.0ˣ	684ˣ	4.0ˣ	1,104ˣ	6.5ˣ	1,623ˣ	9.5ˣ	3,665ʸ	19.8ʸ	...	...
Paraguay	5.0ʸ	19.6ʸ	968ʸ	12.8ʸ	1,092ʸ	14.4ʸ	1,251ʸ	16.6ʸ	...	...	2.8ʸ	64.5ʸ
Peru	3.7	16.2	1,433	12.1	1,475	12.5	1,542	13.0	...	...	0.7	52.5
Saint Kitts and Nevis	...	...	...	...	...	...	...	...	...	...	1.6ᶻ	67.0ᶻ
Saint Lucia	4.8	15.3	349ʸ	3.3ʸ	1,897	18.1	2,743	26.2	1,559**·ˣ	14.5**·ˣ	...	72.9
Saint Martin	...	...	...	...	...	...	...	...	...	...	...	...
St. Vincent and the Grenadines	...	...	450	4.3	1,934	18.3	2,323	22.0	...	...	1.1ʸ	92.2ʸ
Sint Maarten	...	...	...	...	...	...	...	...	...	...	...	...
Suriname	...	...	...	...	...	...	...	...	...	...	...	...
Trinidad and Tobago	...	...	...	...	...	...	...	...	...	...	...	...
Turks and Caicos Islands	3.3*,1	...	...	...	...	...	...	...	...	...	...	...
Uruguay	4.4ˣ	14.9ˣ	...	...	...	...	...	...	...	...	...	...
Venezuela, B.R.	...	...	...	...	...	...	...	...	...	...	...	...
Northern Africa and Western Asia												
Algeria	...	...	...	...	...	...	...	...	...	...	...	94.5ᶻ
Bahrain	2.6ʸ	8.9ʸ	-ˣ	-ˣ	...	...	...	...	...	...	2.0	92.0
Egypt	...	...	...	...	...	...	...	...	...	...	...	...
Iraq	...	...	...	...	...	...	...	...	...	...	...	...
Israel	5.9ᶻ	14.3ᶻ	3,901ᶻ	11.9ᶻ	7,239ᶻ	22.1ᶻ	5,282ᶻ	16.2ᶻ	6,535ᶻ	20.0ᶻ	...	...
Jordan	...	...	193ˣ	1.7ˣ	1,428ˣ	12.2ˣ	1,757ˣ	15.1ˣ	...	...	...	93.7ˣ
Kuwait	...	...	16,026ˣ	21.4ˣ	13,370ˣ	17.8ˣ	16,690**·ˣ	22.2**·ˣ	...	...	5.0ˣ	73.9ˣ
Lebanon	2.6ᶻ	8.6ᶻ	...	...	...	...	877ᶻ	5.1ᶻ	2,670ᶻ	15.6ᶻ	...	...
Libya	...	...	...	...	...	...	...	...	...	...	...	...
Morocco	...	...	-ᶻ	-ᶻ	1,411ᶻ	19.3ᶻ	2,558ʸ	36.1ʸ	...	...	...	...
Oman	5.0ᶻ	11.1ᶻ	-ˣ	-ˣ	6,770ˣ	15.4ˣ	8,617ᶻ	21.5ᶻ	...	...	1.4ˣ	61.7ˣ
Palestine	...	...	...	...	...	...	...	...	...	...	...	...
Qatar	3.5	11.1	...	...	...	...	...	...	...	...	...	...
Saudi Arabia	...	...	...	...	...	...	...	...	...	...	...	...
Sudan	...	...	...	...	...	...	...	...	...	...	...	...
Syrian Arab Republic	...	...	-ʸ	-ʸ	...	18.3ʸ	...	15.4ʸ	...	...	...	...
Tunisia	6.2ʸ	21.6ʸ	...	...	...	...	...	...	6,053	53.7	...	...
Turkey	...	...	...	...	...	...	...	...	...	...	...	89.3ˣ
United Arab Emirates	...	...	6,868ʸ	11.1ʸ	6,456ʸ	10.4ʸ	11,024ʸ	17.8ʸ	...	...	0.6ˣ	62.2ˣ
Yemen	...	...	1,483ˣ	39.7ˣ	723ˣ	19.4ˣ	471ˣ	12.6ˣ	...	...	3.4ᶻ	93.0ˣ
The Pacific												
Australia	5.3ᶻ	14.0ᶻ	4,318ᶻ	10.0ᶻ	8,142ᶻ	18.8ᶻ	7,321ᶻ	16.9ᶻ	9,851ᶻ	22.7ᶻ	...	63.5ᶻ
Cook Islands	3.9	...	...	9.7ᶻ	...	9.9ᶻ	...	10.2ᶻ	.ˣ	5.8	...	...
Fiji	3.9ᶻ	14.0ᶻ	...	...	1,024ᶻ	12.5ᶻ	442ˣ	5.7ˣ	...	...	...	...
Kiribati	...	...	...	...	...	...	...	...	...	...	...	...
Marshall Islands	...	...	...	...	...	...	...	...	...	...	...	...

TABLE 14

(Continued)

Country or territory	Government expenditure on education as % of GDP 2014	Expenditure on education as % of total government expenditure 2014	Government expenditure on pre-primary education per pupil in constant 2013 PPP$ 2014	Government expenditure on pre-primary education per pupil as % of GDP per capita 2014	Government expenditure on primary education per pupil in constant 2013 PPP$ 2014	Government expenditure on primary education per pupil as % of GDP per capita 2014	Government expenditure on secondary education per student in constant 2013 PPP$ 2014	Government expenditure on secondary education per student as % of GDP per capita 2014	Government expenditure on tertiary education per student in constant 2013 PPP$ 2014	Government expenditure on tertiary education per student as % of GDP per capita 2014	Primary education expenditure on textbooks and teaching materials as % of current expenditure on primary education in public institutions 2014	Primary education teaching staff compensation as % of current expenditure on primary education in public institutions 2014
Micronesia F.S.	…	…	…	…	…	…	…	…	…	…	…	…
Nauru	…	…	…	…	…	…	…	…	…	…	…	…
New Zealand	6.4	17.8	5,700	17.0	6,120	18.3	7,467	22.3	9,167	27.4	…	…
Niue	…	…	…	…	…	…	…	…	…	…	…	…
Palau	…	…	…	…	…	…	…	…	…	…	…	…
Papua New Guinea	…	…	…	…	…	…	…	…	…	…	…	…
Samoa	…	…	…	…	…	…	…	…	…	…	…	…
Solomon Islands	…	…	…	…	…	…	…	…	…	…	…	…
Tokelau	…	…	…	…	…	…	…	…	…	…	…	…
Tonga	…	…	…	…	…	…	…	…	…	…	…	…
Tuvalu	…	…	…	…	…	…	…	…	…	…	…	…
Vanuatu	4.9	21.8	…	…	…	…	…	…	…	…	…	…
Southern Asia												
Afghanistan	4.8**	18.4**	…	…	…	…	…	…	…	…	…	…
Bangladesh	2.0**,z	13.8**,z	-x	-x	…	…	304x	12.2x	437x	17.5x	…	…
Bhutan	5.9	17.8	-x	-x	996	13.7	2,631	36.1	3,930	53.9	…	…
India	3.8y	14.1y	453y	9.5y	443y	9.3y	740y	15.5y	2,563y	53.7y	…	…
Iran, Islamic Republic of	3.0	19.7	137	0.8	1,337	8.2	2,534	15.5	2,247	13.8	…	…
Maldives	5.2y	15.3y	…	…	…	…	…	…	…	…	…	…
Nepal	4.7	22.1	76	3.4	334	15.1	324**	14.6**	723	32.6	…	…
Pakistan	2.5	11.3	…	…	368	8.1	602	13.2	2,353	51.6	…	…
Sri Lanka	1.6z	9.8z	-y	-y	459z	4.3z	665z	6.3z	2,504z	23.6z	…	85.5y
Sub-Saharan Africa												
Angola	…	…	…	…	…	…	…	…	…	…	…	…
Benin	4.4	22.2	306	15.3	213	10.7	272	13.6	1,316z	68.2z	1.2	70.8
Botswana	…	…	…	…	…	…	…	…	…	…	…	…
Burkina Faso	4.5	19.4	6	0.4	319	20.0	254	15.9	3,576z	226.3z	6.7	44.7
Burundi	5.4z	17.2z	2z	0.3z	96z	12.8z	232z	31.0z	2,293z	306.0z	0.6x	87.4x
Cabo Verde	5.0z	15.0z	51z	0.8z	917z	14.5z	1,046z	16.5z	1,959z	30.9z	0.4z	95.5x
Cameroon	3.0z	13.8z	159y	5.8y	166y	6.0y	543y	19.7y	1,076y	39.8x	2.0x	81.9z
Central African Republic	1.2x	7.8x	…	…	…	…	…	…	1,056x	114.3x	…	…
Chad	2.9x	12.5x	77x	4.0x	113x	5.9x	409x	21.3x	3,573x	185.7x	…	71.0x
Comoros	5.1y	18.5y	…	…	245x	17.6x	…	…	702y	50.1y	…	…
Congo	…	…	…	…	…	…	…	…	4,971z	83.7z	…	…
Côte d'Ivoire	4.7	20.7	701	21.8	413	12.9	880	27.4	4,000	124.5	4.7	68.7
Democratic Rep. of the Congo	2.2z	16.8z	41z	5.9z	55z	8.0z	41z	5.9z	562z	80.7z	…	…
Djibouti	…	…	…	…	…	…	…	…	…	…	1.1	…
Equatorial Guinea	…	…	…	…	…	…	…	…	…	…	…	…
Eritrea	…	…	…	…	…	…	…	…	…	…	…	…
Ethiopia	4.5z	27.0z	15y	1.2y	100y	8.4y	317y	26.7y	4,008y	337.9y	1.3z	…
Gabon	…	…	…	…	…	…	…	…	…	…	…	…
Gambia	2.8z	10.3z	-z	-z	172z	10.5z	…	…	1,765y	108.8y	…	89.2z
Ghana	6.0z	21.7z	257z	6.5z	382z	9.6z	1,286z	32.5z	3,496z	88.3z	…	80.0z
Guinea	3.5z	14.1z	-x	-x	126z	10.2z	124y	10.0y	1,649z	133.9z	…	59.4z
Guinea-Bissau	2.4z	16.2z	…	…	…	…	…	…	…	…	1.4y	89.1z
Kenya	…	…	…	…	…	…	…	…	…	…	…	…
Lesotho	…	…	…	…	…	…	…	…	603**,y	80.9**,y	…	…
Liberia	2.8y	8.1y	…	…	…	…	…	…	…	…	…	…
Madagascar	2.1z	14.0z	…	…	93y	6.6y	119y	8.4y	1,457y	102.6y	…	71.0z
Malawi	6.9	16.3	-	-	105	13.4	232	29.8	13,164x	1,725.5x	1.0	…
Mali	4.3	18.2	30	1.9	232	14.7	416	26.4	2,163y	141.1y	4.0	75.6
Mauritania	3.3z	11.4z	-z	-z	358z	9.6z	642z	17.3z	2,835z	76.3z	…	…
Mauritius	5.0	20.9	440z	2.5z	2,476	13.5	5,334	29.1	2,009	11.0	2.1	…
Mozambique	6.5z	19.0z	…	…	163z	15.3z	739z	69.2z	1,957z	183.3z	19.1z	65.6z
Namibia	…	…	…	…	…	…	…	…	…	…	…	…
Niger	6.8	21.7	380	41.1	274	29.7	677	73.2	5,535y	617.7y	7.5	81.6z
Nigeria	…	…	…	…	…	…	…	…	…	…	…	…
Rwanda	5.0z	16.6z	9z	0.6z	103z	6.8z	589z	39.0z	1,493z	98.9z	…	…
Sao Tome and Principe	3.9	12.3	386	12.3	366	11.7	264	8.4	1,292	41.3	…	…
Senegal	…	…	…	…	…	…	…	…	…	…	…	…
Seychelles	3.6x	10.4x	…	…	2,025x	8.7x	1,572**,x	6.7**,x	126,427x	542.5x	1.5x	68.7x
Sierra Leone	2.8	15.1	-	-	106z	5.6z	150z	7.9z	…	…	…	87.8x
Somalia	…	…	…	…	…	…	…	…	…	…	…	…
South Africa	6.1	19.1	761	6.0	2,242	17.7	2,532	20.0	4,802	37.9	1.8	76.9
South Sudan	0.8x	3.9x	…	0.4x	…	3.6x	…	…	…	…	…	…
Swaziland	8.6x	22.4x	62x	0.8x	1,617x	20.8x	3,321x	42.7x	…	…	…	…
Togo	4.8	19.4	72	5.1	202	14.4	203x	15.6x	1,581	112.2	0.3	85.5
Uganda	2.2z	11.8z	-z	-z	104y	6.2y	318y	19.0y	1,280y	76.3y	3.0z	…
United Republic of Tanzania	3.5	17.3	…	…	…	…	…	…	…	…	…	…
Zambia	…	…	…	…	…	…	…	…	…	…	…	…
Zimbabwe	…	…	…	…	…	…	…	…	…	…	…	…

TABLE 14

(Continued)

Country or territory	Government expenditure on education as % of GDP	Expenditure on education as % of total government expenditure	Government expenditure on pre-primary education per pupil in constant 2013 PPP$	Government expenditure on pre-primary education per pupil as % of GDP per capita	Government expenditure on primary education per pupil in constant 2013 PPP$	Government expenditure on primary education per pupil as % of GDP per capita	Government expenditure on secondary education per student in constant 2013 PPP$	Government expenditure on secondary education per student as % of GDP per capita	Government expenditure on tertiary education per student in constant 2013 PPP$	Government expenditure on tertiary education per student as % of GDP per capita	Primary education expenditure on textbooks and teaching materials as % of current expenditure on primary education in public institutions	Primary education teaching st compensat as % of current expenditu on primar education in public institution
	2014	2014	2014	2014	2014	2014	2014	2014	2014	2014	2014	2014
World[2]	4.6	14.2	1,038	10.1	1,979	16.8	2,546	19.7	3,721	29.7	...	...
Countries in transition	4.1	12.3	1,531	24.3	...	...	...	...	2,017	17.3	...	...
Developed countries	5.1	12.1	5,665	15.7	7,723	20.6	8,232	22.8	9,167	25.1	...	64.4
Developing countries	4.4	16.2	...	...	...	14.2	...	...	...	...	...	
Caucasus and Central Asia	2.8	12.9	1,088	15.9	...	...	...	...	918	17.3	...	
Eastern and South-eastern Asia	3.9	15.4	812	5.9	2,502	19.9	7,609	19.3	8,977	22.4	...	
Eastern Asia	3.8	13.2	2,266	6.7	7,908	19.8	9,650	21.5	8,977	18.9	...	
South-eastern Asia	4.1	17.5	227	4.4	1,240	19.9	...	...	2,778	22.4	...	
Europe and Northern America	5.0	12.1	5,460	16.5	7,543	20.8	8,232	23.2	7,195	25.4	...	64.5
Latin America and the Caribbean	4.9	16.1	...	9.9	...	15.2	1,972	17.3	...	...	...	
Caribbean	...	...	...	...	...	...	...	...	...	...	...	
Latin America	4.7	16.2	968	12.0	1,385	14.7	1,582	16.6	2,985	21.7	...	81.0
Northern Africa and Western Asia	...	...	...	...	...	...	...	...	...	...	...	
Northern Africa	...	...	...	...	...	...	...	...	...	...	...	
Western Asia	...	...	838	6.4	...	17.8	5,282	15.8	...	...	...	89.3
Pacific	...	...	...	...	...	...	...	...	...	...	...	
Southern Asia	3.8	15.3	38	0.4	451	8.7	665	14.6	2,353	32.6	...	
Sub-Saharan Africa	4.3	16.6	46	1.2	208	10.7	412	19.8	1,959	102.6	...	
Conflict-affected countries	3.8	16.6	...	1.6	351	10.8	537	15.5	2.353	53.7	...	
Countries with low income	3.9	16.7	15	0.9	144	10.5	272	19.0	1.615	113.3	...	
Countries with middle income	4.5	15.7	663	9.4	...	...	...	...	...	...	...	
Lower middle	4.1	15.6	453	9.3	...	12.9	...	17.3	...	...	...	
Upper middle	4.6	15.7	...	...	...	...	...	...	...	...	...	
Countries with high income	4.9	11.9	5,409	15.3	7,812	19.1	8,368	22.2	9,614	24.0	...	

Source: UIS database.

Note: The country groupings by level of income are as defined by the World Bank but include countries listed in the table only. They are based on the list of countries by income group as revised in July 2015.

1. World Bank WDI database, December 2015 release.

2. All regional values shown are medians.

Data in bold are for the school year ending in 2015.

(z) Data are for the school year ending in 2013.

(y) Data are for the school year ending in 2012.

(x) Data are for the school year ending in 2011.

(*) National estimate.

(**) UIS partial estimate.

(-) Magnitude nil or negligible

(...) No data available.

Somali students walk to attend classes at Shabelle Boarding School in Mogadishu.

CREDIT: Kate Holt/GEM Report

Aid tables

INTRODUCTION[1]

The data on aid used in this Report are derived from the Organisation for Economic Co-operation and Development (OECD) International Development Statistics (IDS) databases, which record information provided annually by all member countries of the OECD Development Assistance Committee (DAC), as well as a growing number of donors that are not members of the committee. In this Report, total figures for net official development assistance (ODA) comes from the DAC database while those for gross ODA, sector-allocable aid and aid to education come from the Creditor Reporter System (CRS). Both are available at www.oecd.org/dac/stats/idsonline.

ODA is public funds provided to developing countries to promote their economic and social development. It is concessional; that is, it takes the form of either a grant or a loan carrying a lower rate of interest than is available on the market and, usually, a longer repayment period.

A more extensive version of the aid tables including ODA per recipient is available on the Report's website, www.unesco.org/gemreport.

AID RECIPIENTS AND DONORS

Developing countries are those in Part 1 of the DAC List of Aid Recipients: all low and middle income countries except twelve Central and Eastern European countries and a few more advanced developing countries.

Bilateral donors are countries that provide development assistance directly to recipient countries. Most are members of the DAC, a forum of major bilateral donors established to promote aid and its effectiveness. Bilateral donors also contribute substantially to the financing of multilateral donors through contributions recorded as multilateral ODA.

Multilateral donors are international institutions with government membership that conduct all or a significant part of their activities in favour of developing countries. They include multilateral development banks (e.g. the World Bank and Inter-American Development Bank), United Nations agencies and regional groupings (e.g. the European Commission). The development banks also make non-concessional loans to several middle and higher income countries; these are not counted as part of ODA.

TYPES OF AID

Total ODA: bilateral and multilateral aid for all sectors, as well as aid that is not allocable by sector, such as general budget support and debt relief. In Table 1, total ODA from bilateral donors is bilateral aid only, while aid as a percentage of gross national income (GNI) is bilateral and multilateral ODA.

Sector-allocable ODA: aid allocated to a specific sector, such as education or health. It does not include aid for general development purposes (e.g. general budget support), balance-of-payments support, debt relief or emergency assistance.

Debt relief: includes debt forgiveness, i.e. the extinction of a loan by agreement between the creditor (donor) and debtor (aid recipient), and other action on debt, including debt swaps, buy-backs and refinancing. In the DAC database, debt forgiveness is reported as a grant and therefore counts as ODA.

Country programmable aid: defined by subtracting from total gross ODA aid that:

- is unpredictable by nature (humanitarian aid and debt relief);

- entails no cross-border flows (administrative costs, imputed student costs, and costs related to promotion of development awareness, research in donor countries);

- is not part of cooperation agreements between governments (food aid and aid from local governments);

- is not country programmable by donor (core funding of non-governmental organization).

Country programmable aid is not included in the aid tables, but is used in a few places in the Report.

EDUCATION AID

Direct aid to education: aid to education reported in the CRS database as direct allocations to the education sector. It is the total of direct aid, as defined by the DAC, to:

- basic education, defined by the DAC as covering primary education, basic life skills for youth and adults, and early childhood education;

- secondary education, both general secondary education and vocational training;

- post-secondary education, including advanced technical and managerial training;

- education, 'level unspecified', which refers to any activity that cannot be attributed solely to the development of a particular level of education, such as education research and teacher training. General education programme support is often reported within this subcategory.

Total aid to education: direct aid to education plus 20% of general budget support (aid provided to governments without being earmarked for specific projects or sectors) to represent the estimated 15% to 25% of budget support that typically benefits the education sector.

Total aid to basic education: direct aid to basic education, plus 10% of general budget support, plus 50% of education, 'level unspecified'.

Commitments and disbursements: A commitment is a firm obligation by a donor, expressed in writing and backed by necessary funds to provide specified assistance to a country or a multilateral organization. Disbursements record the actual international transfer of financial resources or of goods and services. Starting with the 2011 Report, disbursement figures are used in the text and tables, while in previous years commitments were reported. As the aid committed in a given year can be disbursed later, sometimes over several years, the annual aid figures based on commitments cannot be directly compared to disbursements. Reliable figures on aid disbursements have only been available since 2002, which consequently is used as the base year.

Current and constant prices: Aid figures in the DAC databases are expressed in US dollars. When comparing aid figures between years, adjustment is required to compensate for inflation and changes in exchange rates. Such adjustments result in aid being expressed in constant dollars, i.e. in dollars fixed at the value they held in a given reference year, including their external value in terms of other currencies. This Report presents most aid data in constant 2014 US dollars.

Source: OECD-DAC, 2016.

ENDNOTES

1. A full set of statistics and indicators related to the introduction is posted in Excel format on the *Global Education Monitoring Report* website at www.unesco.org/gemreport.

TABLE 1

Bilateral and multilateral ODA

	TOTAL ODA				ODA AS % OF GNI				SECTOR-ALLOCABLE ODA			DEBT RELIEF AND OTHER ACTIONS RELATING TO DEBT		
	CONSTANT 2014 US$ MILLIONS								CONSTANT 2014 US$ MILLIONS			CONSTANT 2014 US$ MILLIONS		
	2002–2003 annual average	2013	2014	2015*	2002–2003 annual average	2013	2014	2015*	2002–2003 annual average	2013	2014	2002–2003 annual average	2013	2014
Australia	1,887	3,889	3,498	3,216	0.25	0.33	0.31	0.27	1,294	2,999	2,916	12	10	7
Austria	481	552	637	789	0.23	0.27	0.28	0.32	224	344	327	29	46	109
Belgium	1,662	1,316	1,321	1,338	0.52	0.45	0.46	0.42	739	865	913	740	18	10
Canada	2,498	3,334	3,278	3,454	0.26	0.27	0.24	0.28	1,066	2,191	2,091	6	…	…
Czech Republic**	94	55	63	83	0.09	0.11	0.11	0.12	…	35	37	0	…	…
Denmark	1,687	2,150	2,131	2,217	0.90	0.85	0.86	0.85	276	1,311	1,264	0	53	0
Finland	438	835	938	826	0.35	0.54	0.59	0.56	299	526	621	0	…	…
France	6,581	6,836	6,514	6,327	0.39	0.41	0.37	0.37	3,037	5,759	6,272	3,482	1,172	108
Germany	5,438	9,616	11,589	16,324	0.28	0.38	0.42	0.52	4,108	9,538	11,367	1,877	623	1,110
Greece	246	42	46	139	0.21	0.10	0.11	0.14	213	14	16	…	…	…
Iceland**	11	32	31	33	0.16	0.25	0.22	0.24	…	27	24	…	…	…
Ireland	411	546	519	497	0.40	0.46	0.38	0.36	291	340	327	…	0	0
Italy	1,627	874	1,371	1,958	0.18	0.17	0.19	0.21	212	383	432	959	39	28
Japan	6,630	8,071	6,012	7,024	0.22	0.23	0.19	0.22	3,348	10,454	10,341	622	3,768	…
Kuwait**	91	186	229	…	…	…	…	…	…	490	525	…	…	…
Luxembourg	241	301	300	288	0.82	1.00	1.06	0.93	…	200	207	…	…	…
Netherlands	3,989	3,673	4,027	5,069	0.80	0.67	0.64	0.76	1,755	2,933	2,588	473	62	63
New Zealand	230	362	409	419	0.22	0.26	0.27	0.27	150	258	298	…	…	…
Norway	2,558	4,045	3,889	4,273	0.90	1.07	1.00	1.05	1,282	3,043	2,765	14	22	18
Poland**	23	128	82	117	0.02	0.10	0.09	0.10	…	69	96	…	…	…
Portugal	289	305	246	168	0.25	0.23	0.19	0.16	252	185	206	…	9	12
Republic of Korea	323	1,369	1,396	1,534	0.06	0.13	0.13	0.14	…	1,299	1,286	…	…	…
Slovak Republic**	13	16	16	21	0.03	0.09	0.09	0.10	…	12	9	…	…	…
Slovenia**	…	21	20	28	…	0.13	0.12	0.15	…	13	13	…	…	…
Spain	1,681	941	464	681	0.25	0.17	0.13	0.13	983	643	432	173	243	…
Sweden	2,335	3,777	4,343	5,799	0.82	1.01	1.09	1.40	1,104	2,268	2,327	118	…	…
Switzerland	1,450	2,520	2,779	2,903	0.34	0.46	0.50	0.52	769	1,328	1,627	29	…	…
United Arab Emirates**	1,037	5,401	4,950	4,852	…	1.34	1.26	1.09	…	2,308	2,353	…	…	…
United Kingdom	5,113	11,289	11,233	12,534	0.33	0.70	0.70	0.71	2,101	9,098	8,822	511	89	5
United States	15,948	26,804	27,509	26,473	0.14	0.18	0.19	0.17	8,904	17,843	18,137	1,887	338	47
Estonia	1	12	15	19	…	0.13	0.14	0.15	…	7	9	…	…	…
Hungary	10	34	30	47	…	0.10	0.11	0.13	…	…	17	…	…	…
Kazakhstan	…	5	27	…	…	-	0.02	…	…	2	19	…	…	…
Lithuania	1	18	6	11	0.02	0.11	0.10	0.11	…	…	2	…	…	…
Romania	…	20	70	…	…	0.07	0.11	…	…	…	69	…	…	…
TOTAL bilaterals****	**68,632**	**108,593**	**117,955**	**115,364**	**0.25**	**0.31**	**0.31**	**0.32**	**32,406**	**76,783**	**78,753**	**10,933**	**6,492**	**1,518**
African Development Bank	131	144	137	…	…	…	…	…	9	13	131	134	124	
African Development Fund	787	2,188	1,904	…	…	…	…	…	715	1,851	1,791	157	1	0
Arab Fund for Economic and Social Development	…	388	358	…	…	…	…	…	…	894	878	…	…	…
Asian Development Bank Special Funds	1,234	1,008	1,477	…	…	…	…	…	…	2,696	2,773	…	5	6
Asian Development Fund**	…	…	…	…	…	…	…	…	…	…	…	…	…	…
BADEA	…	82	56	…	…	…	…	…	…	133	126	…	…	…
Climate Investment Funds [CIF]	…	152	350	…	…	…	…	…	…	152	349	…	…	…
EU Institutions	8,780	15,757	16,389	…	…	…	…	…	1,531	13,254	13,854	4	2	1
World Bank (IDA)	8,324	8,202	10,262	…	…	…	…	…	10,073	11,956	13,337	529	101	10
Inter-American Development Bank Special Fund	320	1,937	1,720	…	…	…	…	…	…	1,309	1,222	…	…	…
International Monetary Fund (Concessional Trust Funds)	936	623	180	…	…	…	…	…	…	…	…	490	…	…
OPEC Fund for International Development	102	214	249	…	…	…	…	…	…	402	447	…	…	11
UNDP	405	467	459	…	…	…	…	…	…	417	391	…	…	…
UNICEF	847	1,234	1,295	…	…	…	…	…	510	764	834	…	…	…
UN Peacebuilding Fund	…	43	64	…	…	…	…	…	…	47	64	…	…	…
UN Relief and Works Agency for Palestine Refugees	583	541	680	…	…	…	…	…	…	441	499	…	…	…
World Food Programme	477	365	309	…	…	…	…	…	…	71	53	…	…	…
TOTAL multilaterals****	**26,165**	**42,395**	**43,151**	**…**	**…**	**…**	**…**	**…**	**13,696**	**42,167**	**42,684**	**1,311**	**245**	**154**
TOTAL	**94,797**	**150,988**	**161,105**	**…**	**…**	**…**	**…**	**…**	**46,102**	**118,950**	**121,437**	**12,245**	**6,738**	**1,671**

Source: OECD-DAC, DAC and CRS databases (2015).

*Preliminary data.

**Kuwait and the United Arab Emirates are not part of the Development Assistance Committee (DAC) but are included in its Creditor Reporting System (CRS) database. Iceland became a member of the DAC in 2012 and now reports to the CRS. The Czech Republic, Poland, the Slovak Republic and Slovenia became members of the DAC in 2013.

***The Asian Development Fund is a donor to education but does not report to the OECD on disbursements.

**** The total includes ODA from other bilaterals and multilaterals not listed above.

(…) indicates that data are not available, (-) represents a nil value

Total ODA data represent net disbursements. Sector-allocable ODA and debt relief and other actions relating to debt represent gross disbursements

Total ODA from DAC donors is bilateral ODA only, while ODA as % of GNI includes multilateral ODA.

TABLE 2

Bilateral and multilateral aid to education

| | TOTAL AID TO EDUCATION | | | TOTAL AID TO BASIC EDUCATION | | | DIRECT AID TO EDUCATION | | | DIRECT AID TO BASIC EDUCATION | | | DIRECT AID TO SECONDARY EDUCATION | | |
| | CONSTANT 2014 US$ MILLIONS | | | CONSTANT 2014 US$ MILLIONS | | | CONSTANT 2014 US$ MILLIONS | | | CONSTANT 2014 US$ MILLIONS | | | CONSTANT 2014 US$ MILLIONS | | |
	2002–2003 annual average	2013	2014	2002–2003 annual average	2013	2014	2002–2003 annual average	2013	2014	2002–2003 annual average	2013	2014	2002–2003 annual average	2013	2014
Australia	198	391	529	64	221	306	195	390	529	43	116	126	30	19	9
Austria	71	145	147	6	3	3	71	144	146	3	0	0	3	23	20
Belgium	154	109	101	29	34	30	149	109	101	16	17	18	18	31	29
Canada	258	262	245	107	137	140	254	255	242	74	92	95	11	53	34
Czech Republic*	...	8	10	...	1	1	...	8	10	...	1	0	...	1	1
Denmark	28	150	122	15	67	72	26	138	114	5	22	37	1	5	4
Finland	43	59	80	24	28	42	41	52	74	9	11	14	2	3	3
France	1,444	1,519	1,477	185	224	125	1,399	1,466	1,433	25	141	47	37	147	211
Germany	851	1,770	1,815	136	279	297	850	1,762	1,808	105	152	167	74	120	149
Greece	58	11	11	28	1	1	58	11	11	23	...	...	20	...	...
Iceland*	...	4	2	...	3	2	...	4	2	...	3	2	...	0	0
Ireland	70	53	48	40	25	25	64	48	46	16	8	13	1	5	6
Italy	48	56	72	18	22	31	45	54	71	1	12	15	2	11	13
Japan	492	1,139	588	139	471	181	440	657	515	79	102	54	36	49	70
Kuwait*	...	29	42	...	5	4	...	29	42	...	0	...	...	12	13
Luxembourg	...	48	53	...	14	25	...	48	53	...	9	21	...	29	24
Netherlands	337	229	170	222	92	55	305	224	170	185	81	52	1	22	11
New Zealand	98	83	77	27	28	25	96	79	74	11	24	21	11	3	3
Norway	205	291	305	120	214	216	191	275	291	93	179	181	10	5	8
Poland*	...	29	46	...	1	9	...	29	46	...	0	1	...	1	0
Portugal	76	54	57	11	12	11	76	53	56	7	0	0	8	7	6
Republic of Korea	...	226	227	...	48	45	...	226	227	...	23	25	...	69	78
Slovak Republic*	...	5	4	...	1	1	...	5	4	...	0	0	...	1	1
Slovenia*	...	5	7	...	1	1	...	5	7	...	0	0	...	0	0
Spain	197	80	53	65	35	21	197	78	53	43	11	8	45	12	9
Sweden	114	137	178	74	79	112	95	115	169	46	46	85	3	6	8
Switzerland	72	98	120	34	42	53	65	91	113	26	32	42	29	34	43
United Arab Emirates*	...	713	184	...	356	94	...	100	140	...	1	22	...	1	4
United Kingdom	308	1,582	1,374	212	801	636	189	1,536	1,356	126	382	326	8	233	302
United States	428	977	1,084	271	714	878	241	858	1,049	166	604	820	0	30	15
Estonia	...	1	2	...	0	0	...	1	2	...	...	0	...	0	0
Hungary	...	-	8	...	-	0	...	...	8	...	...	0	...	...	0
Kazakhstan	...	0	18	...	0	8	...	...	18	...	...	...	...	...	...
Lithuania	...	-	1	...	-	0	...	...	1	...	...	...	...	...	0
Romania	...	-	57	...	-	17	...	...	57	...	...	0	...	...	0
Total bilaterals	**5,549**	**10,260**	**9,315**	**1,829**	**3,957**	**3,467**	**5,046**	**8,853**	**9,039**	**1,103**	**2,067**	**2,192**	**352**	**930**	**1,076**
African Development Bank	...	0	0	...	-	0	...	0	0	...	...	...	...	...	...
African Development Fund	98	182	112	53	56	26	75	95	69	11	...	...	2	53	37
Arab Fund for Economic and Social Development	...	5	4	...	1	2	...	5	4	...	...	...	...	0	...
Asian Development Bank Special Funds	...	222	223	...	80	61	...	222	223	...	31	21	...	74	99
Asian Development Fund**	...	...	...	...	-	-	...	...	...	...	...	...	...	...	...
BADEA	...	8	5	...	2	1	...	8	5	...	0	0	...	0	1
Climate Investment Funds [CIF]	...	-	0	...	-	-	...	...	0	...	...	...	...	...	0
EU Institutions	220	1,050	1,016	105	400	429	78	862	773	26	166	161	14	90	71
World Bank (IDA)	1,153	1,149	1,629	775	477	737	1,153	1,148	1,622	646	339	546	105	366	520
Inter-American Development Bank Special Fund	...	42	54	...	36	40	...	42	54	...	34	30	...	1	1
International Monetary Fund (Concessional Trust Funds)	421	243	166	211	122	83	...	...	...	...	...	...	...	...	...
OPEC Fund for International Development	...	17	21	...	7	5	...	17	21	...	6	3	...	6	13
UNDP	...	2	2	...	1	1	...	2	2	...	0	0	...	0	0
UNICEF	75	74	82	74	54	53	75	74	82	74	35	25	0	0	0
UN Peacebuilding Fund	...	-	-	...	-	-	...	...	...	...	...	...	...	...	...
UN Relief and Works Agency for Palestine Refugees	...	351	395	...	351	395	...	351	395	...	351	395	...	...	...
World Food Programme	...	41	31	...	41	30	...	41	31	...	41	30	...	...	...
Total multilaterals	**1,967**	**3,386**	**3,740**	**1,218**	**1,628**	**1,863**	**1,381**	**2,867**	**3,281**	**757**	**1,003**	**1,211**	**121**	**591**	**742**
Total	**7,516**	**13,646**	**13,055**	**3,047**	**5,585**	**5,330**	**6,427**	**11,720**	**12,320**	**1,860**	**3,070**	**3,403**	**473**	**1,520**	**1,818**

Source: OECD-DAC, CRS database (2015).

* Estonia, Hungary, Kazakhstan, Kuwait, Lithuania, Romania and the United Arab Emirates are not part of the DAC but are included in its CRS database. Iceland became a member of the DAC in 2012 and now reports to the CRS. The Czech Republic, Poland, the Slovak Republic and Slovenia became members of the DAC in 2013.

** The Asian Development Fund is a donor to education but does not report to the OECD on disbursements.

Aid from France, the United Kingdom and New Zealand includes funds disbursed to overseas territories (see Table 3).

(...) indicates that data are not available, (-) represents a nil value

All data represent gross disbursements. The share of ODA disbursed to the education sector is as a percentage of gross ODA disbursements as reported in the CRS statistical tables. Total ODA figures in Table 1 represent net disbursements as reported in the DAC statistical tables.

DIRECT AID TO POST-SECONDARY EDUCATION			DIRECT AID TO EDUCATION, LEVEL UNSPECIFIED			SHARE OF EDUCATION IN TOTAL ODA (%)			SHARE OF DIRECT AID TO EDUCATION IN TOTAL SECTOR-ALLOCABLE ODA (%)			SHARE OF BASIC EDUCATION IN TOTAL AID TO EDUCATION (%)		
CONSTANT 2014 US$ MILLIONS			CONSTANT 2014 US$ MILLIONS											
2002–2003 annual average	2013	2014	2002–2003 annual average	2013	2014	2002–2003 annual average	2013	2014	2002–2003 annual average	2013	2014	2002–2003 annual average	2013	2014
83	47	34	39	209	359	11	10	15	15	13	18	32	56	58
60	116	120	5	5	6	15	26	23	32	42	45	8	2	2
92	28	31	23	33	22	9	8	8	20	13	11	19	31	29
106	27	26	62	84	86	10	8	7	24	12	12	42	52	57
...	6	8	...	1	1	...	15	16	...	24	27	...	14	7
1	32	10	19	80	62	2	7	6	9	11	9	56	45	59
2	11	7	28	28	50	10	7	9	14	10	12	56	48	52
1,062	1,066	1,062	274	112	113	22	22	23	46	25	23	13	15	8
611	1,244	1,239	61	247	253	16	18	16	21	18	16	16	16	16
4	9	9	10	1	1	23	25	24	27	78	67	49	6	7
...	...	...	...	0	0	...	11	7	...	13	9	...	90	92
4	6	6	43	29	21	17	10	9	22	14	14	57	47	51
11	12	11	31	20	32	3	6	5	21	14	16	38	40	43
257	250	211	68	257	180	7	14	10	13	6	5	28	41	31
...	8	21	...	10	9	...	16	18	...	6	8	...	17	10
...	0	0	...	9	8	...	16	18	...	24	26	...	29	47
77	104	101	42	17	7	8	6	4	17	8	7	66	40	32
43	48	46	30	4	4	42	23	19	64	31	25	28	34	32
49	36	46	39	56	57	8	7	8	15	9	11	58	74	71
...	27	28	...	1	16	...	23	56	...	42	48	...	3	21
52	23	28	9	23	22	26	18	23	30	29	27	15	22	20
...	83	84	...	50	41	...	16	16	...	17	18	...	21	20
...	3	3	...	1	1	...	30	27	...	42	49	...	19	15
...	3	5	...	1	1	...	24	32	...	37	51	...	12	10
64	9	10	45	46	26	12	8	11	20	12	12	33	43	40
8	19	31	37	44	45	5	4	4	9	5	7	65	58	63
1	11	12	10	13	15	5	4	4	8	7	7	47	43	44
...	1	13	...	96	101	...	13	4	...	4	6	...	50	51
1	129	126	53	792	602	6	14	12	9	17	15	69	51	46
53	123	133	22	102	81	3	4	4	3	5	6	63	73	81
...	0	1	...	0	1	...	7	11	...	12	19	...	13	25
...	...	7	...	...	0	...	-	25	...	...	44	...	...	3
...	...	1	...	...	17	...	2	65	...	...	91	...	50	47
...	...	1	...	...	1	...	-	22	...	...	58	...	...	29
...	...	22	...	...	34	...	-	82	...	...	83	...	...	30
2,641	**3,484**	**3,497**	**950**	**2,373**	**2,274**	**8**	**9**	**8**	**16**	**12**	**11**	**33**	**39**	**37**
...	0	0	...	...	0	...	0	0	...	1	4	...	-	10
0	17	24	61	25	8	12	8	6	10	5	4	54	31	23
...	3	...	...	2	4	...	1	1	...	1	0	...	16	50
...	20	22	...	98	81	...	22	15	...	8	8	...	36	27
...	...	...	...	...	...	...	...	...	...	...	...	...	...	...
...	3	3	...	5	2	...	9	10	...	6	4	...	32	19
...	...	...	...	...	...	...	-	0	...	...	0	...	...	-
22	325	249	17	281	293	3	7	6	5	7	6	48	38	42
145	168	182	257	274	374	14	14	16	11	10	12	67	41	45
...	2	2	...	5	21	...	2	3	...	3	4	...	86	75
...	...	...	...	...	...	45	39	93	...	...	...	50	50	50
...	3	1	...	2	4	...	8	8	...	4	5	...	41	23
...	0	0	...	1	1	...	0	0	...	1	0	...	50	42
0	...	...	...	38	56	9	6	6	15	10	10	99	74	65
...	...	...	...	...	...	...	-	-	...	...	...	...	...	...
...	...	...	...	...	...	...	65	58	...	80	79	...	100	100
...	...	...	...	...	0	...	11	10	...	57	57	...	100	100
167	**541**	**483**	**336**	**732**	**844**	**8**	**8**	**9**	**11**	**8**	**9**	**62**	**48**	**50**
2,809	**4,025**	**3,980**	**1,286**	**3,105**	**3,119**	**8**	**9**	**8**	**14**	**11**	**11**	**41**	**41**	**41**

TABLE 3
Recipients of aid to education

	TOTAL AID TO EDUCATION (CONSTANT 2014 US$ MILLIONS)			TOTAL AID TO BASIC EDUCATION (CONSTANT 2014 US$ MILLIONS)			TOTAL AID TO BASIC EDUCATION PER PRIMARY SCHOOL-AGE CHILD (CONSTANT 2014 US$)			DIRECT AID TO EDUCATION (CONSTANT 2014 US$ MILLIONS)			DIRECT AID TO BASIC EDUCAT (CONSTANT 2014 US$ MILLIC)		
	2002–2003 annual average	2013	2014	2002–2003 annual average	2013	2014	2002–2003 annual average	2013	2014	2002–2003 annual average	2013	2014	2002–2003 annual average	2013	
Caucasus and Central Asia	94	239	213	30	45	47	5	7	7	59	224	208	8	15	
Unallocated within the region	-	20	18	-	1	3	...	...	...	-	20	18	-	0	
Armenia	18	40	29	7	8	6	43	...	...	8	31	28	1	1	
Azerbaijan	12	24	20	4	5	4	7	9	7	6	24	20	1	2	
Georgia	26	47	42	6	9	11	23	36	43	20	47	42	3	4	
Kazakhstan	6	25	21	1	3	1	1	3	1	6	25	21	1	1	
Kyrgyzstan	12	32	40	4	10	14	9	24	35	5	26	37	0	2	
Tajikistan	8	13	13	4	5	4	6	8	7	2	13	13	1	4	
Turkmenistan	1	4	4	0	0	0	1	0	0	1	4	4	0	0	
Uzbekistan	12	35	27	2	5	5	1	3	2	11	35	27	1	2	
Europe and Northern America	195	426	503	68	54	110	15	12	26	184	422	411	38	19	
Unallocated within the region	20	119	70	5	17	14	...	...	...	19	118	70	1	4	
Albania	75	36	37	36	7	7	140	36	40	73	33	31	24	2	
Belarus	-	31	32	-	2	3	-	5	9	-	31	32	-	0	
Bosnia and Herzegovina	31	38	38	10	4	4	...	...	...	31	38	38	6	1	
Croatia	9	-	-	0	-	-	1	-	-	9	-	-	-	-	
Montenegro	-	9	5	-	1	1	-	37	22	-	9	5	-	0	
Republic of Moldova	9	21	73	2	4	21	9	25	...	7	21	73	0	2	
Serbia	36	64	58	10	9	9	29	30	31	34	64	56	4	2	
TFYR Macedonia	13	21	15	5	3	3	37	26	24	9	21	15	2	2	
Ukraine	-	88	174	-	8	49	-	5	30	-	88	89	-	5	
Eastern and South-eastern Asia	869	2,104	1,601	164	644	420	1	4	3	825	1,624	1,562	97	174	
Unallocated within the region	11	30	21	3	4	4	...	...	...	12	33	21	2	2	
Cambodia	47	85	93	18	28	30	8	15	16	39	85	93	7	12	
China	364	518	490	17	30	21	0	0	0	364	518	490	10	4	
DPR Korea	2	4	13	0	2	0	0	1	0	2	4	13	0	2	
Indonesia	149	373	238	49	150	90	2	5	3	142	305	238	35	28	
Lao PDR	28	68	69	8	22	15	10	30	20	23	67	68	5	14	
Malaysia	15	32	33	1	2	2	0	1	1	15	32	33	0	0	
Mongolia	27	57	46	9	18	11	37	81	45	25	57	46	6	11	
Myanmar	11	463	103	6	236	60	1	45	12	11	81	103	5	27	
Philippines	36	61	99	8	31	62	1	3	5	35	61	99	5	23	
Thailand	30	47	45	2	7	6	0	1	1	30	47	45	0	3	
Timor-Leste	20	34	34	4	12	14	26	64	76	16	34	34	2	2	
Viet Nam	128	332	318	39	100	105	4	15	16	112	300	280	20	45	
Latin America and the Caribbean	575	899	882	224	330	306	5	7	6	554	882	866	169	203	
Unallocated within the region	48	86	65	12	14	14	...	...	...	48	86	65	8	8	
Antigua and Barbuda	0	0	0	0	0	0	7	0	0	0	0	0	-	-	
Argentina	19	31	28	2	6	4	1	1	1	19	31	28	1	2	
Aruba	...	...	...	...	...	...	...	...	...	...	...	...	...	...	
Barbados	0	-	-	-	-	-	-	-	-	0	-	-	-	-	
Belize	0	2	1	0	1	0	5	26	11	0	2	1	0	1	
Bolivia, P.S.	87	44	48	56	16	16	44	12	11	84	43	48	46	6	
Brazil	39	119	113	4	18	17	...	...	...	39	119	113	2	5	
Chile	15	30	30	1	7	5	1	5	3	15	30	30	0	3	
Colombia	33	78	77	5	23	19	1	...	...	33	78	77	2	10	
Costa Rica	3	16	11	0	5	4	1	11	9	3	16	11	0	3	
Cuba	12	7	7	3	1	1	3	1	1	12	7	7	3	0	
Dominica	1	2	1	0	1	0	34	107	43	0	0	0	-	0	
Dominican Republic	19	39	53	12	21	24	10	17	19	19	37	53	12	8	
Ecuador	17	38	37	3	15	14	2	8	8	17	38	37	2	6	
El Salvador	8	19	24	3	10	12	4	14	17	8	17	24	2	8	
Grenada	0	1	3	-	0	1	-	2	115	0	1	0	-	0	
Guatemala	30	27	27	16	13	13	8	6	6	29	26	27	13	11	
Guyana	17	4	4	6	1	1	51	13	15	15	4	4	3	1	
Haiti	24	72	107	12	37	64	9	26	45	24	68	97	9	23	
Honduras	37	51	44	28	43	33	26	41	32	36	51	42	24	42	
Jamaica	12	15	9	9	7	6	27	...	...	9	10	9	7	4	
Mexico	31	60	63	2	10	8	0	1	1	31	60	63	1	3	
Nicaragua	59	53	36	33	33	13	41	45	18	50	53	36	22	27	
Panama	5	4	4	0	2	2	1	4	...	5	4	4	0	1	
Paraguay	7	25	15	4	18	8	4	23	11	7	25	15	3	16	
Peru	33	44	47	9	16	19	3	5	6	33	44	47	7	10	
Saint Kitts and Nevis	0	1	-	0	1	-	2	97	-	0	1	-	0	0	
Saint Lucia	1	6	3	0	2	1	10	...	...	1	6	2	0	0	
Saint Vincent and the Grenadines	0	3	1	0	1	1	5	99	52	0	3	1	0	0	
Suriname	3	2	3	1	0	1	19	2	16	3	2	3	1	0	
Trinidad and Tobago	1	-	-	0	-	-	0	-	-	1	-	-	-	-	
Uruguay	3	5	5	1	2	1	2	7	4	3	5	5	0	1	
Venezuela, B.R.	9	16	16	1	4	2	0	1	1	9	16	16	1	2	
Northern Africa and Western Asia	1,071	2,731	2,108	216	1,179	889	5	25	19	912	2,002	1,948	99	630	
Unallocated within the region	11	115	49	4	27	18	...	...	...	12	104	47	3	22	
Algeria	135	136	127	1	3	2	0	1	1	135	136	127	0	1	
Bahrain	0	-	-	0	-	-	0	-	-	0	-	-	0	-	
Egypt	106	832	154	56	388	49	7	37	5	87	191	154	45	22	
Iraq	8	60	68	1	19	20	0	4	4	8	60	68	1	14	
Jordan	131	254	365	58	178	254	80	181	252	21	210	267	0	138	
Lebanon	41	160	180	1	95	92	3	195	180	41	159	180	1	89	
Libya	-	11	10	-	1	1	-	1	2	-	11	10	-	0	
Morocco	286	343	311	17	88	45	4	25	13	286	342	311	6	50	
Oman	0	-	-	0	-	-	0	-	-	0	-	-	0	-	

DIRECT AID TO SECONDARY EDUCATION			DIRECT AID TO POST-SECONDARY EDUCATION			DIRECT AID TO EDUCATION, LEVEL UNSPECIFIED			SHARE OF EDUCATION IN TOTAL ODA (%)			SHARE OF DIRECT AID TO EDUCATION IN SECTOR-ALLOCABLE ODA (%)			SHARE OF BASIC EDUCATION IN TOTAL AID TO EDUCATION (%)		
NSTANT 2014 US$ MILLIONS			CONSTANT 2014 US$ MILLIONS			CONSTANT 2014 US$ MILLIONS											
-2003 ual rage	2013	2014	2002–2003 annual average	2013	2014	2002–2003 annual average	2013	2014	2002–2003 annual average	2013	2014	2002–2003 annual average	2013	2014	2002–2003 annual average	2013	2014
8	**43**	**23**	**35**	**121**	**114**	**8**	**45**	**52**	**5**	**9**	**8**	**5**	**9**	**8**	**32**	**19**	**22**
-	*4*	*4*	-	*13*	*11*	-	*2*	*1*	...	*9*	*8*	...	*9*	*9*	...	*6*	*15*
0	8	1	4	18	19	3	3	6	5	12	9	3	11	10	39	19	20
0	1	0	4	16	14	1	5	4	4	9	7	4	9	7	36	19	19
3	9	1	14	24	25	1	10	12	7	7	6	8	7	7	25	19	25
0	2	2	4	18	17	1	4	2	3	18	23	4	19	24	21	11	6
1	5	7	2	10	8	1	10	18	5	8	10	3	8	10	39	30	35
0	3	2	0	4	5	0	3	3	5	3	3	3	3	4	52	40	35
0	1	1	0	2	2	0	0	0	3	15	13	6	15	14	35	5	3
3	10	5	6	16	14	2	7	7	6	11	7	9	11	7	17	15	17
8	**28**	**29**	**69**	**309**	**272**	**49**	**66**	**92**	**4**	**9**	**9**	**8**	**9**	**9**	**35**	**13**	**22**
1	*9*	*9*	*10*	*79*	*36*	*6*	*26*	*23*	*3*	*8*	*5*	*6*	*10*	*6*	*25*	*14*	*20*
0	7	6	8	18	20	21	6	4	19	11	10	24	11	10	48	18	19
-	0	0	-	27	27	-	4	4	...	30	27	...	30	28	...	6	10
2	4	3	15	27	29	9	5	6	6	6	5	8	7	6	33	10	10
0	-	-	8	-	-	0	-	-	6	...	...	9	...	...	2	...	...
-	1	1	-	5	3	-	2	1	-	7	4	-	7	4	...	17	16
0	1	4	5	14	30	2	3	37	6	6	13	7	6	14	23	18	28
3	3	3	18	46	40	9	13	11	2	7	8	4	7	9	27	13	15
1	0	1	4	17	11	2	2	1	4	8	5	4	8	5	36	15	19
-	1	2	-	76	78	-	7	6	...	11	12	...	12	10	...	9	28
6	**152**	**170**	**563**	**846**	**814**	**90**	**457**	**364**	**9**	**10**	**10**	**14**	**12**	**12**	**19**	**31**	**26**
2	*4*	*2*	*6*	*28*	*18*	*3*	*4*	*2*	*6*	*5*	*3*	*11*	*6*	*4*	*25*	*15*	*17*
3	18	14	16	23	29	14	31	40	10	10	11	10	10	11	37	33	32
0	21	35	320	443	416	13	51	35	15	30	35	20	32	36	5	6	4
1	-	0	1	2	13	0	0	0	1	5	15	3	9	23	14	47	4
2	23	7	63	77	80	22	177	123	7	16	11	15	16	12	33	40	38
2	21	33	14	16	17	2	15	8	10	15	14	10	16	15	29	33	21
3	0	0	10	28	28	2	4	4	8	17	23	33	18	26	5	8	7
0	11	10	16	20	22	2	15	7	12	12	13	16	13	13	32	32	23
0	4	14	4	13	15	1	37	28	10	6	5	16	5	13	54	51	58
5	5	4	20	16	15	4	16	36	3	6	6	8	9	11	23	52	63
2	1	2	24	34	33	3	8	7	4	6	7	8	6	8	6	15	14
5	5	4	7	7	7	2	20	19	7	14	14	7	14	15	22	34	41
0	38	45	60	139	121	22	78	55	8	7	6	9	7	6	30	30	33
5	**99**	**107**	**221**	**342**	**333**	**89**	**239**	**255**	**8**	**8**	**8**	**12**	**9**	**9**	**39**	**37**	**35**
2	*4*	*4*	*31*	*62*	*42*	*7*	*11*	*8*	*8*	*3*	*3*	*11*	*5*	*4*	*24*	*16*	*22*
-	0	-	0	0	0	0	0	0	3	4	3	3	5	3	40	4	8
1	4	5	14	16	15	3	10	8	17	38	35	27	41	36	12	21	15
..	...	...	...	...	...	...	...	...	...	...	...	...	...	...	...	...	...
-	-	-	0	-	-	-	-	-	4	...	...	5	...	...	-	...	...
0	0	0	0	0	0	0	0	1	3	4	3	5	4	4	60	62	41
5	10	12	7	8	8	16	19	24	8	6	7	13	6	7	64	37	33
4	10	4	29	78	79	5	26	26	9	9	10	16	9	10	11	15	15
1	2	4	11	17	16	2	9	10	19	32	11	21	35	12	9	24	17
3	6	8	21	36	38	6	26	24	4	9	6	5	10	6	15	29	24
0	4	2	3	5	4	0	4	3	5	22	13	7	24	14	11	30	33
1	0	1	7	5	5	1	2	1	15	7	6	18	8	7	26	14	12
0	0	-	0	0	0	-	0	-	8	7	4	4	2	3	29	42	34
3	1	2	2	3	13	2	25	29	10	18	23	16	19	24	66	55	45
5	3	4	9	10	10	1	20	19	6	17	16	8	18	18	18	41	38
2	4	6	2	3	3	1	2	6	4	8	16	6	9	18	38	53	49
0	1	-0	0	0	0	-	0	0	2	6	7	2	7	1	-	3	49
5	8	9	6	4	3	4	3	4	9	5	9	12	5	9	53	49	49
7	0	0	1	2	2	4	1	1	19	3	2	26	3	3	33	40	36
1	8	8	7	13	12	6	24	37	12	6	10	17	8	11	52	51	60
2	5	5	2	1	2	9	3	5	9	8	6	15	8	7	77	85	76
0	4	1	0	1	1	2	1	1	11	11	7	12	10	7	75	48	69
5	4	6	22	39	42	1	13	14	14	8	7	15	8	7	6	17	13
3	11	16	13	3	3	12	11	9	8	10	8	13	11	8	55	63	36
3	1	0	1	2	2	0	1	1	11	8	10	14	9	11	9	42	42
1	3	3	2	2	2	2	3	3	8	13	11	14	14	11	49	74	57
7	4	5	15	17	17	5	12	12	5	8	9	8	9	10	27	37	41
-	0	-	0	0	-	0	0	-	1	9	...	1	2	...	28	47	...
0	2	0	0	0	0	0	4	2	4	20	16	4	21	19	31	33	42
0	0	-	0	0	0	0	2	1	4	22	15	7	34	25	25	50	47
0	-	-	1	2	1	0	0	1	7	8	21	7	8	21	43	5	32
0	-	-	1	-	-	0	-	-	15	...	...	15	...	...	1	...	...
0	1	1	2	1	1	1	2	2	20	12	5	23	12	5	16	37	25
1	1	2	6	9	9	1	5	5	11	41	40	15	46	45	10	24	14
8	**171**	**164**	**677**	**832**	**803**	**73**	**374**	**355**	**13**	**10**	**8**	**20**	**12**	**11**	**20**	**43**	**42**
1	*3*	*4*	*3*	*80*	*30*	*1*	*4*	*4*	*7*	*8*	*4*	*12*	*13*	*6*	*36*	*23*	*37*
1	3	3	131	129	120	2	4	3	51	43	50	80	49	55	1	2	2
0	-	-	0	-	-	0	-	-	54	...	...	57	...	...	1	...	...
2	13	8	27	66	74	4	90	45	6	14	3	9	7	6	53	47	32
1	18	17	6	19	27	0	9	11	1	4	5	1	4	9	18	31	29
3	14	3	12	22	35	5	36	46	13	16	13	6	21	18	44	70	70
2	10	15	36	50	49	2	10	47	30	21	19	39	32	31	3	59	51
-	2	0	-	7	7	-	1	3	...	8	5	...	8	8	...	6	13
4	59	66	253	160	168	22	74	63	36	13	11	54	13	11	6	26	15
0	-	-	0	-	-	0	-	-	10	...	...	11	...	...	26	...	...

TABLE 3

Recipients of aid to education (Continued)

| | TOTAL AID TO EDUCATION | | | TOTAL AID TO BASIC EDUCATION | | | TOTAL AID TO BASIC EDUCATION PER PRIMARY SCHOOL-AGE CHILD | | | DIRECT AID TO EDUCATION | | | DIRECT AID TO BASIC EDUCATION | |
	CONSTANT 2014 US$ MILLIONS			CONSTANT 2014 US$ MILLIONS			CONSTANT 2014 US$			CONSTANT 2014 US$ MILLIONS			CONSTANT 2014 US$ MILLIO	
	2002–2003 annual average	2013	2014	2002–2003 annual average	2013	2014	2002–2003 annual average	2013	2014	2002–2003 annual average	2013	2014	2002–2003 annual average	2013
Palestine	51	334	354	21	271	293	48	592	629	51	310	343	15	237
Saudi Arabia	2	-	-	0	-	-	0	-	-	2	-	-	-	-
Sudan*	21	27	30	11	11	16	2	2	3	18	27	30	7	7
Syrian Arab Republic	32	96	72	1	32	19	1	16	...	32	96	72	1	22
Tunisia	100	146	170	2	21	34	2	22	35	100	139	136	1	2
Turkey	101	127	124	17	10	8	3	2	2	76	127	124	3	2
Yemen	44	89	95	23	37	37	6	9	9	43	89	80	17	24
Pacific	**221**	**269**	**228**	**84**	**106**	**105**	**72**	**66**	**64**	**180**	**225**	**226**	**32**	**44**
Unallocated within the region	12	25	21	2	3	3	...	...	...	12	25	21	1	2
Cook Islands	4	4	4	1	3	3	568	1,542	1,631	4	4	4	0	3
Fiji	11	19	18	3	5	4	28	55	37	11	19	18	2	2
Kiribati	10	11	12	3	5	8	242	395	540	10	11	12	0	5
Marshall Islands	12	15	9	6	7	9	797	857	979	1	2	9	0	0
Micronesia, F.S.	24	24	38	12	13	29	696	864	1,994	2	2	38	0	1
Nauru	0	5	4	0	1	0	16	484	149	0	5	4	-	-
Niue	6	4	2	2	2	1	14,094	10,932	4,541	4	3	0	0	0
Palau	4	4	1	2	2	1	1,069	1,366	370	1	2	1	0	0
Papua New Guinea	89	66	55	40	27	23	47	21	18	88	66	55	24	2
Samoa	13	20	15	5	6	4	157	194	125	13	18	15	2	2
Solomon Islands	8	33	19	2	14	11	34	156	118	7	33	19	0	12
Tonga	8	11	7	2	7	2	130	415	137	8	10	7	1	6
Tuvalu	2	7	5	1	3	2	619	1,919	1,144	2	6	5	0	0
Vanuatu	17	20	19	3	9	8	109	266	213	17	20	19	0	9
Southern Asia	**953**	**2,178**	**2,687**	**589**	**967**	**1,234**	**3**	**5**	**7**	**766**	**2,092**	**2,660**	**457**	**606**
Unallocated within the region	14	50	40	6	13	14	...	...	...	13	48	40	3	10
Afghanistan	39	443	388	25	239	278	7	44	50	33	442	388	16	131
Bangladesh	148	528	449	97	311	207	6	19	13	139	444	421	89	227
Bhutan	9	4	2	5	2	1	44	16	6	9	4	2	3	1
India	376	384	806	277	28	270	2	0	2	355	384	806	257	9
Iran, Islamic Republic of	39	79	77	1	2	1	0	0	0	39	79	77	1	1
Maldives	9	2	2	3	1	1	52	...	...	9	2	2	3	0
Nepal	51	137	165	33	74	77	10	22	24	49	137	165	25	55
Pakistan	218	454	643	126	252	342	7	12	16	77	454	643	48	148
Sri Lanka	51	97	116	17	47	43	11	26	25	44	97	116	12	23
Sub-Saharan Africa	**2,810**	**3,395**	**3,233**	**1,478**	**1,627**	**1,489**	**13**	**11**	**9**	**2,224**	**2,854**	**2,841**	**922**	**896**
Unallocated within the region	86	114	115	65	40	44	...	...	...	84	108	102	50	24
Angola	41	18	31	23	4	15	12	1	3	41	18	31	16	2
Benin	44	75	42	16	38	17	13	23	10	39	59	35	11	21
Botswana	3	19	38	0	9	19	1	29	59	3	19	38	0	0
Burkina Faso	90	105	89	54	65	52	27	22	17	63	76	66	35	44
Burundi	14	38	32	6	18	15	5	12	9	10	30	25	2	6
Cameroon	99	97	101	18	7	5	6	2	1	86	97	101	10	4
Cape Verde	38	27	29	5	3	3	59	49	49	36	24	26	2	0
Central African Republic	9	6	21	1	1	9	2	2	12	9	6	4	1	0
Chad	28	13	18	14	7	8	9	3	3	19	13	14	5	5
Comoros	13	16	16	4	3	1	44	22	10	13	14	16	4	1
Congo	26	21	21	2	2	2	5	3	3	26	21	21	1	2
Côte d'Ivoire	93	84	81	33	30	27	12	9	8	55	40	41	9	7
D. R. Congo	123	132	103	55	87	58	6	7	5	31	131	103	5	74
Djibouti	30	25	18	8	11	5	63	119	53	27	20	12	5	8
Equatorial Guinea	9	2	2	5	1	0	62	9	4	9	2	2	3	0
Eritrea	19	14	9	8	0	1	16	0	2	19	14	9	5	0
Ethiopia	104	359	439	58	211	259	5	14	16	80	325	422	31	104
Gabon	31	27	25	5	1	1	27	8	5	30	27	25	4	0
Gambia	10	5	9	6	3	5	29	11	16	8	5	9	5	2
Ghana	127	146	88	81	92	42	26	24	11	79	132	85	47	73
Guinea	45	43	54	27	13	20	18	7	11	41	37	35	23	7
Guinea-Bissau	10	10	19	4	7	10	19	24	38	10	10	15	4	5
Kenya	86	152	99	57	80	57	11	11	8	81	108	99	51	45
Lesotho	24	10	3	12	5	3	34	16	7	20	3	3	7	2
Liberia	3	41	48	2	24	29	5	34	41	3	36	33	2	14
Madagascar	84	65	85	37	35	37	15	11	12	66	65	58	21	29
Malawi	75	72	87	44	44	51	21	16	18	70	64	83	30	23
Mali	101	107	102	54	51	48	29	19	17	78	50	67	30	20
Mauritania	35	31	25	14	9	2	30	16	4	30	20	25	8	3
Mauritius	17	21	14	0	6	1	3	53	13	17	14	13	0	2
Mozambique	153	223	218	85	121	121	22	23	22	110	170	166	45	51
Namibia	27	68	47	14	30	17	39	79	43	27	68	47	12	3
Niger	56	49	89	29	26	45	15	8	14	35	33	62	8	15
Nigeria	33	157	147	17	63	56	1	2	2	32	157	147	12	40
Rwanda	64	129	87	28	64	36	21	37	20	44	119	86	5	20
Sao Tome and Principe	6	7	7	1	1	1	47	43	17	6	7	7	1	0
Senegal	117	146	172	37	59	63	22	26	27	111	130	162	19	44
Seychelles	1	3	1	0	1	0	49	155	41	1	3	1	-	0
Sierra Leone	24	29	44	15	17	27	21	17	26	11	18	21	7	11
Somalia	5	28	33	4	20	23	3	11	13	5	28	33	3	18
South Africa	119	68	45	54	24	14	7	3	2	119	54	45	43	6
South Sudan*	-	64	55	-	36	37	...	20	19	-	64	55	-	16
Swaziland	3	5	6	2	4	5	7	20	23	3	5	6	0	4
Togo	15	23	23	1	6	2	2	6	2	14	19	23	1	4
U. R. Tanzania	299	262	135	228	120	67	33	13	7	225	165	108	178	36

DIRECT AID TO SECONDARY EDUCATION CONSTANT 2014 US$ MILLIONS			DIRECT AID TO POST-SECONDARY EDUCATION CONSTANT 2014 US$ MILLIONS			DIRECT AID TO EDUCATION, LEVEL UNSPECIFIED CONSTANT 2014 US$ MILLIONS			SHARE OF EDUCATION IN TOTAL ODA (%)			SHARE OF DIRECT AID TO EDUCATION IN SECTOR-ALLOCABLE ODA (%)			SHARE OF BASIC EDUCATION IN TOTAL AID TO EDUCATION (%)		
2002–2003 annual average	2013	2014	2002–2003 annual average	2013	2014	2002–2003 annual average	2013	2014	2002–2003 annual average	2013	2014	2002–2003 annual average	2013	2014	2002–2003 annual average	2013	2014
8	9	10	15	21	19	13	43	51	8	13	15	11	17	21	41	81	83
1	-	-	2	-	-	0	-	-	49	...	...	51	...	...	4	...	...
0	4	1	6	9	7	3	8	9	5	2	3	16	5	7	50	40	55
0	3	0	29	51	52	1	20	2	28	5	4	41	31	24	5	33	26
16	9	10	81	97	94	2	32	30	23	14	15	34	14	15	2	15	20
3	9	10	66	99	98	4	17	16	19	4	3	28	4	3	17	8	6
6	15	15	8	23	22	12	27	25	13	8	7	19	11	9	52	42	39
9	23	17	66	77	65	63	82	81	19	13	13	20	13	13	38	40	46
1	0	0	9	20	17	0	2	2	14	10	9	18	11	10	13	14	12
1	0	0	1	1	1	1	0	0	42	21	13	44	21	13	32	67	76
0	1	2	6	9	9	3	7	7	21	21	20	27	23	21	28	28	20
0	3	2	3	2	2	6	1	1	37	17	16	37	17	16	32	51	62
0	-	-	0	1	0	0	1	0	18	16	15	10	6	17	47	48	97
0	-	-	1	0	0	0	0	17	18	17	32	7	5	33	48	53	77
-	3	3	0	1	0	0	1	0	0	19	17	1	19	18	46	14	6
-	-	0	1	1	0	3	2	0	42	23	12	64	25	6	45	41	43
0	0	-	1	1	0	0	1	1	14	13	5	7	8	5	45	45	50
7	2	2	26	12	9	31	51	41	19	10	9	19	10	9	45	41	42
1	2	2	4	9	8	6	5	3	24	16	15	25	18	17	36	28	25
1	9	2	3	9	6	3	4	2	7	12	9	8	12	10	29	41	56
1	0	0	4	4	3	2	1	2	24	13	8	26	13	9	26	60	32
0	0	-	1	1	2	1	5	3	20	25	14	21	27	14	36	39	32
5	3	3	5	7	7	6	2	1	34	22	18	37	23	19	20	47	42
57	410	655	176	431	505	76	638	551	8	11	13	11	12	14	62	44	46
2	5	5	4	20	14	3	7	5	3	5	4	6	7	5	40	27	35
1	37	39	4	59	50	12	215	43	3	9	8	5	10	9	64	54	72
24	81	141	18	53	46	7	83	82	10	15	14	12	16	15	65	59	46
2	1	0	1	1	1	3	1	1	14	3	1	17	3	1	53	38	31
13	227	356	66	111	157	19	37	44	11	9	16	13	9	16	74	7	33
1	0	1	38	77	74	0	2	2	27	62	59	41	71	68	2	2	1
2	0	0	3	1	1	0	1	2	41	5	7	57	5	8	33	35	36
3	19	41	8	26	29	13	37	34	11	13	16	12	14	16	64	54	47
1	26	37	12	72	120	16	209	287	6	15	15	7	18	16	58	56	53
7	15	34	21	12	13	3	46	52	7	11	12	11	13	13	34	48	37
42	412	454	637	623	617	526	918	943	9	7	7	15	8	8	53	48	46
3	13	12	7	45	35	28	21	24	4	3	2	8	3	3	75	35	38
1	7	3	11	4	4	13	4	17	8	5	11	18	6	11	56	24	48
4	5	3	19	14	16	4	19	4	12	11	7	16	10	6	37	51	42
1	0	0	1	1	1	1	18	37	6	15	32	8	15	33	14	48	49
7	9	11	10	10	10	11	12	9	13	9	8	15	9	7	60	62	58
0	4	4	3	4	5	4	15	11	5	7	6	7	6	6	44	48	45
2	6	11	71	82	83	3	5	4	9	12	11	25	15	13	18	7	5
3	11	10	28	10	14	2	3	2	27	10	11	31	12	12	12	11	10
1	0	0	7	4	3	1	2	1	13	3	3	18	7	2	11	22	42
1	1	2	5	4	4	7	3	4	8	2	4	7	5	6	48	53	44
1	0	1	8	12	13	0	1	2	36	9	22	40	24	23	31	15	7
0	3	4	22	15	15	3	1	1	24	12	16	43	17	21	9	11	9
2	6	8	34	24	25	10	2	1	8	4	7	17	9	6	35	36	33
4	17	20	14	15	15	9	25	19	3	5	4	4	7	6	45	66	57
6	1	3	14	9	6	2	2	2	31	15	10	36	18	11	25	45	29
1	0	0	1	1	1	4	2	0	28	25	16	35	34	22	49	39	29
3	10	3	3	3	4	8	0	2	6	17	11	11	19	13	45	2	13
5	24	38	15	17	17	29	180	233	6	9	12	8	11	14	55	59	59
2	2	3	22	22	21	1	3	2	20	25	19	40	26	20	18	6	4
1	1	0	1	1	1	1	1	6	13	4	9	15	5	9	63	59	54
2	23	30	10	13	12	20	23	5	11	10	7	12	10	7	64	63	48
4	1	2	11	24	22	3	5	2	13	7	9	18	13	9	60	30	37
1	0	0	5	2	3	0	2	7	7	10	16	17	11	18	41	64	56
5	20	13	18	17	22	7	26	14	12	4	3	16	4	4	66	53	58
5	1	-	2	0	0	6	1	0	21	3	2	23	1	2	50	56	89
0	6	2	0	2	3	1	14	13	3	8	6	15	8	6	70	58	61
2	6	8	30	18	17	14	12	20	12	10	14	15	14	13	44	54	43
16	6	9	2	2	5	23	33	38	12	6	8	17	7	9	59	61	59
6	9	14	17	17	17	24	4	12	14	7	8	16	6	8	54	48	47
2	2	5	14	13	17	6	2	2	9	9	8	16	10	11	38	30	8
-	3	3	17	9	8	0	1	1	35	12	11	37	10	11	2	27	10
4	20	22	26	11	12	36	88	74	6	9	10	10	9	9	55	54	55
7	10	13	4	1	3	4	54	29	18	22	17	20	24	18	52	44	35
3	8	12	4	4	5	20	6	28	11	6	9	13	7	11	51	52	50
2	40	31	10	29	16	9	48	88	8	6	6	9	6	6	51	40	38
5	11	19	7	10	14	27	77	36	13	12	8	16	12	9	44	50	42
1	2	2	3	3	4	0	2	0	14	14	17	19	17	19	18	18	8
3	12	28	59	61	59	30	13	32	17	14	14	20	15	15	32	40	37
0	0	-	0	1	1	1	2	0	18	10	7	18	10	6	37	43	34
1	3	3	1	1	1	2	3	3	5	5	5	6	5	5	63	61	61
-	5	3	0	1	1	2	5	13	2	3	3	9	7	6	78	71	69
9	3	4	45	23	19	22	21	13	21	5	3	24	4	3	46	35	32
-	4	4	-	4	3	-	40	22	-	5	3	...	9	9	...	57	67
0	0	0	0	0	0	3	1	1	11	4	6	15	4	6	46	82	86
0	4	10	12	10	11	1	2	1	17	10	10	25	11	11	9	28	8
6	27	5	15	32	30	25	71	39	15	7	5	21	6	6	76	46	50

TABLE 3

Recipients of aid to education (Continued)

	TOTAL AID TO EDUCATION			TOTAL AID TO BASIC EDUCATION			TOTAL AID TO BASIC EDUCATION PER PRIMARY SCHOOL-AGE CHILD			DIRECT AID TO EDUCATION			DIRECT AID TO BASIC EDUCAT...	
	CONSTANT 2014 US$ MILLIONS			CONSTANT 2014 US$ MILLIONS			CONSTANT 2014 US$			CONSTANT 2014 US$ MILLIONS			CONSTANT 2014 US$ MILLI...	
	2002–2003 annual average	2013	2014	2002–2003 annual average	2013	2014	2002–2003 annual average	2013	2014	2002–2003 annual average	2013	2014	2002–2003 annual average	2013
Uganda	222	122	126	156	47	40	29	6	5	190	122	120	109	43
Zambia	134	55	77	84	34	47	38	12	15	92	45	72	46	18
Zimbabwe	14	59	62	6	44	44	2	16	16	14	59	62	4	37
Overseas territories**	**247**	**75**	**72**	**123**	**25**	**24**	**2,198**	**7,180**	**7,262**	**241**	**71**	**69**	**1**	**12**
Anguilla (UK)	1	1	-	0	0	-	...	...	...	1	0	-	-	0
Mayotte (France)	173	-	-	86	-	-	...	...	...	173	-	-	-	-
Montserrat (UK)	5	4	3	3	2	1	6,525	...	...	0	2	2	0	0
Saint Helena (UK)	0	1	1	0	0	0	...	...	...	0	1	1	-	0
Tokelau (New Zealand)	6	2	2	3	1	1	13,883	7,180	7,262	5	-	0	0	-
Turks and Caicos Islands (UK)	1	-	-	1	-	-	242	...	...	1	-	-	1	-
Wallis and Futuna (France)	61	67	66	31	21	22	...	...	...	61	67	66	-	12
Unallocated by region or country	*482*	*1,329*	*1,528*	*72*	*607*	*705*	*...*	*...*	*...*	*481*	*1,324*	*1,528*	*35*	*471*
Total	**7,516**	**13,646**	**13,055**	**3,047**	**5,585**	**5,330**	**5**	**9**	**9**	**6,427**	**11,720**	**12,320**	**1,860**	**3,070**
Low income countries	1,786	2,831	2,810	1,029	1,488	1,509	14	15	15	1,352	2,468	2,487	631	832
Lower middle income countries	3,048	6,133	5,504	1,368	2,658	2,267	5	9	7	2,578	4,702	5,256	934	1,305
Upper middle income countries	1,669	2,620	2,655	346	660	694	2	4	4	1,495	2,519	2,511	183	367
High income countries	327	173	158	138	52	41	10	4	3	320	167	154	7	22
Unallocated by income	685	1,888	1,927	167	727	818	...	...	...	682	1,865	1,912	105	544
Total	**7,516**	**13,646**	**13,055**	**3,047**	**5,585**	**5,330**	**5**	**10**	**9**	**6,427**	**11,720**	**12,320**	**1,860**	**3,070**
Caucasus and Central Asia	94	239	213	30	45	47	5	9	9	59	224	208	8	15
Europe and Northern America	195	426	503	68	54	110				184	422	411	38	19
Eastern and South-eastern Asia	869	2,104	1,601	164	644	420	1	4	3	825	1,624	1,562	97	174
Latin America and the Caribbean	575	899	882	224	330	306	5	8	8	554	882	866	169	203
Northern Africa and Western Asia	1,071	2,731	2,108	216	1,179	889	5	25	20	912	2,002	1,948	99	630
Pacific	221	269	228	84	106	105	73	68	66	180	225	226	32	44
Southern Asia	953	2,178	2,687	589	967	1,234	3	5	7	766	2,092	2,660	457	606
Sub-Saharan Africa	2,810	3,395	3,233	1,478	1,627	1,489	13	11	10	2,224	2,854	2,841	922	896
Overseas territories	247	75	72	123	25	24	...	...	...	241	71	69	1	12
Unallocated by region or country	482	1,329	1,528	72	607	705	...	...	...	481	1,324	1,528	35	471
Total	**7,516**	**13,646**	**13,055**	**3,047**	**5,585**	**5,330**	**5**	**10**	**9**	**6,427**	**11,720**	**12,320**	**1,860**	**3,070**

Source: OECD-DAC CRS database (2014).

* Aid disbursement figures for 2002–2003 refer to the former Sudan, before the separation of the South in 2011. Aid disbursements for 2011 onwards have been separated out by the OECD and refer to Sudan and South Sudan.

** As defined on the OECD-DAC list of ODA recipients.

(…) indicates that data are not available, (-) represents a nil value

The share of education in total ODA does not match that in Table 2 because the DAC database is used for donors and the CRS database for recipients in total ODA figures.

Malta and Slovenia are not listed in the table because they were removed from the OECD-DAC list of ODA recipients in 2005. However, the aid they received in 2002–2003 is included in the totals.

The classification by income is based on the World Bank list as of July 2014.

All data represent gross disbursements.

DIRECT AID TO SECONDARY EDUCATION (CONSTANT 2014 US$ MILLIONS)			DIRECT AID TO POST-SECONDARY EDUCATION (CONSTANT 2014 US$ MILLIONS)			DIRECT AID TO EDUCATION, LEVEL UNSPECIFIED (CONSTANT 2014 US$ MILLIONS)			SHARE OF EDUCATION IN TOTAL ODA (%)			SHARE OF DIRECT AID TO EDUCATION IN SECTOR-ALLOCABLE ODA (%)			SHARE OF BASIC EDUCATION IN TOTAL AID TO EDUCATION (%)		
2002-2003 annual average	2013	2014	2002-2003 annual average	2013	2014	2002-2003 annual average	2013	2014	2002-2003 annual average	2013	2014	2002-2003 annual average	2013	2014	2002-2003 annual average	2013	2014
6	60	65	13	11	13	62	8	11	19	7	7	25	7	7	70	39	31
4	1	2	9	3	3	33	23	48	10	5	7	15	4	7	62	62	61
0	5	8	5	5	5	4	12	11	6	7	8	10	8	9	44	73	71
1	37	35	1	1	1	238	20	20	64	22	25	69	22	25	50	33	34
0	-	-	0	-	-	0	-	-	23	12	...	23	1	...	18	50	...
-	-	-	0	-	-	172	-	-	76	...	...	77	...	...	50	...	...
-	0	0	0	0	0	-0	2	1	10	6	7	1	5	5	52	46	43
0	0	-	-	0	0	0	1	1	7	1	0	7	1	0	6	32	47
-	-	-	1	-	-	4	-	-	52	8	11	68	-	0	49	50	51
-	-	-	-	-	-	-	-	-	19	...	...	19	...	...	100	...	...
-	37	35	0	1	0	61	18	18	75	63	66	75	64	67	50	32	33
9	144	163	365	443	456	71	265	407	5	4	5	10	9	10	15	46	46
73	1,520	1,818	2,809	4,025	3,980	1,286	3,105	3,119	9	8	8	14	10	10	41	41	41
37	325	371	271	361	381	363	951	774	8	8	8	13	9	9	58	53	54
20	773	1,005	1,026	1,349	1,442	397	1,275	1,331	10	9	9	14	10	11	45	43	41
37	190	191	1,024	1,477	1,452	151	485	493	10	12	11	15	12	12	21	25	26
8	45	48	51	48	44	255	52	45	36	25	19	43	26	19	42	30	26
20	187	204	436	791	660	120	343	476	5	5	4	10	8	8	24	38	42
73	1,520	1,818	2,809	4,025	3,980	1,286	3,105	3,119	9	8	8	14	10	10	41	41	41
8	43	23	35	121	114	8	45	52	5	9	8	5	9	8	32	19	22
28	28	29	69	309	272	49	66	92	4	9	9	8	9	9	35	13	22
6	152	170	563	846	814	90	457	364	9	10	10	14	12	12	19	31	26
5	99	107	221	342	333	89	239	255	8	8	8	12	9	9	39	37	35
68	171	164	677	832	803	73	374	355	13	10	8	20	12	11	20	43	42
9	23	17	66	77	65	63	82	81	19	13	13	20	13	13	38	40	46
7	410	655	176	431	505	76	638	551	8	11	13	11	12	14	62	44	46
42	412	454	637	623	617	526	918	943	9	7	7	15	8	8	53	48	46
1	37	35	1	1	1	238	20	20	64	22	25	69	22	25	50	33	34
9	144	163	365	443	456	71	265	407	5	4	5	10	9	10	15	46	46
73	1,520	1,818	2,809	4,025	3,980	1,286	3,105	3,119	9	8	8	14	10	10	41	41	41

TABLE 4

ODA recipients

	TOTAL ODA			PER CAPITA ODA			SECTOR-ALLOCABLE ODA			DEBT RELIEF AND OTHER ACTIONS RELATED TO DEBT		
	CONSTANT 2014 US$ MILLIONS			CONSTANT 2014 US$			CONSTANT 2014 US$ MILLIONS			CONSTANT 2014 US$ MILLIONS		
	2002–2003 annual average	2013	2014	2002–2003 annual average	2013	2014	2002–2003 annual average	2013	2014	2002–2003 annual average	2013	2014
Caucasus and Central Asia	**1,879**	**2,809**	**2,727**	**26**	**35**	**33**	**1,144**	**2,589**	**2,584**	**6**	**-**	**-**
Unallocated within the region	-	221	210	...	...	...	-	214	197	-	-	-
Armenia	338	326	309	111	109	103	246	273	291	-	-	-
Azerbaijan	352	272	268	42	29	28	159	267	264	-	-	-
Georgia	345	714	676	75	172	165	237	642	622	-	-	-
Kazakhstan	224	135	93	15	8	5	141	131	90	-	-	-
Kyrgyzstan	212	388	402	42	69	70	143	338	379	6	-	-
Tajikistan	171	399	370	26	50	46	82	376	353	-	-	-
Turkmenistan	26	24	26	6	5	5	13	23	25	-	-	-
Uzbekistan	211	331	373	8	12	13	123	326	362	-	-	-
Europe and Northern America	**4,387**	**4,971**	**5,790**	**50**	**59**	**69**	**2,245**	**4,549**	**4,733**	**1,177**	**1**	**17**
Unallocated within the region	627	1,482	1,496	...	...	...	307	1,154	1,188	33	-	-
Albania	400	326	354	128	113	123	305	293	315	-	-	-
Belarus	-	104	119	-	11	13	-	102	114	-	-	-
Bosnia and Herzegovina	536	583	706	141	152	185	382	571	617	7	1	1
Croatia	145	-	-	33	-	-	99	-	-	-	-	-
Montenegro	5	133	148	9	213	236	5	129	120	-	-	17
Republic of Moldova	146	353	551	35	87	135	106	342	535	1	-	-
Serbia	2,223	966	724	239	108	81	806	948	652	1,137	-	-
TFYR Macedonia	295	257	293	145	124	141	225	253	290	0	-	-
Ukraine	-	767	1,399	-	17	31	-	759	901	-	-	-
Eastern and South-eastern Asia	**10,014**	**20,706**	**15,571**	**5**	**10**	**8**	**6,059**	**13,566**	**12,957**	**373**	**3,663**	**1,175**
Unallocated within the region	177	592	679	...	...	...	112	536	588	-	-	-
Cambodia	484	853	854	38	57	57	368	835	825	-	1	-
China	2,500	1,713	1,389	2	1	1	1,842	1,633	1,354	-	-	-
DPR Korea	191	78	88	8	3	4	76	43	60	-	-	-
Indonesia	2,023	2,334	2,104	9	9	8	972	1,912	1,997	347	9	32
Lao PDR	276	451	488	50	70	74	231	427	451	2	-	-
Malaysia	185	186	144	8	6	5	46	179	126	-	-	-
Mongolia	218	469	358	89	167	125	150	449	344	-	-	-
Myanmar	111	7,302	2,125	2	139	40	67	1,521	794	14	3,650	1,136
Philippines	1,180	1,019	1,544	14	11	16	424	653	940	9	3	6
Thailand	766	822	628	12	12	9	355	755	569	-	-	-
Timor-Leste	268	249	246	294	226	218	229	244	232	-	-	-
Viet Nam	1,634	4,639	4,923	20	51	54	1,186	4,379	4,676	0	0	0
Latin America and the Caribbean	**7,208**	**11,518**	**11,339**	**13**	**19**	**18**	**4,764**	**9,747**	**9,867**	**707**	**31**	**19**
Unallocated within the region	607	2,594	2,348	...	...	...	423	1,579	1,483	1	-	-
Antigua and Barbuda	7	3	2	83	29	23	7	2	2	-	0	-
Argentina	110	82	81	3	2	2	70	76	79	6	2	-
Aruba	...	...	...	...	...	...	-	-	-	-	-	-
Barbados	3	-	-	11	-	-	2	-	-	-	-	-
Belize	13	50	35	47	149	103	8	44	32	3	0	0
Bolivia, P.S.	1,144	728	714	131	71	69	621	705	700	392	-	-
Brazil	422	1,339	1,132	2	7	6	245	1,320	1,116	-	4	1
Chile	77	94	260	5	5	15	69	85	255	1	-	-
Colombia	832	904	1,282	20	19	27	728	816	1,205	0	0	0
Costa Rica	64	74	84	16	16	18	46	67	79	-	5	1
Cuba	79	102	104	7	9	9	65	88	91	-	-	5
Dominica	15	24	19	212	331	259	11	16	16	-	-	-
Dominican Republic	183	211	231	21	21	23	119	193	217	-	-	-
Ecuador	308	226	228	23	15	15	227	207	205	10	-	-
El Salvador	239	231	158	41	38	26	130	192	137	4	1	1
Grenada	11	15	40	107	138	378	11	12	17	-	-	-
Guatemala	335	550	323	27	36	21	253	519	291	-	0	0
Guyana	90	118	168	121	156	221	57	117	165	17	-	-
Haiti	202	1,140	1,058	23	111	101	139	858	847	1	1	1
Honduras	430	659	676	65	85	86	237	621	638	59	1	-
Jamaica	114	130	125	43	47	45	69	96	120	11	6	0
Mexico	222	790	940	2	6	8	212	782	932	0	-	-
Nicaragua	708	519	460	136	88	77	376	482	434	179	1	-
Panama	46	52	38	14	14	10	35	47	35	5	0	0
Paraguay	94	185	136	17	29	21	54	179	133	-	0	0
Peru	685	527	519	26	17	17	408	491	477	13	8	9
Saint Kitts and Nevis	5	15	-	101	287	-	5	9	-	-	-	-
Saint Lucia	17	27	17	107	151	92	17	26	11	-	-	-
Saint Vincent and the Grenadines	7	12	10	68	105	88	5	8	6	3	-	-
Suriname	41	32	14	84	60	26	38	31	13	-	-	-
Trinidad and Tobago	6	-	-	4	-	-	5	-	-	0	-	-
Uruguay	17	46	97	5	13	28	15	44	96	2	-	-
Venezuela, B.R.	77	39	40	3	1	1	59	36	35	-	-	-
Northern Africa and Western Asia	**8,023**	**26,282**	**26,293**	**23**	**63**	**62**	**4,501**	**17,017**	**17,520**	**455**	**142**	**99**
Unallocated within the region	164	1,450	1,361	...	...	...	102	800	796	2	0	2
Algeria	264	319	254	8	9	7	170	280	229	-	-	-
Bahrain	1	-	-	1	-	-	1	-	-	-	-	-
Egypt	1,678	5,937	4,490	23	69	51	1,021	2,576	2,480	187	131	97
Iraq	1,450	1,487	1,343	57	45	39	784	1,329	758	-	-	-
Jordan	1,039	1,618	2,897	208	231	401	331	1,001	1,459	68	-	-
Lebanon	138	775	961	38	157	182	104	496	581	-	-	-
Libya	-	142	198	-	23	32	-	130	130	-	-	-
Morocco	803	2,590	2,794	27	79	84	532	2,541	2,759	179	9	-

TABLE 4
ODA recipients (Continued)

	TOTAL ODA			PER CAPITA ODA			SECTOR-ALLOCABLE ODA			DEBT RELIEF AND OTHER ACTIONS RELATED TO DEBT		
	CONSTANT 2014 US$ MILLIONS			CONSTANT 2014 US$			CONSTANT 2014 US$ MILLIONS			CONSTANT 2014 US$ MILLIONS		
	2002–2003 annual average	2013	2014	2002–2003 annual average	2013	2014	2002–2003 annual average	2013	2014	2002–2003 annual average	2013	2014
Oman	5	-	-	2	-	-	5	-	-	-	-	-
Palestine	635	2,518	2,411	186	586	546	472	1,826	1,661	-	0	-
Saudi Arabia	5	-	-	0	-	-	5	-	-	-	-	-
Sudan*	423	1,556	928	14	41	24	107	541	443	5	1	0
Syrian Arab Republic	112	2,041	1,901	7	102	98	76	309	294	1	-	-
Tunisia	432	1,045	1,101	44	96	100	292	973	900	-	0	0
Turkey	525	3,624	4,366	8	48	57	266	3,444	4,160	-	-	-
Yemen	348	1,181	1,287	18	47	50	234	772	868	14	1	-
Pacific	**1,186**	**2,031**	**1,815**	**153**	**215**	**189**	**892**	**1,731**	**1,719**	**1**	**0**	**-**
Unallocated within the region	85	262	236	...	...	...	68	227	204	-	-	-
Cook Islands	9	19	29	474	938	1,418	8	19	28	-	-	-
Fiji	51	89	93	63	102	106	40	83	89	-	-	-
Kiribati	28	63	80	315	593	733	27	63	79	-	-	-
Marshall Islands	66	97	58	1,261	1,834	1,095	10	25	52	-	-	-
Micronesia, F.S.	136	145	119	1,270	1,405	1,148	21	30	116	-	-	-
Nauru	29	27	22	2,909	2,699	2,169	4	27	21	-	-	-
Niue	13	18	14	7,409	11,416	8,436	7	12	7	-	-	-
Palau	31	34	23	1,554	1,654	1,114	14	21	23	-	-	-
Papua New Guinea	481	672	617	84	94	84	459	666	612	-	-	-
Samoa	53	125	101	297	664	528	51	101	88	-	0	-
Solomon Islands	110	279	205	250	508	366	95	269	194	1	-	-
Tonga	32	82	82	319	781	781	29	76	72	-	-	-
Tuvalu	12	26	35	1,289	2,671	3,530	11	23	33	-	-	-
Vanuatu	51	91	102	258	368	403	46	88	100	0	0	-
Southern Asia	**12,145**	**19,254**	**20,871**	**8**	**11**	**12**	**6,825**	**17,115**	**19,059**	**1,344**	**43**	**25**
Unallocated within the region	443	958	1,048	...	...	...	231	715	812	-	-	-
Afghanistan	1,545	5,179	4,826	70	174	157	693	4,556	4,219	38	7	10
Bangladesh	1,515	3,413	3,164	11	22	20	1,134	2,834	2,813	141	3	3
Bhutan	62	137	147	103	184	195	53	129	144	-	-	-
India	3,384	4,515	5,185	3	4	4	2,666	4,432	5,052	2	-	-
Iran, Islamic Republic of	146	127	131	2	2	2	96	111	112	-	-	-
Maldives	21	32	37	72	93	104	15	32	33	-	-	-
Nepal	483	1,041	1,040	20	38	37	409	996	1,010	13	1	1
Pakistan	3,846	2,990	4,343	26	17	24	1,115	2,541	3,966	1,142	31	11
Sri Lanka	699	863	951	37	42	46	413	768	897	8	-	-
Sub-Saharan Africa	**29,960**	**49,350**	**48,051**	**44**	**56**	**53**	**14,690**	**37,536**	**37,449**	**8,173**	**2,764**	**271**
Unallocated within the region	1,944	4,092	5,750	...	...	...	1,117	3,220	3,861	1	19	9
Angola	536	339	290	33	15	12	226	272	273	-	-	-
Benin	366	687	632	49	68	61	246	564	566	65	2	6
Botswana	51	127	116	28	59	53	39	125	115	2	1	0
Burkina Faso	679	1,107	1,177	54	67	69	426	819	944	70	10	10
Burundi	254	567	524	35	56	50	131	461	432	5	3	14
Cameroon	1,146	781	927	67	36	42	345	645	784	705	82	-
Cape Verde	141	268	257	308	535	507	114	191	221	0	0	0
Central African Republic	69	208	618	18	45	131	51	92	240	13	5	5
Chad	366	514	442	40	40	34	256	269	237	39	6	5
Comoros	38	176	76	65	240	100	33	59	69	3	103	2
Congo	111	178	127	34	42	29	61	121	99	26	43	0
Côte d'Ivoire	1,137	2,103	1,219	66	100	56	316	444	637	582	1,356	2
D. R. Congo	4,766	2,634	2,487	92	37	34	699	1,981	1,816	3,390	138	145
Djibouti	97	162	178	129	190	206	76	114	114	0	0	0
Equatorial Guinea	34	10	10	58	13	12	27	7	7	5	1	1
Eritrea	316	83	82	82	17	16	172	72	69	-	-	-
Ethiopia	1,841	3,937	3,639	26	43	38	1,013	3,047	2,932	119	2	0
Gabon	159	106	130	122	66	79	76	101	126	75	3	3
Gambia	75	124	109	56	69	59	56	101	99	6	0	0
Ghana	1,184	1,411	1,186	59	55	45	645	1,310	1,160	217	9	-
Guinea	358	655	588	39	56	49	232	277	404	55	324	5
Guinea-Bissau	142	106	113	103	62	64	58	88	82	65	12	4
Kenya	688	3,626	2,977	21	85	68	513	2,959	2,612	16	15	6
Lesotho	117	346	133	62	168	64	89	296	125	0	2	0
Liberia	99	535	755	32	128	176	20	450	562	8	1	-
Madagascar	690	655	627	41	29	27	439	450	460	125	175	2
Malawi	598	1,173	1,020	50	75	63	427	984	913	60	11	3
Mali	744	1,448	1,294	63	90	78	497	843	849	87	19	13
Mauritania	377	337	311	129	89	80	189	189	238	123	6	1
Mauritius	49	180	122	40	143	97	47	141	116	-	-	-
Mozambique	2,395	2,423	2,202	122	94	83	1,070	1,929	1,844	966	90	11
Namibia	152	306	273	77	133	116	135	287	268	-	-	-
Niger	527	808	947	43	46	52	264	471	568	122	7	6
Nigeria	413	2,695	2,613	3	16	15	343	2,654	2,548	27	-	-
Rwanda	478	1,101	1,036	55	102	93	281	1,002	1,007	38	2	1
Sao Tome and Principe	43	53	40	294	296	218	31	42	35	9	0	0
Senegal	688	1,054	1,190	65	76	84	542	859	1,072	89	11	10
Seychelles	7	30	15	78	315	155	7	30	14	-	-	-
Sierra Leone	493	530	929	109	88	150	189	344	434	90	97	-
Somalia	194	948	1,038	24	95	101	52	426	521	2	1	1
South Africa	556	1,473	1,312	12	28	25	489	1,381	1,295	-	-	-
South Sudan*	-	1,405	1,961	-	128	171	-	699	593	-	-	-
Swaziland	32	126	97	30	102	77	23	123	92	-	-	-

TABLE 4

ODA recipients (Continued)

	TOTAL ODA			PER CAPITA ODA			SECTOR-ALLOCABLE ODA			DEBT RELIEF AND OTHER ACTIONS RELATED TO DEBT		
	CONSTANT 2014 US$ MILLIONS			CONSTANT 2014 US$			CONSTANT 2014 US$ MILLIONS			CONSTANT 2014 US$ MILLIONS		
	2002–2003 annual average	2013	2014	2002–2003 annual average	2013	2014	2002–2003 annual average	2013	2014	2002–2003 annual average	2013	2014
Togo	84	228	237	16	34	34	57	179	218	15	4	4
U. R. Tanzania	1,951	3,637	2,710	54	75	54	1,059	2,871	2,507	392	203	1
Uganda	1,179	1,844	1,731	46	52	47	754	1,736	1,608	89	0	-
Zambia	1,356	1,157	1,042	120	78	68	622	1,085	1,003	471	0	0
Zimbabwe	246	858	762	19	59	51	138	727	662	-	-	-
Overseas territories**	385	346	289	1,723	1,189	969	352	319	272	1	-	-
Anguilla (UK)	3	8	-	252	576	-	3	0	-	-	-	-
Mayotte (France)	226	-	-	1,378	-	-	226	-	-	-	-	-
Montserrat (UK)	53	59	39	12,067	11,640	7,722	25	51	33	1	-	-
Saint Helena (UK)	6	148	131	1,344	36,218	32,561	6	147	131	-	-	-
Tokelau (New Zealand)	11	25	19	8,187	21,187	15,646	8	15	9	-	-	-
Turks and Caicos Islands (UK)	3	-	-	118	-	-	3	-	-	-	-	-
Wallis and Futuna (France)	82	107	100	5,676	7,993	7,526	82	106	100	-	-	-
Unallocated by region or country	10,040	29,712	32,730	...	...	...	4,630	14,781	15,278	8	95	66
Total	85,226	166,979	165,476	17	29	28	46,102	118,950	121,437	12,245	6,738	1,671
Low income countries	21,850	36,682	35,603	48	62	59	10,304	28,228	27,596	5,876	1,224	249
Lower middle income countries	31,754	65,490	59,130	13	23	21	18,152	46,345	48,207	4,976	5,367	1,307
Upper middle income countries	16,622	22,744	24,048	8	10	10	9,909	20,510	20,432	1,335	30	38
High income countries	912	703	836	8	5	6	748	641	795	14	4	1
Unallocated by income	14,088	41,361	45,858	...	...	...	6,990	23,226	24,407	44	114	76
Total	85,226	166,979	165,476	17	29	28	46,102	118,950	121,437	12,245	6,738	1,671
CCA	1,879	2,809	2,727	26	35	33	1,144	2,589	2,584	6	-	-
ENA	4,387	4,971	5,790	50	59	69	2,245	4,549	4,733	1,177	1	17
ESEA	10,014	20,706	15,571	5	10	8	6,059	13,566	12,957	373	3,663	1,175
LAC	7,208	11,518	11,339	13	19	18	4,764	9,747	9,867	707	31	19
NAWA	8,023	26,282	26,293	23	63	62	4,501	17,017	17,520	455	142	99
P	1,186	2,031	1,815	153	215	189	892	1,731	1,719	1	0	-
SA	12,145	19,254	20,871	8	11	12	6,825	17,115	19,059	1,344	43	25
SSA	29,960	49,350	48,051	44	56	53	14,690	37,536	37,449	8,173	2,764	271
Overseas territories	385	346	289	1,723	1,189	969	352	319	272	1	-	-
Unallocated by region or country	10,040	29,712	32,730	...	...	...	4,630	14,781	15,278	8	95	66
Total	85,226	166,979	165,476	17	29	28	46,102	118,950	121,437	12,245	6,738	1,671

Source: OECD-DAC CRS database (2014).

* Aid disbursement figures for 2002–2003 refer to the former Sudan, before the separation of the South in 2011. Aid disbursements for 2011 onwards have been separated out by the OECD and refer to Sudan and South Sudan.

** As defined on the OECD-DAC list of ODA recipients.

(...) indicates that data are not available, (-) represents a nil value

The share of education in total ODA does not match that in Table 2 because the DAC database is used for donors and the CRS database for recipients in total ODA figures.

Malta and Slovenia are not listed in the table because they were removed from the OECD-DAC list of ODA recipients in 2005. However, the aid they received in 2002–2003 is included in the totals.

The classification by income is based on the World Bank list as of July 2014.

All data represent gross disbursements.

Glossary

Adjusted net enrolment ratio (ANER). Enrolment of the official age group for a given level of education either at that level or the levels above, expressed as a percentage of the population in that age group.

Adult literacy rate. Number of literate persons aged 15 and above, expressed as a percentage of the total population in that age group.

Age-specific enrolment ratio (ASER). Enrolment of a given age or age group, regardless of the level of education in which pupils or students are enrolled, expressed as a percentage of the population of the same age or age group.

Child or under-5 mortality rate. Probability of dying between birth and the fifth birthday, expressed per 1,000 live births.

Completion rate by level. Percentage of children aged three to five years older than the official age of entry into the last grade of an education level who have reached the last grade of that level. For example, the primary attainment rate in a country with a 6-year cycle where the official age of entry into the last grade is 11 years is the percentage of 14 -16 year olds who have reached grade 6.

Conflict affected country. For a given year, any country with 1,000 or more battle-related deaths (including fatalities among civilians and military actors) over the preceding 10-year period and/or more than 200 battle-related deaths in any one year over the preceding 3-year period, according to the Uppsala Conflict Data Program Battle-Related Deaths Dataset.

Constant prices. Prices of a particular item adjusted to remove the overall effect of general price changes (inflation) since a given baseline year.

Dropout rate by grade. Percentage of students who drop out of a given grade in a given school year.

Early childhood care and education (ECCE). Services and programmes that support children's survival, growth, development and learning – including health, nutrition and hygiene, and cognitive, social, emotional and physical development – from birth to entry into primary school.

Early Childhood Development Index (ECDI). Index of fulfilment of developmental potential that assesses children aged 36-59 months in four domains: literacy/numeracy, physical, socio-emotional, and cognitive development. The information is collected through the UNICEF Multiple Indicators Cluster Surveys. A child is 'on track' overall if it is 'on track' in at least three of the four domains.

Education levels according to the International Standard Classification of Education (ISCED), which is the classification system designed to serve as an instrument for assembling, compiling and presenting comparable indicators and statistics of education both within countries and internationally. The system, introduced in 1976, was revised in 1997 and 2011.

■ Pre-primary education (ISCED level 0). Programmes at the initial stage of organized instruction, primarily designed to introduce very young children, aged at least 3 years, to a school-type environment and provide a bridge between home and school. Variously referred to as infant education, nursery education, pre-school education, kindergarten or early childhood education, such programmes are the more formal component of ECCE. Upon completion of these programmes, children continue their education at ISCED 1 (primary education).

■ Primary education (ISCED level 1). Programmes generally designed to give pupils a sound basic education in reading, writing and mathematics, and an elementary understanding of subjects such as history, geography, natural sciences, social sciences, art and music.

■ Secondary education (ISCED levels 2 and 3). Programmes made up of two stages: lower and upper secondary. Lower secondary education (ISCED 2) is generally designed to continue the basic programmes of the primary level but the teaching is typically more subject- focused, requiring more specialized teachers for each subject area. The end of this level often coincides with the end of compulsory education. In upper secondary education (ISCED 3), the final stage of secondary education in most countries, instruction is often organized even more along subject lines and teachers typically need a higher or more subject-specific qualification than at ISCED level 2.

- Post-secondary non-tertiary education (ISCED level 4). It provides learning experiences building on secondary education, preparing for labour market entry as well as tertiary education.

- Tertiary education (ISCED levels 5-8): It builds on secondary education, providing learning activities in specialized fields of education. It aims at learning at a high level of complexity and specialization. It comprises:

  - Level 5: Short-cycle tertiary education, often designed to provide participants with professional knowledge, skills and competencies. It is practically based, occupationally-specific and prepares students to enter the labour market.

  - Level 6: Bachelor's, often designed to provide participants with intermediate academic and/or professional knowledge, skills and competencies, leading to a first degree or equivalent qualification.

  - Level 7: Master's or equivalent level, often designed to provide participants with advanced academic and/or professional knowledge, skills and competencies, leading to a second degree or equivalent qualification.

  - Level 8: Doctoral or equivalent level, designed primarily to lead to an advanced research qualification.

Education for Sustainable Development (ESD). A type of education that aims to enable learners to constructively and creatively address present and future global challenges and create more sustainable and resilient societies.

Global Citizenship Education (GCED). A type of education that aims to empower learners to assume active roles to face and resolve global challenges and to become proactive contributors to a more peaceful, tolerant, inclusive and secure world.

Gross domestic product (GDP). The value of all final goods and services produced in a country in one year (see also Gross national product).

Gross enrolment ratio (GER). Total enrolment in a specific level of education, regardless of age, expressed as a percentage of the population in the official age group corresponding to this level of education. The GER can exceed 100% because of early or late entry and/or grade repetition.

Gross intake rate (GIR). Total number of new entrants to a given grade of primary education, regardless of age, expressed as a percentage of the population at the official school entrance age for that grade.

Gross national income (GNI). The value of all final goods and services produced in a country in one year (gross domestic product) plus income that residents have received from abroad, minus income claimed by non-residents.

Gross national product (GNP). Former denomination of gross national income.

Information and communications technology (ICT) skills. Individuals possess such skills if they have undertaken certain computer-related activities in the last three months: copying or moving a file or folder; using copy and paste tools to duplicate or move information within a document; sending e-mails with attached files (e.g. document, picture, video); using basic arithmetic formulae in a spreadsheet; connecting and installing new devices (e.g. a modem, camera, printer); finding, downloading, installing and configuring software; creating electronic presentations with presentation software (including text, images, sound, video or charts); transferring files between a computer and other devices; and writing a computer program using a specialized programming language.

Literacy. According to UNESCO's 1958 definition, the term refers to the ability of an individual to read and write with understanding a simple short statement related to his/her everyday life. The concept of literacy has since evolved to embrace several skill domains, each conceived on a scale of different mastery levels and serving different purposes.

Net attendance rate (NAR). Number of pupils in the official age group for a given level of education who attend school at that level, expressed as a percentage of the population in that age group.

Net enrolment ratio (NER). Enrolment of the official age group for a given level of education, expressed as a percentage of the population in that age group.

Net intake rate (NIR). New entrants to the first grade of primary education who are of the official primary school entrance age, expressed as a percentage of the population of that age.

New entrants. Pupils entering a given level of education for the first time; the difference between enrolment and repeaters in the first grade of the level.

Never been to school rate. Percentage of children aged three to five years older than the official entrance age into primary education who have never been to school. For example, in a country where the official entrance age is 6 years, the indicator is calculated over the age group 9 to 11 years.

Out-of-school adolescents and youth: Those of lower or upper secondary school age who are not enrolled either in primary, secondary, post-secondary non tertiary or tertiary education.

Out-of-school children. Children in the official primary school age range who are not enrolled in either primary or secondary school.

Over-age for grade rate. The percentage of pupils in each level of education (primary, lower secondary, and upper secondary) who are 2 years or more above the intended age for their grade.

Parity index. It is a measure of inequality defined as the ratio of the values of an education indicator of two population groups. Typically, the numerator is the value of the advantaged group and the denominator is the value of the advantaged group). An index value between 0.97 and 1.03 indicates parity. A value below 0.97 indicates a disparity in favour of the advantaged group. A GPI above 1.03 indicates a disparity in favour of the disadvantaged group. Groups can be defined by:

- Gender: Ratio of female to male values of a given indicator.

- Location. Ratio of rural to urban values of a given indicator.

- Wealth / income. Ratio of the poorest 20% to the richest 20% of a given indicator.

Private institutions. Institutions that are not operated by public authorities but are controlled and managed, whether for profit or not, by private bodies such as non-governmental organizations, religious bodies, special interest groups, foundations or business enterprises.

Public expenditure on education. Total current and capital expenditure on education by local, regional and national governments, including municipalities. Household contributions are excluded. The term covers public expenditure for both public and private institutions.

Pupil/teacher ratio (PTR). Average number of pupils per teacher at a specific level of education.

Pupil/qualified teacher ratio. Average number of pupils per qualified teacher at a specific level of education.

Pupil/trained teacher ratio (PTTR). Average number of pupils per trained teacher at a specific level of education.

Purchasing power parity (PPP). An exchange rate adjustment that accounts for price differences between countries, allowing international comparisons of real output and income.

Repetition rate by grade. Number of repeaters in a given grade in a given school year, expressed as a percentage of enrolment in that grade the previous school year.

School age population. Population of the age group officially corresponding to a given level of education, whether enrolled in school or not.

Skills. Non-innate capabilities that can be learned and transmitted, and have economic or social benefits both to individuals and their societies.

Technical and vocational education and training (TVET). Programmes designed mainly to prepare students for direct entry into a particular occupation or trade (or class of occupations or trades).

Transition rate to secondary education. New entrants to the first grade of secondary education in a given year, expressed as a percentage of the number of pupils enrolled in the final grade of primary education in the previous year. The indicator measures transition to secondary general education only.

Youth literacy rate. Number of literate persons aged 15 to 24, expressed as a percentage of the total population in that age group.

Abbreviations

AAPS	Association of African Planning Schools
AES	Adult Education Survey
AHELO	Assessment of Higher Education Learning Outcomes
AIDS	Acquired immunodeficiency syndrome
ALLS	Adult Literacy and Lifeskills Survey
ASER	Annual Status of Education Report (India, Pakistan)
ATM	Automatic teller machine
BADEA	Banque Arabe pour le Développement Economique en Afrique
BRAC	(formerly) Bangladesh Rural Advancement Committee
BRN	Big Results Now (United Republic of Tanzania)
BRT	Bus rapid transit
CALOHEE	Measuring and Comparing Achievements of Learning Outcomes in Higher Education in Europe
CAPIEMP	Certificat d'Aptitudes Pédagogiques d'Instituteur de l'Enseignement Maternel et Primaire (Cameroon)
CEDAW	Convention on the Elimination of all forms of Discrimination Against Women
CGS-LGA	Conditional Grants Scheme to Local Government Areas (Nigeria)
CLASS	Classroom Assessment Scoring System
CLTS	Community-led total sanitation
COP21	21st Conference of the Parties to the UN Framework Convention on Climate Change
CRS	Creditor Reporting System (OECD)
CSO	Civil society organization
DAC	Development Assistance Committee (OECD)
DFID	Department for International Development (United Kingdom)
DHS	Demographic and Health Survey
EAP-CDS	East Asia Pacific Child Development Scales
ECCE	Early childhood care and education
ECDI	Early Childhood Development Index
ECERS	Early Childhood Environment Rating Scale
ECERS-R	Early Childhood Environment Rating Scale Revised in 1998
ECERS3	Early Childhood Environment Rating Scale Revised in 2015
EDI	EFA Development Index
EFA	Education for All
EGMA	Early Grade Mathematics Assessment
EGRA	Early Grade Reading Assessment

ENADE	Exame Nacional de Desempenho dos Estudantes
ESD	Education for sustainable development
EU	European Union
Eurostat	Statistical office of the European Union
F/M	Female/male
FAO	Food and Agriculture Organization of the United Nations
GCED	Global citizenship education
GDP	Gross domestic product
GEI	Gender-specific EFA Index
GEM Report	Global Education Monitoring Report
GER	Gross enrolment ratio
GET	Global Employment Trends (ILO)
GGA	Global Guidelines Assessment
GME	GET Model Extension (ILO)
GMR	Global Monitoring Report
GNI	Gross national income
GNLC	Global Network of Learning Cities
GNP	Gross national product
GPE	Global Partnership for Education
GPI	Gender parity index
GRALE	Global Report on Adult Learning and Education
GSHS	Global School-based Student Health Survey
HIV	Human immunodeficiency virus
HLPF	High-Level Political Forum on Sustainable Development
HRLS	Human Rights and Legal Aid Services
IAEG-SDGs	Inter-agency and Expert Group on SDG Indicators
IALS	International Adult Literacy Survey
IAR4D	Integrated Agricultural Research for Development
IBE	International Bureau of Education (UNESCO)
ICCA	Indigenous and Community-Conserved Areas
ICCS	International Civics and Citizen Survey
ICF	International Classification of Functioning, Disability and Health
ICILS	International Computer and Information Literacy Study
ICLEI	Local Governments for Local Sustainability
ICT	Information and communication technology
IDA	International Development Association (World Bank)
IDP	Internally displaced people
IEA	International Association for the Evaluation of Educational Achievement
IIEP	International Institute for Educational Planning (UNESCO)

ILO	International Labour Office/Organization
IMF	International Monetary Fund
INES	Indicators of Education Systems (OECD)
ISCED	International Standard Classification of Education
ISSA	International Step By Step Association
LAMP	Literacy Assessment and Monitoring Programme (UIS)
LEARNigeria	Let's Assess, Engage and Report Nigeria
LFS	Labour Force Survey (European Union)
LLECE	Laboratorio Latinoamericano de Evaluación de la Calidad de la Educación (Latin American Laboratory for Assessment of the Quality of Education)
MDG	Millennium Development Goal
MELQO	Measuring Early Learning Quality and Outcomes
MICS	Multiple Indicator Cluster Survey
MLA	Monitoring Learning Achievement
NALABE	National Assessment of Learning Achievement in Basic Education (Nigeria)
NEA	National education account
NEET	Not in education, employment or training
NER	Net enrolment ratio
NESLI	Network for System-Level Indicators (OECD, INES)
NGO	Non-government organization
ODA	Official development assistance
OECD	Organisation for Economic Co-operation and Development
OHCHR	Office of the United Nations High Commissioner for Human Rights
OWG	Open Working Group
PAL	People's Action for Learning
PASEC	Programme d'Analyse des Systèmes Educatifs de la CONFEMEN (Programme of Analysis of Education Systems of the CONFEMEN – Conference of Education Ministers of Countries Using French as a Common Language)
PCEP	Pacific Islands Climate Education Partnership
PEFA	Public Expenditure and Accountability
PEPFAR	President's Emergency Plan For AIDS Relief (United States)
PIAAC	Programme for the International Assessment of Adult Competencies (OECD)
PIRLS	Progress in International Reading Literacy Study
PISA	Programme for International Student Assessment (OECD)
PPP	Purchasing power parity
PRIDI	Regional Project on Child Development Indicators
RCE	Regional Center of Expertise
R&D	Research and development
SABER	Systems Approach for Better Education Results (World Bank)

SACMEQ	Southern and Eastern Africa Consortium for Monitoring Educational Quality
SDG	Sustainable Development Goal
SDI	Shack/Slum Dwellers International
SERCE	Segundo Estudio Regional Comparativo y Explicativo (Second Regional Comparative and Explanatory Study)
SIGI	Social Institutions and Gender Index
SNA	System of National Accounts (United Nations)
STEM	Science, technology, engineering and mathematics
STEP	Skills Toward Employment and Productivity (World Bank)
SULITEST	Sustainability Literacy Test (United Nations)
TALIS	Teaching and Learning International Survey (OECD)
TEDS-M	Teacher Education and Development Study in Mathematics
TERCE	Tercer Estudio Regional Comparativo y Explicativo (Third Regional Comparative and Explanatory Study)
TIMSS	Trends in International Mathematics and Science Study
TVET	Technical and vocational education and training
UCLG	United Cities and Local Governments
UIL	UNESCO Institute for Lifelong Learning
UIS	UNESCO Institute for Statistics
UK	United Kingdom
UN	United Nations
UNAIDS	Joint United Nations Programme on HIV/AIDS
UNDP	United Nations Development Programme
UNESCO	United Nations Educational, Scientific and Cultural Organization
UNGEI	United Nations Girls' Education Initiative
UNICEF	United Nations Children's Fund
UNPD	United Nations Population Division
UNSC	United Nations Statistical Commission
UNU-IAS	United Nations University Institute for the Advanced Study of Sustainability
UOE	UIS/OECD/Eurostat
US	United States
USAID	United States Agency for International Development
WEF	World Education Forum
WEI	World Education Indicators
WFP	World Food Programme (United Nations)
WHO	World Health Organization (United Nations)
WIDE	World Inequality Database on Education
WSSD	World Summit on Sustainable Development
WVS	World Values Survey

Index

This index covers the Introduction and Chapters 1 to 24. It is in word-by-word order which takes account of spaces, so 'teacher training' comes before 'teachers''. Page numbers in italics indicate figures and tables; those in **bold** refer to material in boxes and panels; ***bold italics*** indicates a figure or table in a box or panel..

Subheadings are arranged alphabetically by the significant term, ignoring prepositions and insignificant words (e.g. 'effect on achievement' is alphabetized as 'achievement').

Definitions of terms can be found in the glossary, and additional information on countries can be found in the aid tables and statistical annex.

see also traditional knowledge
Curaçao, ICT facilities in schools *313*
Curitiba (Brazil), green city initiative *126–127*, **127**
curricula see school curricula
Cyberabad Development Authority (India) *119*
cyberbullying *315*
cycling, for urban sustainability **121**
cyclones **33**, *310*
Cyprus
    adult education *238*
    civic education *100*
    education expenditure *233, 234*
    household expenditure *233*
    human rights education *300*
    ICT facilities *314*
    political participation *100*
    primary education *187, 314*
    school completion *187*
    secondary education *187, 238, 314*
    socio-economic background and
        perseverance *249*
    special educational needs *266*
    student support *233, 234*
    tertiary education *229, 231, 233, 234, 238*
Czech Republic
    adult education *238*
    civic education *100*
    digital literacy skills *247, 247*
    early childhood care and education *331*
    education expenditure *233*
    environmental education *301*
    financial literacy *251*
    gender disparity *230*
    HIV education *292*
    household expenditure *233*
    human rights education *300*
    language of instruction *269*
    literacy *282*
    political participation *100*
    primary education completion *187*
    secondary education completion *187, 238*
    socio-economic background and
        perseverance *249*
    special educational needs *266*
    student support *233*
    teacher contracts *336*
    teacher education *331, 336*
    tertiary education *228, 229, 230, 233, 238*

D

Dalit children *108*
Dalit populations *68, 73*
data needs for education monitoring *383*
debt relief, application of aid to achieve MDGs
    141
decent work
    defined *55–56*, **55**, *244, 245*
    and educational attainment *58, 58, 88*
    see also employment; employment skills
Deer Leap programme (Georgia) *313*
deforestation *45*
    management by traditional communities *28*
democracies, regime change *101*
democracy, importance of education *101*
Democracy for All programme (South Africa) *102*
Democratic People's Republic of Korea
    home learning environment *215*
    literacy, numeracy and child development
        219
Democratic Republic of the Congo
    agriculture *47*
    attacks on schools *317*
    child development *219*
    civic education *98*
    early childhood care and education *213, 213*
    education expenditure *347*
    educational attainment *74, 186, 371*
    electricity provision *29–30, 86, 312*

equity improvement *352*
gender disparity *74, 74, 75*
gendered attitudes *264*
global citizenship education **290**, *294*
HIV education *292*
home learning environment *215*
internally displaced persons *272*
literacy *74, 75, 219, 281*
literacy programme participation *278*
malaria prevalence *371*
numeracy *219*
out-of-school children *182*
political participation *98*
pre-primary education *209*
primary education *182, 186, 312*
rural areas *74, 75*
school completion *186*
school curriculum **290**
secondary education *186, 312*
solar lighting project *29–30*
students abroad *323*
teaching methods **191**
tertiary education *231*
underweight children *80*
within country disparity *186, 231*
years of education *186*
Demographic and Health Survey (DHS) *263, 277*
Denmark
    adult education *238*
    aid donor *137*
    civic education *100*
    education expenditure *233*
    environmental concern *304*
    environmental education *301*
    gender disparity *230*
    household expenditure *233*
    human rights education *297, 300*
    ICT facilities *314*
    language of instruction *269*
    literacy *282*
    political participation *71, 100*
    primary education *186, 314*
    school completion *186*
    scientific researchers *372*
    secondary education *186, 238, 314, 338*
    socio-economic background and
        perseverance *249*
    special educational needs *266*
    student support *233*
    sustainable transport **121**
    teacher education *297*
    teacher salaries *337, 338*
    teacher skills **333**
    teaching methods **298**
    tertiary education *228, 229, 230, 232, 233, 238*
    women in politics *71*
deprivation see extreme poverty; inequality;
        marginalization; poverty; wealth
        disparities
desegregation of schools *123–124*
    see also integrated schools
deskilling of migrants *117–118*
developed countries
    employment and education *57*
    ethnic immigrant enclaves *124*
    food waste *45*
    gender disparity *60*
    listed *398*
    scholarship funding beneficiaries *320*
    water and sanitation provision *309*
    see also advanced economies; high income
        countries; OECD countries
developing countries
    economic growth *40*
    effect of educational attainment *55–56*
    employment *51, 56, 119–120*
    food waste *45*
    gender disparity *60*
    green industry development *41*
    ICT facilities *313*
    informal employment *119–120*

listed *398*
manufacturing *51*
scholarships *323*
'split site' university education *321*
students abroad *322, 322*
tax revenue *135*
teacher training requirements *333*
technological transfer *42–43*
tertiary education and political activism *100*
urban planning *125*
voter education campaigns *98, 99*
water and sanitation provision *309, 372*
working poverty *52*
see also emerging economies; least
    developed countries; low income
    countries; middle income countries;
    poorer countries; small island
    developing States
deworming campaigns *79, 85, 140*, **140**
DHS (Demographic and Health Survey) *263, 277*
difficulties category, OECD special needs
    monitoring *266*
digital literacy skills *246–247, 247*
    adaptation of monitoring to digital
        development *247*
    see also ICT skills
disabilities category, OECD special needs
    monitoring *266*
disability see people with disabilities
disadvantages category, OECD special needs
    monitoring *266*
disasters
    disaster preparedness *34, 157*
    GEM policy recommendations *164*
    risk reduction through education *157*
    see also conflict; conflict-affected areas;
        natural disasters
discrimination
    against girls in education *87, 87*
    against marginalized groups *72–73, 123*
    by teachers *123*
    elimination for social development *68*
    gender-biases legislation *87, 89*
    see also gender disparity; prejudice;
        stereotyping
disease
    from poor sanitation and hygiene *68*
    malaria reduction *371*
disparity see gender disparity; inequality; parity
        index
displaced persons
    due to conflict *106*
    urban populations *117*
    see also internally displaced persons;
        refugees
Displacement Tracking Matrix of the
    International Organization for
    Migration *272*
distance learning *232–233, 321, 322*
Djibouti
    educational attainment *74*
    gender disparity *74*
    global citizenship education *294*
    HIV education *292*
    out-of-school children *183*
    primary education *183, 335*
    secondary education *183*
    students abroad *323*
    teacher education *335, 336*
doctor/patient relationships, effect of education
    78
domestic abuse see intimate partner violence
domestic expenditure on education see
        education expenditure; public
        education expenditure
domestic resources for education *135–137*
    support from development aid *137–138*
domestic violence see intimate partner violence
domestic workers
    in economy *120*
    unpaid workers *89, 89*

role of education 61, 78, 88, 165
green energy
    consumer initiatives **31**
    education for 35, 78, 88
    renewable sources 35, 40–41
    solar lighting initiatives 29–30
green industries 40–43, **42**, 61–62
green revolution 44
Grenada
    electricity provision 313
    global citizenship education 294
    HIV education 292
    ICT facilities and internet access 313
    primary education 313
    secondary education 313
Grenadines *see* Saint Vincent and the Grenadines
Grit Scale 248–249
gross domestic product(GDP) *see* GDP
gross enrolment ratio
    pre-primary education 207, 208
    tertiary education 228, 229, 230–231
gross intake rate, survival to final grade 184
Gruma populations, educational attainment
    75, 76
Guatemala
    child health 82
    climate change 34
    conflict 104, 105
    curriculum 107
    early childhood care and education 212
    education expenditure 347
    educational attainment 74, 76, 105, 186
    electricity provision 313
    environmental education 26
    ethnic minorities 76, 102, 105
    gender disparity 74, 76
    global citizenship education 294, 300
    HIV education 292
    human rights education 300
    indigenous peoples 102, 105
    internet access 313
    language of instruction 104, 270
    literacy 82, 195
    mathematics achievement 195
    multicultural attitudes 304
    national assessments 200
    natural disasters 33
    out-of-school civic activities 26
    political participation 102
    primary education 34, 186, 195
    psychological bullying in schools 315
    reading proficiency 195
    rural areas 102
    school completion 34, 186
    school construction 310
    secondary education 34, 186
    teaching methods 102, 107
    tertiary education 231
    violence in schools 315
    within country disparity 76, 186, 231
    years of education 186
Guinea
    agriculture 136
    computer/pupil ratio 313, 314
    discrimination and secondary completion 87
    early childhood care and education 213, 213
    education expenditure 136, 347
    educational attainment 74, 82, 186, 280, 371
    electricity provision 312, 313
    female genital mutilation 82
    gender disparity 74, 74, 75, 87
    HIV education 292
    ICT facilities 314
    internet access 313
    literacy 74, 75, 281
    literacy programme participation 278
    malaria prevalence 371
    national education accounts 343
    out-of-school children 183
    primary education 183, 186, 280, 312, 314
    rural areas 74, 75
    school completion 87, 186

secondary education 87, 183, 186, 312, 314
tertiary education 228, 231
under-5 mortality rate 370, 371
within country disparity 186, 231
years of education 186
youth literacy 280
Guinea-Bissau
    child development 219
    early childhood care and education 210
    home learning environment 215
    literacy and numeracy 219
    primary education 335
    teacher induction 335
    within country disparity 210
Guyana
    child development 219
    early childhood care and education 210
    education expenditure 136
    educational attainment 74, 186
    gender disparity 74
    home learning environment 215
    literacy 195, 196, 219, 281
    literacy programme participation 278
    numeracy 219
    pre-primary education 209
    primary education 186, 196, 335
    reading proficiency 195, 196
    school completion 186
    secondary education 186
    students abroad 322
    teacher induction 335
    tertiary education 231
    within country disparity 186, 210, 231
    years of education 186

H

Haiti
    basic education 138
    climate change 34
    disaster preparedness 34
    education aid 138
    educational attainment 74, 81, 186
    gender disparity 74, 75
    global citizenship education 294
    HIV education 292
    integrated programmes **140**
    intimate partner violence 81
    late entry into primary education 183
    literacy 75, 281
    literacy programme participation 278
    natural disasters 33, 310
    over-age children 183, 184
    police training 110–111
    primary education 34, 183, 184, 186
    rural areas 75
    school completion 34, 186
    school health programmes **140**
    secondary education 34, 184, 186
    tertiary education 231
    underweight children 80
    within country disparity 184, 186, 231
    years of education 186
'handprint' programme (India) 26
handwashing facilities 308, 309
Harlem Children's Zone (United States) 125
Haussa populations, educational attainment
    75, 76
heads of schools, preparation and training 332,
    332
Health Behaviour in School-Aged Children
    Survey 315
health care
    aid 137, 138
    capacity building for crises 372
    community health workers 85, 372
    domestic resource mobilization 138
    effect of improvement 78, 84–85
    integrated approaches 77–80, 82–84, 85,
      140, **140**, 141

multistakeholder finance partnerships 147
national health accounts for financing 343,
    345
need for improved maternity provision 72
role of education 77–80, 87–88
school-based interventions 78–80, 85, 140,
    140
see also sanitation; water provision
health education 79, 165
    HIV/AIDS 79, 85, 87, 291, 292, 297
    need for educational campaigns 373
    sex education 79, **140**
health professionals, global employment 372
Herzegovina *see* Bosnia and Herzegovina
high income countries
    basic skills for economic growth 49
    child mortality rate 83
    childhood obesity 79, 80
    countries listed 399–400
    early childhood education quality 211
    ecological footprint 19, 21–22
    education aid disbursements 354
    education expenditure 136, 136, 234, **234**,
      239, 346, 346, 349
    education outcomes 68, 69
    educational attainment 59, 59, 75
    employment 49, 53, 53, 59, 59, 81
    gender disparity 81, 259, 262
    government incapacity for urban planning
      129
    gross intake rate 184
    health interventions 69
    household expenditure on education 234,
      234
    income inequality 53, 81
    intimate partner violence 82
    literacy 280
    literacy monitoring 280
    marginalized groups 75
    migrants 21, 271
    occupation and earnings 59
    out-of-school children 259
    parental gender attitudes 90
    population growth 20, 116
    primary completion rate 69, 184
    primary education 185, 259, 262
    pupil/teacher ratio and class size 328, 329
    school completion 184, 185, 259
    school meal policies 79
    secondary education 182, 182, 183, 184, 185,
      185, 259, 262
    teacher attrition 339
    tertiary education 229, 232, 234
    under-5 mortality 69
    wealth disparities 259
    working poverty 52
High Level Political Forums (HLPF) 2016 and
    2019 182, 386–387, 388
high skilled employment
    definition 50
    and educational level 59–60, 59
    effect on higher education 41
    green industry needs 41, **42**, 292
High-Level Political Forum on Sustainable
    Development 182
higher education
    and adolescent birth rate 370, 370
    disbursement of aid to scholarships abroad
      325, 325
    and gender-based violence 81, 82
    human rights education 290
    and knowledge of justice 110
    need to produce innovators 42
    scholarships 320–325
    see also post-secondary education; technical
      and vocational education and
      training (TVET); tertiary education
Higher Education for Sustainable Development
    initiative 27
history teaching, post conflict 107
HIV education 79, 87, 291, 292, 297
    see also AIDS epidemic

perseverance 249
tertiary education 231
within country disparity 186, 210, 231
years of education 186
Montserrat, electricity provision, ICT and internet access in schools 313
Morocco
  educational attainment 74, 186
  electricity provision 312
  equity improvement 351, **352**
  female literacy 83
  gender disparity 74
  literacy 83
  primary education 186, 312
  scholarship aid 324, 324
  school completion disparities 186
  secondary education 186, 312
  under-5 mortality rate 83
  violence in schools 316
  years of education 186
mortality
  children 68, 82, 83, 91, 156, 370–371, 371
  from disaster related deaths 157
  increased life expectancy through education 155, 156
mother tongue, and educational attainment 76
mother tongue instruction
  early childhood education 211
  in early education 267, 268–269, 268, 270
  effect in national learning assessments 202, 203
  monitoring 377
  segregated schools 107
  for traditional knowledge acquisition 28–29
  training for 164, 166
mothers
  effect of gender attitudes on children 90
  effect of maternal education 82–84, 85, 91, 165, 217
motor development, young children 216, 217
Mozambique
  adult education 240
  agriculture 46
  early childhood development 217
  education aid 138, 355
  education expenditure 347
  educational attainment 74, 81, 186, 371
  gender disparity 74, 75
  gender-based violence 81, 109
  health interventions **140**
  integrated programmes **140**
  intimate partner violence 81
  literacy 75, 281
  malaria prevalence 371
  national assessments 200
  out-of-school children 183
  over-age children 183
  primary education 183, 183, 186
  rural areas 75
  scholarships 321
  school completion 186
  secondary education 183, 186
  students abroad 323
  teacher absenteeism **191**
  teacher skills 198, **333**
  teaching methods **191**
  tertiary education 231
  violence in schools 316
  voter education 98
  within country disparity 186, 231
  years of education 186
multiculturalism
  attitudes towards 304
  extracurricular activities 299
multilateral aid mechanisms 137
multilingual education 269
  see also language of instruction; mother tongue instruction
Multiple Indicator Cluster Surveys (MICS) 196, **197**, 208, 209, **215**, 219, 257, 263, 278, 280
  Module on Child Functioning 267, 267

multisectoral aid programmes 144–145
multisectoral approaches see integrated approaches
municipal development plans, incorporation of SDGs 141
Muscat Declaration on EFA targets 180
Myanmar
  early childhood care and education 210
  education expenditure 346, 348, **348**
  electricity provision 312
  gender disparity 230
  income level 354
  national school census 309
  natural disasters 33
  out-of-school children 183
  pre-primary education 209
  primary education 183, 312
  secondary education 183, 312
  students abroad 323
  tertiary education 230
  within country disparity 210
MyWorld survey 6

N

NALABE **198**
Namibia
  basic education 138
  climate change education 34–35
  education aid 138
  educational attainment 74, 81, 186
  electricity provision 312
  gender disparity 74, 75
  global citizenship education 290, 294
  intimate partner violence 81
  literacy 75, 281
  pre-primary enrolment 207
  primary education 186, 312
  rural areas 75
  school completion 186
  secondary education 186, 312
  sexuality education 297
  teacher education 297
  teaching methods 102
  tertiary education 231
  textbooks 189
  within country disparity 186, 231
  years of education 186
National Assessment of Educational Progress (United States) 300
National Assessment of Learning Achievement in Basic Education (NALABE) **198**
national development plans
  incorporation of SDGs 141
  see also education planning; national plans
national education accounts 234, 342–346
  for monitoring 379
National Foundation for Education Research, citizenship education 299
National Geographic–Roper 2002 Global Geographic Literacy Survey 302–303
National Geographic–Roper Public Affairs 2006 Geographic Literacy Study 303
national indicators 181
national learning assessments 198–203, **198**, 199
  characteristics 198–199, 199
  citizen-led 196, **201**
  on environmental knowledge 301–302
  frameworks 200
  funding 201
  in inequality measurement 257
  monitoring 378, 380
  in mother tongue 202, 203
  organization and delivery 200
  primary education **198**
  quality 199–201
  reliability 360
national plans, implementation 80, 142–143, 147
national qualifications frameworks 142, 227
national reviews 387

National School Lunch Program (United States) 79
National Survey on Household Living Conditions and Agriculture (Niger) **279**
native language see mother tongue; mother tongue instruction
natural disasters
  disaster preparedness initiatives 34, 157
  education for resilience 157
  effects **33**, 273, 310
natural resources decline 22
nature conservation education 24, 25
Nauru
  violence in schools 316
neighbourhood management projects 125
Nepal
  adolescent birth rate 370
  child development 219
  child health 82
  climate change **33**
  conflict 104
  early childhood care and education 210, 213, 213
  education aid 355
  educational attainment 81, 186, 370
  electricity provision 86, 312, 313
  female literacy 83
  gender disparity 75, 230
  gender equality initiatives 92
  HIV education 292
  home learning environment 215
  internet access 313
  intimate partner violence 81
  language of instruction 104
  literacy 75, 82, 83, 196, 219, 281
  literacy programme participation 277, 278
  national education accounts 343, 344, 344, 345
  natural disasters 33, **33**, 310
  numeracy 219
  peacebuilding 108
  pre-primary education 209
  pregnancy education 84
  primary education 186, 187, 196, 312
  private education 187
  reading proficiency 196
  rural areas 75, 122
  school completion 186
  secondary education 186, 312
  students abroad 323
  tertiary education 229, 230
  TVET participation 224
  under-5 mortality rate 83
  underweight children 80
  urban areas 122
  wealth disparities 122
  within country disparity 186, 210
  years of education 186
NESLI 364, **364**
net enrolment ratio, pre-primary education 207–208, 208
Netherlands
  adult education 238
  education aid donor 355
  education expenditure 233
  education funding 351
  environmental education 301
  equity improvement 351, 352
  gender disparity 230
  household expenditure 233
  integrated interventions 125
  literacy 282
  parent governors 294
  primary education 187
  private education 232
  school completion 187
  secondary education 187, 238
  socio-economic background and perseverance 249
  special educational needs 266
  student support 233
  sustainable transport **121**